ESSENTIAL COMPONENTS OF A QUALITY PROGRAM

COMPONENT 1   A quality physical education program is organized around content standards that offer direction and continuity to instruction and evaluation.

COMPONENT 2   A quality program is student centered and based on the developmental urges, characteristics, and interests of students.

COMPONENT 3   Quality physical education makes physical activity and motor-skill development the core of the program.

COMPONENT 4   Physical education programs teach management skills and self-discipline.

COMPONENT 5   Quality programs emphasize inclusion of all students.

COMPONENT 6   In a quality physical education setting, instruction focuses on the process of learning skills rather than the product or outcome of the skill performance.

COMPONENT 7   A quality physical education program teaches lifetime activities that students can use to promote their health and personal wellness.

COMPONENT 8   Quality physical education teaches cooperative and responsibility skills and helps students develop sensitivity to diversity and gender issues.

DYNAMIC PHYSICAL EDUCATION

FOR SECONDARY SCHOOL STUDENTS

SIXTH EDITION

PAUL W. DARST

ARIZONA STATE UNIVERSITY

ROBERT P. PANGRAZI

ARIZONA STATE UNIVERSITY

PEARSON
Benjamin Cummings

SAN FRANCISCO BOSTON NEW YORK CAPE TOWN
HONG KONG LONDON MADRID MEXICO CITY MONTREAL
MUNICH PARIS SINGAPORE SYDNEY TOKYO TORONTO

Sponsoring Editor: Sandra Lindelof
Assistant Editor: Emily Portwood
Managing Editor: Wendy Earl
Production Supervisor: Janet Vail
Text and Cover Designer: Riezebos Holzbaur Design Group
Compositor: The Left Coast Group
Copyeditor: Michelle Gossage
Proofreader: Martha Ghent
Indexer: Sylvia Coates
Senior Manufacturing Buyer: Stacey Weinberger
Marketing Manager: Neena Bali

Cover images, left to right: basketball player: Rubberball; runner: Photodisc; kickboxer: iStockPhoto/redbaron_on_stockphoto; tennis player: Comstock; volleyball player: Photodisc; hockey player: iStockPhoto/walik

Photo on page 262: Jose Carrillo/PhotoEdit

Library of Congress Cataloging-in-Publication Data
Darst, Paul W.
Dynamic physical education for secondary school students/Paul W. Darst, Robert P. Pangrazi.—6th ed.
    p. cm.
    ISBN-13: 978-0-321-53679-2
    ISBN-10: 0-321-53679-7
1. Physical education and training—Curricula—United States. 2. Physical education and training (Secondary)—United States. 3. Physical education and training—Curricula—Canada. 4. Physical education and training—Study and teaching (Secondary)—Canada. I. Pangrazi, Robert P. II. Title
    GV365.P36 2009
    613.7071'2—dc22
                                                                                        2007051101

The Authors and Publisher believe that the activities and methods described in this publication, when conducted according to the descriptions herein, are reasonably safe for the students to whom this publication is directed. Nonetheless, many of the described activities and methods are accompanied by some degree of risk, including human error. The Authors and Publisher disclaim any liability arising from such risks in connection with any of the activities and methods contained in this publication. If students have any questions or problems with the activities and methods, they should always ask their instructor for help before proceeding.

PEARSON
Benjamin
Cummings

ISBN 0-321-53679-7
ISBN 978-0-321-53679-2

3 4 5 6 7 8 9 10—MAL—12 11 10
www.aw-bc.com

BRIEF CONTENTS

Preface   xi

SECTION 1   JUSTIFYING A PHYSICAL EDUCATION PROGRAM

Chapter 1   Physical Education in the Secondary School   3
Chapter 2   The Impact of Physical Activity on Adolescents   27

SECTION 2   DESIGNING A PHYSICAL EDUCATION PROGRAM

Chapter 3   Steps in Developing a Curriculum   47
Chapter 4   Curriculum Approaches   69

SECTION 3   TEACHING A PHYSICAL EDUCATION PROGRAM

Chapter 5   Planning for Effective Instruction   101
Chapter 6   Improving Instructional Effectiveness   129
Chapter 7   Management and Discipline   147
Chapter 8   Teaching Styles   175
Chapter 9   Improving Instruction Systematically   203
Chapter 10   Assessment, Evaluation, and Grading   229

SECTION 4   DEVELOPING A TOTAL PROGRAM

Chapter 11   Students with Disabilities   263
Chapter 12   Liability and Safety   279
Chapter 13   Intramurals, Sport Clubs, and Athletics:
              Furthering the Opportunity for Physical Activity   295

SECTION 5   IMPLEMENTING INSTRUCTIONAL ACTIVITIES

Chapter 14   Introductory Activities   311
Chapter 15   Promoting and Monitoring Lifestyle Physical Activity   325
Chapter 16   Physical Fitness   343
Chapter 17   Healthy Lifestyles: Activities for Instruction   383
Chapter 18   Promoting Motivation, Cooperation, and Inclusion:
              Nontraditional Ideas for Instruction   403
Chapter 19   Sports   423
Chapter 20   Lifestyle Activities   473
Chapter 21   Outdoor Adventure Activities   521

Index   539

CONTENTS

Preface   xi

SECTION 1   JUSTIFYING A PHYSICAL EDUCATION PROGRAM

CHAPTER 1   PHYSICAL EDUCATION IN THE SECONDARY SCHOOL   3
Chapter Summary   3
Student Outcomes   3
What Is Physical Education?   5
Rationale for Physical Education   6
Major Outcomes for Physical Education   7
Physical Education Content Standards   7
Perspectives Influencing Physical Education   12
Issues Affecting Physical Education Programs   13
Essential Components of a Quality Program   17
Characteristics of Successful Physical Education Programs   19
Study Stimulators and Review Questions   24
References and Suggested Readings   24
Web Sites   25

CHAPTER 2   THE IMPACT OF PHYSICAL ACTIVITY ON ADOLESCENTS   27
Chapter Summary   27
Student Outcomes   27
Growth and Development of Adolescents   30
The Impact of Activity on Health   36
Physical Education Dropouts   38
Academic Achievement and Physical Education   39
Long-Term Effect of Physical Activity   39
Safety Guidelines for Exercise and Physical Activity   40
Study Stimulators and Review Questions   43
References and Suggested Readings   43
Web Sites   45

SECTION 2   DESIGNING A PHYSICAL EDUCATION PROGRAM

CHAPTER 3   STEPS IN DEVELOPING A CURRICULUM   47
Chapter Summary   47
Student Outcomes   47
Designing a Quality Curriculum   49
An Articulated Curriculum: Grades K–12   64
Study Stimulators and Review Questions   66
References and Suggested Readings   66
Web Sites   67

CHAPTER 4   CURRICULUM APPROACHES   69
Chapter Summary   69
Student Outcomes   69
Promoting Physical Activity/Skill Development Approach   70

Sports Education Approach   84
Knowledge Concepts Approaches   86
Fitness Education Approaches   86
Personal and Social Responsibility Approach   93
Study Stimulators and Review Questions   98
References and Suggested Readings   98
Web Sites   99

SECTION 3   TEACHING A PHYSICAL EDUCATION PROGRAM

CHAPTER 5   PLANNING FOR EFFECTIVE INSTRUCTION   101

Chapter Summary   101
Student Outcomes   101
Develop Departmental Policies   102
Consider Pre-Instructional Decisions   110
Teach Each Student as a Whole Person   114
Plan for Optimal Skill Learning   116
Design Comprehensive Unit Plans   120
Create Quality Lesson Plans   121
Reflect on the Completed Lesson   124
Study Stimulators and Review Questions   126
References and Suggested Readings   126
Web Sites   127

CHAPTER 6   IMPROVING INSTRUCTIONAL EFFECTIVENESS   129

Chapter Summary   129
Student Outcomes   129
Maintain Student Interest   130
Develop Effective Listening Skills   132
Communicate Effectively with Your Class   133
Demonstrate a Caring Attitude Toward Students   134
Use Nonverbal Communication   136
Demonstrate and Model Skills   136
Facilitate Learning with Instructional Cues   137
Use Effective Instructional Feedback   138
Consider the Personal Needs of Students   140
Study Stimulators and Review Questions   144
References and Suggested Readings   145
Web Sites   145

CHAPTER 7   MANAGEMENT AND DISCIPLINE   147

Chapter Summary   147
Student Outcomes   147
Strive for a Well-Managed Class   148
Use Effective Class Organization Strategies   148
Teach Responsible Student Behavior   154
Implement a Proactive Behavior Management Approach   156
Maintain and Promote Acceptable Behavior   161
Decrease Unacceptable Behavior   164
Deal with Severe Misbehavior   169
Use Criticism Cautiously   171
Make Punishment a Last Resort   171
Know the Legal Considerations of Expulsion   172
Study Stimulators and Review Questions   172
References and Suggested Readings   173
Web Sites   173

CHAPTER 8   TEACHING STYLES   175
             Chapter Summary   175
             Student Outcomes   176
             Direct Style   177
             Task (Station) Style   177
             Mastery Learning (Outcomes-Based) Style   182
             Individualized Style   190
             Cooperative Learning Style   191
             Inquiry Style   193
             Teaching Styles and Student Learning   197
             A Framework for Using Multiple Teaching Styles   198
             Dynamic Instruction: Elements Common to All Styles   199
             Study Stimulators and Review Questions   200
             References and Suggested Readings   200
             Web Sites   201

CHAPTER 9   IMPROVING INSTRUCTION SYSTEMATICALLY   203
             Chapter Summary   203
             Student Outcomes   203
             Defining Effective Instruction   204
             Improving Teaching Skills   204
             Explaining the Need for Goals and Feedback   205
             Explaining the Need for Systematic Evaluation   205
             Evaluating Effective Teaching   205
             Introducing Methods for Systematically Observing Instruction   207
             Systematically Observing for Self-Improvement   208
             Improving the Quality of Instruction   208
             Observation Systems for Research and Supervision   220
             Study Stimulators and Review Questions   227
             References and Suggested Readings   227
             Web Sites   227

CHAPTER 10   ASSESSMENT, EVALUATION, AND GRADING   229
             Chapter Summary   229
             Student Outcomes   229
             ASSESSMENT OF STUDENT PERFORMANCE   230
             Objective Assessment of Physical Skills   231
             Assessment of Performance Outcomes   237
             Assessment of Knowledge   247
             Assessment of Attitudes and Values   250
             EVALUATION OF STUDENT PERFORMANCE   254
             Norm-Referenced Evaluations   254
             Criterion-Referenced Evaluations   255
             Uses for Student Evaluation   255
             GRADING—DIFFERING VIEWPOINTS   257
             Educational Objectives versus Administrative Tasks   257
             Process versus Product   258
             Relative Improvement   258
             Grading On Potential   259
             Negative versus Positive Grading   259
             Pass-Fail versus Letter Grades   259
             Study Stimulators and Review Questions   260
             References and Suggested Readings   260
             Web Sites   261

SECTION 4 DEVELOPING A TOTAL PROGRAM

CHAPTER 11 STUDENTS WITH DISABILITIES 263

Chapter Summary 263
Student Outcomes 263
Least-Restrictive Environment 265
Mainstreaming 265
Screening and Assessment 266
Development of the IEP 267
A Systematic Approach to Successful Mainstreaming 271
Fitness and Posture for Students with Disabilities 275
Use of Computers 276
Parental Support 276
Recruiting and Training of Aides 276
Study Stimulators and Review Questions 276
References and Suggested Readings 277
Web Sites 277

CHAPTER 12 LIABILITY AND SAFETY 279

Chapter Summary 279
Student Outcomes 280
Torts 281
Negligence and Liability 281
Areas of Responsibility 283
Equipment and Facilities 286
Sports Programs 287
Safety 288
Personal Protection: Minimizing the Effects of a Lawsuit 290
Study Stimulators and Review Questions 293
References and Suggested Readings 293
Web Sites 293

CHAPTER 13 INTRAMURALS, SPORT CLUBS, AND ATHLETICS: FURTHERING THE OPPORTUNITY FOR PHYSICAL ACTIVITY 295

Chapter Summary 295
Student Outcomes 296
Intramurals 296
Sport Clubs 303
Interscholastic Athletics 305
Study Stimulators and Review Questions 308
References and Suggested Readings 309
Web Sites 309

SECTION 5 IMPLEMENTING INSTRUCTIONAL ACTIVITIES

CHAPTER 14 INTRODUCTORY ACTIVITIES 311

Chapter Summary 311
Student Outcomes 311
Agility Activities 313
Sport Movement Challenges 316
Individual Activities 317
Partner and Small-Group Activities 318
Study Stimulators and Review Questions 322
Web Sites 323

CHAPTER 15 PROMOTING AND MONITORING LIFESTYLE PHYSICAL ACTIVITY 325
Chapter Summary 325
Student Outcomes 326
Physical Activity for Adolescents 327
The Physical Activity Pyramid 328
Pedometers and Physical Activity 330
Walking: The "Real" Lifetime Activity 336
Study Stimulators and Review Questions 340
References and Suggested Readings 340
Web Sites 341

CHAPTER 16 PHYSICAL FITNESS 343
Chapter Summary 343
Student Outcomes 344
The Fitness of America's Youth 344
Health-Related and Skill-Related Physical Fitness 346
Creation of a Positive Fitness Experience 348
Exercises for Developing Balanced Fitness Routines 350
Avoidance of Harmful Practices and Exercises 351
Activities and Routines for Developing Fitness 356
Health Club Workouts 368
Study Stimulators and Review Questions 380
References and Suggested Readings 381
Web Sites 381

CHAPTER 17 HEALTHY LIFESTYLES: ACTIVITIES FOR INSTRUCTION 383
Chapter Summary 383
Student Outcomes 384
Integrating Health Concepts 385
How Does the Body Work? 385
Barriers to Healthy Living 392
Teach Health Maintenance Behaviors 398
Study Stimulators and Review Questions 400
References and Suggested Readings 400
Web Sites 401

CHAPTER 18 PROMOTING MOTIVATION, COOPERATION, AND INCLUSION:
NONTRADITIONAL IDEAS FOR INSTRUCTION 403
Individual, Partner, and Small-Group Units of Instruction 403
Novel Team Games and Activities 416
Recreational Activities 419
Relays 419
Cooperative Activities 420
References and Suggested Readings 421
Web Sites 421

CHAPTER 19 SPORTS 423
Archery 423
Badminton 426
Basketball 432
Field Hockey 437
Flag Football 441
Gymnastics 445
Lacrosse 446

Soccer   449
Softball   457
Speed-a-Way   461
Team Handball   462
Track and Field   466
Volleyball   466
References and Suggested Readings   470
Web Sites   471

CHAPTER 20   LIFESTYLE ACTIVITIES   473
Bowling   473
Frisbee   477
Golf   484
In-line Skating Mini-Unit   488
Jogging   489
Racquetball   491
Rhythmic Activity   495
Rope Jumping   495
Strength Training   499
Swimming/Aquatics   504
Tennis   511
References and Suggested Readings   517
Web Sites   519

CHAPTER 21   OUTDOOR ADVENTURE ACTIVITIES   521
Ropes Course Activities   521
Group Initiative Activities   525
Orienteering   529
Transverse Climbing Wall Activities   536
References and Suggested Readings   538
Web Sites   538

Index   539

PREFACE

This revision of *Dynamic Physical Education for Secondary School Students* continues to reflect the national concern for public health. The activity habits of middle and high school students have continued to receive attention from governmental agencies and health experts. From top governmental agencies to local state school boards, the physical activity levels of youth are being scrutinized; physical education programs are receiving national attention and many experts are calling for major reforms in how and what professionals offer students. We continue to maintain that physical education should be a basic component in every student's daily education. Youth inactivity is a major problem that does not always receive attention because most people want to focus on overweight issues, not inactivity. However, physical education professionals are trained to deal with physical activity, not weight issues. There is strong evidence to show that regular physical activity has a positive impact on weight management. This revision focuses on not only increasing the activity level of students in physical education, but also promoting activity both in and out of the school setting. Because there are many factors that influence lifestyle, we have focused this edition on delivering knowledge, developing positive attitudes, and increasing daily activity levels of students.

HIGHLIGHTS OF THE SIXTH EDITION

The Sixth Edition of *Dynamic Physical Education for Secondary School Students* has been revised in many areas. The changes we have made reflect an increasing understanding of the rudiments of quality curriculum and instruction in secondary physical education. This edition includes information on recent trends and issues such as the essential components of a quality curriculum, healthy lifestyles promotion, creating healthy and active schools, and activities that can be performed throughout the lifespan. New information on diversity and gender issues are included to help enhance an effective learning environment. We continue to emphasize that students with disabilities should be integrated into instructional settings, and have included increased information on promoting and monitoring lifestyle activity in Chapter 15. New activities and innovative fitness routines found in health clubs, including kick-boxing, stability balls, medicine balls, yoga, Pilates, and body bars, have been added to Chapter 16. All chapters have been updated to reflect new trends and innovations in secondary school physical education. Because we feel that middle and high school programs have unique characteristics and outcomes, there has been a strong attempt to create different identities for each level. At the high school level, we have placed special emphasis on the ninth grade transition year; a year which, unfortunately, is often the last year of physical education for students.

Pedagogy: Web Sites, Study Stimulators, and Review Questions

At the beginning of each chapter, we present a chapter summary followed by key student outcomes. In addition, the beginning of each chapter identifies which essential components of a quality curriculum are discussed. Each chapter closes with a set of Study Stimulators and Review Questions that precede the References and Suggested Readings section. In addition, when appropriate, relevant web sites for each of the chapters are listed to help students find additional information when necessary. The essential components, chapter summaries, student outcomes, study stimulators, and review questions help focus study and application on important concepts covered in the chapters.

Section 1: Justifying a Physical Education Program

Section 1 places emphasis on designing a program that will be attractive to students. Evidence shows that required daily physical education only occurs in about five percent of high schools. This means physical educators have greater pressure on them to create attractive elective programs. Many schools are offering a "health club" approach in which activities and instruction meet the current needs of students. When students are able to learn "in vogue" activities such as Pilates and kick boxing at school, the odds of them continuing their active lifestyles will be raised. Programs must be as dynamic and changing as dictated by the needs of students and society.

With the continued emphasis on accountability and test scores in school programs, it is important to determine what should be taught, what students should know, and what they should be able to do when they leave the school environment. Chapter 1 contains a review of the NASPE content standards that offer direction to quality physical education programs. The standards identified in Chapter 1 encourage the development of a program that stresses lifetime activity, competency in a wide variety of physical skills, the need for strong social and personal responsibility skills, and the requisite knowledge needed to maintain personal health and an active lifestyle.

Chapter 1 also discusses the essential components of a quality program. Across the country, a wide variety of curriculum approaches and instructional procedures characterize physical education. We believe that while differences may exist among programs, there are many similarities that exist in quality programs. The essential elements of a quality physical education program have been delineated so teachers can include their own unique elements in a program while maintaining the essential elements for quality.

Section 2: Designing a Physical Education Program

Chapter 3 focuses on curriculum construction and how the characteristics of students affect the development of a meaningful curriculum; it includes information on new flexible scheduling ideas and the need for teachers to factor varying lengths of class time into their lesson plans. Chapter 4, which is devoted to helping students and teachers understand different curriculum approaches, has been updated. Suggestions are offered as to how the approaches can be used in a middle school or high school setting. Strengths and weaknesses for each of the curriculum approaches are covered and curriculum maps have been updated for teachers to give a clear overview of the approaches. Both Chapters 3 and 4 focus on middle and high school, with an emphasis on students' growth and development characteristics and the impact that those characteristics have on the design of the curriculum. An understanding of these chapters gives teachers an understanding of the philosophical framework that undergirds the curriculum. New activities have been added and evaluated by a large cadre of new and practicing teachers.

Section 3: Teaching a Physical Education Program

We felt this section needed to be enriched beyond our thinking so we asked Dr. Mary Jo Sariscsany, professor at CSU, Northridge, to contribute to many of the chapters in this section. Her contributions will encourage teachers to perform their teaching skills in a manner that is technically correct and in line with current research. The chapters on pedagogy reflect a body of knowledge related to effective teaching and indicate the science involved in instruction.

Planning has always played an important role in effective teaching. Chapter 5 focuses on planning for success with daily lesson plans and unit plans within the curriculum. Information is provided on preinstructional decision-making and the designing of instructional sequences for recommended parts of a lesson. Practical strategies are offered to help both beginning and experienced teachers organize meaningful and sequential learning experiences. Chapter 6 presents organizational material for improving the instructional atmosphere. Advice for effective supervision and communication with students is presented in a step-by-step approach. Important facets of teaching are presented, such as the development of instructional cues and the demonstration, observation, and maintenance of class performance. A large section of this chapter is devoted to helping teachers adapt instructional tasks to the individual needs of students. The effective use of instructional feedback is important for motivation and learning and much emphasis is placed on this topic. Professor Sariscsany has contributed much to the section on teaching for gender differences and diversity. Diversity issues are extremely important for teachers, considering the growing number of cultures that are a part of the school population.

In Chapter 7, a positive and caring approach is offered for managing and disciplining students. This area is always a major concern of teachers and parents and is rarely covered in detail in physical education textbooks. Teachers are shown how to reinforce desired behavior and develop a positive, yet assertive, discipline style. Punishment, although discouraged, is discussed, and guidelines for acceptable use are presented. Chapter 8 on teaching styles has been updated with new ideas, particularly in the area of peer teaching ideas and analysis. New information on teaching styles and how they can be used to facilitate student learning is included.

Chapter 9 has been revised to feature new instruments and techniques for analyzing instruction. Many of the instruments are a result of work by Dr. Hans van der Mars and his Oregon State University students. This chapter is now up to date and offers new ways of examining the effectiveness of instruction. Chapter 10 has been updated and includes a broad and comprehensive examination of the assessment, evaluation, and grading ideas for secondary schools. There is a review of protocols that have a process focus to help develop authentic assessment instruments. Directions and guidelines for implementing the latest "Fitnessgram" are given. New sections on portfolios and tactical game-playing assessments are also included. In addition, there is a presentation on the pros and cons of grading as well as different points of view on grading to help teachers make important decisions in this area.

Section 4: Developing a Total Program

New ideas have been added to Chapter 11, "Students with Disabilities," by offering a step-by-step approach to the development of an individualized education program (IEP) and the presentation of guidelines for screening and assessment. Criteria are offered to help place students in the least-restrictive environment possible, with emphasis on a positive and constructive approach. Also available are practical ideas for modifying activities that assure inclusiveness to increase the effectiveness of a program.

The important aspects of legal liability are seldom covered in secondary school physical education textbooks, but legal liability continues to be a major concern of teachers. Because teachers are often in a supervisory situation, guidelines in this area are also covered. Chapter 12 provides a new set of liability vignettes for students and teachers to discuss and analyze. It also describes situations teachers should avoid, focuses on safety, and offers a checklist for analyzing possible situations that might result in a lawsuit. Chapter 13 has been updated with new ideas for getting students engaged in various important after-school programs, including intramurals, sports clubs, and athletics. A strong case is made for making these programs an extension of the physical education program with the purpose of keeping students engaged in an active lifestyle.

Section 5: Implementing Instructional Activities

Chapter 14 on introductory activities has been updated with the addition of new activities in various categories to challenge students and get them warmed up for the fitness activities that follow. Many new games with variations for integrating academic concepts have been added.

Chapters 15 and 16 separate and define the differences between fitness and activity and explore how physical education programs can be successful in emphasizing both areas. The focus is on allowing students to select their primary purpose for being active. Emphasis in Chapter 15 is on teaching students self-

management skills to increase their personal activity levels. A new and comprehensive section on pedometers discusses how to begin using them in a class setting and moves toward students independently monitoring their activity levels. Walking, the most overwhelming choice of adults for personal activity, is discussed and a variety of class activities are offered. Chapter 16 includes new information on physical fitness as well as new fitness routines and activities that offer the widest possible range of fitness options for students. A new section on fitness activities found in the health club setting is included to help teachers prepare for activity outside of school. We feel schools should prepare students in a manner that makes it easy for them to join a health club when they are no longer in a school-based physical education setting.

Chapter 17 offers activities for maintaining health and developing an understanding of the basic components of lifetime health and wellness. It is important that these concepts be incorporated into the physical education curriculum wherever possible.

The instructional units are packaged into three chapters: sports, lifestyle activities, and outdoor adventure activities. These chapters are designed to help teachers create meaningful units of instruction by focusing on skills, drills, and lead-up games. It is important that content knowledge be shared with students during the skill development stage. After they have learned a skill, drills are offered so students can practice in a constructive setting. Lead-up games isolate the skills and place them in a competitive setting so students can apply what has been learned. New activities such as inline skating and rock wall climbing have been added. The references, suggested readings, and web sites for each activity are updated so students and teachers can secure in-depth information written by activity experts.

KUDOS

Our work together at Arizona State University has given us this opportunity to continue with the development of an effective, meaningful product that improves the quality of secondary physical education. We are most appreciative for the supportive and positive environment that has benefited us in many ways. Mary Jo Sariscany, CSU, Northridge and Michael Wright, CSU, Sacramento served as consultants and contributed much to a number of chapters in this edition. Hans van der Mars and Connie Pangrazi Orlowicz, Arizona State University and Barbara Ewens Cusimano, Oregon State University and their students field-tested many of the ideas in this book, and we thank them. Belinda Stillwell at California State University, Northridge added valuable information to the field hockey section.

A number of teachers helped field-test and evaluate the instructional units and fitness routines. They include Jessica and Jim Richardson (Paul's daughter and son-in-law) at Smith Jr. High in Mesa, Arizona; Ron Schoenwetter, Sean Jonaitis, and Danny Ortega at Greenfield Jr. High in Gilbert, Arizona; Billie Mautino, Mesquite Jr. High in Gilbert and Tom Calendo at San Tan Middle School in Chandler, Arizona; Harold Bull at McClintock High School in Tempe, Arizona; and Maria Corte at Mesa High School in Mesa, Arizona.

An uncompromising sense of appreciation goes to our wives, Charlene and Debbie, for their constant support and patience. They are both excellent physical education teachers and provided us with many ideas for quality physical education. We would also like to thank our sons and daughters, their spouses, and our grandchildren for their constant support and love, which is an extremely important part of our lives.

Useful textbooks are the result of cohesive teamwork among the publishing company, reviewers, and the authors. We are most appreciative of the professional staff at Benjamin Cummings for their major contributions to this text. Special thanks go to Sandra Lindelof, acquisitions editor, who has provided ongoing support and encouragement. We appreciate Emily Portwood, the project editor, for her persistence, guidance, and new ideas. In addition, special thanks to Janet Vail, production supervisor, for her professionalism and attention to detail. We also want to thank the many reviewers who helped guide our revision efforts.

P.W. Darst and R.P. Pangrazi

REVIEWERS

MELANIE CROY
Angelo State University

MARK KATUME
Chicago State University

MARLA LINDENMEYER
Wichita State University

TAMMY SCHIEK
Rockford College

JIM SYLVIS
Canisius College

DYNAMIC PHYSICAL EDUCATION

FOR SECONDARY SCHOOL STUDENTS

ESSENTIAL COMPONENTS OF A QUALITY PROGRAM

COMPONENT 1 A quality physical education program is organized around content standards that offer direction and continuity to instruction and evaluation.

COMPONENT 2 A quality program is student centered and based on the developmental urges, characteristics, and interests of students.

COMPONENT 3 Quality physical education makes physical activity and motor-skill development the core of the program.

COMPONENT 4 Physical education programs teach management skills and self-discipline.

COMPONENT 5 Quality programs emphasize inclusion of all students.

COMPONENT 6 In a quality physical education setting, instruction focuses on the process of learning skills rather than the product or outcome of the skill performance.

COMPONENT 7 A quality physical education program teaches lifetime activities that students can use to promote their health and personal wellness.

COMPONENT 8 Quality physical education teaches cooperative and responsibility skills and helps students develop sensitivity to diversity and gender issues.

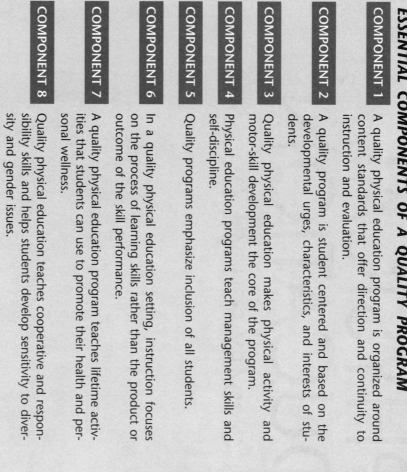

Physical Education in the Secondary School

CHAPTER SUMMARY

Physical education is that phase of the general educational program that focuses on movement experiences to contribute to the total growth and development of each student. Program objectives provide the framework and direction to the physical education curriculum. Systematic and properly taught physical education can help achieve the major content standards, such as movement competence including skills and knowledge, participation in physical activity and maintenance of physical fitness, exhibition of personal and social behavior that respects self and others, and a value of physical activity for health, enjoyment, challenge, self-expression, and/or social interaction. Modern programs of physical education have been influenced by cultural and educational factors. There are many issues that impact physical education programs. Quality programs include essential components and specific characteristics.

STUDENT OUTCOMES

After reading the chapter, you will be able to:

- Describe why people have misconceptions about physical education.
- Define physical education and describe how it functions as part of the secondary school experience.
- List program objectives and recognize the distinctive contributions of physical education.

Student Outcomes, continued

- Cite the content standards of secondary physical education.
- Verbally portray how a variety of societal influences and federal mandates have impacted secondary school physical education.
- Describe various trends and issues in secondary physical education.
- Describe the educational reasons for including physical education as part of the school experience.
- Identify essential components of a quality physical education program.
- Describe the characteristics of successful physical education programs.

Physical education can be a positive and exciting experience for students. A quality program can offer the opportunity to choose between activities such as mountain bicycling, skating with Rollerblades, golf, rock climbing, tennis, racquetball, group activities on a ropes course, and wilderness survival. Some high schools offer elective choices, including sailing, scuba diving, martial arts, Frisbee games, and water aerobics. Modern fitness centers with indoor climbing walls are becoming more common, providing access to a variety of machines and equipment for working on the various components of health-related physical fitness. Two- or 3-week mini-courses as well as semester-long, in-depth units are being designed by creative teachers to meet student needs and desires. New program offerings include adventure and wilderness courses that teach caving, rock climbing, stream fishing, and backpacking as part of the physical education program. Middle schools are offering a wide variety of units—including cardio kickboxing, step aerobics, walking activities using pedometers, team handball, new games, initiative challenges, ropes course activities, modified lacrosse, Frisbee skills, bicycling, and orienteering—so students can explore and find activities they enjoy. Many of the physical activities are at times being integrated with academic concepts from math, science, writing, and geography.

Many programs are emphasizing a positive and humane atmosphere. Strict dress codes have been relaxed to provide students with more choices. Instructional procedures include learning stations in which students work on different tasks at different ability levels. Teachers move about the gymnasium, giving information to, correcting, encouraging, and praising students. Students have more input about the type of activities they would like to see offered. Physical fitness activities include innovative visual materials and music. Choices may include work with exercise balls; fitness scavenger hunts; rope jumping; circuit training; activity routines; partner resistance activities; use of stationary bicycles, rowing machines, or stair-climbing

machines (Figure 1.1); or participation in orienteering courses. These activities are arranged and presented so all students can find personal satisfaction and success. Students at all ability levels are provided with challenging and successful activities that encourage them to expand their physical limits and develop a level of personal success and confidence.

So, is this how the public perceives physical education today? What is physical education? Ask this question and an infinite number of answers will be the result. People have varied images of the physical education environment. Some envision a class in which students dress in a required uniform and exercise in straight lines under the watchful eye of a regimental instructor. Accompanying this image is a negative atmosphere where running laps and exercise are used as punishment for dress code infractions or misbehavior. Others might view physical education as a subject to be avoided because of crowded classes, smelly locker rooms, forced showers, and a lack of time for changing clothes. Athletically inclined participants often remember physical education as a time for playing sports on a daily basis with little or no instruction.

These memories of physical education create a public perception package that might be described as follows: Students are hurried into their gym clothes only to wait at attention for dress inspection. Next, never-changing group calisthenics and stretching are followed by a lap around the track. Students then choose up sides and play the traditional team sport or game of the day (e.g., flag football, basketball, softball, or volleyball). The final activity of the day involves showering in 4 minutes, with a mandatory shower inspection to make sure that all students are wet. Curriculum variety, student input, activity choices, coed activities, and individualized instruction are seldom a part of the program most people remember.

Sadly, the public's perception of physical education often diminishes the importance of the program in the total school curriculum. Even though physically

FIGURE 1.1 Fitness center activities

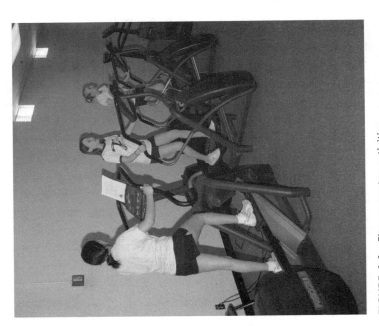

FIGURE 1.2 Teacher and student

active forms of sport and play can have a positive impact on students, many adults still hold a negative view of physical education. Even more unfortunate, unsatisfactory physical education classes still exist in some schools across the country. Physical miseducation is a dragon that rears its ugly head for various reasons, and it is extremely tough to slay. These negative programs create a situation where young adolescents never get the valuable opportunity to experience a quality physical education that could significantly impact their lives (Pangrazi, 2007).

Clearly, the term *physical education* implies widely differing experiences to the public. It is easy to see why many people have misunderstood physical education. Programs vary significantly from place to place and situation to situation. Knowledge, attitudes, and behaviors toward physical activity are strongly influenced by the type of physical education program students experience. Consequently, in developing an effective physical education program, teachers must have a clear understanding of what physical education is and what it should be doing in school settings.

WHAT IS PHYSICAL EDUCATION?

Physical education is a learning process that focuses on knowledge, attitudes, and behaviors relative to physical activity. Physically educating oneself can occur inside or outside the schools. It can be formal or informal. It might include a mother teaching her son or daughter

how to play golf or a player receiving information from the coach of the youth soccer team. It can be a family walking together with pedometers and keeping track of their steps or a mother explaining pacing to her children during a 10-k run. It can be a youth explaining the rules of football to his grandfather or a wife teaching her husband how to play racquetball. It is a group of seventh graders learning to play badminton in a middle school or high school students learning the concepts of health-related fitness in a classroom setting. Physical education is the passing of information, attitudes, and skills from one person to another (Figure 1.2).

Physical education is an important component of the overall school program. It is an integral part of the total educational program that contributes, primarily through physical activity experiences, to the total growth and development of all students. Physical education programs make four unique contributions to the lives of students. The first is the achievement of **daily physical activity** for all students. The second is the achievement of a **personalized level of physical fitness.** Third is the development of **competency in a variety of physical skills** to ensure successful functioning in lifetime physical activities. The fourth contribution requires that students acquire **requisite knowledge for living an active and healthy lifestyle.** If these contributions are not accomplished in physical education classes, they will not be realized elsewhere in the school curriculum. Physical education instructors have a responsibility to develop and teach a systematically organized curriculum for kindergarten through grade 12 that favorably influences all students and enhances their physical activity habits. Students deserve a thoughtful program of physical education that contributes to their quality of life and an active lifestyle. The transmission of knowledge, skills, and attitudes toward this end is physical education.

RATIONALE FOR PHYSICAL EDUCATION

There is certainly a need for quality physical education in the schools. The Youth Risk Behavior Surveillance System (YRBSS) is a nationwide survey conducted by the Centers for Disease Control and Prevention (CDC, 2005). The 2005 survey showed that only 36 percent of youth were active at least 60 minutes a day on 5 or more of the past 7 days. At the same time, the number of youth who attended daily high school physical education classes decreased to 29 percent and 37 percent for boys. To further compound the lack of physical activity issue, students in the 11th and 12th grades are rarely required to take physical education classes. A study by Ogden et al. (2006) showed that 31.7 percent of girls and 36.8 percent of boys, ages 12–19, were at risk of being overweight or were overweight during the 2003–2004 time period. Unfortunately, studies show that adolescents who are overweight will be more likely to be overweight as adults (Ferraro, Thorpe, & Wilkinson, 2003). It is becoming clear that the strong push for academic performance is surging while concern for the health of students is lagging.

Schools are places where physical activity is often discouraged. A physical education class can provide 2,000 or more steps (nearly a mile) of moderate to vigorous physical activity for students (Morgan, 2004). National health goals for the year 2010 (U.S. Department of Health and Human Services [USDHHS], 2000) are designed to increase daily levels of physical activity. Many of the goals directly target schools or programs that take place within the school setting. These goals emphasize reducing inactivity and increasing moderate to vigorous physical activity. The need is clear: Physical education programs can teach youth how to live an active and healthy lifestyle. Currently, many studies offer a strong rationale for increasing the amount of physical education contact offered to students:

- *The percentage of youth who are overweight has more than tripled in the past 30 years* (USDHHS, 2002). A recent study suggested that the prevalence of being overweight is more strongly related to decreases in energy expenditure than to increases in energy intake (Jebb & Moore, 1999). The school environ-

ment discourages physical activity. Students are asked to sit most of the day and walk between classes, which results in decreased energy expenditure. A 30-minute physical education class can offer 1,200 to 2,000 steps of moderate to vigorous physical activity to counteract the effects of an inactive day (Morgan, Pangrazi, & Beighle, 2003). This is a substantial contribution to the daily energy expenditure of students, particularly those students who are inactive. For example, for a student who is averaging 8,000 steps a day, a quality physical education class could increase their number of steps by 20 percent, a substantial increase in physical activity.

- *A positive experience in physical education classes can encourage youngsters to be active as adults.* In a survey sponsored by the Sporting Goods Manufacturers Association (2000), 60 percent of respondents, age 18–34, reported that a positive experience in physical education classes encouraged them to be active in later life. On the other hand, of those respondents who said they were sedentary, only 10 percent said their physical education classes encouraged them to be active. It should be added here that the high school years are usually the last contact students have with physical education. Their opinion of physical education will primarily be based on the type of experience they received.

- *Overweight youth grow into overweight adults.* Studies (Guo, Roche, Chumlea, Gardner, & Siervogel, 1994; Must, Jacques, Dallal, Bajema, & Dietz, 1992) show that adolescent weight is a good predictor of adult obesity. A study by Whitaker et al. (1997) showed that the risk of obesity persisting into adulthood is much higher among adolescents than younger children. The chance for childhood overweight persisting into adulthood increases from 20 percent at 4 years of age to 80 percent by adolescence (Guo & Chumlea, 1999). Considering a quality program encourages active behavior, it makes sense that a program be in place to help youngsters understand the importance of proper weight management and an active lifestyle.

- *A quality physical education program educates youngsters physically but does not detract from the academic performance of the school.* An argument often made is that spending time on physical education will lower the academic performance of students because they have less time to study and learn. To the contrary, studies have shown that students who spend time in physical education classes do equally well or better in academic classes. Two major studies that looked at this issue are the Three Rivers Study (Trudeau, Laurencelle, Tremblay, Rajic, & Shephard, 1998) and a SPARK (Sports, Play and Active Recreation for Kids) related activity program study (Sallis et al., 1999). In both cases, students received the health benefits of physical education without any negative impact on their academic performance.

Physical education gives students the skills they need to be active as adults. One commodity that youth have in contrast to adults is the time to practice and learn new skills. Few adults learn an entire new set of physical skills. More often than not, they practice and enhance skills they have learned earlier in childhood. Considering many adults like to participate in activities that require a requisite skill level (golf, tennis, racquetball, etc.), learning such skills during their school years makes it more likely they will feel able and competent to participate in later life.

Physical activity (which most often occurs in physical education classes) provides immediate and short-term health benefits for youth (Bar-Or, 1995). For overweight students, increased physical activity results in a reduction of the percentage of body fat. Additionally, increased activity reduces blood pressure and improves the blood lipid profile for high health-risk students. Finally, evidence shows that weight-bearing activities performed during the school years offer bone mineral density benefits that carry over into adulthood (Bailey, Faulkner, & McKay, 1996).

Active youth have a tendency to become active adults. Telama, Yang, Laasko, and Viikari (1997) looked at retrospective and longitudinal tracking studies and concluded that the results "indicate that physical activity and sport participation in childhood and adolescence represent a significant prediction for physical activity in adulthood." The relationship is weak but still indicates that activity during youth has an impact on adult activity levels. Another study (Raitakari et al., 1994) showed how strongly inactivity patterns track. In that study, the probability of an inactive 12-year-old remaining sedentary at age 18 was 51–63 percent for girls and 54–61 percent for boys. This clearly shows how we perpetuate the ongoing inactivity patterns of youth by placing them in an inactive school environment.

MAJOR OUTCOMES FOR PHYSICAL EDUCATION

Two words often used in education are outcomes and standards. Many use the terms interchangeably; however, in this text, they have different meanings. **Outcomes** are defined here as lifetime behaviors that impact the lifestyles of individuals. In physical education, the two major outcomes that should override everything else are **physical activity** and **health**, particularly **healthy eating habits**. In other words, all the activities and content of a physical education program are targeted to improve health and increase the activity levels of students. Additionally, these outcomes are reached through behavior-based activities so that students live what they learn in school throughout life. If a physical education program can increase the amount of moderate to vigorous physical activity students achieve and improve their eating habits, more than likely the issue of being overweight in our society can be stemmed.

It makes sense to monitor and evaluate the success of a physical education program in terms of physical activity and healthy behaviors because they can be achieved by all students regardless of genetic limitations and ability levels. All students can learn to live an active lifestyle and increase the amount of activity they perform on a daily basis. Physical educators now have pedometers available that monitor total daily activity and the amount of moderate to vigorous physical activity students accomplish. Teachers can assign activity homework that can be monitored and logged into notebooks and Internet programs. In terms of healthy eating habits, schools and physical education programs can take a much more active role in helping students learn how to fuel their bodies. Eating to live rather than living to eat is an important distinction students have to learn. Physical educators can spearhead efforts to improve the quality of food offered in the cafeterias, improve the quality of brown-bag lunches students carry to school, and monitor the types of celebratory foods that are offered to students. In addition, the current push to offer healthy drinks and snacks in vending machines has not resulted in reduced funds for schools as once was feared. Instead, students learn to choose from a healthy assortment of attractive and healthy snacks. In short, if the physical education successfully graduated students who were active and possessed healthy eating habits, few would doubt the worth of such a program.

PHYSICAL EDUCATION CONTENT STANDARDS

Content **standards** dictate the curriculum and what skills, knowledge, and behavior will be taught to students. They are the framework of a program; they determine the focus and direction of instruction. Standards specify what students should know and be able to perform, with the purpose of reaching the activity and health outcomes. Physical education teaches skills and behaviors taught nowhere else in the school curriculum. When these standards are not accomplished in physical education classes, students leave school without skills, knowledge, and attitudes related to an active lifestyle.

The National Association for Sport and Physical Education (NASPE) professionals have identified a set of standards that give direction to physical education. NASPE published these standards in a booklet (2004) that is most useful for teachers designing, implementing, and evaluating physical education curricula.

There is a general description of the standards and specific information for the standards according to the following grade-level ranges: kindergarten–second, third–fifth, sixth–eighth, and ninth–twelfth. Student expectations are delineated for each standard and show what students should know and be able to do at the end of each grade-level range. Examples of sample student performance outcomes are included to give teachers ideas about how their students should be progressing toward the achievement of each standard.

The standards not only give direction to instruction but also form the framework for assessment and accountability in the program. NASPE publications also offer an assessment series (see Chapter 10) with a wide range of strategies for assessing progress toward the standards. A wide range of strategies is recommended in the assessment series, including teacher observations, written tests, student logs, student projects, student journals, class projects, and portfolios. The assessment strategies show teachers examples of many forms of assessment, with the expectation that each teacher will modify and select assessment tools that are meaningful in his or her setting. The following sections show how the *Dynamic Physical Education for Secondary School Students* program addresses the NASPE National Standards for Physical Education.

Competency in Motor Skills and Movement Patterns

STANDARD 1: Demonstrates competency in motor skills and movement patterns needed to perform a variety of physical activities.

All people want to be skilled and competent in the area of motor performance. The secondary school years are an opportune time to teach motor skills because students have the time and the predisposition to learn. People tend to repeat activities they do well or find rewarding. Success is a great motivator. If students improve their volleyball bumps, Frisbee sidearm throws, or tennis serves, chances are great that they will repeat the activity and incorporate it into their lifestyles. Skill development does not occur overnight or in a 3-week unit. Students should be counseled about how to find opportunities for developing physical skills outside the school program. Teachers provide a support system for students as their skills improve, and the positive benefits of physical activity begin to appear. Students change their attitudes toward physical activity when personal skill levels improve. Students expect instant success, and teachers can help them learn that physical skill development is not easy and demands long, continuous effort. The role of teachers is to help students find individual levels of success—success that is unique to each person.

The range of skills presented in physical education should be unlimited. Because students vary in genetic endowment and interest, it is important that they have an opportunity to explore and learn about their abilities in many types of physical skills. The hierarchy of skill development progresses from fundamental motor skills to specialized skills. Components of motor skill development and movement competence follow.

Fundamental Motor Skills

Fundamental skills are those utilitarian skills that people use to enhance the quality of life. The designation *fundamental skills* is used because skills are basic to a fully functioning individual. These skills help students to function in the environment around them. These skills are divided into three categories: locomotor, nonlocomotor, and manipulative. The majority of these skills should be learned during the elementary school years.

1. *Locomotor Skills* Locomotor skills are used to move the body from one place to another or to project the body upward, as in jumping and hopping. These skills also include walking, running, skipping, leaping, and galloping.

2. *Nonlocomotor Skills* Nonlocomotor skills are performed in place, without appreciable spatial movement. They include bending, stretching, pushing and pulling, raising and lowering, twisting and turning, shaking, bouncing, circling, and so on.

3. *Manipulative Skills* Manipulative skills are developed through object handling. This manipulation of objects leads to hand-eye and foot-eye coordination, which are particularly important for tracking items in space. Manipulative skills form the important basis for many game skills and lifetime activities. Propulsion (throwing, striking, kicking), receipt (catching), rebounding, or redirection of objects (such as volleyball) are basic to this set of skills.

Rhythmic Movement Skills

Individuals who excel in movement activities possess a strong sense of rhythmic ability. Rhythmic movement involves motion that possesses regularity and a predictable pattern. The aptitude to move rhythmically is basic to skill performance in all areas. A rhythmic program that includes aerobic dance, folk and square dancing, rope jumping, and rhythmic gymnastics offers a set of experiences that help attain this objective.

Specialized Motor Skills

Specialized skills are used in various sports, games, and other areas of physical education, including adventure activities, apparatus activities, tumbling, cooperative activities, swimming, dance, and so on. When developing specialized skills such as tennis strokes, racquetball serves, or softball fielding techniques, progression is attained through planned instruction and drills. These skills have critical points of technique, and proper teaching emphasizes correct performance. In most cases, these skills are not well learned until the middle and high school years.

Understanding of Movement Concepts, Principles, Strategies, and Tactics

STANDARD 2: Demonstrates understanding of movement concepts, principles, strategies, and tactics as they apply to the learning and performance of physical activities.

A physical education program should provide students with a wide range of knowledge about many areas. A knowledge component is intertwined with all objectives. Indeed, accomplishing any objective is difficult if students do not have a certain amount of knowledge. For example, getting students to enjoy tennis without understanding rules, strategies, and etiquette is difficult, and most people will not incorporate an aerobic activity into his or her lifestyle without understanding the possible health-related benefits.

Students need to learn about the classification of movement concepts, which includes body awareness, space awareness, qualities of movement, and relationships. It is not enough to learn only the fundamental skills; students need to perform these skills in a variety of settings. For example, students are asked to run in different directions, at different levels, and along different pathways. They can learn to move slowly or quickly or to make a series of strong movements. Movement themes form the foundation of movement experiences necessary for developing specific fundamental skills. Through this process, students develop an increased awareness and understanding of the body as a vehicle for movement and for the acquisition of a personal vocabulary of movement skills. These skills are usually taught in elementary and middle school years. They are used in the secondary school years without instruction and practice; it is usually assumed they have been learned in the earlier grades.

The school years should be the years of opportunity—the opportunity to explore and experience many different types of physical activity. Students should be able to find physical activities that provide personal satisfaction and success. The curriculum should be expansive rather than restrictive. It should allow students to better understand their strengths and limitations and to establish the types of activities they prefer and dislike. Related to this experience is the opportunity to learn basic concepts of movement and physical activity. Students should leave school knowing about center of gravity, force, leverage, stability, and other factors related to efficient movement. Learning basic principles and concepts of physical activity, especially with reference to how physical activity contributes to good health and wellness, is important in this knowledge objective. Understanding the genetic diversity among people, such as body physiques, muscle fibers, cardiovascular-respiratory endurance, and motor coordination, is requisite for helping students evaluate their physical capabilities. (See Chapters 2 and 16 for evidence.) Specifically learning how to assess personal fitness and activity levels, how to plan activity levels, and how to make informed decisions about physical activity and fitness are all important objectives in this domain.

Related to understanding principles of human performance is knowing how to safely participate in activity. The school has both a legal and moral obligation to provide a safe environment. Safety must be actively taught, and activities must be conducted in a safe environment. Instructional procedures in activity must include safety factors, and active supervision is necessary to guide students in safe participation. Students must leave school with an understanding of safety principles of human movement.

Regular Physical Activity

STANDARD 3: Participates regularly in physical activity.

An important objective of a secondary school physical education program is to help students incorporate physical activity into their lifestyles. This requires that curriculum, instruction, and teachers have a positive impact on students' knowledge, attitudes, and skill behaviors relative to physical activities. A successful physical education program is not measured by the current level of knowledge, the physical fitness level, or the physical skills of students, nor is it measured by the number of participants on the varsity athletic teams. Certainly it is not the number of victories that the football or basketball teams accumulate. **The ultimate measure of success is the number of students who participate in daily physical activities such as exercise, sports, dance, and outdoor adventure activities throughout their lives.**

There are several basic considerations for lifetime activity. Sallis (1994) classifies the factors that influence people to be active in four categories: psychological, social, physical-environmental, and biological. Physical education programs should foster those factors that are often referred to as the determinants of active learning. Psychological determinants are among the most powerful. For example, students must derive enjoyment through activity so they will seek further participation. To this end, students must become proficient in a variety of motor skills. Also, most adults will not participate in activities unless they have an adequate level of perceived competence. Because learning new motor skills takes a great deal of time and repetition, everyday life often prohibits busy adults from developing a level of skill competence to ensure play without embarrassment. Students also need a rational basis for play. This can be established through activity orientations that can be transferred to other situations. Such activities should include a variety of games suitable for small groups and sport activities adapted to local situations.

Social influences include factors such as having family and peer role models, having encouragement from significant others, and having the opportunities to participate in activity with others in one's social group. Physical-environmental factors include adequate programs and facilities, adequate equipment and supplies, safe outdoor environments, and available opportunities near home and at school. Included are adequate school opportunities in physical education, intramural sports, and after-school recreation and sports programs. Biological factors include age, gender, ethnic, and/or socioeconomic status (Sallis, 1994).

Without proper planning and systematic arrangement of the learning environment, the probability of developing positive student attitudes and physically active lifestyles is greatly reduced. Secondary curriculum plans and instructional strategies should be concerned with developing learning environments that help students enjoy physical activities for a lifetime.

Achievement and Maintenance of Health-Enhancing Physical Fitness

STANDARD 4: Achieves and maintains a health-enhancing level of physical fitness.

Physical educators provide experiences for students that lead to successful encounters with exercise and regular physical activity. Proper development in this

area implies a focus on regular physical activity that results in a fitness level that motivation and heredity allow. This emphasis leads to improved health-related physical fitness (Corbin, Pangrazi, and Welk, 1994). This includes cardiovascular efficiency, flexibility, body fat reduction, and muscular strength and endurance. Recent physical fitness test batteries focus on the development of criterion-related health standards associated with reduced health risk rather than skill-related fitness based on normative standards (Cooper Institute, 2007).

Students need to experience activities that demonstrate the benefits of physical fitness firsthand. Student participation in activity choices and the opportunity to offer input about the fitness program help create a personalized program. Learning how to develop and arrange suitable fitness routines that positively impact health is an important higher-order objective. Physical fitness development is similar to physical skill development in that it requires time, energy, and self-discipline. Students need to be aware of the factors that influence fitness development. Eating habits, types of activities, heredity, and frequency of activity are just a few of the factors that students must learn. Physical education programs play an important role in helping students develop activity habits that will benefit their physical health.

Allotting a portion of each class to fitness activities helps students understand what is necessary for fitness enhancement. Learning about fitness is much more than facts; students need the participation experience in order to make fitness activities a habit. Many people know the facts about fitness but are not participating in regular physical activity. This is not to say that knowledge is unimportant, but rather that regular physical activity in a person's lifestyle is a top priority for a physical education program. A positive experience in fitness activities can help students develop attitudes that ensure active adult lifestyles. Programs are not successful if students leave school with a dislike for physical activity. Establishing a desire in students to maintain fitness and wellness throughout their adult years is the most important outcome.

Responsible Personal and Social Behavior

STANDARD 5: Exhibits responsible personal and social behavior that respects self and others in physical activity settings.

Responsible behavior involves behaving in a manner that doesn't negatively impact others. Hellison (2003) and others have developed methodology for teaching responsible behavior. It is generally accepted that if responsible behavior is to be learned, it must be taught

FIGURE 1.3 Students working cooperatively

through experiences where such behavior is reinforced on a regular basis. Accepting consequences for one's behavior is learned and needs to be valued and reinforced by responsible adults. Responsible behavior occurs in a hierarchy of behavior, ranging from acting irresponsibly to caring and behaving in a responsible manner. Physical education classes are an excellent setting for teaching responsibility because most behavior is highly visible. Youngsters in a competitive setting may react openly in an irresponsible fashion, offering instructors a "teachable moment" to discuss such unacceptable behavior. Additionally, students have to learn to win and lose in an acceptable manner and assume responsibility for their performances. Accepting the consequences of one's behavior is a lesson that arises regularly in a cooperative/competitive environment.

Cooperation precedes the development of competition, which makes it an important behavior to teach in physical education settings (Figure 1.3). Without cooperation, competitive games cannot be played. The nature of competitive games demands cooperation, fair play, and "sportspersonship," and when these are not present, the joy of participation is lost. Cooperative games teach students that all teammates are needed to reach group goals.

Physical activity environments provide a number of unique opportunities for students to experience and develop social-emotional skills. Getting along with other people, being part of a team, accepting an official's judgment, losing the final game of a tournament, dealing with peers who have varying levels of ability, or changing clothes in a crowded locker room are just a few of the many experiences that may occur in a physical education class. These are important experiences for students. Physical educators have a responsibility to help guide and direct students in understanding these various social-emotional behaviors.

All students need to understand and internalize the merits of participation, cooperation, competition, and tolerance. Good citizenship and fair play help define a desirable social atmosphere. A teacher who listens, shows empathy, and offers guidance can help students differentiate between acceptable and unacceptable ways of dealing with others and expressing feelings. Students need to develop an awareness of how they interact with others and how the quality of their behavior influences others' responses to them. If students do not receive feedback about negative behavior from teachers and peers, they may not realize that the behavior is inappropriate. Establishing reasonable limits of appropriate student behavior followed by consistent enforcement of those limits will help students understand the parameters of acceptable behavior.

Teachers help students develop positive attitudes toward learning by teaching an understanding of various student ability levels, the role of winning and los-

ing, and the value of making an effort to succeed. Positive and concerned instruction has a powerful impact on students' attitudes and self-concepts. A positive teacher communicates to students that they are loved, capable, and contributing individuals. Not only must teachers understand students, but students should understand themselves because self-understanding has a powerful influence on human behavior. The self-concept that a student develops is vital to the learning process. If students believe they belong, that they are important people, and that their successes outweigh their failures, they are given momentum toward developing a desirable self-concept. Encouraging students to provide positive feedback to each other will help students feel positive about their efforts.

The ability to move with grace, confidence, and ease helps students perceive themselves in a positive manner. Achieving self-satisfying levels of skill competency and fitness can also make students feel confident and assured. The self-concept is related to perceived physical skill competence. If students perceive themselves to be competent in a physical activity setting, they will want to participate in physical activity outside of the school environment. On the other hand, if they feel incompetent, they will avoid activity at all costs in an attempt to maintain their self-esteem and avoid embarrassment.

Valuing Physical Activity for Many Reasons

STANDARD 6: Values physical activity for health, enjoyment, challenge, self-expression, and/or social interaction.

This standard focuses on the development of students' awareness of the wide variety of benefits that can be obtained from leading a physically active life. The benefits can take many forms and be perceived differently by individuals. Students need to know about the variety of benefits and be able to look at all the options involved with different types of physical activity and how they relate to their personal interests. They need the knowledge necessary to make thoughtful decisions about which activities impact an individual's health and wellness (see Chapters 2, 15, 16, and 17). They need to know which activities will be more fun for them. Some students will select activities because of the challenge or the opportunity for self-expression. There are many, many activity opportunities for a lifetime of regular physical activity, and a quality program will help students value the activities that meet their own needs. As students develop this understanding of all the benefits of physical activity participation, they will pursue activities that are meaningful to them.

PERSPECTIVES INFLUENCING PHYSICAL EDUCATION

Though physical education programs vary widely across the United States, most endorse similar outcomes. Programs are greatly influenced by current social and professional perspectives. Most curricula (see Chapter 4) are based on a wide variety of goals and objectives emanating from a wide variety of sources. Nevertheless, some schools orient their programs more closely to one perspective than another. Therefore, an understanding of these perspectives will help the reader better understand how curricula reflect the social needs of a culture.

The Social-Historical Perspective

European gymnastics and highly organized and disciplined calisthenics programs dominated early physical education in the United States. Many of the early leaders were European immigrants, primarily from Germany and Sweden, who brought these formal programs with them and implemented them first in colleges and then in the public schools. These systems included formal and structured exercises centered on development of the body. Some have called this an "education of the physical" focus.

In the early 1900s, a major shift in perspective began to occur. As education in general altered its perspective based on the teachings of John Dewey and others, physical education shifted as well. Two of Dewey's cardinal aims of education stressed the promotion of health and a worthy use of leisure time. People became interested in using sports and games to foster these two aims. The school curriculum became a logical place to include these sports and games. Jesse F. Williams, whose text (1927) was published in numerous editions, was one of several leaders who did much to change the perspective of American physical education at this time. Williams and others championed democratic ideals and the concepts of sportspersonship and teamwork. Thus, the strong focus on team sports in physical education was started. This focus is called an "education through the physical" approach. This perspective did not negate the importance of physical fitness and "education of the physical," but it did place a strong emphasis on social development through physical education. This perspective was perpetuated by followers of these early leaders and continues to have currency in the secondary physical education field.

The Cultural-Sports Perspective

Since the turn of the century, sports have become a diversion not only for millions of Americans who are participants, but for millions of Americans who are spectators (Eitzen & Sage, 1986). Youth sports are now highly organized and have large participant rates. Collegiate and professional sports have become big business. Title IX of the Education Amendments Act of 1972 was enacted to provide greater access for girls and women in sports. With the shift from more formal gymnastics to more "American" activities such as football, basketball, and softball, sports became central to the programs of physical education. Because sports are part of the American culture, the development and appreciation of sports skills was logically accepted as a part of American education. This perspective accounts for the emphasis on sports in the expanded curriculum, which includes interscholastic and intramural programs.

The Public Health Perspective

A renewed emphasis on physical fitness occurred in the 1950s, caused by the publication of the Kraus-Weber tests comparing fitness levels of American and European students on strength and flexibility. The public became concerned about the comparable weakness of U.S. students. In response to this concern, President Dwight Eisenhower established the President's Council on Physical Fitness and Sport, an agency that promotes physical fitness not only for students, but also for citizens of all ages. This was the beginning of a fitness boom that has continued to this day. In recent years, more and more evidence indicates that the lack of regular physical activity among adults is a primary risk factor for heart disease and a major contributor to other diseases as well. Data now exist to show that students who are active are more likely to be active later in life, and those who are active during school years have health benefits that extend to later life (Raitakari et al., 1994).

The document Healthy People 2000: National Health Promotion and Disease Objectives (U.S. Public Health Service, 1990) was released by the government with goals to improve the health of all Americans. Many of the target goals were directed toward improving the health status of American youth. All of the objectives in the physical activity area emphasized increasing the amount of time students participate in light to moderate activity. Based on this evidence, several public health experts called for the use of physical education as a public health tool (Sallis & McKenzie, 1991). They suggested that implementation of programs designed to promote lifetime physical activity in the school would reap important public health benefits, including reduced morbidity and mortality from hypokinetic conditions such as heart disease, back pain, obesity, diabetes, high blood pressure, and cancer. The public health perspective has had considerable impact on curriculum and instruction in physical education. This perspective gave impetus to the recommendation within *Healthy People 2000* that there be an increase in physical education in schools by the year 2000.

The release of *Physical Activity and Health: A Report of the Surgeon General* (USDHHS, 1996) documented many health benefits achieved through moderate and regular activity. The report showed that people of all ages, both male and female, benefit from regular physical activity. Never before had a body of research been compiled to show the strong need for activity and fitness in the lives of youth. Activity programs are a requisite for healthy youngsters. Yet in spite of the strong emphasis the report placed on regular and daily activity, many physical education programs continue to emphasize physical fitness goals instead of lifestyle physical activity goals.

Primarily based on the Surgeon General's report promoting physical activity, a new set of goals for America emerged: *Healthy People 2010: National Health Promotion and Disease Objectives* (U.S. Public Health Service, 2000). This document once again continued to focus on physical activity goals that would increase the years of healthy life and eliminate health disparities. These major goals are supported with enabling goals concerned with promoting healthy behaviors, protecting health, achieving access to quality health care, and strengthening community prevention. The objectives are grouped into a number of focus areas similar to those described in *Healthy People 2000*. New focus areas in this document include disability, people with low income, race and ethnicity, chronic diseases, and public health infrastructure.

ISSUES AFFECTING PHYSICAL EDUCATION PROGRAMS

A number of trends and related issues impact the development of secondary school physical education

programs. Some of the factors to be considered when developing a program are discussed in the following section.

State and Local Physical Education Requirements

Most state departments of education set some type of requirement for physical education (NASPE, 2002). Policies differ dramatically from state to state. Some require a number of minutes per week for each grade level, whereas others specify a number of days per week. Several states do not have any physical education requirement. Each school district usually sets requirements designed to fit within the requirements defined by the state department of education. Consequently, district policies can vary dramatically and still be within state guidelines. As an example, in Arizona (which has standards and recommendations by grade level), there is no requirement at the state level for physical education. Most Arizona high schools have a 1-year physical education requirement, others have a 2- or 3-year requirement, and some offer only an elective physical education program. The state requirement significantly affects the curriculum, the students, and the teachers. Physical educators have always been involved to ensure that physical education is a basic part of the school district's requirements.

Designing local requirements can often be a positive practice for physical education programs because it lends stability and credibility at the district level. Some districts have developed requirements that facilitate a selective or elective type of curriculum. This involves specifying requirements by activity category, such as team sports, lifetime sports, gymnastics, aquatics, recreational activities, and dance. For example, students might be required to complete 12 activities in 1 year. The requirement might be that three of the activities must be team sports, three must be lifetime sports, and one each must be selected from the areas of dance, aquatics, and gymnastics. The remaining activity choices would be left to the student. This procedure gives students **choice within a requirement** and ensures that students will receive a variety of activities as well as the opportunity to choose according to their interests. Students have choice but not total freedom, so a balanced curricular approach is ensured.

Coeducational Classes

Title IX of the Educational Amendments Act of 1972 has had a significant impact on most secondary school physical education programs. The law is based on the principle that school activities and programs are of equal value for both sexes. Students should not be denied access to participation in school activities on the basis of sex. This law has stirred up much debate and controversy. Interpretations and details continue to be studied by school districts, state departments of education, and the judicial system.

Legal ramifications mandate equal access to physical education activities for both boys and girls (Figure 1.4). Separate classes for males and females have been reduced in most schools. This does not imply that both sexes must wrestle together, share locker facilities, or have the same activity interests. It does not mean that males can participate in a dance class or females can elect a strength training class when they have interest in these respective areas. In principle, the law also means that instruction is provided by the most qualified person regardless of sex.

The law does allow schools to group students by ability, even if the result is groups consisting of primarily one sex. The law also allows teachers to segregate sexes during the game or competitive aspect of contact sports such as wrestling, basketball, football, ice hockey, and others. Teachers must also be sure that grading standards or procedures are not having an adverse effect on one sex, a specified regulation of Title IX. Standards must be equally fair to both sexes.

Amidst all of the controversy, it is important to examine the objectives of the physical education program and to focus on developing a situation that will meet the requirements of Title IX. There are challenges, but this is a small price to pay for inequalities that have existed in terms of opportunities for learning and participation in sports and physical education. Law or no law, physical education is important to all students regardless of sex. There are also clear advantages to coeducational programs in the areas of social development, activity offerings, and instructional quality. Teachers should be responsible for all students in their classes, regardless of ability or gender.

FIGURE 1.4   Coed class

Students with Disabilities

Public Law (PL) 94-142, the Education of All Handicapped Children Act, was signed in 1975 by President Ford. This law ensures that all youngsters with disabilities receive an appropriate public education that serves their unique needs. A 1990 amendment, PL 101-476 (also known as *IDEA*—Individuals with Disabilities Education Act), continues with the objective of providing disabled individuals with the least restrictive environment in the school setting. Autism and traumatic brain injury have been added to the list of handicapping conditions that should receive the least restrictive environment. IDEA provides that an individual transition plan be developed no later than age 16 as a component of the individualized education program (IEP) process. Rehabilitation and social work services are included as related services.

The law has compelled physical educators to develop specialized classes and programs for many students with disabilities. Other students are mainstreamed into the regular physical education program as part of the least restrictive environment advocated by PL 94-142. School districts are required to hire qualified instructors for these programs, as well as to encourage current teachers to develop skills for providing meaningful experiences for mainstreamed children with disabilities. Physical education has been specified as an important part of the disabled student's curricula or IEP. The IEP contains extensive information covering the student's present status, program objectives, learning activities, and evaluation procedures.

The law can create challenges for physical educators in planning, organizing, managing, and evaluating daily and yearly programs for the disabled. In most situations, the teacher must establish learning environments concurrently for students with and without disabilities. Regardless of the law, the issue is a moral necessity. Physical education is as important to disabled students as it is to other students. All students deserve physical education experiences regardless of their abilities or disabilities.

Conceptual Physical Fitness Programs

A program that started at the college level and has filtered down to many secondary schools is called the conceptual approach. An example of the conceptual approach for secondary schools is the *Fitness for Life* text by Corbin and Lindsey (2007). This approach has been called a lecture–laboratory method. Students spend time receiving information in a lecture situation and then try out or test the information on themselves or on peers in a laboratory setting. Emphasis is placed on information, appraisal procedures, and program planning. Students are expected to understand the "how, what, and why" of physical activity, physical fitness, and exercise. They learn to use diagnostic tests in areas such as cardiovascular endurance, muscular strength and endurance, flexibility, body composition, and motor ability.

A variety of conceptual programs have been field-tested in various situations. In some schools, concepts make up the entire physical education program, while in other programs, the concepts may be only a portion of the requirement, such as a semester class or 6-week unit. Several books are available with lesson sequences and other instructional materials such as slide-tape lectures, scripts, review questions, tests, handouts, overhead transparencies, and laboratory experiments.

The conceptual approach is currently popular for several reasons. First, many believe that an academic approach focused on knowledge and cognitive growth instead of on physical skill is a more respectable educational endeavor. Others believe that when student knowledge is increased, attitudes and behaviors also change, causing physical activity to be incorporated into the student's lifestyle. This is not a proven phenomenon. Increasing a person's knowledge does not ensure a change in behavior, and students must also experience physical activity as well as understand it conceptually. Conceptual learning is an important part of a physical education program, but physical skill development must also receive strong emphasis.

Interdisciplinary Courses

In some secondary schools, physical education is combined with other disciplines, such as health, biology, geology, and geography. In these programs, students have opportunities to learn about subjects such as drugs, alcohol, diseases, safety, first aid, hunting and fishing, taxidermy, rock formations, and environmental concerns. Emphasis is placed on combining physical skill development with knowledge. For example, students can learn about the flora and fauna of an area while concurrently learning camping and backpacking skills. This is the basic thesis of many outdoor education programs in which several disciplines are integrated to teach students about the outdoors.

This approach also balances the acquisition of knowledge and physical skill development, and it offers interesting opportunities for students and teachers. Teachers can take advantage of geographical locations, different learning environments, and the interests of students living in these areas. The physical education teacher can team-teach with teachers from other subject areas such as biology, zoology, or geogra-

phy. In this way, many interesting learning experiences can be developed. A downside of this approach is that the time available for physical skill development is usually reduced in favor of more knowledge time, thus reducing the opportunity to become competent in physical skills.

Virtual (Online) Physical Education Classes

Off-campus physical education programs give students an opportunity to earn credit for advanced study or off-campus courses that are not available in the basic curricula. Students are offered the opportunity to earn credit for off-campus study involving surfing, ice-skating, horseback riding, bowling, golf, and other disciplines. These programs are available to students after they have completed basic requirements. Some type of monitoring and weekly check-in procedure is arranged, with the student, parent, and teacher agreeing to a contract. Many of these programs also contain a fitness component requiring that students show some evidence of maintenance or improvement in fitness (e.g., body composition or cardiovascular endurance).

A more common model, being used in Florida and Minnesota, involves offering personal fitness classes to students in an unstructured environment. Students can sign up for the class, receive instruction from videos and class materials, and do their workouts at home or in other settings. There are no walls, no whistles, and no teachers on-site. Instead, students design their fitness programs based upon personal needs and desires. One of the requirements is that students keep a log of their daily activity with a record of exercises and activities that they completed. Students can record their progress in a personal log or online. Jan Braaten, curriculum coordinator for physical education and health for the Minneapolis Public Schools (MPS), explained why her district began offering online physical education classes in the spring of 2005: "Things have changed in the 21st century in many ways, and one change is the wide variety of options and lifestyles for our students." In the Minneapolis courses, students are asked to perform 30 minutes of vigorous activity 3 days a week. These students record the type of activity they did, their heart rate, and perceived exertion. The students in these online courses must have their log signed off by a parent, coach, trainer, or other adult. The Florida program is slightly different in that students record their activity on the Web and can interact with a number of sources, including the instructor who will give advice and answer student questions throughout the day by e-mail, instant messaging, phone, or fax.

These online programs offer possibilities for advanced study and can add an exciting dimension to the curricula. Students often develop self-management skills and become self-motivated because they select activities that appeal to them and are primarily responsible for what they learn from the experience. Both program leaders admit that it is possible to cheat. However, the majority of students view such programs as a privilege and usually respond in a mature manner. The bottom line is that if students learn to direct their own physical activity experiences without adult supervision, they are a step closer to a lifetime of activity and better health.

Instruction in Community Facilities

Another trend that can be positive for school programs is the use of community facilities. This approach allows schools to use community bowling alleys, golf courses, ski slopes, and skating rinks to enhance the physical education program. Many schools bus students to a bowling alley or golf course once a week. Sometimes schools provide transportation and participation funds; in other cases, students pay the expenses. Funding can also be provided through car washes, candy sales, and raffles. Programs and procedures are limited only by a teacher's ingenuity and creative direction.

Community facilities can add a valuable dimension to secondary programs. Physical educators can broaden their areas of competency or find other professionals who have requisite expertise. A noted physical educator once asked a physical education teacher who taught at a school situated near a beautiful lake, "Do you teach swimming, boating, and sailing here?" "No," replied the teacher, "we don't have the facilities." Finding a way to use community resources for the betterment of students is surely possible. Qualified personnel from the community often want to share their expertise.

Private Sports Instruction

Opportunities for sports and fitness instruction in the private sector continue to expand rapidly. These programs are responsive to the demands of consumers. Indoor climbing walls, YMCA basketball, gymnastics clubs, soccer leagues, Pop Warner football, motocross bicycle racing, Little League Baseball, and racquet clubs are a few examples of programs that are available to students. Students receive in-depth instruction, practice with adequate equipment, have many competitive opportunities, and receive trophies, T-shirts, and similar rewards. Private instruction programs must meet the demands of consumers or lose their clientele.

Often, such programs use quality equipment, the newest techniques, and instructors who are highly skilled and excellent teachers. Many of these instructional programs offer strong competition for physical education programs because of their ability to provide personalized instruction.

Private sector instructional programs can create challenges for school-based physical education programs. The first challenge is that private instruction creates a wide range of backgrounds, experiences, and abilities among students who are participating in school physical education. Students from middle- and upper-class families may have a wealth of experience in sports such as tennis, golf, soccer, and gymnastics, whereas students from lower-income families might not be able to finance private instruction. Another problem is that it can be difficult to develop a gymnastics unit that is meaningful to eighth-grade students who have had 5 years of intensive training at a private sports academy. This same point can be illustrated by comparing students involved in a soccer league for several years with students who have never played the game. Teachers face a difficult challenge when trying to motivate students with such diverse backgrounds.

A second concern relates to public opinion. As opportunities in the private sector increase, public support for the school physical education curricula may lessen. Some people currently believe that secondary school physical education programs can be eliminated because there are adequate opportunities available in the private sector. "Let students learn physical activities outside the school setting so there is more time and money for academic subjects" is a viewpoint often voiced. An opposing viewpoint argues that private instruction opportunities are available only to the upper-middle class and that lower socioeconomic groups will have limited opportunities. Physical educators need to find ways to use the specialized private sector opportunities to enhance the physical education experience for all students in their programs. There are ways to take students to these opportunities and bring these programs to the schools. The trend toward private instruction is continuing to grow, and the possibility is strong that the private sports industry may become a serious competitor of school programs. Physical educators face the challenge of developing quality programs that provide meaningful learning experiences for all students regardless of background.

Equipment, Facilities, and Class Size

A continuing problem that physical educators at all levels face is inadequate equipment and facilities. For some reason, many administrators believe that physical education classes can be larger in number and yet manage with less equipment than an academic class. They fail to realize that it is impossible to learn to dribble a basketball without having access to a basketball on a regular basis. Students become frustrated and bored when standing in line waiting for a turn to dribble the ball. Teachers have a difficult situation with 40 students on six tennis courts. Economic conditions make these problems difficult, and physical educators must strive to get a fair share of the budget. Students are not asked to learn to read and write without books, paper, and pencils. Physical education is as important as other discipline areas and should receive an equal share of the budget dollar.

Legal Liability

Many lawsuits appearing in various aspects of society concern physical educators. Teachers are not immune to liability lawsuits, as evidenced by an increasing number of cases involving parents and students suing teachers, administrators, and school boards. This situation is unnerving when teachers attempt new activities or use new teaching techniques that involve any type of risk. Many teachers and administrators have become extremely cautious and conservative about activities that contain an element of risk, yet often many of these activities are actually safer than those traditionally included in the curriculum. Teachers may refuse to offer new activities for fear of a lawsuit. Ultimately, students become the victims in this process because programs become limited in scope.

Teachers certainly need to acquire adequate knowledge about safety and instructional procedures before implementing a new activity. Legal ramifications must be understood when developing a broad and balanced curriculum. With proper information and careful planning, the instructional risks of various activities can be minimized. If sound policies and procedures are followed on a daily basis, teachers should not worry about legal liability. An in-depth discussion of legal liability can be found in Chapter 12.

Teaching and Coaching Conflicts

The public often has a difficult time separating the physical education program from the athletic program. The athletic program is concerned with recruiting, coaching, and administering teams that will compete against other school teams. These goals are significantly different from the goals of the secondary school physical education program, yet athletics and physical education are often linked because the programs share facilities, equipment, fields, and teachers.

In addition, pressure often comes from the local community to produce winning teams. Pressure to develop outstanding physical education programs is not nearly as strong, and the visibility of the two programs is markedly different. This creates a difficult situation for the physical education teacher who is also a coach. The coach may support the concept of an outstanding curriculum but may not find enough time and energy to do both, causing physical education to take a backseat. This problem has no simple solution. Many teachers want to work in both programs. The pressure to produce winners is apparent, and the individual instructor will determine the quality of the physical education program that is implemented. Many people do excellent work in both areas, but it is not an easy task.

ESSENTIAL COMPONENTS OF A QUALITY PROGRAM

Physical education teachers need to know the essential components of a quality physical education program. In other words, what are critical elements that should be included to ensure that youngsters receive a quality physical education experience? The following components interlock to form a comprehensive physical education program that will be valued by parents, teachers, and students. Each of the components is described briefly in this section. In-depth coverage is offered in the referenced chapters under each point. Figure 1.5 identifies eight essential components of a quality program.

■ *A quality physical education program is organized around content standards that offer direction and continuity to instruction and evaluation.* A quality program is driven by a set of content standards. These standards are defined by a number of competencies youngsters are expected to accomplish. Standards are measurable so both teachers and students know when progress has been made. Previously in this chapter you read about a comprehensive set of physical education content standards. Chapter 10 offers a number of assessment strategies for checking to see if you and your students are meeting the standards.

■ *A quality program is student centered and based on the developmental urges, characteristics, and interests of students.* Students learn best when the skills and activities they must learn match their physical and emotional development. Including activities in the program because they match the competencies of the teacher is not a criterion. Teachers have to teach new activities

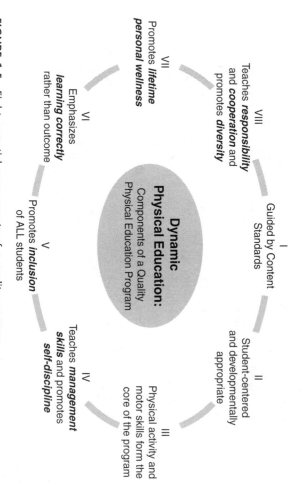

outside their comfort zone if they are going to present a comprehensive program. See Chapter 3 to learn about the characteristics and interests of students and how they impact the creation of a quality physical education program. Chapter 5 offers many ideas for understanding and teaching to the personal needs of students. A quality program focuses on the successes of students so there is motivation to continue. Developing a positive set of behaviors toward physical activity is a key goal of physical education. Chapter 5 also discusses essential elements of teaching and how to positively reinforce students during learning situations.

■ *Quality physical education makes physical activity and motor-skill development the core of the program.* Physical education is the only place in the total school curriculum where instruction is focused on teaching motor skills. Physical education is a unique discipline that focuses on physical activity to ensure the physical development of students. It is mandatory that the program focus on skill development and quality physical activity. Chapters 2, 15, and 16 explain the importance of physical activity for the optimal growth and development of youngsters.

■ *Physical education programs teach management skills and self-discipline.* Physical education teachers are usually evaluated based on how students in their classes behave. Administrators and parents look to see that students are on task and receiving many opportunities to learn new

FIGURE 1.5 Eight essential components of a quality program
Reprinted from R. P. Pangrazi, *Dynamic Physical Education for Elementary School Children*, 15th ed. (p. 20), with permission from Benjamin Cummings. Copyright © 2007 by Pearson Benjamin Cummings.

Dynamic Physical Education: Components of a Quality Physical Education Program

I Guided by Content Standards

II Student-centered and developmentally appropriate

III Physical activity and motor skills form the core of the program

IV Teaches *management skills* and promotes *self-discipline*

V Promotes *inclusion* of ALL students

VI Emphasizes *learning correctly* rather than outcome

VII Promotes *lifetime personal wellness*

VIII Teaches *responsibility* and *cooperation* and promotes *diversity*

skills. When a class is well managed and students work with self-discipline, the experience compares to classroom instruction, bringing credibility to the program. Chapter 7 offers many different methods for teaching management skills and promoting self-discipline.

■ *Quality programs emphasize inclusion of all students.* Instruction is designed for students who need help the most, less-skilled youngsters, and students with disabilities. Students who are skilled and blessed with innate ability have many opportunities to learn. They have the confidence to take private lessons, join clubs, and play in after-school sport programs. Unskilled youngsters or children with disabilities may lack confidence and often are unable to help themselves. Physical education is most likely the last opportunity youngsters will have to learn skills in a caring and positive environment. Instructional progressions designed to help youngsters whose ability places them in the lower 70 percent of the class ensure a positive experience for all. Students who aren't naturally gifted must feel successful if they are expected to enjoy and value physical activity. See Chapter 11 for dealing with youngsters who have disabilities and modifying activities so all children can be successful.

■ *In a quality physical education setting, instruction focuses on the process of learning skills rather than the product or outcome of the skill performance.* When youngsters are learning new motor skills, performing the skill correctly is more important than the outcome of the skill. Youngsters need to learn proper techniques first and then focus on the product of the skill performance. This means teaching a youngster to catch a softball properly rather than worrying about how many he or she catches or misses. Chapter 5 offers strategies for optimizing skill learning. Chapter 10 helps explain when to focus on the process or product evaluation of motor skills.

■ *A quality physical education program teaches lifetime activities that students can use to promote their health and personal wellness.* Quality physical education programs prepare youngsters to participate in activities that they can perform when they become adults. If a program is restricted to team sports, the program will be of little value to the majority of adults. Participation in sport activities declines rapidly with age. Less than 5 percent of adults above the age of 30 report playing a team sport (USDHHS, 1996). By far, walking is the most often reported activity in adulthood. Other activities such as stretching exercises, bicycling, strength development exercises, jogging, swimming, and aerobics are also popular with adults. Quality physical education looks to the future and offers activities youngsters can enjoy and use as adults. Chapters 15 and 16 offer information about the importance of teaching lifetime physical activity skills in a physical education setting. Chapter 17 offers instructional strategies for teaching health and wellness.

■ *Quality physical education teaches cooperative and responsibility skills and helps students develop sensitivity to diversity and gender issues.* Cooperative skills precede competitive skills. Students have to agree to follow rules in order to enjoy group activities. The majority of fights and physical violence occur when youngsters are in a physical activity setting. Physical education is an effective laboratory for learning to behave responsibly because behavior is so observable to others. Situations in physical activity give rise to the need to resolve conflicts in a peaceful manner. Chapter 7 presents ways to teach youngsters responsible behavior and conflict resolution techniques. Students need to learn about similarities and differences between cultures. Competitive activities such as the Olympics often bring cultures together and offer students the opportunity to see different cultures compete with respect and dignity. Coeducational activities help students understand how activities cut

across gender and stereotypes. When gender differences occur in physical activities, it is an excellent time to point out that individuals differ regardless of race or gender. Chapter 6 offers a number of strategies for dealing with gender and diversity issues.

CHARACTERISTICS OF SUCCESSFUL PHYSICAL EDUCATION PROGRAMS

There are many ways to design and implement a quality physical education program. As discussed earlier, a number of factors impact physical education programs. A wide spectrum of possibilities makes the accomplishment of a quality program possible. The following are characteristics that seem to be found in successful programs regardless of the model or design of the curriculum.

A Positive Learning Environment Exists

The instructor is the most important factor in the learning environment. Regardless of the teaching method or curriculum design, a perceptive, analytical teacher is paramount to student learning. An effective teacher creates a teaching–learning atmosphere that is both positive and caring. Instructional procedures are planned carefully so students experience immediate success. The instructor's reactions to student failure are kept minimal and momentary. Instruction focuses feedback and reactions on positive student behaviors rather than using a "correction complex" that responds only to students' mistakes. Effective teachers realize they must take an active role in the teaching–learning process by demonstrating, participating, encouraging, giving feedback, and hustling. Teachers who incorporate physical activities into their lifestyles influence students significantly.

Competent teachers use positive methods to discipline, teach, and motivate. Students are taught to enjoy physical education instead of learning to avoid the environment. Running and exercise are not used as a form of punishment. Students are rewarded for competitive efforts even if their team happens to lose on a given day. Teachers use students' first names and interact with all students on a daily basis. Students are offered a degree of choice and freedom in the learning process in an effort to increase student motivation.

Research on teaching continues to provide information about ways effective teachers impact the teaching–learning process (Siedentop and Tannehill, 2000). Modeling behavior is an effective strategy for influencing specific types of student behavior. Guidelines concerning how to model have long been available. Students want to see models of persons who have incorporated physical activity in their lifestyles. Teachers can discuss their exercise habits with students and allow students to see them participating in and enjoying physical activity. Influential teachers are aware of the powerful effect their behavior has on students and use modeling to help students develop healthy activity habits.

Enthusiasm is another behavior that promotes a positive environment. Evidence shows that this difficult-to-define behavior is a teaching skill that is associated with student learning. Teachers need to display their love of and excitement for physical activity and their joy in teaching. Expecting students to perform well is another critical factor in developing a positive atmosphere for teaching. If students are expected to be unmotivated and troublesome, then the possibility is strong that these behaviors will occur. If students are expected to learn and work hard, then the chance is better that they will perform at a higher level.

Physical educators need to look carefully at the effects of policies and procedures used in programs. If procedures discourage students from being active, they should be reevaluated. If dress codes and grading procedures are causing students to develop avoidance behaviors, acceptable alternatives must be developed. The overall atmosphere of the physical education environment has a strong impact on students and on their attitude toward physical activity. When students leave the physical education environment, they should have a good feeling about physical activity and a desire to return for more.

Student Choice Is Offered

The elective approach to physical education curricula refers to allowing student choice for an optional or elective year of physical education or allowing students to select between several activity options during each activity interval. For example, students can select tennis, weight training, or soccer during the first 3-week unit, and racquetball, archery, or flag football during the second 3 weeks, and so on. The choice can occur not only during the optional class, but also during a required class. The choice process starts in some schools as early as the middle school, while in others it does not begin until high school. This type of program gives students an opportunity to choose activities of personal interest to them and to avoid activities in which they have little interest. Surveys have shown that some students would not elect to take an extra class of physical education because they wanted to avoid one or two specific units of activity, such as swimming, gymnastics, or wrestling. These students

would sacrifice an entire year of physical education to avoid certain activities. To circumvent this behavior, curriculum planners design elective programs so students can choose from a number of activities.

Another advantage of the elective approach is that students will be more motivated when they have influenced the selection of learning activities (Prusak, Treasure, Darst, and Pangrazi, 2004). Fewer problems occur in the areas of participation and discipline. Having more students involved in the program can also mean more support for teachers, equipment, and facilities. Flexibility in class size is yet another advantage. Certain activities can easily accommodate more students, depending on the equipment and facilities. For example, golf and tennis might have smaller classes than soccer and flag football.

Finally, considering these advantages, many teachers are motivated and enthusiastic about teaching in this type of program. An elective program can improve the motivational level of both students and teachers. Any educational practice that can affect the teaching–learning environment should be considered when developing programs in secondary school physical education. Problems do have to be worked out concerning grades, registration procedures, teaching attitudes, and class-roll procedures. However, several solutions are available to a teaching staff that believes in the advantages of the approach.

Elective programs can be an influence in a positive direction. A number of secondary school physical education programs in secondary school physical education programs that have converted to elective programs have experienced an increase in students. Teachers point out that an elective program offers advantages such as increased student participation, enthusiasm, and motivation, as well as increased enthusiasm and motivation of teachers. Students in the 10th grade and above should be able to select all of their physical activities and not be forced into activities that they are not interested in learning or dislike. Students in middle school might be restricted to choosing from categories of activities such as team sports, lifetime sports, fitness activities, dance, aquatics, and adventure activities to ensure a measure of breadth in activity experiences. If possible, they should be permitted to choose from a number of activities in each category. In the fitness area, for example, they might choose aerobic dance, weight training, or jogging. In the lifetime sport area, the choices might be tennis, golf, or bowling.

A Wide Variety of Activities Are Available

The variety of physical activities available to consumers continues to expand. New and exciting activities such as Frisbee, step aerobics, cooperative games, and rock climbing are included in programs across the country. A broad-based program increases the possibility that all students will find an enjoyable physical activity. Physical education programs should offer as many activities as possible. A balance among team sports, lifestyle sports, dance, aquatics, outdoor activities, and physical-conditioning activities should be a major program goal. The following categories illustrate the wide range of activities that can be incorporated into an exemplary program.

Lifestyle Sports and Activities

This area of activities in the secondary school physical education curriculum continues to grow and evolve. These sports and activities are primarily individual or dual activities that can be used for a lifetime as opposed to team sports that are difficult to continue after the school years. These activities are easily incorporated into a person's lifestyle. An early factor in the development of this concept was the Lifetime Sports Education Project (LSEP), sponsored by the American Alliance for Health, Physical Education, Recreation, and Dance (AAHPERD). LSEP originally focused on bowling, archery, badminton, tennis, and golf. Instructional materials and teaching clinics were developed by LSEP to encourage physical educators to expand their curricula.

Today, lifestyle sports and activities have become tremendously popular and have been expanded to include a host of new activities, such as walking, Frisbee, racquetball, sand volleyball, and even lunchtime basketball. AAHPERD estimates that 75 percent of the nation's secondary schools emphasize lifestyle sports in their physical education programs. This expanded offering has provided many participation opportunities for students and adults who are not interested in traditional team sports. Secondary school physical education programs are better able to serve **all** students when a wide variety of lifestyle sports and activities are offered, considering different students are successful and motivated with different activities.

Outdoor Adventure Activities

Another category of activity that has continually gained popularity in the past 30 years is the outdoor adventure or wilderness sports. Backpacking, rock climbing, various ropes course activities (Figure 1.6), orienteering, and mountain bicycling are just a few of the activities in this category. These activities are similar to the lifestyle sports or activities and are primarily individual or dual activities that can be enjoyed over a lifetime. The emphasis is on risk and excitement in using the earth's natural environments, such as snow,

FIGURE 1.6 Adventure activities

water, mountains, ice, rivers, and wilderness areas. Exploration, travel, and adventure are important elements in these activities. To train students in outdoor adventure skills, many schools are developing on-campus facilities such as climbing walls, ropes courses, and orienteering sites, as well as using nearby community environments such as ski slopes, parks, rivers, and mountains. These activities emphasize competition with oneself and the environment in contrast to competition with other people. This is an attractive feature for many students. Outdoor adventure activities can also be enjoyed with family and friends during expanded leisure hours. They give people an opportunity to get away from the city and experience the natural environment in a time of vanishing wilderness areas.

Health-Related Physical Activities

The combination of many publications, such as *Physical Activity and Health: A Report of the Surgeon General* (USDHHS, 1996), *Healthy People 2010: National Health Promotion and Disease Objectives* (U.S. Public Health

Service, 2000), and *Physical Activity for Children: A Statement of Guidelines for Children Ages 5–12* (Corbin & Pangrazi, 2004), and the high visibility of the media on leading an active lifestyle has continued to focus attention across the nation on a variety of physical activities and the importance of an active lifestyle for all ages. Aerobic rhythmic exercise, aerobic kickboxing, walking activities, step aerobics, jogging, weight training (Figure 1.7), and weight-control classes are extremely popular with secondary students and adults. Modern fitness centers are being built in high schools and shared with community partners after school hours. Schools are offering a variety of classes called step aerobics, Pilates Method, exercise balls, and aerobics that emphasize topics such as nutrition, weight maintenance, coronary heart disease, flexibility, and strength. Human Kinetics, the Cooper Institute, and AAHPERD joined forces and created the American Fitness Alliance, with updated materials including the Fitnessgram/Activitygram K–12 program (Cooper Institute, 2007), which includes an updated fitness education program that focuses on increasing activity in everyday activities. Also accompanying the Fitnessgram is a program called the Activitygram. This program emphasizes monitoring and recording the amount of moderate physical activity accumulated each day for 3 days. The program prints out a view of the student's activity patterns after all the data have been entered.

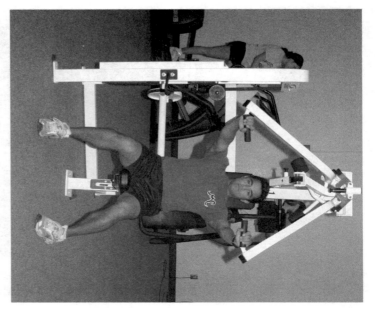

FIGURE 1.7 Weight-lifting class

Novel or Modified Team Sports

Finally, the development of novel or modified team sports is continuing in many schools. Activities such as team handball, Ultimate Frisbee, floor hockey, speed-a-way, broomball, flickerball, angleball, modified lacrosse, and pillow polo are some of the newer team sports variations that are popular in various areas of the country. Some of these are new activities, whereas others are modifications of existing sports. They add another positive dimension to programs because of the increased variety and opportunities for success with certain types of students.

New team sport activities provide many interesting and exciting challenges for both students and instructors. In teaching almost any activity, there may be problems with safety, liability, competent instruction, equipment, and teacher's comfort zones, but the advantages of offering new team sports are well worth the encountered problems. A wide variety of activities should enhance the objective of developing in all students a positive attitude toward a lifetime of physical activity.

Students Receive In-Depth Instruction

Some high schools offer different levels of instruction, such as beginning and intermediate classes. Some schools use the classifications *beginning, team,* and *recreational.* Three-week units are being offered for beginning basketball, team basketball, and recreational basketball. The beginning class covers dribbling, passing, pivoting, rebounding, and so forth, while the team class includes such areas as offensive strategy, zone defenses, and techniques on beating a half-court trap. The final recreational class allows opportunity for team play and tournaments. Students can take three units in a progressive, systematic procedure. An advantage of this approach is that teachers can do a better job of instruction because classes are more homogeneous in motivation and ability. Students usually feel more comfortable in a group in which similar attitudes and abilities prevail.

In grades 10–12, programs should offer intermediate and advanced levels of instruction. Students at these developmental levels choose one or two activities in which they want to excel. Advanced instruction is different from a free-play recreational situation that is commonly found in many programs. Depth refers to organized instruction rather than simply increasing the amount of participation time. Physical educators must move away from the notion that physical education programs should focus only on beginning levels. Many students do not participate in intramural sports, sport clubs, athletics, or outside-school programs; therefore, the physical education program may be the only opportunity to receive in-depth instruction for students. A high level of skill development usually increases a person's tendency to repeat and enjoy an activity.

The length of activity units has shortened over the past decade, especially at the middle school level. In quality programs, 6- to 9-week units are becoming obsolete. In most middle school programs, 2- to 3-week units are the norm. These shorter units enable physical educators to expand the breadth of their programs and to give students an introduction to a wider variety of activities. Some people question this trend because of the reduction in depth of instruction, but students can choose to develop depth in an activity in the high school years. Short units also reduce boredom and frustration, which are common problems among middle school students. With increased program breadth, educators have a better opportunity to provide students with some type of physical activity that they can enjoy and continue to use.

Depth in an activity is made available in high school curricula by allowing students to choose a semester-long unit. This specialized approach is part of an elective or optional program instead of a required program. Semester-long classes give students a chance to gain in-depth skill in an activity of their choice after they complete the required program. Many schools are offering semester- or year-long units focusing on popular activities such as fitness center classes, cardio combinations, lifetime racquet sports, and weight training. The middle school program provides breadth of activity while the high school program gives students the opportunity to develop a high level of skill competency.

Diagnostic and Counseling Practices Are Evident

Students in middle school need guidance and counseling to direct them toward activities that match their interests and physical abilities. Teachers can help students understand their physical strengths and short-comings and the possibilities for alleviating problems. This means data collection and the procedures for interpreting the data to students and parents. Obese and overweight students, for example, might be channeled into activities in which they can find success and feel competent. Students with strong upper bodies might be encouraged to try activities that involve strength. Activity counseling can help students make wise decisions about activities that are well suited to their abilities and will help them address problem areas.

High school students also need to learn about the benefits of physical activity and the types of activities

available. They can use counseling in several other areas, such as behavioral self-modification techniques to aid them in the change and maintenance of activity habits. Students should understand environmental factors and obstacles that work against their attempts to participate in physical activities. Employment parameters, marriage, children, and climate are factors that affect activity lifestyles. Learning to keep records, set goals, and establish reinforcement procedures can help students with their activity habits. Another important area of activity counseling deals with changing interests and activities of people as they grow older. Many adults have been conditioned to think that physical activity is only for the young. This attitude needs to change in light of the revelation that numerous benefits are derived from being active at all age levels. Fitness and play activities are important regardless of age.

Some secondary schools have designed a series of compulsory units that require students to assess their physical abilities and make decisions about physical activities that offer them success and remediate weaknesses. A counseling program helps channel students into physical education activities that can enhance their strengths and alleviate weaknesses. The testing and counseling procedures should be set up in a systematic, organized fashion. A physical education advisor should be assigned to each student to guide her or him through the process in an attempt to give students information on which they can base sound decisions about their future. Counseling students combined with implementing the previously described elective program is an effective way to fuse students' interests with their physical ability requirements. This model provides a blend of information about physical activity and gives students experiences in improving physical skills and physical fitness. Students should leave the program with approach tendencies for physical activity instead of avoidance behaviors.

All Activity Programs Are Integrated

Activity programs such as sport clubs, intramural sports, and interscholastic athletics can effectively help students improve their skills and become more proficient. Such programs also provide opportunities for young people to meet others with similar interests. A variety of important qualities can be experienced through these programs (e.g., teamwork, dedication, perseverance, deferred rewards, and loyalty). These qualities should be nurtured in today's youth.

School activity programs include youth sport, YMCA, Parks and Recreation, and private sport programs. When possible, physical educators should contribute to the leadership aspects of programs that augment physical education. Strong leadership ensures the quality of these programs and guards against possible abuses. Unqualified leaders with inappropriate program goals can lead to a discouraging experience for young, immature students. Programs must be developed with the idea of fostering a love of physical activity in students (rather than promoting escape or avoidance behaviors). Physical educators should help parents, other teachers, and adults organize these programs with the proper goals in mind.

STUDY STIMULATORS AND REVIEW QUESTIONS

1. Describe the public's general perception of physical education.

2. Explain physical education's unique contribution to the lives of students.

3. What is the role of the National Standards for Physical Education?

4. Describe the relationship between "knowing about fitness" and "engaging in physical activity."

5. Explain why physical education is an excellent environment for teaching students about responsible behavior.

6. How would you use the public health perspective to defend physical education as a subject in the schools?

7. Describe four essential components of a quality physical education program.

8. Explain the limitations of a curriculum dominated by team sports.

9. List and discuss strategies that teachers can use to develop positive attitudes toward physical activity in their students.

10. Describe five characteristics of successful physical education programs.

REFERENCES AND SUGGESTED READINGS

American Alliance for Health, Physical Education, Recreation, and Dance and Cooper Institute for Aerobics Research. (1995). *The you stay active handbook*. Reston, VA: AAHPERD and Dallas, TX: The Cooper Institute for Aerobics Research.

Bailey, D. A., Faulkner, R. A., & McKay, H. A. (1996). Growth, physical activity, and bone mineral acquisition. *Exercise and Sport Science Reviews, 24,* 233–266.

Bar-Or, O. (1995). Health benefits of physical activity during childhood and adolescence. *Physical Activity and Fitness Research Digest, 2*(4), 1–6.

Burgeson, C. R., Wechsler, H., Brener, N. D., Young, J. C., & Spain, C. G. (2001). Physical education and activity: Results from the school health policies and programs study (SHPPS) 2000. *Journal of School Health, 71*(7), 279–293.

Centers for Disease Control and Prevention. (2006). Youth risk behavior surveillance—United States, 2005. *Morbidity & Mortality Weekly Report (MMWR), 55*(SS5), 1–108.

Cooper Institute, Meredith, M. & Welk, G., (Eds.). (2007). *Fitnessgram/Activitygram test administration manual* (3rd ed.).

Corbin, C., & Lindsey, R. (2007). *Fitness for life* (updated 5th ed.). Champaign, IL: Human Kinetics Publishers.

Corbin, C., & Pangrazi, R. (2004). *Physical activity for children: A statement of guidelines for children ages 5–12.* Reston, VA: NASPE.

Corbin, C. B., Pangrazi, R. P., & Welk, G. (1994). Toward an understanding of appropriate physical activity levels for youth. *Physical Activity and Fitness Research Digest, 2*(2), 1–8.

Darst, P., & Armstrong, G. (1991). *Outdoor adventure activities for school and recreation programs.* Prospect Heights, IL: Waveland Press.

Eitzen, D. S., & Sage, G. (1986). *Sociology of North American sport.* Dubuque, IA: W. C. Brown.

Ferraro, K. F., Thorpe, R. J., Jr., & Wilkinson, J. A. (2003). The life course of severe obesity: Does childhood overweight matter? *Journal of Gerontology, 58B*(2), S110–S119.

Fitness Products Council (1999). *U.S. participation in fitness activities, 1987–1998.* North Palm Beach, FL: Sporting Goods Manufacturers Association.

Gortmaker, S. L., Must, A., Sobol, A. M., Peterson, K., Colditz, G. A., & Dietz, W. H. (1996). *Archives of Pediatric Adolescent Medicine, 150,* 356–362.

Guo, S. S., & Chumlea, W. C. (1999). Tracking of body mass index in children in relation to overweight in adulthood. *American Journal of Clinical Nutrition, 70,* 145S–148S.

Guo, S. S., Roche, A. F., Chumlea, W. C., Gardner, J. D., & Siervogel, R. M. (1994). The predictive value of childhood body mass index values for overweight at age 35 y. *American Journal of Clinical Nutrition, 59,* 810–819.

Hellison, D. (2003). *Teaching responsibility through physical activity* (2nd ed.). Champaign, IL: Human Kinetics Publishers.

Jebb, S. A., & Moore, M. S. (1999). Contribution of a sedentary lifestyle and inactivity to the etiology of overweight and obesity: Current evidence and research issues. *Medicine and Science in Sports and Exercise, 31,* S534–S541.

Morgan, C. (2004). *A longitudinal study of the relationships between physical activity, body mass index, and physical self-perception in youth.* Unpublished dissertation, Arizona State University.

Morgan, C. F., Pangrazi, R. P., & Beighle, A. (2003). Using pedometers to promote physical activity in physical education. *Journal of Physical Education Recreation and Dance, 74*(7), 33–38.

Must, A., Jacques, P. F., Dallal, G. E., Bajema, C. J., & Dietz, W. H. (1992). Long-term morbidity and mortality of overweight adolescents: A follow-up of the Harvard Growth Study of 1922 to 1935. *New England Journal of Medicine, 327,* 1350–1355.

National Association for Sport and Physical Education. (1992). *Outcomes of Quality Physical Education Programs.* Reston, VA: AAHPERD.

National Association for Sport and Physical Education. (1995). *Moving Into the Future—National Standards for Physical Education: A Guide to Content and Assessment.* St. Louis, MO: Mosby.

National Association for Sport and Physical Education. (2002). *Shape of the Nation 2001: A Survey of State Physical Education Requirements.* Reston, VA: AAHPERD.

National Association for Sport and Physical Education. (2004). *Moving into the future: National standards for physical education* (2nd ed.). Reston, VA: Author.

National Association for Sport and Physical Education. (2004). *Physical activity for children: A statement of guidelines* (2nd ed.). Reston, VA: Author.

National Association for Sport and Physical Education. (2005). *Physical Best Activity Guide: Middle and High School Levels.* (2nd ed.) Champaign, Il: Human Kinetics Publishers.

National Center for Health Statistics. (2004). *Health, United States, 2004 with chartbook on trends in the health of Americans.* Hyattsville, MD.

Ogden, C. L., Carroll, M. D., Curtain, L. R., McDowell, M. A., Tabak, C. J., & Flegal, K. M. (2006). Prevalence of overweight and obesity in the United States, 1999–2004. *Journal of the American Medical Association, 295,* 1549–1555.

Pangrazi, R. P. (2007). *Dynamic physical education for elementary school children* (15th ed.). San Francisco: Benjamin Cummings.

Prusak, K., Treasure, D., Darst, P., & Pangrazi (2004). The effects of choice on the motivation of adolescent girls in physical education. *Journal of Teaching in Physical Education, 23*(1), 19–29.

Raitakari, O. T., Porkka, K. V. K., Taimela, S., Telama, R., Rasanen, L., & Viikari, J. S. A. (1994). Effects of persistent physical activity and inactivity on coronary risk factors in children and young adults. *American Journal of Epidemiology, 140,* 195–205.

Sallis, J. F. (1994). Influences on physical activity of children, adolescents, and adults or determinants of active learning. *Physical Activity and Fitness Research Digest, 1*(7), 1–8.

Sallis, J. F., & McKenzie, T. L. (1991). Physical education's role in public health. *Research Quarterly for Exercise and Sport, 62,* 124–137.

Sallis, J. F., McKenzie, T. L., Kolody, B., Lewis, M., Marshall, S., & Rosengard, P. (1999). Effects of health-related physical education on academic achievement: Project SPARK. *Research Quarterly for Exercise and Sport, 70,* 127–134.

Siedentop, D., and Tannehill, D. (2000). *Developing teaching skills in physical education* (4th ed.). Mountain View, CA: Mayfield Publishing.

Sporting Goods Manufacturers Association. (2000, May/June). *Fitness and Sports Newletter.*

Telama, R., Yang, X., Laakso, L., & Viikari, J. (1997). Physical activity in childhood and adolescence as predictors of physical activity in young adulthood. *American Journal of Preventative Medicine, 13,* 317–323.

Trudeau, F., Laurencelle, L., Tremblay, J., Rajic, M., & Shephard, R. J. (1998). A long-term follow-up of participants in the Trois-Rivieres semi-longitudinal study of growth and development. *Pediatric Exercise Science, 10,* 366–377.

U.S. Department of Health and Human Services. (1996). *Physical activity and health: A report of the surgeon general.* Atlanta, GA: U.S. Department of Health and Human Services, Centers for Disease Control and Prevention, National Center for Chronic Disease Prevention and Health Promotion.

U.S. Department of Health and Human Services. (2002). *Prevalence of overweight among children and adolescents: United States, 1999.* Atlanta, GA: Centers for Disease Control and Prevention, National Center for Health Statistics.

U.S. Department of Health and Human Services. (2000). *Healthy people 2010: National health promotion and disease objectives.* Washington, DC: U.S. Government Printing Office.

U.S. Public Health Service. (1990). *Healthy people 2000: National health promotion and disease objectives.* Washington, DC: U.S. Government Printing Office.

Whitaker, R. C., Wright, J. A., Pepe, M. S., Seidel, K. D., & Dietz, W. H. (1997). Predicting obesity in young adulthood from childhood and parental obesity. *New England Journal of Medicine, 337,* 869–873.

Williams, J. F. (1927). *The principles of physical education.* Philadelphia: W. B. Saunders.

WEB SITES

American Alliance for Health, Physical Education, Recreation and Dance
www.aahperd.org

American Heart Association
www.americanheart.org

Centers for Disease Control and Prevention
www.cdc.gov

Fitness for Life
www.FitnessforLife.org

Fitnessgram/Activitygram
www.Fitnessgram.net

Human Kinetics
www.HumanKinetics.com

National Association for Sport and Physical Education
www.aahperd.org/naspe

Physical Education Teaching and Curriculum Information
www.pecentral.com
www.pelinks4u.org
www.pe4life.org

ESSENTIAL COMPONENTS OF A QUALITY PROGRAM

COMPONENT 1 A quality physical education program is organized around content standards that offer direction and continuity to instruction and evaluation.

COMPONENT 2 A quality program is student centered and based on the developmental urges, characteristics, and interests of students.

COMPONENT 3 Quality physical education makes physical activity and motor-skill development the core of the program.

COMPONENT 4 Physical education programs teach management skills and self-discipline.

COMPONENT 5 Quality programs emphasize inclusion of all students.

COMPONENT 6 In a quality physical education setting, instruction focuses on the process of learning skills rather than the product or outcome of the skill performance.

COMPONENT 7 A quality physical education program teaches lifetime activities that students can use to promote their health and personal wellness.

COMPONENT 8 Quality physical education teaches cooperative and responsibility skills and helps students develop sensitivity to diversity and gender issues.

2

The Impact of
Physical Activity
on Adolescents

CHAPTER SUMMARY

This chapter offers an overview of the impact of physical activity on the growing adolescent. The chapter also looks at important research and cites empirical evidence supporting the value of an active lifestyle in promoting optimum growth and development of secondary school students. Differences in growth patterns and maturation rates of students impact the physical performance of youth. Additionally, the needs of overweight youth are discussed and methodology is presented for teaching them in a manner that promotes increased physical activity. Promoting lifestyle activity is an important outcome for quality physical education programs.

STUDENT OUTCOMES

After reading the chapter, you will be able to:

- Discuss how physical maturity affects the physical skills of students.

- Identify the impact of regular physical activity on adolescent students.

- Describe the general health and activity status of students in American schools.

- Explain the harmful effects that being overweight can have on the health and well-being of a student.

- Defend physical education with research and empirical evidence that is available.

Student Outcomes, continued

- Identify principles to follow for exercising safely in warm climates.
- Describe a safe approach for distance running with adolescent students.

With the publication of *Healthy People 2000* (U.S. Public Health Service, 1990), members of the public health community in the United States began to focus on physical activity as a method of chronic disease prevention. The emphasis on physical activity apparent in this statement of goals led public health experts to propose a change in focus for physical education programs (Sallis & McKenzie, 1991; Simons-Morton, Taylor, Snider, Huang, & Fulton, 1994). Subsequently, a host of public statements have focused on the "health foundations" or "public health" approach.

- *NASPE National Standards for Physical Education* (2004). NASPE has defined a physically educated person with six major standards. These standards emphasize being active, knowing the benefits of physical activity, and developing skills to support physical activity.

- *American Heart Association Statement on Lifestyle Physical Activity* (1992). This early statement focused the attention of the medical and public health communities on the importance of physical activity for good health.

- *Physical Activity and Health: A Report of the Surgeon General (U.S. Department of Health and Human Services [USDHHS], 1996).* This report describes the importance of physical activity in chronic disease prevention and the importance of physical education in promoting physical activity among youth. The report notes a decrease in physical education programs in the United States in the last decade of the 20th century.

- *Centers for Disease Control and Prevention Guidelines for Physical Activity Promotion for Children and Youth* (1997). These guidelines outline methods of promotion of physical activity for children and youth. Promoting activity in the school setting is central to these guidelines.

- *NASPE Physical Activity Guidelines for Children* (2004). This statement extends public health goals and outlines activity guidelines based specifically on the needs of children and youth (see Chapter 16).

- *Health Education Authority Statement on Physical Activity for Children* (1998). This British governmental statement provides guidelines for children similar to those proposed by NASPE.

- *Physical Activity Guidelines for Adolescents: Consensus Statement (Sallis & Patrick, 1994).* This consensus statement (from an international conference) outlines physical activity guidelines for adolescents.

- *Healthy People 2010: National Health Promotion and Disease Objectives (U.S. Public Health Service, 2000).* As was the case for the earlier goals for the year 2000, this report contains physical activity goals central to health promotion and chronic disease prevention. Included are national goals for physical activity promotion for youth and national goals for increasing physical education in the schools.

- *American College of Sports Medicine Guidelines for Exercise Testing and Prescription (2000).* This most recent set of guidelines places new emphasis on the importance of lifestyle physical activity to healthy living.

These statements provide the basis for a consistent and repeated challenge for physical education programs, especially if the goal is to teach youngsters how to maintain an active lifestyle that promotes health and vitality. Administrators and school boards often feel physical education is a subject to be taught only after all other subjects have received adequate coverage and support. Schools teach youth how to achieve academically in order to live a productive life, and few question the importance of learning to read and write. However, there is no higher priority in life than health. Without it, all other skills lack meaning and utility. The science is clear and is well documented in the reports noted in the list presented in the previous section. However, the Surgeon General's report on *Physical Activity and Health* (USDHHS, 1996) documents the health benefits of physical activity as evidenced by these major conclusions:

- People of all ages, both male and female, benefit from regular physical activity.

- Significant health benefits can be obtained by adults who perform moderate physical activity (e.g., 30 minutes of brisk walking or raking leaves, 15 minutes of running, or 45 minutes of playing volleyball) on most, if not all, days of the week (see Chapter 16 for guidelines for children and adolescents).

Physical Fitness	Physical Activity
Youth who fail an item on a fitness test are labeled unfit even though they may not be able to rectify the situation.	Youth who are inactive can become active. Becoming more active is easy to understand and achieve.
Physical fitness performance is strongly impacted by genetic endowment.	All youngsters can become physically active regardless of their physical limitations.
Physical fitness performance is usually reviewed in a comparative manner.	Physical activity goals can be reached in many different ways, making them personal accomplishments.
Physical fitness is usually a short-term goal for youngsters.	Physical activity focuses on long-term lifestyle goals.
Physical fitness is difficult to assess. Even the best tests are not highly reliable and valid.	Physical activity goals can be monitored in many ways, such as amount of time, number of steps, and activity recall.
It is difficult to assign physical fitness workouts as homework since the workloads are very dependent on the individual.	Physical activity can easily be assigned to students, and they can personalize it to fit their needs.

FIGURE 2.1   Physical fitness versus physical activity outcomes for youth

- Additional health benefits are gained through greater amounts or intensities of physical activity. People who can maintain a regular regimen that is of longer duration or of more vigorous intensity are likely to derive the greatest benefit.

- Physical activity reduces the risk of premature mortality in general and of coronary heart disease, diabetes mellitus, hypertension, and colon cancer in particular. Physical activity also improves mental health and is important for the health of muscles, bones, and joints.

Never before has a body of research been compiled to show the strong need for physical activity in the lives of youth. Activity programs are a requisite for healthy youngsters. Physical education today has a clearer mandate than ever to play an important role in the total school curriculum. The fitness and activity program must produce an enjoyable and positive social experience so youth develop a positive attitude toward activity.

For years, schools have focused on training students and raising their fitness levels. As we have shown, this has been an unsuccessful venture because of genetic limitations and the emotional makeup of youngsters. Promoting and encouraging physical activity is an outcome that can be accomplished by all youth regardless of ability or personal interests. Participating in moderate activity decreases the risk of morbidity and mortality if continued throughout the life span (Kujala, Kaprio, Sarna, & Koskenvuo, 1998). Additionally, youth who are active at 3 or 4 years of age are more active as adults (Pate, Baranowski, Dowda, & Trost, 1996). Regular activity for youth increases the probability of an active adult lifestyle (Raitakari et al., 1994). Finally, physical activity benefits those youngsters who need it the most—the unskilled and overweight youngsters. These students often find it difficult to play in sports that demand coordination, speed, and quickness. However, they can be successful in walking, swimming, and biking programs that promote a level of participation to be maintained throughout the life span. Figure 2.1 compares and contrasts the focus on physical fitness versus physical activity.

While we know a lot about physical activity and how to promote it, especially among adults, we know little about the effectiveness of secondary school physical education in promoting physical activity among adolescents. There has been a decrease in physical education programs in high schools in the United States (USDHHS, 1996; Morrow, Jackson, & Payne, 1999). This suggests that most parents and school officials do not value physical education programs and do not see physical education as an effective means of achieving national health goals. Results of Project Active Teen (Dale, Corbin, & Cuddihy, 1998; Dale & Corbin, 2000) provide evidence that secondary programs can promote long-term activity adherence. High school students who completed a health-based physical education program including classroom study and physical activity participation were more likely to meet national health goals for activity several years after completing their physical education requirement than those who took traditional physical education. Stone, McKenzie, Welk, and Booth (1998) describe other school-based interventions that were designed to promote life-span physical activity. Several large-scale intervention projects designed to promote physical activity are currently being conducted under governmental grant sponsorship to test the activity promotion capabilities of physical education. One such project, Targeting Teenaged Girls, is designed to focus on promoting physical activity among teenage girls, a population that has been shown to be susceptible to inactivity as compared to other school-age groups (Centers for Disease Control and Prevention, 1998).

GROWTH AND DEVELOPMENT OF ADOLESCENTS

Adolescence is a time of rapid growth and development. Adolescence is defined here as occurring somewhere between the ages of 8 and 19 for females and 10 to 22 years for males (Malina, 1986). There is much variation in the actual onset of adolescence and entry into adulthood. However, it is during that period of time when the body matures physically and sexually.

Growth patterns are generally controlled by genetic makeup at birth. Although unhealthy parents or poor dietary practices can have a negative impact on proper growth and development, the focus in this section is on normal maturation common to the majority of youngsters. Youngsters follow a general growth pattern; however, each individual's timing is unique. Some students will be advanced physically for their chronological age, whereas others will be identified as slow maturers. Only when aberration from the norm is excessive should teachers and parents become concerned.

Growth Patterns

Growth patterns have a strong impact on success in physical activities. Youngsters who mature early are often better athletes at a young age. However, this may not be the case when all youngsters reach full maturity. Teachers and parents usually want to understand how a youngster is growing compared to others the same age. New weight- and stature (he'ight)-for-age percentiles have been produced for this purpose. Figures 2.2 and 2.3 display stature and weight percentiles that have been developed by the Centers for Disease Control and Prevention (2000). Another method of examining growth patterns is to look at a growth velocity curve for height and weight. The velocity curve is quite useful because it reveals how much a youngster grows on a

year-to-year basis (Figures 2.4 and 2.5, page 33). It is important to note that the growth of boys and girls slows down during the ages of 3 to 7. Slow growth is usually a good time to learn motor skills because learning is not confounded by the changing body parameters such as center of gravity and limb length. In girls, at the age of 9, growth velocity increases rapidly and slows at 12 years. For boys, growth velocity increases at age 11 and peaks at 13. With girls, growth slows down and levels off around the age of 13, as contrasted with boys, who continue to grow rapidly until they are nearly 15. What does all this mean for physical educators?

First, because females reach the adolescent growth spurt first, they often grow taller and heavier during the sixth- and seventh-grade years. Males catch up, however, and grow larger and stronger. When the growth velocity increases in large amounts, the ability to learn motor skills decreases. Because the growth of boys and girls moves at different times and rates, it implies that different strategies for instruction should be used.

Boys continue to grow rapidly through the sophomore year of high school. This often makes it a difficult time for them to learn and perform motor skills. On the other hand, the growth of girls has slowed by the end of the seventh grade, making them more able to learn new skills. Focusing on learning new motor skills should be reduced during periods of rapid growth. It is probably a time to place emphasis on maintaining positive attitudes by focusing on the program and successful performance of skills learned during the earlier years in school.

This rapid growth spurt also brings students a "new" body. They inherit a new center of gravity as they grow "into their head" and their arms and legs increase in length in proportion to their trunk. The head is about 90 percent developed by the age of 6, so as youth enter adolescence, they become much less topheavy. In addition, muscle fiber differentiation now occurs, meaning that adolescents now have slow (aerobic)- and fast (anaerobic)-twitch muscle fibers. The implication is that they may or may not excel at certain types of activities as their muscle physiology changes. Elementary-school-age youngsters do not have muscle fiber differentiation, so youngsters who excel at anaerobic activities also excel at aerobic activities. This is usually not the case in mature individuals; those with more slow-twitch fibers will tend to do better at aerobic activities, while those with a higher proportion of fast-twitch fibers will perform better in anaerobic activities.

These changes make the middle school teacher a major key in helping students continue to feel competent in physical activities. Considering these students have a much different body than they had in elementary school, they must relearn all the skills they were

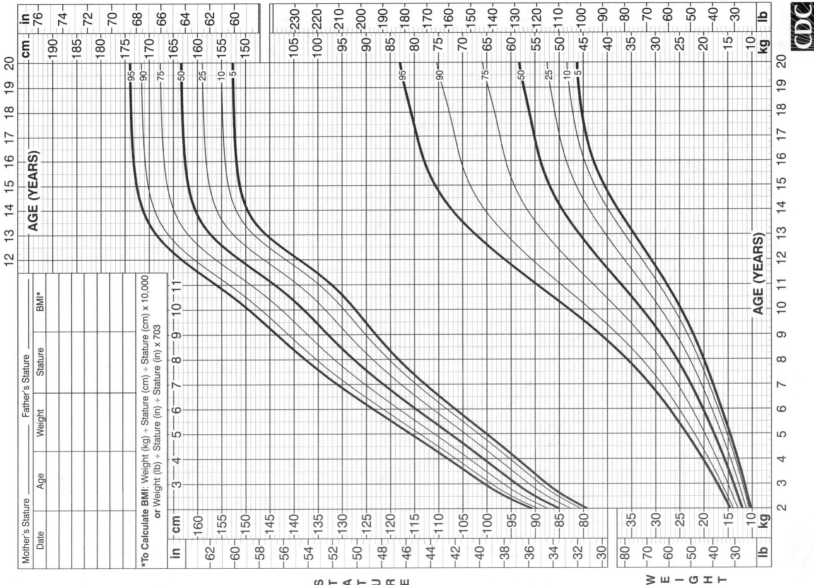

FIGURE 2.2   Stature-for-age and weight-for-age percentiles for girls

Developed by the National Center for Health Statistics in collaboration with the National Center for Chronic Disease Prevention and Health Promotion, 2000.

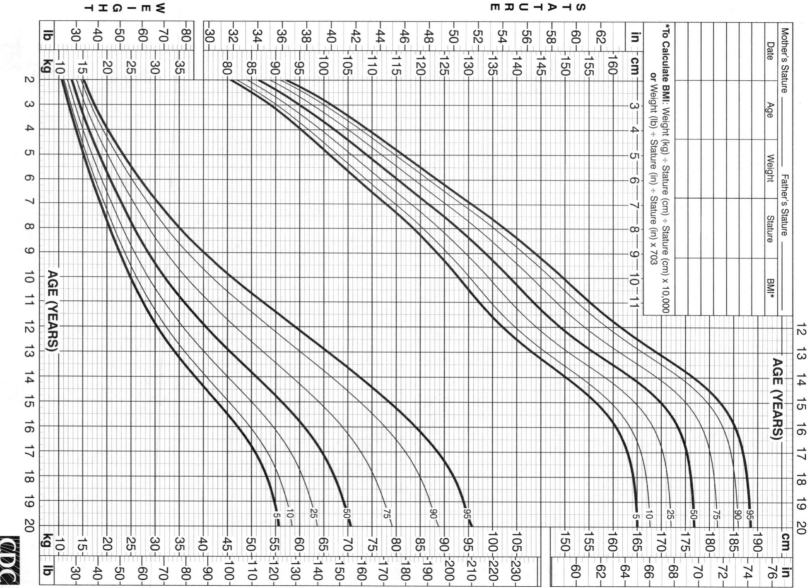

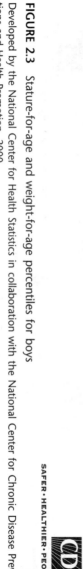

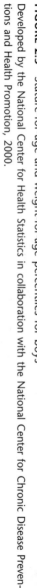

FIGURE 2.3 Stature-for-age and weight-for-age percentiles for boys

Developed by the National Center for Health Statistics in collaboration with the National Center for Chronic Disease Prevention and Health Promotion, 2000.

SAFER · HEALTHIER · PEOPLE™

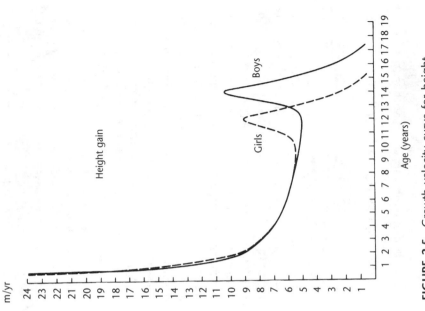

Stature
— Male
-- Female

Weight
— Male
-- Female

FIGURE 2.4 Distance curves for height and weight

From Malina, R. (1975). *Growth and Development: The First Twenty Years in Man.* Minneapolis, MN: Burgess. p. 19.

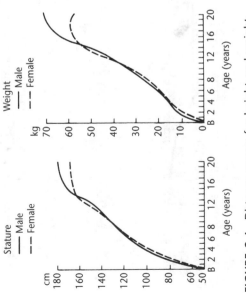

FIGURE 2.5 Growth velocity curve for height

From Tanner, J. M., Whitehouse, R. H., and Takaishi, M. (1966). *Archives of Diseases in Childhood,* 41: 466.

taught previously. Sometimes, it is common to criticize students and elementary physical education teachers by assuming skills were not taught. This is seldom the case; what is a truism is that maturity has changed the perception and performance of previously learned skills. This is a time when middle school teachers must understand what needs to be taught and then proceed to teach the basic skills of throwing, catching, striking, and kicking. With good skill instruction, the middle school years can be a time when students learn what their true abilities are.

Physical Maturity

The concept of maturity is used often by teachers in physical education. Usually, students are identified as being early, late, or average maturers, with teachers referring to social maturity rather than the physical maturity of the youngster. Physical maturity, however, has a strong impact on a student's performance in physical education. The most commonly used method to identify the degree of physical maturity is to compare chronological age with skeletal age. Ossification (hardening) of the bones occurs in the center of the bone shaft and at the ends of the long bones (growth plates). The rate of ossification gives an accurate indication of a youngster's degree of maturation. Physical maturation or skeletal age (which can be identified by X-raying the wrist bones and comparing the development of the subject's bones with a set of standardized X-rays) gives a truer sense of the student's physical maturity (Gruelich & Pyle, 1959; Roche, Chumlea, & Thissen, 1988). If chronological age is greater than skeletal age, the youngster is said to be a late (or slow) maturer. On the other hand, if skeletal age is advanced

beyond chronological age, the student is labeled an early (or fast) maturer.

Early-maturing students of both sexes are generally heavier and taller for their age than average- or late-maturing students. Overweight youngsters are often more mature for their age than are normal-weight youngsters. Early-maturing youngsters also have larger amounts of muscle and bone tissue because of their larger body size. However, the early maturer also carries a greater percentage of body weight as fat tissue (Malina, 1986). Late-maturing youngsters usually catch up to early maturers in height but not in weight. In addition, an early-maturing student in elementary school will also be an early maturer in secondary school. Generally, early-maturing males have mesomorphic physiques, and early-maturing females are characterized by endomorphy. These differences in body size and composition probably account for male-female performance differences in activities that require strength and power.

The motor performance of males is related to skeletal maturity, and more mature youngsters usually perform better on motor tasks (Clarke, 1971). For females, however, motor performance appears to be unrelated to physiological maturity. In fact, a study by Malina (1978) found that in females, late maturation is commonly associated with exceptional motor performance. Because many sports require size and strength, it is likely that male early maturers have a strong advantage in athletic endeavors. This points out the need to design a physical education curriculum that meets the needs of both early and late maturers. Units of instruction that emphasize activities relying less on strength and size and more on aerobic capacity, agility, balance, and coordination need to be included. Instruction often forces students to learn at the same rate or participate in activities with other students regardless of skill level, even though this practice may be detrimental to students who are developing at a faster or slower rate. Teachers sometimes expect youngsters to be capable of performing the same activity at the same time, regardless of maturation. Students do not mature at the same rate and are therefore not at similar levels of readiness to learn. If physical education is for all students, the curriculum needs to offer successful experiences for less-mature youngsters.

The Effect of Activity on Growth Patterns

It appears that activity has little or no impact on the stature of maturing students (Malina, 1986). Some people have theorized that strenuous physical activity disrupts normal developmental patterns, but there is no consistent evidence to support such concerns. Involvement in activity impacts the body composition of participants. The long-term effect of such activity is not known, however, and it is quite possible that once students quit participating, they may return to a body type similar to nonexercisers. A number of studies with teenagers show that short-term training has a strong impact on muscular development (Rowland, 1990). Strength training causes muscular hypertrophy in teenagers in a manner similar to adults. However, if the activity is not continued, lean body mass decreases and fat levels slowly increase.

Physical activity that is high impact (in contrast to swimming) affects skeletal growth by increasing the bone mineral density (Kannus, Haapasalo, Sievanen, Oja, & Vuori, 1994). Vigorous high-impact activity improves internal bone structure so that bones are much more resistant to pressure, tension, and ultimately, to breakage. The bones increase in diameter and density in response to activity. Inactivity for prolonged periods causes demineralization and makes the bones more prone to fracture. This increased bone density developed during adolescence can help guard against osteoporosis in adult life (Haymes, 1986). Peak gain in bone mineral density occurs at 13 to 14 years of age,

and 90 percent of adult bone mineral content is established by the end of adolescence (Bailey, Faulkner, & McKay, 1996). Osteoporosis is a major cause of death and disability in older adults because of skeletal fractures and disfigurement.

Even though activity enhances skeletal density, it does not appear to affect the rate of skeletal maturity. Youngsters who are most mature at an early age will be most mature when evaluated later in adolescence. Exercise ensures optimum growth of bones in maturing youngsters. Care must be taken to ensure that injury to the growth plates of the bones does not occur because of excessive pressure. Strength development should be administered in a progressive and reasonable manner.

Aerobic Capacity

Maximal aerobic power is an individual's maximum ability to use oxygen in the body for metabolic purposes. The oxygen uptake of an individual, all other factors being equal, determines the quality of endurance-oriented performance. Aerobic power increases with chronological age during the elementary school years in males and females at a similar rate, even though males exhibit higher levels as early as the age of 5 (Bar-Or, 1983). At the age of 12, oxygen uptake continues to increase in males and stops improving in females after the age of 14. Because maximal aerobic power is closely related to lean body mass, this tapering off in aerobic power among older females is explained by an increase in reproductive body fat. When aerobic power is related to muscle mass and adjustments are made for body-fat differences, differences in aerobic power are virtually nonexistent between the sexes.

Another method for viewing aerobic power in youngsters is to adjust their maximum oxygen uptake on a per-kilogram-of-body-weight basis. When adjusted in this manner, it shows little change for males (no increase) and a continual decrease for females (Bar-Or, 1983). Again, this decrease among females is in large part caused by an increase in body fat and a proportionate decrease in lean body mass. This lack of increase raises the question as to whether training youngsters increases their aerobic performance.

It appears that, in adolescents, aerobic power can be increased 10 to 20 percent through training. However, not all students respond to training in a similar fashion. In a study by Lortie et al. (1984), 47 young men (17 to 29 years of age) were trained 15 to 20 weeks. Some exhibited almost no change in VO_2 max, while others gained nearly 1 liter of O_2 uptake. This research shows that it is possible to train two youngsters with exactly the same workload and end up with dramatically different results. Often, youth are told they aren't working hard enough when the real issue is their inherited lack of response to training. It points out why focusing on fitness gains is a difficult issue at best. Not all youngsters have the genetic predisposition to improve through training. Grading or rewarding students for improvement that is somewhat out of their control is a simplistic approach to a complicated issue. A better approach is to focus on lifestyle activity and cultivate a positive attitude toward moderate to vigorous physical activity that is accumulated on a daily basis. Positive attitudes toward fitness and activity are more important than training and testing youngsters to see if they can reach their maximum capacity and physical limits. Few adults ever exercise for a lifetime using high-intensity activity that is physically exhausting. A final thought: If physical fitness testing is an important outcome for life, how many adults do you know that test their physical fitness levels on a regular basis?

The Impact of Being Overweight on Aerobic Capacity

Overweight students seldom perform physical activities on a par with leaner youngsters (Bar-Or, 1983). In part, this is because of the greater metabolic cost for an overweight youngster. Overweight students require a higher oxygen uptake cost to perform a given task as compared to lean youngsters. Unfortunately, their capacity is usually lower than that of normal-weight youngsters, making it necessary for them to perform at a higher percentage of their maximum capacity. Because overweight students have to move at a higher percentage of their aerobic capacity, they have less reserve and perceive greater exertion (Bar-Or & Ward, 1989). This lack of reserve probably explains why these youngsters perceive aerobic tasks as demanding and unenjoyable. The task not only feels more demanding, it is more demanding for overweight students.

This increased demand leads to the well-known belief among teachers that "overweight youngsters don't like to run." Some teachers take the approach that the best thing for overweight youngsters is to run hard so they can burn more calories and lose weight. A better first step is to accept that most overweight students are working hard and that workloads must be adjusted accordingly. Because overweight students are often working harder than the normal-weight youngsters, their aerobic demands will be greater. There is no acceptable premise, physiological or psychological, for asking all youngsters to run the same distance regardless of ability. In fact, for many overweight youth, running may be a poor choice of physical activity because of the risk of joint injury.

Workloads for all students need to be based on time rather than distance. Aerobically gifted runners should be expected to move farther than overweight youngsters during a stipulated time period. All students do not and should not have to do the same amount of exercise. Just as one would not expect seventh graders to perform the same workload as that of high school seniors, it is unreasonable to expect all students to perform similar workloads. Exercise programs for overweight subjects should be designed to increase caloric expenditure (emphasize duration of movement) rather than improve cardiovascular fitness (intensity of the movement) (Rowland, 1991). The intensity of the activity should be secondary to the amount of time the student is involved in some type of moderate activity.

Strength

During the elementary school years, muscular strength increases linearly with chronological age (Beunen, 1989) until adolescence, at which time a rapid increase in strength occurs. Strength is related to body size and lean body mass. When differences in strength between the sexes are adjusted for height, there is no difference in lower body strength from age 7 through 17. When the same adjustment between the sexes is made for upper-body strength, however, males have more upper extremity and trunk strength. Males and females can compete on somewhat even terms in activities demanding leg strength, particularly if size and mass are similar. On the other hand, in activities demanding arm or trunk strength, males have a definite advantage, even if they are similar to females in height and mass. These considerations are important when pairing students for competition. Problems can occur if a student is paired with another who is considerably taller and heavier and therefore stronger.

Muscle Fiber Type and Performance

The number of muscle fibers that an individual possesses is genetically predetermined. An increase in muscle size is accomplished by an increase in the size of each muscle fiber. The muscled look of an individual is determined first by the number of fibers and second by the size of the fibers. Skeletal muscle tissue contains fibers that are fast contracting (fast twitch [FT]) and others that are slow contracting (slow twitch [ST]) (Saltin, 1973). The percentage of fast- versus slow-contracting fibers varies from muscle to muscle and among individuals. The percentage of each type of muscle fiber is determined during the first weeks of postnatal life (Dubowitz, 1970). Most individuals are believed to possess about a 50:50 split; that is, half of the muscle fibers are FT and half are ST. A small percentage of people have a ratio of 60-40 (in either direction), and researchers have verified that some people possess an even more extreme ratio.

What is the significance of variation in the ratio of muscle fiber type for physical educators? The ST fibers have a rich supply of blood and related energy mechanisms. This results in a slowly contracting, fatigue-resistant muscle fiber that is well suited to endurance-type (aerobic) activities. In contrast, the FT fibers are capable of bursts of intense activity but are subject to rapid fatigue. These fibers are well suited to activities demanding short-term speed and power (such as pull-ups, the standing long jump, and the shuttle run). The ST fibers would facilitate performance in the mile run or other endurance-oriented activity. On the other hand, the same student may do poorly in a physical education program dominated by team sports that places a premium on quickness and strength. Designing a program that offers activities demanding a wide range of physical attributes (that is, endurance, balance, flexibility) is essential if all students are going to have a successful experience.

Strength and Motor Performance

Strength is an important factor in performing motor skills. A study by Rarick and Dobbins (1975) identified and ranked the factors that contribute to the motor performance of students. The factor identified as most important was strength or power (or both) in relation to body size. Youngsters who demonstrated high levels of strength in relation to their body size were more capable of performing motor skills than were those with lower strength levels.

Deadweight (fat) was the fourth-ranked factor in the motor performance study and was weighted in a negative direction. The more overweight students were, the less proficient they were at performing motor skills. Deadweight acts as a negative factor in motor development because it reduces the student's strength in relation to body size. Overweight students may be stronger than normal-weight youngsters in absolute terms, but they are less strong when strength is adjusted for body weight. This lack of strength causes overweight students to perceive a strength-related task (such as push-ups or sit-ups) as much more difficult than the same task might seem to normal-weight peers. The need for varied workloads accompanied by teacher understanding and empathy is important to ensure that all students have the opportunity for success in strength-related activities. Strength must be developed so youngsters have the tools to find success in motor-development activities.

THE IMPACT OF ACTIVITY ON HEALTH

During the past decade, the interest in physical fitness and increased awareness of the benefits derived from an active lifestyle have spawned a wide assortment of health clubs, a vast array of books and magazines concerning exercise and fitness, and a weekly smorgasbord of distance runs and triathlons. Exercise equipment has been streamlined, and apparel is available for virtually any type of physical activity. Unfortunately, the nation's enthusiasm for physical activity has not affected physical education programs. In 2001, less than 30 percent of high school boys and less than 20 percent of girls had physical education on a daily basis (Grunbaum et al., 2002). Only 32 percent of students reported being active 50 percent of the time while in a physical education class (U.S. Public Health Service, 2000). The discouraging part is that daily physical education continues to decrease, particularly at the high school level. Currently, only 6 percent of middle school students and 5 percent of high school students participate in daily physical education for the entire school year (Burgeson, Wechsler, Brener, Young & Spain, 2001).

The need for activity as an integral part of a healthy lifestyle is strong. Rather than encourage increased activity among youth, many schools have focused on physical fitness testing. This excessive concern about the fitness levels of youth has resulted in a need to "train students to pass fitness tests" to meet district standards. When fitness results become more important than participation in regular activity, students learn that it is more important to focus on short-term goals (fitness test results) rather than a long-term lifestyle (daily activity). Health goals for the nation for the year 2010 (U.S. Public Health Service, 2000) are primarily based on increasing daily levels of physical activity, not fitness levels. Many of the goals directly target schools or programs that can take place within the school setting. These goals are stated in terms of activity objectives rather than fitness objectives, and emphasis is placed on reducing inactivity and increasing light to moderate physical activity.

Emphasis needs to be placed on developing physical education programs that cause lifestyle changes related to increased physical activity to improve health-related fitness (Simons-Morton, Parcel, O'Hara, Blair, & Pate, 1988; Sallis & McKenzie, 1991). Whereas fitness testing has anointed a few gifted students and failed the majority of others, developing programs that change the activity patterns of youth will allow all the opportunity for success and long-term health. Youngsters should be recognized for their willingness to participate rather than their reticence to be tested.

Heart Disease

Coronary heart disease affects more than 5 million people and accounts for 1.5 million heart attacks each year (McGlynn, 1990). The yearly medical costs associated with heart disease in America amount to more than $26 billion (Freedson, 1986). Surely, there can be no greater rationale for increasing the amount of exercise for junior and senior high school students. It has long been believed that heart disease is of geriatric origin and manifests itself only in older adults. In a study by Glass (1973), 5,000 youngsters in the Iowa public schools were examined over a 2-year period. Of these students, 70 percent had symptoms of coronary heart disease, including 7 percent who had extremely high cholesterol levels, a large percentage with high blood pressure, and at least 12 percent who were excessively overweight.

In examining the developmental history of heart disease in humans, Dr. Kenneth Rose (1968) identified the first signs as appearing around the age of 2. The good news is that he also determined that the disease process is reversible until the age of 19. Unfortunately, if youngsters' exercise habits are not altered, they may be burdened with high blood pressure and/or being overweight as they mature into adults. There are no longitudinal studies to document that early control of coronary heart disease risk will reduce the onset of premature death in adult life (Gilliam, MacConnie, Greenen, Pels, & Freedson, 1982). However, it appears that youngsters with high blood pressure, high lipids, and excessive weight tend to retain those high levels into adulthood.

Gilliam, Katch, Thorland, & Weltman (1977) conducted a study that showed the school environment decreases the physical activity of youngsters. Compared to summer activity, youngsters' activity patterns decreased during the school year. A related finding showed that if females were given the opportunity, they would increase their activity to those levels comparable to or above those of most moderately active males. The authors concluded that daily activity patterns can be changed and coronary heart disease decreased through increased cardiovascular activity.

Excessive Weight

Body composition refers to the varying amounts of muscle, bone, and fat within the body. More than half of the fat stored in the body is stored in a layer just below the skin. This is the reason that skinfolds are used to estimate the amount of fat carried within the body. Data gathered for a large study conducted between 1988 and 1994 (U.S. Public Health Service,

2000) showed that 11 percent of adolescents (ages 12–17) are overweight. This is an increase of 6 percent since the last period of observation (1976–1980). Body mass and height directly measured in the National Health and Nutrition Examination Survey (NHANES) shows a 10-percent increase in overweight of 6 through 19 year olds, from approximately 5 percent in 1988–1994 to nearly 15 percent in 1999–2000 (Ogden, Flegal, Carroll, & Johnson, 2002). This increase is occurring at all ages and shows the need to increase the amount of activity youth receive in the school environment.

Being overweight not only decreases a youngster's aerobic performance, but it also has a negative impact on motor performance. The study of overweight issues in adolescents has produced some disturbing findings. Many overweight people appear to have a decreased tendency for muscular activity. As weight increases, the impulse for physical exertion decreases further. As youngsters gain exessive weight, they find themselves in a cycle that appears to be out of control. In most cases, physical activity appears to be the crucial factor in dealing with weight management.

Lack of physical activity is common among overweight youngsters. In a study of ninth-grade females weight youngsters (Johnson, Burke, & Mayer, 1956), females who were overweight ate less but also exercised two-thirds less (in total time) than did normal-weight females. Movies taken of normal-weight and overweight teenagers (Corbin & Fletcher, 1968) demonstrated a great difference in the activity level of the two groups, even though diets were quite similar. A number of researchers have identifed the effectiveness of increased activity in weight management (Eisenman, 1986). Wilmore (1994) identifies inactivity as a far more significant factor in the development of excessive weight gain than overeating. Increasing activity is a key factor and must be accompanied by an attitudinal shift. Students need to develop positive feelings about the role of exercise in maintaining an optimum weight level. Many educators feel it is best to deal with overweight youngsters in a positive fashion rather than trying to solve their problem through increased and mandated exercise. If the treatment is not successful, students may feel as though they are failures and be strongly opposed to future activity programs.

Adults often make this statement: "Don't worry about excessive weight; it will come off when the student reaches adolescence." The opposite is usually true, however. Eighty percent of overweight preadolescents grow into obese adults; however, 96 percent of overweight teenagers become obese adults (Johnson, Burke, & Mayer, 1956). Youngsters clearly do not grow out of obesity; they grow into it. Weight management issues need to be challenged at an early age, and this challenge must come from increased movement and activity. In addition, many overweight students are victims of their home environment. Students are not in total control of their destiny because parents often control much of what they eat and do at home. There are no easy answers, and to solve such complex problems as weight management, parents, nutritionists, counselors, nurses, and physicians need to be involved in the process.

The advantage of using physical activity to treat overweight problems is that it increases energy expenditure and may suppress appetite (Wilmore, 1994). In contrast to rigid diets, exercise minimizes the loss of lean body mass and stimulates fat loss. Physical activity is inexpensive, easy to do in a variety of situations, and often a positive social experience.

Overweight and Type 2 Diabetes

There are other diseases associated with a lack of physical activity. One of the areas of grave concern is the high incidence of overweight youngsters. Closely related to these weight problems is that of type 2 diabetes. About 1.7 per 1,000 youngsters (ages 0 to 19 years) are afflicted with this serious ailment. Properly administered exercise programs can be an effective approach for positively influencing this chronic disorder among youth. Diabetic youth who are physically active show lower levels of blood glucose and a more stable metabolism than sedentary youngsters (Larson, 1984). The fitness of diabetic teenagers, caused by lack of exercise, is lower than that of nondiabetic students. This probably occurs because nurses and teachers fear exercise-induced hypoglycemia (Larson, 1984). Proper management of diet and insulin is a key factor, which usually means ensuring that the energy intake is increased while the insulin dose is maintained. Unfortunately, teenagers usually decrease the amount of their voluntary activity on entering middle and senior high school.

Flexibility and Trunk Strength

A lack of flexibility and trunk strength has been a recurring problem regardless of the source of testing and research. This lack often leads to poor posture and lower back pain (Plowman, 1993). Programs have to accomplish more than aerobic fitness; the need for strength and flexibility is equally important. The need is clear: Develop healthy youngsters today who are capable of maintaining a healthy lifestyle during adulthood.

The evidence shows that many youngsters are not healthy. Even though few youngsters die of heart disease and related health problems such as excessive weight and diabetes mellitus, there is a need for con-

cern. For too long, parents and teachers have assumed that because teenagers seldom complain about their health status, they are healthy. Physical educators owe youngsters a legacy of personal fitness. A physical education program without a strong fitness component is taking away the only opportunity that youngsters will have to learn to maintain their health.

PHYSICAL EDUCATION DROPOUTS

Students who feel physically incompetent usually drop out of physical education, and when they leave school, they have a negative opinion of an active lifestyle. Dropping out of physical education commonly occurs at the middle school level, although the process often begins in the elementary school years. Dropping out of activity because of lack of skill competency during elementary school is most unfortunate. Predicting who will be an outstanding athlete in junior or senior high school by observing elementary school performance is, in fact, quite difficult. In a study by Clarke (1968), coaches rated males who were outstanding athletes. Of the males who were rated as outstanding between the ages of 9 and 15 years, only 25 percent received this rating at the elementary and middle school age. Of the males, 45 percent were rated as outstanding at the elementary school level but not at the middle school level, and 35 percent of the group were rated as outstanding in middle school but not in elementary school. Thus, only 25 percent of the predictions were correct. Most people would not take a risk if the odds were against them 75 percent of the time. Teachers, however, often label youngsters at an early age, even though their predictions may be incorrect three out of four times.

One of the problems with predicting who will be an outstanding athlete at an early age is that it places early maturing youth in skilled positions. For example, youngsters who are selected as outstanding athletes at 10 years of age receive extra amounts of reinforcement from teachers and peers. Additionally, they are placed in skilled positions, allowing them to receive much more practice (e.g., pitching in baseball versus playing right field). This self-fulfilling prophecy results in youngsters practicing more to live up to the expectations of those who selected them. On the other hand, youth who develop more slowly and at a later age often become discouraged and drop out of the sporting experience.

This lack of predictive ability among teachers emphasizes the need for physical education programs to focus on keeping youngsters enthusiastic until they are capable of performing successfully. The purpose of a physical education program is not to develop athletes, and the program should not be presented so that it allows the athletically gifted to excel and prosper at the expense of less-talented youngsters. Physical education is for all youngsters. Gifted youngsters have a myriad of opportunities to enhance their skills. However, students who are less skilled have only the physical education program to help them develop and improve. To reiterate, trying to identify athletes at an early age in a physical education setting is difficult at best, and it may be detrimental to students' future development.

ACADEMIC ACHIEVEMENT AND PHYSICAL EDUCATION

For years, physical educators have attempted to demonstrate a relationship between physical education and improvement in a student's intellectual development. If intellectual development or academic achievement could be linked to physical education, the profession might rank higher as an educational priority. However, according to Shephard (1984a), "Strong proof is lacking." Shephard identifies the many limitations of such investigations, which include the following:

- Studies of special populations, such as the mentally disabled or athletes

- "Halo" effects, because teachers reward star performers with higher marks

- Self-image gains by athletes caused by teacher and peer praise

- Short duration of training programs

- Possible side effects from curtailment of academic instruction

- Use of retrospective data relating observed academic performance to measures of activity or physical ability

Thomas and Thomas (1986) offer a clear and concise summary statement about activity and intellectual ability: " . . . attempts to improve or remediate cognitive function through the use of movement are not theoretically sound, nor does this approach have any empirical support in the research literature." A relationship to other academic areas should not be a requisite for a physical education program. Physical education makes unique contributions to the total school curriculum: motor-skill development and the understanding and maintenance of physical fitness. Considering these contributions cannot be developed elsewhere in the curriculum and contribute to the physical well-being of youngsters, convincing administrators and parents that intellectual development is enhanced by physical education should not be neces-

sary. Physical educators can justify inclusion of the program on the basis of its unique contributions. The public has shown support for a physical education program if it aids, nurtures, and shows concern for the physical development of all students.

A study that has created much interest is the Trois Rivieres regional experiment (Shephard, 1984b). The study provides a well-conceived design for increased physical education programming. Even though students received more time for physical education (and less for academics), their academic performance did not decrease. These results counter the objection that more physical education will result in poorer academic performance because less time is spent in the classroom. Additionally, a follow-up study of participants in the Trois Rivieres study 20 years later suggested that students who had more physical education time in school were more likely to be active later in life (Trudeau, Laurencelle, Trembley, Rajic, & Shephard, 1998). Administrators need to consider this study, particularly today, when many schools have a back-to-basics emphasis. This emphasis usually means "back to the classroom," without physical activity or the arts. One wonders if this lack of concern for the body, our "home to the brain," is detrimental to total development of students. The ability to read is less important if one's health has degenerated. No priority in life is higher than physical well-being.

LONG-TERM EFFECT OF PHYSICAL ACTIVITY

Many experts believe that the physical activity undertaken during the school years has a lifetime impact. Saltin and Grimby (1968) conducted a research project to learn whether the benefits of childhood activity carried over to adult life. They compared the ability to adjust to effort of three groups of participants aged 50 to 59. One group comprised former athletes who had not participated in activity for more than 20 years and who worked in sedentary jobs. A second group consisted of former athletes who kept up a regular training and exercise program during their adult years. The third group consisted of individuals who were not athletes in youth and who were inactive as adults. Results showed that the nonathlete group was capable of the least effort (measured by maximal oxygen uptake). The group that was active during youth but took part in little activity during adulthood scored significantly higher than did the nonathlete group. The athlete group that had maintained training scored a great deal higher than the other two groups. This study shows that functional capacity as an adult is partly a result of activity performed during the growing years.

Relative Humidity Level (%)	Air Temperature (°F)
40	90
50	85
60	80
70	75
80	70
90	65
100	60

FIGURE 2.6 Weather guide: When the humidity and air temperature exceed the corresponding levels, intense activity should be curtailed

SAFETY GUIDELINES FOR EXERCISE AND PHYSICAL ACTIVITY

Two areas of concern for physical educators who are responsible for exercising youngsters are (1) the avoidance of physical injury or harm and (2) the maintenance and development of positive attitudes and feelings about exercise. Few, if any, healthy students are permanently injured by exercise. However, when exercise is not conducted properly or is pushed to excess, emotional problems can arise. The following sections present guidelines for offering students exercise in a safe and positive manner.

Moderation

Moderation is a good way to ensure that youngsters grow up enjoying different types of physical activity. Moderate exercise, coupled with opportunities to participate in recreational activity, helps develop a lasting desire to move. Educators are sometimes concerned that a student may be harmed physiologically by too much or too vigorous activity. To date, there is no evidence that a healthy student can be harmed through vigorous exercise. This does not mean that a student is capable of the same unadjusted physical workload as an adult. Evidence does indicate, however, that youngsters can withstand a gradual increase in workload and are capable of workloads comparable to those of adults when the load is adjusted for height and size.

Exercise and Heat

It is possible to exercise youth in hot weather. The arrival of warm weather does not mean that exercise must stop, but certain measures should be used to avoid heat-related illness. Adolescents do not adapt to extremes of temperature as effectively as adults for the following physiological reasons (Bar-Or, 1983; American Academy of Pediatrics, 2000):

■ Youth have a higher surface area/mass ratio than adults. This allows a greater amount of heat to transfer between the environment and the body.

■ When walking or running, adolescents produce more metabolic heat per unit mass than adults produce. Middle and high school students are not as efficient in executing movement patterns, so they generate more metabolic heat than do adults performing a similar task.

■ The ability to convey heat by blood from the body core to the skin is reduced in youth because of a lower cardiac output at a given oxygen uptake.

■ Sweating capacity is not as great in some teenagers as in adults, resulting in a lowered ability to cool the body.

These physiological differences demonstrate that teenagers are at a disadvantage compared to adults when exercising in an environment where the ambient air temperature is higher than the skin temperature. In addition, the physical maturity of teenagers varies a great deal, so it is quite possible that some youngsters are similar to adults, whereas others are still childlike in terms of their maturation levels.

Individuals can and do acclimatize to warmer temperatures. However, youngsters appear to adjust to heat more slowly than adults (Bar-Or, 1983). Often, teenagers do not instinctively drink enough liquids to replenish fluids lost during exercise. The American Academy of Pediatrics (2000) offers the following guidelines for exercising youngsters in hot weather:

■ The intensity of activities that last 30 minutes or more should be reduced whenever relative humidity and air temperature are above critical levels. Figure 2.6 shows the relationship between humidity and air temperature and when it is necessary to moderate activity demands.

■ When beginning an exercise program in warm weather, the intensity and duration of exercise should be restrained initially and then increased gradually over a period of 10 to 14 days to accomplish acclimation to the effects of heat.

■ Before prolonged physical activity, participants should be fully hydrated. During the activity, periodic drinking (e.g., 5 ounces of cold tap water every 30 minutes for a student weighing 88 pounds) should be enforced.

■ Clothing should be lightweight and limited to one layer of absorbent material to facilitate evaporation of sweat and to expose as much skin as possible. Sweat-saturated garments should be replaced by dry ones. Rubberized sweat suits should never be used to produce weight loss.

The academy identifies youngsters with the following conditions as being at a potentially high risk for heat stress: excessive weight, febrile (feverish) state, cystic fibrosis, gastrointestinal infection, diabetes, type 2 diabetes, chronic heart failure, caloric malnutrition, anorexia nervosa, sweating insufficiency syndrome, and mental retardation.

Distance Running

The question often arises as to how much and how far youngsters should be allowed to run, particularly in a competitive or training-for-competition setting. Because parents, teachers, and coaches seldom see the long-term effects of distance running, they often show little concern or willingness to limit the amount of activity. However, the American Academy of Pediatrics (2000) has identified possible problems that could arise. Lifetime involvement in a sport often depends on the type of early participation and gratification gained. Psychological problems can result from setting unrealistic goals for distance running by youngsters. A student who participates in distance running primarily for parental gratification may tire of the activity after a time and quit, or the student may continue and chafe under the coaching or parental pressure. In either case, psychological damage can occur, causing the student to become discouraged and unwilling to participate—either immediately or in the long run. Participants should be allowed to participate for the enjoyment of running, without fear of teacher, parental, or peer rejection or pressure. A student's sense of accomplishment, satisfaction, and appreciation by peers, parents, and coaches will foster involvement in running and other sports during school years and in later life.

A position taken by the International Athletics Association Federation (IAAF) Medical Committee (1983) states: "The danger certainly exists that with overintensive training, separation of the growth plates may occur in the pelvic region, the knee, or the ankle. While this could heal with rest, nevertheless definitive information is lacking whether in years to come harmful effects may result." In view of this position, it is the opinion of the IAAF Medical Committee that training and competition for long-distance track and road-running events should not be encouraged. Up to the age of 12, it is suggested that not more than 800 meters (½ mile) be run in competition. An increase in distance can be introduced gradually, with a maximum of 3,000 meters (nearly 2 miles) in competition for 14 year olds.

FIGURE 2.7 The PACER fitness test avoids many of the pitfalls of the mile run

Fitness Testing Considerations

A common practice is to test students at the start of the school year in the mile run/walk. Many students may not have ample conditioning to participate safely in the activity. In addition, in many parts of the country, the start of the school year is hot and humid, adding to the stress placed on the cardiovascular system. If testing is deemed necessary, it is recommended that the test be done near the end of the school year after youngsters have had the opportunity to be conditioned. If this is not possible, at least allow youngsters 4 to 6 weeks of activity to achieve proper conditioning. Rowland (1990) recommends starting with a ⅛-mile run/walk and gradually building to a mile run/walk over a 4-week period. A better alternative is to use the PACER (Progressive Aerobic Cardiovascular Endurance Run) aerobic fitness test (Figure 2.7). This test can be administered indoors and does not require completing a mile distance run. The PACER offers similar validity and reliability as the mile run/walk.

Resistance (Strength) Training

Resistance training refers here to a method of conditioning that involves a wide range of resistive loads including free weights, weight machines, stretch bands, medicine balls, and even traditional exercises such as push-ups and sit-ups. It is not competitive body building or power lifting, which involve maximum efforts in an attempt to dramatically increase strength and muscle size. The American Academy of Pediatrics (2001) recommends that adolescents should avoid competitive weight lifting, power lifting, body building, and maximal lifts until they reach skeletal maturity. In physical education, the goal is to teach students the fundamentals of resistance training as part of a total fitness program.

Resistance training for youth often generates concern among educators. Many worry about safety and stress-related injuries, while others question whether such training produces significant strength gains. Many teachers have avoided resistance training in middle school physical education because of safety issues and the wide variation in maturity. Accepted thinking for years was that since many middle school students are just entering adolescence, they are incapable of making significant strength gains because they lack adequate levels of circulating androgens. Evidence is continuing to build that contradicts this point of view (Faigenbaum, 2003) and shows that students of any age and stage of development can increase strength through resistance training. Strength gains of roughly 30 to 50 percent occur in 8–12 weeks with untrained adolescents. Resistance training is an excellent fitness activity for overweight youth because they are often stronger than their smaller and leaner peers. This allows for success and competence in an activity that is less aerobic based. Another concern that females often have is that they will develop excess muscle mass from resistance training. Boys increase in fat-free mass because of hormonal influences; however, girls show less muscular development because of lower levels of androgens (Faigenbaum, 2003).

Safety and prevention of injury are paramount considerations for those interested in weight training for youth. When injuries are reported in a school setting, most have occurred because of inadequate supervision, lack of proper technique, or competitive lifting. The majority of weight-lifting injuries are caused by the major lifts: the power clean, the clean and jerk, the squat lift, or the dead lift (Tanner, 1993). These lifts often are competitive and performed in an uncontrolled (ballistic) manner; they should not be used in a physical education setting. A resistance training program is only one component of a comprehensive fitness program for youth. The National Strength and Conditioning Association (NSCA, 1996) recommends that a young athlete's training include a variety of different exercises such as agility exercises (basketball, volleyball, tennis, and tumbling) and endurance training (distance running, bicycling, and swimming). There are many ways to enhance strength besides using weights if safety is an issue. See Chapters 16 and 20 in this text for a number of alternatives that may solve the safety issue and add variety to the program. In addition, Chapter 20 identifies the basic skills and techniques for implementing a strength training program.

If a decision is made to include a weight-training program in the physical education program, it should be done in a thoughtful and studied manner. Focus on correct lifting techniques instead of the amounts of weight lifted. Proper supervision and technique are key ingredients in a successful program. Program prescription guidelines recommended by Faigenbaum (2003) and NSCA (1996) are as follows:

■ Training is recommended two or three times a week on nonconsecutive days for 20- to 30-minute periods. High repetitions (10–15) at low resistance appear to be most safe for middle-school-age youth.

■ Ensure the activities and exercises are developmentally appropriate. Stretch bands or medicine balls might be more attractive to less motivated youth and are safer alternatives to weights. Weight machines are expensive but also help ensure proper lifting form and easily adjusted resistance.

■ No resistance should be applied until proper form is demonstrated.

■ Start gradually with light weights that ensure success. There is little point in students trying and failing at workloads that were excessive. When beginning a training program, a single set of 10–15 repetitions is a good starting point (Faigenbaum, 2003). After a program has been established, one to three sets per exercise should be done.

■ Increase weight or resistance in 1- to 3-pound increments when 15 repetitions are performed with good form and under control.

■ Maximal lifts should not be performed until youngsters are at least 16 to 17 years old. Some students will want to lift their max, but this often increases the risk of accidents and failure. As a teacher, it is important to help students progress according to sound training principles.

■ Focus on the positive aspects of fitness workouts. Students should learn to chart their exercises, workloads, and repetitions. Young students have the benefit of growth and maturity that help to ensure most will improve—a surefire path to adherence and motivation.

■ One goal does not fit all makes and models of students. Boys and girls will have different reasons for resistance training and fitness regimens. A major instructional objective should be to counsel individuals and help them identify reasonable and meaningful goals.

STUDY STIMULATORS AND REVIEW QUESTIONS

1. Explain the reasons behind the recent efforts to make the promotion of physical activity engagement a central goal for school physical education programs.

2. Explain why efforts to raise physical fitness levels in youth have largely been unsuccessful.

3. Discuss the reason behind the recent efforts to promote activity in female students.

4. Describe the relationship between chronological age and skeletal age.

5. Why is learning new and more complex skills difficult for students between the ages of 9 and 15?

6. Discuss why overweight youngsters perceive aerobic tasks as overly demanding and unenjoyable.

7. Discuss the rationale for basing fitness workloads on time rather than distance or number.

8. Discuss why physical activity, as compared to rigid diets, is a much more attractive intervention to treating overweight students.

9. Explain why physical education professionals should be concerned when the emphasis on "back to the basics" continues.

10. List and explain two strategies to follow when having students exercise in extreme heat.

REFERENCES AND SUGGESTED READINGS

American Academy of Pediatrics. (2000). Policy statement: Climatic heat stress and the exercising child and adolescent. *Pediatrics, 106*(01), 158–159.

American Academy of Pediatrics. (2001). Policy statement: Strength training by children and adolescents. *Pediatrics, 107*(6), 1470–1472.

American College of Sports Medicine. (2000). *ACSM's guidelines for exercise testing and prescription* (6th ed.). Philadelphia, PA: Lippincott Williams & Wilkins.

American Heart Association. (1992). Medical/scientific statement on exercise: Benefits and recommendations for physical activity for all Americans. *Circulation, 85*(1), 2726–2730.

Bailey, D. A., Faulkner, R. A., & McKay, H. A. (1996). Growth, physical activity, and bone mineral acquisition. *Exercise and Sport Science Reviews, 24*, 233–266.

Bar-Or, O. (1983). *Pediatric sports medicine for the practitioner.* New York: Springer-Verlag.

Bar-Or, O., & Ward, D. S. (1989). Rating of perceived exertion in children. In O. Bar-Or (Ed.), *Advances in Pediatric Sport Sciences: Vol. 3.* Champaign, IL: Human Kinetics Publishers.

Beunen, G. (1989). Biological age in pediatric exercise research. In O. Bar-Or (Ed.), *Advances in pediatric sport sciences: Vol. 3.* Champaign, IL: Human Kinetics Publishers.

Burgeson, C. R., Wechsler, H., Brener, N. D., Young, J. C., & Spain, C. G. (2001). Physical education and activity: Results from the School Health Policies and Programs Study (SHPPS) 2000. *Journal of School Health, 71*(7), 279–293.

Centers for Disease Control and Prevention. (1997). Guidelines for school and community programs to promote lifelong physical activity among young people. *Morbidity and Mortality Weekly Report, 46,* 1–36.

Centers for Disease Control and Prevention. (1998). Youth risk behavior surveillance United States, 1997. *Morbidity and Mortality Weekly Report, 47,* 1–36.

Centers for Disease Control and Prevention. (2000). *CDC growth charts—United States.* Washington, DC: U.S. Department of Health and Human Services.

Clarke, H. H. (1968). Characteristics of the young athlete: A longitudinal look. *Kinesiology Review, 3,* 33–42.

Clarke, H. H. (1971). *Physical motor tests in the Medford boy's growth study.* Englewood Cliffs, NJ: Prentice-Hall.

Corbin, C. B., & Fletcher, P. (1968). Diet and activity patterns of obese and non-obese elementary school children. *Research Quarterly, 39*(4), 922.

Dale, D., & Corbin, C. B. (2000). Physical activity participation of high school graduates following exposure to conceptual or traditional physical education. *Research Quarterly of Exercise and Sport, 71,* 61–68.

Dale, D., Corbin, C. B., & Cuddihy, T. F. (1998). Can conceptual physical education promote physically active lifestyles? *Pediatric Exercise Science, 10,* 97–109.

Dubowitz, V. (1970). Differentiation of fiber types in skeletal muscle. In E. J. Briskey, R. G. Cassens, & B. B. Marsh (Eds.), *Physiology and biochemistry of muscle as a food: Vol. 2.* Madison, WI: University of Wisconsin Press.

Eisenman, P. (1986). Physical activity and body composition. In V. Seefeldt (Ed.), *Physical activity and well-being.* Reston, VA: American Alliance for Health, Physical Education, and Dance (AAHPERD).

Faigenbaum, A. D. (2003). Youth resistance training. *President's Council on Physical Fitness and Sports Research Digest 4*(3), 1–8.

Freedson, P. S. (1986). Cardiorespiratory diseases. In V. Seefeldt (Ed.), *Physical activity and well-being.* Reston, VA: AAHPERD.

Gilliam, T. B., Katch, V. L., Thorland, W. G., and Weltman, A. W. (1977). Prevalence of coronary heart disease risk factors in active children, 7 to 12 years of age. *Medicine and Science in Sports and Exercise, 9*(1), 21–25.

Gilliam, T. B., MacConnie, S. E., Greenen, D. L., Pels, A. E., & Freedson, P. S. (1982). Exercise program for children: A way to prevent heart disease? *The Physician and Sportsmedicine, 10*(9), 96–101, 105–106, 108.

Glass, W. (1973). Coronary heart disease sessions prove vitally interesting. *California AHPER Journal* (May–June), 7.

Gruelich, W., & Pyle, S. (1959). *Radiographic atlas of skeletal development of the hand and wrist* (2nd ed.). Stanford, CA: Stanford University Press.

Grunbaum, J. A., Kann, L., Kinchen, S., Williams, B., Ross, J. G., Lowry, R., et al. (2002). Youth risk behavior surveillance—United States, 2001. *Morbidity and Mortality Weekly Report, 51*(SS-4), 1–64.

Haymes, E. M. (1986). Nutrition and ergogenic aids. In V. Seefeldt (Ed.), *Physical activity and well-being.* Reston, VA: AAHPERD.

Health Education Authority. (1998). *Young and active?* London: Author.

International Athletics Association Federation. (1983). Not kid's stuff. *Sportsmedicine Bulletin, 18*(1), 11.

Johnson, M. L., Burke, B. S., & Mayer, J. (1956). The prevalence and incidence of obesity in a cross section of elementary and secondary school children. *American Journal of Clinical Nutrition, 4*(3), 231.

Kannus, P., Haapasalo, H., Sievanen, H., Oja, P., & Vuori, I. (1994). The site-specific effects of long-term unilateral activity on bone mineral density and content. *Bone, 15,* 279–284.

Kujala, U. M., Kaprio, J., Sarna, S., & Koskenvuo, M. (1998). Relationship of leisure-time physical activity and mortality: The Finnish twin cohort. *Journal of the American Medical Association, 279*(6), 440–444.

Larson, Y. (1984). Physical performance and the young diabetic. In R. A. Boileau (Ed.), *Advances in pediatric sport sciences.* Champaign, IL: Human Kinetics Publishers.

Lortie, G., Simoneau, J. A., Hamel, P., Boulay, M. R., Landry, F., and Bourchard, C. (1984). Responses of maximal aerobic power and capacity to aerobic training. *International Journal of Sports Medicine, 5,* 232–236.

Malina, R. (1975). *Growth and development: The first twenty years in man.* (p. 19). Minneapolis, MN: Burgess.

Malina, R. M. (1978). Physical growth and maturity characteristics of young athletes. In R. A. Magill, M. H. Ash, & F. L. Smoll (Eds.), *Children and youth in sport: A contemporary anthology.* Champaign, IL: Human Kinetics Publishers.

Malina, R. M. (1986). Physical growth and development. In V. Seefeldt (Ed.), *Physical activity and well-being.* Reston, VA: AAHPERD.

McGlynn, G. (1990). *Dynamics of fitness.* Dubuque, IA: William C. Brown Publishers.

Morrow, J. R., Jackson, A. W., & Payne, V. G. (1999). Physical activity promotion and school physical education. *President's Council on Physical Fitness and Sports Research Digest,* Series 3, No. 7.

National Association for Sport and Physical Education. (1992). *NASPE Outcomes Project.* Reston, VA: Author.

National Association for Sport and Physical Education. (2004). *Physical activity for children: A statement of guidelines for children ages 5–12* (2nd ed.). Reston, VA: AAHPERD and NASPE Publications.

National Association for Sport and Physical Education. (2004). *Moving into the future—National standards for physical education* (2nd ed.). Reston, VA: Author.

National Strength and Conditioning Association. (1996). Youth resistance training: Position statement paper and literature review. *Strength and Conditioning, 18*(6), 62–76.

Ogden, C. L., Flegal, K. M., Carroll, M. D., & Johnson, C. L. (2002). Prevalence and trends in overweight among U.S. children and adolescents, 1999–2000. *Journal of the American Medical Association, 288,* 1728–1732.

Pate, R. R., Baranowski, T., Dowda, M., & Trost, S. G. (1996). Tracking of physical activity in young children. *Medicine and Science in Sports and Exercise, 28*(1), 92–96.

Plowman, S. A. (1993). Physical fitness and healthy low-back function. *Physical Activity and Fitness Research Digest, 1*(3), 1–8.

Raitakari, O. T., Porkka, K. V. K., Taimela, S., Telama, R., Rasanen, L., & Viikari, J. S. A. (1994). Effects of persistent physical activity and inactivity on coronary risk factors in children and young adults. *American Journal of Epidemiology, 140,* 195–205.

Rarick, L. G., & Dobbins, D. A. (1975). Basic components in the motor performances of children six to nine years of age. *Medicine and Science in Sports, 72,* 2.

Roche, A. F., Chumlea, W. C., & Thissen, D. (1988). *Assessing the skeletal maturity of the hand-wrist: Fels Method.* Springfield, IL: Thomas Publishing Co.

Rose, K. (1968). To keep people in health. *Journal of the American College Health Association, 22,* 80.

Ross, J. G., Pate, R. R., Corbin, C. C., Delpy, L. A., & Gold, R. S. (1987). What is going on in the elementary physical education program? *Journal of Physical Education, Recreation, and Dance, 58*(9), 78–84.

Rowland, T. W. (1990). *Exercise and children's health.* Champaign, IL: Human Kinetics Publishers.

Rowland, T. W. (1991). Effects of obesity on aerobic fitness in adolescent females. *American Journal of Disease in Children, 145,* 764–768.

Sallis, J. F., & McKenzie, T. L. (1991). Physical education's role in public health. *Research Quarterly of Exercise and Sport, 62,* 124–137.

Sallis, J. F., & Patrick, K. (1994). Physical activity guidelines for adolescents: Consensus statement. *Pediatric Exercise Science, 6,* 302–314.

Saltin, B. (1973). Metabolic fundamentals of exercise. *Medicine and Science of Sports, 5,* 137–146.

Saltin, B., & Grimby, G. (1968). Physiological analysis of middle-aged and old former athletes, comparison with still active athletes of the same ages. *Circulation, 38*(6), 1104.

Shephard, R. J. (1984a). Physical activity and child health. *Sports Medicine, 1,* 205–233.

Shephard, R. J. (1984b). Physical activity and "wellness" of the child. In R. A. Boileau (Ed.), *Advances in pediatric sport sciences.* Champaign, IL: Human Kinetics Publishers.

Simons-Morton, B. B., Parcel, G. S., O'Hara, N. M., Blair, S. N., & Pate, R. R. (1988). Health-related physical fitness in childhood: Status and recommendations. *American Review of Public Health, 9,* 403–425.

Simons-Morton, B. B., Taylor, W. C., Snider, S. A., Huang, I. W., & Fulton, J. E. (1994). Observed levels of elementary and middle school children's physical activity during physical education classes. *Preventive Medicine, 23,* 437–441.

Stone, E. J., McKenzie T. L., Welk, G. J., & Booth, M. L. (1998). Effects of physical activity interventions in youth: Review and synthesis. *American Journal of Preventive Medicine, 15,* 298–315.

Tanner, J. M., Whitehouse, R. H., & Takaishi, M. (1966). Growth velocity curve for height. *Archives of Diseases in Childhood, 41,* 467.

Tanner, S. M. (1993). Weighing the risks: Strength training for children and adolescents. *The Physician and Sportsmedicine, 21*(6), 105–116.

Thomas, J. R., & Thomas, K. T. (1986). The relation of movement and cognitive function. In V. Seefeldt (Ed.), *Physical activity and well-being.* Reston, VA: AAHPERD.

Thomas, J. R., & Tennant, L. K. (1978). Effects of rewards on changes in children's motivation for an athletic task. In F. L. Smoll & R. E. Smith (Eds.), *Psychological perspectives in youth sports.* New York: Hemisphere Publishing.

Trudeau, F., Laurencelle, L., Trembley, J., Rajic, M., & Shephard, R. J. (1998). A long-term follow-up of participants in the Trois-Rivieres semi-longitudinal study of growth and development. *Pediatric Exercise Science, 10,* 366–377.

U.S. Department of Health and Human Services. (1996). *Physical activity and health: A report of the surgeon general.* Atlanta, GA: U.S. Department of Health and Human Services, Centers for Disease Control and Prevention, National Center for Chronic Disease Prevention and Health Promotion.

U.S. Public Health Service. (1990). *Healthy people 2000: National health promotion and disease prevention objectives.* Washington, DC: U.S. Government Printing Office.

U.S. Public Health Service. (2000). *Healthy people 2010: National health promotion and disease objectives.* Washington, DC: U.S. Government Printing Office.

Wilmore, J. H. (1994). Exercise, obesity, and weight control. *Physical Activity and Fitness Research Digest, 1*(6), 1–8.

WEB SITES

Children and Physical Activity
www.cdc.gov/nccdphp/dash/presphysactrpt/index.htm
www.kidsource.com/kidsource/content4/promote.phyed.html
www.americanheart.org/presenter.jhtml?identifier=4596

Children's Health
www.aap.org

Fitness Tests
www.cooperinst.org
www.presidentschallenge.org

Obesity
www.cdc.gov/nccdphp/dnpa/obesity/index.htm

Presidential Active Lifestyle Award
www.presidentschallenge.org/educators/program_details/active_lifestyle/implementation.aspx

Strength Training and Children
www.acsm.org

Youth Sports
www.nays.org

ESSENTIAL COMPONENTS OF A QUALITY PROGRAM

COMPONENT 1   A quality physical education program is organized around content standards that offer direction and continuity to instruction and evaluation.

COMPONENT 2   A quality program is student centered and based on the developmental urges, characteristics, and interests of students.

COMPONENT 3   Quality physical education makes physical activity and motor-skill development the core of the program.

COMPONENT 4   Physical education programs teach management skills and self-discipline.

COMPONENT 5   Quality programs emphasize inclusion of all students.

COMPONENT 6   In a quality physical education setting, instruction focuses on the process of learning skills rather than the product or outcome of the skill performance.

COMPONENT 7   A quality physical education program teaches lifetime activities that students can use to promote their health and personal wellness.

COMPONENT 8   Quality physical education teaches cooperative and responsibility skills and helps students develop sensitivity to diversity and gender issues.

3

Steps in Developing a Curriculum

CHAPTER SUMMARY

This chapter offers a systematic approach for developing a curriculum, with suggested formats for organization and evaluation. A written curriculum gives direction to the instructional program. A sequence of steps is offered for planning and designing a comprehensive curriculum. The concepts of scope, sequence, breadth, depth, and balance help ensure that the curriculum will meet the needs of all students. The chapter also provides a discussion on the importance and advantages of articulating the curriculum from kindergarten through 12th grade.

STUDENT OUTCOMES

After reading the chapter, you will be able to:

- Discuss the common value orientations in physical education curriculum approaches.

- List and discuss the steps of curriculum construction.

- Describe the issues that must be considered in developing a philosophy and conceptual framework.

- Describe various environmental factors that must be considered when developing a physical education curriculum.

- Analyze the content standards that should guide curriculum development.

- Explain how to write the three parts of student-centered objectives. →

Student Outcomes, continued

- Discuss the desires of adults and students with regard to physical education activities.

- Explain the physical, social, emotional, and intellectual differences between middle and senior high school students.

- Discuss the following concepts as they relate to curriculum construction: scope, sequence, breadth, depth, and balance.

- Give several examples of how curriculum can be evaluated.

- Explain the advantages of an articulated K–12 curriculum.

Curriculum is a framework of student-centered physical activities that promotes physical activity and skill development. A curriculum is a delivery system that gives sequence and direction to the learning experiences of students. The development of a curriculum includes a set of beliefs and goals that evolves from a theoretical framework or value orientation. Value orientation is a set of personal and professional beliefs that provides a basis for determining curricular decisions. Most often, physical educators have several value orientations, and physical education programs reflect a blend of different values. For example, a chosen curriculum approach might include establishing lifetime participation in physical activities, developing sports skills, acquiring fitness knowledge, improving social skills, acquiring disciplinary knowledge, or combining a variety of orientations.

When developing or revising an existing curriculum, the value orientation of the physical education staff toward the existing curriculum and toward proposed changes is a necessary consideration (Jewett, Bain, & Ennis, 1995). Determining the value orientation of the curriculum involves consideration of three major components: the subject matter to be learned, the students for whom the curriculum is being developed, and the society that has established the schools. Priorities in curriculum vary depending on the value orientations of the physical educators involved in the planning. Physical educators who place highest priority on subject matter mastery include an emphasis on sports, dance, outdoor adventure activities, physical fitness activities, and aquatic activities. This orientation places strong emphasis on learning skills and gaining knowledge so students have the opportunity to learn the subject matter and continue active participation for a lifetime. In contrast, instructors who favor

a student-centered approach prize activities that develop the individual student. They emphasize helping students find activities that are personally meaningful. Other physical educators see student autonomy and self-direction as the most important goals. They focus instruction and curricula on lifetime sport skills and nontraditional activities, such as cooperative games, trust-building procedures, and group activities, in an attempt to foster problem solving and interpersonal skills.

These examples illustrate a few of the different value orientations of physical educators. Usually, most curricula in the secondary schools are put together by committee and therefore reflect a **number** of value orientations. Teachers need to know the value orientations that drive their curriculum so there is consistency in instructional goals. Finding common ground among value orientations makes it easier for a staff to present lessons that teach common goals and objectives. Before accepting a new teaching position, ask the following questions about the school's curriculum. If you answer "no" to most of the questions listed here, it may be difficult for you to work comfortably in such a setting because it conflicts with your value orientation:

- Will the curriculum express a point of view about subject matter that is consistent with mine?

- Does the curriculum express a point of view about student learning that I believe?

- Does the curriculum express a point of view about the school's role in accomplishing social-cultural goals that is similar to my beliefs?

- Can I implement instructional strategies I value within this model?

DESIGNING A QUALITY CURRICULUM

The steps that follow offer a sequential approach for constructing a meaningful, well-planned curriculum guide. The first four steps are designed to establish the framework that guides selection of activities for the curriculum. These steps are often ignored because the focus is on activities that are easily implemented regardless of whether they contribute to content standards. The result is a curriculum with little direction, a situation similar to building a house without blueprints.

Step One: Develop a Guiding Philosophy

The initial step in curriculum design is to define a philosophy of physical education that reflects the beliefs that guide the developmental process. A philosophical statement defines how physical education fits into the total school curriculum and what it will accomplish for each student. The following is an example of a philosophical platform for physical education.

Physical education is that portion of the student's overall education that is accomplished through physical activity. Schools foster the process of educating the entire person: the body and the mind. Physical education is responsible for developing the body through instruction that is predominantly focused on physical activity and skill development. A high-quality program teaches students how to live an active and healthy lifestyle. The overriding goal of education—to develop an individual who can live effectively in a democracy—guides the development of this and all educational programs. The major and unique contributions of a quality physical education program are to help students in the following ways:

- **Develop personal activity and fitness behaviors.** The program must be experiential, that is, it must immerse students in a large variety of activities so they develop an understanding of their personal strengths and weaknesses. Knowledge is not enough—many adults have plenty of knowledge related to the need for fitness and activity but don't practice what they know. Taking time for personal health activity is a habit that is learned during the middle and high school years. Physical education at this level may be the last learning experience for many students as they enter adulthood. Personal physical activity behaviors and fitness are learned through regular participation in daily physical activity.

- **Learn motor skills that can be used for recreational activity throughout life.** Movement competency is rooted in developing a broad base of motor skills. Instruction should focus on learning motor skills in a positive and nurturing environment that assures students the joy of activity. Personal competency in a wide variety of skills gives students the tools they need to lead an active and rewarding life.

- **Develop an understanding of the concepts related to active and healthy behaviors.** It is not enough to be active without understanding the reasons for being active and healthy. Moving efficiently requires understanding anatomical and mechanical principles of skill performance. Physical education instruction integrates knowledge about physical activity and skill performance so students learn how to maintain personal fitness.

Step Two: Define a Conceptual Framework for the Curriculum

A conceptual framework is a series of statements that characterize the desired curriculum. These concepts establish the criteria that will be used to select activities and experiences included in the curriculum. The framework not only directs the activities, but also reflects beliefs about education and the learner. Following are some conceptual statements that define a student-centered, developmental curriculum.

- **Curriculum goals and objectives are appropriate for all students.** This implies a balanced curriculum that covers fundamental skills, sport skills, games, rhythms and dance, gymnastics, and individual and dual activities. Emphasis is placed on developing a broad foundation of motor skills for all students.

- **Activities in the curriculum are selected based on their potential to help students reach content standards.** The secondary school years are a time of experimentation, exploration, practice, and decision making with many movement possibilities. The criterion for inclusion of activities is not based on whether teachers or students prefer certain activities. Activities are included in the curriculum because they contribute to student progress toward content standards.

- **The curriculum helps students develop lifelong physical activity habits and understand basic fitness concepts.** Regardless of the philosophy of the curriculum, it should be designed so students leave school with active lifestyle habits. Fitness is an important component of the curriculum and should be varied, positive, and educational. The fitness program is experiential—that is, students participate in fitness activities rather than just being told the facts of fitness. A meaningful curriculum helps students understand that physical activity and fitness are personal in nature, need to be maintained throughout life, and contribute to better health.

- *The curriculum includes activities that enhance cognitive and affective learning.* Students are whole beings and need to learn more than the physical performance of skills. They must understand skill performance principles and develop cognitive learning related to physical activity and wellness. Affective development, the learning of cooperative and social skills, is fostered through group activities that include all students regardless of their widely varying skills and abilities.

- *The curriculum provides experiences that allow all students to succeed and feel satisfaction.* Quality programs focus on minimizing failure and emphasizing success. Activities that emphasize self-improvement, participation, and cooperation encourage the development of positive self-concepts. Physical education instruction focuses on learning in an environment without being labeled a winner or loser.

- *The curriculum is planned and based on an educational environment that is consistent with other academic areas in the school.* Physical education teachers need the same working conditions as other teachers in the school setting. Class sizes similar to those of other classroom teachers (20 to 35 students) and an assigned teaching area (e.g., gym space, outdoor fields, or exercise rooms) are needed for physical education instruction. Enough equipment for maximum activity and participation implies one piece of individual equipment for each student and ample apparatuses to limit long lines while waiting for a turn. A daily program ensures maximum opportunity for learning and retention.

- *Activities in the curriculum are presented in an educationally sound sequence.* Progression is the center of learning, and the curriculum should reflect progression vertically (between grade and developmental levels) and horizontally (within each level and within each activity). The sequence should be from simple to more complex, both vertically and horizontally.

- *The curriculum includes an appropriate means of assessing student progress.* Student assessment includes health-related fitness, skill development, cognitive learning, and attitude development toward physical activity. Any assessment program should enhance the effectiveness of the program and should help teachers individualize instruction, communicate with parents, and identify students with special needs.

Step Three: Consider Environmental Factors

Environmental factors are all those conditions within the community and school district that limit or extend the scope of the curriculum. Examples of environmental factors are the amount and type of equipment, budget size, and cultural makeup and interests of the community. Other factors, such as the support of school administrators, can affect the type of scheduling or amount of required physical education in the school. Different communities may value certain types of activities or experiences for their students. Although environmental factors need to be examined carefully, they should not circumvent and limit curriculum scope and sequence. Rather, these factors should give direction to the curriculum development process. A well-designed curriculum provides a goal, direction, and destination for the future, a high road to instructional success. Consider various environmental factors and try to use them to enhance the creativity and scope of the curriculum.

Following are examples of environmental factors that limit the development of a quality curriculum. Although these factors can sometimes be limiting, they can be handled creatively to ensure an effective curriculum. Think big; develop a comprehensive and ideal curriculum that is as varied, broad, and creative as possible. Seek to expand and develop the curriculum beyond these limiting factors.

School Administrators

The support of school administrators has a significant impact on the curriculum. It is important to interpret program goals to administrators. Like the general public, administrators may have misconceptions about physical education and its contribution to the overall education of students. In most cases, administrators will support physical education if they perceive that the program is built on sound educational principles that are documented and evaluated. The support of school administrators yields positive dividends over time because administrators have the power to influence situations and implement strategies. Areas where administrative support is necessary include the following:

- Determining the number of staff members and class size.

- Hiring staff to fill specific departmental needs.

- Constructing or developing facilities and teaching areas (e.g., racquetball courts, weight rooms, exercise trails, or swimming pools).

- Purchasing equipment and teaching aids (e.g., golf clubs, jump bands, Rollerblades, medicine balls, body bars, physioballs, or jump ropes).

- Supporting innovative ideas or new activities (e.g., a pilot unit on orienteering, an off-campus cross-country skiing lesson, or a team-teaching presentation of a golf unit).

- Maintaining existing teaching stations (e.g., watering the fields, cleaning the gymnasium, or repairing weight machines).

- Supporting professional development with in-service workshops, professional conferences, and current literature.

- Providing useful and meaningful feedback to teachers on their teaching performance (e.g., collecting data on management time, productive time, active learning time, or behavior patterns).

The Community: People and Climate

Occupations, religions, educational levels, cultural values, and physical activity habits within the community are factors that might affect curriculum development. Parents have a strong influence on the activity interests and habits of their children. The geographical location and the climate of the area are also important factors for consideration. The terrain (mountains, deserts, plains, and so on), combined with the weather conditions particular to each area, have an effect on people's activity interests. Extremely hot or cold climates markedly influence what activities are included in the curriculum and at what time of the year they should be scheduled.

Facilities and Equipment

Available teaching facilities dictate activities that can be offered. Facilities include on-campus as well as off-campus areas in the neighboring community. Off-campus facilities might be a community swimming pool or park. Equipment must be available in quality and quantity. One piece of equipment per child is

necessary if students are to learn at an optimum rate. Equipment can be purchased with school funds or with special funds raised by students through demonstration programs. Some types of equipment can be constructed by school maintenance departments or as industrial arts projects. Another possibility is to ask students to bring equipment, such as jump ropes, soccer balls, and basketballs, from home.

Laws and Requirements

Laws, regulations, and requirements at the national, state, and local levels may restrict or direct a curriculum. Programs must conform to these laws. Examples of two national laws affecting physical education programs are Title IX of the Educational Amendments Act of 1972 and Public Law 94-142. The former enforces equal opportunities for both sexes, and the latter mandates equal access to educational services for students with disabilities. Individual states also may have various laws that affect physical education programming.

Scheduling

The schedule or organizational pattern of the school has an impact on curriculum development. How many times per week classes meet, the length of class periods, and who teaches the classes are factors to consider. Many scheduling alternatives exist: daily, two or three times per week, every other week, and other variations. Regardless of the various parameters, most secondary schools put together a scheduling committee consisting of administrators, teachers, parents, and students in order to develop a workable schedule for all parties. There are two basic types of schedules: the traditional schedule and the **flexible or block schedule**. The traditional plan (Figure 3.1) divides the school day into five or six equal time periods. Each class, such as math, science, or physical education, meets for the same length of time on each day of the school week. The advantage of the traditional schedule is that it is easier to set up, more economical, and easier to administer. Students are in the same class at the same time each day. This provides students and administrators with a stable routine.

Flexible or block schedules (Figure 3.2) provide a varying length of time for classes depending on the nature of the subject matter and the type of instruction given. Usually, the block schedule is twice as long as the regular schedule. Seventy to 90 minutes is a common length for a block schedule. A block schedule would allow physical education students to travel to a local ski slope, a rock-climbing center, or a local Frisbee golf course and meet for a longer block of time. Schools use

Period	Time	Monday	Tuesday	Wednesday	Thursday	Friday
Homeroom	8:00–8:15	→				
1	8:15–9:10	General math	→			
2	9:15–10:10	English	→			
3	10:15–11:10	Biology	→			
Lunch	11:15–11:45					
Study hall	11:45–12:15	→				
4	12:15–1:10	Physical education	→			
5	1:15–2:10	History	→			
6	2:15–3:10	Home economics	→			

FIGURE 3.1 Traditional schedule

Block	Time	Semester 1	Semester 2
1	8:00–9:30	Math	History
2	9:35–11:05	Physical Education	Computers
3	11:05–11:30	Lunch	Lunch
3	11:35–1:05	Biology	Geography
4	1:10–2:40	English 1	English 2

FIGURE 3.2 Example of a 4-by-4 block schedule

different flexible schedules to meet the needs of students and teachers involved. There are a number of popular block schedules such as the 4-by-4 format where students take only four classes each semester, usually two 90-minute classes in the morning and two classes in the afternoon. Another variation is called an alternating block plan where students go to four classes one day and then four different classes the next day. This rotates every day and gives the students eight classes for the year. A flexible or block schedule provides time for travel off-campus, more time for skill development, the option of grouping students for different types of instruction (large or small groups), or the use of limited and specific types of equipment. Most physical education teachers feel that block schedules improve the learning in their classes (Hastie, 2003).

Budget and Funding

Budget and funding procedures differ among school districts. However, the physical education department head is usually involved in developing and submitting the budget. Understanding the funding procedures and planning an aggressive strategy for obtaining an adequate budget is a necessity for a quality program. Physical educators should seek parity with other school departments in terms of class size and equipment. Students cannot learn to read and write without materials and supplies, and they cannot learn physical skills without the necessary equipment.

In addition to the basic departmental budget, funds may be available through outside sources. Sometimes the athletic and physical education departments can share equipment. With tight budgets, this is an effective way to cut costs. Various community and parent groups, like the Lions or Rotary Club, may help with short-term funding for special facility or equipment needs, such as a weight room, racquetball courts, or tennis racquets. Some schools allow departments to have special fund-raising campaigns involving students and faculty. Car washes, candy sales, or admission to special sports demonstrations are useful projects for generating funds. Some states offer tax incentives for contributions to school programs. The best programs are not always the ones with the most funding, but adequate funding is necessary to produce a quality curriculum.

Step Four: Determine Content Standards and Student Objectives

Content standards determine the direction of the program as dictated and desired by the state, district, or individual school. Such standards are fixed goals for learning. They determine what students should know and be able to do when they complete their schooling. Student progress is dictated by how students compare to the fixed standards rather than how they compare with other students. Content standards determine what criteria will be used to select instructional activities for the curriculum. NASPE standards (2004) should be looked at carefully as well as state and local standards.

Write Student-Centered Objectives

After content standards have been defined, student-centered objectives are written. Objectives dictate the specific activities students will need to learn throughout the school year. Student-centered objectives are usually written in behavioral terms. Behavioral objectives contain three key characteristics: (1) a desired behavior that is observable and measurable, (2) the conditions or environment where the behavior should occur, and (3) a criterion for success that can be measured. Objectives are written for all three of the learning domains: psychomotor, cognitive, and affective. A description of each domain follows.

1. *Psychomotor domain.* This domain is the primary focus of instruction for physical educators. The seven levels in psychomotor domain taxonomy are movement vocabulary, movement of body parts, locomotor movements, movement implements and objects, patterns of movement, movement with others, and movement problem solving. This graduated list progresses in line with the developmental level of learners. Students learn the vocabulary of movement before proceeding to simple body-part movements and then on to more complex sport skills. More complex movements are learned to enable students to participate in activities with others and to solve personal movement dilemmas.

2. *Cognitive domain.* The cognitive domain includes six major areas: knowledge, comprehension, application, analysis, synthesis, and evaluation. The focus of the cognitive domain for physical education is knowing rules and strategies, health information, safety, and so on, and being able to understand and apply such knowledge. As students mature, they learn to analyze different activities, develop personalized exercise routines (synthesis), and evaluate their fitness/activity levels.

3. *Affective domain.* The affective domain deals with feelings, attitudes, and values. The major categories of learning in this area are receiving, responding, valuing, organizing, and characterizing. The affective domain changes more slowly than do the psychomotor and cognitive domains. How teachers treat students and the feelings students develop toward physical education are ultimately more important than the knowledge and skills developed in physical education programs.

Behavioral objectives are time consuming to write. Some teachers become bogged down and discouraged because the number of objectives appears overwhelming. The following are examples of behavioral objectives related to NASPE content standards (2004):

Psychomotor Domain

1. Move efficiently using a variety of locomotor skills, such as walking, sliding, carioca, running, and backward running.

2. Bump the volleyball 12 consecutive times against a wall above a 10-foot line.

Cognitive Domain

1. Identify five stretching exercises that develop low-back and hamstring flexibility.

2. Understand how warm-up and cooldown periods prevent injuries.

Affective Domain

1. Show empathy for the concerns and limitations of peers.

2. Demonstrate a willingness to participate with peers regardless of diversity or disability.

Step Five: Select Student-Centered Activities

When selecting activities for a student-centered curriculum, a clear understanding of students is requisite. The task of designing a program that flows with students rather than runs contrary to their desires, characteristics, and interests requires a clear view of their nature. It makes little sense to gather activities for instruction if they are not developmentally appropriate or do not appeal to students. The major criterion to follow when selecting activities for the curriculum is, "Do the activities contribute to content standards and student-centered objectives?" This approach contrasts with selecting activities because they are fun or because you enjoy them. Some teachers fail to include activities in the curriculum if they lack confidence or feel incompetent with regard to the activity (such as rhythms). This results in a curriculum that is designed for the teacher's benefit rather than students'. If an activity contributes to content standards, it is necessary to develop requisite instructional competency. Imagine a math teacher choosing not to teach fractions or multiplication tables to students because of feelings of incompetence. It is your responsibility to learn to teach new activities so students experience and learn all requisite physical skills.

As many activities as possible that contribute to content standards should be gathered in the planning stage. The greater the number of activities considered, the more varied and imaginative the final program. In this step, place emphasis on brainstorming, creating, and innovating without restriction. The finished curriculum will be deficient if it is limited at this step. Later steps will offer an opportunity to delete inappropriate activities.

An important consideration in selecting activities for the program is to look at the desires of parents and students in your area. Years ago, people banded together and decided to set aside land and build schools because they wanted their children to acquire certain information, attitudes, and skills in a systematic manner from professionally prepared teachers. These parents had certain ambitions for their youth. Even though society has changed dramatically since that time and much new information has been discovered, parents and students still have a number of desires in this area. Physical education curriculum planners need to analyze the following desires of society.

Desires of Parents and Students

Desire to Be Physically Fit, Healthy, and Attractive Being fit, healthy, and attractive is especially important to physical educators because of the contribution that physical activity makes in these areas. Proof that activity aids in achieving weight control, cardiovascular efficiency, flexibility, and strength is well documented. The public is aware of the humiliation and problems that individuals face throughout life if they are overweight, weak, or unattractive. Physically fit people feel positive and successful, and they portray a positive image to others. These successes add up to a positive self-concept. In contrast, overweight people often have difficulty with simple daily activities like dressing, sitting, and walking. They may have a negative self-image and often cannot participate in or enjoy many activities.

Desire to Play Play has been frequently discussed as an important behavior that permeates all cultures in a

variety of forms. Sports, dance, and various types of physical activity are serious forms of play. Many other forms of play, including music, drama, and art, are also important in society. Indeed, play is as important to most people as work, and an enjoyable play life is as valuable as a productive work life. In fact, to many, play is the most important aspect of their lives. It is what they would call "paradise" or "the good life." They look forward to a round of golf, a jog along a canal, or a backpacking trip in the mountains. Physical education can make a significant contribution to this universal desire to play.

Desire for Knowledge The human race continues to search for knowledge in all areas. People are curious about the world around them. Physical education has an extensive body of knowledge that comes from the various subfields, including exercise physiology, kinesiology, motor learning, sport psychology, and sport sociology.

Desire for Success, Approval, and Satisfaction People tend to repeat activities that provide them with success. They also tend to avoid activities in which they are not successful. Various types of success usually lead to recognition, approval, or self-satisfaction. People participate in activities in which they are successful because feelings of success lead to satisfaction and happiness. Physical activities are in this category and thus make a significant contribution to one's life.

Desire for Social and Emotional Competence Most people are concerned about how other people feel about them. People want to be accepted, respected, and liked. Adults want their children to develop acceptable social and emotional skills so that they can enjoy life. Schools are the major social agency in our culture. Information is imparted in the school setting regarding dating, mental health, sex education, nutrition, driver education, and many other important areas. Physical education offers unique opportunities in this social-emotional area because of the nature and arrangement of its subject matter. Competitive situations (involving winning, losing, and accepting referee decisions) and coeducational activities (with emphasis on movement skills) provide a rich source of social and emotional experiences for youth. Physical education teachers can have a tremendous impact on students in these areas.

Desire to Compete Most societies are competitive. Indeed, competition is present in almost all aspects of our culture. People learn to compete at an early age, and many employers believe that the best competitors

Developmental Levels and Characteristics of Students

In addition to the desires of parents and students, the developmental levels and characteristics of students should also be examined. Characteristics are those typical or distinctive features of students that represent a given developmental or age level. As students grow and develop, certain characteristics appear and disappear. Within a specific age range, most students will exhibit similar characteristics. There will always be extreme ends of the normal curve regarding developmental levels. Students will vary in height, weight, social abilities, and in many other areas at each chronological age.

Developmental characteristics are usually defined by chronological age. The problem with this approach is that four or five different developmental age levels may exist within a given chronological age range (e.g., seventh grade may contain students who have developmental ages ranging from 10 to 14 years old). Most schools, however, group students by chronological age rather than developmental level because of administrative ease. Physical education teachers must be aware of the wide range of developmental levels that exist at a given grade level. These developmental differences affect physical abilities and performance in physical activities.

Student characteristics are categorized into physical, social, emotional, and intellectual areas. Curriculum planners carefully consider all areas because physical education programs contribute to all four. Some physical educators mistakenly believe their program contributes only to the physical area, but physical activities are not learned in a vacuum; students are also involved mentally, socially, and emotionally. The characteristics of students are important to understand when determining the types of activities, the length of units, the amount of student choice, and the content to be emphasized.

The characteristics of middle school students are different from those of senior high students, and their developmental levels need to be considered as separate entities. It is difficult to sort out characteristics by each of the four categories. In the following sections on middle and senior high school students, two areas will be discussed: the physical area, and a combination of the social, emotional, and intellectual areas.

The middle school curriculum is an important link in the total school curriculum. There is plenty of data to support the importance of physical education (see Chapter 1 discussion). The middle school years represent the first time students are able to make personal decisions about what they like and dislike. Decisions made are often irreversible and last a lifetime. Middle school is a time when students may choose to avoid physical activity whenever possible. Teachers and

are the most successful workers in the business world. Adults want their children to be competitors and winners. In many youth sport leagues, children are forced at an early age to compete for league championships, trophies, and adult approval. Some people believe that this early competitive experience is beneficial for youngsters, but others seriously question these practices. Regardless of the stand taken, most societies are competitive. The competitive nature of sports and physical activity requires physical educators to take a stand on competition. Physical education programs can have a strong influence on youngsters and their ability to compete.

Desire for Risk, Adventure, and Excitement Perhaps because of increased urbanization, mechanization, and impersonal, fast-paced lifestyles, many people are turning to high-risk adventurous activities for fun. Physical activities such as rock climbing, skiing, white-water canoeing, and backpacking are increasing in popularity and give people an opportunity to do something new, risky, and exciting. The physical education curriculum can provide many experiences to satisfy this desire.

Desire for Rhythmic Expression Most people enjoy listening to and moving to rhythmic sounds. Many forms of rhythmic activity have been popular in a wide variety of cultures throughout history. They can include many forms of dance, such as folk, square, and aerobic dancing, as well as sport movements, such as jumping rope, running hurdles, or exercising to music. Rhythms can be both enjoyable and motivational. A variety of rhythmic activities are an important part of a physical education curriculum.

Desire for Creative Expression People look for ways to express their autonomy and individuality. Clothes and hairstyles are popular ways to reveal oneself to the world. Play and leisure time is another opportunity for self-expression. The work world often puts limits on individuality, stimulating people to channel their creative and individual desires into play or leisure pursuits. Physical activities provide numerous possibilities for creative outlets structured by the rules that govern the activities. In basketball, students enjoy trying to develop acrobatic shots or creative drives to the basket, passes, and assists. In gymnastics, the opportunity to develop a creative routine to music or to perfect new moves may be challenging. New plays and defenses are created in football. The challenges are unlimited, and the opportunities for creative expression appeal to students. Physical education curricula should be planned carefully to help satisfy this desire.

administrators know this is a difficult time for youngsters, so it is important to keep students turned on to ward activity through a well-organized and expertly taught program. It is often difficult to find a curriculum that is designed expressly for the adolescent student. Curricula for middle school students may be a watered-down high school programs or an extension of the elementary school curriculum. Neither program suits adolescents; they need a program that is designed to meet traits and characteristics that are unique to their stage of development.

Never again will youngsters have to experience as many major changes as they do during middle school. Youngsters at this level want to be independent but still desire the security of authority. This places teachers in a situation where they are consistently challenged and questioned but expected to exert direction when necessary. Understanding the developmental characteristics of these youngsters is requisite to effective instruction. The following sections examine characteristics and follow with a discussion of the implications of various traits.

Physical Characteristics: Middle School

RAPID AND UNEVEN GROWTH. Middle school students go through a rapid and uneven growth spurt. Girls enter this spurt about 18 months earlier than boys and are usually taller and more mature early in this period. Once boys experience the growth spurt, they pass girls in height and weight. The final result is a wide range of physical maturity, which did not exist in the elementary school years.

IMPLICATIONS: *Teachers need to recognize the number of problems caused by the rapid and uneven growth. Girls are often stronger, faster, and larger than boys. Boys may feel uneasy about this growth difference between the sexes as well as among themselves. Activities have to be adjusted to account for the size and skill differences. Teachers can expect that boys who have not entered puberty will not be as strong and quick as more mature youngsters and will feel uneasy about competing in physical contact sports. Girls who are developmentally advanced or retarded may feel insecure and not want to participate in physical education activities. Teachers must take time to discuss this wide variation in maturity and help youngsters understand they are normal. In addition, students need to be nurtured as they learn how their physical size and development influences their choice of participation in various physical activities.*

DECREASED EFFECTIVENESS TO LEARN MOTOR SKILLS. The range of motor ability levels increases among students, and the skill level differences of students become increasingly apparent. Motor abilities develop slowly because of the increase in growth velocity. Awkwardness, poor coordination, low strength, and low endurance are common during rapid growth spurts. As students go through puberty, they develop secondary sexual characteristics. Boys experience facial hair, pubic hair, a voice change, and genital and shoulder development. Girls develop breasts, pubic hair, a widening of the hips, and an accumulation of body fat.

IMPLICATIONS: *When growth velocity is high, the predisposition to learn motor skills is decreased. This makes the middle school years a difficult time to teach new skills that are tough to master. Combined with an unwillingness to fail in front of peers, students try to avoid activity or avoid learning new skills if they fear embarrassment. A focus on individual and dual activities will help minimize the risk of public failure. In addition, all units of instruction should be started in a manner that ensures student success. This helps minimize the tendency of adolescents to speak negatively (and loudly) about their dislike of the unit when they are failing. Finally, students develop musculature and add body fat, which changes the body's center of gravity and perceptual awareness. The result of these changes is decreased performance in activities requiring balance and body coordination.*

CHANGES IN PHYSICAL TRAITS. Boys become stronger and gain endurance. Females often gain an advantage over boys in the areas of balance and flexibility. Posture is sometimes a problem with youngsters who are embarrassed about their height. Ossification of the bones is usually not complete.

IMPLICATIONS: *Physical performance differences between sexes is obvious to students. This increased awareness of physical differences demands that teachers discuss the differences and the importance of posture and lifetime fitness. An understanding of different body types and their impact on physical performance is important so students can begin to select activities that are well suited to their particular build and physique. Because of incomplete bone ossification, it may be a good time to avoid heavy physical contact sports in order to avoid permanent damage to the skeletal system. Learning to participate with others regardless of ability level is an important outcome because this is a time when students form cliques. This can lead to a separation of sexes and friends with differing skill levels, which is undesirable and may be self-limiting as students mature.*

Social, Emotional, and Intellectual Development: Middle School

INDEPENDENCE AND PEER GROUPS. Students have a strong need for independence and are often torn between adult and peer values. Peer groups, providing the standards for behavior, represent independence because of the absence of adults. Leaders, followers, and loyalty start to evolve through group dynamics. Fighting with parents and peers is common at this age, as is competitiveness.

IMPLICATIONS: Independence is an important trait that students need to learn. If students do not learn independence, they become liabilities to society because they cannot make decisions that contribute to the betterment of the society. Thus, it is important to provide situations that will allow youngsters to make decisions in a somewhat structured setting. They can learn the consequences of their decisions and behaviors without finding themselves in a life-threatening situation. Offering opportunities for leadership skill development helps youngsters develop their decision-making skills. Participation in game and sport activities fosters an understanding of the importance of rules in maintaining an environment that is acceptable to all participants.

EMOTIONAL INSTABILITY. Moods change quickly, for this is an emotional and unpredictable period. Students often become angry, fearful, and easily upset.

IMPLICATIONS: The moodiness of middle school students is often precipitated by their rapid development and lack of experience in dealing with new social situations. Teachers must strive to be even-tempered and unruffled by students' consistent mood changes. Students want great freedom to express their behaviors and desires, but they expect teachers to be perfect models. It is a time when teachers must display patience and direction without excessive force. Teacher modeling of desirable behavior helps avoid troubling double standards—expecting students to do as they are told regardless of the teacher's behavior.

SOCIAL AWARENESS. Students are interested in improving themselves, especially in the physical area. Weight training, bodybuilding, and figure control or body sculpting are of special interest. Strong concerns about size and abilities are common. Grooming, clothes, and appearance become important because students are overly self-conscious about their bodies. Romantic interests begin at this age range, and students try to impress each other in various ways. Girls are usually ahead of boys socially and begin to date older boys. Social activities become important, and dances, movies, parties, and athletic events serve as social meeting places.

IMPLICATIONS: Discussions about physiological changes help students accept varying student sizes and limitations and to accept these individual differences. Allowing students to express themselves without ridicule or embarrassment encourages self-acceptance. A number of social activities can be provided for students so they learn proper social behavior in a variety of settings.

INTELLECTUAL DEVELOPMENT. Intellectual development continues throughout this period. Students can concentrate longer, are able to understand more complex concepts, and are better able to follow directions. An interest in the "why" of physical activity occurs. Daydreaming and fantasizing are lessening for many students. The variety of student activities decreases continually throughout this period and into adulthood. Students begin to make decisions about areas in which they want to specialize. This has strong implications for future sport and physical activity participation. A strong interest in risk, excitement, and adventure is common.

IMPLICATIONS: Intellectual development among students can be exciting for teachers considering interaction can be meaningful and challenging. Teachers need to explain why they are teaching certain activities rather than telling students to do it "because I said so." Helping students become familiar with their physical abilities so they can make wise and thoughtful choices about activities that match their skills increases understanding. Students in middle school often try high-risk activities and end up making poor decisions because of their desire to show off and impress others. It is important that safety procedures have been thoroughly covered so students understand the consequences of their behaviors.

Middle school is often a challenging and difficult time for students. They are confused by their changing physical appearance and the transition process from childhood to adulthood. Many important decisions are being made about their careers and goals for life. For physical education teachers, the situation is extremely challenging and can be quite frustrating and demanding as well as rewarding. Physical education can play a significant role in these students' lives.

Physical Characteristics: High School

INCREASED MOTOR ABILITY AND COORDINATION. Most students have finished their growth spurt and are approaching physical maturity. Bone growth and the ossification process are complete for most students. Sexual characteristics reach maturity for both boys and girls. Students are beyond the period of physical awkwardness and become more comfortable with their physical abilities. Motor ability and coordination improve quicker during this time period.

IMPLICATIONS: This is an excellent time for students to improve existing motor skills and learn new skills. Students are more comfortable trying new physical skills and performing in front of peers. Teachers can move students through instructional progressions at a much faster rate.

MODIFICATION OF PHYSICAL TRAITS. Strength, endurance, and speed continue to increase. Boys surpass girls in height and weight. Boys continue to develop muscularity while most girls level off in this area.

IMPLICATIONS: Teachers need to help students understand that physical differences among students impact skill performance. Students need guidance toward activities they will be able to successfully participate in within their physical limits. Developing sensitivity for participation with others at various ability levels is an important learning.

Social, Emotional, and Intellectual Development: High School

SOCIAL AWARENESS. Social activities such as going to dances, parties, athletic events, and clubs dominate the lives of high school students. Students are concerned with dating, going steady, getting a job, getting married, and starting a career. Peer groups are important and help provide behavioral standards in areas such as dress, grooming, and interests. Peer groups teach students loyalty to a group yet independence from adults. Students still have a difficult time deciding between adult and peer values, and conflicts exist between adults and students. Competition increases with an emphasis on grades, athletics, and dating. There is continued concern about size, strength, and physical ability, but students show more interest in cosmetic fitness than health-related fitness.

IMPLICATIONS: High school is not a time to force students into activities that do not interest them. There should be many opportunities for choice. Dress requirements, time for changing clothes, and grooming time are important issues where students should have input into the physical education course requirements. Students enjoy opportunities to express their opinions and ideas with regard to various issues. Weight lifting, aerobics, Pilates exercises, figure control, and other popular fitness activities are attractive to these students.

EMOTIONAL DEVELOPMENT. Most students have completed the puberty cycle and are comfortable with their bodies and the direction of their lives. There are fewer mood swings, and students seem to be more stable emotionally. Problems with fighting, extreme competitiveness, and arguing over issues start to diminish.

IMPLICATIONS: Students need additional experiences with emotional control. They need to understand the necessity of emotional control in physical education environments and in other aspects of life. Effective adult models of emotional control allow students to witness acceptable behavior patterns. Teachers who talk about emotional control in class and behave differently during an interscholastic basketball game offer little credibility to their students.

INTELLECTUAL DEVELOPMENT. Students are approaching their intellectual potential. Their memories and their abilities to reason, concentrate, imagine, and think conceptually have improved and continue to develop. Students have experienced the knowledge explosion and changing American values. Many students experience broken homes, single-parent families, multiple moves, drugs, and early sexual activity. Students look for risk, excitement, and adventure. They have a large base of knowledge and experience by the time they reach this period. Students express strong concern about security, attention, affection, self-worth, and intellectual improvement. There is a continued narrowing of interests and an emphasis on specialization in activities where they perceive themselves to be competent.

IMPLICATIONS: Teachers need to be sensitive to the increasing intellectual abilities of their students. A focus on the "why" of physical education and the objectives of the program is often demanded. Students need to be able to choose activities they want to learn. Units should be longer to ensure in-depth instruction. The curriculum should include units that incorporate risk, excitement, and adventure. Students also want to understand the cognitive concepts of activities as well as improve their physical skills. The senior high school years are important in transforming adolescents into adults. Students must face the realities of the world and make decisions about education, careers, marriage, religion, politics, and lifestyles. Teachers have a responsibility for imparting information, attitudes, and skills.

Consideration of the Activity Interests of Students

Program planners should examine student interests with activities being offered. Too often, programs are based on the activity interests of teachers, administrators, and parents, rather than students. Often, teachers will not teach activities in which they are not skilled. The activity comfort zone of teachers can be narrow and the curriculum limited. Lack of variety may cause students to develop escape or avoidance behaviors in physical education. They may like physical activity, but not like the activities presented or the methods of instruction. Effective teachers learn to expand their teaching repertoire of activities and methods to better meet students' interests.

When the activity interests of students are not considered, students may avoid taking physical education, especially at the high school level, where the program should be consumer driven. For example, teachers at a particular school may try offering units on lifetime activities such as golf, bowling, and archery and then find out that only a few students may register because of the lack of student interest or expense of the activities. In another example, if all of the units in the curriculum are required during an optional year of physical education, some students may avoid the entire year because they do not wish to take one or two of the specific units. In other words, students will avoid an entire year because of one or two compulsory activities. As a minimum, the high school program should offer students four or five activity choices. The high school program is not the time to force students into activities in which they have little or no interest.

Surveys or checklists can be used to gather data about student activity interests. Surveys completed in the spring help determine the curricular offerings for the following fall and spring semesters. The survey can be administered every other year to all demographic groups within the schools (i.e., boys, girls, athletes, nonathletes, various racial groups, and various grade levels). As many students as possible should be surveyed to ensure valid information. Ideally, the survey can be administered in a class or homeroom period (math, science, or English) so all students have the opportunity to respond. Student interests can be analyzed by age, sex, or racial group.

A survey instrument should include all possible physical activities that contribute to the content standards and objectives of physical education. It is important to avoid restrictive thinking when listing activity offerings in a survey. For example, the lack of a pool, racquetball courts, ski slopes, or various types of equipment for specific activities need not prohibit an educator from including these activities on the survey. Travel to off-campus facilities in the nearby community may be possible in the future. Most communities have nearby golf driving ranges, racquet clubs, bowling alleys, pools, ski slopes, or wooded areas that can be used for the school program. Data collected from surveys can be used to support the need for expanding physical facilities, such as adding a pool, racquetball courts, tennis courts, or a weight-lifting room. If student interest is evident, administrators may be convinced that facilities and equipment, course offerings, or new teachers should be added to the physical education program.

An example of an interest survey is shown in Figure 3.3. The instrument can be revised every other year, and new activity trends included. Professional and popular literature help provide information about the new activity patterns and habits. Interests in the community can be determined by looking at various recreation programs offered through the YMCA, the parks and recreation department, private clubs, community leagues, and corporations. Facilities available, such as bowling alleys, golf courses, ski slopes, health clubs, and swimming pools, provide additional information about interests in the community.

Step Six: Organize Selected Activities into Instructional Units for a Yearly Plan

After appropriate activities that contribute to content standards have been selected, design a delivery system that ensures all activities are taught. Activities are most often grouped by grade level and put into units that are arranged in a weekly format. When using this approach, instruction is focused on an activity over an entire week. The weekly plan has three major advantages. First, a comprehensive lesson plan for the week can be developed and divided into the appropriate number of days for your school schedule. This will keep planning duties manageable. The objective for each week is to move students along the path of learning at an optimal rate. What cannot be covered one day is taught in the next lesson. Second, less orientation instruction is needed after the first day. Safety factors, teaching hints, and key points need only a brief review each day, and equipment needs are similar from day to day. Third, progression and learning sequences are evident; both teacher and students can see progress.

Determine Length of Activity Units

The length of an activity unit can vary from 2 weeks to 1 year. For example, a 2-week unit on Frisbee or a 1-year course on weight training or dance could be offered. Developmental levels and interests of students affect the length of a unit, as does the school schedule and the number of days per week that a class meets. The number of class meetings per week is a key factor in deciding the length of a unit. A 3-week unit that meets daily offers 15 sessions, while a 3-week unit that meets twice a week allows only six sessions. Although both are 3-week units, there is a big difference in the amount of actual class time for instruction.

At one end of the spectrum is an arrangement of long units of activity (depth) focused on a few activities. Students take four to eight activities in a year. An example is the following:

First 9 weeks—Flag football or soccer
Second 9 weeks—Basketball or volleyball
Third 9 weeks—Wrestling or gymnastics
Last 9 weeks—Softball or track and field

Another design uses 6-week units:

First 6 weeks—Swimming
Second 6 weeks—Volleyball
Third 6 weeks—Basketball
Fourth 6 weeks—Gymnastics/Wrestling
Fifth 6 weeks—Track and field
Last 6 weeks—Softball

Physical Activity Interest Survey

Name _____

Grade _____ Age _____ Sex _____

Athletic team _____

Instructions: Which of the following physical activities or sports would you be most interested in taking as a course in the physical education program? Please list your top 5 choices on the lines provided. Place a number 1 in front of your highest choice, a number 2 in front of your next choice, and so on, until you reach choice number 5. Remember to make only 5 choices.

Aquatic Activities

____ Lifesaving, water safety
____ Skin and scuba diving
____ Surfing
____ Swimming, diving
____ Water sports (polo, volleyball, basketball)

Individual Activities

____ Archery
____ Badminton
____ Fencing
____ Frisbee
____ Golf
____ Gymnastics
____ Handball
____ Racquetball
____ Recreational games (bowling, horseshoes, shuffleboard, etc.)
____ Roller-skating
____ Skateboarding
____ Squash
____ Tennis
____ Track and field

Physical Conditioning Activities

____ Aerobic dance
____ Body conditioning, weight control
____ Cardio kickboxing
____ Martial arts (judo, karate, kendo, etc.)
____ Medicine balls
____ Physioballs
____ Pilates
____ Walking activities
____ Weight training
____ Yoga

Outdoor Adventure Activities

____ Backpacking
____ Canoeing, kayaking

____ Cycling (bicycling)
____ Fishing
____ Horseback riding
____ Hunting
____ Ice-skating
____ Orienteering
____ Outdoor survival
____ Rock climbing
____ Sailing
____ Skiing (cross country)
____ Skiing (downhill)
____ Snowshoeing

Rhythmic Activities

____ Ballet
____ Country swing dance
____ Disco
____ Folk and square dance
____ Jazz dance
____ Modern dance
____ Social dance

Team Activities

____ Baseball
____ Basketball
____ Eclipse ball
____ Field hockey
____ Flag football
____ Ice hockey
____ Lacrosse
____ Soccer
____ Softball
____ Speedball/speed-a-way
____ Team handball
____ Volleyball
____ Wrestling

Directions for the teacher: Remind students to select only 5 choices, using the numbers 1–5 on the lines beside the activities. When analyzing the data, it is helpful to transpose numbers 1 and 5 and numbers 2 and 4. In other words, a 1 becomes a 5 and a 5 becomes a 1. A 2 is worth 4 and a 4 worth 2. The numbers are added for each activity. The activities with the most points are the most popular, and those with the least points are the least popular.

FIGURE 3.3 Physical activity interest survey

Still another design is to offer two units during each 9-week grading period. One unit is 5 weeks and the other 4 weeks. In this way, students take eight units per year. Two examples of this approach are as follows:

Program A

First 9 weeks
Soccer (5 weeks)
Flag football (4 weeks)

Second 9 weeks
Tennis (5 weeks)
Basketball (4 weeks)

Third 9 weeks
Volleyball (5 weeks)
Health club activities (4 weeks)

Last 9 weeks
Track and field (5 weeks)
Softball (4 weeks)

Program B

First 9 weeks
Field hockey (5 weeks)
Speed-a-way (4 weeks)

Second 9 weeks
Volleyball (5 weeks)
Dance (4 weeks)

Third 9 weeks
Basketball (5 weeks)
Fitness center activities (4 weeks)

Last 9 weeks
Tennis (5 weeks)
Track and field (4 weeks)

At the opposite end of the spectrum is an arrangement using short 1-, 2-, and 3-week units (breadth) that offer students 12 to 18 different activities during the year. The following is an example:

Weeks	Activity
1–3	Swimming/Water polo
4–6	Flag football/Soccer
7–9	Tennis/Raquetball
10–12	Volleyball/Eclipse Ball
13–15	Dance Variations
16–18	Basketball/Team handball
19–21	Badminton/Fishing
22–24	Tumbling/Orienteering
25–27	Frisbee games/Frisbee golf
28–30	Speed-a-way/Flickerball
31–33	Track and field/Golf
34–36	Softball/Over-the-Line

Each unit starts with basic skills and progresses to a point where instruction and skill practice is necessary because students cannot perform adequately. Starting each unit with the easiest activity ensures success and

review for all students. Instructional sequences for each day are built on the preceding lesson.

Check the Scope, Sequence, Breadth, Depth, and Balance of the Curriculum

An important step in creating a quality program is to review and monitor the scope, sequence, breadth, depth, and balance of the curriculum. These are important concepts that ensure that a quality curriculum is being implemented for the students in the specific situation.

Scope is the content of the curriculum for each year. Monitoring the scope of the curriculum ensures that the entire content of the program will be covered in a systematic and accountable fashion for each year. In middle school physical education, the scope of the curriculum is broad; many activities are presented to ensure that a breadth of activities is included. Student interest wanes if units are too long. Also, middle school physical education is designed to help students learn about and explore all the available types of physical activity. There is in-depth coverage of fewer activities in the high school program. High school students are ready to choose longer activity units that will help them increase their skills dramatically. Figure 3.4 shows an example of a yearly plan with a four-part lesson for seventh graders that focuses on breadth with 18 to 20 units in the yearly curriculum.

The **sequence** of the activities in the curriculum is arranged progressively throughout the year and from year to year. Yearly and year-to-year curriculum plans serve as guides for teachers. Curricula are articulated in two planes, **horizontal** and **vertical**. Horizontal articulation includes the yearly plan and defines the skills and activities for that year. Vertical articulation is concerned with scope and sequence for all years K–12. Sequence ensures that students receive different instruction and activities at each grade or developmental level. Of particular importance is the articulation of program material throughout elementary, middle, and high school programs. Figure 3.5 is an example of a page from a scope and sequence chart for a K–12 curriculum. Notice how the different units of instruction are added throughout the grades 4–12 on the chart. Different units and skills are introduced[I], reviewed and reinforced[R], and taken to proficiency[P] at the indicated grade levels.

Balance ensures that all objectives in the program receive adequate coverage. When reviewing the scope and sequence of the curriculum, checking for balance avoids a skewing toward one particular area. To ensure balance, major areas of emphasis are determined based on program objectives. These areas can be allotted a percentage of program time based on the characteristics and interests of students. This determination

Unit No.	Introductory	Fitness	Lesson Focus	Game
1	Move and Freeze	Orientation	Orientation	Simple Games
2	Basic Movements	Teacher Leader	Soccer Skills	Lead-up Soccer Games
3	Walk, Trot, Jog	Stretching	Soccer Skills	Soccer Game
4	Fugitive Tag Variations	Form Running	Football Skills	Lead-up Football Games
5	Pivot Variations	Racetrack Fitness	Football Skills/Throton	Small-Sided Football Games
6	Flag Grab	Aerobic Fitness and Partner Resistance	Group Team Building	Paper, Scissors, Rock
7	Marking	Walking Activities	Pedometer Activities	Pedometer Game
8	Run, Stop, and Pivot	Circuit Training	Volleyball Skills	Lead-Up Volleyball Games
9	Flag Grab Variations	Astronaut Drills	Volleyball Skills/Eclipse Ball	Small-Sided Volleyball Games
10	Marking Variations	Jump Rope Continuity	Rope Jumping Skills	Chicken Baseball
11	Move and Change Directions	Squad Leader	Floor Hockey	Lead-up Hockey Games
12	Quick Hands	Step Aerobics	Floor Hockey/Roller Hockey	Small-Sided Hockey Games
13	Partner Over and Around	Dyna-Bands	Team Handball	Lead-up Team Handball Games
14	Flash Drills	Cardio Choice	Team Handball	Small-Sided Team Handball Games
15	Agility Drills	Jump and Jog	Tennis Skills	Lead-up Tennis Games
16	Moving Throw and Catch	Fortune Cookie	Tennis Skills	Eclipse Ball Variations
17	Clothespin Tag	Scavenger Hunt	Basketball Skills	Lead-up Basketball Games
18	File Running	Basketball Circuit	Basketball Skills	Small-Sides Basketball Games
19	Moving High Fives	Monopoly Fitness	Rhythms	Dances
20	Jumping and Plyometrics	Squad Leader Variations with Task Cards	Rhythms	Dances
21	Fastest Tag Variations	Kickboxing Aerobics	New Games	New Game Activities
22	Standing High Fives	Novel Walking Activities	Track and Field	Running Relays
23	Loose Caboose	Pacer Run	Track and Field	Running Relays
24	Leaping Lena/Rooster Hop	Long Jump Rope Fitness	Gymnastics	Pyramid Building
25	Move and Change Directions	Scavenger Hunt	Frisbee Skills/Spinjammers	Ultimate Frisbee
26	Triangle and One	Circuit Training with a Jog	Softball Skills	Frisbee Softball
27	Spider Tag Variations	Yoga/Pilates	Softball Skills	Over-the-Line Softball
28	Marking Variations	Walking Activities	Golf Skills	Golf Skills
29	Blob Tag	Cardio Choice/Medicine Balls	Badminton Skills	Lead-up Badminton Games
30	Quarter Eagle Agility	Frisbee Fitness	Badminton Skills	Badminton Games
31	Triangle and Two	Scavenger Hunt	Orienteering Skills	Orienteering Meet
32	Power Walk Variations	Rope Jumping and Partner Resistance	Flickerball Skills	Flickerball Game
33	Move and Perform a Stretch	Cardio Choice/Physioballs	Speed-a-way	Speed-a-way Game
34	Tag Games	Monopoly Fitness	Juggling Skills	Partner Juggling
35	Fitness Self-Testing	Fitness Self-Testing	Fitness Self-Testing	Fitness Self-Testing
36	Teacher Choice	Teacher Choice	Cageball Games	Relays/Tag Games

FIGURE 3.4 Yearly curriculum plan for seventh graders

FIGURE 3.5 Scope and sequence example

Handwritten annotations: "Weeks" (with arrow to the number row); "USE X's on the weeks progression is taking place."

Activity	K	1	2	3	4	5	6	7	8	9	10	11	12
Archery													
1. History	✓	✓	✓	✓							—	I	R
2. Safety—Rules—Strategy											—	I	R
3. Equipment											—	I	R
4. Shooting											—	I	R
Badminton													
1. History											—	I	R
2. Safety—Rules—Strategy					I	R				P	—	I	R
3. Equipment					I	R				P	R	R	R
4. Skills					I	R				P	R	R	R
a. Grip					I	R				P	R	R	R
b. Serves					I	R				P	R	R	R
c. Strokes					I	R				P	R	R	R
Bowling													
1. History											—	I	R
2. Safety—Rules—Strategy								I	R	R	—	I	R
3. Equipment								I	R	R	—	I	R
4. Skills								I	R	R	—	I	R
a. Grip								I	R	R	—	I	R
b. Approach								I	R	R	—	I	R
c. Delivery								I	R	R	—	I	R
Cross-Country Skiing													
1. History											—	I	R
2. Safety—Rules—Strategy								I	R	R	—	I	R
3. Equipment								I	R	R	—	I	R
4. Skills								I	R	R	—	I	R
a. Kick glide								I	R	R	—	I	R
b. Stop								I	R	R	—	I	R
c. Turns								I	R	R	—	I	R
d. Poling								I	R	R	—	I	R
e. Climb								I	R	R	—	I	R
Curling													
1. History											—	I	R
2. Safety—Rules—Strategy											—	I	R
3. Equipment											—	I	R
4. Skills											—	I	R
a. Delivery											—	I	R
b. Sweeping											—	I	R
Golf													
1. History											—	I	R
2. Safety—Rules—Strategy											—	I	R
3. Equipment											—	I	R
4. Skills											—	I	R
a. Grip											—	I	R
b. Full swings											—	I	R
c. Approach shots											—	I	R
d. Putting											—	I	R

I—Introduce: initial instruction of psychomotor, cognitive, and affective skills that are explained, demonstrated, and practiced.
R—Review and reinforce: continued instruction of skill-level improvement and increased knowledge of techniques.
P—Proficiency: the attainment of an individual's maximum skill level through instruction and practice.

FIGURE 3.5 Scope and sequence example

Courtesy of LaCrosse, WI, Public Schools.

reveals to administrators, teachers, and parents the direction and emphasis of the program. All areas have a proportionate share of instructional time, and the percentage of time allotted to each area reflects the needs and characteristics.

Common categories of activities emphasized are team sports, lifetime sports, physical conditioning or fitness activities, dance activities, gymnastics activities, aquatic activities, and adventure activities. An important point is to ensure that all students have experience with a variety of activities selected from as many categories as possible in the middle school setting. Too often, the curriculum is heavily tipped toward team sports because of class size, facilities, equipment, or the instructor's lack of interest or ability in other areas. An unbalanced curriculum is not appropriate for students who are interested in activity categories not offered. For example, many students enjoy Frisbee, orienteering, dance, or skin diving. They may not enjoy football, basketball, wrestling, or volleyball. If the curriculum is unbalanced, these students will not have access to potentially fulfilling activities. Teachers must make every effort to offer a balanced program.

The skillful curriculum planner arranges activities in the program to influence the habits of students with regards to physical activity, rhythms, and sports areas. Initially, students who are not interested in physical activity may have to be positively directed toward those activities. They may need a gentle push to engage in the activities until the reinforcing aspects of physical activities have developed a "positively addicted" person. All students need to find activities for fun and health-related fitness in the physical education curriculum. Physical education programs can take a leadership role in trying to shape activity preferences, and teachers should select and arrange activities with this goal in mind.

The most often found category of activity in the schools is team sports. Many physical educators claim these are the most popular activities with students and are the most economical activities in terms of facilities and equipment. More often than not, they are popular with vocal students who are skilled in such sports. Less-skilled students are intimidated and afraid to admit that they don't like team sports for fear their more skilled peers will not like them. In addition, team sports units are only more economical (in terms of required equipment) when they are improperly taught. To teach basketball or softball with three or four balls ensures that the majority of students will be standing rather than practicing skills in a semi-individualized manner.

More teachers are including a variety of lifetime activities, such as walking, jogging, hiking, step aerobics, kickboxing, Pilates, yoga, weight training, racquetball, tennis, badminton, bowling, and golf. These activities have more carryover value for later life be-

cause they do not require a number of teammates for participation. Successful programs develop a balance of team sports, lifetime sports, physical fitness, gymnastics, dance, aquatics, and currently popular activities. Curricula that offer an activity balance have a higher potential for positively affecting all students within the school.

Step Seven: Evaluate and Modify the Curriculum

Evaluation schedules and suggested techniques for modifying the curriculum are an integral part of the curricular structure. A number of sources can supply evaluative data: pupils, teachers, consultants, parents, and administrators. The type of data desired can vary. Achievement test scores can supply hard data to compare preassessments and postassessments with those of other programs. Subjective assessments might include likes and dislikes, value judgments, problem areas, and needed adjustments. The evaluation schedule can select a limited area for assessment, or assessment can be broadened to cover the entire program. Collecting information is only the first step; the information must be translated into action. Modification of possible program deficiencies is based on sound educational philosophy. If the program has weak spots, identifying the weaknesses and determining the causes are important steps to take.

A pilot or trial project can be instituted if the new curriculum represents a radical change. One school in the district might be chosen to develop a pilot program. Site selection should offer the program a strong opportunity to succeed, for success depends in large part on the educational climate of the school. In some cases, the experimental program might be implemented with only one class in a school. Enthusiastic, skilled direction is necessary for such projects. Much information can be derived from this pilot process before an entire program is implemented throughout the school system.

AN ARTICULATED CURRICULUM: GRADES K–12

Often, physical education curricula are developed in parts. There is usually a curriculum for the elementary school level, one for middle school, and another for the high school. Each curriculum is written and organized independently of the others. A district-wide K–12 plan that considers all of the steps mentioned is seldom developed. In many cases, elementary physical education specialists do not know middle and high school physical education teachers, let alone have an understanding of the curriculum taught at each level.

Teachers operate autonomously, without concern for or knowledge of what is done at other levels. This leads to a fragmented program that shows little articulation between levels. Time, energy, and learning of activities may be wasted, duplicated, or omitted in a curriculum that is not vertically articulated.

Curriculum planners need an understanding of the impact these curriculum steps have on students in terms of overall program objectives. An articulated curriculum with consistent policies and procedures on instruction, management, discipline, grading, student choices, dress codes, and so forth will impact students in a positive manner and improve participation in the program. This approach will also impact students' attitudes toward physical education and physical activity participation now and in the future. For example, a teacher who does not look carefully at the scope, sequence, and balance of the curriculum may repeat or omit important aspects of the program. A well-developed K–12 curriculum plan will provide fitness activities, lifetime sports, rhythmic activities, gymnastics, and outdoor adventure-type activities as well as team sports. An articulated physical education program should also consider the after-school participation opportunities for students, such as activity clubs, intramural sports, or athletic programs. An articulated quality physical education curriculum can lead students into these after-school participation opportunities. Physical educators must carefully consider these curriculum steps and elements when policies, procedures, yearly plans, daily plans, and other aspects of dealing with students are formulated. Specific suggestions are made throughout this text with respect to each of these program steps.

The Elementary School Program

Elementary school physical education programs place emphasis on expanding the activity experiences of students. Youngsters enter kindergarten with similar skills. The elementary curriculum strives to offer a wide variety of activities to ensure that students have the opportunity to experience success. In addition, a wide variety of activities ensures that students will be involved in short units of instruction in order to minimize long bouts of failure. If units are short, students who don't like a certain activity or feel like failures know they will not have to continue the activity for an extended time. In addition, the wide variety of short units ensures that all students will find some activity they enjoy, increasing their opportunity to experience success.

The Middle School Program

In middle school, this variety of units continues, and the units are short to ensure that students will not have to excessively endure an activity they dislike. A balanced curriculum places equal emphasis on all activities in the curriculum consistent with the program objectives and goals. Activities are included if they meet the needs and interests of all learners and contribute to program standards. For example, a design that offers only four or five team sports during the year does not meet the needs of students who do not like team sports, are uninterested in the sports offered, or prefer individual activities.

Another important consideration in organizing the middle school curriculum is the matter of sequence. Organized correctly, sequence ensures that students receive instruction in a progressive manner from kindergarten to graduation. Skills and knowledge are learned in a sequential manner, so previous material taught contributes to current learning. An example of a lack of sequence is teaching youngsters basketball skills in the first grade and continuing to teach these same skills until students leave school. It would be unthinkable to give youngsters a calculus book in first grade, ask them to repeat the material for 12 years, and then assume they have learned calculus through repetition.

Sequence in the middle school years ensures that units of instruction are organized and designed expressly for this level. Emphasis on strategy and advanced skill should be minimized because students at this age enter a rapid growth curve that reduces the ability to learn motor skills. Asking students to split their concentration on skill performance and strategy reduces the odds they will learn either. As an example, think back to learning to drive a car for the first time. It was difficult to concentrate on the fine motor skills involved in driving while thinking about the rules of the road. After driving skills were overlearned, it was possible to think about many other things (e.g., putting on makeup and talking on a cell phone). Frustration and fear can be the result of this type of overload. Until a skill is overlearned, concentration should be on skill performance. When the skills become overlearned, students can concentrate on the cognitive aspect of sport strategy. Most middle school students have not overlearned skills, so strategy should be a minor part of instruction.

When developing scope and sequence for middle school students, it is difficult to design a sequence that is perfect for all youngsters. Students are grouped (whether it be by grade, age, or developmental level), and every group is characterized by a range of differences. To expect students to strictly follow a predetermined sequence is unrealistic. Effective teachers modify the sequence depending on the capabilities of the student. The best teaching is one-on-one, when activities and instruction are in line with student ability level. Regardless, scope and sequence are important because they lend general direction to instruction.

The High School Program

Senior high school physical education curricula vary greatly from state to state and from large urban schools with six to eight physical education teachers to the small rural schools with one or two teachers. Local school districts have the ultimate responsibility for developing a program that meets state guidelines. State requirements are different, and some school districts allow a number of substitutions for physical education. Some districts have a 4-year requirement, while others do not have any requirements. Another district may have a 3-year requirement but allow substitutions such as cheerleading, athletics, orchestra, or band to fulfill the requirement. The variations and possibilities are endless. Nevertheless, the high school program should build upon the middle school program.

At the high school level, quality programs come in many sizes and shapes. A small high school in upstate New York, a large urban high school in eastern Pennsylvania, or a medium-sized high school in central Arizona can all have quality programs within their existing frameworks. Some programs will have more students, more teachers, more facilities, and better equipment. Requirements, schedules, and administrative support may be quite different in each situation. Quality programs are not, however, a function of large facilities, abundant equipment, extensive physical education requirements, numerous teachers, or small class sizes. Outstanding high school programs are developed by a group of hardworking, dedicated professionals who are doing their best with given resources. There is strong leadership and purpose found in successful programs. A continual effort must be made to improve programs and to change those aspects that are detrimental to accomplishing goals. A sense of excitement and enthusiasm must be found within the program. Curriculum developers can work positively within the existing framework to change existing parameters that cause difficulties.

The high school years offer the educational system an opportunity to polish and improve its product: students who are productive individuals in society. To ensure that the physical education program contributes to this long-term objective, it is important to understand the growth and development of students and the implications these characteristics have on designing a well-planned curriculum. A quality experience for the entire K–12 sequence emphasizes individual success, self-testing, monitoring, physical skill development, requisite knowledge, wellness concepts, choice, and preparation for a lifetime of physical activity. It is important that the high school curriculum build vertically on the middle school curriculum and the middle school curriculum build on the elementary curriculum.

1. Explain the role of a teacher's value orientation when developing a curriculum.

2. List and explain three environmental factors that will influence the scope and general focus of a curriculum.

3. Discuss possible concerns that administrators might have when implementing a flexible schedule.

4. Explain the focus of the affective learning domain.

5. What are the three central components of a behavioral objective?

6. List and briefly explain two societal influences that should be considered when designing a curriculum.

7. Discuss the implication of students' rapid and often uneven growth patterns for physical education teachers.

8. Compared to middle school students, why do high school students generally have less difficulty learning new skills?

9. Explain what is meant by the "scope" of a curriculum.

10. Discuss the importance of periodically evaluating the curriculum.

REFERENCES AND
SUGGESTED READINGS

Buck, M. M., Lund, J. L., Harrison, J. M., & Blakemore Cook, C. L. (2007). *Instructional strategies for secondary physical education* (6th ed.). Boston: McGraw-Hill.

Ennis, C. (1993). Can we really do it all? Making curriculum choices in middle and high school programs. In J. E. Rink (Ed.), *Critical crossroads: Middle and secondary physical education* (pp. 13–23). Reston, VA: NASPE.

Hastie, P. (2003). *Teaching for lifetime physical activity through quality high school physical education.* San Francisco: Benjamin Cummings.

Himberg, C., Hutchinson, G. E. & Roussell, J. M. (2003). *Teaching secondary physical education preparing adolescents to be active for life.* Champaign, IL: Human Kinetics.

Jewett, A., Bain, L., & Ennis, K. (1995). *The curriculum process in physical education*. Dubuque, IA: W. B. Brown and Benchmark.

Kelly, L. & Melograno, V. J. (2004). *Developing the physical education curriculum: An achievement based approach*. Champaign, IL: Human Kinetics Publishers.

National Association for Sport & Physical Education. (2004). *Moving into the future—National standards for physical education* (2nd ed.). Reston, VA: Author.

Rink, J. (2006). *Teaching physical education for learning* (5th ed.). Boston: McGraw-Hill.

Siedentop, D., Mand, C., & Taggart, A. (1986). *Physical education—Teaching and curriculum strategies for grades 5–12*. Mountain View, CA: Mayfield Publishing Co.

Siedentop, D., & Tannehill, D. (2000). *Developing teaching skills in physical education* (4th ed.). Mountain View, CA: Mayfield Publishing Co.

van der Mars, H., Darst, P. W., Vogler, E. W., & Cusimano, B. (1995). Novice and expert physical education teachers: Maybe they think and decide differently . . . but do they behave differently? *Journal of Teaching in Physical Education, 14*(3), 340–347.

Wuest, D., & Lombardo, B. (1994). *Curriculum and instruction: The secondary school physical education experience*. St. Louis, MO: Mosby.

WEB SITES

Curricula Examples
www.sasked.gov.sk.ca/docs/physed/physed1-5/index.html

Physical Education Curriculum Information
www.pecentral.com
www.pelinks4u.org
reach.ucf.edu/~pezone

Research for Education and Learning
www.mcrel.org

ESSENTIAL COMPONENTS OF A QUALITY PROGRAM

COMPONENT 1 A quality physical education program is organized around content standards that offer direction and continuity to instruction and evaluation.

COMPONENT 2 A quality program is student centered and based on the developmental urges, characteristics, and interests of students.

COMPONENT 3 Quality physical education makes physical activity and motor-skill development the core of the program.

COMPONENT 4 Physical education programs teach management skills and self-discipline.

COMPONENT 5 Quality programs emphasize inclusion of all students.

COMPONENT 6 In a quality physical education setting, instruction focuses on the process of learning skills rather than the product or outcome of the skill performance.

COMPONENT 7 A quality physical education program teaches lifetime activities that students can use to promote their health and personal wellness.

COMPONENT 8 Quality physical education teaches cooperative and responsibility skills and helps students develop sensitivity to diversity and gender issues.

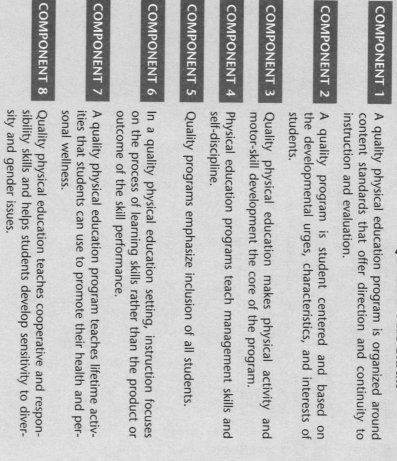

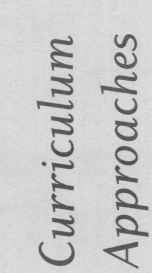

4

Curriculum Approaches

CHAPTER SUMMARY

This chapter focuses on the various curriculum approaches in use today. There are many approaches being used and many variations of these. Allied to this purpose is an analysis of the characteristics and strengths of the various approaches.

STUDENT OUTCOMES

After reading the chapter, you will be able to:

- Describe curriculum approaches and explain the various ways they are used by physical educators.

- List and discuss commonly used organizing centers in secondary school physical education.

- List and describe the popular categories of activities commonly used in the approach known as promoting physical activity/skill development.

- Discuss the advantages and disadvantages of the popular promoting physical activity/skill development approach.

- Discuss the problems of implementing an outdoor adventure activity approach in a high school.

- Describe the pros and cons of a sports education approach for secondary school physical education..

Student Outcomes, continued

- Explain the characteristics of a knowledge concepts curriculum approach.
- Understand how fitness education can be integrated into a knowledge concepts curriculum approach.
- List the different levels of social development in Hellison's approach.

Curriculum approaches developed by following the seven steps in Chapter 3 provide an overall philosophy and scheme that underlies the physical education curriculum. Curriculum approaches include a set of beliefs and goals that evolve from a theoretical framework or value base. These approaches provide the basis for organizing objectives and content, structuring and sequencing activities, and evaluating the curriculum plan. The scope and sequence of activities for the instructional program evolve from the curriculum approach (see Chapter 3). Approaches provide interrelationships between content and the instructional process. An understanding of popular curriculum approaches and how they can be adapted to unique situations facilitates the development process. When building a quality physical education curriculum, different approaches can be used:

1. A curriculum approach that is functioning in another school can be incorporated into a new setting. The program can be accepted in total with only minor changes for local school or community preferences.

2. Adaptation of an existing curriculum approach to meet the local interests, preferences, and school priorities is a second alternative. The existing approach is modified by incorporating local interests, preferences, and school philosophies into a restructured program.

3. A new approach is constructed, coordinating ideas from many sources to form a unified program. This is the most difficult and time-consuming challenge and requires a breadth of experience and clear understanding of the curriculum process.

Formal curricula are usually organized around a major theme, often called an organizing center. The most common organizing centers for physical education curricula are the following:

- Physical skills that are involved in various movement forms, sports, and physical activity. Commonly included are units on basketball, tennis, square dancing, volleyball, weight training, walking, and jogging.

- Physical fitness components such as cardiovascular efficiency, strength, and control of body fat.

- Health and wellness knowledge and activities involving stress management, nutrition, weight control, substance abuse, personal safety, physical fitness, environmental awareness, and behavioral self-control.

- Movement themes such as propelling, catching, striking, and balancing.

- Analysis of movement elements such as force, time, space, and flow.

- Student motives such as appearance, health, and achievement.

- Disciplinary knowledge from such areas as biomechanics, motor learning, exercise physiology, and sport philosophy.

- Social development themes, such as competition, emotional control, sportspersonship, and cooperation.

PROMOTING PHYSICAL ACTIVITY/ SKILL DEVELOPMENT APPROACH

The most commonly used curriculum approach at the secondary level is a broad-based multiple activity approach that focuses on promoting physical activity and developing physical skills with students. A wide variety of activities are included from several categories. These include fitness activities such as jogging or walking; sport units including tennis, basketball, gymnastics, aquatics, and dance; and nontraditional activities like Frisbee or new games. This system uses units of physical activity or sport as the basic core of the curriculum. The primary focus is promoting activity and learning motor skills. These skills and activities provide the content of the model and the structure or format of the curriculum. Units vary in length from 2 weeks to 1 full school year, depending on program philosophy and the school level of the student. Middle schools usually offer shorter units that ensure variety and introduction to skills, while high schools have longer units with an in-depth focus on activities. Included activities change depending on the desires of society and needs and interests of the students. Most often, activities are classified in the following categories:

- Team sports: basketball, volleyball, flag football, softball, or soccer

- Lifetime sports: golf, tennis, bowling, archery, or racquetball

- Dance: folk, square, modern, or country swing

- Fitness activities: jogging, walking, aerobics, weight training, use of exercise machines, Pilates exercises, exercise balls, and kickboxing

- Recreational games: horseshoes, shuffleboard, or table tennis

- Outdoor adventure activities: bicycling, rock climbing, skiing, or orienteering (Figure 4.1)

- Aquatics: swimming, diving, skin and scuba diving, or water sports

- Nontraditional activities: Frisbee variations, modified sports or games, Eclipse Ball, throtons, martial arts, cooperative activities, or new games (Figure 4.2)

This type of curriculum is usually arranged with a balance of activities from these categories. However, it is possible to concentrate the focus on one or more categories of activity, such as the outdoor adventure activities or fitness activities. In most cases, activities are included on the basis of a number of mediating factors, such as student interest, teacher interest and expertise, community interest, class size, facilities, equipment, and climate. Activities in the curriculum generally follow the preferences of society, usually with a significant time lag. The arrival of the "new" units and skills in physical education curricula—such as step aerobics, power walking, skating with Rollerblades, mountain biking, Spinjammer Frisbees, or throtons—are usually indicative of the desires of the people whom the program serves. Instructors have to stay aware of student activity interests and trends of society in order to update the curriculum. This approach is popular because it allows for diversity and flexibility in meeting the changing interests and desires of today's students. To attract students to this program, a variety of "current and popular" activities with "cool new equipment" need to be offered. Because students have different competencies and interests, most want to be able to participate in activities related to their personal abilities. Offering a wide range of instructional units makes the program more appealing to the entire student body.

This approach provides the opportunity for students to explore, experiment, and experience a wide variety of physical skills and physical activities. The approach also provides in-depth units that help students gain sufficient experience and skill competency for

FIGURE 4.1   Adventure activity

adult participation. There are many opportunities for students to learn lifetime skills and compete with others, the environment, or against themselves in different units.

Some experts argue that the promotion of physical activity with a skill-based model using short units offers exposure to a variety of activities but does not allow ample time to develop competency or mastery of skills and knowledge (Taylor & Chiogioji, 1987; Ennis, 1993). They believe that units should be a minimum of 10 to 12 weeks, with in-depth instruction available for those activities of interest to students. They argue that short units (2 to 4 weeks) offer minimal time and provide little change in skill level. At the high school level, short units restrict learning opportunities, and many educators advocate semester-long classes as a minimal time requirement to ensure development of adequate levels of competency.

The authors have advocated short units for middle school students and longer units for high school students because of their students' interests and developmental characteristics. Middle school youngsters who are going through puberty, a rapid growth spurt, and a period of slow motor development need successful experiences with a wide variety of activities. At a time when students find it difficult to tolerate failure, longer units can lock students into a frustrating or boring experience for a long period of time. Variety and novelty in a success-oriented atmosphere are important motivational keys for this age group. Short units of instruction are usually presented in middle school so that students can experience many different activities and learn about their areas of personal interest and competency. The flow of the curriculum from middle school to high school goes from short units to long units—from searching for areas of competency to consumer-driven choices for achieving high levels of interest and competency.

Students can find success in short units when emphasis is on exploring and learning about one's personal strengths and weaknesses. Finally, because a majority of students are still trying to identify their strengths and weaknesses, this is possibly the last opportunity they will have to experience a wide variety of activities. Nontraditional units of instruction (see Chapter 18) can be used to offer variety and help maintain student interest. The middle school years should not be a time of specialization and refinement, but rather a time of exploration and discovery.

Learning environments can be productive when units are changed often. Students and teachers are excited when a new activity begins. Long units can turn into a prolonged class tournament without variety and structured skill work. Some students, usually unskilled, may feel they are placed in tournament play and forced into highly competitive situations without the opportunity to develop an adequate skill level. This only adds to the frustration for less-skilled students. Finally, some teachers advocate long units to minimize their preparation duties and requisite instructional competency. The fewer units taught, the less planning and knowledge needed. This rationale is difficult to ac-

FIGURE 4.2 Frisbee activity SpinJammers

cept if the needs and interests of all students are kept in focus.

Choice in the Approach

Instruction in a promoting physical activity/skill development curriculum proceeds from introductory lessons to advanced and specialized courses. Students are most often grouped by grade level than by ability or developmental level. In most situations, students proceed through a sequence of required physical activities throughout the school year in the middle school and continue on to an elective program at the high school level.

The choice concept can be used in a number of ways with any length unit and any type of organizational schedule in the skills-based curriculum. This strategy in the curriculum can increase the level of motivation of both students and teachers and help create a more positive environment for both teachers and students. Allowing for choice offers the following advantages:

- Increased student motivation and enthusiasm and a desire to take more physical activity because of a higher interest level

- Fewer problems with dressing, participation, and discipline

- Better use of teaching expertise and the development of specialists

- Improved instruction over a period of time

- Increased teacher motivation and enthusiasm

This trend of incorporating choice into the curriculum, which started at the college level and filtered down to high school and middle school programs, allows students a degree of choice for activities in the program. Classes are open to both genders, and the gender composition of the class will depend on personal interests in the activities. Using this approach, male and female teachers work together and decide who is better qualified to teach a specific activity. Each teacher develops two or three specialties and teaches those specialties to different classes of students, rather than teaching all activities to the same students.

Many schools are on a 9-week grading schedule. Students could choose physical education units at the beginning of each semester. An example of this design with three teachers has been used coeducationally, with males and females allowed to select all activities. If more than three teachers are available, students have the opportunity to make choices from a broader selection. An example of alternating 4- and 5-week units in a coeducational curriculum with choices for students follows:

First Semester

First 9 weeks

Eclipse Ball/volleyball, yoga/Pilates, or soccer (4 weeks)

Flag football, archery, or tennis (5 weeks)

Second 9 weeks

Eclipse Ball/volleyball, badminton, or lacrosse (4 weeks)

Basketball, team handball, or field hockey (5 weeks)

Second Semester

Third 9 weeks

Aerobics, speed-a-way, or basketball (4 weeks)

Wrestling, orienteering, or volleyball (5 weeks)

Fourth 9 weeks

Softball, track and field, or badminton (4 weeks)

Swimming, Frisbee games, or cardio kickboxing/physioballs (5 weeks)

Some schools vary this approach by developing requirements by activity categories to ensure that breadth across categories is provided. For example, students take a certain number of team sports, lifetime sports, physical fitness activities, dance units, aquatics, or recreational activities. This concept is referred to as a **choice within a requirement**. Depending on the number of units offered, students are required to take a specified number of units from each category. For example, if the program offers 24 3-week units over a 2-year period, the requirements might include the following:

1 unit of Fitness for Life: Middle School (Corbin, LaMasurier, & Lambdin, 2007) concepts

2 units of aquatics

2 units of dance

4 units of physical fitness

5 units of lifetime sports

5 units of team sports

5 units of elective activities

24 units total

Consideration of Proficiency Levels in the Approach

Many high schools are attempting to offer different proficiency levels for various activities. This implies sections for beginning, intermediate, and advanced levels of instruction for the most popular activities. Grouping students by ability and experience can offer

efficient teaching and learning situations for teachers and students. Students may be more comfortable with others who are near their ability level. Students can skip a level if they are proficient at the earlier level. Teachers can provide more specialized and in-depth instruction when students are similar in experience and ability with the activity. The following are descriptions that can be used for different levels of instruction:

- Beginning level: introductory units for the development of the basic skills and knowledge of the activity

- Intermediate level: more advanced skills and knowledge about the activity and the team concepts of the team sports

- Advanced level: advanced units that allow the students to continue pursuing higher skill levels and to focus more on competitive or challenging levels of activities

A Suggested Middle School Curriculum for the Promoting Physical Activity/Skill Development Approach

The daily lesson plan format for this approach in the middle school should include an introductory or warm-up activity (3 to 5 minutes), a physical fitness routine (10 to 15 minutes), and a lesson focus and game segment (25 to 35 minutes). (See Chapters 5 and 6 for details of the lesson plan format, as well as the text *Lesson Plans for Dynamic Physical Education for Secondary School Students* by Casten, 2009.) This format should be consistent and an outgrowth of the elementary physical education program. A consistent instructional format within each class provides teachers and students with an important measure of stability and routine. Each of the four areas in the lesson plan should be planned out for the year so that all activities will be covered. If activities are not planned, teachers will find that they forgot to include certain activities or that they don't have enough activities for the remainder of the year. In addition, trying to design a scope and sequence is impossible if activities are not in a written format. How does one modify the curriculum when the activities presented cannot be recalled?

Introductory Activities

The introductory activity occupies 3 to 5 minutes of the total lesson format. The purpose of this is to

Week	Introductory Activity	Week	Introductory Activity
1	Move and freeze	18	Form running
2	Basic movements (walk, slide, carioca, step-hop)	19	Jumping and plyometric drills
3	Fugitive tag with a variety of movements	20	Fastest tag variations
4	Walk, trot, sprint	21	Seat rolls and wave drill
5	Basic movement (pivots, slide and pivot, carioca and pivot)	22	Standing high fives
		23	Loose caboose
6	Run, stop, and pivot	24	Spider tag variations
7	Flag grab with a variety of movements	25	Leaping Lena
8	Marking variations	26	Rooster hop
9	Move and change directions	27	Move, change directions, and freeze
10	Quick hands with beanbags	28	Triangle and one
11	Flash drills	29	Making variations
12	Partner over and under	30	Power-walk variations—Add 'em up
13	Throw and catch on the move	31	Throwing and catching variations on the move
14	Clothespin tag variations	32	Follow the leader
15	File running variations	33	Triangle and two
16	Quickness drills	34	Wave drill variations
17	Movements with high fives	35	Standing high fives
		36	Blob tag

FIGURE 4.3 Yearly sequence of introductory activities for middle school students

prepare students physiologically for strenuous activity. An allied purpose is to psychologically ready students for activity. Students usually take a few minutes to become emotionally involved in activity after a day of sitting in classes. The introductory activity requires minimal organization and demands large muscle movement. It may be an integral part of the fitness routine or can be a separate entity. In either case, the introductory activity should raise the heart rate, warm up the body, and stretch the muscles in anticipation of the fitness development activity. Teachers should change the introductory activity each week to add variety to the warm-up procedure. The sixth-, seventh-, and eighth-grade students can perform similar introductory activities. Figure 4.3 shows a recommended yearly sequence (36 weeks). An in-depth discussion of introductory activities is found in Chapter 14.

Fitness Routines

The fitness routines use 10 to 15 minutes of the lesson, and their primary purpose is the development of physical fitness and positive attitudes toward lifetime activity and fitness. Fitness routines should offer total fitness development to the students. In other words, an attempt should be made to develop and enhance major components of fitness, especially flexibility, muscular strength and endurance, body composition, and cardiovascular endurance. The activities should be

demanding, progressive in nature, and useful after graduation and into the future. Students must experience a wide variety of fitness routines so they can learn to select methods acceptable to them for a lifetime. They should leave school with an understanding that there are many ways to develop and maintain an active lifestyle and that the responsibility for doing so lies with them.

Students in the middle school should stay with the same routine for 2 weeks in order to get a good feel for a routine over a 10-day period. Minor changes and variations can be used with each routine to provide success, variety, and a challenge for all the students. Variations for each routine are discussed in Chapters 15 and 16. Success in the fitness routines will help motivate students and serve as a basis for future skill development in the lessons. Students need to experience and learn that fitness is individual and relative to their genetic and trainability background. Teachers need to remind students that through continued efforts in the fitness area, all students can be successful. The Fitnessgram (Cooper Institute, 2007) can be used to educate and monitor students in the fitness area. A fitness report and "Activitygram" can be used for self-testing, goal setting, and communication with parents. A printout graphically reveals the student's fitness profile. It can be a positive part of the fitness segment of the class and a good way to involve students and parents by collecting information, entering it in the

like football, they can always look forward to Frisbee the next day.

Middle school students should have some choice as to which units they take. They should be required to take at least one unit from each of the following categories: team sports, lifetime sports, nontraditional activities, rhythms, and aquatics. Physical fitness routines should be required in all units of instruction on a daily basis. Teachers should decide which activities in their program will fit the various categories. The category requirement then ensures a measure of breadth for each student in the program. Students should not be allowed to repeat the same unit because the emphasis of the model is to ensure that students explore and receive a breadth of activities. Students should have the opportunity to learn the fundamentals of personal fitness and physical activity before they leave the middle school in case the high school they attend does not have a physical education requirement. Each student will thus have five required categories of activity. The remaining units would then be chosen by each student in any category where they have an interest. Students should be allowed to take advanced-level units after meeting their basic requirements.

The specific activity units that are offered should be determined jointly by students through a student interest survey and the physical education staff. Activity units must be used to accomplish NASPE and state standards and should be updated from year to year, depending on the interests of the students and the opinions of the staff. This approach should provide a balance of activities from the required categories.

A school with four physical education teachers might offer the curriculum design shown in Figure 4.5. During the first unit of each semester, students would make their eight choices based on the required categories and their personal interests. At that time, students would be reminded to select activities based on their interests and curriculum requirements, rather than on the teacher or on who else is in the class. The composition of the class should be determined by student interests and course requirements. The first unit of the semester is a required unit that focuses on an introduction to the program and a discussion and practice of all rules, routines, and policies.

Previous learning is considered in the sequence of the **horizontal** or yearly curriculum. Activities that use common skills can be placed later in the year (e.g., team handball, speed-a-way, and floor hockey can build on basketball, volleyball, and soccer). Within the **vertical** arrangement, the seventh grade should build on the sixth grade in terms of skills, cognitive learning, and lead-up games. The eighth-grade curriculum should then build on the seventh grade. Increased

Weeks	Fitness Routines
1–2	Teacher-leader activities
3–4	Stretching and form running
5–6	Four corner fitness
7–8	Partner race track fitness
9–10	Exercise to music
11–12	Jump bands fitness
13–14	Circuit training fitness
15–16	Step aerobics
17–18	Jump and jog fitness
19–20	Monopoly fitness
21–22	Power-walking variations
23–24	Partner resistance and aerobic fitness
25–26	Long jump-rope fitness
27–28	Fortune cookie fitness
29–30	Squad leader fitness
31–32	Cardio kickboxing
33–34	Jump-rope fitness
35–36	Group fitness scavenger hunt

FIGURE 4.4 Yearly sequence of fitness routines for middle school students

computer, and analyzing it for future use. Fitness self-testing should not take a lot of class time and maintains the purpose of teaching students skills that they can use for a lifetime.

Fitness routines recommended for the middle school are shown in Figure 4.4. An in-depth discussion with samples and variations are included in Chapters 15 and 16 and in the text *Lesson Plans for Dynamic Physical Education for Secondary School Students* (Casten, 2009).

Lesson Focus and Game

The lesson focus and game should last 25 to 35 minutes, depending on the length of the period. This is the instructional part of the lesson, with the major emphasis on skill development, cognitive learning, and enhancement of the affective domain. This phase of the lesson contains skills to be taught, drills, and lead-up activities necessary for skill practice, all of which culminate in games and tournaments. The length of activity units in the lesson focus should be short, in the range of 2 to 3 weeks if the classes meet daily. Two-week units are recommended with a daily format. Three-week units can be a combination of two activities, such as football and Frisbee. The combination-type unit allows a daily alternation of the two activities. This combination can be an effective way to keep all students involved; if they don't

Weeks	Lesson Focus Choices
First Semester (Weeks 1–18)	
1–2	Introduction and orientation to physical education
3–4	Swimming, volleyball, Eclipse Ball, Frisbee games, or flag football
5–6	Swimming, tennis, badminton, or soccer
7–8	Weight training, tennis, basketball, or lacrosse
9–10	Gymnastics, badminton, soccer, or Frisbee games
11–12	Aerobics, basketball, field hockey, or lacrosse
13–14	Orienteering, basketball, team handball, or lacrosse
15–16	Jogging, yoga, speed-a-way, or wrestling
17–18	Modern dance, step aerobics, team handball, or golf
Second Semester (Weeks 19–36)	
19–20	Dance: folk, square, line and country; aerobics and cardio kickboxing; weight training; or cooperative activities
21–22	Orienteering, speed-a-way, weight training, or new games
23–24	Frisbee games, basketball, soccer, or volleyball
25–26	Gymnastics, badminton, tennis, or field hockey
27–28	Track and field, softball, volleyball, or physical conditioning
29–30	Modern dance, self-defense, lacrosse, or Frisbee games
31–32	Track and field, walking activities, team handball, or new games
33–34	Swimming, modern dance, recreational games, or flag football variations
35–36	Swimming, speed-a-way, group team building, or team handball

FIGURE 4.5 Middle school lesson focus sequence for a four-person physical education department

knowledge, more in-depth strategies, and higher skill levels are the focus of the eighth grade. Because of scheduling problems, some schools must put seventh- and eighth-grade students together in the same class. This is unfortunate because of the wide range of developmental levels of students in these two grades. Principles of individualized instruction are discussed in Chapters 5 and 6, and they can help individual physical skill development instruction within these classes. Teachers are always faced with many different physical skill levels within their classes no matter what the organizational scheme. Teachers must be aware of the developmental differences and provide a variety of learning activities for different levels within each unit.

This curriculum approach for middle school students can be implemented effectively with a variety of adaptations depending on the number of students and teachers, the school requirements, the teaching facilities, the equipment available, the school schedule, and other environmental factors discussed in Chapter 3. This framework serves as the basis for the Dynamic Secondary School Curriculum Approach used with many middle school physical education programs across the country.

A Suggested Ninth-Grade Curriculum for Promoting Physical Activity/Skill Development: The Transition Year for Students to High School

The ninth-grade year is the last required class of physical education in many schools. Consequently, it is important for ninth graders to leave with positive attitudes toward physical activity, a desire to return for additional physical education classes, and a desire to pursue a lifetime of physical activity.

Ninth graders are usually in a transition from middle school to senior high school. Some districts put the ninth graders with the seventh and eighth graders, while most other districts place them with the 10th-, 11th-, and 12th-grade students. Both arrangements have advantages and disadvantages, and decisions are usually based on such factors as historical arrangements, class size, building space, and projected district growth. The ninth-grade curriculum design usually resembles that of the other grades with which the students are grouped. The requirements, schedules, length of units, types of activities, amount of choice, and other factors are usually the same as the middle school programs. A major difference is that the length of the ninth-grade units tends to be longer than the middle school units. Some schools also allow ninth graders to take longer, specialized units in a few popular activities such as dance, gymnastics, aerobics, or weight training. Different proficiency levels may also be available for some ninth graders (e.g., beginning, intermediate, and advanced units).

The grade 9 curriculum design for physical education should be especially attractive to students because it may be their last organized physical activity experience. Making a curriculum attractive does not mean compromising educational objectives. The curricula must be designed with specific, valuable objectives in mind, and students should not be allowed to make all their curricular decisions in any situation.

A curriculum approach can be made both attractive and educationally sound by incorporating a number of factors. First, students should have some activity choices for each unit. At this grade level, they need continued opportunities to explore different activities. Second, the arrangement should incorporate organized self-testing, personal counseling, and a wellness orientation to give students additional information for making decisions about physical activity and their lifestyles. Third, the choices of activity should include a wide variety of different categories of physical activity, especially new and popular units such as skating with Rollerblades, mountain biking, rock climbing, Frisbee, walking, cardiovascular machines, weight training, physioballs, cardio kickboxing, and aerobics. Fourth, the program should lead students into more depth in their selected activities so that they can develop a higher skill level. This means having different proficiency levels, such as beginning, intermediate, and advanced sections, or at least the opportunity to repeat favorite units. Finally, efforts should be made to develop a positive learning environment so that students will enjoy the process and have a desire to return for additional learning during the remainder of their high school years.

Classes should meet daily, and units should be 2–3 weeks in length. Ninth graders should be required to take units from the following categories:

2 units of Fitness for Life (Corbin & Lindsey, 2007) and wellness concepts
1 unit of team sports
1 unit of lifetime sports
1 unit of rhythms
1 unit of aquatics
1 unit of novel activities or adventure activities
5 units of electives from any category

This requirement ensures a measure of breadth by category. The electives can be used for greater depth in an activity or for additional breadth, depending on the interests of the student. Ninth graders should be able to repeat a unit or take an intermediate-level class as part of their electives. Because students at this age have started to narrow their activity interests, they should be able to start specializing in favorite activities. Their developmental level will allow them to improve faster than the sixth, seventh, or eighth graders in the motor-skills area. Students who take two 3-week units of the same activity should demonstrate visible improvement in skill-level development.

Introductory Activities

A short introductory or warm-up activity (3 to 5 minutes) is useful to prepare students for the physical fitness routine (see Chapters 15 and 16). These activities should be attractive and challenging with lots of variety. Low organization and large muscle type activities that get students moving quickly should dominate this segment of the lesson. An example is the popular "high-five" activity in which football, baseball, and basketball teammates slap hands together overhead or down low after performing some feat of excellence. Ninth graders can be challenged to warm up by alternating various locomotor movements (walking, jogging, sliding, and doing carioca) with giving classmates a "high five," a "low five," or a "medium five." A music tape can be programmed with 15-second intervals on and off to change the movements of the students. Another example is to have student partners give each other a high-five after a 90-, 180-, 270-, or a 360-degree turn and jump to the right or left. These are good ways to prepare students for the vigorous fitness routines in a novel and interesting manner.

The introductory activity should be changed at least every week. There are many ways to add variety and challenge with each weekly introductory activity. The yearly sequence suggested for middle school students can serve as the basis for the ninth graders. The ninth-grade sequence should be developed with many additional examples from Chapter 14. For

Week	Activity
1	Basic movements (walk, slide, carioca, triple jump)
2	Stretching and flexibility exercises
3	Form running variations
4	Basic sport movement (pivots, slide and pivot, carioca, run backwards)
5	Fugitive tag variations
6	Flag grab with a variety of movements
7	Marking variations
8	Move and change directions
9	Quick hands with Throtons
10	Flash drills
11	Movements with high fives
12	Jog and stretch variations
13	Throw and catch on the move
14	Clothespin tag variations
15	File running variations
16	Quickness drills
17	Form running
18	Jumping and plyometric drills
19	Fastest tag variations
20	Seat rolls and wave drill
21	Standing high fives with a turn
22	Loose caboose variations
23	Spider tag variations
24	Flexibility challenges
25	Quarter eagle footwork
26	Move, change directions, and freeze
27	Triangle and one
28	Making variations
29	Power walk variations (Chapter 15)
30	Throwing and catching variations on the move
31	Blob tag variations
32	Triangle and two
33	Wave drill variations
34	Student choice
35	Student choice
36	Student choice

FIGURE 4.6 Yearly sequence of introductory activities for ninth graders

Week	Activity
1–3	Teacher–leader activities and form running
4–6	Weight training stations
7–9	Partner race track fitness
10–12	Step aerobics
13–15	Exercise machines
16–18	Circuit training stations
19–21	Jump and jog fitness
22–24	Fitness scavenger hunt
25–27	Power-walk variations
28–30	Cardio kickboxing fitness
31–33	Partner jump-rope activities
34–36	Fortune cookie fitness/Monopoly fitness

FIGURE 4.7 Yearly sequence of fitness routines for ninth graders

added interest, modified or new warm-up activities can be created, depending on the season, the type of fitness routine that follows (strength, endurance, or flexibility focus), or the type of lesson focus activity that follows (basketball, golf, or tennis). The yearly sequence of introductory activities for ninth graders shown in Figure 4.6 is suggested.

Fitness Routines

A vigorous and demanding physical fitness routine (10 to 15 minutes) should follow the introductory segment of the lesson. A different routine every 3 weeks gives students a final chance to explore many different fitness activities. Emphasis should be placed on imparting knowledge to students so they understand which activities affect various parameters of fitness. Students need to be taught and encouraged to make decisions relative to physical fitness and their personal fitness routine choices. Students should self-test their fitness level at least once a year with the Fitnessgram system (Cooper Institute, 2007) and be educated on the various components of health-related fitness. Teachers need to ensure that students understand the role that genetics and training factors play in the results of fitness testing (see Chapters 2 and 16 for evidence) and make sure that students understand the importance of regular activity relative to the results of the fitness test.

The 3-week physical fitness routines in Figure 4.7 are suggested for the ninth-grade curriculum. Instructors should carefully explain and demonstrate progression and overload principles to the students. Within each of the 3-week routines, teachers should vary the activities as much as possible to provide variety, success, and a challenge for all students.

Lesson Focus and Games

Results of a student interest survey combined with the opinions of teachers can be used to determine the activity units offered during the lesson focus segment (25

Weeks	Lesson Focus Choices

First Semester (Weeks 1–18)

1–3	Fitness for Life concepts (required: 6 sections) (Corbin & Lindsey, 2007)
4–6	Swimming 1 & 2, novel activities (Eclipse Ball), dance 1, badminton, or soccer
7–9	Swimming 1 & 2, volleyball, dance 1 & 2, or fitness walking
10–12	Dance 1 & 2, Frisbee games, speed-a-way, team handball, or volleyball
13–15	Dance 2, tennis, basketball, field hockey, novel activities (Eclipse Ball), or combatives
16–18	Aerobic and weight training 1 & 2, tennis, golf, badminton, or lacrosse

Second Semester (Weeks 19–36)

19–21	Fitness for Life concepts (required: 6 sections) (Corbin & Lindsey, 2007)
22–24	Soccer, basketball, tennis, weight training, orienteering, or field hockey
25–27	Gymnastics, basketball 2, Frisbee games, lacrosse, speed-a-way, or tennis
28–30	Dance 2, volleyball, recreational games, softball 1 & 2, or weight training
31–33	Soccer, team handball, dance (2 sections), weight training, or new games
34–36	Swimming 1 & 2, Frisbee games 1 & 2, or orienteering games 1 & 2

FIGURE 4.8 Ninth-grade lesson focus sequence for a six-person physical education department

to 35 minutes). Classes should meet daily, and the units should be 3 weeks long. When feasible, the curriculum should be extended into the community to use nearby facilities, such as Frisbee golf courses, local climbing gyms, golf ranges, bowling alleys, ski slopes, and rivers or lakes. Community resources can become an important part of the program both in terms of facilities and instructional personnel. Schools must work in concert with the private sport and recreation groups in the community. Students need to be socialized into the activities available in the local community.

Physical skills can be taught and monitored with performance objectives written for each unit. Programmed practice sheets can also be added to structure skill work during the lesson focus. Examples are provided in the activity Chapters 19–21. A strong knowledge component should also be incorporated into all units. A written test should be given every 9 weeks after completing three units. Students should be given reading assignments, written work for portfolios, and outside-of-class projects to enhance their attitudes toward physical activity. Ideas for student assessment and the programmed practice sheets are included in Chapter 10.

Instructors must take care to organize the curriculum activities horizontally throughout the year and ensure vertical articulation with the eighth-grade program. Opportunities should be available to increase skill levels and knowledge of activities included in previous years. The sequence of activity units in Figure 4.8 is suggested for a ninth-grade curriculum with six

teachers. The first unit of each semester is required for all students. It should consist of a Fitness for Life concepts class (see the Fitness Education Approach section later in this chapter). The remaining units are choices for the students based on the category requirements and the students' interests. Students must meet the category requirement, and then the remaining units are electives.

A Suggested High School Curriculum for Promoting Physical Activity/Skill Development: A Total Elective Program with a Health Club/Fitness Center Emphasis (10th, 11th, and 12th Grades)

At these grade levels, students continue to narrow their range of interests in many areas, including the physical activity area. Students are capable and should be allowed to choose the physical activities they want to pursue. By the 10th grade, the program should be totally elective and consumer driven. This is not the time to force students into certain activity settings where they have no interest. It is a time for growing student independence and choice. Students should decide what activities to take under the structure and guidance of a well-developed physical education elective approach.

Classes should meet daily and last 6 to 9 weeks, depending on the school schedule. Units offered and class composition should be determined by student interest. These longer units allow for in-depth instruction and the development of a high level of skill competency. High school students have the ability to persist at tasks for a longer period and can benefit from the long units of instruction. After 6 to 9 weeks of instruction, students should have a sufficient level of skill and knowledge so that the reinforcing aspects of the activity will motivate them to continue outside the school environment. The curriculum should emphasize a health club or fitness center approach of lifetime or lifestyle-type activities that are usually available in a community health club or elsewhere in the community. This could include such activities as walking, jogging, step aerobics, yoga, Pilates, cardio kickboxing, physioballs, body bars, medicine balls, swimming, tennis, racquetball, weight training, bicycling, hiking, and so on. The program should also offer as many proficiency levels of instruction as possible to accommodate different students' abilities.

Students switch lesson focus activities only after a minimum of 6 to 9 weeks of instruction and practice. They can repeat a lesson focus unit at a higher skill level if it is offered, or they can take different units for another 6 to 9 weeks. Facilities, student interest, and faculty expertise will determine which activities are taught each period. Community facilities and programs should be used as much as possible within the existing parameters available for funds, travel arrangements, and legal liability. Sometimes the students can go into the community for units, and sometimes the community programs can be brought to the schools. The community facilities might include swimming pools, fitness centers, rock-climbing gyms, hiking or cycling trails, martial arts centers, orienteering sites, ski slopes, bowling alleys, golf ranges, or canoeing areas.

The fitness portion of the lesson (15 to 20 minutes) should also be elective in nature. It could be organized in several ways. One format would have each available teacher coordinating a different fitness activity at a different teaching site. Specific activities might include stretching, weight lifting, walking and jogging variations, step aerobics, box aerobics, or rope jumping. Students could pursue their preferences on certain days of the week and then switch to different activities on alternate days. The only requirement is that students must maintain a balance of cardiovascular activities and muscular strength or flexibility activities. Students could switch instructors and activities depending on their needs and interests. After the fitness portion of the lesson, students and teachers move on to their selected lesson focus unit. This allows students to select the type

and variety of fitness activity they desire, as long as they maintain the balance we've described. Details for switching from activity to activity and keeping track of student attendance would be worked out among teachers.

Another format could have students going to the fitness activities for the entire class period on Tuesday and Thursday while going to the lesson focus activities for the entire period on Monday, Wednesday, and Friday. Still another format could have students rotating between fitness days and lesson focus days every other day of the week so that the time eventually equalizes with 3 days one week and then 2 days the next week. No matter which format is used, teachers must emphasize the importance of a daily and balanced program of physical activity for all students.

FIGURE 4.9 Tenth-, 11th-, and 12th-grade lesson focus sequence for a six-person physical education department

Weeks	Elective Class Offerings
1–9	Fitness for Life concepts (Corbin & Lindsey, 2007) Tennis Golf Dance Fitness center activities Novel cooperative activities and new games
10–18	Racquetball Volleyball/Eclipse Ball Fitness center activities Rock climbing Frisbee Soccer
19–27	Bowling Bicycling Badminton Fitness center activities Orienteering Basketball
28–36	Fitness center activities Dance Water sports and activities Tennis Racquetball Hiking and camping

A school that has six teachers available per period and appropriate facilities could offer the following fitness stations:

- Stretching and brisk walking
- Slow jogging and interval training
- Aerobic dance (beginning level)
- Aerobic dance/cardio kickboxing (intermediate level)
- Weight training (beginning and intermediate)
- Yoga/Pilates exercise and work with physioballs or medicine balls

If facilities are limited and certain fitness activities are extremely popular (weight training or aerobic dance), then a rotation schedule might allow students whose last names start with letters A–M to participate on Monday and Wednesday, while N–Z would participate on Tuesday and Thursday. In any of these formats, teachers have to solve potential problems with attendance and rotation procedures for students who might ride a bus to a ski slope or walk to a local bowling alley. There may be times when some students would have to miss the fitness portion of the lesson because of the logistics of the situation.

Figure 4.9 is an example of a yearly lesson focus sequence for a high school promoting a physical activity/skill development program with a health club focus that has six teachers available. Teachers can become specialists in certain popular activities that students elect each year. The quality of instruction should be at the highest possible level. Activities in the program will change as often as students desire. Communities with strong interests in specific activities (golf, tennis, sailing, horseback riding, hockey, rock climbing, lacrosse, etc.) will dictate the activity choices of students. The schools will then be cooperating with the private sector by preparing students for lifestyle activities available in the surrounding community. The physical education profession can no longer afford to offer programs that show little or no concern for student preference.

Articulation in Promoting Physical Activity/Skill Development: Elementary School through High School

The approach presented here is carefully articulated from elementary school through high school. It is built on the popular elementary (K–6) physical education

	Grades											
K	*1*	*2*	*3*	*4*	*5*	*6*	*7*	*8*	*9*	*10*	*11*	*12*
Required units -------------------------------- Elective units
Variety and exploration ------- Specialized units
Balance and breadth ---------------------- Depth
Physical fitness/activity ------ Physical fitness/activity
Required and varied ------------------------- Choice
Health/Wellness concepts -- Health/Wellness concepts
Required -------------------------------------- Choice

FIGURE 4.10 K–12 curriculum components

model developed by Pangrazi (2007). It follows the same daily format and uses arrangements of learning activities appropriate for the developmental levels of students. The entire K–12 sequence emphasizes skill development, individual success, a process focus, regular physical activity, exploration, guidance, self-monitoring, knowledge, and a lifetime of physical activity. The components of this model are shown in Figure 4.10. This model provides school districts with a sound, progressively arranged physical education curriculum that has been field-tested by the authors in many districts. Options have been used depending on the specific factors involved. The model is built on educational theory and research, as well as on practical environmental factors influencing learning environments. It gives students many successful encounters with physical activity so they will leave school with positive approach tendencies toward learning in general and physical activities in particular.

Outdoor Adventure Activities Approach

Another variation of the promoting physical activity/skill development approach is the outdoor adventure activities approach. Popular activities in this approach are bicycling, orienteering, backpacking, skin or scuba diving, canoeing, cross-country skiing, downhill skiing, caving, rock climbing or rappelling, group initiatives, and ropes course activities. Some schools include a limited number of short units (either elective or required) of adventure activities as part of the program, while others offer an entire semester course of adventure activities. Most often, high schools offer a yearlong elective course designed with a variety of outdoor adventure pursuits. The program might include a yearlong elective wilderness adventure class in the physical education program that includes instruction and field trips for rock climbing, rappelling, caving, beginning and advanced backpacking, and day hikes. Usually, the focus of these programs is on the development of basic skills requisite for participation in these activities. Another approach is to offer group initiative and cooperative activities that help students learn group and individual problem-solving skills under stressful situations.

Adding outdoor adventure activities to the program creates significant change for teachers, students, administrators, and parents. Many of the activities must be done off-campus. For example, rock-climbing areas, wooded or desert locations, caves, rivers, and lakes can be used. Establishing a nearby off-campus environment with various outdoor facilities can provide a variety of teaching areas for these activities. The units can culminate with an off-campus trip during the school day or as an after-school or weekend trip with parents involved. The trips give students an opportunity to learn and experience activities that are different from regular school offerings. After-school, weekend, and vacation period times are often used for these classes.

Safety and liability problems related to these activities require special safety and insurance arrangements. Many administrators and parents show little concern about injuries related to athletic programs such as football, wrestling, and gymnastics, but they are extremely cautious about implementing adventure activities that appear risky. Most of the activities require funding for specialized equipment, such as compasses, climbing ropes, and camping gear. Teachers must show evidence of having proper qualifications because of the expertise required for high-risk activities.

With the problems created by outdoor adventure activities, why take the time to do the extra work? Because, in most cases, secondary students are highly motivated and enthusiastic about the activities. There are many reasons for this increased interest. Some students enjoy the novelty of the activities; others like the risk and excitement, the challenge of the environment, or the opportunity to make decisions; while still others like the social opportunities without competition between people. Other students are attracted to the lifetime participation emphasis and the opportunities that exist within the community. The activities offer the opportunity to travel, explore new areas, and enjoy competition with an environment of wind, water, snow, mountains, and woods. These activities satisfy the objectives of physical education and make it worth the extra effort.

Physical educators continually need to dispel the following four myths that often block the introduction of outdoor pursuits into the physical education curriculum (Parker & Steen, 1988).

1. The school must be located near major outdoor areas or state parks.

2. The teacher must have advanced skill levels in outdoor activities.

3. There are insurmountable obstacles regarding safety, legal liability, and insurance.

4. The cost of outdoor pursuits is too expensive for schools.

Schools and physical educators can overcome these problems in a number of ways. By starting small and being creative and innovative, much can be accomplished. Many of the activities are easy to implement and can be started on campus with a limited budget. With proper training and supervision, students can experience a safe and rewarding experience with outdoor activities.

Some schools have offered an elective outdoor adventure curriculum with two different levels. The first level is an introductory course that gives students an opportunity to enjoy and learn about the local outdoor areas. Students learn the fundamental skills of backpacking, fishing, hunting, camping, and wilderness first aid. Field trips are set up during the school day, after school, and over weekends. Students make choices on which and how many field trips they are going to take. Examples of activities and trips that have been used in Phoenix, Arizona, include hiking in a riparian area, fishing and camping in the high desert, participating in desert awareness activities at the Arizona-Sonora Desert Museum in Tucson, learning trap or skeet shooting and gun safety at a shooting range, hunting pheasants at a local hunting club, shooting arrows at an archery range, and learning basic horsemanship skills at a local horse stable.

Another more advanced and demanding course could include skills in rock climbing, backpacking, caving, orienteering, and skiing. Arizona students could select field trips from the following choices: hiking at Mount Humphrey in Flagstaff, backpacking into the Havasupai Falls area of the Grand Canyon, orienteering at North Mountain Park in Phoenix, rock climbing in the McDowell Mountains, cave exploring in the Tucson area, cross-country and downhill skiing in Flagstaff, and backpacking and rock climbing at Weaver's Needle in the Superstition Mountains. These classes could be elective and meet daily to work on the skills involved and prepare for the various field trips. Students may have to pay a special class fee for travel expenses and extra equipment (see Figure 4.11).

Austin O'Brien High School in Calgary, Alberta, Canada, has offered a variety of outdoor adventure-type activities as part of their curricular offerings. Students elect units on canoeing, sailing, kayaking,

FIGURE 4.11 Course sequence for an outdoor adventure class in Arizona

Outdoor Adventure Schedule

Date(s)	Day(s)	Activity	Destination	Depart	Return Approx.	Fee	Comments	Type of Tran.*
Sept. 19	Friday	Day hike	Wet Beaver Creek—Sedona	7 A.M.	5 P.M.	Paid	Bring a swimming suit and old tennis shoes. Don't forget water and your lunch.	SB
27-28	Sat.–Sun.	Fishing/camping trip	Payson area	8 A.M.	8 P.M.	$20	Great place to fish and swim—may need license.	CV
Oct. 7	Tuesday	Desert awareness	Arizona-Sonora Desert Museum—Tucson	8 A.M.	5 P.M.	Paid	This is the best desert museum in the Southwest.	SB
24	Friday	Gun safety	Black Canyon Range	8 A.M.	2 P.M.	Paid	Bring your own shells—adults needed.	SB
25	Saturday	Trap/skeet competition	Black Canyon Range	8 A.M.	2 P.M.	$10	Includes 2 rounds of shooting and prizes.	SV
Nov. 15	Saturday	Pheasant hunt	Salt Cedar Preserve	7 A.M.	2 P.M.	$15	Bring own gun and shells—must have adult with each student—you keep pheasants you shoot.	CV
26	Wednesday	Field archery	Black Canyon Range	8 A.M.	2 P.M.	Paid	Compound bows OK—adults needed. Wear tennis shoes.	SB
Dec. 9	Tuesday	Horsemanship	Pointe Stables	8 A.M.	1 P.M.	Paid	Wear jeans and tennis shoes or boots.	SB
12	Friday	Horsemanship	Pointe Stables	6 P.M.	10 P.M.	Paid	All parents are invited and needed for potluck under the stars—guests of students are welcome.	None
Jan. 31	Saturday	Downhill skiing	Flagstaff	6 A.M.	8 P.M.	$???	Rent boots, skis, and poles in Phoenix.	CB
Feb. 7	Saturday	Cross-country skiing	Flagstaff	6 A.M.	6 P.M.	Paid	Bring gloves, hat, change of clothes—overdress.	CV
March 6	Friday	Rock climbing	South Mountain Park	8 A.M.	5 P.M.	Paid	Bring chocolate chip cookies for instructor.	SB
28	Saturday	Rock climbing	McDowell Mts.	6 A.M.	6 P.M.	Paid	Bring chocolate chip cookies for instructor.	SV
April 4-5	Sat.–Sun.	Caving/day hike	Tucson Area	6 A.M.	8 P.M.	$25	Bring change of clothes and plastic bag.	PV
16	Thurs.	Map and compass	North Mountain Park	8 A.M.	2 P.M.	Paid	Bring water, lunch, hat, sunglasses, notebook, ruler, and pencil.	SB
25	Saturday	Day hike	Superstitions	6 A.M.	5 P.M.	Paid	Bring water, hat, sunglasses, and lunch.	SB
May 8	Friday	Day hike	Mt. Humphreys	5 A.M.	9 P.M.	Paid	Bring warm clothing, rain gear, water, hat.	SB
14-18	Thurs.–Mon.	Backpacking trip	North Rim—Grand Canyon	4 P.M.	4 P.M.	$30	Advanced hike—30 miles—qualifying hike will be Thurs., May 7th, 6 P.M., Squaw Peak Park.	CV

*SB—School bus   CB—Commercial bus   SV—School van   CV—Commercial van

REMINDER!! Unless someone takes your place, there will be *no refunds* on nonpaid field trips for *any reason*. Nonpaid field trips are limited by number. Participants will be selected by physical conditioning and/or class grade point average.

Austin O'Brien High School

1. Learn-to-sail program—Lake Wabamum
2. Walleyball
3. Bicycle mechanics course and Elk Island Tour
4. Curling
5. Archery
6. Rifle target shooting (trap and skeet)
7. Camping and hiking program
8. Cross-country skiing
9. Tennis
10. Social dance
11. Badminton
12. Racquetball
13. Bowling
14. Downhill skiing
15. Volleyball and pickleball
16. Coaching certification level-1 theory

FIGURE 4.12   Austin O'Brien adventure program

basic rock climbing, orienteering, outdoor survival, wilderness camping, backpacking, and cross-country skiing. A senior-level elective physical education class includes the yearly sequence of activities shown in Figure 4.12, including outdoor adventure activities and several popular lifetime activities.

SPORTS EDUCATION APPROACH

The sports education curriculum was developed to promote a positive sport experience for all students regardless of their ability level (Siedentop, Hastie, & van der Mars, 2004; Bulger, Mohr, Rairigh, & Townsend, 2007). The curriculum includes a combination of physical education, intramural sports, and interscholastic athletics. It allows students, regardless of ability level, to experience the positive values of sports in a manner similar to being involved in an interscholastic sports program. The goal of the sports education approach is to help students experience such qualities as working to reach deferred goals, teamwork, loyalty, commitment, perseverance, dedication, and concern for other people. The approach emphasizes the importance of teams, leagues, seasons, championships, coaches, practice, player involvement, formal records, statistics, and competitive balance. These characteristics are usually emphasized in sport programs but not in a physical education program. This model gives all students a chance to experience a quality competitive sports program that is organized and supervised by an unbiased physical educator who will protect the important values of

sports. Students learn to compete and be good competitors. A desired outcome is that students become competent, literate, and enthusiastic sports participants who want to play sports at local, national, and international levels.

The model uses the following six characteristics that make the sports education approach different from more traditional approaches to physical education.

1. Sports education involves **seasons** rather than units.

2. Students quickly become members of teams—**affiliation.**

3. There is a **formal schedule of competition.**

4. There is usually a **major culminating event.**

5. **Records** are kept and publicized.

6. **Festivity** is included to provide for excitement, meaning, and a social element.

Each season begins with instruction and development of team strategies according to the teams' strengths and weaknesses. The teacher helps organize the class into teams and elect a student captain; then he or she instructs team members about skill development. Teams take the initiative to organize practice, decide on players' positions, and determine strategies for playing other teams. Students assume more responsibility as the program evolves and they begin to understand its goals.

The program can be implemented in several ways, depending on the situation and the comfort zone of the teacher. It might be accomplished in a single class, with one teacher and one class. It could involve several classes that meet during the same period of the day. It could also be implemented with classes that meet during different periods of the day, with competition scheduled at a common time. Another implementation style involves practice during the regular class period followed by competition outside of class.

Depending on student interests, available facilities, and school schedules, different activities can be selected for the program. Traditional team sports and individual sports such as basketball, volleyball, flag football, soccer, softball, badminton, gymnastics, cross-country running, or track and field can be selected. The sports could be modified into activities such as three-person volleyball, three-person basketball, or over-the-line softball. Lifetime sports such as tennis, bowling, or golf are popular choices, with other possibilities being less common activities such as Ultimate Frisbee, bicycling courses, orienteering meets, speed-a-way, team handball, floor or field hockey, or modified lacrosse.

If several teachers are working together, students have several choices for leagues that are of interest to them. The leagues vary in length from 3 to 4 weeks to 9 to 10 weeks depending on student interest, facilities, and the school schedule. Students have the opportunity to participate in approximately five to 12 leagues in a year of physical education. The seasonal schedule for a school could adhere to grading periods. For example, 6- or 9-week grading periods could drive seasons for the leagues (see Figure 4.13).

All leagues include aspects of sports (Siedentop, Hastie, & van der Mars, 2004; Bulger, Mohr, Rairigh, & Townsend, 2007), including seasons, team affiliation, formal competition, culminating events, record keeping, and festivity. Leagues and rules of competition can be modified to ensure students are successful. For example, volleyball and basketball leagues could have choices for three-on-three competition in addition to the five-on-five format. There could be a boys' league, girls' league, or a coed league. Participation is required for all students, and developmentally appropriate competition that is equated is implemented. Students handle all roles in the units, including coaching, scorekeeping, keeping statistics, managing equipment, and refereeing. The teacher's role is to ensure that the sports environment is protected and that students learn the values of fair play and equal competition, as well as the skills, rules, and etiquette of the sport. Students are involved as coaches and instructors for their teams. Students select uniforms, team names, starting lineups, substitution patterns, and practice arrangements and times. Records are kept and posted in public areas, and awards are given for a variety of student accomplishments in addition to winning games or matches. Research on this model has revealed that many students enjoy this approach because they feel that there are more opportunities for socializing and having fun (Carlson & Hastie, 1997; Hastie, 2003). Many students point out the development of leadership skills, and other students express an increased sense of belonging and trust with peers in the model. Siedentop, Mand, and Taggart (1986) offer an example of using three-person teams in a volleyball league setting.

Seasonal Sport Education Schedule

Season	Team Sports	Individual Sports
Autumn	Flag football Cross country	Tennis Archery Table tennis
Early winter	Volleyball Soccer	Fencing Bowling Badminton Racquetball
Late winter	Basketball Swimming	Fencing Bowling Racquetball Riflery
Spring	Baseball Softball Track and field	Badminton Golf Archery

FIGURE 4.13 Seasonal sports education schedule
Reprinted from Siedentop, Hastie, & ven der Mars, *Complete Guide to Sport Education*, with permission from Human Kinetics Publishers. Copyright © 2004.

One league is for skilled players, and the other is for less-skilled players. (Note that there are other legitimate ways of dividing students for competition.)

The first week is devoted to practice and instruction. Four students of varying levels of skill are selected to assist the teachers in assigning students to teams. After 3 days of observation, the students are assigned to teams, four students to each team. The teams are then assigned to two leagues of eight teams each. On the fourth day of class, students begin to receive instruction and practice as a team. One teacher takes administrative responsibility for each league.

During the second week, the students have 2 practice days and 2 scrimmage days. Scrimmage days allow teachers to make sure that rules are understood and to teach refereeing as a skill. During the third week, a double round-robin league play begins for each league; there are 2 match days and 2 practice days. From the third through the seventh weeks, students have 3 match days and 1 practice day per week. During the eighth week, there is a championship tournament involving all 16 teams.

During match days, students participate in a warm-up period followed by a timed match; the duration of the match is determined by the length of the teaching period, for example, 22 minutes. All matches start and stop at the same time. There is a signal every 5 minutes for substitutions. Students referee their own games, with referees being those students not playing at the moment.

Three-Person Volleyball

This model is for a middle or junior high school setting in which two teachers share classes that total 50 to 70 students. Three-person volleyball is played with a junior-size volleyball, with a 7-foot net, and a 15-by-40 foot court.

The class meets 4 days per week, and the volleyball season is designed for 8 weeks or a total of 32 sessions. With 64 students, this class has two volleyball leagues.

Referees also keep score. The winner of each match is the team with the most points at the final time signal. Standings can be kept in terms of total points scored or win-loss records (or some combination of the two). The teachers observe games and make notes for individual players and teams in terms of skills and strategies to be worked on at subsequent practice sessions. Team captains are responsible for seeing that a certain portion of practice sessions is devoted to those notes. In other practice sessions, all teams and players practice certain skills and strategies as directed by the teachers.

Students get to choose a name for their team and adopt a uniform (as long as it meets the standards set by the teachers for physical education clothing). Each Monday, the league standings are posted along with other items concerning the league. If team play in any league is very unequal, the teachers and the four student representatives can, at the end of the first round of play, make personnel changes in teams to equalize competition for the second round. (pp. 196-197)

KNOWLEDGE CONCEPTS APPROACHES

In a knowledge concepts approach, more emphasis is on knowledge and cognitive understanding of the various subdisciplines of physical education/kinesiology. Students learn the how and the why of physical activity through involvement in problem-solving experiments. There is less emphasis on doing activities in this scheme. Students still spend time with activities in the gym and on playing fields, but they also spend time in a classroom with lectures, PowerPoint presentations, study guides, work sheets, and videos similar to those a classroom teacher prepares in a more academic subject. There is time set aside for laboratories designed to help students discover important conceptual knowledge (see Figures 4.14 through 4.17). Knowledge objectives become an important concern in this approach. The rules, strategy, knowledge concepts, and history of a sport or physical activity are discussed throughout each unit. There are experts who believe school physical education will survive only if it becomes more academically oriented (Buck, Lund, Harrison, & Blakemore Cook, 2007). The argument is for more academic rigor in our physical education curriculums.

Several variations for implementing concepts into a curriculum are possible: (1) Integrate the concepts into regular activity-based units; (2) include several separate units on concepts to supplement activity-based units; and (3) teach concepts only on special occasions, such as rainy days or shortened periods. Some argue that a curriculum based on concepts is easier to defend to a school board. Other educators feel knowledge-based discussions divert too much time from promoting activity and physical skill development. Balancing these areas of emphasis is important because instructional time for knowledge and skill is limited. If one area is emphasized, then another area has to be reduced or eliminated. Knowledge concepts are important, but if the increased emphasis reduces time available for physical skill development and physical activity time, an important program objective may be slighted. Knowing about physical activity is not the same as experiencing them. If students are going to incorporate activities into their lifestyles, they need an opportunity to gain knowledge and develop competency in several physical activities.

FITNESS EDUCATION APPROACHES

The fitness education idea is most consistent with the public health perspective of physical education and is an example of a knowledge concepts approach. This idea has gained popularity in many universities, colleges, and high schools (Corbin & Lindsey, 2007). The model focuses on imparting physical fitness concepts to students. The theory is that at some point in a student's education, it is important to devote a course to the knowledge concepts related to the physical education objectives: is active, has knowledge, values regular activity, and is fit (see Chapter 1, Physical Education Content Standards section). Evidence suggests that fitness education courses promote knowledge, improve attitudes about activity, and alter lifestyle activity patterns later in life (Brynteson & Adams, 1993; Dale, Corbin, & Cuddihy, 1998; Dale & Corbin, 2000).

A popular fitness education approach is the Fitness for Life approach (Corbin & Lindsey, 2007). This approach to physical education and fitness development places instructional emphasis on lecture, laboratory experiments, and exercise programs for use in adulthood. This model uses the HELP philosophy, which specifies the goal of promoting health for everyone with an emphasis on lifetime activity designed to meet personal needs. Lessons help students learn facts about fitness and physical activity so they can be good consumers, program planners, and problem solvers. Students participate in both classroom activities and gymnasium or outdoor fitness activities. They receive experiences with self-testing procedures in order to establish a fitness profile. A variety of fitness activities and routines are taught that can be done individually or in groups for a lifetime of regular activity. The Fitness for Life program answers the following questions:

■ Why is physical activity important to every person?

■ How should physical activity take place?

■ What forms of physical activity are available?

Basketball Dribbling Work Sheet

Student's Name _____

Practicing, Observing, and Evaluating Basketball Dribbling

Dribbling skill in basketball can be observed in two different ways. One way is to look at the **process** of performing the skill. This involves looking at the mechanics of performing the skill during the process. How efficient was the performer in using his or her body to perform the skill? The second way to observe is to look at the results or the **product** of the performance. How fast did the student dribble to half-court and back? How fast did he or she dribble around the cones?

Use the checklist below and practice with a classmate. Watch him or her dribble a basketball and check each component of the skill listed below.

1. Head is up and looking at the defenders.   Yes ___   No ___

2. Fingertips are used to control the ball.   Yes ___   No ___

3. Knees are bent and center of gravity is low.   Yes ___   No ___

4. Nondribbling hand protects the ball.   Yes ___   No ___

5. Height of the dribble is below the waist.   Yes ___   No ___

After each dribbling trial, explain to your partner how you evaluated each segment of the skill. Repeat the process so that each of you has an opportunity to work on all elements of the the dribbling skill. After working on the checklist of skill components, move on to dribbling around a set of cones to see how fast you can dribble in and out of the cones. Use a stopwatch to record the time of each trial.

6. How did it feel to make corrections on your partner's dribbling skill?

7. How did your partner feel about being corrected on the elements?

8. Can you explain the difference between the process and product of a physical skill?

9. Do you feel like this helped you to understand and improve your dribbling skill?

FIGURE 4.14 Basketball dribbling work sheet

Orienteering Skills Practice Sheet

1. Stand on the 50-yard line of the football field. Find north and write down what you are facing.

2. Stand at the east field-goal pole. Find 40° and write down what you are facing.

3. Start at the east 20-yard line. Take 20 paces west. What yard line are you standing on?

4. Shoot a bearing at the baseball batting cage from the west 40-yard line. What angle are you standing at?

5. Start at the trash can in front of the bleachers. Take 15 paces east. Where are you standing?

6. Stand at the east end zone of the football field. What is directly south of you?

7. Stand at the drinking fountain. Take 10 paces north. Where are you standing?

8. Face 40°, walk 40 paces. Add 120°, walk 40 paces. Add 120°, walk 40 paces. What shape am I?

9. Face 360°, then walk 20 paces. Turn to 90°, and then walk 20 paces. Turn to 180°, and then walk 20 paces. Turn to 270°, and then walk 20 paces. What shape am I?

10. Turn to 120°, then walk 30 paces. Turn to 240°, and then walk 30 paces. Turn to 360°, and then walk 30 paces. What shape am I?

11. Stand under the football scoreboard facing east. Shoot a bearing at the closest corner of the bleachers. What is your bearing?

FIGURE 4.15 Orienteering skills practice sheet
From Jessica Richardson, Smith Junior High School, Mesa, Arizona.

Student's Name: _____

Practice several overhand and underhand volleyball serves. Try putting different types of spins on both of the serves. Complete the following questions:

1. Where do you have to contact the ball to make it spin to the right? _____

_____

2. Where do you have to contact the ball to make it spin to the left? _____

_____

3. Can you serve the volleyball with backspin toward you? _____

_____

4. Can you serve the volleyball with topspin away from you? _____

_____

5. Can you serve the volleyball with no spin? _____

_____

6. Please explain where you must strike the volleyball in order to get the proper spin as described in questions 3, 4, and 5. _____

_____

7. Please describe the flight of the volleyball with the spins described in questions 3, 4, and 5. _____

_____

8. How can these different spins impact your ability as a volleyball player? _____

_____

9. Please relate this concept of spin to baseball, softball, racquetball, tennis, or basketball and give a specific example of the use of spin in these activities. _____

_____

10. What conclusion can you make about the use of force in creating spin on an object? _____

_____

FIGURE 4.16 Volleyball serves—problem-solving questions

Jump Bands Work Sheet

Name _____   Date _____

Partner _____

Group Members _____

_____

Place a check beside each skill that your partner is successful in performing.

1. My partner can move the jump bands to the rhythm of the music. _____

2. My partner can move to the single foot pattern of in, in, out, out on one side _____ or

    both sides _____ of the jump bands.

3. My partner can move to the double foot pattern of in, in, out. _____

4. My partner can dance from one side of the jump bands to the other using one of the methods

    taught. _____

Answer the following questions.

5. Why are jump bands considered an excellent cardiovascular endurance activity?

6. Why is it critical to work together when using the jump bands in class?

7. How could the jump bands be used as part of a fitness circuit in class?

FIGURE 4.17   Jump bands work sheet
From Char Darst, Mesa Public Schools, Mesa, Arizona.

The objectives for this approach are arranged in a hierarchical order called the "stairway to lifetime fitness" (Figure 4.18). The rationale is that if students climb the lifetime fitness stairway, they will be more likely to be active throughout life. Information and activities are provided on a number of topics, including cardiovascular fitness, strength, endurance, flexibility, fat control, skill-related fitness, correct ways to exercise, and how to plan an exercise program. Students learn to diagnose and solve personal fitness problems.

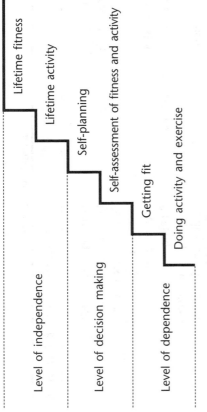

FIGURE 4.18 Stairway to lifetime fitness

Reprinted from C. B. Corbin and R. Lindsey, *Fitness for Life*, 5th ed. (p. 14), with permission from Human Kinetics Publishers. Copyright © 2005 by Human Kinetics Publishers.

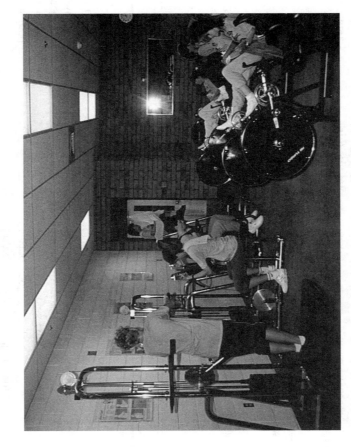

FIGURE 4.19 Gilbert High School super circuit class

They have opportunities to develop exercise programs to remediate health concerns.

Several options are available for incorporating Fitness for Life into a school curriculum. Common alternatives are to offer a one- or two-semester program using the Fitness for Life model. Some schools, such as Mainland High School in Daytona Beach, Florida, combine teaching knowledge concepts with participation in a modern school fitness center equipped with the latest fitness machines and technology (Wood, Fisher, Huth, & Graham, 1995). Gilbert High School, in Gilbert, Arizona, offers an elective "super circuit" class using a fitness circuit (see Figure 4.19) developed by the Universal Company in Iowa. Students work out on the super circuit every other day and participate in lifetime sports such as tennis, golf, and racquetball during other days. Students take a Fitness for Life section of the class 1 or 2 days per week.

Many states have adopted a statewide requirement or a recommendation for a fitness concepts-type course to address many of the state standards for physical education. In addition, several provinces in Canada and the Department of Defense Dependent Schools worldwide have added such a requirement or recommendation (Watson, Sherrill, & Weigand, 1994). A wide variety of curriculum and instructional materials is available to teachers, such as books for students, lesson plans for teachers, work sheets and study guides,

Discussion Topics		Activity-Based Topics		
Table of Contents	Self-Management/Group Discussion	Fitness Focus	Self-Assessment	Activity
Fitness and wellness for all	Learning to self-assess	Starter program	Exercise basics	Skill/health-related fitness
Safe and smart physical activity	Building self-confidence	Fitness games	Fitnessgram 1	Safe exercise
Benefits of physical activity	Reducing risk factors	Cooperative games	Healthy back test	Back-exercise circuit
How much is enough?	Choosing a good activity	Line exercise	Posture	Circuit workout
Learning self-management skills	Setting goals	Fitness trail	Fitnessgram 2	Elastic-band circuit
Lifestyle physical activity and positive attitudes	Building positive attitudes	School stepping	Walking test	Walking for wellness
Cardiovascular fitness	Learning to self-monitor	Aerobic dance	Step test and mile run	Cardiovascular fitness
Active aerobics and recreation	Finding social support	Step aerobics	Fitnessgram 3	Jogging principles
Active sports and skill-related fitness	Building performance skills	Orienteering	Skill-related fitness	The sports star program
Flexibility	Building intrinsic motivation	Jump and stretch routine	Arm, leg, and trunk flex	Flexibility circuit
Muscle fitness: basic principle and strength	Preventing relapse	Partner resistance exercises	Modified 1 rep max/grip strength	Weight training
Muscle fitness: endurance and general info	Managing time	Homemade weights	Muscular endurance	Endurance circuit
Body composition	Improving physical self-perceptions	Exercise circuit	Skinfolds and Ht/Wt charts	Muscular fitness exercises
Choosing nutritious food	Saying "no"	Jollyball	Body measurements	Cooperative aerobics
Making consumer choices	Learning to think critically	Rhythmical exercise	Body comp/flex/strength	Isometric exercise circuit
A wellness perspective	Thinking success	Cooper's aerobics	Cardio and muscular endurance	Health and fitness club
Stress management	Controlling competitive stress	Frisbee golf	Signs of stress	Relaxation exercises
Personal program planning	Overcoming barriers	Exercising at home	Evaluating personal program	Performing your plan

FIGURE 4.20   Contents for a Fitness for Life class

Reprinted from D. Dale, K. McConnell, and C. B. Corbin, *Fitness for Life Lesson Plans*, 5th ed., with permission from Human Kinetics Publishers. Copyright © 2007 by Human Kinetics Publishers.

vocabulary cards, activity cards, PowerPoint presentations, overhead transparencies, review questions, laboratory experiments, and test materials (Corbin & Lindsey, 2007). The recommended content for a high school Fitness for Life class is shown in Figure 4.20. This approach is based on 2 days per week in the classroom and 3 days in an activity setting. Students learn the concepts of healthy activity and apply these concepts by designing fitness activities and self-assessing personal fitness. This program is compatible with the Fitnessgram/Activitygram (Cooper Institute, 2007) and the Physical Best materials from National Association for Sport and Physical Education (2005). The newest edition has Web icons that direct students to a variety of Internet sites from the Fitness for Life site (www.fitnessforlife.org).

Another similar knowledge concepts approach to secondary curriculum focuses on the components of human health (see Chapter 17 for a variety of health and wellness activities). The model is more comprehensive than the fitness concepts approach. Units of instruction in health and wellness include stress management, alcohol and drug abuse, nutrition, weight control, physical fitness, coping skills, personal safety, environmental awareness, behavioral self-control, and problem-solving skills related to these specific topics. Health and wellness is viewed by many as an important area that should be an ongoing part of the educational process throughout life. It is a preventive approach and expands the fitness concepts approach. To maintain health and wellness, students need requisite information and skills. Advocates of this program point to numerous health problems that abound in our society. A healthy lifestyle for all students is the major objective of this model.

Both the health and wellness and the fitness education models focus primarily on knowledge. People who advocate these models find the emphasis on knowledge to be an advantage because it adds credibility to a program. The downside is the increase in time spent on lecture and analysis, resulting in less time for learning physical skills and promoting physical activity. Students need information, but they also need successful encounters with physical activity and time allotted for practicing and performing physical skills. Determining exactly how much time should be spent on knowledge acquisition and how much on physical skill development is difficult. Schools using a concepts approach offer a balance of physical activity and knowledge concepts. For example, a common approach is to offer several units on health activities (including fitness) to supplement or complement physical activities units.

PERSONAL AND SOCIAL RESPONSIBILITY APPROACH

Hellison (2003) developed a set of ideas and a curriculum approach that focuses on enhancing social competence, self-control, responsible behavior, and concern for others within the physical education class environment. Emphasis on fitness and the development of sports skills and knowledge is reduced in order to accomplish the primary goal of personal and social competence. Sports and physical activities are used as a means of accomplishing personal and social goals. The basic philosophy of the personal and social development approach is that personal and social problems in society have created situations that require schools to offer this type of focus. Professionals subscribing to this approach believe that many students are disruptive and difficult to manage, making it the school's responsibility to provide better personal and social development training. This approach has been field-tested with troubled or alienated youth and general student populations over a 30-year period. The approach has been used in many different forms and with different terms for the various levels of responsibility.

In one variation of this approach, students proceed through six developmental levels of social competence. Different students enter at different levels and proceed upward through the steps. Students are encouraged to rate themselves on each of the levels and compare their ratings with their teacher's ratings (see Figure 4.21). Discussion between the teacher and students examines perceptions of how students are progressing. The following are examples of levels of personal and social development:

- **Level 0: Irresponsibility.** Students do not participate and are totally unmotivated and undisciplined. They interrupt and intimidate other students and teachers. They make excuses and blame others for their behavior. Teachers find it difficult to manage or accomplish much with these students.

- **Level 1: Self-control.** Students at the self-control level can control themselves without the direct supervision of the teacher and do not infringe on the rights of other students or the teacher. They can begin to participate in class activities and enhance their learning.

- **Level 2: Involvement.** Level 2 involves student self-control and desired involvement with the subject matter of fitness, skills, and games. Students are enthusiastically involved in the program without constant prompting or supervision of the teacher.

Definition of Ratings

0   Little self-control
Not involved
Uses put-downs
Irresponsible
Disruptive

1   Under control, not involved
Not participating
Not prepared
Nonproductive

2   Under control, involved when teacher directed
Frequently off task
Needs prompting
Needs frequent reminders

3   Self-responsibility
Works independently
Self-motivated
Needs frequent reminders

4   Caring
Cares about others
Involved with others
Sensitive to needs of others

5   Going beyond
Leadership
Additional responsibility
Helping teacher

Student			Teacher
Date	Rating	Rating	Comments

FIGURE 4.21   Social development checklist

■ *Level 3: Self-responsibility.* Students at Level 3 begin to identify their interests and start to make choices within the parameters of the program. Motivation and responsibility are characteristics of these students. They start to take more responsibility and explore options for their lives outside the program. This stage represents a start of their own identity.

■ *Level 4: Caring.* The caring stage has students moving outside themselves and showing concern for other students and the teacher. Students are cooperative and helpful and show a genuine interest in the lives of others. There is a real concern about the world around them.

■ *Level 5: Going Beyond.* The highest level is characterized by student leadership and additional responsibility for program decisions. Students get involved with the teacher on decisions that will affect all students in the program. Students become coworkers with teachers.

This model can be implemented in different ways depending on the specifics of the school situation and the type of students. Hellison (2003) suggests an option that uses a day-to-day consistency with the following five parts to the lesson:

Self-Responsiblity Checklist

Name _____

Date _____

My Self Control

—— I did no name-calling

—— If I got mad, I tried to have self-control

—— I didn't interrupt when someone else was talking

—— My self-control was not that good today

My Involvement

—— I listened to all directions

—— I tried all activities

—— I worked even when I didn't feel like it

My Self-Responsibility

—— I followed all directions

—— I did not blame others

—— I was responsible for myself

My Caring

—— I helped someone today in class or out of class

—— I said something nice to someone today

—— I did not help anyone at all

Comments

FIGURE 4.22 Self-responsibility checklist

1. Counseling time for connecting with students

2. An awareness talk about the responsibility levels

3. The physical activity lesson with integrated personal and social discussions

4. A group meeting for students' opinions

5. Reflection time to self-evaluate personal and social responsibility for the day (see Figures 4.22 and 4.23 for examples).

Examples of strategies available to the teacher for implementing personal and social responsibility are teacher talk, modeling, reinforcement, self-reflection, reflection-in-action (snap judgment based on previous experiences), student sharing, sport court (small group of students making a decision for the class), the talking bench (where two students go to work out a problem), journal writing by students, student checklists, student achievement records, and behavior contracts between the student and the teacher. Many specific strategies have been used and are available to the teacher for each of the social development levels (0–5). For example, rubrics for assessment of students can be developed to provide students with feedback or to grade them on their personal and social responsibility in physical education classes (see Figure 4.24). Refer to Chapter 10 for a discussion on developing rubrics. Finally, Figure 4.25 (page 97) is a form that could be used with student personal development plans in Level 3 (self-responsibility).

Self-Evaluation

Date _____

Self-control

How well did you control your temper and mouth today?	0	1	2

Effort

How hard did you try today?	0	1	2

Self-Coaching

Did you have a self-improvement or basketball goal and work on it today?	0	1	2

Coaching

Did you help others, do some positive coaching, or help make this a good experience for everyone today?	0	1	2

Outside the gym

Self-control?	0	1	2
Effort?	0	1	2
Goal-setting?	0	1	2
Helping others?	0	1	2

One comment about yourself today:

FIGURE 4.23 Self-evaluation form

Reprinted from D. R. Hellison, *Teaching Responsibility Through Physical Activity* (p. 51), with permission from Human Kinetics Publishers. Copyright © 2003 by Donald R. Hellison.

Responsibility Rubric

	Consistently	Sporadically	Seldom	Never
Contributes to own well-being:				
Effort and self-motivation	___	___	___	___
Independence	___	___	___	___
Goal setting	___	___	___	___
Contributes to others' well-being:				
Respect	___	___	___	___
Helping	___	___	___	___
Leadership	___	___	___	___

FIGURE 4.24 Rubric on assessment of personal and social responsibility

Reprinted from D. R. Hellison, *Teaching Responsibility Through Physical Activity* (p. 111), with permission from Human Kinetics Publishers. Copyright © 2003 by Donald R. Hellison.

My Personal Plan #1

1. Fitness: Choose at least one

   My flexibility goal is _____.

   My strength goal is _____.

   My aerobic goal is _____.

   Today in fitness I did _____.

2. Motor skills: Choose at least one skill from one activity

   My basketball goal is _____.

   My volleyball goal is _____.

   My soccer goal is _____.

   My _____ goal is _____.

   Today in motor skill development I did _____.

3. Choose one

   The creativity/expressive activity I did was _____.

   I spend my "pal time" with _____ doing _____.

   The stress management activity I did today was _____.

   The self-defense activity I did today was _____.

4. During my Level III time

   My respect for others was

   _____ good   _____ OK   _____ not OK

   My effort was

   _____ high   _____ medium   _____ low

   My plan was

   _____ my own   _____ somewhat my own   _____ not my own

   My self-discipline in carrying out my plan was

   _____ good   _____ fair   _____ poor

   I helped someone else.

   _____ Yes!   _____ A little   _____ No!

FIGURE 4.25 My personal plan #1

Reprinted from D. R. Hellison, *Teaching Responsibility Through Physical Activity* (p. 70), with permission from Human Kinetics Publishers. Copyright © 2003 by Donald R. Hellison.

STUDY STIMULATORS AND REVIEW QUESTIONS

1. List and explain the common organizing centers for physical education curricula.

2. Why do the authors advocate shorter units for the middle school and longer units for the high schools?

3. What are the advantages to offering choice to students in the physical education curriculum?

4. Discuss the unique features of the promoting physical activity/skill development approach that is widely used today.

5. How does the promoting physical activity/skill development approach change from middle school to high school?

6. List examples of culminating events in an outdoor adventure curriculum approach.

7. What is the fundamental goal of the sports education approach?

8. Briefly describe and explain the "stairway to lifetime fitness."

9. What tends to be the dilemma for teachers who wish to emphasize both the teaching of knowledge concepts and physical skills?

10. Provide the underlying rationale for the personal and social responsibility curriculum.

REFERENCES AND SUGGESTED READINGS

Brynteson, P., & Adams, T. M. (1993). The effects of conceptually based physical education programs on attitudes and exercise habits of college alumni after 2 to 11 years of follow-up. *Research Quarterly for Exercise and Sport, 64,* 208–212.

Buck, M. M., Lund, J. L., Harrison, J. M., & Blakemore Cook, C. L. (2007). *Instructional strategies for secondary school physical education* (6th ed.). Boston: McGraw-Hill.

Bulger, S. M., Mohr, D. J., Rairigh, R. M., & Townsend, J. S. (2007). *Sport education seasons.* Champaign, IL: Human Kinetics Publishers.

Carlson, T. B., & Hastie, P. A. (1997). The student social system within a unit of sport education. *Journal of Teaching in Physical Education, 16,* 243–257.

Casten, C. (2009). *Lesson plans for dynamic physical education for secondary school students* (3rd ed.). Boston: Allyn and Bacon.

Cooper Institute, Meredith, M. & Welk, G. (Eds.). (2007). *Fitnessgram/Activitygram test administration manual* (4th ed.). Champaign, IL: Human Kinetics Publishers.

Corbin, C., LeMasurier, G., & Lambdin, D. (2007). *Fitness for life: Middle school.* Champaign, IL: Human Kinetics Publishers.

Corbin, C., & Lindsey, R. (2007). *Fitness for life* (updated 5th ed.). Champaign, IL: Human Kinetics Publishers.

Dale, D., & Corbin, C. (2000). Physical activity participation of high school graduates following exposure to conceptual or traditional physical education. *Research Quarterly of Exercise and Sport, 71,* 61–68.

Dale, D., Corbin, C. & Cuddihy, T. (1998). Can conceptual physical education promote physically active lifestyles? *Pediatric Exercise Science, 10,* 97–109.

Ennis, C. (1993). Can we really do it all? Making curriculum choices in middle and high school programs. In J. E. Rink (Ed.), *Critical Crossroads: Middle and Secondary Physical Education* (pp. 13–23). Reston, VA: NASPE.

Hastie, P. A. (2003). *Teaching of lifetime physical activity through quality high school physical education.* San Francisco: Benjamin Cummings.

Hellison, D. R. (2003). *Teaching responsibility through physical activity* (2nd ed.). Champaign, IL: Human Kinetics Publishers.

Jewett, A., Bain, L., & Ennis, K. (1995). *The curriculum process in physical education.* Dubuque, IA: W. C. Brown and Benchmark.

Johnson, D. J., & Harageones, E. G. (1994). A health fitness course in secondary physical education: The Florida experience. In R. R. Pate and R. C. Hohn (Eds.), *Health and fitness through physical education.* Champaign, IL: Human Kinetics Publishers.

Melograno, V. J. (1996). *Designing the physical education curriculum.* Champaign, IL: Human Kinetics Publishers.

National Association for Sport and Physical Education. (2004). *Moving into the future—National standards for physical education* (2nd ed.). Reston, VA: Author.

National Association for Sport and Physical Education (2005). *Physical best activity guide: Middle and high school levels* (2nd ed.) Champaign, IL: Human Kinetics Publishers.

Pangrazi, R. P. (2007). *Dynamic physical education for elementary school children* (15th ed.). San Francisco: Benjamin Cummings.

Parker, M., & Steen, T. (1988). Outdoor pursuits and physical education: Making the connection. *Newsletter of the Council on Outdoor Education, 30*(1), 4.

Portman, P., & McCollum, R. (1995). *Teaching High School lifetime P.E. Teaching High School Physical Education, 1*(2), 9.

Siedentop, D. (1994). *Sports education.* Champaign, IL: Human Kinetics Publishers.

Siedentop, D., Hastie, P., & van der Mars, H. (2004). *Complete guide to sport education.* Champaign, IL: Human Kinetics Publishers.

Siedentop, D., Mand, C., & Taggart, A. (1986). *Physical education—Teaching and curriculum strategies for grades 5–12.* Mountain View, CA: Mayfield Publishing Co.

Siedentop, D., & Tannehill, D. (2000). *Developing teaching skills in physical education* (4th ed.). Mountain View, CA: Mayfield Publishing Co.

Taylor, J., & Chiogioji, E. (1987). Implications of education reform on high school programs. *Journal of Physical Education, Recreation, and Dance, 58*(2), 22–23.

Vickers, J. (1993). While Rome burns: Meeting the challenge of the new reform movement in education. In J. E. Rink

(Ed.), *Critical crossroads: Middle and secondary physical education* (pp. 47–59). Reston, VA.: NASPE.

Watson, E. R., Sherrill, A., & Weigand, B. (1994). Curriculum development in a worldwide school system. *Journal of Physical Education, Recreation, and Dance, 65,* 17–20.

Wood, K., Fisher, C., Huth, T., & Graham, P. (1995). Opening the door to tomorrow's classroom. *Teaching High School Physical Education, 1*(1), 3–5.

WEB SITES

Action for Healthy Kids
www.actionforhealthykids.org

American Hiking Society
www.americanhiking.org

Fitness for Life
www.FitnessforLife.org

Physical Education Teaching and Curriculum Information
www.pecentral.com
www.pelinks4u.org
www.pe4life.org
reach.ucf.edu/~pezone

Project Adventure
www.pa.org

ESSENTIAL COMPONENTS OF A QUALITY PROGRAM

COMPONENT 1 A quality physical education program is organized around content standards that offer direction and continuity to instruction and evaluation.

COMPONENT 2 A quality program is student centered and based on the developmental urges, characteristics, and interests of students.

COMPONENT 3 Quality physical education makes physical activity and motor-skill development the core of the program.

COMPONENT 4 Physical education programs teach management skills and self-discipline.

COMPONENT 5 Quality programs emphasize inclusion of all students.

COMPONENT 6 In a quality physical education setting, instruction focuses on the process of learning skills rather than the product or outcome of the skill performance.

COMPONENT 7 A quality physical education program teaches lifetime activities that students can use to promote their health and personal wellness.

COMPONENT 8 Quality physical education teaches cooperative and responsibility skills and helps students develop sensitivity to diversity and gender issues.

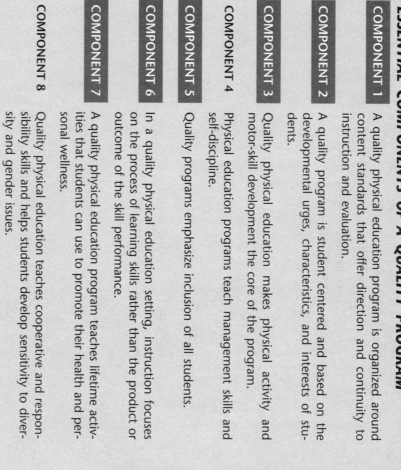

5

Planning for Effective Instruction

CHAPTER SUMMARY

Policies and procedures need to be defined prior to planning for instruction. Such policies and procedures give direction to the program and offer the framework for planning quality lessons for students. Pre-instructional decisions must be considered as part of planning a lesson that considers space, equipment, and a safe environment. Various stages of planning ensure quality instruction. In addition, the components of a three-part lesson plan ensure that students receive a balanced approach to instruction. After a lesson has been presented, reflection is a necessary component of quality instruction.

STUDENT OUTCOMES

After reading this chapter, you will be able to:

- Write and define policies and procedures that will guide your physical education program.

- Describe the role of planning in preparing for quality instruction.

- Understand how arousal impacts skill learning.

- Give meaningful skill feedback.

- Identify the characteristics of effective practice sessions.

- List pre-instructional decisions that must occur before the actual delivery of the lesson, including use of space, equipment, time, and pace.

Student Outcomes, continued

- Articulate how students can become involved in developing the learning experience.

- Describe ways in which learning in the affective domain can be enhanced.

- Discuss the various parts of a meaningful unit plan.

- Understand the rationale for the three components of a lesson and describe the characteristics of each.

- Analyze and reflect on completed lesson plans.

DEVELOP DEPARTMENTAL POLICIES

The development and implementation of a quality physical education program require that policies and procedures are determined, communicated, and applied consistently to all students. In order to ensure consistency in the program, all members of the physical education department need to sit down and come to general agreement on a number of issues. These issues not only guide the staff, they guide students and parents. Over time, the goal should be to design a set of written guidelines that are presented to students on the first day of school and reinforced continually throughout the year. An excellent curriculum is not effective without a well-developed set of policies and procedures and an ongoing revision process.

After the policies have been agreed upon by the faculty members and administration, a letter or handbook for students and parents should be created. The letter or small booklet should be brief, clear, and succinct and sent to all students, parents, and administrators. Discuss the information in the letter with the class and ask students to discuss the information with their parents. Ask students to have their parents read the guidelines, sign an approval form, and return it within 1 or 2 days (Figure 5.1). Students and parents can have misconceptions about the nature of physical education, and clarifying all aspects of the program limits future problems.

The physical education handbook should cover the following areas:

- Uniforms and dress requirements

- Attendance and participation

- Excuses and makeup procedures

- Showers and towels

- Locks and lockers

- Equipment

- Grading procedures

Uniforms and Dress Requirements

Students should be encouraged to change into activewear for physical education classes. The comfort, safety, and hygiene of uniforms selected by students are important. Many schools still require a specific uniform and enforce strict dress codes. Uniforms and dress codes can create problems and be a source of controversy. Students often avoid physical education environments simply because of a dress-code requirement, yet these same students will admit they enjoy physical activities and would take a class if no dress code existed. The benefits of having all students dress alike may not be worth developing escape and avoidance behaviors in students.

Controversy over uniforms and dress codes should not develop into a "make or break" issue. If the school favors a dress code, a student committee can be formed each year to select a new uniform. Clothing companies can provide several available options with school colors, emblems, or mascots. Students can decide the uniform they desire or have the option of buying a different type of uniform. Several choices should be offered. Adolescence is a time of growing independence, and allowing students to select their physical education attire is not detrimental to the accomplishment of program objectives. There are times when specialized clothing is necessary for certain activities, such as rock climbing or horseback riding. Aerobics, yoga, and the martial arts often necessitate specialized clothing for freedom of movement.

Another problem is the legality of an imposed dress code. Some states stipulate that if a specific dress code is required, the school must purchase uniforms

---

Ovation High School Physical Education Department
Ovation, AZ

Dear Parents:

This booklet contains the policies and procedures of the physical education department. We would like you to carefully read and discuss the program regulations with your son or daughter. These policies and procedures are important for making the learning environment a pleasant experience for all students.

We desire to have all students leave physical education classes with a positive attitude and the urge to be physically active throughout their lifetime. If you have any questions about the curriculum or the policies and procedures of the department, please call me at 555-4724.

Please sign the slip at the bottom of the sheet and have your child return it to school.

Thank you.

Sincerely,

Physical Education Teacher

- -

We have read the booklet and understand the policies and procedures.

_____   _____
Parent   Student

_____
Date

FIGURE 5.1 Letter to parent regarding policies and procedures

---

for those students unable to do so. Dress codes can create problems for students with specific religious beliefs that forbid wearing gym attire. Other students may have physical deformities or embarrassing conditions they wish to keep covered. For example, a student who has a severe case of acne on his back may not want to go swimming without a shirt.

These problems reveal why a flexible policy on uniforms and dress requirements may be the best approach. The perceived advantages of a strict dress code—developing discipline, school spirit, and cooperation; enhancing the identification of teams; reducing discrimination against poorer or wealthier students; and reducing unit cost of attire because of large orders—are debatable and seldom worth the problems generated. Teachers and students should both influence the decisions on dress requirements, and teachers should have the flexibility to make decisions that facilitate the learning process of each individual in each situation.

A department policy regarding students who cannot afford a uniform or a change of clothes is necessary. Often, a special fund can be made available through school fund-raisers. The parent–teacher association may be able to provide funds through one of

its projects. Sometimes used or unclaimed clothes can be cleaned and worn by students who cannot afford to buy a uniform. A policy on the laundering of gymnasium clothes is probably one of personal choice, as is the laundering of regular street clothes. If hygiene problems occur, students (and, if necessary, parents) can be confronted. Students should identify their gym clothes with permanent ink or name tags because of the numerous opportunities for mix-ups, losses, or pilferage.

Teachers need to model appropriate attire for physical activities. An active teaching role is certainly enhanced by appropriate dress, and students are strongly influenced by the behavior of their teachers. It is difficult to defend teaching in blue jeans when students are not allowed to participate in similar attire.

Attendance and Participation Policies

If students enjoy physical education, there will be fewer problems with attendance and participation. The overall curriculum and instructional procedures will have more of an effect on students than policies

School Nurse Excuse Form

Student _____ Date _____

Please excuse the above-named student from physical education class for the following day(s):

_____

The reason the student is excused is: _____

_____

_____

Thank you,

_____

School Nurse

FIGURE 5.2 School nurse excuse form

and procedures on attendance and participation. Some teachers spend so much time and energy on these latter concerns that they lose sight of the importance of curriculum and instruction. Students are more enthusiastic about physical education if a quality curriculum and an effective instructional program exists.

Nevertheless, there do need to be policies for attendance, participation, and excuses from class. A system that allows students to earn reinforcers (e.g., points, activity time, privileges) for attending and participating is an effective strategy. Too often, a negative or "chop" system is used, in which students lose points or privileges or receive lower grades for inappropriate behavior. This approach creates a negative environment, while the positive approach has the opposite effect. Students can be awarded one point per day for attendance, one point for dressing, and points for participating, rather than subtracting or cutting points for not attending and participating.

All medical excuses and notes from parents should be presented to the school nurse at the beginning of the school day rather than during class time. The nurse is a health professional and is probably more objective than the physical educator to make decisions about medical problems requiring special attention. The nurse should make the final decision on participation and should communicate with the physical education teacher both verbally and in writing. A form can be developed to facilitate this communication (Figure 5.2). If students cannot participate for 3 consecutive days, it

is common practice in most schools to recommend they visit a physician. A physician's report form (Figure 5.3) can be sent to the student's doctor. This type of form helps improve communication between the school nurse, the physician, and the physical educator. Students need to understand that credit for physical education is not awarded to people who cannot participate in the class sessions.

Students who have minor problems, such as being tired or having a sore throat, headache, or cramps, should be handled on an individual basis. Some students can participate with these problems, whereas others cannot. Teachers must become knowledgeable about the backgrounds and personalities of their students. A policy that treats all students the same is usually misdirected. Religious beliefs relative to participating on various holidays or holy days often result in students asking to be excused. This should be handled individually through the school administration. If confusion arises about excuses related to minor illness or religious beliefs, students should be allowed to see the school nurse for illnesses and a guidance counselor or administrator about preferences and beliefs.

Students also have bad days, headaches, cramps, family problems, and other concerns that affect their daily performance. Sometimes students need a little extra encouragement to participate, and at other times, they may need a day off. Effective teachers get to know their students so they have some basis for judging individual situations. In contrast, some teachers believe

Physician's Report Form

Date _____

Dear Dr. _____

The following student, _____, has requested that he/she be excused from physical education activities. We would like your help in designing a program that is appropriate for this student's physical condition. Our program offers a wide variety of physical activities. Please complete the following information to enable us to develop a personalized program.

Thank you for your time.

Sincerely,

_____

Physical Education Department Head

- -

1. Type of illness, injury, or handicap _____

2. Restrictions _____

3. Activities to be avoided _____

4. Duration of restriction _____

5. Other important information _____

6. Physician's name _____

   Address _____ Phone _____

7. Signature _____ Date _____

Please send form to: Person _____

   School _____

   Address _____

FIGURE 5.3 Physician's report form

that students are "cheating" if the student does not want to participate on a given day. Initially, students should be given the benefit of the doubt because they may indeed have a problem. If the same student continues to have participation problems, contact the parents or apply some alternative procedures.

Develop a policy for tardiness. Start each class at a precise time, and let students know exactly what time the class begins. Excessive tardiness should be integrated into the makeup policies and procedures for grades.

Class Makeup Procedures

Usually students have the right to make up missed classes because of excused absences. Try to focus the makeup work on activities that were missed. Attending another physical education class is an option. Possibilities for makeup work can focus on knowledge activities, performance activities, or spectator activities. Depending on the objectives of the lessons missed, some activities will be more valuable than others. The following are examples that can be used in each area.

Makeup Work: Knowledge Activities

The following alternatives might be offered to students who missed a knowledge activity. Students complete one of the following assignments and turn it in to the instructor:

- Read an article in the sports section of the newspaper and write a 1-page analysis (form provided).
- Read an article in any sports magazine and write a 1-page analysis (form provided).
- Read a short biographical sketch about a noted sports figure and write a 1-page analysis (form provided).
- List and define 15 terms from any of the following activities: basketball, field hockey, flag football, lacrosse, orienteering, physical conditioning, recreational games, running techniques, soccer, swimming, team handball, and volleyball.
- Diagram the playing area of any of the activities listed previously.
- List and explain 10 rules from any sport.
- Read a book related to a sport and write a 1-page analysis (form provided).
- Choose a project (with teacher approval).

The form shown in Figure 5.4 can be used for student reports on these knowledge activities.

Makeup Work: Performance Activities

Students who have missed performance activities might be asked to participate in any of the following activities and to write a 1-page analysis (form provided):

- Run a mile for time or jog for 15 minutes.
- Run a parcourse.
- Ride a bike for 30 minutes.
- Attend an aerobics class.
- Lift weights for 30 minutes.
- Play 18 holes of disc golf.
- Play one set of tennis.
- Play two games of racquetball.
- Play 18 holes of regular golf.
- Engage in a workout at a health club.
- Choose an activity (approved by instructor).

The form in Figure 5.5 can be used for the analysis of the performance.

Makeup Work: Spectator Activities

Students observe one of the following events and write a 1-page analysis (form provided). Events can take place at the middle or senior high school, community college, college, or professional level. Any of the following event activities is acceptable: football, soccer, cross-country running, tennis, volleyball, basketball, softball, baseball, wrestling, track and field, swimming, and student choice (approved by instructor). However, students should be encouraged to make up classes by engaging in physical activity rather than being a spectator. Figure 5.6 is an analysis sheet that can be used for reporting spectator activities.

Hygiene Issues

Students should be encouraged, but not forced, to shower after all vigorous activity sessions. Discuss hygiene and why showering is important. Students should understand the importance of developing lifetime health habits. However, showering, like the uniform issue, should not evolve into a polarizing conflict. Many physical educators have developed avoidance behaviors in students because of inflexible or poorly managed showering policies. For example, one teacher required students to shower after every class, including golf, archery, and discussion sessions. Showering is surely not necessary after every physical education class. Others give students only 5 to 7 minutes to shower and change clothes. This is not enough time for students to dry their hair, change clothes, and return to the classroom. Appearance is an important aspect of personal development. Teachers who overlook this fact often alienate students and stimulate adverse reactions to physical education.

Analyze the nature of each lesson and the allotted time schedule. Swimming, for example, requires more preparation time at the end of class, whereas an archery activity does not necessitate showering. Showering policies should be flexible so teachers can make appropriate exceptions for students. Many students are uncomfortable showering in front of peers because of menstruation, underdeveloped bodies, acne problems, deformities, or various other problems. Private showers can help alleviate this concern. Teachers need to be sensitive to the fact that poorly planned and poorly administered showering and dressing procedures can cause students to identify physical education as a negative experience.

Give students a say in matters of personal health and cleanliness. If teachers make all of the decisions for students, little is learned about making decisions in later life. If students complain about peers who possess strong

---

Article Report

Name _____

Date _____

Publication _____

Author _____

Major idea of article:

Your opinion of the material:

What are the benefits of this material to you?

Parent or guardian signature _____

FIGURE 5.4 Knowledge analysis sheet

Performance Analysis

Name _____

Activity _____

Date _____

Explain the activity you performed.

Explain the physical benefits of this activity.

What were your scores, time repetitions, and so forth?

Parent or guardian signature _____

FIGURE 5.5 Performance analysis sheet

body odor, the matter will need to be discussed with the student and, possibly, with his or her parents. Teachers should try to avoid incorporating showering and dressing behaviors into the grading system.

It should be noted that many schools are now taking the policy that showering is optional for all students, particularly in the middle school years. The wide-ranging levels of maturity among middle school students can lead to much embarrassment and teasing. If students choose to shower, policies are put in place that facilitate their choice. In most cases, these students will need to bring their own towels and be responsible for seeing that they are laundered regularly. If students choose not to shower, that is their choice and they are

openly given that option. Most students will shower when it becomes important to them. Showering should not be an issue that turns youngsters away from a lifetime of physical activity. A little perspective will go a long ways in creating positive attitudes among students.

Towels

If showers are required, a policy on towels should also be determined. A simple procedure is to have students bring towels from home along with their activity clothing. Students are then responsible for changing towels and uniforms on a regular basis. Mark names on the towels to minimize loss. Some districts provide students

Spectator Analysis

Name _____

Event _____

Date, place _____

Opponents _____

Final score _____

Type of offense and defense of each team: _____

How the scoring occurred:

Strengths and weaknesses of each team:

Your reactions to the event:

Parent or guardian signature _____

FIGURE 5.6 Spectator analysis sheet

with towels for physical education class. The towels can be purchased by the school and laundered on a regular basis in school facilities. This arrangement helps reduce mildew and odor problems created by students leaving wet towels in their lockers. Towels need to be checked out and in each day, and a security system must be developed. This approach creates a number of additional problems for teachers.

Another approach is to use a towel service company that provides freshly laundered towels on a daily basis. This approach is usually more expensive but easier to manage. Funding for a towel service can come from the school's general budget, a student fee, a booster club project, or a physical education department project, such as selling candy or sponsoring car washes. Each school district has fund-raising and budget procedures that need to be followed. The physical education staff can weigh the advantages and disadvantages of each towel supply procedure before making a decision.

Locker Room Supervision

Some schools assign students a combination lock and a small wire basket or metal locker for their activity clothes. A longer, larger locker is usually available for street clothes during each activity period. Longer lockers commonly alternate with the shorter lockers throughout the locker room. This helps spread students around the entire area. Older students are usu-

ally assigned upper locker rows because they can reach them. A master list of which student occupies which locker should be maintained. This can be done with a student locker assignment sheet. Problems such as forgotten combinations or misplaced locks can be readily solved when the teacher has a master list of combinations and the locker assignment sheet.

Supervision procedures for the locker room can be arranged to ensure safety and theft prevention. The room should be locked during class time to prevent thefts. Teachers should walk through the locker room regularly to check for unlocked lockers and clothes and towels that are left out accidentally. This routine reduces loss caused by theft. In some situations, teacher aides can be hired to supervise the locker room, distribute towels, and help maintain management policies.

Equipment

Proper types of equipment in adequate amounts are a must for quality programs. Students cannot learn various physical skills without proper equipment. Physical education departments need basketballs, tennis racquets, and Frisbees, just as math and reading departments need books, paper, and pencils. Students cannot learn to play tennis without racquets and balls. In many instances, physical education departments are asked to get along without proper amounts of equipment. A class of 35 students needs more than five basketballs, six volleyballs, or 10 tennis racquets. Administrators need to be convinced that physical education is more than one or two games of a specific activity.

Equipment Purchasing

An adequate budget is necessary for purchasing equipment for the physical education program. The physical education budget needs to be separate from the athletic budget. Coaches don't like to share equipment they use for their athletic teams with the physical education program and vice versa.

Equipment priorities should be based on student interest surveys and the number of students who will use the equipment. If certain activities are offered more frequently than others, equipment for these should be a higher priority. The quality and price of equipment should be studied carefully before making a purchase. Usually, equipment orders will go out on bid. If the order doesn't contain clear specifications, cheap and poorly made equipment may be the end result. Check with other schools to see what experiences they have had with specific equipment. The cheapest price is not always the best deal. Durability and longevity are especially important. Write a justification that includes desired specifications so the buyer understands the importance of meeting your needs. Understand that buyers will accept the lowest price if there are no specifications, leaving you with equipment that is not satisfactory.

Using a multiyear approach for buying expensive equipment is useful for negotiating with budget committees or school boards when a large amount of capital is necessary for equipment. If several thousand dollars are needed to add equipment for a new activity, it may be possible to implement the activity in three phases over 3 years. Student interest and willingness to bring in personal equipment for particular activities is also an effective strategy for gaining administrative support. Offering a cycling unit with each student bringing in his or her own bicycle or offering golf classes where students use their own clubs are effective strategies for generating student and administrative interest in new activities. A word of caution, however: If you find ways of creating new units without district support, you may never get funded in the future. Administrators may assume that you can always solve the funding issues.

Another source of equipment involves the physical education staff, the maintenance department, or the industrial arts classes. Starting blocks, relay batons, soccer goals, team handball goals, and jump ropes are examples of equipment that can be constructed. Take

care to ensure that all safety specifications have been met. Several books and articles describe how to make homemade equipment (Pangrazi, 2007a).

Physical education equipment can also be purchased jointly with other schools, city parks and recreation departments, and the athletic department. Many districts, for example, jointly purchase free weights and weight machines for the use of athletes, physical education classes, and adult community education programs. Joint purchases are an excellent way to share costs and involve the entire community. This method can be used for purchasing tennis, racquetball, badminton, volleyball, softball, basketball, and aerobic dance equipment.

Storage, Distribution, and Maintenance of Equipment

An accurate equipment inventory should be completed at the beginning and the end of each school year. Records kept year to year help determine the needs of the department and facilitate the purchasing process. Documenting the type and amount of equipment lost each year provides information for improving security and distribution procedures.

A storage area that is easily accessible to both male and female teachers is desirable. The storage area should be close to the teaching stations (e.g., the gym, fields, and courts). It is inconvenient to pick up and return equipment to an area far from the station. The storage area should be designed with labeled shelves, bins, and containers for all pieces of equipment. All teachers, student leaders, and students who have access to the area need to cooperate fully in keeping the area clean and orderly. It is easy to become disorganized when many people are sharing equipment. Transporting equipment to and from the teaching areas requires that a variety of ball bags, equipment carts, and portable ball carts are available. These will reduce the amount of class time expended on equipment transport. Students can be given responsibilities for the movement of equipment if they are trained properly.

Develop a system for using equipment that is not designated on the yearly curriculum. A sign-up and checkout list can be posted in the storage area along with the yearly sequence of activities. The department head or equipment coordinator is notified if any changes are made in the schedule with regard to equipment. This prevents problems with teachers not having necessary equipment for their classes. Equipment should not be loaned to outside groups without following designated procedures. If equipment is shared or loaned to other groups, it must be marked or identified with some regulation code to prevent losses or mix-ups with equipment from other sources.

These decisions are all part of the ongoing process of implementing a quality physical education curriculum. Equipment is part of a program's lifeblood. Without adequate equipment, the effectiveness of the teaching–learning environment is reduced because students without equipment become bored, unmotivated, and troublesome for the teacher. How can students learn to dribble, pass, and shoot a basketball when they stand in line and take turns sharing a ball with five or six other students? The goal of a program should be to provide every student with a piece of equipment. Productive learning time can thus be greatly enhanced.

Grading Procedures

Grading is an important part of the policies and procedures described in the department handbook and should be determined and discussed with students during the first week of classes. Teachers within the department should generally agree on the components and application of grading guidelines. If one teacher grades differently than the rest, students will soon communicate to other students about the aberration. Parents should also be made fully aware about how their youngster will be graded. Evaluation and grading recommendations are discussed in detail in Chapter 10.

CONSIDER PRE-INSTRUCTIONAL DECISIONS

Pre-instructional decisions are basic to the success of a lesson. They are rather mundane, which causes many teachers to forget to plan for them. However, they are as important as planning the content of the lesson. In fact, if this phase of the lesson is not carefully considered, it may be impossible to effectively present the content.

Determine the Instructional Format

How students are grouped for instruction is a decision that is made early in the lesson-planning process. More than one arrangement can be used in a single lesson. The objectives and nature of the instructional experiences, plus the space and equipment available, determine the type of grouping. There are three basic schemes, with numerous variations and subdivisions.

Large-Group Instruction

Large-group instruction demands that all students respond to the same challenge, whether as individuals, partners, or members of a group. This format allows the teacher to conduct the class in a guided progression. The single-challenge format is convenient for

group instruction and demonstration because all students are involved in similar activities. Pacing is a problem with no easy solution, considering effective instruction must be personalized to meet each student's needs. Student differences are recognized, yet the assumption is made that a central core of activity is acceptable for students of the same age.

Small-Group or Station Instruction

In the small-group (or station) format, the class is divided into two or more groups, each working on a different skill or activity. Some system of rotation is provided, and the students change from one activity to another (Figure 5.7). Dividing a class into groups for station teaching is valuable at times, particularly when supplies and apparatuses are limited. This arrangement can save time in providing apparatus experiences because once the circuit is set, little change in apparatuses is needed. The participants are changed, not the apparatuses. Some system of rotation is instituted, with changes either by signal or at will. Sometimes all stations are visited during a single class session, and in other cases, students make only a few station changes per session.

Class control and guidance may be a problem with the small-group format, considering stopping the class to provide instruction and guidance is not practical. Posting written guidelines at each station can help students be more self-directed. The instructions should include rearranging the station before moving on to the next. These measures preclude the teacher from dividing his or her efforts over a number of stations. If a station has a safety hazard (e.g., rope climbing), the teacher may wish to devote more attention there.

Individual Skill Instruction

In the individual skill format, students select their skills from a variety of choices and rotate at will to new skills. They can get equipment themselves or choose from pieces provided. The most effective format is when students work independently. It allows everyone to work on skills at a comfortable rate. In addition, it allows students to select a variety of skills and activities based on their competency levels.

Determine the Use of Space

A common error is to take a class to a large practice area, give students a task to accomplish, and fail to define or limit the space in which the task should be performed. The class spreads out in an area so large it is impossible to communicate and manage the class. The type of skills being practiced and the ability of the teacher to control the class dictate the size of the space.

FIGURE 5.7 Students practicing at stations

Delineating a small area for participation makes it easier to control a class because students can see and hear better. As students become more responsive, the size of the area can be enlarged. Regardless of the size of the space, delineate the practice area. An easy way is to set up cones around the perimeter of the area. Chalk lines, evenly spaced equipment, or natural boundaries can also serve as restraining lines. Starting the lesson by having the class jog throughout the delineated area is an excellent way to communicate to students the boundaries for participation.

A factor affecting the size of the practice area is the amount of instruction needed. When students are learning a closed skill (only one way to perform or respond) and need constant feedback and redirection, it is important to stay near the instructor. Establish a smaller area where students move for instruction and then return to the larger area for practice.

Available space is often divided into smaller areas to maximize student participation. An example is a volleyball game where only 12 students can play on one available court. In most cases, it is more effective to divide the area into two smaller courts to facilitate a greater number of students.

A related consideration when partitioning space is safety. If the playing areas are too close together, players from one area might run into players in the other area. For example, a softball setting is unsafe if a player on one field can hit a ball into another play area.

Determine the Use of Equipment

Equipment can be a limiting factor. Teachers need to know exactly what equipment is available and in

working condition. The amount of equipment available will determine how to structure the lesson and group students. For example, if there are only 16 racquets for a class of 30, some type of sharing or station work will have to be organized.

How much equipment is enough? If it is individual-use equipment, such as racquets, bats, and balls, there should be one per student. If it is group-oriented equipment, such as gymnastics apparatuses, there should be enough to ensure waiting lines of no more than four students. Too often, teachers settle for less equipment because they teach the way they have been taught. For example, a teacher is teaching volleyball and has plenty of volleyballs. Rather than have students practice individually against the wall or with a partner, the students are divided into two long lines, and only one or two balls are used. Most of the time is spent waiting in line rather than practicing.

If equipment is limited, it is necessary to adapt instruction. Be careful about accepting limited equipment without expressing concern because many administrators believe that physical educators are always capable of "making do." Communicate with your educational leader regularly, and explain the importance of equipment for effective instruction. Ask parent–teacher groups to help with fund-raising to purchase necessary equipment. Math teachers are not expected to teach math without a book for each student, and physical educators should not be expected to teach without adequate equipment. When teachers settle for less, they get less.

How can you get by with a dearth of equipment? The most common solution is to teach using the small-group format. This implies dividing students into stations where each group has enough equipment. For example, in a softball unit, some students practice fielding, others batting, others making the double play, and so on. Another approach is to divide the class in half and allow one group to work on one activity while another is involved in an unrelated activity. For example, because of a shortage of racquets, one-half of the class could be involved in practice while the other half plays half-court basketball. This approach is less educationally sound and increases the demands made on the instructor.

Another approach is to use the peer review approach. While one student practices the activity, a peer is involved in offering feedback and evaluation. The two share the equipment and take turns in practice and evaluation. The final approach is to do what is most commonly done: Design drills that involve standing in line and waiting for a turn. This is least acceptable from an educational standpoint.

The initial setup of equipment depends on the focus of the lesson. For example, the height of the basket can be reduced to emphasize correct shooting form. The height of the volleyball net can be lowered to allow spiking practice. Nets can be placed at different heights to allow different types of practice. Equipment and apparatuses can be modified to best suit the needs of the learner. There is nothing sacred about a 10-foot basket or regulation-sized ball. If modifying the equipment improves the quality of learning, do it.

Determine the Use of Time and Pace

A number of decisions related to time need to be made prior to instruction. How time allotted for a lesson is used influences instructional outcomes. The amount of time allowed for fitness and skill development impacts what is accomplished in a physical education program. For example, if a teacher decides to use 10 additional minutes per lesson for fitness development, the result will be an increase of nearly 30 hours of time devoted to physical fitness during the school year.

The pace of a lesson is related to time. Skillful teachers know when to terminate practice sessions and move on to new activities. Students become bored and begin to display off-task behaviors if practice sessions are excessively long. Knowing when to refocus on a different task is important. In most cases, it is better to err on the short side than to allow practice to the point of fatigue and boredom. A rule of thumb is to refocus or change the task when five or more students go off task. If it is necessary to extend the length of the practice session, try the following:

1. Refocus the class. Ask the class to observe another student's performance, or explain the importance of the skill and how it will help their game-time performance.

2. Refine or extend the task. Stop the class and ask them to improve their technique by focusing on a phase of their performance. Try challenging them with a more difficult variation. This approach redefines the challenge and is a more difficult variation of the skill they were practicing.

3. Stop and evaluate. Stop the class and take time to evaluate performance. Students can work with a partner and check for key points. Emphasis is placed on evaluating and correcting performance. Practice resumes after a few minutes of evaluation.

Pacing is affected depending on who directs the lesson: teacher or student. When the teacher directs the pace, the instructor controls timing, and students are expected to perform the task at the same time. Determining whether a presentation should be teacher or student paced depends on the type of skill being taught. If the skill is closed in nature, teacher pacing appears to be most effective. Teacher pacing can be accompanied by verbal cues and modeled behavior. It is effective for learning new skills because cues and visual imagery help learners develop a conception of the pattern to be performed. Student pacing allows learning to progress at different rates. It is effective when open skills (variety of correct responses) are being learned and a variety of responses are preferred or encouraged.

Determine the Use of Instructional Devices

Instructional devices include a variety of materials, equipment, or people—any of which supplement, clarify, or improve certain instructional procedures. These devices can be used to present information, stimulate different senses, provide information feedback, restrict movements, control practice time, or aid in evaluation and motivation. The devices may be simple, such as targets taped on the wall or cones to dribble around in basketball (Figure 5.8), or they may be more sophisticated, such as videotapes, videotape recorders, or ball machines for tennis.

Instructional devices help impart more information and improve the motivational aspects of the class. Because most public school environments have a large student-to-teacher ratio, it is difficult to find enough time for each student. A number of challenging and success-oriented activities can be developed using instructional devices. The following are examples:

- In basketball, tape targets on a wall for various types of passes. Use a stopwatch to time students dribbling through a course of boundary cones. Pictures, diagrams, and handouts can provide students with graphic information on various skills and rules.

- In volleyball, hoops, jump ropes, or tape on the floor can be used as targets for setting, bumping, or serving. Extend a rope across the top of the net to help students hit serves above or beneath the rope to ensure height, accuracy, or velocity. Videotapes are available to provide instruction for various volleyball skills.

- In tennis, use empty ball cans as targets when working on serves. A tennis ball suspended on a small rope that can be adjusted up or down on a basketball hoop teaches students the "feel" of extending the arm for serves and overhead shots. A list of performance objectives for partners can give direction to a tennis class.

- In track and field, a student leader can run a station on low hurdles by timing heats and providing corrective feedback. A string stretched between two chairs can help students practice jumping for height in the long jump. Laminated diagrams of the release angle of the shot put combined with a discussion can give students important information.

- In badminton, targets can be placed in various sections of the court. Suspend shuttlecocks on a light rope to practice overhand shots. A rope suspended on high-jump standards will force students to get the proper height on clear shots.

- In flag football, a punting station can use a goalpost for height and accuracy, boundary corners for placement accuracy, and a stopwatch for hang time. A swinging tire or a hoop suspended from a tree or goalpost can be used for passing accuracy, and boundary cones can be used for passing distance. Blackboards, magnetic boards, and overhead projectors are useful for diagramming plays and defensive strategy. Student leaders can supervise each station, record the completion of various skills, and provide corrective feedback for each student.

A creative teacher uses instructional devices in many different ways. These devices certainly do not replace the teacher but help supplement the teaching–learning environment. Effective teachers continually try to add devices that motivate students, provide more feedback, or increase practice attempts.

FIGURE 5.8   Instructional devices

Teachers with a limited budget can create instructional devices with such basic components as a roll of tape, several ropes, string, and hoops. An extensive budget does not always produce the best learning environments. Students seem to enjoy the challenge related to practicing with various types of instructional devices.

Create a Safe Environment

A safe environment is a prerequisite for effective teaching. Safety results from behaviors taught by the teacher. "Safety first and everything else second" should be the motto of every teacher. It is possible a teacher will be removed from the teaching profession if accidents occur because of faulty planning and lack of foresight. More than half the injuries in schools occur in physical education classes; if they result from poor planning and preparation, a teacher may be found liable and responsible for such injuries (see Chapter 12).

Teachers must foresee the possibility of hazardous situations that result in student injury. Safety inspections should be conducted at regular intervals (see Chapter 12). An apparatus that has not been used for awhile should be inspected. Rules are only the beginning with students; safe and sensible behavior needs to be taught and practiced. For example, if students are in a gymnastics unit, they must receive instruction and practice in developing proper methods for absorbing momentum and force. It may be necessary to practice safety, as in taking turns, spotting, and using the apparatus as directed.

Safety occurs when curricular presentations are listed in proper progression. Injuries are avoided when students perform only those activities for which they are prepared. A written curriculum can reassure a safety committee or court of law that proper sequencing of activities was used. In addition, proper progression of activities generates a feeling of confidence in students because they feel they have the necessary background to perform adequately.

TEACH EACH STUDENT AS A WHOLE PERSON

When planning learning experiences, consider that people are whole beings. They do not learn a new skill in the psychomotor domain without developing some allied cognitive and affective outcomes. For example, if people are taught a new soccer drill, they will wonder why they need to learn it. They are integrating the activity cognitively into their total selves. At the same time, they are developing a related feeling about the skill (e.g., "I'm good at this drill," or "I'm never going to use this").

Teachers can enhance the effectiveness of instruction by integrating educational goals in all domains. Tell students why they are learning new skills or performing them in a certain fashion. Learning in the cognitive area may involve knowing when to use a certain skill or how to correct errors in an activity. It involves decision making based on facts and information gathered from various sources. Cognitive development emphasizes the importance of helping students understand as contrasted to just "doing it because I told you to" (Figure 5.9).

The performing arts (physical education, music, and drama) offer a number of opportunities for affective domain development. There are many occasions to learn personal responsibility, share, express feelings, set personal goals, and function independently. Working as a team, learning to be subordinate to a leader, and being a leader can be taught. Teach the whole person. It is discouraging to hear teachers say, "My job is just to teach skills. I'm not going to get involved in developing attitudes. That's someone else's job." Physical educators have an excellent opportunity to develop positive attitudes and values. The battle may be won, but the war lost if teachers produce graduates with good skill development and negative attitudes toward physical activity and participation.

Experiences can be enriched by encouraging students to discover ways of improving techniques or remedying problems they are having in skill performance. They can be given opportunities to help each other diagnose and improve techniques. Strategies for game situations can be developed through group discussions and planning. The point is to enrich and enhance learning situations so students are able to

internalize them in a personalized and meaningful manner. A golden rule does not have to be taught in every lesson, but little is learned if teachers fail to offer integrated presentations on a regular basis.

Teach for Cognitive Development

Involving students in organizing the content and implementation of the lesson can enhance cognitive development. This is not to suggest that students will decide what, when, and how learning will take place, but rather they will be involved in improving the structure of the learning tasks. The following are some of the advantages to involving the learner in the instructional process:

- Learners usually select experiences that are within their abilities and skill levels.

- When learners help make a decision, they accept some of the responsibility for learning. It is easy to blame others for failure if a learner is not involved in some of the decisions. Personal involvement means accepting the responsibility to make decisions and see that they are implemented.

- Most people feel better about an environment in which they have some input and control. Self-concepts can be enhanced when learners help determine their destiny.

- When lessons fail because incorrect decisions were made, the learner shoulders some of the blame. This helps develop decision-making skills that focus on personal responsibility.

Decision making and involvement in one's learning process are learned. Students need an opportunity to make decisions and be placed in a situation where they can realize the impact of their decisions. The opportunity to make incorrect as well as correct decisions is an important part of the learning process. There is no decision making involved when correct decisions are the only conclusions accepted and approved by the teacher. Soon, students begin to choose not to make decisions at all rather than risk making an incorrect choice.

Responsibility is learned by making wise decisions that impact the future of the individual and others. Decision making at a young age teaches students to learn from their mistakes at a time when the consequences are not as great. Responsibility training involves allowing the learner to make decisions and to choose from alternatives. Allowing students to make choices should be done in a gradual and controlled manner by using some of the following strategies.

FIGURE 5.9   Checking for understanding

1. Limit the number of choices. This allows some control over the ultimate outcome of the situation but offers students a chance to help decide how the outcome will be reached. This may be a wise choice when learners have had little opportunity for decision making in the past. New teachers who have little understanding of their students may want to select this method until they are more familiar with the class.

2. Allow students the opportunity to modify an activity. The learner is allowed to modify the difficulty or complexity of the skill being practiced. If used effectively, this strategy allows learners to adapt the activity to suit their individual skill levels. Involving them in this process can actually reduce the burden of deciding about exceptions and student complaints that "It is too hard to do" or "I'm bored." It becomes the student's responsibility to personalize the task. Options allowed might be to change the rules, the equipment being used, the number of players on a team, or the type of ball or racquet. Some examples are as follows:

   a. Using a slower-moving family ball rather than a handball.
   b. Increasing the number of fielders in a softball game.
   c. Lowering the basket in a basketball unit.
   d. Decreasing the length of a distance run or the height of hurdles.

3. Offer tasks that are open ended. This approach allows students the most latitude for deciding the content of the lesson. In this situation, they are given a task, and it is their responsibility to solve it. The teacher decides the educational end, and students decide the means. As students become adept at using

this approach, they can develop a number of alternatives. These examples could be used at this level:

   a. "Develop a game that requires four passes before a shot at the goal."
   b. "Develop a floor exercise routine that contains a forward roll, backward roll, and cartwheel."
   c. "Develop a long rope-jumping routine that involves four people and two pieces of manipulative equipment."

This approach is called problem solving because there is no predetermined answer (see Chapter 8). This technique is effective in helping students apply principles they have learned previously to new situations. Ultimately, the problem is solved through a movement response guided by cognitive involvement.

Enhance the Affective Domain

How each student feels about the physical education experience has an impact on his or her level of motivation to be active throughout life. Little is gained if students participate in a class yet leave hating it. It is possible to design experiences that improve the opportunity for positive attitudes and values to develop. When developing a lesson plan, evaluate its impact on the attitudes of students. Will the planned lesson result in a positive experience for students? Few people develop positive feelings after participating in an activity where they were embarrassed or failed. Ponder some of the following situations and the attitudes that might result:

■ Think of the situation where a teacher asks everyone to run a mile. Overweight students are slowest and run for the longest time, while the rest of the class waits for them to finish. These students cannot change the outcome of the run even if they want to.

Failure and belittlement occur every day. It's a small wonder they come to dislike running and exercise.

■ How do students feel who have been asked to perform in front of the rest of the class even though they are unskilled? For example, a student is asked to dribble a soccer ball through a set of cones for a timed performance. The added stress probably results in a poorer-than-usual response. They may not want to play soccer anymore.

■ What feelings do students have when asked to pitch in a softball game and they are unable to throw strikes? Might they do everything possible to avoid playing softball in the future?

Students need to know that teachers care about their feelings and want to prevent placing them in embarrassing situations. Sometimes, teachers have the idea that caring for students indicates weakness. This is seldom the case. Teachers can be firm and demanding as long as they are fair and considerate. To knowingly place students in an embarrassing situation is never justified and results in the formation of negative attitudes.

Attitudes and values are formed based in large part on how students are treated by teachers and peers. When enhancing the affective domain, how one teaches is more important than what one teaches. Students want to be acknowledged as human beings with needs and concerns. They want to be treated in a courteous and nonderogatory manner. If teachers choose to avoid how students feel, they teach without concern for others' feelings. More often than not, the best way to discover how students feel is to ask them. The majority will be honest. If a teacher can accept student input, the result is an atmosphere that produces positive attitudes and values.

PLAN FOR OPTIMAL SKILL LEARNING

A major objective of physical education is to improve skill performance. Students in physical education want to become physically educated. If they go to a math class, they expect to learn math. Students deserve an educational experience rather than a recreational one, where playing rather than learning is the goal. When developing a lesson plan, the following points help form the underlying foundation of the planning effort.

Know the Purpose of the Lesson

The lesson should be designed to improve the skill performance of students so they are able to meet program standards. What is the purpose of the total program, the unit, and the lesson plan? If the lesson presentation does not contribute to the skill development of participants, it probably denotes a recreational approach rather than an educational lesson. The lesson must contribute to positive lifestyle changes that carry over to adulthood. Knowing program standards and desired outcomes (NASPE, 2004) and how instruction contributes to those outcomes gives direction to the program.

Include Instruction as Part of Every Lesson

Instruction is an observable action. There are many different ways to accomplish instructional outcomes, but all of the methods demand instruction. Instruction can take many forms, such as working individually with students, evaluating a student's progress on a mastery learning packet, developing task cards, or conducting group instruction. Regardless of the method used, instruction must be a regular and consistent part of each lesson. Physical education must go beyond the recreational aspects of activity and be instructive in nature. A major problem with a recreational approach is that "the rich get richer and the poor get poorer." For example, if "the ball is rolled out" and students are left on their own for basketball games, skilled players will handle the ball more and dominate less-skilled players. Unskilled students may feel pressure during competitive situations and find it difficult to think about technique and proper performance when they are concentrating on strategy and not making mistakes.

Integrate the Lesson with Past and Future Instruction

A sound secondary school physical education program should build on the foundation built by the elementary school physical education experience. Many school districts lack adequate communication between elementary and secondary program organizers. Each section may act autonomously, without regard for what is taught in other grades. Secondary curriculum planners should consider elementary school program goals, activities, and teaching procedures. The transition from elementary to secondary programs is smoother if learning activities and teaching procedures progress with continuity. High school teachers who know the previous experiences of students in elementary and middle school programs can present instruction that is not repetitious or too difficult because of lack of previous experience in the activity.

Well-planned lessons reflect a progression of activities between lessons. Skill development activities taught throughout a unit help ensure that practice opportunities are sequential and regular. An unacceptable but common approach is to bunch all instruction into the first day or two of a unit. This makes it difficult for unskilled students to develop motor skills because there is little instruction and opportunity for skill feedback and correction after the start of the unit.

The philosophy of the teacher determines whether there is a plan for effective instruction. Does the teacher believe that youngsters must learn on their own and that responsibility for learning is solely the student's? Or does the teacher believe that student and teacher share the burden of learning in an environment where both are determined to reach educational outcomes? A teacher's plan for skill development will strongly affect student learning. If instructors fail to assume responsibility for teaching and refining skills, who will?

Helping students effectively learn physical skills requires that teachers understand a few basic principles of motor learning. Teaching motor skills is not a difficult task when teachers understand the basic tenets of proper performance techniques.

Understand Arousal

Arousal is the level of excitement stress produces (Schmidt & Lee, 2005). The level of arousal can have a positive or negative impact on performance of motor skills. The key to proper arousal is to find the "just right" amount. Too little arousal and youth are uninterested in learning. On the other hand, too much arousal fills youth with stress and anxiety, resulting in a decrease in motor performance. The more complex a skill is, the more arousal can disrupt learning. On the other hand, if a skill is simple, such as running, a greater amount of arousal can be tolerated without causing a reduction in skill performance. Optimally, youth should be aroused to a level at which they are excited, confident, and positive about participation.

Competition affects the arousal level of students. When competition is introduced in the early stages of skill learning, stress and anxiety reduce a performer's ability to learn. On the other hand, if competition is introduced after a skill has been overlearned, it can improve the level of performance. Overlearning a skill is characterized as performing the skill without having to think about it. Because many middle and high school youth have not overlearned skills, teachers should minimize competitive situations when teaching skills. For example, assume the objective is to practice basketball dribbling. Students are placed in squads to run a relay requiring that they dribble to the opposite end

of the gym, shoot a basket, and return. The first squad finished is the winner. The result is that instead of concentrating on dribbling form, students focus on winning the relay. They are overaroused and determined to run as quickly as possible. Dribbling is done poorly (if at all), the balls fly out of control, and the teacher is dismayed by the result. In this case, the relay competition overaroused those youth who had not yet overlearned dribbling skills.

Give Meaningful Skill Feedback

Feedback is important in the teaching process because it impacts what is being learned, what should be avoided, and how the performance can be modified. Skill feedback is any kind of information about a movement performance. There are two types of skill feedback: intrinsic and extrinsic. Intrinsic feedback is internal and inherent to the performance of the skill and travels through the senses, such as vision, hearing, touch, and smell. Extrinsic feedback is external and comes from an outside source, such as a teacher, a videotape, a stopwatch, and so on. Feedback from the instructor should be encouraging (or constructive), frequent, public (so all students benefit), and contingent on performance or effort.

Knowledge of Results

Knowledge of results is extrinsic feedback given after a skill has been performed. It involves information about the skill outcome so students know whether their attempts were successful (or not). Knowledge of results provides information about an incorrect or unsuccessful performance. Learners need feedback about outcomes so they can adjust the practice trials that follow. This type of feedback need not be negative, but rather a statement of fact telling whether the skill performance resulted in a successful outcome. Often, there is little need for feedback because the task outcome is obvious, such as making a basket or jumping a rope.

Knowledge of results originates externally from a teacher, peer, or other source. It is external feedback that is most often delivered by the teacher to stimulate effective skill performance. Knowledge of results is critical in the early stages of learning motor skills. After performers start to master a skill, they can analyze their performance and develop a personal system of internal feedback rather than depending on knowledge of results from a teacher or peer.

Knowledge of Performance

This type of feedback is similar to knowledge of results in that it is verbal, is extrinsic in nature, and occurs after the performance. Knowledge of results focuses on the outcome (product) of a skill, whereas knowledge of performance relates to the process (mechanics) of the skill performance. When using this type of feedback, refer to specific components of the learner's performance. For example, "I like the way you kept your chin on your chest during the forward roll," or "That's the way to step toward the target with your left foot when throwing."

Knowledge of performance can increase a student's level of motivation because it provides feedback about improvement. Frustration often sets in when a student finds it difficult to discern improvement. Feedback provides a lift and a rededication to continued practice. Knowledge of performance is a strong reinforcer, particularly when an instructor mentions something performed correctly. This feedback motivates youngsters to repeat the same pattern, ultimately resulting in improved performance. The most important aspect of this feedback is that it provides information for future patterns of skill performance.

Make performance feedback short, content filled, and concise. Explain exactly what was correct or incorrect (e.g., "That was excellent body rotation"). Concentrate on one key point to avoid confusion. Imagine a performer who is told, "Step with the left foot, rotate the trunk, lead with the elbow, and snap the wrist on your next throw!" Excessive feedback confuses anyone trying to improve a skill.

When working with students new to a skill, focus on knowledge of performance. Knowledge of results focuses solely on the skill outcome and doesn't consider whether the skill was performed correctly. An unskilled youth who manages to throw a ball into a basket might believe that the task was performed correctly even though the technical points of the throw were performed incorrectly. The goal of physical education is to teach skills correctly, with less emphasis placed on the outcome of the skill performance. In contrast, strong emphasis is placed on product (performance) rather than process (technique) when youngsters choose to enter the competitive world of athletics.

A final point about knowledge of performance: Allow time for performers to internalize feedback. Often, teachers give feedback and then ask a youth to "try it again." It is possible that the same mistake will be repeated because the youngster did not have time to internalize the feedback. Offer knowledge of performance feedback and move to another youngster. Observe how students perform following your feedback. Follow up on your feedback at a later time. This allows students a chance to relax, internalize the feedback, and modify future practice attempts.

Provide Effective Practice Sessions

Practice is a key part of learning motor skills. It is not enough that students receive the opportunity to practice; they must practice with emphasis on quality of their mechanics (practicing correctly). This section explains how to design practice sessions that optimize motor-skill learning.

Focus Practice on Process

Practice can be focused in two directions—product or process. Product-based practice places emphasis on the desired outcome of skill performance. For example, when teaching hitting, reinforcement is offered only when the student hits the ball for a base hit. Process-based practice, however, has the teacher encouraging students to perform the skill correctly with little emphasis on the outcome. This leads to a product–process conflict. Students who think the teacher is only interested in the product may not concentrate on performing with the proper technique. Overemphasis on product or skill outcome decreases a student's willingness to take risks and learn new ways of performing a skill. Focus practice on correct skill technique when youth are in the learning and practice phase of skill development.

Use Mental Practice Techniques

Mental practice involves practicing a motor skill in a quiet, relaxed environment. The experience involves thinking about the activity and its related sounds, colors, and other sensations. Students visualize themselves doing the activity successfully and at regular speed. Images of failure should be avoided (Schmidt & Lee, 2005). Mental practice stimulates performers to think about and review the activity they are to practice. Some experience or familiarity with the motor task is requisite before the performer can derive value from mental practice. Mental practice is used in combination with regular practice, not in place of it. Before performing the task, prompt students to mentally review the critical factors and sequencing of the act.

Decide on Whole versus Part Practice

Skills can be taught by the whole or part method. The whole method refers to the process of learning the entire skill or activity in one dose. The part method breaks down a skill into a series of parts followed by combining the parts into the whole skill. For example, a simple gymnastics routine might be broken into component parts and put back together for the performance.

Whether to use the whole or part method depends on the complexity and organization of the skills to be learned. Complexity refers to the number of serial skills (parts) or components there are in a task. Organization defines how the parts are related to each other. High organization means the parts of the skill are closely related to each other, making separation difficult. An example of a highly organized and complex skill is throwing; it is difficult to develop proper mechanics without going through the complete motion at normal speed. A low-organized skill is a line dance, in which footwork and arm movements can be rehearsed separately. Generally, if the skills are high in complexity but low in organization, they can be taught in parts. If complexity is low but organization high, the skills must be taught as a whole. A final consideration is the duration of the skill. If the skill is of short duration, such as throwing, batting, or kicking, trying to teach the skill in parts and at reduced speed is probably counterproductive. Imagine trying to slow down kicking a soccer ball while teaching it part by part. The performer would find it impossible to develop proper pattern and timing.

When skill components are learned separately, give students time to practice putting the parts together. For example, in a gymnastics routine, students might perform the activities separately but find difficulty sequencing them because they have not learned how to modify each activity based on the previous one.

Determine Length and Distribution of Practice Sessions

Short practice sessions usually produce more efficient learning than do longer sessions because they avoid both physical and mental fatigue (boredom). The challenge is to try to offer as many repetitions as possible within short practice sessions. Use varied approaches, challenges, and activities to develop the same skill in order to maintain motivational levels. For example, using many different drills helps maintain motivation but still focuses on the skills to be learned.

Another way to determine the length of practice sessions is to examine the tasks being practiced. If a skill causes physical fatigue, demands intense concentration, or has the potential to become tedious, practice sessions should be short and frequent, with an adequate rest pause between intervals. Stop practice when students are bored or tired and focus on a different activity until they regain their enthusiasm to learn.

Practice sessions that are spread out over many days are usually more effective than sessions crowded into a short time span. The combination of practice and review is effective because activities can be taught in a short unit and practiced in review sessions throughout the year. In the initial stages of skill learning, it is particularly important that practice sessions

be distributed in this way. Later, when success in skill performance increases motivation, individual practice sessions can be lengthened.

Use Random Skill Practice

There are two basic ways to organize skill instruction. The first is blocked skill practice, where all the trials of one task are completed before moving on to the next task. Because blocked practice is effective during the early stages of learning a new skill, learners usually make rapid improvement because they are practicing the same skill over and over. This success encourages learners to continue practicing. However, there is a drawback to blocked practice. It makes learners believe they are more skilled than they actually are. When the skill is applied in a natural setting, performance level lowers because there are many variations of the skill. This creates an increased failure rate that may cause a decrease in motivation.

The other method is random skill practice in which the order of task presentations is mixed and no task is practiced twice in succession. Goode and Magill (1986) showed that random practice was the most effective approach to use when learning skills. Blocked practice gave the best results during the acquisition phase of skill learning; however, students who learned a skill using random practice demonstrated a much higher level of retention.

The reason random practice results in better skill retention is related to mentally generating solutions. When the same task is practiced over and over, youngsters not only become bored, they don't think about how to perform the skill. Because the same motor program is used over and over to complete the task, little effort or thinking is required. In contrast, students using random practice forget the motor program used and have to consciously re-create the solution to be successful. Because students become bored quickly when doing the same task over and over, random practice helps minimize this negative side effect.

Offer Variable Skill Practice

Motor tasks are usually grouped into classes of tasks. For example, throwing is a collection of a class of movements. Throwing a ball in a sport can be performed in many different ways, such as at different speeds, different trajectories, and varying distances. Even though throwing tasks are all different, the variations have fundamental similarities. Movements in a class usually involve the same body parts using a similar rhythm, but they are performed with many variations. These differences create the need for variable practice in a variable setting.

Practice sessions should include a variety of skills in a movement class with a variety of situations and parameters in which the skill is performed. If a skill to be learned involves one fixed way of performing it (a "closed" skill), such as placekicking a football or striking a ball off a batting tee, variability is much less important. However, most skills are "open," and responses are somewhat unpredictable, which makes variability in practice important (e.g., catching or batting a ball moving at different speeds and from different angles). Motor skills should be practiced under a variety of conditions so students can respond to a wide variety of novel situations.

DESIGN COMPREHENSIVE UNIT PLANS

Units of instruction offer a method for organizing and presenting activities over a stipulated period of time. Without units, it is difficult to offer scope and sequence for various instructional activities throughout the year. Units vary in length depending on the age and ability of students and the design of the curriculum. Most units focus on physical activity or movement forms, such as team sports, lifetime sports, dance, or physical conditioning. However, some units are developed to emphasize a concept or idea, such as cardiovascular efficiency, body composition, flexibility, or strength.

When unit plans are developed, a wide variety of sources should be reviewed to ensure that the unit is comprehensive. Units of instruction usually reflect a range of activities gathered from materials produced by experts. Another plus of unit plans is that they give teachers a plan for how instruction should proceed. This prevents fragmentation. An instructor with a coherent unit plan does not simply teach from day to day and hope that everything will somehow fit together by the end of the unit.

There are many different ways to write and organize units of instruction. Most plans contain the following elements, even though they may be titled differently or listed in a different order.

Objectives or Standards for the Unit

Objectives should be written before organizing the activities and experiences. The objectives state what the students are expected to know on completion of the unit. Students should be made aware of what they are expected to learn. Objectives are usually listed for the three learning domains. For example, what cognitive understandings should students have, and will they be tested in these areas? What are the social and emotional concepts students should develop through par-

ticipation in this unit? Finally, what skills, techniques, and game strategies should be learned on completion of the unit?

Many districts are now asking that teachers include the national standards for physical education (NASPE, 2004) into the unit and lesson plans. The standards give direction to the entire physical education program and help clarify what students should learn. Note that many of the chapters of this text open with the national standards that are being met through activities in the current chapter.

Skills and Activities

This section is the instructional core of the unit and is organized according to unit objectives. Specific skills to be developed, drills to facilitate skill development, lead-up games to be taught, and culminating experiences are listed in this section. Scope and sequence are also integrated into this section to ensure a meaningful presentation. When activities are listed in proper sequence, instructionally sound and legally safe lessons are more easily written. Students and teachers may list the learning experiences as desirable student outcomes to ensure simple translation.

Instructional Procedures

Instructional procedures determine how activities will be presented to ensure the maximum amount of learning. Points included are instructional techniques, observations on the efficient use of equipment, necessary safety procedures, and teaching formations.

Equipment, Facilities, and Instructional Devices

Listing equipment and facilities needed for instruction makes it easy to quickly see what is available and whether other teachers are using these items or facilities for a unit being taught concurrently. If facilities or equipment need to be prepared prior to the start of the lesson (e.g., lowering goals or deflating balls), this should be listed on the lesson plan.

Culminating Activities

This section identifies how the unit will be concluded. A tournament between selected teams, an intraschool contest, or a school demonstration play day could be implemented. In any case, the unit should finish with an activity that is enjoyable to students and leaves them with a positive feeling toward the unit of instruction.

Evaluation

The final section outlines how student progress is monitored. The instructor can carry out monitoring,

I. Title and grade level
II. Analysis and description of setting
   A. Previous experiences and exposure to activity
   B. Limiting factors: class size, class organization, mixed grades, facilities and equipment, period of day class meets
   C. Rationale for including the activity
III. Objectives
   A. General unit objectives (NASPE, 2004)
   B. Specific objectives
     1. Psychomotor (physical performance) skills
     2. Knowledge, rules, and strategies
     3. Attitudes and values
IV. Organization
   A. Time (length of unit)
   B. Space available
   C. Equipment and supplies
   D. Basic grouping of students
   E. Number of groups
V. Content
   A. Introduction of the activity
   B. Rules
   C. Skills (diagram all drills)
   D. Activities and lead-up games
   E. Skills tests
   F. Written tests
   G. Block plan for entire unit
   H. Grading procedures
VI. References and resources

or students can be given guidelines for self-evaluation. Written tests can be administered to evaluate the knowledge gained through instruction. Skill tests can be selected to assess the level of performance and skill development. An attitude inventory can measure the impact of the unit on the affective area of learning.

Another phase of evaluation involves asking students to comment on the unit and its method of presentation. This should be done in writing (anonymously) rather than verbally because some student comments may anger or belittle the teacher. Student evaluations offer direction for modifying the unit and making it more effective in the future.

Suggested Weekly (Block Plan) Schedule

The purpose of a block plan is to distribute the activities of the unit into weekly segments. This gives the teacher a sense of timing and an indication of what should be taught and when. A block plan alleviates problems such as insufficient time to teach the desired activities or insufficient activities to fill up the time frame. It eases the burden of writing lesson plans because the material to be taught is identified and sequenced into a meaningful time frame. Daily lesson plans are developed by following the outline of the block plan.

Figure 5.10 is an example of a block plan for a unit on racquetball. This textbook has an accompanying lesson plan book that has been field-tested and written by Dr. Carole Casten (2009). Professor Casten, of California State University (CSU-Dominguez Hills), designed a model high school program, and the information in *Lesson Plans for Dynamic Physical Education for Secondary School Students* is an outgrowth of her creativity and planning. This book offers lesson plans for a wide-ranging set of units. For example, there are block plans and lesson plans for units such as orienteering, archery, Frisbee golf, rock climbing, kickboxing, and weight training. The lessons are written in an easy-to-use format so teachers can quickly implement some new and innovative approaches to their programs. Chapters 19 to 21 in this text also include a number of sample block plans.

Bibliography and Resources

The bibliography contains materials used by students and teacher. Students are given a list of materials they can peruse if they desire more information. Location of materials should be identified. Teachers may have a separate list and collection of resources they use for instruction. For example, pamphlets on nutrition or physical fitness, available films, bulletin-board materials, and textbooks could be included in the resource section.

The following outline is an example of a skeleton structure for designing unit plans.

CREATE QUALITY LESSON PLANS

The importance of lesson planning cannot be overemphasized. Instructors at the middle and high school level are, at times, criticized for their lack of planning. A cycle of not planning often begins early in a teacher's career when student teachers observe master teachers doing little, if any, planning. The emphasis placed on developing meaningful lesson and unit plans in professional preparation courses appears unnecessary when a master teacher teaches without the aid of thoughtful planning. The beginning teacher is unable to meaningfully judge the effectiveness of the master teacher because of a lack of perspective and experience. The master teacher has taught the material for many years and has evolved a method of presentation through trial and error. It is possible to present a lesson without planning, but the quality of any lesson can be improved through research, preparation, and a well-sequenced plan.

Planning helps teachers present quality instruction and maintain meaningful interaction with students.

Introduction What is racquetball? Grips—ready position Forehand stroke Backhand stroke Class procedures Practice bounce and hit Rule of the day	*Review* Grip, forehand, backhand Equipment *Teach* Serves—Drive, Z Lob *Activities* Serves—practice Bounce and hit Rule of the day	*Review* Serves, rules *Teach* Back-wall shots Hinders Kill shots *Activities* Back-wall practice or short game Rule of the day	*Review* Forehand, backhand *Teach* Court position Passing shots Kill shots *Activities* Performance objectives or short game Rule of the day	*Review* Back-wall shots *Teach* Ceiling shots Passing shots Kill shots *Activities* Ceiling games 1, 2, or 3 shots
Review Problem rules Serve strategy Court coverage *Activities* Accuracy drills Drive serve Lob serve Backhand Backhand games 1 or 2 shots	*Teach* Cutthroat Doubles *Activities* Performance objectives 8-ball rally Rotation workup	*Review* Problem areas *Activities* Performance objectives 5 and out Ceiling games	*Review* Rules *Activities* Performance objectives Regular game Cutthroat or doubles	*Review* Kill shots *Activities* Rotation workup
Activities Performance objectives Backhand games Regular game Tournament games	*Written exam* *Activities* Performance objectives Tournament games	*Review* Rules, strategy, shots serves *Activities* Performance objectives Tournament games	*Activities* Performance objectives Tournament games Cutthroat or doubles	*Final performance* **Objectives work** *Review course* **Objectives** Final games Return exam

FIGURE 5.10 Racquetball block plan

Teachers, regardless of experience and ability, have many things to remember while teaching. When presenting a lesson, situations occur that are impossible to predict. For example, dealing with discipline problems; modifying lessons spontaneously; relating to students by name; offering praise, feedback, and reinforcement; and developing an awareness of teaching behavior patterns need to be done regularly. If the content of the lesson is planned, written, and readily available, greater emphasis can be placed on other equally important phases of teaching.

When planning a lesson, the skills and abilities of students need to be considered if success is going to be an integral part of the presentation. This understanding results in drills and activities that are challenging but not threatening. Remember that an activity is challenging or threatening based on the student's perception, not the instructor's. An activity is challenging if the learner believes it is difficult but achievable. It is threatening if the learner perceives it to be impossible. The same drill could be challenging to some students and threatening to others. Trying to sort out how students perceive various activities makes teaching a difficult task.

Regular success is necessary if students are expected to enjoy an activity for a lifetime. An instructor can force students to do just about anything within the educational setting. If forced into activities that result in frequent failure, students will probably learn to dislike or avoid them in the future. To give students lifetime skills and attitudes, monitor and adjust lessons regularly. Maintain sensitivity to the learner's perceptions and feelings, and teach with concern for each student as an individual.

Lesson planning is unique to each teacher. The competency of the individual in various activities will determine the depth of the lesson plan. More research and reading will need to be done for a unit in which a teacher has little experience. When a teacher is unfamiliar with a unit and still refuses to plan, the quality of instruction is compromised. Solid planning helps overcome a lack of competency and demonstrates the willingness to change and learn new skills and knowledge. Planning increases the effectiveness of the instructor. Regardless of the content, consider the following points when planning a lesson:

■ Learning physical skills takes practice and repetition. Each lesson should be organized to maximize the amount of meaningful participation and to minimize the amount of teacher verbalization and off-task student behavior.

■ Practice combined with instruction and meaningful feedback ensures skill development. Instructional sequences and procedures that increase the amount of feedback in a lesson are part of the written lesson plan. Key points to be learned may require regular and specific feedback to ensure that correct learning patterns occur.

■ Lesson plans allow for differing ability levels of the students. Build a range of activities into each lesson plan so that students can progress at varying rates, depending on their levels of skill. List the activities in progression to simplify presentation and enhance learning.

■ Requisite equipment should be listed in the lesson plan. This prevents the problem of being in the middle of a lesson only to find that needed equipment was not procured. The initial placement of equipment and how it is distributed and put away are tasks that are planned before teaching.

■ Time needed for management activities can be minimized with prior planning. List whether students are to be in small groups or partnered, the type of formation required, and how these procedures will be implemented.

■ Outcomes of the lesson should be listed. The outcomes of the lesson are easier to reach when both the instructor and students know where they are going. Outcomes can be written in brief form and stated clearly so that students know what they are expected to learn.

■ Because lesson plans are personal, they can be written in code. All information need not be written out in longhand. For example, many teachers often write their lesson plans on 4- by 6-inch cards, which can be carried easily and used with minimal

distraction. The card contents reflect the instructor's thoughts and planning, which have occurred before the actual teaching session.

■ Time should be estimated for various activities needed in the lesson. For example, the amount of time for roll call, a warm-up activity, fitness development, and the lesson's focus should be estimated. The time schedule need not be inflexible, but it should be followed closely enough so that planned activities are taught.

■ Planning is an important phase of teaching. Few teachers instruct for more than 4 to 5 hours per day. If an 8-hour day is expected of other workers, instructors should use some of their remaining work time for planning. Consider a comparison with coaching. All successful coaches spend a great deal of time planning, observing films, and constructing game plans. The game may not last more than an hour or 2, but many hours of planning take place before the contest. Teachers of physical education should recognize the need to spend time each day planning for 4 to 5 hours of teaching. The results of a well-planned lesson are rewarding to both students and the teacher.

■ Successful experiences should be planned for students. The plan should include enough challenge to motivate and enough variety to maintain interest. A balance of safety and challenge is required in the school setting.

Major Instructional Components of the Lesson

A daily lesson-plan format provides teachers and students with a measure of stability. A consistent daily instructional format offers routine and structure. Lesson plans offer a systematic approach to teaching so all activities are covered during the year. When planning a lesson, the skills and abilities of students need to be considered if success is going to be an integral part of the presentation. This understanding results in drills and activities that are challenging but not threatening. Whether an activity is challenging or threatening is based on the student's perception, not the instructor's. In effect, because the least gifted students may find difficulty in learning, it is usually best to gear instruction based on the ability levels of such students. Students can get discouraged when they find tasks too difficult to learn. The amount of time spent on different parts of the lesson can be predetermined. Most lesson plans cover three parts: a warm-up activity, a fitness component, and the lesson focus.

Introductory (Warm-Up) Activity

The introductory activity occupies 3 to 5 minutes of the total lesson. The purpose is to prepare students for activity. Students require a few minutes to become emotionally involved in the activity after sitting in classes. Introductory activities (Chapter 14) require minimal organization and place demands on large muscle movement. The activities may be an integral part of the fitness routine or a separate entity. In either case, the introductory activity is used to raise the heart rate, warm up the body, and stretch the muscles in anticipation of a fitness development activity. Teachers can change the introductory activity each week to add variety to the warm-up procedure.

Fitness Development Activity

Fitness activities take 15 to 20 minutes and focus on the development of physical fitness. Instruction centers focus on developing major components of fitness, especially flexibility, muscular strength and endurance, body composition, and cardiovascular endurance. A wide variety of fitness activities are offered so students can learn to select methods acceptable to them in adulthood. Graduating from school knowing many ways to develop and maintain physical fitness is a program objective that will allow students to select lifetime fitness activities. A successful experience in fitness activities is motivating and creates positive attitudes. An in-depth discussion of physical fitness and examples of routines are found in Chapter 16.

Lesson Focus and Game or Closing Activity

The lesson focus and game activity is 25 to 30 minutes in duration depending on the length of the period. This is the instructional part of the lesson, which emphasizes skill development, cognitive learning, and enhancement of the affective domain. This phase of the lesson contains skills to be taught, drills, and lead-up activities, all of which culminate in games and tournaments.

In elementary schools, games are often played at the end of the lesson so students leave with a positive feeling about physical activity. These games are often unrelated to the lesson focus activity because students often desire a new and exciting activity to renew their enthusiasm. As students mature into the middle and high school years, the game or closing activity is often an extension of the lesson focus. For example, in an orienteering lesson, students could use the last part of the lesson for completing an activity. On the other hand, if students show they are ready for a new activ-

ity, it is often beneficial to introduce a cooperative or competitive game activity.

Content of the Lesson Plan

Instructional Activities

Specific skills and activities to be taught need to be listed in the lesson plan. These are listed in proper progression to ensure that instruction builds on previously learned skills. Progression also helps ensure that activities are presented in a safe manner. The skills and related activities need not be written out in detail. Write enough so it is easy to comprehend the activities when teaching.

Teaching and Organization Hints

A list of instructional procedures can help teachers conceptualize prior to the lesson what details need to be prepared, including how the equipment is organized, what formations to use, key points of instruction to share with students, and the specific feedback used. New instructional procedures can be recorded after a lesson and maintained for the next time the lesson is taught.

Expected Student Outcomes

Prior to the lesson, establish what students are expected to experience, learn, and perform. Curriculum objectives can be listed to give direction to instruction. With careful planning of expected student outcomes, teachers can offer a wide variety of experiences throughout the school year to help students develop in all domains—psychomotor, cognitive, and affective.

REFLECT ON THE COMPLETED LESSON

Teaching is a full-time job. Teachers who excel and impact the lives of their students put a great deal of time and energy into their teaching. Obviously, all who teach physical education work hard to accomplish goals. But, it is always easy to identify a truly outstanding teacher who seems to gets students to perform at a high level. One of the elements that is obvious among great teachers is their level of caring and thinking. They spend a great deal of time thinking about the lessons they have presented in order to find new and better ways to get students to respond. This process is often referred to as reflection—the act of sitting back and asking the question, "How could I have done that better so students would learn more?"

Many things make teaching difficult (e.g., accommodating the weather, having to teach outside,

Questions to Aid the Reflection Process

Planning

- Did I prepare ahead of time? Mental preparation prior to a lesson ensures continuity occurs in a lesson.
- Did I understand the "whys" of my lesson? Knowing why you are teaching something will give you greater strength and conviction in your presentation.
- Did I state my instructional goals for the lesson? Students are more focused if they know what they are supposed to learn.
- Did I plan the lesson so students can participate safely, such as creating safe areas for running, with no slippery spots, broken glass, objects to run into, and adequate room for striking activities?

Equipment

- Was my equipment arranged prior to class? Proper equipment placement reduces management time and allows more time for instruction and practice.
- Did I use enough equipment to keep all students involved and assured of maximum practice opportunities?
- Did I notify the principal about equipment that needs to be repaired or replaced? On a regular basis, do I record areas where equipment is lacking or insufficient in quantity? Do I inform the principal of these shortcomings?
- Did I select equipment that is appropriate for the developmental level of the students (e.g., proper size and types of balls, basketball hoop height, hand implements)?

Methodology

- Did I constantly move and reposition myself during the lesson? Moving allows you to be close to more students so you can reinforce and help them. It usually reduces behavior problems.
- Did I teach with enthusiasm and energy? Energy and zest rubs off on students.
- Did I try to show just as much energy for the last class of the day as I did for the first class of the day? Did I work just as hard on Friday as I did at the start of the week?
- Did I keep students moving during lesson transitions? Did I plan my transitions carefully so little time was needed to proceed to the next part of the lesson?

Instruction

- Was I alert for children who were having trouble performing the activities and needed some personal help? Youngsters want to receive relevant but subtle help.
- Did I praise youngsters who made an effort or improved? Saying something positive to children increases their desire to perform at a higher level.
- Did I give sufficient attention to the personalization and creativity of each student? Everybody feels unique and different and wants to deal with learning tasks in a personal manner.
- Did I teach for quality of movement or just offer a large quantity of activities in an attempt to keep students on task? Repetition is a necessary part of learning new skills.

Discipline/Management

- Did I teach students to be responsible for their learning and personal behavior? Students need to learn responsibility and self-direction skills.
- Did I evaluate how I handled discipline and management problems? Did I preserve the self-esteem of my students during behavior correction episodes? Did I yell out my corrective feedback for the entire class to hear? What are some ways I could have handled situations better?
- Did I make positive calls home to reinforce students who are really trying and working hard?

Assessment

- Did I bring closure to my lesson? This gives feedback about the effectiveness of instruction. It also allows students a chance to reflect on what they have learned. Did I ask for answers in a way that allows me to quickly check that all students understand?
- Did I evaluate the usefulness of the activities I presented? Did I make changes as quickly as possible to ensure my lessons were improving and better at meeting the needs of my students?
- Did I communicate with teachers and the principal about things that need to be improved or better understood? Did I leave my office and meet other teachers on a regular basis for the sake of goodwill and program support?

FIGURE 5.11 Questions to aid the reflection process

having a limited amount of equipment, not knowing how certain youngsters will respond to your discipline techniques). There are no simple answers to be found. What works one time may not work the next. Some teachers like to put in an 8:00-to-3:00 day, and you better not be in their way when the "clock strikes three." These teachers will teach the same way and the same thing year after year without change. It is often said that these teachers have been "teaching 20 years and have 1 year of experience." That approach is the opposite of reflecting and trying to improve.

Quality teachers find time to reflect on all the factors related to their lessons. Most teachers admit that their first lesson of the week is not as polished and effective as one taught near the end of the week. A lesson taught during the first period of the day does not include all the finer points learned through trial and error. Instruction improves when teachers reflect on why some things worked and others didn't. Leave time at the end of the day to reflect and note ways the lesson can be improved. Try keeping a portfolio related to inspiration and insight you uncover during the reflection process. Write down personal growth indicators and situations that offer evidence you are growing professionally. Continue to reflect and see it as a dynamic and ongoing process. Examine Figure 5.11 on the previous page for a list of questions that aid the reflection process. Add other questions that are specific and related to your professional growth.

STUDY STIMULATORS AND REVIEW QUESTIONS

1. Explain why students should not be allowed to get physical education credit for band or athletics.

2. Discuss the pros and cons of a dress code for physical education classes.

3. Discuss the difference between knowledge of results and knowledge of performance by using an example involving volleyball or any other sport activity.

4. Which of the two practice schedules, blocked or random, can help minimize boredom for students. Explain your choice.

5. What are the practical implications of physical and mental fatigue on the planning of learning tasks?

6. What is the rationale for imbedding a culminating activity at the end of lessons and units?

7. Other than purchasing new equipment, what are two effective strategies programs can employ to increase the amount of equipment available for instruction?

8. What benefits are there to having students share in some of the decision-making processes?

9. Provide an example of a makeup assignment in fitness that includes a knowledge, performance, and spectator task.

10. How are lower-skilled students shortchanged when most of the instruction is limited to the first 2 days of a unit?

REFERENCES AND SUGGESTED READINGS

Buck, M. M., Lund, J. L., Harrison, J. M., & Blakemore Cook, C. L. (2007). *Instructional strategies for secondary physical education* (6th ed.). Boston: McGraw-Hill.

Casten, C. M. (2009). *Lesson plans for dynamic physical education for secondary school students* (6th ed.). San Francisco: Pearson Benjamin Cummings.

Goode, S., & Magill, R. A. (1986). The contextual interference effects in learning three badminton serves. *Research Quarterly for Exercise and Sport, 57*, 308–314.

Harrison, J. M. (1987). A review of the research on teacher effectiveness and its implications for current practice. *Quest, 39*, 36–55.

Kelly, L. E., & Melograno, V. J. (2004). *Designing the physical education curriculum: An achievement based approach.* Champaign, IL: Human Kinetics Publishers.

National Association for Sport and Physical Education. (2004). *Moving into the future: National standards for physical education* (2nd ed.). Reston, VA: Author.

Pangrazi, R. P. (2007a). *Dynamic physical education for elementary school children* (15th ed.). San Francisco: Benjamin Cummings.

Pangrazi, R. P. (2007b). *Lesson plans for elementary physical education for elementary school children* (15th ed.). San Francisco: Benjamin Cummings.

Parker, J. (1995). Secondary teachers' views of effective teaching in physical education. *Journal of Teaching in Physical Education, 14(2)*, 127–139.

Rink, J. E. (2006). *Teaching physical education for learning* (5th ed.). Boston: McGraw-Hill.

Sariscsany, M. J., Darst, P., & van der Mars, H. (1995). The effects of three teacher supervision patterns on student on-task and skill performance in secondary physical education. *Journal of Teaching in Physical Education, 14(2)*, 179–197.

Schmidt, R. A., & Lee, T. (2005). *Motor control and learning* (4th ed.). Champaign, IL: Human Kinetics Publishers.

Siedentop, D., & Tannehill, D. (2000). *Developing teaching skills in physical education* (4th ed.). Mountain View, CA: Mayfield Publishing Co.

van der Mars, H., Vogler, W., Darst, P., and Cusimano, B. (1994). Active supervision patterns of physical education teachers and their relationship with student behavior. *Journal of Teaching in Physical Education, 14*(1), 99–112.

Wuest, D. A., & Bucher, C. A. (2003). *Foundations of physical education, exercise science, and sport* (14th ed.). Boston: McGraw-Hill.

Wuest, D. A., & Lombardo, B. (1994). *Curriculum and instruction, the secondary school physical education experience.* St. Louis, MO: Mosby.

WEB SITES

Unit and Lesson Planning

www.hcc.hawaii.edu/intranet/committees/FacDevCom
/guidebk/teachtip/lesspln1.htm

www.hcc.hawaii.edu/intranet/committees/FacDevCom
/guidebk/teachtip/lesspln3.htm

www.hcc.hawaii.edu/intranet/committees/FacDevCom
/guidebk/teachtip/lesspln2.htm

www.pecentral.org

www.pelinks4u.org

www.pe4life.org

www.masterteacher.com

www.masterteacher.com/p.cfm?mt_item_number=1765

ESSENTIAL COMPONENTS OF A QUALITY PROGRAM

COMPONENT 1 A quality physical education program is organized around content standards that offer direction and continuity to instruction and evaluation.

COMPONENT 2 A quality program is student centered and based on the developmental urges, characteristics, and interests of students.

COMPONENT 3 Quality physical education makes physical activity and motor-skill development the core of the program.

COMPONENT 4 Physical education programs teach management skills and self-discipline.

COMPONENT 5 Quality programs emphasize inclusion of all students.

COMPONENT 6 In a quality physical education setting, instruction focuses on the process of learning skills rather than the product or outcome of the skill performance.

COMPONENT 7 A quality physical education program teaches lifetime activities that students can use to promote their health and personal wellness.

COMPONENT 8 Quality physical education teaches cooperative and responsibility skills and helps students develop sensitivity to diversity and gender issues.

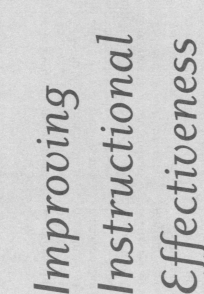

6

Improving Instructional Effectiveness

CHAPTER SUMMARY

This chapter presents effective methods for being an active and connected teacher. Quality instruction demands effective communication between teacher and student that can be enhanced by using instructional cues, demonstrating, modeling, and providing meaningful feedback. An important part of teaching is to understand the personal needs of students, which includes teaching for diversity and understanding gender differences.

STUDENT OUTCOMES

After reading this chapter, you will be able to:

- Identify various ways to stay connected with students, including using active supervision and maintaining the flow of the lesson.

- Speak effectively to a class using proper techniques.

- Understand procedures needed to develop effective instructional cues.

- Cite various ways to enhance the clarity of communication between the teacher and the learner.

- Effectively use instructional cues to facilitate student learning.

- Describe demonstration and modeling skills that facilitate an environment conducive to learning.

Student Outcomes, continued

- Articulate strategies and techniques used to supply students with meaningful feedback regarding performance.
- Teach effectively for diversity and gender differences.

Competent teachers create a learning environment where students want to learn and practice skills, as well as feel safe and receive equitable treatment. Such an environment is characterized by a sensitive and caring teacher who uses a variety of techniques to foster learning in all students. It is a fallacy that teachers treat all students alike. More often than not, students know they are unique, and each would like to be treated as a special individual. The challenge is to better understand what makes each student "tick."

This section helps teachers develop a repertoire of teaching skills and strategies that allows them to meet the needs of all students in a class. Notice the word *all* in the previous sentence. Many teachers can help students who want to learn; however, only the best teachers are capable of motivating students who don't particularly like the subject matter. This is the challenge: Teach all students regardless of their intrinsic desire to learn. A good place to begin is with the skill of listening. Few traits enhance the learning environment more than effective listening by the teacher. A student's self-worth is enhanced when a teacher listens and acknowledges his or her feelings and concerns.

MAINTAIN STUDENT INTEREST

A component of effective teaching is a learning environment that facilitates student learning and maintains interest. Environmental and instructional planning ensure that students have an opportunity to learn skills in a positive setting. Active teacher supervision and instructional flow will make students feel as though the teacher is involved and cares about the learning environment.

Use Active Supervision

Observation of class performance is critical in ensuring that students stay on task and practice activities correctly (van der Mars, Vogler, Darst, & Cusimano, 1994). This requires supervision of students in an active manner—that is, positioning oneself so that eye contact can be maintained with all students. Students have a tendency to stay on task if they know someone is

watching. This mandates staying out of the center of the area. It is common to observe teachers placing students in a circle and then standing in the center of the formation. Not only is it impossible to see all students, but it is difficult for students facing the back of the teacher to hear. Because students cannot hear and there is little eye contact with half of the class, the teacher may not be aware of an accident or misbehavior.

Some teachers assume they must move to the same location in the teaching area when giving instructions because students will listen only when they are on or near this spot. Not only is this incorrect, but it can result in negative consequences. Students who choose to exhibit deviant or off-task behavior usually move away from the instructor. Because the teacher's movement patterns are predictable, deviant students are farthest from the teacher in a position that is difficult to observe. In addition, it is possible the teacher may never move into certain areas, causing some students to believe the teacher does not like them. Active supervision requires the instructor to move around the perimeter of the area. Another reason for moving in an unpredictable manner is to keep students on task. For example, when using a number of teaching stations, some teachers move from station to station in a predictable manner. Students may perform the tasks while the teacher is watching but move off task as soon as the teacher moves to the next station. Here's the bottom line: Actively move in a random fashion so students cannot anticipate where you will be observing next.

Active supervision demands movement and effective observation. If you develop a plan for reaching all students, they will come to believe you are concerned about them. In addition, it is important to place yourself in an optimum position to observe skill performance. For example, if you are observing kicking, stand to the side rather than behind the student. A judgment that needs to be made when observing performances is how long to stay with a single group or student. If you get overly involved with a student, the rest of the class may move off task. On the other hand, if contacts are short and terse, the student may not benefit from the interaction. Learn to pace instructional feedback by giving one or two pointers and moving to another student.

Develop a Plan for Active Supervision

Experts who work with beginning teachers know they often "look at students but do not see." When teachers do not have a plan for actively supervising behavior, they usually are not able to recall whether students exhibited desired behaviors. To keep all students on task, it is important to develop a plan for monitoring this behavior. A practical plan might be to scan the class from left to right at regular intervals and observe the number of students who are performing the assigned task. When teaching a class of 25 to 35 students, it usually takes 4 to 6 seconds to scan an entire class. If done faster, it is difficult to internalize the results of the scan. A number of variables can be evaluated through systematic observation: students responding to a start or stop signal (response latency), key points of skill performance, adherence to safety procedures, and on-task performance.

Design a plan for active supervision. This plan should include where to stand for observation, how long to stay with each student, and how to move through the instructional area. One approach to ensure that all students receive personal contact is to check off the names of students who were addressed during the lesson. This can be done immediately after the lesson with a roll sheet or at a later time if the lesson is recorded. Often, teachers find they do not make regular contact with certain students and make excessive contact with others. This leads to feelings of favoritism or concern that "the teacher does not like me." It is difficult to interact with all students in a single physical education lesson, but in a 1- or 2-week period, all students should receive feedback and attention.

Teacher movement should be planned considering it affects supervisory effectiveness. To facilitate learning to move, divide the teaching area into four equal parts and set a goal of moving into each area a certain number of times. Give instructions and reinforcement from all quadrants. A nonparticipating student can be used to chart movement. See pages 217–222 to create an objective measurement plan for active supervision and student contact.

Maintain the Flow of the Lesson

An important phase of effective instruction is pacing the lesson to keep students interested in learning, yet not frustrated. The following points offer ways to improve the flow of a lesson and maintain student motivation to reach desired goals.

Minimize Verbalization and Increase Activity

It is easy to become engrossed in instruction and lose sight of student interest. Students enter class expecting to be involved in activity. If a teacher spends 5 minutes with roll call followed by 5 or 10 minutes of lecture, students lose interest and motivation. Move the class into activity first and give instructions later. This gets students immersed in the activity so they will be more receptive to listening. As a general rule, if instruction is going to take longer than a minute or two, it should be broken into a number of short sessions. Alternating instruction with application of the information will keep students on task. The following are suggestions for effective instruction:

1. **Focus instruction on one or two key points.** It is difficult to remember a series of instructions. Telling students a number of points related to skill performance leaves them baffled and frustrated. In a series of points, most learners remember the first and the last point. Strong emphasis on one or two key points makes it easier for students to focus their concentration.

2. **Refrain from lengthy skill descriptions.** When instructions last longer than 30 to 60 seconds, students become listless because they can't comprehend and remember all of the input. Develop a pattern of short, concise presentations, alternated with practice sessions. Short practice sessions offer an opportunity to refocus on key points of a skill many times.

3. **Present information in its most basic, easy-to-understand form.** If a class does not understand the presentation, you have failed your students. Check for understanding to see if students comprehend the material.

4. **Separate management and instructional episodes.** Consider the following instructions during the presentation of a new game: "In this game, we will break into groups of five. Each group will get a ball and form a small circle. On the command 'Go,' the game will start. Here is how you play the game. . . . " A lengthy discussion of game rules and conduct follows. Because the instructions are long, students will usually forget what they were asked to do earlier. Or, they will think about whom they want in their group rather than the game rules. Instead, move the class into game formation (management) and then discuss the activity to be learned (instruction). This serves two purposes: It reduces the length of the episode, and it makes it easier to conceptualize how the game is played.

Maintain the Focus of Instruction

It is easy to become derailed when an interesting event occurs in class. Lesson plans are designed to guide the instruction toward desired objectives. When teachers constantly allow students to "sidetrack" them and get them to talk about subjects unrelated to instructional outcomes, goals may not be reached. Experienced teachers know some students will intentionally try to move them away from the tasks at hand in order to participate in activities they prefer. Effective teachers maintain their momentum toward objectives, yet they are able to show interest in student ideas. Sometimes it is necessary to deviate from planned objectives and take advantage of the "teachable moment." However, this should be the exception, not the rule. Students know the teacher is responsible for guiding the content of the lesson, and they expect it.

Maintain the Pace and Continuity of Instruction

Effective lessons flow in a consistent and well-planned manner. There are many transitions during a lesson: organizing students into groups, changing from one part of the lesson to another, and issuing and putting away equipment. Students should perceive transitions as an integral part of the instruction. If a transition is excessively long, it interrupts instructional momentum and students may begin to misbehave. Minimize time spent on transitions considering they detract from accomplishing the lesson's goals.

Pace of instruction affects the flow of the lesson (Siedentop & Tannehill, 2000). How often should a teacher break into practice sessions to clarify a point or refocus instruction? Usually, there is a natural break in practice episodes where students become bored or fatigued and begin to move off task. This is a signal for the teacher to refocus on the same or a new goal. If most of the students are not performing correctly after an instructional episode, stop and restate the situation.

Activity instruction demands continuity so learners understand the purpose of performing various activities. For example, instructors often break activities into parts but clearly know how the skill as a whole is performed. Students also need to know how the various parts of a skill fit together. Skills are performed in a sequence (e.g., a throw is followed by a catch, a double play follows a pattern). Students should experience the various parts in a sequence within the same lesson and in a variety of contexts. It is expecting too much of students to have them practice parts for 1 or 2 weeks and then put them together as a whole. Integrate the activity or drill into the ultimate focal point: the accomplishment of the skill or activity.

DEVELOP EFFECTIVE LISTENING SKILLS

For most teachers, listening skills are more difficult to learn than speaking skills. Instructors are taught to impart knowledge to students and have practiced speaking for years. Many students view teachers as people who teach you but do not care about your point of view. Poor communication is usually caused by a breakdown in listening rather than speaking. There is a lot of truth in the adage, "People were given two ears and one mouth so they could listen twice as much as they speak." The following activities will help you become a more effective listener.

1. *Be an active listener.* Good listeners convince the speaker that they are interested in what is being said. Much of this is done through nonverbal behavior such as maintaining eye contact, nodding the head in agreement, using facial expressions, and moving toward the speaker. Active listening shows students that their ideas and thoughts count and that they have some input into their destiny.

2. *Determine what the student is really trying to say.* Many students are not capable of clearly expressing their feelings, particularly if they have deep concerns. The words expressed may not clearly signal what the student is feeling. For example, a teenager may say, "I hate PE." In most cases, students do not hate all phases of physical education; rather, it may be that something more immediate is the problem. An effective response might be, "You sound upset; are you having a problem you want to discuss?" This makes students feel as though their feelings are important and gives them an opportunity to clarify their concerns. It also prevents the teacher from internalizing the student's emotion and responding in a heated manner, such as, "I don't care whether you like it or not; get with it!"

3. *Paraphrase what the student said.* Paraphrasing is restating what was said to you, including the feelings detected, in your own words. For example, the teacher might respond, "Do I hear you saying that you are frustrated and bored with this activity?" If the paraphrasing is correct, it makes the student feel validated and understood. If the interpretation is incorrect, the student has an opportunity to restate the problem. In addition, it offers the teacher an opportunity to clearly understand how students perceive various situations.

4. *Allow students to tell you how they feel.* Teachers who listen to students learn more about their feelings. It is important to let students know that you

will listen and then to practice doing so. If you are an effective listener, you hear things that are not always positive. For example, students may tell you honestly which activities they enjoy and which they do not. They may tell you how you made them feel when you criticized them. This type of communication is constructive only if you are able to accept it objectively and not be threatened by the feedback. Such feedback can be important for improving instruction. Even though it may not be a valid criticism of the program or procedures, it does offer opportunity for program and instructional improvement. Here's a word of caution: If you find it difficult to accept such communication, it is probably best to tell students that you prefer not to hear about it. It may be best to avoid such interaction with students if it affects your confidence or starts a confrontation.

5. **Avoid situations that undermine effective communication.** Certain types of verbal interaction convince students that the teacher is unwilling to listen. These are some of the more common examples:

a. *Preaching or moralizing.* This is often manifested by telling others they "should know better than that!" Obviously, students make mistakes because they are immature and learning. A big part of learning is making mistakes and knowing how to avoid such situations in the future. Teachers who expect such mistakes are not shocked by student misbehavior and are able to deal with it in a rational manner.

b. *Threatening.* Threats are often used to control students. They are usually ultimatums given to students to terminate undesirable behavior, even though the teacher knows that they will be impossible to implement. For example, the threat "If you do not stop that, I'm going to kick you out of class" is difficult to enforce. Most teachers are not in a position to expel students. If students hear enough idle threats, they soon learn to ignore and mock the teacher. As a reminder, it is not a threat if the misbehavior can and will be rectified consistently.

c. *Ordering and commanding.* If teachers appear to be bossy, students begin to think they are nothing more than pawns to be moved around the area. Try to develop patterns of communication that ask students to carry out tasks. Courtesy and politeness are requisites for effective teacher–student relationships. In addition, if teachers want to be treated with respect, they need to treat others similarly.

d. *Interrogating.* When there is a problem, such as a fight between students, teachers often try to figure out who started the fight rather than deal with the feelings of the combatants. Little is gained by trying to solve "who started it." Students will usually shirk the blame and suggest that it was not their fault. A much better solution is to begin by acknowledging feelings: "You know fighting is not accepted in my class; you must have been very angry to place yourself in this predicament." This allows students to talk about their feelings rather than place the blame on the other person. It also tells them that even when they do something wrong, the teacher cares about them.

e. *Refusing to listen.* This technique usually manifests itself by saying, "Let's talk about it some other time." There are situations when this response is necessary. However, if it is always the case, students will begin to avoid interaction with the instructor.

f. *Labeling.* In this situation, the teacher tells students, "Stop acting like fools," or "You're behaving like a bunch of animals." This is not only degrading, but it also dehumanizes students. In most cases, labeling is done because teachers think it will improve performance. In actuality, it is usually destructive and leaves a person with a negative feeling about the teacher.

g. *Sarcasm.* This is frequently used as humor in day-to-day interactions among peers. Within the classroom, sarcasm is often misunderstood and can create hard feelings between the teacher and students. If the listener has to ask, "What did she mean by that?", it is clear that the message was not understood as intended. It is best to respond to students in a caring and respectful manner. Sarcasm will not create the positive learning environment needed for students to feel safe and accepted.

COMMUNICATE EFFECTIVELY WITH YOUR CLASS

Many words can be spoken, but little is accomplished if students do not understand what has been said. Communication implies more than words; it assumes understanding has occurred. The following points can enhance the effectiveness of instruction:

1. *Develop a stimulating speaking style.* It is not necessary to be an outstanding speaker, yet it is important to be interesting and exciting. The chance for effective communication improves if students want to listen to a teacher. Use the voice effectively; alter

the intensity, raise and lower the pitch, and change the speed of delivery. Use nonverbal behavior to emphasize important points. In addition, keep discussions short and to the point so that students are willing to stop what they are doing and listen.

2. *Use a "teaser" to create interest.* If a concept is somewhat difficult to comprehend, set the stage by briefly describing what is to follow and why it is important. A teaser is a sentence or two that makes it seem important to learn forthcoming information. The teaser usually tips students off that something important will follow. This helps get students ready to listen so they don't miss the first part of the discussion. Use current events to set the stage, such as offensive or defensive strategies applied during the school's recent basketball tournament.

3. *Build on previous learning experiences.* Whenever possible, try to tie the discussion to previous skills and knowledge students have mastered. It can be effective to show students how a skill is similar (or dissimilar) to one learned earlier. Transfer of learning can be optimized if students understand the relationship to their previous experiences. Using the inquiry teaching style (see Chapter 8) can help students link past experiences to upcoming activities. Using questions based upon this teaching strategy can also provide opportunities for teachers to check for student understanding.

4. *Present the material in proper progression.* Teach skills in the sequence in which they will be performed. There are exceptions where a teacher may want to focus on a critical step first and then build around it. For example, in dance, a teacher may teach step patterns and then put them together to complete the dance. However, in most cases, the progression should mimic the sequence of performance. Adolescents usually assume that the order in which activities are presented is the correct progression.

5. *Model correct and incorrect examples.* Most adolescents learn physical skills quicker by observing rather than listening. This mandates modeling desirable and incorrect examples. For example, students will comprehend quicker if they are shown the correct way to pivot and one or two incorrect examples of pivoting. Often, teachers talk students through all skills and movements. When possible, combine instruction with demonstration to improve the efficiency of the communication, and demonstrate each skill in the playing area where students will perform or practice the skill.

6. *Check for understanding.* Monitor student understanding through active responses to efficiently assess instructional clarity. Asking a question and/or having students respond with an observable behavior allows the teacher to monitor effective communication. For example, you might say, "Raise your hand if you do not understand how to land correctly," or "See me if you do not understand how the game is played," or "Show me the triple threat position."

7. *Separate management and instructional episodes.* Much emphasis has been placed on maintaining short episodes of communication and focusing on cues that are easily understood. Here's a special point of attention: Teachers often combine management activities with instructional activities. For example, during a presentation of a new game, the teacher says the following: "In this game, we will break into groups of five. Each group will get a ball and form a small circle. On the command *go*, the game will start. Here is how you play the game. . . ." At this point, a lengthy discussion of game rules and conduct is given. By this time, most students have forgotten the management strategies. It is more effective to move the class into the game formation and then discuss the activity. This serves two purposes: It reduces the length of the episode and makes it easier for the class to conceptualize how the game is played. In addition, it avoids the tendency for students to become unfocused, thinking about whom they want for a partner instead of listening to the rules. Teach students one thing at a time. Remember to "manage first, instruct second."

DEMONSTRATE A CARING ATTITUDE TOWARD STUDENTS

The communication techniques a teacher uses will impact how students feel toward them. Teachers who take a positive approach to communication with students and establish a warm, caring environment are effective. A positive approach to student motivation is recommended because of the long-term effects on both students and teachers. Teaching and learning are more enjoyable when students and instructors can look forward to participating in a positive environment and feel better about learning, teaching, and the overall school atmosphere at the end of the day. The positive approach seems to enhance the overall motivation of both teachers and students over a longer period of time.

Students often judge the quality of a teacher on attributes unrelated to the teacher's knowledge of subject matter. The teacher's style of presentation can influence how students feel about physical education.

Students eventually tune out teachers who shout commands, speak like drill sergeants, or repeat certain phrases. Students want to understand and be understood. The following points will help students feel that you care about them.

1. **Speak about the behavior of students, not about their personal character.** The following is an example of speaking *about* a student's behavior: "Talking when I am talking is unacceptable behavior." Such feedback identifies behavior that can be improved upon and avoids questioning the self-worth of the student. This approach helps students feel you are interested in helping rather than belittling them. In contrast, saying something like, "Why do you always have to act like a fool?" reflects on the student's character and undermines his or her self-esteem. It is also nonspecific, making it difficult to determine what behavior concerns you. Focus on specific misbehavior followed by the type of behavior that should be displayed.

2. **Put yourself in the student's shoes.** How would you feel if someone embarrassed you in front of the class? How do you feel when you are inept and trying to learn a new skill? These and other emotions often make listening difficult for youths. What conditions are necessary to make it easy for you to accept constructive feedback? Excessive feedback may stress a student and cause a reduction in performance. Offer feedback in small doses. If you are going to suggest ways to improve performance, do so on a personal basis and leave the student to practice without scrutiny. To ask students to change and then stand over them until they do so may cause resentment and internal pressure.

3. **Identify your feelings about students.** At times teachers send mixed messages to students. They may be unhappy with students because of situations unrelated to class performance yet unwilling to discuss the real issues. Instead, they respond with unkind feedback about skill performance. Their negative feelings are then transferred to the students regarding their performance in class. This was not the teacher's intent but the result of pent-up feelings over an unrelated issue. Students perceive negativity from a teacher. Take responsibility for communicating how you feel (albeit negative), but make sure that it is directed toward the undesirable behavior.

4. **Accentuate the positive.** When phrasing the instructional points of a lesson, stress the positive. For example, tell students to "Make a sharp cut," rather than saying, "Don't round off your cut." An

easy way to emphasize the "why" of an activity is to say, "Do this because. . . ." If there are several different and acceptable ways to perform the movement patterns, be explicit. Show students various ways and discuss reasons for the differences. Students like to know the correct technique, even if it is beyond their sphere of accomplishment. Explain only enough, however, to get the activity underway successfully.

5. **Speak precisely.** Limit the use of open-ended directives, and substitute those with precise goals. Instead of saying, "How many times can you . . . ?" or "See how many times you can . . . ," give students a definite target goal. Use directives like, "See if you can . . . five times without missing," or "Show me five different ways you can. . . . " Ask students to select a target goal. Using measurable and attainable goals is especially important when teaching slow learners or special education students.

6. **Optimize speech patterns.** Avoid sermonizing at the least provocation. Excessive reliance on certain words and phrases, such as "okay," "all right," and the irritating "and uh," are unappealing to students. Many adolescents begin to listen for repetitive speech patterns rather than listening to what the teacher is expressing. Acquire a broad vocabulary of effective phrases for indicating approval and good effort, and vary verbal patterns.

7. **Conduct cognitive discussions in the classroom.** Whenever possible, lengthy discussions should be held in the classroom for reasons of comfort and student expectations. Students expect to move in the activity area, whereas they have learned to sit and interact cognitively in the classroom. Rules can be explained, procedures and responsibilities outlined, and formations illustrated on the blackboard. If discussions will last longer than 1 or 2 minutes, it is best to place students in a comfortable setting and use instructional aids such as overheads, handouts, and films.

8. **Treat all responses to questions with dignity.** Respect students' responses and opinions and avoid humiliating a student who gives a wrong answer. Pass over inappropriate answers by directing attention to more appropriate responses. Or, tell students that they have offered a good answer, but the question is not the right one. Remind them to save the answer and then go back to the students when it is correct for another question. Refrain from injecting personal opinion into the instructional question–answer process. At the end of the discussion, summarizing important points may be valuable.

FIGURE 6.1 Nonverbal reinforcement for a job well done

USE NONVERBAL COMMUNICATION

Using nonverbal communication is an important way of telling students what behavior is acceptable. Nonverbal communication is effective because it is interpreted by students and often perceived as more meaningful than words. For example, beginning teachers often have a difficult time making their feelings align with their body language. They may be pleased with student performance yet portray a less-than-pleased message (e.g., frowning or placing hands on hips). Another common example occurs when teachers want to assert themselves and gain control of a class. They often place their hands in their pockets, stand in a slouched position, and back away from the class. This nonverbal behavior signals anything but assertiveness and gives students mixed messages.

Nonverbal behavior can be used to praise a class effectively, including thrusting of a finger into the air to signify "number 1," giving a thumbs-up or a high five, shaking hands, and so on (Figure 6.1). Nonverbal behavior can also be negative, including placing hands on the hips, holding a finger to the lips, frowning, and staring. In any case, effective use of nonverbal behavior can increase the validity and strength of verbal communication.

When using nonverbal communication, consider the customs and mores of different cultures. It is the teacher's responsibility to learn how students respond to different types of gestures. For example, Hmong and Laotian adolescents may be touched on the head only by parents and close relatives. A teacher who pats a student on the head for approval is interfering with the student's spiritual nature. The okay sign (touching thumb and forefinger) is an indication of approval in the United States. However, in several Asian cultures, it is a "zero," indicating the student is not performing properly. In many South American countries, the okay sign carries a sexual connotation. Teachers new to an area should ask for advice when expressing approval to students from other cultures.

To make nonverbal behavior convincing, teachers can watch their behavior and then practice necessary modification. An effective method is to practice in front of a mirror and display different emotions. Another is to work with someone who does not know you well. If this person can identify the emotions demonstrated by the nonverbal behavior, they most likely will be effective in a teaching situation. Using a videotape recorder is an effective tool for self-analysis. Analyze yourself to see how you look when teaching under stress, disciplining a student, or praising a class.

DEMONSTRATE AND MODEL SKILLS

Most students learn more easily if they see a demonstration of a skill or technique. The adage "a picture is worth a thousand words" holds true in physical education. Demonstrations can illustrate variety or different depth of movement, show something unique or different, point out items of technique or approach, illustrate different acceptable styles, and show progress. Another important reason for demonstrating is to help develop credibility with students. For example, many students may question whether a skill can be performed until they see the teacher or another student do it. Secondary school students are notorious for their "show me" attitudes; a demonstration will help show that the skill is in their range of abilities.

Teacher Demonstration

Be sure that the class can see and hear the performance. Demonstrate the performance in the correct location; for example, if the triple threat position for basketball is being performed, the demonstration should be located in the appropriate location at a basket. When explaining technique, highlight key points of performance. Show the proper starting position and verbalize the instructions from that point on, or provide a more complete, point-by-point demonstration. Terminology should be clear and include the use of visual words, such as "tabletop," "belly button to the target," or "flat platform"; techniques should be demonstrated within the student's skill level. The more complex a skill is, the more demonstration is needed. Questions can be raised during the demonstration, but avoid allowing the question–answer period to take up too much time. Effectiveness of teacher demonstration depends on a combination of visual cues, proper location, and clarity of verbal instruction.

Student Demonstration

Student demonstration is an effective teaching technique because it interjects the students' ideas into the lesson. Using students to demonstrate provides others with opportunities to see one of their own performing the skill. Involving students also demonstrates accountability of the task.

As students practice and move, the class can be stopped for a demonstration. It is rarely acceptable to pick out a student and ask him or her to demonstrate in front of the class without asking the student if he or she wants to demonstrate. A safe way to avoid embarrassing a student is to check his or her performance while the class is engaged in activity. If the demonstration is unsatisfactory, you can quietly tell him or her, "That's close to what I had in mind; let me see if I can find someone else who knows this activity." If partner or small-group work is undertaken, the same principle applies (Figure 6.2).

If You Can't Demonstrate

Because of physical and skill limitations, some teachers cannot demonstrate. Few teachers can perform all physical activities well, so don't feel like you have to be an expert at every activity. Even a skilled teacher needs to devise a backup plan when he or she is unable to offer an effective demonstration. Through reading, study, and analysis of movement, teachers can develop an understanding and knowledge of the activities. Even if performing the activity is impossible, study and understand how the activity is done. In addition, use videotapes or teaching signs to offer meaningful orientation.

FACILITATE LEARNING WITH INSTRUCTIONAL CUES

Instructional cues are words that quickly and efficiently communicate to the learner proper technique and performance of skills or movement tasks. When

FIGURE 6.2 Demonstrating skills with a partner

learning skills, youngsters need a clear understanding of critical skill points. Students often understand mentally how to perform a skill prior to successful application. Cues provide students a clear mental and physical understanding of performance stages.

Motor learning and cognitive understanding of a skill must be developed simultaneously. Sometimes, teachers carefully plan skill and movement activities but fail to plan for the instructional cues to be used during skill practice. The result may be a class that does not clearly understand technique and points of performance. When developing instructional cues, consider the following points.

Use Accurate Cues

If the cue is going to help the learner perform a skill correctly, it must be precise and accurate. It needs to lead the learner in the proper direction and be part of a comprehensive package of cues. All instructors have to teach activities they know little about. Few, if any, teachers know everything about all activities. Textbooks and media aids are available for reference. These resources delineate the key points of the skill (Fronske, 2008; Fronske & Wilson, 2002). Other options include asking other teachers who have specific knowledge or videotaping an activity and analyzing points of performance where students have the most difficulty. In any case, cues are developed through study, practice, and experience. Even a beginning teacher needs to possess ample learning cues for teaching preliminary experiences.

Use Short, Descriptive Cues

Sometimes cues are made more comprehensive and lengthy than necessary. Many teachers teach as they were taught in high school. They remember a class where the teacher told them everything they needed to know at the start of the unit and let them practice without instruction for the rest of the period. This assumes students can comprehend a long list of instructions and correctly apply them to skills. If this is not the case, students spend the rest of the unit performing skills incorrectly. An incorrect motor pattern practiced for a long period is difficult to correct later.

To avoid confusing and overwhelming the learner, choose a small number of cues for each lesson. The cues should be short and contain keywords. They should help the learner focus on one phase of skill during practice. Integrating several small movement patterns into one explicit cue reduces the number of cues needed and their length. For example, when teaching batting, a cue might be "Squish the bug." The purpose of this cue would be to rotate the hips and complete the follow-through. Other examples of hitting cues follow:

"Step toward the target."
"Keep your elbows away from your body."
"Shift weight from the rear to front foot."

One way to examine the effectiveness of the cues is to see if they totally communicate the skill. Have all the critical points of batting been covered, or is the skill being done incorrectly in certain phases? In most skills, the performance can be broken into three parts: preparing to perform, performing the skill, and following through. Focus cues on one phase at a time because it is difficult for students to remember more. Descriptive words are most effective with adolescents, particularly if they have an exciting sound. Examples of this are "Snap your wrists," "Twist the upper body during the follow-through," or "Explode off the starting line." In other situations, make the voice influence the effectiveness of the cue. For example, if a skill is to be done smoothly and softly, the teacher can speak in a soft tone and ask students to "let the movement flooooow" or to "move smoooooothly across the balance beam." Cues are most effective when voice inflections, body language, and action words are used to signal the desired behavior.

Integrate Cues

Integrate cues to combine parts of a skill and to use words that focus on the skill as a whole. These cues depend on prior cues used during the presentation of a skill and assume that concepts delineated in earlier phases of instruction were correctly understood. Examples of integrating cues might be the following:

"Step, rotate, throw."
"Run, jump, and forward roll."
"Stride, swing, follow through."

Integrated cues are a set of action words that help students sequence and time parts of a skill. These cues are reminders of the proper sequence of skills and the mental images of the performance. Depending on the rhythm of the presentation, the cues can signal the speed and tempo of the skill performance. In addition, they can serve as a specialized language that allows the student and teacher to communicate effectively.

USE EFFECTIVE INSTRUCTIONAL FEEDBACK

Effective teachers use instructional feedback to promote student learning. Used properly, it can enhance a student's self-image, improve the focus of performance, result in individualized instruction, increase the rate of on-task behavior, and improve understanding. Proper feedback can be used to affect skill performance or the results of skill performance (see pages 213–215). The following points offer direction for improving the quality of feedback used in the instructional setting.

Know When to Use Positive, Corrective, and Negative Feedback

Most teachers use corrective feedback to alter student performance. In most cases, unless a teacher focuses totally on mistakes and failures, negative feedback (e.g., "That was a lousy throw") is seldom used. Instead, corrective feedback is used to focus on the incorrect part of the performance (or related behavior). Students usually expect this; however, if it is the only type of feedback offered, students begin to perceive it as negative. The danger of overusing corrective feedback is that it creates a climate where students worry about making errors for fear the instructor will embarrass or belittle them. In addition, excessive correction may cause students to think that no matter what they do correctly, the teacher never sees the positive aspect of their efforts.

Focus on the positive points of student performance. This creates a positive atmosphere where students are willing to accept a challenge and risk error or failure. Teachers who use positive feedback usually feel better about their students because they look for strengths in performance and use this as a foundation for skill improvement. Many physical education instructors rely heavily on corrective feedback, leading to the observation that they have a correction complex. Corrective statements are appropriate if the learning environment has a balance of positive and corrective feedback. Siedentop & Tannehill (2000) recommend that an educational environment have a 3:1 or 4:1 ratio of positive feedback to corrective feedback. A higher ratio of positive feedback certainly enhances the overall positive atmosphere of the class. Because the use of corrective feedback comes easily for most teachers, it is important to practice increasing the amount of positive feedback used.

Understand Different Types of Information Feedback

Information feedback is given when students have completed a skill attempt. Feedback on the results of many skill attempts is obvious, as in the case of golf swings, basketball shots, or baseball swings. It is inherent in the activity, and students immediately know the results of the skill attempt. Feedback on the form or topography of skill behavior is, however, difficult to attain. Feedback can easily be tied to the instructional cues developed for each skill performance. Using feedback that integrates skill cues provides students with useful information on how well they are performing a skill.

Plan carefully for information feedback delivered in classes. This should include determining the specific skill behaviors that you are trying to foster. The feedback should be prescriptive in nature so that it helps eradicate errors. There are different ways to tell students that they are performing at an acceptable level. Feedback statements can be general, specific, verbal, or nonverbal. Including a student's first name with the feedback is a meaningful way to help students realize the teacher is aware and sincere about their skill development. The following are some examples of different types of feedback:

Corrective or Prescriptive

"Get the shot–put angle up to 42°."
"Bend your knees more and uncoil."
"Adjust your grip by spreading your fingers."
"Accelerate through the ball."
"Keep your wrists stiff and start the action with your shoulders."
"Transfer your weight as you contact the ball."

Positive General

"Good job."
"Way to go."

"Nice defense."
"All right, Jim."
"Very nice hustle."
"Interesting question, Mary."
"Okay, class."

Positive Specific

"Good angle of release."
"Perfect timing on the outlet pass."
"Way to hit the soft spot in the 1-3-1 zone."
"Great job looking off the undercoverage."
"That's the way to vary your serves. It keeps them off balance."
"Karen, good job keeping your head down."

Nonverbal Positive or Corrective

Winking or smiling.
Thumbs up or down.
Pat on the back.
Clapping the hands.
Facial gestures.
Making a "V" sign.
Shaking the fist.

Plan a variety of feedback options, including statements that use first names, specific positive information, and nonverbal messages. Variety is necessary to avoid satiation and redundancy. Feedback should be directed at key points of the specific skill and appropriate to the student's age and developmental level.

Give Feedback to All Class Members

Teachers have many students in class and must decide on the length of feedback episodes and the number of students to contact. It may depend on the skill being taught. For example, if it is a skill that students will learn quickly, movement from student to student will ensure there are no major dysfunctions. This ongoing approach allows contact with many students during the lesson. In addition, it helps keep students on task because they know the teacher is moving and watching the class regularly. The drawback to this approach is that little opportunity occurs for in-depth feedback.

If skills are complex and refinement is a goal, taking more time to observe students is more effective. This means watching a student long enough to offer highly specific and information-loaded feedback. The end result is high-quality feedback to a fewer number of students.

Avoid Scrutiny after Feedback

When giving feedback to students, avoid close scrutiny of the student at the completion of your input. Students become tense if a teacher tells them how to perform a skill correctly and then watches to see if they do it exactly as instructed. Students are allowed to practice without being closely observed by the teacher or class. In short, observe carefully, offer feedback, move to another student, and recheck progress at a later time.

Use Peer Feedback to Increase Quality Performance

Secondary students are capable of enhancing their understanding of skill performance when they are given opportunities to serve as peer coaches. Using peer coaches can address the large class sizes frequently seen in physical education. For example, students work in groups of three where one person serves as the coach and focuses on a second student's skill performance, while the third person is the support player passing the ball or rebounding. During the skill performance, the peer coach focuses on the cues previously highlighted during the instructional part of the lesson and shares feedback on the strengths and weaknesses of the skill performance. Students rotate through each position. Feedback can be both oral and written and focuses on the key points of the specific skill. (See Figure 6.3.)

Know When to Use Group or Individual Feedback

In school settings, much feedback is group oriented. The most common method is to stop and offer feedback to all students. This is the fastest method, but it also allows the most room for misinterpretation. Some students may not understand the feedback, while others may not listen because it does not seem relevant to them. It is effective to direct feedback (positive only) to a student so the rest of the class can hear it. This allows feedback to "ripple" through the class, offering instruction to the rest of the class. An example would be, "Sarah is hitting the tennis ball at its peak when she serves."

In addition, feedback should focus on the desired task. For example, if students are asked to catch a batted ball in front of their body, it clouds the issue if the teacher offers feedback on the quality of the throw. If catching is the focus, feedback should be on catching so that students continue to concentrate on that skill. An example of feedback in this setting is, "Watch the way Michelle keeps her body in front of the ball when catching ground balls." As a final clarification, it is not necessary to have students watch other students to accomplish the desired outcome. In fact, it is effective only if the performer is capable of showing the skill correctly. If this approach is used exclusively, less skilled (or shy) performers will seldom have an oppor-

tunity to receive feedback from the class. It can be just as effective to tell the class how well a student was doing and then move on, for example, "Mike always keeps his head up when dribbling."

Offer feedback to students as soon as possible after the performance. If the feedback is delayed, allow opportunity for immediate practice so students can apply the information. Little is gained and much lost if students are told how to improve and then leave class without opportunity for practice. Few, if any, students will remember the suggestions. If the end of class is approaching, it is probably best to limit feedback and work on situations that can be practiced immediately. Other problems can be solved at the next class.

CONSIDER THE PERSONAL NEEDS OF STUDENTS

If teaching only involved presenting physical activities to students, it would be a simple endeavor. The uniqueness of each student in a large class is a factor that makes teaching complex and challenging. This section focuses on ways to make instruction meaningful and personal. Teachers who are able to make each student feel important impact the lives of their students. Empowering students to take responsibility for their learning can be accomplished through positive interactions and acknowledgment of effort and improvement. Understanding the diversity of classes, allowing students to make educational decisions, and encouraging student creativity are some of the ways to make a lesson feel like it was "specifically designed for each student."

Teach for Diversity and Equity

Multicultural education allows all students to reach their potential regardless of the diversity among learners. Four major variables of diversity influence how teachers and students think and learn: race/ethnicity, gender, social class, and ability. Multicultural education creates an educational environment in which students from a variety of backgrounds and experience come together to experience educational equality (Manning & Baruth, 2004). Multicultural education assumes that children come from different backgrounds and helps them make sense of their everyday lives. It emphasizes the contributions of various groups that make up our country and focuses on how to learn rather than on what to learn.

Current trends in growth in the United States are causing changes in classrooms. Children who were previously excluded from classes because of language, race, economics, and abilities are now learning to-

Peer Feedback

Passer _____   Coach _____

Practice Task: Three people: 1 passer, 1 shooter, 1 coach

The passer will pass four balls from the top of the key by using either a bounce pass or chest pass; the coach will provide the passer with feedback based on the critial elements and cues listed below. Rotate roles after four passes.

Goal: Effective layups using the correct form

Layup

Essential Elements:
(Reverse for left/right hand layup)
1. Carry the ball with the left hand in front and under the ball
2. Place the right hand on top and slightly behind
3. Carry the ball to shoulder and head height as the left foot pushes off
4. Lift the body with the right knee
5. Direct the ball to the backboard with right hand
6. Place the ball rather than throw against backboard
7. Follow through with the palm of the right hand high in direction of backboard

Cues:
- Scoop
- Lift (right/left leg)
- Flick to target (square on backboard)

Things My Partner Did Well:

Things for my partner to focus on to help improve the layup:

FIGURE 6.3 Example of peer feedback to increase quality performance

gether. Teaching now requires a pluralistic mindset and the ability to communicate across cultures. It is the responsibility of educators to teach children to live comfortably and to prosper in this diverse and changing world. It is important that students celebrate their own cultures while learning to integrate into the diversity of the world. For most students, classroom interaction between teachers and students is the major part of multicultural education they will receive. Teachers can do a number of things to teach and value diversity.

1. Help students learn about the similarities and differences between cultures.

2. Encourage students to understand that people from similar cultures share common values, customs, and beliefs.

3. Make children aware of acts of discrimination and teach them ways to deal with inequity and prejudice.

4. Help youngsters develop pride in their family's culture.

5. Teach youngsters ways to communicate effectively with other cultures and races and with the other gender.

6. Instill respect for all people regardless of race/ethnicity, gender, social class, and ability.

7. Help students understand that people learn differently.

8. Teach students strategies for dealing effectively with diverse skill levels and creating equitable experiences.

How teachers perceive students strongly impacts student performance. Teachers who effectively teach for diversity hold high expectations for all students, including ethnic minority children and youth. Research shows that teachers tend to have lower expectations for ethnic minority youth (Vasquez, 1988). These low expectations occur in interpersonal interactions and in how students are placed in opportunities for enrichment and personal growth. At-risk youth need a rich curriculum that allows no room for failure and provides the necessary support for success.

Teachers have to know and educate themselves so they better understand the needs of all students. Diversity implies differences within and between cultures. Learning about other cultures ensures that working with students will be done with an increased understanding of the past experiences each student has endured. When working with different cultures, the focus should be on understanding the culture and the individuals. This contrasts with learning about a culture and then stereotyping them as "all the same." It is important to gather information about the cultures that are diverse and different than the teachers. Teachers almost always teach like they have been taught and often with inadequate knowledge about other cultures. Fuller (2001) offers a number of questions to answer when working with a different group or culture.

1. *What is their history?* Certainly few teachers can become experts in the history of all cultures they teach. However, they can recognize and be familiar with major events and important names within the culture.

2. *What are their important cultural values?* Different cultures interact with and discipline students in different ways. Ask parents and students how they work with children and what values are particularly important in their households.

3. *Who are influential individuals in their group?* Students will identify with local individuals who are held in high esteem in their community. Teachers who are aware of these important people will have insight into their students by the role models they admire.

4. *What are their major religious beliefs?* Many groups belong to similar religions that drive many of their beliefs. Often, many values of children in a community area will be driven by religious beliefs.

5. *What are their important political beliefs?* Important political issues are often discussed at home. By making an effort to learn about these issues, teachers show they are interested in how their students live in their communities.

6. *What political, religious, and social days do they celebrate?* Students will discuss these important days and expect teachers to understand why they celebrate them. Talking about these days with students creates goodwill and makes students feel like their cultures are valued.

Another way to facilitate student diversity in group instruction is to vary teaching presentations. Students learn through a variety of styles, and each can differ widely. Some learn orally, others visually, and many others through firsthand experiences. Group instruction through problem-solving/cooperative, reciprocal/peer, and guided discovery instructional strategies can be used to facilitate a better understanding of diversity. Each strategy focuses on clear interactions between small groups of students in order to answer a question, solve a problem, or achieve a goal. Providing opportunities for students to engage in a mix of individual and interactive classroom tasks can deepen understanding of people from diverse backgrounds. Group problem solving can develop skills such as teamwork, collaboration, and a basic understanding of diverse backgrounds. Some students learn easily through auditory methods, while others learn better using visual means. Cooperative learning (see Chapter 8) offers students the opportunity to work together toward common goals and to feel positive about the different contributions of each of the members of the group.

Diversity can also be increased through discussion sessions. Using small groups or small-sided teams provides a larger number of students to offer individual perspectives, and this allows for a greater array of diverse points of view. When students are involved in decision making and leadership opportunities followed by facilitated discussions, increased attention and participation in the learning process occur. Students are motivated by sharing, using different approaches, and feeling an increased acceptance because they come from varied backgrounds. Students are provided with opportunities to get to know other students through varied instructional practices that employ a variety of student skills to solve problems and communicate well

Avoid Biases in Gender Differences

Teachers play a large role in how children learn to behave. Adults model gender-specific behaviors for children and youngsters who, in turn, copy the behavior. Research shows that teachers tend to treat boys and girls differently (Grossman & Grossman, 1994). For example, teachers pay more attention to boys and give boys more encouragement. Teachers give more praise for achievement to boys and call on girls less often than they call on boys. Teachers also respond to inappropriate behavior from boys and girls in different ways. Aggression is tolerated more in boys than in girls. However, disruptive talking is tolerated more in girls than in boys. Boys are reprimanded more than girls, and teachers use more physical means of disciplining boys.

The expectations a teacher has for boys and girls strongly impact how they interact with them. These expectations are frequently based on stereotypes and social expectations. For example, teachers expect boys to be more active and more precocious and not to be as good academically. As a result, they pay closer attention to them, and when they do well, they are more likely to get positive attention. Girls, on the other hand, are expected to be more reserved and to do well academically, so they tend to be overlooked when they are doing "what they are supposed to do." When they misbehave, teachers see this as an aberration and are more negative to the female than they might be to the male. This is a common, yet unacceptable, pitfall among teachers. It takes a concerted effort to overcome these biases. Some teachers believe that girls aren't able to perform at a level similar to boys, even though research shows otherwise. Particularly in elementary school, differences in strength, endurance, and physical skills are minimal. It is common for teachers to harbor their own gender beliefs and expectations that may directly or indirectly affect their interactions with boys and girls as well as their expectations of appropriate and inappropriate behaviors. Therefore, it becomes even more critical to develop an effective physical education environment that helps all youngsters find success when teachers become aware of how specific behaviors can impact students and address them in a positive and equitable manner. Using the following teaching behaviors minimizes stereotyping by gender:

- Reinforce the performances of all students regardless of gender.

- Provide activities that are developmentally appropriate and allow all students to find success.

- Design programs that ensure success in coeducational experiences. Boys and girls can challenge

---

in diverse settings and groups, thus increasing the possibility of being able to effectively help them learn.

The following teaching tips can help increase instructional effectiveness in a diverse setting:

- At the start of the school year (and at regular intervals thereafter), speak about the importance of encouraging and respecting diversity.

- When using group activities, insist that groups be diverse with regard to race, gender, and nationality.

- Be aware of how you speak about different groups of students. Do you refer to all students alike? Do you address boys and girls differently? Develop a consistent style for addressing all students regardless of their differences.

- Encourage all students to participate in discussions. Avoid allowing some students from certain groups to dominate interaction. Use a random method of picking students so all have an equal chance of contributing.

- Treat all students with respect and expect students to treat each other with dignity. Intervene if a student or group of students is dominating.

- When a difficult situation arises over an issue with undertones of diversity, take a time-out and ask students to think about their thoughts and ideas. Allow all parties time to collect their thoughts and plan a response.

- Make sure evaluations and grades are written in gender-neutral or gender-inclusive terms.

- Encourage students to work with different partners every day. Students need to get to know other students in order to appreciate their differences.

- Invite guest speakers to class who represent diversity in gender, race, and ethnicity even if they are not speaking about multicultural or diversity issues.

- When students make comments that are sexist or racist, ask them to restate their ideas in a way that is not offensive to others. Teach students that it is all right to express one's opinion but not in an inflammatory manner.

- Rotate leaders when using groups. Give all students the opportunity to learn leadership skills.

Developing a classroom environment free from inequity in diverse settings will take preplanning. Figure 6.4 will provide you some practice time to think and develop specific strategies to address issues of diversity in a fair and equitable manner.

Instructions: Respond to the following questions and develop an inclusive list of strategies.

1. Do I have a plan to handle negative comments based upon race, gender, sexual orientation, skill abilities, and/or ethnic diversity?

   Write down any comments you have heard and list possible strategies for addressing these comments that will ensure the development of a positive learning environment.

2. Do I systematically select students to demonstrate, speak, or lead?

   List the type of strategies you would use to ensure that all students have opportunities to interact with other students, demonstrate, express their opinions, and serve as a captain or squad leader.

3. Do I use equitable language, pictures, activities, and instructional tools?

   List the terms you can use to address students; develop task cards, bulletin boards, and study guides; and check selected activities for skill or gender biases.

4. Would my interactions with students be rated as inclusive, neutral, and equitable?

   Make audio or video recordings of your verbal interactions with students and colleagues for equity and diversity.

5. Do I ensure that all students have an opportunity to be selected and work with different individuals on a regular basis?

   Develop strategies that ensure all students have several opportunities to be selected; rotate partners, teams, and individuals that are selected to demonstrate or lead in a way that is equitable and not based on stereotypes or gender bias.

6. Do my teaching style, strategies, and teaching content present opportunities for all students to learn and participate equitably?

   Identify strategies that will assess your teaching styles based on student success across diverse student populations.

FIGURE 6.4 Developing an equitable learning environment in diverse settings

each other to higher levels if the atmosphere is positive.

- Don't use and don't accept students' stereotypical comments, such as, "You throw like a girl."

- Include activities in the curriculum that cut across typical gender stereotypes, such as rhythms are for girls and football is for boys.

- Arrange activities so the more aggressive and skilled students do not dominate. Little is learned if students are taught to be submissive or play down their abilities.

- Arrange practice sessions so all students receive equal amounts of practice and opportunity to participate. Practice sessions should not give more

practice opportunities to the skilled while the unskilled stand aside and observe.

- Expect all boys and girls to perform equally well. Teacher expectations communicate much about a student's ability level. Students view themselves through the eyes of their teacher.

STUDY STIMULATORS AND REVIEW QUESTIONS

1. Describe the types of behaviors that teachers exhibit when they actively supervise their students.

2. Discuss the importance of developing a plan for actively supervising students.

3. Discuss the strategies available to teachers to effectively manage the need to individualize instruction.

4. List and briefly explain four ways in which good teacher-to-student communication can be undermined.

5. Discuss the importance of teachers matching their nonverbal expressions with their words.

6. Give an example of a physical skill that has a distinct rhythm and provide a possible cue.

7. What are the problems of overusing corrective feedback?

8. Discuss the teacher's dilemma between attending to all students and providing in-depth feedback to individual students.

9. Discuss the influence of teachers' perceptions regarding cultural and ethnic differences on their ability to be successful at teaching diverse groups of students.

REFERENCES AND SUGGESTED READINGS

Banks, J. A. (2003). *Teaching strategies for ethnic studies* (7th ed.). Boston: Allyn & Bacon.

Bennett, C. L. (2003). *Comprehensive multicultural education: Theory and practice.* (5th ed.). Boston: Allyn & Bacon.

Cushner, K. H. (2003). *Human diversity in action: Developing multicultural competencies for the classroom* (2nd ed.). Boston: McGraw-Hill.

Fronske, H. (2008). *Teaching cues for sport skills for secondary school students* (4th ed.). San Francisco: Benjamin Cummings.

Fronske, H., & Wilson, R. (2002). *Teaching cues for basic sport skills for elementary and middle school students.* San Francisco: Benjamin Cummings.

Fuller, M. L. (2001). Multicultural concerns and classroom management. In C. A. Grant & M. L. Gomez, *Campus and classroom: Making schooling multicultural* (pp. 109–134). Upper Saddle River: Prentice Hall.

Grant, C. A. (Ed.). (1995). *Educating for diversity: An anthology of multicultural voices.* Boston: Allyn & Bacon.

Grossman, H., & Grossman, S. H. (1994). *Gender issues in education.* Boston: Allyn & Bacon.

Harrison, J. M. (1987). A review of the research on teacher effectiveness and its implications for current practice. *Quest, 39,* 36–55.

Harrison, J. M., Blakemore, C. L., & Buck, M. M. (2001). *Instructional strategies for secondary physical education* (5th ed.). Boston: McGraw-Hill.

Koppelman, K., & Goodhart, L. (2005). *Understanding human differences: Multicultural education for a diverse America.* Boston: Allyn & Bacon.

Manning, M. L., & Baruth, L. G. (2004). *Multicultural education of children and adolescents* (4th ed.). Boston: Allyn & Bacon.

Pang, V. O. (2005). *Multicultural education: A caring-centered, reflective approach* (2nd ed.). Boston: McGraw-Hill.

Pangrazi, R. P. (2004). *Dynamic physical education for elementary school children* (14th ed.). San Francisco: Benjamin Cummings.

Parker, J. (1995). Secondary teachers' views of effective teaching in physical education. *Journal of Teaching in Physical Education, 14*(2), 127–139.

Rink, J. E. (2006). *Teaching physical education for learning* (5th ed.). Boston: McGraw-Hill.

Sariscsany, M. J., Darst, P., & van der Mars, H. (1995). The effects of three teacher supervision patterns on student on-task and skill performance in secondary physical education. *Journal of Teaching in Physical Education, 14*(2), 179–197.

Schmidt, R. A., & Wrisberg, C. (2004). *Motor learning and performance* (3rd ed.). Champaign, IL: Human Kinetics Publishers.

Siedentop, D., & Tannehill, D. (2000). *Developing teaching skills in physical education* (4th ed.). Mountain View, CA: Mayfield Publishing Co.

Tiedt, P. L., & Tiedt, I. M. (2002). *Multicultural teaching: A handbook of activities, information, and resources* (6th ed.). Boston: Allyn & Bacon.

van der Mars, H., Vogler, W., Darst, P., & Cusimano, B. (1994). Active supervision patterns of physical education teachers and their relationship with student behavior. *Journal of Teaching in Physical Education, 14*(1), 99–112.

Vasquez, J. (1988). Contests of learning for minority children. *Educational Forum, 52*(3), 243–253.

Wardle, F., & Cruz-Janzen, M. I. (2004). *Meeting the needs of multiethnic and multiracial children in schools.* Boston: Allyn & Bacon.

WEB SITES

Activity Cues
www.pecentral.org/climate/monicaparsonarticle.html

Communication
http://crs.uvm.edu/gopher/nerl/personal/comm/e.html
http://nonverbal.ucsc.edu/
www.pecentral.org/climate/monicaparsonarticle.html
www.bizmove.com/skills/m8g.htm

Elements of Instruction
www.humboldt.edu/~tha1/hunter-eei.html

Enhancing Teacher Effectiveness
www.hcc.hawaii.edu/intranet/committees/FacDevCom/guidebk/teachtip/enhance.htm

Multicultural Education
www.ncrel.org/sdrs/areas/issues/educatrs/leadrshp/le4pppme.htm
www.inclusiveeducation.ca

ESSENTIAL COMPONENTS OF A QUALITY PROGRAM

COMPONENT 1 A quality physical education program is organized around content standards that offer direction and continuity to instruction and evaluation.

COMPONENT 2 A quality program is student centered and based on the developmental urges, characteristics, and interests of students.

COMPONENT 3 Quality physical education makes physical activity and motor-skill development the core of the program.

COMPONENT 4 Physical education programs teach management skills and self-discipline.

COMPONENT 5 Quality programs emphasize inclusion of all students.

COMPONENT 6 In a quality physical education setting, instruction focuses on the process of learning skills rather than the product or outcome of the skill performance.

COMPONENT 7 A quality physical education program teaches lifetime activities that students can use to promote their health and personal wellness.

COMPONENT 8 Quality physical education teaches cooperative and responsibility skills and helps students develop sensitivity to diversity and gender issues.

7

Management and Discipline

CHAPTER SUMMARY

This chapter covers many ways of teaching class organization skills through physical activity. Emphasis is on a positive and constructive approach to moving students quickly into instructional settings. Responsible behavior is an important part of teaching, and students are expected to know what acceptable behavior is and how to resolve conflict in a nonphysical manner. Preventing behavior problems is always more important than dealing with problems after they occur. Organizing an environment that offers a behavior management component helps students become good citizens. Much discussion and instructional advice is given to maintain and increase desirable behavior while decreasing undesirable behavior at the same time. Finally, when all else fails, behavioral correction techniques must be implemented. A number of strategies are offered, from reprimands to behavior contracts.

STUDENT OUTCOMES

After reading this chapter, you will be able to:

- Manage a class by delivering instruction efficiently and moving students into instructional settings quickly.

- Teach students responsible behavior by using responsibility-development techniques and conflict resolution.

- Minimize behavior problems in your classes by creating a behavior plan and establishing rules and consequences.

Student Outcomes, continued

- Increase desirable behavior by using social reinforcers effectively.

- Decrease undesirable behavior by designing a behavioral response plan. This includes a range of teacher behaviors including reprimands, removal of positive consequences, and behavior games.

- Avoid the use of criticism when interacting with students.

- Know when to resort to punishment (rarely) to stifle undesirable behavior.

M anagement and discipline are requisite and closely related parts of effective instruction. Management here refers to moving, organizing, and grouping students for instruction. Management requires working with students in such a manner that discipline problems are minimized because there is little "dead" or "stand around" time. Discipline in this text is defined as dealing with unacceptable behavior and behavior that disrupts the flow and continuity of the lesson. In most cases, strong management techniques will minimize discipline problems because students learn to move in an efficient and self-directed manner. Management strategies also involve modifying and maintaining desirable behavior as well as decreasing undesirable behavior.

Successful teachers effectively manage student behavior. Management skills may vary among teachers in emphasis and focus, but collectively they characterize quality teaching. Effective teachers make three assumptions: Teaching is a profession, students are in school to learn, and the teacher's responsibility is to facilitate student learning. These assumptions indicate that teachers will teach a range of students, both those who accept instruction and those who do not. Competent teachers maintain faith in students who have not yet found success and expect them to do so eventually. The majority of students in a class are relatively easy to teach, but making appreciable gains among low-aptitude and indifferent students is the mark of a great teacher.

STRIVE FOR A WELL-MANAGED CLASS

A well-managed class occurs when teacher and students assume dual responsibility for reaching targeted learning goals. Presentations and instructional strategies match students' development levels. Teacher's application of instructional styles, more than the characteristics of a particular teaching style, determines how and what students learn. Effective class management and organizational skills create an environment

that gives students opportunities to learn free from discord. Effective teachers have the ability, skills, and strategies to prevent problems before they occur and create a learning environment where little time is spent dealing with deviant behavior.

A teacher's behavior and personal conduct does not occur in a vacuum. Students reflect the personality, outlook, ideals, and expectations of their teacher. Teachers should examine and reflect upon their personal habits and attitudes to see if their behaviors may negatively impact students. Effective teachers model the behavior expected of their students. This means moving quickly if the request is that students hustle. It implies listening carefully to students or performing required fitness activities from time to time. Modeling desired behavior has a strong impact on students. The phrase "Your actions speak louder than your words" is true because students often make judgments about teachers based on their nonverbal behaviors. Too often, physical education teachers model nonactive behaviors and are viewed as authoritative figures carrying a clipboard, whistling, and ordering students to do things they are unwilling to do.

Effective instruction can help students become more capable and self-sufficient, offering experience to promote success and develop a positive self-concept. Teachers who make clear expectations for learning and behavior develop classes that function with little wasted time and disruption. Lessons run smoothly and are characterized by instructional routines students expect and follow. A productive class setting is work oriented and on task, yet relaxed and pleasant. The next section shows how to organize and move a class quickly and effectively.

USE EFFECTIVE CLASS ORGANIZATION STRATEGIES

Successful teachers organize students quickly for instruction. Moving and organizing students efficiently requires understanding of various techniques and strategies, coupled with student acceptance of those techniques. If a class is poorly managed, the result is a lesson with excessive time wasted on nonlearning-oriented tasks. Students appreciate a learning environment that is organized and efficient, allowing for a maximum amount of class time to be devoted to learning and practicing skills.

Management techniques can be seen as skills that students need to practice and learn. Viewing class management strategies in this light makes it easier to understand that students need time to develop classroom management skills. Just as students need time to improve physical skills, they will need repeated practice of management routines. A simple statement such as, "It appears we have forgotten how to freeze quickly. Let's practice," reminds students of expected behavior in a constructive manner. Regardless of the educational setting, effective teachers have students practice management skills to reach expected behavior outcomes.

Alternate Instruction and Practice Episodes

Student disinterest during the teacher's instruction frequently occurs when the instruction is delivered as a long and involved technical monologue. Little learning occurs when students don't listen or have forgotten most of the information. Information regarding skill performance often includes a list of items to complete: because people usually remember the first and the last point, most students are only able to integrate and concentrate on one or two points following the instructional episode. Instructions should be specific and rarely last longer than 30 to 45 seconds. Deliver instructions in small doses, focusing on one or two points at a time. An effective approach is to alternate short instructional episodes with periods of activity. Have students model what was just emphasized, such as how to hold the racket, stand in ready position, or follow through. Minimizing the amount of content per instructional episode allows them to focus clearly on stated goals and attain a better understanding. This is not to suggest that information should not be delivered to students, but the "tell-it-all-at-the-start" style should be replaced by integrated instruction: input, practice, feedback. New units of instruction can be introduced using an interactive instructional period involving questions, modeling, and short periods of practice. Beginning with 30 minutes of instruction on the first day followed by student practice or play results in limited understanding of the new content. Engage students through activity and build interest and understanding.

Middle school and high school students are anxious to move and as a result may not hear all the in-

structional information. An effective strategy is to manage first prior to giving instructions. If students are to be in groups of two or a small team, divide them quickly using the "when before what" technique. This technique is also effective to get students ready for skill practice or game play. Tell students **when** to perform before stating **what**. For example, "When I say start, I'd like you to get a partner . . ." or, "When I say 'Go!,' I want you to jog over and get a volleyball and practice volleying against the wall." When you have finished giving necessary instructions, students start on the word, "Go." Because the keyword is not given until all directions have been issued, students must be attentive.

Stop and Start a Class Consistently

Starting and stopping activity during a class ensures valuable time will be spent learning and practicing, not waiting or performing off-task behaviors. Effective teachers will select start and stop signals that ensure students respond in a timely fashion. Pick a consistent signal that all students can easily hear to stop a class. It does not matter what the signal is, as long as it always means the same thing: "Stop quickly." A basketball lesson may produce a high level of noise as compared to tumbling and may need a loud signal such as a whistle. Music can also be an effective stop signal during quieter activities. For instance, when the music stops, students know they are to stop and listen. Stop signals are important because they may have to be used for safety purposes (e.g., a student injury). Including a visual signal (such as raising the hand overhead) with the audio signal is effective because some students may not hear the audio signal if they are engrossed in activity or are hearing impaired. The start signal should be different from the stop signal to avoid confusion. Voice signals can frequently be used to start the class. Reinforcement of students' responses to start and stop signals ensures that students know classroom expectations and are held accountable. If students do not respond to the signal to stop, take time to practice the procedure and reinforce students when they perform management behavior properly. Oftentimes, skill performance is reinforced regularly, but correct management behavior is not. Behavior that is not reinforced often will not be performed often.

It is reasonable to expect 100-percent compliance when asking students to stop. If some students stop and listen to directions and others do not, accountability is lost. Students quickly begin to wonder why they have to stop but other students don't. Scanning the class to see if all students are stopped and ready to respond to the next set of directions provides teachers with needed information, confirming that all students are prepared to listen, and ensures that the stop signal is clear and students know what is expected of them. Teachers who settle for less than full attention will soon have a class that ignores stop signals. Students must be held accountable for responding appropriately to an instructor's expectations.

Many variables affect a class's rate and speed of response. The nature of the activity, the students' motivational level, their feelings about the teacher, the time of day, and the weather are a few examples. Teachers control some of these variables, while others are fixed. A positive, success-oriented atmosphere helps decrease response time. Positive teacher reactions focused on appropriate student managerial behaviors are effective. Examples of such responses include the following:

1. "Way to go class—everyone dressed and ready in 4 minutes."

2. "Jim, great hustle back to your squad."

3. "Thank you for getting quiet so quickly."

4. "Look at squad 1 line up quickly."

5. "Hey, I'm impressed how quickly you all got in position."

6. "Way to stop on the whistle; thank you."

Expedite Instructional Transitions

Instructional transitions involve a change in instructional focus that, in turn, demands a reorganization of the class. Discipline problems frequently occur during transitions, often because disorganization creates time to stand around and visit with peers while students wait for the next task. Instructional momentum is lost, and teachers often become frustrated when students must be redirected. Students will also stray off-task when the activity lasts longer than is desirable. Transitions can add to the pace of the lesson when they result in effective flow of instruction. Transitions are planned episodes and should be written and thought out in a manner similar to instructional content.

Errors in instructional planning can create situations where students finish early and become off task waiting to see what is next. Activities need to support choice and to allow student to guide themselves in learning new tasks. Specifying the number of repetitions offers an end in sight; some students will finish early, while others may talk and move at a slow pace. Anytime the numbers of repetitions are stipulated, completion time will vary among students. Here is an example: Instructions are given to students to practice chipping 20 golf balls. Obviously, the speed at which

students will carry out this task will differ. A better approach is to give students an amount of time to complete the task. When time is up, instruction moves on to the next task. This approach is similar to station teaching where students work for a specified amount of time. This also has the side effect of teaching students to maximize the amount of practice they get in a certain amount of time. Certainly, this is a lesson they can use throughout life to "make the most of their time." An option is to have another task that students must complete when they finish early. However, this often becomes a negative approach because some students perceive they have to do more than others because they were efficient in completing the previous task. Repetition and refinement determine the amount of skill learning that takes place, so the more better repetitions, the better.

Group Students Effectively

The nature of physical education requires moving students into small groups and instructional formations on a regular basis. Simple techniques can be used to accomplish this in rapid fashion. For example, use a technique such as "toe to toe" to teach students to find partners quickly. The goal of the game is to get toe to toe with a partner as fast as possible. Other challenges are to find someone your approximate height or to touch fists with a partner. Students without a partner go to the center of the teaching area (marked by a cone or spot and called the "friendship pot") and find someone else without a partner. This gives students a designated spot to locate a partner as opposed to feeling unwanted and running around the area searching for (or avoiding) a partner. Emphasize finding a partner within two giant steps rather than looking for a favorite friend or snubbing someone. Students often stay near a friend. If you prefer a different mix, tell the class to move throughout the area and find a different partner each time "toe to toe" is called.

Many activities require the class to be divided in half for skill practice. An efficient way to achieve this is to have students get toe to toe with a partner. One partner then takes a knee while the other remains standing. Those standing are asked to go to one side of the area, while those kneeling move to the other side. This strategy divides partners into opposing sides and can address the problem that may arise when friends select each other. A quick game of rock-paper-scissors can be used to designate which person in a pair will get equipment, go to a specific side, or be captain.

Another technique that is effective when the goal is quickly placing students into small groups is to signal (whistle blasts or loud hand claps) a certain number of times. Students form groups that correspond to

FIGURE 7.1 Students in squads

An effective approach for moving a class into a single-file line or circle is to have students run randomly throughout the area until a signal is given. On the signal "fall in," students continue jogging (in the same direction as the teacher) while moving toward the perimeter of the area and fall in line behind someone until a circle is formed. This exercise can be done while students are running, jogging, skipping, or walking. As long as students continue to move behind another person, a circle forms automatically.

Use Squads to Expedite Class Organization

Some teachers find that placing students into squads (Figure 7.1) helps them manage a class effectively. Squads offer a place for students to assemble, a way to group students into prearranged teams of equal ability, and a method to expedite learning students' names.

Guidelines for Forming Squads

The following are guidelines for using squad formation to maximize teaching effectiveness.

1. Avoid selecting squads or groups in a manner that embarrasses a student who might be chosen last. In all cases, avoid using an "auction" approach where student leaders look over the group and visibly pick those whom they favor.

2. Establish a designated location where students are to assemble into squad formation. On signal,

the number of signals and sit down to signify that they have the correct number in their group. Students who can't find a group in their immediate vicinity go to the center of the area and find the needed number of members. The use of hand signals (three fingers, etc.) to show the size of the desired group can be an effective way to signal the class to move into small groups.

Upon entering the facility, students also can be given a piece of paper or a token with a number or color. While the music is playing, they will exchange the paper with several different people. When the music stops, they must find the person or people in the class with the same number or color. This technique can be used to select partners or teams. Using hula hoops of various colors can be another fun and effective approach to creating small groups. Similar to musical chairs the music plays and when stopped students will quickly place a foot into the closest hula hoop with other people to form the designated number (e.g., groups of three, four, or five). All students must find a hoop and place one foot inside, but the number cannot go above the designated number. Hoops can be color-coded, and the red hoop will join a blue hoop, green will join yellow, and purple will join white.

When different techniques are used frequently to form groups, students accept this as a regularly occurring routine and will know that they will be expected to work with a variety of people for short periods of time. Students will also learn that working with a variety of classmates provides opportunities to work with individuals they might not otherwise get to know. This practice can contribute to a positive learning environment.

students move to the designated area, with squad leaders in front and the rest of the squad behind.

3. Use squads to provide opportunities for leadership and following among peers by appointing squad leaders. Examples of leadership activities are moving squads to a specified location, leading squads through exercises or introductory activities, and appointing squad members to certain positions in sport activities. Rotate squad leaders every 2 to 3 weeks so all students have an opportunity to lead.

4. Consider predetermining the composition of squads. It may be important to have equal representation of ability levels on each squad. Squads can also be used to separate certain students so they don't have the opportunity to disrupt the class. To ensure students get to work with all students in the class, change squad members on a regular basis. In most cases, an even number of squads should be formed. This allows the class to be broken quickly into halves for games.

Home Base and Station Teaching

Creating a home base is a way of using squads to facilitate the management of students in a variety of educational settings. Place a number of marking spots around the area that corresponds to the number of squads. Upon the command "home base," squad leaders move to the nearest marking spot, and their respective squad members line up behind them. Once this basic skill is learned, it can be used to facilitate instruction. For example, prior to the start of the lesson, station teaching signs and a marking spot are put out around the perimeter of the area. Students complete the initial parts of the lesson. When instruction at the stations is about to start, the teacher calls out "home base," and squad leaders hustle to a marking spot at each of the stations. The result is a rapid transition; a squad of students at each station is ready to begin. This activity can also be used to split the class in half by placing an equal number of marking spots in each half of the area.

Learn Students' Names

Learning the names of students not only personalizes instruction, it makes it much easier to manage students. Praise, feedback, and correction go unheeded when students are addressed as "Hey, you!" Develop a system to expedite learning names. One approach is to memorize three or four names per class period. The names are written on a note card, and those students are identified at the start and throughout the period. At the end of the period, identify the students again.

Once the first set of names has been memorized, a new set can be learned. At the start of class when the meeting occurs, those names learned previously can be reviewed and new students identified. Don't be shy about telling students you are trying to learn their names. Asking students to say their name before performing a skill or answering a question can help you learn students' names. Once learned, you may precede the question or skill performance with the student's name (e.g., "Mary, it's your turn to try it").

Another effective way to learn names is to take a photograph of each class in squads and identify students by keying names to the picture. Identification is easier with students in squads because they will be in the same location. Identify a few students whom you know and do not know before the start of the period. Set personal goals by calculating the percentage of students whose names you know after each period.

Establish Class Procedures and Expectations

Students enjoy the sense of security that comes from knowing what to do from the time they enter the instructional area until they leave. A number of procedures need to be handled routinely. The following are situations that arise often and need to be planned for ahead of time.

Motivate Students to Dress for Activity Quickly

Students must change into activity clothes in locker rooms located some distance from where attendance will be taken. This can lead to a rather slow and unorganized start. Students also dress at different times. Inappropriate activity can occur when the students who have dressed quickly are waiting for slower students to arrive. This dressing time difference also means that students are in two different and separate places, both of which require supervision. How a lesson starts often determines how a lesson finishes (good start—good finish). A positive approach is to allow students who dress quickly to participate in activities they enjoy until the entire class is assembled. This gives students a reason to change quickly because they know they will have time to participate in activities they enjoy. It is effective to allow students to select things they like to do from a list of safe activities such as shooting baskets, juggling objects, jumping rope, and practicing floor hockey. Developing an award system for individuals or squads is another effective way to expedite the dressing process. "Free time" points are awarded each time individuals or all squad members are dressed and ready to participate by a specific time. The responsibility for getting students ready can shift from the teacher to students when positive reinforcement is provided.

Dealing with Nonparticipation

Identifying students who are not to participate in the lesson should be done in a consistent and efficient manner. A routine that addresses this issue is effective when the decision for nonparticipation is made by someone (nurse or classroom teacher) other than the physical education teacher before students arrive at the lesson area. If a school nurse is not available, a written policy approved by the school administrator should be in place. This prevents a situation where the physical education teacher encourages students to participate even though they are not supposed to do so. The physical education teacher needs a note from the school nurse listing student's name, health problem, and reason why he or she must sit out or take part in modified activity. This information must be accepted at face value, thus avoiding questioning students to determine what the problem is and what the solution should be. Because most teachers are not health agents, they are not qualified to determine which students should participate based on a health problem. A student with a note from home or a physician should never be allowed to return to participation without parental permission.

Taking Roll Call

Roll call (attendance) is a daily routine that could lead to students becoming bored. While waiting to participate they may begin to socialize or get involved in horseplay, resulting in a class getting off to a noisy and disorganized start. An effective method for taking attendance each day helps reduce time spent in management of behavior problems. An effective technique is to use squads and squad leaders. Each squad leader reports any absentees to the teacher orally or by filling out an attendance sheet. Another approach is to paint numbers on the floor and assign each student a number. The teacher or a student leader glances quickly through the numbers and records the absentees while the students are exercising. Some teachers post a sign-in sheet for attendance, which students quickly initial. Yet another approach is to check attendance while students are beginning the first class activity. Regardless of the method used, the technique should save time and foster self-management qualities in students.

Closing a Lesson

A regular routine for closing the lesson is beneficial. Closure provides opportunities to check for student understanding of the day's lesson, review material for the next day, or record achieved outcomes. For example, ask the class to verbally identify (or physically demonstrate) the key points of a skill learned, give the results of games being played, or discuss new ideas learned during a strategy session. Closure can also be used to prepare students for the next lesson, for example, tomorrow we will apply the skills you learned today in a game setting. It is also a good time to have discussions related to their quality efforts and willingness to work on their own. Closure may be done while lined up at the door, in closed squad formation, or while kneeling in a semicircle, allowing time for closure related to the instructional content and a procedure for leaving the teaching area.

Use Equipment Effectively

Today's physical education is characterized by every student having a piece of equipment for practice and skill development. Acceptable teaching practices ensure that students spend limited time waiting for a turn to practice and perform expected skills. Having a specific routine for placement of equipment during instruction can reduce off-task behavior and lack of attention. Placing the equipment in a home position avoids the problem of students' striking one another with the equipment, dropping it, or practicing activities when they should be listening. To avoid students playing with the equipment when it is placed on the floor, ask them to put down the equipment and take a large step away from it. For example, hockey sticks are placed on the floor, basketballs between the feet, and jump ropes folded in half and placed behind the neck.

Distribution of numerous pieces of equipment in large classes can reduce the amount of time students have to develop and understand skills and create more time spent in noninstruction. Therefore it is necessary to distribute equipment to students as quickly as possible, yet in a safe manner. When students have to wait for a piece of equipment, time is wasted and behavior problems occur. A common practice that often results in many students waiting is to assign leaders to get the equipment for their squad. A better and faster method is to have the equipment placed around the perimeter of the practice area. Following clear instructions and a predetermined signal, students acquire a piece of equipment, take it to their personal space, and begin practicing an assigned task. This approach takes advantage of the natural urge to try the equipment and reinforces students who procure equipment quickly. Equipment is put away using the same routine. Placing equipment in the middle of the area in one container and telling students to "run and get a ball" creates an unsafe situation as well as wastes valuable time.

Regardless of the method used to distribute equipment, clearly state what students are supposed to do with it once they have a piece of equipment. Unless safety is a problem, get students engaged with their piece of equipment immediately. Asking students to hold their equipment until everybody is ready may reinforce students who lag behind to get their equipment. Having students start practicing once they get their equipment can act as a prompt to those students who are slow responders.

TEACH RESPONSIBLE STUDENT BEHAVIOR

Physical education should be a positive experience for all students. To create a learning environment that ensures students will experience the benefits of physical education, students must accept that they are mutually responsible for contributing to a positive learning environment. Increased emphasis on teaching responsible behavior to students has been placed with teachers. A basic premise for learning responsible behavior is that it must be planned for, taught, and reinforced. Responsible behavior takes time and practice to learn, much like any other skill. Don Hellison (2003) developed strategies and programs for teaching responsibility to older students. Hellison suggests there is a hierarchy of responsible behavior. The focus in this section is on the idea that there are different levels of responsible behavior that can be learned. Teaching responsible behavior described here involves five levels of behavior. Each is defined in the following text, accompanied by examples of typical student behavior at each level. One point to note is some teachers take issue with identifying a level as "zero." If that is a problem, renumber the levels or letter them. The important point is not the label but the process of trying to behave at a higher level of responsibility.

Levels of Responsibility
Level 0: Irresponsibility

Level 0 students are unmotivated and undisciplined. Their behavior includes discrediting other students' involvement and interrupting, intimidating, manipulating, and verbally or physically abusing other students and perhaps the teacher.
Behavior examples include the following:

- At home: Blaming brothers or sisters for problems; lying to parents
- During free time: Calling other students names; laughing at others
- In physical education: Talking to friends when the teacher is giving instructions; pushing and shoving when selecting equipment

Level 1: Self-Control

Students at this level do not participate in the day's activity or show much mastery or improvement. These students control their behavior enough so they do not interfere with the other students' right to learn and the teacher's right to teach.
Behavior examples include the following:

- At home: Keeping self from hitting a brother or sister even though angry
- During free time: Not getting angry at others because they did something to upset them
- In physical education: Waiting until an appropriate time to talk with friends; having control and not letting behavior of others bother them

Level 2: Involvement

These students show self-control and are involved in the subject matter or activity.
Behavior examples include the following:

- At home: Helping with chores around the house
- During free time: Visiting with friends; participating in a game
- In physical education: Listening and performing an activity; trying an activity even if it isn't a favorite; participating in an activity without complaining

Level 3: Self-Responsibility

Level 3 students take responsibility for their choices and for linking these choices to their own identities. They are able to work without direct supervision, eventually taking responsibility for their intentions and actions.
Behavior examples include the following:

- At home: Cleaning up without being asked
- During free time: Taking the initiative to involve others in activities
- In physical education: Following directions; practicing a skill without being told; trying new activities without prompting

Level 4: Caring

Students behaving at this level are motivated to extend their sense of responsible behavior by cooperating, giving support, showing concern, and helping.

Behavior examples include the following:

- At home: Helping take care of a younger brother or sister or a pet
- During free time: Asking students who they don't know or who feel left out to join them in play
- In physical education: Helping someone who is having trouble; helping a new student feel welcome; working with all students; showing that all people are worthwhile

Responsible behavior is taught using a number of strategies. Post the levels of responsibility in the teaching area. Explain the different levels of behavior and identify acceptable behaviors at each level. After students have received an introduction to responsible behavior, implement the program by reinforcement of desired behavior and redirection of inappropriate behavior. The program is based on this two-pronged approach: (1) **Catch** students using responsible behavior and reinforce them; and (2) **redirect** students behaving at level 0 by asking, "At what level are you performing, and what level would be more acceptable?" An example is the following discussion between teacher and student: You see a student behaving at level 0 and open dialogue with the student in a **nonconfrontational and nonadversarial** manner:

"Matt, it appeared you were making fun of someone."

"I wasn't making fun of anyone!"

"Maybe not, but if you were, what level of behavior would it be?"

"Zero!"

"Is that the kind of person you want to be or the level of behavior you want to show?"

"No!"

"If you were at level 0, do you think you could make some changes? Perhaps you could move to level 1 and have self-control even if someone else makes you mad or even if you do not like that person."

Teacher feedback forms the core of the responsibility approach; however, there are many strategies for increasing responsible behavior in the instructional setting. The following are some strategies that can be used:

- *Model desirable behavior*—Interact at a high level with your students to encourage responsible behavior. Students do not care about how much you know until they know how much you care. Treat youth with dignity and respect and follow through with responsible actions and words. In return, expect them to treat you and others with the same dignity and respect.

- *Use reinforcement*—Give students specific feedback about the quality of their behavior. If corrective feedback is given, make sure it identifies the desired level of behavior. If reinforcing desirable behavior, be specific in identifying why the behavior is desirable and conveying that you appreciate such acts. In some cases, it may be beneficial to identify a super citizen or give a "happygram" for special behavior.

- *Allow student sharing*—Offer students a chance to give their opinions about responsible behavior. Accept all students' feelings as important. Focus on ways to encourage higher levels of responsible behavior. Brainstorming to identify consequences of high- and low-level behavior is an effective approach. Another practice is to ask students to give examples of responsible behavior at different levels. Allow students time to share how they feel when someone uses a high- or low-level behavior around them.

- *Encourage goal setting*—Help students set goals for the responsible behavior they want to exhibit. This can be done at the start of a lesson by asking students to tell a partner the level of behavior they want to use today. At the end of the lesson, partners evaluate each other to see if the behavior was exhibited. Examples of behaviors are listening, hustling, following directions, being courteous, and complimenting others.

- *Offer opportunities for responsibility*—Give students responsibility in a class setting. Being a group leader, team captain, referee, scorekeeper, rule maker, or dispute arbitrator encourages students to exhibit high-level behavior. Because responsible positions affect other students, effective leaders have to behave responsibly.

- *Allow student choice*—Realize responsible behavior is best learned when students make choices. The natural consequences of self-selected choices are often the best teachers. Students can make choices about games they choose to play, fitness activities they select, and friends they choose. Discussing how to make meaningful choices (see Chapter 17) is an important phase of learning to make responsible choices.

Conflict Resolution

Conflict between students often occurs, resulting in aggression and violence. About one in seven students is either a bully or victim (Beane, 1999). Nobody wants to create a world where the strong dominate and the weak live in fear and submission. Conflict is a part of daily life, and students should understand that it is necessary to deal with conflict in an effective manner. Students can learn ways to respect others' opinions and feelings while maintaining their own worth and dignity.

There are a number of ways to solve conflicts, but the most common methods identified involve three types of behavior—dominating, appeasing, and cooperating. Students who use the dominating style are often unsure about their standing in the group. They want things to be done in their way but are afraid others will reject them. They often lack confidence and try hard to get others to accept their way of doing things. Youth who are appeasers lack confidence but want to be accepted by others. They do not like conflict and are willing to put down their feelings in order to placate others.

Neither the dominating nor the appeasing approach is effective for solving conflicts in the long run. No one likes to be dominated or placed in the position of having to appease others. Conflict resolution can help students learn to solve conflicts in a peaceful manner with no apparent losers. This approach takes a cooperative approach to solving problems. Such an approach often builds positive feelings between students and leads to better group cohesiveness. The following are steps typically followed to resolve conflicts (Gordon & Brown, 1996). If youth are experienced at conflict resolution, they may be able to carry out the steps without instructor intervention.

1. *Stop the aggressive behavior immediately.* Separate students in conflict immediately and give them an opportunity to cool down. A predesignated cooldown area is an excellent place to send students to relax and calm down.

2. *Gather data about what happened and define the problem.* Find out what happened, who was involved, and how each person feels about the conflict. Open the discussion with a feeling-oriented statement such as, "You must have really been angry to get involved in a fight." This allows students to talk about their emotions and the incident.

3. *Brainstorm possible solutions.* Keep in mind that brainstorming is a nonjudgmental process where all solutions are accepted regardless of their perceived value. Encourage the students to think of as many options as possible by asking open-ended questions, such as "How could we solve this problem?" and "What other ways could we deal with this?"

4. *Test the solutions generated through brainstorming.* Ask a question such as, "What solutions might work best?" Help students understand the implications of the solutions and how the solutions can be implemented. Accept solutions that may differ from your way of solving the problem.

5. *Help implement the plan.* Walk students through the solution so they develop a perception of the approach. Guide them through the steps by asking, "Who goes first?" or "Who will take the next step?" As the solution is implemented, there may be a need to change it, which can be agreed on by the involved students.

6. *Evaluate the approach.* Observe to see that the plan is accomplishing the desired outcome. Encourage students to change the plan if necessary.

The conflict resolution process takes practice and time. Teachers who take time for conflict resolution live with the knowledge that they are teaching students to solve problems without violence or excessive emotion. It demands an objective approach to resolution. Facilitating the conflict resolution process demands certain behaviors from the instructor. Empathetic listening to both parties is necessary. Both sides of the problem must be explored, and students must feel as though the process was equitable. Blame is not assessed in this process. Placing blame only encourages self-defense behavior, such as appeasing or being aggressive. Students must trust that the process will be fair and objective and that they will receive a fair shake if they deal with the issue cooperatively.

IMPLEMENT A PROACTIVE BEHAVIOR MANAGEMENT APPROACH

Many class management and discipline problems can be prevented through anticipation and planning. Anticipate the types of problems that might occur and have a plan for dealing with them when they do. Teachers worry that a situation will occur that they are not able to handle. Developing a plan of attack for dealing with problems offers a sense of confidence and peace of mind. The first phase of an effective behavior management plan is beginning the year on a proactive and positive note. Developing a comprehensive behavior management approach is a systematic way to deal with problems that affect all teachers and are generally ranked as the most serious concerns of teachers and parents.

Create a Behavior Plan for Yourself

The old adage "know thyself" is never more important than when having to manage a class of students. How are you going to respond when misbehavior occurs? Are you going to be threatened, angry, sad, or unmoved? What types of behaviors are going to set you off and anger you quickly? How do you behave and respond to students when you are angry? These and many other questions arise when teachers assume the responsibility for a class. The one thing to assume is that management and discipline skills will be needed regardless of what age or type of class is being taught. How a teacher responds to misbehavior will make a huge difference in how students respond to the teacher. Generally, there are three ways a teacher communicates to students when various types of misbehavior occur.

- *Passive communicator.* A passive teacher "hopes" to make all students happy in order to avoid being upset. Passive means trying to avoid all conflict and please others. Directly or indirectly the passive teacher is constantly saying, "Like me; appreciate what I do for you." Many passive teachers want to be perfect so everybody will like them and hope that students will behave perfectly. When students behave like students and go off task, Mr. Passive becomes upset and angry. A common pattern is for the passive teacher to let behavior slide until he or she "can't take it anymore." Then he or she loses composure and lashes out at the class in anger. When the anger subsides, Mr. Passive now wants to make up again and restarts the cycle of letting things go and "blowing up."

Passive teachers often turn over their power to students, particularly the least cooperative students. For example, they will say things like, "We are not going to start until everyone is listening!" Interpreted concretely, students may hear, "This is great. We don't have to start until we are finished with our conversation." Passive teachers also ignore unacceptable behavior and hope it will disappear. Ignoring seldom causes behavior to disappear; rather such behavior often becomes worse over time. Passive teachers often make threats but never follow through with them. For example, this teacher might say, "If you do that one more time, I am going to call your parents." When there is no follow-through or it is impossible to follow through, the words are empty and meaningless and students soon learn disrespect for the teacher. Another common trait of a passive teacher is to ask questions that will result in information that is

meaningless, for example, "What did you do that for?" or "Why are you doing this?" or "Don't you know better than that?" These questions do not elicit useful information, and the teacher soon becomes frustrated and angry at all of the "I don't know" responses.

- *Aggressive communicator.* An aggressive teacher wants to overpower others by coming on strong. Aggressive instructors feel it is a competition, and they must win at all costs whenever communication occurs. A common trait with aggressive communicators is that they use the word "you" all the time. A number of statements keep students feeling defensive and attacked. Examples are, "You never listen to me; you are always the one in trouble; you are the problem here; you are always talking." Aggressive responders often have all the answers and express others' viewpoints (which are often wrong). For example, they may say something like, "You think that because you did that last year, you can do it in my class." Obviously, no one knows what another is thinking, and it serves no purpose to communicate this way.

Aggressive communicators often use the words "always" and "never." These words are labeling words. They make students feel as if they are bad people who always behave in certain ways or never do anything right. Words that generalize and label create communication problems and can result in alienation rather than respect. Aggressive communicators often see students as personally attacking them and focus on labeling the other person rather than dealing with the behavior. Often, they don't reveal how they feel about things and are unwilling to express their own thoughts and feelings. If students never know how a teacher feels, it is likely they will not develop much empathy for their instructor. A good rule of thumb is this: Any statement about the other person rather than telling them how **you** feel will give your communication an attacking and aggressive flavor.

- *Assertive communicator.* An assertive teacher does not beg, plead, or threaten. Rather, the approach is straightforward and focused on feelings and expectations. An assertive person is not afraid to say what he or she wants and does not worry about what others will think of him or her. A teacher who wants to be liked is quite concerned about what students think of him or her. An assertive teacher wants what is best for students and doesn't worry about what they think. Assertiveness comes across to students as a "no-nonsense" approach that needs to be carried out. It is clear and direct, and it is concrete (requires little interpretation to carry out). For example, an assertive teacher might say to a student who has been talking out of turn, "It bothers me when you talk while I am talking." You are expressing your feelings and making the unacceptable behavior clear. Now follow that statement with an assertive statement that expresses the desired behavior: "That is your second warning; I'd like you to stop immediately." Assertive communication places great emphasis on clarity without anger. High emotion is not part of assertive responding because it turns assertion into aggressiveness.

An excellent way to make messages more assertive is to make them using the word "I" instead of "you." Talking about your own feelings and emotions will make the messages sound much more reasonable and firm, for example, "When you are playing with your equipment while I am talking, it bothers me and makes me forget what I planned on saying. Please leave your equipment alone when I talk." Such messages always identify the behavior that is disruptive or annoying, offer how you feel, and direct the student to behave in a proper manner. An excellent reference on discipline is *Conscious Discipline* (Bailey, 2001). This is a valuable reference if you are unsure of how to become an assertive communicator.

One of the key elements to effective management of students is being aware of your behavior when disciplining students. Serious misbehavior can cause some teachers to become angry, others to feel threatened, and others to behave in a tyrannical manner. Part of your behavior plan is to remind yourself of how you will behave when misbehavior occurs. Personal behavior plans usually include the following points.

1. *Maintain composure.* Students don't know your trigger points unless you reveal them. If you "lose it," students lose respect for you and believe you are an ineffective teacher.

2. *Acknowledge your feelings when student misbehavior occurs.* Do you feel angry, threatened, challenged, or fearful? How do you typically respond when a student defies you? Know yourself.

3. *Design a plan for yourself when such feelings occur.* When you feel anxiety building inside because of student misbehavior, use a calming approach such as counting to 10 before responding, or taking five deep breaths, or avoiding dealing with the student misbehavior until you feel your emotions are in control.

4. *Know the options you have for dealing with the deviant behavior.* Talking with students is best done after class if it is going to take more than a few seconds. Limited time options are quietly warning the student, quietly removing the student from class, or quietly sending another student for help if the situation is severe.

Determine Rules and Procedures for the School Year

Rules are an expected part of the school environment. Most teachers want students to be respectful to them and other students. It is not unreasonable to expect students to behave. If you can't manage students, you can't teach them anything. In fact, most school administrators judge your effectiveness by how well you manage students. Accept the fact that managing students is a necessary and important part of teaching; in fact, it is a requisite to the delivery of content. When creating your rules, select general categories rather than specific behavior. For example, the rule "respect your peers" includes many things, from not physically abusing someone to not swearing. Post rules in the teaching area where all students can easily read them. The following are examples of general rules:

- *Stop, look, and listen.* This implies stopping on signal, looking at the instructor, and listening for instructions.

- *Take care of equipment.* This includes caring for, distributing, gathering, and using equipment properly.

- *Respect the rights of others.* This includes behavior such as not bothering others, leaving their equipment alone, and not fighting and arguing.

Minimize the number of rules. Try not to exceed three to five rules; more rules make it difficult for students to remember all the details and make the teacher appear overly strict. Numerous rules also make students rule specific. A student may choose to chew gum in the gym room because the school rule is "no gum chewing in the halls or classrooms." When students become rule specific, they often fail to think about right and wrong and only follow stipulated rules. Rules are guidelines for desired behavior rather than negative statements telling students what they can't do. Consider the following points when designing rules:

- Select major categories of behavior rather than a multitude of specific rules.

- Identify observable behavior. This makes it easy to determine whether a person is following a rule and does not involve subjective judgment.

- Make rules reasonable for the age level of students. The best rules are those that cut across all ages and situations.

- Try to limit the number of rules to three to five.

- State rules briefly and positively. It is impossible to write a rule that covers all situations and conditions. Make the rule brief, yet broad. An important part of teaching is to get students to think about the moral implications of the rule rather than seeing it as someone telling them what they can't do.

Communicate the Consequences of Misbehavior

When rules are broken, students have to learn to accept the consequences of their behaviors. A sign of a mature student is the willingness to accept the consequences of improper behavior. Immature students argue, try to place the blame on others, or refuse to accept the need for such rules. List and post the consequences of misbehavior in a prominent place in the teaching area. Discuss your rules with students to ensure they understand and see the necessity of having behavior guidelines. Be sure you apply rules and consequences consistently to ensure no students are punished excessively or unfairly. For example, if you like one student more than another, you may inadvertently punish each student differently for the same misbehavior. This leads students to believe you are unfair (which you are). Giving students a say in the development of rules and consequences helps them create an environment in which they feel some sense of ownership. When consequences have been mutually agreed on, don't feel upset, disappointed, or angry when you have to discipline students. They chose to break rules they helped create, and you are only administering predetermined consequences. This process reduces anger and guilt so both teacher and students feel better about each other.

Implement Your Management Plan

A number of things can be done during the first week or two of teaching to ensure classes begin successfully. The first few days of school are a time to communicate expectations in a manner that leaves students with a positive first impression. Students want to develop a positive relationship with you, and a meaningful start leaves them confident and excited about the experience. Consider the following points.

Develop Awareness and the Ability to Coprocess

Teachers have to be aware of what is going on in their class if they are going to be effective managers. It is common to find beginning teachers who don't even see students misbehaving or going off task. Research done years ago (Kounin, 1970) found that the quality of "withitness" and "overlappingness" were common traits of effective teachers. Withitness is defined as the ability to be aware of what is going on in class regardless of what you are doing or teaching. Kounin described overlappingness (being able to process many things at once in an effective manner [coprocess]) as a critical trait of effective teachers. What this means is that teachers have to do many things at once. It is not a profession for those who have a single goal in mind and tend to be able to concentrate on one thing at a time. Rather, you will have to see how students are behaving regardless of what you are teaching. "Juggling many balls at one time" is a descriptive catchphrase for an effective teacher.

Be a Leader, Not a Friend

Students want a teacher who is a knowledgeable, personable leader. They are not looking for a friend; in fact, most students feel uncomfortable if they perceive that you want to be "one of them." Let students know what they will learn during the semester. Don't look to be a part of their personal discussions. There must be a comfortable distance between you and your students. This is not to say that you shouldn't be friendly and caring; it is important to be concerned about students as long as your concern is expressed in a professional manner. Being a leader means knowing it is your charge to direct a class. You are responsible for what is learned and how it is presented. Student input is important, but ultimately, it is your responsibility to lead a class to desired objectives.

Communicate High Standards

Students respond to your expectations. If you expect students to perform at high levels, the majority of them will strive to do so. A common but accurate expression is, "You get what you ask for." If you expect students to perform to the best of their abilities, they probably will do so. On the other hand, if you act like you don't care whether they try to achieve to the best of their abilities, some students will do as little as possible.

Use Activities that Involve the Entire Class

To minimize class management problems, select instructional activities that keep the entire group involved in simultaneous activity. As you develop rapport with a class, different styles of teaching and class organization can be used. It is usually better to use a more direct style of teaching (see Chapter 8) in the first few weeks of teaching. This allows you to view the entire class and see how students respond to the educational setting. Less directed teaching styles and varied organizational schemes are usually implemented after class management skills have been developed and students have shown the ability to work independently. Station teaching, peer teaching, and other approaches are most effective when the teacher and students feel mutual respect.

Give Positive Group Feedback

Positive feedback delivered to a class develops group morale and points the class toward common goals. Classes should learn to view themselves as units that work together and are rewarded when they meet group goals. Students have to work within groups as adults, so learning about group cooperation and pride in accomplishment helps ensure a smoothly running class and prepares them for adulthood.

Discipline Individually and Avoid Group Negative Feedback

When negative feedback is delivered, it should be done privately and personally to individual students. Few people want to have negative comments delivered globally for others to hear. In addition, never punish all students for the behavior of a few misbehaving students. This approach leads to resentment and contrary results. If you criticize the entire group, there is a strong possibility of losing the respect and admiration of students who were behaving properly.

Avoid Feedback that Offers the Possibility for Backlash

Some verbal types of interactions work in the short term but cause long-term and negative consequences. The following types of feedback often work immediately but cause greater problems over the long haul. If students grow resentful, they will become deviant when the teacher is not around. Some examples of counterproductive feedback follow:

- *Preaching or moralizing.* The most common example of moralizing is telling students they "should know better than that!" Quite frankly, if they knew better, they may not have behaved in an unacceptable manner. They make mistakes because they are immature and learning on the job. A part of learning is making mistakes. Correct mistakes in a quiet and caring manner.

- *Threatening.* Threats are ultimatums given in an attempt to terminate undesirable behavior even though you know you cannot carry out the threat. For example, the threat, "If you do not stop that, I'm going to kick you out of class," sounds tough but is usually impossible to enforce. You are not in a position to expel students, and some students are aware of your inability to carry out the threat. If students hear enough idle threats, they start to tune out and respect gradually wanes.

- *Ordering and commanding.* If you are bossy, students begin to think they are nothing more than pawns to be moved around the area. Use patterns of communication that ask students to carry out tasks. Courtesy and politeness are requisites for effective teacher-student relationships.

- *Interrogating.* When there is a problem (e.g., an argument between students), an initial reaction is to try and figure out who started the argument rather than deal with the feelings of the students. Little is gained by trying to solve "who started it." Students often shirk the blame and suggest it was not their fault. Try calmly saying, "You know loud arguing is not acceptable behavior in my class. You must have been very angry to place yourself in this situation." This encourages students to talk about their feelings rather than place blame on others. It also communicates a caring and concerned attitude toward students even when they misbehave.

- *Refusing to listen.* This commonly manifests itself as "Let's talk about it some other time." At times, during instruction, this response is necessary. However, if you always refuse to listen, students will avoid interaction and believe you don't care.

- *Labeling.* Labeling is characterized by telling students, "Stop acting like babies" or "You're behaving like a bunch of loonies." On an individual level, it might sound like, "You're always the problem or trouble in this class." This is degrading and dehumanizes students. Often, labeling is done with the intent of improving performance. In actuality, it is usually destructive and leaves students with negative feelings.

Give Clear and Specific Instructions

There are times when students misbehave because they don't understand the instructions. Give instructions and then proceed with the activity. Monitor to see if a majority of students don't perform correctly. If more than half of your students seem to be unsure or confused as to what they should do, it is time to stop the entire class and reinstruct. When the majority of students follow the instructions given, your instructions were clear and the remaining students can observe or gain clarity from others. Clarity of instruction rests with the teacher; if students are focused and listening yet confused when it is time to participate, it is time to monitor and adjust.

MAINTAIN AND PROMOTE ACCEPTABLE BEHAVIOR

Managing student behavior is an ongoing task. A class of students is really a group of individuals, each of whom must be uniquely treated and understood. Some teachers question the importance of instructional discipline. The most basic of reasons for teaching discipline is that it allows students to learn effectively without encroaching on the rights of others. Our society is based on freedom hinged to self-discipline. Americans have much personal freedom as long as they do not encroach on the rights of others. In similar fashion, students can enjoy freedom as long as their behavior is consistent with educational objectives and does not prevent other students from learning.

Most students choose to cooperate and participate positively in the educational setting. In fact, learners are largely responsible for allowing the teacher to teach. No one can be taught who chooses not to cooperate. Effective management of behavior means maintaining an environment in which all students have the opportunity to learn. It is a teacher's responsibility to fashion a learning environment where all students learn and feel comfortable. Students who choose to be disruptive and off task infringe on the rights of students who choose to cooperate. If a teacher has to spend a great deal of energy working with students who are disorderly, students who want to learn are shortchanged.

The purpose of this section is to offer a plan for modifying and maintaining desired behavior. The overall approach is two pronged and straightforward: first, increase levels of desired behavior, and second, eliminate or reduce undesirable behavior by focusing on a positive and constructive approach that teaches students responsible behavior.

Increase Desired Behavior

Behavior that is followed by appropriate positive reinforcement will occur more often in the future. This principle is a key for increasing desired behavior. The strength of this simple principle is that it focuses on positive and desired educational outcomes. A critical

component of increasing desired behavior through reinforcement is that such behavior must occur. For example, if a student often makes negative comments about his peers, it may be a difficult and slow process because reinforcement can only be given when a positive comment is made. Arranging the environment is often necessary to stimulate the desired behavior to be reinforced. Some suggested ideas that are discussed in detail later in the chapter are to use the Premack Principle, use behavioral contracts, use failure-proof activities, and prompt students for the desired behavior. Key points for increasing desired behaviors lie in deciding what to use as reinforcers, selecting those that effectively reinforce individuals, and properly using the reinforcers.

Social Reinforcers

With secondary school students, it is best to use social reinforcers to increase desired behavior. Teachers and parents most often use this class of reinforcers, such as praise, physical contact, and facial expressions to acknowledge desirable and acceptable behavior. The following are examples of reinforcers that can be used with students in a physical education setting:

Words of Praise

Great job	Nice going
Exactly right	I really like that job
Perfect arm placement	That's the best one yet
Way to go	Nice hustle

Physical Expressions

Smiling	Winking
Nodding	Clenched fist overhead
Thumbs-up	Clapping

Physical Contact

Handshake	High five

An early step is to identify the social reinforcers that different age students find acceptable in the school setting. As students mature, they become much less willing to accept certain types of reinforcers. To pick out individual students for praise in front of peers may embarrass them or make them feel uncomfortable. With such students, it is best to deliver praise on a personal basis whenever possible to avoid any negative spin. Some students may not want to be touched even to the point of receiving a high five, and those of the opposite sex may interpret a hug or pat on the back incorrectly. If unsure of how students will react, it is best to ask the school administrator to define the social reinforcers that are acceptable and to which students respond positively.

Effective use of social reinforcers requires giving praise and making positive statements. Many teachers feel uncomfortable when learning to administer positive reinforcement to students because such behavior feels inauthentic. A common complaint from teachers learning how to reinforce is, "This is not who I am; students will know I am a fake." Any change in communication patterns feels uncomfortable at first. Trying new ways of communicating with a class requires a period of adjustment. New patterns of praise and reinforcement often feel contrived and insincere. (Fortunately, students don't know the difference because they don't know who you "really are.") There is no way to avoid discomfort if you want to improve your teaching effectiveness. Teachers who are unwilling to experience this initial period of uneasiness will not improve. The assumption that patterns of speech learned during youth and into college are naturally suited for teaching is false. Teachers are made, not born, and they find success through hard work and dedication. If practiced regularly, new behavioral patterns soon become a natural expression of who you are in a short time.

Praise is most effective when it identifies and reinforces specific behavior. This contrasts with general statements, such as "Good job" or "You are an excellent performer." General and nonspecific statements do not communicate to students what was done well, leaving the student to guess what you had in mind. If the student guesses incorrectly, he or she may actually think he or she is being reinforced for a behavior you deem unacceptable. To improve the specificity and effectiveness of feedback, describe the exact behavior you want reinforced. At the same time, do not make your feedback judgmental in nature. Describing behavior identifies the specifics of performance and makes no judgment about the individual as a whole. Judging the person, however, is general and often criticizes the individual as a whole instead of the desired behavior. For example, compare the following:

Describing: "I saw your excellent forward roll, James; you tucked your head just right."

Judging: "That's a good job; however, I think you can accomplish it at a much higher level."

In the first example, James is identified by name, and a specific behavior he performed is reinforced. In the second situation, it is impossible to identify what is good, and it leaves the student with an empty feeling. In most cases, if a question can be asked about delivered praise or criticism (e.g., what was good, or how can it be performed at a higher level), the feedback is open to misinterpretation. To increase desired behavior, verbally or physically describe what makes the performance effective, good, or noteworthy. This reinforces the student and communicates to the rest of the class the performance expected by the instructor.

Extrinsic Reinforcers

Social reinforcers are by far the best method when changing or maintaining student behavior. However, there are times when the teacher's ability to reinforce behavior intrinsically is seriously compromised. For example, a new or substitute teacher has not established a relationship with students. Students have to value and respect a teacher before their social reinforcers become meaningful and filled with value to students. In this case, extrinsic reinforcers may have to be used. For example, free time that allows students to participate in their choice of activities can be used as reinforcement. One of the best ways to identify activities students want to do is to ask them. Give a quick informal poll of two or three choices. When students get to vote and choose an activity that is reinforcing to them, it is usually accepted by the entire class. Free time usually ranks highest among middle and high school students' preferences. Some examples of activities that might be used to reinforce a class are free time to practice a skill, the opportunity to play a game, the chance to act as a teacher's aide, the chance to be a teacher in a cross-aged tutoring situation, or the opportunity to be a team captain. Prudent use of free time as a reinforcement can get students to participate in a self-selected activity.

Access to novelty activities, competitive games, and class tournaments can be used as reinforcers. Frisbee games such as golf, baseball, Guts, and Ultimate are Frisbee recreational activities that may be highly desirable for some classes. By analyzing the likes and dislikes of students, teachers can develop a set of activity reinforcers that work.

The Premack Principle. Teachers often unknowingly use the Premack Principle (Premack, 1965) to increase desired behavior. The principle states that when a high-frequency behavior (preferred) is contingent on completion of a lower-frequency behavior (less desirable), it is likely to increase the occurrence of the lower-frequency behavior. This implies that when the less desirable behavior is completed, a more desirable behavior is allowed. An activity that students enjoy is used to increase the occurrence of an activity that students are reticent to perform.

Learning activities can be planned using the Premack Principle. The Premack Principle is sometimes referred to as "Grandma's Principle, "Grandma's law," or "Eat your spinach; then you may have dessert." Teachers can arrange the environment so that students must spend a certain amount of time completing a certain number of attempts at a less popular activity before they can gain access to a preferred activity. For example, seventh-grade students would have to complete the nine skill

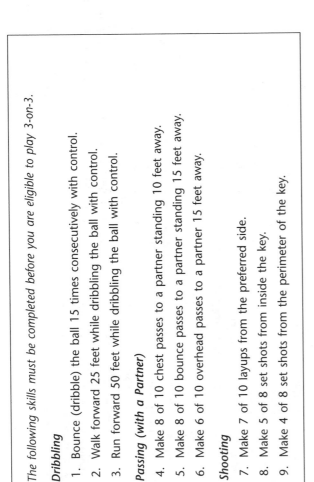

The following skills must be completed before you are eligible to play 3-on-3.

Dribbling

1. Bounce (dribble) the ball 15 times consecutively with control.
2. Walk forward 25 feet while dribbling the ball with control.
3. Run forward 50 feet while dribbling the ball with control.

Passing (with a Partner)

4. Make 8 of 10 chest passes to a partner standing 10 feet away.
5. Make 8 of 10 bounce passes to a partner standing 15 feet away.
6. Make 6 of 10 overhead passes to a partner 15 feet away.

Shooting

7. Make 7 of 10 layups from the preferred side.
8. Make 5 of 8 set shots from inside the key.
9. Make 4 of 8 set shots from the perimeter of the key.

FIGURE 7.2 Basketball skill objectives

objectives shown in Figure 7.2 before being allowed to participate in a three-on-three class tournament. The skill objectives demand practice and are less favorable activities, while the three-on-three tournament is the favorable activity.

It is best to select reinforcing activities that are related to the physical education class setting. In some situations, when student motivation and interest are low, teachers may choose to use reinforcements outside the physical education area. These might include enjoying free time, talking with peers, or going to a sporting event. Such rewards are harder to defend educationally but may be necessary in extreme situations.

Extrinsic Reinforcers—A Word of Caution. The question here is whether to use extrinsic reinforcers on a regular basis with students to shape their behavior. Consider the example where the physical education teacher gives points that lead to a special day of free activity. Students in this setting earn points when they wear the proper uniform, get to class on time, and behave properly. The strategy is to increase desirable behavior by offering a reward that is given when a specified number of points are earned. The theory is that students will choose to perform the desired behavior because they want to earn points and ultimately receive the reward. However, what if they find themselves in a setting where points are not assigned; they may be less motivated to behave in a desirable manner. It is quite possible that students will see little "payoff" in behaving properly because they do not receive any reward for their behavior. The result is that that their level of internal motivation and

self-discipline has been undermined. Evidence shows that overuse of extrinsic rewards can decrease a student's intrinsic motivation (Greene & Lepper, 1975; Whitehead & Corbin, 1991). In most cases, limit the use of extrinsic reinforcers to situations where social reinforcers are ineffective. As soon as possible, remove the extrinsic reinforcers so students are motivated to perform for the personal satisfaction of accomplishment. Nothing is more rewarding to most students than to accomplish a goal they didn't think possible. Education doesn't get any better than when students are motivated to perform for their own personal reasons—true intrinsic motivation.

Prompt Desired Behavior

Prompts are used to remind students to perform desired behavior. They encourage the development of new patterns of behavior. There are a number of ways to prompt students in the physical education setting. The most common are the following:

1. *Modeling.* You or another student performs the behavior desired, with the expectation that students respond in similar fashion. For example, placing your piece of equipment on the floor when stopping the class will remind the class to do likewise. Modeling is an effective prompt for desired behavior because students often emulate a teacher they respect.

2. *Verbal cues.* This is a common method of prompting and involves using words such as *hustle* and *keep going.* The purpose is to remind students of

desired behavior. Usually, verbal cues are used to maintain the pace of the lesson, increase the intensity of the performance, or motivate students to stay on task.

3. **Nonverbal cues.** Many physical cues are given through body language to communicate concepts such as "hustle," "quiet down," "move over here," "great performance," "quiet down," and so on. When you're teaching skills, nonverbal physical cues can prompt students by moving them into proper position, helping them through the correct pattern, or placing body parts in proper alignment.

Prompts should not be used to the point where students will not perform without them. The goal is to gradually remove the prompt so that behavior is self-motivated. This process is called *fading* and involves gradual removal of the prompt. It is likely you will use prompts at opportune times; however, the major purpose of prompting is to increase the occurrence of desired behavior. The weakest (least intrusive) prompt possible should be used to stimulate the behavior. For example, when students are not staying on task, one could give students a long lecture (longer than 30 seconds often becomes a lecture) about the importance of staying on task. However, this approach is time consuming and overreactionary. It is not suited to repetitive use and is ineffective in the long run. Select a cue that is short and concise and closely linked to the desired skill.

In addition to these points, be sure the prompt identifies the desired task. For example, if you prompt the class to "hustle" and it is not linked to the desired behavior, there may be confusion. Some students may think the prompt means to perform the skill as fast as possible; others may think they should stop what they are doing and hustle to the teacher. Link the prompt to the desired behavior in a consistent manner to ensure students clearly understand the meaning of your prompt.

Shape Desired Behavior

Shaping techniques can be used to build new and desired behavior. When desired behavior does not exist, shaping—which uses extinction and reinforcement—is used to create new behavior. Shaping tends to be slow and inefficient and is used only if prompting is not possible. Two principles form the foundation for shaping behavior.

1. *Differential reinforcement is used to increase the incidence of desired behavior.* Responses that reach a predetermined criterion are reinforced, while behaviors that do not meet the criterion are ignored (extinction). An example of this principle involves asking a class to put their equipment down quickly. You decide that students should put the equipment on the floor within 5 seconds. Using differential reinforcement, reinforce the students whenever they meet the 5-second criterion and ignore their performance when it takes longer than 5 seconds.

2. *The criterion that must be reached for reinforcement to occur is increased.* In this step, you gradually shift the criterion standard toward the desired goal. For example, if the desired behavior is for the class to become quiet within 5 seconds after a signal has been given, it might be necessary to start with a 12-second interval. Why the longer interval? In all likelihood, it is not reasonable to expect that an inattentive class will quiet down quickly. If a 5-second interval is selected initially, there is a strong possibility that you and your students will be frustrated by the lack of success. In addition, this stringent standard of behavior will not be achieved often, resulting in few opportunities to reinforce the class. The result is a situation in which both you and the class feel they have failed. To avoid this possibility of failure, gradually move toward the desired terminal behavior. In this case, start with 12 seconds until the class performs as desired. Next, shift to a 10-second interval and ask the class to perform to this new standard. The process is gradually repeated until the terminal behavior is reached.

DECREASE UNACCEPTABLE BEHAVIOR

Society is based on personal freedom hinged to self-discipline. Individuals have freedom as long as they do not encroach on the rights of others. In similar fashion, students can enjoy freedom as long as their behavior is consistent with educational objectives and does not prevent other students from learning. Discipline teaches students what behaviors are appropriate in the teaching-learning situation. Discipline is used when attempts to increase desirable behavior have failed.

Know Your Options for Dealing with Unacceptable Behavior

One of the more important things for a teacher to know is what options are available when students behave in an unacceptable manner. What is acceptable and unacceptable in dealing with a student who has misbehaved? A surprising issue for most beginning teachers is that there are many options for stopping student misbehavior. Check with administrators and fellow teachers to see what they use and/or accept for dealing with student misbehavior. Then decide the order in which those behavior response steps are to be administered. What follows are some general steps that most school districts allow when dealing with inappropriate behavior. Each of these steps is described in detail later. The first three steps assume you can get the student to work with you, and the last three steps are based on needing outside help to rectify the situation. It is always best to try and handle the discipline yourself because invoking parents or administrators and suspending students ultimately doesn't solve the problem between you and the student.

1. *Ignore or gently reprimand the behavior.* Minor behavior that doesn't seem to disrupt the class or harm anybody can often be ignored. If this works, maybe a look in the direction of the student will terminate the behavior. A word of caution about ignoring behavior is that sometimes a teacher can only ignore the behavior for so long before it gets the best of them. At that point, tempers flare and the teacher does something that actually reinforces the misbehaving student. Sometimes, if a teacher "goes off" on a youngster, that student will actually be sort of a folk hero outside of class. The caution here is to make sure you can ignore the behavior over the long haul.

Another method to use in this step is a quiet reprimand to "get back on task." It is a quiet warning that is delivered personally so it is not within earshot of other students. The purpose is to quietly remind a student to get back on task. It is always a good idea to try and get students to behave in acceptable ways by using the least forceful manner first. Many students will respond, and there will be little emotional cost for teacher or student.

2. *Give a time-out.* This step involves giving a quiet and personal warning and sending a student to time-out until he or she is ready to return and behave properly. The purpose of this step is to gently and quietly remind the student in an unobtrusive manner. This step is used for rather minor behavior that is not a serious issue and doesn't bother others. More on time-out is discussed later in the chapter.

3. *Remove from the activity.* This step occurs for behavior that occurred earlier but has not stopped as requested. The student is asked to leave class and sit on the side somewhat out of sight from the rest of the class. In this case, the student's behavior will not be discussed outside of class and remains an issue between the teacher and student. This step is

used when the behavior occurs a number of times or has escalated in seriousness.

4. *Make a phone call home.* This approach may be taken when the misbehavior occurs a number of times and the previous steps have not caused it to desist. Phoning parents or guardians at home is a step that must be carefully considered before it is done. Many parents do not want to hear about their student's misbehavior. They feel it is the school's responsibility to handle their youngster. This step could actually backfire depending on how the parents react. For example, maybe the parent severely punishes the youngster at home because the parent has been embarrassed. The punishment could range from long-term grounding to physical punishment. The result is that the student might blame his or her teacher for the punishment he or she received at home and take it out on the teacher. Behavior might actually get worse rather than better. Before calling parents, talk to administrators and other teachers to find out whether calling home will be an effective approach.

5. *Send the student to the principal.* This step must be thought about carefully before being invoked. Think of all the possibilities that might make this an ineffective approach. The principal may not want to discipline students or may start to believe that you are not capable of effectively dealing with students. In either case, when one of your students shows up at the office, the principal may have a brief discussion with the student but internally think you are the problem. Another problem with this approach is that administrators are not emotionally involved in the situation. The student's misbehavior may have upset you, but the administrator has not been a part of that emotion. The student is asked what he or she did wrong and states, "Nothing." Now where is the discussion going to lead? The principal realizes that the quickest way to get the student out of his or her office is to ask the student to behave in the future. The student verbally agrees (but may still feel negative toward the teacher) and returns to class—very little has been accomplished.

If this approach is going to work, the principal should be tipped off ahead of time about what is going on in class and what the misbehavior was. In most cases, the behavior has been going on for some time, and the teacher finally decides that he or she can't tolerate it any longer. Another approach is to call the office and tell the principal's secretary what has happened. This will help the principal get tuned in to the problem and will make it difficult for the student to say that "nothing" happened.

6. *Suspend or reassign the student.* Suspension from school is not possible in some states and/or school districts. This is a serious issue, and totally suspending a student may actually give a student who dislikes school exactly what he or she wants. A more effective approach is in-school suspension, which takes away all the free time the student has. The student usually is sent to a room where he or she has no friends and is asked to do his or her work without much input from others. Sometimes the student is sent to another nearby school for in-school suspension for a preestablished time frame. The purpose is to remove the student from his or her familiar environment that is filled with a number of reinforcers and issues that get in the way of learning. A student can also be reassigned to another teacher's class if there appears to be an obvious conflict with the teacher. These are serious approaches that can become complex because they involve the parents, other teachers, other school administrators, and the legal ramifications of the state. Hopefully, behavior is not allowed to escalate to this level and will be changed much earlier in the sequence of discipline alternatives.

Identify Acceptable and Unacceptable Behavior

An important step in behavior control is to decide exactly which behaviors are acceptable and which are unacceptable in the learning environment. These can be listed in a handout and discussed with students at the beginning of the year. The list should be posted in the locker room and in the gymnasium and sent to parents and administrators. How teachers react to student behavior plays a powerful role in managing student behavior and establishing a positive learning environment. There should be a personal plan in place for responding to different types of misbehavior. Determine specific student behaviors that will be praised, reprimanded, or ignored. Each teacher should develop a list of specific student behaviors and accompanying reactions. An instructor's list might look like this:

Praise	*Reprimand*	*Ignore*
Listening	Arguing	Talking out
Following directions	Embarrassing others	Raising a hand
Hustling	Interrupting others	Snapping fingers
Being on time	Going off task	Showing off
Dressing properly	Talking during instructions	Constantly asking questions

Negative student behavior is often reinforced by the teacher and the peer group. For example, assume a student misbehaves and the teacher publicly reprimands the student. The friends of the student will laugh at the situation. Unfortunately, peer laughter is reinforcing to this student, and the behavior occurs more often in the future. When an undesirable behavior is not seriously distracting, ignoring it and showing a positive reaction to a simultaneously occurring appropriate behavior is effective. If necessary, explain to the students that they also should ignore the student's inappropriate behavior. In this way, the misbehaving student does not receive attention from either the teacher or peers.

Use Behavior Correction Techniques

Behavior correction techniques can be used to decrease undesirable behavior after positive reinforcement has failed. Using positive reinforcement to increase desired behavior is done with the hope that it will replace negative behavior. A rule of thumb to follow before correcting behavior is to reinforce the desired behavior twice. For example, assume a student keeps talking while the other students are listening properly. Reinforce the students who are behaving correctly. Often, the misbehaving student will emulate those being reinforced in order to receive similar positive feedback. If not, the use of corrective feedback is warranted. Figure 7.3 is a checklist that outlines the points found in this discussion.

Corrective Feedback (Reprimands)

Corrective feedback should be clear and specific. Apply the correction as near to the misbehavior as possible. Just as positive reinforcement should be delivered immediately following the desired behavior, so should negative consequences. Negative consequences can be anything the student does not want or need as long as there is no violation of the rights or dignity of the student. Just as teachers need to know what reinforces students, they need to know what a negative experience is for students who misbehave.

Remind yourself that behavior correction is designed to teach students how to behave properly rather than to punish them. There should be no punitive measures involved. Focus on natural consequences that occur when students behave improperly. When students are disciplined, they can respond in a negative manner, causing class disruption. The following steps help prevent teacher-student conflict in front of the class.

Corrective Feedback Checklist

☐ Make a positive statement to the class.

☐ Use proximity—move to the area of deviancy.

☐ Get the entire class involved in a physical activity (preferably moving around the area or using a piece of equipment). The class should be unaware that a warning is being delivered.

☐ **Quietly, individually, and unemotionally** deliver the statement redirecting the student (warning).

— State the behavior that needs to change (the student is okay; it is the behavior that needs changing).

— State how to correct the behavior.

— Avoid **visual confrontation** with the student.

— Move away.

— **Never** touch the student.

☐ Say something positive to another student or to the class to help you refocus on the positive things going on in class.

☐ Give the student a chance to change the behavior.

— Go back to the student to positively reinforce progress toward the desired behavior.

— Remember that shaping the correct behavior will take time.

— Reinforce even small steps in the right direction.

FIGURE 7.3 Checklist for delivering corrective feedback

1. ***Do not reprimand the student publicly.*** Putting down a student in front of the class is never productive and can stir up resentment toward the teacher. Buy 10 to 20 seconds for talking with the student privately by assigning the class a task to perform. It may be as simple as quickly reengaging them in the activity they just completed. This keeps the class engaged while you quickly discuss the situation with the misbehaving student.

2. ***Isolate the student and yourself.*** Discipline a student where others can't hear what you are saying. The problem is a private matter between you and the student. Often, a couple of students may be misbehaving together. Separate them and deal with their behavior one on one.

3. ***Speak about the behavior, not the person.*** Ask that the behavior be stopped rather than telling a student, "You are always causing problems in this class." Avoid general and negative statements related to the personality of the student.

4. ***State your position once; repeat it once if you believe the student didn't understand.*** Don't argue or try to prove your point. Take no more than 10 to 15 seconds to tell the student what the unacceptable behavior was and what acceptable behavior is

that you would like to see. For example, "John, you were talking while I was talking; I need you to listen when I am explaining things." If you go on for more than 10 seconds or so, you start to lose control of the class, and it turns into a lecture rather than a correction.

5. ***Walk away after you have delivered the behavior you desire.*** Eyeballing students after you have reprimanded them is confrontational. To get yourself back on track, positively reinforce one or two other students.

6. ***Don't threaten or bully the student.*** These actions build resentment and may cause greater problems at a later time. Don't be sarcastic. Instead, state clearly what you desire from the student in terms of acceptable behavior.

7. ***Avoid touching the student when correcting behavior.*** Even if you have positive intentions, it can send mixed messages. Some students don't want to be touched and will aggressively pull away and make a scene in front of the class.

8. ***Reinforce acceptable behavior.*** Be vigilant in looking for the desired behavior because reinforcing such behavior will cause it to occur more often in the future.

Removal of Positive Consequences

This is a common approach used by parents, so many students are already familiar with it. The basic approach is to remove something positive from the student when misbehavior occurs. For example, students give up some of their free time because of misbehavior. They lose points related to a grade. They are not allowed to participate in an activity that is exciting to them. For removal of positive consequences to be effective, make sure students really want to participate in the removal activity. It wouldn't work to keep a student out of a game if the student didn't like the game. A few key principles should be followed when using this technique:

- Make sure the magnitude of the removal fits the crime. In other words, students who commit a minor infraction shouldn't have in-school suspension for a week.

- Be consistent in removal among all students and with the same students. Students believe teachers are unfair if they are more severe with one student than another. In addition, a student penalized for a specific misbehavior should receive the same penalty for a later repetition.

- Make sure students understand the consequences of their misbehaviors before the penalties are implemented. This avoids applying penalties in an emotional, unthinking manner. If students know what the consequences will be, they are making the choice to accept the consequences when they choose to misbehave.

- Regardless of the method used, if the behavior is not decreasing or is increasing, change methods until a decrease in frequency occurs.

- At times, it is helpful to chart a student's misbehavior to see if the frequency is decreasing.

Time-Out

In "time-out," students are removed from a positive (reinforcing) situation. It is similar to the penalty box in an ice hockey game. If a student is behaving inappropriately, he or she is asked privately to go to the time-out area. The area should be far enough away from the class to avoid the ridicule of peers but close enough to be within the supervision of the teacher. The area can be specifically designated in the gymnasium, or it can be an area in an outside field, such as under a tree, on a bench, or in a baseball dugout.

Being placed in time-out should communicate to students that they have disrupted the class and must be removed so that the rest of the class can participate

as desired. Students can also use the time-out area as a "cooling-off" spot so that they can move to voluntarily if they are angry, embarrassed, or frustrated. If students have been placed in the time-out area for fighting or arguing, they should be placed at opposite ends of the area so the behavior does not escalate. In addition, it can be mandated that they stay in their own half of the gymnasium until the next meeting of the class. This prevents the possibility of continued animosity.

Time-out does not stifle misbehavior if the student receives reinforcement for being there. Time-out means receiving no reinforcement. If class is a negative experience for students, taking them out of class is not a punishment and may be a reward. The class must be an enjoyable experience and be reinforcing to students. Too often, having a student sit out of class results in an experience that is reinforcing to him or her. For example, the student who is sent to the office gets to avoid activity while visiting with friends who come into the office. Notoriety can be achieved among peers for surviving the office experience and being able to tell others, "It doesn't matter one bit what that teacher does to me." Don't put students in time-out and then let them sit on the side of the gymnasium, watching peers participate. Being a spectator is more reinforcing than participating in class activities for some students. One of the ways to avoid this problem is to penalize students for nonparticipation (when they are in time-out). This means they will lose credit for that day, and it will impact the grade they earn in class. A set of consequences for unacceptable behavior might be as follows:

- *First misbehavior.* To avoid embarrassment, the student is warned quietly on a personal basis. This could be a peer or teacher warning. At times, students are not aware that they are bothering others, and a gentle reminder by a peer or teacher will refocus the student.

- *Second misbehavior.* The student is quietly asked to go to the time-out area until he or she is ready to participate properly. Some teachers ask students to stay for a specified amount of time or tell them to stay until they allow them to return. The problem with this approach is that the teacher will find it difficult to keep track of when each student entered time-out if there are a number of students involved. Also, the arbitrary approach of telling a student when they can reenter is often discriminatory. A student who is usually on task may be kept out for less time than a student who is a chronic offender. This means that there are different punishments for students who have misbehaved in a similar manner. Punishment should be equal for all students regardless of how you feel about the student.

■ *Third misbehavior.* The student goes to time-out for the remainder of the period and loses points for nonparticipation. If the behavior continues, the student will lose free-time privileges. Serving an in-school suspension is effective with chronic offenders. The in-school suspension time is served during the student's free time in a study hall atmosphere supervised by teachers on a rotating basis.

If these consequences are ineffective, the last alternative is to call the parents for a conference with the principal and teacher. Participating in educational endeavors is a privilege, and people who choose to disrupt society ultimately lose their privileges (e.g., incarceration in reform school, prison). The attempt must be to teach students that they are not bigger than the system—that rules and laws pertain to all people.

Implement a Behavior Change Plan

Changing behavior is possible but a slow process. Teachers want to change behavior quickly and on the spot, and at times, they make incorrect decisions because they don't have time to think out an effective solution. In-class misbehavior can be temporarily stopped, but it may often go unchanged for the future. Understand that change will require action that must be planned and repeated a number of times. The following steps can be used to develop a plan for changing behavior.

1. Identify a single behavior that needs to be changed, improved, or strengthened. Don't pick more than one behavior as it will make it much more difficult to monitor change and may decrease the student's chance for success.

2. Identify a behavior that will be substituted for the behavior to be modified.

3. Determine what positively reinforces the student. Have a discussion with the student to see what is reinforcing.

4. Decide whether a negative reinforcer (see the following section) is needed to give momentum to the change process.

5. Develop a plan for getting the desired behavior to occur (see Prompt and Shape Desired Behavior, pp. 163–164). This will generate a behavior that can be reinforced and used to replace the undesirable behavior.

6. Put the plan into effect and set a time frame for evaluation of the plan. Decide what modifications

are needed to make the plan more effective. This modification may demand a different set or schedule of reinforcers or negative consequences. If an entirely different plan is needed (because the behavior hasn't decreased or changed), make such changes and proceed.

7. Continue evaluating and modifying the plan.

Create Behavior Contracts

A behavior contract is a written statement specifying certain student behaviors that must occur in order to earn certain rewards or privileges. The student and teacher sign the contract that is generated after a private conference to decide on the appropriate behaviors and rewards. Letting the student make some decisions dealing with the contract is often useful.

The behavior contract may be a successful strategy for students with difficult behavior problems. Make every attempt to use rewards that occur naturally in physical education class (such as Frisbee play, jump rope games, aerobics, and basketball). In some cases, however, different types of rewards may have to be used. For example, a student who is interested only in rock music and motorcycles could be allowed to spend some time reading, writing about, or discussing one of these topics. As behavior improves, and the student's attitude becomes more positive, the rewards are switched to physical education activities. The contract is gradually phased out over a period of time as the student gains control of his or her behavior and demonstrates the ability to participate in normal class environments.

Contracts can be written for a small group of students or for an entire class with similar problems, but teachers must be careful about setting up a reward system for too many students. The system can become too complex or time consuming to supervise properly. The contract is best used with a limited number of students. An example of a behavior contract that can be used with an individual, a small group, or an entire class of students is shown in Figure 7.4.

DEAL WITH SEVERE MISBEHAVIOR

At times, corrective behavior techniques don't work. Many strategies may have been tried with a student with little success. At this time, teachers must go beyond their own resources. As a note of caution, all the previous techniques have assumed that a teacher is working individually to solve the problem. This is the first and best approach. It is easier to send the student to the office and ask someone else to solve the problem. Unfortunately, this does not solve the problem

Behavior Contract

	Points
I. Class Preparation	
A. Attendance	1
B. On time	1
C. Properly dressed	1
II. Social Behavior	
A. Showering	1
B. Lack of inappropriate behaviors	
Cursing	
Fighting	
Disrupting	5
	9 points per day
	(36 points per week)

During Friday's class, points may be exchanged for time in aerobics, weight training, Frisbee, or basketball.

I agree to these conditions.

Student _____

Teacher _____

FIGURE 7.4 Behavior contract

between the student and the teacher. Also, administrators may feel that the teacher is incapable of dealing effectively with students. The steps listed here assume that all other avenues have been tried and have failed.

Most secondary schools have some type of disciplinary referral form for severe problems. The form is used to keep an accurate record of behavioral problems and is a part of the communication process among students, teachers, parents, administrators, and counselors. The referral form is an effective tool for documenting student behavior. A disadvantage is that the approach is time consuming so some teachers are unwilling to use it. However, there are few shortcuts to a well-disciplined class. The following is a four-step approach for dealing with behavior that is difficult and continuous.

Step 1. Initiate an informal, private conference between the teacher and student, focusing on the behavioral aberration. An agreement should be reached regarding the consequences of future behavior.

Step 2. Check with other teachers and administrators to see if a telephone call to the parents will help the situation. As discussed earlier, it might not, depending on the situation. The nature of the call home should be to find solutions for the existing problem. The focus of the conversation should be to solicit help and advice rather than to denounce their youngster. If you alienate the parents, they may side with the student and make it even more difficult for you to deal with the student. During this discussion, ask the parents if they would like to participate in a conference with their youngster, the school counselor, and yourself.

Step 3. Schedule a conference with the teacher, parents (if they are willing), student, and principal or counselor to discuss the problem and develop a plan for changing the behavior. A written copy of the plan should be distributed to all people involved.

Step 4. If necessary, use severe disciplinary actions, such as these:

a. *Loss of privileges:* Privilege losses could include access to the cafeteria, clubs, athletics, or dances. Parents are notified in writing about the procedures used.

b. *In-school suspension:* Students are sent to a designated area with a supervisor who enforces strict rules and guidelines for school-work.

c. *Short- and long-term suspensions from school:* The student is suspended from school for 3 to 10 days, depending on the severity of the behavior and the student's history. Strict policies and procedures are arranged and followed carefully to ensure due process. Parents must be notified in writing as to the steps that have been followed.

d. *Expulsion:* The final step used in extremely severe instances is expulsion. The principal initiates the action with a letter to the student and parents. An official action from the Board of Education may be required to expel a student. Due process and appeal procedures must be used and made available to the student.

USE CRITICISM CAUTIOUSLY

Criticism must be used with caution and judgment. Criticism is often used with the belief that it will improve the performance of students. Scolding and criticism are often the behavior control tools of choice because they give the impression that the results are effective and immediate. Usually, misbehavior stops and you assume the situation has been rectified. Unfortunately, this is not always the case. Criticism and punishment lend a negative air to the instructional environment and have a negative impact on both students and teacher. The old saying "It hurts me more than you" is often the case. Many teachers feel uncomfortable when they must criticize or punish students. It makes them feel as though they cannot handle students and that the class is incorrigible. This feeling of incompetence leads to a destructive cycle where students feel negative about the instructor and the instructor feels negative about the class. In the long run, this is one of the most debilitating effects of criticism and punishment.

As mentioned earlier, another negative aspect of criticism is that it does not offer a solution. In a study by Thomas, Becker, and Armstrong (1968), a teacher was asked to stop praising a class. Off-task behavior increased from 8.7 percent to nearly 26 percent. When the teacher was asked to increase criticism from 5 times in 20 minutes to 16 times in 20 minutes, more off-task behavior was demonstrated. On some days, the percentage of off-task behavior increased to more than 50 percent. The point is that when attention is given to off-task behavior and no praise is offered for on-task accomplishment, off-task behavior increases dramatically. The criticism shows results (students respond to the request of the criticism), but students do not change. In fact, the students are reinforced (they receive attention from the teacher) for their off-task behavior. In addition, because their on-task behavior is not praised, it decreases. The net result is exactly the opposite of what is desired.

MAKE PUNISHMENT A LAST RESORT

A difficult question is whether punishment should be used in an educational setting. Punishment can have negative side effects because fear is the primary motivator. Consider the long-term need for punishment. If the long-term effects of using punishment are more beneficial than not using it, it is unethical not to use punishment. In other words, if a student is going to be in a worse situation because punishment was not used to deter self-destructive behavior, it is wrong not to use it. It may be necessary to punish a student for protection from self-inflicted harm (e.g., using a certain apparatus without supervision). Punishment may be needed to teach students not to hurt others. Punishment in these situations can cause discomfort to the teacher and student in the short run, but it may allow the student to participate successfully in society later.

Most situations in the educational setting do not require punishment because they are not as severe as those described previously. A major reason for avoiding punishment is that it can have undesirable side effects. When students are punished, they learn to avoid the source of punishment. It forces them to be more covert in their actions. They spend time finding ways to be devious without being caught. Instead of encouraging students to discuss problems with teachers and parents, punishment teaches them to avoid these individuals for fear of being punished. Another side effect is that it teaches students to be aggressive toward others. Students who have been physically or emotionally punished by parents act in similar fashion to others. The result is a student who is secretive and aggressive with others—certainly less-than-desirable traits. Finally, if punishment is used to stop certain behavior, as soon as the punishment stops, the behavior will return. Thus, little has been learned; the punishment has just led to short-term change.

If it is necessary to use punishment, remember the following points:

1. **Be consistent and make the "punishment fit the crime."** Students quickly lose respect for a teacher who treats others with favoritism. They view the teacher as unfair if punishment is extreme or unfair. Peers quickly side with the student who is treated unfairly, causing a class morale problem for the instructor.

2. *Offer a warning signal, as discussed previously.* This may prevent excessive use of punishment as students often behave after receiving a warning. In

addition, they probably view the teacher as caring and fair.

3. **Do not threaten students.** Offer only one warning. Threats have little impact on students and make them feel that you cannot handle the class. One warning gives students the feeling that you are not looking to punish them and are fair. Follow through; do not challenge or threaten students and then fail to deal with the behavior.

4. **Follow the misbehavior with the punishment as soon as possible.** It is much less effective and more often viewed as unfair when it is delayed.

5. **Punish softly and calmly.** Do not seek revenge or be vindictive. If responsible behavior is expected from students, make sure you reprimand and punish in a responsible manner. Studies (O'Leary & Becker, 1968) show that soft reprimands are more effective than loud ones.

In addition, try to avoid having negative feelings about a student and internalizing student misbehavior. Being punitive when handling deviant behavior destroys any chance for a worthwhile relationship. Misbehavior should be handled in a manner that contributes to the development of responsible, confident students who understand that people who function effectively in society must adjust to certain limits. Forget about past bouts of deviant behavior and approach the student in a positive fashion at the start of each class. If this is not done, students are labeled, making behavioral change more difficult. Students may also learn to live up to the teacher's negative expectations.

If punishment is used, make sure that only those students who misbehaved are punished. Punishing an entire class for the deviant behavior of a few students is unfair and may trigger undesirable side effects. Students become hostile toward those who caused the loss of privileges, and this peer hostility lowers the level of positive social interaction with the deviants.

KNOW THE LEGAL CONSIDERATIONS OF EXPULSION

If serious problems occur, discuss the problems with the classroom teacher and principal. Many times, deviant behavior is part of a larger, more severe problem that is troubling a student. A cooperative approach may provide an effective solution. A group meeting involving parents, classroom teacher, principal, counselor, and physical education specialist may open avenues that encourage understanding and increase productive behavior.

Legal concerns involving the student's rights in disciplinary areas are an essential consideration. While minor infractions may be handled routinely, expulsion and other substantial punishments can be imposed on students only after due process. The issue of student rights is complicated, and most school systems have established guidelines and procedures for dealing with students who have been removed from the class or school setting. Students should be removed from class only if they are disruptive to the point of interfering with the learning experiences of other students and if all other means of altering behavior have not worked. Sending a student out of class is a last resort and means that both teacher and student have failed.

STUDY STIMULATORS AND REVIEW QUESTIONS

1. Explain how effective class management and discipline are related.

2. Discuss how the teaching of management skills is similar to the teaching of physical skills.

3. What would be an appropriate strategy to use if students do not respond to a signal to stop?

4. Design a motivating strategy aimed at encouraging students to dress quickly and immediately enter the gym.

5. Briefly describe Hellison's hierarchy of responsible behavior.

6. Why should class rules be stated in more general terms?

7. List and explain the negative consequences of teacher comments that students interpret as preaching or threatening.

8. Briefly explain and give a practical teaching application of the Premack Principle.

9. List and explain two essential characteristics of effective praise.

10. Why should prompts be gradually faded out?

11. Provide three examples of the strategy called "removal of positive consequences."

12. Explain the negative consequences of using verbal criticism.

REFERENCES AND SUGGESTED READINGS

Bailey, B. A. (2001). *Conscious discipline.* Oviedo, FL: Loving Guidance, Inc.

Beane, A. (1999). *The bully free classroom.* Minneapolis: Free Spirit Publishing.

Canter, L., & Canter, M. (1997). *Assertive discipline: Positive behavior management for today's classroom.* Santa Monica, CA: Lee Canter and Associates.

Charles, C. M. (1989). *Building classroom discipline* (3rd ed.). New York: Longman.

Curwin, R. L., & Mendler, A. N. (1988). *Discipline with dignity.* Washington, DC: Association for Supervision and Curriculum Development.

Darst, P. W., & Whitehead, S. (1975). Developing a contingency management system for controlling student behavior. *Pennsylvania Journal of Physical Education and Recreation, 46*(3), 11–12.

Gordon, A., & Brown, K. W. (1996). *Guiding young students in a diverse society.* Boston: Allyn & Bacon.

Greene, D., & Lepper, M. R. (1975). Turning play into work: Effects of adult surveillance and extrinsic rewards on students' internal motivation. *Journal of Personality and Social Psychology, 31,* 479–486.

Hellison, D. (2003). *Teaching responsibility through physical activity* (2nd ed.). Champaign, IL: Human Kinetics Publishers.

Kounin, L. S. (1970). *Discipline and group management in classrooms.* New York: Holt, Rinehart & Winston.

McBride, R. (1992). Critical thinking—An overview with implications for physical education. *Journal of Teaching in Physical Education, 11,* 112–125.

Nelson, J. (1996). *Positive discipline.* New York: Ballantine.

O'Leary, K. D., & Becker, W. C. (1968). The effects of intensity of a teacher's reprimands on students' behavior. *Journal of School Psychology, 7,* 8–11.

Paese, P. (1982). Effects of interdependent group contingencies in a secondary physical education setting. *Journal of Teaching in Physical Education, 2*(1), 29–37.

Premack, D. (1965). Reinforcement theory. In D. Levine (Ed.), *Nebraska symposium on motivation.* Lincoln: University of Nebraska Press.

Siedentop, D., & Tannehill, D. (2000). *Developing teaching skills in physical education* (4th ed.). Mountain View, CA: Mayfield Publishing Co.

Thomas, D. R., Becker, W. C., & Armstrong, M. (1968). Production and elimination of disruptive classroom behavior by systematically varying teachers' behavior. *Journal of Applied Behavior Analysis, 1,* 35–45.

Whitehead, J. R., & Corbin, C. B. (1991). Effects of fitness test type, teacher, and gender on exercise intrinsic motivation and physical self-worth. *Journal of School Health, 61,* 11–16.

Wolfgang, C. H. (1996). *The three faces of discipline for the elementary school teacher.* Boston: Allyn & Bacon.

Xiang, P., McBride, R., & Guan, J. (2004). Children's motivation in elementary physical education: A longitudinal study. *Research Quarterly for Exercise and Sport, 75*(1),71–80.

WEB SITES

Classroom Management
www.glencoe.com/sec/teachingtoday/tiparchive.phtml/4
www.honorlevel.com/techniques.html
www.inclusiveeducation.ca

Discipline
www.disciplinehelp.com
www.pecentral.org/climate/disciplinelinks.html#classroombehaviormanagementsites

Management Styles
http://education.indiana.edu/cas/tt/v1i2/what.html

Responsibility Materials
www.teachinglearning.com/showCategory.php?category_id=10

ESSENTIAL COMPONENTS OF A QUALITY PROGRAM

COMPONENT 1 A quality physical education program is organized around content standards that offer direction and continuity to instruction and evaluation.

COMPONENT 2 A quality program is student centered and based on the developmental urges, characteristics, and interests of students.

COMPONENT 3 Quality physical education makes physical activity and motor-skill development the core of the program.

COMPONENT 4 Physical education programs teach management skills and self-discipline.

COMPONENT 5 Quality programs emphasize inclusion of all students.

COMPONENT 6 In a quality physical education setting, instruction focuses on the process of learning skills rather than the product or outcome of the skill performance.

COMPONENT 7 A quality physical education program teaches lifetime activities that students can use to promote their health and personal wellness.

COMPONENT 8 Quality physical education teaches cooperative and responsibility skills and helps students develop sensitivity to diversity and gender issues.

8

Teaching Styles

CHAPTER SUMMARY

The purpose of this chapter is to explore the variety of instructional styles that exist and how they can be used to enhance instruction. There is no one best style for all situations. Each style has advantages that will be effective depending on the type of students, specific activities, desired objectives, and various conditions.

The teaching styles covered in this chapter include the direct style, task (station) style, mastery learning style, individualized style, cooperative learning style, and inquiry style. Direct instruction, as a teaching style, is probably the most common approach used in the secondary schools. It can be effective depending on the learning outcomes to be accomplished and how it is implemented. The task style of instruction involves selecting and arranging tasks for students to practice in specific learning areas called *stations*. Students usually rotate through each learning area in small groups and work on the preselected tasks. The mastery learning style takes terminal target skills and divides them into progressive sub-skills. Individualized styles of teaching use learning packets, resource centers, and self-paced learning activities. Cooperative learning places students in groups with common goals. Students are interdependent in order to achieve group goals. The inquiry model of instruction focuses on the process of instruction rather than the product of instruction. Students are placed in situations where they have to inquire, speculate, reflect, analyze, and discover. Guided discovery is an inquiry style of instruction in which the teacher leads students to discover one planned solution to a given problem. Problem solving is another inquiry style. With this style, students are led to the discovery of multiple correct answers to a problem.

There is mounting evidence from teacher effectiveness research indicating that many teaching styles can be effective if certain characteristics are present in the teaching situation.

STUDENT OUTCOMES

After reading this chapter, you will be able to:

- Discuss the specific areas where an instructional style provides direction for the teacher.

- Explain in detail the characteristics of an effective educational environment as indicated by current teacher effectiveness research.

- Plan and teach an appropriate secondary school physical education lesson using each teaching style discussed.

- Describe the advantages and disadvantages of each teaching style.

- Give examples that illustrate when a particular teaching style should be used.

- Discuss the reasons why a physical education teacher should be able to use a variety of instructional strategies.

Different teaching styles and models have been used successfully in secondary school physical education classes (Mosston & Ashworth, 2002; Metzler, 2005; Rink, 2006; Buck, Lund, Harrison, & Blakemore, 2007; Siedentop & Tannehill, 2000). Professionals label and categorize styles in many ways. Many of the labels overlap and can be confusing to the beginning teacher. A teaching style is an instructional strategy used to organize the educational environment. Using a particular style of teaching provides direction for presenting information, organizing practice, providing feedback, keeping students engaged in appropriate behavior, and monitoring progress toward selected goals or objectives. Teaching styles are defined in terms of the teacher's approach during the lesson, and expected student learning outcomes.

There is no single "best" universal teaching style. Even though educators endorse their favorite approach, evidence does not suggest that one style is more effective than another. A repertoire of styles that can be used with different objectives, students, activities, facilities, and equipment is the mark of a master teacher. In addition, a teacher may decide to combine various styles during the course of one unit or even one lesson (see Sports Education Approach in Chapter 4, pp. 84–86). Making the most appropriate choice of teaching styles is a crucial decision that should be given much thought. The following variables have to be considered before an appropriate style can be selected:

- Specific student learning outcomes based upon state and district standards, as well as daily objectives of the lesson, such as physical skills, physical fitness, knowledge, and social behaviors.

- The nature of the activities involved, such as tennis, volleyball, swimming, or fencing.

- The nature of students, including individual characteristics, interests, developmental level, socioeconomic status, motivation, and background.

- The total number of students in the class.

- The equipment and facilities available, such as tennis racquets and courts.

- The abilities, skills, and comfort zone of the teacher.

Instructional effectiveness is enhanced by the selection and implementation of various teaching styles. Both teachers and students maintain interest and enthusiasm when a variety of styles is used. Too often, a favorite teaching style becomes the norm. Perhaps the use of a different teaching style in an appropriate setting would improve the learning environment for students and teachers. A new or modified teaching style is not a panacea for all the ills of every school environment or setting, and a teaching style is not selected without considering all variables. Different styles do, however, offer advantages in certain situations. A teacher who has developed a quality instructional program can keep the program exciting by implementing various teaching styles.

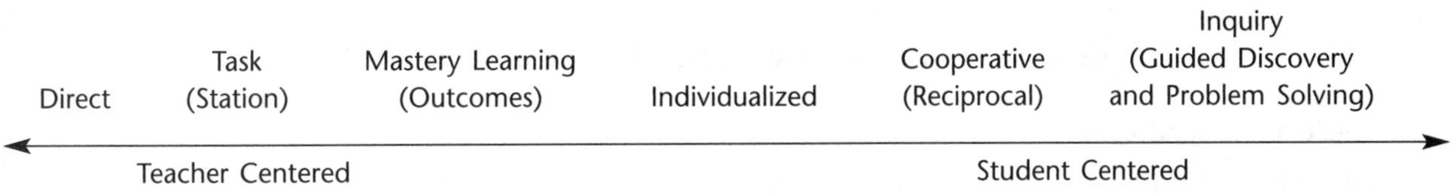

Direct	Task (Station)	Mastery Learning (Outcomes)	Individualized	Cooperative (Reciprocal)	Inquiry (Guided Discovery and Problem Solving)

Teacher Centered

Student Centered

FIGURE 8.1 Continuum of teaching styles

Teachers can use combinations of styles in a lesson or unit plan; they do not have to adopt just one style at a time. Mosston's continuum of teaching styles (Mosston & Ashworth, 2002) identifies a teacher-centered approach at one end of the spectrum and a student-centered approach at the other. A continuum of teaching styles based on the degree of teacher control exercised in a lesson is shown in Figure 8.1. Although the continuum appears to work in a linear direction, where the teacher controls learning at one end and the student at the other, each of the teaching styles is designed to enhance the learning of all students. A lesson using a particular teaching style or one that uses multiple styles must have student learning outcomes as its end product. It is best to remember that students are the key participants and recipients of each style.

DIRECT STYLE

The direct teaching style is sometimes looked upon with disfavor by some teachers because they identify it with Mosston and Ashworth's (2002) command style, in which all actions performed by students are commanded by a teacher signal or demonstration. However, the direct teaching style has more flexibility and variations than the command style. The direct style, like any other type of instruction, can be effective or ineffective depending on how it is used and administered. It is effective for teaching beginning levels of physical skills and fitness activities such as aerobic routines and martial arts. When activities present an inherent hazard or danger, such as fencing, archery, or rock climbing, instruction needs to be well organized and activities highly supervised. It is the teacher's responsibility to direct all learning outcomes and facilitate the timing and selection within each lesson. Students are given little freedom until they understand the hazards and demonstrate responsibility. The direct style may also be effective in situations where student discipline is a problem. Because the teacher controls student activities, this style offers greater control and class management. For a beginning teacher with new students, large classes, or high rates of inappropriate student behavior, the direct style is an excellent choice until he or she becomes more familiar with the classes.

When using this teaching style, the teacher provides instruction to either the entire class or small groups in the class. The teacher guides the pace and di-

rection of the class. Direct instruction is followed by guided practice so errors can be corrected. Guided practice is then followed by independent practice that is supervised by an actively involved teacher. Students spend most of class time engaged in appropriate subject matter. Specific learning outcomes are communicated to students, and much time is devoted to practice while the teacher actively supervises and provides frequent feedback. Even though instruction is direct, it should be conducted in a positive and supportive manner.

A common model of direct teaching begins with the teacher explaining and demonstrating skills to be developed. Students are organized into partners, small groups, or squads for practice. As students practice, the teacher moves around the area, correcting errors, praising, scolding, encouraging, and asking questions. On the signal to stop, students gather around the teacher for evaluative comments and a redirection toward another skill. The teacher serves as the major demonstrator, lecturer, motivator, organizer, disciplinarian, director, and error corrector.

The direct teaching style emphasizes instruction in a controlled class environment that ensures safety. Although the teacher is in direct control of the learning outcomes and pace of the activities, emphasis is placed on minimizing the amount of time students passively watch, listen to a lecture/demonstration, or wait in line. Learning for all students must be an impending result of the direct teaching style. Students need to be active, participate at a high level of success, and experience a variety of practice opportunities that support learning outcomes. Higher-skilled and lower-skilled students are hindered when learning activities are too easy and unchallenging or too difficult, resulting in repeated failure. Offer enough options to cover various ability levels. Direct instruction provides limited opportunities for student choice, social interaction, and self-pacing.

TASK (STATION) STYLE

Student skill levels differ widely in physical education classes. This range of ability must be addressed if students are to achieve a high level of success. In order to provide opportunities for success, the task or station style of teaching can provide students with challenging yet appropriate tasks. When teachers encounter large classes, the task style provides multiple activity areas and addresses the problem of minimal equipment and supplies.

Baseball or Softball Skill Station Task-style Worksheet

1. Fielding Ground Balls

a. One partner will roll or hit, and the other will field the ball. Switch after the allotted time. Distance will increase as the fielder becomes highly successful.

b. The hitting partner will also assess the fielder based on the critical elements listed below and use the cues to assist your partner.

Critical Elements:

a. Position feet so the body is centered toward the incoming ball.

b. Lower the hips to position the glove to the ground.

c. Focus the eyes on the ball and the throwing hand over the mitt and in position to trap the incoming ball.

d. Extend the arm with the mitt and follow (with your eyes) the ball into the mitt.

Cues for feedback:

a. Center the ball.

b. Keep hips down.

c. Watch the ball into your hand.

Partner Assessment:

1. Where were most of the mistakes made?

2. What area needs to improve?

3. What can you do to help your partner improve?

2. Leading Off and Stealing a Base

a. One player acts as the pitcher while the other takes a lead from first base. The base runner must "read" the pitcher in order to get a good start. The pitcher watches the runner to assess performance based on the critical elements listed below. Feedback is given using the specified cues. Switch positions after the allotted time.

Critical Elements:

a. Begin in a comfortable "ready" position with both feet a shoulder-width apart and both knees bent. Place hands out in front of the chest with the arms slightly bent.

b. First, swing the arms. Swing the left arm toward the desired base and pump back the right arm. Simultaneously plant the left foot and thrust the right foot forward.

c. Keep the body low and the knees bent while initiating the first explosive movements toward the base.

FIGURE 8.2   Example of a task-style worksheet used at baseball or softball skill stations

---

The task style of teaching focuses on arranging and presenting learning tasks at several learning areas or stations. Students rotate between learning stations to work on assigned tasks. At each station, students have a number of tasks to learn and practice. They work on the tasks without specific teacher directions. Moving students from one station to another can be signaled with preset time intervals controlled by the teacher or music. For example, students may be given 5 minutes to work at stations that have four or five predetermined tasks. A cue (music stopping) or signal (whistle, drumbeat) to rotate to a new station is given after time has elapsed. An option is to allow students to pace themselves and monitor their progress. Providing students with task sheets containing a series of activities and variations based on difficulty is a means for developing ownership of learning. Students complete the tasks selected and continue to another station.

There is more freedom with this style as compared to the direct approach because students work individually on the tasks. Student accountability and ownership of his or her learning can be developed through the task style.

Cues for Feedback:

a. Bend the knees; keep the feet wide

b. Explode toward the other base, out not up.

c. Drive forward using the arms.

Partner Assessment:

1. Were the knees bent?

2. Did your partner stay loose and in a ready position?

3. Did your partner swing his or her arms and stay low through the first steps of stealing (explode)?

4. Give suggestions for two specific areas.

3. **Throwing to a Target (second to first)**

a. Two players will practice throwing from a second base position to first base. Distance will be extended after five successfully completed throws.

b. A third player will begin the task by throwing a grounder from home plate to the second-base person, throwing to the first-base side. After five successful completions players will rotate from first base, to home plate, to second base.

Critical Elements:

a. Gather the ball as in the fielding task. Pivot and step with the nondominant foot toward the target, and aim at the desired target.

b. Extend the arm, releasing the ball.

c. After releasing the ball, follow through by allowing the arm to swing freely.

Cues for feedback:

a. Gather.

b. Step.

c. Extend.

d. Follow through.

Partner Assessment:

1. Did he or she step toward the target?

2. Was the throw on-line?

3. Did he or she follow through?

4. Where did most of the throws end up and why?

FIGURE 8.2 Continued

Work sheets, content development, and peer coaching can be integrated at each station (see Figure 8.2).

Some teachers are uncomfortable with the task style because there appears to be less order and control compared to direct instruction. Visually, the task style appears more chaotic because students are engaging in a variety of activities at the same time. With proper planning, organization, and supervision, however, teachers can effectively order and manage the environment. In fact, a well-organized lesson relieves the teacher of some organizational duties during in-class participation. The task style is motivating to students because of the variety and levels of learning tasks. Having multiple tasks representing low to high levels of challenges at each station provides opportunities for students to select activities that match their comfort zones. Junior and senior high students enjoy opportunities to select activities and demonstrate learning to themselves and others. Students are provided opportunities to be responsible for their learning. Students often need time to adjust to the increased freedom, flexibility, and opportunities to make decisions, but the end result is better self-management skills. The task style is flexible in terms of its use across the curriculum. This style can be used for aspects of skill development, fitness engagement, social interactions, and cognitive learning. The design, planning, and implementation of appropriate task stations are the only aspects that limit the use of this style.

This instructional style allows teachers to move off center stage and away from being the central figure in the instructional process because students assume more responsibility. Teachers become agents of feedback and facilitate learning by visiting various learning stations and interacting with students who need help with tasks. Predetermined cues become the focus of the feedback and interactions. Less time is spent directing and managing the entire group and more time is focused on learning. This approach does require preparation time for planning and designing tasks that meet the needs of all students. Tasks must be designed that provide all students with a high level of success and accountability. During the lesson, teachers may need to use strong supervision and active movement skills to facilitate on-task behavior and learning at all of the different stations. Teachers who stand in one spot or move in ways that keep them from

seeing all of their students may face tough managerial tasks. Adequate facilities, equipment, and instructional devices are necessary to keep students productive and working on appropriate tasks. Consider the following guidelines when selecting, writing, and presenting tasks for secondary school physical education classes:

• Select tasks that cover the basic skills of an activity.

• Select tasks that provide students with success and challenge. The tasks should be designed for the appropriate ability range of the students. The highest-skilled student should be challenged, and the lowest-skilled student should be successful.

• Avoid tasks that demand excessive risk and possible injury.

• Tape task cards on the wall, strap them to boundary cones, or place them on the floor if students can avoid stepping on them. Another alternative is to give students a copy of the tasks on a sheet of paper that they carry from station to station. The task

---

Basketball Tasks

Dribbling Tasks (*What to do*)
1. Standing—right and left hand—25 times
2. Half speed—right and left hand—baseline to midcourt
3. Full speed—right and left hand—baseline to midcourt
4. Around the cones—25 sec

Ball Handling (*What to do*)
1. Around head—left and right—5 times each
2. Around waist—left and right—5 times each
3. Around each leg—left and right—5 times each
4. Figure 8 around legs—10 times
5. Hand switch between legs—10 times
6. Bounce between legs and switch—10 times

Jump Shots (*What to do*)
1. 3 ft away—right angle, center, left angle
2. 9 ft away—right angle, center, left angle
3. 15 ft away—right angle, center, left angle
4. 20 ft away—right angle, center, left angle

Passing Skills (*What to do*)
Strike the target from 8 ft, 10 ft, 12 ft, 15 ft
1. Chest—10 times
2. Bounce—10 times
3. Overhead—10 times
4. One hand overhead (baseball)—10 times

Dribbling Cues (*How to do*)
1. Fingertips
2. Lower center of gravity
3. Opposite hand in front
4. Eyes on opponents

Jump-Shot Cues (*How to do*)
1. Straight-up jump
2. Wrist position
3. Elbow position
4. Slight backspin on ball
5. Follow-through

Passing Cues (*How to do*)
1. Use your peripheral vision—do not telegraph.
2. Step toward target.
3. Transfer your weight to the front foot.
4. Aim for the numbers.

FIGURE 8.3   Basketball tasks

Peer Feedback

Assessment:

Passer _____   Coach _____

Practice Task: Three people: 1 passer, 1 shooter, 1 coach

The passer will pass four balls from the top of the key, by using either a bounce pass or chest pass; the coach will provide the passer with feedback. Rotate roles after four passes.

Goal: Effective layups using the correct form

Layup

Essential Elements:
(Reverse for left-handed layup)

1. Carry the ball with the left hand in front and under the ball.
2. Place the right hand on top and slightly behind.
3. Carry the ball to shoulder and head height as the left foot pushes off.
4. Lift the body with the right knee.
5. Direct the ball to the backboard with the right hand.
6. Place the ball rather than throw it against the backboard.
7. Follow through with the palm of the right hand high in the direction of the backboard.

Cues:
- Scoop.
- Lift.
- Flick to target (square on backboard).

Things my partner did well:

Things for my partner to focus on to help improve the layup:

FIGURE 8.4   Peer assessment basketball layup

sheets can be maintained by students and taken home for practice after school.

- Write the tasks so they are easy to comprehend. Use keywords or phrases that students have learned previously. Effective task descriptions using both words and pictures explain what to do and how to do it (see the examples in Figure 8.3). Check to see if students understand the tasks and are able to practice unsupervised. In situations where there are reading or language barriers, pictures and/or symbols can clarify the tasks students are to perform.

- Incorporate a combination of instructional devices that add feedback, variety, and challenge to the environment. Examples of such devices include targets, cones, hoops, ropes, and stopwatches.

    Figure 8.3 shows a list of basketball tasks with descriptions of what to do and how to perform each task. Task lists can be printed on one or two cards at each station.

- Include individual and/or peer assessment sheets to increase accountability and student learning (Figure 8.4).

MASTERY LEARNING
OUTCOMES-BASED WORKSHEET

Hockey

Slap Shot Practice

- Work in pairs to develop skill (must receive the pass from your partner) once you know how to correctly perform a slap shot. Practice the slap shot, focusing on the cues and checking that the shot is being performed appropriately according to the cues listed below.

- Each performer must have mastery of the skill before he or she moves on to the higher-level assessments listed below.

- Each of you will take turns being the coach/teacher, and the performer will suggest to you when he or she is ready to move to the next level based on success rate of both the skill performance and the outcome of the performance.

- If he or she does not complete each level of the assessment at the minimum standard, he or she must stay with that level and continue to practice until criteria are successfully met.

Slap Shot Assessment (use spots to mark the appropriate distances)

- From 6 feet away, right angle, center, left angle, three out of four times, receive pass from partner, and shoot between cones.

- From 12 feet away, right, center, and left, four out of six times, receive pass from partner.

Cues: One hand high, one hand low, elbow at right angle (on take back), puck low and fast—extend to waist

FIGURE 8.5 Mastery learning outcomes-based worksheet

The task style of instruction can be used with a variety of grouping patterns. Students can work alone, with a partner, or in a small group. The partner or reciprocal pattern is useful with large classes, limited amounts of equipment, and with skills where a partner can time, count, record, or analyze the skill work. For example, one student can dribble through a set of cones while the other is timing and recording. In a group of three students, one student might bump a volleyball against the wall while another analyzes the form with a checklist and the third records the performance. The social aspect of being able to work on tasks with a partner or friend is a form of cooperative learning discussed later. Arrange tasks so students find success and challenge by offering a progressive arrangement of experiences, from simple to complex with small steps along the way. Allow students to progress at their own speed through the activities, challenging themselves by choice. As they build a backlog of success, learning activities become more challenging.

An effective instructional approach using learning stations for soccer follows. The soccer field practice area is arranged with four learning stations and learning outcomes written on a card at each station. Students spend 3 to 5 minutes working on the activities designed to achieve the outcomes at each station and

rotate to the next station. Station activities are arranged so students experience success quickly and frequently at first and then are challenged by later tasks. Student learning outcomes can be changed daily or repeated depending on the how the class progresses. Points earned through successful completion of the learning outcomes can be used to signal a degree of competency in the area.

MASTERY LEARNING (OUTCOMES-BASED) STYLE

Mastery learning is an instructional strategy that breaks down a complex skill (terminal outcome) into a series of smaller and progressive subskills. The assumption is that when the subskills are learned, the desired terminal outcome will be reached. Each of the subskills becomes the focus of learning. The subskills are usually written as objectives that must be mastered to achieve the target outcome. The continuum of subskills must be mastered at a high level of success (usually 80- to 90-percent correct) and contain all the critical elements, as determined by the cues, before students attempt more complicated tasks (see Figure 8.5).

	Yes	No	% Correct
Ready Position			
Hips to net	1 2 3 4 5 6 7 8 9 10	1 2 3 4 5 6 7 8 9 10	
Racquet between belly button and chest	1 2 3 4 5 6 7 8 9 10	1 2 3 4 5 6 7 8 9 10	
Medium body posture	1 2 3 4 5 6 7 8 9 10	1 2 3 4 5 6 7 8 9 10	
Execution			
Racquet taken back	1 2 3 4 5 6 7 8 9 10	1 2 3 4 5 6 7 8 9 10	
Feet to the ball	1 2 3 4 5 6 7 8 9 10	1 2 3 4 5 6 7 8 9 10	
Swing low to high	1 2 3 4 5 6 7 8 9 10	1 2 3 4 5 6 7 8 9 10	
Follow-through			
Finishes by shoulder	1 2 3 4 5 6 7 8 9 10	1 2 3 4 5 6 7 8 9 10	
Return to ready position	1 2 3 4 5 6 7 8 9 10	1 2 3 4 5 6 7 8 9 10	

FIGURE 8.6 Readiness checklist for performing a tennis forehand

The number of subskills depends on the complexity of the skill. If mastery is not achieved, corrective activities are offered so the student has the opportunity to learn from alternative materials, peer tutoring, or any type of learning activity that meets personal preferences. For an in-depth discussion of mastery learning, see Lawrence, Lawrence, and Samek (2006).

Mastery learning as an instructional strategy is useful in a number of ways. First, students move at an individualized pace and master preliminary skills needed for the desired learning outcome. The style is well suited for students who are low-skilled or have disabilities. It also provides homework, when necessary, enabling youngsters to work during their spare time on areas needing improvement. The process of the style can be outlined as follows:

1. The target skill or outcome is divided into sequenced, progressive units.

2. Prerequisite competency is evaluated.

3. Performance objectives for each of the successive learning units are established.

4. Informal progress testing can be done by the performer to determine readiness for more formal testing by the teacher or a peer (see Figure 8.6).

5. When a student has determined his or her readiness, testing by the teacher determines pass or fail for a particular subskill. A student who passes the task moves up to the next student learning outcome.

6. If the student is unable to pass the particular subskill, practice continues, incorporating alternative or corrective measures designed by both the teacher and student.

A mastery learning breakdown for soccer skills follows. The target outcome is soccer proficiency and the ability to play soccer. Accomplishing the outcomes ensures that students have a basic level of competency in dribbling, trapping, kicking, heading, and making throw-ins.

Dribbling Tasks

1. Dribble the soccer ball under control a distance of 20 yards three consecutive times, keeping the ball within 5 feet of your feet each foot touch.

2. Dribble the soccer ball under control through an obstacle course of six pylons over a distance of 30 yards in 25 seconds or less.

3. With a partner, pass the soccer ball back and forth five times while in a running motion for a distance

of 50 yards two consecutive times. Maintain control by keeping the ball between your knee and the ground and using no more than three foot touches before you pass.

Trapping Tasks

4. When the ball is rolled to you by a partner 10 yards away, trap it four of five times, using the instep method with the right and then the left foot, and use no more than two foot touches to control the ball.

5. With a partner tossing the ball, trap four of five shots using the chest method.

Kicking Tasks

6. Kick the ball to a partner who is standing 10 yards away five consecutive times with a push pass using the right and left side of the foot; the ball should remain below the knee on each pass, which should occur after trapping and controlling the ball from your partner.

7. Repeat task 6 using the instep kick. Loft the ball to your partner; the ball should be above the knee as it travels.

8. Kick four of five shots that enter the goal in the air from a distance of 20 yards using an instep kick from both the right, left, and middle of the goal.

Heading and Throw-In Tasks

9. From a partner toss, head three consecutive balls in the air at a height of at least 10 feet in a soft arch.

10. Beginning with a partner toss, head six consecutive balls back and forth with a partner, resulting in a soft arch to the ball.

11. Make four of five throw-ins from out-of-bounds into a hula hoop placed 15 yards away; keep your back foot on the ground.

Designing Mastery Learning Units of Instruction

The first step in designing any type of mastery learning unit is deciding what is to be learned. This procedure is called content analysis (Siedentop & Tannehill, 2000). Content analysis is a technique for determining all aspects important to student learning outcomes. There are two types of content analysis. First, there is *procedural analysis*. This is simply creating a list of all the subskills that must be performed for an event to be considered successful. Students can work on these subskills in any particular order, and the order of the subskills does not have an impact on a student's ability to complete the overall task. This can be thought of as a "to do" list without priority for any of the components on the list. A procedural analysis of a social dance unit might look like the following:

1. Procedure for asking a partner to dance
   a. Hello, my name is _____. May I have this dance?

2. Procedure for accepting an invitation to dance
   a. Thank you. My name is _____, and I would like to have this dance with you.

3. Escorting dance partners to and from the dance floor
   a. Asking
   b. Extending/accepting elbow
   c. Bow and curtsy

4. Dance steps
   a. Fox-trot
   b. Waltz
   c. Swing
   d. Tango
   e. Cha-cha

5. Participating in a social dance
   a. Filling out a dance card

Although this list looks like it follows a progression, none of the tasks are relevant to learning the next one, and students can learn and work on any task independent of the others. In contrast to this approach is another type of content analysis called *hierarchical analysis*. In this type of analysis, teachers produce a sequential chain of events that define a particular skill or event. Many times this type of analysis is used in describing the learning components of a physical skill because the components must be learned in the proper order. A hierarchical analysis of spiking a volleyball might look like the following:

1. Preliminary movements
   a. Knees bent and feet slightly staggered
   b. Eyes tracking ball from setter
   c. Beginning movements starting from 8-10 feet behind the net
   d. Body aligned with ball so no adjustments need to be made in air

2. Backswing/recovery
   a. Directional step with opposite foot is taken to ball
   b. Hitting side foot is swung even with guidance foot

c. Body is gathered to jump with bent knees

d. Arms start in front and are swung to behind body in extended position

3. Force producing movements

a. Heels are planted and jump is generated off of both feet, straight up, with extension of hips, knees, and ankles

b. Arms are swung forward and extended upward

c. Striking arm is cocked with elbow higher than shoulder

d. Elbow is extended, and wrist is flexed to contact ball downward

4. Critical instant

a. Contact of ball occurs between heel and lower palm of hand

b. Ball is contacted slightly above center

c. Contact with ball is slightly above head in front of contact shoulder

d. Contact with fingers is over the top of ball

5. Follow-through

a. Contact arm moves through the ball from the shoulder

b. Wrist snaps after contact, and arm continues to opposite hip

c. Player lands on toes with feet a shoulder-width apart

d. Knees bend to absorb impact and maintain balance

This list provides teachers and students with a learning progression that is ordered and followed for optimal learning. Performing these types of analyses on all aspects of the curriculum is crucial for matching student learning outcomes with students' developmental levels for optimal student success. Teachers have the autonomy to decide what their definition of success is and which subskills students must master. The challenge is to determine how the subskills must be performed in order to reach the student learning outcomes based on an appropriate match between subskill and student developmental levels. It is a good idea to review references to determine how it should be done if you are unsure or lack sufficient knowledge about certain aspects of the curriculum.

Another way to use mastery learning is to develop units of instruction. Such instructional units have been used successfully in secondary schools for many activities, including badminton, volleyball, soccer, tennis, racquetball, aquatics, and gymnastics. Middle and high school students are gradually given opportunities to make decisions and control their practice behaviors. This type of instruction is effective with physical activities that require the development of individual skills (e.g., volleyball passes, forehands, backhands).

The following steps define the process for developing instructional units for mastery learning:

1. Define the specific tasks or behaviors in observable, measurable terms (e.g., volleyball passes, badminton clears, tennis serves, and soccer kicks, rather than vague, hypothetical terms such as positive attitudes, physical fitness, or self-concept).

2. Clearly specify the final learning outcomes for the end of the unit. Knowing the specific final goal will increase student motivation. Final goals, such as perform 10 consecutive forearm passes, serve three of four into a target area using either underhand or overhand serves, or successfully kick three of four goals from a minimum of 20 feet, can serve as personal challenges for students. Adding more authentic outcomes, such as two successful forearm passes during game play, is a way to add realism to the goals.

3. Develop a monitoring and measuring system. This enables students to see daily improvement and set goals that progress toward the final, terminal objective. Skill rubrics provide a clear understanding of how skills will be assessed and when mastery is achieved (Figure 8.7). In addition to teacher assessment, peer assessment and self-assessment should be encouraged.

4. Develop meaningful learning outcomes that consider the various parameters of successful performance. These include speed, strength, endurance, accuracy, and consistency. For example, volleyball serves require a combination of speed and accuracy. An objective should include both parameters. For example, have students hit serves between the net and a rope strung 10 feet higher than the net. The serves must land inbounds and 10 feet or less from the back line. This ensures both speed and accuracy. Many other physical skills, such as dribbling in soccer, pitching in baseball, or dribbling in basketball, require similar combinations. Combinations can also be developed in similar sequences as those performed in game play.

5. Arrange performances in a progressive sequence so students can experience success quickly and frequently. As students build a backlog of success, the tasks will become more difficult and challenging.

Figure 8.8 is a volleyball mastery learning unit that is appropriate for high school students. The core objectives are required, but students can choose from optional objectives. Figure 8.9 on page 188 is a flag

Features Levels of Learning	Control	Foot Contact	Visual Focus	Balance
Exceeding	Always contacts the ball so that it stays within 3–4 feet of self.	Always appropriately uses the inside and outside of both right and left feet.	Always watches opponents with the head looking up.	The body is in balance with a smooth flow to the dribbling pattern.
Accomplished	Most often contacts the ball so that it stays within 3–4 feet of self.	Often uses both inside and outside of feet. Often uses both right and left feet.	Often watches opponents with the head looking up. Looks at feet occasionally.	The body is most often in balance. The dribbling pattern is sometimes uneven.
Developing	Sometimes contacts the ball so that it stays within 3–4 feet of self.	Sometimes uses both inside and outside of feet. Sometimes uses both right and left feet.	Sometimes looks up at opponents. Looks at feet often.	The body is sometimes in balance. The dribbling pattern is very uneven.
Emerging	Rarely contacts the ball so that it stays within 3–4 feet of self.	Rarely uses both inside and outside of feet. Rarely uses both right and left feet.	Rarely looks up at opponents. Looks at feet most of the time.	The body is out of balance most of the time. The dribbling does not have a pattern.

FIGURE 8.7 Skill rubric for soccer dribbling, a personal and/or peer assessment
(Printed with permission from Joleen Bailey, City University of New York, Cortland.)

football unit that can be used with middle school students. It follows the same format as the volleyball unit, with core and optional performance objectives.

In Chapters 19 through 21, a number of mastery learning units are provided. The units are general units, and objectives can be modified depending on the particular situation. They may be too difficult for certain students and too easy for others. It is important that all students find success and challenge with some of the objectives. Another excellent source for units is the lesson plan book by Casten (2009) that accompanies this text.

Performance objectives that are listed focus primarily on physical skills rather than on cognitive activities. Teachers may want a specific combination of cognitive and physical skills to be built into the unit. For example, the unit could provide a balance of learning outcomes related to teamwork, participation, phys-

ical skills, and cognitive activities. The mastery learning style allows teachers and students the flexibility of choice and allows opportunities to select activities that match students' developmental level.

Using Mastery Learning Units of Instruction

When using mastery learning units, students need to understand the learning outcomes, performance activities, and the importance of self-direction. Units are given to students so they can explain them to their parents, work on the objectives at home in their free time, or keep records of their performance at school. Students have to respect how involvement in this strategy is different from other instructional strategies. Some students take longer to adapt and become comfortable with this

Volleyball

Core Objectives

Forearm Pass (Bump)

1. Bump 12 consecutive forearm passes against the wall at a height of at least 10 ft.
2. Bump 12 consecutive forearm passes into the air at a height of at least 10 ft.
3. Bump 10 consecutive forearm passes over the net with the instructor or a classmate.

Overhead Set Pass

4. Hit 15 consecutive set passes against the wall at a height of at least 10 ft.
5. Hit 15 consecutive set passes into the air at a height of at least 10 ft.
6. Hit 12 consecutive set passes over the net with the instructor or a classmate.

Serves

7. Hit 3 consecutive underhand serves into the right half of the court.
8. Hit 3 of 4 underhand serves into the left half of the court.
9. Hit 3 consecutive overhand serves inbounds.

Attendance and Participation

10. Be dressed and ready to participate at 8 a.m.
11. Participate in 15 games.
12. Score 90% or better on a rules, strategies, and techniques test (2 attempts only).

Optional Objectives

1. Standing 2 ft from the back line, bump 3 of 5 forearm passes into an 8-ft circle surrounding the setter's position. The height must be at least 10 ft, and the ball must be thrown by the instructor or a classmate.
2. Bump 3 of 5 forearm passes over the net at a height of at least 12 ft that land inbounds and not more than 8 ft from the backline.
3. Standing in the setter's position, hit 3 consecutive overhead sets at least 10-ft high that land in a 5-ft circle where the spiker would be located. The ball will be thrown by the instructor or a classmate.
4. Hit 3 of 5 overhead passes over the net at least 12-ft high that land inbounds and not more than 8 ft from the backline.
5. Standing in the setter's position, hit 3 of 5 back sets at least 10-ft high that land in a 5-ft circle where the spiker would be located. The ball will be thrown by the instructor or a classmate.
6. Volley 12 consecutive times over the net with the instructor or a classmate by alternating forearm passes and overhead passes.
7. Alternate forearm passes and overhead passes in the air at a height of 10 ft or more for 12 consecutive times.
8. Spike 3 of 4 sets inbounds from an on-hand position (3-step approach, jump, extended arm, hand contact).
9. Spike 3 of 5 sets inbounds from an off-hand position.
10. Recover 3 consecutive balls from the net. Recoveries must be playable (8-ft high in the playing area).
11. Hit 3 consecutive overhand serves into the right half of the court.
12. Hit 3 of 4 overhand serves into the left half of the court.
13. Hit 3 of 5 overhand serves under a rope 15-ft high that land in the back half of the court.
14. Officiate at least 3 games, using proper calls and signals.
15. Coach a team for the class tournament. Plan strategy, substitution, and scheduling.
16. Devise and carry out a research project that deals with volleyball. Check with the instructor for ideas.

FIGURE 8.8 Volleyball mastery learning example

instructional format. Students have not had much experience controlling the pace of their learning, and it is important to be actively engaged in the learning process by monitoring student progress, developing personal and peer assessments, facilitating the pace of the learning experience, and designing activities that demonstrate student progress toward selected learning outcomes. Explain and demonstrate expected outcomes to students in the learning areas where they will be practicing. Introduce various instructional devices and targets. Arrange

Flag Football

Core Objectives

Passing Tasks

1. Throw 10 passes to the chest area of a partner standing 10 yd away.
2. Throw 3 of 4 consecutive passes beyond a target distance of 20 yd.
3. Throwing 5 passes, knock over 3 targets from a distance of 10 yd.
4. Throw 4 of 6 passes through a tire from a distance of 10 yd.

Centering Tasks

5. With a partner 5 yd away, execute 10 over-the-head snaps to the chest area, using correct holding, proper rotation, and follow-through techniques.
6. Facing the opposite direction from a partner, 5 yd away, execute a proper center stance with feet well spread and toes pointed straight ahead, knees bent, and two hands on the ball. Snap the ball back through the legs for 10 consecutive times.
7. Perform task 6 but move back 10 yd.
8. Center snap 4 of 6 times through a tire a distance of 5 yd away.

Punting Tasks

9. With a partner centering the ball, from a distance of 10 yd away, punt the football using proper technique to another set of partners 15 yd away 3 consecutive times.
10. Perform task 9 but at a distance of 20 yd.
11. Punt the ball 3 consecutive times within the boundary lines of the field and beyond a distance of 20 yd.
12. Punt the ball 3 consecutive times for a hang time of 2.5 sec or better (use stopwatch).

Catching Tasks

13. With a partner, run a "quick" pass pattern and catch the ball 2 of 3 times (5–7-yd pattern).
14. With a partner, run a 10–15-yd "down and in" pass pattern and catch the ball 2 of 3 times.
15. With a partner, run a 10–15-yd "down and out" pass pattern and catch the ball 2 of 3 times.
16. With a partner, run a 5–7-yd "hook" pattern and catch the ball 2 of 3 times.

Attendance and Participation

1. Be ready to participate in football activities 5 min after the last bell rings each day.
2. Use proper locker-room behavior (will be discussed or posted) at all times.
3. Score at least 90% on a written test (2 attempts only).

Optional Objectives

1. Attend two football games (flag or regular) during the grading period.
2. Throw 3 of 4 passes through a tire from a distance of 10 yd.
3. Throw 3 of 4 passes through a tire from a distance of 15 yd.
4. Throw 3 of 4 passes through a moving tire from a distance of 10 yd.
5. Throw 3 of 4 passes through a moving tire from a distance of 15 yd.
6. Catch 2 passes in a game.
7. Intercept a pass in a game.
8. Write a 1-page report on a fiction or nonfiction book related to the topic of football.

FIGURE 8.9 Flag football mastery learning example

the gymnasium or playing field with learning areas for specific objectives, such as the dribbling area, passing area, shooting area, or ball-handling area.

A rotational scheme can be incorporated using small groups placed at learning stations. Depending on class size, multiple stations supporting the same learning outcomes may be needed to prevent overcrowding and allow students continued control of their learning and practice pace. An alternative is to allow students to

rotate to any learning area they need to practice. A variety of grouping patterns (individual, partners, or small groups) can be used depending on available facilities, equipment, objectives, and student choice. Consider the amount of freedom, flexibility, and choice students can handle and yet be productive. It is best to start with small amounts of freedom and then gradually increase choices and options as students get used to self-selection and monitoring their learning.

Performance Objectives: Beginning Racquetball

Name _____

Instructor Checked	Class Member Checked	
		1. Stand approximately 6 ft from the back wall and in the center of the court. Bounce the ball against the sidewall and hit 3 of 4 shots below the white line with a forehand shot.
		2. Perform objective 1 but hit 3 of 5 balls with the backhand shot.
		3. Hit 3 of 5 power serves that land within 2 ft of the sidewall and are otherwise legal.
		4. Hit 3 of 4 lob serves within approximately 3 ft of the sidewall that do not bounce out from the back wall more than 8 ft.
		5. Stand approximately 6 ft from the back wall, bounce the ball against the back wall, and hit 3 of 4 shots below the white line on the front wall with a forehand shot.
		6. Perform objective 5 but hit 3 of 5 balls with the backhand shot.
		7. Hit 3 of 4 diagonal or "Z" serves that hit the front, side, floor, and opposite side, in that order. (The ball may hit but need not hit the back wall for the serve to be effective.)
		8. Hit 3 of 4 Scotch serves or "Scotch toss" serves that hit the front, side, floor, back, and side, in that order. This is similar to the "Z" serve in execution, except that the ball hits the back wall after bouncing on the floor.
		9. Return 3 of 4 serves hit to you by the instructor. (One of each of the following will be used: power, lob, diagonal, and Scotch.)
		10. Execute 3 of 4 attempts at "3-hit drill." (Instructor will explain in detail.)
		11. Execute 3 of 4 attempts at "4-hit drill." (Instructor will explain.)
		12. Hit 3 of 5 ceiling shots with a forehand shot. The ball will be thrown or hit by instructor and must be returned to the ceiling, front wall, and floor, in that order.

Note: Entry into ladder tournament is contingent on completion of any 8 of the 12 objectives. To receive a grade of A for the class, you must exhibit proficiency in all 12 objectives.

Objectives 1–8 may be checked by a class member; however, the instructor may spot-check any objectives at his or her discretion.

Objectives 9–12 will be checked by instructor. Performance objectives may be tested in courts 1 and 4.

FIGURE 8.10 Performance objectives for racquetball

Successful completion of learning outcomes can be monitored by the teacher, peers, or individually. If class size is small and the number of outcomes is small, the teacher may be able to do all of the monitoring. Otherwise, a combination of procedures is recommended. Student involvement in the monitoring process enhances their understanding of learning ex-pectations and increases their level of personal responsibility. Students can use a performance chart to monitor learning outcomes at each practice station or carry a master list from station to station. Another approach is to develop a performance sheet for each student that combines teacher and peer monitoring (Figure 8.10). Peers monitor easy-to-interpret outcomes, while the teacher monitors more difficult ones. A third method allows students to privately monitor their progress in attaining specified learning outcomes (Figure 8.11). Teachers can experiment with several monitoring approaches depending on the activity, the number of learning outcomes, the students' abilities, the size of the class, and the available equipment and facilities.

INDIVIDUALIZED STYLE

Learning packages that incorporate a learning laboratory-resource center are used in the individualized style. An example of a learning center is shown in Figure 8.12. The individualized style is based on student-centered learning through an individualized curriculum. Students select the level of proficiency they want to pursue and proceed at their desired rate of learning. Learning packets with objectives, study guides, learning activities, and assessment procedures are developed as independent study guides. Students work independently on objectives, view videotapes and slides, work on computer software, look at overhead materials, read books and articles, and prepare for the assessment procedure. Assessment usually progresses from self to peers and finally to the teacher. This approach requires that teachers develop learning materials and procedures for supervising the distribution and return of those materials.

The individualized style of teaching follows five basic steps:

1. **Diagnosis.** Preassessment is done to determine the student's current level of cognitive knowledge and psychomotor skill.

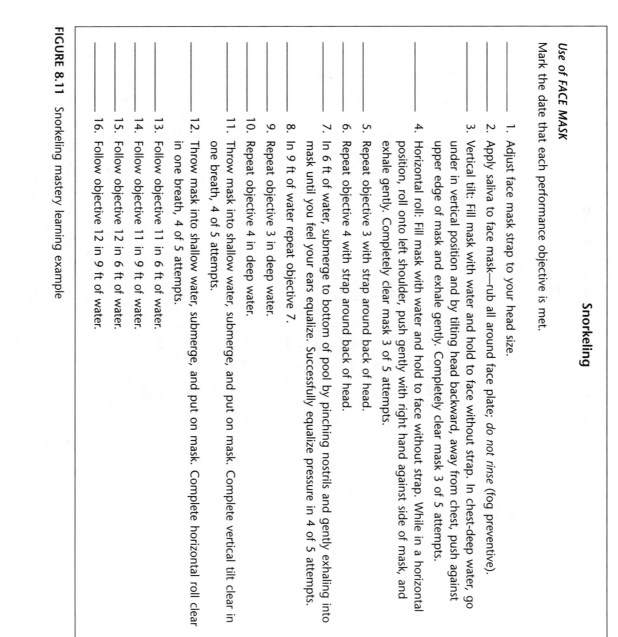

Snorkeling

Use of FACE MASK

Mark the date that each performance objective is met.

_____ 1. Adjust face mask strap to your head size.

_____ 2. Apply saliva to face mask—rub all around face plate; *do not rinse* (fog preventive).

_____ 3. Vertical tilt: Fill mask with water and hold to face without strap. In chest-deep water, go under in vertical position and by tilting head backward, away from chest, push against upper edge of mask and exhale gently. Completely clear mask 3 of 5 attempts.

_____ 4. Horizontal roll: Fill mask with water and hold to face without strap. While in a horizontal position, roll onto left shoulder, push gently with right hand against side of mask, and exhale gently. Completely clear mask 3 of 5 attempts.

_____ 5. Repeat objective 3 with strap around back of head.

_____ 6. Repeat objective 4 with strap around back of head.

_____ 7. In 6 ft of water, submerge to bottom of pool by pinching nostrils and gently exhaling into mask until you feel your ears equalize. Successfully equalize pressure in 4 of 5 attempts.

_____ 8. In 9 ft of water repeat objective 7.

_____ 9. Repeat objective 3 in deep water.

_____ 10. Repeat objective 4 in deep water.

_____ 11. Throw mask into shallow water, submerge, and put on mask. Complete vertical tilt clear in one breath, 4 of 5 attempts.

_____ 12. Throw mask into shallow water, submerge, and put on mask. Complete horizontal roll clear in one breath, 4 of 5 attempts.

_____ 13. Follow objective 11 in 6 ft of water.

_____ 14. Follow objective 11 in 9 ft of water.

_____ 15. Follow objective 12 in 6 ft of water.

_____ 16. Follow objective 12 in 9 ft of water.

FIGURE 8.11 Snorkeling mastery learning example

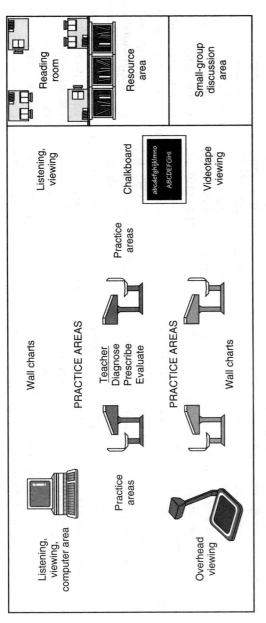

FIGURE 8.12 Organization of a learning center

From R. P. Pangrazi, *Dynamic Physical Education for Elementary School Children* (13th ed., p. 44). Copyright © 2001 by Allyn & Bacon. Reprinted with permission.

2. **Prescription.** Individual students begin at a level related to their performance on the initial assessment.

3. **Development.** All students receive a learning package that guides them toward successful completion of the predetermined criterion level. Students proceed to the next learning level after completing a level.

4. **Evaluation.** Each student receives a final evaluation by a peer or the teacher after completing the steps in the learning package. Evaluation includes both cognitive and psychomotor skills.

5. **Reinforcement.** As students complete the learning packages, accomplishments are recorded. New packages are prescribed, and teaching is given for key points of the material.

Individualized instruction offers the following advantages:

- Students, parents, and administrators know exactly what is expected and accomplished by students.

- Self-direction enhances the motivational level of most students.

- Students at most competency levels find success and challenge with objectives.

- Students progress through the learning outcomes at their own rate.

- Students can choose and sequence learning activities.

- Students have some choice concerning the grouping arrangement of skill practice (e.g., alone, with a partner, or in a small group).

- Students accept a large degree of responsibility for learning.

- Teachers have more freedom to give individual attention and offer feedback.

Problems to be solved when using the individualized approach include the following:

- Performance outcomes are time consuming to write and require constant revision.

- A monitoring and assessment system needs to be developed that does not take up too much class time.

- Instructional devices are necessary to provide variety and feedback. These increase the setup and takedown time of each class for the teacher.

- Many teachers and students need time to get used to the contract format. Students and teachers are often more comfortable with the direct approach. Changing to an individualized format will require time for adjustment.

COOPERATIVE LEARNING STYLE

Cooperative learning places students in groups to work together toward common goals using problem-based learning (PBL). Through cooperative learning activities, individuals achieve outcomes that are beneficial in solving predetermined problems through group interaction and participation. Student work is arranged so there is interdependence in the achievement of group goals but also an accountability procedure for all individual members of the group (Johnson, Johnson, & Holubec, 1990). When cooperative strategies are used appropriately in diverse settings, students usually develop a better understanding of how their peers' skill levels differ from their own. Social gains can develop in the areas of communication, compromise, and acceptance of diverse ideas. Learning outcomes are achieved through group interactions including participation through different roles, such as performer, observer, recorder, or evaluator. Physical educators can impact students in a positive way in the social, cognitive, and psychomotor areas by using cooperative learning formats.

Teachers who want to foster constructive relationships among students and improve skills and knowledge use cooperative learning strategies. Emphasis is placed on group outcomes rather than on individual outcomes. Students are placed in groups or teams and are given an opportunity to work together to solve problems in a team approach. Groups are usually heterogeneous (i.e., containing a mix of skill level, knowledge, socioeconomic level, race, and gender). Small teams with two to five students participate in an effort to successfully complete the goal. The focus is on working together with peers rather than competing against them and hoping they fail. Students learn that the problems cannot be solved without the cooperation of their peers. All members of the group must reach established goals. Success occurs when teams have completed their assignments through cooperation and participation of all team members. The content to be learned and the social interaction criteria expected within each team are developed by the teacher prior to student implementation. Selected content allows students to develop and apply appropriate and successful solutions through application and refinement (trial and error). Problem-based learning provides opportunities for members of each team to creatively develop, select, and implement a variety of strategies for solving each problem.

The following roles can be assigned to group members:

- A performer who does the skills or tasks.
- A recorder who keeps track of statistics, trials, or key points made by the group.
- A coach who provides feedback to the performer or times practice trials.
- A presenter who communicates key points to the class.
- A motivator who encourages and provides positive feedback to all group members.

Students should switch roles often, and stated group tasks should be organized so they proceed from

simple to complex. Observe and facilitate team member participation so all members contribute. Selected content activities require the knowledge and effort of all members of the group. While each member may contribute based on his or her personal strengths and abilities, if one student is allowed to dominate and direct the team, other members may feel their contributions are not necessary to complete the task. Make it clear that all members of the team are needed, even if in varying amounts of involvement. Students can be provided with personal and team assessments that highlight expectations while a team member is attaining the selected tasks (Figure 8.13), and they can convey these expectations to team members and provide the teacher with levels of contribution made by each team member. Cooperative learning tasks can include cognitive or psychomotor skills.

The following are examples of class activities that can be used with the cooperative learning style:

- Make teams responsible for developing a warm-up or physical fitness routine appropriate for a specific sport (e.g. soccer, water polo). Each member of the team can focus on a different component of fitness as he or she addresses each sport or activity (e.g., upper body flexibility, abdominal strength, cardiovascular efficiency, upper body strength, or lower back flexibility).

- Ask each member of a team to be responsible for teaching others a skill that is a part of a sport unit and a specific offense or defense. For example, in basketball, team members teach dribbling, passing, free throws, layups, rebounding, setting a pick, using a give-and-go, or playing defensive rebounding position.

- In a dance unit, have teams develop a dance that includes a variety of dance steps or skills. Each member of the team is responsible for incorporating the specific skills into the routine. Ask each dance team to teach other teams their routines.

- Set up a class tournament in a sport unit such as volleyball. Each team is responsible for some aspect of the tournament, such as creating tournament brackets, producing media guides, training and assessing scorekeepers and game officials, reporting each team's statistics, announcing game play-by-plays, and analyzing team strategy for offense or defense. Switch roles on a regular basis.

- In a tumbling or gymnastics unit, assign students to develop a small group stunt or routine and then teach another team the same stunt. Another example is to have an "expert" from each team get together with "experts" from other teams for a

Using a check mark, rate the following expectations based on your involvement today.

	Always	Sometimes	Never
Listened when others offered ideas			
Accepted others' ideas without disagreement or questioning			
Congratulated team members' efforts			
My teammates would agree I was a team player			
Give examples(s) that support why you rated yourself as you did for each category			

FIGURE 8.13 Team member expectations—A self-evaluation

short clinic on a particular stunt. These experts then return to their teams and teach the stunt.

- Have team members modify or redesign a sport or activity to make it more inclusive or success oriented. The goal is to allow more participation and success for all team members. Using a larger ball, more bounces, a lower net, and a larger goal are examples of game modifications.

- Have teams work with a study sheet that focuses on three to five key elements of a skill, such as serving in volleyball or tennis. Teams design several drills that emphasize each of the key points of the skill. Examples of student roles are drill planner, director of the drill, coach for the skill points, and recorder of the attempts and successful trials.

The learning process is enhanced when team members depend on their peers for both individual and team success. Students can develop many of the behaviors and leadership skills needed to create a positive learning environment. Cooperative learning also reflects the social behaviors and patterns expected of individuals in the working environment. As students learn to problem solve as a member of a team, they can develop an appreciation for the benefits of shared successes. The old adage "two heads are better than one" reflects the added knowledge potential available to solve a task.

Reciprocal Teaching Style

Mosston and Ashworth (2002) describe a similar style they label *reciprocal*. Reciprocal teaching is a form of cooperative learning because several students are in-

volved with different roles, such as a doer, retriever, and observer. The primary difference between the two styles is that in reciprocal teaching, it is not crucial that all students walk away with the same learned outcomes. Students have more freedom to work at their own level and receive appropriate feedback on their performance rather than on a group performance. Figures 8.14 and 8.15 are examples of reciprocal style sheets that can be used with badminton and soccer. The doers are the performers, and the observers are watching and providing feedback to the doers. The retriever is returning the balls for more trials. The tosser is helping with the setup of the drill.

INQUIRY STYLE

The inquiry style is process oriented, rather than product oriented. A student's experience during the process is considered more important than the final outcome or solution. Students experience learning situations that require them to inquire, speculate, reflect, analyze, and discover. They are cognitively active in this type of instruction. The teacher guides and directs students, rather than commanding or telling. Students discover their own answers and solutions.

The teacher is responsible for stimulating student curiosity about the subject matter. A combination of questions, problems, examples, and learning activities leads students toward one or more final solutions. This is called the "ask, don't tell, principle." The steps follow a sequence and are arranged logically so students can move from one step to the next after a certain amount of thinking. The steps should not be too large or small to prevent students from becoming frustrated or bored. The instructional environment is one of

Name _____   Style   B   Ⓒ   D

Class _____

Date _____

Partner _____

Badminton—forehand overhead clear

To the students: This task is performed in groups of three: doer, tosser, and observer.

The tosser: Throw a high, clear service to the doer.

The doer: Practice the forehand overhead clear 10 times.

The observer: Analyze the doer's form by comparing the performance to the criteria listed below. Offer feedback about what is done well and what needs to be corrected.

Rotate roles after each inning of 10.

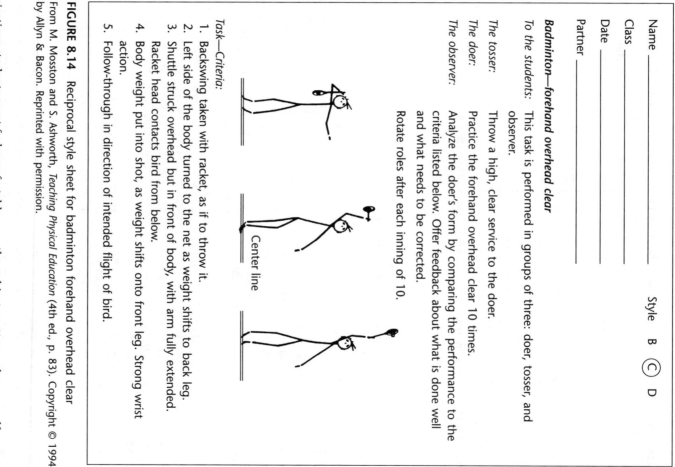

Center line

Task—Criteria:

1. Backswing taken with racket, as if to throw it.
2. Left side of the body turned to the net as weight shifts to back leg.
3. Shuttle struck overhead but in front of body, with arm fully extended. Racket head contacts bird from below.
4. Body weight put into shot, as weight shifts onto front leg. Strong wrist action.
5. Follow-through in direction of intended flight of bird.

FIGURE 8.14   Reciprocal style sheet for badminton forehand overhead clear

open communication; students must feel comfortable experimenting and inquiring without fear of failure.

Some educators believe inquiry methods of instruction should play a more prominent role in educational methodology (Mosston & Ashworth, 2002). They posit that students need opportunities to inquire, solve problems, and discover, instead of primarily experiencing approaches that emphasize listening, absorbing, and complying. Arguments have been made to expand the focus of physical education methodology to include the inquiry style. Proponents of this style believe that it enhances students' ability to think, improves creativity, creates a better understanding of

the subject matter, enhances self-concept, and develops lifelong learning patterns. Students develop ownership of the answers and solutions. Students who actively engage in solving the problem are more likely to remember at a later date. Some educators argue that students who do not experience inquiry methods may become dormant, unchallenged, and unused.

Inquiry is used when students have a basic understanding of the game. Teachers can use this style to help students understand when to apply certain skills. What to do when they don't have the ball, the best place to be to receive a pass, and how to split the defense are just a few examples that teachers can use to

Style B Ⓒ D

Name _____

Class _____

Date _____

Partner _____

Soccer—long throw-in

Work in groups of three—doer, retriever, and observer. Doer executes the task 10 times to a distance of approximately 15 yards. The retriever returns the ball, while the observer offers feedback to the doer by comparing the performance to the criteria listed below.

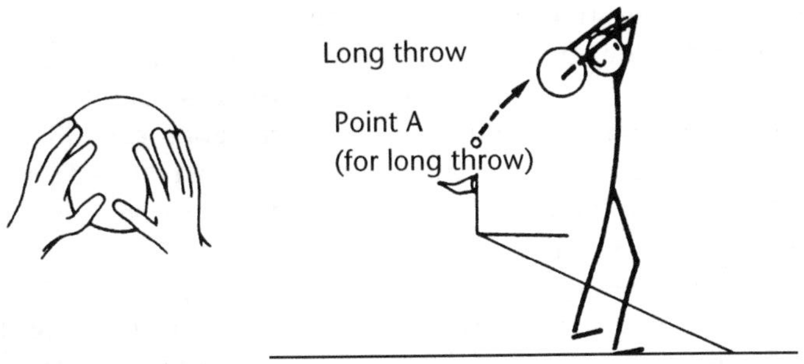

Long throw

Point A
(for long throw)

Criteria:

1. Both hands are used as ball is swung to point A behind the head.
2. Player takes one or two quick steps forward to gain momentum.
3. Body is bent backward, with a slight bend at the knees.
4. A whipping action of the body and a forceful straightening of legs develops thrust.

Note: Both feet must stay on the ground until ball is released, and it must be thrown in the direction the thrower is facing.

FIGURE 8.15 Reciprocal style sheet for soccer long throw-in

From M. Mosston and S. Ashworth, *Teaching Physical Education* (4th ed., p. 95). Copyright © 1994 by Allyn & Bacon. Reprinted with permission.

develop areas of critical thinking necessary to be successful in game play. If students do not have basic understanding and application of motor skills, the inquiry style may not be successful.

Once they acquire these skills, however, inquiry helps foster higher-level thinking skills such as application, integration, refinement, and other examples of critical thinking. Application and best practice can frequently be discovered using inquiry related to problem solving. Most beginning teachers are practiced in telling students information rather than fostering critical thinking. It is a complex skill that needs time and training to develop and should be considered when choosing these styles. Depending on the situation, these methods offer advantages when learning about cognitive issues. The inquiry style offers teachers another teaching tool in their repertoire of skills.

Guided Discovery (Convergent)

The inquiry style in physical education is generally characterized by two approaches: guided discovery (or convergent) and problem solving (or divergent) (Mosston & Ashworth, 2002). Teachers using guided discovery lead students through a series of preplanned tasks in order to guide students toward a specific solution (convergent) or an effective solution (divergent). Activities are designed so that students reach the answer desired by the teacher. Guided discovery can be used to help students discover knowledge about some of the following:

- Court coverage strategies that prevent scoring in tennis, badminton, racquetball, and handball.

- Effective angles of release for distance throwing with the shot put, discus, football, and softball.

- Batting stance and foot pattern alterations for hitting the baseball or softball to the open space in various fields or through the gaps in the infield.

- Specific offensive strategies for scoring in the key depending on the defenders and the type of defense.

- Dribbling techniques in soccer used to fake out a defender and move the ball upfield.

- When to use a give-and-go in certain situations to advance the ball in a game of team handball.

- The role of a person's center of gravity and momentum in performing activities in gymnastics such as the balance beam or the side horse.

It is possible to arrange the learning environment for these activities in many different ways. Give students an activity that asks them to solve a problem, ask a series of questions, and then have students participate in several learning activities based on their answers. After allowing students to practice using their solutions and strategies, hold a brief discussion to see if they have grasped the application of the strategies. The following are examples of learning activities:

In basketball, students analyze and determine the best offensive solution when a defender is playing tight defense. Often, the best solution is to fake a shot and then drive to the basket. If the defender is playing off them, the offensive player should shoot the ball. Students should have the opportunity to practice defense playing tight and off the ball, as well as the opportunity to reverse roles and play offense. This gives them a chance to discover different solutions.

In soccer, students can experiment with long and short passes with defenders in certain positions. Long, high passes are necessary to get the ball over a defender, whereas quick, short passes that stay on the ground are necessary to keep the defender from intercepting the ball, and they are easier for a teammate to receive and trap.

In the shot-put and discus throws, students might experiment with various release angles to see how they affect the flight and distance of the throws. The objective is to discover the best angle of release for maximum distance.

Problem-Solving (Divergent) Style

The second inquiry style involves a divergent approach, rather than converging on one solution. Students move through a series of experiences and attempt to devise as many acceptable solutions to the problem as possible. Many times, these activities are posed in terms of a student challenge where teachers give students an opportunity to solve problems or activities in different ways. Assessment of learning takes place through demonstration. Encourage students to be creative and develop unique solutions while analyzing the pros and cons of each solution. This style is useful for discussions and assignments dealing with values, social issues, wellness concepts, and controversial topics related to sport and physical education. Honesty in sports, cooperation with teammates, competition, violence in sports, amateur versus professional sports, athletes taking drugs to improve performance, arguing with officials, women participating in sports, and masculine and feminine roles are examples of topics that can be researched, explored, discussed, and debated in a physical education class.

Wellness is an area that lends itself to the problem-solving approach. Many different approaches and methods can be used for maintaining good health. Students can learn to solve their personal fitness problems with physical activity programs that are personalized to meet their needs. Problem-solving approaches are also useful in resolving the issues of proper diet and weight control. Stress reduction, alcohol and drug abuse, and tobacco use are areas that can be addressed effectively with problem-solving techniques.

When using this style, the teacher is responsible for creating an open environment where students are encouraged to explore all aspects of these controversial topics. Books, articles, movies, interviews, questions, and discussions are possibilities for accumulating and sharing information. Students are encouraged to gather information and weigh all alternatives before making a decision. The teacher's opinion does not carry more weight or emphasis than student opinion. An effective strategy for starting the problem solving involves using a "trigger story." The following are example of stories you could read aloud to students to prompt discussion:

- You and your partner are involved in a tightly contested golf match with another pair of students. Your partner hits his drive into the woods. While you are getting ready for your second shot, you turn and see your partner kick his ball out of the woods into an area where there is a clear shot to the green. His kick was not visible to either of your opponents. What would you do in this situation?

- You are playing on a Pop Warner football team. During the game, you make an aggressive, yet legal tackle on your opponent's best running back. The running back receives a leg injury as a result and has to be carried off the field. Your teammates cheer and praise you for injuring the star player. Your coach also praises you when you come off the field. What should you do?

TEACHING STYLES AND STUDENT LEARNING

Remember that these styles were developed as a means to produce student learning. Sometimes teachers lose sight of why things are taught in a certain manner, and the information about all of the different teaching styles becomes confusing. Sometimes a style is used based on constraints such as space and equipment, but in reality this decision still is made because it uses these items in order to produce an environment that is better suited for learning. Ultimately, that is why we choose certain styles over others. Teachers are encouraged to remember the following when it comes to teaching styles and student learning:

• One style does not cover all situations. All styles offer various strengths and obstacles in a physical education setting. The list for choosing a style (p. 176) should be regularly reviewed in order to ensure that the correct style is being used for the situation.

• A combination of styles can be an effective way to reach more students. When choosing a teaching style, one does not need to choose just one and design the entire lesson's experiences around it. By using different styles for different parts of a lesson or unit, it may be possible to provide better learning opportunities for students.

• Student diversity is an issue that faces every teacher, and the use of various teaching styles may appeal to a diverse group of students. Student diversity occurs in ethnicity, socioeconomics, language, gender, ability, or learning styles, to name a few. With this amount of diversity, one teacher may not be able to meet the demands of all students. Allowing for different teaching styles where students take on some of the instructional roles may allow diversity issues to be met. Certain styles are better suited for different learning styles, language skills, and so on. By using a variety of styles, there is a greater chance of reaching more students.

• The abilities of the teacher should be considered when choosing a style. Many times teachers choose a style because literature states that it would be effective in a specific situation. If it works for the teacher, that is the style of choice. However, if the teacher feels uncomfortable, the lesson will suffer regardless of the style used. It is best to use each style in small amounts until there is a comfort level that shows students you are confident and comfortable. This might be the most crucial decision you make with regard to teaching styles.

• At a bicycle motocross race, you hear the father of a 5-year-old criticizing his daughter for losing the championship race. The daughter is crying. You hear the father say to the mother, "She has to learn to compete. That's what life's all about." How do you react?

• You are coaching a freshman volleyball team. The game is close, and everyone is excited. The mother of a member of your team is being obnoxious. She yells mean things at players on both teams, at the coaches, and at the officials. During a time-out, the referee comes over and says, "Can't you do something about her?" What would you do?

• Your team is warming up when the referee walks in. Everybody recognizes him. He refereed your last game that you lost because he called a foul every time you moved. A member of your team says loudly, "Not him again!" What would you say?

• Right after the fourth game of the season, which your team just lost by four points, you are walking out of the locker room when you hear a parent say to a player on your team, "Boy, did you embarrass me tonight. You were terrible!" How would you react in this situation?

The problem-solving approach is also useful when physical skills can be performed or developed in more than one way. Teachers can allow students to experiment briefly with these skills to determine which approach is most effective for them. In this example, an individualized style and a divergent style would work nicely in combination. In many case, a skill can be adapted for certain situations. Some examples are the batting stance in baseball, golf grips and swing, putting grip and stroke, starts for sprints, high-jumping technique, and training methods for distance running. A problem-solving style can also be used to develop routines for gymnastics, including many different ways to correctly perform on pieces of apparatus. Students can experiment with many ways to mount the equipment, make various turns or swings, travel across the equipment, and perform various dismounts. In team sports, have students design several offenses that work against a particular defense and several defenses that will work against a specific offensive strategy. In basketball, a defender can experiment with options against a taller or quicker player. Students can also determine their options against opponents in various individual sports. In racquetball, there are several serves that can be used to counter an opponent's strong forehand or extreme quickness. If a lob serve does not work, maybe a power serve or a Z-serve will be more effective.

A Tactical Framework

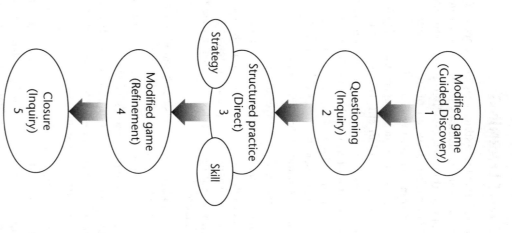

FIGURE 8.16 Tactical framework using multiple teaching styles

A FRAMEWORK FOR USING MULTIPLE TEACHING STYLES

Adolescent students should be moving from teacher-dependent learning toward independent learning styles. Providing students with multiple opportunities to create an understanding of how to be successful in physical movement can support progress toward such independence. Multiple teaching styles encourage students to make decisions and problem-solve. In *Teaching Games for Understanding* (TGFU), authors Griffin and Butler (2005) and later Mitchell, Oslin, and Griffin (2006) developed a student-centered approach to learning game play. This framework builds upon the use of a modified game approach using guided discovery and inquiry styles to develop tactical understanding and skill development. Within this framework,

teachers are encouraged to be facilitators of learning and focus activities using a discovery-based approach. Each step of the framework is shown in Figure 8.16.

Step one of the framework is the application of a modified game in which students play and discover the solution to a task that allows the best strategy to surface. The solution could be understanding specific skills or using a specific strategy. An example of a modified game of 3-on-3 basketball would be how to score multiple times from inside the basketball key and below the last hash mark. Each game is developed with specific rule modifications that help focus students' play toward discovering the correct solution (as predetermined by the teacher). Using this problem, the rules state that players may not dribble the basketball, all passes must be either a chest or bounce pass, players may not hold the ball for more than 3 seconds, all shots must be made inside the key and below the last hash mark (block), and defense cannot "reach in."

Step two of the framework is then completed after students have had an opportunity to play the game (step 1). Questions are used to guide the students toward the correct responses. For instance, a teacher may ask students: "How was your team able to score from inside of the key?"; "What did you do to try and get the ball if you didn't have the ball?"; "How did you help your teammates get the ball?"; or "What was the best way to shoot the ball from inside the key?" Focusing on a specific skill should lead students to identify that a basketball layup is the most effective shot to use from inside the key. If the teacher's goal was to focus on a specific strategy, the questions would lead students toward identifying setting screens or a give-and-go.

Once students have a clear understanding of which skill or strategy allows for successful accomplishment of the problem defined in step 1, students move on to practice either the skill or strategy in a game-like situation (step 3). For instance, if the solution was to get team players open, then practice would focus on the give-and-go. Each team would select one side of the basket, one player would be placed at the top of the key with the ball, one player would be on the wing, and the third member would be a defender on the point player only (levels of defense start from a shadow level to competitive as players improve). The point passes the ball to the wing and then cuts to the basket to receive the ball and attempt a layup (with no dribble). Key phrases such as *scoop, lift,* and *flick* can be used to focus on the layup technique. If the focus is the give-and-go, phrases can include *fake, cut,* and *target hand.*

Active engagement is the key to learning and refining a task. Step 4 has players returning to a modified game to re-apply the skill or strategy after practice. By

The Framework

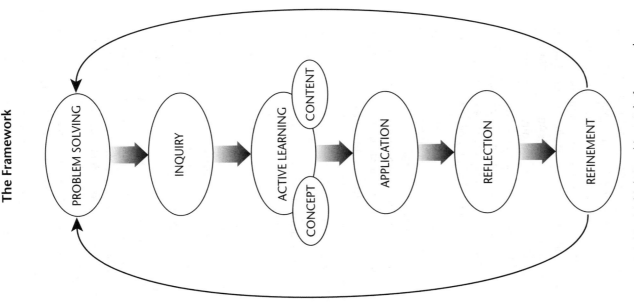

FIGURE 8.17 Multiple teaching style framework

playing the game after practice, students should have a better understanding of which skill to use, when to use it, and why. During closure, teachers can use inquiry to affirm that students understood and were able to apply the solutions they developed and practiced.

Students are actively engaged in this multiple-stage process that applies multiple teaching styles (see Figure 8.17).

Steps 1 and 2 (Figure 8.16) apply forms of guided discovery-based learning (divergent and convergent), while steps 3 (direct instruction) and 4 (application and integration of what was learned in step 3) engage learners in understanding and refinement of skills and/or strategies through active learning. Students can apply previously learned skills and knowledge to solve the problem designed for step 1. Students are actively engaged in each stage, and the teacher facilitates student learning. This is an excellent example of how teachers "ask and don't tell" and illustrates instructional practices that are indirect. Students are able to understand why certain skills and strategies are used in certain situations, and the new content, skills, and knowledge have meaning. Applying multiple teaching styles within a specific framework based on TGFU can enhance students' long-term understanding and retention.

DYNAMIC INSTRUCTION: ELEMENTS COMMON TO ALL STYLES

Regardless of the teaching style used, an effective learning environment can be identified by a set of instructional behaviors that occur regularly. These behaviors do not describe a specific method or style and provide significant room for individual approaches to teaching content. The focus is less on what the teacher does and more on what students are doing. For example, any style of teaching that produces high rates of student engagement and positive attitudes toward the subject matter is considered an effective learning environment. Evidence from teacher effectiveness research (Siedentop & Tannehill, 2000) indicates that regardless of the teacher's instructional style, an educational environment is most effective when the following elements are present:

- Students are engaged in appropriate learning activities for a large percentage of class time. Effective teachers use class time wisely. Little time is wasted on noninstructional activities such as taking attendance, dressing, checking lunch tickets, or taking yearbook photos. Teachers plan carefully and insist on appropriate learning activities that deal with the subject matter. Students need time to learn; effective teachers make sure that students use class time to receive information and practice

skills. Learning activities are matched to students' abilities and contribute to overall class objectives.

- The learning atmosphere is success oriented, with a positive, caring climate. Evidence clearly shows that teachers who develop a positive and supportive atmosphere are more effective in terms of student learning and student attitudes toward school. The old idea of creating a harsh, negative, "tough guy" climate has proven not to be the best way to foster learning and positive attitudes toward physical activity. Appropriate social and organizational behavior needs to be supported by teachers. Students and

- teachers should feel positive about working and learning in the physical education environment.

- Students are given clear objectives and receive high rates of information feedback from the teacher and the environment. Students need to know what they are going to be held accountable for in the physical education class. Class activities should be arranged so students spend large amounts of time on the required objectives. Activities should be meaningful, with a clear tie to the class objectives. Positive and corrective feedback should be available from the teacher. The environment is designed so students can receive feedback on learning attempts even when the teacher is not available. Peers and instructional devices are used to provide feedback.

- Student progress is monitored regularly, and students are held accountable for learning in physical education. Students are expected to make progress toward class objectives. Records are kept relative to various objectives. Students know exactly what is expected of them and how the expectations are tied to the accountability system. Reward students for small steps of progress toward larger goals. If progress is not monitored regularly, students cannot be held accountable, and the environment will be less effective.

- Low rates of management time and smooth transitions from one activity to another characterize the environment. Effective teachers are efficient managers of students. Students move from one learning activity to another smoothly and without wasting time. Time-saving procedures are planned and implemented efficiently. Students spend little time waiting during class transitions. Equipment is organized to facilitate smooth transitions. Attendance procedures, starting and stopping procedures, and instructional procedures are all tightly organized with little wasted time.

- Students spend a limited amount of time waiting in line or participating in other unproductive behaviors. Effective environments are characterized by high rates of time engaged in subject matter. In physical education, this means high rates of time spent practicing, drilling, and playing. Physical education is activity based, and students need to spend class time doing the activity, not waiting for an opportunity.

- Teachers are organized with high, but realistic expectations for student achievement. Structured learning activities should challenge students. The activities must not be too easy or too difficult. Students need success and challenge from learning activities. Expect students to learn, and hold them accountable for their progress.

- Teachers are enthusiastic about what they are doing and are actively involved in the instructional process. Students need an enthusiastic model—someone who has incorporated physical activity into his or her lifestyle. Active involvement means active supervision, enthusiasm, and high interaction rates with students. These characteristics enhance learning regardless of the teaching style used; they are important for ensuring student achievement and positive attitudes.

STUDY STIMULATORS AND REVIEW QUESTIONS

1. Discuss the various factors that should be considered when choosing a teaching style.

2. Explain why problem solving is not a good approach to teaching rock climbing.

3. Provide an overview of what teachers need to do from a planning perspective to effectively use the task style of teaching.

4. Discuss the attractive features of mastery learning.

5. What is the main focus of a teacher's monitoring effort when using mastery learning?

6. Explain the various roles of students in the cooperative learning style.

7. Discuss the various criticisms that have been voiced about inquiry styles of teaching.

8. Develop a short "trigger story" with a focus on ethical behavior in sport.

9. Why should a teacher develop a large repertoire of teaching styles?

10. Discuss the dynamic instruction elements that are common to all styles.

REFERENCES AND SUGGESTED READINGS

Buck, M. M., Lund, J. L., Harrison, J. L., & Blakemore, C. L. (2007). *Instructional strategies for secondary school physical education with NASPE: Moving into the future* (6th ed.). Boston: McGraw-Hill.

Byra, M., & Jenkins, J. (2000). Matching instructional tasks with learner ability: Teaching style E. *Journal of Physical Education, Recreation, & Dance, 71*(3), 26–30.

Casten, C. M. (2009). *Lesson plans for dynamic physical education for secondary students* (6th ed.). San Francisco: Pearson Benjamin Cummings.

Dyson, B., & Grineski, S. (2001). Using cooperative learning structures in physical education. *Journal of Physical Education, Recreation, & Dance, 72*(2), 28–31.

Ernst, M., & Byra, M. (1998). What does the reciprocal style of teaching hold for junior high school learners? *Journal of Physical Education, Recreation, & Dance, 55*(1), 24–37.

Griffin, L. L., & Butler, Joy. (2005). *Teaching games for understanding—Theory, research, and practice.* Champaign, IL: Human Kinetics.

Johnson, D. W., Johnson, R. T., & Holubec, E. J. (1990). *Circles of learning: Cooperation in the classroom* (3rd ed.). Edina, MN: Interaction.

Lawrence, C. M., Lawrence, G., & Samek, L. S. (2006). *Organizing classrooms for small-group instruction: Learning for mastery.* Lanham, MD: Rowman & Littlefield Publishing Group.

Melograno, V. J. (1996). *Designing the physical education curriculum.* Champaign, IL: Human Kinetics.

Metzler, M. W. (2005). *Instructional models for physical education* (2nd ed.). Scottsdale, AZ: Holcomb Hathaway, Publishers.

Mitchell, S. A., Oslin, J. L., & Griffin L. L. (2006). *Teaching sport concepts and skills: A tactical games approach* (2nd ed.). Champaign, IL: Human Kinetics.

Mosston, M., & Ashworth, S. (2002). *Teaching physical education* (5th ed.). San Francisco: Benjamin Cummings.

Pangrazi, R. P. (2007). *Dynamic physical education for elementary school children* (15th ed.). San Francisco: Benjamin Cummings.

Rink, J. E. (2006). *Teaching physical education for learning* (5th ed.). Boston: McGraw Hill.

Siedentop, D., & Tannehill, D. (2000). *Developing teaching skills in physical education* (4th ed.). Mountain View, CA: Mayfield Publishing Co.

Torp, L., & Sage, S. (1998). *Problems as possibilities: Problem-based learning for K–12 education.* Alexandria, VA: Association for Supervision and Curriculum Development.

WEB SITES

Physical Education Teaching and Curriculum Information (styles information)
http://www.pecentral.com
http://www.pelinks4u.org
http://www.pe4life.org
http://www.reach.ucf.edu/~pezone

Research for Education and Learning
http://www.mcrel.org

Research on Teaching Physical Education
http://www.UnlockResearch.com

Teaching Styles and Learning Styles
http://www2.ncsu.edu/unity/lockers/users/f/felder/public/Learning_Styles.html

ESSENTIAL COMPONENTS OF A QUALITY PROGRAM

COMPONENT 1 A quality physical education program is organized around content standards that offer direction and continuity to instruction and evaluation.

COMPONENT 2 A quality program is student centered and based on the developmental urges, characteristics, and interests of students.

COMPONENT 3 Quality physical education makes physical activity and motor-skill development the core of the program.

COMPONENT 4 Physical education programs teach management skills and self-discipline.

COMPONENT 5 Quality programs emphasize inclusion of all students.

COMPONENT 6 In a quality physical education setting, instruction focuses on the process of learning skills rather than the product or outcome of the skill performance.

COMPONENT 7 A quality physical education program teaches lifetime activities that students can use to promote their health and personal wellness.

COMPONENT 8 Quality physical education teaches cooperative and responsibility skills and helps students develop sensitivity to diversity and gender issues.

202

Improving Instruction Systematically

CHAPTER SUMMARY

The chapter will establish that teaching is a skill that can be improved by using a systematic, data-based approach in an ongoing manner. Teachers can identify areas that need to be modified and improved and develop a system of self-evaluation to improve the instructional process. The methods of systematic observation include event recording, duration recording, interval recording, and planned activity checks (placchecks). Evaluation is kept simple by focusing on one specific area at a time. Attempting to record and change too many behaviors frustrates and confuses teachers. Areas that teachers can evaluate include the following: practice time, instruction time, class management, response latency, student performance, instructional feedback, student contacts, and active supervision. After mastering the simple single behavior systems in this chapter, teachers may want to use one of the combination systems explained later in the chapter for looking at multiple teaching and student behaviors.

STUDENT OUTCOMES

After reading this chapter, you will be able to:

- Discuss the problems of evaluating instruction by using checklists and rating scales.

- Explain the advantages of self-evaluation concerning instruction in physical education.

- Describe the use of the specific systematic observation methods.

Student Outcomes, continued

- Define specific teacher and student behaviors that are part of an ongoing evaluation scheme.

- Set up a systematic observation plan for analyzing a specific teaching or student behavior.

- Complete a self-evaluation and set future goals for instructional improvement.

- Complete an evaluation of a taped or live lesson and make recommendations for improvement.

Few professionals question the need for trying to improve instructional effectiveness. Most teachers want to be respected for their ability to impart knowledge and change behavior patterns of their students. University classes in teacher education strive to impart teaching skills to students. Those students who become effective instructors have one thing in common: They are motivated to improve and excel. It is not enough, however, to be motivated. Motivation without proper teaching skills leaves teachers in a predicament. They want to change and grow but do not know what needs to be changed and learned. Therefore, a systematic approach for evaluating instruction is advocated so teachers can assess when they are improving or need to improve.

DEFINING EFFECTIVE INSTRUCTION

Effective instruction is a broad and general term that can be defined many ways. Simply put, it is probably best characterized by what students learn through contact with a teacher. The goal of an instructor is to teach new skills, refine previously learned skills, change attitudes, and leave students with a positive feeling about what they have learned. If students do not learn, instruction has not occurred. Some teachers feel they are successful if they teach students all the key points of skill performance. If, in spite of the presentation of key points, students do not perform differently than they did prior to the skill analysis, instruction was ineffective.

A common saying in education is "students learn when teachers teach." This is probably true if teachers are effective in their teaching methods. On the other hand, learning is not guaranteed. Teaching effectively demands that positive changes in behavior occur. The changes may be attitudinal, skill oriented, or knowledge based. Regardless of the learning domain affected, learning occurs and teaching is effective only when

observable changes result. Think about it! If noticeable changes in students do not occur, how can teachers say they have taught effectively? This speaks to the need for systematic evaluation of instruction.

IMPROVING TEACHING SKILLS

Teaching is learned just like any other skill. If you want to learn to play racquetball, you practice racquetball. Most people who have learned sport skills have followed the process of setting goals, diagnosing their problems, prescribing methods for improving, and evaluating their progress. This approach is needed to improve teaching skills as well. To learn to teach, a cyclical process must occur; teach, analyze the results, prescribe changes, and evaluate progress made. It is not enough to listen, read, and observe. Active participation in teaching is necessary.

The second part of improving teaching skills requires that teachers do more than teach. Many teachers have taught the same thing for years without changing. They have not incorporated new skills and ideas into their teaching methods. This results in a teacher who is stagnant and unchanging. What if athletes never tried to change or use newly discovered techniques? Quite likely they would not remain competitive. When teachers fail to update their techniques, the public may believe they do not care about being effective.

Practice and improvement goes hand in hand. Teachers need to evaluate their performances so they know whether they are improving or becoming stagnant. Ask teachers you know whether they are better teachers this year as compared to last year. If they say yes, ask them to prove it. If they can't give you anything more than a belief that they are better, you probably have found teachers who have never used the process of systematic instructional improvement.

EXPLAINING THE NEED FOR GOALS AND FEEDBACK

Teachers need goals aimed at improving their teaching effectiveness. Establishing goals and not evaluating them is like driving down a highway without a map. How can you know when you have reached your goals if you do not establish some method of evaluation? Goals and feedback need to be developed concurrently. It is necessary to have an objective way of evaluating whether teachers have improved. This is feedback: information gathered for the purpose of modifying future responses.

Feedback about teaching can be used to guide improvement in instructional methods. Assume you have a goal of improving volleyball skills. For comparative purposes, you want to try teaching the volleyball set using a reciprocal teaching method for instruction. You allow half the class to teach a friend the set while you teach the other half using a teacher-centered, direct style of instruction. After a week of practice, you evaluate the performance level of the volleyball set. Comparing the reciprocal style versus the direct style generates feedback about the effectiveness of the method.

This example illustrates goal setting and data gathering related to instructional outcomes. Later in the chapter, systematic approaches for improving instruction will be offered. All the approaches involve setting goals and establishing a database of information to see if they were accomplished. Learning to collect meaningful data about teaching is necessary for improvement.

EXPLAINING THE NEED FOR SYSTEMATIC EVALUATION

Instruction has most often been evaluated using inexact and insensitive methods such as intuition, checklists, rating scales, and observation. Over time, these methods have proven to be relatively ineffective for improving the quality of instruction. The use of intuition relies on the expertise of a supervisor, who observes the instructor, recommends changes, and reinforces the result. Improvement is difficult to identify because the evaluation process offers little or no quantification. It is possible the supervisor will forget what the quality of the first lesson was compared with the present teaching episode. In this situation, evaluating whether improvement has occurred is next to impossible.

Checklists and rating scales are used as evaluation tools and give the appearance of an objective, quantified method (Figure 9.1). However, rating scales are unreliable and become more so when the number of

rating points is increased. Scales and checklists are open to a wide spread of interpretation depending on who is performing the evaluation. Most evaluation that is done using checklists and rating scales is subject to the impressions and opinions of the evaluator.

This lack of objectiveness indicates the need for a systematic method of observing teaching effectiveness. Siedentop and Tannehill (2000) have developed a number of systematic methods for teacher evaluation and research. These techniques have led to increased educational research in the area of pedagogy. This chapter discusses methods that are systematic in nature and feasible for self-evaluation of instructional effectiveness.

Methods described here use systematic observation for self-improvement. If the reader chooses to conduct research projects and to study this area in depth, the Siedentop and Tannehill text *Developing Teaching Skills in Physical Education* (2000) is an excellent resource. This chapter shows how systematic evaluation can be implemented in a typical school setting.

EVALUATING EFFECTIVE TEACHING

What should be evaluated in the teaching process? Three major areas can be observed and evaluated. The first is teacher behavior. This includes evaluation of areas such as teacher movement, instruction presentation, the praise-to-criticism ratio, use of first names, and the length of instructional episodes. Focus is on the performance of skills that are managed by the teacher. The responsibility for performing behaviors in this category rests solely with the teacher.

The second category of observable behavior is student behavior. Examples of student behavior are the rate of deviant behavior, the amount of time students stay on task, the number of students on task, the number of practice trials students receive, and the amount of time that students are engaged in physical activity. These variables can be evaluated through direct observation; they link to student learning more closely than teacher behavior variables. Note that these behaviors are process oriented. Emphasis is placed on increasing or decreasing the occurrence of student behavior rather than measuring the actual performance of a skill.

Another important indication of learning is done by the evaluation of student skill performance, knowledge, and attitudes toward physical activity and physical education. Chapter 10 provides ideas and examples for evaluating these areas. This third category focuses primarily on the product of learning. How students learned is not the issue; if they learned is the concern. On the surface, this seems to many teachers to be the only important evaluative area. Either students learn

Student _____ Activity _____ Grade _____

	5	4	3	2	1	Comments
1. Use of language						
2. Quality of voice						
3. Personal appearance						
4. Class management						
5. Presentation and teaching techniques						
6. Professional poise						
7. Enthusiasm, interest						
8. Adaptability, foresight						
9. Adequate activity						
10. Knowledge of subject						
11. Appropriate use of student help						
12. Demonstration (if any)						
13. Progression (if applicable)						
14. General organization						

General evaluation
5–Superior
4–Above average
3–Average
2–Below average
1–Poor

Evaluating Teacher _____

Date _____

FIGURE 9.1 Example of a rating scale

The best evaluation system includes behavior from all three categories. It is important to look at teaching behavior. It is also necessary to evaluate how students respond in a class setting. If both teachers and students are demonstrating effective behavior patterns, the evaluation of skill performance is appropriate. All three areas are interrelated, and all three need to be evaluated.

the skill or they don't. If they learn the skill, teachers have taught. However, things are not always so simple. It may be that students have learned the skills but leave physical education with a negative attitude toward activity. What would be gained if students learned skills they never wanted to use again? What about unskilled students? Can they ever find success in physical education classes?

INTRODUCING METHODS FOR SYSTEMATICALLY OBSERVING INSTRUCTION

Instruction can be systematically observed using a variety of methods to gather information. The instruments are easy to use. A key is to clearly define the area to be evaluated. Definitions should be written and followed to make the data meaningful. The methods require little more than pencil, paper, video recorder, and stopwatch. A videotape recorder can add the dimensions of replay and privacy, which are especially important for the beginning teacher.

Event Recording

In simplest terms, event recording involves noting how many times an event occurs during a specified time period. Event recording identifies the frequency with which certain behavior occurs. It measures the quantity of events, not the quality. For example, event recording might be defined as the number of times a teacher interacts with students or the number of times a positive statement is made. A teacher might tally the number of practice attempts students receive after a skill has been introduced or the number of times the class is asked to stop and come to attention. Event recording results are usually divided by the number of minutes in the evaluation session to give an event rate per minute. This enables the teacher to compare lessons that involve different content or teaching styles.

To lessen the time needed for analysis, use a sampling technique. For example, if the lesson is 30-min long, four bouts of recording, each lasting 2 min at evenly distributed points in the lesson, reduce the burden of recording and yield representative results. Any observable behavior of teachers, students, or between teachers and students can be recorded when the behavior has been clearly defined.

Duration Recording

While event recording offers insight into the frequency of certain behavior, duration recording reveals how long behavior occurs in terms of minutes and seconds. Time is the measure used in this type of recording. As with event recording, duration recording does not have to be done for an entire lesson. Representative sampling of three or four bouts of observation, 3 min per bout, can be used to generalize about the entire session.

These data are usually converted to percentages so comparisons can be made from lesson to lesson. This is done by dividing the entire observation time into the amount of time devoted to the specific observed behavior. For example, if activity was observed for 20 min and the student was active for 10 of the 20 min, the result would be 50 percent. This would be expressed as "50 percent of the total time was spent in activity." This approach is used to identify the duration of certain behaviors, such as practice, managerial, or instructional behaviors.

Interval Recording

Interval recording analyzes behavior patterns for short periods of time. When conducting interval recording, intervals should be 6–12 sec, with one interval for observing and the other for recording. If a teacher used 6-sec intervals during a 1-min session, five intervals would be devoted to observing and five to recording the results. According to Siedentop and Tannehill (2000), it is important to have at least 90 data points (observe–record = 1 point) to establish the validity of the technique. This would generate 100 data points in 20 min using 6-sec intervals.

Data generated from this technique are usually converted to a percentage of the data points in which the behavior occurred. If, for example, the behavior occurred in 40 of 100 data points, the figure is 40 percent. Percentages can be compared lesson to lesson. A simple way to keep track of intervals is to wear a recorder headset that "beeps" every 6 sec. The observer can alternate between observing and recording with each signal. This technique is reliable, particularly when the intervals are short, and it can be used to record instructional time, managerial time, academic learning time, and other types of observable behavior.

Placheck Recording/ Group Time Sampling

Placheck (planned activity check) recording is similar to interval recording in that behavior is observed at different intervals. This technique is used to observe group behavior. At regular intervals during a lesson, the observer scans the group for 10 sec. The scan begins at the left side of the instructional area and moves to the right side, taking note of which students are not on task. The observer makes one observation per student and does not go back or change the decision, even if the student changes behavior during the 10-sec interval.

The technique is used to identify student effort, productive activity, and participation. It is usually best to record the less frequently occurring behavior to speed counting. For example, if the teacher is interested in identifying the percentage of students involved in the assigned activity, recording the number of students who are not participating is easier. Intervals should last 10 sec and be spaced randomly throughout the lesson. There should be eight to 10 observation intervals. Again, signals to observe can be recorded on a tape recorder at random intervals to cue the observer. This technique will yield information concerning the behavior of the group, thus it is referred to as *group time sampling*.

SYSTEMATICALLY OBSERVING FOR SELF-IMPROVEMENT

Each teacher has different strengths and weaknesses and different concerns for improvement. The approach used for systematic observation directed at self-improvement varies greatly from teacher to teacher. Instructors decide which variables they want to evaluate and determine the best possible way to record and monitor the data. Evaluating one area at a time is usually best. Trying to record more than one variable at a time may be frustrating and confusing. It may also confound the picture by making it difficult to decide how to change the teaching behavior in question.

After deciding which behavior needs to be changed, a plan for meaningful evaluation is developed. Identifying the behavior that affects the desired educational outcome is necessary, as well as deciding which method of observation to use. A coding form is developed to facilitate recording the data. Coding sheets should be specific to each situation and suited to the teacher. Areas on the sheet can provide for recording the teacher, the date, the focus and content of the lesson, the grade level and competency of the students, the duration of the lesson, and a short description of the evaluation procedure. The sheets should be consistent for each type of behavior so the instructor can compare progress throughout the year.

Deciding what behavior will be recorded depends on the instructor's situation. For example, can the data be gathered by students who are not participating? Can another teacher easily gather the data? Can the data be gathered from an audiotape, or is a videotape necessary? Is the instructor willing to let others gather the information, or does the teacher believe that it is important to keep the data confidential? These and other questions determine what areas the teacher is willing to evaluate. In most cases, the teacher is least

threatened by self-evaluation techniques and more willing to change when it is not required by outside authorities. Another advantage of self-evaluation is that teaching behavior changes least when outside observers are not present. Self-evaluation techniques can better reveal actual patterns exhibited in day-to-day teaching.

IMPROVING THE QUALITY OF INSTRUCTION

Quality instruction results when an effective teacher implements a well-planned lesson. Successful teachers have learned how to do this over a period of years through a somewhat inefficient method of trial and error. Unfortunately, sheer experience does not guarantee an outstanding teacher. Witness the fact there are many experienced yet mediocre teachers. A key to improving teaching ability is experience coupled with meaningful feedback about the teacher's performance.

Teachers may find it difficult to find someone capable of offering evaluative feedback. Principals and curriculum supervisors may be too busy or may not possess skills necessary for systematically observing teaching behavior. This accentuates the importance of learning to self-evaluate. Teachers have long been told to talk less, move more, praise more, learn more names, and increase student practice time—primarily without documented methods of measurement. This section shows a number of teacher behaviors that are observable and measurable. The data can be gathered by the teacher, by teaching peers, or by selected students.

Take a do-it-yourself approach to evaluation. Feedback gained in the privacy of one's office is easier to digest and less threatening. Teachers can set personal goals and chart their performance without others knowing. When teachers evaluate their teaching procedures, they are usually willing to change. This attitude contrasts with a resistant attitude when principals or department heads impose external evaluation.

Instructional Time

The educational process requires that teachers instruct. The throw-out-the-ball approach is nothing more than leisure time activity in a school setting. Instructors need to know the amount of instruction they offer students. Instructional time refers to initial demonstrations, cues, and explanations to get students started on an activity. This time deals directly with physical education content.

Instructional Time

Teacher _Charlene Darst_ Observer _B. Pangrazi_

Class _1st period_ Grade _10_ Date and time _3/22—9:05_

Lesson focus _Golf_ Comments _1st class meeting of unit_

Starting time _9:15_ End time _10:00_ Length of lesson _45 min_

15	10	8	35	17	1:03	31	9	8
14	21	10	21	43	3:19	7	25	

Total instructional time _8 min 56 sec_

Percent of class time devoted to instruction _19%_

Number of episodes _17_ Average length of episodes _31.5 sec_

FIGURE 9.2 Sample form for instructional time

Find a meaningful balance between instruction and practice. An observer can tally the number of instructional episodes and the length of each episode occurring in a daily class. At a later time, the average length of instruction can then be evaluated, as well as the proportion of the lesson that was used for instruction. Instructional episodes should be short and frequent, with an attempt made to limit episodes to 45 sec or less.

How to Determine Length of Instruction

1. Design a form for duration recording.

2. Have a colleague or a nonparticipating student turn on the stopwatch every time an instructional episode begins and stop the watch when instruction ends. Record the episode on the form, clear the watch, and be ready to time the next instructional episode. An alternative method is to record the lesson using an audiotape recorder and rerun the tape at the end of the day. Establish a criterion for identifying the difference between instructional and management episodes. (For a description of management episodes, see Chapter 7.)

3. Total the amount of time spent on instruction.

4. Convert the amount of time to the percentage of lesson time devoted to instruction by dividing the length of the lesson into the time spent on instruction. The average length of an instructional episode can be determined by dividing the total instructional time by the number of instructional episodes. Figure 9.2 is an example of a recording form.

Class Management Episodes

Effective teachers efficiently manage students. Management time is when no instruction or practice is taking place. Management occurs when students are moved into various formations, when equipment is gathered or put away, and when directions are given about these tasks. It also includes taking roll, keeping records, recording fitness scores, and changing clothes (see Chapter 7 for a description of management skills). Figure 9.3 is an example of a form for duration recording using a stopwatch.

Understanding the amount of time being used for class management, and the length and number of

Management Time

Teacher _____ Don Hicks _____ Observer _____ Connie Pangrazi _____

Class _____ 5th period _____ Grade _____ 10 _____ Date and time _____ 11/7—2:05 _____

Lesson focus _____ Frisbee _____ Comments _____

Starting time _____ 2:13 _____ End time _____ 2:50 _____ Length of lesson _____ 37 min _____

55	10	21	1:15	19	18	55	33	16	
43									

Total instructional time _____ 5 min 45 sec _____

Percent of class time devoted to instruction _____ 15% _____

Number of episodes _____ 10 _____ Average length of episodes _____ 34.5 sec _____

FIGURE 9.3 Sample form for management time

episodes, is useful. The number of episodes and the length of each can be recorded by an observer. These data are useful for analyzing how much lesson time is devoted to the area of management. A high percentage of management time can indicate an inefficient organizational scheme or students' slow response to explanations.

How to Determine Length of Management Time

1. Design a form that gathers the data desired (Figure 9.3).
2. Record the lesson with a video recorder. Time the length of each management episode, and record each episode in a box on the form.
3. Total the amount of management time and divide it by the length of the period to compute the percent of management time during the lesson.
4. Total the number of episodes and divide this number into the amount of time devoted to management to find the average length of a management episode.

Response Latency

Response latency is the amount of time it takes a class to respond to commands or signals. It occurs when instructions are given to begin practicing an activity or to stop an activity. An observer can evaluate the amount of time that elapses from the moment a command is given to start or stop an activity to the moment when the students actually begin or stop. The amount of time that elapses is response latency. An accompanying criterion needs to be set for the percentage of students who are expected to be on task. It is reasonable to expect 100 percent of the students to respond to the command. If less than 100 percent of the class is expected to respond, a gradual loss of class control can occur. The average amount of response latency can be calculated so the instructor can set a goal for improving student behavior. A certain amount of response latency should be expected. Few groups of students stop or start immediately, and most instructors have a strong feeling about the amount of latency that they are willing to tolerate.

Response Latency

Teacher __Paul Dant__ Observer __Reid Wilcox__

Class __5th period__ Grade __9__ Date and time __2/5—12:45__

Lesson focus __Team Handball__ Comments _____

Starting time __12:50__ End time __1:33__ Length of lesson __43 min__

Starting Response Latency

3	12	17	5	5	11	18	9	7
11	3	5	6	14				

Stopping Response Latency

12	13	8	18	5	5	14	12	11
3	10	19	18	17				

Total amount of starting response latency __2 min 6 sec__

Percent of class time devoted to response latency __4%__

Number of episodes __14__ Average length of episode __9 sec__

Total amount of stopping response latency __2 min 45 sec__

Percent of class time devoted to stopping response latency __6%__

Number of episodes __14__ Average length of episode __11.8 sec__

FIGURE 9.4 Sample form for response latency

After more than a 5-sec response latency, teachers usually become uneasy and expect the class to stop or start.

How to Determine Length of Response Latency

1. Develop a form for gathering the data (see Figure 9.4).
2. Have a nonparticipating student or colleague time the response latency each time the class is asked to stop or start. The clock should run from the time the command to stop is given until the next command is given, or until the class is involved in productive behavior. For example, the teacher gives the command to stop the activity and return to squads (watch is started). Students stop the game and slowly return to squads. The teacher waits until all students are sitting quietly before giving the next direction (watch is stopped). Starting and stopping response latency are two separate behaviors and should be recorded separately.

			Inactive,
Parts of the Lesson	Practicing	Listening	Off Task,
Introductory activity	2.5 min	1.0 min	
Fitness development	11.5 min	2.5 min	
Lesson focus	15.0 min	7.5 min	
Total	29.0 min	11.0 min	

Teacher: Debbie Massoney
School: Jason Junior High

FIGURE 9.5 Results of a duration recording for practice time

3. Add up all of the episodes of response latency (in seconds) and then divide this by the total number of seconds in the observation. This gives you the percentage of response latency.

4. Identify the number of response latency episodes and divide this number into the total amount of time logged for response latency to calculate the average.

Practice and Activity Time

To learn physical skills, students must be involved in meaningful physical activity. Physical education programs deal with a finite amount of scheduled time per week. High-success, engaged time with motor activities is defined as Academic Learning Time-Physical Education (ALT-PE). ALT-PE is defined as activity where students are practicing skills in a setting that enables them to experience success. Learning is related to the amount of time students are involved in productive, on-task activity. In a well-regarded school district, the average amount of activity time per 50-min period was only 9–12 min. Evidence shows teachers can significantly increase the amount of ALT-PE for students. This component of physical education classes has been studied in many ways and with many different instruments (McKenzie, 2005; Randall & Imwold, 1989).

To evaluate activity or practice time, duration recording is an effective procedure. A student or fellow teacher can observe a lesson and time the intervals when students are involved in practicing skills. The chart in Figure 9.5 is an example of the results of a duration recording for practice time. The goal is to increase the amount of time students receive for meaningful practice. A teacher could increase the amount of practice time by using more or different equipment, selecting drills that require a minimum of standing in line, or streamlining the amount of verbal instruction.

There are many ways to increase and improve activity time and practice time depending on the unit and the teaching environment.

How to Evaluate Practice Time

1. Design a form for collecting the data (Figure 9.6).

2. Have a nonparticipating student or colleague identify students who will be used for the evaluation. These are the students that the evaluator will observe to see when they are involved in practice and for how long.

3. Turn on the stopwatch when the students are engaged in practice activity, and record the interval of practice.

4. Total the amount of time for student practice (in minutes) and divide it by the length of the lesson. This will compute the percent of practice time in a given lesson.

Student Performance

Some classes have a greater percentage of students performing at optimum levels than others. Reasons for this vary. A class may be poorly motivated, have difficulty understanding instructions, or be out of control. In any case, instructors can evaluate the percentage of students who are performing in a desired manner. This can be accomplished by using the placheck observation technique. Examples of areas that can be evaluated are students performing the stipulated activity, productive behavior, effort, and interest in the activity. Once baseline data are gathered, teachers can strive to increase the percentage of students involved in the desired observable behavior.

How to Calculate Student Performance

1. Design a form for recording the desired data. Figure 9.7 is an example of a form that can be used for placheck observation. The example can be used to identify three different areas of student performance.

2. Place 8–10 audio signals (whistles) at random intervals on a tape recorder to signal when a placheck should be conducted.

3. Scan the area in a specified and consistent direction from left to right every time the tape-recorded signal sounds. The class is scanned for 7 to 10 sec while the number of students who are not engaged in the desired behavior is recorded.

4. Convert the data to a percentage by dividing the total number of students into the average number

Practice Time

Teacher _Eugene Petersen_   Observer _P. W. Darst_

Class _2nd period_   Grade _8_   Date and time _11/15—9:15_

Lesson focus _Basketball_   Comments _Week two_

Starting time _9:25_   End time _10:00_   Length of lesson _35 min_

35	10	2:04	25	29	1:39	17	55	34
43	1:55	1:01	33	10	10	18	1:17	4:50
24	39	31	34					

Total instructional time _20 min 13 sec_

Percent of class time devoted to instruction _57.8%_

Number of episodes _22_   Average length of episodes _55.1 sec_

FIGURE 9.6   Sample form for collecting data on practice time

of unproductive students and multiplying the result by 100. Eight to 10 placbecks spaced randomly throughout a class period will yield valid information about the conduct of the class.

Instructional Feedback

The feedback teachers offer to students influences instructional effectiveness. It is possible for instructors to analyze their interaction patterns and set meaningful goals for improvement. Few teachers enter the profession with the ability to communicate with clarity. The process of changing communication behaviors can create discomfort and concern but will ultimately pay rewarding dividends. Evaluation in the following areas can create improvement in feedback delivery.

Praise and Criticism

When students are involved in activity, teachers deliver feedback dealing with student performance. This feedback can be positive and constructive, or negative and critical. It is easy to measure the occurrences of praise and criticism. The occurrences can be tallied and evaluated at the end of the day. Calculate the number of instances and the ratio of positive-to-negative comments. Using these data, begin to set goals for increasing the number of comments per minute and modifying the ratio of positive-to-negative comments. A teacher can expect to average one to two comments per minute with a positive-to-negative ratio of 3 or 4 to 1.

General Versus Specific Feedback

Feedback given to students can be specific or general. Comments like "Good job," "Way to go," and "Cut that out" are general in nature. General feedback can be either negative or positive and does not specify the behavior being reinforced. In contrast, specific feedback identifies the student by name, mentions the behavior being reinforced, and can be accompanied by a valuing statement. An example is, "Michelle, that's the way to keep your head tucked! I really like that forward roll!"

To evaluate this area, teachers can tally the number of general and specific feedback instances. Considering both types of feedback can be negative or positive, this

Student Performance

Teacher ___Bob Pangrazi___

Class ___2nd period___ Grade ___12___ Observer ___Norma Pike___

Lesson focus ___Weight Lifting___ Comments ___ Date and time ___1/26 – 9:20___

Starting time ___9:28___ End time ___10:12___ Length of lesson ___44 min___

Active/inactive

On task/off task

5	4	12	7	8	5		
9	2	1	8				

Effort/noneffort

Number of plachecks ___10___

Total number of students in class ___33___

Average number of students not on desired behavior ___6.1___

Percentage of students not on desired behavior ___18%___

FIGURE 9.7 Placheck observation of student performance

can also be counted. Using first names personalizes the feedback and directs it to the right individual. Total the number of times first names are used. The number of valuing statements can also be monitored. Divide the totals in all of the categories by the length of the lesson (in minutes) to render a rate per minute. Figure 9.8 is an example of a form that can be used to tally the feedback behaviors described in this section.

Positive feedback should be specific whenever possible so students know exactly what it was they did well. An instructor might say, "Your throw to second base was exactly where it should have been!" This type of feedback creates a positive feeling in a class. Sometimes, however, teachers use this type of feedback to such an extent that it becomes a habitual form of communication (e.g., "good job, nice serve"). These comments do not identify specific desirable behavior and may be ignored by students. It is also possible that an undesirable behavior may be reinforced when feedback is general.

Corrective Instructional Feedback

Effective teachers coach students to higher levels of performance. This involves giving performers meaningful corrective feedback. Corrective feedback focuses on improving the performance of the participant. Teachers should ignore poor performances if students are already aware of them. Corrective instructional feedback is specific whenever possible, so performers know what it is they must correct. An example of corrective instructional feedback might be, "Your throw to second base was too far to the left of the base! Try to throw the ball directly over the base." This type of feedback tells the student what was incorrect about the skill attempt and how the skill should be performed.

Instructional Feedback

Teacher _____   Observer _____

Class _____   Grade _____   Date and time _____

Lesson focus _____   Comments _____

Starting time _____   End time _____   Length of lesson _____

Interactions unrelated to skill performance	+	
	–	
General instructional feedback	+	
	–	
Specific positive instructional feedback		
Corrective instructional feedback		
First names		
Nonverbal feedback	+	
	–	

Ratio + to –/nonskill related _____

Ratio + to –/skill related _____

FIGURE 9.8   Sample form for tallying feedback behaviors

Nonverbal Feedback

Much performance feedback can be given nonverbally. This is certainly meaningful to students and may be equal to or more effective than verbal forms of communication. Examples of nonverbal feedback that could occur after a desired performance are a pat on the back, a wink, a smile, a nod of the head, the thumbs-up sign, and clapping the hands. Nonverbal feedback can also be negative: frowning, shaking the head in disapproval, walking away from a student, or laughing at a poor performance.

It is possible to tally the number of positive and negative nonverbal behaviors exhibited by a teacher. A student or another instructor can do the tallying. Students may be better at evaluating the instructor in this domain because they are aware of what each of the instructor's mannerisms means.

How to Tally Instructional Feedback and Related Behaviors

1. Design a form to collect the data. Figure 9.8 is an example of a form that can be used.

2. Record a lesson for playback and evaluation at a later time.

3. Mark the data to be analyzed. Analyze one category at a time when beginning. For example, analyze the use of first names during the first playback, and then play the tape again to evaluate corrective feedback.

4. Convert the data to a form that can be generalized from lesson to lesson (e.g., rate per minute [rpm], rate per lesson, or ratio of positive-to-negative interactions).

Active Supervision and Student Contact

Contact and active supervision are important in maintaining students' involvement with learning tasks (van der Mars, Vogler, Darst, & Cusimano, 1994). Contact means moving among and offering personalized information feedback to the students. To evaluate student contact, count the number of times an instructor interacts with a student. This type of feedback differs

Teacher Movement—Active Supervisor and Student Contact

Teacher ___Danny Marcello___　　Observer ___Ken Coyle___

Class ___5th period___　Grade ___9___　Date and time ___3/17 – 1:05___

Lesson focus ___Volleyball___　　Comments _____

Starting time ___1:15___　End time ___2:01___　Length of lesson ___46 min___

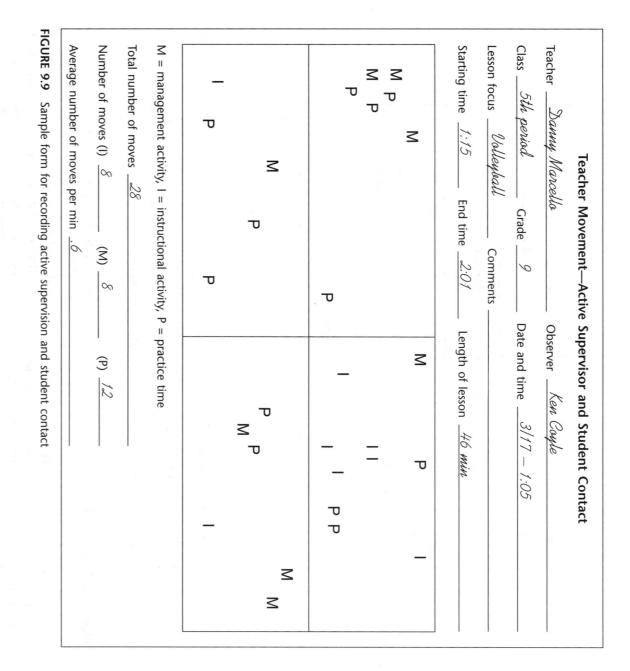

M = management activity, I = instructional activity, P = practice time

Total number of moves ___28___

Number of moves (I) ___8___　(M) ___8___　(P) ___12___

Average number of moves per min ___.6___

FIGURE 9.9　Sample form for recording active supervision and student contact

from total class interaction and demands that the instructor have keen insight into each student's behavior and particular needs.

Related to this area is teacher movement and supervision. Instructors often have a particular area in the gymnasium from which they feel comfortable teaching. Before instruction begins, the teacher moves back to this area. The teacher's movement pattern causes students to drift to different areas, depending on their feeling about the activity or the instructor. Students who like the instructor will usually move closer, whereas students who dislike the teacher or are uneasy about the activity may move away from the teacher or to an area where they are less visible. This results in a configuration where competent performers are near the instructor, and students who are deviant or less competent move away and become difficult to observe.

These problems can be decreased by actively moving throughout the teaching area. Teacher movement can be evaluated by dividing the teaching area into quadrants and tallying the number of times the instructor moves from quadrant to quadrant. A tally is made on the form only if the teacher speaks to a student or to the class as a whole while in the quadrant. Do not tally when the teacher merely passes through a quadrant.

Another measure is the amount of time a teacher stays in a quadrant. Teachers should try to spend the same amount of time in each teaching quadrant. The length of time can be recorded on the form in relationship to where the teacher stands. At the end of the lesson, analyze the amount of time spent in each quadrant. This can be difficult if the teacher is an active mover and does not stay in the same quadrant for very long.

FIGURE 9.10 Completed Class Time Management Analysis Form

Source: van der Mars, H. (2007). Unpublished material. Arizona State University-Polytechnic, Mesa, Arizona.

TIME CATEGORY DEFINITIONS:

Instruction (I):	Time devoted to transmitting information regarding subject matter content (i.e., rules, technique, tactics, strategy, etiquette, history, etc.)
Mgm't (M):	Time devoted to organizational activities as well as class business unrelated to the lesson.
Warm-up (Wu):	Time devoted to routine execution of physical activities whose purpose is to prepare individuals for engaging in further activity, but not designed to alter the state of the individuals on a long-term basis.
Fitness (F):	Time devoted to activities whose major purpose is to alter the physical state of the individual in terms of strength, cardiovascular capacity, or flexibility.
Techn. Pr. (P):	Time devoted to the practice of gross-motor or sport skills, and strategy outside the applied context with the primary goal of technique development.
Game (G):	Time devoted to the application of skills and strategies in a competitive setting.

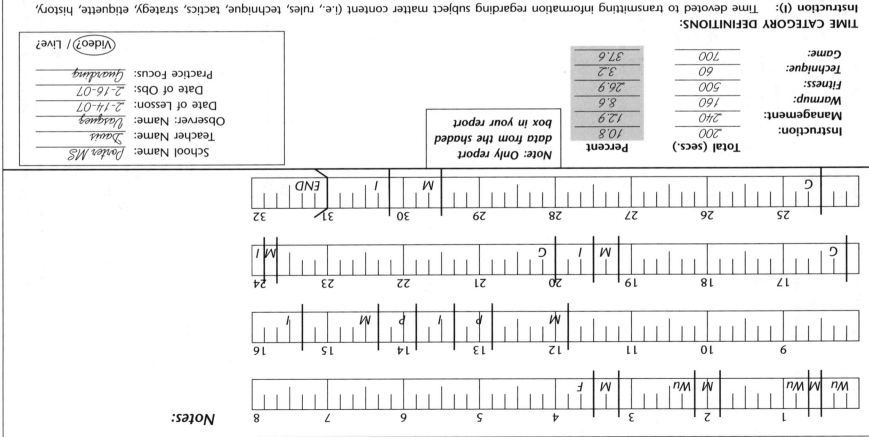

School Name: _Porter MS_
Teacher Name: _David_
Observer Name: _Vazquez_
Date of Lesson: _2-14-07_
Date of Obs: _2-16-07_
Practice Focus: _Guarding_

(Video?) / Live?

Note: Only report data from the shaded box in your report

	Total (secs.)	Percent
Instruction:	200	10.8
Management:	240	12.9
Warmup:	160	8.6
Fitness:	500	26.9
Technique:	60	3.2
Game:	700	37.6

Notes:

Based on the observation you just completed, respond to the following questions. Your responses to these questions will become the basis for your profile report, so be thoughtful and complete.

Answer immediately following your video analysis!

1. The results of this assessment serve as appropriate supporting evidence for which NASPE Beginning Teacher Standard(s) (BTS)?

2. Defend your choice! Why is this evidence appropriate to show that you are meeting this particular BTS?

3. Judge the quality of the evidence you collected (i.e., does this evidence reflect "unacceptable-," "acceptable-," or "target-" level performance on your part).

4. How did you collect the data?

5. What contributed to or hampered the success of your lesson related to this observation?

POSITIVES:

AREAS FOR DEVELOPMENT?

FIGURE 9.11   Reflective observation comments

Another suggested technique is to code the type of teacher behavior that occurs each time the instructor moves into a new quadrant. For example, an "M" might signify management activity, an "I" might indicate instructional activity with the entire class, and a "P" might stand for practice time interactions with individual students. This tally reveals the number of these three types of instructor interactions with students and also where the teacher moved to conduct the different types of class or individual interactions.

How to Quantify Active Supervision and Student Contact

1. Develop a coding form similar to the one in Figure 9.9 on page 216.

2. Ask a nonparticipating student or a colleague to videotape the lesson so that you can evaluate it later.

3. Evaluate the data by calculating the number of moves per lesson and the number of moves that

Observation __2__ of __4__ .
Date of lesson: __4-3-07__
Date of Obs.: __same__

Teacher name: _L. Swanson_
Observer Name: _T. Brown_
Lesson Content: **1.** _Team Wu_
2. _Team Conditioning_
3. _3 v. 2 (Ball Mgmt)_
4. _Competition Games 6–7_

Video / (Live Obs.)

DEFINITIONS:

Elapsed Time: The time during the lesson during which the signal occurred.

Response Latency: Time from the teacher's signal until students are quiet and in "home position." If the teacher starts with direction before attention is established (e.g., continued movement/chatting), record that duration and circle that number.

Teacher Reaction: Teacher's reaction to students' performance on freezing in "home position" and getting quiet.

Can be: **Positive (+):** "Thanks for freezing so quickly."
No reaction (O): No comment . . . On to new directions.
Neg./Corr. (–) "You should be doing better on those freezes."

RECORD ONLY THOSE SIGNALS THAT YOU USED TO START NEW INSTRUCTIONS!!

Signal	Elapsed Time (Min:sec)	Response Latency (sec)	Teacher Reaction			COMMENTS:
			+	–	O	
Sample > 3	4:40	8				
1	:56	7			0	
2	5:33	6	+			
3	12:48	12		–		
4	21:14	4	+			
5	21:43	(2)			0	
6	31:58	6	+			
7	42:18	7	+			
8	44:56	4	+			
9						
10						

Data Summary:		
Average Response Latency	_6 Sec_	
Teacher Reactions:	Positive: _5_ (total #)	62.5% of total
	Negative: _1_ (total #)	12.5% of total
	No reaction: _2_ (total #)	25.0% of total

FIGURE 9.12 Completed Signal for Attention Analysis Form

Source: van der Mars, H. (2007). Unpublished materials. Arizona State University-Polytechnic, Mesa, Arizona.

Based on the observation you just completed, respond to the following questions. Your responses to these questions will become the basis for your profile report, so be thoughtful and complete.

1. The results of this assessment serve as appropriate supporting evidence for which NASPE Beginning Teacher Standard(s) (BTS)?

2. Defend your choice! Why is this evidence appropriate to show that you are meeting this particular BTS?

3. Judge the quality of the evidence you collected (i.e., does this evidence reflect "unacceptable-," "acceptable-," or "target-" level performance on your part). Defend your choice!

4. How did you collect the data?

5. What contributed to or hampered the success of your lesson related to this observation?

POSITIVES:

AREAS FOR DEVELOPMENT?

FIGURE 9.13 Reflective observation comments

OBSERVATION SYSTEMS FOR RESEARCH AND SUPERVISION

After practicing these introductory observation systems that focus on one or two teaching behaviors, more sophisticated systems can be used that focus on multiple teaching or multiple student behaviors. Some systems include the simultaneous observation of teacher and student behaviors. Many instruments have been field-tested in middle and senior high

school settings for research and supervision purposes. The more sophisticated systems require more practice time in order to code data that are valid and reliable.

Class Time Management Analysis Form

Teachers can use the Class Time Analysis Form shown in Figure 9.10 on page 217 (van der Mars, 2007) to look at multiple segments of class time. Six segments of class time and corresponding definitions of each are listed on the front of the form. Duration recording can be used in a live setting or from a videotape of the lesson.

involved instruction, management, and practice interactions.

Directions: Each time one of the behaviors occurs, place a tally in the appropriate coding box. At the end of the observation, figure the total frequencies and rate per minute for each observed behavior.

Beh. 1 1st Name	Beh. 2 I with demo	Beh. 3 I w. out demo	Beh. 4 +Beh. Feedb.	Beh. 5	Beh. 6
~~IIII~~ ~~IIII~~ ~~IIII~~ ~~IIII~~ ~~IIII~~ ~~IIII~~ ~~IIII~~ ~~IIII~~ ~~IIII~~ II	IIII	~~IIII~~ ~~IIII~~ ~~IIII~~ ~~IIII~~ II	~~IIII~~ ~~IIII~~ I		
Total: 47	Total: 4	Total: 22	Total: 11	Total:	Total:
(47/33)	(4/33)	(22/33)	(11/33)		
Rate**: 1.42	Rate**: .12	Rate**: .66	Rate**: .33	Rate**:	Rate**:

**Rate = total freq/length of obs. in min.   NOTE: Technique- or tactics-related feedback and/or prompt totals should be divided by the total class time spent in activity.

Beh. 1 def.:	Use of student first name when interacting
Beh. 2 def.:	Instructional task statement accompanied w. a demo
Beh. 3 def.:	Instructional task statement not accompanied w. a demo
Beh. 4 def.:	Positive reaction (verbal) on students' class conduct.
Beh. 5 def.:	
Beh. 6 def.:	

FIGURE 9.14 Completed Event Recording Form

Source: van der Mars, H. (2007). Unpublished materials. Arizona State University-Polytechnic, Mesa, Arizona.

Teacher name: P. Martinez
Date of class: 4-26-07
Date of obs.: 4-27-07
Lesson content: Wu: over/under
　　　　　　　Fitn.: Squad Ldr.
　　　　　　　Skill: Throw/Catch
　　　　　　　Game: Fastest Tag
Length of obs.: 33 min
　　Observation: 4 of 6
　　　　　　　(Video?) / Live?

The first letter of each segment of the lesson is coded as it occurs. A line is drawn across the timeline when the segment ends and a new segment begins. A total number of seconds is recorded for each segment, and the percentage of each segment is calculated for the lesson. The back of the form (Figure 9.11, page 218) is used for reflective analysis of various teaching skills and to focus on the National Association for Sport and Physical Education (NASPE) Beginning Teaching Standards.

Signal for Attention Analysis Form

The Signal for Attention Analysis Form shown in Figure 9.12 on page 219 (van der Mars, 2007) can be used to analyze a teacher's signals for attention, the student's response latency, and the teacher's reaction to the students' behavior. The data show teachers how many signals were used, the time when the signals occurred in the lesson, how long the response latency lasted, and the teacher's reaction to the situation. Average lengths of time for the response latencies and the percentages of the teacher's reaction behaviors can be calculated. The back of the form (Figure 9.13) has the same questions for reflective analysis of the involved teaching skills.

Event Recording Form

The Event Recording Form shown in Figure 9.14 (van der Mars, 2007) gives the teacher the opportunity to

Based on the observation you just completed, respond to the following questions. Your responses to these questions will become the basis for your profile report, so be thoughtful and complete.

Answer immediately following your video analysis!

1. The results of this assessment serve as appropriate supporting evidence for which NASPE Beginning Teacher Standard(s) (BTS)?

2. Defend your choice! Why is this evidence appropriate to show that you are meeting this particular BTS?

3. Judge the quality of the evidence you collected (i.e., does this evidence reflect "unacceptable-," "acceptable-," or "target-" level performance on your part).

4. How did you collect the data?

5. What contributed to or hampered the success of your lesson related to this observation?

POSITIVES:

AREAS FOR DEVELOPMENT:

FIGURE 9.15 Reflective observation comments

Oregon State University MS-PETE Supervision Coding Form

This coding form (van der Mars, 2007), shown in Figure 9.16, can be used by school principals, college or school district physical education supervisors, or athletic supervisors for specific supervision of student teachers, beginning or advanced teachers, coaches, or researchers focusing on the teaching of physical education classes. The form is much more sophisticated than the previous forms because multiple teaching and stu-

select six different teaching behaviors to be analyzed in the lesson. For example, the teacher could select positive feedback, corrective feedback, nonverbal behavior, idiosyncratic behaviors, or mention of first names. This data helps the teacher focus on his or her behaviors and skills that need extra analysis and attention. It also gives the teacher some choice in developing a personal growth plan for his or her skills and teaching situation. The back of the form (Figure 9.15) is the same as the back of the previous two forms and should be used in a similar manner.

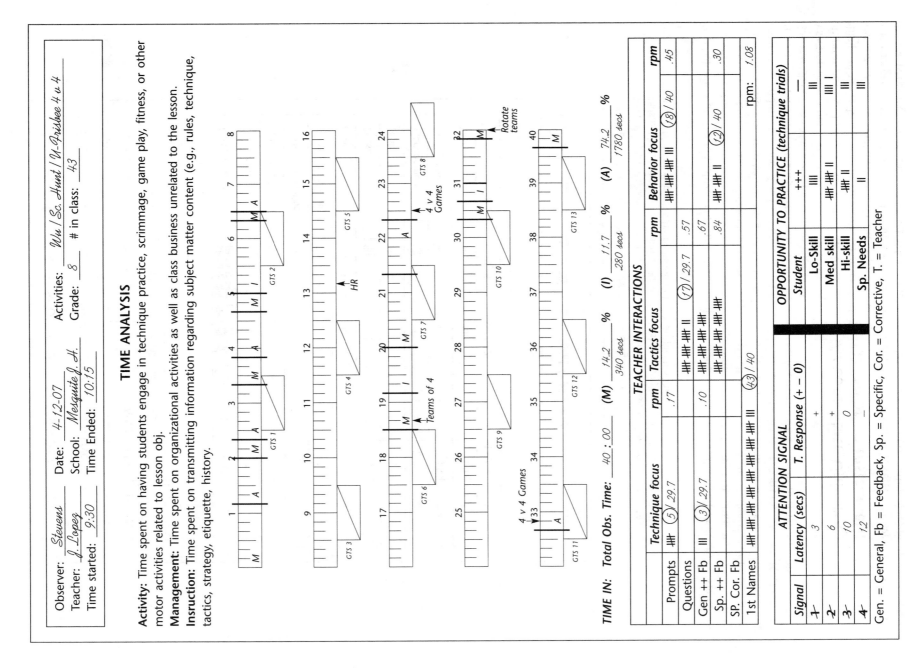

FIGURE 9.16 Completed Oregon State University MS-PETE Supervision Coding Form

Arizona State University Observation Instrument (ASUOI)

Date _11-15_   Coach _Darst_   Sport _Basketball_   Observer _Lacy_

Categories	Time	Time	Total	RPM	Percentage
Use of first name	IIII HHH IIII	HHH HHHI I	30	1.5	12.9
Preinstruction	HHH	II	7	.35	3
Concurrent instruction	III	I	4	.2	1.7
Postinstruction	HHH HHH HHH HHH HHH HHH HHH II	HHH HHH HHH HHH HHH HHH HHH III	81	4.05	35.1
Questioning	III	II	6	.3	2.6
Physical assistance	II	III	2	.1	.9
Positive modeling	III	III	7	.35	3
Negative modeling	II	I	3	.15	1.3
Hustle	HHH HHH	HHH III	18	.9	7.8
Praise	IIII	HHH I	10	.5	4.3
Scold	III	III	7	.35	3
Management	HHH HHH HHH HHH II	HHH HHH HHH III	46	2.3	20
Uncodable	II	I	3	.15	1.3
Silence	III	III	7	.35	3
Total	119	112	231	11.55	

Comments ___ _Preseason Practice—20 minutes total observation_ ___

FIGURE 9.17 Completed ASUOI event recording sheet
From *Analyzing Physical Education and Sport Instruction* by P. Darst, D. Zakrajsek, and V. Mancini (Eds.), 1989. Champaign, IL: Human Kinetics Publishers. Copyright 1989 by P. Darst, D. Zakrajsek, and V. Mancini. Reprinted by permission of Human Kinetics Publishers.

dent behaviors are being analyzed concurrently during the same lesson.

Specific definitions for all categories and teacher/student behaviors need to be learned and practiced by supervisors and the teachers. The form includes a timeline analysis for activity, management, and instruction. (See the Class Time Management Form in Figure 9.10). A section for teacher or coach interactions with students on prompts, questions, general positive feedback, specific positive feedback, specific corrective feedback, and first name use is included (see Figure 9.8). These teacher/coach interactions are looked at according to the focus on technique, tactics, or behavior. Finally,

there are sections on the teacher's attention signals (see form in Figure 9.12) and the students' opportunities to practice according to the students' skill level. This is a great supervision form for final student teaching observations, growth plan reports for first-year teachers, or research on teaching/coaching environments.

Arizona State University Observation Instrument

The Arizona State University Observation Instrument (ASUOI) is an observation system that focuses on

Arizona State University Observation Instrument (ASUOI)

12	14	14	7	4	13	4	14	10	1/12	4	3	14	5	14	5	14	14	
12	14	14	12	4	13	10	14	1/10	11	4	14	14	14	14	14	14	14	
12	14	14	12	6	12	14	14	9	6	14	14	14	4	13	4	11	14	
13	14	11	4	12	14	14	2	4	1/3	14	4	13	4	4				
12	14	1/3	7	12	1/10	14	14	2	5	4	14	4	14	10	4			
12	3	5	4	14	12	9	14	14	14	4	12	14	14	4	4			
1/5	4	14	6	14	2	9	14	14	14	5	12	14	14	14	14			
2	4	14	4	14	2	6	14	Rest	14	5	14	12	1/9	14	14	14		
2	14	4	4	14	2	7	14	1/10	14	14	14	14	1/2	14	10			
2	14	4	14	14	4	7	14	14	10	9	14	14	2	14	4			
7	14	4	14	14	14	3	1/3	14	14	4	14	4	14	14	4			
2	1/10	9	14	14	14	4	14	12	14	7	4	1/6	3	14	14			
7	9	7	14	14	1/11	4	14	12	1/4	14	14	8	4	14	1/10	14		
1/5	10	8	14	4	14	14	14	1/4	14	14	12	7	4	14	14			

Coach _Claxton_ Date _4–15_ Observer _Lacy_

School _Grand Canyon H.S._ Sport _Tennis (varsity boys)_

Comments _Record (10 min) – Rest (2 min) – Record (10 min)_

Midseason – Day after match.

Behavior Codes

1. Use of first name
2. Preinstruction
3. Concurrent instruction
4. Postinstruction
5. Questioning
6. Physical assistance
7. Positive modeling
8. Negative modeling
9. Hustle
10. Praise
11. Scold
12. Management
13. Uncodable
14. Silence

FIGURE 9.18 Completed ASUOI interval recording sheet

From *Analyzing Physical Education and Sport Instruction* by P. Darst, D. Zakrajsek, and V. Mancini (Eds.), 1989. Champaign, IL: Human Kinetics Publishers. Copyright 1989 by P. Darst, D. Zakrajsek, and V. Mancini. Reprinted by permission of Human Kinetics Publishers.

14 categories of teacher behavior (Lacy & Darst, 1989). The system has been expanded and modified several times to create an instrument that is sensitive to the instructional category of behavior. The system can be used with event or interval recording.

The teacher behaviors include the following:

1. Use of First Name—Use of a student's first name or nickname.

2. Preinstruction—Information that is given to students prior to participation, such as explaining a skill, drill, or strategy.

3. Concurrent Instruction—Specific instructional cues or prompts given during practice or playing time.

4. Postinstruction—Information or feedback that is given to students after a skill attempt.

Arizona State University Observation Instrument (ASUOI)

Categories	Number of intervals	Percentage of intervals
1. Use of first name	18	7.5
2. Preinstruction	11	4.6
3. Concurrent instruction	8	3.3
4. Postinstruction	34	14.2
5. Questioning	8	3.3
6. Physical assistance	4	1.7
7. Positive modeling	8	3.3
8. Negative modeling	2	0.8
9. Hustle	8	3.3
10. Praise	12	5.0
11. Scold	8	3.3
12. Management	19	7.9
13. Uncodable	4	1.7
14. Silence	114	47.5
Total	240	100

FIGURE 9.19 Completed ASUOI recording worksheet

From *Analyzing Physical Education and Sport Instruction* by P. Darst, D. Zakrajsek, and V. Mancini (Eds.), 1989. Champaign, IL: Human Kinetics Publishers. Copyright 1989 by P. Darst, D. Zakrajsek, and V. Mancini. Reprinted by permission of Human Kinetics Publishers.

5. Questioning—Questions that are asked about skills, strategies, or assignments.

6. Physical Assistance—Manually moving a student's arms or legs to get them into the proper position or to move through the proper range of motion.

7. Positive Modeling—Teacher demonstration of the correct way to perform a skill.

8. Negative Modeling—Teacher demonstration of the incorrect way to perform a skill.

9. Hustle—Teacher statements that are intended to intensify the efforts of the students.

10. Praise—Verbal or nonverbal compliments or statements of acceptance.

11. Scold—Teacher behaviors that express displeasure with the students, which can be verbal or nonverbal.

12. Management—Teacher behaviors that focus on organizational aspects of a class such as lining up, taking attendance, and rotating between stations.

13. Uncodable—Behavior that does not fit into the remaining categories.

14. Silence—Teacher behavior that is used with interval recording and focuses on periods of time where the teacher is monitoring without any verbal interactions.

The event recording procedure involves placing a tally within a behavior category as the behavior occurs. Figure 9.17 on page 224 is an example of a completed event recording sheet for a basketball session. The behaviors can be totaled, a rate per minute established (RPM), and a specific percentage for each behavior calculated. Figure 9.18 on page 225 is an example of an interval recording sheet for ASUOI. A 5-sec interval is used, and the appropriate number assigned to the behavior is entered in the block. If a student's first name is used with a behavior, then a 1 is entered with the number of the other behavior, such as ½ to show a first name with a praise. The number of intervals for each behavior is tallied and a percentage determined (see Figure 9.19).

Teachers use feedback from this instrument to analyze and set goals for their teaching behaviors in the various categories. Examples of behavior teachers analyze include the use of the various instructional categories, praise-to-scold ratios, management procedures, or hustle behaviors.

STUDY STIMULATORS AND REVIEW QUESTIONS

1. Discuss the stages involved in the systematic process of improving your teaching skills.

2. Define feedback and goal setting in the context of improving your teaching skills.

3. Describe the major shortcomings of evaluation techniques such as rating scales and checklists.

4. List and discuss the three major areas of the teaching–learning process that can be defined, observed, and evaluated.

5. A teacher completed a self-assessment and determined that there was 50 percent of class time spent in activity, during which the rate of skill-related feedback was 1.3 per minute. Which observation techniques did the teacher employ?

6. List and discuss four student behaviors that are best assessed using event recording.

7. Explain the fundamental difference between event recording, duration recording, and placheck recording.

8. Why do the authors advocate that teachers engage in self-evaluation as opposed to assessment only by a principal?

9. Explain what is meant by "the teacher has a praise-to-scold ratio of 3:2."

10. Discuss the reasons why it is important that teachers continuously move throughout the entire teaching area.

11. Explain how activity time or practice time is different from ALT-PE.

12. Why do teachers at all levels of experience need to evaluate their instructional behaviors?

REFERENCES AND SUGGESTED READINGS

Darst, P. W., Zakrajsek, D. B., & Mancini, V. H. (Eds.). (1989). *Analyzing physical education and sport instruction* (2nd ed.). Champaign, IL: Human Kinetics Publishers.

Lacy, A., & Darst, P. (1989). The Arizona State University Observation Instrument (ASUOI). In P. W. Darst, D. B. Zakrajsek, & V. H. Mancini (Eds.), *Analyzing physical education and sport instruction* (2nd ed., pp. 369–377). Champaign, IL: Human Kinetics Publishers.

McKenzie, T. L. (2005). *System for Observing Fitness Instruction Time (SOFIT) procedures manual.* Unpublished manuscript, San Diego State University.

Randall, L., & Imwold, C. (1989). The effect of an intervention on academic learning time provided by preservice physical education teachers. *Journal of Teaching in Physical Education, 8*(4), 271–279.

Siedentop, D., & Tannehill, D. (2000). *Developing teaching skills in physical education* (4th ed.). Mountain View, CA: Mayfield Publishing Co.

van der Mars, H. (2007). Instructional analysis Forms. Unpublished materials. Arizona State University-Polytechnic, Mesa, Arizona.

van der Mars, H., Vogler, W., Darst, P., & Cusimano, B. (1994). Active supervision patterns of physical education teachers and their relationship with student behavior. *Journal of Teaching in Physical Education, 14*(1), 99–112.

Welk, G. (2002). *Physical activity assessments for health-related research.* Champaign, IL: Human Kinetics Publishers.

WEB SITES

Assessment Ideas
http://pe.central.org/assessment/assessment.html

Physical Education General Information and Assessment Ideas
www.pecentral.com
www.pelinks4u.org
www.pe4life.org
www.reach.ucf.edu/~pezone/

Self-Assessment/Reflection
www.utexas.edu/academic/cte/getfeedback/selfref.html

Video as Assessment Tool
http://www.teaching.berkeley.edu/bgd/videotape.html

ESSENTIAL COMPONENTS OF A QUALITY PROGRAM

COMPONENT 1   A quality physical education program is organized around content standards that offer direction and continuity to instruction and evaluation.

COMPONENT 2   A quality program is student centered and based on the developmental urges, characteristics, and interests of students.

COMPONENT 3   Quality physical education makes physical activity and motor-skill development the core of the program.

COMPONENT 4   Physical education programs teach management skills and self-discipline.

COMPONENT 5   Quality programs emphasize inclusion of all students.

COMPONENT 6   In a quality physical education setting, instruction focuses on the process of learning skills rather than the product or outcome of the skill performance.

COMPONENT 7   A quality physical education program teaches lifetime activities that students can use to promote their health and personal wellness.

COMPONENT 8   Quality physical education teaches cooperative and responsibility skills and helps students develop sensitivity to diversity and gender issues.

10

Assessment, Evaluation, and Grading

CHAPTER SUMMARY

This chapter offers a broad overview of assessment, evaluation, and grading techniques. This chapter will address assessment, evaluation, and grading issues for the psychomotor (physical), cognitive (knowledge), and affective (social) learning domains. Examples of existing evaluation techniques for physical skills are offered. Examples of assessment techniques for performance outcomes include scoring rubrics, checklists, rating scales, personal interviews, and self-evaluation logs. Also covered is how to evaluate the knowledge and social components of physical education. Grading is always a difficult issue for physical education teachers, so both sides of the grading issue are covered so teachers can see the many viewpoints that must be considered.

STUDENT OUTCOMES

After reading this chapter, you should be able to:

- Explain the difference between assessment, evaluation, and grading.

- Administer a sport skills assessment to a class of secondary school students in physical education.

- Know how to assess performance outcomes using a variety of instruments including rubrics, checklists, rating scales, anecdotal record sheets, and self-evaluation logs.

Student Outcomes, continued

- Devise a knowledge assessment for secondary school students on specific sports units.

- Create a study guide and related exam for students.

- Know how to administer the national physical education test.

- Discuss issues related to assessment, evaluation, and grading, including educational objectives versus administrative tasks, process versus product, improvement and potential, negative versus positive, and pass–fail versus letter grades.

- Explain the pros and cons of specific methods of grading in physical education.

- Develop a grading scheme that is in line with stated objectives for secondary school physical education.

A ssessment, evaluation, and grading are areas teachers are expected to integrate into the teaching process. Regardless of how these processes are managed, the emphasis on accountability continues to place more importance on this area. National, state, and district standards are becoming the norm. No longer are school boards willing to support a program that does not document its impact on students. Teachers must demonstrate that each student meets specific learning outcomes specified by content standards. Student learning, achievement of content, assessment, and grading can be means of accountability that inform parents and the public how well their child's school is achieving. Similarly, students are much less willing to accept a grade in physical education if it is not grounded on principles similar to those in other academic areas.

Assessment, evaluation, and grading are three different entities. *Assessment* is defined as the measurement or collection of information regarding the student performance of skills, knowledge, and attitudes taught in physical education classes. Assessment should answer the question: "What does this student know how to do?", and instructionally, assessment should answer the question: "What does the student need to learn next?" *Evaluation* is defined as the process of using the assessment information to make a judgment on student performance. *Grading* is a composite score that incorporates the information and data gathered through the assessment and evaluation process. Used together, assessment, evaluation, and grading offer students a view of how they are performing in different areas under the physical education umbrella. For example, a student might earn high marks in volleyball and basketball skills but lower marks in soccer and team handball. A grade is assigned as a composite score for all the areas measured in physical education; to some degree, it is an average report of all data gathered through the process of assessment and evaluation.

ASSESSMENT OF STUDENT PERFORMANCE

Assessment, defined as the collection of information about student performance, has always been a tough subject for teachers to tackle. Traditionally, assessment in physical education has been directed at functions of compliance (e.g., dressing, participation, attendance) and not on components that reflect student learning (Lund, 1993). Even when performance is considered, it is done in ways that are suspect in recording true learning. Matanin and Tannehill (1994) suggest the use of ongoing, daily assessments (process) to obtain measures that reliably reflect student learning.

Two types of assessments are performed in physical education: formal assessment, defined as assessment with the intent to affect grading procedures, and informal assessment, defined as assessment done to obtain knowledge about student performance but not for use in the determination of grades. The latter of these two is the measure of choice for most physical educators. As a profession, physical education teachers tend to perform an incredible amount of informal assessments daily. Where they can improve is in using this information to evaluate or even grade students because there is currently little formal assessment in physical education that targets student performance (Lund, 1993; Matanin & Tannehill, 1994).

Within the field of physical education, assessment is an area of varying difficulty. Classes are bigger than traditional classroom settings, students have various skill abilities, there are multiple content areas, and there is often no formal protocol established to collect student work and develop permanent records, such as standardized testing results used in mathematics or literature. Assessment and evaluation in physical education is left to individual teachers and departments. This is often true even if state standards provide the content to be covered at each grade level in predetermined areas. Given multiple obstacles, teachers are faced with the challenge of developing and implementing assessment techniques and strategies that are authentic representations of what students have learned and can do. The following sections are designed to give teachers the framework and tools to perform more meaningful and accurate assessments of their students.

OBJECTIVE ASSESSMENT OF PHYSICAL SKILLS

Physical skill development is a primary purpose of physical education. Knowledge and attitude development can be addressed in other areas of the curriculum, but physical skill development only occurs through an effective physical education program. Physical skills can be divided into two subsets: The first set contains the general components of skill such as agility, balance, coordination, power, reaction time, and speed. These components are often referred to as skill-related fitness. The second set of skills relates to the ability to perform specific sport skills, such as those found in basketball, tennis, or team handball.

General Components of Skill

Individuals who are skilled usually display ability in a number of skill components. The more a person excels in each of the components, the greater the possibility they will perform well in sport skills. Teachers can more effectively develop instructional lessons and related assessments when a clear understanding of movement principles and concepts are understood. Adolescent students can begin to understand the relationship of these skill performances to their own abilities and establish attainable goals and outcomes based on their own perception of their ability within the skill components. The following discussion identifies each of the components of skill and offers an example of a test commonly used to measure each component.

Agility

Agility is the ability of the body to change position rapidly and accurately while moving in space. Most sports require agility and the ability to move in different directions quickly.

Sample Test. In the shuttle run (American Association for Health, Physical Education, and Recreation, [AAHPER], 1976), two blocks of wood are placed side by side on a line 30 feet from the starting line. On the command to start, the student runs from behind the starting line to retrieve one of the blocks. After placing

it behind the starting line, the student runs to pick up the second block and carries it back across the starting line. Two trials are given, with a rest allowed between them. The score is recorded as the number of seconds required to retrieve both blocks.

Balance

Balance is usually classified into two types: static and dynamic. Static balance occurs when the person is in a fixed position, such as doing a handstand or balancing on a balance beam. Dynamic balance is the ability to move in a stable manner without falling and is used in activities such as skating, gymnastics, and most locomotor sports.

Sample Tests. In the stork stand for static balance (Safrit, 1990), the student stands erect on the dominant foot, placing the opposite foot flat on the medial part of the supporting knee, with the hands on hips. The score is the amount of time the balance position can be held.

In the balance beam walk for dynamic balance (Jensen & Hirst, 1980), the student is instructed to stand at one end of a 4-inch-wide balance beam. When ready, the student begins to slowly walk (one foot in front of the other) the full length of the beam, pausing at the end for 5 seconds, turning 180°, and returning to the starting point. Three trials are given. The test is a scored as pass-fail.

Coordination

Coordination is the ability to smoothly integrate a number of motor patterns together to produce a complete and effective skill. Coordination is most often required for complex skills such as throwing, catching, striking, and kicking.

Sample Test. In the stick test of coordination (Corbin, Welk, Corbin, & Welk, 2008), the student juggles three wooden wands. One wand is held in each hand, and the third wand rests across the other two. The resting wand is flipped a half turn (1 point) or full turn (2 points) and caught using the wands in each hand. Five attempts are allowed for a half turn and five attempts for a full turn. The test is scored by adding the points earned for the number of successful flips (15 points possible).

Speed and Reaction Time

Speed and reaction time are closely related components. Speed is the ability to move quickly in the shortest time possible. Reaction time is the amount of time necessary to respond to a signal. Even though both can be measured separately, it is most common to group them and measure them singly in a dash. Running a sprint for time requires rapid reaction time and speed.

Sample Test. In the 50-yard dash (AAHPER, 1976), the student is timed while running the 50-yard distance as fast as possible.

Power

Power is the ability to exert high muscular forces in a minimum amount of time.

Sample Test. In the standing long jump (AAHPER, 1976), the student assumes a starting position behind the takeoff line. The student takes off using both feet simultaneously and jumps as far as possible. The long jump is scored on the best of three trials to the nearest inch.

Integrating Assessment of General Skill Components

Results from the formal testing found previously can frequently provide students with perceptions of their abilities, but assessment must go beyond an understanding of these basic concepts. Students will begin to understand and place added meaning to the results if they understand the bigger picture of how these concepts are used in the world of sports, fitness, and games. These results will provide students with a baseline for success, but the relationship and implications of these concepts will be more thoroughly constructed through active engagement, interaction, and analysis of the movement environment.

Specific Sport Skills Tests

Standardized testing is frequently used to communicate student learning outcomes. A wide number of formal tests have been designed to objectively evaluate sport skills. These tests are usually carefully designed and score high in validity and reliability. Norms are usually available for the tests so teachers can compare the performance of their students with a larger number of students who have been tested. This section is not meant to be comprehensive but to give a few examples of the types of objective tests that are available to teachers. Two excellent textbooks that contain a wide variety of tests are *Measurement and Evaluation in Physical Education and Exercise Science* (Lacy & Hastad, 2007) and *Assessing Sport Skills* (Strand & Wilson, 1993).

Bear in mind that these *formal assessments* evaluate components of specific sport skills in isolation and do not evaluate actual performance in game situations. An

actual performance assessment would be called an *authentic assessment*, which determines how successful a student is in the application of skills in a "real" setting. The complexity of the skill application can limit such testing, resulting in teachers finding them unacceptable in the instructional setting. Another drawback is that some tests require a large number of trained personnel for administration, which may not be feasible in large secondary classes. Regardless of these restrictions, an effective teacher will arrange his or her instructional environment to include both formal and authentic skill assessments and evaluation. It is important that students know that learning is an integral part of physical education. Assessment should answer this question: "What does this student know how to do?"

Cornish Handball Test

This test (Cornish, 1949) consists of five test items: the 30-second volley, the front-wall placement, the back-wall placement, the service placement, and the power test. When the tests were analyzed for validity, however, the power test and the 30-second volley alone predicted handball performance almost as effectively as all five items together. To conserve time, it is therefore recommended that only the two items be used.

Equipment. Several handballs are required. The service line is the only marking necessary for the volley test. For the power test, a line is drawn on the front wall at a height of 6 feet. Lines are also drawn on the floor as follows: The first line is 18 feet from the front wall; the second line is 5 feet behind the first; and the third, fourth, and fifth lines are each 5¾ feet apart. These lines form six scoring zones. The area from the front wall to the first line scores 1 point, as does the first of the five zones behind. The second, third, fourth, and fifth zones score two, three, four, and five points, respectively. A stopwatch is needed for the volley test.

Power Test Directions. The subject stands in the service zone and throws the ball against the front wall. The subject lets the ball hit the floor on the rebound before striking it. The subject then hits the ball as hard as possible, making sure that it strikes the front wall below the 6-foot line. Subjects must throw the ball against the wall before each power stroke. Five trials are given with each hand. A retrial is allowed for an attempt in which the subject steps into the front court or fails to hit the wall below the 6-foot line.

Scoring. The value of the scoring zone, in which each trial first touches the floor, is recorded. The subject's score is the total points for the 10 trials.

Thirty-Second Volley. The subject stands behind the service line, drops the ball, and begins volleying it against the front wall for 30 seconds. The subject should hit all strokes from behind the service line. If the ball does not return past this line, the subject is allowed to step into the frontcourt to hit the ball but must then get back behind the line for the succeeding stroke. If the subject misses the ball, the instructor hands over another ball and volleying continues.

Scoring. The score is the total number of times the ball hits the front wall in 30 seconds.

Kemp-Vincent Tennis Rally Test

This test (Kemp & Vincent, 1968) evaluates rallying ability in tennis under game conditions. Two students of similar ability assume ready positions on opposite sides of the net on a singles tennis court. Each player has two tennis balls on his or her side of the court. On signal, one student bounces a ball behind the baseline and with a courtesy stroke, puts the ball into play. The two students rally the ball as long as possible. When a ball is hit into the net or out of bounds, either player starts another ball into play with a courtesy stroke from behind the baseline. Any type of stroke may be used during a rally. If all four balls are hit out of play, the testing students are responsible for retrieving them to continue the test. One 3-minute trial is allowed.

Scoring. For a 3-minute rally, the combined number of hits for the two players are counted, including any erroneous hits. The courtesy stroke to put a ball in play counts as a hit. Errors committed by each player are counted. From the combined number of hits for both players, each individual player subtracts the number of his or her errors to arrive at a final rally score.

AAHPERD Basketball Test

The American Alliance for Health, Physical Education, Recreation, and Dance (AAHPERD) basketball test (AAHPER, 1984) evaluates a number of basketball skills, including dribbling, passing, shooting, and defensive ability. Each of the areas is briefly described.

Speed Spot Shooting. Five spots are laid out around the key. The shooter must shoot, retrieve the ball, dribble to another spot, and shoot again. The student must attempt at least one shot from each spot. All students get three trials of 60 seconds each.

Passing. Six targets are placed on a wall with a restraining line 8 feet away from the wall. On signal, the student performs a chest pass to the first target, recovers the ball, drops the ball, and moves to the second target. This action continues until he or she reaches the last target. While at the last target, the student throws two chest passes, and then repeats the sequence moving to the left. This pattern continues until time runs out (30 seconds). Three trials are given.

Control Dribble. Five cones are placed in the key, one in each corner and the fifth in the middle. On signal, the student weaves in and out of the cones and completes the course as fast as possible. The score is recorded as number of seconds required to complete the course. Three trials are given.

Defensive Ability. The student slides in defensive position from marker to marker without crossing the feet. Each time a marker is reached, the student must touch the floor. The score is recorded as number of seconds required to complete the course.

Johnson Soccer Test

The purpose of this test (Johnson, 1963) is to evaluate general ability in soccer. A wall marked with the same dimensions as a soccer goal and a supply of soccer balls are needed. The student starts behind a restraining line that is 15 feet from the wall. On signal, the student kicks a ball against the wall so that it rebounds back on the fly or after bouncing. The objective is to return the ball against the backboard as many times as possible during a 30-second timed interval. All kicks must be initiated from behind the restraining line. If a ball goes out of control, the student can retrieve another from the supply. Three 30-second trials are given. The score is the number of legal kicks made during the three trials.

Health-Related Fitness

Physical fitness testing has occurred for decades in physical education. Some experts make an argument for placing less emphasis on fitness testing and more on activity evaluation (Pangrazi, 2007). There is much to be said, however, for using a standardized test that is administered to many students. Currently the Fitnessgram System (Cooper Institute, 2007) is the most popular test being used to measure health-related physical fitness and is the recommended test by the AAHPERD. The test items have been checked for validity and reliability. The Fitnessgram offers a variety of fitness test items so teachers can develop a customized test battery. The focus of the Fitnessgram is on teaching students about the importance of activity for good health. Students are not compared to one another but are given feedback about their fitness and whether it meets the minimum standard for good health.

The Fitnessgram is based primarily on exercise behaviors rather than students' attempts to demonstrate that they are the "best." The Fitnessgram program acknowledges and commends performance; however, it places its highest priority on the development and reinforcement of health-related behaviors that are attainable by all students. These behavior programs are used to recognize participants for any of the following activities: completion of exercise logs, achievement of specific and personalized goals, and fulfillment of a contractual agreement (with a responsible adult). A text that is helpful for understanding fitness and activity topics is *Toward a Better Understanding of Physical Activity and Fitness: Selected Topics, Volume Two,* (Corbin, Pangrazi, & Franks, 2004).

Fitnessgram Test Items

The suggested test items in the Fitnessgram are briefly described in the following text. Other test items are included in the manual to give teachers a choice of designing a different test battery. A comprehensive test administration manual, related materials, and software can be ordered from Human Kinetics Publishers, P.O. Box 5076, Champaign, IL 61825-5076 (www.Fitnessgram.net).

Aerobic Capacity. The Progressive Aerobic Cardiovascular Endurance Run (PACER) test is an excellent alternative to the mile—it involves a 20-meter shuttle run (a 15-meter pacer is also included) and can be performed indoors. The test is progressive and starts out at a level that allows all youngsters to be successful and gradually increases in difficulty. The objective of the PACER is to run back and forth across the 20- or 15-meter distance within a specified time limit that gradually decreases. The 20- or 15-meter distance is not intimidating to youngsters (compared to the mile) and avoids the problem of trying to teach students to pace themselves rather than running all out and fatiguing rapidly.

Body Composition. Body composition is evaluated using percent body fat, which is calculated by measuring the triceps and calf skinfolds or body mass index (calculated using height and weight).

Abdominal Strength. The curl-up test uses a cadence (one curl-up every 3 seconds). The maximum limit is 75. Students lie in a supine position with the knees bent at a 140° angle. The hands are placed flat on the mat alongside the hips. The objective is to gradually sit up and move the fingers down the mat a specified distance.

Upper-Body Strength. The push-up test is done to a cadence (one every 3 seconds) and is an excellent substitute for the pull-up. A successful push-up is counted when the arms are bent to a 90° angle. This item allows many more students to experience success as compared to the pull-up and flexed-arm hang. Other alternative test items to the push-up are the modified pull-up, the pull-up, and the flexed-arm hang.

Trunk Extensor Strength and Flexibility. The trunk lift test is done from a facedown position. This test involves lifting the upper body 6 to 12 inches off the floor using the muscles of the back. The position must be held until the measurement can be made.

Flexibility. The back-saver sit and reach is similar to the traditional sit-and-reach test except that it is performed with one leg flexed to avoid encouraging students to hyperextend. Measurement is made on both the right and left legs.

Criterion-Referenced Health Standards

A major reason for doing health-related fitness evaluation is to provide students, teachers, and parents with information about good health. The Fitnessgram (Cooper Institute, 2007) uses **criterion-referenced health standards** that represent good health instead of traditional percentile rankings. These standards represent a level of fitness that offers some degree of protection against diseases resulting from sedentary living. The Fitnessgram uses an approach that classifies fitness performance into two categories: needs improvement and healthy fitness zone (HFZ). All students are encouraged to score in the HFZ; however, there is little advantage to scoring beyond the healthy fitness zone.

Criterion-referenced health standards do not compare students against each other as do percentile rankings. Instead, youngsters are concerned with personal fitness and minimizing possible health problems by trying to score within the HFZ. Criterion-referenced health standards for aerobic fitness are based on a study by Blair and colleagues (1989). A significant decrease in risk of all-cause mortality occurred when people were active enough to avoid classification in the bottom 20 percent of the population. The risk level continues to decrease as fitness levels increase but not significantly when compared to moving out of the least active group. The aerobic performance minimums (mile run or PACER) for the Fitnessgram HFZ require

FIGURE 10.1   Self-testing health-related fitness

achieving a fitness level that is above the least-active portion (bottom 20 percent) of the population.

Criterion-referenced health standards for percent of fat are calculated from equations reported by Slaughter and colleagues (1988). Detailed information on the development of these equations and other issues related to the measurement and interpretation of body composition information is available in Lohman (1992). Williams and colleagues (1992) reported that students with body-fat levels above 25 percent for boys and 30 to 35 percent for girls are more likely to exhibit elevated cholesterol and hypertension levels. The lower limit for the Fitnessgram HFZ corresponds to these levels of body fat. In other words, students who are fatter may be at risk for future health problems.

Criterion-referenced health standards have not been established for abdominal strength, upper-body strength, and flexibility. For example, it is difficult to determine whether a lack of upper-body strength is important for quality health. Instead, criterion-referenced training standards are used for these areas of fitness. The lower limit represents a performance level that youngsters should be able to accomplish if they are reasonably active and exercise. These standards reflect how many push-ups active students should be able to perform. Stated another way, these standards reflect a reasonable expectation for students who are sufficiently active.

Effective Uses of Fitness Tests

Fitness tests are designed to evaluate and educate students about the status of their physical fitness. In spite of continued research and improvement, fitness tests have limitations and usually show low validity (that is, they do not measure what they purport to measure). It is important to bear in mind that the results of fitness

evaluation are often flawed or inaccurate. Therefore, how the tests are used becomes an important issue. The three major ways to use fitness tests are (1) to teach personal self-testing, (2) to establish personal best fitness performances, and (3) to evaluate institutional fitness goals. The personal self-testing program is most strongly advocated in the physical education program. It can be done in the least amount of time, is educational, and can be done frequently. In addition, little instructional time is lost, and students learn how to evaluate their fitness, a skill that will serve them for a lifetime.

Personal Self-Testing. The personal self-testing program is an approach that is student centered, is concerned with the process of fitness testing, and places emphasis on learning to self-evaluate (Figure 10.1). When using this technique, students can work individually or find a friend with whom they would like to self-test. With a partner, they evaluate each other and develop their own fitness profiles. The goal is to learn the process of fitness testing so students will be able to evaluate their health status during adulthood. Students are asked to do their best, but the teacher does not interfere in the process. The results are the property of the student and are not posted or shared with other students. The personal self-testing program is an educational endeavor; it also allows for more frequent evaluation because it can be done quickly, privately, and informally.

Figure 10.2 is an example of a self-evaluation form that can be used by students. It contains a column to check off whether the minimum criterion-referenced health standard for each test item has been met. The purpose of recording the data is to help students learn to evaluate themselves without the stigma of others having to view or know about it. As a final note, it is acceptable for some students to choose not to be tested on a certain item because they fear embarrassment (skinfolds) or failure (PACER). It is worse to be tested and embarrassed than to not be tested at all.

Personal Best Testing. The personal best testing approach appeals to gifted performers and to students who are motivated by achieving a maximum performance. The objective is to achieve a maximum score in each of the test items. This approach has been used for years with most fitness tests. In addition, several awards (President's Council on Physical Fitness and Sports, 2004) are issued to high-level performers. This is a formal testing program as compared to the self-testing approach discussed previously. Test items must be performed correctly, following test protocol to the letter. It requires a considerable amount of time to administer.

Name _____   Age _____   Grade _____   Room _____

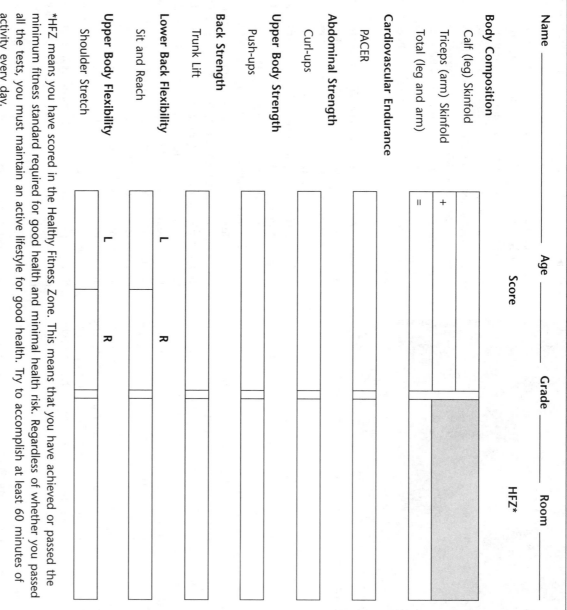

	Score			HFZ*
Body Composition				
Calf (leg) Skinfold				
Triceps (arm) Skinfold	+			
Total (leg and arm)	=			
Cardiovascular Endurance				
PACER				
Abdominal Strength				
Curl-ups				
Upper Body Strength				
Push-ups				
Back Strength				
Trunk Lift				
Lower Back Flexibility				
Sit and Reach	L	R		
Upper Body Flexibility				
Shoulder Stretch	L	R		

*HFZ means you have scored in the Healthy Fitness Zone. This means that you have achieved or passed the minimum fitness standard required for good health and minimal health risk. Regardless of whether you passed all the tests, you must maintain an active lifestyle for good health. Try to accomplish at least 60 minutes of activity every day.

You do not have to share the results of your personal fitness record. It is for your information and should help you determine your health status. Ask your teacher if you need ideas for increasing your physical activity level.

Students are learning the process of evaluating their fitness. The scores recorded may not be accurate.

FIGURE 10.2   My personal fitness record (Fitnessgram)

Personal best testing is an elective program. It requires maximal performance and usually is not motivating to less-capable students. Some students are threatened and fear the embarrassment of failing to perform well in front of peers. A way to avoid embarrassing students who are less capable is to administer the test outside of class time. Testing opportunities can be offered after or before school and on a weekend when school is not in session. Some city recreation departments can offer fitness testing opportunities outside the physical education program as another elective option.

This approach is much less threatening; students can choose to participate in the personal best testing session or decide to entirely avoid such situations.

Institutional Evaluation. The institutional evaluation program involves examining the fitness levels of students to see if the institution (school) is reaching its desired objectives. Institutional objectives are closely tied to the physical education curriculum. If the curriculum being taught to students is adequate and the goals meaningful, the majority of students should be able to reach institutional goals. A common approach for institutional goal setting is to establish a percentage of the student body that must meet or exceed criterion-referenced health standards for a fitness test. If the percentage is below established institutional standards, it may indicate that the curriculum needs to be modified in order to meet the objective.

Because this type of testing impacts teachers and curriculum offerings, it is done in a formal and standardized manner. A common approach is to train a team of parents to administer tests throughout the system. This ensures accuracy and consistency across all schools in the district. Each test item is reviewed separately because it is possible that objectives are reached for some but not all of the items. To avoid testing all students every year, some districts evaluate only during entry level years (i.e., the seventh and ninth grades). This minimizes the amount of formal testing youngsters have to endure during their school career.

ASSESSMENT OF PERFORMANCE OUTCOMES

Assessment in physical education is often difficult because of the nature of the subject matter. There is seldom a perfect and correct performance. Even outstanding athletes who have practiced for years make performance errors. However, there are ways to assess student performance that allows for a continuum of performance levels between good and poor. Assessment of student performance is an important issue that can be accomplished in many different ways. Assessment can become more than an end product, resulting in evaluation of good and poor; it can be used as an integral part of student learning and understanding. Assessment can be used as a tool to guide the instructional process and develop in-depth student understanding.

What students are to learn is directed by national, state, and/or content-specific standards. These standards serve as a guide to what can be expected upon completion. Expectations and outcomes are clarified with standards; yet it is often unclear if the learning outcomes based on these standards are achieved without input derived from alternative and authentic assessment. When authentic assessment is used, teachers can state that students "know" and "do" what is stated in the standards. Information collected from alternative and authentic assessment makes it clear what students have learned. Standards direct the learning, giving it a framework; objectives are more immediate outcomes and can be developed to focus on the progressive nature of learning as well as outcomes. Stu-

dent learning objectives are written so that both the teacher and students know what they can do at the end of the course or upon completion of the lesson.

A looming question is this: "How do teachers help students engage in assessment that is meaningful?" It is this question that drives the principles of using assessment as tools to assess student skill level and understanding and provide opportunities to involve the student with outcomes-based learning. Meaningful information should result from systematic and ongoing assessment that involve all three learning domains. Assessment can occur throughout multiple levels of learning, including knowledge, comprehension, application, analysis, synthesis, and evaluation.

Traditionally, assessment in physical education has been accomplished informally, often done on the spot when a teacher corrects or reinforces a student's performance. Visual monitoring of students' performance has also been accepted as a form of assessment. Teachers visually scan to see if students are successfully accomplishing specific tasks. Informal assessment typically produces no documented evidence to show students or parents that objectives have been attained. Standards-based content highlights what students should know and be able to do at the end of specific grade levels (NASPE, 2004). Standards provide guidelines for teachers and departments to communicate and give direction to physical education.

With the introduction of physical education content standards, more formal, yet alternative assessments are becoming popular because teachers are expected to assess and report student progress toward program standards (Chepko & Arnold, 2000). While similar to alternative assessment, another aspect to assessing student performance is making sure that the assessment is authentic. Authentic assessment is defined as measuring student performance in a real-world application of knowledge or skills. Unlike many of the skills tests listed in the previous section, authentic assessment allows for students to perform in a normal setting rather than a contrived testing environment. What good is performing a skill well if a student is not able to perform it when it counts? Student outcomes on a written rules test will mean little if they can not be applied appropriately during game play. By assessing students during normal participation, a teacher ensures that the assessment will reflect actual knowledge or ability. In all of the following examples of assessment instruments, it is relatively easy to ensure that each have at least some authentic components to them. Examples of conditions that represent authentic assessment can include the following:

- Adherence to rules during play
- Strategy formulation and execution

Levels of Learning	Elements of Learning		
	Punting within a limited time	Punting to a Partner	Punting at Angles
Professional	■ Watches the ball and not the partner ■ Only 2 steps are taken, then ball is punted	■ Eyes are on the ball ■ Distance is adjusted to location of receiving partner; partner does not move more than 10 feet ■ The step-hop technique is used	■ Eyes are on the ball ■ Leg angle extends toward the intended target ■ Ball is within 15 feet of target
Collegiate	■ Eyes are on the ball ■ 3 or more steps are taken	■ Eyes are on the ball ■ Distance is adjusted to location of receiving partner; partner moves no more than 15 feet ■ The step-hop technique is used	■ Eyes are on the ball ■ Leg angle extends toward the intended target ■ Ball is within 20 feet of the target
Varsity	■ Eyes are taken off the ball ■ 3 or more steps are taken	■ Eyes are on the ball ■ Distance is adjusted to location of receiving partner; partner moves no more than 20 feet ■ The step-hop technique is not used	■ Eyes are on the ball ■ Leg angle extends toward the intended target ■ Ball is not catchable
Junior Varsity	■ Eyes are taken off the ball ■ Ball is dropped ■ Ball is not kicked	■ Eyes are taken off the ball ■ Ball is not catchable for partner ■ The step-hop technique is not used	■ Eyes are taken off the ball ■ Leg angle does not extend toward the intended target ■ Ball is not catchable

FIGURE 10.3 High school rubric for punting a football

- Skill selection and application during play
- Performance of physical skills under gamelike or competitive situations
- Self-monitoring for performance indicators of activity involvement, fitness, and appropriate social engagement

Scoring Rubrics

A rubric is an alternative way to evaluate a specific outcome. Rubrics can be used to objectively score a student according to the level of achievement he or she has accomplished based upon specific criteria. Effective rubrics focus on specific learning outcomes or objectives that students are expected to achieve. Scores are assigned for each level of attainment. Rubrics can be used as both process and product assessments. When a rubric is used as a process assessment, information is shared with the student and becomes an excellent tool to self-diagnose both strengths and weaknesses and develop a practice plan (Figure 10.3).

Students are given the rubric prior to assessment so they understand how they will be assessed and held

Name: _____ Date: _____

Outstanding

A. Participates in weight training activities over and above class requirements.

B. Expresses positive views toward safety in the weight room.

C. Participates in three intramural or extramural weight training competitions.

D. Gives examples of proper techniques for five basic lifts.

E. Leads by example in the weight room by taking turns and encouraging peers.

F. Can self-analyze each lift and explain what part of the body is being developed.

G. Records all lifts by weight and repetitions into log.

Satisfactory

A. Participates in all class requirement activities.

B. Shows concern for safety but is not overt about safe practices.

C. Participates in two intramural or extramural weight training competitions.

D. Usually, but not always, able to demonstrate proper technique for five basic lifts.

E. Displays primary interest in self-development rather than helping others.

F. Usually knows what body part each lift develops.

G. Usually records all lifts by weight and repetitions into log.

Needs Improvement

A. Doesn't always complete class requirement activities.

B. Usually shows concern for safety but at times lifts using unsafe practices.

C. Participates in one intramural or extramural weight training competition.

D. Often not able to demonstrate proper techniques when a new lift is introduced.

E. Rarely tries to help others.

F. Rarely knows what body part is developed by a lift.

G. Often fails to record all lifts by weight and repetitions into log.

Unsatisfactory

A. Demonstrates spotty record of completing class requirement activities.

B. Considers safety a low priority and needs correction regularly.

C. Does not participate in intramural or extramural weight training competition.

D. Fails to use proper techniques when lifting.

E. Often fails to allow peers to "work-in" and share weights.

F. Displays unorganized total weight program.

G. Does not maintain a log of lifts by weight and repetition.

FIGURE 10.4 Scoring rubric for a weight training class

accountable. The scoring system and the criteria assigned each level must be objective and attainable and answer a basic question common to most assessments: "Does the student consistently meet the stated criteria required for completion of the course requirement?" Figure 10.4 is an example of an outcomes-based product rubric for grading a weight training class.

Another use of rubrics is to list criteria that need to be completed for successful performance of a skill. The criteria are performance levels students are expected to achieve as they practice skills. Students obtain a clear and objective picture of how they are performing and can develop future practice tasks based on those areas still needing development. This type of skill evaluation helps students focus on the process of correct performance as compared to product evaluation. Basic to the skill evaluation rubric is the question of whether the student can perform the motor skills using correct technique. Figure 10.5 is an example of a bowling rubric using videotape analysis. In this case, students work together in groups of three and analyze their own

and their peers' skill performance. The performer receives the average of three scores, his or her own score and the scores of two peers.

Checklists

Subjective evaluation leads to inconsistency in assessment and evaluation. Students are unclear as to what is to be graded and, just as importantly, *how* it is to be graded. Specifying the performance criteria to be graded can be improved using a check sheet or scorecard. Criteria are listed and ranked on a scale of points. Even though using the checklist increases the reliability of the data, the overall approach remains subjective. A score sheet can be used to evaluate skill development or successful application of skills in an authentic setting. For example, teachers select the types of skills they believe a student should learn in a basketball unit.

Checklists are useful for reporting progress to students and parents and identifying students who are in

This assignment will require that you evaluate yourself using videotape analysis. Over the next 3 weeks, have one of the members of the group videotape you while you are performing the following skills. You must be taped at least twice doing the same skills. Make sure everyone in your group has been videotaped performing all the skills listed below. Evaluate your tape at home or at school. Then give your tape to each of the members in your group and ask them to evaluate it. When you have completed all the skills, turn in the tape (label it with your name) and your evaluation sheet.

	Always 2 pts	Usually 1 pt	Rarely 0 pts
Approach			
Push away on first step			
Push away: out and down—elbow straight			
Backswing: straight—in line with boards			
Steps: smooth, gliding, even rhythm			
Steps: increase in length and speed			
Slide on left foot			
Release			
Shoulders: parallel to foul line			
Shoulders: level			
Upper body: inclined forward			
Left foot: in line with boards			
Weight balanced on left foot			
Thumb in 12 o'clock position			
Ball first strikes alley 1.5 ft in front of left foot			
Follow-through: straight and to shoulder height			
Aim			
Approach: straight, in line with boards			
Release: proper dot to dots at foul line			
Crosses proper dart			
Where does ball strike pins? (e.g., 1–3, 1, 3, 1–2)			

Scoring: Total points accumulated in each area above.

Self-evaluation:	Approach	Release	Aim
Trial 1			
Trial 2			
Peer #1 evaluation of me	Approach	Release	Aim
Trial 1			
Trial 2			
Peer #2 evaluation of me	Approach	Release	Aim
Trial 1			
Trial 2			
Total Score:			

Write a short evaluation of how you will improve your bowling skills based on your evaluation of your bowling form.

FIGURE 10.5 Bowling rubric using videotape evaluation

Work with a partner. Each of you has a task sheet and will be responsible for evaluating each other. You will have to find other peers to complete some of the tasks. Record the date the task was tried and whether it was successfully accomplished (yes/no). Then initial the sheet.

Date	Score	Initials	Description of task
			Stand 45 ft from a partner who is inside a hoop and complete 5 consecutive underhand pitches to that person without causing him/her to move outside the hoop.
			Stand 60 feet from a partner who is inside a hoop and complete 5 overhand throws to that person without forcing him or her to move more than 1 foot outside the hoop.
			Demonstrate the proper stance, windup, and delivery of the windmill pitch.
			From a designated area of the outfield, situated 150 feet (boys) or 100 feet (girls) away, throw the softball through the air directly to a 10-foot-wide circle chalked in front of home plate. To count, the throw must bounce only once before landing or going through the circle. Make 3 of 5 throws.
			Display pitching skills by striking out 3 or more batters or by allowing no more than 5 base hits in an actual game.
			Using the correct fielding stance, cleanly field 5 consecutive ground or fly balls hit by partner.
			Play a game of Pepper with a group of no more than 6 players, demonstrating good bat control, hand–eye coordination, and fielding skills.
			Play a game of 500 with no more than 5 players and demonstrate skills in catching flies and line drives and in fielding ground balls.
			Using a batting tee, hit 5 consecutive softballs, on the fly or on the ground, past the 80-foot semicircle line marked off in chalk.
			Execute proper bunting form and ability by dumping 3 of 5 attempts into designated bunting areas along the first or third baselines.
			In an actual game, make 2 or more base hits.

Bonus Requirements (You may substitute the following for tasks above you didn't accomplish.)

			Make a diagram of an official softball diamond on poster board. Illustrate proper field dimensions.
			On a piece of paper, show how batting average and earned run average are compiled.
			Umpire a game for 3 or more innings.
			Keep accurate score in an official score book for 3 or more innings.

FIGURE 10.6   Softball peer assessment task checklist

need of special help. Using a class list with skills displayed across the top of the sheet is a common method used for recording class progress. If grading is based on the number of activities students master, the checklist can deliver this information. Checklists are usually most effective when skills are listed in the se-

quence in which they should be learned. In this way, the teacher can gear the teaching process to diagnosed needs. To avoid disrupting the learning process, teachers can record student progress informally while students are practicing. Figure 10.6 is an example of a pass–fail task checklist that is used in softball. In this

Work with a partner. See the course syllabus for the days when you should evaluate the following skills. If you successfully pass the skill, have your partner verify your performance by dating and initialing this sheet. When finished, calculate the total number of points you have earned.

Skill to Be Tested:	Points Possible	Date Passed	Partner's Initials
Wall sets: Set ball 12–15 inches above a 10 ft-line against the wall 25 times (try to make them consecutive).	5		
Quick hands sets: Set ball 12–15 inches above hands in air or against wall for 30 seconds.	5		
Partner sets: Set 25 sets with your partner 15 ft apart (try to make them consecutive).	10		
Hoop sets: Set 10 balls into a hula hoop 12 ft away from a partner-tossed ball from a right angle to the net or wall.	15		
Wall bumps: Bump the ball above a 10-ft line against the wall 25 times (try to make them consecutive).	5		
Partner bumps: 25 bumps with a partner 15 ft apart (try to make them consecutive).	10		
Hoop bumps: Bump 10 balls into a hula hoop 12 ft away from a partner-tossed ball. The ball should be tossed at a 30°–45° angle to the net.	15		
Overhand serves: Make 10 successful overhand serves.	10		
Wall spikes: 10 consecutive floor-to-wall spikes.	5		
Four-step approach: Perform 5 dry approaches.	5		
Spikes: Do 5 successful spikes.	10		
Blocking fundamentals: 5 static jumps, 5 crossover step jumps to the right and left.	5		
Total Score:			

FIGURE 10.7   Volleyball skills peer assessment checklist

example, students work with a partner and are responsible for evaluating each other. When a task is evaluated, the form is dated, scored, and initialed.

Figure 10.7 is an example of a volleyball skills peer-assessment checklist. In this situation, a partner observes and completes the assessment. Points are earned by completing tasks. At the end of the unit, a grade is assigned based on the number of points accumulated. If there is some concern about the accuracy of evaluation, students can be spot-checked on different skills. In most cases, the strength of a checklist is that it gives direction to instruction. Students know what is expected of them and how they will be evaluated.

Rating Scales

Teachers can use rating scales to evaluate the performance of a class of students. The rating scale should list the tasks that need to be completed by students. To some degree, these tasks form the outcomes for the unit. Figure 10.8 is an example of a team handball teacher rating scale. Rating is done on a four-point scale; the required tasks are awarded for a task completed successfully. The required tasks should be posted in the teaching area so students know what skills they are expected to learn and how they will be evaluated. In a longer unit of instruction, ratings can be done at the

Students will be rated on the following team handball skills. The following rating scale will be used for evaluation purposes.

1 = Student unable to complete the task
2 = Student usually does not complete the task successfully
3 = Student usually completes the task successfully
4 = Student always completes the task successfully

Name of Students

Skill Task													
Dribble the ball with the right hand (standing position) for 10 consecutive times.													
Same as task above, but with the left hand.													
Dribble the ball with the right hand (moving forward) from the centerline to the goal line without losing the dribble.													
Same as task above, but with the left hand.													
Pass the ball to a partner standing 10 feet away with a 2-handed chest pass to the chest area (between chin and waist) 8 of 10 times.													
Pass the ball to a partner standing 10 feet away with a 2-handed bounce pass to the waist area 8 of 10 times.													
Pass the ball to a partner standing 10 feet away with a 2-handed overhead pass to the chest area 8 of 10 times.													
Pass the ball to a partner standing 10 feet away with a 1-handed overhead pass to the chest area 8 of 10 times.													
While running from the centerline, alternately pass a 2-handed chest and bounce pass that can be caught by a partner running at a parallel distance of 12 feet with 3 of 4 passes hitting the partner in the hands.													
While standing 7 meters from the goal, hit 3 of 5 goals.													
Defend 3 of 5 attempted shots taken by a partner from a distance of 7 meters.													
Dribble the ball with the right hand (moving forward) from the centerline to the goal area without losing the dribble. Jump up and make a goal 3 of 5 times.													
From 6 meters, hit a target 5 consecutive times with the following passes: roller, hook, jump, shovel, 1-handed shoulder, sidearm, and behind-the-back.													
From 9 meters away, hit 2 of 5 goals.													
From 9 meters away, defend 4 of 5 goal shots.													
Dribble through a set of 6 cones in 25 seconds.													

FIGURE 10.8 Team handball teacher rating scale

end of each week. Using students' peers to assist in the assessment process can be a valuable tool. Large class numbers can prevent in-depth assessment from being completed in a timely manner, but by developing peer assessment tasks, teachers are relieved of being the sole individual determining students' level of success. Peer assessment can also increase communication and observation skills and add to a student's understanding of effective skill performance. Time can be effectively used when peers assist in the assessment process.

Anecdotal Record Sheets

A record sheet that contains student names and has room for comments about student performance can be used to assess student progress. Anecdotal records of student progress can be reinforcing to both student and teacher as it is often difficult to remember how much progress has been made over a period of time. With anecdotal records, teachers can inform students of their initial skill levels compared with their present performances. When making anecdotal records, record the performance as soon and accurately as possible. If background information is needed to put the performance in proper context, it should be included.

A tape recorder is useful for recording anecdotal information. The teacher may record comments during observation and transcribe them later. This process helps teachers learn the names and behavior patterns of students and leads to an increased understanding of student performance. Observations should be recorded at the start of the unit and compared with observations made at a later date as instruction proceeds.

Personal Interviews

Student input is a valuable tool to gain information about student knowledge, understanding, and interests. Establishing an interview system to monitor students can develop added value and an important component within the educational environment. A personal interview can make students feel wanted and cared for, considering few students have the opportunity to share with an instructor how much they have learned in a class. Personal interviews may seem like an overwhelming task given large class sizes and limited time. Using a focus group, where students of similar abilities are interviewed at the same time, can produce similar insights. Grouping students with those of similar abilities can provide a safe environment for students to share how they feel, what they understand, and their strengths and weaknesses. Caution must be used, however, if the interview goal is to assign grades.

Quality of responses must be based on a clearly defined set of standards and criteria develop prior to the interview. Less subjectivity will occur when checklists of questions and skill evaluations are developed and followed with each student.

Even if this approach cannot be used on a broad scale, interviewing can be a useful tool for evaluating the effectiveness of the program and the instruction. Teachers can select key students to interview to see how well they are learning, how they feel about the instructional approach, and what they might like to have added to the program. Seldom do teachers sit down and discuss the wants and concerns of students. This approach can enhance this important phase of instruction. The following is an example of questions that might be covered in an interview:

1. Did you enjoy the unit of instruction?
2. What new skills did you learn?
3. Did you improve your skill level? Did you have adequate time to practice?
4. Did you receive adequate instruction during the unit?
5. How did your peers interact with you during the unit?
6. Describe how you felt participating in this activity.
7. Describe three things that you liked least in this unit.
8. Explain why you would or would not take this course again.
9. What type of activities would you like to see offered in physical education?
10. Why do you think physical education should be (or not be) offered for juniors and seniors?

Self-Assessment Logs

Developing personal ownership for one's success is an important goal during the secondary years. Teaching students how to personally assess their performances can be a useful tool in helping students develop independence and also providing a component of the grading system. Goal setting is a common approach used to assist students in developing strategies for attaining success and assessing their performance. In order for self-assessment to be valid and reliable, students must be taught how to assess themselves and be given multiple opportunities to practice. Even though instructional time will be spent teaching and practicing self-assessment, meaningful information and knowledge can be developed. Teachers who use this

Your assignment is to keep track of the physical activity you do when you are not in school. It is best to accumulate at least 60 minutes of physical activity each day to maintain good health. However, 30 minutes is acceptable. Not only will you look better if you are active each day, but you will be healthier and have more energy.

Activities Done This Week

	Amount of Time (Minutes)						
	M	Tu	W	Th	F	Sa	Su
Walking							
Jogging							
Bicycle riding							
Rope jumping							
Playing or practicing a team sport with friends							
In-line skating							
Playing Frisbee							
Hiking							
Practicing martial arts							
Practicing cheerleading skills							
Swimming or playing a water sport							
Playing or practicing tennis							
Playing or practicing golf							
Playing or practicing racquetball							
Going to a health club for a workout							

Other Activities (list below)

Number of days I was active for at least 60 minutes: _____
Number of days I was active for at least 30 minutes: _____
Number of days I was not active for at least 30 minutes: _____

Grading: You will receive 5 points for each day you are active for at least 30 minutes. If you are active for at least 60 minutes, you will receive 10 points for that day. If you are active for more than 30 minutes at least 5 of the 7 days, you will receive a bonus of 30 points.

My weekly score: _____ points

FIGURE 10.9 Weekly physical activity log

approach also assess and evaluate these students. The final grade will be a composite of student and teacher assessments and evaluation.

Figure 10.9 is an example of a weekly physical activity log. Students are expected to monitor the physical activity they accumulate outside of the school day and record it in the log. Goals can be set for how much activity should be accumulated. In this case, the goal is at least 30 to 60 minutes a day. This log could also be used for extra credit or homework so students could augment their in-class grade by participating in activities outside of school.

Authentic Assessment Sheet

Date _____   Activity Observed *Badminton Doubles*

Observer _____   Performer _____

Phase of Skill	Description of Important Elements	Errors Observed	Possible Causes	Corrective Feedback
Court Positioning	• Remains in critical portions of the court for participation • Recognizes when offensive and defensive positions should be assumed • Attempts to move opponents from good court positioning			
Court Movement	• Quickly moves to position for shot returns, coverage of court, etc. • Following court event, moves back to neutral position • Begins to anticipate where opponents will hit shuttle and moves in anticipation			
Strategy	• Recognizes strengths and weaknesses of opponents and attempts to exploit each • Attempts to use "front and back" or "side-to-side" strategy when appropriate • Uses variety of shots when appropriate			
Skills	• Serves • Clears • Drives • Lobs • Smashes			
Partner Recognition	• Attempts to support partner through communication, movement, and encouragement • Displays positive sporting behaviors			

FIGURE 10.10   Authentic assessment in badminton

Another variation of the self-evaluation approach is to allow students to develop goals they want to achieve based on specific standards and outcomes. The class decides democratically how students will accomplish these outcomes. Students are also responsible for completing the assessment materials used to ensure that the specified learning outcomes are achieved. At the end of the instructional session, both students and the teacher evaluate the progress made and the final grade.

Some teachers add a third phase to the self-evaluation process by having students evaluate each other, resulting in a three-pronged evaluation scheme: teacher, student peer, and self-evaluation. One of the strongest reasons given for using this approach is that it makes students feel more involved in the educational process. Students are more likely to believe that the grading system is fair when it manifests itself through teacher, peer, and self-evaluation.

Portfolios

Portfolios are also an effective tool in assessing student performance and demonstrating that students have accomplished specific objectives in an authentic manner. They are a collection of multiple assessments made throughout a certain segment of the class. They can include measures of all three learning domains and serve as an excellent tool to holistically assess a student. One of the main advantages of using portfolios is that it allows for students who may not excel physically to demonstrate learning and competence in physical education. Melograno (1994) provides good information for teachers interested in developing assessments through the use of portfolios. Examples of items to include in a student portfolio include but should not be limited to the following:

- Tests, assignments, and projects completed in class and as homework

- Fitness score results

- Journal entries

- Performance results on skill tests

- Self-assessments and reflections

- Goals of students

Tactical/Game-Play Assessment

One of the most authentic forms of assessment in physical education occurs in the form of Games Performance Assessment (Mitchell & Olsin, 1999). This type of assessment is authentic in nature because it focuses on the two main aspects of game play: physical performance and decision making. These two components define the nature of game play and will provide a teacher and student with accurate information about a student's ability to participate in an authentic setting. Tactical assessments focus on a student's knowledge of what to do during participation and will tell a teacher if a student can leave his or her class with the ability to engage in that activity outside the world of physical education. In just about every sporting adventure that students tackle, there is a tactical component. Everything from water polo to cricket has tactical problems to solve. In many cases, this type of assessment can

provide information critical to the success of a student. For instance, it is just as important for the student to know what club to use while golfing as it is for them to know how to swing the club. Figure 10.10 is an observation sheet that can be used to evaluate a student's ability to solve tactical problems during a game of badminton.

ASSESSMENT OF KNOWLEDGE

Cognitive assessment is an integral part of evaluating the whole child. A combination of all three learning domains (cognitive, psychomotor, and affective) influence students' desire to participate in movement activities. Traditional evaluation of content knowledge through written tests has been viewed in a controversial light. Students may feel that it is enough to learn skills, and they should not have to take written exams in physical education. Some parents resent it when their youngsters receive a lower grade because of poor performance on written tests. Teachers have often been unwilling to administer written tests in physical education because of the amount of time it takes from skill practice. Regardless of feelings, it is apparent that knowledge is involved in the application of all motor skills. An individual must know rules, regulations, and proper etiquette to participate fairly and enjoyably with others. Proper skill performance is knowledge based, and skill improvement will not occur if the individual does not know proper skill technique. To minimize concern, teachers need to explain to students and parents why cognitive achievement is as important in physical education as in any other academic area.

Evaluating the cognitive domain through alternative assessment can be done efficiently and authentically. Physical education should always be focused on maximizing activity and ensuring that students learn physical skills; in addition, they also need to know the "whys" of physical movement. Cognitive assessment of physical education content does not have to be an endeavor that occurs only in the physical education classroom. Academic content teachers can deliver and measure requisite knowledge as effectively as physical educators through integration. Examples of this can include analysis of exercise heart-rate zones in math class, or biomechanical impact on sport skills in physics, or nutritional analysis and its impact on calorie consumption in aerobic sports. Including the cognitive component as a part of a total program indicates that effective skill learning requires knowledge.

Assessing knowledge of the rules, strategy, and history of a sport or activity can be accomplished through alternative and more authentic unique techniques. For example, students can, individually or in small groups,

Racquetball Exam

I. In the blanks below, fill in the name of the area of the court designated by each letter. (10 points)

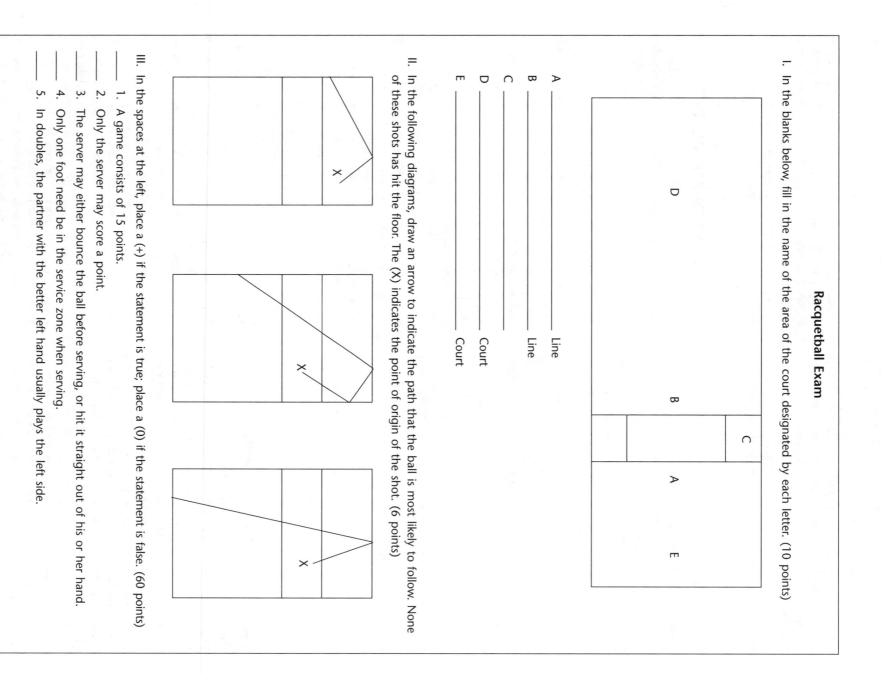

A _____ Line

B _____ Line

C _____ Court

D _____ Court

E _____ Court

II. In the following diagrams, draw an arrow to indicate the path that the ball is most likely to follow. None of these shots has hit the floor. The (X) indicates the point of origin of the shot. (6 points)

III. In the spaces at the left, place a (+) if the statement is true; place a (0) if the statement is false. (60 points)

___ 1. A game consists of 15 points.

___ 2. Only the server may score a point.

___ 3. The server may either bounce the ball before serving, or hit it straight out of his or her hand.

___ 4. Only one foot need be in the service zone when serving.

___ 5. In doubles, the partner with the better left hand usually plays the left side.

FIGURE 10.11   Knowledge test for racquetball

_____ 6. The choice for the right to serve is decided by the toss of a coin, and the side winning the toss starts the first and third games.

_____ 7. If a player swings and misses on the serve, he or she is given only one more chance.

_____ 8. A legal serve must bounce in the backcourt on a fly or after touching one sidewall.

_____ 9. In doubles, only one person serves in the first and second service. After that, both players on each team serve.

_____ 10. A player is out if he or she is hit with his or her own shot on the fly, but it is a hinder if his or her own shot hits him or her on one bounce.

_____ 11. It is common courtesy to alternate serves to each court, but in tournament play, there is no such rule.

_____ 12. The more walls that a shot hits, the deader the rebound will be.

_____ 13. When playing a "lane shot," it is usually best to hit the ball underhand.

_____ 14. It is good to use the sidewall when using the "lob serve."

_____ 15. The "kill shot" should be attempted when the ball is chest high.

_____ 16. The most advantageous court position is just behind the short line.

_____ 17. It is often wise to let a waist-high shot bounce off the back wall so that it can be returned from a lower height.

_____ 18. In doubles, a player may call a hinder when he or she is obstructed from hitting the ball by his or her partner.

_____ 19. In doubles, the server's partner must lean against the sidewall until the ball passes the service line.

_____ 20. The ball should be contacted at the junction between the fingers and the palm.

IV. In the spaces at the left, place the letter of the answer that best completes the statement. (24 points)

_____ 1. Which of the following is *not* a serve?
  A. Scotch-toss serve
  B. Ceiling serve
  C. Power serve
  D. Z serve

_____ 2. All of the following concerning body position for hitting the "kill shot" are correct *except*:
  A. Bend the knees and waist.
  B. Weight transfer is from the front foot to the rear foot.
  C. Contact should be at shin level or lower.
  D. The forearm should be parallel to the floor.

_____ 3. All of the following are "shorts" *except*:
  A. Hitting the sidewall and then the front wall.
  B. Hitting the front wall and then having the ball bounce in front of the short line.
  C. Hitting the front wall and then the two sidewalls.
  D. Hitting the front wall and then the ceiling.

_____ 4. All of the following statements concerning receiving the serve are true *except*:
  A. The receiver must be behind the short line while the ball is being served.
  B. The receiver may return the service on either the volley or the first bounce.
  C. A short may be returned if so desired.
  D. The receiver does not have the option of returning the service on a foot fault.

_____ 5. How many bounces are permitted on the serve?
  A. 2
  B. 3
  C. 4
  D. unlimited amount

FIGURE 10.11 Continued

develop a crossword puzzle based on the rules of a specific sport. These crossword puzzles are then exchanged with classmates to be completed and used to document cognitive understanding. (See units on archery, badminton, and bowling in Chapter 20 for examples of puzzles and word searches.) Students can demonstrate their understanding of rules by performing referee duties during game and tournament play. Accuracy of decisions and calls can be determined by a peer assessment. Both of these alternative methods of assessment represent cognitive understanding in an authentic setting.

Application of fitness formulas, concepts, and principles (e.g., exercise heart rate, overload, FITT) and development of personal exercise programs can be documented through completion of fitness portfolios. Students include goals, records of participation, and activity tracking scores (e.g., with a pedometer) to support their outcomes. Fitness portfolios can be an authentic representation of knowledge and application.

Regardless of the cognitive assessments used, teachers must match the developmental levels of the students at the different grade levels. When developing written test questions using multiple choice, true–false, completion, or essay options, teachers can use a combination to effectively meet student abilities. When using essay questions, it is important to remember that grading time will be increased, as compared to multiple choice and/or true–false questions. Figure 10.11 on the preceding page is an example of a test that might be administered to freshmen at the completion of a unit on racquetball.

When designing written tests, observing a few key points can make the examinations more effective.

Pointers for Effective Written Tests

1. Group different types of questions by format. True–false, multiple-choice, and matching questions should be in separate sections.

2. Place all instructions on the test. Particular instructions for different types of questions should precede each section.

3. Place the test items in increasing order of difficulty. Students may give up on the exam if the first question or two is high in difficulty.

4. Ensure that there is not an obvious pattern to the exam, such as alternating true-and-false items or keywords that tip off the answer (e.g., using *always* or *never* in true–false questions).

5. Carefully monitor the exam. Students feel the instructor is unfair if it is easy to cheat or share answers. Also, when monitoring the exam, teachers

can listen to student questions. Similar questions about similar items often tip off an instructor to a poorly designed or written item.

Another approach to check knowledge outcomes is to give students a study guide. The study guide should contain knowledge that students need to know to participate successfully in a unit of instruction. Figure 10.12 is an example of a rugby study guide and exam developed for entry-level high school students. It contains the basic formations, terminology, and rules necessary to participate in a touch rugby unit.

Sources of Knowledge Test Questions

A publication (Zhu, Safrit, & Cohen, 1999) offers a national health-related physical fitness knowledge test. The *FitSmart Test User Manual* is designed to accurately measure students' knowledge of basic fitness concepts at the high school level. This test comes with software so students can take an online test or complete a hard copy of the exam. One advantage of using this test is that it is a formal test designed by test and measurement experts and offers credibility to the knowledge component of physical education. Instructions for administering the test are similar to other national test batteries.

A few sources are available that contain test questions. "Canned" questions are seldom adequate for most teachers because they do not cover all desired areas. Most teachers have favorite areas of emphasis and know what students need to know. However, these sources can give direction to test writing and offer an indication of what others deem important in the way of knowledge. Such questions can also be modified to meet the specific needs of teachers. The text by McGee and Farrow (1987) includes 250 to 400 multiple-choice questions for each of 15 different physical education activities. Questions range from beginning to advanced performance level and are appropriate for junior and senior high school students.

ASSESSMENT OF ATTITUDES AND VALUES

Standard 6 of the NASPE National Standards for Physical Education states that students will "value[s] physical activity for health, enjoyment, challenge, self-expression, and/or social interaction" as a learning outcome (2004). There is a clear relationship between participation and value, enjoyment and social interac-

The following is information you are expected to know when the written exam is given at the end of the week. We will discuss any questions you have prior to the exam.

Rugby is a game played by two teams of 15 players who are allowed to carry, kick, and throw the ball. Players attempt to score points by placing the ball over the opponents' goal line (a try) or by kicking the ball over the crossbar (a goal).

Team formations and positions (for this class)

```
                            Goal line

                                              X

       X         X

                 X

            XXX (these players interlock)
            1 2 3 (these players interlock)

         4
                      5
                               6
   7
                            Goal line
```

Names of players by position: 1 = prop forward; 2 = hooker; 3 = prop forward; 4 = scrum halfback; 5 = center; 6 = wing (strong side); 7 = wing (weak side)

Terminology

Try (touchdown)—worth 4 points. When the ball is touched down in the opponents' end zone.

Conversion (extra point)—2 points. Attempted kick after the try is scored. The ball is kicked from any distance beyond 10 yards and directly out from where the ball was touched down.

Penalty goal—3 points. This follows an infraction of the rules and is kicked from the point of infraction or anywhere behind it. It may be placekicked or drop-kicked over the bar of the goalpost.

Drop goal—3 points. This is a dropkick that is taken at any time while the game is in progress. The ball must go over the bar.

Lineout—Formed by the two teams of the scrum forwards in opposing lines wherever the ball goes into "touch" (out of bounds); both teams jump to try to obtain possession, and then the ball is thrown between them by the wing.

Scrum—Forwards bind together against each other while the scrum half throws or rolls the ball directly between the two rows. Both sides try to gain possession by "hooking" the ball back with their feet so that the backs start a running movement.

Rules

1. Seven players make up a team.
2. Match begins with a kickoff, which must travel at least 10 yards.
3. Play is continual and is only stopped when the ball is out of bounds (like soccer).
4. When the player with the ball is tagged, that player must stop, place the ball on the ground, and quickly line up in position.
5. Three players (on each team) will form a scrummage by the two forwards and the hooker. These players will interlock. This group of three players is called "the pack."
6. As "the pack" forms a scrum, the other players remain behind them.
7. The scrum should be steady until the ball is put in by the scrum half of the non-offending team. If the ball runs straight through the scrum, it must be put in again.

(continues)

FIGURE 10.12 Rugby study guide and exam

8. The three front players must not raise a foot until the ball touches the ground. These players cannot handle the ball.

9. The scrum half is expected to pick up the ball smartly and pass it sharply back to the next person in line. Following this, a series of backward laterals occurs, each pass made just before the ball carrier is tagged.

10. A ruck occurs when one or more players from each team close around the ball when it is on the ground between them. Players must be on their feet and must bind with at least one arm around a teammate.

11. A maul occurs when one or more players from each team close around a player who is carrying the ball.

Name: _____

Rugby Test
(20-point unit test)

Multiple Choice (1 point each)

1. In the game of rugby played in class, each team has _____ players.
   a. 10
   b. 7
   c. 22
   d. 14

2. The game begins with a kickoff, which must travel at least _____ yd.
   a. 40
   b. 30
   c. 20
   d. 10

3. Play is continual and is only stopped when:
   a. A player calls "time-out"
   b. The ball is out of bounds
   c. A player falls down
   d. The ball is kicked

4. A _____ is formed by the two teams' forwards and hookers in opposing lines wherever the ball goes into "touch" (out of bounds); both teams jump to try to obtain possession as the ball is thrown in bounds.
   a. Conversion
   b. Scrum
   c. Lineout
   d. Ruck

5. In class, when the player with the ball is _____, that player must stop, place the ball on the ground, and quickly line up into position.
   a. Scared
   b. Tackled
   c. Tagged with either hand
   d. Tagged with both hands

Matching

		Positions
1. Known as "the pack" _____		A. 2 forwards and hooker
2. Puts the ball in and takes it out _____		B. Scrum halfback
3. Must not raise a foot until the ball touches the ground _____		C. Center and 2 wings
4. Fastest-running player(s) on the team _____		
5. These players will interlock _____		

FIGURE 10.12 Rugby study guide and exam (Continued)

True/False

_____ 1. A 98-lb player will most likely play the position of a "prop forward."

_____ 2. A "try" is scored as soon as the player carrying the ball crosses the opponents' end zone.

_____ 3. A player can pass the ball forward, sideways, and behind.

_____ 4. Rugby is a team sport played at many colleges that may even offer scholarships to both male and female students.

_____ 5. A 280-lb player will most likely play the position of a "wing."

FIGURE 10.12 Continued

Attitude Check Sheet

Assign 0 to 5 points during each observation with 5 being the highest score. A number of observations should be made during the semester in order to reveal consistency and improvement.

Student   Date _____   Lesson focus _____

Student						
1. Tries all activities	0	1	2	3	4	5
2. Is on time	0	1	2	3	4	5
3. Consistently gives a maximum effort	0	1	2	3	4	5
4. Shows concern for others	0	1	2	3	4	5
5. Listens to and applies criticism	0	1	2	3	4	5
6. Shows enthusiasm	0	1	2	3	4	5
7. Participates with all students	0	1	2	3	4	5
8. Shares ideas with teacher and class	0	1	2	3	4	5
9. Demonstrates leadership	0	1	2	3	4	5
10. Volunteers to help others	0	1	2	3	4	5

FIGURE 10.13 Student attitude check sheet

tion. Traditional assessment tools such as grading on attendance, dressing, and written tests give little support to students' affective growth and development. Assessment in the affective domain supports the positive impact physical education has on students' feelings toward movement. Few educators measure the impact their program and instruction have on this important area. Usually, teachers agree about what to do for students in the affective learning domain. Most teachers want to do the following:

1. Develop positive attitudes toward physical activity. If students learn physical skills but develop a negative feeling about activity, it is quite likely they will not participate when left on their own. Feeling positive about one's ability and competency in physical activities will increase the possibility of participation.

2. Enhance a positive self-concept. If students learn physical skills and are able to perform them adequately, they will be viewed positively by peers. Self-concept is reinforced through feedback from others. When teachers and peers respond positively, individuals learn that they are worthy individuals.

3. Develop proper social skills. Students need to learn to play fair and with proper respect for others. The opportunity to cooperate and compete with peers offers students a chance to learn what personal behavior is acceptable or unacceptable. Because most behavior in physical education is visible to others, feedback about proper social behavior is effective and immediate.

Behavioral attitudes can be informally monitored with a checklist similar to the one in Figure 10.13.

This instrument is informal and relates specific behaviors to attitude. Teachers often view a "good attitude" as one where the student does what the teacher tells them to do. This approach deals more with behavior than attitude toward physical education. If such a tool is used, it offers the advantage of listing specific criteria. At times, teachers will tell a student he or she has a "bad attitude" but not define why he or she is being chastised. A checklist defines what behavior is expected and helps prevent making snap judgments about attitudes.

A number of instruments are available for measuring attitudes and values. A few examples are offered here. For a review of a wide variety of instruments, see the text by Lacy and Hastad (2007). Such instruments have been evaluated over time and are somewhat more accurate in evaluating long-term attitudes and values. Regardless of the instrument used, teachers should use caution; personality traits change and are difficult to measure.

Edgington Attitude Scale

This scale (Edgington, 1968) measures the attitude of high school students toward physical education. The inventory consists of 66 statements about physical education class. Students are asked to place a mark next to the response option that best reflects their feelings about the statement. A Likert scale is used, and students can respond with six options, from very strongly agree to very strongly disagree.

Adams Physical Education Attitude Scale

On this scale (Adams, 1963), attitudes toward physical education are measured using statements about physical education. The student reads the statement and then indicates agreement or disagreement, for example, "I suppose physical education is all right, but I don't much care for it."

Using Affective Assessment

Assessing the affective development of students is important information that can be used to develop a physical education program that will have positive long-term effects. Caution must be issued when evaluating a student's emotional side. Adolescence is a time filled with great change, and students are often viewed as moody, self-absorbed, confrontational, and even "know-it-alls." This changing and emotional time will not always provide objective results that can be incorporated in to an overall evaluation score. Yet assessing how students feel about physical education and ensuring that students engage in positive experiences that help build self-esteem and self-confidence is critical. Students' perceptions can be used to address changes in content or instructional delivery. There is no better assessment tool regarding students' attitudes and beliefs than those gathered from the students.

EVALUATION OF STUDENT PERFORMANCE

Now that we have collected information about our students in all aspects of physical education, it is time to do something with that information. The evaluation process is crucial in providing feedback to students, teachers, and parents. Teachers are provided with information to make judgments about student performance based on certain criteria. These criteria usually fall under two separate categories: norm-referenced and criterion-referenced evaluations.

NORM-REFERENCED EVALUATIONS

Performing a norm-referenced evaluation of student performance requires a teacher to use assessment information to rank a student in comparison to other student performances on a similar event. Standardized tests, such as the President's Challenge on Physical Fitness (President's Council on Physical Fitness and Sports, 2004), are reported in this fashion. This information will allow a student to know where his or her performance stands in comparison to his or her peers. On a smaller level, teachers may implement this type of evaluation within their own classes. "Grading on a curve" is an example of norm-referenced evaluation that teachers might implement. The benefits of this type of evaluation are as follows:

- Allows for performance evaluation in relation to peers.

- Is easily administered and collected because most of the measures are outcomes such as number of times and timed events.

- Usually focuses on performance outcomes rather than processes; therefore, it is useful to rank students amongst themselves and to evaluate overall program effectiveness.

There are also disadvantages to this method, including the following:

- Students often feel that they are being unfairly compared to others and that components like improvement and effort are lost in this method.

- Usually little information about why a performance was good or bad is communicated with this type of evaluation.

- In this method, there will always be a student who comes in first and one that comes in last in regards to their performance. In other words, at least one student will fail the task no matter how well they do because in relation to his or her peers' performance, he or she performed the worst.

CRITERION-REFERENCED EVALUATIONS

The other method of evaluating student performance is using criterion-referenced evaluations. Criterion-referenced evaluation involves comparing a student's performance against a preexisting set of criteria or guidelines. Standardized tests such as the Fitnessgram are reported in this fashion. Much of what is done in a typical physical education class falls under this type of evaluation. When students perform in class to preestablished requirements, criterion-referenced evaluations are being performed. In this type of evaluation, it falls upon the teacher to make appropriate choices in determining the criteria for evaluation. This is not always an easy task as some students will easily surpass the criteria, while others will fail the same criteria. Most of the controversy of grading in physical education can be attributed to choosing appropriate criteria for evaluation. Using this type of evaluation, every student in your class can receive an "A" for his or her performance; likewise all of them can fail. This is why it is so important for a teacher to choose correct criteria. The benefits of criterion-referenced evaluations are as follows:

- Evaluation is custom fit for the specific groups or students with whom a teacher is working.

- The information provided is informative in relation to what a student can and cannot do instead of how he or she compares to others.

- These evaluations can provide reasons why students are performing at a certain level.

- It is possible for every student to be successful in regards to mastering content.

The drawbacks to criterion-referenced evaluations are as follows:

- The criteria chosen to evaluate performance may not represent appropriate standards.

- Levels of acceptance or quality may be set too high or low for the majority of students. When all students in a class receive an "A" on a test, it might

be that the evaluation is not sensitive enough to discriminate differences in performance.

Teachers are urged to weigh all the advantages and disadvantages of both of these types of evaluations in order to judge which type is the most appropriate for their specific situation. This decision can be crucial in evaluating student and program performance.

USES FOR STUDENT EVALUATION

Many components are evaluated in physical education. A major part of evaluation is examining the skill learning and development that occurs through the instructional process. Even though skill development is a primary focus of physical education, it is not enough; students need to learn about strategy, skill performance techniques, sport etiquette, and positive attitudes toward physical activity. Written exams and alternative assessments can evaluate whether students have requisite knowledge for successful participation. Finally, the area of attitudes and values is important to the program. Students will choose not to participate if their attitudes and values have not developed concurrently with skills and knowledge.

Using assessment instruments serves a number of purposes (Strand & Wilson, 1993). Some of the more common reasons for evaluation include the following:

Grading. Performance on valid and realiable instruments offers objective data for grading. Communicating with students and parents is more effective when an objective and systematic tool has been used for evaluation (e.g., rubrics, Fitnessgram). Parents and students can see how they compare to others or established criteria and are given a realistic view of their performance. Grades based on objective data carry more credibility and respect both inside and outside the profession.

Motivation. Nothing motivates students more than improvement based on individual effort. When improvement can be documented through evaluation, it can be clear evidence that effort has been rewarded. It is difficult to know the extent of improvement (or lack of) if both process and product assessment are not a part of the program. Another factor that motivates students is the setting of achievable goals. It is difficult to know what is reasonable and reachable if students are unaware of their performance levels and abilities.

Diagnosis. Process assessment often reveals problems or deficiencies. When teaching an entire class, it is difficult to sense the ability and progress of each student. Often more energy is placed on monitoring student behavior than student performance. Assessment performed throughout a unit will focus energy on progress of individual students and reveal those students whose skills are deficient or performed incorrectly.

Placement and equalization. At times, it is effective to group students homogeneously, that is, students with equal ability are placed in groups. On the other hand, using a peer tutoring method can be done if assessment reveals some skilled performers and others having problems. Student evaluation will help teachers place students with mentor coaches and balance small groups' ability levels when it enhances learning.

Program evaluation. Evaluation of students can reveal the effectiveness of the program and the relevancy of objectives. If all students pass the evaluation, it may mean that the goals of the program are too low. If many fail, the quality of instruction may be inadequate or the standard of performance may be out of reach. Over time, evaluation of students can give direction to the program as objectives and instructional strategies are modified to increase student success.

Program support. Results of regular evaluation can be used to validate and support the program. Data gained through evaluation are objective and can reveal what students are expected to learn and how effectively they are learning. Accountability is a buzzword among educators as schools try to document what students are learning in order to gain public support. When administrators need to make cutbacks in programs, they usually ask faculty members to justify continuation of their programs. Data gained through consistent assessment and evaluation of students are strong and effective means to defend the program.

To Grade or Not to Grade?

Another issue related to grading is whether physical education should be graded. Some feel that the most important purpose of a physical education program is to offer students the opportunity to recreate and exercise. Others feel that education should be a primary focus, and a grade is needed to reflect how much students have learned. Arguments are offered on each side of the issue—to grade or not to grade—to help teachers better understand and defend the approach they choose. For an in-depth review of grading, the text by Lacy and Hastad (2007) is recommended.

Arguments Against Using a Grading System

- Grades are difficult to interpret. A grade means one thing to one teacher and another to a different teacher. When moving to a different school, the meaning of the grade does not transfer, and teachers at the new school may view the grade differently.

- Physical education does not place emphasis on content and product. Rather, it judges success by improvement of skills. Grades in academic areas reflect achievement and accomplishment; because grades in physical education reflect improvement and effort, they may be interpreted incorrectly.

- Often, time is limited in physical education, and classes only meet a few days a week. Testing for the purpose of assigning a grade is time consuming and takes away from learning opportunities. Physical educators try to squeeze as much learning as possible into a minimal amount of time, and grading dramatically reduces their instructional time.

- Physical education is diverse and broad by definition. Instruction covers all three learning domains, that is, skill development, attitude formation, and content knowledge. Trying to grade all three of these areas is difficult and demands a great deal of time. In addition, which of these three domains is most important, and can any of them be overlooked?

- Grading is done only in areas where standardized instruments have been developed. Fitness testing is the major area in physical education where a variety of standardized tests have been developed. Because of the dearth of standardized tests in other areas, excessive attention is given to fitness testing.

- Physical education emphasizes physical fitness and skill performance. Performance in these areas is strongly controlled by genetics, making it difficult for all students to achieve, even when they "give it their best effort." In addition, when grades are given for physical fitness performance, some youngsters feel discouraged because they train and still do not reach standards of high performance (see Chapter 16).

Arguments for Using a Grading System

- Giving grades makes physical education similar to other academic areas in the school curriculum. This gives physical education credibility and gains respect from parents, teachers, and administrators.

- Grades communicate the performance of students to parents. Parents have a right to know how their youngsters perform in physical education. Grades are used by teachers in other areas and are easily understood and interpreted by parents; therefore, they should be used in physical education.

■ When grades are not given, academic respect is lost. Physical education already suffers from the misguided perception that physical educators don't teach anything; they just "roll out the ball." Lack of a grading system may make it appear to others that little teaching or learning is occurring.

■ A grading system gives accountability. When grades are given, administrators and parents often assume that teaching and student accomplishment have occurred.

■ A grading system rewards skilled students. Students are rewarded in academic areas for their intelligence and performance and should be similarly rewarded for accomplishment in physical education settings.

■ Grading systems where teachers choose appropriate criteria for assessment allow for a greater success than many other academic areas where success and failure are only determined through performance outcomes.

GRADING—DIFFERING VIEWPOINTS

Many approaches are used for grading students. Grading methods vary depending on the philosophies of teachers and districtwide school regulations. This section examines different viewpoints, offers insight into each, and challenges readers to defend the grading procedure they choose.

EDUCATIONAL OBJECTIVES VERSUS ADMINISTRATIVE TASKS

There is general agreement that physical education should help students achieve in four areas: skill development, physical fitness, personal values, and cognitive development. Some grading systems assign weight to each of these areas when compiling a grade. Regardless of the amount of emphasis given to each area, the final grade depends on accomplishment of educational objectives. This contrasts with grading on completion of administrative tasks where students earn a part or all of their grade by showering, attending, participating, being prompt, and wearing the proper uniform. This latter approach grades students on tasks that have little to do with accomplishment of physical education objectives. Furthermore, these tasks are usually docu-

mented at the beginning of the period and will serve little in holding students accountable for their in-class performances.

Consider the conflicts arising when students are graded on achievement of educational objectives versus accomplishment of administrative tasks. Assume a student in a math class regularly forgets to bring a pencil and is tardy but earns an A grade on all math exams. Does this student earn a final grade of A, or is the student penalized for doing poorly on administrative tasks (tardiness, and so on) and given a C grade? Reverse the situation and assume the student has an outstanding attitude, is never tardy, and always brings the proper supplies to class. At the end of the semester, the student has earned a C grade on exams yet performed all administrative tasks at a high level. Does this student receive a final grade of A? If grades in other curricular areas of the school are earned through accomplishment of educational objectives or performance of administrative tasks, it is probably wise to follow suit in the physical education area.

Administrative tasks are usually enforced through school or districtwide regulations. For example, most districts have procedures for dealing with excessive absences or tardiness. Usually, teachers need not further penalize students through a grade reduction. Sometimes students are graded on participation, which is similar to receiving a grade just because one is physically present in class. On the other hand, students should be able to choose not to participate in class only when they are excused by the administration or by the school nurse (for sickness or injury). Participation alone should not be used as a factor in assigning grades. Rather, all students should be expected to participate unless excused by administrative edict.

If a student does not attend class, it is defensible to ask the student to repeat the class. This is usually done by assigning a failing grade. Because instructors do this in other academic areas, excessive absences are usually an acceptable criterion for failing the student. The major theme to remember is that grading systems in physical education should be in line with the grading systems in other subject-matter areas. If physical educators choose to grade otherwise, the grade may be meaningless to other teachers, parents, and students. Differences in grading approaches have caused some school districts to not calculate physical education grades in the overall grade point average nor include them in graduation requirements. When grades earned in physical education become unimportant to school requirements, it makes it easy to say that physical education should no longer be required of all students considering the grade is meaningless. The bottom line is to grade in a manner that is compatible with other subject-matter areas.

PROCESS VERSUS PRODUCT

Another area of concern when evaluating is whether the process or the product of education is more important. Those who emphasize the process of education stress the importance of students leaving school with warm and positive feelings toward physical activity. These educators state their beliefs in the following manner: "I am not concerned about how many skills my students learn, I just want them to walk out of my class with positive feelings about physical activity." The assumption is that students who feel positive about physical activity will be willing to be active throughout their lifetimes. These teachers assign grades based on the process of trying rather than the product of performance. Students who receive higher grades may not be the most skilled but have shown improvement and effort throughout the semester.

Teachers who reside in the product camp focus primarily on student accomplishment and see effort as something that is laudable but not part of the grading process. Their philosophy might be stated as follows: "I don't really care whether students like me or physical education. What is ultimately important is their performance. After all, the students who are best in math earn the highest grades, so why should it be any different in physical education?" Teachers who focus on product give the highest grade to the best performer, regardless of other factors. Less-skilled students, no matter how hard they try, will not receive an above-average grade.

This is a difficult problem to resolve in physical education and is always hotly debated. One point of view is that students should learn how society works from the grading system. People are not rewarded in life based on how hard they try, but rather, on their performance. For example, if real estate agents try hard but never sell a house, they will not make any money. The payoff is for selling houses, not for trying hard to sell houses. An opposing viewpoint is that many people in society are rewarded for effort, and "doing your best" should be rewarded.

The need to develop competency in various physical skills offers support for the product point of view. Research shows (AAHPER, 1954) that 78 percent of all hobby interests are established before the age of 12. Interests are established based on competency in different areas. A relatively low percentage of adults select new hobbies in areas where they feel incompetent. To ensure lifetime activity, school physical education programs need to graduate students whose skill competencies allow them to feel comfortable in public view. A grading system that focuses on skill development and performance will encourage the quest toward competency.

A solution to consider is to grade on performance while teaching in a manner that focuses on the process of learning. Much is to be said for teaching in a manner that helps students develop a positive attitude toward activity. Attitude development depends largely on how teachers present the material rather than on actual performance. Students, with the help of the instructional process, need to understand that they perform differently from each other as in math or science and receive a respectively higher or lower grade. This would make physical education similar to other academic areas in that those who perform best would receive the highest grade.

RELATIVE IMPROVEMENT

Some physical educators believe that effort, or "just doing the best that you can," should be the most important factor in assigning grades. To reward effort, these teachers base student grades on the amount a student improves. This involves pretesting and posttesting to determine the amount of progress made throughout the grading period. This approach contrasts with basing the grade on absolute performance; it is quite possible that the best performer in the class will not receive the highest grade because of lack of improvement.

Grading on improvement is time consuming and requires that the same test be given at the beginning and end of the semester or unit. The test may or may not be a valid reflection of what has been learned in the class and may not be sensitive enough to reflect improvement made by both poor and outstanding performers. Testing at the beginning of a unit can be discouraging and demoralizing if a student performs poorly in front of peers. It can also be hazardous in some activities, such as gymnastics or archery, which require intensive instruction to prevent accidents or injuries.

Another factor to consider is the issue of performing for a grade. Students learn quickly that if they perform too well on the pretest, they will be penalized at posttest time. It is thus important to perform at a low level in order to demonstrate a higher degree of improvement on the posttest. A related problem is that improvement is sometimes easier at beginning levels of a skill than at high levels of performance. Most teachers are aware of the rapid improvement beginners make before reaching a learning plateau. A skilled performer may be at a level where improvement is difficult to achieve. Lack of improvement in this situation would result in a skilled performer receiving a lower grade than a beginner.

GRADING ON POTENTIAL

Some teachers choose to grade on potential. These teachers may lower a student's grade because the student did not reach his or her potential. On the other hand, a grade may be raised because the teacher felt the student didn't have much ability but did reach his or her potential. In other words, the teacher decides what a student's potential performance level should be and then assigns a grade based on whether he or she reached this level. The grade a student receives depends on the teacher's subjective perception of that student's genetic limitations. How can any teacher really know the absolute potential of any student? This approach results in students being assigned a grade based on an unknown factor: potential.

This approach depends on the teacher's feelings about the student in question. It is based on intangibles and may result in a grade being assigned because the student is "just like her brothers or sisters." Grades are difficult to defend when they are based on the teacher's subjective beliefs rather than on criteria that can be measured and evaluated. How would a parent react to a teacher's statement that, "Your youngster received a failing grade because he just didn't live up to his potential"? To be defensible, grading systems need to be based on tangible data gleaned from observable behavior and performance.

NEGATIVE VERSUS POSITIVE GRADING

To make the grading system defensible and concrete, some teachers have used point systems. In most point systems, both performance objectives and administrative factors are listed as grade components. A student earns a grade through performance, attitude, and knowledge. Point systems can become a negative influence if handled incorrectly. For example, some teachers give students 100 points at the start of the semester and then "chip off" points for various unsatisfactory levels of performance. A student may lose points for not trying, not performing, or not knowing answers on a test. Students soon realize that energy should be spent on concentrating on negative behaviors that lose points rather than educational objectives.

This contrasts with a system that rewards positive behavior. When the student performs well, points are assigned and the student can earn his or her grade through self-direction. In a negative system, teachers make all the judgments about points lost and receive, in turn, the negative feelings of the student. In a positive system, students can behave in a positive manner to earn points. Teachers are constantly rewarding their behavior, which fosters positive feelings toward physical education and teachers. Rewarding positive behavior makes students feel that the teacher cares about their welfare and growth.

A negative system tends to make teachers focus on what students cannot do rather than on what they should or can do. Energy is spent on "policing" students and threatening to take away points if they do not behave. Students do not respond well to this approach, considering a loss of points does not require an immediate change in behavior and a redirection. The loss of points results in a reduction of the final grade, a consequence that is usually 6 to 9 weeks away. Few students respond positively to grade leverage through a negative system. Students who care about their grades are performing well in the first place. Threatening to lower the grade of a student who does not like physical education or school in general only further alienates the student and is based on a system of negative reinforcement. The grading system should positively encourage students to perform.

PASS–FAIL VERSUS LETTER GRADES

Another approach to grading involves assigning a pass–fail grade instead of a letter grade. Pass–fail has become more common today because of the push to avoid having physical education grades count in the academic grade point average. This approach prevents students from receiving a low grade in physical education while earning high grades in subject matter areas.

When using a pass–fail grading system, no method is available for rewarding outstanding performers. A student who earns a grade of C or D receives the same final grade as the top performer in the class. This approach reinforces making a minimal effort to accomplish goals because differing levels of performance are not rewarded. The pass–fail system also does little to show students that they have improved. For example, if a student is performing at the C level and earns a B by the end of the next quarter, the pass grade reflects no change in performance. Grading systems are most effective when they reward improved standards of performance.

Some teachers endorse pass-fail grading because it eases the burden of evaluation. They no longer have to worry about bookkeeping chores because the grade is only grossly indicative of student progress. Recording anything more than the minimum performance required for passing the class becomes unnecessary. Some teachers, therefore, support this grading system because of ease of implementation.

Once again, when the grading system in physical education differs from those in other subject matter areas, defending the program in the school setting becomes difficult. If physical education does not require grading integrity, the subject probably should not be counted in the grade point average. The problem lies in the final outcome. If the physical education department chooses to operate autonomously from the rest of the school system, it then becomes vulnerable to nonsupport and abandonment. Physical education should be considered an integral part of the school system and should be graded in a manner consistent with other subject matter areas.

STUDY STIMULATORS AND REVIEW QUESTIONS

1. Differentiate between assessment, evaluation, and grading.

2. From a teacher's perspective, explain why the use of "positive grading" is preferred over "negative grading."

3. Briefly describe the basic procedure of doing the Fitnessgram PACER test.

4. What are the advantages of doing the PACER test over the 1-mile run?

5. Explain what criterion-referenced health standards indicate for students.

6. Why is authentic assessment preferred in a physical education environment?

7. Explain why physical educators should follow the lead of classroom teachers and grade students on performance in class.

8. What is the "process versus product" dilemma faced by teachers in terms of their grading procedures?

9. Explain the potential long-term effects of a negative type of grading scheme.

10. Why are there so many different points of view regarding grading in physical education?

REFERENCES AND SUGGESTED READINGS

Abendroth-Smith, J., Kras, J., & Strand, B. (1996). Get aboard the B-BOAT (Biomechanically based observation and analysis for teachers). *Journal of Physical Education, Recreation, and Dance, 67*(8), 20–23.

Adams, R. S. (1963). Two scales for measuring attitude toward physical education. *Research Quarterly, 34,* 91–94.

American Association for Health, Physical Education, and Recreation. (1954). *Children in focus.* Reston, VA: AAHPERD.

American Association for Health, Physical Education, and Recreation. (1976). *Youth fitness test manual.* Reston, VA: AAHPERD.

Blair, S. N., Kohl, H. W., Paffenbarger, R. S., Clark, D. G., Cooper, K. H., & Gibbons, L. W. (1989). Physical fitness and all-cause mortality: A prospective study of healthy men and women. *Journal of the American Medical Association, 17,* 2395–2401.

Block, M. E., Lieberman, L. J., & Connor-Kuntz, F. (1998). Authentic assessment in adapted physical education. *Journal of Physical Education, Recreation, and Dance, 69*(3), 48–55.

Chepko, S., & Arnold, R. K. (Eds.). (2000). *Guidelines for physical education programs: Grades K–12 standards, objectives, and assessments.* San Francisco: Benjamin Cummings.

Cooper Institute, Meredith, M., & Welk, G. (Eds.). (2007). *Fitnessgram/Activitygram test administration manual* (4th ed.). Champaign, IL: Human Kinetics Publishers.

Corbin, C. B., Pangrazi, R. P., & Franks, B. D. (Eds.). (2004). *Toward a better understanding of physical activity and fitness: Selected topics, Volume Two.* Scottsdale, AZ: Holcomb Hathaway Publishers.

Corbin, C. B., Welk, G. J., Corbin, W. R., & Welk, K. A. (2008). *Concepts of physical fitness and wellness: A comprehensive lifestyle approach* (14th ed.). Boston: McGraw-Hill.

Cornish, C. (1949). A study of measurement of ability in handball. *Research Quarterly, 20,* 215–222.

Cutforth, N., & Parker, M. (1996). Promoting affective development in physical education. *Journal of Physical Education, Recreation, and Dance, 67*(7), 19–23.

Edgington, C. W. (1968). Development of an attitude scale to measure attitudes of high school freshman boys toward physical education. *Research Quarterly, 39,* 505–512.

Fay, T., & Doolittle, S. (2002). Agents for change: From standards to assessment to accountability in physical education. *Journal of Physical Education, Recreation, and Dance, 73*(3), 29–33.

Grehaigne, J., & Godbout, P. (1998). Formative assessment in team sports in a tactical approach context. *Journal of Physical Education, Recreation, and Dance, 69*(1), 46–51.

Hastie, P. A., Sanders, S. W., & Rowland, R. S. (1998). Where good intentions meet harsh realities: Teaching large classes in physical education. *Journal of Teaching in Physical Education, 18,* 277–289.

Jensen, C. R., & Hirst, C. C. (1980). *Measurement in physical education and athletics.* New York: Macmillan.

Johnson, J. R. (1963). The development of a single-item test as a measure of soccer skill. Unpublished master's thesis, University of California, Los Angeles.

Kemp, J., & Vincent, M. F. (1968). Kemp-Vincent rally test of tennis skill. *Research Quarterly, 39,* 1000–1004.

Kleinman, I. (1997). Grading: A powerful teaching tool. *Journal of Physical Education, Recreation, and Dance, 68*(5), 29–32.

Lacy, A. C. (1995). Assessment activities in physical education: Help for overloaded teachers. *Journal of Physical Education, Recreation, and Dance, 66*(6), 8–9.

Lacy, A. C., & Hastad, D. N. (2007). *Measurement and evaluation in physical education and exercise science* (5th ed.). San Francisco: Benjamin Cummings.

Lohman, T. G. (1992). *Advances in body composition.* Champaign, IL: Human Kinetics Publishers.

Lund, J. (1993). The role of accountability and assessment in physical education. In J. Rink (Ed.), *Critical crossroads: Middle secondary school physical education* (pp. 102–112). Reston, VA: NASPE.

Lund, J. L. (2000). *Creating rubrics for physical education.* Reston, VA: NASPE.

Matanin, M., & Tannehill, D. (1994). Assessment and grading in physical education. *Journal of Teaching in Physical Education, 13,* 395–405.

McGee, R., & Farrow, A. (1987). *Test questions for physical education activities.* Champaign, IL: Human Kinetics Publishers.

Melograno, V. J. (1994). Portfolio assessment. Documenting authentic student learning. *Journal of Physical Education, Recreation, and Dance, 65*(8), 50–55, 58–61.

Mitchell, S. A., & Olsin, J. L. (1999). *Assessment in games teaching.* Reston, VA: NASPE.

National Association for Sport and Physical Education. (2004). *Moving into the future: National standards for physical education* (2nd ed.). Reston, VA: Author.

Pangrazi, R. P. (2007). *Dynamic physical education for elementary school children* (15th ed.). San Francisco: Benjamin Cummings.

President's Council on Physical Fitness and Sports. (2004). *The president's challenge handbook.* Washington, DC: Author.

Safrit, M. J. (1990). *Introduction to measurement in physical education and exercise science* (2nd ed.). St. Louis: Times Mirror/Mosby.

Slaughter, M. H., Lohman, T. G., Boileau, R. A., Horswill, C. A., Stillman, R. J., Van Loan, M. D. & Benben, D. A. (1988). Skinfold equations for estimation of body fatness in children and youth. *Human Biology, 60,* 709–723.

Strand, B. N., & Wilson, R. (1993). *Assessing sport skills.* Champaign, IL: Human Kinetics Publishers.

Williams, D. P., Going, S. B., Lohman, T. G., Harsha, D. W., Webber, L. S., & Bereson, G. S. (1992). Body fatness and the risk of elevated blood pressure, total cholesterol and serum lipoprotein ratios in children and youth. *American Journal of Public Health, 82,* 358–363.

Wood, T. (1996). Evaluation: The road less traveled. In S. Silverman & C. D. Ennis (Eds.), *Student learning in physical education* (pp. 171–198). Champaign, IL: Human Kinetics Publishers.

Wood, T. (2003). Assessment in physical education: The future is now! In S. Silverman & C. D. Ennis (Eds.), *Student learning in physical education* (pp. 187–203). Champaign, Il: Human Kinetics Publishers.

Zhu, W. (1997). Alternative assessment: What, why, how. *Journal of Physical Education, Recreation, and Dance, 68*(7), 17–18.

Zhu, W., Safrit, M. J., & Cohen, A. (1999). *FitSmart test user manual.* Champaign, IL: Human Kinetics Publishers.

WEB SITES

Assessment Ideas
www.pecentral.org/assessment/assessment.html

Fitnessgram/Activitygram
www.Fitnessgram.net

National Association for Sport and Physical Education
www.aahperd.org/naspe

Physical Education Teaching and Curriculum Information
www.pecentral.com
www.pelinks4u.org
www.pe4life.org
www.reach.ucf.edu/~pezone/

Presidents Council on Physical Fitness and Sports
www.fitness.gov

Research for Education and Learning
www.mcrel.org

ESSENTIAL COMPONENTS OF A QUALITY PROGRAM

COMPONENT 1 A quality physical education program is organized around content standards that offer direction and continuity to instruction and evaluation.

COMPONENT 2 A quality program is student centered and based on the developmental urges, characteristics, and interests of students.

COMPONENT 3 Quality physical education makes physical activity and motor-skill development the core of the program.

COMPONENT 4 Physical education programs teach management skills and self-discipline.

COMPONENT 5 Quality programs emphasize inclusion of all students.

COMPONENT 6 In a quality physical education setting, instruction focuses on the process of learning skills rather than the product or outcome of the skill performance.

COMPONENT 7 A quality physical education program teaches lifetime activities that students can use to promote their health and personal wellness.

COMPONENT 8 Quality physical education teaches cooperative and responsibility skills and helps students develop sensitivity to diversity and gender issues.

11

Students with Disabilities

CHAPTER SUMMARY

This chapter focuses on the most common types of disabilities and the ways to modify activities and determine categories of placement for students with disabilities. Every state is required by federal law to develop a plan for identifying, locating, and evaluating all students with disabilities. Due process for students and parents is an important requisite when conducting formal assessment procedures. Assessment plays a vital part in determining proper placement of the disabled student into physical education. Moving a student to a less restrictive learning environment should be based on achievement of specified competencies that are necessary in the new environment. Mainstreaming involves the practice of placing students with disabilities into classes with able peers. An individualized learning environment increases opportunities for successful mainstreaming. The special student should not be permitted to use a disability as a crutch or as an excuse for substandard work.

STUDENT OUTCOMES

After reading this chapter, you will be able to:

- Understand the implications of Public Law (PL) 94–142 and the Individuals with Disabilities Education Act (IDEA) on physical education.

- Develop a plan for identifying, locating, and evaluating all students with disabilities.

Student Outcomes, continued

- Cite standards associated with assessment procedures for special students.

- Identify essential elements of an individualized educational program and list the stages of development.

- List guidelines for successful mainstreaming experiences.

- Describe ways to modify learning experiences in physical education to accommodate students with disabilities.

The Education for All Handicapped Children Act (PL 94–142) was passed by Congress in 1975. It was the 142nd act of legislation passed by the 94th Congress. This legislation introduced new requirements, vocabulary, and concepts into physical education programs across the United States. These concepts include individualized educational programs (IEPs), mainstreaming, least restrictive environments, zero reject, and progressive inclusion. The purpose of the law is clear and concise:

It is the purpose of this act to assure that all handicapped children* have available to them a free appropriate public education which emphasizes special education and related services designed to meet their unique needs, to assure that the rights of handicapped children and their parents or guardians are protected, to assist States and localities to provide for the education of all handicapped children, and to assess and assure the effectiveness of efforts to educate handicapped children. (PL 94–142)

In short, the law requires that all youth with disabilities, ages 3 to 21, receive a free and appropriate education in the least restrictive environment. The law includes youngsters in public and private care facilities and schools. Youth with disabilities who can learn in regular classes with the use of supplementary aids and services must be educated with youngsters who are able. Physical education is the only specific area mentioned in PL 94–142. The law indicates that the term special education "means specially designed instruc-

*The term *handicapped* is used in PL 94–142 to include youngsters who are mentally retarded, hard of hearing, deaf, speech impaired, visually handicapped, seriously emotionally disturbed, orthopedically impaired, other health impaired, blind, multihandicapped, or specific learning disabled. More appropriate wording is *students with disabilities*, which will be used throughout this chapter.

tion, instruction in physical education, home instruction, and instruction in hospitals and institutions." A 1997 amendment, PL 105-17 (also known as the Individuals with Disabilities Education Act [IDEA]), continues with the objective of providing handicapped individuals with the least restrictive environment in the school setting. The Individuals with Disabilities Education Act states, *"Physical education services, specially designed if necessary, must be made available to every child with a disability receiving a free appropriate public education."* Autism and traumatic brain injury have been added to the list of handicapping conditions that should receive the least restrictive environment. IDEA provides that an individual transition plan be developed no later than age 16 as a component of the IEP process. Rehabilitation and social work services are included as related services.

To comply with PL 94–142, secondary schools must locate, identify, and evaluate all students who might have a disability. A screening process must be followed by a formal assessment procedure. An assessment must be made and an IEP developed for each student before placement into a special program can be made. The law states who will be responsible for developing the IEP and what the contents of the IEP will include.

The passage of PL 94–142 shows that a strong commitment has been made to equality and education for all Americans. Prior to 1970, these students had limited access to schools and did not have an equal opportunity to participate in school programs. The government also ensured that funding would be made available for quality instruction. The law authorizes a payment to each state of 40 percent of the average per-pupil expenditure in U.S. elementary and secondary schools, multiplied by the number of youngsters with disabilities who are receiving special education and related services. The federal mandate reveals the concern of the public for comprehensive education programs for all students regardless of disability.

LEAST RESTRICTIVE ENVIRONMENT

PL 105–17 uses the term *least restrictive environment* to help determine the best placement arrangement of students with disabilities. This concept refers to the idea that not all individuals can do all of the same activities in the same environment. However, the concept of "zero reject" entitles everyone of school age to some aspect of the school program. No one can be totally rejected because of a disability. The focus should be on placing students into settings that offer the best opportunity for educational advancement. It is inappropriate to place a youngster in an environment where success is impossible. However, it is debilitating to put a student in a setting that is more restrictive than necessary. Special educators speak about mainstreaming options that offer a variety of opportunities, from participation in regular physical education classes to physical education in a full-time special school. Figure 11.1 shows a series of options that might be available for physical education.

The least restrictive environment varies depending on the unit of instruction and the teaching style. For example, for a student in a wheelchair, a soccer or football unit might be restrictive, whereas in a basketball or Frisbee unit, the environment would not be as restrictive. For a student with emotional disabilities, the direct style of instruction might be the least restrictive environment, while a problem-solving method with group cooperation may be too difficult and would be more restrictive. Consistent and regular judgments need to be made considering curriculum content and teaching styles change the type of environment the student enters. It is shortsighted to place students into a situation and then forget about them. Evaluation and modification of environments need to be ongoing. The concept of "progressive inclusion" focuses on the idea that as students make progress, they should have the opportunity to progress to less restrictive environments and experience more of the mainstream of schools and programs.

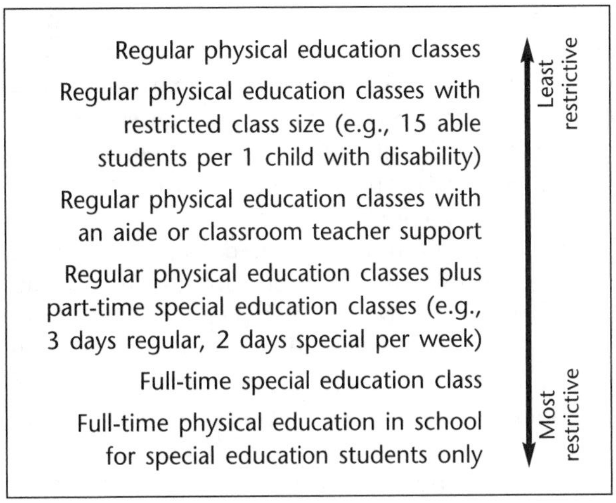

MAINSTREAMING

Physical educators usually speak in terms of mainstreaming rather than least restrictive environments. Mainstreaming means that students with disabilities must have opportunities to integrate with other students in public schools. Prudent placement in a least restricted educational environment means that the setting must be as normal as possible (normalization) while ensuring that the student can fit in and achieve success in that placement. The placement may be mainstreaming but is not confined to this approach.

Regular physical education classes

Regular physical education classes with restricted class size (e.g., 15 able students per 1 child with disability)

Regular physical education classes with an aide or classroom teacher support

Regular physical education classes plus part-time special education classes (e.g., 3 days regular, 2 days special per week)

Full-time special education class

Full-time physical education in school for special education students only

Least restrictive ← → Most restrictive

FIGURE 11.1 Physical education mainstreaming options, least to most restrictive environments

There are several categories of placement relative to physical education classes.

1. Full mainstreaming. Students with disabilities function as full-time members of a regular school routine. They go to all classes with able students. Within the limitations of their disabilities, they participate in physical education with able peers. An example may be auditory-impaired students who, with a minimal amount of assistance, are able to participate fully.

2. Mainstreaming for physical education only. Students with disabilities are not members of the regular academic classes in the secondary schools but can still participate in physical education with able peers. This setting may include students with emotional disabilities who are grouped in the classroom and are separated into regular physical education classes.

3. Partial mainstreaming. Students participate in selected physical education experiences but do not attend on a full-time basis because they can be successful in only a few of the offerings. Their developmental needs are usually met in special classes.

4. Special developmental classes. Students with disabilities are in segregated special education classes.

5. Reverse mainstreaming. Able students are brought into a special physical education class to promote intergroup peer relationships.

Segregation can be maintained only when it is in the best interests of the student. The purpose of segregated programs is to establish a level of skill and social proficiency that will eventually enable the special student to be transferred to a less restricted learning environment. The goal of the process is to place students in the least restrictive environment, where they can benefit most. Students with disabilities, working on their own, have often been denied opportunities to interact with peers and to become a part of the social and academic classroom network.

Students with disabilities need support personnel during mainstreaming. Even though the physical education teacher is responsible for the mainstreamed students during class time, these students may still require access to special education teachers, school psychologists, and speech therapists. Support personnel often view physical education as a time to get rid of their students; however, they are a source of information and support for the physical education teacher in charge.

SCREENING AND ASSESSMENT

Every state is required to develop a plan for identifying, locating, and evaluating all students with disabilities. Generally, screening involves all students districtwide and is usually conducted at the start of the school year. Screening tests include commonly used test batteries such as the Fitnessgram (Cooper Institute, 2007). In most situations, screening tests may be administered without parental permission. They are used to make initial identification of students who need special services.

Assessment is conducted after screening evaluations have been made and appropriate students are referred to special education directors. Assessment is performed by a team of experts, which often includes the physical education specialist. Due process for students and parents is important during formal assessment procedures. Due process ensures that parents and students are informed of their rights and have the opportunity to challenge educational decisions they feel are unfair or incorrect.

Due Process Guidelines

To ensure that due process is offered to parents and students, the following guidelines must be followed:

1. **Written permission.** A written notice must be sent to parents stating that their child has been referred for assessment. The notice explains that the district requests permission to conduct an evaluation to determine if special education services are required for the child. Also included in the permission letter must be reasons for testing and the tests to be used. Before assessment can begin, the letter must be signed by the parents and returned to the district.

2. **Interpretation of the assessment.** Results of the assessment must be interpreted in a meeting that includes the parents. Persons who are knowledgeable of test procedures need to be present to answer questions parents ask. At the meeting, parents are told whether their child has any disabilities and what services will be provided.

3. **External evaluation.** If parents are not satisfied with the results of the assessment, an evaluation outside of school can be requested. The district must provide a list of agencies that can perform such assessments. If the results differ from the school district evaluation, the district must pay for the external evaluation. If the results are similar, parents have to pay for the external testing.

4. **Negotiation and hearings.** If parents and the school district disagree on the results of the assessment, the district is required to negotiate the differences. When negotiations fail, an impartial hearing officer listens to both parties and renders an official decision. This is usually the final review; however, both parties do have the right to appeal to the state department of education, which renders a binding and final decision. Civil action through the legal system can be pursued should the district or parents still disagree. However, few cases ever reach this level of long-term disagreement, and educators should not hesitate to serve the needs of youngsters with disabilities based on this concern.

5. **Confidentiality.** As is the case with other student records, only parents of the child or authorized school personnel can review the student's evaluation. Review by other parties can be done only after written permission has been given by the student's parents.

Procedures for Ensuring Assessment Standards

PL 94-142 ensures that assessment will be held to certain standards to provide fair and objective results. The following areas are specifically delineated in the law.

Selection of Test Instruments

The test instruments used must provide a valid examination of what they purport to measure. When selecting instruments, it must be clear to all parties how the tests were developed and how they will measure the area of disability. More than one test procedure must be used to determine the student's status. Both formal and informal assessment techniques should be used to ensure that the results measure the student's impairment rather than simply reflect the student's shortcomings.

Unfortunately, youngsters must be labeled as "disabled" in order to reap the benefits of a special education program. The stigmatizing effect of labels and the fallibility of various means of testing students are dilemmas that must be faced. Although current pedagogical practices discourage labeling, in this case, it is necessary because school districts have to certify the disability to receive funding.

Administration Procedures

Many disabilities interfere with standard test procedures. For example, many students have communication problems and must be tested in a manner that ensures testing of motor ability rather than communication skills. Many students have visual and hearing disabilities that prevent using tests that rely on these faculties.

A possibility of misdiagnosing and incorrectly classifying students as mentally retarded can occur with certain ethnic groups, such as Native Americans, African Americans, and Spanish-speaking students. These youngsters, often victims of poor and impoverished living, may be only environmentally retarded and in need of cultural enrichment. It is subtle discrimination, but it must be replaced with understanding that students differ because of culture, poverty, migrant lifestyle, and language. Many of the tests are based on White, middle-class standards. Minority students need to be carefully assessed to determine the validity of the testing procedure.

Team Evaluation

A number of experts are used for assessment to help ensure that all facets of the student will be reviewed and evaluated. Evaluation professionals who are well trained and qualified administer the various tests. It is the responsibility of the school district to ensure that this will occur.

Role of the Physical Education Specialist

The physical education specialist is the point person for assessing and developing an **individualized educational program (IEP)**. An example of an IEP is presented in Figure 11.2. It is the physical educator's responsibility to review all student's health folders to see if any students have previously been recommended for differing support in the past. Students with differing needs are first observed in the regular physical education setting. Similarly, the physical education teacher should visit with these students to see how they perceive the situation and how they would like to proceed. Usually, an adapted physical educator who specializes

in working with students with different needs is called in to do the assessment. However, the physical education teacher is expected to offer feedback about how the student participates in regular physical education classes. The physical education teacher teams with the special education teacher to develop the IEP. It then becomes the responsibility of the physical education specialist to implement the IEP strategies.

Standards for placing students into special programs are necessary so parents feel that well-defined criteria have been used. Several states have adopted criteria for determining eligibility of students for adapted physical education classes. State guidelines differ but should be followed closely if they exist. Often, standards are based on the administration of standardized tests for which norms or percentiles have been developed. This procedure helps ensure that objective guidelines are used and avoids subjective judgment that may be open to disagreement and controversy.

If a student is determined not to be eligible for special education services, it may be beneficial to refer the student to programs for secondary students with special needs. These programs deal with areas that are not delineated by PL 94–142, such as obesity, physical fitness, and motor deficiencies. Unfortunately, few secondary schools offer such programs, and eligible students must survive in the regular programs. Physical educators need to show concern for helping students with these problems because obesity and physical fitness are areas with long-term health consequences and are especially important to students and their parents.

DEVELOPMENT OF THE IEP

PL 94–142 requires that an IEP be developed for each student receiving special education and related services. The IEP must be developed by a committee as stipulated by the law. Included on the committee are the following members: a local education association representative who is qualified to provide and supervise the administration of special education, the student's parents, the teachers who have direct responsibility for implementing the IEP, and when appropriate, the student. Other individuals, such as an independent evaluator, may be included at the discretion of the parents or school district. This program identifies the student's unique qualities and determines educationally relevant strengths and weaknesses. A plan is then devised based on the diagnosis. The IEP needs to contain the following material:

1. Current status of the student's level of educational performance.

Individualized Educational Program

☐ Initial Placement
☐ Reevaluation
☐ Change of Placement
☐ Review

A. STUDENT INFORMATION:

Student Name _____ _____ _____   Student No. _____   Home School _____
                        Last   First   Middle

Date of Birth _____   Chronological Age _____ (M _____ or F _____)   Present Placement/Grade _____

Parent/Guardian Name(s) _____   Receiving School _____

Home Address _____ _____ _____   Program Recommended _____
                        Street   City/State   Zip

Home Phone _____   Work Phone _____   Starting Date _____

Emergency Phone _____   Three (3) Year Reevaluation Due Date ___/___/___

Primary Language (Home) _____ (Child) _____   Interpreter Needed: Yes _____ No _____

B. VISION SCREENING RESULTS: Pass _____ Fail _____   **HEARING SCREENING RESULTS:** Pass _____ Fail _____

Date: _____ Comments: _____   Date: _____ Comments: _____

C. REQUIRED OBSERVATION(S): (All categories other than regular teacher)

Date(s) _____ By: _____   Date(s) _____ By: _____   Date(s) _____ By: _____
                        Name(s)   Name(s)   Name(s)

D. SUMMARY OF PRESENT LEVELS OF PERFORMANCE:

Educational:
_____
_____
_____
_____
_____
_____

Behavioral:
_____
_____
_____
_____

E. Additional justification. See comments _____ Initial   See addendum _____ Initial

F. PLACEMENT RECOMMENDATION INDICATING LEAST RESTRICTIVE ENVIRONMENT:

Related services needed: Yes _____ No _____ (*List below.)

Placement Recommendation	Person Responsible	Amount of Time (Range)	Entry Date On/About	Review Reports On/About	Projected Ending Date	IEP Review Date
Primary:						
*Related Services:						

Transportation Needed? Yes _____ No _____ (If Yes, submit MPS Special Education Transportation Request Form.)

Describe extent student will participate in regular program. _____

FIGURE 11.2 Example of an individualized educational program (IEP)

Student Name _____

Date Held _____
Student No. _____

G. PROGRAM PLANNING:

Long-Term Goals:

_____
_____
_____
_____
_____

Short-Term Objectives (Goals):

_____
_____
_____
_____
_____

H. EVALUATION:

Evaluation criteria are described in the Individual Implementation Plan (IIP), which is available in the classroom file.

I. PLACEMENT COMMITTEE:

The following have been consulted or have participated in the placement and IEP decisions:

Names of Members	Position	Present (Initial)	Oral Report	Written Report	Signatures
	Parents/Guardian				
	Parents/Guardian				
	School Administrator				
	Special Ed Administrator				
	School Psychologist				
	Nurse				
	Teacher(s) Receiving				
	Teacher(s) Referring				
	Interpreter				

Dissenting Opinion: Yes _____ No _____ If Yes, see comments _____ *Initial* See addendum _____ *Initial*

J. PARENT (OR GUARDIAN) STATEMENT:

We agree to the placement recommended in this IEP. Yes _____ No _____

We give our permission to have our child counseled by the professional staff, if necessary. Yes _____ No _____

We understand that placement will be on a continuing trial basis and we will be contacted if any placement changes are contemplated. We are aware that such placement does not guarantee success; however, in order to help our child, we accept the responsibility to cooperate in every way with the school program. We acknowledge that we have been notified of and have received a copy of our due process rights pertaining to special education placement and have a basic understanding of these rights. We acknowledge that we have received a copy of the completed IEP Form.

_____   _____
Parent or Guardian Signature   Date

Comments: _____
_____
_____

FIGURE 11.2 Continued

2. A statement of long-term goals and short-term instructional objectives.

3. A statement of special education and related services to be provided to the youngster. Also, a report as to what extent the student will be able to participate in regular educational programs.

4. The dates for initiation of services and anticipated duration of the services.

5. Appropriate objective criteria for determining annually whether the short-term objectives are being reached.

Developing and sequencing objectives for the student is the first step in formulating the IEP. Short-range and long-range goals are delineated, and data collection procedures and testing schedules are established to monitor the student's progress. Materials and strategies to be used in implementing the IEP are established followed by a determination of the methods of evaluation to be used in order to monitor the student's progress and effectiveness of the program. Movement to a less restrictive environment is based on achievement of specified competencies that are necessary in the new environment.

The IEP must contain a section determining whether specially designed physical education is needed. If not, the student is held to the same expectations as his or her peer group. A student who needs special physical education might have an IEP with specified goals and objectives and still be mainstreamed in regular physical education with goals that do not resemble those of classmates.

Continued and periodic follow-up of the student is necessary. Effective communication between special and regular teachers is essential because the student's progress needs careful monitoring. At the completion of the designated time period or school year, a written progress report is filed along with recommendations for action during the coming year or time period. A summer program is often an excellent prescription to ensure that school year improvement is maintained. Comprehensive records are maintained so that information about the youngster's problem and the effects of long-term treatment are always available.

Assistive Technology

As part of the IEP process, IDEA stipulated that assistive technology (AT) must be offered for children with disabilities if it is needed to receive "free and appropriate public education." AT is defined as any piece of equipment, device, or system that helps bypass, work around, or compensate for an individual's specific learning deficits. It is the school district's responsibility

to accept and supply the technology at no cost to parents. The IEP team is responsible for determining whether an assessment for AT is required. Either school district employees or an outside agency may conduct the assessment. Just about any learning problem can be reviewed to see if AT can compensate for the learning difficulty. For example, a youth who has trouble writing might be allowed to record it and have it converted to a typed paper. A person who has trouble with math could be allowed to use a calculator in a variety of settings so he or she learns to easily manipulate numbers. Students who have difficulty reading because of dyslexia can be helped by AT that reads aloud a manual or book.

Many different types of AT tools are available for students with learning deficits. They range from low-technology items, such as pencils, planners, highlighters, glasses, magnifying glasses, large-print books, and special lighting, to more high-tech equipment. Examples of higher technology aids are electronic work sheets, optical character recognition, radio listening systems, word processors, speech recognition programs, spell checkers, and talking calculators and dictionaries. In addition, vibrating pagers, hearing aids, classroom amplification, closed captioning, screen magnification software, braille keyboards, and translation software are just a few of the many types of AT available. Certainly, many different instructional software packages can be used to augment learning in different academic areas. The software focuses on instruction rather than assistance to help students find success.

Using AT has to be a thoughtful and well-planned process where all involved parties clearly understand that they must be "on board" and supportive. Certainly, it makes much sense to consider the student's strengths and special needs as well as his or her motivation to use the AT. If a student sees little value in using the technology, he or she more than likely will not follow through with it. The student is the end user, and he or she must find the AT valuable, not embarrassing or worthy of ridicule from peers. Even though it seems obvious that the AT must meet the developmental characteristics of the student, there is a possibility that parents or teachers may be overzealous in prescribing technology that is inappropriate. It is appropriate to try a trial period with the student and AT to see if it is suitable. Parents also can be critical of the success of the prescribed AT. If they don't see a need or are embarrassed that their youngster needs such help, odds are high they will undermine the student at home. This points out the need for the student and parents to be involved in the process of diagnosis and prescription. The following steps help ensure the successful implementation of AT.

than to "normal" peers. Proper levels of fitness and skill are vital for healthful living. Such levels enable them to compete with peers. It is important to accept responsibility for meeting the needs of students, including those with disabilities that permit some degree of mainstreaming. Teachers need to be able to judge when referral for special assistance or additional services is in order. Physical education teachers must be able to do the following: (1) analyze and diagnose motor behavior of the students with disabilities, (2) provide appropriate experiences for remediation of motor conditions needing attention, and (3) register data as needed on the student's personal record. Record keeping is important. A short period, perhaps 5 minutes between classes, could be set aside to accomplish the task promptly. When time between classes is short, the teacher may want to use a portable tape recorder for recording evaluative comments during class time.

To work successfully with students with disabilities, teachers have to understand specific impairments and how they affect learning. Also, it is necessary to know how to assess motor and fitness needs and how to structure remediation to meet those needs. Teachers should have alternative strategies in reserve in case the original method fails. Referral to the special education teacher then becomes a last resort. When giving explanations and directions, couch them in terms that all students, including those with disabilities, can understand. Be sure everyone understands what is to be accomplished before the learning experiences begin, especially when working with the hearing impaired. Concentrate on finding activities where students can excel. Avoid placing students with disabilities in situations where they could easily fail. Give them opportunities that make the best use of their talents. Stress the special objectives of those with disabilities. Obvious increments of improvement toward terminal objectives are excellent motivators for both students and teachers. Let youngsters know that you as a teacher are vitally interested in their progress.

Step Two: Make Modifications to the Curriculum

This step involves reviewing the existing physical education curriculum and determining how it will impact students who have differing needs. An important point to consider is whether certain activities completely exclude certain students. Many students with disabilities have severe developmental lags that become insurmountable if the curriculum is not modified. On the other hand, if the student is going to be included, they must be able to accomplish a portion of the program. It also may be that certain activities are

1. Identify the needs of the student. Do they need help with listening, reading, organization, memory, math, etc.? Being as specific as possible in identifying the special need(s) of the student will make prescription much more accurate and effective.

2. Review the AT that is available to meet those needs. SchwabLearning.org has an excellent list of tools and a booklet that explains this approach in detail. It contains a checklist of steps that make the job much easier.

3. Use a trial period to see how (or if) the youth and parents adapt to the AT. Did the AT improve the performance of the child? If not, it may have been incorrect technology or used incorrectly (if at all) by the student.

4. Review the AT instruments to see if they are user friendly, reliable, and somewhat maintenance free. Another important consideration is technical support when help is required. It is commonplace to find much variation in the quality of support. There is much competition among companies that supply AT, and if one product isn't satisfactory, certainly other options should be considered.

A SYSTEMATIC APPROACH TO SUCCESSFUL MAINSTREAMING

Mainstreaming is a moral issue. Educators have the responsibility to see that all students have the opportunity to experience activity and related social experiences. All parents desire the maximum of experiences for their youngsters, and the goal of teachers should be to meet this need. The issue is not whether to mainstream, but how to mainstream effectively. The physical educator has to teach a number of students, some with disabilities and diverse impairments. Learning strategies that the instructor is familiar with and has been using successfully may not be appropriate for students with disabilities. The teacher must accept the student as a full-fledged participant and assume the responsibilities that go along with special education. Few disagree that mainstreaming increases the difficulty of offering instruction for all students; however, teachers who support it show their concern for the human spirit regardless of condition.

Step One: Determine How to Teach

The success or failure of the mainstreaming process depends largely on the interaction between the teacher and the student with a disability. There is no foolproof, teacher-proof system. Purposes and derived goals are perhaps more important to students with disabilities

limiting, and inclusion is not in the best interest of the student with special needs. A compromise must be reached where the physical education teacher has made changes in his or her curriculum, and mainstreamed students realize that there may be activities that are not suited to their participation. It should always be the intent and responsibility of the teacher to try and individualize activities as much as possible so youngsters with disabilities are smoothly integrated.

Step Three: Find Ways to Modify Instruction and Activities for Student Success

Special education students need additional consideration when participating in group activities, particularly when the activity is competitive. Much depends on the physical condition of the student and the type of disability. Students like to win in a competitive situation, and resentment can be created if a team loss is attributed to the presence of a student with a disability. Equalization helps reduce this source of friction. Rules can be changed for everyone so that the student with a disability has a chance to contribute to group success. On the other hand, students need to recognize that everyone, including the disabled and the inept, has a right to play.

Be aware of situations that might devalue the student socially. Avoid using the degrading method of having captains choose from a group of waiting students. Elimination games should be changed so that points are scored instead of players being eliminated (this is an important consideration for all youngsters). Determine the most desirable involvement for students with disabilities by analyzing participants' roles in game and sport activities. Assign a role or position that will make the experience as natural or normal as possible.

Students with disabilities have to build confidence in their skills before they want to participate with others. Individual activities give them a greater amount of practice time without the pressure of failing in front of peers. The aim of these techniques is to make students with disabilities less visible and not set apart from able classmates. Using students with disabilities as umpires or scorekeepers is a last resort. Overprotectiveness benefits no one and prevents the special student from experiencing challenge and personal accomplishment. Avoid the tendency to underestimate students' abilities.

Many instructional modifications can be made that will not be obvious to other students but will improve the opportunity for student success. For example, factors such as teaching styles, verbal instructions, demonstrations, and the elimination of distractions might easily be manipulated in a manner that improves the lesson for all.

A Reflection Check

Making modifications to the lesson impacts many people. It impacts youngsters with differing needs, other students in the class, and the teacher. It is relatively easy to modify activities, but it can be quite difficult to make modifications that add to the total environment rather than create unsafe conditions or reduce the educational value of the experience. When thinking about ways to accommodate all students, take some time to reflect on the total experience. The following questions should be considered as you formulate modifications.

■ Do the changes allow students with differing needs to participate successfully yet still be challenged?

■ Does the modification make the setting unsafe for students with differing needs as well as for those students without disabilities?

■ Does the change negatively impact the quality of the educational experience? Is learning seriously hampered because of the changes made?

■ Does the change cause an undue burden on the teacher? This is important because many teachers come to resent students with differing needs because they feel the burden is too great. Certainly, change needs to be made, but it has to be reasonable for all parties.

Activities need to be modified because all students have differing needs. In fact, when a teacher seldom or never modifies activities, he or she probably is not meeting the needs of many students. Effective teachers always examine an activity and know that it is their responsibility to make the environment better for all students. The idea of "doing the most good for the most students" is a good adage to follow. The following are ways to modify curriculum activities.

Modifications for Students Lacking Strength and Endurance

■ Lower or enlarge the size of the goal. In basketball, the goal can be lowered; in soccer, the goal might be enlarged.

■ Modify the tempo of the game. For example, games might be performed using a brisk walk rather than running. Another way to modify tempo is to stop the game regularly for substitution. Autosubstitutions can be an excellent method for allowing students to determine when they are fatigued; they ask predetermined substitutes to take their places.

■ Reduce the weight and/or modify the size of the projectile. A lighter object will move more slowly and inflict less damage upon impact. A larger object will move more slowly, making it easier for students to track visually and catch.

■ Reduce the distance that a ball must be thrown or served. Options are to reduce the dimensions of the playing area or add more players to the game. In serving, others can help make the serve playable. For example, in volleyball, other teammates can bat the serve over the net as long as it does not touch the floor.

■ In games that are played to a certain number of points, reduce the number required for a win. For example, volleyball games could be played to seven or 11, depending on the skill and intensity of the players.

■ Modify striking implements by shortening them and reducing their weight. Racquets are much easier to control when they are shortened. Softball bats are easier to control when the player "chokes up" and selects a lighter bat.

■ If possible, slow the ball by letting out some air. This will reduce the speed of rebound and make the ball easier to control in a restricted area. It will also keep the ball from rolling away from players when it is not under control.

Modifications for Students Lacking Coordination

■ Increase the size of the goal or target. Increasing the size of a basketball goal will increase the opportunity for success. Another alternative might be to offer points for hitting the backboard near a goal. Because scoring is self-motivating, modification should occur until success is ensured.

■ Offer protection when appropriate. The lack of coordination will make the student more suscep-

tible to injury from a projectile. Use various types of protectors (such as glasses, chest protectors, or face masks).

■ When teaching throwing, allow students the opportunity to throw at maximum velocity without concern for accuracy. Use small balls that can be grasped easily. Fleece balls and beanbags are easy to hold and release.

■ Use a stationary object when teaching striking or hitting. The use of a batting tee or tennis ball fastened to a string can offer the student an opportunity for success. In addition, a larger racquet or bat can be used, and "choking up" on the grip can be tried.

■ Make projectiles easily retrievable. If a great deal of time is spent on recovering the projectile, students will receive few practice trials and feel frustrated. Place them near a backstop or use a goal that rebounds the projectile to the shooter.

■ When teaching catching, use a soft, lightweight, and slow-moving object. Beach balls and balloons are excellent for beginning catching skills because they allow the student to track his or her movement visually. In addition, foam rubber balls eliminate the fear of being hurt by a thrown or batted projectile.

Modifications for Students Lacking Balance and Agility

■ Increase the width of rails, lines, and beams when practicing balance. Carrying a long pole will help minimize rapid shifts of balance and is a useful lead-up activity.

■ Increase the width of the base of support. Students should be taught to keep the feet spread at least to shoulder width.

■ Emphasize use of many body parts when teaching balance. The more body parts in contact with the floor, the easier it is to balance the body. Beginning balance practice should emphasize controlled movement using as many body parts as possible.

■ Increase the surface area of the body parts in contact with the floor or beam. For example, walking flat-footed is easier than walking on tiptoes.

■ Lower the center of gravity. This offers more stability and greater balance to the youngster. Place emphasis on bending the knees and slightly leaning forward.

■ Play the games in a different position. Some games may be played in a sitting or lying position, which is easier and less demanding than standing or running.

■ Provide matching or substitution. Match another student on borrowed crutches with a student on braces. Two players can be combined to play one position. A student in a desk chair with wheels can be matched against a student in a wheelchair.

■ Allow students to substitute skills. For example, a student may be able to strike an object but may lack the mobility to run. Another student can be selected to run.

■ Make sure that surfaces offer good friction. Floors and shoes should not be slick or students will fall. Carpets or tumbling mats will increase traction.

■ Provide balance assistance. A barre, cane, or chair can be used to keep the student from falling.

■ Teach students how to fall. Students with balance problems will inevitably fall. Practice in learning how to fall should be offered so that they gradually learn how to absorb the force.

Step Four: Determine What Support and Aid Is Necessary

When a student is deemed ready for placement, consultation between the physical education teacher and the special education supervisor is of prime importance. In a setting where emotions and feelings can run high, it is important to ensure that communication and planning occur on a regular basis. The reception and acceptance of special students cannot be left to chance. A scheduled plan has to be instituted before the student is mainstreamed. Special and physical education professionals must discuss the needs of the student and the needs of the physical education teacher in order to develop realistic expectations. It is quite possible that the special education teacher may have to participate in a physical education class to ensure a smooth transition. The thrust should center on what students can do rather than on what they cannot do. Any approach that treats students with disabilities as cripples is dehumanizing.

Full information about the needs of the student is due to the physical education teacher before the student participates. Physical education teachers must feel able to tell support personnel what kind of help they need. Negative feelings toward students with differing needs will occur if the physical educator feels students are dropped into class without asking what kind of help they need. This procedure should also be implemented when the student moves from one mainstreaming situation to another. Both able students and students with disabilities need opportunities to make appropriate progress. The educational needs of students with disabilities must be met without jeopardizing the progress of other students. This does not rule out activity modifications so that those with disabilities can be included.

Step Five: Teach Tolerance to All Students

The teacher is advised to help all students understand the problems related to being disabled. A goal should be to have students understand, accept, and live comfortably with persons with disabilities. They should recognize that students with disabilities are functional and worthwhile individuals who have innate abilities and can make significant contributions to society. The concept of understanding and appreciating individual differences is one that merits positive development and should concentrate on three aspects:

■ Recognizing the similarities among all people: their hopes, rights, aspirations, and goals.

■ Understanding human differences and focusing on the concept that all people are disabled. For some, disabilities are of such nature and severity that they interfere with normal living.

■ Exploring ways to deal with those who differ without helping too much, and stressing the acceptance of all students as worthwhile individuals. People with disabilities deserve consideration and understanding based on empathy, not sympathy.

Tolerance Training

A number of activities can be conducted to help students better understand the feelings, differences, and similarities of students with disabilities. Teach students that everybody has a number of areas where they feel a deficit or lack confidence in their ability to perform. Talking about similarities rather than differences is a good starting point. Often some type of disability will cause students to focus on the deficit, which dehumanizes that person. A number of strategies can be used to teach better tolerance and understanding of others. The following are some suggestions that can be modified to help students increase their sensitivity to others.

■ Ask students to brainstorm as many words or images that come to them when they think of or hear the words *disability, impairment, handicap,* etc. Write the words on the board and continue to discuss the words mentioned throughout the week. As discussion and feelings about such words continue to surface, create a new list of words and images that occur.

■ Discuss a number of celebrities who had some type of disability, for example, Helen Keller, Ray Charles, Winston Churchill, Abraham Lincoln, and Franklin D. Roosevelt. Discuss how these celebrities succeeded despite serious disabilities. Try to focus on how they used their existing strengths to succeed. Identify peers with disabilities and how these students are more similar than different.

■ Discuss behaviors that teachers and students can use to make students with disabilities feel a part of the class setting. Approach these peers and give them a high five or word of encouragement. Identify activities where they may excel or feel competent. Ask students how they could modify success for all students. Often students have a good idea of how an activity should be changed or modified to ensure success for all students regardless of disability.

- Discuss how to behave toward students with disabilities. For example, if you are chatting with someone in a wheelchair, seat yourself first and then begin the discussion. If you see a blind person, identify yourself and ask if you can be of assistance. Use a normal tone of voice to avoid startling or treating them in a manner different than you use with others.

- Check out the school for modifications that have been made to make the school accessible for all. For example, is there a sink at the right height for students in a wheelchair? Are there automatic doors; are the curbs ramped in places? Borrow some wheelchairs and have students try to get around the school without leaving the chair.

- Discuss why a society passes laws to aid those with disabilities. Ask them the purpose of the laws and how such laws reflect on our society. Identify the handicapped parking laws and ask students how they feel when someone without a disability parks in these spots. How do their parents feel about this law? Do they sometimes park in a handicapped spot?

Step Six: Integrate Students with Differing Needs into the Class

Once the mainstreamed student, able students, and teacher have undergone preliminary preparation, consideration can be given to integrating the disabled youngster into the learning environment. When correctly implemented, mainstreaming allows the student to make educational progress, achieve in those areas outlined in the IEP, learn to accept limitations, observe and model appropriate behavior, and become socially accepted by others. Some guidelines for successful integration of students with disabilities into physical education follow.

- Expect students with disabilities to meet target goals specified in the IEP in addition to participating in the regular program of activities. This can involve resources beyond the physical education class, including special work and homework.

- Build ego strength; stress abilities. Eliminate established practices that unwittingly contribute to embarrassment and failure.

- Foster peer acceptance, which begins when the teacher accepts the student as a functioning, participating member of the class.

- Concentrate on the student's physical education needs and not on the disability. Give strong attention to fundamental skills and physical fitness qualities.

- Provide continual monitoring and periodically assess the student's target goals. Anecdotal and periodic record keeping are implicit in this guideline.

- Be constantly aware of students' feelings and anxiety concerning their progress and integration. Provide positive feedback as a basic practice.

FITNESS AND POSTURE FOR STUDENTS WITH DISABILITIES

The normalization process has directed attention to posture as a factor in peer acceptance. Because many secondary students with disabilities have low physical fitness levels, posture problems occur in this group. One aim of mainstreaming is to make special students less visible, hence the need to help them achieve acceptable posture. Values received from an attractive appearance include better acceptance by peers and more employment opportunities later.

Physical fitness is also important for these students. To compete with and gain respect from peers, the goal of fitness is a justified thrust of the physical education program. Adequate physical fitness helps the student move through the school day, which may be complicated by a sensory deficit, a mobility problem, or a mental deficiency.

Special care must be given to students who have been excluded from physical education programs. Wheelchair-bound students need special attention given to their cardiovascular development through activities that stimulate deep breathing. Arm development is important so that they can move in and out of the wheelchair easily.

An idiosyncratic gait or an appearance that gives the impression of abnormality is often a problem for mentally retarded youngsters. Early identification of a problem and inclusion of a posture correction program are important. The physical educator is often best qualified to initiate and supervise this program. Informal screening includes several tasks: walking, sitting, and stair climbing. Obesity may need to be considered in amelioration. Once identification is made, a more detailed analysis of the subject's posture can follow. The degree of postural abnormality governs whether referral is indicated. Videotaping can provide baseline data from which to monitor corrections. Achieving acceptable posture is both a short-term (progress) and long-term (achievement) goal to be included in the student's IEP. Referral for severe conditions or for postural conditions that are difficult to correct usually involves the support services of a physician or an orthopedic specialist.

The psychosocial aspects of posture should be considered, with attention focused on the establishment of a good self-concept and effective social relations. Behavior management can focus on motivation toward better postural habits when standing, walking, sitting, lifting, and general movement. Proper posture should become a habit.

USE OF COMPUTERS

Computers are becoming increasingly available in schools all over the country. The computer is a time-saving device that can take over record-keeping chores required by the provisions of PL 94–142. Printouts of present and past status reports can be made available on demand. The computer can also provide comparisons with established norms, especially in physical fitness areas, and it can record progress toward the target goals set by the IEP. The computer minimizes the time necessary for recording student progress. In addition, computerized graphic compilations facilitate quick comprehension of progress reports. Several computer programs are available for writing and updating the IEP.

Another significant computer service is related to informational printouts. The due process regulations of PL 94–142 might be one such topic. Information concerning specific disabilities could be made readily available. Guidelines for formulating the IEP are another possibility. Long- and short-term objectives can be retrieved from a growing data bank.

Making relevant progress information available to students can be excellent motivation and stimulates a systematic approach to the attainment of specific achievements. The same information can also be the basis for reports to parents and other adults who are interested in the student. These reports can enhance parental cooperation.

PARENTAL SUPPORT

Having parents on the IEP committee spurs their involvement and establishes a line of communication between home and school. Home training or homework may be recommended for many students. If home training is indicated, parents must be committed in terms of time and effort. Their work need not be burdensome but must be done regularly in accordance with the sequenced learning patterns. Also, the school must supply printed and sequenced learning activities for a systematic approach to the homework. Materials should be understandable and goals clear. Parents should see obvious progress in their youngsters as assignments unfold.

Older students with disabilities may accept some responsibility for home training, relegating the parent to the role of an interested, encouraging spectator. Even if homework is not feasible, parental interest and support are positive factors. The parents can help their youngster realize what skills have been learned and what progress has been made.

RECRUITING AND TRAINING OF AIDES

The use of aides can be an effective way of increasing the amount of instruction and practice for students who are disabled. Volunteers are easy to find among various community organizations, such as parent-teacher associations, foster grandparents, and community colleges. High school students who volunteer have proven effective with middle school students.

An initial meeting with volunteer aides should explain the type of youngsters with whom they will work and clarify their responsibilities. Aides must learn how to be most effective in assisting the instructor. Training could include learning how to work effectively with individuals, recording data, and developing special materials and instructional supplies. In addition, the potential aides should receive experience in working with youngsters to see if they are capable and enjoy such work. Physical education specialists must also learn how to work with aides. In some cases, physical educators find the task of organizing and supervising aides to be burdensome if they have not learned to supervise and organize.

Aides can assume many roles that increase the effectiveness of the instructional situation. For example, the aide may gather and locate equipment and supplies prior to the lesson. They may officiate games and ensure that they run smoothly. Seasoned aides enjoy and are capable of offering one-on-one or small-group instruction to youngsters. Aides should not reduce the need for involvement of the physical education instructor because they only implement instruction strategies that have been organized and developed by the professional educator. In addition, the physical educator must monitor the quality of the presentations made by the aide.

STUDY STIMULATORS AND REVIEW QUESTIONS

1. Explain the term *least restrictive environment*.
2. Cite the steps associated with development of an individualized educational program (IEP). Indicate

the phases of development most important to ensure success.

3. Explain the moral dimension of the mainstreaming process.

4. Discuss four strategies that will contribute to a successful integration of students with disabilities.

5. What is the central purpose of modifying practice or game conditions for students with disabilities?

6. Provide four examples of how activities can be modified for students who lack strength and endurance.

7. Discuss the recommended teaching strategies for instructing students with mental retardation.

8. Visually impaired students cannot benefit from demonstrations or other visual cues. Explain what alternative strategies can be used for these students.

9. Why is it especially important to have consistency and routine in the learning environment when students with emotional disabilities are mainstreamed?

10. How can a physical education teacher increase the parental involvement when instructing a student with a disability?

REFERENCES AND SUGGESTED READINGS

Auxter, D., Pyfer, J., & Huettig, C. (2005). *Principles and methods of adapted physical education and recreation* (10th ed.). Boston: McGraw-Hill.

Block, M. E. (2000). *A teacher's guide to including students with disabilities in regular physical education* (2nd ed.). Paul H. Brookes Publishing Co.: Baltimore, MD.

Cooper Institute. (2007). *Fitnessgram/activitygram test administration manual* (4th ed.). Champaign, IL: Human Kinetics.

Davis, R. W. (2002). *Inclusion through sports: A guide to enhancing sport experiences.* Champaign, IL: Human Kinetics.

Dobbins, D. A., Garron, R., & Rarick, G. L. (1981). The motor performance of educable mentally retarded and intellectually normal boys after covariate control for differences in body size. *Research Quarterly, 52*(1), 6–7.

Dunn, J. M., & Leitschuh, C. (2006). *Special physical education* (8th ed.). Dubuque, IA: Kendall/Hunt Publishing Co.

Friend, M. (2008). *Special education: Contemporary perspectives for school professionals* (2nd ed.). Boston: Allyn & Bacon.

Henley, M., Ramsey, R. S., & Algozzine, R. F. (2006). *Characteristics of and strategies for teaching students with mild disabilities* (5th ed.). Boston: Allyn & Bacon.

Horvat, M., Eichstaedt, C., Kalakian, L., & Croce, R. (2003). *Developmental/adapted physical education: Making ability count* (4th ed.). San Francisco: Benjamin Cummings.

Sherrill, C. (2004). *Adapted physical activity, recreation and sport* (6th ed.). Boston: WCB/McGraw-Hill.

Ulrich, D. A. (1983). A comparison of the qualitative motor performance of normal, educable, and trainable mentally retarded students. In R. L. Eason, T. L. Smith, & F. Caron (Eds.), *Adapted physical activity.* Champaign, IL: Human Kinetics.

Vogler, E. (2003). Students with disabilities in physical education. In Silverman, S., & Ennis, C. (Eds.) *Student learning in physical education* (2nd ed.). Champaign, IL: Human Kinetics.

Winnick, J. P. (2005). *Adapted physical education and sport* (4th ed.). Champaign, IL: Human Kinetics.

Winnick, J. P., & Short, F. X. (1999). *The Brockport physical fitness test manual.* Champaign, IL: Human Kinetics.

Yun, J., Shapiro, D., & Kennedy, J. (2000). Reaching IEP goals in the general physical education class. *Journal of Physical Education, Recreation, and Dance, 71*(8), 33–37.

WEB SITES

Adapted Physical Education
www.palaestra.com/
www.pecentral.org/adapted/adaptedmenu.html
www.pelinks4u.org/sections/adapted/adapted.htm
www.twu.edu/inspire/

Adapted PE Assessment Tools
www.pecentral.org/adapted/adaptedinstruments.html

Assistive Technology
www.rfbd.org
www.ataccess.org
www.ctcnet.org

Children's Disabilities Information
www.childrensdisabilities.info/

Inclusion Programs that Work
www.ed.gov/pubs/EPTW/eptw12/index.html
www.palaestra.com/Inclusion.html

Legal Issues
asclepius.com/angel/special.html
www.ed.gov/offices/OSERS/Policy/IDEA/the_law.html

National Standards
www.cortland.edu/apens/

Weight-Control Information Network
http://win.niddk.nih.gov/

ESSENTIAL COMPONENTS OF A QUALITY PROGRAM

COMPONENT 1 A quality physical education program is organized around content standards that offer direction and continuity to instruction and evaluation.

COMPONENT 2 A quality program is student centered and based on the developmental urges, characteristics, and interests of students.

COMPONENT 3 Quality physical education makes physical activity and motor-skill development the core of the program.

COMPONENT 4 Physical education programs teach management skills and self-discipline.

COMPONENT 5 Quality programs emphasize inclusion of all students.

COMPONENT 6 In a quality physical education setting, instruction focuses on the process of learning skills rather than the product or outcome of the skill performance.

COMPONENT 7 A quality physical education program teaches lifetime activities that students can use to promote their health and personal wellness.

COMPONENT 8 Quality physical education teaches cooperative and responsibility skills and helps students develop sensitivity to diversity and gender issues.

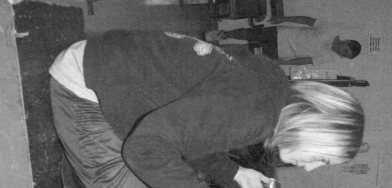

12

Liability and Safety

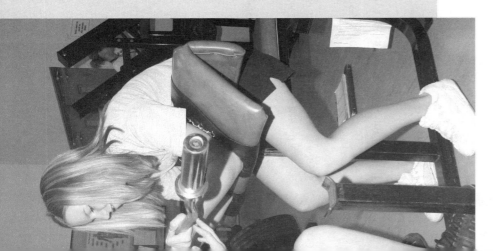

CHAPTER SUMMARY

This chapter focuses on the concepts of liability and negligence and how each area affects methods of instruction. Liability is a responsibility to perform a duty to a particular group, namely students in an education setting. Tort liability is a lawsuit for breach of duty. Money is given to the offended individual when the breach of duty was flagrant. Negligence involves four major areas: (1) duty to the individual, (2) breach of duty or failure to carry out the required duty, (3) injury to the student, and (4) proximate cause (whether the accident was caused by the teacher not carrying out the duty). There are many types of negligence: malfeasance, misfeasance, nonfeasance, contributory negligence, and comparative or shared negligence. The major areas of neglect tha t often lead to lawsuits are supervision of students, instruction of students, equipment and facilities, and athletic participation. Written policies and guidelines in these areas need to be developed and integrated into the educational process.

The practice of safety involves preventing accidents. Teachers need to understand the health status of students and have a plan for emergency care when an accident occurs. Using a safety and liability checklist is a preventive approach to avoiding the possibility of a lawsuit. Safety primarily involves preventing accidents before they occur. Written procedures need to be developed in the area of safety and continuously updated and reviewed. A written plan for emergency care should be established, approved by the school district, and followed to the letter by teachers. The administration of first aid should be undertaken by the physical

Chapter Summary, continued

education instructor only for saving a life. Accident reports should be filled out immediately while the results of the accident are fresh. A safety and liability checklist can be used to monitor the physical education environment.

STUDENT OUTCOMES

After reading the chapter, you will be able to:

- Clearly delineate the different types of negligence and give an example of how each situation might occur in the physical education setting.

- Identify the different types of defense arguments that are made to prove that the instructor was not negligent. Allied to this is understanding why each defense leaves the teacher at the mercy of the court.

- Explain why careful planning is a prelude to adequate instruction.

- List several guidelines a teacher should incorporate when planning for meaningful and safe instruction.

- Describe the features of athletic participation that make it a high-risk activity. Define a set of guidelines that will help minimize the chance of a lawsuit.

- Develop a working definition of safety that represents the risks inherent in physical education.

- Write a plan for emergency care when an accident occurs in a physical education class.

- Dictate the need for effective record keeping of accidents and purchase of liability insurance.

- Write a comprehensive safety checklist for a physical education or athletic program.

School district personnel, including teaching and nonteaching members, are obligated to exercise ordinary care for the safety of students. This duty is manifested as the ability to anticipate reasonably foreseeable dangers and the responsibility to take necessary precautions to prevent problems from occurring. Failure to do so may cause the district to be the target of lawsuits.

Compared with other subject-matter areas, physical education is particularly vulnerable to accidents and resultant injuries. More than 50 percent of all accidents in the school setting occur on the playground and in the gymnasium. Even though schools cannot be held financially accountable for costs associated with treatment of injuries, they can be forced to pay these expenses if the injured party sues and wins judgment. Legal suits are conducted under respective state statutes. Principles underlying legal action are similar, but certain regulations and procedures vary among states. Teachers should acquire a copy of the legal lia-

bility policy in their district. Districts usually have a written definition of situations in which teachers can be held liable.

All students have the right to freedom from injury caused by others or participation in a program. Courts have ruled that teachers owe their students a duty of care to protect them from harm. Teachers must offer a standard of care that any reasonable and prudent professional with similar training would apply under the given circumstances. A teacher is required to exercise the teaching skill, discretion, and knowledge that members of the profession in good standing normally possess in similar situations. Lawsuits usually occur when citizens believe that this standard of care was not exercised.

Liability is the responsibility to perform a duty for a particular group. It is an obligation to perform in a particular way that is required by law and enforced by court action. Teachers are bound by contract to carry out their duties in a reasonable and prudent manner. Liability is always a legal matter. It must be proved in a court of law that negligence occurred before one can be held liable.

TORTS

In education, a tort is concerned with the teacher–student relationship and is a legal wrong that results in direct or indirect injury to another individual or to property. The following legal definition is from *Black's Law Dictionary* (Garner, 2004):

[A tort is] a private or civil wrong or injury, other than breach of contract, for which the court will provide a remedy in the form of an action for damages. Three elements of every tort action are: existence of legal duty from defendant to plaintiff, breach of duty, and damage as proximate result.

As the result of a tort, the court can give a monetary reward for damages that occurred. The court can also give a monetary reward for punitive damages if a breach of duty can be established. Usually, the court rewards the offended individual for damages that occurred because of the negligence of the instructor or other responsible individual. Punitive damages are much less common.

NEGLIGENCE AND LIABILITY

Liability is usually concerned with a breach of duty through negligence. Lawyers examine the situation that gave rise to the injury to establish if liability can be determined. Four major points must be established to determine if a teacher was negligent.

Determination of Liability

1. Duty. The first point considered is that of duty owed to the participants. Did the school or teacher owe students a duty of care that implies conforming to certain standards of conduct? When examining duty or breach of duty, the court looks at reasonable care that a member of the profession in good standing would provide. In other words, to determine a reasonable standard, the court uses the conduct of other teachers as a standard for comparison.

2. Breach of Duty. The teacher must commit a breach of duty by failing to conform to the required duty. After it is established that a duty was required, it must be proved that the teacher did not perform that duty. Two situations are possible: (a) the teacher did something that was not supposed to be done (e.g., putting boxing gloves on students to resolve their differences), or (b) the teacher did not do something that should have been done (e.g., failing to teach an activity using proper progressions).

3. Proximate Cause. The failure of the teacher to conform to the required standard must be the proximate cause of the resulting injury. It must be proved that the injury was caused by the teacher's breach of duty. It is not enough to simply prove that a breach of duty occurred. It must simultaneously be shown that the injury was a direct result of the teacher's failure to provide a reasonable standard of care. The plaintiff's expert will try to convince the court that there was a requisite standard and that standard was not met. In contrast, the defendant will try to show that the teacher met the proper standard of care.

4. Damages. Actual harm must occur if liability is to be established. If no injury or harm occurs, there is no liability. It must be proved that the injured party is entitled to compensatory damages for financial loss or physical discomfort. Actual damages can be physical, emotional, or financial, but the court will only award financial remuneration.

Foreseeability

A key to the issue of negligence is foreseeability. Courts expect that a trained professional is able to foresee potentially harmful situations. Was it possible for the teacher to predict and anticipate the danger of the harmful act or situation and to take appropriate measures to prevent it from occurring? If the injured party can prove that the teacher should have foreseen the danger involved in an activity or situation (even in part), the teacher will be found negligent for failing to act in a reasonable and prudent manner. This points out the necessity of examining all activities, equipment, and facilities for possible hazards and sources of accident.

Sample Case: A Case of Foreseeability?

A common game (unfortunately) in many school settings is bombardment, or dodgeball. During the game, a student is hit in the eye by a ball and loses vision in that eye. Was this a foreseeable accident that could have been prevented? Were the balls being used capable of inflicting severe injury? Were students aware of rules that might have prevented this injury? Were the abilities of the students somewhat equal, or were some capable of throwing with such velocity that injury was predictable? Were all students forced to play the game? These questions would likely be considered in court in an attempt to prove that the teacher should have been able to predict the overly dangerous situation.

Types of Negligence

Negligence is defined by the court as conduct that falls below a standard of care established to protect others from unreasonable risk or harm. Several types of negligence can be categorized.

Malfeasance

Malfeasance occurs when the teacher does something improper by committing an act that is unlawful and wrongful, with no legal basis (often referred to as an act of commission). Malfeasance can be illustrated by the following incident. A male student misbehaved on numerous occasions. In desperation, the teacher gave the student a choice of punishment—a severe spanking in front of the class or running many laps around the field. The student chose the former and suffered physical and emotional damage. Even though the teacher gave the student a choice whereby he could have avoided the paddling, the teacher is still liable for any physical or emotional harm caused.

Misfeasance

Misfeasance occurs when the teacher follows the proper procedures but does not perform according to the required standard of conduct. Misfeasance is based on performance of the proper action but not up to the required standard. It is usually the subpar performance of an act that might have been otherwise lawfully done. An example would be the teacher offering to spot a student during a tumbling routine and then not doing the spotting properly. If the student is injured following a faulty spot, the teacher can be held liable.

Nonfeasance

Nonfeasance is based on lack of action in carrying out a duty. This is usually an act of omission: The teacher knew the proper procedures but failed to follow them. Teachers can be found negligent if they act or fail to act. Understanding and carrying out proper procedures and duties in a manner befitting members of the profession is essential. In contrast to the misfeasance example, nonfeasance occurs when a teacher knows that it is necessary to spot certain gymnastic routines but fails to do so. Courts expect teachers to behave with more skill and insight than parents. Teachers are expected to behave with greater competency because they have been educated to give students a higher standard of professional care than parents.

Sample Case: Does Size Make a Difference?
Students are playing in a middle school game of diagonal soccer. When their numbers are called, three students

from each team come running to the center to try and get the ball first and gain scoring advantage. One of the students is a small student who weighs about 70 lb. A student on the other team is mature and weighs nearly 160 lb. As they approach the ball, the larger student basically runs over the smaller student, knocking him down and causing a head injury. Within 2 weeks, the student has a seizure, and the parents plan to sue. Should the students have been matched for maturity and ability? Does gender make a difference? Could the game have been modified to avoid this injury? Is the teacher guilty of malpractice?

Contributory Negligence

The situation is different when the injured student is partially or wholly at fault. Students are expected to exercise sensible care and to follow directions or regulations designed to protect them from injury. When the injured party exhibited improper behavior that caused the accident, it is usually ruled to be contributory negligence because the injured party contributed to the resulting harm. This responsibility is directly related to the maturity, ability, and experience of the youngster. For example, most states have laws specifying that a child under 7 years of age is incapable of contributory negligence (Baley and Matthews, 1988).

Sample Case: "I told them not to, but they did it anyway!"

A physical education instructor teaching a class of freshmen students has thoroughly explained the shot put and related safety rules and marked restraining lines that are easy for students to see. During class, students are engaged in practicing a number of events. One of the students runs through the restricted area and is hit by a shot put. Who is to blame? Was the student old enough to know better? Were there too many events being taught at the same time? Should the teacher have foreseen that an accident might happen even if students were prewarned? Is the shot put an appropriate event for physical education classes? Is there an assumption of risk in all physical education activities, causing these situations to happen from time to time?

Comparative or Shared Negligence

Under the doctrine of comparative negligence, the injured party can recover damages only if he or she is found to be less negligent than the defendant (the teacher). Where statutes apply, the amount of recovery is generally reduced in proportion to the injured party's participation in the circumstances leading to the injury.

Common Defenses Against Negligence

Negligence must be proven in a court of law. Many-times, teachers are negligent in carrying out their du-ties, yet the injured party does not take the case to court. If a teacher is sued, some of the following de-fenses are used in an attempt to show that the teacher's action was not the primary cause of the accident.

Act of God

The act of God defense places the cause of injury on forces beyond the control of the teacher or the school. The defense is made that it was impossible to predict an unsafe condition, but through an act of God, the in-jury occurred. Typical acts would be a gust of wind that blew over a volleyball standard or a cloudburst of rain that made a surface slick. The act of God defense can be used only in cases in which the injury still would have occurred even though reasonable and prudent ac-tion had been taken.

Proximate Cause

The defense of proximate cause attempts to prove that the accident was not caused by the negligence of the teacher. There must be a close relationship between the breach of duty by the teacher and the injury. This is a common defense in cases dealing with proper supervi-sion. The student is participating in an activity super-vised by the teacher. When the teacher leaves the playing area to get a cup of coffee, the student is in-jured. The defense lawyer will try to show that the ac-cident would have occurred regardless of whether the teacher was there.

Assumption of Risk

Clearly, physical education is a high-risk activity when compared with most other curriculum areas. Assump-tion of risk implies the participant assumes the risk of an activity when choosing to be part of that activity. The assumption of risk defense is seldom used by phys-ical education teachers because students are not often allowed to choose to participate or not participate. An instructor for an elective program that allows students to choose desired units of instruction might find this a better defense than one who teaches a totally required program. Athletic and sport club participation occurs by choice, and players must assume a greater risk in ac-tivities such as football and gymnastics.

Contributory Negligence

Contributory negligence is often used by the defense in an attempt to convince the court that the injured

party acted in a manner that was abnormal. In other words, the injured individual did not act in a manner that was typical of students of similar age and matu-rity. The defense attempts to demonstrate that the ac-tivity or equipment in question was used for years with no record of accident. A case is made based on the manner of presentation—how students were taught to act in a safe manner—and that the injured student acted outside the parameters of safe conduct. A key point in this defense is whether the activity was suit-able for the age and maturity level of the participants.

AREAS OF RESPONSIBILITY

A two-tiered approach for analyzing injuries is useful for determining responsibility. The first tier includes the duties that the administration must assume in sup-port of the program. The second tier defines the duties of the instructor or staff member charged with teach-ing or supervising students. Each party has a role to fill, but some overlap occurs. The following example illus-trates the differences.

A student is hurt while performing a tumbling stunt. A lawsuit ensues, charging the teacher with neg-ligence for not following safe procedures. The adminis-tration is usually included in the suit, being charged with negligence for hiring an incompetent (not quali-fied) instructor and not implementing proper safety factors. When delegating responsibility, the two levels of responsibility should be considered for the follow-ing reasons:

1. They identify different functions and responsibili-ties of the teaching staff and administration.

2. They provide a framework for reducing injuries and improving safety procedures.

3. They provide perspective for following legal prece-dents.

For the responsibilities that are described in the following sections, both administrative and instruc-tional duties are presented.

Supervision

All activities in a school setting must be supervised, in-cluding recess, lunch times, and field trips. The re-sponsibilities of the school are critical if supervision is to function properly.

Administration

Two levels are identified in supervision: general and specific. General supervision (study hall, lunchroom, and so on) refers to broad coverage, when students are not under direct control of a teacher or a designated individual. A plan of supervision should be made, designating the areas to be covered and including where and how the supervisor should rotate through these areas. This plan, kept in the principal's office, should cover rules of conduct governing student behavior. Rules should be posted prominently on bulletin boards, especially in classrooms. In addition to the plan, administrators must select qualified personnel, provide necessary training, and monitor the plan properly.

The general supervisor must be concerned primarily with student behavior, focusing on the student's right to a safe and unthreatening experience. Supervisors should observe the area, looking for breaches of discipline, particularly when an individual or group "picks on" another youngster. If it becomes necessary to leave the area, a qualified substitute must be found to prevent the area from going unsupervised.

Staff

General supervision is necessary during times when students congregate but are not involved in instruction. The supervisor should know the school's plan for supervision and emergency care procedures to follow in case of an accident. Supervision is a positive act that requires the supervisor to be actively involved and moving throughout the area. The number of supervisors should be determined by the type of activity, the size of the area, and the number and age of the students.

Specific supervision requires that the instructor be with a certain group of students (i.e., a class). An example is spotting students who are performing challenging gymnastic activities. If certain pieces of apparatus require special care and proper use, rules and regulations must be posted near the apparatus. Students should be made aware of the rules and should receive appropriate instruction and guidance in applying the rules. When rules are modified, they should be rewritten in proper form. There is no substitute for documentation when the need to defend policies and approaches arises.

When teaching, arrange and teach the class so that all students are always in view. This implies supervising from the perimeter of the area. Teachers who are at the center of the student group with many students behind them will find it impossible to supervise a class safely and effectively. Equipment and apparatuses should not go unsupervised at any time when left accessible to students in the area. An example would be equipment that is left on the playing field between classes. If other students in the area have easy access to the equipment, they may use it in an unsafe manner, and the teacher can be found liable if an injury occurs.

Instruction

Instructional responsibility rests primarily with the teacher, but administrative personnel have certain defined functions.

Administration

The administration should review and approve the curricular plan. The curriculum should be reviewed regularly to ensure that it is current and updated.

Sample Case: "I know we had a supervisor out there!"

At lunch, middle school students have 20 minutes of free time to play on the activity field and in the gymnasium. One teacher is assigned to supervise the students on the playing field, and one is supervising the gym. The playing field is large, and there is an injury opposite of where the teacher is standing. The teacher hustles to aid the student. While the teacher is attending the student, a fight breaks out and goes unnoticed by the teacher because she is busy with the injured student. A smaller student is severely beaten by a larger student. Is the teacher liable because she didn't see the fight? Can one teacher adequately supervise a playground full of students? Is the administrator the one who is responsible because only one teacher was assigned to supervise? Did the teacher have a way to communicate with the front office to ask for additional help?

Teachers should not agree to supervise activities for which they are unqualified to anticipate possible hazards. If this situation arises, a written memo should be sent to the department head or principal stating such lack of insight and qualification. Teachers should maintain a copy for their files.

Merriman (1993) offers five recommendations to ensure that adequate supervision occurs:

1. The supervisor must be in the immediate vicinity (within sight and hearing).

2. If required to leave, the supervisor must have an adequate replacement in place before departing. Adequate replacements do not include paraprofessionals, student teachers, custodial help, or untrained teachers.

3. Supervision procedures must be preplanned and incorporated into daily lessons.

4. Supervision procedures should include what to observe and listen for, where to stand for the most effective view, and what to do if a problem arises.

5. Supervision requires that age, maturity, and skill ability of participants must always be considered, as well as the inherent risk of the activity.

Activities included in the curriculum should be based on contributions they make to the growth and development of youngsters. It makes little sense in a court of law to say that an activity was included "for the fun of it" or "because students liked it." Instead, activities should be placed in the curriculum because they meet program objectives. Administrators are obligated to support the program with adequate finances. The principal and higher administrators should visit the program periodically. Familiarity with program content and operation reduces the possibility that practices were occurring without adequate administrative supervision.

Instructional Staff

With regard to instruction, the teacher has a duty to protect students from unreasonable physical or mental harm. This includes avoiding any acts or omissions that might cause such harm. The teacher is educated, experienced, and skilled in physical education and must be able to foresee situations that could be harmful.

The major area of concern involving instruction is whether the student received adequate instruction before or during activity participation. Adequate instruction means (1) teaching students how to perform activities correctly and use equipment and apparatuses properly, and (2) teaching youngsters necessary safety precautions. If instructions are given, they must be correct and understandable and include proper technique, or the instructor can be held liable. The risk involved in an activity must be communicated to the learner.

The age and maturity level of students play an important role in the selection of activities. Younger students require more care, instructions that are easy to comprehend, and clear restrictions in the name of safety. Some students have a lack of appropriate fear in activities, and the teacher must be aware of this when discussing safety factors. A daredevil may have little concern about performing a high-risk activity, even if an instructor is nearby. This places much responsibility on the instructor to give adequate instruction and supervision.

Careful planning is a necessity. Written curriculum guides and lesson plans should offer a well-prepared approach that can withstand scrutiny and examination by other teachers and administrators. Written lesson plans should include proper sequence and progression of skill instruction. Teachers are on defensible grounds if they can show that the progression of activities was based on presentations designed by experts and was followed carefully during the teaching act. District and state guidelines enforcing instructional sequences and restricted activities should be checked closely.

Sample Case: The Need for a Curriculum and Lesson Plan

In a gymnastics unit being taught in a high school, one of the teachers is a former gymnast. Because of her knowledge level, she convinces the rest of the physical education team to teach gymnastics to their students as well. This school does not have a curriculum guide, and none of the teachers write lesson plans. One of the less competent (in the gymnastics area) teachers decides to have students try a headspring over a tumbling mat. A student is seriously hurt (severe neck injury that causes paralysis), and the parents of the student file a $1.5 million lawsuit. How would you defend yourself in this situation? Would it help if you were able to say gymnastics was part of the school curriculum? What if the plaintiff's lawyer brings in an expert witness who says the instructional sequence was inappropriate? Could you show your lesson plan that shows the proper instructional sequence based on what expert instructors recommend? Can you be an expert in every activity you teach, or do you need to rely on other experts for the proper sequence of activities to teach?

Proper instruction demands that students not be forced to participate. If a youngster is required to perform an activity unwillingly, the teacher may be open to a lawsuit. In a lawsuit dealing with stunts and tumbling, the court held the teacher liable when a student claimed that she was not given adequate instruction in how to perform a stunt called "roll over two." The teacher was held liable because the student claimed she was forced to try the stunt before adequate instruction was offered. Gymnastics and tumbling are areas in which lawsuits are prevalent because of a lack of adequate instruction. Posting the proper sequence of skills and lead-up activities may be useful to ensure that they have been presented properly. Teachers need to tread the line carefully between helpfully encouraging and forcing students to try new activities.

For teachers who incorporate punishment as a part of the instructional process, the consequences of its use should be examined carefully before implementation. Physical punishment that brings about permanent or long-lasting damage is indefensible. Using some type of physical activity (push-ups or running) is an unacceptable practice that increases the risk of being sued. Any punishment used must be in line with the physical maturity and health of the student involved. A teacher's practice of having students perform laps when they have misbehaved might go unchallenged for years. However, making students perform physical activity for misbehavior is indefensible under any circumstance. If a student is injured while performing physical punishment, teachers are usually found liable and held responsible for the injury.

Sample Case: Running for Punishment—The Right Choice?

- Youngsters are participating in a physical education class and are unruly. They are talking when they shouldn't and generally not cooperating. The teacher, in a fit of controlled anger, tells the two students to go run laps around a large field until they decide to behave. It is a hot fall day, and after 15 minutes of running, one of the students falls and goes into convulsions on the far side (a third of a mile away) of the field. The teacher doesn't see the child go down until a student tells him about it. Is this malfeasance? Is running an acceptable choice for punishment? Were the weather conditions considered? Did the youth have some preexisting health condition? Were the students under the watchful eye of the teacher or out of sight? Could you defend yourself in this situation?

The following points can help teachers plan for meaningful and safe instruction:

- Sequence all activities in units of instruction and develop written lesson plans. Many problems occur when snap judgments are made under the daily pressure and strain of teaching.

- Scrutinize high-risk activities to ensure that all safety procedures have been implemented. If in doubt, discuss the activities with other experienced teachers and administrators.

- Ensure that activities used in the curriculum are within the developmental limits of the students. Considering the range of maturity and development of youngsters in a class is usually wide, activities may be beyond the ability level of some students.

- Remember, if students' grades are based on the number of activities in which they participate, some students may feel forced to try all activities. Teachers should make it clear to students that the choice to participate belongs to them. When they are afraid of getting hurt, they can elect not to perform an activity.

- Include in written lesson plans necessary safety equipment. The lesson plan should detail how equipment should be arranged, where mats will be placed, and where the instructor will carry out supervision.

- If a student claims injury or brings a note from parents requesting that the student not participate in physical activity, honor the communication. Excuses are almost always given at the start of the period when the teacher is busy with many other duties (e.g., getting equipment ready, taking roll, and opening lockers). It is difficult to make a thoughtful judgment at this time. The school nurse is qualified to make these judgments when they relate to health and should be used in that capacity. If the excuses continue over a long period of time, the teacher or nurse should have a conference with the parents to rectify the situation.

- Make sure that activities included in the instructional process are in line with the available equipment and facilities. An example is the amount of space available. If a soccer lead-up activity is brought indoors because of inclement weather, it may no longer be a safe and appropriate activity.

- If spotting is required for safe completion of activities, always do it yourself or train students to spot others. Teaching students how to spot is as important as teaching them physical skills. Safe conduct must be learned.

- If students are working independently at stations, distribute carefully constructed and written task cards to help eliminate unsafe practices.

- Have a written emergency care plan posted in the gymnasium. This plan should be approved by health care professionals and should be followed to the letter when an injury occurs.

EQUIPMENT AND FACILITIES

School responsibility for equipment and facilities is required for both noninstructional and class use.

Administration

The principal and the custodian should oversee the fields and playground equipment that are used for recess and outside activities. Students should be instructed to report broken and unsafe equipment, as well as hazards (glass, cans, rocks), to the principal's office. If equipment is faulty, it should be removed from the area. A regular inspection of equipment and facilities, preferably by the physical education specialist, should be instituted, perhaps weekly. If a specialist is not employed, the inspection will have to be performed by the principal or the custodian. Results of the inspection should be filed with the school district safety committee. Replacement of sawdust, sand, or other shock-absorbing material must be done regularly. Administrators should develop a written checklist of equipment and apparatuses for the purpose of recording scheduled safety inspections. The date of inspection should be noted to show that inspection occurs at regular intervals. If a potentially dangerous situation exists, rules or warnings should be posted so that students and teachers are made aware of the risk before participation is allowed.

Proper installation of equipment is critical. Climbing equipment and other equipment that must be anchored should be installed by a reputable firm that guarantees its work. When examining apparatuses, inspection of the installation is important. Maintenance of facilities is also important. Grass should be kept short and the grounds inspected for debris. Holes in the ground should be filled and loose gravel removed. A proper finish that prevents excessive slipping should be used on indoor floors. Shower rooms should have a roughened floor finish applied to prevent falls when the floors are wet.

Equipment and facilities used in the physical education program must ensure safe participation. The choice of apparatuses and equipment should be based on the growth and developmental levels of the students. For example, allowing middle school students to use climbing equipment that was designed for high school students may result in a fall that causes injury. Hazards found on playing fields need to be repaired or eliminated. The legal concept of an "attractive nuisance" implies that some piece of equipment or apparatus, usually left unsupervised, was so attractive to youngsters that they could not be expected to avoid it. When an injury occurs, even though students may have been using the apparatus incorrectly, teachers and school administrators are often held liable because the attractive nuisance should have been removed from the area when unsupervised.

Instructional Staff

Indoor facilities are of primary concern to physical education instructors. While the administration is charged with overall responsibility for facilities and equipment, including periodic inspections, the instructor should make a regular safety inspection of the instructional area. If corrective action is needed, the principal or other designated administrator should be notified in writing. Verbal notification is not enough, considering it offers little legal protection to the instructor.

Facilities should be used in a safe manner. Often, the sidelines and end lines of playing fields for sports such as football, soccer, and field hockey are placed too close to walls, curbing, or fences. The boundaries for the game should be moved to allow adequate room for deceleration, even though the size of the playing area may be reduced. In the gymnasium, students should not be asked to run to a line that is close to a wall. Another common hazard is baskets positioned too close to the playing area. The poles that support the baskets must be padded.

Proper use of equipment and apparatuses is important. Regardless of the state of equipment repair, if it is misused, it may result in an injury. If equipment has the potential for misuse, students must receive instruction about acceptable ways to participate. Safety instruction should be included in the written lesson plan to ensure that all points are covered. Equipment should be purchased on the basis of quality and safety as well as potential use. Many lawsuits occur because of unsafe equipment and apparatuses. The liability for such equipment may rest with the manufacturer, but this has to be proven, which means that the teacher must state, in writing, the exact specifications of the desired equipment. The process of bidding for lower-priced items may result in the purchase of less-safe equipment. If teachers have specified proper equipment in writing, however, the possibility of being held liable for injury is reduced.

SPORTS PROGRAMS

A common problem for administrators of school sports programs is providing qualified coaches. The administration should set minimum requirements for coaches and ensure that incompetent individuals are removed from coaching duties (see Chapter 13). When students are involved in extracurricular activity, teachers (coaches) are responsible for the safe conduct of activities. The following areas often give rise to lawsuits if they are not handled carefully.

Mismatched Opponents

A common error that gives rise to lawsuits is the mismatching of students on the basis of size and ability. Just because the competitors are the same sex and choose to participate does not absolve the instructor of liability if an injury occurs. The question that courts examine is whether an effort was made to match students according to height, weight, and ability. Courts are less understanding about mismatching in the physical education setting compared with an athletic contest, but mismatching is a factor that should be avoided in any situation.

Waiver Forms

Participants in extracurricular activities should be required to sign a responsibility waiver form. The form should explain the risks involved in voluntary participation and briefly discuss the types of injuries that have occurred in the past during practice and competition. Signed waiver slips do not waive the rights of participants; teachers and coaches still can be found liable if injuries occur. However, the waiver form does clearly communicate the risks involved and may be a strong "assumption of risk" defense.

Medical Examinations

Participants must have a medical examination before participating. Records of the examination should be kept on file and should be identified prominently when physical restrictions or limitations exist. It is common to place a "red dot" on the folders of students who have a history of medical problems. Students must not be allowed to participate unless they purchase or show proof of medical insurance. Evidence of such coverage should be kept in the folders of athletic participants.

Preseason Conditioning

Preseason conditioning should be undertaken in a systematic and progressive fashion. Coaches should be aware of guidelines dealing with heat and humidity (see Chapter 2). For example, in Arizona, guidelines are to avoid strenuous activity when the temperature exceeds 85°F and the humidity exceeds 40 percent. When these conditions are exceeded, running is curtailed to 10 minutes and active games to 30 minutes. Drinking water should be available and given to students on demand.

Sample Case: All Students Were Given a Summer Conditioning Regimen

Students in a successful football program are given a summer conditioning program to follow during summer vacation. When the players return to formal football practices, the first thing the coach does is ask all players to run a mile. The coach says that this will show who followed the conditioning regimen during the summer. It is a hot August day, and while the players are running, one of them suffers a serious seizure. Can coaches assume all students will follow the regimen? Do athletes respond differently to training? Are linemen more susceptible to overheating? Does it make sense to assign the same workload to all athletes regardless of body type? Should practices be started with a physical test (run a mile)? How will you defend your decision to have them all run a mile on the first day of practice?

Transportation of Students

Whenever students are transported, teachers are responsible for their safety, both en route and during the activity. Transportation liability can be avoided by not providing transportation but instead requiring participants to meet at the site of the event (Pittman, 1993). If the school must provide transportation, li-

censed drivers and school-approved vehicles should always be used. Travel plans should include official approval from the appropriate school administrator. One special note to consider is if the driver receives pay or reimbursement for the trip, the possibility of being held liable for injury increases dramatically. To make the matter worse, many insurance policies do not cover drivers who receive compensation for transporting students. If teachers are transporting students and receiving reimbursement, a special insurance rider should be purchased that provides liability coverage for this situation.

SAFETY

The major thrust of safety should be to prevent situations that cause accidents. It is estimated that more than 70 percent of injuries that occur in sports and related activities could be prevented through proper safety procedures. On the other hand, some accidents occur despite precautions, and proper emergency procedures should be established to cope with any situation. A comprehensive study of injuries received in sports and related activities was conducted by the U.S. Consumer Product Safety Commission (1997). This study involved a network of computers in 119 hospital emergency rooms that channeled injury data to a central point. The sports and activities that produced the most injuries were, in order, football, touch football, baseball, basketball, gymnastics, and skiing. The facility that produced the most disabling injuries was the swimming pool.

Learning to recognize potential high-risk situations is an important factor in preventing accidents. Teachers must possess a clear understanding of the hazards and potential dangers of an activity before they can establish controls. Instructors must not assume that participants are aware of the dangers and risks involved in various activities. Students must be told of all dangers and risks before participation.

Guidelines for Safety

1. In-service sessions in safety should be administered by experienced and knowledgeable teachers. Department heads may be responsible for the training, or outside experts can be employed to undertake the responsibility. Giving in-district credit to participating teachers offers strong indication that the district is concerned about using proper safety techniques.

2. Medical records should be reviewed at the start of the school year. Atypical students should be identified and noted within each class listing before the

first instructional day. If necessary, the teacher or school nurse can call the doctor of a student with disabilities or activity restrictions to inquire about the situation and discuss special needs. Physical education teachers should be notified by the classroom teacher or school nurse about youngsters who have special problems (e.g., epilepsy) or temporary problems (e.g., medication).

3. Throughout the school year, safety orientations should be conducted with students. Discussions should include potentially dangerous situations, class conduct, and rules for proper use of equipment and apparatuses. Teachers should urge students to report any conditions that might cause an accident.

4. Safety rules for specific units of instruction should be discussed at the onset of each unit. Rules should be posted and brought to the attention of students regularly. Posters and bulletin boards can promote safety in an enjoyable and stimulating manner.

5. If students are to serve as instructional aides, they should be trained. Aides must understand the techniques of spotting, for example, and must receive proper instruction if they are to be a part of the educational process. Caution must be used when using student aides because teachers are still responsible even if an aide performs a duty incorrectly.

6. Instructional practices need to be monitored for possible hazards. For example, students in competitive situations should be matched by size, maturity, and ability. Proper instruction necessary for safe participation should occur prior to activity. Instructors should receive a competence check to ensure that they are adequately trained to give instruction in various activities. The instructional area should be properly prepared for safe participation; if the area is lacking necessary apparatuses and safety devices, instruction should be modified to meet safety standards.

7. An inventory of equipment and apparatuses should include a safety checklist. Whenever necessary, equipment in need of repair should be sent to proper agents. If the cost of repair is greater than 40 percent of the replacement cost, discarding the equipment or apparatus is usually a more economical choice.

8. When an injury occurs, it should be recorded and a report placed in the student's file. An injury should also be filed by type of injury, such as ankle sprain or broken arm. The report should list the activity and the conditions to facilitate analysis at regular intervals. The analysis may show that injuries are occurring regularly during a specific activity or on a

certain piece of equipment. This process can give direction for creating a safer environment or for defending the safety record of a sport, activity, or piece of equipment.

9. Teachers need to maintain up-to-date first-aid and cardiopulmonary resuscitation (CPR) certification. Administrators should ensure that teachers meet these standards and should provide training sessions when necessary.

Safety Committee

Safety should be publicized regularly throughout the school, and a mechanism should exist that allows students, parents, and teachers to voice concerns about unsafe conditions. A safety committee can meet at regular intervals to establish safety policies, rule on requests for allowing high-risk activities, and analyze serious injuries that have occurred in the school district. This committee should develop safety rules that apply districtwide to all teachers. It may determine that certain activities involve too high a risk for the return in student benefit. Acceptable criteria for sport equipment and apparatuses may be established by the committee.

The safety committee should include one or more high-level administrators, physical education teachers, health officers (nurse), parents, and students. School administrators are usually indicted when lawsuits occur because they are held responsible for program content and curriculum. Their representation on the safety committee is therefore important. Students on the committee may be aware of possible hazards, and parents may often voice concerns overlooked by teachers.

Emergency Care Plan

Before any emergency arises, teachers should prepare themselves by learning about special health and physical conditions of students (Gray, 1993). Most schools have a method for identifying students with special health problems. If a student has a problem that may require treatment, a consent-to-treat form should be on file in case the parent or guardian is unavailable. Necessary first-aid materials and supplies should be available in a kit and be readily accessible. Establishing procedures for emergency care and notification of parents in case of injury is of utmost importance in providing a high standard of care for students. To plan properly for emergency care, all physical education teachers should have first-aid training. First aid is the immediate and temporary care given at an emergency before a physician is available. Its purpose is to save life, prevent aggravation of injuries, and alleviate severe suffering. If there is evidence of life-threatening bleeding or if the victim is unconscious or has stopped breathing, the teacher must administer first aid. When already injured persons may be further injured if they are not moved, then moving them is permissible. As a general rule, however, an injured person should not be moved unless absolutely necessary. If back or neck injury is indicated, the head must be immobilized and should not be moved without the use of a spine board. The purpose of first aid is to save life. The emergency care plan consists of the following steps:

1. Administration of first aid to the injured student is the number-one priority. Treat only life-threatening injuries. The school nurse should be called to the scene of the accident immediately; Emergency care procedures should indicate whether the student can be moved and in what fashion. It is critical that the individual applying first aid avoid aggravating the injury.

2. Parents should be notified as soon as possible when emergency care is required. Each student's file should list home and emergency telephone numbers where parents can be reached. If possible, the school should have an arrangement with local emergency facilities so that a paramedic unit can be called immediately to the scene of a serious accident.

3. In most cases, the student should be released to a parent or a designated representative. Policies for transportation of injured students should be established and documented.

4. A student accident report should be completed promptly while the details of the accident are clear. Figure 12.1 is an example of an accident form that covers the necessary details. The teacher and principal should both retain copies, and additional copies should be sent to the administrative office.

PERSONAL PROTECTION: MINIMIZING THE EFFECTS OF A LAWSUIT

In spite of proper care, injuries do occur, and lawsuits may be initiated. Two courses of action are necessary to counteract the effects of a suit.

Liability Insurance

Teachers may be protected by school district liability insurance. Usually, however, teachers must purchase their own policies. Most policies provide for legal services to contest a suit and will pay indemnity up to the limits of the policy (liability coverage of $500,000 is most common). Most policies give the insurance company the right to settle out of court. Unfortunately, when this occurs, some may infer that the teacher was guilty even though the circumstances indicate otherwise. Insurance companies usually settle out of court to avoid the excessive legal fees required to try to win the case in court.

Record Keeping

The second course of action is to keep complete records of accidents. Many lawsuits occur months or even years after the accident, when memory of the situation is fuzzy. Accident reports should be filled out immediately after an injury. The teacher should take care to provide no evidence, oral or written, that others could use in a court of law. Do not attempt to make a diagnosis or to specify the supposed cause of the accident in the report.

If newspaper reporters probe for details, the teacher should avoid describing the accident beyond the basic facts. When discussing the accident with administrators, the teacher should describe only the facts recorded on the accident report. School records can be subpoenaed in court proceedings. The point here is not to dissemble, but to be cautious and avoid self-incrimination.

Safety and Liability Checklist

The following checklist can be used to monitor the physical education environment. Any situations that deviate from safe and legally sound practices should be rectified immediately.

Supervision and Instruction

1. Are teachers adequately trained in all of the activities that they are teaching?

2. Do all teachers have evidence of a necessary level of first-aid training?

3. When supervising, do personnel have access to a written plan of areas to be observed and responsibilities to be carried out?

4. Have students been warned of potential dangers and risks and advised of rules and the reasons for the rules?

5. Are safety rules posted near areas of increased risk?

6. Are lesson plans written? Do they include provisions for proper instruction, sequence of activities, and safety? Are all activities taught listed in the district curriculum guide?

Student Accident Report

_____ School

In all cases, this form should be filed through the school nurse and signed by the principal of the school. The original will be forwarded to the superintendent's office, where it will be initialed and sent to the head nurse. The second copy will be retained by the principal or the nurse. The third copy should be given to the physical education teacher if accident is related.

Name of Injured _____ Address _____

Phone _____ Grade _____ Home Room _____ Age _____

Parents of Injured _____

Place of Accident _____ Date of Accident _____

Hour _____ A.M. / P.M. Date Reported _____ By Whom _____

Parent Contact Attempted at _____ A.M. / P.M. Parent Contacted at _____ A.M. / P.M.

DESCRIBE ACCIDENT, GIVING SPECIFIC LOCATION AND CONDITION OF PREMISES _____

_____

NATURE OF INJURY _____
(Describe in detail)

CARE GIVEN OR ACTION TAKEN BY NURSE OR OTHERS _____

_____

REASON INJURED PERSON WAS ON PREMISES _____
(Activity at time—e.g., lunch, physical education, etc.)

STAFF MEMBER RESPONSIBLE FOR STUDENT SUPERVISION AT TIME OF ACCIDENT _____

IS STUDENT COVERED BY SCHOOL-SPONSORED ACCIDENT INSURANCE? _____ YES _____ NO

MEDICAL CARE RECOMMENDED _____ YES _____ NO

WHERE TAKEN AFTER ACCIDENT _____
(Specify home, physician, or hospital, giving name and address)

BY WHOM _____ AT WHAT TIME _____ A.M. / P.M.

FOLLOW-UP BY NURSE TO BE SENT TO CENTRAL HEALTH OFFICE _____

REMEDIATION MEASURES TAKEN _____
(Attach individual remarks if necessary)

School _____ Principal _____

Date _____ Nurse _____

On the back of this sheet, list all persons familiar with the circumstances of the accident, giving name, address, telephone number, age, and location with respect to the accident.

FIGURE 12.1 Sample Student Accident Report Form

7. When a new activity is introduced, are safety precautions and instructions for correct skill performance always communicated to the class?

8. Are the activities taught in the program based on sound curriculum principles? Could the activities and units of instruction be defended on the basis of their educational contributions?

9. Do the methods of instruction recognize individual differences among students, and are the necessary steps taken to meet the needs of all students, regardless of sex, ability, or disability?

10. Are substitute teachers given clear and comprehensive lesson plans so that they can maintain the scope and sequence of instruction?

11. Is the student evaluation plan based on actual performance and objective data rather than on favoritism or arbitrary and capricious standards?

12. Is appropriate dress required for students? This does not imply uniforms—only dress (including shoes) that ensures the safety of the student.

13. When necessary for safety, are students grouped according to ability level, size, or age?

14. Is the class left unsupervised for teacher visits to the office, lounge, or bathroom? Is one teacher ever asked to supervise two or more classes at the same time?

15. If students are used as teacher aides or to spot others, are they given proper instruction and training?

Equipment and Facilities

1. Is all equipment inspected regularly, and are the inspection results recorded on a form and sent to the proper administrators?

2. Is a log maintained recording the regular occurrence of an inspection, the equipment in need of repair, and the date when repairs were made?

3. Are "attractive nuisances" eliminated from the gymnasium and playing field?

4. Are specific safety rules posted on facilities and near equipment?

5. Are the following inspected periodically:
   a. Playing field for presence of glass, rocks, and metal objects?
   b. Fasteners holding equipment, such as climbing ropes, horizontal bars, or baskets?
   c. Goals for games, such as football, soccer, and field hockey, to be sure that they are fastened securely?
   d. Padded areas, such as goal supports?

6. Are mats placed under apparatuses from which a fall is possible?

7. Are playing fields arranged so participants will not run into each other or be hit by a ball from another game?

8. Are landing pits filled and maintained properly?

Emergency Care

1. Is there a written procedure for emergency care?

2. Is a person properly trained in first aid available immediately following an accident?

3. Are emergency telephone numbers readily accessible?

4. Are telephone numbers of parents available?

5. Is an up-to-date first-aid kit available? Is ice immediately available?

6. Are health folders maintained that list restrictions, allergies, and health problems of students?

7. Are health folders reviewed by instructors on a regular basis?

8. Are students participating in extracurricular activities required to have insurance? Is the policy number recorded?

9. Is there a plan for treating injuries that involves the local paramedics?

10. Are accident reports filed promptly and analyzed regularly?

Transportation of Students

1. Have parents been informed that their students will be transported off campus?

2. Are detailed travel plans approved by the site administrator and kept on file?

3. Are school vehicles used whenever possible?

4. Are drivers properly licensed and vehicles insured?

5. If teachers or parents use their vehicles to transport students, are the students, driver, and car owner covered by an insurance rider purchased by the school district?

STUDY STIMULATORS AND REVIEW QUESTIONS

1. Explain what standard of duty a teacher has from a legal standpoint.

2. Explain what is meant by contributory negligence and provide an example of such.

3. Discuss the responsibilities of the school district administration in the areas of supervision and instruction.

4. Discuss the importance of having a well-laid-out lesson plan from a legal defense perspective.

5. Define "attractive nuisance" and explain how it might pose a risk for teachers.

6. Cite the four elements that must be present to confirm negligence.

7. Explain why it is important to have a high-ranking district administrator on the safety committee.

8. Describe the basic emergency care process that should be followed when a student suffers a serious injury.

9. Differentiate between malfeasance, misfeasance, and nonfeasance. Cite examples of each as they might occur in the physical education setting.

10. Why is a decision to "settle out of court" often a mixed blessing for the teacher?

REFERENCES AND SUGGESTED READINGS

Appenzeller, H. (Ed.) (1998). *Risk management in sport: Issues and strategies.* Durham, NC: Carolina Academic Press.

Appenzeller, H. (2003). *Managing sports and risk management strategies* (2nd ed.). Durham, NC: Carolina Academic Press.

Baley, J. A., & Matthews, D. L. (1988). *Law and liability in athletics, physical education, and recreation.* Dubuque, IA: William C. Brown Publishing.

Blucker, J. A., & Pell, S. W. (1986). Legal and ethical issues. *Journal of Physical Education, Recreation, and Dance, 57,* 19–21.

Clement, A. (2004). *Law in sport and physical activity* (3rd ed.). Dania, FL: Sport and Law Press.

Dougherty, N. J. (Ed.) (2002). *Principles of safety in physical education and sport* (3rd ed.). Reston, VA: American Alliance for Health, Physical Education, Recreation and Dance (AAHPERD).

Dougherty, N. J., Golberger, A. S., & Carpenter, A. S. (2002). *Sport, physical activity, and the law.* Champaign, IL: Sagamore Publishing.

Gallup, Elizabeth M. (1995). *Law and the team physician.* Champaign, IL: Human Kinetics Publishers.

Garner, B. A. (Ed.) (2004). *Black's law dictionary* (8th ed.). St. Paul, MN: West.

Gray, G. R. (1993). Providing adequate medical care to program participants. *Journal of Physical Education, Recreation, and Dance, 64(2),* 56–57.

Hart, J. E., & Ritson, R. J. (2002). *Liability and safety in physical education and sport: A practitioner's guide to the legal aspects of teaching and coaching in elementary and secondary schools* (2nd ed.). Reston, VA: AAHPERD.

Institute for the Study of Educational Policy, Law Division. (1986). *School athletics and the law.* Seattle, WA: University of Washington Press.

Merriman, J. (1993). Supervision in sport and physical activity, *Journal of Physical Education, Recreation, and Dance, 64(2),* 20–23.

Pittman, A. J. (1993). Safe transportation—A driving concern. *Journal of Physical Education, Recreation, and Dance, 64(2),* 53–55.

U.S. Consumer Product Safety Commission. (1997). *Handbook for public playground safety.* Washington, DC: U.S. Government Printing Office.

van der Smissen, B. (1990). *Legal liability and risk management of public and private entities.* Cincinnati, OH: Anderson.

WEB SITES

Legal Issues and Physical Education

www.kin.sfasu.edu/finkenberg/kin511/Liability.html

www.nils.com/rupps/comparative-negligence.htm

www.pecentral.org/booksmusic/bookstore/books/liabilitytexts.html

Playgrounds

www.cpsc.gov/CPSCPUB/PUBS/playpubs.html

www.playdesigns.com/

School Safety and Security

www.schoolsecurity.org/

www.sasked.gov.sk.ca/docs/physed/safe/

ESSENTIAL COMPONENTS OF A QUALITY PROGRAM

COMPONENT 1 A quality physical education program is organized around content standards that offer direction and continuity to instruction and evaluation.

COMPONENT 2 A quality program is student centered and based on the developmental urges, characteristics, and interests of students.

COMPONENT 3 Quality physical education makes physical activity and motor-skill development the core of the program.

COMPONENT 4 Physical education programs teach management skills and self-discipline.

COMPONENT 5 Quality programs emphasize inclusion of all students.

COMPONENT 6 In a quality physical education setting, instruction focuses on the process of learning skills rather than the product or outcome of the skill performance.

COMPONENT 7 A quality physical education program teaches lifetime activities that students can use to promote their health and personal wellness.

COMPONENT 8 Quality physical education teaches cooperative and responsibility skills and helps students develop sensitivity to diversity and gender issues.

13

Intramurals, Sport Clubs, and Athletics: Furthering the Opportunity for Physical Activity

CHAPTER SUMMARY

This chapter summarizes the role of intramurals, sport clubs, and athletics in the total school program. These programs should be available for all students and be conducted in a manner that contributes to educational objectives. The intramural program is a voluntary laboratory situation that enables students to develop interest and competence in a wide range of physical activities. Intramurals offer something of interest to all students in the school. The programs offer a balance of competitive and recreational activities. Student interest surveys give direction to activity offerings in intramural and sport club programs. Leadership of the program is a joint arrangement that includes students and faculty.

Many motivational devices can be used to encourage and reward students' participation in intramurals. Facilities, equipment, officials, and equating competition are critical elements in developing a successful intramural program. Types of tournaments include round-robin, ladder pyramid, and elimination. Properly organized tournaments are important to a successful program. Sport clubs include students who have a common interest in a particular sport or physical activity. These clubs are usually organized and funded by students. Important matters for a sport club to consider are membership rules, funding procedures, use of equipment and facilities, supervision, legal liability, and transportation.

The school athletic program should contribute to educational goals. How an athletic program is conducted determines whether a program is a positive or negative experience for students. The recruitment of qualified coaches is the cornerstone of a high-quality athletic program. The ability to perform well as a physical educator and an athletic coach is a difficult challenge.

STUDENT OUTCOMES

After reading this chapter, you will be able to:

- Explain the relationship and the differences between intramurals, sport clubs, and athletics.

- Set up a student interest survey that could be used for determining the activities to be offered in an intramural program.

- Discuss the issues regarding intramural programs, such as leadership, motivation, facilities, officials, competition, and tournament construction.

- Discuss the issues regarding sport clubs, such as objectives, regulations, facilities, liability, budget, coaching, and transportation.

- Defend the values of a properly organized and conducted athletic program.

- Explain many possible detrimental effects of an athletic program.

- Identify procedures for developing a high-quality athletic program.

- Defend the implementation of intramural, sport club, and athletic programs in an educational setting.

S chool-sponsored cocurricular programs that focus on sports, games, and physical activities are especially important to students. Valuable lessons are learned that enhance and shape physical skills, knowledge, social skills, and attitudes. Physical educators should be involved in the overall planning and delivery of these programs to ensure that the educational value of these programs is enhanced. Many school districts that have cut back offerings in these areas are reconsidering their previous position and planning to reinstitute after-school programs (Wright, 1995; Hall, 1995). These programs serve a valuable function for students. They provide adolescents with positive alternatives to youth crimes, gangs, violence, dropout problems, discipline problems, and drug experimentation, and they also provide further opportunities for engagement in physical activity for health-related benefits. The activities are important for middle school students who are exploring and searching for programs where they can be involved.

Intramural programs and sport clubs are rarely priority items in middle and high schools. In school districts, the athletic program is the number-one after-school activity and gets most of the facilities, money, and qualified personnel. Even in districts where athletics are strong at the high school level, many middle school athletic programs are inadequate or nonexistent. Quality programs should be offered in all three areas. A well-developed model for athletics,

intramurals, and sport clubs can serve the needs of many students while offering activity and recreation in a school-sanctioned setting.

Studies have revealed that a high percentage of students who participate in athletics in elementary school drop out or are eliminated during the secondary school years. This would not be such an alarming figure (considering that athletic programs are for the elite) if there were other avenues for students to enjoy sports and physical activities. One of the best and most economical approaches is the intramural and sport club program. If, however, the school district does not hire qualified personnel to administer them, these programs soon become second rate and fail to attract participants. The ensuing discussion offers direction for developing quality intramurals, sport club programs, and athletic programs, which are based on student interest and conducted through student input and energy.

INTRAMURALS
What, Who, and Why of Intramural Programs

An intramural program is an organized activity for students that is an extension of the physical education program. Student attendance and participation are voluntary, and the program is limited to the boundaries of a specific school. The intramural program can be a laboratory, as recommended by the National Intramural-Recreational Sports Association (2004), for engagement in physical activity for health-related benefits, skill development, social interaction, recreational participation, and application of knowledge gained in the physical education program. In terms of supervisory personnel, equipment, and facilities, the intramural program should be funded by the school district. In some cases, fees might be required if the activity involves private facilities such as climbing walls, bowling alleys, skating rinks, or horseback riding stables.

When a broad variety of activities are offered in the intramural program, physical education teachers can delegate more class time to instruction because the opportunity to play sports can occur in the intramural setting. Also, a teacher conducting each program may use one program to spark interest in the other. The intramural program is a social meeting ground for students. Youngsters participate in activities they may enjoy and use throughout their lives.

Who participates in an intramural program? Hopefully, every student in the school. The program should offer something of interest to all students and provide appropriate competitive experiences for students of all sizes, shapes, and skill levels. All students need to have ample opportunity to find success and enjoyment in the program, regardless of their physical stature or ability level.

Why have an intramural program? An intramural program offers students an opportunity to develop interest and competence in a wide range of recreational activities. The program also gives students an opportunity to develop and maintain a reasonable level of fitness. Evidence has shown that if people do not develop competence and confidence during their school years in their ability to participate in recreational activities, they seldom participate in later life. In the intramural program, students learn to compete against and cooperate with each other in an environment that has little at stake in terms of winning and losing. The program can be a setting for developing lifelong friendships.

The intramural program can also be a place to learn leadership and followership skills. Students learn to compromise and assert themselves. Through these programs, students, parents, and teachers become closer friends. Finally, the program offers students a place to spend some of their out-of-school time in a supervised setting, rather than walking the streets with nothing to do. Few programs for youth offer so many benefits at such a low cost to society.

Recreation Versus Competition

Considering a successful intramural program should attract all types of students, the question arises as to

whether competition or recreation should be featured. If competition is the overriding concern, then tournaments that identify champions and reinforce winners are featured. Competition emphasizes practicing as much as possible, only playing participants who are the best and avoiding mistakes as much as possible.

If recreation is featured, emphasis is placed on participation and playing all teams an equal number of times. Tournament and league standings are avoided or not posted, and students play each game as an entity in itself. Rewarding recreation emphasizes attendance and participation, and all students are expected to play the same amount. Awards and trophies are not offered, but in some cases, certificates of participation are given.

Which direction should the intramural program take? As usual, no easy answer exists, but several points need to be considered. Because many students may have been cut from an athletic program, they may still want to compete. However, many of the participants may not have participated on an athletic team after the elementary school years, and they may simply desire a positive experience. It appears that most high school students prefer an intramural program that is a mixture of both recreation and competition. Students want the opportunity to match skill and wits with an opponent in a competitive setting. They also want to have an opportunity to relax, play, and communicate with peers. The best programs probably offer students a balance of competition and recreation.

Types of Activities

The types and varieties of activities offered to students are the heart of the intramural program. There should be activities to meet the desires of all students. In some cases, the intramural program has been an outgrowth of the athletic program rather than the physical education program and has been directed by athletic coaches. The result is probably a program that is conducted in a manner similar to the athletic program. In most cases, this type of program may be inappropriate. The scope of intramural activities should be unlimited and dictated by students. If students are expected to participate in the program during their free time, it must cater to their desires and wants. The intramural program should not be regarded as "minor "league for athletes who might make the varsity team at a later date.

A student survey is a good idea to determine student interests and to establish the magnitude of those interests. Surveys can be conducted by homeroom teachers and returned when they are completed. A compilation of results should then be posted so students can clearly see that the activities offered are a result of their expressed interests. The survey is a strong tool when bargaining with the administration for program facilities and equipment. When principals understand that many students desire certain activities, the physical educator then has some leverage to gain program support. Figure 13.1 is a sample of the type of survey that could be administered. The survey will also indicate to students the number and variety of activities that can be offered. After a survey has been administered and compiled, information about desired activities, times to offer the program, and qualified supervisors are identified. A program that matches student interests is easier to develop if a diagnostic instrument similar to the one in Figure 13.1 is administered.

Leadership

Leadership of an intramural program is a joint obligation. School districts should fund personnel to supervise the program and to minimize liability problems. However, students also have a responsibility to organize committees and to implement a successful program. They should develop the policies, rules, and procedures that guide the program.

Forming the Intramural Council

An effective way to ensure student input and energy for implementing the intramural program is to develop an intramural council. The council consists of six to 10 students and is balanced by gender and grade level. This group makes the final decisions about the wide-ranging aspects of the program. Committees that report to the council are developed and maintained with productive students. Some of the following committees might be organized to serve the intramural council.

- Activity Development. The activity development committee is responsible for selecting intramural activities as well as facilities, equipment, and personnel necessary for implementation.

- Rules and Regulations. The rules and regulations committee develops guidelines for administering the program. This committee is also the enforcement body when rule infractions occur.

- Scheduling and Statistics. The scheduling and statistics committee schedules games and contests, maintains school intramural records and league standings, and oversees other related matters.

- Referees. The officiating committee recruits referees, trains them, and interprets and makes rulings dealing with protests.

- Public Relations. The public relations committee develops all materials for promoting the program, seeks funding from private organizations, and sponsors car washes, raffles, and other fund-raising activities.

- Safety. The safety committee develops an approved list of procedures for first aid and emergency situations and provides a trained student capable of administering first aid and able to be present at activities.

- Eligibility for Participation and Guidelines for Continued Participation. One of the primary roles for leadership in any intramural program is developing the standards for participation. Although the rules committee will be charged with enforcing the rules of the program, it will be up to the leader of the program to determine minimum qualifications for participation. Some schools use criteria such as grade point averages or student status in regard to school discipline or attendance as criteria for participation. The program should reflect the values of the school but should not make participation criteria so difficult that it excludes a majority of students. An effective intramural leader will find the right balance between punitive restrictions and unlimited participation.

The formation of the student intramural council should not supersede the need for qualified adult personnel, and the school district should be willing to hire adequate help. Without district funding, there is usually little administrative commitment to the program, and a lack of administrative commitment ultimately leads to program failure.

Motivating Students to Participate

Many methods are available for promoting intramural programs and encouraging participation. Regardless of the method used, students must see the benefits of participating to have the program work. The program must exude a spirit and be an "in" thing to do. Some of the following suggestions have been used with success in varying situations and can be modified to meet the needs of a particular school.

- Intramural Bulletin Board. Bulletin boards, located throughout the school, display schedules, standings, and future activities. Pictures of champions can also be posted and labeled.

- Patches. Winners are awarded arm patches with a school designation, the year, and activity. Some successful programs have awarded patches for participating in a certain number of activities regardless of winning or losing.

Humerus High School Intramural Survey

Student name _____ Grade _____

1. Would you participate in the intramural program if activities were offered that interest you?

   Yes _____ No _____ If no, why not?

2. What do you like most about the present intramural program?

3. What do you like least about the present intramural program?

4. If you choose not to participate, would you be willing to help out in the program in other roles? Check those ways in which you could offer your aid.

   Officiating _____ Publicity _____ Secretarial _____ Scorekeeping _____ Other (identify) _____

5. It is possible to develop a program that emphasizes competition, recreation, or a combination of both. Which would you desire?

   Competition _____ Recreation _____ Both _____

6. What days and what time of the day would be best for your participation?

   Day   Time

   Monday _____

   Tuesday _____

   Wednesday _____

   Thursday _____

   Friday _____

   Saturday _____

7. Should awards be given to winning participants?

   Yes _____ No _____ Please justify your answer.

8. Please list any other points that would make the program better suit your needs.

9. The following is a list of activities that might be offered. Please circle 5 that you would most like to be offered in the intramural program. If an activity that you want is not offered, please write it in the blank at the end of the form.

Archery	Checkers	Frisbee golf	Orienteering	Steeplechase
Badminton	Chess	Golf	Paddle tennis	Swimming
Bait and fly	Cooperative games	Driving	Relays	Table tennis
casting	Croquet	Putting	Riflery	Tennis
Basketball	Cross country	Gymnastics	Roller hockey	Tetherball
One on one	Darts	Handball	Roller skating	Track and field
Two on two	Decathlon	Horseshoes	Shuffleboard	Tumbling
Other	Deck tennis	Ice hockey	Skiing	Volleyball
Free-throw	Fencing	Judo	Soccer	Two player
shooting	Field hockey	Kite flying	Softball	Volley tennis
Billiards	Figure skating	Lacrosse	Fast pitch	Water basketball
Bowling	Flag football	Lawn bowling	Slow pitch	Water polo
Box hockey	Flickerball	Marbles	One pitch	Weight lifting
Cards	Floor hockey	New games	Speed-a-way	Wrestling

   Others

10. Do you know of any experts who could teach and help organize any of the activities designated above? If so, please describe how they can be contacted.

FIGURE 13.1 Sample high school intramural survey

- T-shirts. T-shirts can be given to winners or participants. The school can hold a T-shirt day on which teachers and participants wear their shirts to school.

- Point-Total Chart. Points are given for winning first, second, third, or fourth place in an activity, or points can be awarded simply for participation. The points may be awarded to homeroom teams or on an individual basis. The point-total chart keeps a running tally throughout the year.

- Trophies. Trophies are awarded to homerooms based on point totals at the end of the school year. An excellent idea is to award an "outstanding participant trophy" to those who earned the most participant points.

- Newspaper Reports. These articles are written by students and are placed in the school or local newspaper. They motivate best when they explicitly name students.

- Field Trips. Field trips are awarded to all participants at the end of the activity. For instance, at the end of the basketball tournament, all participants might attend a college or professional game together.

- Extramural Competition. A play-day activity can be organized between one or more schools that have similar activities. The participants meet at one school on a Saturday and compete against each other. These students are nonathletes; the play-day provides an opportunity for them to compete in a setting similar to athletic competition.

- Committee Acknowledgment. Volunteers that serve on the various committees for the program are rewarded with the recognition they deserve. Student participants will be more likely to serve on committees if they feel appreciated for doing so.

Two schools of thought are involved in promoting intramural programs. One awards notoriety and trophies to winners, while the other offers awards and equal publicity to all participants. A case can be made for both approaches. A consideration is that winners already receive reinforcement, but others of lesser accomplishment may need additional positive strokes to ensure equal publicity for all students in the program.

Facilities and Equipment

Without proper facilities and equipment, an intramural program has little chance for success. A major problem is the conflict between athletics and intramurals. Much time and money has been poured into athletic programs, and athletics can be expected to take priority in terms of facility use. At best, the programs should compromise on the use of facilities at opportune times, such as during the final game of the intramural tournament.

Another way to work through the facility problem is to schedule program activities out of season. For example, scheduling intramural basketball programs in the fall or spring would alleviate the conflict. Or, schedule intramural activities during low-demand times such as before school, during noon hour, and later in the evening. Community facilities such as churches, the YMCA or YWCA, and city park and recreation areas, can be used at times to increase the number of participants who can be accommodated. Scheduling becomes paramount in ensuring that facilities will be available. The scheduling committee should work with the athletic director and staging director to avoid conflicts.

Equipment should be provided by the district. Some successful programs have been funded by student activities such as car washes or raffles, but in general, when the district chooses not to give funding, the program is held in low esteem. If the program involves private facilities (such as bowling alleys, golf courses, or skating rinks), club members will usually receive reduced rates. Having an equipment committee to determine how and when money will be spent is effective. The committee is responsible for maintaining and repairing equipment. The school provides a storage area for intramural equipment that is used solely by intramurals. It usually creates conflict when physical education program equipment is used for the intramural program. When equipment is lost or damaged, hard feelings or loss of program support may occur.

Officials

Critical to the success of any athletic endeavor is the quality of the officiating. The intramural program should be officiated by students. It is unrealistic to think teachers will be willing to work ball games. A sound approach is to develop an officiating committee with the responsibility for acquiring and training officials. Many students who do not play competitively are willing to officiate and enjoy being an integral part of an event.

Students should be recruited as soon as possible so they can acquire experience and work confidently with experienced officials. They should be trained in rules and game mechanics prior to a tournament and be allowed to practice with as little pressure as possible. The word of the officials is absolute. If a disagreement arises, it is filed and resolved through proper protest channels.

Scheduling officials and being sure that they make their assignments is crucial. An organized plan needs to be implemented with a master chart posted where student officials can initial to verify that they have accepted the assignment for the game.

Officials can be given points for the number of games they work; they can also be awarded patches, T-shirts, and trophies for their accomplishments in a fashion similar to participants. Without some recognition, students will have little motivation for carrying out the thankless obligations of officiating.

Equating Competition

All participants need to know that they have an opportunity to succeed in the intramural setting. Students fail to participate if they foresee a constant diet of losing or other negative experiences. Grouping by ability has both advantages and disadvantages. It can be awkward to have skilled and unskilled players together when the activity demands a great deal of progression and skill performance. In those cases, having similarly skilled students play together and compete against teams of similar ability is probably better. However, placing less-skilled athletes with skilled athletes may improve the performance level of the unskilled students and enhance their confidence. It also provides opportunities for skilled persons to aid the less skilled.

When grouping for teams, try the following methods. Allow students to choose competition levels. Provide the opportunity for both recreation and competitive games. This will allow students to choose the intensity at which they would like to participate. By allowing students to choose this level of competition, they will be more likely to choose one that is comfortable to them. There is also less embarrassment for them than if they were placed in a game where the rest of the participants did not match their ability level.

Homerooms can compete against homerooms. This is the most heterogeneous method of grouping. Students of varying skill levels will then play on the same team. Grouping by homeroom may be effective if students are randomly placed there. Another method is to use divisions of competition. Depending on the activity, students are grouped by ability, size, or age. Homerooms could sponsor two or more teams of different ability that play in different leagues. The advantage of homeroom sponsorship lies in the camaraderie developed among students and the possibility of enhancing the classroom relationships. Probably the best solution is to equalize the competition regardless of homeroom assignments or other segregating factors. Choosing teams that are somewhat equal can be done in the following ways:

1. Leaders are elected by the students. The leaders then choose teams in a private session held away from the rest of the participants. To further strengthen the idea of fair play, leaders might even choose teams without knowing which team they will be on. In so doing, leaders will ensure that each team is equally strong.

2. Students are arranged by height or weight. The names of students within a certain range are put in one box, and a different range of heights in another box. Teams are then selected by drawing the names of an equal number of students of similar size for each team.

Whatever method is used to form teams, be sensitive to maintaining a balance of competition and preventing embarrassing situations. Teams should never be selected in such a fashion that the poorest player is chosen last. The intramural experience should be a positive experience that all students anticipate it with enthusiasm. If the program is to succeed, participants are needed and should be treated as important and meaningful people.

Tournaments

A variety of tournaments can be organized to carry out the intramural program. The type will depend on the number of entries, the number of sessions or how many days the tournament will continue, the facilities and equipment available, and the number of officials, scorers, and other helpers on hand. The following types of tournaments are often used with success.

Round-Robin Tournament

The round-robin tournament is a good choice when adequate time is available for play. In this type of tournament, every team or individual plays every other team or individual once. Final standings are based on win–loss percentages. To determine the amount of time the tournament will take, the following formula can be used:

TI(TI − 1)/2
where TI = number of teams or individuals
For example, if there are five teams in a softball unit, 5(5 − 1)/2 = 10 games are to be scheduled.

To arrange a tournament for an odd number of teams, each team should be assigned a number. (Number the teams down the right column and up the left column.) All numbers rotate, and the last number each time draws a bye. An example using seven teams follows:

Round 1
7—1 (bye)
6—1
5—2
4—3

Round 2
6—1 (bye)
5—7
4—1
3—2

Round 3
5—1 (bye)
4—6
3—7
2—1

Round 4
4—1 (bye)
3—5
2—6
1—7

Round 5
3—1 (bye)
2—4
1—5
7—6

Round 6
2—1 (bye)
1—3
7—4
6—5

Round 7
1—1 (bye)
7—2
6—3
5—4

Round 1
1—2
8—3
7—4
6—5

Round 2
1—8
7—2
6—3
5—4

Round 3
1—7
6—8
5—2
4—3

Round 4
1—6
5—7
4—8
3—2

Round 5
1—5
4—6
3—7
2—8

Round 6
1—4
3—5
2—6
8—7

Round 7
1—3
2—4
8—5
7—6

To arrange a tournament for an even number of teams, the plan is similar except that the position of Team 1 remains stationary and the other teams revolve around it until the combinations are completed. There are no byes in this plan. An example of an eight-team tournament follows.

Ladder Tournament

A ladder format is used for an ongoing tournament that is administered by a teacher or informally by students. Competition occurs by challenging a higher-ranked opponent and is supervised minimally. Various arrangements are possible, but participants usually challenge only those opponents who are two steps above a participant's present ranking. If the challenger wins, that person changes places with the loser. The teacher can establish an initial ranking, or positions can be drawn out of a hat. Figure 13.2 shows an example of a ladder.

Pyramid Tournament

A pyramid tournament is similar to a ladder tournament, but more challenge and variety are possible because there is a wider choice of opponents (Figure 13.3). In the pyramid tournament, any player challenges any opponent one level above his or her present ranking. In another variation, any player challenges someone at his or her level and beats that person before he or she can challenge a person at a higher level.

Elimination Tournament

The disadvantage of the elimination tournament is that poorer teams are eliminated first and do not get to play as many games as more proficient teams. The skilled thus get better, and less-skilled students sit out without an opportunity to improve. The advantage of the elimination tournament is that it can be completed in a shorter amount of time than, for example, the round-robin tournament. Double-elimination tournaments are somewhat better than single elimina-

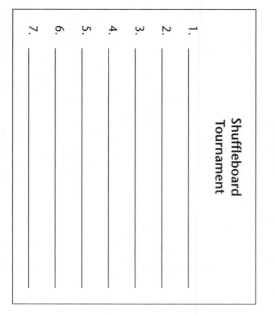

**Shuffleboard
Tournament**

1. _____
2. _____
3. _____
4. _____
5. _____
6. _____
7. _____

FIGURE 13.2 Ladder tournament chart

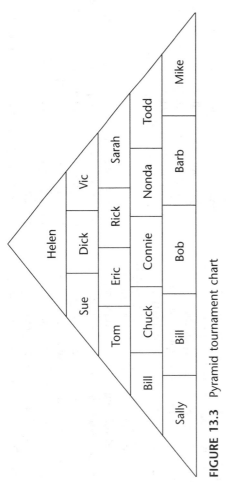

FIGURE 13.3 Pyramid tournament chart

tion because two losses are required before a team is relegated to the sidelines. Students come to intramurals to play rather than sit on the side and watch others play. Figure 13.4 is an example of a simple single-elimination tournament with six teams.

SPORT CLUBS

Sport clubs are filled with students who are bonded by their common interest in some sport or activity. The concept originated in Europe and has become more common in the United States, largely because of the inability of school districts to fund a wide variety of activities. The clubs are for students, are run by students, and are often funded by the students. They offer young people the chance to organize a club that meets the specific needs of a group and the opportunity to socialize with friends.

Developing a Sport Club Network

Sport clubs are often administered by guidelines set by the intramural director in a school district. The clubs can be an outgrowth of either the intramural or athletic program. The types of sport clubs to be developed are usually dictated by students. The following steps are typical of a system for developing a sport club network in the school setting.

1. **Determine the interests of students.** A survey instrument (see Figure 13.1) is used to determine student interests in and concerns for sport clubs. It is usually best to develop one or two clubs first to demonstrate the effectiveness of this approach to the district administrators.

2. **Meet with interested students.** Before the meeting with students, find a faculty member or some other person to serve as the club's advisor. The advisor

should have a keen interest in the area and at least a minimal amount of expertise. For example, it is foolish to appoint someone as an advisor to the backpacking club if he or she has never backpacked. During the first meeting, dues necessary for conducting club activities should be discussed. If the cost is prohibitive, many students may choose not to participate. Students should also discuss the joys and dangers of participating in the activity. Discuss school guidelines for clubs so students understand the parameters involved.

3. **Develop a constitution.** After the initial meeting, students who are interested meet again to develop a constitution. This document delineates membership requirements, the function and selection of officers, and meeting dates. An outline form can be used to aid in the development of similar club constitutions.

4. **Establish rules and regulations.** Clubs need to determine the scope of their organization and the requirements of club members to retain active

Round 1	*Round 2*	*Round 3*	
Team 1	Team 1		
Bye		Team 3	
Team 2	Team 3		Team 4
Team 3			Champion
Team 4	Team 4	Team 4	
Team 5			
Bye	Team 6	Finals	
Team 6	Semifinals		

FIGURE 13.4 Single-elimination tournament chart

membership. If competition with other clubs is involved, travel funding and housing requirements are explicitly outlined. The need for adult chaperones and drivers and the need for a waiver of responsibility signed by parents are vital parts of the rules. The basic premise of rules is to eliminate misunderstandings and to encourage a safe, liability-free club setting.

5. *Seek funding, facilities, and equipment.* With the help of the advisor, students should determine what facilities and equipment are available and when they can be scheduled. Seeking outside funding from private organizations and service clubs is important. In some cases, school time may be given for clubs to conduct meeting and planning sessions. Appropriate facilities such as bowling alleys or swimming pools need to be contacted to see if 1 or 2 hours per week can be reserved for club activities.

6. *Organize participation and competition.* Once facilities, equipment, and participants have been determined, a participation event will need to be organized. No matter if the event is intramural or extramural, careful planning should occur to provide the participants a rich and rewarding experience.

7. *Conduct a periodic evaluation.* Clubs should be evaluated on a regular basis to see if interest is waning, whether the needs of students are being met, and whether the manner of club conduct needs to be modified. Sometimes when clubs are developed based on the interests of students, that interest can decrease to such an extent that the club should be discontinued. New student interests may also develop and result in a new club advisor, better ways to facilitate club goals, or an attempt to stimulate renewed interest in the club.

Implementing a Sport Club

The following areas should be considered when developing a sport club. They are considerations that school district personnel need to be aware of if a successful program is to be implemented.

Liability

Students who participate in the club should have liability insurance. Depending on the activity, regular school insurance may cover the student during participation. However, if the activity is exceptionally risky (e.g., skiing or rugby), supplementary insurance is usually needed. Parents must certify that the student is covered by their insurance policy if students choose not to purchase insurance offered by the district's carrier.

A signed parental responsibility waiver form is necessary for participation in club activities. Even though the form does not waive the student's right to sue and seek redress, a signed form communicates to the school district that the parents approve and are aware of their student's participation in the program.

Instructors and advisors to the program must be competent to administer the activity. If the school district advisor lacks proper training, experts outside the school should be secured. These may be parents or interested community volunteers. In most cases, the responsibility for supplying a safe environment falls on the school district.

Procedures for handling injuries are important and may involve having a physician on call. Written procedures should be available and understood by all club members in case an accident occurs. For example, what steps will be taken if someone is injured on a backpacking trip? Accidents do happen, and there is much less trouble if proper emergency procedures have been planned for such an occurrence.

Budget

It is ideal when the school district funds sport clubs. In some cases, student fees are assessed at the start of the school year and distributed on an equal basis to all clubs. This provides a financial foundation, but almost all clubs require additional funding. The most common methods used are cake sales, car washes, rummage sales, sales of old and outdated equipment, candy sales, and donations. When travel and lodging are necessary, students are usually expected to absorb the cost. School districts will often provide a bus if the activity is scheduled when buses are available. Travel by private car is the least acceptable method of transport because of the possibility of an accident and subsequent liability problems.

Many clubs have an equipment bank where equipment is stored for use year after year. The club develops an adequate source of equipment over a period of years. Used equipment from local colleges and high school athletic programs can sometimes be secured to augment the equipment bank.

Coaching

Qualified coaches and other school-affiliated advisors are usually involved in administration of the athletic and intramural programs. This means club advisors and coaches may have to be selected from the community. Some type of screening should be undertaken by the school district to see that the advisors are properly qualified. The club programs have to be conducted at a time when these people are available considering many potential advisors are employed during the school day. If the activity is recreational in nature, interested parents may carry out the supervisory responsibilities. All adults involved should be approved by the school district and required to sign a form agreeing to abide by district policies.

Facilities

Facilities usually have to be scheduled at low-use times. Sport clubs are often last in line for facilities, after the athletic and intramural programs. Facilities need to be found in the community if the clubs involve sports that are offered interscholastically. For example, city parks have softball fields that can be used. Some school districts choose not to approve clubs dealing with sports that are offered at the intramural and interscholastic level. The philosophy behind this ruling is that club sports should offer opportunities that are not available through other avenues. If that is the case, then most sport club programs will be conducted in private facilities such as bowling alleys, swimming pools, ski areas, skating rinks, riflery and archery ranges, and racquetball clubs.

Achievement Clubs

Many of the activities suggested in the intramurals section for motivating students can be used with sport club activities. In addition, some clubs can be formed for which students are eligible only after they have met predetermined standards of achievement. Examples might be a jogging club, bike-riding club, distance swimming club, and a weight-lifting club. In each case, students join the club and are a part of the group only after they have met the minimum standards.

INTERSCHOLASTIC ATHLETICS

The interscholastic athletic program usually stands at the top of the pyramid in terms of attention, time, and money focused on the program. Sports in the school setting should contribute to the educational purposes of the institution. Arguments abound as to whether the athletic program is a negative or positive influence on students. Athletics are not inherently good or bad. How the athletic program is conducted makes it a positive or negative experience for participants. It is possible to create a positive experience for students through a competitive sports program

Values of an Athletic Program

A strong athletic program can develop a sense of belonging among the participants. Students like to see what they can accomplish by themselves and with the help of peers. Team sports teach them that goals can be reached only if teammates are willing to cooperate. It quickly becomes apparent that cooperation precedes competition. Conducting a competitive game is impossible when teammates do not cooperate and follow the established rules.

Athletics teach students that the journey is more important than the destination. The work done to reach a goal is the essence of an athletic experience, and students learn that after the victory, continued hard work is still necessary. This lesson may carry over to adult life and help the participant continue to succeed.

Athletics give students something to talk about and something to do. Many of the problems of youth arise because of boredom and little to do when the school day is over. Athletics give status to participants and make them feel important. The program allows students to share their positive accomplishments with others and appreciate the accomplishments of friends.

The athletic program serves as a laboratory for gifted students. It offers students a chance to perfect their skills to a high level with the aid of a knowledgeable coach. Students who are athletically gifted are appreciated and rewarded for their accomplishments. The athletic program brings a community of people together for a common cause. Parents and businesspeople begin to develop pride in their communities and find a common ground for communication. The athletic team can be a unifying factor that brings together people of all backgrounds.

Participation in athletics can teach students how to maintain a level of physical fitness and to care for their bodies. They learn about the need for self-discipline when one desires to reach a goal. The importance of making sacrifices, following training rules, and practicing regularly become an attitudinal set of the participants. Sportsmanship and self-control must be practiced if students are to find success. Rules and regulations become an integral part of sport participation and illustrate to students the importance of following predetermined rules. Students learn they are penalized when rules are broken, and those unwilling to cooperate are seldom welcome to participate. Finally, the athletic program shows students how highly regarded and important excellence is to people. Athletics should try to embody excellence and the Olympic ideal. Students set goals and make sacrifices in an attempt to achieve excellence without any guarantee of success.

Detrimental Effects of an Athletic Program

The athletic program mobilizes large amounts of time, energy, and money to aid a relatively small number of participants. This sometimes leads to neglect of less-skilled performers. In contrast, an athlete who receives special attention can develop the attitude that athletes are better than others and are eligible for personal favors and special attention. This can lead to a situation whereby student athletes develop a value set that is detrimental when their playing days are over.

Participation in athletic programs often interrupts the educational environment. Athletes leave school to go on trips or receive released time to practice during a final-period physical education class. The athlete may begin to believe that it is more important to be a successful athlete than a competent student. Another possible effect of the athletic program is a loss of personal identity. Athletes are told when to eat, when to practice, when they can have free time, and when to study. They may soon begin to wonder if they can make any important decisions for themselves and whether they have the right to live their own lives.

The pressures of coaching are apparent to all who have filled a head coaching position in a major sport. This pressure is often unjust and can lead to unacceptable coaching behavior. Athletic coaching is a good example of holding an individual accountable for the end result (winning) regardless of how that individual reaches the goal. When this occurs, students may suffer from the coach's lack of concern and caring about personal problems and injuries. Until an equal emphasis is placed on the process of coaching as well as on the product, the athletic setting will be less than a positive and developmental experience (Steinberg, Singer, and Murphy, 1999).

At times, parents and community members can become so deeply involved in the athletic program that they apply pressure on students to win at all costs. Student athletes begin to feel that if they do not win, they will not be accepted as an integral part of the community. The athletic program then becomes an incessant effort on the part of students to achieve the adults' goals. In these situations, adults forget that the athletic program was developed for students in an effort to contribute to the youngsters' personal growth. When the program becomes an adult program with adult goals, students cannot separate what is important from what is not. Another concern for athletes is injury. All participants assume the risk of injury through involvement. If the desire to win exceeds the desire to provide a safe environment, then some students may be ordered to play with an injury or may receive injuries caused by lack of proper care and treatment. Concern for the health of participants is the paramount program goal.

Developing a Quality Athletic Program

Depending on how it is organized and presented, an athletic program can be a positive or negative experience for students. The following guidelines, if heeded, help ensure meaningful experiences for participants. All districts have to interpret the guidelines based on their specific situations, but it is difficult to imagine that a worthwhile program will result if districts deviate from the guidelines to a large degree.

Guidelines to Ensure a Quality Experience

1. The athletic program should be voluntary. All students who choose to participate should have an opportunity to compete. All athletes should have the opportunity to play if they have practiced and disciplined themselves. Cutting players from a squad is an accepted practice, but there should be another arena in which players can compete. This may mean a junior varsity, C squad, or strong intramural or sport club program. If athletics is regarded as an educational experience, all students have the right to receive that experience.

2. The program should be based on the maturation level of participants. This is particularly important at the middle school level because these students exhibit a wide range of development. Grouping by age, ability, or size may be necessary if the program is to be meaningful.

3. The athletic program should be an after-school program. The practice of giving a period of school time for practice is discriminatory and runs counter to the established rule that an academic education is the school's priority. Along the same lines, excusing athletes from physical education is difficult to justify. If the program is educational, then all students, regardless of background, should benefit from it.

4. The athletic program should offer a broad spectrum of activities for participants; the fewer activities offered, the fewer participants. The program should also be balanced in offering activities to all groups—skilled and unskilled, boys and girls, able-bodied students and those with disabilities.

5. Organization of the athletic program should meet the needs of students. The concerns of the specta-

tors should be met only after the program has been developed. Many sports are dropped because they do not draw large numbers of spectators and make money. If this trend continues, football and basketball might represent the total athletic program.

6. All participants should be certified as medically healthy by a physician. The program should be evaluated regularly in terms of safety practices to ensure that proper procedures are being conducted.

7. Procedures to be followed should an accident occur must be written, posted, and sent to parents. Most districts ask that parents sign a waiver of responsibility form before a student can participate. This is an opportune time to explain the safety and first-aid procedures being followed. Insurance for all participants is a must. Many states have specific guidelines and requirements, such as having an automated external defibrillator (AED) on site for all athletic contests (e.g., New York).

8. As idealistic as it may sound to many coaches, the program should emphasize enjoyment and participation. Skill development and a positive experience are benefits that students can take with them after graduation. One might well question what has been gained if students win most of their games but lose the desire to participate in sports once they leave school.

9. Physical conditioning should be an important phase of the program. Preconditioning is essential to the safety and welfare of players and should precede intense, early-season practice sessions.

10. Facilities should be shared by all facets of the athletic, intramural, and sport club programs. It is understandable that athletics are expected to take priority, but someone needs to direct the situation so that all programs are given acceptable use of the facilities and equipment.

11. Awards, trophies, and other incentives used to identify outstanding achievement should be minimized. This is not to avoid rewarding excellence but to encourage proper discretion. If awards are given in excess, they become meaningless.

12. The athletic program should be constantly evaluated. In some cases, the program is seldom scrutinized until an infraction occurs. Periodic evaluations by the athletic director, principal, and coaching staff can aid in preventing problems. Evaluation can serve to improve offerings for both boys and girls, upgrade scheduling efficiency, and show the need for in-service training.

The Athletic Council

To help ensure that a quality athletic program is maintained, many school districts organize an athletic council. The council is a districtwide body composed of the superintendent (or a representative), principals, the athletic director for the district, coaches from each of the schools, and student representatives from each school. All schools, sports, and genders should be equally represented.

The athletic council plans and evaluates the total district athletic program and deals with problems such as finances, facilities, and personnel. The council promotes the athletic program and serves as a screening body when outside parties become involved with the program. This body is responsible for evaluating coaches and hearing grievances. Sometimes, for example, parents have a concern but are hesitant to approach the coach involved. The council hears such cases confidentially without revealing the plaintiff's identity. The council can enhance the image of the coaching community. It can be a place where coaches work together to achieve the highest ideals and to reach common goals. In summary, the council should be a valuable asset for coaches, administrators, and athletes.

Securing Qualified Coaches

Qualified coaches are the cornerstone of a sound athletic program. Most coaches are highly motivated and dedicated. In most cases, they have to be motivated by their enjoyment of sport rather than the financial remuneration, for coaching is one of the lowest-paid professions. An athletic director recently calculated that assistant coaches were receiving about 50 cents per hour. Most coaches enter the profession because they were successful athletes and found positive experiences in the athletic program. Being an outstanding athlete seldom guarantees success in coaching, however. Coaches need to have a wide range of abilities. The following attributes are characteristics of successful coaches:

■ Strong Character. The coach should be a model for athletes to emulate. How the coach relates to others, the individual's physical appearance, and whether he or she displays honesty, integrity, and other personal qualities often teach students more about athletics than the actual participation experience (Alberts, 2003). Many administrators find cause for concern when coaches swear, drink, or smoke excessively, and most students cannot deal with the double standard of a coach who advocates team fitness but does not practice fitness, who tells them to be respectful but yells when a mistake is made, and who preaches honesty but shows them how to foul without being caught. Many athletes remember their coach much longer than they remember the actual playing experience.

■ Knowledge of Growth and Development Patterns. The coach must have a strong background in motor development and motor learning. Understanding the physical limits of athletes is as important as understanding their capabilities under pressure. The coach should also have some knowledge of psychology and the emotional development of secondary-level students. Knowing when to reinforce, when to scold, and when to praise are key components of a successful coaching career.

■ Knowledge of the Activity. Coaches should know the fundamentals of the sport that they are coaching and the best ways to present and teach the basic skills. A good coach understands strategy and knows when to use various types of game plans. The coach must be an excellent teacher, and in many cases, the best coaches are also regarded as the best teachers. Concurrent with a knowledge of the sport is the ability to plan carefully. Both teaching and coaching demand a high degree of planning to succeed. Effective coaches always attempt to account for every minute of practice time so that idle or wasted time is minimized.

Coaching Certification

The need for certification in the coaching profession is great. The belief is still widely held that anyone can coach—regardless of background or training. Unfortunately, almost anyone can find the opportunity to coach because of the lack of certification requirements and standards. Each state sets the specific requirements for coaches within the schools in that state. Some states have an age requirement only, whereas others require a teaching certificate or a specific coaching education program, such as the American Sport Education Program (available through Human Kinetics) (Martens, 2004).

Training of Coaches

Training in many areas is necessary for coaches to be productive and motivating. A National Association for Sport and Physical Education (NASPE) task force of the American Alliance for Health, Physical Education, Recreation and Dance (AAHPERD) has developed a second edition on coaching standards called *Quality Coaches, Quality Sports: National Standards for Sport Coaches* (2006). The task force identified 40 standards in the following eight domains:

1. Philosophy and Ethics
2. Safety and Injury Prevention
3. Growth and Development
4. Physical Conditioning
5. Organization and Administration
6. Sport Skills, Tactics, and Strategies
7. Teaching and Communication
8. Evaluation

Coaching is an impressive responsibility, and regardless of certification, coaches should make an attempt to seek the best possible training.

The Teaching-Coaching Conflict

A personal conflict often occurs when teachers choose to coach. Particularly in physical education, a teacher who is required to coach long hours has a difficult task. Many physical education instructors are not hired for their expertise in teaching but rather for their ability to coach more than one sport. This policy can result in a situation where teaching takes second place to coaching, and most of the teacher's planning and energy are dedicated to the coaching assignment.

Teachers who also coach often end up working 10- to 12-hour days. The pay is low, but the rewards can be great. Coaching ability is scrutinized regularly in terms of the winning and losing record, and teachers may become caught up in the pressure of trying to be winning coaches for fear of losing their positions. In this situation, it takes a strong and gifted person to place equal emphasis on teaching and coaching. Physical educators should not lose sight of the fact that about 90 percent of their salary comes from teaching and the remaining 10 percent from coaching. Many more students are affected by the outstanding teacher than by the effective coach. The ability to perform well in both roles is a difficult challenge, particularly when the majority of contingencies apply to the coaching role (Darst & Pangrazi, 1996).

STUDY STIMULATORS AND REVIEW QUESTIONS

1. Outline the components of a total physical education program and explain which types of students each serves.

2. Discuss why the authors are adamant about advocating for intramural and sport club programs for students after school.

3. Explain why an intramural program that offers both recreational and competitive opportunities has greater appeal to the student population.

4. Discuss the importance of having students dictate the direction and focus of the intramural program.

5. Defend an intramural program that is about to be eliminated because of a district budget crisis.

6. Construct a round-robin tournament with 10 teams.

7. What are the differences between an intramural program and a sport club?

8. Explain why it is less likely to see a basketball sport club than a bowling sport club.

9. Discuss the possible values and detrimental effects of an interscholastic athletic program.

10. Why do secondary teachers often experience the teaching–coaching role conflict?

REFERENCES AND SUGGESTED READINGS

Alberts, C. (2003). *Coaching issues & dilemmas: Character building through sport participation*. Reston, VA: NASPE.

Bucher, C., & Krotee, M. (2002). *Management of physical education and sport*. Boston, MA: McGraw Hill.

Carr, G. (2004). *Sport mechanics for coaches* (2nd ed.). Champaign, IL: Human Kinetics.

Cassidy, T., Jones, R., & Potrac, P. (2004). *Understanding sports coaching*. New York, NY: Routledge.

Darst, P., & Pangrazi, R. (1996). The teaching/coaching challenge. *Teaching Secondary Physical Education, 2*(6), 4–5.

Flegel, M. (2004). *Sport first aid* (3rd ed.). Champaign, IL: Human Kinetics.

Hall, M. (1995). Interscholastic sports on way this year, insiders predict. *Albuquerque Journal*, September 3(1), 8–9.

Martens, Rainer. (2004). *Successful Coaching* (3rd ed.). Champaign, IL: Human Kinetics.

National Association for Sport and Physical Education. (2006). *Quality coaches, quality sports: National standards for sport coaches* (2nd ed.). Reston, VA: AAHPERD.

National Association for Sport and Physical Education. (2002a). *Co-curricular physical activity and sport programs for middle school students*. Reston, VA: AAHPERD.

National Association for Sport and Physical Education. (2002b). *Guidelines for after school physical activity and intramural programs*. Reston, VA: AAHPERD.

National Intramural-Recreational Sports Association. (2004). *Mission and bylaws*. Retrieved from www.nirsa.org

Sharkey, B., & Gaskill, S. (2006). *Sport physiology for coaches*. Champaign, IL: Human Kinetics.

Siedentop, D. (2007). *Introduction to Physical Education, Fitness, and Sport* (6th ed.). Boston, MA: McGraw Hill.

Steinberg, G. M., Singer, R. N., & Murphy, M. (1999). Lack of control in coaching: Potential complications and strategies to help coaches. *Journal of Physical Education, Recreation, and Dance, 70*(8), 39–42.

Wright, R. (1995). Plotting a comeback at APS. *Albuquerque Journal, 3*(1), 8–9.

WEB SITES

American Sport Education Program
www.asep.com

Character Counts
www.charactercounts.org

National Alliance for Youth Sports
www.nays.org

National Association for Girls and Women in Sports
www.aahperd.org/nagws

National Association of Sports Officials
www.naso.org

National Federation of State High School Associations
www.nfhs.org

National Intramural-Recreational Sports Association
www.nirsa.org

Physical Education Information
www.pecentral.com
www.pelinks4u.org
www.reach.ucf.edu/~pezone

Positive Coaching Alliance
www.positivecoach.org

Research for Education and Learning
www.mcrel.org

NATIONAL STANDARDS FOR PHYSICAL EDUCATION*

STANDARD 1   Demonstrates competency in motor skills and movement patterns needed to perform a variety of physical activities.

STANDARD 2   Demonstrates understanding of movement concepts, principles, strategies, and tactics as they apply to the learning and performance of physical activities.

STANDARD 3   Participates regularly in physical activity.

STANDARD 4   Achieves and maintains a health-enhancing level of physical fitness.

STANDARD 5   Exhibits responsible personal and social behavior that respects self and others in physical activity settings.

STANDARD 6   Values physical activity for health, enjoyment, challenge, self-expression, and/or social interaction.

ESSENTIAL COMPONENTS OF A QUALITY PROGRAM

COMPONENT 1   A quality physical education program is organized around content standards that offer direction and continuity to instruction and evaluation.

COMPONENT 2   A quality program is student centered and based on the developmental urges, characteristics, and interests of students.

COMPONENT 3   Quality physical education makes physical activity and motor-skill development the core of the program.

COMPONENT 4   Physical education programs teach management skills and self-discipline.

COMPONENT 5   Quality programs emphasize inclusion of all students.

COMPONENT 6   In a quality physical education setting, instruction focuses on the process of learning skills rather than the product or outcome of the skill performance.

COMPONENT 7   A quality physical education program teaches lifetime activities that students can use to promote their health and personal wellness.

COMPONENT 8   Quality physical education teaches cooperative and responsibility skills and helps students develop sensitivity to diversity and gender issues.

*Reprinted from *Moving Into the Future: National Standards for Physical Education*, 2nd ed. (2004), with permission from the National Association for Sport and Physical Education (NASPE), 1900 Association Dr., Reston, VA 20191–1599.

14

Introductory Activities

CHAPTER SUMMARY

This chapter establishes a justification for introductory activities in the daily lesson plan for secondary school physical education and provides teachers with a variety of activity ideas that can be used with students as introductory activities. Introductory activities are vigorous in nature, consist primarily of gross locomotor movement, are not rigidly structured, and allow for considerable freedom of movement. Introductory activities serve as a psychological and physiological warm-up for the ensuing portion of the lesson. They are characterized by a minimum of instruction and a maximum of movement. Introductory activities should be selected with the interests, development levels, and physical abilities of the students in mind. Introductory activities can be novel and challenging. They can also allow students to be creative. The introductory activity period lasts 2 or 3 minutes and emphasizes enthusiasm and motivation. Students should learn to develop introductory activities that will be useful to them as a lead-up for activities they intend to pursue for a lifetime. As long as the activities are vigorous and emphasize large muscle movement, they can be used in this part of the lesson.

STUDENT OUTCOMES

After reading this chapter, you will be able to:

- Discuss the objectives of introductory activities for secondary school physical education.

Student Outcomes, continued

- Select appropriate introductory activities for students taking a specific unit of activity.
- Characterize the various features of the introductory phase of the lesson.
- Develop a new or modified introductory activity.

The beginning of the lesson is important in ensuring a successful experience for students and teacher. Even though the introductory activity takes the least amount of time in the lesson, it helps ensure a positive start. All classes come to PE after a break. They have been talking with friends and want to continue chatting and enjoying each others' company. Successful teachers know that if they can get the class with them immediately, it sets the tone for the rest of the lesson. On the other hand, if all students aren't on task and ready to participate after the introductory activity, chances are the lesson and student behavior will go downhill from that point.

All lessons should start by getting the class quickly on the floor with nothing more than a "jog around the area" command. When a signal is given, the class freezes in the ready position and stops talking. A good "rule of thumb" is to jog and freeze a class three times to discourage inattentive behavior. If the entire class is on task, then an enjoyable introductory activity is played. In a sense, it is a reward for the class being attentive and ready to learn. If the class is not attentive, then it is often best to skip the introductory activity and work on class management skills (see Chapter 7). Another way to look at it is that it may be unwise to start a class that is out of control with an exciting introduction because it will only make the problem worse. By ensuring the class is well managed and on task, you express your personal expectation that "before we can enjoy class activities, you need to be attentive and ready to participate properly."

Most students desire immediate activity when they arrive for class, and introductory activities meet this need. Introductory activities are vigorous and incorporate large muscle activity in their execution. An objective of introductory activities is to use movements basic to sport and leisure pursuits. When appropriate, explain how the activities apply to their personal activity interests. Introductory activities serve as a psychological and physiological warm-up for the rest of the lesson. Introductory activities should be selected with the interests and developmental levels of the students in mind. Junior high school students, because of their rapid growth spurts, need activities that emphasize body control, coordination, and agility. Although not necessary, senior high school students like

to know how introductory activities are related to activities in which they have developed competency and interest.

To teach leadership skills, ask students to direct introductory activities they have learned. They need opportunities to lead and become independent thinkers. Inform the class of the goal and the desired outcome. Students can develop introductory activities suited to their needs. As long as the activities are vigorous and emphasize large muscle movement, they can be used in this part of the lesson. It is also entirely possible that the introductory activity may place large demands on the cardiovascular system and can be used for this purpose after the fitness portion of the lesson. A large variety of introductory activities should be taught and presented to show students that there are many acceptable methods to prepare for ensuring physical activity.

The introductory activities in this chapter are roughly grouped into the following categories:

- Agility Activities—The activities in this group are designed to improve the aerobic power and agility of students. They are demanding and should be done in short bouts so excessive fatigue doesn't become an issue. Emphasis is placed on quick feet and fast response to different commands.

- Sport Movement Challenges—This set of activities features giving students a variety of challenges while performing sport movements that include but are not limited to sliding, leaping, jumping and hopping, and the grapevine step. Students should be encouraged to perform the sport movements in an athletic position.

- Individual Activities—These activities are based on individual challenges while competing against other students. Students are encouraged to see how many times they can perform an activity.

- Partner and Small Group Activities—These are cooperative activities that require working with a partner or small group. This group includes a variety of tag games that can be played in small groups or as a single class. Some of the activities may excite a class, so they should be used only if you are able to get the attention of the class back quickly when the activity is over.

FIGURE 14.1   Wave drill

AGILITY ACTIVITIES

Seat Roll

Students begin on all fours with their heads up, looking at the instructor. When the teacher gives a left- or right-hand signal, students respond quickly by rolling in that direction on their seat. Seat rolls can be alternated with running in place or with rope jumping to increase the aerobic challenge.

Arkansas Flip

Begin in the same position as the seat roll. Students flip over to the left or right, without touching their seats to the floor, so they are in a crab position (half flip). The flip should be a quick, continuous movement. Students can wait for the next signal in the crab position or, if the teacher designates, can continue over to an all-fours position with the head up (full flip).

Quarter Eagle

Students are in a ready position with the head up, arms flexed in front of the body, knees slightly bent, and feet straight ahead and a shoulder width apart. The instructor gives a hand signal left or right. The class responds by making a quarter jump turn in that direction and returning to the starting position as quickly as possible.

A variation involves having participants move on a verbal signal such as "go." The students then make a quarter turn to the left or right and wait for the next signal. They continue to make quarter turns on each signal.

Wave Drill

In the wave drill (Figure 14.1), students are in ready position. They shuffle (without a crossover step) left, right, backward, or forward on signal. A useful variation is to place an obstacle (boundary cone) for students to shuffle over.

Variation 1. Same as original, except use a crossover step.

Variation 2. Same as original, except that students are on all fours.

Variation 3. Students are between two cones or bags while rapidly running in place. On a hand signal to the left or right, the performer steps over the obstacle in the corresponding direction and moves the feet in place while waiting for the next signal.

Variation 4. Same as variation 3 except that students move left or right with both feet together (ski hop). Emphasis is on watching the signal and moving quickly.

Log Roll (Three-Person Roll)

Students are in groups of three and on all fours to start the log roll. The instructor gives a signal left or right. The middle person does a roll (with the body extended) in that direction, while the person on that side rolls up and over the top of the middle person. The drill continues with each person rolling several times. The objective is to roll with the body straight, get up quickly, and barely touch anybody while going over them.

Square Drill

The class forms several 10-yard squares with boundary cones. Students stand in the middle of each side of the square and face the center. On signal, they shuffle around the square to the left or right, depending on the signal of the teacher. A student can be in the center of the square to give a direction signal.

Lateral Shuffle

Place two cones about 5 yards apart. A student stands in the middle and shuffles quickly back and forth between the cones, touching the cone each time. Students try to make as many touches as possible in 15 seconds. Set up enough pairs of cones so all students can participate simultaneously.

Rooster Hop Drill

Students hop 10 yards on one leg in the following sequence: (1) left hand touching the right toe, which is

FIGURE 14.3 Weave drill

FIGURE 14.4 Running weave drill

FIGURE 14.2 Rooster hop drill

on the ground; (2) right hand touching the left toe on the ground; (3) right hand touching the right toe on the ground; and (4) left hand touching the left toe on the ground (Figure 14.2). Students can be challenged to develop different combinations and tasks.

Weave Drill

The weave drill is similar to the wave drill except that students shuffle in and out of a series of obstacles, such as cones, blocking dummies, or boards (Figure 14.3). A shuffling step is used rather than a crossover step.

Running Weave Drill

Students run through the maze of obstacles with a regular running stride (Figure 14.4). A stopwatch can be used to challenge students to improve their times, and the maze can be arranged in many different ways. Let students set up the maze and time each other. Use the carioca (or grapevine) step as a variation.

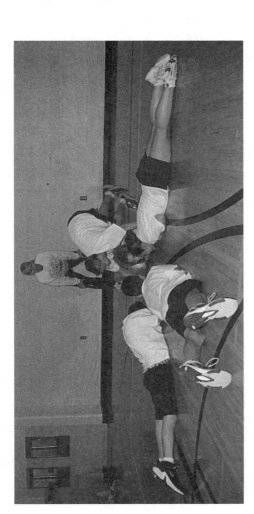

FIGURE 14.5 All-fours circle

Leaping Lena with a Forward Roll

Students stand in a ready position rapidly running in place. On the first command, students leap forward as far as possible and begin moving the feet again. Two more leaps are repeated and then a forward roll is performed if mats are available. Students return to the end of the line when finished.

Burpee-Flip Drill

The burpee-flip can be done in small groups or in unison with the entire class. The teacher calls out the number, and students yell the number while performing the movement. The sequence is as follows:

1. Standing position

2. Bend the knees, hands on the floor or ground

3. Legs kick back into an all-fours position, head up

4. Half flip right to a crab position

5. Half flip right to an all-fours position

This drill can also be done with a left flip or with two flips, one left and one right, and so forth. Let students try this drill with a small group. Challenge them to stay together and to continue enlarging the group. Participants must call the numbers for their group.

Another variation is to put in a push-up before the flip. Step 4 would be the down motion, and Step 5 would be the up motion. Use caution to ensure that students are far enough apart in case one student flips the wrong way.

All-Fours Circle

Students lie on their stomachs with heads close together and legs extended outward like the spokes of a wheel (Figure 14.5). One person starts by placing the

hands in the center and moving around the circle over the other students without touching anyone. The last person who is passed is the next participant. The drill can be done with four to 12 people.

Coffee Grinder Square

With the coffee grinder square (Figure 14.6), students start at one corner of the square, run to the next corner, and perform a coffee grinder on the right arm (arm extended on the ground, supporting the body weight, while the feet walk 360° around the arm). At the next corner, they put their left arms down and do another coffee grinder. This continues through the four corners. The square should be marked with something flat, such as beanbags or spots. Students should move in the same direction around the square.

Flash Drill

To begin the flash drill (Figure 14.7), students stand in a ready position facing the teacher. The teacher

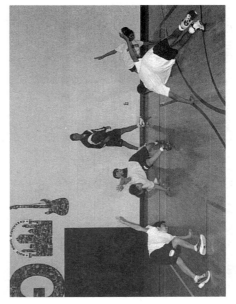

FIGURE 14.6 Coffee grinder square

FIGURE 14.7 Flash drill

exclaims "feet," and students stutter the feet. The teacher then "flashes" the following hand signals:

1. Hands up: Students jump up and return to stuttering feet.

2. Hands down: Students touch the floor and return to stuttering feet.

3. Hands right: Students shuffle right with hands in defensive position.

4. Hands left: Students shuffle left with hands in defensive position.

5. Hands make a circle: Students do a forward roll and get up stuttering.

SPORT MOVEMENT CHALLENGES

The following activities can be done with sport movements such as sliding, carioca steps, power skipping, running, and jumping. The locomotor movement is then combined with a challenging activity that is used in sport such as a pivot, stop, or change of direction.

Move and Change Direction

Students run in any direction and change direction on signal. The change in direction can be specified or student selected. If specified, the commands might be "reverse, right angle, 45 degrees," or "left turn." The change in direction should be made quickly in pivot-like fashion.

Move and Change Speed or Level

Students move throughout the area. On signal, they are challenged to lower their centers of gravity or to

move slower or faster. They can be challenged to touch the floor or give a high five while moving. Combinations of changing the level (as well as changing the speed of the movement) can be developed.

Move and Change the Type of Locomotion

Students move using a specified sport movement. On signal, they change to another type of movement. Challenges can be given to do the movements forward, backward, sideways, or diagonally.

Move and Quickly Stop

Students move throughout the area and quickly stop under control. Emphasis should be placed on stopping using proper technique. Students should lower the center of gravity, widen the base of support, and place one foot in front of the other to absorb the force.

Move and Perform Athletic Movement

Students move and stop on signal. They then perform an athletic skill move, such as a basketball jump shot, leaping football pass catch, volleyball spike, or soccer kick. Students should place emphasis on correct form and timing. A variation of the activity is for students to move with a partner and throw a pass on signal, punt a ball, or shoot a basket. The partner catches the ball or rebounds the shot.

Move, Stop, and Pivot

Students move under control throughout the area. On signal, they stop, pivot, and resume moving. Emphasis should be placed on making a sharp pivot and a rapid acceleration. The skill is similar to running a pass pattern in football.

Move and Perform a Fitness Task

The class moves throughout the area. When a signal is given, students perform a predesignated fitness task. Examples of tasks are push-ups, sit-ups, squat thrusts, and crab kicks. The fitness tasks can be written on a card and flashed to the class to signal the next challenge.

Move and Perform a Stretch

The class is challenged to run throughout the area. On signal, students stop and perform a designated stretching activity. (See Chapter 16 for a comprehensive list of stretching exercises.) A list of stretches that covers all body parts can be posted so students perform a different stretch after each signal.

INDIVIDUAL ACTIVITIES

Number Challenges

Students are challenged to move and perform to a set of three to four numbers. For example, the given set of numbers might be 25, 10, and 30. The first number would signify some type of sport movement, the second number a set of stretching exercises, and the last an activity with equipment. Implemented, this challenge might be 25 running steps, 10 repetitions of a stretching activity, and 30 rope-jumping turns.

Four Corners

A square or rectangle is marked using four boundary cones. Students spread out around the perimeter of the square or rectangle. On a signal, they move in the same direction around the perimeter. As they pass a corner, they change the movement they are doing. On the short side, some of the challenges would be to move on all fours, in crab position, or with a bear crawl to focus on the upper body area.

Gauntlet Run

Students line up at one end of a football field or an area of similar size. Challenges are placed every 10 yards. Examples of challenges might be to jump over hurdles, crawl through hoops, run through tires, perform a long jump to a certain distance, hop backwards, high-jump over a bar, do a forward roll, or perform a sport movement. Students can begin with different challenges so the activity does not become a race. Emphasis should be placed on warming up and achieving quality movement.

Rubber Band

Students begin from a central point with the instructor. On signal, the students move away from the instructor using a designated movement such as a jump, run, power skip, slide, carioca movement, or walk. On the second signal, students sprint back to the instructor's position where they form a tight circle around the teacher. The cycle is repeated with different movements. As a variation, students can perform one or two stretching activities when they return to the teacher.

Rope Jumping

Each student has a jump rope. On the first signal, they begin jumping rope. On the second signal, they drop the rope and perform a stretching activity. A third signal can be used to designate performing a light, easy run. Emphasis should be placed on warming up students for fitness activity rather than offering an intense workout.

Ball Activities

Each student has a ball and dribbles it throughout the area while moving. On signal, students stop and move the ball behind the back, around each leg, and overhead. Emphasis is on learning to handle the ball as well as on moving. A variation is to drop one ball on signal and play catch with a partner until the signal to resume dribbling is given.

Beanbag Touch and Go

Spread different colored beanbags throughout the area. On signal, students run to a beanbag, touch it, and resume running. To increase the challenge, the color of the beanbag can be specified, and the touch must be made with a designated body part. An example might be, "Touch six yellow beanbags with your left hand." Students can also move to a beanbag, perform a 90° pivot (or 180°), and resume running.

Vanishing Beanbags

Spread beanbags throughout the area to allow one per student. Students move around the area until a signal is given. On the signal, they find a beanbag and kneel on it. The instructor then signals for the class to move again, and one or more beanbags are removed during this interval. Now when students are signaled to find a beanbag, some will be left without one. A challenge is offered to not be left out more than five times. Locomotor movements and different body parts can be specified to add challenge and variety.

Hoops and Plyometrics

Each student has a hula hoop and rolls it alongside or carries the hoop while jogging. On the signal, the hoops are dropped, and students are challenged to move in and out of as many hoops as possible during the time given. The number and color of hoops to move in and out of can be specified, as well as the type of activity to perform. Students can be asked to do plyometric-type movements with two feet, one foot, or alternating feet. When the teacher gives the next signal, the students pick up the hoop and resume jogging with the hoop or rolling it.

Musical Hoops

This activity is similar to musical chairs. Hoops are spread over the floor space with each student putting one foot or two feet in a hoop (depending on how many hoops are available). Play a musical tape with random pauses. The teacher collects some of the hoops during the music so that some students will be eliminated when the music stops. The eliminated students go to the perimeter and perform a designated stretch or some type of exercise until the music stops and then return to the game. The sport movement can be changed each round.

Animal Walks and Sport Movements

Two parallel lines marked with boundary cones are placed 10 to 20 yards apart. Half of the class lines up on one line and the other half on the opposite line. On signal, students walk like an animal or perform a locomotor movement from one line to the other. Students must be careful as they cross over in the middle of the cones. Examples of walks that can be done are the forward crab walk, the backward crab walk, forward bear crawls, and sideways bear crawls. Movements include sliding, doing carioca, walking, doing crossover steps, or performing power skips.

PARTNER AND SMALL-GROUP ACTIVITIES

Marking

Marking is an excellent activity for learning to elude an opponent and also for learning to stay defensively near someone. Partners are selected, and one elects to stay near the other. On the first signal, the challenge is to stay as close as possible to the partner who is attempting to get away. When a second signal is given, both partners must immediately freeze. If the chaser can reach out and "mark" the partner, the chaser scores a point. Roles are reversed each time a signal is given. Sport movements can be changed for each round, for example, walking, fast walking, jogging, sliding, and doing carioca.

Marking with Addition or Multiplication

With a partner, students perform a rock, paper, scissors sequence and then display a number from one to five with one hand. Students quickly add or multiply the numbers. Whoever calls out the correct sum or product of the two numbers first runs and tries to get away from their partner. Students can line up with their partners in a scattered formation or in a line at midcourt facing their partners. The teacher can control all of the starts and stops or allow students to start and stop on their own.

Pac-Man

Students must walk on any line on the gym floor. About five students are given a Pac-Man designation (carrying a ball or rubber chicken, etc.). The Pac-Men are the taggers. Students move along the lines and try to avoid being tagged. Pac-Men try to tag the others and give them the piece of equipment after tagging them. Locomotor movements can be changed for each round.

Pentabridge Hustle

To start the pentabridge hustle (Figure 14.8), students form groups of five. They spread out as far as possible in the playing area and form individual bridges that another person can move under. On signal, the first person in the group of five moves under the other four bridging students and runs ahead 6–10 steps and forms a bridge. The next person in sequence moves under the four bridges. This becomes a continuous movement activity. Activity success depends on making sure that students form bridges that are quite a distance apart so that enough running occurs to ensure warm-up.

Over, Under, and Around #1

To begin this activity (Figure 14.9), students find a partner. One person gets in position on all fours while the other stands alongside, ready to begin the movement challenge. The challenge is given to move over, go under, and run around the partner a certain number of times. For example, move over your partner five times, go under eight times, and run around 10 times. When the task is completed, partners change positions and the challenge is repeated. To increase motivation, the challenge can be made to move over, under, and around different students. For a more difficult challenge, the students move on all fours slowly throughout the area.

FIGURE 14.8 Pentabridge hustle

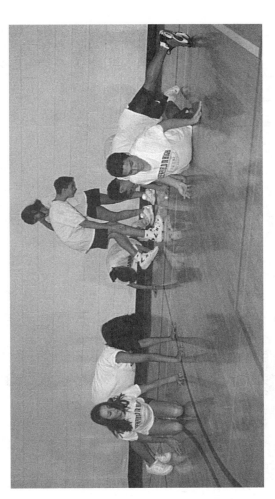

FIGURE 14.9 Over, under, and around

Over, Under, and Around #2

A variation of the previous activity is to have three students work together. Two students hold hands and the third student goes over the hands, around the group and then under the hands for 15 seconds; then everyone changes places. This variation is excellent for a situation where students cannot get on all fours because of the grass, heat, or teaching area.

New Leader

Students work in small groups. The task is to continuously move in a productive fashion that will warm up the group. One person begins as the leader. When a signal is given, a new leader steps up and leads the next activity.

One Behind

Students are in groups of three. One person is the leader, and he or she begins an exercise. The leader moves on to a second exercise, and the next person begins the first activity. Each person in the group is one behind the person in front of them in terms of the activity.

Tag Games

A variety of tag games can be used to motivate students to move. They are excellent for teaching students to elude and chase each other while staying under control. Examples of tag games include the following:

1. **Balance tag.** To be safe, balance in a stipulated position (e.g., one hand and one foot on the floor or one foot on the floor).

2. **Push-up tag.** Assume the push-up or another designated position to avoid being tagged.

3. **Blob tag.** Two people begin by being "it." When they tag someone, they hold hands or lock elbows. As a number of people are tagged, the chain or blob of people becomes long, and only those at the end of the chain are eligible to tag.

4. **Addition tag.** This is similar to blob tag, but students try to move across the gym floor (or a rectangle area) with their partners and avoid the taggers in the middle of the floor. If tagged, the partners trade places or stay in the middle to make it more difficult for others to cross the floor. Locomotor movement is changed to add variety and more of a challenge.

5. **Frozen tag.** When tagged, the person must freeze in a designated position (e.g., stork stand or straddle stretch position). To be able to resume play, a classmate must "high-five" the "frozen" person.

6. **Spider tag.** Students stand back to back with a partner with the elbows hooked. A pair of people are "it" and chase the other pairs. If a pair is tagged (or becomes unhooked), they are "it."

7. **Triangle-plus-one tag.** Three students hold hands to form a triangle. One person in the triangle is the leader. The fourth person outside the triangle tries to tag the leader. The triangle moves around to avoid getting the leader tagged. Leader and tagger are changed often.

8. **Fugitive tag.** One person is the fugitive and is given a head start. The partner is a police person trying to tag the fugitive. Flag belts can be used by the fugitive. Various movements can be used.

9. **Fastest tag.** All students are "it" at the same time. Use only short bouts of activity to be safe. Start a new bout often in this warm-up period. Start students with a walk, then slide, then skip, and then carioca steps. When students are tagged, they can kneel and tag others from that position. Focus students on safety and have them watch where they are moving and be under control at all times.

10. **Triangle-and-two tag.** Students are in groups of five. Three students hold hands and form a trian-
gle. One other student is the chaser, and the other student is a fugitive trying to keep from being tagged. The triangle tries to help the fugitive stay untagged by moving around and blocking the chaser. Rules include no jumping over the triangle or pushing the triangle out of the way. The triangle must stay together. The chaser must go around the triangle to tag. Students switch roles after a tag or a certain amount of time.

11. **Clothespin tag.** Students place two or three clothespins on the back of their shirts. The game starts in a scatter formation with specific boundaries, usually marked by boundary cones. When the game is started, students try to grab other students' clothespins and try to avoid getting their clothespins taken. As students acquire other clothespins, they place them on the front of their shirts. The game should be stopped and started often, and the means of locomotion (walk, jog, slide, carioca steps) should be changed.

12. **Heads-and-tails tag.** The teacher flips a large coin or floor spot with the picture of a head and a tail of a donkey taped on opposite sides of the spot. Half the students are heads (they put a hand on their head) and half are tails (they put a hand on their tail). Whichever side comes up is the winner and chaser of the opposite group. Modify the type of movement to add a variation.

13. **Help-me tag.** Start with four or five taggers in a large area. Three or four students hold a rubber chicken as a safe area. Three students can be touching a chicken at one time. The chicken must be passed on before 30 seconds or the holder becomes a tagger. Students can yell "help me" for a chicken when they are about to be tagged.

14. **Hospital tag.** Four or five taggers have some type of soft ball or equipment for tagging (no throwing or hard hitting). If a student is tagged, he or she must hold the injury with the other hand. If tagged twice, the two wounds are held with each hand. On the third tag, student must go to one knee and wait for a rehab high five from a classmate. Change the taggers often.

15. **True or false partner tag.** Students face a partner down the middle line in the gym. A safe zone is about 10 yards behind each line. The teacher calls out a true or false question, and the line that has the correct answer (either the true line or the false line) chases the other group and tags them before the safe zone. If a student gets tagged outside the safe zone, he or she changes sides.

FIGURE 14.10 Mirror drill

Follow the Leader

Students are grouped by pairs. On signal, the leader performs all types of movements to elude his or her partner. Zigzags, rolls, 360° turns, and jumps are encouraged. Partners switch after 30 seconds. The same drill can be done with one leader and two or more followers.

Hoops on the Ground

Students run around the area where hoops are spread. When the teacher calls a number, students must get that number of students inside one hoop in 5 seconds or less.

Mirror Drill in Place

Each student faces a partner (Figure 14.10). One person is the leader and makes a quick movement with the hands, head, legs, or body. The partner tries to be a mirror and perform the exact movement. The leader must pause briefly between movements. Leader and partner exchange places after 30 seconds.

Formation Rhythmic Running

The class begins in a circular formation. Students move to a drumbeat or other steady beat. They attempt to run rhythmically to the beat, lifting the knees and maintaining a formation or line with even spacing between students. Challenges can be added, such as clapping hands on the first beat, stamping the feet on the third beat, and thrusting a hand into the air on the fourth beat of a four-count rhythm.

As students become experienced at maintaining the formation and rhythm of the activity, they can be led into different formations such as a rectangle, square, triangle, or line. Students can also "wind up" and "unwind" the line and can learn to cross in front of each other to "break a line."

Loose Caboose

All students are hooked together in groups of two or three by having the rear person put their hands on the waist of the front person. The teacher picks several students to move without a partner. These students are termed the loose cabooses. The loose cabooses try to hook on with another set of students by grabbing the waist of the rear student. When this happens, the front student is now loose and attempts to hook on with another pair of students. The teacher can vary the means of locomotion for the students.

Flag Grab

All students have a flag belt and are scattered around the gym. On the start signal, students try to grab the flags of others while trying to avoid getting their flag taken. Students drop the flags they took immediately, and the other students put the flags back on and continue in the game. Teachers vary the movements to include walk, jog, slide, and carioca steps.

Running High Fives

Use a music interval of 15 seconds on and 15 seconds off. When the music is playing, students walk the first interval, then jog, slide, skip, do carioca, or stretch. When the music goes off, students give high fives to other students. After a couple of intervals, students can give low fives, then alternate between high and low fives, then medium fives, then alternate between right hand and left hand, and so on as the teacher varies the activity.

Standing High Fives

Students get a partner about the same height. Students start with a jump and right-hand high five, then use the left hand, and then use both hands. Next, students add a quarter turn and the various high fives. Next, students add a half turn and then the high fives. Then they add a three-quarter turn and finally a full turn. Students should try turning to the right and left and using both hands with each turn. Encourage body control and teamwork.

Quick Hands with Beanbags

Students sit facing a partner with legs crossed or extended. One beanbag is placed on the floor equally between the two partners. The teacher calls out "right" or "left," and the students try to quickly grab the beanbag with the appropriate hand that was called by the teacher. The same activity can be performed from a push-up position or a sit-up position with partners facing each other and then quickly trying to grab the beanbag as the right or left hand is called by the teacher.

Builders/Destroyers

Place about 30 cones on the gym floor in a scatter formation with half the cones tipped over. Half of the students are the builders that are trying to set up all of the cones, and the other half of the students are the destroyers that are tipping over the cones. After 15–20 seconds, stop the activity and see how many cones are in each position. Challenge the groups to improve that number during the next time frame.

Hoops Circle Pass

Divide the class into three or four groups that form circles while holding hands. A hula hoop is started between two connected hands. The hoop is passed around the circle without letting go of hands. Students need to work together to help others through the hoop in the most efficient manner. After a couple of practice runs, a race can be held to see which group performs the passing techniques the fastest.

Quick Lineup

The class is divided into four equal groups. Each group decides on a team name and lines up single file, facing one assigned side of the teacher (front, back, right side, or left side). All students close their eyes, and the teacher moves to a new position and rotates her or his body position. On the teacher's signal, students run to the new position and line up in the same order, facing the same side of the teacher and yell out their team name as they finish. The first team finished gets a point.

Moving Throw and Catch

Move and play catch with your partner under control from about 5 yards apart. Any type of ball, beanbag, throton, rubber chicken, etc., can be used for this activity. Students need to remain safe and under control with their movements and equipment. Teachers can stop the action often and do a large group stretch or exercise to maintain control. The locomotor movements can be changed to add variety for this activity. Challenge students to add different pivots, such as front, back, 90°, 180°, or 360° during this activity.

STUDY STIMULATORS AND REVIEW QUESTIONS

1. Explain the primary purposes of introductory activities.

2. Describe the characteristics of an effective introductory activity.

3. Cite four reasons for using introductory activities in secondary school lessons.

4. Why should the interests, physical abilities, and developmental levels of students be considered in the selection of introductory activities?

5. Discuss the transition from introductory activities to physical fitness activities. Why is this transition important in secondary classes?

6. Why should the introductory activity be short in length (2–3 minutes) with an atmosphere of enthusiasm, motivation, and fun?

7. What can a teacher do to make an introductory activity novel and challenging for students?

WEB SITES

Human Kinetics (Books and Materials)
www.humankinetics.com

National Association for Sport and Physical Education (Books, Materials, and Workshops)
www.aahperd.org/naspe

Physical Education Teaching and Curriculum Information
www.pecentral.com
www.pelinks4u.org
www.pe4life.org

NATIONAL STANDARDS FOR PHYSICAL EDUCATION*

STANDARD 1 Demonstrates competency in motor skills and movement patterns needed to perform a variety of physical activities.

STANDARD 2 Demonstrates understanding of movement concepts, principles, strategies, and tactics as they apply to the learning and performance of physical activities.

STANDARD 3 Participates regularly in physical activity.

STANDARD 4 Achieves and maintains a health-enhancing level of physical fitness.

STANDARD 5 Exhibits responsible personal and social behavior that respects self and others in physical activity settings.

STANDARD 6 Values physical activity for health, enjoyment, challenge, self-expression, and/or social interaction.

ESSENTIAL COMPONENTS OF A QUALITY PROGRAM

COMPONENT 1 A quality physical education program is organized around content standards that offer direction and continuity to instruction and evaluation.

COMPONENT 2 A quality program is student centered and based on the developmental urges, characteristics, and interests of students.

COMPONENT 3 Quality physical education makes physical activity and motor-skill development the core of the program.

COMPONENT 4 Physical education programs teach management skills and self-discipline.

COMPONENT 5 Quality programs emphasize inclusion of all students.

COMPONENT 6 In a quality physical education setting, instruction focuses on the process of learning skills rather than the product or outcome of the skill performance.

COMPONENT 7 A quality physical education program teaches lifetime activities that students can use to promote their health and personal wellness.

COMPONENT 8 Quality physical education teaches cooperative and responsibility skills and helps students develop sensitivity to diversity and gender issues.

*Reprinted from *Moving Into the Future: National Standards for Physical Education,* 2nd ed. (2004), with permission from the National Association for Sport and Physical Education (NASPE), 1900 Association Dr., Reston, VA 20191–1599.

15

Promoting and Monitoring Lifestyle Physical Activity

CHAPTER SUMMARY

This chapter explains the differences between physical fitness and physical activity and how different students will choose one over the other based on their personal needs. The Physical Activity Pyramid gives students a concrete explanation of how they should plan for and incorporate physical activity into their daily lifestyles. The focus is on adding at least 60 minutes of moderate to vigorous activity to their daily routine.

Pedometers can be an important tool for teachers and students in promoting adequate amounts of physical activity. Pedometers are accurate when students learn how to find the best placement point on their bodies. Goal setting can be easily done using pedometers, which measure either steps or activity time. Students can set personal goals that are within reach to ensure continued motivation. Guidelines for teachers are offered for using pedometers in physical education classes. Finally, teachers are urged to used pedometers to measure the effectiveness of their physical education programs. Showing an increase in physical activity outside the school environment may be one of the most positive aspects of a quality physical education program.

Walking is the "real" lifestyle activity. It can be done anywhere with a minimum of equipment, and all youth can walk. Walking is also an effective tool for teaching students to deal with weight management issues. A schoolwide walking program can be implemented to help create an "active school." Many walking activities are included for use in and outside of physical education classes.

STUDENT OUTCOMES

After reading this chapter, you will be able to:

- Describe why activity is more important than fitness in ensuring health.

- Know the different parts of the Physical Activity Pyramid and why each level is important for optimal health.

- Understand how to identify moderate to vigorous physical activity.

- Know how to use pedometers and to help students learn where to place the pedometer for highest accuracy.

- Help students design personal goals for activity.

- Implement the use of pedometers in a physical education setting.

- Understand why pedometers can be used to measure program activity outcomes.

- Express the role of physical activity in maintaining proper body weight.

- Implement a schoolwide walking program.

P hysical activity or physical fitness? Which of these outcomes should physical education focus upon in its quest to better serve students? The answer is that it depends on each student's needs and desire. For too long, physical education teachers determined they knew what was best for all students regardless of their condition, ages, maturity levels, or abilities. What was best for all was to try and improve their level of physical fitness as measured by fitness testing. To this day, when teachers are asked to assume accountability for their programs, the majority fall back on fitness testing. However, fitness for all students has been a failing proposition. Obesity continues to increase across the country, and fitness levels show little if any improvement (Corbin & Pangrazi, 1992). Students who are overweight, unskilled, or not predisposed to physical fitness do all they can to avoid physical education classes in middle school and high school. What could be done differently to better meet the needs of all youth? Is it possible that we are failing the youth we want to help the most?

Based on an examination of the problems described in the previous paragraph, it is clear that there are two distinctly different outcomes for physical education that serve students with different needs. That is why this book separates physical fitness and physi-

cal activity into two separate and distinct chapters. **Physical activity** is defined as bodily movement that is produced by the contraction of skeletal muscle and that substantially increases energy expenditure (Corbin & Pangrazi, 2004). Physical activity is an umbrella term that looks at the process of moving. Such movement could take on different forms, such as exercise, sports, and leisure activity. In contrast, **physical fitness** is a set of attributes that people have or achieve relating to their ability to perform physical activity (U.S. Department of Health and Human Services [USDHHS], 1996). Whereas physical activity is a process-oriented outcome related to behavior and lifestyle, physical fitness is a product outcome with an emphasis on achieving a higher state of being. The vast majority of people are not interested in achieving a high level of physical fitness but may be more receptive to learning to live an active lifestyle in order to maintain health-related fitness. In similar fashion, most students who are nonathletes are not interested in the product of physical fitness but are receptive to learning to enjoy their bodies through lifestyle physical activities (see Chapter 20). Therefore, Chapter 15 focuses on the process of being physically active for good health, while Chapter 16 is written to promote a higher state of skill-related physical fitness.

PHYSICAL ACTIVITY FOR ADOLESCENTS

A consensus statement developed by a board of experts serves as a guide for teachers. This statement delineates the amount of activity adolescents (ages 11 to 21) need and contains two basic guidelines (Sallis & Patrick, 1994). Guideline 1 states, "All adolescents should be physically active daily, or nearly every day, as part of play, games, sports, work, transportation, recreation, physical education, or planned exercise, in the context of family, school, and community activities." Guideline 2 states, "Adolescents should engage in three or more sessions per week of activities that last 20 minutes or more and require moderate to vigorous levels of exertion."

Meeting Guideline 1 should be a priority and a minimum. Participation in 30 minutes of daily physical activity is a reasonable goal, even for sedentary youth. Beyond this, Guideline 2 is a most desirable goal. The consensus statement includes brisk walking, jogging, stair-climbing, basketball, racquet sports, soccer, dance, lap swimming, skating, strength (resistance) training, lawn mowing, and cycling as some examples of activities that meet Guideline 2. Maintaining the heart rate at a target heart rate for the full 20 minutes is not necessary to meet Guideline 2, and many of the activities listed do not produce such a result.

Moderate to Vigorous Physical Activity (MVPA)

What is moderate to vigorous intensity activity? Experts generally agree on what constitutes light, moderate, and vigorous physical activity. Metabolic equivalent of tasks (METs) (resting metabolic rate) are used to quantify activity. One MET equals calories expended at rest (resting metabolism). Two METs indicate activity that is twice as intense. Three METs require three times

as much energy and so on. Activities of three METs or less are considered to be light activities. Examples are strolling (slow walking), slow stationary cycling, stretching, golfing with a motorized cart, fishing (sitting), bowling, carpet sweeping, and riding a mower (Pate et al., 1995). Activity that expends four to six times the energy expended at rest (four to six METs) is considered to be moderate to vigorous in nature. Examples of activity at this level are brisk walking, racquet sports, and lawn mowing with a power mower.

The **activity prescription** for adolescents does not discourage or downplay the value of vigorous activity. Activities done at seven METs or higher are considered vigorous in nature. They include very brisk walking, walking uphill, jogging, relatively fast cycling, active involvement in many sports, lawn mowing with a hand mower, and doing exercise routines such as aerobic dance. For years, students have been told that aerobic activity must be continuous to be beneficial. A major implication of the new recommendation is that activity can be beneficial even if accumulated in several shorter bouts of activity throughout the day. For example, 15 minutes of walking and 15 minutes of aerobic dance done at different times of the day, or three 10-minute intervals of continuous cycling done at different times of the day would meet the physical activity prescription.

Expending calories in activity that equals 60 minutes of MVPA (walking briskly) each day (1,000 to 2,000 kcal per week) achieves health benefits similar to performance-related fitness training (see Chapter 16). There is more than one way to prescribe physical activity for good health. Different forms of activity have different benefits; it is appropriate to use one set of guidelines or recommendations to achieve good health while using another set of guidelines to enhance the fitness levels of those interested in performance (see Figure 15.1).

The activity prescription recommendations cover a broad range of moderate to vigorous activities,

	Skill-Related Fitness Prescription Model	Health-Related Fitness Prescription
Frequency	Three days per week	Physical activity every day or almost every day (walking, climbing stairs, gardening, doing housework, exercising)
Intensity	65%–85% of predicted maximum heart rate	Moderate intensity activity (equivalent to brisk walking)
Time	Minimum of 20 minutes per exercise session	Accumulate 30 minutes or more of activity throughout the day

FIGURE 15.1 Guidelines for skill-related and health-related fitness

including those that can be done as part of work or normal daily routines as well as during free time. These recommendations are useful for students who do not like highly intense physical activity. Many people remain sedentary or drop out of activity because they believe that exercise is only beneficial when it is vigorous, high-intensity activity. The new recommendations make it easier for sedentary people to see the value in participation in moderate activity.

THE PHYSICAL ACTIVITY PYRAMID

The Physical Activity Pyramid (Figure 15.2) is a prescription model for good health that helps students understand how much and what type of activity they need. The activity pyramid offers a visual approach to activity prescription. It is useful because people have become confused in recent years by scientific reports concerning the amount of physical activity necessary to produce health and fitness benefits. The Physical Activity Pyramid helps students understand that there are many different types of beneficial activity. It classifies activity into six different types and shows how each type has its own unique FIT (frequency, intensity, and time) formula and benefits.

Describing Types of Physical Activities in the Pyramid

Level 1: Lifestyle Physical Activities

At the base of the Physical Activity Pyramid is lifestyle physical activity. Lifestyle physical activities are those people can do as part of their regular everyday work or daily routine. Examples of such activities are doing yard work and delivering the mail. Of course, there are ways of doing lifestyle physical activity other than working at an active job. For example, someone who sits at a desk for most of the day can get lifestyle activity by walking or riding a bicycle to work rather than driving a car. Other lifestyle physical activities can be done in or around the home. For teens, raking the leaves, mowing the lawn, walking to the store, and carrying the groceries are lifestyle activities. Housework that requires using the large muscles of the body is also lifestyle physical activity.

Level 2: Active Aerobic Activities

Level 2 of the pyramid includes active aerobic activities. Aerobic activities are those performed at a pace for which the body can supply adequate oxygen to meet the demands of the activity. Because lifestyle activities meet this criterion, they are aerobic in nature. However, in the pyramid, *active aerobics* refers to those aer-obic activities that elevate the heart rate to a relatively high level. In other words, this level includes aerobic activities using the skill-related fitness formula for target heart rate. Examples of popular moderate-to-vigorous active aerobics are aerobic dance, step aerobics, jogging, brisk walking, moderate-to-vigorous swimming, and biking. Middle and high school students should perform the more vigorous activities at Level 2 three days a week for at least 20 minutes.

Level 2: Active Sports and Recreational Activities

Also on Level 2 of the Physical Activity Pyramid are active sports and recreation. Some examples of active sports are basketball, tennis, hiking, racquetball, and volleyball. Like active aerobics, this type of activity is typically more vigorous than lifestyle physical activity. Sports involve vigorous bursts of activity with brief rest periods. Though they are often not truly aerobic in nature, when they are done without long rest periods they have many of the same benefits as aerobic activities.

Some sports are not vigorously active and should be considered lifestyle physical activities. For example, golf is more like the activity received from walking to work rather than the more vigorous activity generated in tennis or basketball. It is beneficial but not vigorous in nature. Recreational activities such as rock climbing or canoeing are not considered to be sports by some people. Nevertheless, they can be used to meet the moderate-to-vigorous activity recommendation if performed vigorously.

Level 3: Flexibility Activities

Flexibility is the ability to use joints through a full range of motion as a result of having long muscles and elastic connective tissues. There are, no doubt, some activities from Level 1 and Level 2 of the pyramid that help build flexibility to some extent. Still, to develop this part of fitness, it is necessary to do special flexibility exercises that involve stretching the muscles and using the joints through their full range of normal motion. For this purpose, stretching exercises are best.

Flexibility exercises should be done at least 3 days a week and can be done every day. The intensity requires a stretch beyond normal to a point of mild discomfort. Each exercise is performed several times for 10 to 30 seconds. It is important to perform exercises for each of the body's major muscle groups.

Level 3: Muscle Fitness Activities

Muscle fitness includes strength and muscular endurance. Some of the activities from Levels 1 and 2 of the pyramid, such as sports, can contribute to the

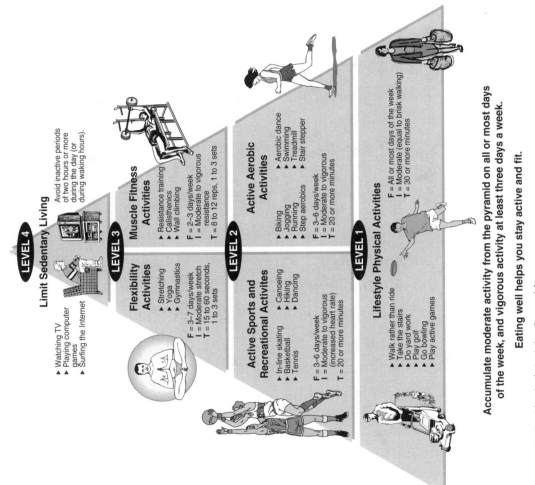

Limit Sedentary Living

LEVEL 4

▲ Watching TV
▲ Playing computer games
▲ Surfing the Internet

Avoid inactive periods of two hours or more during the day (or during waking hours).

LEVEL 3

Flexibility Activities

▲ Stretching
▲ Yoga
▲ Gymnastics

F = 3–7 days/week
I = Moderate stretch
T = 15 to 60 seconds, 1 to 3 sets

Muscle Fitness Activities

▲ Resistance training
▲ Calisthenics
▲ Wall climbing

F = 2–3 days/week
I = Moderate to vigorous resistance
T = 8 to 12 reps, 1 to 3 sets

LEVEL 2

Active Sports and Recreational Activites

▲ In-line skating
▲ Basketball
▲ Tennis

▲ Canoeing
▲ Hiking
▲ Dancing

F = 3–6 days/week
I = Moderate to vigorous (increased heart rate)
T = 20 or more minutes

Active Aerobic Activities

▲ Biking
▲ Jogging
▲ Running
▲ Step aerobics

▲ Aerobic dance
▲ Swimming
▲ Treadmill
▲ Stair stepper

F = 3–6 days/week
I = Moderate to vigorous
T = 20 or more minutes

LEVEL 1

Lifestyle Physical Activities

▲ Walk rather than ride
▲ Take the stairs
▲ Do yard work
▲ Play golf
▲ Go bowling
▲ Play active games

F = All or most days of the week
I = Moderate (equal to brisk walking)
T = 30 or more minutes

Accumulate moderate activity from the pyramid on all or most days of the week, and vigorous activity at least three days a week.

Eating well helps you stay active and fit.

FIGURE 15.2 Physical Activity Pyramid

Reprinted, with permission, from C. B. Corbin and R. Lindsay (2007). *Fitness for Life*, updated 5th ed., p. 64, Human Kinetics, Champaign, IL.

development of the two parts of muscle fitness. But most experts agree that if you want to improve muscle fitness, you need to do some exercises especially designed to build it.

The American College of Sports Medicine (ACSM, 2000) recommends that muscle fitness exercises be done at least 2 days a week. Exercises for several different muscle groups (eight to 10) should be done using a percentage of the maximum weight you can lift. The percentage (intensity) depends on the type of muscle fitness to be developed. Each exercise should be performed eight to 12 times (a set). The ACSM notes, "While more frequent training and additional sets or combination of sets and repetitions elicit larger strength gains, the additional improvement is relatively small" (2000, p. 160).

Level 4: Inactivity–Sedentary Living

At the top of the pyramid is inactivity. Some inactivity is not necessarily bad. For example, we need adequate amounts of sleep, and after vigorous exercise, rest is important. Also, there are benefits associated with activities that are fairly sedentary. Nevertheless, the Physical Activity Pyramid is designed to provide information about the benefits of regular physical activity. Sedentary living as a lifestyle is discouraged. Long periods of inactivity during the hours of the day when you are awake should be limited. People who excessively sit and watch television or who spend all of their free time playing video games are not getting the activity they need for good health.

Understanding the Levels of Physical Activity

The primary reason for arranging the pyramid into six types and four levels is associated with the benefits that result from each activity type. Those activities having broad general health and wellness benefits for large numbers of people are placed at the base of the pyramid.

Lifestyle activity is placed at the base of the pyramid because scientific evidence indicates that inactive people who begin regular exercise have the most to gain. *Physical Activity and Health: A Report of the Surgeon General* (USDHHS, 1996) points out that our nation could reap great health and economic benefits if the 24 percent of our population who are totally sedentary would begin modest amounts of regular physical activity. Further, those who are only occasionally active could also benefit by meeting the standards for lifestyle activity suggested in Level 1 of the pyramid. The benefits at this level are wide ranging, including reduced risk of various diseases such as heart disease, diabetes, and cancer. The extra calories expended in doing these activities are also useful in controlling body fat and reducing the risk of obesity. Wellness benefits include increased functional capacity as well as improved quality of life.

At Level 2 are the more vigorous activities. Scientific reports suggest that for those people who are already active, active aerobics and active sports and recreation provide health and fitness benefits in addition to those provided by regular lifestyle activity. For those with little free time, regular activity from Level 2 can substitute for lifestyle activity, though participation at both levels is encouraged. Like lifestyle activities, the activities at this level provide broad general health benefits. It is for this reason that these activities are placed at Level 2. It should be noted that the more vigorous nature of the activities make them difficult for some people to perform, and for this reason, they may not be as appealing to as many students as activities at Level 1.

At Level 3 are exercises designed to build flexibility and muscle fitness. Performing exercises of either type builds physical fitness that contributes to improved performance in various jobs and in active sports. Muscle fitness has also been associated with reduced risk of osteoporosis (Shaw & Snow-Harter, 1995), and both types of exercises when prescribed and performed appropriately are thought to contribute to reduced rate of injury and less risk of back problems (Plowman, 1993).

It is obvious why rest and inactivity are at the top of the pyramid (Level 4). In general, they do not provide health benefits.

A secondary reason guiding the placement of activities is frequency of the activity. As the level in the pyramid increases, the frequency of participation decreases. Those activities at Level 1 should be performed daily. Those at Levels 2 and 3 can be performed fewer days per week, and inactivity (Level 4) is something that should be limited on all days of the week.

PEDOMETERS AND PHYSICAL ACTIVITY

Pedometers are a natural fit for a chapter on the promotion of physical activity because that is their primary function—to measure the daily amount of physical activity a person accumulates. Pedometers generally measure the quantity of physical activity, although newer models can measure the intensity and duration of activity. Early pedometers were mechanical and used a moving lever arm to count steps. Electronic pedometers now detect movement through a spring-loaded, counterbalanced mechanism that records vertical acceleration at the hip. Pedometers are small, unobtrusive, and easily fastened to a belt or waistband. In their most basic form, pedometers measure the number of steps a person takes. Counting steps is an effective way to measure how active a person is throughout the day, even though pedometers can't measure all types of activity. Because pedometers are not waterproof, they can't measure swimming activity. Also, pedometers don't accurately measure activities on wheels such as bicycling, skateboarding, and in-line skating. However, considering most of the physical activity people accumulate is overland, pedometers are still one of the best ways to measure physical activity for young and old alike. Using pedometers to measure the physical activity levels of youth is now an accepted instructional and research methodology (Beighle, Pangrazi, & Vincent, 2001; Crouter, Schneider, Karabulut, & Bassett Jr, 2003; Kilanowski, Consalvi, & Epstein, 1999).

A number of pedometers on the market have features other than just the counting of steps. Some of the more common measures include distance covered and caloric expenditure. To measure distance covered, the length of the step must be entered into the pedometer. The pedometer then calculates distance covered by multiplying the step length times the number of steps. To measure energy expenditure, a number of factors must be entered into the pedometer such as weight and stride length. Based on the number of steps taken, the pedometers calculate the number of kilocalories expended. Newer pedometers have a function that measures exercise time. Every time a person moves, the pedometer starts accumulating time. When the person stops moving, the timing function stops. This function shows the total hours and minutes of exercise time accumulated throughout the day. The measurement of activity time is a more accurate indicator of a person's activity level.

Considering the Accuracy of Pedometers

Activity recommendations in terms of daily minutes of physical activity for youth (Corbin & Pangrazi, 2004) and adults (USDHHS, 1996) have created an interest in accurately measuring personal movement. When people are asked to recall and report the amount of activity they performed throughout the previous day, most find it difficult to quantify how active they were. Additionally, it may be that the recall was done on a day that is not typical, resulting in an underestimation or overestimation of physical activity. With children, some type of objective measuring tool is helpful for documenting activity levels because it avoids dependency on recollection and reading of questionnaires. The pedometer is an objective activity-measuring instrument that has been studied by a number of researchers. A recent study (Crouter, Schneider, Karabulut, & Bassett Jr., 2003) evaluated the validity of 10 different electronic pedometers and found them to be "most accurate." A similar study (Schneider, Crouter, Lukajic, & Bassett Jr., 2003) examined the reliability and accuracy of 10 pedometers over a 400-m walk with similar results.

A limitation of pedometers is that they are less accurate when people move slowly (less than 4 km/h) or walk with an uneven gait (Crouter, Schneider, Karabulut, & Bassett Jr., 2003). Pedometers depend on a fairly consistent up and down motion with each step, and an uneven or slow gait may not create enough movement for the pedometer to measure. Pedometers overestimated distance covered at slower speeds and underestimated actual distance at higher speeds. Caloric expenditure was most often overestimated (Crouter, Schneider, Karabulut, & Bassett Jr., 2003). These errors in distance and energy expenditure are not surprising considering they are all based on consistency of step length and walking speed. Throughout a day of activities, it is most likely that both step length and walking speed will vary. Another factor that contributes to the error is that some pedometers require the stride length to be entered in 3-inch intervals, thus resulting in overestimating or underestimating distance covered.

Undercounting errors may also occur with highly overweight students because of the placement of the pedometer. On these students, the orientation of the pedometer is often tilted away from the vertical plane and moved toward the horizontal plane by excess body fat around the waist. If the pedometer is not parallel with the upright plane of the body, its accuracy is affected. The next section explains how to find an accurate placement point for difficult cases. In spite of these limitations, pedometers are still one of the most accurate and reasonably priced tools for measuring physical activity.

Using Pedometers in a Class Setting

There are a number of things to work through after making the decision to use pedometers. The first step is to get a set of pedometers to use in physical education classes. A set of 36 pedometers will cost $300 to $500, depending on the number of functions and accompanying materials. Many schools have been successful in asking parent–teacher groups to fund pedometers. Interest can be created by making a presentation to the group and asking for support. Another option is a "shareware" program where companies sell pedometers at a reduced price to school empoyees, who in turn sell the pedometers to parents and others to raise money. Certainly, selling pedometers is a much healthier fund-raising activity than selling candy or cookie dough.

Using pedometers in physical education requires teaching proper protocol to students. Teachers become frustrated when students fuss with their pedometers, which usually occurs when they don't have a set of standard procedures to follow. Here is an often-used procedure that minimizes pedometer preparation time. Prior to distribution, permanently number each pedometer and store no more than six pedometers in a small plastic container. Make sure you have the same number of pedometers (not more than six) in each container so it is easy to see when a pedometer (and corresponding student) is missing. Students arrive and, on signal, go to their assigned box, secure a pedometer, and put it on while moving around the area. On signal, they freeze, reset their pedometers, and class begins, as usual. At the end of class, students remove their pedometers, put them back in the same container, record their steps or activity time on the sheet next to their container, and prepare to exit class. This procedure of learning to secure, fasten, and put away the pedometer is critical for successful integration of pedometers into the program. Allied to this procedure are two basic rules:

1. "You shake it, we take it." The pedometer can be damaged by hard shaking and requires a very small up and down motion to record steps. The purpose of using pedometers is to accurately record steps,

and falsely recording steps is strongly discouraged. In most cases, the pedometer is taken from the student, but he or she can use it the next time the student comes to class.

2. "Once off, forever off." This rule stipulates that once the pedometer is placed on the waistband (at the start of class), it is not to be removed for the remainder of the period. The pedometer can be read from the waistband. If students are allowed to take their pedometers on and off, they will drop and break them or destroy the accuracy of their recordings. As in rule 1, the pedometer is available again at the next class period.

Another important thing to consider when introducing pedometers is the novelty phase. It is natural for a student to want to learn how a pedometer works. Give them time to open and close it, move it gently up and down to watch it count, and learn what causes the pedometer to stop counting steps and time. A related problem in the introduction phase is that there may be an excessively high rate of pedometer loss. Therefore, the pedometers should be introduced in a controlled setting, i.e., physical education class, where students can be closely observed returning the pedometers. Use the following schedule to overcome the high-interest or novelty period. For the first 6 to 8 weeks of school, use the pedometers in physical education classes only. From that point up to the winter break, use the pedometers to evaluate how much activity students get during the school day. Students put on the pedometers in the morning and return them at the end of the school day. After winter break, those students who have been responsible up to this point can use the pedometers to carry out 24-hour activity surveillance. They put on the pedometers each morning and clear them. The next morning, students record their activity and reset the pedometers. Recording is conducted Monday through Friday mornings to avoid the weekends. In most cases, pedometers are lost if they leave school over the weekends. Once the pedometers become a regular part of each student's lifestyle, fewer pedometers will be lost or misplaced. Many schools put in place a replacement policy before giving students the freedom to take the pedometers out of the school environment. A letter is sent home explaining the activity program and the use of pedometers. If a pedometer is lost, the student must pay a fee to replace it.

Teaching Students about Pedometer Placement and Accuracy

Pedometers are usually worn at the waistline, directly over the midpoint of the front of the thigh and kneecap. This positioning has long been recommended as a standard placement. However, an article by Vincent-Graser, Pangrazi, and Vincent (in press) showed that the right (or left) side (midaxillary line) is a slightly better place for the initial position. Regardless, the first thing that should be taught to students is to find the placement point for them that offers the most accurate counting of steps. The following protocol is designed to teach students how to find the waistband point where the pedometer measures accurately.

1. Place the pedometer on the waistband on the right side of the body, midway between the front and back of the body (over the hip). The pedometer must be parallel to the body and upright. If it is angled in any direction, it will not measure accurately. To accurately measure the number of steps, the pedometer must be started at zero steps each time. To do this, teach students to open the pedometer without removing it from the waistband, reset it to zero steps, and then gently close the pedometer without moving. Begin walking at a normal cadence while counting the number of steps they are taking. Ask students to stop immediately when they have counted 30 steps. Gently open the pedometer without removing it and check the step count. If the step count is within 1-2 steps of 30, this placement is an accurate location for the pedometer. If the step count is less accurate, try the next step.

2. Move the pedometer so it is positioned over the midpoint of the right (or left) thigh. Open the pedometer, clear it, and take 30 steps as described in step 1. Again, if the step count is within 1-2 steps of 30, this new placement is your most accurate measurement spot. If not, try another placement (see the next step) and repeat the step test.

3. Pedometers must remain in an upright plane (with the pedometer display perpendicular to the floor and parallel to the body) in order to accurately register step counts. Loose-fitting clothing will impact accuracy because the clothing absorbs the slight vertical force that occurs with each step. Excess body fat can tilt the pedometer and negate accuracy. In these cases, placement at waist level behind the hip and on the back often results in an accurate measurement. Research (Vincent-Graser, Pangrazi, & Vincent, in press) showed that placing the pedometer on an adjustable Velcro belt resulted in more accurate readings because more precise adjustments could be made. Repeat the 30-step process outlined in step 1 until an accurate placement point has been identified.

Pedometers and Personal Goal Setting

A common approach in physical education is the "one-standard-fits-all" approach. For example, we often have all students run a mile, do 25 push-ups, and walk 10,000 steps without considering that they are all unique and differently talented individuals. Application of this approach is based on a single standard and assumes that it will work for all types of people regardless of age, gender, or health. This practice of "mass prescription" often turns off students who need activity the most. An often-referenced standard is 10,000 steps per day (Hatano, 1993). This standard was designed for cardiovascular disease prevention but has grown to be the most-often-quoted standard for daily activity. A standard for youth that is often mentioned is 11,000 steps/day for girls and 13,000 steps/day for boys. This standard is used for the Presidential Active Lifestyle Award (President's Council on Physical Fitness and Sports [PCPFS], 2004) which is awarded to students who meet these daily standards over a 6-week period.

The problem with a **single standard goal** is that it doesn't take into account the substantial differences between people of all ages and gender. A predisposition to be active may make it much easier for some students to reach the step criteria, while others may find it next to impossible because they are naturally less active. Some individuals may have shorter stride lengths, so they reach 10,000 steps sooner than a taller youngster. How many steps *should* be set as a standard? Should it be set high so only those already active individuals can reach it? Should it be set low so the majority of people are able to reach the goal? Should it be set high enough to provide a proven health-related benefit? If you accumulate more than 11,000 steps, is there any point in moving beyond the 11,000-step threshold? If you accumulate 4,000 steps each day, does 11,000 steps seem an impossible goal? When all is said and done, setting one goal that applies with equivalent efficacy to a large population is a difficult proposition at best.

The approach recommended here is the **baseline and goal-setting** technique (Pangrazi, Beighle, & Sidman, 2007). This method requires that each individual identify his or her average daily activity (baseline) level. For adolescents and adults, 8 days of step counts (or activity time) are required for establishing an average activity level (Trost, Pate, Freedson, Sallis, & Taylor, 2000). Older students have substantial day-to-day variation in their activity patterns, and it takes at least 8 days of activity monitoring to ensure a reliable and valid baseline. Baseline data can be entered in a chart similar to the one shown in Figure 15.3.

After the baseline level of activity has been established by averaging the 8 days of activity, this becomes the reference point for setting personal goals. A personal goal is established by taking the baseline activity level and adding 10 percent more steps (or time in whole minutes) to that level. For example, assume a student has a baseline level of 6,000 steps per day. That student would set a personal goal of 6,000 steps plus 600 steps for a total of 6,600 steps. The student would pursue this goal for 2 weeks. If the goal is reached for a majority of the days (8 or more) during this 2-week period, another 10 percent (600 steps) is added to the goal, and the process is repeated. For most people, a top goal of 4,000 to 6,000 steps above their baseline level is a reasonable expectation. Using the example of 6,000 baseline steps, a goal of 10,000 to 12,000 steps would be this student's ultimate goal. This baseline and goal-setting approach takes into consideration the fact that all individuals are unique. It gradually increases personal goals so they seem achievable to even inactive individuals. Most individuals are interested in determining their baseline level of activity, and this is a way to motivate students to gradually increase their current activity levels.

A third way to establish step levels for youth is to define a **healthy activity zone** (HAZ). In this method, there is not one standard that each youngster has to reach. This approach has been used by the FitnessGram (2004) for specifying a range of scores (the healthy fitness zone [HFZ]) where students should score on fitness test items. Some of the FitnessGram test items (e.g., PACER run and skinfolds) are based on health-related criteria, while others are based on improvement resulting from training. Applied to physical activity, a range of steps (or activity time) can be established for each gender that would serve as the HFZ. This method requires further research, but may be an acceptable way to establish a range of scores that can apply to the vast majority of children and adults. It is also possible that a combination of methods, such as baseline/goal-setting and HFZ standards, could ultimately be the best solution.

Understanding Activity Time and Step Goal Differences

Many pedometers can now measure steps and physical activity time. In other words, they count all steps taken and the number of minutes of moving. Moving time is typically termed *activity time*. Goals for steps have been established. For example, as mentioned earlier, students must accumulate 13,000 steps (boys) or 11,000 steps (girls) in a 24-hour period for 6 weeks to earn the

Step 1: Calculate Your Average Daily Activity Level

Your average daily activity is your current activity level or baseline activity level. This score will be used to calculate your personal activity goal. You may establish a step-count goal or time goal (number of minutes). Each day, record the number of steps and/or time you have accumulated on your pedometer. At the end of 8 days, find your average daily activity score by dividing all the step counts and time by 8.

Day	Step Counts	Time
1		
2		
3		
4		
5		
6		
7		
8		
Average Daily Activity		

Step 2: Calculate Your Personal Daily Activity Goal

A reasonable personal goal is to increase activity 10 percent. This means you will take your average daily activity and add 10 percent to your current level. You will strive to reach your goal each day for 2 weeks. If you reach your goal on any 8 days or more, you should increase your goal by another 10 percent. If you don't reach your goal for at least 8 days, you should stay at your current level of activity. At the end of the 2-week period, check your progress and start a new 2-week period of activity. The following is an example of goal setting based on a student who has a baseline activity level of 7,000 steps and 70 minutes. If you use minutes as a goal, round off the seconds to the nearest minute.

Baseline Activity Level	Personal Goal – 10% over your baseline	Weeks	Goal Met
7000 steps	7700 steps	1–2	Yes
7700 steps	8400 steps	3–4	Yes
8400 steps	9100 steps	5–6	No
8400 steps	9100 steps	7–8	No

FIGURE 15.3 Setting your personalized activity goal

President's Challenge Active Lifestyle Award. Many adults are well aware of the 10,000-step goal, even though they have little idea of why or how it was established. A more common way of expressing goals is in terms of minutes per day. For example, the activity guidelines for adolescents specify a minimum of at least 30 minutes a day. Pedometers that monitor the number of minutes of activity make it easy to interpret these goals. However, 30 minutes of activity is not much activity for teenagers because the intent of these goals was to ensure they were involved in 30 minutes of moderate to vigorous activity over and above their baseline activity level. With pedometers that measure

activity time, it soon becomes apparent that 30 minutes is much below the amount of activity most students should accumulate on a daily basis.

Activity goals are much more meaningful because they are adjusted for size differences among individuals. To use an example, I go for a walk with a friend who is 6 inches taller than me. We put on our pedometers and walk together for 30 minutes. At the end of the walk, my friend has accumulated 3,000 steps while I accumulated 3,600 steps—even though we were walking alongside each other. However, when we compare our activity time, it is the same; both of us have accumulated 30 minutes of physical activity.

Why the difference in steps? My friend has a longer stride length because of his longer legs. Even though we walked the same distance, he had fewer steps, which could be quite discouraging if he didn't understand the reason for the difference. Also, it makes it much easier for me to reach a step goal because I will accumulate more steps in the same amount of time. However, if we establish activity time goals, we will have to walk the same amount of time to reach our desired outcome. Therefore, it makes much more sense to use activity time goals with students so that they have an equal chance of reaching their goals. By the way, because my friend weighed 25 lb more than me, he burned more calories, even though he took fewer steps.

Determining the Distance You Moved

Many pedometer users want to know how far they have walked. It is possible to set personal goals in terms of miles; however, mileage measurements are not as accurate as activity time and steps. To determine distance, it is necessary to measure your stride length. Probably, the easiest method is to use the following steps:

1. Establish two lines that are 30-ft apart and mark them clearly with cones. If you have a volleyball court marked off in your teaching area, its width is 29 ft, 6 in. Add 6 in. to this distance, and you have a 30-ft distance that is easy to use.

2. Have students walk from the starting line to the opposite line and count the number of steps it takes them to cross the finish line. They should walk with the stride and speed they normally use with most of their everyday activities. To make it even more accurate, have students walk 10 to 15 steps around the area and to the start line without stopping. As they step on the starting line, they begin counting and stop as they cross the finish line.

3. Remember the number of steps taken and convert the steps taken to stride length (see Figure 15.4). To convert steps to distance, multiply stride length times the number of steps.

Pedometer Activities

Middle school and high school teachers find pedometers to be a valuable tool for hypothesis testing. Students can be challenged to answer questions such as, "Are students more active than parents?" or "Do you take more steps during a football class or an Ultimate Frisbee class?" A further idea may involve students

Number of Steps over a 30-ft distance	Stride Length (feet, inches)
8	3' 9"
9	3' 4"
10	3' 0"
11	2' 9"
12	2' 6"
13	2' 4"
14	2' 2"
15	2' 0"
16	1' 11"
17	1' 9"
18	1' 8"
19	1' 7"
20	1' 6"

FIGURE 15.4 Calculating stride length

modifying or inventing a game based on pedometer-determined steps. Another use for the pedometer is to help students to determine their leisure time physical activity with an aim to establish personal goals (as described previously) or develop ways to promote daily physical activity in and out of school.

The following activities illustrate a number of ways to use pedometers in a school setting. They are explained in greater detail in the resource book *Pedometer Power* (Pangrazi, Beighle, & Sidman, 2007).

- **Movement across the State or United States.** Students accumulate steps and measure their stride lengths so they can do the math to see how far they have traveled on a state or U.S. map. As they reach different checkpoints, students can participate in class discussions about foods, art, and various cultural sites.

- **Active or Inactive.** Students can participate in a variety of physical education lessons and try to predict which lessons are high activity and which are low activity. An enjoyable related activity is to try and guess how many steps they will take in the activity. Over time, they begin to understand the activity value of different sports and games.

- **A Safe Walk to School.** Walking to school can add 1,000 to 2,000 steps each to a student's activity level. This is a good activity for teaching students about safe walks, walks that increase the distance (and steps), and walks that avoid traffic.

- **School Steps Contest.** This is a schoolwide contest with all classes participating. The step counts of all students in each class, including the teacher, are added and then divided by the number of students. Finding the average number of steps for the entire class makes this a group competition and avoids putting down students who are less active. A gentle reminder here is that students should not reveal their step counts unless they choose to do so. A sensitive approach is to have the students place their step counts anonymously on a tally sheet.

- **Estimation—How Many Steps Does it Take?** Measure a distance that is exactly 1/8- or 1/4-mile in length. Students put on their pedometers, clear them at the starting line, and walk at a normal pace to the end of the distance. Depending on whether they walked a 1/8- or 1/4-mile distance, they multiply the number of steps they accumulated by eight or four. That is the number of steps it takes them to walk 1 mile.

Using Pedometers for Program Accountability

A common issue for physical education teachers is to find criteria for which they can be held accountable. Teachers have chosen fitness or skill development as outcomes they are willing to use as measures of their success. There are a number of issues that teachers might want to consider before choosing fitness or skill development as their success criteria. Fitness is most commonly used because tests have long been used in the school setting. However, such tests may not be a good choice because the increase in obesity among today's youth decreases fitness test performance. Common sense indicates that the increase in body fat in youth directly impacts aerobic endurance and various strength measures. In addition, the ability to respond to training is strongly affected by genetics (Bouchard, 1999), with some individuals showing little or no improvement with training. Another problem in using fitness as an outcome is that the amount of time currently available for physical activity during the school day limits chances of improving fitness to an extent measurable by fitness testing. Although many students will improve their fitness test scores purely as a result of maturation, this is not an accurate representation of the teacher's contribution to student fitness. Using fitness as the focal indicator of actual teaching success may be inviting failure.

Skill development is an important assessment outcome for physical education. However, a large part of skill performance is genetic endowment, much in the same way that some students are born better artists or musicians. Additionally, physical skills can be difficult to evaluate because of time constraints and the overall numbers of students seen by the physical education teacher. Perfection is never reached in the performance of physical skills. For example, even the best basketball and soccer players in the world miss as many shots as they make. Baseball players make an "out" three times out of 10 at bat. Rugby players fumble the ball and miss kicks. This does not imply that skills should not be emphasized or assessed, but considering the nature of physical skill performance is one of imperfection, it is asking a lot of teachers to base the success of their programs on the skill performance of students. Also, when evaluating skill development, it is apparent there are few instruments available that are valid, reliable, and easy to administer in a limited time environment. Teachers are aware of this "catch-22." If they take a lot of time to access skill performance, they will have little time left to teach those same skills for which they are being evaluated.

Why not base program accountability on an average school increase in daily physical activity? What could be more important for health and wellness than increasing the amount of activity students accumulate on a daily basis? All students can move and be physically active in settings both in and out of school. Unless they have a physical disability, all students can monitor their physical activity levels using pedometers. Most parents would be delighted if their youngsters were taught to live an active lifestyle. That might be one of the best legacies a physical education program could leave students.

Pedometers can be used to evaluate the baseline activity levels of students at or near the start of the school year. This can be followed up with regular monitoring a number of times throughout the school year. All students can set goals for increasing daily physical activity regardless of their genetic predisposition. Physical education teachers can establish goals for a number of subgroups including classes, grade levels, and gender. School administrators might accept a 2-percent increase in physical activity accumulated as a schoolwide goal over an 18-week period. Activity levels both in and out of schools could be used as separate outcomes. Out-of-school activity can be regarded as physical education homework. A program designed to increase the amount of physical activity students accumulate on a daily basis makes a valuable contribution to all students in the school environment.

WALKING: THE "REAL" LIFETIME ACTIVITY

Walking is an activity that almost all people can do. In fact, it forms the basis for all lifestyle physical activity. If one can't walk, the quality of life is dramatically impacted. Walking can be done by all, male or female, skilled or unskilled, fit or unfit. Therefore, a strong focus of physical education should be to teach the joy of moving and walking and trying to accumulate physical activity. Students can be taught to maximize the number of steps they take rather than trying to accomplish movement tasks in the fewest possible steps. Allied to this goal should be teaching the many benefits of being a walker. Walking has so many health-related benefits that if it could be put in the form a pill to be swallowed, it would immediately become a best seller on the drug market. Walking has few side effects and the benefits are many:

■ Maintaining weight. When combined with a healthy approach to eating, walking is key to a lifetime approach to weight management. Proper weight management results in decreasing the risks of many hypokinetic diseases, such as type 2 diabetes, heart disease, stroke, cancer, and osteoarthritis.

■ Managing blood pressure. Physical activity strengthens the heart and makes it more efficient so it pumps more blood with less effort. This results in less pressure on the arteries and vital organs. Walking appears to be as effective as some medications in reducing high blood pressure.

■ Boosting high-density lipoproteins (HDLs). This helps reduce low-density lipoproteins (LDLs) or "destructive cholesterol." LDLs increase plaque buildup in the arteries, which is a major cause of heart attacks.

■ Reducing the risk of type 2 diabetes. This disease is increasing at an alarming rate among young people. People at high risk of diabetes cut their risk in half by combining walking with lower fat intake and a 5- to 7-percent decrease in weight.

■ Decreasing the risk of heart attack. Three hours of walking a week was associated with a 30- to 40-percent lower risk of heart disease in women.

Walking has the advantage of not requiring any special equipment and of having a low injury rate. Walking, probably more than any other activity, will be done by students when they reach adulthood. One of the things that makes walking such a valuable skill for health maintenance is its simplicity. To receive the best health results, walking should be done at least five times per week for 30 minutes or more. Certainly, any amount of time for walking is beneficial. The 30 minutes of walking can be accumulated in three bouts of at least 10 minutes, but a 30-minute walk is recommended for youth in middle and high school classes. Only a few things need to be remembered to achieve maximum benefit:

1. Students should walk at a brisk pace with a comfortable stride and a good arm swing.

2. Students' walking pace should allow them to carry on a conversation without difficulty. If students find they can't walk and talk at the same time, encourage them to slow the pace slightly. For most youth in school, this will not be a problem, and the opportunity to socialize will be more important than the walk itself. The most important outcome is that they enjoy the experience and realize the benefits of walking.

3. The walking program in school is a great place to coordinate pedometer use. Students can begin to see how many steps they typically make in a specified amount of time. The Walk4Life pedometers measure both walking time and steps. All things being equal, the more steps gathered in a specified time, the higher the intensity of the walk.

Walking for Weight Management

Currently, it is estimated that nearly 16 percent of adolescents are overweight. Another 15 percent are "at risk" for becoming overweight (Beals, 2003). It is estimated that 70 percent of overweight adolescents will grow to be obese adults. Unfortunately, energy expenditure through physical activity has decreased over the last 10 years, while energy intake has increased. The supersize fast-food meals and high-fat content foods have certainly contributed to this increase in caloric consumption. Weight management always deals with both variables, intake and expenditure. People who are successful in maintaining proper body weight have usually learned to manage intake and increase physical activity. A number of studies show if only diet is managed for weight control, pounds lost in the treatment program will usually be regained as soon as the intervention stops. There is no question that restricting the diet in a highly controlled setting will result in weight loss. However, if this weight loss is not coupled with learning a new and more active lifestyle, success in weight management will be short lived.

Walking is probably the activity of choice for overweight students. It is easy on the joints, doesn't overly stress the cardiovascular system, and is not painful to perform. The old adage, "no pain–no gain" makes absolutely no sense for overweight students. Many of these students have already been turned off to physical activity because of many negative past experiences. Students who have been pushed in the past will push back when they become old enough to make personal decisions, and that usually means a sedentary lifestyle. Rekindling the joy of activity for these students will take an encouraging and kind approach. Walking is usually their choice of activity, and when coupled with pedometers, a new interest in being active can be ignited.

A question often asked is, "Does walking really make a difference in weight management?" The answer is, "Yes, it makes a difference, but you can always outeat the number of calories you burn." Consider the following: The number of calories burned during exercise depends on a number of factors, among them the speed of the walk and body size being two of the more important factors. Figure 15.5 shows the number of calories burned during a 30-minute walk based on body weight.

Assume a 140-lb student takes a 30-minute walk at a moderate pace and burns about 150 calories. Wanting to reward himself, this student decides to buy a typical-size candy bar in a food mart. Without looking at the calories, the student easily eats the candy bar and ingests 300 to 350 calories—a net gain in calories of 150 to 200 calories. In general terms, about 3,500 calories equals a pound of weight gained or lost depending on the energy intake and expenditure balance. Within 2 to 3 weeks, if this student continues to walk 30 minutes a day and add a candy bar to his normal food intake, a pound of weight will be gained. This shows why it is necessary to keep an eye on both physical activity and diet. It also illustrates how easy it is to gain weight even when a person is adding physical activity to his or her day. The one good thing to remember about increasing physical activity and decreasing sedentary behavior is that most people don't eat when they are active. Just being active may make it easier to decrease caloric intake.

Body Weight (lb)	Calories Burned in 30 Minutes
70	75
80	86
90	96
100	107
110	118
120	129
130	139
140	150
150	161
160	172
170	182
180	193
190	204
200	214

FIGURE 15.5 Calories burned in 30 minutes based on body weight

---

Recently, walking poles (similar to ski poles) have come in vogue, and they may be a boon to students who are overweight. They have been used for years in the Scandinavian countries, and research has shown that 25- to 30-percent more calories are burned as compared to walking without poles. The poles increase the heart rate by 10–15 beats and put more than 90 percent of the body's muscle mass to work. Additionally, they help absorb some of the impact on the knees and ankles that results in an increase in upper-body strength and a decrease in hip, knee, and foot injuries. Adding walking poles to the physical education program is another way to motivate students and realize greater results from their walking. An excellent Web site on using and purchasing walking poles can be found at www.walkingpoles.com.

Implementing a School Walking Program

Safety is always a key issue. When initiating a program, the walking should be done where all students are in view of the teacher. However, most people will want more variety than just walking around a track or field. If approved by the administration, walking courses around the school neighborhood can be established so students become familiar with many different walking paths and the time required to complete the circuit. All walking paths should be designed and mapped by the teacher prior to allowing students to follow them. Driving each pathway will allow you to write directions and map the mileage for each trail. Set up safety guidelines that are integrated into each path. Some safety guidelines to consider include the following:

- Always use the sidewalk. If a sidewalk is not available, walk on the left side of the roadway facing traffic.

- Stipulate that students must walk with another person or in a small group. If someone is injured or needs help, one of the group can return to the school for help.

- Do not run from aggressive dogs; this only makes the problem worse. Teach students to stop, face them, and give them a stern, "No!"

- Have students sign out, listing which path they are walking. If someone is missing, it will be much easier to track such students.

- If students have serious health problems, ensure they are cleared by the school nurse. Also, they should be required to wear a "medical tag" in case of an accident requiring emergency care.

■ Strongly encourage students to purchase walking or running shoes with reflective tape built into them. This can make it much easier for automobile drivers to see them.

■ Initiate a warm-up for students before the walk and teach them to cool down when they have finished walking. Walk a short distance, and stop and stretch the arms, legs, and back (see Chapter 16 for suggested stretches). When you have finished your walk, stretch one more time.

■ Drink plenty of water, whether it is cold or hot. Drink 8 ounces of water 15 minutes before the walk. If it is hot and dry, drink 6 ounces every 15 to 20 minutes during the walk. At the end of the walk, drink another 8 to 16 ounces of water. Waiting for the "thirst" signal as a reminder to drink may be too late. The sensation of "thirstiness" usually comes after the body is in need of water.

■ In cold weather, learn to layer clothing so a layer can be removed if it gets too hot. A number of layers of lighter clothing is much more useful than one heavy layer. Wear a hat, gloves, and scarf if necessary. In hot weather, wear loose, light-colored clothing, a hat, and sunglasses. Remember to put on sunscreen regardless of heat or cold; ultraviolet sun rays will quickly cause sun damage. Teachers should emphasize that sunscreen should always be applied when students will be outside for more than a few minutes.

Suggesting Walking Activities

1. "I Spy." Students take a score card with them on their walk. The card has a challenge on it. An example would be: "Identify as many different makes of cars as possible" or "List as many different birds and animals as you can." Different cards can be designed to create varying challenges. When the students complete their walks, the items they have identified can be discussed.

2. "Mixed Up Walks." Add some variations for limited amounts of time. For example, start with a backwards walk for 1 minute, then walk regularly for 1 minute, then do carioca steps for 1 minute, then walking regularly, and so on. Tasks assigned can be different types of movements or varying challenges such as, "Complete your walk by making 10 left turns on your route." The location of where students made a turn must be documented.

3. "Interval Walk." Set up a walking circuit with stretching and strength activities at each corner of the football field. For example, walk a lap, then do a standing stretch for 30 seconds, then walk half of a lap to a sitting stretch, then walk another lap, then do some abdominal activities, and then walk to a push-up station.

4. "Cross-Country Walking." Set up a cross-country walking race with teams in the class. Have a map set up for the walking course so there is a nice variety of walking areas. Students try to walk as fast as possible and receive a number at the finish line. The team with the lowest number of points is the winner. This is a competitive activity, but it can be approached in a positive and fun manner for students' efforts to walk fast.

5. Set up a walking "golf" tournament with hula hoops for holes and a tennis ball to be thrown by each student. Set up the course around your teaching space, with cones for the tees and hoops for the holes. Students throw the ball and then walk with their group to the hoop. Students use a scorecard to keep track of the number of throws for each hole.

6. "Treasure Hunt." Set up a walking course with a set of clues to follow to 10 sites. At the sites, you can tape a set of words that can be found and later arranged in a particular order to come up with a popular saying or jingle. Examples of the clues to follow could include cards with these hints: "A place for extra points on the south side"; "A place for H_2O"; "Fans sit here on the west side"; "Long jumpers take off here"; "Stand under this for the score of the game"; and "A place for trash."

7. "Poker Walk." Set out several decks of cards at various locations around the teaching area. Students walk to the areas and pick up one card without looking at the card. They walk to as many areas as possible within a time limit and then add up the points. Have a prize for high- and low-point totals and then change the rules each time. Set it up so anyone can win by just walking to the card areas, picking up the card, and then adding up the points at the end of the time limit.

8. "Know Your Community." Have the class take different walks and identify different types of businesses and professional offices along their routes. Different challenges can be listed, asking students to find different businesses or locations.

9. "Weekly Walking Calendar." Each week, students can be given a 5-day calendar that stipulates different types of things to do on their walks (e.g., Monday—walk with a friend; Tuesday—walk with walking poles; Wednesday—walk with hand weights; Thursday—walk 15 minutes in one direction and return to

the starting spot by retracing your path; and Friday—walk and use a pedometer to count your steps).

10. "Learn About Your Friend." Give students a series of questions on a card that will help them get to know a friend better. The goal is to walk and discover new things about a friend while moving.

11. "Off-Campus Walks." Students can gain extra credit by taking walks outside of the school day. This can be an excellent opportunity to use pedometers to track their walks. They can record their steps and activity time and report back to class on both measures.

STUDY STIMULATORS AND REVIEW QUESTIONS

1. What is the impact of adding at least 60 minutes of daily physical activity to your lifestyle?

2. What are the levels of the Physical Activity Pyramid? How much time should be spent on each of the components on a weekly basis?

3. What level in the activity pyramid forms the foundation for good health? How can students be taught to change their activity habits to meet the minimum activity requirements?

4. What can pedometers measure? Which of the measurements is most accurate and useful for the majority of students? Why?

5. What are the steps to follow when teaching students to develop personal goals? When should the goals be reset?

6. What are the three most common areas physical educators use to establish the accountability of their programs? Which of the three might be most meaningful to choose as a program outcome?

7. Why is walking often called the "real" lifetime activity?

8. How can walking play an important role in weight management?

9. What are the basic steps to follow when implementing a walking program in physical education?

10. How can student physical activity outside of the school environment be increased?

11. Create three walking activities that could be assigned to students for after-school physical activity.

REFERENCES AND SUGGESTED READINGS

American College of Sports Medicine. (2000). *ACSM's guidelines for exercise testing and prescription* (6th ed.). Philadelphia: Lippincott, Williams and Wilkins.

Beals, K. A. (2003). Addressing an epidemic: Treatment strategies for youth obesity. *ACSM Fit Society Page,* Spring, 9–11.

Beighle, A., Pangrazi, R. P., & Vincent, S. D. (2001). Pedometers, physical activity, and accountability. *Journal of Physical Education, Recreation, and Dance,* 72(9), 16–19.

Bouchard, C. (1999). Heredity and health related fitness. In C. B. Corbin and R. P. Pangrazi (Eds.), *Toward a better understanding of physical fitness and activity.* Scottsdale, AZ: Holcomb Hathaway Publishers.

Cooper Institute. (2004). *Fitnessgram/activitygram test administration manual* (3rd ed.). Champaign, IL: Human Kinetics Publishers.

Corbin, C. B., & Lindsey, R. (2007). *Fitness for life* (5th ed.). Champaign, IL: Human Kinetics.

Corbin, C. B., & Pangrazi, R. P. (1992). Are American children and youth fit? *Research Quarterly for Exercise and Sport,* 63(2), 96–106.

Corbin, C. B., & Pangrazi, R. P. (2004). *Physical activity for children: A statement of guidelines for children ages 5–12.* Reston, VA: National Association for Sport and Physical Education.

Crouter, S. C., Schneider, P. L., Karabulut, M., & Bassett Jr., D. R. (2003). Validity of 10 electronic pedometers for measuring steps, distance, and energy cost. *Medicine and Science in Sports and Exercise,* 35(8), 1455–1460.

Decker, J., & Mize, M. (2002). *Walking games and activities.* Champaign, IL: Human Kinetics Publishers.

Hatano, Y. (1993). Use of the pedometer for promoting daily walking exercise. *International Council for Health, Physical Education and Recreation,* 29, 4–28.

Kilanowski, C. K., Consalvi, A. R., & Epstein, L. H. (1999). Validation of an electronic pedometer for measurement of physical activity in children. *Pediatric Exercise Science,* 11, 63–68.

Morgan, Jr., C. F., Pangrazi, R. P., & Beighle, A. (2003). Using pedometers to promote physical activity in physical education. *Journal of Physical Education, Recreation, and Dance,* 74(7), 33–38.

Pangrazi, R. P., Beighle, A., & Sidman, C. L. (2007). *Pedometer power: Using pedometers in school and community* (2nd ed.). Champaign, IL: Human Kinetics Publishers.

Pate, R. R., Pratt, M., Blair, S. N., Haskill, W. L., Macera, E. A., & Bouchard, C. (1995). Physical activity and public health. *Journal of the American Medical Association,* 273(5), 402–407.

Plowman, S. A. (1993). Physical fitness and healthy low back function. *Physical Activity and Fitness Research Digest,* 1(3), 1–8.

President's Council on Physical Fitness and Sports. (2004). *The President's Challenge Physical Activity and Fitness Awards Program.* Bloomington, IN: Author.

Sallis, J. F., & Patrick, K. (1994). Physical activity guidelines for adolescents: Consensus statement. *Pediatric Exercise Science, 6*(4), 302–314.

Schneider, P. L., Crouter, S. E., Lukajic, O., & Bassett, Jr., D. R. (2003). Accuracy and reliability of 10 pedometers for measuring steps over a 400-m walk. *Medicine and Science in Sports and Exercise, 35*(10), 1779–1784.

Shaw, J. M., & Snow-Harter, C. (1995). Osteoporosis and physical activity. *Physical Activity and Fitness Research Digest, 2*(3), 1–8.

Trost, S. G., Pate, R., R., Freedson, P. S., Sallis, J. F., & Taylor, W. C. (2000). Using objective physical activity measures with youth: How many days of monitoring are needed? *Medicine and Science in Sports and Exercise, 32*(2), 426–431.

U.S. Department of Health and Human Services. (1996). *Physical activity and health: A report of the surgeon general.* Atlanta, GA: U.S. Department of Health and Human Services, Centers for Disease Control and Prevention, National Center for Chronic Disease Prevention and Health Promotion.

U.S. Public Health Service. (2000). *Healthy people 2010. National health promotion and disease objectives.* Washington, DC: U.S. Government Printing Office.

Vincent, S. D., & Pangrazi, R. P. (2002). Does reactivity exist in children when measuring activity levels with pedometers? *Pediatric Exercise Science, 14*(1), 56–63.

Vincent-Graser, S. D., Pangrazi, R. P., & Vincent, W. (in press). Effects of placement, attachment, and weight classification on pedometer accuracy. *Journal of Physical Activity and Health.*

WEB SITES

Walking Programs

http://walking.about.com

http://walking.about.com/cs/measure/tp/pedometerprog.htm

www.accustep10000.org

www.americaonthemove.org

www.steptracker.com

Videos and Instructional Materials

http://walking.about.com/cs/poles/a/polesrutlin_3.htm

www.exrx.net/

Pedometers

http://walk4life.com/

http://walking.about.com/cs/measure/tp/pedometer.htm

walking.about.com/cs/measure/bb/bybpedometer.htm

www.pecentral.org/pedometry/

NATIONAL STANDARDS FOR PHYSICAL EDUCATION*

STANDARD 1 Demonstrates competency in motor skills and movement patterns needed to perform a variety of physical activities.

STANDARD 2 Demonstrates understanding of movement concepts, principles, strategies, and tactics as they apply to the learning and performance of physical activities.

STANDARD 3 Participates regularly in physical activity.

STANDARD 4 Achieves and maintains a health-enhancing level of physical fitness.

STANDARD 5 Exhibits responsible personal and social behavior that respects self and others in physical activity settings.

STANDARD 6 Values physical activity for health, enjoyment, challenge, self-expression, and/or social interaction.

ESSENTIAL COMPONENTS OF A QUALITY PROGRAM

COMPONENT 1 A quality physical education program is organized around content standards that offer direction and continuity to instruction and evaluation.

COMPONENT 2 A quality program is student centered and based on the developmental urges, characteristics, and interests of students.

COMPONENT 3 Quality physical education makes physical activity and motor-skill development the core of the program.

COMPONENT 4 Physical education programs teach management skills and self-discipline.

COMPONENT 5 Quality programs emphasize inclusion of all students.

COMPONENT 6 In a quality physical education setting, instruction focuses on the process of learning skills rather than the product or outcome of the skill performance.

COMPONENT 7 A quality physical education program teaches lifetime activities that students can use to promote their health and personal wellness.

COMPONENT 8 Quality physical education teaches cooperative and responsibility skills and helps students develop sensitivity to diversity and gender issues.

*Reprinted from Moving Into the Future: National Standards for Physical Education, 2nd ed. (2004), with permission from the National Association for Sport and Physical Education (NASPE), 1900 Association Dr., Reston, VA 20191-1599.

16

Physical Fitness

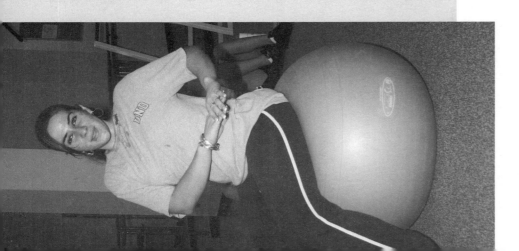

CHAPTER SUMMARY

The purpose of this chapter is to explain the importance of including physical fitness activities in the lesson plan and identifying novel strategies and techniques that could be used to implement fitness into the lesson structure. A variety of exercises and techniques that can be used to develop physical fitness are discussed. Fitness is defined into two categories: health related and skill related. Health-related fitness is selected for the vast majority of people. A selected few who care about their athletic performance or personal accomplishments will choose skill-related fitness as their outcome of choice.

Fitness performance is strongly controlled by genetic factors, including how students respond to training. The relationship between activity and fitness performance is weak and leads to misconceptions about the importance of training and passing fitness tests. Newer fitness tests evaluate the amount of fitness necessary for good health using criterion standards. Secondary school students need the opportunity to experience and select fitness routines that are useful and motivating to them personally. Physical fitness activities should be offered as a positive contribution to total wellness. These activities should not be used as punishment. Using a wide variety of fitness routines helps motivate students toward a lifetime of fitness activities. The school physical education program should help students make the transition into community-based physical activity programs, particularly health and fitness clubs. Instruction and participation relative to physical fitness should be done in a positive atmosphere.

STUDENT OUTCOMES

After reading this chapter, you will be able to:

- Differentiate between skill-related and health-related physical fitness.

- Understand how genetic endowment impacts physical fitness performance on skill-related tests.

- Identify the various components of physical fitness and how they can be measured and evaluated.

- Describe the impact that physical fitness can have upon the overall wellness of a person.

- Explain the relationship between fitness and activity and what impact this relationship has on performance on fitness tests.

- Cite strategies and techniques to motivate students to develop and maintain physical fitness.

- Demonstrate the instructional procedures associated with exercise routines included in this chapter.

- Develop new and different physical fitness routines that will accomplish fitness objectives and motivate students to continue to be active for a lifetime.

A ll students want to be fit and active. Physical education programs that do not make time for fitness development indirectly teach students that fitness is not important for a healthy lifestyle. At the secondary school level, students should have the opportunity to experience and design fitness routines that are useful and motivating to them personally. Physical fitness activity should be offered as a positive contribution to total wellness. It should be something that benefits those who participate and not be used as punishment for misbehavior.

THE FITNESS OF AMERICA'S YOUTH

A popular point of view among physical education teachers is that youth today are less fit than they were in the past. This opinion is often used as a justification for more physical education time in the schools. Comparative research (Corbin & Pangrazi, 1992) suggests that the fitness of today's youngsters has not degenerated, and they perform at a level similar to students 40 years ago. When data were compared from the last four national youth fitness surveys (1957 to 1985) conducted by the American Alliance for Health, Physical Education, Recreation, and Dance (AAHPERD) and the President's Council on Physical Fitness and Sports, the only items used in all four surveys were pull-

ups and the flexed-arm hang. Youngsters, both boys and girls, showed an increase in upper-body strength when these two items were compared over 4 decades. Unfortunately, it is difficult to compare other areas of fitness because the test items were changed on a regular basis. The area where youths have shown a serious and documented decline is body composition. Currently, 16 percent of youth age 6 through 19 years old (1999–2002) are overweight, and another 31 percent are at risk for being overweight (85th percentile of sex-specific body mass index [BMI]-for-age growth charts) (Hedley, et al., 2004). This large increase in overweight youth takes its toll on fitness scores. Common sense would dictate that if someone can do 50 push-ups at normal weight, putting 20 lb of sand on his or her back will decrease the number of push-ups he or she is able to perform. Body fat is dead weight and does not contribute to muscular or cardiovascular performance. Thus, all strength and aerobic performance scores decrease as being overweight increases at a rapid rate among youths.

Genetic Endowment and Fitness Performance

Physical fitness tests often lead students down a path of failure regardless of how much they train to improve. A significant amount of fitness test performance is explained by heredity (Bouchard, Dionne, Simoneau, & Boulay, 1992; Bouchard, 1999). Various factors, such as environment, nutrition, heredity, and maturation, affect fitness performance as reflected in physical fitness test scores. Research clearly shows that heredity and maturation strongly impact fitness scores (Bouchard, Dionne, Simoneau, & Boulay, 1992; Bouchard, 1999; Pangrazi & Corbin, 1990). In fact, these factors may have more to do with youth fitness scores than activity level. Lifestyle and environmental factors can also make a difference. For example, nutrition is a lifestyle factor that can influence test scores, and environmental conditions (heat, humidity, and pollution) strongly modify test performances. Fitness performance is only partially determined by activity and training.

Some youths have a definite advantage on tests because of the types of muscle fibers they inherit. Others inherit a predisposition to perform well on tests. In other words, even in an untrained state, some students score better because of heredity. On the other hand, some youngsters who train will not score as well as others who are untrained because of their genetic predispositions. Beyond heredity lies another genetic factor that predisposes some youngsters to high performance. Recent research has shown that trainability is inherited (Bouchard, Dionne, Simoneau, & Boulay, 1992; Bouchard, 1999), which means some people receive more benefit from training (regular physical activity) than others. As an example, assume that two students perform the same amount of activity throughout a semester. Student A shows dramatic improvement immediately, while Student B does not. Student A simply responds more favorably to training than Student B. Student B inherited a system that is responsive to exercise. Student A not only gets fit and scores well on the test but gets feedback that says, "The activity works—it makes me fit." The less-responsive student scores poorly, receives no feedback, and concludes that, "Activity doesn't improve my fitness, so why try?" The unfortunate thing is that Student B will improve in fitness but to a lesser degree than Student A and will take longer to show improvement. Student B will probably never achieve the fitness level attained by Student A. Trainability and genetic endowment differences limit performance, making it important to have different expectations for students.

Does this mean there is little use in helping students become more fit and active? Certainly not. Whereas heredity plays an important role in fitness, all youngsters benefit from regular physical activity. Even though some students will not show much improvement in their physical performance, physical activity offers them health benefits. Regardless of desired outcomes, less-gifted students will always need more encouragement and positive feedback because their improvement will be in smaller increments and of a lesser magnitude.

The Relationship Between Fitness Results and Activity

Teachers and parents want to believe that fitness in youngsters is primarily a reflection of how active they are. A common belief is that because students excessively watch television and play video games, they score poorly on fitness tests. A weak relationship exists between activity and fitness test performance among adolescents (Morrow & Freedson, 1994). The mistaken belief that being physically active builds fitness may lead teachers to the conclusion that youngsters who score high on fitness tests are active, and those who don't score well are inactive. Physical activity is an important variable in fitness development, but other factors can be of equal or greater importance. If teachers make the mistake of assuming that a student is inactive because of scores on a fitness test, misunderstandings and misinterpretations can result.

For example, consider the problems that occur when teachers mistakenly assume that fitness and activity are highly related. If youngsters are encouraged to do regular exercise and training to improve their fitness scores, many will take the challenge seriously. When fitness tests are given, students will expect to do well on the tests if they have been training regularly, and of course, teachers will also expect them to do well. If, however, they receive scores that are lower than expected, they will be disappointed. They will be especially discouraged if the teacher concludes that their low fitness status is a reflection of not training and being active. Such a conclusion as, "You are not as fit as you should be compared to other students, therefore you have not been active," is often not true. This type of dialogue from teachers will cause a loss of self-esteem and respect between student and teacher.

The other side of this issue can just as easily be untrue, that is, assuming that youngsters who make high scores on fitness tests are training the hardest and being the most active. Youngsters who are genetically gifted may be inactive yet still perform well on fitness tests. Students are always aware of peers who don't train, aren't active, and maintain poor health habits yet still perform well on fitness tests. If teachers do not teach students why these cases occur, students soon question the integrity of the teacher. Teach students that some people are most gifted in the area of fitness performance. It is easier for such students to show fitness improvement over those students who lack the genetic predisposition for fitness performance.

HEALTH-RELATED AND SKILL-RELATED PHYSICAL FITNESS

A general definition regarding the precise nature of physical fitness has never been universally accepted. However, two types of physical fitness are most often recognized: health-related physical fitness and skill-related physical fitness. The differentiation between physical fitness related to functional health and physical performance related to athletic ability makes it easier to develop proper fitness objectives and goals for youngsters. The components of health-related physical fitness are a subset of skill-related fitness components. Health-related fitness is characterized by moderate and regular physical activity as described in Chapter 15. The lifetime activities in Chapter 20 are often used by adults as a medium to maintain health-related fitness. These activities are designed for the masses who are generally unwilling to exercise at high intensities. Health-related activities can be integrated into regular everyday lifestyles.

In contrast, skill-related physical fitness not only includes the health-related components, but also components that are in part controlled by genetic factors. Skill-related fitness is the right choice for people who want to perform at a high level (usually in an athletic setting) but is less acceptable for the masses because it requires training and exercising at high intensities. In addition, many individuals cannot reach high levels of skill-related fitness because of their genetic limitations. The following discussion describes and contrasts the differences between health-related and skill-related fitness.

Health-Related Physical Fitness

Teaching health-related fitness should be the focus in physical education. The benefit of health-related fitness is that all students can improve their health status through daily physical activity. Health-related fitness is one of the few areas where all students can succeed regardless of ability level and genetic limitations. Students can be assured that, "If you are willing to be active, you will enhance your health status." This contrasts with skill-related fitness, which is sport performance oriented and influenced by genetic traits and abilities. A primary reason for teaching health-related fitness is that it gives students activity habits they can use throughout their life spans.

Health-related physical fitness includes those aspects of physiological function that offer protection from diseases related to a sedentary lifestyle. It can be improved and/or maintained through regular physical activity. Specific components include cardiovascular fitness, body composition (ratio of leanness to fatness), abdominal strength and endurance, and flexibility. When measuring health-related fitness, criterion standards are used to indicate levels of good health. The Fitnessgram (Cooper Institute, 2004) uses criterion-referenced health standards that represent good health instead of traditional percentile rankings often found in skill-related fitness tests (see Chapter 10). These standards represent a level of fitness that offers some degree of protection against diseases resulting from sedentary living. The Fitnessgram uses an approach that classifies fitness performance into two categories: needs improvement and healthy fitness zone (HFZ). All students are encouraged to score in the HFZ; however, there is little health advantage to scoring outside the HFZ. Criterion-referenced health standards do not compare students against each other. The goal is for all students to achieve and move their personal performance into the HFZ.

Health-Related Fitness Components

Health-related physical fitness includes aspects of physiological function that offer protection from diseases caused by a sedentary lifestyle. Health-related fitness is often called *functional fitness* because it helps ensure that a person will be able to function effectively in everyday tasks. Such fitness can be improved and/or maintained through daily moderate physical activity. Specific components include cardiovascular fitness, body composition (ratio of leanness to fatness), abdominal strength and endurance, and flexibility. These are the components measured in the Fitnessgram test (Cooper Institute, 2004). The following are the major components of health-related fitness.

Cardiovascular Fitness

Aerobic fitness is important for a healthy lifestyle and may be the most important element of fitness. Cardiovascular endurance is the ability of the heart, the blood vessels, and the respiratory system to deliver oxygen efficiently over an extended period of time. At least 60 minutes of moderate to vigorous aerobic activity should be accumulated daily (Corbin & Pangrazi, 2007) to ensure good health. Activities that stimulate development in this area are walking, jogging, biking, rope jumping, aerobic dance, swimming, and active sports such as basketball or soccer.

The exercise prescription model is best for individuals interested in cardiovascular or aerobic fitness improvement. Among those for whom these guidelines are particularly desirable are athletes and those in jobs requiring great physical demands, such as law enforcement or fire safety. To improve skill-related cardiovascular fitness, the FIT (frequency, intensity, and time) formula is used to identify the necessary exercise prescription. Working out for the sake of fitness improvement should be done at least 3 days per week (frequency), at a heart rate of 70 to 85 percent of predicted maximum heart rate (intensity), and for at least 20 minutes (time) (American College of Sports Medicine [ACSM], 2000). Maximum heart rate is calculated roughly as 220 minus your age. Thus, the maximum heart rate for a 15-year-old student would be $220 - 15 = 205$. For this student, 70 to 85 percent of 205 would mean keeping the heart rate between 144 and 174 beats per minute while participating in aerobic activities.

Body Composition

Body composition is an integral part of health-related fitness. Body composition is the proportion of body fat to lean body mass. After the thickness of selected skinfolds has been measured, the percentage of body fat can be extrapolated from tables. The conversion of skinfold thickness to percent body fat can be a less-accurate measure, but it is easier to communicate to parents than skinfold thickness. Considering the wellness status of individuals is dependent on body composition, students must learn about concepts and consequences in this area.

Another way to determine body composition is by using the body mass index (BMI). BMI is a number calculated by using a person's weight and height. BMI is being used in many states to evaluate body fatness among students. It is generally a reliable method and has the advantage of providing feedback without touching the body, for example, skinfold measurements. Research shows that BMI correlates to direct measures of body fat such as underwater weight. The Centers for Disease Control and Prevention (CDC) and the American Academy of Pediatrics recommend that BMI be used to screen for overweight youth. For teenagers, a sex- and age-specific table of percentiles is used to determine the BMI.

Flexibility

Flexibility is the range of movement through which a joint or sequence of joints can move. Inactive individuals lose flexibility, whereas frequent movement helps retain the range of movement. Through stretching activities, the length of muscles, tendons, and ligaments is increased. The ligaments and tendons retain their elasticity through constant use. People who are flexible may be less subject to injury in sport, usually possess sound posture, and have less lower-back pain.

Muscular Strength and Endurance

Strength is the ability of muscles to exert force; it is an important fitness component that facilitates learning motor skills. Most activities in physical education do not build strength in the areas where it is most needed: the arm–shoulder girdle and the abdominal region. Muscular endurance is the ability to exert force over an extended period. Endurance postpones the onset of fatigue so that activity can be performed for lengthy periods. Most sport activities require that muscular skills, such as throwing, kicking, and striking, be performed many times without fatigue.

Skill-Related Fitness Components

Skill-related fitness includes those physical qualities that enable a person to perform in sport activities. For years, the primary fitness test for teachers was the AAHPERD Youth Fitness Test (1987). Today this test is known as the President's Challenge Youth Fitness Test (President's Council on Physical Fitness and Sports, 2007). Skill-related fitness is closely related to athletic ability. The traits of speed, agility, coordination, and so on form the basis of the ability to excel in sports. Because skill-related fitness is strongly influenced by one's natural or inherited traits, it is difficult for the majority of students to achieve. In contrast to health-related tests, skill-related fitness tests often use norm-referenced standards where students are compared in terms of where they rank compared to their peers. For some students, the goal becomes trying to do better than other students rather than learning to do the best they can regardless of peer scores.

Skill-related fitness components are useful for performing motor tasks related to sports and athletics. The ability to perform well depends largely on the genetic endowment of the individual. Where it is possible for all students to perform adequately in health-related fitness activities, it is difficult, if not impossible, for a large number of youngsters to excel in this area of fitness. Asking students to "try harder" only adds to their frustration if they lack native ability because they see their more-skilled friends perform well without effort. When skill-related fitness is taught, it should be accompanied by an explanation of why some students can perform well with a minimum of effort whereas others, no matter how hard they try, never excel. Many examples can be used to illustrate genetic differences, such as speed, jumping ability, strength, and physical size in individuals. The bottom line for teachers is to understand that some students will want to work hard to improve their fitness performance while a majority will probably be satisfied to play, be active, and enjoy their bodies in a less demanding manner. For these students, health-related fitness will be an important outcome.

Skill-related physical fitness includes the health-related items listed previously plus the following:

Agility

Agility is the ability of the body to change position rapidly and accurately while moving. Wrestling and football are examples of sports that require agility.

Balance

Balance refers to the body's ability to maintain a state of equilibrium while remaining stationary or moving. Maintaining balance is essential to all sports but is especially important in the performance of gymnastic activities.

Coordination

Coordination is the ability of the body to smoothly and successfully perform more than one motor task at the same time. Needed for football, baseball, tennis, soccer, and other sports that require hand–eye and foot–eye skills, coordination can be developed by repeatedly practicing the skill to be learned.

Power

Power is the ability to transfer energy explosively into force. To develop power, a person must practice activities that are required to improve strength but at a faster rate involving sudden bursts of energy. Skills requiring power include high jumping, long jumping, performing the shot put, throwing, and kicking.

Speed

Speed is the ability of the body to perform movement in a short period of time. Usually associated with running forward, speed is essential for the successful performance of most sports and general locomotor movement skills.

CREATION OF A POSITIVE FITNESS EXPERIENCE

How the fitness program is taught increases the possibility of students being "turned on" to activity. Fitness activity in and of itself is neither good nor bad. Instead, how fitness activities are taught influences what youngsters feel about making fitness a part of their lifestyles. Physical educators should keep in mind that the majority of youth (unless it is a class designed for athletes) are more interested in good health than high levels of skill-related fitness. Consider the following strategies to make activity a positive learning experience.

Individualize Fitness Workloads

Students who are expected to participate in fitness activities and find themselves unable to perform exercises are not likely to develop a positive attitude toward physical activity. Allow students to determine personal workloads and capabilities. Use time (instead of repetitions and distance) as the workload variable and ask youngsters to do the best they can within the time limit. People dislike and fear experiences of failure they perceive to be forced upon them from an external source. Voluntary long-term exercise is more probable when individuals are internally driven to do their best. Fitness experiences that give control to students offer better opportunity for development of positive attitudes toward activity.

Present a Variety of Physical Fitness Routines and Exercises

Teaching a variety of fitness opportunities decreases the monotony of doing the same routines week after week and increases the likelihood that students will experience fitness activities that are enjoyable. Most youngsters are willing to accept activities they dislike if they know there will be a chance to experience routines they enjoy in the near future. A yearlong routine of "doing calisthenics and running a mile" forces students, regardless of ability and interest, to participate in the same routine whether they like it or not. When youngsters know a new and exciting routine is on the horizon, their tolerance for routines or activities they dislike will increase. Avoiding potential boredom by systematically changing fitness activities is a significant way to help students perceive fitness in a positive way.

Give Students Meaningful Feedback

Teacher feedback contributes to the way students view fitness activities. Immediate, accurate, and specific feedback regarding performance encourages continued participation. Provided in a positive manner, this feedback can stimulate youths to extend their participation habits outside the confines of the gymnasium. Reinforce everybody, not just those who perform at high levels. All youngsters need feedback and reinforcement, even if they are incapable of performing at an elite level.

Teach Physical Skills and Fitness

Physical education programs teach skill development and fitness. Some states mandate fitness testing, which may make teachers worry that their students "will not pass." This concern can lead to the skill development portion of physical education being sacrificed in order to increase the emphasis on teaching fitness. Skills are the tools that most adults use to attain fitness. The majority of individuals maintain fitness through various skill-based activities, such as tennis, badminton, swimming, golf, basketball, aerobics, bicycling, and the like. People have a much greater propensity to participate as adults if they feel competent in an activity. Skills and physical activity go hand in hand for an active lifestyle.

Be a Positive Role Model

Appearance, attitude, and actions speak loudly about teachers and their values regarding fitness. Teachers who display physical vitality, take pride in being active, participate in fitness activities with students, and are physically fit positively influence youngsters to maintain an active lifestyle. It is unreasonable to expect teachers to complete a fitness routine each period, 5 days a week. However, teachers must exercise with a class periodically to assure students they are willing to do what they ask them to do.

Foster the Attitudes of Students

Attitudes dictate whether youths choose to participate in activity. Teachers and parents sometimes take the approach of forcing fitness on students in order to "make them all fit." This can lead to resentment and insensitivity to the feelings of students. Training does not equate to lifetime fitness. When youngsters are trained without concern for their feelings, it is possible the result will be fit students who dislike physical activity. Once a negative attitude is developed, it is difficult to change. This does not mean that youngsters should avoid fitness activity. It means that fitness participation must be a positive and success-based experience. Avoid funneling youngsters into one type of fitness activity. For example, running may be an inappropriate activity for overweight youth, and lean, uncoordinated students may not enjoy contact activities. The fitness experience must be a challenge rather than a threat. A challenge is an experience that participants feel they can accomplish. In contrast, a threat appears to be an impossible undertaking—one where there is no use trying. As a final note, remember that whether activity is a challenge or a threat depends on the perceptions of the learner, not the instructor. Listen to students express their concerns. Don't tell them to "do it for your own good."

Start Easy and Progress Slowly

Fitness development is a journey, not a destination. No teacher wants students to get fit in school only to become inactive adults. A rule of thumb is to allow students to start at a level they can accomplish. This means offering the option of self-directed workloads within a specified time frame. Don't force students into heavy workloads too soon. It is impossible to start a fitness program at a level that is too easy. Start with success and gradually increase the workload to avoid the discouragement of failure and excessive muscle soreness. When students successfully accomplish activities, they learn a system of self-talk that expresses exercise behavior in a positive light. This avoids the common practice of self-criticism when students fail to live up to their own or others' standards.

Encourage Activities that Are Positively Addicting

Teachers want students to exercise throughout adulthood. Certain activities may be more likely to stimulate exercise outside of school. Some evidence (Glasser, 1976) shows that if the following activity conditions are met, exercise will become positively addicting and a necessary part of one's life. These steps imply that many individual activities, including walking, jogging, hiking, biking, and the like, are activities that students might regularly use for fitness during adulthood.

- The activity must be noncompetitive; the student chooses and wants to do it.

- It must not require a great deal of mental effort.

- The activity can be done alone—without a partner or teammates.

- Students must believe in the value of the exercise for improving health and general welfare.

- Participants must believe that the activity will become easier and more meaningful if they persist. To become addicting, the activity must be done for at least 6 months.

- The activity should be accomplished in such a manner that the participant is not self-critical.

EXERCISES FOR DEVELOPING BALANCED FITNESS ROUTINES

Exercises discussed in this section are divided into four groups. All groups of exercises should be represented when developing routines that exercise all parts of the body. The first group consists of warm-up and flexibility activities. These groups of exercises primarily develop muscular strength and endurance in the upper body, midsection, and lower body. When exercise routines are planned, they should contain a balance of activities from all groups. The following instructional procedures (and exercises to avoid) should be considered carefully when developing exercise routines.

Instructional Procedures

Fitness instruction is exclusively dedicated to the presentation of a variety of fitness activities. The following suggestions can aid in the successful implementation of the fitness module.

1. Fitness instruction should be preceded by a 2- to 3-minute warm-up period. The introductory activity is useful for this purpose because it allows youngsters the opportunity to "loosen up" and prepare for strenuous activity.

2. The fitness portion of the daily lesson, including the warm-up, should not extend beyond 15 to 20 minutes. Some argue that more time is needed to develop adequate fitness. However, there is a limited amount of time for fitness and skill instruction. Because skill instruction is part of a balanced physical education program, compromise is necessary to ensure that all phases of the program are covered.

3. Activities should be vigorous in nature, exercise all body parts, and cover the major components of fitness.

4. A variety of fitness routines comprising sequential exercises for total body development is a recommended alternative to a yearlong program of regimented calisthenics and running. Considering different people like different forms of exercise, a diverse array of routines should replace the traditional approach of doing the same routine day in and day out.

5. The fitness routine should be conducted during the first part of the lesson. Relegating fitness to the end of the lesson does little to enhance the image of exercise. Further, by having the exercise phase of the lesson precede skill instruction, the concept

of getting fit to play sport, instead of playing sport to get fit, is reinforced.

6. Teachers should assume an active role in fitness instruction. Students respond positively to being a role model. This does not imply doing all exercises with all classes; however, students must see an instructor's willingness to exercise.

7. When determining workloads for exercise, the available alternatives are time, speed, or repetitions. It is best to base the workloads on time rather than on a specified number of repetitions so youngsters can adjust their workloads within personal limits. Having students perform as many repetitions as they are capable of in a given amount of time will result in successful and positive feelings about activity.

8. Use audiotapes to time fitness activity segments so teachers are free to move throughout the area and offer individualized instruction. Participation and instruction should be enthusiastic and focus on positive outcomes. If the instructor does not enjoy physical fitness participation, such an attitude will be apparent to students.

9. Fitness activities should never be assigned as punishment. Such a practice teaches students that push-ups and running are things you do when you misbehave. The opportunity to exercise should be a privilege as well as an enjoyable experience. Think of the money adults spend to join a health club. Take a positive approach and offer students a chance to jog with a friend when they do something well. This not only allows them the opportunity to visit with the friend, but to exercise on a positive note. Be an effective salesperson; sell the joy of activity and benefits of physical fitness to students.

10. When a new exercise is introduced, it should be demonstrated and broken into components, and its value should be explained. It should be practiced at a slower-than-normal pace and then accelerated. Proper form should be emphasized.

11. Proper form is important when performing exercises. For instance, in exercises requiring the arms to be held in front of the body or overhead, the abdominal wall needs to be contracted to maintain proper positioning of the pelvis. The feet should be pointed reasonably straight ahead, the chest should be up, and the head and shoulders should be in good postural alignment.

12. Vary the aerobic activity used in classes. Too often, such activity consists of everybody running a lap.

This practice is not only boring, it does little to meet the personal needs of all students. Exercise substitutes for running might be interval training, rope jumping, obstacle courses, astronaut drills, brisk walking, rhythmic aerobic exercise, and parachute movements.

AVOIDANCE OF HARMFUL PRACTICES AND EXERCISES

The following points contraindicate certain exercise practices and should be considered when offering fitness instruction. For in-depth coverage of contraindicated exercises, consult *Concepts of Fitness and Wellness* by Corbin and colleagues (2008).

1. The following techniques (Macfarlane, 1993) should be avoided when performing abdominal exercises that lift the head and trunk off the floor:

   ■ Avoid placing the hands behind the head or high on the neck. This may cause hyperflexion and injury to the discs when the elbows swing forward to help pull the body up.

   ■ Keep the knees bent. Straight legs cause the hip flexor muscles to be used earlier and more forcefully, making it difficult to maintain a proper pelvic tilt.

   ■ Don't hold the feet on the floor. Having another student secure the feet places more force on the lumbar vertebrae and may lead to lumbar hyperextension.

   ■ Don't lift the buttocks and lumbar region off the floor. This also causes the hip flexor muscles to contract vigorously.

2. Two types of stretching activities have been used to develop flexibility. Ballistic stretching (strong bouncing movements) formerly was the most common stretching used, but this has been discouraged for many years because it was thought to increase delayed-onset muscle soreness. The other flexibility activity, static stretching, involves increasing the stretch to the point of discomfort, backing off slightly to where the position can be held comfortably, and maintaining the stretch for an extended time. Static stretching has been advocated because it was thought to reduce muscle soreness and prevent injury. A study (Smith et al., 1993) has disputed the muscle soreness and tissue damage theory with findings that showed ballistic and static stretching both increase muscle soreness. In fact, the static stretching actually induced significantly more soreness than did ballistic stretching. Static stretching is a better choice for improved

flexibility, but ballistic stretching is probably not as harmful as once thought.

3. If forward flexion is done from a sitting position in an effort to touch the toes, the bend should be from the hips, not from the waist, and should be done with one leg flexed. To conform with this concern, the new Fitnessgram sit-and-reach test item is now performed with one leg flexed to reduce stress on the lower back.

4. Straight-leg raises from a supine position should be avoided because they may strain the lower back. The problem can be somewhat alleviated by placing the hands under the small of the back, but it is probably best to avoid such exercises.

5. Deep knee bends (full squats) and the duckwalk should be avoided. They may cause damage to the knee joints and have little developmental value. Much more beneficial is flexing the knee joint to 90° and returning to a standing position.

6. When doing stretching exercises from a standing position, the knees should not be hyperextended. The knee joint should be relaxed rather than locked. It is often effective to have students do their stretching with bent knees; this will remind them not to hyperextend the joint. In all stretching activities, participants should be allowed to judge their range of motion. Expecting all students to be able to touch their toes is an unrealistic goal. If concerned about touching the toes from this position, do so from a sitting position with one leg flexed.

7. Activities that place stress on the neck should be avoided. Examples of activities in which caution should be used are the inverted bicycle, wrestler's bridge, and abdominal exercises with the hands behind the head.

8. The so-called hurdler's stretch should be avoided. This activity is done in the sitting position with one leg forward and the other leg bent and to the rear. Using this stretch places undue pressure on the knee joint of the bent leg. Substitute a stretch using a similar position with one leg straight forward and the other leg bent with the foot placed in the crotch area.

9. Stretches that demand excessive back arching should be avoided. For example, while lying in the prone position, the student reaches back and grabs the ankles. By pulling and arching, the exerciser can hyperextend the lower back. This places stress on the discs and stretches the abdominal muscles (not needed by most people).

Flexibility and Warm-Up Exercises

The exercises in this section increase the range of motion at various joints. They also prepare the body for more strenuous activity that may follow. In the beginning, the stretching positions should be held for approximately 10 seconds. As flexibility increases, the stretches can be held for up to 30 seconds.

Lower-Leg Stretches

Lower-Leg Stretch. Stand facing a wall with the feet about a shoulder width apart. Place the palms of the hands on the wall at eye level. Walk away from the wall, keeping the body straight, until the stretch is felt in the lower portion of the calf. The feet should remain flat on the floor during the stretch.

Achilles Tendon Stretch. Stand facing a wall with the forearms on it. Place the forehead on the back of the hands. Back 2 to 3 feet away from the wall, bend, and move one leg closer to the wall. Flex the bent leg with the foot on the floor until the stretch is felt in the Achilles tendon area. The feet should remain flat on the floor as the leg closest to the wall is flexed. Repeat, flexing the other leg.

Balance Beam Stretch. Place one foot in front of the other, about 3 feet apart. The feet should be in line as though one were walking a balance beam. Bend the forward leg at the knee, lean forward, and keep the rear foot flat on the floor. Repeat with the opposite leg forward. The calf of the rear leg should be stretched.

Upper-Leg Stretches

Bear Hug. Stand with one leg forward and the other to the rear. Bend the forward knee as much as possible while keeping the rear foot flat on the floor. Repeat the exercise with the other foot forward. Variation: Different muscles can be stretched by turning the hips slightly in either direction. To increase the stretching motion, look over the shoulder and toward the rear foot.

Leg Pickup. Sit on the floor with the legs spread. Reach forward and grab the outside of the ankle with one hand and the outside of the knee with the other. Pick the leg up and pull the ankle toward the chin. The back of the upper leg should be stretched. Repeat the stretch, lifting the other leg.

Side Leg Stretch. Lie on the floor on the left side. Reach down with the right hand and grab the ankle. Pull the ankle and upper leg toward the rear of the

body. Pull the ankle as near to the buttocks as possible and hold, stretching the front of the thigh. Repeat with the other side of the body.

New Hurdler's Stretch. Sit on the floor with one leg forward and the other leg bent at the knee with the foot tucked into the crotch. Lean gradually forward, bending at the hips and tucking the head. Allow the forward leg to flex at the knee. This stretches the back of the thigh. Next, lean backward, away from the forward leg, to stretch the top of the thigh. Repeat, reversing leg positions.

Groin Stretch. Sit on the floor with the legs spread as far apart and kept as straight as possible. Slowly lean forward from the hips and reach with the hands. Do not bend at the neck and shoulders because that puts pressure on the lower back. Stretch and hold in three positions: left, right, and directly ahead.

Lower-Back Stretches

Back Bender. Stand with the feet about a shoulder width apart. Bend the knees slightly and gradually bend the lower back, starting at the hips. Relax the arms and neck and let the upper body hang. If more stretch is desired, gradually straighten the legs.

Ankle Hold. From a standing position with the knees bent, reach down and hold both ankles with the hands. Gradually straighten the legs, applying the stretch to the lower back.

Sitting Toe Touch. Sit on the floor with the legs straight and together. Reach forward and grab the lower legs. Gradually walk the hands down the legs toward the ankles; continue to walk the hands down and touch the toes. Bend from the hips, not the upper back.

Feet-Together Stretch. Sit with the knees bent and the soles of the feet touching. Reach forward with the hands and grasp the ankles. Gently bend forward from the hips, applying stretch to the inside of the legs and lower back. To increase the stretching effect, place the elbows on or near the knees and press them toward the floor.

Cross-Legged Stretch. Sit on the floor with the legs crossed and tucked toward the buttocks. Lean forward with the elbows in front of the knees. To stretch the sides of the lower back, lean forward to the left and then the right.

FIGURE 16.1 Body twist

Body Twist. Figure 16.1 shows the body twist. Sit on the floor with the right leg straight. Lift the left leg over the right leg and place it on the floor outside the right knee. Move the right elbow outside the upper left thigh and use it to maintain pressure on the leg. Lean back and support the upper body with the left hand. Rotate the upper body toward the left hand and arm. Reverse the position and stretch the other side of the body.

Table Stretch. Stand facing a table, chair, or similar platform. Place one leg on the table while maintaining the weight on the other leg. Lean forward from the hips to apply stretch to the hamstrings and lower back. Repeat with the other leg on the table. Variation: Stand with the side of the body facing the table. Place one leg on the table and bend toward the table to stretch the inside of the leg. Repeat with the other side of the body facing the table.

Back Stretches

Back Roller Stretch. Curl up by holding the lower legs with the arms. Tuck the head gently on the knees. Tip backward and then roll back and forth gently. The rolling action should be slow and should stretch the length of the back. Variation: Perform the same stretch but cross the legs and tuck them close to the buttocks.

Straight-Leg Roller. In a sitting position, roll backward and allow the legs to move overhead. Support the hips with the hands to control the stretch. The legs can be straightened and moved to different positions to vary the intensity and location of the stretch.

Squat Stretch. Begin in a standing position with the legs a shoulder width apart and the feet pointed outward. Gradually move to a squatting position, keeping the feet flat on the floor if possible. If balance is a problem, the stretch can be done while leaning against a wall.

Side-of-the-Body Stretches

Wall Stretch. Stand with one side toward the wall. Lean toward the wall and support the body with the hand. Walk away until the feet are 2 to 3 feet from the wall. While supporting the weight in the leaning position, bend the body toward the wall, stretching the side. Reverse and stretch the other side.

Elbow Grab Stretch. In a standing position with the feet spread, raise the hands above the head. Grab the elbows with the hands. Lean to the side and pull the elbow in that direction. Reverse and pull to the opposite side.

Standing Hip Bend. Stand with one hand on the hip and the other arm overhead. Bend to the side with the hand resting on the hip. The arm overhead should point and move in the direction of the stretch with a slight bend at the elbow. Reverse and stretch the opposite side.

Sitting Side Stretch. Sit on the floor with the legs spread as far apart as possible. Lift the arms overhead and reach toward one foot. Reverse and stretch in the opposite direction. Try to maintain an erect upper body.

Arm and Shoulder Girdle Stretches

Arm and Shoulder Stretch. Standing, extend the arms and place the palms of the hands together. Move the arms upward and overhead. Lift the arms as high as possible over the head.

Elbow Puller. Bend the right arm and place it behind the head. Reach to the right elbow with the left hand. Pull the elbow to the left to stretch the triceps and the top of the shoulders. Reverse the positions of the arms and repeat.

Elbow Pusher. Place the right arm over the left shoulder. Push the right elbow toward the body with the left hand and hold. Repeat in the opposite direction.

Wishbone Stretch. Move the arms behind the back and clasp hands. Keep the arms straight and raise the hands toward the ceiling to stretch the shoulder girdle. Variation: Stand near a wall (back toward the wall) and place the hands on it. Gently bend at the knees and lower the body while keeping the hands at the same level.

Exercises for Upper-Body Development

Push-Ups. The basic push-up is done from the front leaning rest position. Only the hands and toes are on the floor, and the body is kept as straight as possible. The exercise is a two-count movement as the body is lowered by bending only at the elbows and then returned to the starting position.

As the body is lowered, only the chest touches the floor before the return to starting position. The push-up should be done with controlled movement. The arms can be adjusted together or apart, depending on the desired muscles to be exercised. As the arms are moved closer together, greater demands are placed on the triceps. Spreading the arms beyond shoulder width increases the workload on the muscles across the chest (pectorals). Variation: If it is difficult to perform a full push-up, the half (knee) push-up is excellent. Movement is the same as the push-up, but the body is supported by the hands and knees.

Inclined Wall Push-Ups. This exercise can be done with either the feet or the hands on the wall. The hands version is easier and should precede the push-up with feet on the wall. In the hands version, the hands are placed on the wall while the feet walk as far from the wall as possible. The farther the performer's feet move from the wall, the more inclined and difficult the push-up will be.

When the student is able to do the inclined push-up with the hands on the wall, the feet-on-the-wall version can be attempted. This exercise is similar to doing a push-up in the handstand position and demands a great deal of strength. As the hands are walked closer to the wall, the incline becomes less, and a greater demand is placed on the shoulder girdle muscles.

Reclining Partner Pull-Ups. Students find a partner of similar strength. One partner assumes a supine position on the floor, while the other stands in a straddle position at chest level. Partners use a wristlock grip with both hands. The standing partner stands erect while the partner in the supine position attempts to do a reclining pull-up (Figure 16.2). The upward pull is done completely by the person in supine position bending at the elbows. The standing person's task is to remain rigid and erect.

It is helpful for the person in the supine position to start this exercise with the feet against a wall. This will prevent the person from sliding and will keep the focus of the activity on upper-body development.

Rocking Chair. The exerciser moves to a prone position on the floor. With the arms out to the sides of the body, the back is arched in an attempt to raise the upper body off the floor. While the upper body is elevated, different activities and arm positions can be attempted. For example, arm circling, waving, clapping

FIGURE 16.2   Reclining partner pull-ups

hands, or placing the hands behind the head can add challenge to this upper-back and shoulder development activity. Variation: The lower body can be elevated instead of the upper. Various movements can then be done with the legs. In either exercise, a partner may be required to hold the half of the body not being moved.

Crab Walk. This activity can be modified in several ways to develop trunk and upper-body strength. The crab position is an inverted walk on all fours. The stomach faces the ceiling with the weight supported on the hands and feet. Crab walking can be done in all directions and should be performed with the trunk as straight as possible. Variations: The crab kick can be executed from this position by alternating forward kicks of the left and right leg. The double crab kick is done by kicking both feet forward and then backward simultaneously.

Exercises for the Midsection

Reverse Curl. Lie on the back with the hands on the floor to the sides of the body. Curl the knees to the chest. The upper body remains on the floor. Try to lift the buttocks and lower the back off the floor. To increase the challenge, do not return the feet to the floor after each repetition, lowering them to within 1 or 2 inches off the floor. This activity requires greater abdominal strength as there is no resting period (feet on floor).

Pelvis Tilter. Lie on the back with feet flat on the floor, knees bent, arms out in wing position, and palms up. Flatten the lower back, bringing it closer to the floor by tensing the lower abdominals and lifting up on the pelvis. Hold for eight to 12 counts. Tense slowly and release slowly.

Knee Touch Curl-Up. Lie on the back, with feet flat and knees bent, and with hands flat on top of thighs. Leading with the chin, slide the hands forward until the fingers touch the kneecaps and gradually curl the head and shoulders until the shoulder blades are lifted off the floor. Hold for eight counts and return to the original position. To avoid stress on the lower back, the performer should not curl up to the sitting position.

Curl-Up. Lie on the back with feet flat, knees bent, and arms on the floor at the side of the body with palms down. Lift the head and shoulders to a 45° angle and then back in a two-count pattern. The hands should slide forward on the floor 3 to 4 inches. The curl-up can also be done as an eight-count exercise, moving up on one count, holding for six counts, and moving down on the last count.

FIGURE 16.3 Leg extension

Curl-Up with Twist. Lie on the back with feet flat and knees bent. Arms are folded and placed across the chest with hands on shoulders. Do a partial curl-up and twist the chest to the left. Repeat, turning the chest to the right.

Leg Extension. Sit on the floor with legs extended and hands on hips. With a quick, vigorous action, raise the knees and bring both heels as close to the seat as possible (Figure 16.3). The movement is a drag with the toes touching lightly. Return to the original position.

Abdominal Cruncher. Lie in supine position with feet flat, knees bent, and palms of hands cupped over the ears (not behind the head). An alternate position is to fold the arms across the chest and place the hands on the shoulders. Tuck the chin and curl upward until the shoulder blades leave the floor. Return to the floor with a slow uncurling.

Exercises for the Lower Body

Squat Jumps. Begin in a squatting position with one foot slightly ahead of the other. Assume part of the weight with the hands in front of the body. Jump as high as possible and return to the squatting position. Taking some of the body weight with the hands is important to avoid stressing the knee joints.

Treadmill. Begin on all fours with one foot forward and one behind. Rapidly alternate foot positions while taking the weight of the body on the arms. The movement of the feet can be varied by moving both feet forward and back simultaneously or by moving the feet apart and together.

Jumping Jacks. Begin in standing position with the arms at the sides and feet together. Simultaneously lift the arms overhead and spread the legs on the first count. On the second count, return arms and legs to the starting position. Variations: Feet and arm movements can be varied. The arms can be moved in front of the body, behind the body, and in different patterns. The legs can be split forward and backward, crossed in front of each other, and swung to the front of the body.

Running in Place. Running in place is most beneficial when the upper leg is lifted parallel to the floor. The thighs can touch the hands held slightly above the parallel line to encourage the high lift.

Side-Leg Flex. Lie on your side on the floor. Rest the head in the right hand and place the left hand along the side of the body. On the first count, lift the left leg and arm and point them toward the ceiling. Return to the starting position on the second count. Rotate to the other side of the body after performing the desired number of repetitions. Variation: The double side-leg flex is an exercise that demands more effort. Both legs are lifted simultaneously as far off the floor as possible.

Front-Leg Kick. From standing position, alternately kick each leg forward and as high as possible. This exercise should be done rhythmically so that all movement occurs on the toes. When the leg is kicked upward, the arm on the same side should be moved forward in an attempt to touch the toe of the lifted leg.

ACTIVITIES AND ROUTINES FOR DEVELOPING FITNESS

The following are methods of organizing exercises and aerobic activities to develop total body fitness. All of the routines should enhance muscular strength and endurance, as well as cardiovascular endurance.

Teacher and Student Leader Exercise Routines

During the first part of the school year, teachers should lead and teach all exercises to ensure that they are learned correctly. It is also important that teachers stay involved in fitness activities throughout the year to

demonstrate their willingness to do the activities that they are asking students to perform. In some cases, teachers ask students to exercise and maintain fitness while they choose not to do either. Pushing others to be fit is difficult if the teacher does not make a similar personal commitment.

When a wide repertoire of exercises has been learned, students can begin to lead the exercise routines. Leading not only means starting and stopping the exercises but includes designing well-balanced routines that offer total body development. Students can be guided in the desirable number of repetitions and how to count exercises as they are being performed. In any case, students should not be forced to lead the exercises; leading should be a personal choice.

More than one student leader can be used at a time. For example, if four leaders are selected, each can be thinking of the exercises to choose when it is his or her turn. Leaders can be placed on four sides of the class, with the class rotating one-quarter turn to face a new leader after each exercise. If a leader cannot think of an appropriate exercise, the class can be asked to volunteer one. In any case, emphasis should be placed on learning to weave together a set of exercises that offers total body development. Continuous movement activity should also be added to the exercise routines to ensure cardiovascular endurance development.

Squad Leader Exercises

Squad leader exercises offer students the opportunity to develop fitness routines without teacher intervention. Squad leaders take their squad to a designated area and put the squad through a fitness routine. It is helpful if a blank exercise card is given to each squad leader a few days before the student will lead. The leader can develop a routine and write down the exercises and repetitions or duration of each.

Squad leaders can also assign members of the group to lead or to offer certain activities. A number of exercises can be specified to develop a particular area of the body. For example, ask leaders to develop a routine that has two exercises for the arm-shoulder girdle area, two for the abdominal region, one for the legs, three for flexibility, and 2 minutes of continuous movement. The responsibility for planning a fitness routine that is balanced and developmental should shift gradually from the teacher to the students.

Exercises to Music

Without question, music increases the motivational level of students during exercise. While many commercial exercise-to-music records are available, they all suffer from two major problems: They seldom meet the specific workload requirements of different groups of students, and they cannot provide the necessary systematic overload. Teachers therefore need to develop their own homemade exercise-to-music tapes that can be tailored to meet the needs of a specific class or grade.

Homemade exercise tapes can be developed using a tape recorder. Music that is currently popular can be combined with exercises that students have already learned. Avoid music that might affront some members of the community. Either the teacher or a group of students can make the tapes. When students do the taping, they have control over the selection, sequence, and number of exercises and repetitions. The routines can be adapted to particular needs and characteristics of the group. Procedures for starting and stopping exercises can be incorporated easily in the taping.

Continuous Movement Activities

Jogging

Jogging is running at a slow pace. It is faster than walking but slower than sprinting. Jogging is an excellent conditioner for the cardiovascular system and can be done by virtually all students. It does not require specialized equipment or specialized skill.

Any one of three approaches can be used to develop a jogging program. The first is the jog–walk approach, which emphasizes the amount of time that one is involved in continuous movement. Students determine how far they can jog before they need to slow down and walk. Walking is continued until the exerciser is again ready to jog. The goal is to decrease the length and time of the walking episodes and to increase the jogging.

A second approach to increasing endurance through jogging is to set up definite and measured intervals. An example would be setting up cones to mark jogging intervals of 110 yards and walking intervals of 55 yards. As the fitness level increases, the length of the jogging interval is increased and the walking interval decreased.

Finally, the workload can be increased by increasing either the duration or the pace of the jogging. The goal is either to maintain a constant pace and to increase the distance run or to run the same distance at an increased pace. Increasing the speed is usually the less-desirable alternative because the intensity of the exercise may discourage students.

Jogging is performed in an erect body position with a minimal amount of leaning. Excessive leaning is less efficient and demands a greater amount of energy. The elbows should be bent and the arms carried in a relaxed manner. Most joggers strike the ground with a flat foot. This allows the force of impact to be absorbed over a larger surface area, which seems to be more desirable. Some joggers land on the heel and then rotate to the toe. In either case, trying to change a jogger's foot action is often ineffective.

Jogging should be a noncompetitive activity. Students should be encouraged to look for self-improvement instead of comparing their performance with others. An enjoyable technique is to ask students to jog with a partner who has similar ability. They should be encouraged to talk and visit while they jog. Suggest that if they find it difficult to talk while jogging, they are probably running too fast.

Endurance and continuous activity should be rewarded. Teachers sometimes have a tendency to ask students to run a certain distance, and then they reward those students who complete the distance first. This is discouraging to the majority of the joggers. Students should be permitted to run in any direction they desire until a certain amount of time has elapsed. This prevents the situation in which a few gifted runners finish first and have to sit and wait for the rest of the class to complete a given distance.

A general rule of thumb for beginning a jogging program is to ask students to walk and jog continuously for 5 minutes. Increase the amount of time 1 minute per week up to 15 minutes. Individuals can increase the total amount of time while they also try to reduce the amount of walking. Ideas for an instructional unit on jogging can be found in Chapter 20.

Rope Jumping

Rope jumping is a demanding activity that requires little equipment. For some participants it can be a valuable approach to cardiovascular fitness. The energy demands of rope jumping are similar to jogging. Rope jumping can be performed for a specified amount of time or for a specified number of jumps.

A variety of activities can be done with a jump rope to help avoid the monotony and excessive fatigue of continuous jumping. The rope can be turned at fast or slow speeds while different foot steps are performed. If rope jumping is used for the fitness portion of the lesson, it should be alternated with stretching activities to give students an opportunity to recover from aerobic demands. See Chapter 20 for ideas on developing a unit of instruction on rope jumping.

Four Corners

A large rectangle is formed using four cones as markers. Students move continually around the perimeter of the rectangle. At each corner, a different movement is performed. Examples of activity alternatives that can be performed on the long sides of the rectangle are jogging, power skipping, sliding, jumping, and hopping. On the short sides of the rectangle, movements on all fours (for example, bear walk and crab walk) can be performed. Another interesting variation is to use tumbling activities or use tires and challenge students to go over, around, and through them. The need for continuous movement should be emphasized, and the rectangle should be large enough to provide a challenging workload for the cardiovascular system.

Interval Training

Interval training involves carefully controlling the work and rest intervals of the participant. Intervals of work (exercise) and rest can be measured in distance, repetitions, or time. Interval training is done by monitoring the heart rate. The student first needs to get the heart rate up to 120 to 140 beats per minute with a warm-up routine. Strenuous activity is then performed to push the heart rate into the 170 to 180 beats-per-minute range. At this point, the runner begins the rest interval (usually walking) until the heart rate returns to 120 to 140 beats per minute. Theoretically, the amount of time it takes for the heart rate to return to 120 to 140 beats per minute should not exceed 90 seconds. The major advantage of interval training is that endurance can be increased markedly in a short period of time.

Interval training can be used with various locomotor movements. For example, the following work and rest activities can be alternated. Intervals can be measured in either distance or time.

Work Activities	*Rest Activities*
Brisk walking	Slow walking
Jogging	Walking
Sprinting	Jogging
Rope jumping	Walking
Jumping in place	Walking

Circuit Training

Exercise stations are organized into a circuit for the sake of fitness development. Each of the stations contributes, in part, to the total fitness of the participant. The components of fitness—flexibility, muscular strength and endurance, and cardiovascular endurance—are represented in the circuit.

Development of a Circuit

1. If the circuit is to be used as a group activity, all class members must be capable of performing each of the exercises.

2. Organize the stations so different muscle groups or fitness components are exercised. In other words, consecutive stations should not place demands on the same area of the body.

3. Students should know how to perform all of the activities correctly. Proper form is important. Instruction can be done verbally, or descriptive posters can be placed at each station.

4. Distribute students evenly among the stations at the beginning of the exercise bout. A rotation plan ensures that students move to the correct station.

5. Measure dosage in time or repetitions. Students can move on their own to the next station if they have completed the required number of repetitions. If a time criterion is used, the class moves as a whole when students have exercised for a specified amount of time.

6. To increase the demands on the cardiovascular system, one or two of the stations can include rope jumping or running in place. Another alternative is to have students run around the perimeter of the entire circuit a certain number of times before moving to the next station.

7. The circuit should contain no fewer than 10 stations. The result of participation in the circuit is a total body workout.

Timing and Dosage

Workload at each station should be based on time, and each student should be asked to do their best within that time. Signals to start exercising, stop exercising, and rotate to the next stations are given. This allows accurate timing of intervals. A reasonable expectation for beginning circuit training is 40 seconds per station. The amount of rest between stations can also be monitored to increase or decrease the workload. An effective way of timing the circuit is to use a tape recording of popular music that students enjoy, with signals to stop and start activities interspersed at proper intervals.

Figure 16.4 is an example of a circuit that might be developed for middle school students.

Astronaut Drills

Astronaut drills are continuous movement activities that combine exercises with walking and jogging. Students move randomly throughout the area or follow each other in a circle formation. The drills begin with brisk walking. On signal, the teacher or selected students lead the class in exercises or stunt activities. If a

9. Run, with the knees lifted as high as possible.

10. Stop and perform a treadmill.

11. Repeat the previous steps.

Continuity Exercises

Continuity exercises can be done in squad formation or scatter formation. Because each student has a jump rope, students must have plenty of room to avoid hitting each other. Performers alternate between rope jumping and exercises. Rope jumping is done for timed episodes with music to help maintain the rhythm. At the signal to stop rope jumping, students quickly drop the rope and move into position for the exercise. Selected exercises should be performed in a down position with a leader who says, "Ready," and the students respond, "One-two," while performing the exercise. For each repetition, students wait until the command "Ready" is given. Students are allowed to monitor their own speed and intensity. The following is an example of a routine:

First signal. Begin rope jumping.

Second signal. Stop jumping, drop ropes, and move to the push-up position. On each command of "Ready," do one push-up.

Third signal. Resume rope jumping.

Fourth signal. Drop ropes and move into supine position on the floor with the arms overhead, prepared to do the rowing exercise. On the command "Ready," perform the exercise.

Fifth signal. Resume rope jumping.

Sixth signal. Drop the ropes, and move into crab position. Prepare to do the double crab kick. On the signal "Ready," both feet are extended forward and back.

Seventh signal. Resume rope jumping.

Eighth signal. Move into position for the side-leg flex exercise. On the command "Ready," lift the upper leg and return it to the starting position.

Ninth signal. Resume rope jumping.

Tenth signal. Move into position for the reclining partner pull-up. On signal, pull the body up on count one, and return to the floor on count two. Switch positions with your partner after the proper number of repetitions has been performed.

The number of repetitions and the duration of the rope-jumping episodes should be determined by the fitness levels of the students. More exercises can be added to the routine. Instructors can use a tape

---

Nine-Station Course

1 Rope jumping	2 Push-ups	3 Agility run	4 Arm circles
8 Windmill	7 Treadmill	6 Crab walk	5 Rowing

9
Hula-hooping (or any relaxing "fun" activity)

FIGURE 16.4 Circuit-training stations

movement is not developed immediately, the class runs or walks in place. Combinations of the following activities can be arranged to develop a demanding routine:

1. Performing various locomotor movements such as hopping, running, jumping, leaping, skipping, and running on the toes.

2. Moving throughout the area on all fours in the front crab position, reverse crab position, or the bear crawl position.

3. Performing exercises, such as arm circles, body twists, and trunk and upper-body stretches, while moving around the area.

4. Performing stationary exercises, such as push-ups, sit-ups, and jumping jacks, to stress development of the upper body and abdominal wall.

Students move throughout the area and perform as many exercises as possible. They can also develop individual routines that control the amounts of time allotted for movement activity and stationary activity. The following is an example of an astronaut drill that might be implemented. The duration of the movements is timed, and students are encouraged to do the best they can within the specified time.

1. Walk throughout the area.

2. Run and hurdle.

3. Stop and perform push-ups.

4. Walk and do arm circles.

5. Do a crab walk.

6. Stop, find a friend, and perform partner strength exercises.

7. Hop for a period of time on each foot.

8. Walk on all fours (bear crawl).

recorder to signal the start and finish of the rope-jumping episodes. Continuity exercises are an example of interval training. The rope jumping stresses the cardiovascular system, while the exercises develop strength and allow the performer to recover.

Partner Resistance Exercises

Partner resistance exercises are enjoyable for students because they offer variable workloads and a chance to work with a partner. Partners must be matched in size and strength so they can challenge each other. The exercises should be performed throughout the full range of motion at each joint and take 8 to 12 seconds each to complete. The partner providing the resistance gives the "Begin" command and counts the duration of the exercise. Three sets of each exercise are done by each student as they alternate the exercise and resistance roles.

The following are examples of exercises that can be performed. Challenge students to invent their own partner resistance exercises and to develop a set of exercises that strengthens all body parts.

Arm Curl-Ups. The exerciser keeps the upper arms against the sides of the body, bends the elbows, and turns palms up. The partner puts fists in the exerciser's palms. The exerciser then attempts to curl the forearms upward to the shoulders. To develop the opposite set of muscles, push down in the opposite direction, starting with palms at shoulder level.

Forearm Flex. The exerciser places the hands, palms down, on the partner's shoulders. The exerciser at-

tempts to push the partner into the floor. The partner may slowly lower the body to allow the exerciser to move through the full range of motion. Try the exercise with the palms up.

Fist Pull-Apart. The exerciser places the fists together in front of the body at shoulder level. The exerciser attempts to pull the hands apart while the partner forces them together with pressure on the elbows. Reverse this exercise and begin with the fists apart. Partner tries to push them together by grasping the wrists.

Pec Deck. The exerciser holds the arms up at a 90° angle at shoulder height. The exerciser then pushes the arms together in front of the body, similar to the motion on a Pec-Deck machine. The exercise may be reversed while resistance is provided on the inside or outside of the arms, depending on which direction the exerciser is moving.

Butterfly. The exerciser holds the arms straight, forming a right angle with the side of the body (Figure 16.5). The partner attempts to hold the arms down, while the exerciser lifts with straight arms to the sides. Try the activity with the arms above the head; move them down to the sides against partner's effort to hold them up.

Camelback. The exerciser is on all fours with the head up. The partner sits or pushes on the exerciser's back while the exerciser tries to hump the back like a camel.

Back Builder. The exerciser spreads the legs and bends forward at the waist with the head up. The partner faces

FIGURE 16.5 Butterfly

the exerciser and clasps the hands together behind the exerciser's neck. The exerciser then attempts to stand upright while the partner pulls downward.

Scissors. The exerciser lies on one side while the partner straddles him or her and holds the upper leg down. The exerciser attempts to raise the top leg. The exercise is reversed and performed with the other leg.

Bear Trap. The exerciser performs as in the scissors but spreads the legs first and attempts to move them together while the partner holds them apart.

Knee Bender. The exerciser lies in prone position with legs straight and arms ahead on the floor. The partner places the hands on the back of the exerciser's ankle. The exerciser attempts to flex the knee while the partner applies pressure. Reverse legs. Try this exercise in the opposite direction with the knee joint at a 90° angle.

Resistance Push-Up. The exerciser is in push-up position with arms bent so that the body is halfway up from the floor. The partner straddles or stands alongside the exerciser's head and puts pressure on the top of the shoulders by pushing down. The partner must judge the amount of pressure to apply in order to prevent the exerciser from collapsing.

Aerobic movements such as walking, jogging, sliding, skipping, and so on can be alternated with the partner resistance exercises to create a balanced fitness routine. We suggest devoting 45 seconds to partner resistance and 20 to 30 seconds to aerobic movements. Creative signs can help structure this routine.

Challenge Courses

Challenge courses, or parcourses, are popular throughout the country. Different stations are developed, and the participants move from station to station as they cover the course. The type of movement done between stations can also place demands on the participants' body systems. Courses can be run for time, or repetitions can be increased to ensure balanced fitness development. Courses should be developed to exercise all parts of the body. A variety of activities, such as stretching, vaulting, agility runs, climbing, hanging and chinning, and crawling, can be included to place demands on all aspects of fitness. Figure 16.6 represents an indoor challenge course that might be constructed for students.

ities, students work together to enhance their fitness levels. They should be encouraged to develop personalized group activities. The following are examples of exercises that use the parachute.

Toe Toucher. Sit with the feet extended under the parachute and hold the chute taut with a two-hand grip, drawing it to the chin. Bend forward and touch the grip to the toes. Return the chute to the stretched position.

Curl-Up. Extend the body under the parachute in curl-up position so the chute comes up to the chin when held taut. Do curl-ups, returning each time to the stretched position. Encourage students to work together and snap the chute tight each time they recline.

Dorsal Lift. In prone position, lie with the head toward the chute. Grasp the chute with the arms extended overhead. On signal, raise the chute off the floor while simultaneously raising the head and chest. Encourage students to lift the chute high enough so they can "see a friend" across the way.

Sitting Leg Lift. In a sitting position with the legs under the chute, lift the legs on signal while holding the chute taut, and lift the chute off the floor. Hold the position for 6 to 10 seconds. Try to keep the legs straight. As a variation, start in a supine position with the legs under the chute and do a V-seat.

Sitting Pulls. Sit with the back to the parachute. Grasp the chute and raise it overhead. On signal, try to pull the chute down to the knees. Other variations are done facing the chute and raising it above the head, lowering it to eye level, and lowering it to waist level. Emphasis should be placed on using the arms and shoulder girdle to apply force rather than leaning.

All-Fours Pulls. Get on the floor in a crab-, bear-, or seal-walk position. Grasp the chute with one hand. On signal, pull and hold the contraction for 6 to 10 seconds. Repeat using the other hand and different positions.

Isometric Exercises. A wide variety of isometric exercises can be done using the parachute. Various body parts can be exercised by applying pressure to the chute. The exercises should be held for 6 to 10 seconds. Encourage students to develop new isometric techniques.

Rhythmic Aerobic Activity. The parachute is excellent for stimulating aerobic activity. For example, students can do various locomotor movements while

Parachute Exercises

The parachute can be used to develop fitness activities that are exciting and challenging. Through these activ-

7. Climb to top of a rope or hang for 20 seconds

8. Do a forward roll the length of the mat

9. Vault a 36-inch box or horse

10. Cross the finish line

6. Do an agility run (figure eight) around 3 chairs

5. Do a crab walk the length of the mat, feet first

4. High-jump over a 30-inch-high bar

3. Crawl through 4 tires

2. Hurdle over 3 benches

1. Run around 2 chairs

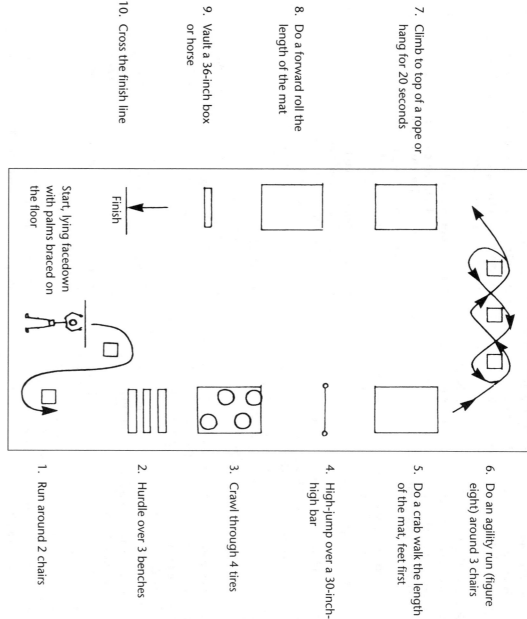

Start, lying facedown with palms braced on the floor

Finish

FIGURE 16.6 Challenge course

holding onto the chute. A sample routine with the chute follows:

1. Skip clockwise.
2. Skip counterclockwise.
3. Jump to the center of the parachute.
4. Hop backward and tighten the chute.
5. Slowly lift the parachute overhead.
6. Slowly lower the parachute to toes.
7. Quickly lift the parachute overhead.
8. Quickly lower the parachute to toes.
9. Repeat steps 5 through 8.
10. Run clockwise with the chute held overhead.
11. Run backward with the chute held at waist level.
12. Make a dome.
13. Repeat steps 10 through 12.
14. Finish with a parachute lift and release the chute.

Running Activities and Drills

A number of running drills and activities can be used to improve running techniques, agility, and fitness levels, depending on how they are administered. Aerobic ability varies widely in classes, and many students may not be able to do much running because of being overweight and other disabilities. Offer other options, or allow them to perform the drill while walking.

Form Running

This drill works well on a football field using the yard lines as markers. A squad of students lines up on the boundary line at the goal line, 10-yard line, 20-yard line, 30-yard line, and so forth. The teacher stands on the hash mark closest to the students, on about the 25-yard line. On signal, the first student in each line runs across the field on the respective yard line. The teacher continues to give a starting signal for each wave of students until all of the students are on the opposite boundary line. The teacher then moves to the opposite hash mark and starts the students running back across the field. Each time the students run across the field, they should be told to concentrate on one aspect of their running form. The following aspects can be emphasized:

1. Keep the head still—no lateral or turning movements. Eyes should be focused straight ahead. Keep the chin down.

2. Relax the hands. Place the thumb on the first pad of the index finger. Put hands beside the front pocket as they move backward.

3. Bend elbows approximately 90°, and move the arms straight forward and back with no lateral movement across the chest. Arms gently brush the sides of the body.

4. Align the feet straight ahead. Knees drive straight ahead rather than upward. High knee action can be used as another variation, although it is not necessary for good running form. The heel of the foot should come close to the buttocks.

5. Align the foot, knee, and hip. The body tilts forward about 5° from the feet, not from the hips.

6. The length of the stride is usually shorter for longer runs (i.e., a longer stride for sprinting and a shorter stride for distance running).

Give students only one aspect of running form to concentrate on during each trip across the field so that they can emphasize and overlearn each point. Beginning slowly and increasing the speed gradually works best. Start the drill at half speed, then proceed to three-quarter speed, and finally, increase to full speed.

This same drill format can also be used with other running activities.

1. *Backwards running.* Stay on the line. Roll the shoulders forward and keep them forward while running. Emphasize the arm movement forward and back. Pull that arm through with each step.

2. *Crossover-step backward.* The teacher stands on the boundary line, and the first wave of students moves 5 yards out on their respective yard lines facing the teacher. The teacher gives a left- or right-hand signal. The students start backward with a crossover step. When the teacher changes the direction signal, students rotate their hips and do a crossover step on the opposite side. Students must keep their eyes on the teacher and concentrate on rotating their hips and staying on the line.

3. *Crossover-step forward.* As students run forward, they concentrate on stepping across the line with each step. It is important to start slowly and to increase the speed gradually.

4. *Carioca step.* Students stand sideways on the line with their arms held out, parallel to the ground. On a signal, the students move sideways down the line by using a crossover step in front and a return step, a crossover step in back, and finally another step. This process is repeated for the length of the field. Students should make sure that they lead with both the right and left shoulder.

5. **Shuffle sideways.** Students stand sideways on the line in a ready position (feet a shoulder width apart, knees bent, head up, arms flexed in front of the body). On signal, students shuffle down the line without a crossover step. Students should also lead with both the left and right sides. A variation is to have students spread out down the line and face the teacher, who is standing in front of the entire group. The teacher gives a left- or right-hand signal to start the group moving.

Form-running drills can be done without lines if necessary. Use boundary cones to mark the beginning and end of each running section. Another variation is to place cones at one third and two thirds of the distance and ask students to vary their speed in each third. For example, students could jog the first third, sprint the second, and ease to three-quarter speed during the last third. Or they can change the type of running during each third. The following combinations might be used:

1. Jog, shuffle right, and shuffle left.

2. Carioca step, shuffle, and sprint.

3. Backward run, crossover left, and crossover right.

4. Form run, crossover front, and form run.

5. Carioca step left, carioca step right, and sprint.

File Running

Divide the class into two or three groups according to cardiovascular fitness level: high, medium, and low. Each group lines up single file and begins to jog around a given distance, such as a quarter-mile track, a field, or a set of boundary cones. Students should keep a 2- to 3-yard distance between each person. The last person in line sprints past the file and becomes the leader. When the new leader is in place, the new last person begins to sprint past the file. This procedure continues for a given distance or a given number of minutes. The high fitness group will cover more distance in a given time.

Walk-Jog-Sprint

This is a continuous movement activity in which the teacher controls the speed of movement with a whistle signal. Three whistles mean sprint, two mean jog, and one means walk. The students start by walking around a given area (track, field, or boundary cone). The teacher then alternates the periods of jogging, sprinting, and walking for a number of minutes or for a given distance. It is important to progressively build up the time or distance.

Pace Work

Students need to practice running at an even pace for a given distance, such as a 6-, 8-, or 10-minute mile. Pacing can be practiced by running shorter segments of the distance at the correct speed. Figures 16.7 and 16.8 show the required time for covering certain distances in order to maintain correct pacing. It is easiest to use a marked track, but a workable track can be developed through placement of boundary cones. Using a rectangle is helpful for ease of measurement. Students are divided into groups and challenged to run distances at a given time. For example, the fast group might work on a 6-minute-mile pace: 110 yards in 22.5 seconds, 220 yards in 45 seconds, and 440 yards in 90 seconds. The medium group could work on an 8-minute pace, and the slow group could focus on a 10-minute-mile pace. It is interesting to have students calculate a world record pace for a given distance and then try to run a small segment of that distance at the record pace. For instance, have them run 50 yards at a 4-minute-mile pace, or 440 yards at a 2.5-hour-marathon pace.

Another strategy for teaching students about pace is to set up a square, 50 yards on a side. Place a cone at every corner and in the middle of each side. Put an equal number of students at each cone. Calculate the 25-yard time for various speeds (such as a 6-, 8-, or 10-minute mile). Have students try to run at a given speed, and blow a whistle each time they should have completed a 25-yard run. The students should be at a cone each time the whistle sounds. This way, they can tell if they are going too fast or too slow.

Random Running

Random running is a simple and effective way to improve cardiovascular fitness. The emphasis is on long,

1. Five to 10 minutes of easy jogging.
2. Steady, intense speed for 1 to 2 kilometers.
3. Five minutes of rapid walking.

Fartlek

Fartlek is a form of training that was developed in Sweden in the 1930s and 1940s. (The term *Fartlek* means "speed play.") The training is aerobic in nature and entails hard but untimed long-distance efforts over topographic challenges. The hilly terrain is run at varied tempos. Fartlek is usually done on soft surfaces. A typical workout for an athlete in training might be as follows:

slow distance (LSD) running. Students are allowed to run randomly throughout the area at a pace that is comfortable for them. They are encouraged to find a partner and to talk while jogging.

Students who need to walk because of their subpar level of fitness can do so without experiencing the stigma of finishing last during a run. The distance each student runs is not charted. Effort is acknowledged rather than speed or distance-running ability. Emphasis is placed on being active, involved, and moving during the entire episode rather than on seeing how far one can run or jog.

Students can begin with a 10-minute random running episode three times per week. The duration of the run can be increased 1 minute per week until a maximum 20-minute episode is achieved. This allows the majority of students to increase their workload in a gradual and palatable manner.

FIGURE 16.7 Pace chart for 40- and 100-yard dashes

Times for 40- and 100-Yard Dashes

To run 1 mi in:	You would have to run the 40-yard dash 44 times, with each dash run in:	Or run the 100-yard dash 17.6 times, with each dash run in:
3:48 min (world record time)	5.18 sec	12.95 sec
5:00 min	6.81 sec	17.04 sec
6:00 min	8.18 sec	20.45 sec
7:00 min	9.55 sec	23.87 sec
8:00 min	10.90 sec	27.25 sec
10:00 min	13.62 sec	34.08 sec

Interval (miles)	To run 1 mile (1760 yd) in: (min)								
	4:00	5:00	6:00	7:00	8:00	9:00	10:00	11:00	12:00
¾ (1320 yd)	3:00	3:45	4:30	5:15	6:00	6:45	7:30	8:15	9:00
½ (880 yd)	2:00	2:30	3:00	3:30	4:00	4:30	5:00	5:30	6:00
¼ (440 yd)	1:00	1:15	1:30	1:45	2:00	2:15	2:30	2:45	3:00
⅛ (220 yd)	:30	:37½	:45	:52½	1:00	1:07½	1:15	1:22½	1:30
1/16 (110 yd)	:15	:18¾	:22½	:26¼	:30	:33¾	:37½	:41¼	:45

FIGURE 16.8 Pace chart for 1-mile run

4. Easy running broken by 50 to 60 meters of accelerated runs that cause moderate fatigue.

5. Easy running with 2 to 5 intermittent swift strides every 100 meters until moderate fatigue results.

6. Full uphill effort for 150 to 200 meters.

7. One minute of fast-paced running on level ground.

8. Easy running for 5 to 10 meters.

This workout illustrates the variation involved in Fartlek. Students can be given a workout that might last 10 to 20 minutes and encompasses the many different tempos and geographic features described. The run challenges can be written on cards, and students select runs of varying difficulty (easy, moderate, difficult, strenuous).

Monopoly Fitness

Place students in groups of two to three at 12 to 14 fitness stations around the perimeter of the area. Station ideas could include stretch-band exercises, stretches, jump-rope activities, strength-development exercises, and jump-band activities. Students perform curls with exercise tubes in Figure 16.9. Have a student roll the dice. All students add the numbers when the dice stop rolling and jog forward the corresponding number of stations. They then perform the exercise listed at that station. Students may repeat some stations. Use music intervals to signal when to exercise and when to roll the dice.

Track and Field Fitness

Position a cardiovascular exercise station in each corner of the teaching area. In each of these corners, there should be a mat or a bench for step-ups and at least five to six jump ropes. Establish a predetermined spot on

the floor for the rope jumping and a designated jogging area. Other signs should be placed within the four corners to complete the circuit. A music tape with intervals of 30 seconds of music followed by a 6-second pause can be used to signal changes. Students perform the exercise challenges while the music is playing and move to the next station on the pauses. This routine provides students with the opportunity to choose an appropriate fitness challenge at each station.

Jump-Bands Circuit

Arrange this fitness routine as a circuit of stations around the area. Place the students in groups of four with two jumpers and two band holders. (See the jump

FIGURE 16.9 Curls with exercise tubes on a fitness circuit

bands section, pp. 405–6.) Exercisers use the basic four-count step of "in, in, out, out." Students are encouraged to make a quick choice while working at each station and to choose an activity that will challenge their own levels of fitness. Other stations that can be integrated into this circuit include abdominal strength choices, upper-body strength choices, and flexibility choices. A tape of 30 seconds of music and 10 seconds of silence can be used to signal station changes.

Cardio-Choice Fitness

Create a circuit with a number of stations around the perimeter of the area. Use four cardio-choice signs, one placed in each corner of the room. Students are encouraged to make a quick choice while working at each station and to choose an activity that will challenge their personal levels of fitness. Other stations in the circuit include abdominal strength choices, upper-body strength choices, and flexibility choices. A tape of 30 seconds of music and 10 seconds of pause can be used to signal rotation to the next station and free the teacher. Cardio-choice signs include the following:

Cardio-choice A (2 of each): Power walk and talk with a friend, jump rope, slide halfway, pivot and do carioca steps; and Cardio-choice B (2 of each): Jog around the perimeter of the area, jump rope, and do step-ups.

Fitness Scavenger Hunt

Students can work together in teams or small groups. The teams stay together and "hunt" for the exercise area of the gym or field space. The teams are given a laminated sheet or card that lists the area to find and the activities to perform at the designated area. The sheets could have eight to 12 activities depending on how long the fitness segment of the lesson is going to last. Each group can be assigned a different starting point to ensure that students are spread across all areas and that a backup of students does not occur at one of the fitness areas. Examples of entries on the exercise sheet or card could be the following:

- Run to each corner of the gym and perform 25 curl-ups. All team members should work together.
- Run to the open set of bleachers and perform 25 step-ups on the first row. The count should be "up, up, down, down," with your steps.
- Do carioca steps to each of the other groups and tell them that they are doing a good job.
- Jog to the tumbling mats and perform two sitting stretches; hold each for 8 counts.
- Run and find the short jump ropes. Complete 25 jumps at a "fast-time" pace.

choices, upper-body strength choices, and flexibility choices. A tape of 30 seconds of music and 10 seconds of silence can be used to signal station changes.

Students can complete all seven activities and then return to their squads and wait for the next activity.

- Jog to the "jumping jacks" sign and perform 25 jumping jacks with at least four different variations in arm or foot patterns.
- Jog and touch five walls, two different red lines, and three different black lines. Stay together with your group.

Fitness Cookie Jar Exchange

A variation of the fitness scavenger hunt is called the "fitness cookie jar." A variety of fitness activities are written on different index cards and then placed in a "cookie jar" (shoe box). The shoe box can then be placed at the center of the gym or at another convenient place for students to pick up and return the cards. Students can work alone or with a partner. Partners take turns selecting the fitness card from the box. The activities can be similar to the fitness scavenger hunt activities or could also include ball handling skills with a specific area designated for the use of equipment. Examples could include the following:

- Dribble the basketball down and back up the length of the gym.
- Jog and shake hands with eight different people. Tell them to have a good day.
- Do a crab walk across the width of the gym.
- Jog over and tell your teacher that physical education is a fun activity.
- Perform a "mirror drill" with a partner for 30 seconds.
- Do carioca steps around the basketball court two times.
- Slide to the drinking fountain and get a drink.
- Perform two layup shots at three different baskets.
- Perform three partner resistance exercises with a different partner.

Music can be programmed on a tape for 30-second intervals to structure the transitions for students. A 10-second interval without music could be used for getting a new card. Students could then perform as many repetitions as possible while the music is playing. This allows more individualization for students with varying fitness and skill abilities. Students should be challenged to do as many as possible and try to improve as the units continue.

Partner Racetrack Fitness

Students begin work with a partner at one of five or six stations in the gym or on a field outside. The stations are arranged in a circle or rectangle around the area. Each station has a sign with five or six exercises or stretches to perform. On the start signal, one partner begins the first exercise or stretch on the card, while the other partner jogs around the perimeter of the stations. Upon returning, the partners switch roles and then move down the list of activities on the cards. The teacher can also change the locomotor movement for the students going around the cones. For example, in addition to jogging, students could do carioca steps, slide, run backwards, skip, or hurdle around the stations. The signs at the stations could include stretches, jumping jacks, crab kicks, treadmills, sit-ups, push-ups, body twists, and other variations. Continuous music could be used to motivate students. Stability balls and medicine balls can be added to the racetrack stations. (See the following sections on the two types of balls and the exercises that can challenge your students.)

The 12 Ways of Fitness

This is an add-on fitness game using 12 student leaders. It follows the same format as the song "The Twelve Days of Christmas." Students could be in groups of 12, or a large group could be used with the student leaders. Each student adds on the next number of exercises. Here is an example:

1 push-up (first student leader)

2 sit-ups (second leader adds on)

3 coffee-grinders (third leader adds on)

4 crab kicks (fourth leader adds on)

5 golden rests (fifth leader adds on)

6 leaping leaps (sixth leader adds on)

7 jumping jacks (seventh leader adds on)

8 forward lunges (eighth leader adds on)

9 carioca steps (ninth leader adds on)

10 skipping skips (10th leader adds on)

11 rooster hops (11th leader adds on)

12 running steps (last student leader adds on)

Long Jump-Rope Fitness Routine

Students are in groups of three with a long jump rope. Two students are turning the rope, and the third student is the jumper. When the music comes on, the jumper makes three jumps and begins running a figure eight around the turners. Jumpers make three jumps each time they enter the center of the figure eight. The focus

is on entering the jumping area with the turning rope, making the three jumps, and then continuing on around the figure eight. When the music stops, a new jumper starts and the old jumper becomes a turner. The music should be programmed for 30 to 45 seconds of music and 10 to 15 seconds of no music for change time.

Jump and Jog Fitness

Set up five or six cones in a circle around the gym with two or three jump ropes at each cone. Students need to get a partner and start at one of the cones. One partner jumps rope at the cone, while the other partner jogs around the circle. Partners switch roles with the completion of each lap. Teachers can vary the student movement around the cones with the following: walk, jog, slide, do carioca steps, power skip, and perform butt kickers (heels hit the butt).

As students improve their rope-jumping skills, the teacher can vary the foot patterns with the following: two-foot basic step, jog step, side swings (left and right), jumping-jack step, ski jump step, scissors step, crossovers, and double jumps. Teachers can also stop the action and lead the class in a strength or flexibility exercise and then return the students to the jump and jog activities.

Circuit Training Fitness with a Jog

Create stations for jumping rope, crab kicks, stretching, and doing sit-ups, treadmills, arm circles, agility runs, and push-ups. Students exercise for 30 seconds at each station for the first week and have 5 to 10 seconds to move up to the next station. During the next week, the station intervals can be longer, and a jog can be added around the circuit stations before moving up. The jog can be varied with a slide, power skip, carioca steps, and backward run. Variations for each station can be added or substituted. Station cards can have two or three variations of the exercise.

Partner Resistance and Aerobic Movement Fitness

Students alternate between a partner resistance activity and an aerobic activity. The intervals for the partner resistance activities should be 45 to 60 seconds and 30 seconds for the aerobic movement intervals. Students can work with a partner at a station that has a card listing the various resistance activities and aerobic activities. The resistance activities can be grouped into upper-body and lower-body activities. Each resistance activity should take 8 to 10 seconds through the full range of motion. Partners should provide enough resistance to allow the exerciser to complete the

HEALTH CLUB WORKOUTS

This group of activities are generally taught in health clubs. An important outcome for quality physical education programs is to graduate students who feel comfortable joining a health club. Students must leave high school having the perceived competence to participate with older adults. Many people will not join community clubs and organizations because they feel they are incompetent and will embarrass themselves. There are many activities that are popular in clubs, including spinning, aerobic dance, kickboxing, and Pilates. The intent of the following activities are to stimulate teachers to teach and stay current with activities taught in nearby health clubs. These activities change regularly, and course instruction in physical education will have to stay current to be relevant to juniors and seniors taking physical education classes.

Aerobics Workouts

At present, many types of aerobic activities are being taught in health clubs. Aerobic dance is the basis for many variations of rhythmic exercise now implemented. These routines develop a high level of cardiorespiratory fitness, as well as strength and flexibility. Popular music is used to increase the activity enjoyment. Rhythmic aerobic exercise consists of a mixture of fundamental movements—dance steps, swinging movements, and stretching exercises. Routines are developed to music that has a definite and obvious beat. Other variations of aerobic dance are step aerobics and low-impact aerobics. These are popular because they eliminate some of the stress on the legs and joints. The height of the steps can help determine the desired workload.

The activities and routines should ease the burden of learning. If the movement patterns are too difficult, students become self-conscious and discouraged. Use the following points as guidelines when teaching new aerobic exercise routines.

- Alternate the intensity of the activities. This allows interval training to be built into the routines. Stretching movements can be alternated with demanding locomotor movements.

- Routines motivate more students when they appear not to be dance activities. The challenge is to develop demanding routines that will increase the

repetition in 8 to 10 seconds. After one repetition, the partners change roles. The aerobic activities can be done in place (jumping-jack variations) or moving around the stations (jog, skip, or slide). Several variations will be demonstrated. The complete descriptions of the partner activities are on pages 360–361.

- Energetic and positive teachers strongly influence the success of the presentations. Students need to see teachers enjoying fitness activities.

The following steps and movements can be used to develop a wide variety of routines. The majority are performed to four counts, although this can be varied depending on the skill level of the students.

Running and Walking Steps

1. Directional runs can be done forward, backward, diagonally, sideways, or turning.

2. Rhythmic runs integrate a specific movement (knee lift, clap, jump, jump-turn) on the fourth beat.

3. Runs with stunts are performed while lifting the knees, kicking up the heels, or slapping the thighs or heels. Runs can also be done with the legs extended, such as the goose step.

4. Runs with the arms in various positions can include the arms on the head, straight up or down, or on the hips.

Movements on the Floor

1. Sit-ups or curl-ups can be used in many ways. For example, use four counts: (1) up to the knees, (2) touch the floor, (3) back to the knees, (4) return to the floor. A V-seat can be held for two counts and rested for two counts.

2. Side-leg raises can be done with a straight leg on the side or the lower leg can be extended while positioned on your back with bent knees.

3. Alternate leg raises are performed in supine position with one leg raised to meet the opposite hand. Repeat using the opposite leg or both legs.

4. Push-ups can be done in two- or four-count movements. A four count would be as follows: (1) halfway down, (2) touch chest to floor, (3) halfway up, (4) arms fully extended.

5. Crab kicks and treadmills can be performed to four-count movements.

Standing Movements

1. **Lunge Variations.** To perform a lunge, step forward onto the right foot while bending at the

endurance level of all participants. All students should feel comfortable performing the routines.

- Follow-the-leader activities work well with students after they have developed a repertoire of movements. Each student can be responsible for leading one activity.

knees and extending arms into the air (counts one and two). Return to the starting position by bringing the right foot back and pulling arms into a jogging position (counts three and four). Vary the exercise by changing the direction of the move or the depth and speed of the lunge.

2. **Side Bends.** Begin with the feet apart. Reach overhead while bending to the side. This movement is usually done to four beats: (1) reach, (2) bend, (3) return, and (4) arm down.

3. **Reaches.** Alternate reaching upward with the right and left arms. Reaches can be done sideways also and are usually two-count movements.

4. **Arm and Shoulder Circles.** Make arm circles with one or both arms. Vary the size and speed of the circles. Shoulder shrugs can be done in similar fashion.

Jumping-Jacks Variations

1. **Arms Alternately Extended.** Jump with the arms alternately extended upward and pulled into the chest.

2. **Side Jumping Jacks.** Use regular arm action while the feet are kept together for jumping forward, backward, and sideways.

3. **Variations with Feet.** Try forward stride alternating, forward and side stride alternating, kicks or knee lifts, crossing the feet, and a heel–toe step.

Bounce Steps

1. **Bounce and Clap.** The step is similar to the slow-time jump-rope step. Clap on every other bounce.

2. **Bounce, Turn, and Clap.** Make a quarter- or half-turn with each jump.

3. **Three Bounces and Clap.** Bounce three times and then clap and bounce on the fourth beat. Turns can be performed using the four counts.

4. **Bounce and Rock Side to Side.** Transfer weight from side to side and forward and backward. Add clapping or arm swinging.

5. **Bounce with Body Twist.** Hold the arms at shoulder level and twist the lower body back and forth on each bounce.

6. **Bounce with Floor Patterns.** Bounce and make different floor patterns such as a box, diagonal, or triangle.

7. **Bounce with Kick Variations.** Perform different kick variations such as knee lift, kick, knee lift, and

kick; double kicks, knee lift, and slap knees; kick and clap under the knees. Combine the kicks with two- or four-count turns.

Activities with Manipulative Equipment

1. **Jump Ropes.** Using the jump rope, perform basic steps such as forward, backward, slow, and fast time. Jump on one foot, cross arms, and jump while jogging. Swing the rope from side to side with the handles in one hand and jump over it.

2. **Beanbags.** Toss and catch the beanbags while performing various locomotor movements. Challenge students using different tosses.

3. **Hoops.** Rhythmically swing the hoop around different body parts. Perform different locomotor movements around and over hoops.

4. **Balls.** Bounce, toss, and dribble balls; add locomotor movements while performing tasks.

Sample Routine

1. March, moving arms in large circles.

2. Hold a side lunge position and circle the right arm. Do reverse circling with the left arm.

3. Bounce forward twice, slapping thighs; then bounce backward twice, thrusting arms in the air.

4. Bounce and clap. Perform a quarter turn on every second bounce. Perform movement clockwise and counterclockwise.

5. Do a grapevine step with a clap on the fourth beat. Repeat it to the left.

6. Perform a jumping-jack variation, extending arms up and out.

7. Bounce and twist.

8. Do a two-count version of side jumping jacks.

9. Bounce, bounce, bounce, and clap to a four-count movement.

10. Do rhythmic running with a clap on the fourth beat. While running, move into a circle formation.

11. Bounce and twist.

12. Perform side leg raises with each leg.

13. Do rhythmic running with a clap on every fourth beat.

Strength Training

Most teachers use strength development through strength training. Physical education programs should instruct students in the use of weights and weight machines for proper development with an emphasis on safety. Using strength training as an instructional unit is often difficult because of lack of equipment and facilities.

Strength-training routines should develop all major body parts. This prevents the excessive development of specific body parts, which can lead to postural or joint problems. Exercises should be performed through the full range of motion. If training is being done for a specific sport, it may be important to analyze the sport and develop exercises that replicate the range of motion it uses.

Strength exercises should be performed at a speed similar to the movements performed in various physical activities. If a student is involved in an activity requiring speed, then the exercises should be performed at a similar speed. Similarly, if a student is training for activities demanding high levels of endurance, the exercises should be designed to increase this attribute. When the sport or activity demands strength, the training program can be geared to develop muscular strength. In each case, students should understand program differences and be able to develop a personal program. For an in-depth discussion of strength training, see Chapter 20 (pages 499–504).

Safety

Students must know and practice necessary safety precautions. The following points should be clear and reinforced regularly. It is wise to post safety rules as a further reminder and to avoid possible lawsuits.

■ Perform warm-up exercises before intense lifting. These may be a set of calisthenics or a set of strength exercises at a lower level.

■ Use correct form to prevent injury as well as to develop strength. When a heavy weight is lifted from the floor, the lift should be done with bent knees, straight back, and head up.

■ Spot weight lifters. Spotters are absolutely necessary when near-maximum weight is being lifted. Exercises such as the bench press, squats, and declined presses should always have two students present to spot.

■ Check the equipment regularly. Weights should be checked by the instructor before each period and by students each time they use them. Collars should be tightly fastened, cables checked, and bolts on machines periodically tightened.

■ Wear wide leather practice belts when heavy lifting is performed. This prevents injury to the lower back and abdominal wall.

■ Explain all exercises in class before implementation. This implies that proper form, points of safety, and necessary spotting be discussed before students participate.

Repetitions and Sets

There are many theories about the proper number of repetitions and sets that need to be performed to achieve optimum results. Repetitions are the number of times a participant performs an exercise to make a set. Each set, in turn, consists of a specified number of repetitions of the same exercise. Determining the proper number of repetitions or sets is difficult. Literally dozens of experts have researched this area without agreement. For physical education classes, a middle-of-the-road approach is probably best. Three sets of 10 repetitions should be performed for each exercise.

Strength or Endurance?

Muscular strength and endurance are developed using different methods. If maximum strength is desired, the exercise program should emphasize heavy strength and fewer repetitions. If endurance is the desired outcome, the program should emphasize a high number of repetitions with less strength. Some strength and endurance will be developed regardless of the type of program, but major gains will depend on the selected emphasis.

Frequency and Rest Intervals

Frequency is the number of workouts per week. The most common pattern is lifting every other day, leaving 3 days to recover and dissipate waste products. Some participants alternate by exercising the upper body and the lower body on different days. This results in a 6-day program while retaining the day of rest between workouts.

The rest interval between repetitions and sets can be timed carefully to increase the intensity of the workout. By organizing the exercises in a circuit stressing different muscle groups, the amount of time needed for a total workout can be reduced. In other words, less recovery time is needed between sets if the next exercise places demands on a different group of muscles.

Body Bar Exercises

Body Bars are new and innovative fitness equipment that can be used to supplement the strength-training component of the health club physical education program. Body Bars are fitness bars that were developed in 1987 and are available in regular length, which is 4-feet long (3, 6, 9, 12, 15, 18, and 24 lb), mini-length, which is 2-feet long (4 and 6 lb), and the heavy model, which is 5-feet long (30 and 36 lb). Flex bars are also available in 3- and 4-foot lengths with varying resistance depending on the students' abilities. Most high school girls should consider the regular length at 18 lb. Boys should consider the 18- or 24-lb versions or the heavier models, but it is still an individual approach, so it is nice to have a variety of lengths and weights.

Body Bars can be combined with stability balls or medicine balls in a variety of lessons and circuit-training situations. We suggest the following lifts with the Body Bars, which are explained in Chapter 20 in the strength-training unit section.

Lower Body

- Squat—quadriceps
- Squats with military press—quadriceps and deltoids
- Squats with toe raises—quadriceps and gastrocnemius muscles
- Lunges—gluteus maximus
- Straight leg dead lift—hamstrings
- Wide leg squats and plies—adductors
- Toe raises—gastrocnemius muscles

Upper Body

Figure 16.10 depicts a student performing pull-ups using a Body Bar with the help of two other students.

- Bench press—pectorals
- Bent-over rows—latissimus dorsi
- Military press—deltoids
- Forward raises—deltoids
- Standing rowing—deltoids
- Arm curls—biceps
- Arm curl 7s—biceps (seven counts halfway up and continue seven counts for the second half of the repetition, followed by seven counts for the full range of motion during the next repetition).
- Tricep extensions—triceps

Core

- Sit-ups with bar at chest

In Figure 16.11, student performs sit-ups using a Body Bar with a partner. The standing partner can perform an arm curl with each repetition.

- Bar on shelf sit-ups (sit-up with bar at the chest and then a military press at the top of the sit-up)

FIGURE 16.10 Pull-ups using a Body Bar and two partners

Unit Planning

Chapter 20 contains several ideas and activities for a unit on strength training that can be modified or augmented to meet the needs of the instructor, the students, and the physical education program.

Cardio Kickboxing

Cardio kickboxing is a popular physical activity that is being offered in many health clubs and fitness centers to attract new participants and motivate continuing members. Cardio kickboxing, which is also sometimes known as aerobic kickboxing, Tae Bo, or cardio karate is a rhythmic repetition of boxing jabs and punches, karate kicks and blows, combined with the movements or elements of aerobic dance. This activity can be used to attract and challenge all levels of students in the schools. Cardio kickboxing can be incorporated into the program as a stand-alone unit or as a part of a variety of fitness routines that are a segment of each day's lesson. There are videotapes available that offer easy-to-understand instruction in developing lessons and kickboxing routines. Start with a direct instruction style with students in a scatter formation by leading students through basic techniques on the boxer's stance and shuffle. Then progress into various punches

FIGURE 16.11 Partner sit-ups with a Body Bar

and kicks. Once the basic skills have been learned and students are comfortable, a variety of routines can be introduced to incorporate all of the skills.

Cardio Kickboxing Basic Skills

Boxer's stance. This is the ready position for most kicks and punching activities. Hands are held about chin high, with the dominant hand slightly behind the opposite hand in most cases. Carry the weight on the balls of the feet, with the feet pointed straight ahead and the dominant foot to the rear of the front foot. Most punches require a weight transfer and a pivot off the rear foot.

Boxer's center jog stance. This stance involves bouncing on both feet, with the hands up to the chin, and the feet even, parallel, and a shoulder width apart. This stance is used to lead into the boxer's stance described previously. It is also an effective position to practice bobbing and weaving to each side by dropping the head and upper body.

Punches and blocks: jab, cross, uppercut, hook, blocks, and flutter jabs. The jab is with the lead arm and it snaps forward and back. The cross is made with the rear arm and involves a shoulder turn and a pivot on the rear foot. The uppercut involves dropping the knee and starting a circular windmill motion with the arm. This is followed by rotating the hips and extending the knee upward as the punch comes up and forward. The hook can be performed with either arm and involves a slight drop of the arm and a rounded hooking motion to hit the side of the target. Blocks involve

moving either arm upward in an L shape to block a punch. Flutter jabs can be done from the center jog stance and involve a burst of continuous jabs.

Kicks: front, side, and roundhouse. The front kick involves a step with the opposite foot followed by bringing the knee up with a flexed ankle and extending the kick forward. The right side kick involves stepping sideways with the right foot, then crossing over with the left foot, bringing the right knee up, and extending the kick to the side, bringing the right knee up, and extending the kick to the side (see Figure 16.12). The roundhouse kick involves stepping forward with the opposite foot, raising the kicking leg to a flexed position, pivoting on the rear foot, and exploding the kick forward with the toes pointed.

An effective lesson sequence would involve the following:

FIGURE 16.12 Side kicks in cardio kickboxing

1. Boxer's jog with bobbing and weaving, jabs and blocks.

2. Left jabs and right jabs.

3. Left hooks and right hooks.

4. Left uppercuts and right uppercuts.

5. Left jab combos (jab, jab, cross) and right jab combos.

6. Left forward kicks and right forward kicks.

7. Left side kicks and right side kicks.

8. Left roundhouse kicks and right roundhouse kicks.

9. Left combo kicks and right combo kicks.

After these skills have been introduced in a scatter formation and students are comfortable performing, all of these combinations can be put into fun and challenging routines with music. One option is to have students moving in waves across the length of the floor in continuous movement. When all students get to the opposite end of the floor, give them a new variation routine

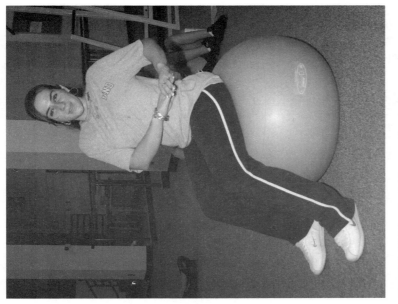

FIGURE 16.14 Stretching on the ball

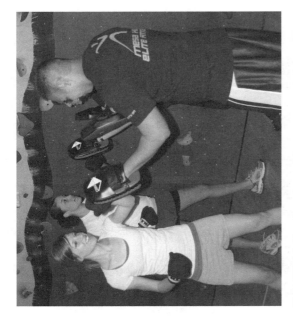

FIGURE 16.13 Sparring with partners wearing sparring mitts

to follow for going back across the floor. Remind students to focus on their skills and to do their best. The next instructional variation is to have partners or small groups work with the sparring mitts so they practice striking the mitts (see Figure 16.13). Remind students that this class is **not** a self-defense class and the focus is on the physical workout. The kicks and punches may be the same as a self-defense class, but students are not taught the overall philosophy of self-defense and need to be careful with these ideas.

Stability Balls

The exercise or stability balls have been gaining popularity with schools and health clubs and offer an activity that can be done at home, work, or in a club. The physical education program is an excellent place to get started and learn the basics of the balls. Activities on the balls can be modified many ways by varying the position of the ball to ensure that all students are being challenged and can find success quickly. The ball provides an unstable base for exercising and adds challenge for the core muscles of the stomach, back, sides, and buttocks. Many stretching and flexibility activities can be done on the balls (see Figure 16.14). Work on the balls helps to remind students about good posture and proper alignment of the body. Work on the balls can tie to other activity programs such as strength training with hand weights or stretch bands, yoga activities, and Pilates. You can even do a line dance using the arms and upper body, such as the "Macarena." Students can use the balls to personalize their workouts and improve their performance in other sports or activities. There are varying sizes and quality of the balls, so it is important to research prices and sizes.

Basic Skills for the Stability or Exercise Ball

Safety. It is important to teach students safety for getting on and off the ball and staying on the ball. Always use two hands and both feet in a stable position and move slowly and carefully. Many activities are performed with the ball against the wall or with a partner for stability. It takes time and practice to get used to the motion of the ball.

Basic Sit, Lie, All Fours. These are basic positions and serve as starting points for many of the exercises. In the sitting position, the feet should be a shoulder width apart with the thighs parallel to the ground and a 90° angle formed with the lower legs. Good posture should always be practiced (head up, shoulders back, stomach in and relaxed). Have students move into the lying position on all fours and move around slightly side to side, forward and back, and in a circular motion to get comfortable on the balls (Figure 16.15).

Hand Walk with the Ball (Push-up Variations). From the all-fours position, move forward by walking the hands forward until the hips and thighs are on the ball. Try to work under control and balance. Continue to move forward until the knees are on the ball and

FIGURE 16.15 Additional challenges on the ball

then forward until your shins and ankles are on the ball. If you can, try some slight push-ups in any of these positions (see Figure 16.16).

Sit-ups on the Ball. Move to a lying position on the ball. Roll forward and lower the buttocks toward the floor while keeping the upper body more vertical. Try crunches from this position. Continue to roll back farther up on the ball to increase the difficulty of the curl-ups. Hold the hands near the ears and add a slight twist to each side as you come up.

Squats with the Ball. Move the feet to a shoulder-width position with the ball pressed against a wall. Position the ball in the lower-back area. Slowly roll down on the ball into a squat position with the thighs parallel to the floor. Small dumbbells can be added to increase the strength.

Superperson Challenge Position. A more challenging skill involving multiple muscle groups begins in the all-fours position while lifting the left arm and the right leg in superperson style. Work on balance and then try the opposite side. Next, try both hands held in the air with one leg and then switch legs. Eventually, try both arms and legs in the air like the "real" super-person.

Additional Stability Ball Exercises

(See also Chapter 20, Strength Training section for strength training ideas.)

Lower Body

- Wall squats—quadriceps

FIGURE 16.16 Push-ups on the ball

- Lunges with Russian twist—gluteus maximus
- Woodchoppers with toe raise—quadriceps and gastrocnemius muscles (Place the ball up, over, and behind the head and then down to the toes.)
- Glute lift (two legs/one leg)—gluteus maximus
- Hamstring press—hamstrings
- Hamstring lift—hamstrings
- Adductor presses—adductors
- Bent-over glute raises—gluteus maximus

Upper Body

- Bench press with Body Bar—pectorals (see Figure 16.17)
- One handed bent-over rows with dumbbell—latissimus dorsi
- Push-ups with legs on ball—pectorals
- Flies with dumbbells—pectorals
- Military press with Body Bar or dumbbells—deltoids
- Lateral raises with dumbbells—deltoids
- Forward raises with Body Bar or dumbbells while performing wall squats—deltoids
- Arm curls sitting or preacher curls—biceps
- Tricep extensions sitting or laying with Body Bar or dumbbells—triceps
- Kickbacks with dumbbells—triceps
- Dips—triceps

Core

- Crunches
- Hand-to-opposite-knee crunches

FIGURE 16.17 Bench press with Body Bar on stability ball

- Plank

- Plank knees to chest

- Plank to V

- Russian twists (In partial sit-up position, twist left and right, and touch the ball to the floor.)

- Ball-on-shelf sit-ups

- Hand-to-feet switch

- Suitcase with ball and barbells (Sit on ball and then tilt left and right as if you are holding a suitcase.)

- Side twists with wall

- Roll outs

- Sit, lay, sit

Stability Ball Fitness Routine

The following is an example of a stability ball fitness routine developed by Ron Schoenwetter at Greenfield Junior High School in Gilbert, Arizona. Students work with a partner and are equipped with a stability ball. Partner A performs any type of locomotor movement once or twice around the perimeter (basketball floor, gymnasium, rectangle of cones, etc.), while partner B performs an exercise on the stability ball.

- Partner A performs sit-ups, balancing on the stability ball, while partner B jogs around the perimeter twice. Upon his or her return, both partners switch roles and repeat the exercise.

- Partner A performs push-ups on the stability ball, while partner B performs a basketball slide around the perimeter once. When partner B returns, partner A then slides while partner B performs push-ups.

- Partner A performs a supine reverse trunk curl, while partner B performs carioca steps around the perimeter once. The reverse trunk curl is done by lying flat on the floor with both feet on top of the

ball; partner A grips the ball with heels and hamstrings and pulls ball in to the body. This is repeated until partner B returns. Partners then switch activities.

- Partner A uses the stability ball to perform wall squats against a wall, while Partner B performs a two-step around the perimeter once. The partners switch roles.

- Partner A performs a hamstring curl, while partner B jogs backward around the perimeter. The hamstring curl is performed by lying facedown on the floor and the stability ball, resting on top of the hamstrings. Partner A uses his or her heels to squeeze the ball against the gluteus maximus for 5–7 seconds. He or she squeezes and releases the ball until partner B returns. The partners switch roles.

- Partner A performs a side-lying abduction, while partner B jogs around the perimeter twice. Abduction is performed by starting in a side-lying position with the bottom leg bent. The top leg is extended out to the side with the foot resting on the floor. Both hands are supported on the front of the ball. Partner A slowly abducts the top leg until it is parallel to the floor then pauses at the top and lowers the leg. Partner A repeats this activity until partner B completes one lap. Partner A then switches sides while partner B jogs the second lap. After that, partners switch roles.

- Partner A performs a side-lying adduction, while partner B skips around the perimeter twice. Adduction starts in a side-lying position on the floor with an elevated leg. The ball is centered under the ankle. The lower leg is flexed to 90 degrees and rests on the floor under the top leg. The head rests on one arm, and the other arm is on the floor in front of the body. Partner A adducts the lower leg until it lifts off the floor 3–4 inches, then pauses at the top and lowers the leg. Partner A repeats this activity until partner B finishes his or her first lap; then switch legs on his or her second lap. After that, partners switch roles.

- Partner A performs a supine leg curl, while partner B performs carioca steps around the perimeter once. This begins in a supine position with the heels on top of the ball. The hands rest on the floor, and the lower back and buttocks are slightly off the floor. Partner A curls the ball in toward the buttocks and rolls it back to the starting position. This is repeated until partner B returns. Then the partners switch roles.

- Partner A performs a Russian twist, while partner B performs power skips around the perimeter once. The twist begins with the performer sitting on the floor and the ball on one side of the body. Partner A begins by touching the ball to the floor on each side of his or her body continuously and as fast as possible. It is important not to sacrifice good technique for speed. (An advanced version requires the performer to keep his or her feet 3 inches off the ground throughout the routine.) Partner A performs this until partner B returns, when the partners switch roles.

Medicine Balls

The medicine ball has gained popularity and can add a nice challenge for students in a fitness workout. They can be used in a variety of ways to focus on all parts of the body. After students become comfortable with them, they can be used in a circuit with combinations of other pieces of equipment such as jump bands, jump ropes, or stability balls. We suggest that students start with a partner who has about the same height or strength ability. Most girls should start with a 2-kg (4.4-lb) ball and boys with a 3-kg (6.6-lb) ball. Organize students in two lines facing each other and use the length of the gym to avoid injuries with overthrows, missed catches, and runaway balls. We suggest a ball that bounces and has a good grip.

The following is a list of exercises for medicine ball routines, developed by Maria Corte at Mesa High School in Mesa, Arizona. Students work in pairs with partners of their choice. Each pair is equipped with a 4-lb medicine ball.

Warm-ups

Around the World. One partner has a medicine ball, while the opposite partner faces him or her. Both partners begin by holding the ball or his or her hands above the head. Partner A rotates in a clockwise direction, bringing the ball all the way to the floor and back above the head. Partner B does the same without the ball. This is done five times and then the partners switch directions for five rotations. Then partners exchange the ball and repeat the activity.

Good Mornings. Partners again face each other about 10 feet apart with one ball. Keeping the back straight and the ball or hands above the head, both partners bend at the waist and back up to a straight position. It is important to keep the head up and back straight.

Wood Choppers. The student holds the ball between the legs, brings it up above the head, and returns it down between the legs (simulating chopping wood).

Lower-Body/Upper-Body Exercises

Overhead Lunges/Power Squats. Partners are side by side with one holding the medicine ball above the head. Both partners perform 10 walking lunges. Partners then exchange the ball, change direction, and continue the activity. This is performed three times each. It is important to keep the knee parallel to the toe when lunging.

Toss Series A. Chest Toss, Overhead Toss, Underhand Toss, Combinations

- *Chest Toss*—Partners face each other approximately 5-10 feet apart. Partners perform a chest pass with the ball back and forth for about 20 seconds. It is important to keep hands out to give the partner a target and to help catch the ball safely.

- *Overhead Toss*—Partners stand approximately 5-10 feet apart. Partners perform the overhead pass back and forth for approximately 20 seconds. It is important to toss the ball above the partner's head.

- *Underhand Toss*—Partners stand approximately 5-10 feet apart. Using both hands, each partner tosses the medicine ball back and forth with an underhand motion for about 20 seconds.

- *Combinations*—After the previous three exercises are completed, they are put into a combination routine. Partners complete 10 repetitions of each, one after the other for 60 seconds.

Toss Series B. Left Lateral Toss, Right Lateral Toss, Chest Squat Toss, Combinations

- *Left Lateral Toss*—Partners face each other approximately 5-10 feet apart. The partner with the ball twists to his or her left and tosses the medicine ball to his or her partner. Upon catching the ball, the next partner twists to the left and tosses the ball back to his or her partner. It is important for both partners to bend down as they twist. This exercise is done for 10 repetitions each.

- *Right Lateral Toss*—Partners face each other approximately 5-10 feet apart. The partner with the ball twists to his or her right and tosses the medicine ball to his or her partner. Upon catching the ball, the next partner twists to the right and tosses the ball back to his or her partner. It is important for both partners to bend down as they twist. This exercise is done for 10 repetitions each.

- *Chest Squat Toss*—Partners face each other approximately 5-10 feet apart. Both partners simultaneously perform a squat. As the partner with the medicine ball comes up out of his or her squat, he or she gives a chest pass to the partner. Both partners perform squats again. As the partner with the ball comes out of his or her squat, he or she gives a chest pass back to the partner. This is repeated for 10 repetitions each.

- *Combinations*—After the previous three exercises are completed, they are put into a combination routine. Partners complete 10 repetitions of each, one after the other for 60 seconds.

Cardiovascular Exercises

1, 2, 3, Switch Chest Passes. Partners face each other approximately 5–10 feet apart. Partners perform three chest passes (total) and then run to switch places with each other. They continue the exercise for 10 repetitions.

Chest Pass Switch. Partners face each other approximately 5–10 feet apart. Partner A gives a chest pass to partner B; then partners switch places. The exercise continues for 20 repetitions.

Roll Pass. Partners form two single-file lines approximately 10 feet apart. The first two partners begin with partner A rolling the medicine ball diagonally down the court or field. Both partners run in a straight line downcourt. Partner B must pick up the ball and make a diagonal pass back to partner A. At this point, the next group of two may begin. This continues until they have reached the end of the exercise area. Upon finishing, both partners move to the outside of the area and hustle back to the original lines. This is done five times each.

Chest Pass. Partners begin in the same formation as the roll pass. Both partners slide downcourt while performing chest passes back and forth. It is important to lead the partner to the spot where he or she will be at the completion of the pass. Upon reaching the end of the designated area, both partners move to the outside of the area and return to the line. This exercise is performed five times each.

1, 2, 3, Switch. This is the same exercise as the chest pass (previous activity) except that partners must switch places after every third chest pass as they slide down the court. Upon reaching the end of the designated area, both partners move to the outside of the area and return to the line. This exercise is repeated for five repetitions each.

Abdominal Exercises

Russian Twists. Partners sit in pairs, facing the same direction about 5 feet apart and keeping their feet slightly off the ground. The partner on the right side starts with the ball. He or she taps the ball on the ground to the right side, left side, and then right side. After the third tap, he or she passes the ball to the part-

FIGURE 16.18 Russian twist with a partner toss using medicine balls

ner on the left. He or she catches the ball and repeats the same exercise (left, right, left), then passes the ball back to his or her partner. This sequence is repeated approximately five times each. Figure 16.18 shows the Russian twist with a partner toss.

Straddle Chest Passes. Partners face each other in a sit-up position. The partner with the medicine ball performs a sit-up and makes a chest pass to his or her partner, who is in the upright sit-up position. The partner catches the ball and performs a sit up. This sequence is repeated approximately 10 times each.

Chest Pass Sit-Ups. This is performed the same way as straddle chest passes with one difference. Both partners perform a sit-up simultaneously as they pass and catch the medicine ball. This sequence is repeated approximately 10–15 times.

Standing Twists. Partners stand back to back. The partner with the ball turns to his or her left and hands the medicine ball off to the partner, who is turning to his or her right. Partners work quickly but must maintain a quality position throughout. This pattern continues about 10–15 times, then partners change the direction of the handoff for another set of 10–15.

Upper Body Exercises

Plank Hold. Partner A assumes the plank position on the floor. Partner B places the medicine ball on his or her partner's back. Partner A must keep the ball steady for approximately 30 seconds. Partners then switch roles and repeat.

Trunk/Plank Rolls. Partners face each other in a push-up position about 3 feet apart. One partner rolls the ball diagonally across to his or her partner. The partner receives the pass with one hand and then rolls the ball to the other hand. The ball is then passed diagonally back to the first partner. The activity continues for 10 transfer passes. Directions of the ball can be changed to use both hands many times. Figure 16.19 shows the trunk/plank roll.

FIGURE 16.19 Trunk/plank roll with a partner

Cooldown

Cooldown/Stretch. Partners sit facing each other on the floor with feet spread in a straddle position. The partner with the medicine ball begins to roll the ball slowly with his or her fingers toward the partner, stretching the hamstrings and lower back. At the peak of the stretch, he or she slowly releases the ball to the partner who receives the ball and repeats the stretch. This sequence is repeated five times each.

Pilates

The Pilates training program originated with Joseph Pilates in Germany more than 80 years ago. The program has evolved over that time into a popular worldwide exercise program that has attracted millions of people of varying ages and physical abilities. It focuses on good posture, proper breathing, and fundamental exercises that stretch and strengthen the muscles. Pilates is a set of exercises done in a dynamic and rhythmic sequence in order to produce a low-intensity, calorie-burning workout that sculpts the muscles. In addition, Pilates works the core muscle groups (abdominal, lower back, hips, and buttocks) to produce a streamlined, longer, leaner body look. Advocates argue that Pilates makes them look and feel great. Pilates can be added to a physical education program in many ways. There are many books and videos with different combinations of Pilates that can be used to get students started on a program.

The following is an example of a beginner sequence of exercises:

Stretch with Knee Sway. On your back, pull your knees up to your chest, flatten your lower back and hold this pose. Then slowly lower your knees to one side and then the other.

Spinal Rotation. Sitting in a slight straddle position with the legs extended and the arms out to the side, slowly rotate the upper body to the left and right.

The Hundred. On your back with the legs at a 90° angle, lift the shoulders and arms up slightly and exhale five times pressing the hands down and then five times pressing the hands upward. Increase the repetitions until this sequence can be done 10 times for 100 breaths.

Abdominal Strengthener. Lie on your back with hands behind the head and knees flexed; exhale and curl up slowly using just the abdominal muscles. Repeat five to six times. Figure 16.20 shows another abdominal strengthener, the crisscross.

Lower Abdominal Strengthener. Use the same position as before with a mat under the hips. Start the knees at 90° with the ankles crossed and slowly curl the hips up towards your chest.

Rolling Ball. Sit curled up by hugging the ankles and curling the spine. Slowly roll backwards while maintaining the position. Repeat five to six times.

Single-Leg Stretch. Lie on your back with one leg extended about 12 inches off the floor. Flex the other leg and bring the knee to the chest. Hold the flexed leg and raise the shoulders slowly. Hold the position while rotating the position of the legs.

Double Straight Leg. Lie on your back, hands behind your head with the legs pointed toward the ceiling while held tight together. Lift the chin and shoulders slightly off the mat and lower the legs about 1 foot. Keep the lower back tight to the floor. Repeat five to six times.

Forward Spine Stretch and Roll-Ups. Start in a sitting position with the legs and arms extended forward. Stretch forward and exhale. Repeat five to six times and then add the roll-up by slowly going backward to the mat with the arms extended.

Bridge. Lie on your back with the arms extended, the palms down, and the knees bent. Lift the upper body upwards using the abdominal muscles only. Hold for eight counts and repeat several times.

Back Strengthener. Start in an all-fours position. Lift and extend the opposite arm and leg and hold the position several seconds and then switch arms and legs. Repeat several times.

FIGURE 16.20 The crisscross abdominal strengthener

FIGURE 16.21 Side plank with twist in (a) the starting position, and (b) the down position

Side Plank with an Oblique Twist. In Figure 16.21, students demonstrate the starting position of Pilates exercise side plank with twist (a), and the twist down to the floor. (b)

Total Rest Pose. Start in an all-fours position. Push the hips to your heels and your stomach to your thighs. Slowly extend the arms forward with your palms flat on the floor and hold for a longer count.

Yoga

Yoga is one of the most popular fitness practices of today. Considering the fast pace and multiple activities of our lives, yoga can provide a mental and physical focus that helps people deal with their lives. It can be implemented into the physical education program as a brief 10- to 15-minute fitness routine as a part of a four-part lesson, as a 2-week unit that meets daily, or as part of a semester unit that combines many health-club–type activities such as Pilates, kickboxing, and stability and medicine ball routines. Yoga has grown in popularity because of the variety of holistic mind-body benefits that it can provide for students of any ability level, from excellent athletes to average-skilled students and anyone in-between those levels. There are many different forms and variations of yoga. Many of these forms focus on multiple topics, including breathing, diet, personal behavior, meditation, relaxation, stress management, and health promotion. It can be a wonderful addition to your program.

Power Yoga

Power yoga is an active form of yoga that links a flowing sequence of poses together in continual succession. The sequence of poses or postures are designed to warm up the body, increase circulation, improve muscular strength and endurance, increase flexibility and range of motion, and relieve mental and physical stress.

Strength Yoga

Strength yoga incorporates more challenging arm-balancing poses into the power yoga sequence to help develop muscular strength in the upper body and improve posture. This workout is effective in improving physical performance and confidence, releasing tension, and promoting peace of mind.

Basic Beginning Poses

The following are recommended beginner poses for your beginning classes. Students need to learn these yoga terms and poses. It will take beginners awhile to get comfortable with them and feel like they are having success. Detailed information on all of these poses is available from many sources, including Internet searches, DVDs, and texts in our suggested readings. Most state and district AAHPERD associations will provide yoga information and certifications.

- Basic Sitting
- Breathing Arms
- Child's Pose
- Downward-Facing Dog
- Mountain Pose
- Stork to Knee
- Stork to Thigh
- Side Bending

- Star (see Figure 16.22)
- Forward Lunge
- Plank
- Seal
- Triangle (see Figure 16.23)
- Forward Lunge with Yoga Arms
- Proud Warrior
- Downward-Facing Dog with Leg Lift
- Side One Arm
- Side One Arm with Leg Lift
- Sun Salutation (see Figure 16.24)
- Triceps Plank
- L Sit
- Rocking Horse
- Relaxation Supine with Breathing
- Yoga Sitting
- Side Leans
- Breathing Arms

FIGURE 16.22　Star position

FIGURE 16.23　Triangle pose

FIGURE 16.24　Sun salutation

STUDY STIMULATORS AND REVIEW QUESTIONS

1. What are the main differences between the criterion-referenced and norm-referenced fitness tests?

2. Identify the different types of standards often used with health-related and skill-related fitness tests.

3. Explain the influence of heredity on students' ability to perform well on physical fitness tests.

4. What are the consequences of the belief that physical activity and fitness performance are highly related?

5. Discuss the basis for the recommendation that every U.S. adult should accumulate 60 minutes or more of moderate to vigorous physical activity on most, preferably all, days of the week.

6. Describe the main purpose for the development of the Physical Activity Pyramid.

7. Explain why "lifestyle activities" make up the base of the Physical Activity Pyramid.

8. Discuss four strategies teachers should employ to create more positive fitness experiences for students.

9. What guidelines are offered for flexibility and stretching exercises?

10. What legacy should a quality physical education program offer its graduates?

REFERENCES AND SUGGESTED READINGS

American Alliance for Health, Physical Education, Research, and Dance. (1987). *Youth fitness test manual*. Reston, VA: Author.

American College of Sports Medicine. (2000). *Guidelines for exercise testing and prescription* (6th ed.). Baltimore, MD: Williams and Wilkins.

Austin, D. (2002). *Pilates for every body*. New York: Rodale.

Bouchard, C. (1999). Heredity and health related fitness. In C. B. Corbin & R. P. Pangrazi (Eds.), *Toward a better understanding of physical fitness & activity*. Scottsdale, AZ: Holcomb Hathaway Publishers.

Bouchard, C., Dionne, F. T., Simoneau, J., & Boulay, M. (1992). Genetics of aerobic and anaerobic performances. *Exercise and Sport Sciences Reviews, 20*, 27–58.

Brown, C. (2004). *The Pilates Program for every body*. Pleasantville, NY: Reader's Digest with Tucker Slingsby Ltd.

Cooper Institute. (2004). *Fitnessgram test administration manual* (3rd ed.). Champaign, IL: Human Kinetics Publishers.

Corbin, C. B., & Pangrazi, R. P. (1992). Are American children and youth fit? *Research Quarterly for Exercise and Sport, 63*(2), 96–106.

Corbin, C. B., & Pangrazi, R. P. (2004). *Physical activity for children: A statement of guidelines for children ages 5–12* (2nd ed.). Reston, VA: National Association for Sport and Physical Education.

Corbin, C. B., Welk, G. J., Corbin, W. R., & Welk, K. A. (2008). *Concepts of fitness and wellness: A comprehensive lifestyle approach* (7th ed.). Boston: McGraw-Hill.

Craig, C. (2003). *Pilates on the ball*. Rochester, VT: Healing Arts Press.

Darst, P. W., Pangrazi, R. P., & Stillwell, B. (1995). Middle school physical education—Make it more exciting. *Journal of Physical Education, Recreation, and Dance, 66*(8), 8–9.

Fronske, H. (2008). *Teaching cues for sport skills* (4th ed.). San Francisco: Benjamin Cummings.

Gallagher-Mundy, C. (2004). *Exercise ball for beginners*. New York: HarperCollins.

Glasser, W. (1976). *Positive addiction*. New York: Harper and Row.

Groves, B. (2002). Weight training. In N. Dougherty (Ed.), *Physical activity and sport for the secondary school student* (5th ed.). Reston, VA: NASPE and AAHPERD.

Hedley, A. A., Ogden C. L., Johnson, C. L., Carroll, M. D., Curtin, L. R., & Flegal, K. M. (2004). Prevalence of overweight and obesity among U.S. children, adolescents, and adults, 1999–2002. *Journal of the American Medical Association, 291*(23), 2847–2850.

Macfarlane, P. A. (1993). Out with the sit-up, in with the curl-up. *Journal of Physical Education, Recreation, and Dance, 64*(6), 62–66.

McCurdy, K. W., Langford, G. A., & Maina, M. P. (2004). Inclusion of appropriate resistance exercises in physical education. *Teaching Elementary Physical Education, 15*(No. 3), 30–34.

Mood, D. P., Musker, F. E., & Rink, J. E. (2007). *Sports and recreational activities* (14th ed.). Boston: McGraw-Hill.

Morrow, J. R., Jr., & Freedson, P. W. (1994). Relationship between habitual physical activity and aerobic fitness in adolescents. *Pediatric Exercise Science, 6*(4), 315–329.

National Association for Sport and Physical Education. (2004). *Physical activity for children: A statement of guidelines* (2nd ed.). Reston, VA: Author.

Pangrazi, R. P. (1994). Teaching fitness in physical education. In R. R. Pate & R. C. Hohn (Eds.), *Health and fitness through physical education* (pp. 75–80). Champaign, IL: Human Kinetics Publishers.

Pangrazi, R. P., & Corbin, C. B. (1990). Age as a factor relating to physical fitness test performance. *Research Quarterly for Exercise and Sport, 61*(4), 410–414.

Pangrazi, R. P., & Corbin, C. B. (1994). *Teaching strategies for improving youth fitness* (2nd ed.). Reston, VA: AAHPERD.

President's Council on Physical Fitness and Sports. (2007). *President's challenge handbook*. Washington, DC: U.S. Government Printing Office.

Sallis, J. F., & Patrick, K. (1994). Physical activity guidelines for adolescents: Consensus statement. *Pediatric Exercise Science, 6*(4), 302–314.

Schmottlach, N., & McManama, J. (2006). *The physical education handbook* (11th ed.). San Francisco: Benjamin Cummings.

Smith, L. L., Brunetz, M. H., Chenier, T. C., McCammon, M. R., Hourmard, J. A., & Franklin, M. E., et al. (1993). The effects of static and ballistic stretching on delayed onset muscle soreness and creatine kinase. *Research Quarterly for Exercise and Sport, 64*(1), 103–107.

U.S. Department of Health and Human Services. (1996). *Physical activity and health: A report of the surgeon general*. Atlanta, GA: U.S. Department of Health and Human Services, Centers for Disease Control and Prevention, National Center for Chronic Disease Prevention and Health Promotion.

U.S. Public Health Service. (1990). *Healthy people 2000: National health promotion and disease preventive objectives*. Washington, DC: U.S. Government Printing Office.

U.S. Public Health Service. (2000). *Healthy people 2010: National health promotion and disease objectives*. Washington, DC: U.S. Government Printing Office.

Walters, R. S. (2002). Aerobic fitness. In N. Dougherty (Ed.), *Physical activity and sport for the secondary school student* (5th ed.). Reston, VA: NASPE and AAHPERD.

WEB SITES

Fitness for Youth

www.americanheart.org/presenter.jhtml?identifier=4596
www.cdc.gov/nccdphp/dash/presphysactrpt/index.htm
www.fitnessgram.net/

Physical Activity Reports

www.cdc.gov/nccdphp/sgr/sgr.htm
www.health.gov/healthypeople/

Physical Fitness Assessment

www.fitnessgram.net/
www.presidentchallenge.org/

NATIONAL STANDARDS FOR PHYSICAL EDUCATION*

STANDARD 1 Demonstrates competency in motor skills and movement patterns needed to perform a variety of physical activities.

STANDARD 2 Demonstrates understanding of movement concepts, principles, strategies, and tactics as they apply to the learning and performance of physical activities.

STANDARD 3 Participates regularly in physical activity.

STANDARD 4 Achieves and maintains a health-enhancing level of physical fitness.

STANDARD 5 Exhibits responsible personal and social behavior that respects self and others in physical activity settings.

STANDARD 6 Values physical activity for health, enjoyment, challenge, self-expression, and/or social interaction.

ESSENTIAL COMPONENTS OF A QUALITY PROGRAM

COMPONENT 1 A quality physical education program is organized around content standards that offer direction and continuity to instruction and evaluation.

COMPONENT 2 A quality program is student centered and based on the developmental urges, characteristics, and interests of students.

COMPONENT 3 Quality physical education makes physical activity and motor-skill development the core of the program.

COMPONENT 4 Physical education programs teach management skills and self-discipline.

COMPONENT 5 Quality programs emphasize inclusion of all students.

COMPONENT 6 In a quality physical education setting, instruction focuses on the process of learning skills rather than the product or outcome of the skill performance.

COMPONENT 7 A quality physical education program teaches lifetime activities that students can use to promote their health and personal wellness.

COMPONENT 8 Quality physical education teaches cooperative and responsibility skills and helps students develop sensitivity to diversity and gender issues.

*Reprinted from *Moving Into the Future: National Standards for Physical Education*, 2nd ed. (2004), with permission from the National Association for Sport and Physical Education (NASPE), 1900 Association Dr., Reston, VA 20191-1599.

17

Healthy Lifestyles: Activities for Instruction

CHAPTER SUMMARY

This chapter focuses on teaching basic concepts of health and the related components that can be enhanced within the physical education setting. The chapter offers the methodology for holding discussions to develop an understanding and insight into behavior necessary to maintain an optimum level of health. A state of general health and personal functioning helps determine the quality of life. Discussion sessions must include the opportunity for students to have the psychological freedom to explore alternative lifestyles. A difficult skill for students to learn is independent decision making based upon careful consideration of alternatives and consequences rather than peer pressure. Teachers can help students understand the requisites of quality health by offering a discussion session that is structured so students can feel comfortable. Focus setting, clarifying, acknowledging, and silence are behaviors teachers need to learn to use when conducting discussion sessions.

To ensure total body development, exercises must follow principles of exercise. Stress affects performance and is not unique to any age group. Being overweight is associated with various degenerative diseases and can be curtailed through a reduction of caloric consumption and increased activity. Substance abuse among students is common and serves to stimulate the onset of emotional problems and degenerative diseases.

STUDENT OUTCOMES

After reading this chapter, you will be able to:

- Conduct a discussion session with students that successfully allows clarification and understanding of healthy lifestyle concepts.

- Describe how concepts for healthy living can be achieved through a properly structured instructional program of physical education.

- Understand the basic function of the skeletal, muscular, and cardiorespiratory systems.

- Explain how health instruction can be integrated into the physical education setting at the middle and high school level.

- Delineate the type of teacher behavior that enhances the development of self-concept among students.

- Identify risk factors that are associated with degenerative diseases.

- Discuss factors that are roadblocks to healthy lifestyles.

- Explain how stress reduction can be accomplished.

- Describe how students can learn to evaluate their levels of physical fitness.

- List a plan for improving self-control by altering behavior.

The need for teaching students how to maintain personal health for a lifetime becomes apparent when one examines the skyrocketing costs of minimal health care. Health insurance policies cost 5 to 10 percent of an individual's gross income. A short stay in the hospital may incur a bill for thousands of dollars, yet in spite of costs, Americans continue to put little or no effort into maintaining a healthy lifestyle.

Being healthy allows an individual to participate fully in life. Having the energy and enthusiasm to undertake activities after a full day's work is characteristic of people who are well. An individual who is healthy is not only free of sickness or other malady, but is happy, vibrant, and able to solve personal problems.

Teaching students how to achieve a lasting state of healthiness lends credibility to the physical education profession. For many years, physical educators were seen solely as teachers of physical skills who had little concern for the knowledge and comprehension involved in physical performance. The various personalities and unique needs of the student participants were often ignored by teachers who appeared to be concerned only about the product (i.e., "Learn the skill or else!"). The age-old argument of product versus process can be moderated by teaching the development of a healthy lifestyle through the process of daily living. There are no trophies

or other extrinsic rewards for achieving it. Health is a personal matter. When it is achieved, the individual is directly rewarded with a full lifestyle. Teachers can no longer ignore the importance of teaching students the what, why, and how of maintaining a healthy profile. Maintaining total health must be considered a primary objective of secondary school physical education.

Why teach health concepts in the physical education setting? Teachers are often skeptical about teaching material other than physical skill activities, yet the ability to develop and maintain personal health will remain with an individual for a lifetime. This is one of the few long-lasting gifts teachers can offer to students. Achieving an optimal level of health is unique and personal. What is useful to one person may be superfluous to another. Teachers must therefore teach students how to search for a healthy lifestyle and then maintain it once found.

At present, the credibility of the physical education profession is strained. Teachers often offer students skills and activities that they will never use again. For example, students may spend 9 weeks each year from junior high through the sophomore year of high school involved in flag football. This is equivalent to 36 weeks of flag football or an entire school year. The possibility is strong that few of these individuals will play football after graduation from high school. Few people play flag football after age 25, yet 1 year of physical education was spent playing and learning a healthy sport that is seldom used for maintaining a healthy lifestyle in adulthood. The point here is not to belittle football or to ask for its elimination; rather, it is to suggest that physical education programs have often shown an inadequate concern for teaching students the skills that are useful after they leave school.

Teaching students how to maintain a state of personal health makes activity purposeful. Students begin to understand why certain activities and games are selected in place of others. Selection of activities for a lifetime of physical involvement can only occur after students have been exposed to a wide range of instructional units. A systematic approach to curriculum development is critical for ensuring that students know the many pathways to personal fitness and health.

INTEGRATING HEALTH CONCEPTS

Few schools offer a comprehensive health education program for students. Often such instruction must be conducted by the physical education teacher. This chapter is designed for physical education teachers who are asked to integrate health education into the physical education program. Most often, this is required of teachers at the middle school level so most of the basic concepts and suggested learning activities are geared to that level. The topics covered in this chapter are divided into three areas:

- **How Does the Body Work**—This includes basics of the skeletal, muscular, and cardiovascular systems. Emphasis is placed on basic concepts that all students should know, followed by some learning activities that can be assigned or discussed in class to further understanding. Much of the information is related to the body in an exercise and activity setting and how it responds to physical activity. Basic principles of training and fitness also are covered in this section.

- **Barriers to Healthy Living**—Whereas the first topic deals with how the body works when it is healthy and fully functioning, this section deals with behaviors that can be harmful to the body if they are not managed or avoided by students. The emphasis is on developing a basic understanding of stress, nutrition and weight management, substance abuse, personal safety, and first aid. The instructional effort is not to preach and mandate what students should do, but rather to help students understand how to make thoughtful decisions that maintain their health status.

- **Health Maintenance Behaviors**—It is important to understand how the body works and how it can be damaged by poor health habits, but knowledge is not enough. Students need to learn how to maintain health-related fitness, manage stress, and learn self-control skills related to behavior. This section is designed to help students evaluate their health status and modify their behavior when necessary. Steps for modifying personal behavior help students monitor, prioritize, and set personal goals.

Each of these areas includes basic concepts students need to understand. This provides direction for both the teacher and students. The concepts should give students a general idea of what is important and which areas must be understood to achieve proper functioning. The concepts, when taken as a whole, offer a framework to help initiate discussions that examine the pros and cons of personal decisions related to health maintenance. This approach contrasts with giving students a set of objectives that must be learned, leaving little room for student input and inquiry.

The suggested learning activities offer minilaboratory experiences that apply the concepts and add substance to basic instructional concepts. The laboratory experiences are simple, yet they clearly illustrate how the body functions in different settings. Many of these experiences can be done in 5 or 10 minutes by a whole class. They are excellent rainy-day activities or homework assignments. Encourage students to develop a notebook of activities and lab experiences that they can use as a reference. An excellent resource for laboratory activities and instructional lesson plans is *Fitness for Life Teacher Resources and Materials CD-ROM* (McConnell, Corbin, & Dale, 2004).

HOW DOES THE BODY WORK?

A basic understanding of how the body functions is important if students are to learn how to maintain a healthy organism. The three major systems discussed here are the skeletal, muscular, and cardiorespiratory system. A brief discussion of each is provided with concepts, and suggested learning activities are offered to enhance student understanding.

Skeletal System

The skeletal system is the framework of the body. The bones act as a system of levers and are linked together at various points called *joints*. The joints are held together by ligaments, which are tough and unable to stretch. In a joint injury, when the bones are moved beyond the normal limits, it is the ligaments that are most often injured.

Joints that are freely movable are called *synovial joints*. Synovial fluid is secreted to lubricate the joint and reduce friction. A thin layer of cartilage also reduces friction at the ends of the bones. A disk, or meniscus, forms a pad between many of the weight-bearing joints and absorbs shock. When the cartilage is damaged, the joint becomes less able to move easily, and arthritis often occurs.

Muscular activity increases the stress placed on bones. The bones respond to this added stress by increasing in diameter, becoming more dense (and more resistant to breakage), and reorganizing their internal structures, which offers more bone strength. The bones act as a mineral reserve for the body and can become deformed as a result of dietary deficiency. The bones also can change shape because of regular stress. This may give athletes, whose skeletal systems are conditioned, a mechanical advantage in performing certain skills. The skeletal system is not a static system but changes and adapts in response to the demands placed on it.

The bones are connected to make three different types of levers, with the joint acting as the fulcrum (Figure 17.1). The muscles apply force to the joints, while the body weight or an external object provides the resistance. The levers are classified as first-, second-, or third-class levers. Examples of third-class lever actions are the movement of the biceps muscle to flex the forearm at the elbow joint, the sideways movement of the upper arm at the shoulder joint by the deltoid muscle, and the flexion of the lower leg at the knee joint by the hamstring muscles. A second-class lever occurs where the gastrocnemius muscle raises the weight of the body onto the toes. The forearm is an example of a first-class lever when it is being extended at the elbow joint (fulcrum) by the triceps muscle.

Basic Concepts

1. The skeletal system consists of 206 bones and determines the external appearance of the body. This network of bones is somewhat malleable and can be reshaped, made denser, and strengthened.

2. Joints are located where two or more bones are fastened together by ligaments to allow movement that is restricted by the range of motion. The range of motion at various joints can be increased by regularly performing flexibility exercises. The most flexible people have the greatest range of motion at a combination of joints.

3. Bones are held together by ligaments and muscle tissue. The stronger the muscles become, the stronger the ligaments and tendons become in response. This makes a stronger joint, which is more resistant to injury.

4. Attractive posture occurs when the bones are in good alignment. Alignment depends on the muscular system to hold the bones in correct position. Poor posture occurs when the muscles are weak and increased stress is placed on the joints.

5. The bones meet at joints to establish levers. Movement occurs when muscles apply force (by contraction only) to the bones.

6. The attachment of the muscle to the bone determines the mechanical advantage that can be gained at the joint. Generally, those muscles that attach farther from the joint can generate more force. There is, however, a trade-off. When the attachment is farther from the joint, the amount of speed that can be generated is less, and vice versa.

7. The human body has three types of lever arrangements. These are classified by the fulcrum, force, and resistance. The majority of levers in the body are third-class levers in which the point of force (produced by the muscles) lies between the fulcrum (joint) and the point of resistance (the weight of the object to be moved) (see Figure 17.1).

Suggested Learning Activities

1. Identify and locate the bones of major significance in movement. (Approximately 167 bones are capable of moving.) Some that can be assigned are as follows:
   a. Arm–shoulder girdle—radius, ulna, humerus, scapula, and clavicle
   b. Back–pelvis—spinal column, pelvis, coccyx
   c. Thigh–leg—femur, tibia, fibula, patella
   d. Chest—sternum, ribs

2. Identify the type of movement possible at selected joints. Use various terms to identify the movements (e.g., extension, flexion, adduction, abduction, pronation, supination, and plantar flexion).

3. Diagram and list the types of levers found in the body. Illustrate the force, fulcrum, and resistance points. Identify muscle attachments and the impact of such in terms of generating force or speed in movement.

4. Obtain animal bones and analyze the various parts of the bone. Identify the bone marrow, growth plates, epiphyses, ligaments, tendons, muscle origins and attachments, and cartilage.

5. Study outdated X-ray films of children to see the different rates of ossification. Note differences in bone shape and structure between individuals.

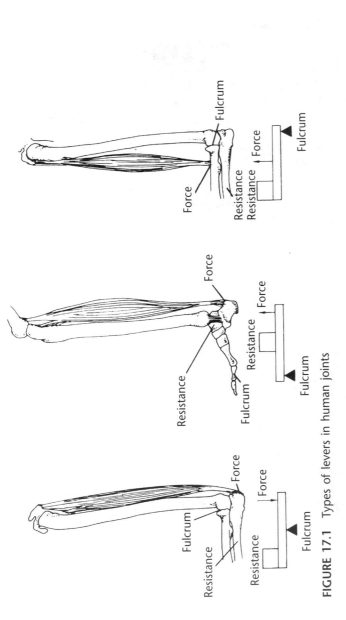

FIGURE 17.1   Types of levers in human joints

Muscular System

The muscular system (Figure 17.2) is complex. Muscles apply force to the bones to create movement and always create movement through contraction. When one set of muscles contracts, the other set relaxes. Muscles are always paired. The muscle (or group of muscles) that relaxes while another set contracts is called the antagonistic muscle. The muscles located on the anterior side of the body are flexors and reduce the angle of a joint while the body is standing. Muscles on the posterior side of the body produce extension and a return from flexion.

People are born with two types of muscle fiber. These are commonly referred to as slow-twitch and fast-twitch fibers. Slow-twitch fibers respond efficiently to aerobic activity, while fast-twitch fibers are suited to highly demanding anaerobic activity. This explains, in part, why people perform physical activities at varying levels. People are born with a set ratio of fast- and slow-twitch fibers. Those with a higher ratio of slow-twitch fibers are better able to perform in endurance activities; those with a greater percentage of fast-twitch fibers might excel in activities of high intensity and short duration.

Strength gains are made when muscles are overloaded, and overload occurs when people do more work than they performed previously. This means that more weight must be lifted on a regular basis if gains are to occur. Exercises should overload as many muscle groups as possible in order to ensure total body development. Both the flexors and extensors should receive equal amounts of overload exercise so a proper balance between the two muscle groups is maintained. Muscu-

lar strength appears to be an important factor in performing motor skills.

Muscular exercises should apply resistance through the full range of motion in order to maintain maximum flexibility. Strenuous exercise such as weight lifting should be done every other day so that the muscles have an opportunity to heal and regenerate. Maintaining muscular strength throughout life is important. If exercises are not done to maintain strength, atrophy will occur rapidly. It has been shown that the average American will gain 1 pound of additional weight per year after age 25. This can result in 30 pounds of excess weight by age 55. During the same period, the bone and muscle mass decrease by approximately 0.5 pound per year, which results in a total gain of 45 pounds of fat (Wilmore, 1999).

Basic Concepts

1. Muscles contract and apply force by pulling only. They never push. When movement in the opposite direction is desired, the antagonistic muscles must contract.

2. A reduction in joint angle is called *flexion;* an increase in the joint angle is *extension.* Generally, the flexor muscles are on the anterior side of the body, and the extensors are on the posterior side.

3. Exercises should focus on developing the flexors and extensors equally if proper posture and joint integrity are to be maintained.

4. Muscles can be attached directly to the bone. A tendon, such as the Achilles, can also be the source of

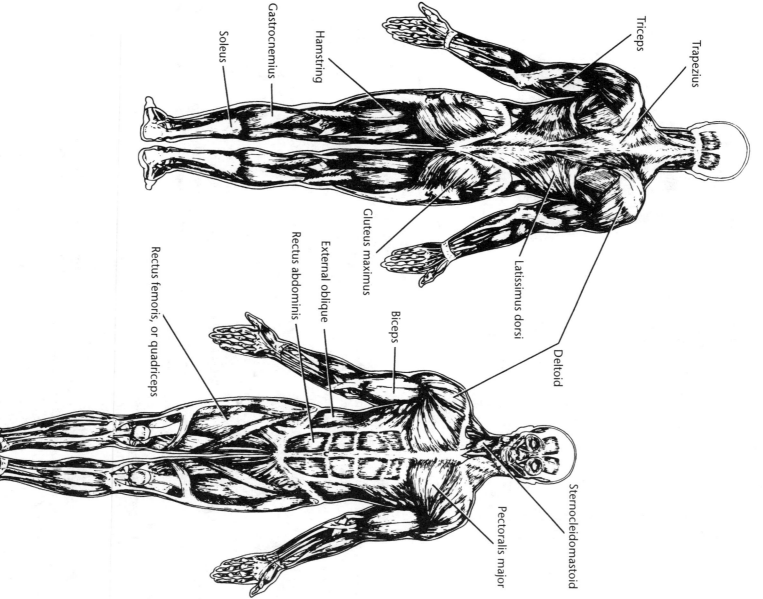

Trapezius

Triceps

Hamstring

Gastrocnemius

Soleus

Gluteus maximus

Latissimus dorsi

Deltoid

Rectus femoris, or quadriceps

External oblique

Rectus abdominis

Biceps

Sternocleidomastoid

Pectoralis major

FIGURE 17.2 The muscular system

attachment. The origin of the muscle is the fixed portion of the muscle; the insertion is the moving part of the muscle.

5. Progression involving gradual overloading of the muscles is necessary to increase muscular strength and endurance. Males find that regular exercise can cause an increase in the girth of a muscle. Females rarely attain similar results from strenuous exercise. This is because the male hormone testosterone is responsible for the increase in muscle size and is present in greater quantities in males.

6. Different types of training are necessary for developing muscular strength and muscular endurance. Larger amounts of weight and fewer repetitions will cause a greater increase in strength; less weight and more repetitions will enhance muscular endurance.

7. There are different types of muscular contractions: isometric (without movement), isotonic (with movement), and eccentric (movement that lengthens the muscle from a contracted state). The contraction most commonly used for developing strength and endurance is the isotonic.

8. Static stretching can increase flexibility. Flexibility (the range of motion at a joint) increases because of a lengthening of connective tissue that surrounds the muscle fibers.

9. Muscle soreness occurs when the workload is applied too intensely. The soreness probably results from muscle tissue damage. Static stretching will alleviate the pain somewhat and will help prepare the body for continued activity.

10. The principle of specificity is important in developing muscular strength. Only those muscles that are exercised will develop. There is no carryover from other muscle groups (i.e., strengthening the arms will not cause an increase in leg strength).

Suggested Learning Activities

1. Identify major muscle groups and their functions at the joints. Discuss the origins and insertions of the muscles.

2. Study muscles from animals under a microscope. Show stained biopsies of human muscle fiber that reveal fast- and slow-twitch muscle fibers.

3. Perform some skill-related activities that might reveal which individuals appear to be endowed with more fast-twitch than slow-twitch fibers. Examples might be the standing long jump, vertical jump, and an endurance activity such as the mile run.

4. Develop a personal strength profile for students. Measure the strength of various muscle groups using a dynamometer, and set goals for well-rounded strength development.

5. Perform an action research project. As an example, pretest students for strength and divide them into equal groups. Have one group train for 12 weeks using muscular endurance techniques while the other trains for 12 weeks using muscular strength techniques. Retest them and compare the results of the two groups after training.

6. Identify various sports and games, and determine what type of training will achieve maximum results.

7. Discuss certain exercises that should be avoided, such as straight-leg sit-ups and deep knee bends.

8. Have students identify why backache occurs in more than 70 percent of Americans. Prescribe a program of exercise that could remedy the majority of these back problems.

Cardiorespiratory System

The cardiorespiratory system consists of the heart (Figure 17.3), lungs, arteries, capillaries, and veins. The heart is a muscle that pumps blood throughout the circulatory system—arteries, capillaries, and veins. The coronary arteries bring the heart a rich supply of blood. Heart disease occurs when fatty deposits block or seriously impede the flow of blood to the heart.

The heart has two chambers and is, in effect, divided in half with each side providing different functions. The left side of the heart pumps blood carrying nutrients and oxygen to the body through the arteries to the capillaries, where the nutrients and oxygen are exchanged for waste products and carbon dioxide. The waste-carrying blood is returned through the veins to the right side of the heart, from which the blood is routed through the lungs to discharge the carbon dioxide and pick up oxygen. This oxygen-renewed blood returns to the left side of the heart to complete the circuit.

Each time the heart beats, it pumps blood through both chambers. The beat is called the pulse; its impact travels through the body. Pulse is measured in number of beats per minute. A pulse rate of 75 means that the heart is beating 75 times each minute. The cardiac output is determined by the pulse rate and the stroke volume, which is the amount of blood discharged by each beat.

The pulse is measured by placing the two middle fingers of the right hand on the thumb side of the subject's wrist while the subject is seated. Taking the pulse at the wrist is usually preferable to using the carotid artery because pressure on the carotid can decrease blood flow to the brain.

The respiratory system includes the entryways (nose and mouth), the trachea (or windpipe), the primary bronchi, and the lungs. Figure 17.4 shows the components of the respiratory system.

Breathing consists of inhaling and exhaling air. Air contains 21-percent oxygen, which is necessary for life. Inspiration is assisted by muscular contraction, and expiration is accomplished by a relaxing of the muscles. Inspiration occurs when the intercostal muscles and the diaphragm contract. This increases the size of the chest cavity, and expansion of the lungs causes air to flow in as a result of reduced air pressure. When the muscles are relaxed, the size of the chest cavity is reduced, the pressure is increased, and air flows from the lungs.

The primary function of the lungs is to provide oxygen to the cells on demand. The amount of oxygen needed will vary depending on activity level.

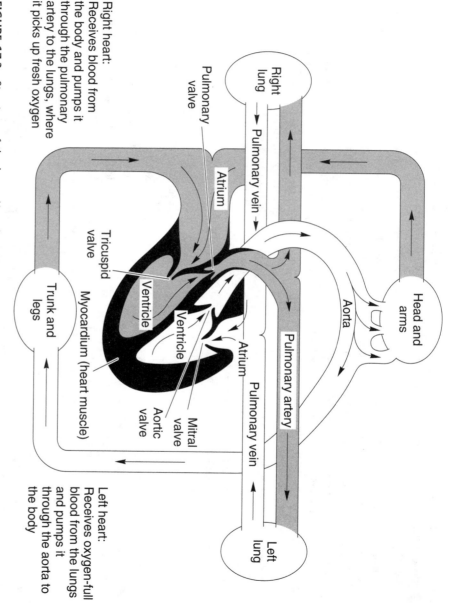

FIGURE 17.3 Structure of the heart (American Heart Association)

Right heart:
Receives blood from the body and pumps it through the pulmonary artery to the lungs, where it picks up fresh oxygen

Left heart:
Receives oxygen-full blood from the lungs and pumps it through the aorta to the body

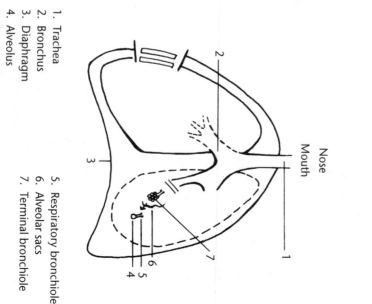

1. Trachea
2. Bronchus
3. Diaphragm
4. Alveolus
5. Respiratory bronchiole
6. Alveolar sacs
7. Terminal bronchiole

FIGURE 17.4 The respiratory system

When an individual exercises strenuously, the rate of respiration increases in order to bring more oxygen to tissues. If the amount of oxygen carried to the cells is adequate to maintain the level of activity, the activity is termed *aerobic*, or *endurance exercise*. Examples are walking, jogging, and bicycling for distance. If, because of high-intensity activity, the body is not capable of bringing enough oxygen to the cells, the body will continue to operate for a short time without oxygen. This results in an oxygen debt, which must be repaid later. In this case, the activity is termed *anaerobic exercise*.

The respiratory rate will return to normal after exercise. The recovery rate will be faster if the oxygen debt incurred during exercise was small. An individual has recovered from the exertion of exercise when blood pressure, heart rate, and ventilation rate have returned to preexercise levels.

Basic Concepts

1. The heart is a muscular organ that must be exercised like other muscles to maintain maximum efficiency. The most effective heart exercise is activity of low intensity and long duration, which is aerobic in nature.

2. Pulse rate varies among individuals. It does slow down at rest, however, as a result of aerobic training. Resting pulse rate is sometimes used as an indicator of the state of training.

3. Cardiorespiratory training appears to decrease the susceptibility of individuals to heart disease. The younger that one begins maintaining fitness, the better the opportunity to retard the onset of cardiovascular disease.

4. Aerobic endurance activities (jogging, brisk walking, bicycling) appear to change the chemistry of the blood and lower the cholesterol level. There are two types of lipoproteins—high-density lipoproteins (HDLs) and low-density lipoproteins (LDLs)—and exercise appears to increase the ratio of HDLs to LDLs. This is important because HDL seems to prevent harmful plaque from building up in the arteries.

5. Hypokinetic diseases are somewhat influenced by gender, heredity, race, and age. Many of these diseases can be prevented, however, by controlling factors such as smoking, being overweight, inactivity, improper diet, and high blood pressure.

6. The heart rate must reach the training state if cardiorespiratory benefits are to be realized. (See item 7 in the following Suggested Learning Activities for calculating the training zone.)

7. The heart grows stronger and larger when the body is involved in aerobic activity (30 minutes or more). A larger and stronger heart results in a greater stroke volume per beat.

8. If weight control is a concern, maintaining muscle mass is important. Severe dieting often results not only in a loss of fat cells, but in a loss of muscle tissue as well. Considering muscle tissue burns twice as many calories as fat tissue, it is important for weight control as well as for cosmetic and performance reasons.

9. The vital capacity of the lungs can be increased through regular aerobic exercise. This makes the oxygen exchange system more efficient.

Suggested Learning Activities

1. Discuss the acronym DANGER, which is defined as follows, in regard to cardiovascular disease:
   - Don't smoke.
   - Avoid foods high in fat and cholesterol.
   - Now control high blood pressure and diabetes.
   - Get medical examinations at least every other year.
   - Exercise moderately each day.
   - Reduce weight if carrying excess fat.

2. Compare resting pulse rates among students. Look for differences between sexes, ages, and states of training. Try taking the resting pulse rate in different positions.

3. Examine the impact that exercise has on heart rate. Record the resting heart rate. Have each person run in place for 1 minute. Take the pulse rate immediately and record it. Continue taking the pulse rate at 2-minute intervals three to five times to demonstrate recovery rate. Discuss individual differences in maximum heart rate and recovery heart rate.

4. Teach students how to take blood pressure. Exercise for 1 minute as described previously and monitor the effect that exercise has on blood pressure.

5. Demonstrate the effects on the cardiovascular system of carrying excess weight. Identify two students who weigh the same, are of the same sex, are in similar training states, and who do not carry excess weight. Monitor their resting heart rate before starting. Ask one person to perform the upcoming task while carrying two 10-pound weights. Set two markers 20 yards apart, and have both students run back and forth between the cones 10 times. Immediately after they finish, monitor their heart rates and recovery rates as described previously.

Discuss the fact that excessive body fat is merely dead weight that must be moved, and note how the excess weight decreases physical performance.

6. Compare heart rates after 2- or 3-minute bouts of different types of exercise. Experiment with walking, jogging, sprinting, rope jumping, bicycling, and performing calisthenics. Discuss the differences.

7. Calculate the heart rate training zone that should be maintained to achieve the training effect and to ensure that the individual is not underexercising or overexercising. To do this, first determine the estimated maximum heart rate by taking 220 minus the student's age; then multiply the difference by 70 percent and 85 percent. An example for a student who is 15 follows:

$$220 - 15 = 205$$
$$205 \times .70 = 144$$
$$205 \times .85 = 174$$

The heart rate training zone for this student would be a heartbeat (or pulse rate) between 144 and 174. Have the students try different modes of exercise and see if they raise their heart rates into the training zone.

8. Identify resting respiratory rates. Have students try different types of exercise and compare the effects each has on the respiratory rate.

BARRIERS TO HEALTHY LIVING

Healthy living involves knowing what activities to avoid as well as what to do. Teaching about these activities should not be done by preaching and telling students what they should or should not do. Emphasis is placed instead on showing students the pros and cons of various practices and the consequences of making certain decisions. The ultimate decision and responsibility rest with the student, not the teacher.

This section covers stress, nutrition and weight control, substance abuse, and personal safety. All are areas where behavior can be modified to enhance the quality of life. Students can make decisions in these areas that affect how they live and, sometimes, whether they will live.

Stress

Stress is the body's reaction to certain situations in life. Everyone experiences some stress. Stress, by itself, is probably not harmful, but handling stress is critical in determining the impact it will have on one's life. Many students are seen as carefree and without worries. Quite the opposite is usually the case. Students live under the stress of others' expectations, peer pressure, sexual mores, and the necessity of becoming an independent being. If teachers appreciate that students are subject to stress, they can begin to deal with them in ways that alleviate possible stressors and allow for stress release. In this way, teachers can have an impact on the students' self-concept and their worldviews.

Psychologically, stress may take the form of excitement, fear, or anger. Physical changes also accompany psychological stress. For example, heart rate increases, blood pressure rises, ventilation rate increases, perspiration increases, body temperature may rise, and the pupils may dilate. This response to stress once aided human beings in survival and is labeled the "fight-or-flight syndrome." When a situation arises that may cause one harm, the body's endocrine system prepares it to fight or to flee the situation. People often speak of the "adrenaline flowing" when they are scared or worried about upcoming situations.

Unfortunately, our society and schools offer few opportunities to relieve tension through activity, and few individuals find the motivation to do so. The resulting tension and stress that build up cause individuals to expend a great deal of energy in unproductive ways. People often feel fatigued when they are unable to release stress. Many nervous habits, such as constant movement while sitting, playing with an item in the hands, and various facial twitches, are the body's attempts to relieve tension.

The ultimate question when dealing with stress might be: "What does it matter if I'm under stress? All people are." It matters because excessive stress has many detrimental effects on the body. It increases the risk of heart disease and can lead to insomnia and hypertension. Indigestion is common in stressed individuals, as is constipation. Many backaches and general body aches originate through stress. Doctors are diagnosing more and more "psychosomatic" diseases, those with no physical prognoses that appear to be caused by stress. Another serious problem associated with unrelieved stress is the tendency of individuals to try to cope by using substances such as alcohol, tobacco, and drugs.

People who feel stressed demonstrate behavior that is characterized by some of the following patterns:

■ Moving everywhere rapidly, even when it is unnecessary.

■ Feeling bored and impatient with classes and how things are being done by others.

■ Trying to do two or more things simultaneously. (This is referred to as polyphasic thought or action.)

- Having to always feel busy and feeling uneasy when time is taken to do nothing or to do something relaxing.

- Needing to do everything faster and more efficiently than everyone else.

- Exhibiting many strong gestures, such as clenching the fists, banging a hand on the table, or dramatically waving the arms.

Learning to cope with stressful situations is important. The first step involves developing an awareness of what types of situations cause stress. Sharing situations with others often releases the tension and allows students to feel that they are "normal" and are maturing properly. In the physical education setting, emphasis should be placed on the role that activity can play in stress reduction. Involvement in enjoyable and success-oriented physical activities can decrease tension. This involvement has a side effect because the required concentration will provide a diversion from worries and stressors. Note, however, that if the activity is not enjoyable and if the student consistently fails to find success, the level of stress may actually increase.

Some experts believe that exercise applies stress to the body in a systematic fashion and thus prepares the individual to deal with other stressful situations. One goal of teachers should be to provide a variety of activities and to help students select activities that will be productive and meaningful ways of relieving tension.

Another beneficial strategy is to teach various relaxation techniques that help relieve general body stress. These are discussed in a later section in this chapter.

Basic Concepts

1. Stress affects all individuals to varying degrees. Some stress is necessary to stimulate performance and increase motivation.

2. The amount of stress with which one is able to cope depends on how it is perceived. Positive self-concepts help people accept threatening situations in a less stressful manner.

3. When people have difficulty dealing with stress through productive methods, such as exercise, relaxation activities, and talks with friends, they often attempt to relieve stress through unhealthy and potentially dangerous means, such as alcohol, tobacco, and drug usage.

4. Stress causes changes in perceptible bodily functions. An awareness of these changes is necessary if students are to recognize when they are under stress and need to cope with its effects.

5. Stress appears to increase susceptibility to many diseases and causes psychosomatic illnesses.

6. Exercise is an excellent way to relieve stress and tension when the activity is perceived as enjoyable and success oriented.

7. Stress is a risk factor that influences the onset of heart disease.

8. There are different ways of relieving stress, including exercising, expressing feelings to friends, developing problem-solving skills, and performing accepted relaxation techniques.

Suggested Learning Activities

1. Hold an isometric contraction at the elbow joint. With the other hand, feel the contraction in the biceps and triceps. Repeat the activity with other muscle groups. Discuss how stress causes generalized body tension that can result in tensed muscles and an increase in general body fatigue. Learning to recognize muscle tension is a desired outcome of this discussion.

2. Discuss the concept of "choking" under pressure. How does this relate to athletic performance? What happens when stress is greater than the individual's ability to cope with it? Discuss how some stress increases performance, while too much decreases it.

3. Discuss the importance of perception in stressful situations. How is stress perceived? Should students admit when they are worried or scared? Is it better to be "tough" and not tell anyone how they feel? Is it better to keep emotions inside or to share feelings with others?

4. Discuss the importance of finding activities in which students believe they are successful. How are positive self-concepts developed? Why are some people able to cope with failure and losing better than others?

5. Discuss situations in physical activity settings that give rise to increased stress, such as failing in front of others, not being selected for a team, being ridiculed for a poor performance, or losing a game that was personally important. How could these situations be handled differently?

6. Identify physical activities that seem to relieve tension and stress. Discuss the relationship between involvement in activity and the reduction of stress.

7. Identify and discuss unproductive attempts to relieve stress such as drinking, smoking, and drug abuse. Why are these methods chosen rather than exercise, discussions, or relaxation activities?

9. Teach relaxation techniques such as deep breathing, progressive muscle relaxation, and personal meditation. Emphasize the importance of taking time for these activities daily. Just as brushing the teeth is necessary for healthy dentition, relaxation is necessary for a healthy body and mind.

8. Discuss the many effects of stress on bodily health. Give students a stress inventory to see how much stress they are under, and discuss ways of reducing this pressure.

FIGURE 17.5 Anatomy of MyPyramid. Individual elements of MyPyramid reinforce important concepts for students planning a healthy diet.

Source: U.S. Department of Agriculture, The New Look and Messages of USDA's MyPyramid, Background. 2005. Available at www.mypyramid.gov.

Nutrition and Weight Management

Proper nutrition is necessary if students are to expect a high level of physical performance from their bodies. An important area of concern deals with the balance between caloric intake and expenditure in order to maintain proper weight. Students should understand the reasons and methods for maintaining an optimum level of body weight. Discuss the impact of empty calories through excessive ingestion of junk foods. Explain the importance of a balanced diet to help the body grow and develop. Point out that the role of exercise in weight control and muscle development is as important as a balanced diet.

It's important for students to understand the elements of a balanced diet. A balanced diet draws from

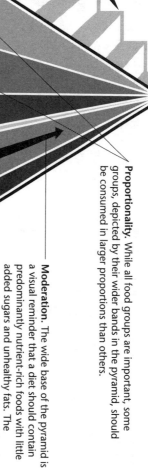

MyPyramid.gov
STEPS TO A HEALTHIER YOU

Grains · Vegetables · Fruits · Oils · Milk · Meat & Beans

Physical activity. Physical activity is important on a daily basis.

Proportionality. While all food groups are important, some groups, depicted by their wider bands in the pyramid, should be consumed in larger proportions than others.

Moderation. The wide base of the pyramid is a visual reminder that a diet should contain predominantly nutrient-rich foods with little added sugars and unhealthy fats. The narrowing of the bands on the top of the pyramid reinforces that sugary food and solid fats should be consumed in moderation.

Variety. The pyramid contains numerous colorful bands to encourage a diet that contains a variety of food groups.

Gradual improvement. The pyramid slogan reinforces that small, gradual changes in both diet and lifestyle can be beneficial.

Personalization. There are several MyPyramids available online that provide a personalized eating plan based on your individual needs.

each of the basic food groups; emphasis should be given to proportionality, moderation, and variety. The revised MyPyramid from the U.S. Department of Agriculture (2005) illustrates that the most food should be eaten from the grain, vegetable, and milk groups, but also shows that eating foods from the fruit, oil, and meat and bean groups is essential to a healthy diet. (Figure 17.5)

Encourage students to moderate the consumption of foods high in cholesterol and fat. Some cholesterol and fat are necessary for proper body function. When too much fat is ingested, however, cholesterol and triglyceride levels in the blood plasma increase. Many studies have shown a relationship between high cholesterol and triglyceride levels and coronary heart disease. (A blood test is needed to determine blood lipid levels.)

Students should be aware of which foods are high in fat and cholesterol. The following are examples of foods high in cholesterol: eggs, cheese, cream, most beef and pork cuts, chocolate milk, shrimp, chocolate candy, cake and cookies, and ice cream.

Depending on the criteria used, anywhere from 30 to 50 percent of students are overweight, meaning that their body weight is over the accepted limits for their ages, sexes, and body builds. It is important for students to begin to develop an awareness of the caloric content of foods as well as the nutritional value. They can then begin to count calories and practice consistency in the amount of calories they ingest. Coupled with this awareness should be some comprehension of the number of calories expended through various types of physical activity (Figure 17.6). Students need to understand that when caloric intake exceeds caloric expenditure, becoming overweight results. A well-documented and common cause of becoming overweight is inactivity. Most experts believe overweight students do not eat more than normal-weight students; rather, they exercise less.

Being overweight is a roadblock to optimal health. Life insurance companies view overweight people as poor risks because of their shorter life expectancy. Excessive body fat makes the heart work harder, increases the chance of having high blood pressure, and lowers the possibility of recovery from a heart attack. Even more detrimental to students is the psychological impact that being overweight has on self-concept development. Students of normal weight find it much easier to perform physical tasks because strength in relationship to body weight is a critical performance factor. Overweight students are often punished more severely than normal-weight students for the same type of deviance and may receive lower grades for a similar quality of work.

Basic Concepts

1. Diet should be balanced and contain foods from each of the four basic groups. This ensures that the body will receive essential nutrients.

2. Caloric expenditure (body functions plus exercise) and intake (eating) must be balanced to maintain a healthy weight. A weight-reducing program should include a reduction in caloric intake and an increase in daily exercise.

3. Activities vary in the energy they require. Individual needs must be considered in the selection of activities to promote weight control and physical fitness maintenance.

4. Junk foods add little if any nutritional value to the diet and are usually high in calories. Foods and beverages such as sugar, margarine and butter, oils, and alcohol are high in calories but make little or no contribution in terms of nutrition.

5. Excessive weight makes performing physical tasks difficult. This results in less success and in less motivation to be active, thus increasing the tendency toward being overweight.

6. Being overweight increases the risk of heart disease and other related diseases such as diabetes.

7. A majority of cases of overweight students are caused by inactivity or lack of sufficient activity.

Activity	Calories per Hour
Moderate activity	*200–350*
Bicycling (5½ mph)	210
Walking (2½ mph)	210
Gardening	220
Canoeing (2½ mph)	230
Golf	250
Lawn mowing (power mower)	250
Lawn mowing (hand mower)	270
Bowling	270
Fencing	300
Rowing (2½ mph)	300
Swimming (¼ mph)	300
Walking (3¾ mph)	300
Badminton	350
Horseback riding (trotting)	350
Square-dancing	350
Volleyball	350
Roller skating	350
Vigorous activity	*Over 350*
Table tennis	360
Ice-skating (10 mph)	400
Tennis	420
Water-skiing	480
Hill climbing (100 ft/hr)	490
Skiing (10 mph)	600
Squash and handball	600
Cycling (13 mph)	660
Scull rowing (race)	840
Running (10 mph)	900

FIGURE 17.6 Caloric expenditure

Adapted from material from the President's Council on Physical Fitness and Sports, Washington, DC.

The majority of overweight students do not consume more calories than normal-weight students; they are simply less active.

8. Vitamins are not nutrients but are catalysts that facilitate metabolic processes. Certain vitamin deficiencies can produce various diseases.

9. Various foods are excellent sources of specific nutrients. Students should be able to identify which foods to ingest to provide a balance of the needed nutrients, vitamins, and minerals.

Suggested Learning Concepts

1. Post a list of activities and their energy demands on the bulletin board. Discuss the need for selecting

activities that will burn enough calories to balance caloric intake.

2. Maintain a food diary. Record all the foods eaten daily and the amount of calories in each. Compare the amount of calories ingested with the amount of calories expended.

3. Maintain a nutritious-food diary. Record all the foods eaten daily and categorize each by food group. Determine the percentage of carbohydrates, proteins, and fats in relation to all the food ingested during each day.

4. Develop a desirable and practical balanced diet that can be followed for 1 week. Arrange with parents to facilitate the diet within their budget restrictions.

5. Calculate the recommended daily balanced allowance (RDA) for various nutrients. Compare a daily intake with the recommendations for various minerals and vitamins.

6. Bring various foods to class that have labels offering nutrition information. Determine which foods are good buys for desired nutrients.

7. Develop an activity diary. For 1 week, record all activity over and above maintenance activities. Calculate the number of calories burned per day.

8. Discuss and analyze the ways in which society rewards physically fit individuals. Contrast these with the ways in which overweight people are discriminated against in various situations.

Substance Abuse

Substance abuse is defined as the harmful use of alcohol, tobacco, or drugs. If students are expected to make wise and meaningful decisions in this area, they must understand the impact of various substances on their physical and psychological being. Facts, both pro and con, should be presented in a nonjudgmental environment, without moralizing and preaching. It is difficult for students to make personal decisions if most of the information they receive is from peers or moralizing adults.

Alcohol, tobacco, and drugs are usually detrimental to total health. The use and misuse of these substances should be discussed objectively with students because much of the information they receive is from biased sources, such as parents, peers, and various media formats. The physical education teacher can promote unbiased discussions and fact-seeking sessions that relate to a healthy lifestyle. Many times, the physical educator is the only person oriented to health promotion. However, if the instructor feels strongly

that an issue has only one acceptable point of view, then discussions should be avoided. Telling students only the reasons why not to do something can result in a strong polarization in the opposite direction.

Alcohol has both short-term and long-term effects. Short-term effects vary as a result of the depressant effect that alcohol has on the central nervous system. Some people become relaxed, others become aggressive, and some become active in differing degrees. Ultimately, a lack of coordination and confusion occur if a great deal of alcohol is ingested. The long-term effects of alcohol abuse may be liver damage, heart disease, and malnutrition. The greatest concern surrounding long-term drinking is the possibility of alcoholism. Most agree that alcoholism has the following components: loss of control of alcohol intake, presence of functional or structural damage (physical and psychological), and dependence on alcohol to maintain an acceptable level of functioning.

Students usually drink for any of the following reasons: curiosity, desire to celebrate with parents, peer pressure, desire to be like adults and appear more mature, rebellion against the adult world, desire to be like their models, or addiction (they are alcoholics). Students are often ambivalent about alcohol. They know its detrimental effects, and yet they see many of their friends and role models using it. The problem is a difficult one, and an understanding of both moderate use and abstinence is needed. An understanding of how to cope with peer pressure to drink alcohol is also needed and is discussed in the next section on basic concepts.

Tobacco use is common among junior and senior high students. Smoking significantly increases the possibility of heart attacks, strokes, and cancer. Chronic bronchitis and emphysema are prevalent diseases among smokers. A recent study revealed that the average life span of long-term smokers is 7 years shorter than that of nonsmokers.

Students need to understand smoking's impact on a healthy body. Along with this knowledge, they should examine why so many people choose to smoke. Today, the fastest growing segment of the smoking population is young girls and women. Students will make the final decision for their individual behaviors, but before they do so, they need to thoroughly understand the ramifications of smoking.

The use of marijuana and of hard-core drugs should also be discussed. Outside agencies are often most helpful in discussing substance abuse in an objective manner with students. The use of steroids, "pep pills," and pain relievers in athletics should also be debated. In each case, the intent should be to enhance students' awareness so they know the alternatives and consequences. Substance abuse is contrary to the whole concept of personal health. Physical educators need to accept the challenge of increasing student understanding and knowledge in these areas.

Basic Concepts

1. The earlier one begins to smoke, the greater the risk to functional health.

2. People smoke for psychological reasons.

3. Young people may choose substance abuse because of curiosity, status, or peer pressure.

4. Choosing a lifestyle independently of peers requires great courage.

5. Wise and purposeful decisions about substance abuse can be made only when all of the alternatives and consequences are understood.

6. Substance abuse is often an attempt to cope with stress. Exercise and relaxation are much more productive, healthy methods of coping.

7. The use of alcohol, tobacco, and drugs always carries the risk of addiction. When people are addicted, they are no longer in charge of their lifestyles. All people, to some degree, are subject to addiction; no one is immune.

8. Spending time and effort on developing personal competencies is more productive than abusing substances. Personal competency in many areas reduces the need to "be like everyone else" and contributes to a positive self-concept.

9. The use of harmful substances frequently reduces the pleasure one can receive from experiencing the world. Physical performance is often reduced because of substance abuse.

10. A person can drink and smoke and still excel at athletics, but their maximum performance level may be reduced and the ultimate effect on the athlete will be harmful. Students see many professional athletes who smoke and drink. They need to be aware that this happens, but they should understand that the choice is undesirable from a health standpoint.

Suggested Learning Activities

1. Identify and discuss the reasons why people choose or choose not to become involved in substance abuse.

2. Discuss the importance of making personal decisions based on what is best for you. Why do we follow others and allow them to influence our decisions, even when those decisions are not in our best interest?

3. Develop a bulletin board that illustrates the many ways used by the tobacco, alcohol, and drug industries to try to get young people to buy their products. Reserve a spot for advertisements (if any can be found) that admonish and encourage students to abstain or moderate the use of various substances.

4. Students often see professional and college athletes smoking and drinking on television while hearing that these habits impair performance. Discuss why these athletes can perform at a high level even though they may drink or smoke.

5. Students often choose to be part of a peer group at any cost. Discuss how our society often respects and honors individuals who have the courage to go their own way. Examples might be Columbus, Helen Keller, Martin Luther King, Jr., and so forth.

6. Identify and discuss the ways in which people in our society choose to relieve and dissipate stress. Discuss productive releases of tension such as recreation, hobbies, and sports.

7. Bring in speakers who are knowledgeable about the effects and uses of alcohol, tobacco, and drugs. If necessary, bring in a pair of speakers who might debate both sides of an issue.

8. Develop visual aids that identify the various effects that alcohol, tobacco, and drugs have on the body.

Safety and First Aid

Safety and first aid have often been part of the physical education program because more accidents occur in physical education than in any other area of the school curriculum. Safety is an attitude and a concern for one's welfare and health. An accident is an unplanned event or act that may result in injury or death. Often, accidents occur when they could have been prevented. The following are the most common causes of accidents: lack of knowledge and understanding of risks; lack of skill and competence to perform tasks safely, such as riding a bike or driving a car; false sense of security that leads people to think that accidents happen only to others; fatigue or illness that affects physical and mental performance; drugs and alcohol; and strong emotional states (e.g., anger, fear, or worry) that cause people to do things they might not otherwise do.

Traffic accidents are an area in which many deaths could be prevented. Wearing seat belts reduces the risk of dying by 50 percent. Drinking alcohol while driving increases the risk of an accident 20-fold compared to not drinking. Another factor that has reduced the number of traffic deaths is the 55-mph speed limit.

Driver education and an awareness of the possibility of serious injury should be a part of the health program.

Bicycles are another source of numerous accidents. Automobile drivers have difficulty seeing bicycles, and the resulting accidents are often serious. The physical education setting is often the only place where bicycle safety training occurs. Classes in bicycling for safety and fitness are usually well received by middle school and high school students.

Swimming-related accidents are the second leading cause of accidental death among young adults. More than 50 percent of all drownings occur when people unexpectedly find themselves in the water. Another major cause of death from drowning is alcohol ingestion. Swimming and drinking do not mix well. Physical education programs should encourage all students to learn to swim and to learn water-safety rules at some time during their school careers.

Physical education and sports are sources of injury in the school setting. Proper safety procedures should be taught, as well as first-aid techniques. Students should know how to stop bleeding, treat shock, and administer mouth-to-mouth respiration and cardiopulmonary resuscitation (CPR). Many physical education programs now include a required unit of instruction dealing with these topics. It is estimated that 100,000 to 200,000 lives could be saved by bystanders if they knew CPR.

Basic Concepts

1. Accidents are unplanned events or acts that may result in injury or death. The majority of accidents could be avoided if people were adequately prepared and understood the necessary competencies and risks involved.

2. Wearing seat belts and not drinking alcohol while driving will dramatically decrease the risk of death by automobile accident.

3. Bicycles are often not seen by car drivers. Bicycling safety classes can help lower the number of bicycle accidents.

4. Swimming-related accidents are the second leading cause of accidental death among young people. Instructional swimming programs and avoiding alcohol will dramatically decrease the risk of death by drowning.

5. Many thousands of lives could be saved if all people knew how to perform CPR.

6. All students should know how to administer CPR.

7. Basic first-aid procedures to prevent further injury to victims are competencies that all students should possess.

Suggested Learning Activities

1. Discuss the causes of different types of accidents and how many accidents could be avoided.

2. Identify the types of accidents that happen to different age groups and why this appears to be the case.

3. Identify the role of alcohol and drugs in causing accidents. Why are these substances used in recreational settings?

4. Develop a bulletin board that illustrates how to care for shock victims. Practice the steps in a mock procedure.

5. Have an "accident day" when various types of accidents are staged that demand such treatments as stopping bleeding, giving mouth-to-mouth respirations, and performing CPR.

6. Outline the steps to follow in case of a home fire. Discuss how many fires could be prevented.

7. Conduct a bicycle safety fair. Have students design bulletin boards and displays that explain and emphasize bicycle safety.

TEACH HEALTH MAINTENANCE BEHAVIORS

It is apparent that the health of students can be seriously impaired when safety issues are dealt with incorrectly. However, consuming proper nutrition, avoiding substance abuse, and practicing proper safety when bicycling or driving a car can protect the health of participants. The purpose of this section is to help students learn maintenance behaviors. Health maintenance focuses on a three-pronged approach: (1) health-related fitness, (2) stress reduction, and (3) self-evaluation. None of these areas are covered entirely because many in-depth sources are available. A highly recommended source for helping students develop lifetime fitness is the text *Fitness for Life* by Corbin and Lindsey (2007).

Health-Related Fitness

Health-related fitness is directly related to the wellness of individuals and generally consists of cardiovascular fitness, strength, muscular endurance, flexibility, and body fatness. Cardiovascular fitness is the most important phase of fitness for wellness. Cardiovascular fitness is a complex concept but, simply put, involves efficient functioning of the heart, blood, and blood vessels in order to supply oxygen to the body during aerobic activity. Strength refers to the ability of a muscle or muscle group to exert force. Without strength, a low standard of performance can be expected because muscles will fatigue before an individual can perform well. Muscular endurance refers to the ability of a muscle or muscle group to exert effort over a period of time. Endurance uses strength and postpones fatigue so the effort can be expended for long periods. Cardiovascular fitness also plays a key role in how long people can perform an activity. Flexibility is a person's range of movement at the joints. It allows freedom of movement and ready adjustment of the body for various movements. Body fatness refers to the percentage of body weight that is fat. People who are physically fit generally have a lower percentage of body fat than those who are unfit. For males in secondary school, 11- to 15-percent fat is a reasonable range, while 20 to 25 percent is acceptable for females (Corbin & Lindsey, 2007).

It is important to help students develop a health-related fitness plan that they can use to monitor themselves throughout their lives. The basic steps for such a plan are as follows:

1. Identify present areas of fitness and weakness through pretesting with the Fitnessgram test (Cooper Institute, 2004). This test will show students the criterion level they need to achieve for good health.

2. Identify the present activities that the students are performing by having them fill out a survey that lists a wide variety of activities. Post a chart that shows the components of health-related fitness enhanced by each activity. A good source for surveys and lists of activity benefits is *Fitness for Life* by Corbin and Lindsey (2007).

3. Select some activities that will build the health-related fitness components that each student needs, as identified in step 1. Each student will begin to have a personalized plan that is meaningful only to him or her.

4. Plan a week-long activity program that contains activities that are enjoyable and help alleviate weaknesses in various component areas. Evaluate the week-long program and develop a month-long program in order to provide longer-range goals. In the program, delineate the frequency of exercise, the intensity, and the amount of time to be spent exercising.

Stress Reduction

Many methods are recommended for learning to cope with stress. Only the most popular and acceptable in the school setting are covered here. The following textbooks are resources to help with this area (Blonna, 2005; Greenberg, 2004; Corbin & Lindsey, 2007).

In an earlier section, exercise was discussed as an excellent method of controlling stress. It appears to allow negative feelings to dissipate and positive feelings to replace them. The relaxed feeling that occurs after an exercise bout is championed by many as the best part of activity.

Many deep-breathing exercises are available. The relaxation response advocated by Benson (1975) is supposed to replicate the effects of Transcendental Meditation. Individuals sit comfortably and quietly and breathe deeply through the nose. The word "one" is said each time the person exhales. Twenty-minute bouts, once or twice a day, are recommended.

Another popular method is progressive relaxation as developed by Jacobson (1968). In this technique, a muscle or muscle group is first tensed and then relaxed slowly and smoothly. All the major parts of the body are in turn relaxed as one works down from the head to the toes.

Regardless of the activity choice selected for relaxation, students should be taught the importance of taking time to relax. It can be an important learning situation to take 4 or 5 minutes at the end of a class to sit down and relax. This communicates to students that relaxation is indeed important considering the instructor allows time for the activity.

Self-Evaluation and Behavior Self-Control

Self-Evaluating

An important step in maintaining good health is being able to evaluate oneself on a regular basis. Individuals ultimately answer to themselves, and thus students need not share the results of their evaluations. Many inventories, such as drinking and smoking scales, are available from various governmental agencies. Students can begin to see the extent of a problem and whether they are improving.

Students should be taught to evaluate their own levels of health-related physical fitness. Each of the health-related fitness items can be evaluated easily using the Fitnessgram (Cooper Institute, 2004). If students are not given time in the physical education program to evaluate their own fitness levels, they will probably not take the time for evaluation once they leave school. An effective technique is to give each student a self-testing card that has room for recording four to five different testing episodes. Students regularly test themselves and record their performances. If desired, instructors can file the cards and return them when it is time for another testing period. This system allows students to monitor their personal health-related fitness in a number of areas.

Modifying Personal Behavior

Students can be taught how to monitor their personal health behavior. Behavior modification is a systematic approach to solving problems. It involves keeping records of behavior in order to understand the positive and negative variables that influence behavior. The following steps can be presented to students to help them learn to manipulate their behavior.

1. Maintain behavior records. Students monitor their activity patterns and record the performances on personal charts. Currently, there are many Web sites that allow activity monitoring online. An example is the President's Challenge award system (http://www.presidentschallenge.org/). These sites allow them to observe their patterns of exercise, the duration of the exercise, and the intensity of effort. Such observation becomes self-reinforcing when, for example, students see clearly that they are exercising only 2 days per week and showing little gain, or when they observe rapid improvement after exercising 5 days per week for several weeks. Another advantage of recording behavior is that the routine act of recording reminds the performer that the behavior must be done. This routine reinforcement causes the behavior performance to improve.

2. Develop a priority schedule. If students want to exercise regularly, they must schedule the activity and make it a high-priority item. In other words, exercise must be done before other less-important tasks are performed. Scheduling the activity for a certain number of days at a specified time is most effective.

3. Analyze restrictive factors. Even after behavior has been analyzed and priorities are set, students may find that desired behavior patterns are not being followed. The reasons for this must then be analyzed and other changes implemented to increase the probability of carrying out the behavior. For example, the time of day for exercise may have to be changed. Exercising for two shorter periods per day, instead of one long period, might be a solution. Exercising with a friend or changing the mode of exercise would be another possible solution.

4. Establish rewards. To continue the activity over a long period of time, it can be helpful to establish personal contingencies that are available after performing the desired behavior. For example, students might relax and watch television immediately after exercise or take a long, hot shower.

Regardless of the reward, it must be meaningful and worthwhile to the individual. Verbalizing internally after each exercise routine is also effective as a contingency. One might say to oneself, "I feel better and look stronger after every bout of exercise." In any case, if students can identify something positive that occurs because of or after the exercise bout, they will have a tendency to continue on the path of wellness.

STUDY STIMULATORS AND REVIEW QUESTIONS

1. Define health education and discuss how it can be integrated into secondary physical education.

2. Describe several ideas for teaching health concepts in physical education.

3. What can teachers do to develop awareness and decision-making skills for students? Specifically, discuss the importance of coping and decision-making skills.

4. Identify several teaching behaviors critical to leading effective class discussions.

5. What are the areas of understanding necessary for students to develop a value for personal health? Include several knowledge concepts and learning experiences for each area.

6. Discuss the importance of proper nutrition for youth.

7. Describe various types of substance abuse as they apply to secondary school students.

8. What concepts of safety and first aid are important for healthy living?

REFERENCES AND SUGGESTED READINGS

Benson, H. (1975). *The relaxation response.* New York: William Morrow and Co.

Blonna, R. (2005). *Coping with stress in a changing world* (3rd ed.). Boston: McGraw-Hill.

Cooper Institute. (2004). *Fitnessgram/activitygram test administration manual* (3rd ed.). Champaign, IL: Human Kinetics Publishers.

Corbin, C., & Lindsey, R. (2007). *Fitness for life* (5th ed., updated). Champaign, IL: Human Kinetics Publishers.

Corbin, C. B., Welk, G., Corbin, W. G., & Welk, K. M. (2007). *Concepts of physical fitness and wellness: A comprehensive lifestyle approach* (7th ed.). Boston: McGraw-Hill.

Fahey, T. D., Insel, P. M., & Roth, W. T. (2005). *Fit and well: Core concepts and labs in physical fitness and wellness* (6th ed.). Boston: McGraw-Hill.

Friedman, M., & Rosenman, R. H. (1974). *Type A behavior and your heart.* New York: Alfred A. Knopf.

Greenberg, J. S. (2004). *Comprehensive stress management* (8th ed.). Boston: McGraw-Hill.

Hoeger, W. W. K., & Hoeger, S. A. (2005). *Lifetime fitness and wellness: A personalized plan* (6th ed.). Belmont, CA: Wadsworth.

Jackson, A. W., Morrow, J. R., Jr., Hill, D. W., & Dishman, R. K. (2004). *Physical activity for health and fitness* (updated edition). Champaign, IL: Human Kinetics Publishers.

Jacobson, E. (1968). *Progressive relaxation* (2nd ed.). Chicago: University of Chicago Press.

McConnell, K., Corbin, C. B., & Dale, D. (2004). *Fitness for life teacher resources and materials CD-ROM* (5th ed.). Champaign, IL: Human Kinetics Publishers.

U.S. Department of Agriculture. (2005). *The Food Guide Pyramid.* Pueblo, CO: Superintendent of Documents.

Wilmore, J. H. (1999). Exercise, obesity, and weight control. In C. B. Corbin & R. P. Pangrazi (Eds.), *Toward a better understanding of physical fitness and activity.* Scottsdale, AZ: Holcomb Hathaway Publishers.

WEB SITES

Healthy Lifestyles
www.actionforhealthykids.org/
www.aap.org/
www.cdc.gov/nccdphp/dnpa/physical/recommendations/index.htm
http://medlineplus.gov/
www.quackwatch.org/index.html

Nutrition
www.chowbaby.com
http://outside.utsouthwestern.edu/chn/index.htm
www.mypyramid.gov
www.utsouthwestern.edu/utsw/cda/dept27712/files/40245.html

Weight Management
www.surgeongeneral.gov/topics/obesity/

Stress Management
www.ericdigests.org/pre-926/stress.htm
www.mindtools.com/smpage.html

Substance Abuse
http://alcoholism.about.com/
www.kidsource.com/kidsource/pages/health.substance.html
www.samhsa.gov/index.aspx
www.thecommunityguide.org/

NATIONAL STANDARDS FOR PHYSICAL EDUCATION*

STANDARD 1 Demonstrates competency in motor skills and movement patterns needed to perform a variety of physical activities.

STANDARD 2 Demonstrates understanding of movement concepts, principles, strategies, and tactics as they apply to the learning and performance of physical activities.

STANDARD 3 Participates regularly in physical activity.

STANDARD 4 Achieves and maintains a health-enhancing level of physical fitness.

STANDARD 5 Exhibits responsible personal and social behavior that respects self and others in physical activity settings.

STANDARD 6 Values physical activity for health, enjoyment, challenge, self-expression, and/or social interaction.

ESSENTIAL COMPONENTS OF A QUALITY PROGRAM

COMPONENT 1 A quality physical education program is organized around content standards that offer direction and continuity to instruction and evaluation.

COMPONENT 2 A quality program is student centered and based on the developmental urges, characteristics, and interests of students.

COMPONENT 3 Quality physical education makes physical activity and motor-skill development the core of the program.

COMPONENT 4 Physical education programs teach management skills and self-discipline.

COMPONENT 5 Quality programs emphasize inclusion of all students.

COMPONENT 6 In a quality physical education setting, instruction focuses on the process of learning skills rather than the product or outcome of the skill performance.

COMPONENT 7 A quality physical education program teaches lifetime activities that students can use to promote their health and personal wellness.

COMPONENT 8 Quality physical education teaches cooperative and responsibility skills and helps students develop sensitivity to diversity and gender issues.

*Reprinted from *Moving Into the Future: National Standards for Physical Education*, 2nd ed. (2004), with permission from the National Association for Sport and Physical Education (NASPE), 1900 Association Dr., Reston, VA 20191-1599.

402

18

Promoting Motivation, Cooperation, and Inclusion: Nontraditional Ideas for Instruction

POSITIVELY
NO CLIMBING
ON WALL WITHOUT
A TEACHER OR
COACH PRESENT

The activities in this chapter offer students and teachers a change of pace. The activities are personally challenging and allow students to develop new skills and to work closely with classmates. Many are useful for rainy days, shortened-period days, for introductory activities, or as a 1- or 2-week unit. The activities require equipment that is not often used in typical secondary physical education programs. They include novel tasks and equipment meant to be presented as different challenges from the more traditional activities in the physical education setting. Because variation in student ability makes little difference in the presentation of these activities, they can be motivating to all students. For example, the proper progression of juggling activities can be taught. After the rudimentary skills are learned, some students may choose to progress to more challenging tasks, whereas others remain at a lower level.

An excellent way to implement nontraditional activities is to present them on a Tuesday or Thursday to break up a longer unit of instruction. Students can be encouraged to help each other master the tasks, with emphasis often placed on cooperation. This creates a different environment that may be more meaningful for some students. The low-key instructional approach is also an inviting variation for instructors.

INDIVIDUAL, PARTNER, AND SMALL-GROUP UNITS OF INSTRUCTION

Activities in this area include the use of beanbags, hoops, and jump bands; juggling; sport stacking, stunts, and combatives; and the use of wands. They focus primarily on individual skill development and allow each student to progress at an optimum rate of development. Students can develop new and different challenges that the rest of the class can try.

Beanbags

The best size beanbag is usually 6 inches by 6 inches because it can be balanced on various body parts and used for many challenges. The advantage of the beanbags is that they can be used for juggling activities as well as for many of the challenge activities listed here. Students should try to master the stunts with both the right and left hands.

The following are challenges that can be taken in any order.

1. Toss the beanbag overhead and catch it on the back of the hand. Try catching on different body parts, such as the shoulder, knee, and foot.

2. Toss the beanbag, make a half-turn, and catch it. Try making a different number of turns (full, double, and so forth).

3. Toss the beanbag, clap the hands, and catch it. Try clapping the hands a specified number of times. Clap the hands around different parts of the body.

4. Toss the beanbag and touch various body parts or objects. For example, toss it and touch the toes, shoulders, and hips before catching it. Specify objects to touch, such as the wall, floor, or a line.

5. Toss the beanbag, move to various body positions, and catch it. Suggested positions are sitting, kneeling, adopting a supine or prone position, and moving to one's side.

6. Reverse task 5 by tossing the beanbag from some of the suggested positions and then resuming the standing position.

7. Toss the beanbag and perform various stunts before catching it, such as heel clicks, heel slaps, a jump with a full turn, and a push-up.

8. Toss the beanbag from behind the back and catch it. Toss it overhead and catch it behind the back.

9. Toss the beanbag, move, and catch it. Cover as much ground as possible between the toss and catch. Move forward, backward, and sideways, using different steps such as the carioca, shuffle, and slide.

10. Toss the beanbag with various body parts (feet, knees, shoulders) and catch it with the hands or other body parts. Try to develop as much height on the toss as possible.

11. Perform some of the stunts with a beanbag in each hand. Catch the bags simultaneously.

12. Play a balance tag game. Specify a body part on which the bag must be balanced while moving. Designate who is "it." If the beanbag falls off or is touched with the hands, the player must freeze and is subject to being tagged.

13. Try partner activities. Play catch with a partner using two or three beanbags. Toss and catch the beanbags using various body parts.

Hoops

Hoops are useful for offering various challenges to students. A 42-inch-diameter hoop is usually the best size. This is a large enough hoop to move through and over and to use for hula-hoop activities. Students should try to master the activities with both sides of their bodies.

Emphasis can be placed on creating new routines with the hoops. The following are suggested ideas:

1. Spin the hoop like a top and see how long the hoop will continue to spin. While the hoop is spinning, see how many times it can be jumped.

2. Twirl a hula hoop using various body parts (waist, knees, ankles, neck, wrist). Twirl a hula hoop from the neck to the knees and back up to the neck. Twirl it on a wrist and then change it to the other wrist. Pass the hoop to a partner while twirling it.

3. Try many of the hula-hooping challenges while using two or more hoops. Twirl a hula hoop with a hoop on two or more body parts.

4. Play catch with a partner while twirling a hula hoop. Catch more than one object and twirl more than one hoop.

5. Jump or hop through a hoop held by a partner. Vary the challenge by altering the angle and height of the hoop. Try jumping through two or more parallel hoops without touching them.

6. Roll the hoop like a spare tire. Change direction on signal. Roll two or more hoops at the same time.

7. Use the hoop in place of a jump rope. Jump the hoop forward, backward, and sideways. Perform various foot stunts like toe touching, a rocker step, and heel-and-toe movement while jumping.

8. Roll the hoop forward with a reverse spin. The spin should cause it to return to the thrower. As the hoop returns, try some of the following challenges: jump the hoop, move through it, kick it up with the toe and catch it, and pick it up with the arm and begin twirling it on your arm.

9. Play catch with the hoop with a partner. Use two or more hoops and throw them alternately as well as simultaneously.

10. Employ the "hoop relay." Break into equal-size groups. Join hands and place a hoop on a pair of joined hands. The object is to pass the hoop around the circle without releasing the hand grip. The first group to get the hoop around the circle is declared the winner.

Jump Bands

Using jump bands is a new, novel physical activity that physical educators can use with their students in a number of fun, challenging ways. The jump bands provide a high rate of physical activity for varying-sized groups of students with three students being the ideal

FIGURE 18.1 Jump-bands position

minimum number. Two students attach the jump bands around the lower legs or ankle area with Velcro and jump rhythmically to music while a third or fourth student jumps in and out of the bands with specific foot patterns (Figure 18.1). The students with the bands on their legs can adjust them up or down depending on the skill and fitness levels of the students jumping in and out of the bands. Beginners should start with the bands as low as possible on the legs. The bands can be moved up on the legs for a more challenging, demanding workout because the jumpers have to jump higher to get over the bands. Students obviously change positions often because of the jumping demands and to develop their skills with the bands on, and as a jumper in and out of the bands. The jump bands demand teamwork for all involved. Many creative opportunities are also possible with different steps and partner activities.

Jump bands can be used as part of a rhythms unit with other rhythms and dances such as tinikling or activities with lummi sticks, or they can be a short stand-alone unit with just the jump bands. There are a wide variety of rhythmic foot pattern skills that can be developed with a group of three students working together, as well as a number of fun, challenging larger-group activities with several groups working together. Another fun variation of the jump bands is to use them as part of a fitness routine in a fitness circuit (see Chapter 16, Jump-Bands Circuit, page 365). In a fitness circuit, students could rotate from a jump-band station for cardiovascular work to a flexibility station, to a strength station, and then back to another cardiovascular station with the jump bands and so on.

Stations could also incorporate medicine balls and stability balls in a variety of ways. Students will enjoy the variety and challenge of jump bands and other equipment for all of these activities.

Beginning Jump-Band Steps

Music should be a 4/4 rhythm with popular, upbeat songs. We suggest songs such as "Hit Me with Your Best Shot" (Pat Benatar), "Settling" (Sugarland), or "Who Says You Can't Go Home" (Bon Jovi). The following steps are suggested to get started:

1. The students with the jump bands on should follow an OUT, OUT, IN, IN pattern. They should practice together without the music and then with the music.

2. The jumper should start with the right side facing the bands. When the bands go apart, the right foot should go in and then hop on the right foot. The left foot should then cross over to the out position and then hop on the left foot in the out position. The right foot should then cross over to the in position and then hop on the right foot. The sequence should be IN, IN, OUT, OUT. After becoming comfortable with one side facing the bands, the opposite side should face the bands.

3. The next sequence should be in on the right, change to the left, out on the right, pause, and start over from the opposite side. Then switch to the left foot, starting the sequence IN, CHANGE, OUT, PAUSE.

4. The next sequence is with two feet together, starting with the right or left side. The sequence is IN, PAUSE, OUT, PAUSE. Switch sides after becoming comfortable.

5. The next variation is to add a spin (90°, 180°, etc.) to each step as you move in and out of the bands. Start with a small spin and then increase the spin as you become comfortable.

Challenging Jump-Band Ideas

Rotating in a circle: Students with the bands on their legs slowly rotate in a circle while the jumper is working on his or her steps. After awhile, the students switch the rotation to the opposite direction.

Tic-tac-toe: Two groups join together and form a tic-tac-toe formation with the jump bands. The jumpers start in one corner and follow single file in a clockwise direction through the four jumping areas, continuing forward to the next set of bands. Then they all change directions and go counterclockwise. Another variation is for the jump-band group to start rotating slowly in a circle as described previously.

Snake the line: A large group activity can set up with two long vertical lines of jump bands covering the length of the gym. The people in the middle of the lines will have two sets of jump bands on their legs (one in front and one in the back). These people should practice as a large group to coordinate their OUT, OUT, IN, IN sequence. The jumpers can begin weaving through the jump bands in a snakelike fashion. If you have enough jump bands for two lines, the students can go down one line and come back crossing the other line for continuous activity.

Juggling

Juggling offers a challenge to secondary school students. If the majority of students have not mastered basic juggling skills, juggling scarves should be purchased. They are lightweight, sheer scarves that move slowly and allow students to master the proper arm and hand movements. Once the movement pattern is learned, beanbags, juggle bags (small, round beanbags), and fleece balls can be used before proceeding to balls, rings, and clubs.

Juggling with scarves does teach students the correct patterns of object movement; however, it does not transfer automatically to juggling with faster-moving objects such as fleece balls, tennis balls, rings, and hoops. Therefore, two distinct sections for juggling are offered: a section on learning to juggle with scarves and a section explaining juggling with balls. Juggling with scarves will bring success to a majority of the class, while youngsters who have mastered the scarves can move to balls and other objects.

Juggling with Scarves

Scarves are held by the fingertips near the center. To throw the scarf, it should be lifted and pulled into the air above eye level. Scarves are caught by clawing, a downward motion of the hand, and grabbing the scarf from above as it is falling. Scarf juggling should teach proper habits (e.g., tossing the scarves straight up in line with the body rather than forward or backward). Many instructors remind students to imagine that they are in a phone booth to emphasize tossing and catching without moving.

Cascading

Cascading is the easiest pattern for juggling three objects. The following sequence can be used to learn this basic technique.

1. *One scarf:* Hold the scarf in the center. Quickly move the arm across the chest and toss the scarf with the palm out. Reach out with the other hand and catch the scarf in a straight, downward motion (clawing). Toss the scarf with this hand using the motion and claw it with the opposite hand. Repeat the tossing and clawing sequence. The scarf should move in a figure-eight pattern as shown in Figure 18.2.

2. *Two scarves.* Hold a scarf with the fingertips in each hand. Toss the first one across the body as described.

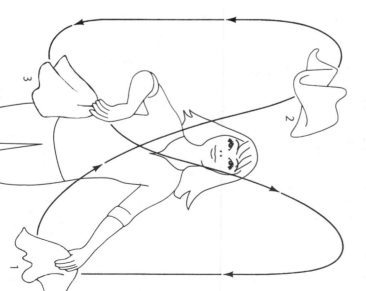

FIGURE 18.2 Making a figure-eight motion with scarves

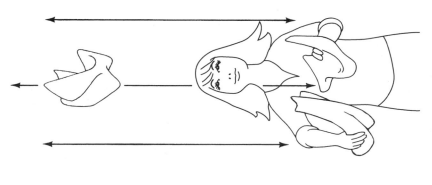

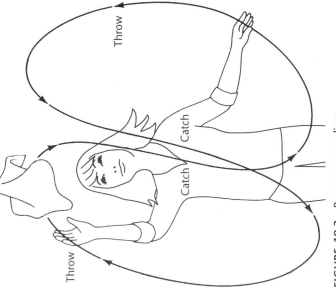

FIGURE 18.3 Reverse cascading

scribed in step 1. When it reaches its peak, look at it, and toss the second scarf across the body in the opposite direction. The first scarf thrown is caught (clawed) by the hand throwing the second scarf and vice versa. Verbal cues such as "toss," "claw," "toss," "claw" are helpful.

3. *Three-scarf cascading.* Hold a scarf in each hand by the fingertips. Hold the third scarf with the ring and little finger against the palm of the hand. The first scarf to be thrown will be from the hand that is holding two scarves. Toss this scarf from the fingertips across the chest as learned earlier. When scarf 1 reaches its peak, throw scarf 2 from the other hand across the body. As this hand starts to come down, it catches scarf 1. When scarf 2 reaches its peak, throw scarf 3 in the same path as that of scarf 1. To complete the cycle, as the hand comes down from throwing scarf 3, it catches scarf 2. The cycle is started over by throwing scarf 1 with the opposite hand. Tosses are always alternated between left and right hands with a smooth, even rhythm.

Reverse Cascading

Reverse cascading involves tossing the scarves from waist level to the outside of the body and allowing the scarves to drop down the midline of the body (Figure 18.3).

1. *One scarf.* Begin by holding the scarf as described in the previous Cascading section. The throw goes away from the midline of the body over the top, so the scarf is released and falls down the center of the

body. Catch it with the opposite hand and toss it in a similar fashion on the opposite side of the body.

2. *Two scarves.* Begin with a scarf in each hand. Toss the first as described in step 1. When it begins its descent, toss the second scarf. Catch the first scarf, then the second, and repeat the pattern in a toss, toss, catch, catch manner.

3. *Three scarves.* Think of a large funnel fixed at eye level directly in front of the juggler. The goal is to drop all scarves through this funnel so that they drop straight down the center of the body. Begin with three scarves as described earlier for three-scarf cascading. Toss the first scarf from the hand holding two scarves.

Column Juggling

Column juggling is so named because the scarves move straight up and down as though they were inside a large pipe or column and do not cross the body. To perform three-scarf column juggling, begin with two scarves in one hand and one in the other hand. Start with a scarf from the hand that has two scarves, and toss it straight up the midline of the body overhead. When this scarf reaches its peak, toss the other two scarves upward along the sides of the body (Figure 18.4). Catch the first scarf with either hand and

FIGURE 18.4 Column juggling

toss it upward again. Catch the other two scarves and toss them upward, continuing the pattern.

Showering

Showering is more difficult than cascading because of the rapid movement of the hands. There is less time allowed for catching and tossing. The scarves move in a circle following each other. It should be practiced in both directions for maximum challenge.

Start with two scarves in the right hand and one in the other. Begin by throwing the first two scarves from the right hand. Toss the scarves in a large circle away from the midline of the body and overhead as high as possible. As soon as the second scarf is released, toss the scarf across to the left hand and throw it in the same path with the right hand. All scarves are caught with the left hand and passed to the right hand.

Juggling Challenges

- While cascading, toss a scarf under one leg.

- While cascading, toss a scarf from behind the back.

- Instead of catching one of the scarves, blow it upward with a strong breath of air.

- Begin cascading by tossing the first scarf into the air with a foot. Lay the scarf across the foot and kick it into the air.

- Try juggling three scarves with one hand. Do not worry about establishing a pattern, just catch the lowest scarf each time. Try both regular and reverse cascading as well as column juggling.

- While doing column juggling, toss up one scarf, hold the other two, and make a full turn. Resume juggling.

- Try juggling more than three scarves (up to six) while facing a partner.

- Juggle three scarves while standing side by side with inside arms around each other. This is easy to do considering it is regular three-scarf cascading.

Juggling with Balls

Juggling with balls requires accurate, consistent tossing, and this should be the first emphasis. The tosses should be thrown to the same height on both sides of the body, about 2 to 2½ feet upward and across the body because the ball is tossed from one hand to the other. Practice tossing the ball parallel to the body; the most common problem in juggling is that the balls are tossed forward, and the juggler has to move forward to catch them.

The fingers, not the palms, should be used in tossing and catching. Stress relaxed wrist action. Encour-

age students to look upward to watch the balls at the peak of their flight, rather than watching the hands. Focus on where the ball peaks, not the hands. Two balls must be carried in the starting hand, and the art of releasing only one must be mastered. Progression should be working successively with one ball, then two balls, and finally three balls.

Recommended Progression for Cascading

1. Using one ball and one hand only, toss the ball upward (2 to 2½ feet), and catch it with the same hand. Begin with the dominant hand, and later practice with the other. Toss quickly, with wrist action. Then handle the ball alternately with right and left hands, tossing from one hand to the other.

2. Now, with one ball in each hand, alternate tossing a ball upward and catching it in the same hand so that one ball is always in the air. Begin again with a ball in each hand. Toss across the body to the other hand. To keep the balls from colliding, toss under the incoming ball. After some expertise has been acquired, alternate the two kinds of tosses by doing a set number (four to six) of each before shifting to the other.

3. Hold two balls in the starting hand and one in the other. Toss one of the balls in the starting hand, toss the ball from the other hand, and then toss the third ball. Keep the balls moving in a figure-eight pattern (Figure 18.5).

Recommended Progression for Showering

1. The showering motion is usually counterclockwise. Hold one ball in each hand. Begin by tossing with the right hand on an inward path, and then immediately toss the other ball from the left directly across the body to the right hand. Continue this until the action is smooth.

2. Now, hold two balls in the right hand and one in the left. Toss the first ball from the right hand on

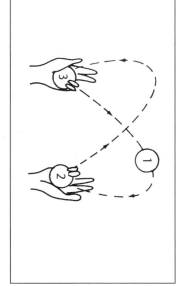

FIGURE 18.5 Cascading with three balls and two hands

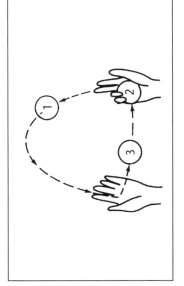

FIGURE 18.6 Showering with three balls and two hands

an inward path and immediately toss the second on the same path. At about the same time, toss the ball from the left hand directly across the body to the right hand (Figure 18.6).

3. A few students may be able to change from cascading to showering and vice versa. This is a skill of considerable challenge.

Sport Stacking with Speed Stacks

Students have been stacking drinking cups in some form or fashion since the invention of paper and plastic cups. In recent years, however, cup stacking has evolved into much more than a pastime on the kitchen floor. Now called sport stacking, it's a full-fledged, challenging, and fun motor-skill activity, while also emerging as a stand-alone sport itself.

With the advent of plastic cups specifically designed for stacking (called Speed Stacks; www .speedstacks.com), students are manipulating cups with extraordinary precision and speed. Much like juggling, sport stacking focuses on hand–eye coordination and dexterity—but with a much higher success rate. It is easy to learn and appeals to all ability levels of students.

Sport stacking is an individual, small-group, or team activity where participants stack and unstack 12 specially made plastic cups in predetermined pyramids. Stackers race against the clock and in relays. Sport stacking helps students use both sides of their bodies and brains, promoting hand quickness and concentration. Sport stacking can challenge students to focus on hand–eye coordination and reaction time—important skills for almost any sport or physical activity.

Every student, no matter what his or her athletic ability, can find success with sport stacking. This developmental activity is based on the inclusion of all students. Sport stacking is taught in a specific progression from the basic 3 Stack to the challenging Cycle Stack, which involves several advanced stacking sequences. It's easy to master, and with practice, students

can progress quickly to the more complicated patterns. Once the basic stacks are taught, there are many activities designed to enhance an entire sport stacking unit.

With sport stacking, there is an opportunity for individual, partner, and team activities, cooperative and competitive. The culmination of a sport stacking unit can include time trials for recording personal records, head-to-head relay matches, or a competitive tournament format. There is also room for creative expression with "freestyle stacking." Sport stacking can include many positive elements such as teamwork, sportsmanship, competition, determination, achievement of personal bests, and world record setting.

Basics of Sport Stacking

Students find the most success when introduced to sport stacking with formal instruction, supplemented with opportunities to compete in relays, race against the clock to set personal records, or have fun stacking with each other. The ideal scenario is to have enough sets of "stacking cups" made specifically for sport stacking (12 cups in each set) to allow every student a hands-on opportunity to stack. The following are five steps to learn the basic stacking patterns. (Please note that for teaching purposes, these instructions are written for a stacker whose right hand is dominant.)

Step 1: The 3 Stack   The 3 Stack is the most basic pyramid in sport stacking. It's the place to start, and once it's learned, you can progress quickly into the next steps.

Up Stacking

1. Start with three cups nested together in front of you.

2. Take the top cup off with your right hand and set it next to the bottom cup.

3. Take the second cup off with your left hand and place it on top to build your first pyramid.

Down Stacking

1. To down stack, place your right hand on the top cup and your left hand on the bottom left cup.

2. Slide the cup in your right hand down over the bottom right cup. Bring the cup in your left hand over the second cup.

3. You are now back to your original stack of three cups and ready to go again.

Step 2: The 3-3 Stack

1. After you have mastered the 3 Stack, place another set of three cups in front of you so you have two

sets of three cups nested and ready to be up stacked.

2. Working from left to right, up stack each set of three cups.

3. Now go back to the first stack on your left and down stack that set. Then down stack the other set. (Remember to always go back to the beginning to down stack.)

Step 3: The 3-3-3 Stack (Beginner Competition Stack)

1. Start with three sets of three cups each nested together in front of you.

2. Working from left to right, up stack each stack.

3. Then *go back to the beginning* to down stack again, working from left to right.

Step 4: The 6 Stack (using the 3-2-1 Method)

The 3-2-1 method is by far the fastest way to build a 6 Stack. Take your time to learn this method and practice it over and over; it's your ticket to really stacking fast.

Up Stacking

1. Start with six cups nested together in one stack in front of you.

2. Take three cups with your right hand and two cups with your left. Hold the cups loose with your pinkies under the bottom cups. Spread the cups apart with your fingers.

3. Release the bottom cup in your right hand down just to the right of the center cup. Release the bottom cup from your left hand to the left of the center cup so you now have three cups forming the base of your pyramid.

4. Release the next cup in your right hand on top of the center and right cups that form the base of the pyramid. Set the cup in your left hand next to it. Set the last cup in your right hand on top.

Down Stacking

1. To down stack, place your right hand on the top cup and your left hand on the second cup on the left.

2. Slide to the right with your right hand and at the same time to the left with your left hand.

3. Take the three cups in your right hand and the two cups in your left and put them back in one stack of six cups.

4. Now that you know the 6 Stack, practice it again and again.

Step 5: The 3-6-3 Stack (Competition Stack)

The 3-6-3 Stack combines the skills learned in the 3 Stack and the 6 Stack. You now get to use your complete set of 12 cups. Working from left to right, stack three, then six, then three cups. Go back to the beginning and down stack. Practice slowly as you develop skill and then speed up your pace. Take your time, use the 3-2-1 method when stacking your 6 Stack, and have fun practicing. It is important to use a light, soft touch. Slide, never slam, your cups. Race a friend, time yourself on a StackMat competition timer, chart your personal best, and try to beat your time. Keep practicing.

1. Start with one stack of three cups, one stack of six and one stack of three, with each stack nested together in front of you.

2. Working from left to right, up stack the three, up stack the six (don't forget the 3-2-1 method), and up stack the remaining three.

3. Then *go back to the beginning* to down stack in the same order.

Step 6: The Cycle Stack (Premiere Competition Stack)

The Cycle Stack is the most complex of the competitive stacks. It consists of a 3-6-3, followed by a 6-6, and then a 1-10-1, with a few fancy maneuvers in between, all ending with a down-stacked 3-6-3. Specific instructions for the Cycle Stack can be obtained through the World Sport Stacking Association (WSSA).*

Beginning Cup-Stacking Activities

Stackers and blasters: Cups are set up around the gym on the floor; half of the sets are up stacked, and half are down stacked. Students are designated as "stackers" or "blasters." When the music starts, stackers go around up stacking (whichever stack type has been designated: 3-3-3, 3-6-3, or Cycle Stack) stacks that are down stacked, and blasters go around down stacking the up-stacked stacks. For an option, pedometers can be used, or various locomotor movements (slide, power skip, etc) can be designated for either stackers or blasters. After 30 seconds to 1 minute of music, the music stops, and the groups may return to a sideline. Stackers and blasters may count their up or down stacks. Repeat, designating a new movement

*The World Sport Stacking Association (WSSA) was formed in 2001 to govern and promote sport stacking worldwide. The WSSA is a nonprofit organization and serves as the official source for rules and regulations to provide a consistent framework for sport stacking tournaments and events. The WSSA can be reached online at www.worldsportstackingassociation.org or by phone at 1-303-917-4171.

form. Basketball dribbling with the left or right hand or soccer ball dribbling could be incorporated.

Follow-the-leader rotations: The equipment should include folding tables or practice mats and four sets of Speed Stacks per table. Place a set of Speed Stacks on each quadrant of the table and arrange to begin a 3-3-3 stack. Leave the first and third stacks in the down-stacked position and the others in the up-stack position. Students should be with a partner side by side. The lead stacker should begin up and down stacking the cups from left to right. The partner then follows the leader. This rotation continues for a certain amount of time or rotations. The stacking should include a variety of stacks (e.g., 3-6-3, 6-6, or two 10 Stacks).

Around the Table: A set of Speed Stacks is placed on each quadrant of a table arranged for a selected stack (e.g., 3-3-3, 3-6-3, 6-6, or Cycle Stack). Assign four stackers per table (one stacker per quadrant). Have each stacker get in a ready position in front of their down-stacked set of Speed Stacks. On the "go" signal, students up stack and down stack the selected sequence at their quadrants. Once his or her pattern is complete, each stacker moves around the table counterclockwise to the next quadrant to stack the next set. Continue to stack around the table for a designated period of time. Consider the following variations:

■ Switcho/Stacko. The students begin stacking in a counterclockwise direction. On a signal, stackers reverse their directions and stack around the table clockwise.

■ Large Group Stacking. Line up a number of 6-foot tables and expand the "Around the Table Stacking" to accommodate a large group that will stack continuously and move from one stack to the next in a clockwise or counterclockwise direction.

■ Hound and Rabbit Table Challenge. Place a set of down-stacked Speed Stacks at each quadrant arranged in a 3-6-3. Two stackers stand at diagonal quadrants across the table from each other in a ready position. Designate one stacker as the "hound" and the other as the "rabbit." On the "go" signal, each stacker begins up and down stacking the set in front of them. When the stack is completed, each stacker moves clockwise to the next stack and repeats the stacking sequence. The objective is for the "hound" to try and catch the "rabbit" as they stack quickly around the table.

Floor Relays: At one end of the teaching area, set up enough 3-3-3 stacks to match the number of teams participating. The stacks should be evenly spread apart and marked by cones or an established line. Form teams made up of three to four students. Establish a starting line across the area from the stacks and have teams line up in file formation behind the starting line, each lined up with a 3-3-3 stack. On the "go" signal, the first person on each team runs to their set of Speed Stacks and properly up stacks and down stacks the 3-3-3. When the stack is properly completed, the student runs back to the relay team, tags the next person, and the process is repeated until all relay members have had one turn. The floor relay is complete once the last stacker returns to their team and crosses the starting line. Consider the following variations:

1. Set up and stack a 3-3-3-3, 3-6-3, or Cycle Stack.

2. Use various locomotor skills and equipment to move from the start line to the stacks, such as slide, skip, juggle, dribble a basketball, dribble a soccer ball, pull on scooters, jump ropes, etc.

3. Pair up with a set of Speed Stacks across the area for each pair. This activity is a continuous two-person relay where students move across the gym, stack the selected stack, and go back to tag their partners' hands. This is repeated until time is called. Use timed music of 2, 3, or 4 minutes in duration. A variety of movements and sports skills can be used. Students can use pedometers to check steps or time.

4. Instead of the Speed Stacks being lined up left to right at the end of the area, rearrange each stack in a line that runs straight ahead of each relay team. If you're doing a 3-3-3 for example, set up three cups about 5 to 8 feet straight ahead from the starting line, move 5 to 8 feet forward, and set up another three cups. Continue this with the other two sets of three. On the "go" signal, the first relay team member runs to up stack the first three cups, continues to the second stack and up stacks them, and continues to the third and fourth stacks to do the same. When all four stacks of three are in an up-stacked position, the student runs back to the beginning, but his or her job is not done yet. He or she must head back down the line to down stack all four stacks in order. Once all the stacks are back to their original position, the student runs back and tags the next relay team member.

There are many other possibilities for sport stacking activities that can be competitive or cooperative. Refer to the speedstacks.com Web site for ideas. The following are just a few examples:

■ Individual races in a group setting

■ Continuous relays

■ Partner stacking

- Team relay races
- Personal record setting with a StackMat competition timer or the use of a stopwatch
- Stacking with eyes closed
- Incorporation of stretches, sit-ups, push-ups, etc., with cup stacking
- Freestyle stacking

Stunts, Pyramids, and Combatives

This unit should emphasize personal challenge and brief competitive episodes. Students enjoy the chance to pit their strength and coordination skills against others. The combatives should be between opponents of approximately the same skill level and size. Partners should be switched often so there is little chance for animosity to develop. The contests start and stop by mutual agreement, with either party able to terminate the contest immediately. There is little point in running tournaments to see who is the class champion in a specific combative. Instead, emphasize enjoying the activity, learning one's strengths and weaknesses, and being able to challenge a number of opponents.

Stunts, on the other hand, require that students work cooperatively to accomplish them successfully and are an excellent way to help students learn more about their peers.

Suggested Individual Stunts

Leg Dip. Extend both hands and one leg forward while balancing on the other leg. Lower the body until the seat touches the heel and then return to the standing position. This must be done without the aid of the arms and without losing balance.

Behind-the-Back Touch. Start in a standing position with the arms extended behind the back and hands clasped. Squat slowly and touch the floor with an extended finger; then return to the standing position.

Knee Jump. Kneel on the floor with the seat on the heels and the toes pointing backward. In one continuous motion, swing the arms forward and jump to the feet. If accomplished, try to perform a half-turn during the jump.

Wall Climb. Take a push-up position with the feet against the wall. Walk up the wall with the feet to a handstand position and then return to the push-up position.

Popover. While in push-up position, propel the body upward and do a half-turn to the inverted push-up position. Pop over to the regular push-up position.

Caterpillar. One student is on his or her hands and knees, acting as the support. Another student, facing

Double Heel Click. Jump upward and click the heels twice. If accomplished, try to perform a triple heel click before landing.

Push-Up Inversion. Begin in a push-up position. Push strongly off the floor and bring the legs through the arms in one smooth motion—assuming the inverted push-up position. Return to the original position with a strong movement backward.

Jump Through. Hold the left toe with the right hand. Jump the right foot through without losing the grip on the toe. Try the stunt with the other foot.

Sitting Liftoff. Sit on the floor with the legs extended forward. Place the hands on the floor somewhere between the hips and knees, depending on the balance point. Lift the entire body off the floor in a balanced position. The stunt can be learned in stages—first with the heels remaining on the floor and then with the heels held off the floor by a friend.

Jumping Toe Touch. Begin in a standing position with the hands held in front of the body, a shoulder width apart, palms down. When ready, jump up and bring the feet quickly forward so the toe tips touch the hands in front of the body. The attempt should be to bring the hands to the feet, lifting the feet as high as possible.

Leg Circling. In a squatting position with both hands on the floor, place the left knee between the arms and extend the right leg to the side. Swing the right leg forward and under the lifted right arm, under the left leg and arm, and back to starting position. Perform several circles in succession. Try circling with the other leg.

Suggested Partner and Group Stunts

Leapfrog. One student forms the base by standing stiff legged, bending over, and placing the hands on the knees. The other student runs and leaps over the base by performing a light push-off on the back of the base. A number of students can form bases to create a series of leaps for the moving student.

Wheelbarrow. One partner is in a push-up position with the legs spread. The other person walks between the legs and grasps and lifts the partner's lower legs. The partner in push-up position then walks while the other person moves forward, backward, or sideways. A double or triple wheelbarrow can be performed with students extending their legs over the shoulders and back of the student in push-up position and placing their hands on the floor.

the same direction, places the hands about 2 feet in front of the support's hands. The second student's legs are then placed on top of the support and locked together at the ankles. Five to six students can continue this process and then begin walking when everyone is in place.

Knee Stand. The base student is in a crab position. The other student stands on the knees of the base. A spotter may be necessary to help the second student come to a balanced position.

Cooperative Scooter. Two students face each other and sit with toes under the seat of the other. The arms are joined by holding the other student's arms at the wrist or above. Students scoot forward or backward by cooperatively lifting the feet when the other lifts the seat. Progress is made by alternately flexing and extending the knees and hips.

Spider Walk. The base student is in a sitting position with his or her back against a wall. The next student backs up and sits lightly on the knees of the base. More students can be added in similar fashion. The hands should be placed around the waist of each person in front. Walking is done by moving the feet on the same side together.

Triple High Jump. Students form groups of three and join hands. One of the students is designated as the performer and jumps over the joined arms of the other two. The performer is assisted in the jump by an upward lift from the others. The hands to be jumped over should be clasped lightly and released if the jumper does not gain enough height.

Octopus. Eight to 12 students work together to develop this activity. Half of the students form a circle with hands joined, while each student in the other half finds a pair of joined hands to lean backward on, placing the weight on the heels. Each of the leaners then joins hands behind the backs of the others, thus creating two separate groups with joined hands. The octopus begins moving slowly around the circle, taking small sidesteps. The stunt is brought to a climax by moving as fast as possible.

Double-Bear Walk. The base student is on his or her hands and knees. The top student assumes the same position with the hands on the shoulders and the knees over the hips of the base. They move slowly throughout the area without losing balance.

Double-Crab Walk. The bottom student moves into a crab position. The top performer straddles the base and also assumes the crab position with the hands on the

FIGURE 18.7 Spotting the back balance

shoulders and the feet on the knees of the base. They move slowly throughout the area.

Back Balance. Students work with a partner. One partner lies in the supine position and becomes the base. The base bends the knees, and the balancer places the small of the back on the soles of the base's feet. The balancer then lies back and balances in a layout position (Figure 18.7).

Sitting Balance. The base assumes a supine position on the floor. The balancer straddles the base so that they are looking at each other. The balancer sits on the soles of the base's feet while the base holds the ankles of the balancer. The legs of the balancer should be extended as much as possible.

Abdominal Balance. The base assumes a supine position on the floor and then raises the legs and positions the feet so the soles are parallel to the floor. The balancer faces the base and places the abdomen on the soles of the base's feet. The base grasps the hands of the balancer and extends the legs to move the performer into a balanced position. The balancer should attempt to arch the back, raise the head, and extend the arms to the sides.

Seat Press. The base lies on the floor with the knees bent and the feet flat on the floor. The balancer straddles the base, facing the feet of the base. The two join hands, and the top partner sits on the joined hands supported by the base. The balancer's legs are placed on the knees of the base.

Mini-Pyramids. Students can work in groups of three to five to develop various types of pyramids.

Some examples are shown in Figure 18.8. Students should be encouraged to develop different types of pyramids and allowed time to share them with the rest of the class. Examples are the hip–shoulder stand, double-crab stand, double-bear stand, and shoulder stand. Students should be cautioned to select a partner of similar size and to stand on the proper points of support.

Combatives

There are many types of combatives. This list should give insight into the many variations but is certainly not exhaustive.

FIGURE 18.8   Mini-pyramids

Arm Wrestling. This popular activity can be done lying on the floor or sitting at a table. The right hands are clasped, and the elbows are bent and rest on the floor or table. When ready, the goal is to force the opponent's hand down to the floor or table surface. The elbows cannot be lifted from the surface.

Leg Wrestling. Opponents are side by side and supine on a mat with their heads in opposite directions. They lock the near elbows and prepare for action. On signal, they lift the inside leg vertically two times before hooking the legs on the third count. They then try to roll the opponent over backwards.

Standing Hand Wrestle. Contestants place the toes of their right feet together and grasp right hands in a handshake grip. The left foot is moved to the rear for support. The goal is to force the opponent to move either foot.

Finger Wrestle. Opponents stand on the right foot and hold the left foot with the left hand. The index fingers of the right hand are hooked, and opponents attempt to push each other off balance.

Flag Grab. Contestants have a flag tucked in the belt and attempt to keep others from pulling it out. At the same time, opponents try to collect as many flags as possible.

Palm Wrestle. Contestants face each other, standing 12 inches apart. The palms of the opponents are placed together and must remain so for the duration of the contest. The goal is to push the opponent off balance.

Toe Dance. Contestants begin by placing their hands on the opponents' shoulders. The goal is to step on top of the toes of the opponents. A variation can be to see how many toe touches can be accumulated in a specified time.

Seat Pull-Up. Opponents sit on the floor, facing each other, with the knees bent, and the soles of the contestants' shoes together. Players bend forward, grasp hands firmly, and attempt to pull their opponents' seats off the floor. The winner must be sitting upright in position when the opponent is lifted from the floor, or the contest is a draw.

Back-to-Back Takedown. Contestants sit back to back and lock elbows. The feet are widely spread to form a broad base of support. Both players attempt to pull the other to the left and touch the opponent's shoulder (or elbow) to the floor. As a variation, attempt the contest by pulling in the opposite direction.

Tug-of-War Activities

Tug-of-war activities can be conducted in pairs. Partners should be changed often so students have a chance to compete with many others and are not subjected to constantly losing or to seldom being challenged. Tug-of-war ropes are easily made from 10 feet of 3/8-inch nylon rope and two sections of 5/8-inch garden hose that is 2 feet long. The rope is threaded through the garden hose, which serves as a handle, and tied with a bowline knot so there is a loop at each end of the rope.

Partners can have contests using some of the following suggested positions and activities.

Different Positions. Facing, back-to-back, side-to-side, one-handed, two-handed, and crab positions are a few suggested variations, with the rope hooked over the foot, in a push-up position, and on all fours.

Balance Pulls. Students begin in a stationary position. The goal is to cause the opponent to move the feet or lose balance.

Pick-Up Contest. Indian clubs or bowling pins are placed behind the contestants. The goal is to pull and move backward in order to pick up the clubs.

Multiple Rope Pulls. Ropes can be twisted together so four to six students can become involved in the contest.

Pick Up and Pull. The ropes are laid on the floor between two contestants. On signal, the two opponents run to the rope, pick it up, and the tug-of-war ensues.

Team Tug-of-War

Small groups and classes can have contests with the large commercially available tug-of-war ropes. Most are 50 feet in length and at least 1 inch in diameter. Many of the ropes have large loops on the end so students can stand inside of them. Caution must be used with the loops, however, because students cannot easily release or step outside the loop when the other team gains momentum.

A suggested manner for conducting team tugs-of-war is to tie a marker in the middle of the rope. Two parallel lines are drawn 10 to 20 feet apart. The pull starts with the marker in the middle of the two lines. The goal is to pull the marker over your team's line. Variations for different types of pulls are to try pulling with the rope overhead, having opponents pull with their backs to each other, pulling with one hand on the ground or in the air, or pulling from a seated position.

Wands

Wands provide challenge through balance and flexibility activities, which can be performed individually. Wands are usually made from 5/8-inch or 3/4-inch dowels and should be 42 inches long. They can be painted, and rubber tips can be placed on the ends to soften the noise they make when falling on the floor.

Wand Whirl. Stand a wand in front of the body, and balance it with one finger. Release the wand, perform a full turn, and catch the wand. Try the activity in both directions. Try catching it with one finger on top of the wand.

Thread the Needle. Hold the wand in both hands near the ankles. Without letting go of the wand, step over the wand and through the space between the arms. Return to the starting position. Try passing the wand under the feet side to side, one foot at a time, with the wand held in front of and behind the body.

Thread the Needle (Jumping). Perform virtually the same stunt as the previous activity, except jump over the stick and pass it under the feet simultaneously.

Wand Kickover. Balance the wand in front of the body with one hand. Release the wand, kick a leg over, and catch the wand. Try kicking in both directions using both legs. Try catching the wand with one finger.

Walk Under. Grasp the wand with the right hand. Twist under the right arm without letting go of the wand, without taking it off the floor, and without touching the knee to the floor. Try using the left arm also.

Wand Walk-down. Start in a straddle stance, with legs straight. Hold a wand near one end, with the other end of the wand above the head and pointed toward the ceiling. Bend backward, place the wand on the floor behind, and walk the hands down the wand. Return to a standing position. If the hands do not have rubber tips, a spotter may have to stabilize the wand end on the floor.

Broomstick Balance. Balance the wand vertically in one hand. Begin by walking while balancing and then attempt to balance the wand in a stationary position. Try walking in different directions, using both hands, and balancing the wand on different body parts.

Partner Exchange. Face a partner, each balancing a wand in front of you. On signal, run to the other's wand and catch it before it hits the floor. Challenge can be added by increasing the distance, using two wands, and performing stunts such as a full turn or heel click before catching the wand.

Reaction Time. Hold the wand horizontally. Your partner places one hand directly above the wand, palm down. Drop the wand, and your partner must try to catch the wand before it hits the floor. This can also be tried holding the wand vertically. The other person forms a "V" with the thumb and fingers and is challenged to catch the wand. Marks can be placed on the wand and students challenged to catch the wand on certain marks.

Wand Wrestle. Hold a wand in the vertical position with a partner. The goal is to move the wand to the horizontal plane. One person is designated to move the wand horizontally while the other resists the attempt. Roles are reversed after each bout.

Wand Release. Sit facing a partner with the legs straight and the soles of the feet together. Together, hold a wand horizontally at chest level. A win occurs when one person causes the other to release the grip on the wand. Neither player is allowed to leave or modify the starting position.

Isometric Exercises. Perform isometric exercises. Examples are attempting to twist the wand, to stretch the wand, to compress the wand, or to pull it against different body parts. Many stretching activities can also be done using the wands.

NOVEL TEAM GAMES AND ACTIVITIES

The following activities are enjoyable for students because they demand few specialized skills yet require teamwork. The games help develop camaraderie among students, and teams can be reorganized periodically to equalize the competition. Rules listed are only starting points; students and teachers can modify any and all of the rules as they desire.

Cageball Games

Cageballs come in many different sizes. The most common size is 2 feet in diameter, which is an easy size to store and inflate. The next size is 4 feet in diameter, which makes the games more interesting at the high school level. Drawbacks to the larger size are storage, expense, and inflation time. The largest cageballs, often termed *earth balls*, are 5 or 6 feet in diameter. These can be kicked, batted, and tossed. Students should not be allowed to mount the ball and roll it, however, because falls in those circumstances are common.

Crab Cageball. Students are divided into four teams. Cones can be used to delineate the corners of a square. One team forms one side of the square, and a different team makes up each side. All players sit with hands behind them for support. Each team is numbered from right to left beginning with the number 1. The cageball is placed in the middle of the square. The instructor or another student calls out a number, and one member from each team (with the number called) performs a crab walk to the center and attempts to kick the cageball over the other teams. A team has a point scored against it when (1) the ball is kicked over or through the team, (2) a team member touches the ball with the arms or hands, or (3) a player stands to block or stop the ball. The team with the fewest points is declared the winner.

Long Team Cageball. Players are divided into two teams. The teams move into sitting positions in two lines facing each other 10 to 15 feet apart. The teacher rolls or throws a cageball between the two lines. The object is for one team to kick the ball over the other team. A point is scored against a team when the ball goes over or through a line. The team with the fewer points wins. Again, a point is awarded if a player stands or touches the ball with the hands. More than one cageball can be used simultaneously.

Cageball Football. The game is played on a large playing field. The class is divided into two teams. The object of the game is to carry the cageball across the goal line. The only way the ball can be advanced, however, is when it is in the air. Whenever the ball is on the ground, it can only be moved backwards or sideways. This game is best played with a 4-foot or larger cageball.

Cageball Target Throw. The cageball is used as a target in this game. Divide the class into two teams and place them on opposite sides of the gym. A center line divides the area in half, and teams are restricted to movement in their half. Use cones to mark the goal line near the ends of the playing area. Center the cageball between the teams. Each team is given a number of playground balls or volleyballs for throwing at the cageball. The object is to move the cageball across the opponent's goal line by hitting the cageball with the volleyballs. The cageball cannot be touched by any player. If it is touched, regardless of intent, the point goes to the other team.

Scooter Cageball Soccer. Each player is given a scooter. The ball may be advanced by using the feet only. The object is to score a goal in a fashion similar to soccer. Penalty shots are awarded for rough play, touching the ball with the hands, and leaving the scooter.

Throton Activities and Games

Throtons are objects that can be used for throwing and catching activities as well as for games similar to football, team handball, or Ultimate Frisbee. The throtons provide a novel and fun change of pace and challenges especially appropriate for secondary school students (Figure 18.9). A variety of throwing and catching skills that can be performed with the throtons include overhand throws, sidearm throws, underhand throws, option-type football pitches with either hand, rugby-type laterals, and centering-type skills. The throtons

FIGURE 18.9 Throtons

are soft and easy for students to catch. Refer to Chapters 19 and 20 for rules and ideas for football, team handball, and Frisbee games that can use the throtons.

Scoops Activities and Games

Scoops can also be used for throwing and catching activities as well as games like modified lacrosse or Ultimate Frisbee (Figure 18.10). (See sections in Chapters 19 and 20.) A variety of challenging throwing and catching skills can be performed with either hand. Examples include overhand throws, sidearm throws, and underhand throws. Catching skills involve a different positioning of the scoop for throws above and below the waist, as well as forehand and backhand position of the scoop. Additional skills include scooping the ball off the ground and cradling the ball while running (Chapter 19, Lacrosse section). Balls of different sizes can be used depending on the skills of the students. Students should start with a softball-sized whiffle ball and then progress to more difficult balls that are smaller, harder, or bounce more. The scoops are an excellent lead-up game for lacrosse because the skills are similar. The rules for Ultimate Frisbee (Chapter 20) can be used for a game with the scoops.

Flickerball Games

Flickerball is a similar game to team handball or Ultimate Frisbee in which a team tries to advance a ball or object down the field or court and score a goal by throwing the object through or into a goal. On an outdoor field, the goals can be 4-foot by 8-foot pieces of plywood permanently placed on poles so that they are about 8 feet high. A 2- or 3-foot square is cut out of the center of the goal. If the ball goes through the hole, more points are awarded than if the ball hits the plywood. Local rules and variations can be applied. Usually a three-point type of basketball crease is set up to keep the players farther away from the goal. The size of the crease can vary according to the situation. A "rules of three" approach can be applied to force students to pass within 3 seconds, to make at least three passes before shooting, and for defenders, to keep back at least 3 feet from the player with the ball. The player with the ball can also take only three steps and then must pass or shoot. Turnovers or free passes occur when any of the rules of three are violated. The players advance the ball up the field by passing to teammates. If the game is played indoors, a target such as a mat on the wall or a standing goal can be substituted for the goals. Various types of footballs, Throtons, foam balls, rugby balls, and Frisbees can be used for the games to add variety to the unit.

Potato Ball Games

Potato ball is usually played with a regular or modified football. Other types of balls can be used, including playground balls, Nerf balls, throtons, or alligator-skin-type balls. The game is similar to Ultimate Frisbee except that you can run or throw the ball. The game involves continuous movement until a touchdown is scored by running or throwing to a teammate across the goal line. The game is usually played on a football field or across a football field. Students advance the ball toward the goal line by running or passing to teammates in any direction: forward, sideways, or backwards. A turnover occurs when a student is tagged while holding the ball, when an incomplete pass occurs, or when an interception occurs. Play starts immediately when the opposing team picks up the ball. The game works best with short, controlled passes while advancing the ball up the field.

Eclipse Ball Games

Eclipse Ball is a racquet game that combines elements from badminton, racquetball, tennis, and volleyball. It is played on a standard volleyball court with a special eclipse ball. A modified tennis racquet or any other similar type racquet is used to serve the ball and hit forehands and backhands. Four to six players can be on a team, depending on the size of the court. The game is designed to foster long rallies with second chances because the ball is allowed to bounce and to be played off of the back walls with special rules for keeping the rally alive. A "play it" situation is possible when one team is at fault and the opposing team desires to gamble for more points. For example, if a player hits the ball out of bounds and an opposing team player feels that he or she can keep a rally alive, an opposing player yells "play it" and continues to play for the point, which is now worth two points instead of the normal one point. Each additional "play it" call adds two points more to the rally so that a rally may be worth many points. Local rules for each school or facility can be developed. For a list of official rules, write to Eclipse Ball, Inc., P.O. Box 333, Grant, Michigan, 49327.

FIGURE 18.10 Scoops

RECREATIONAL ACTIVITIES

Many other recreational-type activities can be used as mini-units or as a change of pace. Rules and regulations usually accompany the purchase of equipment and are specific to the situation. The authors have had success with the following activities:

Shuffleboard
Deck tennis
Tennis volleyball
Table tennis
Pillow polo
Sacket
Horseshoes
Lawn bowling
Global ball
Pickleball

RELAYS

When they are not overused, relays are enjoyable activities for students. To keep the atmosphere vibrant and the students motivated, the teams should be changed often to equalize the ability of various groups. If the same team wins every bout, the outcome is predetermined and the rest of the class will not be motivated. Another motivator is frequent changing of the relay. The relay can be run once to show students how it is to be conducted and then one to three times for competition. All relay teams should have the same number of persons on each squad. It is wise to change the order of the squads so different people get a chance to run starting and finishing legs. Define the signals to start the relay, and tell students what position they must assume when finished (sitting, kneeling, or some alternative position).

Potato Relays. Potato relays have been played for years. A small box to hold the objects (potatoes) is placed in front of each squad. Four circles (hoops can be used) are placed 10 to 15 feet apart in front of each squad. The goal is for the first runner to pick up an object from the box and carry it to one of the hoops, come back, pick up another object, and place it in another hoop. This is done until all the hoops are filled. The next person picks up the objects one at a time from the hoops and places them back in the box. The pattern is repeated until all members of the squad have had a turn.

Wheelbarrow Relay. The wheelbarrow position described earlier in the chapter is used as the means of locomotion. All members of each squad must participate in both the carrying position and the down formation.

Bowling Pin Relay. Four bowling pins per squad are used. They are evenly spaced in front of each squad in a fashion similar to the potato relay. The first person in line lays down all of the pins, and the next person stands them up. Only one hand can be used.

Over and Under Ball Relay. Each team is spread out in open squad formation so players are 10 to 15 feet apart. The first person in line passes the ball backward overhead to the nearest teammate. That person throws it backward between the legs to another teammate, and the pattern repeats. When the ball gets to the end of the squad, that person runs to the front of the squad and passes the ball backward. The process is repeated until all players have had a turn at the end and front of the squad.

Stepping-Stone Relay. Two small carpet squares are used per squad. The first person in line is the mover and helps the next person in line move down and back. The only way to advance in this relay is by standing on a carpet square and moving to another. It is illegal to move or stand on the floor. The mover picks up the rear carpet square and moves it in front of the advancing player so the next step can be taken. All players must play both roles before the relay is completed.

Pass-and-Squat Relay. Players are spread out so they are 10 to 15 feet apart. The first person in line turns around, faces the rest of the squad, and throws a volleyball or soccer ball to the first person in line, who returns the throw and squats. The leader now throws the ball to the next person until all members have received a throw and have squatted. When the ball is thrown to the last player, that person dribbles the ball to the front of the squad and repeats the pattern.

Fetch Relay. Squads line up and place one member at the other end of the playing area, 10 to 20 yards away. This person runs back to the squad and fetches the next person. The person who has just been fetched in turn runs back and fetches the next person. The pattern continues until all members have been fetched to the opposite end of the playing area.

Snowball Relay. This relay is similar to the fetch relay, except that after one person has been fetched, both players run back and pick up another player. The pattern continues until the majority of squad members are running back and forth, picking up the remaining members. This relay can be exhausting for the first few people in line and should not be run too often.

Sport Skill Relays. Many sport skills can be used for relays. For example, dribble the basketball down the court, make a basket, and return. The problem with relays of this type is that success is predicated on the skill level of the participants. If some students are less skilled in basketball, the relay can be a source of embarrassment, causing these students to bear the brunt of losing the relay. An instructor who uses sport skill relays is wise to include a wide variety of skills and to develop many different types of relays.

Spread-Eagle Relay. Break the class into groups of eight to 10 students. They lie down on the floor and form a circle with their heads toward the center. They join hands and spread the legs. Participants in each squad are numbered, beginning with one through the number of squad members. When a number is called, that person stands up, runs around the circle, and then resumes the prone position on the floor. The runner must place both feet between each pair of legs. The first person to return to the starting position earns a point for that squad. The squad with the most points wins.

COOPERATIVE ACTIVITIES

Cooperative activities require students to work together. They can be used early in the year as mixers in an attempt to help students get to know one another. Emphasis is on enjoyment and accomplishment.

Commonalities. Put enough hula hoops out for half the students in the class. The class walks or moves around the gym until the music stops or the teacher blows a whistle. Two students put one foot in the same hoop. They must talk to their partners and come up with two common traits that they have that are not visible to anyone. The students then repeat this activity and find a new partner or group of three and complete the same task. The groups can get bigger and bigger as the teacher decides. This is an excellent way for class members to get to know each other and for the teacher to also learn about the students in the class.

Picnic Name Game. Have your class stand in a circle. The first person starts by saying his or her first name and what he or she is bringing to the picnic; the item must start with the same letter as the person's first name (e.g., Paul is bringing peanut butter or Jessica is bringing jelly). The next person repeats the first name and the item of all the previous people and then adds his or her name and the item that he or she is bringing to the picnic. This procedure continues until the last person has said everyone's name and item.

Group Name Juggling. Ask the class to stand in a circle. The first person calls out the name of one person in the circle and then passes a soft ball (or any piece of appropriate equipment) underhand to that person. This continues until all members of the circle have been called and received a pass. After the group gets the hang of the game, then more pieces of equipment can be added, and the speed of the game can be increased. It is fun with a rubber chicken, pig, or fish or all three at the same time. If your class size is large, start with two or three circles. Periodically rotate several people to a new circle to increase the learning of classmates' names.

Mass Stand Up. Start with two people sitting back to back. They lock elbows and try to stand up. Increase the number to three people, then four, and so forth. See how many people can stand up simultaneously. Try the same thing in a sitting position, facing your partner with hands locked, feet flat, and toes touching. Add people to this position also.

Butt Tug. Stand in two lines back to back. One line moves to the left step. Bend over, cross the arms between the legs, and grasp the hands of two different people from the other team. Now begin tugging. Be careful to maintain your balance, remain under control, and remind students to not let go of their grips. Try forming two teams in the described position and have a race while maintaining the hand grips.

Circle Sit. Have students stand and form a circle holding hands. Close the circle so shoulders are touching. Move the right side of the body toward the center of the circle and move inward, eliminating gaps. Now sit on the knees of the person behind. Try walking in this position when everyone has assumed the sitting position. Put the left side toward the center and sit on a new partner's lap.

Word or Team Sounds. Students all close their eyes. Someone is designated to move throughout the group and assign a word or sound such as "grrr; wow; Colts, Rockets," or other football, basketball, or baseball teams to the players. The number of words assigned will determine the number of groups formed. This is a useful way to organize groups. When the command is given, the only noises that can be made are those that resemble the word. Students must keep their eyes closed and move throughout the area in search of another person who has been assigned the same word. For example, people assigned to be "Buckeyes" or "Sun Devils" search for their counterparts by saying "buckeyes" or "sun devils" and listening for others saying the same words.

Entanglement. Divide the class into two or more groups. Each group makes a tight circle with arms pointing toward the middle. In each group, students hold someone's hand until everybody is holding hands. Each person must hold a hand of two different people and not hold the hands of the people on either side. On signal, the two groups race to see which can untangle first without disjoining hands. The group may end up in either one large circle or in two smaller, connecting circles. People can be facing different directions when finished.

Bulldozer. Students lie in prone position side by side and as close as possible on the floor. The end person rolls on top of the next person and down the line of people. When that person gets to the end of the line, the next person starts the roll. Two teams can be formed and a relay race conducted.

Zipper. Players make a single-file line. Each student bends over, reaches between the legs with the left hand, and grasps the right hand of the person to the rear. This continues on down the line until all hands are grasped. On signal, the last person in line lies down, the next person backs over the last person and lies down, and so forth until the last person lies down, and then immediately stands and reverses the procedure. The first team to zip and unzip the zipper is declared the winner.

Addition Tag. Two are selected to be "it." They must hold hands and can tag only with their outside hands. When they tag someone, that person must hook on. This continues and the tagging line becomes longer and longer. Regardless of the length of the line, only the hand on each end of the line is eligible to tag.

Team Paper, Scissors, and Rock. Two teams huddle up on half of the gym or field space. Team members decide as a group which of the three choices (paper, scissors, or rock) they will reveal as a team when the game begins. The team members come out to the midcourt line and face each other with one foot on the line. The teacher counts, "one, two, three, show." The teams reveal their group decision on the word "show" with the appropriate hand signal, and winning team members chase losing team members and try to tag them before they reach a safe zone, which is about 10–20 yards from the starting line (paper covers rock, rock breaks scissors, and scissors cut paper). If a person gets tagged, he or she must switch teams. After each round, team members rehuddle and decide their next choice.

Chicken Baseball. Two teams of about nine people are competing. The game starts with each team in a single-file line. Team 1 has a rubber chicken with the first person in line. Team 2 has the first person in line ready to run around the line. At the start of the game, the rubber chicken is passed back by alternating over the head of the first person and then between the legs of the next person until the last person gets the chicken and then throws it as far as possible while yelling, "chicken." The first person on team 2 is running around his or her team and getting points for each time around while team 1 is passing the chicken. When "chicken" is yelled, all members of team 2 run to the chicken and begin passing it back in the previously described manner while team 1 is currently accumulating points by having its last person running laps around the group. The teams have to work together to line up quickly and take turns running the laps around the group.

REFERENCES AND SUGGESTED READINGS

Barney, D., & Mauch, L. (2003). Jump bands: Success and fun with rhythms. *Teaching Elementary Physical Education, 14*(6), 14–16.

Darst, P., & Armstrong, G. (1991). *Outdoor adventure activities for school and recreation programs.* Prospect Heights, IL: Waveland Press.

Fluegelman, A. (Ed.). (1976). *The new games book.* Garden City, NY: Doubleday and Co.

Kreidler, W., & Furlong, L. (1995). *Adventures in peacemaking,* Hamilton, MA: Project Adventure.

Orlick, T. (1982). *Cooperative sports and games book.* New York: Pantheon Books.

Pangrazi, R. P. (2007). *Dynamic physical education for elementary school children* (15th ed.). San Francisco: Benjamin Cummings.

Panicucci, J., Constable, N. S., Hunt, L., Kohut, L., & Rheingold, A. (2003). *Adventure curriculum for physical education: High school.* Hamilton, MA: Project Adventure.

Rohnke, K. (1984). *Silver bullets: A guide to initiative problems, adventure games, and trust activities.* Dubuque, IA: Kendall/Hunt Publishing Company.

Rohnke, K. (1989) *Cowstails and cobras II: A guide to games, initiatives, ropes courses, and adventure curriculum.* Dubuque, IA: Kendall/Hunt Publishing Company.

Rohnke, K., & Butler, S. (1995). *Quick silver.* Dubuque, IA: Kendall/Hunt Publishing Company.

WEB SITES

Adventure Activities
www.adventurehardware.com
www.pa.org

Sport Stacking
www.speedstacks.com
www.worldsportstackingassociation.org

Throtons
www.aeroaction.com

NATIONAL STANDARDS FOR PHYSICAL EDUCATION*

STANDARD 1   Demonstrates competency in motor skills and movement patterns needed to perform a variety of physical activities.

STANDARD 2   Demonstrates understanding of movement concepts, principles, strategies, and tactics as they apply to the learning and performance of physical activities.

STANDARD 3   Participates regularly in physical activity.

STANDARD 4   Achieves and maintains a health-enhancing level of physical fitness.

STANDARD 5   Exhibits responsible personal and social behavior that respects self and others in physical activity settings.

STANDARD 6   Values physical activity for health, enjoyment, challenge, self-expression, and/or social interaction.

ESSENTIAL COMPONENTS OF A QUALITY PROGRAM

COMPONENT 1   A quality physical education program is organized around content standards that offer direction and continuity to instruction and evaluation.

COMPONENT 2   A quality program is student centered and based on the developmental urges, characteristics, and interests of students.

COMPONENT 3   Quality physical education makes physical activity and motor-skill development the core of the program.

COMPONENT 4   Physical education programs teach management skills and self-discipline.

COMPONENT 5   Quality programs emphasize inclusion of all students.

COMPONENT 6   In a quality physical education setting, instruction focuses on the process of learning skills rather than the product or outcome of the skill performance.

COMPONENT 7   A quality physical education program teaches lifetime activities that students can use to promote their health and personal wellness.

COMPONENT 8   Quality physical education teaches cooperative and responsibility skills and helps students develop sensitivity to diversity and gender issues.

*Reprinted from *Moving Into the Future: National Standards for Physical Education*, 2nd ed. (2004), with permission from the National Association for Sport and Physical Education (NASPE), 1900 Association Dr., Reston, VA 20191–1599.

19

Sports

Chapters 19 to 21 offer beginning-level units in a wide variety of instructional activities. Rating scales, performance objectives for tasks, station work ideas, block plans, and rainy-day activities are some of the ideas presented in this section. Specific lesson plans are available for many activities in the lesson plan text by Casten (2009). It is important that teachers try new ideas to improve the instructional process. A variety of learning activities helps motivate both students and teachers. The various units serve as frameworks for developing instructional units. These units are not all inclusive but are starting points that stimulate and encourage a wide range of instructional approaches. The ideas can be adapted and shaped into a unit that is unique and meets the needs of students in different areas. This allows teachers to retain control in planning and developing instructional sequences.

Lead-up activities and skills are presented in detail for units where a dearth of resource materials exists. Some units are highly complex and demand in-depth, specialized instruction. In these cases, comprehensive resources have been listed. Such resources are listed for gymnastics and track and field because of the complexity of the areas.

ARCHERY

Archery has long been recognized as an appealing activity for students of both sexes, of all ages, and for those with disabilities. The two most popular forms are target archery and field archery. Target archery involves shooting a specific number of arrows from a given distance at a target with five or 10 concentric circles. Scoring is completed by adding up the points for each arrow striking the target. This is the most popular archery activity taught in secondary school programs. Field archery involves 28 stationary targets of assorted sizes and shapes placed at varying distances. Field shooting requires a larger area and considerable safety procedures. It is especially appealing to those who hunt and bowfish. Many families enjoy participating together, for archery activities can be enjoyed by all family members.

Sequence of Skills
Bracing the Bow

Several methods are used for stringing or bracing the bow. One method involves using a bowstringer device made of a 5-foot rope with a leather cup on each end. The cups are put on both ends of the bow with the string hanging down toward the ground in front of the body. After placing one string loop in position, place one foot on the center of the bowstringer, and pull the bow straight up with one hand. Use the free hand to slide the free string loop into place. To unstring the bow, reverse the process.

Another stringing technique is called the step-through method. Start by placing the bottom string loop in position, and then put the bottom curve of the bow across the top of the right ankle, and step between the string and the bow with the left foot. Use the left hand to bend the bow against the left thigh until the string loop can be moved into place with the right hand. Be sure to keep the face away from the bow tip.

Establishing a Stance

The feet should straddle the shooting line and be a shoulder width apart. The toes should be in a direct line with the target. The knees should be relaxed and a comfortable standing posture maintained.

Nocking the Arrow

The bow should be held horizontally in the left hand, and the nock of the arrow should be placed on the nocking point of the string. The odd-colored feather should face away from the bow. Use the index finger of the left hand to steady the arrow on the arrow rest.

Extending and Draw

The string is on the first joint of three fingers of the right hand. The index finger is above the arrow, and the next two fingers are below the arrow. Rotate the bow to a vertical position with the left arm parallel to the ground. Extend the left arm and draw the string toward the body with the right hand. Keep the right elbow parallel to the ground. Be sure the fingers of the bow hand are loose and relaxed.

Anchoring and Holding

The string should touch the nose, lips, and chin, while the index finger touches under the center of the chin. The anchor point should be the same for every shot.

Aiming

Target archery has two basic methods of aiming—point of aim and bowsights. The beginner should probably use the point-of-aim technique, which involves finding a spot somewhere on a vertical line drawn above, through, and below the middle of the target. This point of aim will vary according to the distance from the target. To locate the point, align the eye and the arrow with an object on the vertical line through the center of the target. Shoot several rounds and then adjust the point of aim up or down accordingly. A mechanical bowsight can be mounted on the bow and used by aligning the center of the target through the aperture. The aperture is then adjusted up or down, or left or right, depending on the pattern of the arrows for that shooting distance. The aperture position is then noted for each distance and is used in the future.

Releasing and Experiencing Afterhold

As the arrow is released, the back muscles remain tight while the string fingers relax. The relaxed drawing hand moves backward slightly along the neck. The bow arm and head remain steady until the arrow hits the target (afterhold).

Retrieving Arrows

Arrows in a target should be removed by placing the arrow between the index and middle finger of the left hand. The palm of the hand should be away from the target facing the archer. The right hand should be placed on the arrow close to the target. The arrow is removed by gently twisting and pulling at the same angle at which the arrow entered. If the fletching (feathers or plastic material used to stabilize the flight of the arrow) is inside the target, the arrow should be pulled through the target. Arrows should be carried with the points together and the feathers spread out to prevent damage.

Ideas for Effective Instruction

Equipment

The composition of bows is primarily wood, fiberglass, or a laminated combination of the two. Both straight and recurved bows are available. The recurved bow has curved ends to provide additional leverage, which increases the velocity of the arrow. Bows also have different weights and lengths. Archers should select a bow based on their strength and skill. Starting with a lighter bow is best and then progressing to a heavier one as skill and strength are developed. In class situations, teachers should try to have a variety of bows available for different ability levels.

Arrow shafts are made of wood, fiberglass, or aluminum. It is important for the beginning archer to get the proper length arrow. A good method for determining proper length is to have someone hold a yardstick against the sternum, perpendicular to the body, while the individual extends the arms with the palms on either side of the yardstick. The point at which the fingertips touch the yardstick is the correct arrow length. For beginners, it is better to have long arrows. Many different types of points and feathers are available.

Many types of finger tabs and shooting gloves are also available to protect fingers and to promote smooth release. An arm guard should be used to prevent the bowstring from slapping the bow arm and to keep long clothing sleeves snug to the body. Movable and stationary quivers are used to transport arrows and sometimes to support the bow while retrieving arrows.

General Rules

1. Archers must straddle a shooting line. Arrows should always be pointed downrange.

2. An end of six arrows is usually shot at one time. A round consists of a number of ends shot at several distances.

3. Values for rings in a target are as follows:

Five-Ring Scoring
Gold = 9
Red = 7
Blue = 5
Black = 3
White = 1

10-Ring Scoring
Gold = 10, 9
Red = 8, 7
Blue = 6, 5
Black = 4, 3
White = 2, 1

4. An arrow that bisects two colors scores the higher of the two values.

5. An arrow that bounces off a target or passes through a target is given seven points if there is a witness.

6. The petticoat, or outside area of the target, counts as a miss.

Organization, Skill Work, and Safety

Beginning students can experience success quickly if the instructor moves the target close to them (10 yards or less). Students can then move away from the target as their skill levels increase. A safe environment is important. Make sure that students follow strict rules for shooting procedures. Partner work is useful for checking form, reminding about safety procedures, and giv-

ing feedback. A form for a rating scale or checklist for shooting can also be useful and motivating to some students. Several checklists are available from the sources listed at the end of the unit.

Time should be spent with partners and observers to make sure that they are actively involved in the learning process and concentrating on the specific shooting skills. Make sure that all students are mentally involved, even when they are not shooting.

Lead-Up Games and Learning Activities

Relays

Each team has one target, and each person has one arrow. The first person in line shoots and then goes to the end of the line. All team members shoot one arrow, and then the team score is tallied. The team with the highest score is the winner.

Turkey Shoot

Each team draws a turkey about the size of a target on a piece of paper. The turkey is placed on the target. Each team tries to hit the turkey as many times as possible.

Tic-Tac-Toe or Bingo

Balloons or a target with squares are placed on the regular target—three rows of three for tic-tac-toe, or five rows of five for bingo. The object is to hit three or five in a row vertically, horizontally, or diagonally. The game can be for individuals or for teams.

Target Work-Up

Start with four or five students on a target. Shoot an end of four arrows and tally the score. The highest scorer moves up one target, and the lowest scorer moves down a target. This can be an individual or partner activity.

Tape Shooting

Place two pieces of masking tape across the target, one vertically and one horizontally. The object is to hit either piece of tape. This can also be an individual or team event.

Suggested Performance Objectives

Core Objectives

Objectives 1, 2, and 3 should be completed before the student is allowed to shoot on the range.

1. On a written test covering safety rules, archery terminology, and scoring, the student will score at least 70 percent (two attempts allowed).

2. The student will demonstrate how to brace and unbrace the bow. Grading is on a pass-fail basis.

3. The student will demonstrate the nine steps of the shooting technique (i.e., stand, nock, extend, draw, anchor, hold, aim, release, and afterhold). Grading is on a pass-fail basis.

4. At a distance of 10 yards, the student will hit the target at least five of six times and score a minimum of 28 points.

5. At a distance of 15 yards, the student will hit the target four of six times and score a minimum of 24 points.

6. At a distance of 20 yards, the student will hit the target four of six times and score a minimum of 24 points.

7. The student will participate in a minimum of two out of three novelty archery events.

Optional Activities (Extra Credit)

1. On a written test covering safety rules, archery terminology, and scoring, the student will score 100 percent.

2. At a distance of 10 yards, the student will hit the target six of six times and score at least 40 points.

3. At a distance of 15 yards, the student will hit the target five of six times and score at least 40 points.

4. At a distance of 20 yards, the student will hit the target five of six times and score at least 38 points.

5. The student will write a two-page report on the history of archery, complete with bibliography.

6. The student will participate in all 3 days of novelty archery events.

7. The student will design and put up a bulletin board about archery.

Reinforcement Menu

1. Ensure core objectives 1, 2, and 3 are met before students are allowed to shoot.

2. Post the checklist of objectives on the bulletin board.

3. Post on the bulletin board the high ends and high rounds for each class.

4. Post on the bulletin board the results tournament for each distance.

5. Give ribbons to winners of novelty eve...

6. Award extra-credit points for exceeding skill requirements.

Rainy-Day Activities

Discussion and practice can focus on these areas:

Eye dominance	Draw
Stance	Anchor
Nock	Tighten-hold
Extension	Aim
Bow hand position	Tighten-release
String hand and arm position	Afterhold

A great resource for archery unit ideas is Bane McCracken's book *It's Not Just Gym Anymore* (2001).

BADMINTON

Badminton is popular in schools, from the middle and high school through college levels. Competition at the college level is popular nationally and internationally. The activity is considered a lifetime sport and can be enjoyed by all in a recreational setting. The game is played with a shuttlecock and racquet on a court with a net set at a height of 5 feet. The court is marked for both doubles and singles competition. A toss of a coin or a spin of the racquet determines service or court choice. The game begins with a serve from the right-hand service court to an opponent standing in the opposite right-hand service court.

Sequence of Skills

Grips

Forehand. With the racquet lying across the palm and fingers of the racquet hand, the index finger should be separated from the rest of the fingers. Wrap the thumb around the other side of the handle. The grip resembles a handshake and is called the "pistol grip." This grip is used for serving and forehand shots.

Backhand. Move the thumb to a straightened position and to the right of the handle. Rotate the rest of the hand one-fourth of a turn to the right (if right handed). Regardless of the grip used, the player should make contact with the shuttlecock as early and as high as possible. This gives the player a better angle for return and for more controlled shots and forces an opponent to move quickly.

Serves

Ready Position and Preparatory Action. Stand with the nonracquet foot forward and the weight mainly on the racquet foot. The feet should be approximately 12 to 15 inches apart. The nonracquet shoulder is toward the receiver, with the racquet held waist high and behind the body. Keep the wrist cocked.

The shuttlecock must be contacted below the waist at the instant of the serve. Either a forehand or backhand shot may be used, but the forehand is most common. Until the serve is delivered, the server and receiver must be in their legal service courts. Part of both players' feet must remain in contact with the ground.

Singles Service. Review the ready position. Extend the nonracquet arm and drop the shuttlecock before starting to move the racquet forward. As weight is shifted to the front foot, rotate the shoulders and hips. As contact is made below the waist, the wrist and forearm rotate. The racquet arm should follow through high and be extended over the left shoulder at completion of service. Most serves will be long and high. A short serve is, however, effective if your opponent is playing too deep.

Doubles Service. The stance is similar to the singles serve. Contact the shuttlecock closer to waist height and slightly more toward the server's racquet-hand side. Guide the shuttlecock instead of hitting it. The wrist does not uncock. Just prior to contacting the shuttlecock, shift the weight from the racquet foot to the nonracquet foot. Little follow-through or rotation occurs. The shuttlecock should peak in height just before the net and be descending as it clears the net.

Forehand Shots

Clear. Get in ready position with the feet and shoulders parallel to the net. Hold the racquet slightly to the backhand side, and bend the knees slightly. Contact the shuttlecock as high as possible and in front of the body. The racquet face should be tilted upward, and the shuttlecock should clear the opponent's racquet and land close to the back line.

Drop. When contact with the shuttlecock is made, the racquet face should be flat and pointing ahead or slightly downward. The shuttlecock is gently guided over the net. Remember to follow through. The shuttlecock should just drop over the net into the opponent's forecourt.

Smash. Extend the arm when the shuttlecock is hit in front of the body. Rotation of the wrist and forearm is performed quickly. The downward angle of the racquet face is more important than the racquet speed. The shot should only be attempted from the front three-fourths of the court.

Backhand Shots

Ready Position. From the forehand position, turn so that the racquet shoulder faces the net. The weight should be on the nonracquet foot, the racquet shoulder up, and the forearm slightly down and across the chest. While shifting the weight to the racquet foot, the body rotates toward the net. As the wrist leads, the racquet extends upward. The racquet arm and elbow should be fully extended at contact. The thumb should not point upward.

Clear. Hitting hard and upward, contact the shuttlecock as high as possible and hit it over the opponent's racquet. Contact should be made in front of the body with the racquet face flat to the target.

Drop. As the shuttlecock is guided over the net, the racquet should be flat and pointed ahead or slightly downward. The shuttlecock should land close to the net.

Underhand Shots

Ready Position. Place the racquet foot forward and the racquet face parallel to the ground. Cock the wrist and make contact as close to net height as possible.

Forehand Net Clear. The forehand net clear is a high, deep shot similar to the singles deep serve. Turn the shoulder slightly toward the net, and cock the wrist. An inward rotation of the wrist and a lifting of the forearm occur just before contact. Proceed to follow-through with the elbow slightly bent.

Backhand Net Clear. The racquet foot is forward, and the racquet shoulder turned to the net. Contact the shuttlecock as close to net height as possible. As the player moves toward the net, the wrist should be cocked. An outward rotation is used for the backhand. The shot is high and deep into the opponent's court.

Forehand Net Drop. Review the forehand net clear. The net drop is guided over the net with a lifting motion. The shuttlecock should drop quickly.

Backhand Net Drop. This is the same motion as the forehand net drop except that the backhand grip is

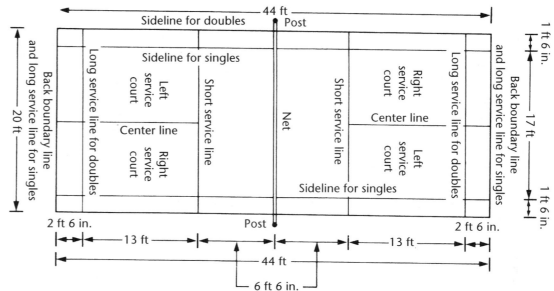

FIGURE 19.1 Badminton court dimensions

used. The shuttlecock should be contacted close to net height.

Ready Position for Receiving. The feet should be parallel and positioned slightly wider apart than the shoulders. Bend the knees slightly with the weight forward. Hold the racquet with the head up and to the backhand side of the body.

Doubles Strategy

Up and Back. One player plays close shots while the partner plays deep shots.

Side by Side. Each partner plays half of the court and is responsible for close or deep shots in his or her half of the court.

Combination. Both side-by-side and up-and-back formations are used. Regardless of the strategy, partners should always call for the shot ("Mine!") to avoid accidental injuries.

Ideas for Effective Instruction

Racquets and Shuttlecocks

The racquet frame can be made of metal or wood. It is usually 26 inches long and weighs between 3.75 and 5.5 ounces. Nylon is commonly the choice of material for stringing the racquet. The metal frame racquets are desirable because they do not warp or require a press for storage.

The weight of the shuttlecock is between 73 and 85 grains, with 14 to 16 feathers. If authentic feathers are used, the shuttlecocks should be stored in a damp place. If nylon feathers are used, the shuttlecocks will be more durable and reasonably priced, which is desirable in the school setting.

Net

The top of the net is 5 feet from the floor at its midpoint. It is 5 feet, 1 inch at the posts. The net is 30 inches in height and 20 feet long.

Court

Figure 19.1 shows the court dimensions for badminton.

Games and Match

Eleven points make a game in women's singles. All doubles and men's singles games are 15 points. A match consists of two games out of three. As soon as a side wins two games, the match is over. The winner of the previous game serves the next game. Players change courts after the first and second games. In the third game, players change after eight points in a 15-point game and after six points in an 11-point game.

Scoring

Only the serving side scores and continues to do so until an error is committed.

Setting

If the score becomes tied, the game may be extended by the player or side first reaching the tied score. In a 15-point game, the set may occur at 13–13 (setting to 5 points) or 14–14 (setting to 3 points). In an 11-point game, the score may be set at 10–10 (setting to 2 points) or 9–9 (setting to 3 points). A set game continues, but the score called is now 0–0, or "love all." The first player or side to reach the set score wins. If a side chooses not to set, the regular game is completed.

Singles Play

The first serve is taken from the right service court and received crosscourt (diagonally) in the opponent's right service court. All serves on 0 or an even score are served and received in the right-hand court. All serves on an odd score are served and received in the left service court.

Doubles Play

In the first inning, the first service is one hand only. In all other innings, the serving team gets to use two hands. At the beginning of each inning, the player in the right court serves first. Partners rotate only after winning a point.

Even and odd scores are served from the same court as in singles play. If a player serves out of turn or from the incorrect service court and wins the rally, a let will be called. The let must be claimed by the receiving team before the next serve.

If a player standing in the incorrect court takes the serve and wins the rally, it will be a let, provided the let is claimed before the next serve. If either of these cases occurs and the side at fault loses the rally, the mistake stands, and the players' positions are not corrected for the rest of the game.

Faults

A fault committed by the serving side (in-side) results in a side out, while a fault committed by the receiving side (out-side) results in a point for the server. A fault occurs in any of the following situations:

1. During the serve, the shuttlecock is contacted above the server's waist, or the racquet head is held above the hand.

2. During the serve, the shuttlecock does not fall within the boundaries of the diagonal service court.

3. During the serve, some part of both feet of the server and receiver do not remain in contact with the court, inside the boundary lines, until the shuttlecock leaves the racquet of the server. Feet on the boundary lines are considered out-of-bounds.

Organization and Skill Work

An effective way to add variety and skill work to classes is to create a series of stations. The stations can be arranged to use the space available in the gymnasium and can focus on badminton skills, conditioning activities, or a combination of both (Figure 19.2).

Partner activities are helpful with accompanying rating scales or checklists like the one following.

Partner Activities: Low doubles serve.

Equipment: One badminton racquet and five shuttlecocks per couple.

Procedure: One person is the server, and the other is the helper with a trained eye. The server follows these steps, and the helper checks off the skills as they are completed.

1. Standing behind the 6-foot, 6-inch line from the wall, drop the bird and hit it underhand against the wall. Repeat this at least five times. The trained eye must be looking for and giving feedback on the following criteria:

   a. Keep both feet on the ground until after the shuttlecock is contacted.

   b. Hold the shuttlecock at chest height.

   c. Contact the shuttlecock below the waist level.

   d. Keep the racquet head below the wrist at the point of contact.

   e. Keep the wrist firm and cocked throughout the stroke.

   f. Guide the shuttlecock instead of hitting it.

2. From the same position behind the line, direct three of five serves above the 5-foot, 1-inch line on the wall and below the 18-inch line above it. Switch positions, and if you were serving, become the helper. Help your partner, and remember that you are the trained eye who sees what your partner is doing. Partners repeat the first two steps.

3. Move to the court and take about five practice serves. Keep the serve under the 18-inch line. Now do five serves and have your partner record your score. This score is to help you determine your accuracy. Switch positions again and repeat step 3.

4. Now try step 3 using your backhand.

Tournament play works well for badminton. Ladder, pyramid, or round-robin tournaments can add a competitive flavor to the class. The use of marking tape on the floor and walls, jump ropes on the court, fleece balls, and task cards can give the teacher more stations for a circuit. This enables the student to progress at a personalized skill level. Mini-games or lead-up games played on the courts allow for skill work, competition, and enjoyment. Regulation games and tournament play can gradually replace the lead-up games. Students should also be trained as scorekeepers and line or service judges.

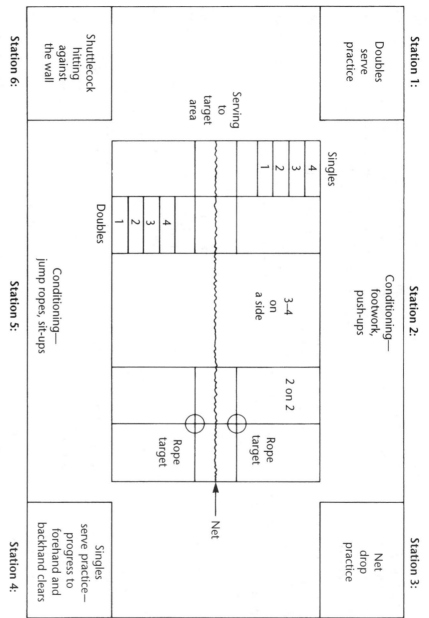

Station 1: Doubles serve practice

Station 2: Conditioning—footwork, push-ups

Station 3: Net drop practice

Singles

4
3
2
1

Doubles

4
3
2
1

Serving to target area

3–4 on a side

2 on 2

Rope target

Rope target

Net

Station 6: Shuttlecock hitting against the wall

Station 5: Conditioning—jump ropes, sit-ups

Station 4: Singles serve practice—progress to forehand and backhand clears

FIGURE 19.2 Station skill work—badminton

Lead-Up Games and Learning Activities

Doubles Drop

After the short serve and underhand drop are taught, a "doubles drop game" can be played between the net and the short service line.

Overhead Clear

After the long serve and the overhead clear are taught, an overhead clear "rally" could be attempted. Try to keep the shuttlecock in play at least five times in a row; then try 10 times in a row, 15 times, and so forth.

Designated Shots

After the underhand clear is taught, work on a "designated shots rally." Start with a short serve, return with an underhand drop, return with an underhand clear, and return with an overhead clear. Keep performing clear with overhead and underhand clears.

Server Versus Receiver

After the "flick" serve and "push" return are taught, play a server versus receiver game. The receiver must

try to return as many as possible of the server's 20 serves in a row—10 from the right and 10 from the left. The server gets a point each time the receiver misses the return. The receiver gets a point if the server misses the serve. Reverse the server and receiver roles.

Clear–Smash

After the smash is taught, play a long serve and overhead clear game. Start with a long serve, return with an overhead clear, and keep hitting clears until someone makes a short clear shot; then smash the short clear. The server is awarded one point if the smash is not returned or loses one point if the smash is returned. Repeat the rally and try to make points by well-placed smashes.

Drive Rally

After the drive shot is taught, organize a drive rally with four players. Drive crosscourt and down the alley. If the drive shot is too high, smash it.

Advanced Combination Drill

Start the rally with a long serve and return with an overhead drop, return with an underhand drop, return with an underhand clear to the opponent's backhand side, return with a backhand overhead clear, and return with an overhead clear unless the return shot is short. If the shot is short, use a smash.

Volleyball Badminton

Four players are on each team. Assigned positions rotate as in volleyball.

Three per Team

Alternate servers, and the "up" player plays the net shots.

Name the Shot

After 5 days of the badminton unit, challenge students to name the shots (Figure 19.3).

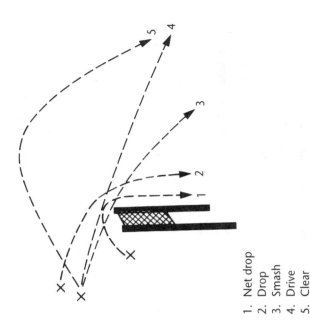

1. Net drop
2. Drop
3. Smash
4. Drive
5. Clear

FIGURE 19.3 Name the shot—badminton

Suggested Performance Objectives
Core Objectives

All directions given are for right-handed players.

Short or Low Serves

1. Standing 6 feet, 6 inches from the wall, serve the shuttlecock 10 times in a row between the 5-foot and 6-foot marks on the wall.

2. Standing behind the short service line on the right side of the court, serve the shuttlecock crosscourt over the net 10 times and get seven out of 10 in the court.

3. Repeat step 2 from the left side of the service court.

4. Standing behind the short service line, next to the center line in the right court, serve the shuttlecock crosscourt over the net, between the net and a rope 1 foot above it. Repeat this five times in a row from the right and then five times from the left.

5. Standing behind the short service line, next to the center line in the right-hand court, serve 10 short serves in a row to the receiver's backhand side on the court.

6. Repeat step 5, standing in the left-hand court.

Long Serves

7. Standing to the right of and next to the center line, 12 feet from the net, serve 10 long serves in a row to the opposite court.

8. Repeat step 1 from the left service court.

9. Repeat step 1, but the serves must land in the backhand area marked on the court. Serve five long serves in a row to this area.

Underhand Clears: Forehand and Backhand

10. Standing between the net and the short service line, drop the shuttlecock and hit 10 underhand clears in a row on the forehand side, to the back 4 feet of the court marked for doubles.

11. Repeat step 1 on the backhand side.

12. Standing 6 feet behind the short service line, hit five underhand clears in a row on the forehand side to the back 4 feet of the doubles court.

13. Repeat step 3 on the backhand side.

Drops

14. Standing just behind the short service line on the right court, hit a tossed shuttlecock from your partner in an underhand drop on the forehand side. Return 10 drops in a row from the forehand side.

15. Repeat step 1 on the backhand side.

16. Repeat steps 1 and 2 from the left court.

17. Standing anywhere just behind the short service line, hit a shuttlecock barely tossed over the net by your partner, alternating between your forehand and backhand on the toss. Hit 10 underhand drops in a row back between the net and a rope stretched 1 foot above the net.

Optional Objectives

1. Standing next to the center line on the right court and just behind the short service line, "flick" serve the shuttle five times in a row to the back 3 feet of the doubles service court. Repeat on the left.

2. Standing in the right receiving court for doubles, "push" return five short serves in a row either to the server's backhand side or down the side alley next to server. Repeat on the left.

3. Standing 6 feet from the short service line next to the center line on the right court, return five long serves in a row to the backhand side of the server with an overhead clear.

4. Repeat step 3, standing in the left court.

5. A server sets up short, high shots 6 to 8 inches from the net. Standing 6 feet from the short service line, smash five in a row within 15 feet of the net.

6. Repeat step 5, smashing five in a row down the left side of the court.

7. Repeat step 5, smashing five in a row down the right side of the court.

8. Standing within 10 feet of the short service line, return 10 of your opponent's smashes back over the net as smashes.

9. Standing within the last 5 feet of the back court, hit an overhead drop off your opponent's clears to you. Hit five shuttlecock drops to the right court side between the net and the short service line.

10. Repeat step 9 on the left court between the net and the short service line.

11. Stand on the center line, 6 feet from the short service line. Your partner sets up low, flat serves down the forehand alley. Hit five forehand drives in a row down that alley.

12. Repeat step 11, hitting five backhand drives down the backhand-side alley.

13. Standing within 12 feet of the net, from a high clear setup by a partner, backhand five overhead clears in a row to the back 6 feet of the doubles court.

14. Standing 15 feet or farther from the net, backhand five overhead clears in a row to the back 4 feet of the doubles court.

Overhead Clears: Forehand

18. Standing within 12 feet of the net, your partner hits underhand clears. Return 10 shuttlecocks in a row with an overhead forehand clear into the doubles court, at least 10 feet from the net.

19. Repeat step 1, returning 10 in a row to the back 4 feet of the doubles court.

20. Repeat step 1, returning 10 in a row, alternating from right court to left court at least 10 feet from the net.

Attendance and Participation

21. Arrive on time for class, dressed and ready to participate (one-third of a point per day, up to six points maximum).

22. Participate in 15 games: 13 doubles and two singles.

Skill Tests

Badminton courts can be marked in many different ways to provide students with a challenge in perfecting their skills (Figure 19.4). Using white shoe polish or masking tape, number portions of the target area in an ascending manner, from the easiest to the most difficult shots. Courts can be marked for deep serves, low serves, clears, drops, and drives. The teacher determines the number of attempts that each student is allowed.

BASKETBALL

Basketball is a popular game played on school yards by many participants. It was invented in 1891 at Springfield College by Dr. Naismith, who used peach baskets and a soccer ball. The game offers reinforcement to participants when a basket is made and is one of the few team sports requiring skills that can be practiced individually. The game demands great cardiorespiratory endurance and fine-motor development.

Basketball instruction should focus on developing skills and competence so students leave school with the ability to participate in recreational games later in life. At the middle school level, emphasis should be on lead-up games that allow all students to find success and enjoyment. As students develop the skills necessary to play the game well, instruction during the high school years can concentrate on strategy and teamwork. Highly skilled and interested students should be offered additional opportunities to play through intramural programs, recreational leagues, or interscholastic competition.

Sequence of Skills

One of the attractive components of basketball is that little equipment is necessary for participation. Students should be required to wear a gym shoe made for the activity. Running shoes are a poor substitute for

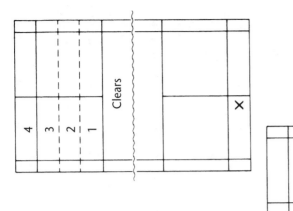

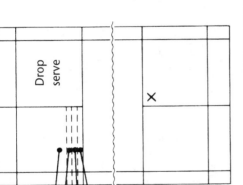

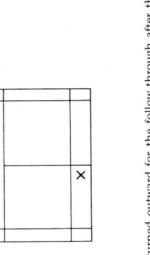

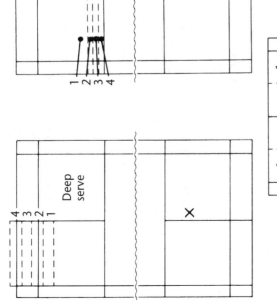

Deep serve

Drop serve

Clears

Smashes

Drops

FIGURE 19.4 Badminton skills test

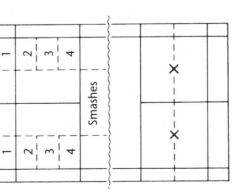

basketball shoes because they often leave black marks on the floor, do not offer adequate support, and wear out quickly.

The following skills are basic to the game of basketball. Students never learn these skills to perfection, so offer time for regular practice. For example, players can always make a better pass, develop more efficient dribbling skills, or shoot a higher percentage of baskets.

Passing

Regardless of the pass used, certain points should be emphasized. The ball should be handled with the fingertips. As the ball makes contact with the hands, the elbows should bend and the hands move toward the body in order to "give" with the ball and absorb the force. The passer should step forward in the direction of the receiver. The ball is released with a quick straightening of the elbows and a snap of the wrists. The arms and fingers are fully extended with the palms

turned outward for the follow-through after the ball has been released. A passer should anticipate where his or her teammate is going to be when the ball reaches the receiver. Many of the passing drills should therefore focus on passing while moving.

Chest Pass

The chest pass is used frequently in basketball for passes up to 20 feet. The ball is held at chest level with the fingers spread on both sides of the ball. One foot is ahead of the other in a stride position. The elbows remain close to the body, and the ball is propelled by extending the arms, snapping the wrists, and stepping toward the target.

Bounce Pass

The bounce pass is used to transfer the ball to a closely guarded teammate. It is directed to a spot on the floor that is closer to the receiver than the passer. The ball should rebound to waist level of the receiver. Passing form is similar to the chest pass.

Flip Pass

This pass is used for a close-range exchange. The ball is flipped somewhat upward to a teammate. It is used often as a pass to a player cutting to the basket for a layup shot.

Two-Handed Overhead Pass

This pass is used against a shorter opponent, usually in back court. The passer is in a short stride position with the ball held overhead. The momentum of the pass comes from a forceful wrist and finger snap. The upper arms remain relatively in place.

Catching

For effective catching, it is important to keep the eyes on the ball, follow the ball into the hands, and concentrate on the catch before beginning the next task. The receiver should move toward the ball and reach for it with the fingers spread. When the pass is at waist level or above, the thumbs should be pointed in and the fingers up. When the ball is to be caught below waist level, the thumbs are out and the fingers down. The hands should "give" and move toward the body to absorb the force of the throw and thus make the ball more catchable.

Dribbling

Dribbling requires bent knees and crouching. The forearm of the dribbling hand is parallel to the floor, and the ball should be pushed toward the floor, rather than slapped. The ball is controlled with the fingertips. Most of the force supplied to the ball should be from the wrist, so arm movement is minimized. Emphasis should be placed on controlling the ball.

Shooting

Certain points are common to all shooting. The body should be squared up with the basket whenever possible. The ball is held with the fingers spread, and the elbow of the shooting hand should always be directly behind the ball. The eyes are fixed on the rim, and the ball is shot with a slight backspin on it. The arm is extended on follow-through with the wrist flexed.

Layup Shots

For a right-handed layup, the player approaches the basket from the right side at an angle of about 45°. The ball is released with the right hand, and the weight is on the left foot. As the body is elevated off the floor by the left foot, the ball is released 12 to 18 inches above the basket on the backboard. For a left-handed shot, the sequence is the opposite. The shooter should always reach toward the spot on the backboard with the shooting hand, and students should practice shooting with either hand.

One-Hand Push Shots

The push shot is used primarily for shooting free throws. Few people shoot a one-hand shot from a set position. The ball is held at shoulder level in the non-shooting hand. The shooting hand is behind the ball, the fingertips touching the ball, and the wrist is cocked. The legs are a shoulder width apart, and the knees are slightly bent. To shoot, straighten the legs and push forward with the forearm and wrist. The wrist should be bent over on follow-through and the arm straight.

Jump Shots

The jump shot is the most popular shot in basketball because it is difficult to block. The hands are in the same position as described for the one-hand push shot. After the shooter jumps, the ball is placed just above and in front of the head. The elbow must be kept under the ball so the shooting hand moves in a straight line toward the basket. The wrist snaps on release. The shot should be performed using a jump in an upward plane. Leaning forward, sideways, or backward will make the shot much less consistent. The jump shot is sometimes difficult for middle school students. They often learn the wrong motor pattern of throwing the ball instead of shooting it. If this is the case, use a smaller ball, a lower basket, or both to develop the correct pattern.

Ideas for Effective Instruction

Drills used in basketball should simulate game conditions as closely as possible. There are few situations in basketball where players are standing still. Passing drills, therefore, should include player movement, shooting drills should require movement and pressure, and drills for dribbling under control should include looking away from the ball.

Baskets can be lowered to 8.5 to 9 feet to increase the amount of success. This will also help develop better shooting patterns in the weaker, smaller players. Note that almost all students will select the lower basket when they have a choice of a basket at regulation height and another, lowered basket. Most people are motivated by being able to dunk the shot and thus shoot a higher percentage.

The program should concentrate on skill development and include many drills. Basketball offers endless drill possibilities, and using many drills gives variety and breadth to the instructional program. The drills should offer each student as much practice as possible in a stipulated amount of time. Lining up a squad of eight players to take turns makes little sense. Use as many balls as possible. In some cases, students may be willing to bring one from home for class use. More baskets and balls mean that more students will have an opportunity to practice and learn skills.

There are many basketball drills to enhance passing, dribbling, and shooting, but the lead-up games in the following section encourage skill practice while introducing competition and game play. When possible, therefore, isolate skills and practice them in lead-up games to maintain a high level of student motivation.

Lead-Up Games and Learning Activities

Keep-away

The essence of the game is to make as many consecutive passes as possible without losing control to the opposite team. Teams may consist of five to 10 players. Use colored vests so players can identify their teammates. The game is started with a jump ball, and the goal is to maintain control. Each defensive player must stay with a designated opponent, rather than the defensive team swarming in a zone defense. As soon as possession is lost, counting of passes is started by that team. The team that makes the most consecutive passes within a designated time is the winner.

Five Passes

This game is similar to keep-away, but the object is to make five consecutive passes. As soon as these have been made, the ball is turned over to the other team. Students are not allowed to travel with the ball. Two or three dribbles may be allowed between passes. Players may hold the ball for only 3 seconds.

Dribble Tag

The playing area is divided into two equal parts. All players begin dribbling in one-half of the area. The object of this game is to maintain a continuous dribble while avoiding being tagged by another player. If tagged or if control of the ball is lost, the player must move to the other half of the playing area and practice dribbling without the pressure of competition.

Dribble Keep-away

The area is divided into two equal parts. All players start in one-half of the area and begin dribbling. The goal is to maintain control of the dribble while trying to disrupt the dribble of an opponent. If control of the ball is lost, the player moves to the other side of the area and practices.

Around the World

Shooting spots are marked on the floor with tape. Players are in groups of three. A player begins at the first spot and continues until a shot misses. The player can then wait for another turn or take a second "risk" shot. If the risk shot is made, the player continues "around the world." If the shot is missed, the player must start over on the next turn. The winner is the player who goes around the world first. A variation is to count the number of shots that players take to move around the world. The person who makes the circuit with the fewest shots is the winner.

Twenty-One

Players are in groups of three or four. Each player receives a long shot (distance must be designated) and a follow-up shot. The long shot, if made, counts two points, and the follow-up shot counts one point. The follow-up shot must be taken from the spot where the ball was recovered. The first player to score 21 points is the winner. A variation is to play team 21, in which the first team of players to score 21 is declared the winner.

Horse

Players work in groups of two to four and shoot in a predetermined order. The first player shoots from any place on the court. If the shot is made, the next player must make the same type of shot from the same position. If the shot is missed by the next player, that player receives an "H," and the following player can shoot any shot desired. No penalty is assigned for a missed shot unless the previous player has made a shot. A player is disqualified if the letters spelling HORSE are accumulated. The winner is the last remaining player.

Sideline Basketball

The class is divided into two teams, each lined up along one side of the court, facing the other. The game is played by three or four active players from each team. The remainder of the players standing on the sideline can catch and pass the ball to the active players, but they may not shoot or enter the playing floor. They must keep one foot completely out-of-bounds at all times.

Active players play regular basketball with one variation; they may pass and receive the ball from sideline players. The game starts with the active players occupying their own half of the court. The ball is taken out-of-bounds under its own basket by the team that was scored upon. Play continues until one team scores or until a period of time (2 or 3 minutes) elapses. The active players then move to the left side of their line, and three new active players come out from the right. All other players move down three places in the line.

No official out-of-bounds on the sides is called. The players on that side of the floor simply recover the ball and put it into play without delay with a pass to an active player. Out-of-bounds on the ends is the same as in regular basketball. If one of the sideline players enters the court and touches the ball, it is a violation, and the ball is awarded out-of-bounds on the other side to a sideline player. Free throws are awarded when a player is fouled. Sideline players may pass to each other and should be well spaced along the side.

Half-Court Basketball

Teams of two to four work best for this variation. The game is similar to regulation basketball with the following exceptions. When a defensive player recovers the ball, either from a rebound or an interception, the ball must be taken back to midcourt before offensive play can begin. After a basket is made, the ball must again be taken to midcourt. For out-of-bounds and ball-handling violations, the ball is awarded to the opponents' out-of-bounds at a spot near the place where the violation occurred. The ball, in this case, does not have to be taken to midcourt. If a foul occurs, the ball is given to the offended team, or regulation foul shooting can be done.

Three on Three

There are many lead-up games in which the number of players on a team varies. The advantage of playing half-court basketball with only two or three players on a team is that each player gets to handle the ball more. Regulation rules are followed.

The game 3 on 3 can be played with four or five teams. An offensive team of three stands forward of the midcourt line while another team is on defense. The other teams wait behind midcourt for their turns. A scrimmage is over when one team scores. The defensive team then goes on offense, and a new team comes in to play defense. The old offensive team goes to the rear of the line of waiting players. The game can be varied so that the winning team stays on after a basket is scored. Caution must be used with the winner-stay-on approach as it sometimes means that the better players get much more practice than the less-skilled performers. Make the teams as equal as possible so all have a chance to win.

Suggested Performance Objectives

The following are examples of performance objectives that might be used in a beginning basketball class. The standards may have to be adjusted depending on the skill level and age of the students.

Core Objectives

Dribbling Tasks

1. In a stationary position, execute a right-hand dribble 10 consecutive times.

2. Perform task 1 except use the left hand.

3. Using a reduced speed, dribble the ball with the right hand from the baseline to the midcourt line without losing control.

4. Using a reduced speed, dribble the ball with the left hand from the midcourt line to the baseline without losing the dribble.

Passing Tasks

5. Standing 10 feet away from the target on the wall, throw 10 consecutive two-hand chest passes.

6. Standing 10 feet away from a partner, execute eight of 10 consecutive two-hand passes.

7. Standing 10 feet away from the target, throw 10 consecutive two-hand bounce passes.

8. Standing 10 feet away from a partner, execute eight of 10 consecutive bounce passes.

9. Standing 10 feet away from the target, throw 10 consecutive two-hand overhead passes.

10. Standing 10 feet away from a partner, execute eight of 10 consecutive two-hand overhead passes.

Shooting Tasks

11. Starting from the right side about 20 feet from the basket, dribble the ball toward the basket and make four of six lay-ups using the backboard.

12. Perform task 11, but start from the left side.

13. Standing 6 feet from the basket (right side), make four of six bank shots.

14. Perform task 13, but use the left side.

15. Standing at the free-throw line, make five of 10 consecutive set shots.

16. Standing 10 feet from the basket, make five of 10 jump shots.

Rebounding Tasks

17. Standing with the feet a shoulder width apart and with both hands at shoulder level, jump up and touch the target on the wall three consecutive times using both hands.

18. Standing 2 to 3 feet away from the basket, toss the ball off the right side of the backboard and rebound it with both hands five consecutive times.

19. Perform task 18, but use the left side.

20. Standing 2 to 3 feet from the basket, toss the ball off the right side of the backboard, rebound it using both hands, and pivot right using the overhead pass or chest pass to a partner. Repeat five consecutive times.

21. Perform task 20, but use the left side and pivot left.

Optional Objectives

1. Officiate at least one regulation game during class time, using correct calls and signals.

2. Write a 1-page report on the game of basketball.

3. Make a list of 15 basketball terms and define them.

4. Write a 1-page report on a basketball article or book.

5. Perform a figure-eight ball-handling technique by weaving the ball around one leg and then around the other leg—forming a figure eight—successfully for 10 seconds.

6. Make eight of 10 bank shots from anywhere outside the foul lane.

7. Make nine of 10 free throws.

FIELD HOCKEY

Field hockey is a popular team sport that has been played predominately by females in the United States. Many clubs across the country are affiliated with the United States Field Hockey Association and offer playing experiences for participants ages 6 to 60 years old. In other countries, the game is also played by males and is a popular Olympic sport. Many high schools and colleges offer field hockey competition for girls and women.

The regulation game is played with 11 players on each team. The object of the game is to move a ball with a stick into the opponent's goal, which is 12 feet wide and 7 feet high. The game is started with a pass back to teammates in the center of the field. Besides the goalkeeper, a team usually has three forwards, three links, three backs, and one sweeper. The field is 60 yards by 100 yards with a 16-yard striking circle (Figure 19.5).

Hockey equipment includes the ball, sticks, shin guards, mouth guards, and the goalkeeper's helmet with mask, chest protector, gloves, full-length leg pads, and kickers for the shoes. The ball is composed of cork

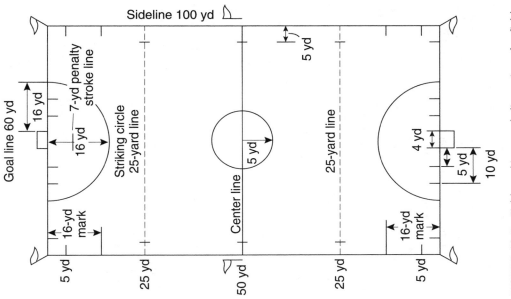

FIGURE 19.5 Field markings and dimensions for field hockey

and twine and is covered in leather. Sticks vary in length from 30 to 37 inches. Middle school students use sticks that are 30 to 34 inches long, and high school students use sticks that are 35 to 37 inches. All regulation sticks have a flat surface on one side and a rounded surface on the other. Only the flat side can be used for legal hits.

The game can be modified in several ways for secondary physical education units. The number of players and the field size can be reduced. Goals can be improvised by using boundary cones, high-jump standards, or even soccer goals. A whiffle ball or a rubber or plastic ball can be used, and plastic sticks that are flat on both sides are available. A flat plastic puck is recommended for play on the gymnasium floor. Goalies should wear a face mask, chest protector, and shin guards from softball or lacrosse equipment. If the goalie equipment is not available, then the game should be played without a goalie. Both boys and girls can enjoy the game in a coeducational unit. Field hockey can be played indoors, outdoors, or on a cement surface.

Sequence of Skills

Gripping

Grip in is the basic grip. The left hand is placed on the top of the stick as though "shaking hands." The right hand is placed 6 to 8 inches below the left hand. The palms of the hands will face each other in most situations. The right hand can slide up the stick for a drive shot and for a reverse stick. The lower position is used for dribbling and for most passes.

Dribbling

Dribbling is propelling the ball downfield in a controlled manner. It can be done straight down the field or zigzagging to the left and right. In straight dribbling, the arms are kept in front of the body. The flat side of the stick faces forward. Short, controlled taps on the ball are used. The ball should remain in front of the body. The zigzag dribble moves the ball left and right by using a forehand tap to the left and a reverse stick tap to the right. In the reverse stick, the stick is turned over, with the toe of the stick pointing down. This type of dribble requires a lot of practice and stick control. The taps to the left and right should be short and controlled. Dribbling can also include dragging the ball with the flat side of the stick. The stick stays in contact with the ball as it is being dragged downfield.

Passing and Shooting

The drive shot is the most forceful pass for longer distances and goal shots. The hands are together, and the stick comes back and forward in a manner similar to a shortened golf swing. The stick cannot be lifted higher than the shoulder in either the backswing or follow-through. Drive shots can be straight, to the left, or to the right.

The push pass is used for shorter, more accurate passes. The pass is usually executed quickly off the dribble. There is no backswing. The right hand is lower on the stick, and the ball is pushed or swept along the ground.

The scoop is a pass or shot that is lofted into the air using a shoveling motion for a shot or to get over an opponent's stick. The top of the stick must be tilted backward so the blade is behind and under the ball to give it loft as the force is applied. The flick pass or shot is the most popular aerial shot, which gets off the ground about knee high and is an extension of the push pass. The flick is a popular shot on goal.

A slap hit is a modified drive shot or pass that uses a short backswing and does not require a change in the position of the hands. The pass can be used with the hands apart in the normal hand position for ball handling.

Fielding

Fielding refers to stopping and controlling a moving ball and must be practiced with balls coming from the right, left, and center. The face of the stick and the body position need to be adjusted according to the direction in which the ball is traveling. The front fielding position is similar to the straight dribbling position and is used for balls rolling straight toward a person. Balls coming from the left require a regular forehand position with the blade facing to the left. For balls coming from the right, the stick must intercept the ball before it reaches the body. The blade must be turned so that it is facing to the right. Fielding requires the ability to absorb the ball's momentum by "giving" with the stick, depending on the speed of the ball.

Tackling and Dodging

Tackling is attempting to take the ball away from an opponent. Tackles can be made straight on or from the left or the right side of an opponent. Timing is important because the ball must be picked off while it is away from the opponent's stick. The stick is carried low, and the tackler must concentrate on the ball and on the opponent's stick. The speed of the opponent and the ball must be considered. The tackle should not be a reckless striking of the stick.

Dodging is a skill for evading a tackler and maintaining control of the ball. A dodge can be executed to the left or right side of the tackler, and a scoop shot can also be used to go over an opponent's stick. If a dodge is made to the left, the dodger should move the ball 90° to the left just before the tackle. A dodger moving around to the left is on the stick side, which is the right, of the opponent. This maneuver is a stick-side dodge. A dodge to the right involves moving the ball to the right of the opponent, but the dodger's body must move around the other side of the tackler, that is, the ball goes to the right but the person goes to the left (nonstick-side dodge). A reverse stick technique can also be used for a nonstick-side dodge. The player uses the reverse stick to pull the ball across the body to the nonstick side of the defender and then steps forward with the left foot and pushes the ball past the defender.

Doing a Bully or Face-Off

The bully is used only when simultaneous fouls occur. Two players face each other in the middle of the field with their respective sticks facing the direction of the goal where they can score. The bully starts with the two players striking the ground on his or her own side of the ball and then touching sticks above the ball. This is repeated three times, and then players attempt to control the ball or to pass it to a teammate.

Goalkeeping

The goalkeeper can kick the ball or block the ball with the body, hands, or stick. Most balls are blocked with the legs or feet, hence the padding on these areas. Most clears away from the goal are with a kick. The goalie cannot hold the ball or throw the ball away from the goal.

Ideas for Effective Instruction

Drills can be set up for partner work at several stations. Dribbling, passing, fielding, shooting, tackling, dodging, and goalkeeping can be specific stations with varying tasks to be practiced. Use the performance objectives detailed here for the tasks at each station. Set up boundary cones, stopwatches, targets, baskets, and other instructional devices for challenging skill work. Arrange classes so that students spend several minutes working at each of four stations. The station work can then be followed by several small group drills, such as 3 on 3, keep-away, or three-person weave. A modified or regulation game could follow the group work. This variety of learning activities helps to keep students active and motivated.

Remind students continually about the importance of safe stick handling. High sticking (when stick comes above the waist) is extremely dangerous, and rules must be enforced tightly. Body checking, tripping, and hooking with the stick should also be forbidden. A free hit or penalty corner can be used as a penalty for these violations, depending on where the penalty occurs. The teacher must be clear about the rules, regulations, and penalties that are going to be enforced in the game.

Lead-Up Games and Learning Activities
Sit-Up Sticks

This activity is a fun warm-up and fitness idea where partners face each other in a typical sit-up position. On

the start signal, partners perform a sit-up and pass one hockey stick back and forth at the top of each sit-up. A challenge would be to see how many passes could be made in 30 seconds.

Three-Person Weave

The ball is started by the center person and passed to either the person on the left or right. The person making the pass always runs behind the person who receives the pass. The person receiving the pass then dribbles to the center to become the middle person. This procedure continues downfield.

Partner Passing

Partners stand apart and try to hit and complete as many passes as possible in 30 seconds. Each hit is counted. For variations, try the same activity with three people in a triangle, four in a square, or five in a circle.

Circle Keep-away

Students form a circle with one person in the middle. The people in the circle try to keep the ball away from the center person. This can also be played with only three people. The person in the middle is rotated after 1 minute.

Circle Dribble

A student dribbles the ball around the circle as fast as possible, concluding the dribble at the next person in the circle. All members of the circle go around quickly. Circles compete against each other or against the clock. A variation of this is to dribble in and out of the players standing in the circle.

Star Drill

Five classmates make a star formation. Number 1 passes to 2, and 2 to 3, and so forth. After passing the ball, the passer runs and takes that person's spot. The passer always follows the pass, and more than one person can be in line. The game can also be played against another team or against the clock.

Defensive Squares Drill

Several squares are set up with boundary cones. The size of the squares can vary depending on the ability of the students. Smaller squares will make the drill more demanding for the offensive player. A defensive player is in the square, and an offensive player tries to dribble through the square. The defensive player tries to keep the offensive player from dribbling through the square.

Dribble and Hit for Distance

Half of the class or group lines up 5 yards behind a drive line. A partner is downfield about 50 yards. On signal, the hitters dribble the 5 yards and hit a drive shot as far as possible. The partner stands over the ball, and a winner is determined. Partners change places after several hits.

No-Goalie Field Hockey

The game is played without a goalie. Person-to-person defense can be used. The goal size can also be modified if necessary.

End Zone Hockey

The entire end line of the field is the goal area. Each team designates a certain number of goalies and field players. The goalies must spread out over the entire goal line in order to cover it properly. Goalies and field players change places after a specified number of minutes.

Sideline Hockey

Part of each team lines up on one sideline, while the rest of each team is on the field. The sideline players keep the ball from going out-of-bounds, and they can also pass to the field players. A regulation goal and goalie are used in the game. The sideline and field players switch after 3 minutes of play. This game can be varied by putting members of each team on both sidelines, thus adding another challenge to the game.

Square Hockey

The game is played on a large square. Each team defends two sides of the square. Some team members are on the square sides as goalies, and others are on the field trying to hit the ball past either of the two end lines. At the start of the game, the teacher can have all students stand on the square and count off. Several numbers can then be called, and those students become the field players.

Half-Circle Hockey

This is similar to square hockey, but each team forms one-half of a circle. The half circles connect, and the object is to push the ball through the opponent's half circle. If the ball comes to rest inside the circle, it belongs to the team nearer the ball. That team can take a shot from the point where the ball stopped.

Modified Coed Field Hockey

This modified game is recommended for coeducational physical education classes. The rules and penalties are as follows:

1. A pass back is used to start the game and after each goal.

2. A legal hit is used when the ball goes out-of-bounds.

3. A short corner shot is awarded to the offense when the ball goes past the end line within the striking circle, last touching off a defender.

4. A long corner shot is awarded to the offense when the ball goes past the end line outside the striking circle, last touching off a defender.

5. A defensive hit is awarded to the defensive team when the ball goes over the end line off an offensive player.

6. The striking circle is the 16-yard half circle around the goal. A free shot is awarded for a foul occurring anywhere outside the striking circle. All players must be 5 yards away when the shot is hit.

7. A penalty corner is awarded for a defensive foul inside the striking circle.

8. Offside occurs when an offensive player gains an advantage within the 25-yard line. A defensive hit is awarded at the top of the circle.

9. High sticking occurs when the stick is raised above the shoulder. The penalty is a free hit or a penalty corner if it occurs in the striking circle.

10. Advancing is when a player uses any part of the body to advance the ball. The penalty is a free hit or a penalty corner.

11. Hooking, tripping, or dangerous stick use involves using the stick to slow down or trip an opponent. The penalty is a free hit or penalty corner.

12. Body checking is vigorous use of the body for blocking and other maneuvers. The penalty is a free hit or penalty corner.

Suggested Performance Objectives

These performance objectives can be used to structure the learning activities for station work. They can also be tied to a motivational scheme for earning grades or winning an entry into a playing situation. Teachers might develop a contract from these objectives, which can be modified according to the ability levels of the students in a specific situation. If the objectives are too hard or too easy, they should be rewritten to provide a fair challenge and a successful experience for students.

1. Dribble the ball for 30 yards, three consecutive times, using proper technique at all times (straight dribble).

2. Dribble the ball through an obstacle course and back in 30 seconds or less (straight dribble).

3. Dribble the ball toward a target and execute a non-stick dodge in three of five attempts without losing control.

4. Dribble the ball toward a target and execute a stickside dodge around the target in three of five attempts without losing control.

5. With a partner, push pass the ball back and forth (jogging speed) for 30 yards, two consecutive times.

6. Use a push pass to direct the ball to a target three of five times from a distance of 10 yards.

7. Shoot three of five drive shots into the goal from 10 yards (no goalie).

8. Scoop the ball over an obstacle into a basket three consecutive times from within a stick-length distance.

9. Dribble the ball from the center of the field toward the goal, and hit three drive shots three consecutive times without a goalie.

10. Execute proper fielding of the ball from the front, right, and left sides, passed by a partner from 10 to 15 yards away (five times from each side).

11. Dribble the ball for 30 yards, three consecutive times, using proper technique at all times (zigzag dribble).

12. Dribble the ball through an obstacle course and back in 30 seconds or less (zigzag dribble).

13. Dribble the ball toward a goal and score two of five drive shots past a goalie from 10 yards.

14. Execute a three-person weave passing drill from a distance of 15 to 30 yards, two consecutive times.

15. Hit two of five penalty shots past a goalie.

16. Execute a proper tackle from the left, right, and center.

17. Scoop and run with the ball for 25 yards.

18. Dribble 5 yards, and then execute a scoop shot. Repeat five consecutive times.

19. Flick three of five balls into the left and right corners of the goal.

Rainy-Day Activities

Many of the drills and modified games can be played indoors with a flat plastic puck and an indoor stick. Teachers can set up station activities for working on performance tasks. Modified games, such as sideline hockey, end zone hockey, and square hockey, can be played indoors with large numbers of students. Strategies, terminology, and penalties can be discussed at indoor sessions.

FLAG FOOTBALL

Football is America's favorite spectator sport. Professional football players are held in high esteem by students. The shape of the football makes throwing and catching more difficult and challenging than similar maneuvers in other sports. Flag and touch football are variations of the game of football, modified so the game can be played without the padding and equipment necessary for tackle football. Flag football is usually the more enjoyable sport because it eliminates the arguments about whether someone was touched.

Sequence of Skills

Passing

Passing is used to advance the ball downfield to a teammate. The passer looks at the receiver and points the shoulder opposite the throwing arm toward the receiver. The ball is brought up to the throwing shoulder with both hands. The fingers of the throwing hand are placed across the laces of the ball. The weight is transferred to the rear leg in preparation for the throw. On throwing, the weight is transferred forward, and a step is taken with the front foot in the direction of the receiver. The throwing arm is extended and the wrist flicked upon release of the ball. The longer the throw to be made, the higher the angle of release needs to be.

Lateral Pass

Lateral passing is pitching the ball underhand to a teammate. The ball must be tossed sideways or backwards to be a legal lateral that can then be passed again. There is no attempt to make the ball spiral as it does in a pass.

Catching

Because the football is a large and heavy object and can be thrown with great velocity, the catcher must "give" and bring the ball in toward the body. In a stationary position, the catcher faces the thrower and plants the feet about a shoulder width apart. To catch a ball on the run, the catcher observes the ball by looking over the shoulder. The fingers should be spread and the arms extended to meet the ball. This allows "giving" with the ball and bringing the ball in toward the body in an attempt to absorb the force of the throw. Students should develop the habit of tucking the ball in close to the body after each catch.

Carrying the Ball

The ball is carried with the arm on the outside, and the end of the ball is tucked into the notch formed by the elbow and arm. The fingers cradle the forward part of the ball.

Centering

The center moves into position with the feet well spread and the toes pointed straight ahead. The knees are bent in preparation for forward movement. The dominant hand reaches forward slightly and is placed across the laces of the ball, which is resting on the ground before him or her. The other hand is on the side near the back and guides the ball. The head is between the legs; the center's eyes are on the receiver. The arms are extended, and the ball is propelled by pulling both arms backward and upward. The ball should spiral on its way to the quarterback.

When centering in T formation, only one hand is used. The quarterback places the throwing hand in the crotch of the center and the other hand below with the hands touching at the base of the palms. The ball is given a one-quarter turn as it is centered and placed sideways in the quarterback's hands.

Developing a Stance

The 2-point stance is used by ends and backs so they can see downfield. The feet are spread a shoulder width, and the knees are bent slightly. The hands can be placed just above the knees.

The 3-point stance is used as a down position in order to move quickly forward or sideways. The feet are spread a shoulder width apart with the toes pointing straight ahead. The player leans forward and places the desired hand on the ground while keeping the back parallel to the playing surface. The weight is on the balls of the feet; the head is up. Little weight is placed on the down hand.

The 4-point stance is used to move forward quickly. Lateral movement is sacrificed with this stance. It is similar to the 3-point stance, but both hands are on the ground and more weight is placed on the hands.

Blocking

The purpose of blocking is to prevent the defensive player from getting the flag of the ball carrier. It is accomplished by keeping the body between the defensive player and the ball carrier. Knocking the defensive player down is not necessary to accomplish a successful block.

Shoulder Blocking

The shoulder block starts from a 3- or 4-point stance. The blocker moves forward and makes shoulder contact at the chest level of the opponent. The head should be placed between the opponent and the ball carrier in order to move the defensive player away from the ball carrier. The elbows are out and the hands are held near the chest.

Pass Blocking

The pass block is used when the quarterback is dropping back to throw a pass. The block can begin from any of the described stances. The blocker moves slightly backward with the rear foot as the opponent charges. The blocker should attempt to stay between the quarterback and the rusher.

Exchanging the Ball

The handoff is made with the inside hand (nearest the receiver). The ball is held with both hands until the ball carrier is about 6 feet away. It is then shifted to the hand nearer the receiver, with the elbow bent partially away from the body. The receiver comes toward the quarterback with the near arm bent and carried in front of the chest, the palm down. The other arm is carried about waist high, with the palm up. As the ball is exchanged, the receiver clamps down on the ball to secure it.

Punting

The punter starts in standing position with both arms fully extended to receive the ball. The kicking foot is placed slightly forward. After receiving the ball, the kicker takes two steps forward, beginning with the dominant foot. The ball is slightly turned in and held at waist height. The kicking leg is swung forward, and at impact, the knee is straightened to provide maximum force. The toes are pointed and the long axis of the ball should be dropped rather than tossed into the air. The drop needs to be mastered before effective punting can occur.

Ideas for Effective Instruction

Because many drills are available for flag football, the authors have devoted this section to delineating the rules and equipment necessary for them. Most of the prerequisites for developing a sound flag football program are listed and discussed.

Uniforms

Rubber-soled shoes should be worn. Metal cleats or spikes are not allowed, nor is any hard surface padding or helmets.

Flags

Flags are available in two colors for team play. All flags should be similar in terms of pulling the flags loose from players. The flag belts have two flags attached, one at each hip. Either flag pulled downs the ball carrier.

Downed Ball

To down a ball carrier, either flag must be withdrawn from the waist by a tackler. The tackler must stop at the point of tackle and hold up the hand with the withdrawn flag. It is illegal for ball carriers to deliberately touch their own flags or to defend them in any manner. These acts would cause a penalty of 15-yard loss from the point of the foul and loss of a down.

Dead Ball

The ball is ruled dead on a fumble when it hits the ground or on a wild center when it hits the ground. When a fumble rolls out-of-bounds, the ball is returned to the team that had last full possession of it.

Loss of Flags

If the flag is inadvertently lost, that player is ineligible to handle the ball. The ball then becomes dead if the player is behind the line of scrimmage or the pass is called incomplete. It is illegal for a player to deliberately withdraw an opponent's flag unless that opponent is in possession of the ball. Such conduct is penalized as unsportsmanlike for a penalty of 15 yards.

Charging and Tackling

The ball carrier may not run through a defensive player but must attempt to evade the tackler. The tackler must not hold, push, or run through the ball carrier, but he or she must play the flag rather than the person. The officials decide these judgment calls and may award a penalty of 15 yards and loss of a down offensively, and 15 yards defensively.

Tackling

Tackling is not permitted. The ball is declared dead when a defensive player pulls one of the runner's flags. Action against the runner, other than pulling the flag, is unnecessary roughness and carries a penalty of 15 yards from

the point of the foul and loss of a down offensively, and 15 yards from the point of the foul defensively.

Hacking

It is a foul for the ball carrier to hack, push, or straight-arm another player. This results in a penalty of 15 yards from the point of the foul and loss of a down.

Blocking

Line blocking is the same as in regulation football. In open-field (out-of-the-line) line blocking, no part of the blocker's body, except the feet, shall be in contact with the ground during the block. Blocking is a type of body checking, with the blocker in an upright position and without the use of hands or extended arms. Any rough tactics, such as attempting to run over or batter down an opponent, must be penalized as unnecessary roughness. Unnecessary roughness may be declared if the blocker uses knees or elbows in blocking, carrying a penalty of 15 yards and loss of a down offensively, and 15 yards and first down defensively.

Passing

A forward pass may be thrown from any point behind the line of scrimmage. The passer is declared down if a flag is withdrawn by a defensive player or if a flag falls out on its own before the passer's arm is engaged in the throwing motion. It is the responsibility of the officials to make this decision.

Downs

A team has four downs to advance the ball from wherever the team takes over to score. If the team fails to score in four downs, its opponents gain possession of the ball at the spot where the ball is declared dead on the fourth down. To obtain a first down, the offensive team must complete three forward passes out of four downs. A forward pass is a pass thrown from behind the line of scrimmage past the line of scrimmage.

Miscellaneous Penalties

The following penalties should be explained and discussed with students.

Illegal use of flags	15 yards
Offensive use of hands	15 yards
Defensive illegal use of hands	15 yards
Offsides	5 yards
Pushing ball carrier out-of-bounds	15 yards
Ball carrier pushing the interference	15 yards
Ineligible person downfield	5 yards
Illegal procedure	5 yards

Lead-Up Games and Learning Activities

The following lead-up games can be enjoyable ways to broaden the variety of activities in a football unit. They also avoid one student dominating a skilled position while others simply go through the motions of blocking.

Five Passes

The game can be played on a football field, but the size of the field is not critical; any large area is satisfactory. Players scatter on the field. The object of the game is for one team (identified by pinnies) to make five consecutive passes to five different players without losing control of the ball. This scores one point. The defense may play the ball only and may not make personal contact. No player is allowed to take more than three steps when in possession of the ball, or the ball is given to the other team.

There is no penalty when the ball hits the ground. It remains in play, but this interrupts the five-pass sequence, which starts over. Students should call the number of consecutive passes out loud.

Kick Over

The game is played on a football field with a 10-yard end zone. Teams are scattered at opposite ends of the field. The object is to punt the ball over the other team's goal line. If the ball is caught in the end zone, no score results. A ball kicked into the end zone and not caught scores a goal. If the ball is kicked beyond the end zone on the fly, a score is made regardless of whether the ball is caught.

Play is started by one team with a punt from a point 20 to 30 feet in front of its own goal line. On a punt, if the ball is not caught, the team must kick from the point of recovery. If the ball is caught, the team also kicks from the point of recovery. When the ball is caught, three long strides are allowed to advance the ball for a kick. It is a good idea to number students and to allow them to kick in rotation so all receive equal practice.

Fourth Down

Six to eight players are on a team and play in an area roughly half the size of a football field. Every play is a fourth down, which means that the play must score or the team loses the ball. No kicking is permitted, and players may pass at any time from any spot in any direction. There can be a series of passes on any play, either from behind or beyond the line of scrimmage.

The teams start in the middle of the field with possession determined by a coin toss. The ball is put into

play by centering. The quarterback receiving the ball runs or passes to any teammate. The receiver has the same options. No blocking is permitted. After each touchdown, the ball is brought to the center of the field and the nonscoring team resumes play. The ball is downed when the player's flag is pulled. If a player makes an incomplete pass beyond the line of scrimmage, the ball is brought to the spot from which it was thrown.

Positions are rotated so everyone has a chance to be the quarterback. The rotation occurs after every down. The quarterback rotates to center, which ensures that everyone plays all positions.

Captain Football

The game is played on half of a football field. Five yards beyond each goal is a 6-foot by 6-foot square, which is the box. The teams must be identified with pinnies. The object of the game is to complete a pass to the captain in the box.

To begin, the players line up at opposite ends of the field. One team kicks off from its 10-yard line to the other team. The game then becomes keep-away, with one team trying to secure possession of the ball and the other team trying to retain possession until a successful pass can be made to the captain in the box. To score a touchdown, the captain must catch the ball on the fly and still keep both feet in the box.

A player may run sideways or backwards when in possession of the ball. Players may not run forward but are allowed momentum (two steps) if receiving or intercepting a ball. More than two steps is penalized by loss of possession.

The captain is allowed three attempts to catch a pass or one successful goal before a new player is rotated into the box. A ball hitting the ground inbounds remains in play. Players may not bat or kick a free ball. The penalty is the awarding of the ball to the other team out-of-bounds.

Aerial Ball

Aerial ball is similar to flag football with the following differences. The ball may be passed at any time. It can be thrown at any time beyond the line of scrimmage; immediately after an interception, during a kickoff, or during a received kick. Players have four downs to score a touchdown. If the ball is thrown from behind the line of scrimmage and an incomplete pass results, the ball is returned to the previous spot on the line of scrimmage. If the pass originates otherwise and is incomplete, the ball is placed at the point from which the pass was thrown.

Because the ball can be passed at any time, no downfield blocking is permitted. A player may screen the ball carrier but cannot make a block. Screening is defined as running between the ball carrier and the defense.

Suggested Performance Objectives

Core Objectives

1. Throw 10 overhand passes to the chest area of a partner who is standing 10 yards away. Practice correct holding, point of release, and follow-through techniques of passing.

2. Throw three or four consecutive passes beyond a target positioned 20 yards away.

3. Facing the opposite direction from a partner 5 yards away, execute a proper center stance with feet well spread and toes pointed straight ahead, knees bent, and two hands on the ball. Snap the ball back through the legs 10 consecutive times.

4. With a partner centering the ball, punt the ball one time from a distance of 10 yards using proper technique, to another set of partners 15 yards away.

5. Perform task 4 except at a distance of 20 yards.

6. Punt the ball three consecutive times within the boundary lines of the field and beyond a distance of 20 yards.

7. With a partner, run a "quick" pass pattern (5- to 7-yard pattern) and catch the ball two of three times.

8. With a partner, run a 10- to 15-yard "down and in" pass pattern and catch the ball two of three times.

9. With a partner, run a 10- to 15-yard "down and out" pass pattern and catch the ball two of three times.

10. With a partner, run a 5- to 7-yard "hook" pattern and catch the ball two of three times.

Optional Objectives

1. With a partner centering the ball, punt the football three consecutive times from a distance of 10 yards using proper technique, to another set of partners 15 yards away.

2. Perform task 1 but at a distance of 20 yards.

3. As a center, snap the ball four of six times through a tire positioned 5 yards away.

4. Throw three of four consecutive passes beyond a target positioned 20 yards away.

5. Throw four of six passes through a tire from a distance of 10 yards.

GYMNASTICS

Gymnastics refers to the performance of a routine on a piece of heavy apparatus or on a large mat. The routines are evaluated on a 10-point scale by a panel of judges. The gymnastics events for men include parallel bars, horizontal bar, long-horse vaulting, still rings, pommel horse, and floor exercise. Women's events include the uneven parallel bars, balance beam, side-horse vaulting, and floor exercise. In many major gymnastics competitions, the participants must perform a compulsory or set routine and an optional or original routine.

Varying forms of gymnastics were the most common activity in early physical education programs. These different forms of gymnastics were brought to the United States primarily from Germany and Sweden. Gymnastics became popular through clubs formed in the communities, YMCAs, and the public schools. Private gymnastics clubs and sport schools are still popular, and gymnastics is still taught in some secondary schools and colleges in the United States. Many adults continue to enjoy gymnastics as a lifetime recreational activity. In some geographic areas, competition is available through the private clubs for various age groups.

Instructional units in gymnastics and tumbling are an excellent way to achieve a balanced secondary physical education curriculum. Unfortunately, many school districts do not have the heavy apparatus. In these situations, an extensive unit on tumbling should be incorporated in the program. Gymnastics activities offer students an interesting variety of challenges and should be available for students to explore and experience.

Sequence of Skills

Each gymnastics event is a highly specialized area that incorporates many specific skills and techniques. A sequence of skills should be taught on each piece of apparatus and for the floor exercise. In a coeducational class, eight pieces of apparatus and two different floor exercise routines can be offered if the equipment is available. Comprehensive texts are listed in the suggested readings, with in-depth information on the sequence of skills for each event. Gymnastics teachers need to have an extensive background in the teaching strategies and safety procedures for all of the individual events. Teachers should carefully analyze the abilities and characteristics of their students, the time allotted to the gymnastics unit, and the pieces of equipment available for instruction. Safety is especially important because of the hazards posed by many of the gymnastics events.

Ideas for Instruction

Each piece of apparatus and the floor exercise can be arranged as a specific learning area for students. After students are introduced to each area and given introductory tasks to perform, they can be distributed evenly throughout the area. This ensures that students will have maximum opportunity to attempt the various skills. Each student can be given a performance card to record the completion of tasks. The tasks can be written as performance objectives or as simple cues. These objectives and the recording forms will help motivate students to use class time in a productive manner.

A gymnastics meet with student judges is an enjoyable culminating activity. Teams can be organized, and students can select their favorite events. Students work with a partner or in groups of three for safety purposes. One person performs, and the partner spots. Spotting must be explained carefully to students, and the importance of spotting must be continually reinforced.

LACROSSE

Lacrosse is played in the United States, Australia, and England, and it is the national sport of Canada. In the United States, lacrosse is most popular in the Middle Atlantic States. The game was originated by Native Americans as early as the 16th century. The Native Americans played each game with more than 100 players and often with as many as 1,000 players.

Lacrosse is a wide-open game that offers aerobic activity for players. The game can be easily modified to suit all skill and age levels. Examples of modified games are soft lacrosse, which is played in a gym or on a field with a lacrosse stick, ball, and goals; plastic lacrosse, which is played with modified plastic sticks and does not require as much skill as regulation lacrosse; box lacrosse, which is played in an arena or lacrosse box and requires the highest skill; and field lacrosse, which is played on a soccer-size field with a playing area behind each goal.

Sequence of Skills

Gripping the Stick

Position the dominant hand at least halfway down the handle of the stick, palm up. The other hand grips the stick at the end with the palm down. The stick should be held close to the body with relaxed hands and wrists.

Throwing

Bring the head of the stick backwards while keeping the eyes focused on the target. Step with the opposite foot in the direction of the throw. Keep the elbows high and throw overhand to improve accuracy. The hands should be kept a shoulder width apart (don't push the ball). Break the wrists on follow-through, with the head of the stick pointing to the target at the end of the throw.

Catching

Reach to meet the ball and "give" with the arms when the ball makes contact with the stick. Move the feet and align the body with the path of the oncoming ball. When catching, allow the dominant hand to slide on the handle for better stick control. The following techniques are used for catching balls at various levels:

1. *Above the shoulders.* Extend the crosse in the path of the ball. When the ball is caught, rotate the dominant hand sharply inward to protect it from a defender.

2. *Between the shoulders and knees.* Extend the face of the stick directly toward the ball. When caught, move the head of the crosse upward.

3. *Below the knees.* Rotate the handle outward and upward following the reception.

4. *Head high.* Put the face of the crosse directly in the path of the ball with the head and shoulders dropping to the left. Rotate the crosse inward with the dominant hand upon reception.

5. *Ball on the weak-hand side of the body.* Bring the dominant hand across the body to put the crosse in the path of the ball. Cross the leg on the dominant side in front of the other leg while turning the body. After the catch, move the head of the crosse upward.

Scooping

When fielding ground balls, bend the knees and the back. Keep the butt end of the stick away from the midline of the body. Scoop up the ball with a slight shovel motion. As soon as the ball enters the stick, the player needs to break to the right or left to elude the defender.

Dodging

There are four basic dodges used by an offensive player who has the ball in an attempt to evade the defender:

1. *Face dodge.* The player with the ball fakes throwing the ball. When the crosse is about even with the head, it is twisted to the nondominant side. The offensive player then drops the shoulders and head slightly to the nondominant side, brings the leg on

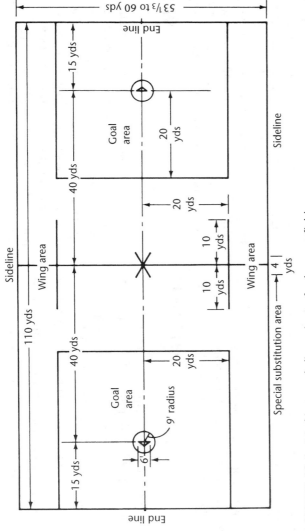

FIGURE 19.6 Markings and dimensions of a lacrosse field

the dominant side across the other leg, and runs around the defender.

2. *Change-of-pace dodge.* The offensive player runs quickly in one direction, stops suddenly, and reverses directions. This pattern of movement is continued until the opportunity arises to move past the defender.

3. *Toss dodge.* When the offensive player meets the defender, the ball is tossed on the ground or in the air past the defender. The player then moves past the defender and recovers the ball.

4. *Force dodge.* The offensive player approaches the defender with the back side of the body. This causes the defender to retreat. The offensive player fakes to the left and right until an opportunity occurs to run past the defender.

Goaltending

The main duties of the goalie are to stop the ball, direct the defense, and start the offense by passing the ball out to the side or down the field. The goalie should be positioned as follows: feet a shoulder width apart with the knees bent. Decrease the shooting angle for the offensive player by moving in an arc about 3 feet from the goal mouth with short shuffle steps. When the ball is behind the goal, the goalie should operate in the same arc, favoring the ball side. If regulation equipment is lacking, it is highly recommended that the goalie wear a softball catcher's mask and chest protector during shooting drills and games.

Ideas for Effective Instruction

Equipment

The lacrosse ball is solid rubber and white or orange in color. It is slightly smaller than a baseball, but just as hard. When dropped from a height of 6 feet above a solid wooden floor, it must bounce 43 to 51 inches. The lacrosse stick may be 40 to 72 inches long with the exception of the goalie's stick, which may be any length. For physical education, plastic sticks and balls are recommended. The net of the stick is between 6½ and 10 inches. The net is made of gut, rawhide, or nylon. Players wear gloves and a helmet with a face mask in regulation lacrosse.

Game Play

Lacrosse is often played in a football stadium. In physical education classes, it can be played on any field, gym, or court with portable goals. The regulation field is 110 yards long with the goals 80 yards apart, leaving 15 yards behind each goal. The field is 60 yards wide, but current rules allow for the width to be reduced to 53⅓ yards, which is the width of a football field (Figure 19.6). A rectangular box, 35 by 40 yards surrounds each goal and is called the goal area. The goal consists of two vertical posts joined by a top crossbar. The posts are 6 feet apart, and the top crossbar is 6 feet from the ground.

There are 10 players on a team, including a goalie, three midfielders, three attackers, and three defenders. The goalie guards the goal and receives support from the defenders. The defenders must remain in their half of the field. The midfielders serve as "rovers" and roam the entire field, operating as both offensive and defensive players. One of the midfielders handles each face-off and is called the center. The attackers remain in the offensive half of the field and attempt shots on goal. The attackers, defenders, and the goalies often play the entire game, but the midfielders are often substituted.

Basic Rules

Face-Off. Play begins with a face-off (a draw) at the start of each quarter and after a goal is scored. The ball is placed between the back side of the opponents' sticks. All players must be in their assigned positions for the face-off. On signal, players in the wing areas are released, but all other players are confined until a player gains possession of the ball, the ball goes out-of-bounds, or the ball crosses either of the goal-line areas.

Off-Side Rule. Each team must have three players located on its attack half and four players on its defensive half of the field. This prevents piling up around the goal.

Out-of-Bounds. When a player throws or carries the ball out-of-bounds, the opposing team gets possession. However, when a loose ball goes out-of-bounds as a result of a shot taken at the goal, it is awarded to the team whose player is closest to it at the exact time it rolls out-of-bounds.

Checking. Body checking is allowed in regulation play in an attempt to dislodge the ball. Football blocks can be legally made on the player with the ball or on those who are going for a loose ball 5 yards away. Checking an opponent with the body or stick is a common practice.

Illegal Procedure. This occurs when (1) an offensive player steps in the opponent's crease when the ball is in the attacking half of the field, or (2) a defending player with the ball runs through the crease.

Penalty Box. There are two types of fouls: personal and technical. Personal fouls are more serious than technical fouls and result in suspension for 1 to 3 minutes based on the severity and intention of the foul. Personal fouls are assigned for illegal personal contact, tripping, and unsportsmanlike conduct. Technical fouls usually result in a 30-second suspension from the game if the player does not have the ball. If the offending team has the ball, it loses possession of the ball. Technical fouls are assigned for the following infractions:

- Interfering with an opponent without the ball.
- Holding any part of the opponent's body.
- Pushing, particularly from the rear.
- Acting illegally with the stick or playing the game without the stick.
- Withholding the ball from play by lying on it or trapping it longer than necessary to gain control.

Modified Rules

The regulation rules for lacrosse can be modified for use in a physical education setting where equipment and facilities are limited. The following are various modifications:

1. The number of players can be reduced to less than 10 so players have more opportunity to handle the ball. Try assigning players to zones so all students have the opportunity to play the ball. This helps prevent the most dominant players from always "hogging" the ball.

2. No stick or body contact is allowed. Encourage students to play the ball rather than the opponent. If a violation occurs, a penalty shot is awarded at the spot of the infraction.

3. Players must keep both hands on their sticks at all times. A penalty shot is awarded at the spot of an infraction.

4. If a ball goes out-of-bounds, the team that did not touch it last may run it in or pass it in.

5. To steal the ball from an opponent, only stick-on-stick tactics may be used (no body contact).

6. To encourage teamwork and passing skills, two passes must be made before each shot on goal.

7. Play should be continuous without any stalling tactics. If problems develop in this area, add a time limit for holding the ball. For example, if the ball is held more than 5 seconds, it is turned over to the other team at the point of infraction.

8. The ball is a "free ball" when it is on the ground or in the air. Stick contact is allowed at these times without body contact.

Organization and Skill Work

A number of drills and lead-up games can be used to teach the fundamentals of lacrosse. See the units on basketball, soccer, and field hockey for additional activities that can be modified for lacrosse.

held longer than 3 seconds or it is turned over to the other team.

Half-Court Lacrosse. The offensive team gets five attempts to score. Each shot on goal counts as an offensive attempt. Offense and defense switch roles after the five attempts.

Five Touch. At least five members of a team must touch the ball before a goal can be scored.

SOCCER

Soccer, the most popular game in the world, is now rapidly gaining popularity among youth in the United States. Many sport clubs and programs run by organizations such as the YMCA, YWCA, Boys Clubs, and municipal recreation departments now sponsor soccer teams, and many school districts are now including soccer in their intramural and athletic programs. Soccer is known throughout the rest of the world as "football." The game is said to have originated in England around the 10th century, but in fact, the Romans played a game similar to soccer. Soccer was brought to the United States about 1870 and was played by women in an organized fashion in 1919. From a physical education standpoint, one of the advantages of soccer is that it is one of the few sports that depends primarily on foot–eye coordination for success. Many kickers in American football are soccer-style kickers. The long hours of kicking practice have contributed to their success.

The object of the game is to move the ball down the field by foot, body, or head contact to score goals and to prevent the opposing team from scoring. Soccer demands teamwork and the coordination of individual skills into group goals. Position play becomes important as students become more skilled. It is an excellent game for cardiovascular development because it demands a great deal of running and body control.

Sequence of Skills

The skills of soccer are difficult to master, so instructors should teach the skills through short practice sessions. Many drills and lead-up games can be used to make the practice sessions interesting and novel.

Dribbling

The purpose of dribbling in soccer is similar to basketball—to maintain control of the ball and advance it before passing it off to a teammate or shooting on goal. The ball is advanced by pushing it with the inside or outside of the front of the foot. The player

Drills

Throwing and Catching

1. Practice throwing the ball against a wall.

2. With a partner, begin throwing and catching in close proximity. Gradually move apart until longer passes are made.

3. Play keep-away in groups of three.

4. Use the jack-in-the-box drill. The "jack" is located midway between the two other players, each with a ball. The "jack" receives a pass from one of the end players, who is about 10 yards away. The "jack" passes the ball back to that player, rotates 180 degrees, and receives a pass from the other end player. Change "jack" players frequently.

5. Use buddy passing for learning to pass on the move. Buddies jog around the area and pass back and forth to each other. Increase the challenge by giving each a ball.

6. Use the three-person rush and three-person weave, similar to the common basketball drills.

Scooping. Organize the class into groups of three. Two students are positioned on one side with the third student across from them, 30 feet away. The ball is placed in the middle. One of the two students positioned on the same side runs to the ball, scoops it up, and carries it a few steps before dropping it. Continuing forward, the student runs behind the player on the opposite side. This player runs forward, scoops up the ball, carries it a few steps, drops it, and moves forward behind the remaining student. The pattern continues.

Shooting. A line of four to five students face the goal. A "feeder" behind the goal passes the ball to a shooter who cuts toward the goal or moves to a different position. After the shot on goal, the shooter becomes the "feeder." Rotate goalies frequently.

Lead-Up Games

Dodging. Practice all types of dodges with a partner, using one ball per two students.

Defending. Three offensive players try to keep the ball away from the defensive player while remaining in the circle.

Three-Seconds, No Steps. Players cannot take any steps with the ball. In addition, the ball may not be

should keep the ball close during the dribble, rather than kicking it and then running after it. Practice should involve learning to run in different patterns, such as weaving, dodging, and twisting or turning with the ball.

Kicking

The purpose of the kick is to pass the ball to a teammate or to take a shot on goal. When passing, the performer plants the nonkicking foot alongside the ball with the foot pointing in the desired direction of the kick. The ball is contacted with the inside portion of the instep of the foot. The body weight shifts forward after the kick. The pass can also be made with the outside of the foot, although this kick will not move the ball as great a distance or with as much velocity. It is an excellent kick for passing without breaking stride or for passing to the side.

In kicking for a shot on goal, the procedure is similar to the inside-of-the-foot kick. The nonkicking foot is planted alongside the ball with the toes pointing in the direction of the goal. The ball is contacted on the instep, followed by a snap of the lower leg and follow-through.

Trapping

The purpose of trapping is to deflect a moving ball and bring it under control so it may be advanced or passed. Any part of the body may contact the ball except the hands or arms. Effective trapping will result in the ball dropping in front of the body in position to be advanced. The sole-of-the-foot trap is most commonly used and is often called *wedging*. The ball is contacted between the foot and the ground just as the ball hits the ground. The shin trap is done by moving to meet the ball just as it hits the ground in front of the lower legs. The ball is trapped between the inside of the lower leg and the ground. The chest trap is executed by arching the trunk of the body backwards and giving with the ball on contact. The giving occurs with the body collapsing so the ball does not rebound and instead drops in front of the player.

Heading

Heading can be an effective way of propelling a ball in the air to a teammate or on goal. The player should strike the ball with the head, rather than waiting for the ball to hit the head. The player leans backward as the ball approaches. The head is up, with the eyes following the ball. On contact, the head moves forward and strikes the ball near the hairline on the forehead. The body also swings forward as the follow-through is completed.

Tackling

Tackling is used defensively to take the ball away from an offensive player who is dribbling or attempting to pass. The single-leg tackle is used when approaching an opponent directly, from behind, or from the side. Effective tackling depends, in large part, on being able to anticipate the opponent's next move with the foot. One leg reaches for the ball while the weight is supported on the other. The knees should be bent so good balance is maintained. Focus should be on a clean tackle rather than on body contact. The object is to reach out and bring the ball to the body, or to kick the ball away and then continue to pursue it.

Goalkeeping

Goalkeeping involves stopping shots by catching or otherwise stopping the ball. Goalkeepers should become adept at catching low, rolling balls; at diving on rolling balls; at catching airborne balls waist high and below; and at catching airborne balls waist high and above. The diving movements are the reason the goalie may choose to wear knee, elbow, and hip pads.

Students should get in the habit of catching low, rolling balls in much the same manner as a baseball outfielder: get down on one knee, with the body behind the ball to act as a backstop, and catch it with both hands, fingers pointing toward the ground. If diving for a ball is necessary, the goalie must throw the body behind it and cradle it with the hands. The body should always be between the goal and the ball.

The goalie may also punch the ball in order to deflect it if the ball is not catchable. The ball can be deflected off other body parts if it cannot be punched.

After a ball is caught by the goalkeeper, it is thrown to a teammate. The ball can also be kicked, but this is less desirable because it is less accurate. Effective throws allow teammates to place the ball in action immediately.

Ideas for Effective Instruction

Soccer is played with two teams of 11 players each. For young players, however, decreasing the size of the teams is more effective. This results in each player handling the ball more often and feeling an integral part of the soccer team.

Many of the drills, such as dribbling, kicking, and punting, can be learned individually. This means that one ball per player will ensure the maximum amount of practice time. Many types of balls can be used besides a regulation soccer ball. Playground balls (8½ inches in diameter) can be used if they are deflated slightly. Many students will play a more aggressive game of soccer if a foam-rubber training ball is

Lead-Up Games and Learning Activities

The following lead-up games are excellent for getting students involved in soccer activities. They emphasize participation and action. The lead-up activities are often more fun for the majority of students than an actual soccer game because these activities develop specific skills in which students may lack expertise.

Circle Kickball

Players are in circle formation. They kick the ball with the side of the foot back and forth inside the circle. The object is to kick the ball out of the circle beneath shoulder level. A point is scored against each of the players where the ball left the circle. If the lost ball is clearly the fault of a single player, however, then the point is scored against that player only. Players who kick the ball over the shoulders of the circle players have a point scored against them. Players with the fewest points scored against them are the winners. The game works well with a foam training ball because the ball can be kicked at someone from a short distance.

Soccer Croquet

The game is similar to croquet in that the object is for one ball to hit another. One player kicks a ball and tries to hit another ball lying ahead. Kickers alternate until a hit is made, which scores one point for the kicker. The game continues until a player scores a specified number of points.

Soccer Keep-away

Players are spaced evenly around a circle about 10 yards in diameter with one player in the center. The object of the game is to keep the player in the center from touching the ball. The ball is passed back and forth as in soccer. If the center player touches the ball with a foot, the person who kicked the ball goes in the center. If there is an error, the person responsible changes places with the person in the center.

Diagonal Soccer

Two corners are marked off with cones 5 feet from the corners on both sides, outlining triangular dead areas. Each team lines up and protects two adjacent sides of the square. The size of the area depends on the size of the class (more students require more playing area) and must be adjusted accordingly. Dead areas on opposite corners mark the opposing team's goal line. To begin competition, three players from each team move into the playing area in their own half of the space.

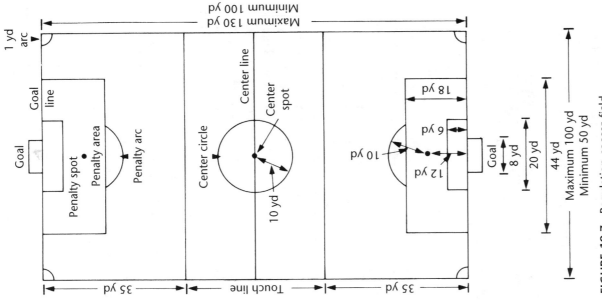

FIGURE 19.7 Regulation soccer field

used. They become less fearful of being hit by the ball and are willing to kick it with maximum velocity.

Field sizes can be reduced in order to increase the activity level of the game. The regulation game is played on a field with dimensions illustrated in Figure 19.7. Soccer is meant to be played on grass. If a hard surface is used, deflate the ball so that it is not as "live" and will not bounce so readily.

The drills used for developing soccer skills should help all participants in achieving proper form. For example, if students are asked to pass and trap together, drills should focus on developing both skills; yet students are sometimes asked to kick with velocity, so the students trapping are fearful of getting hurt. Those students then develop an improper trapping style.

These are the active players. During play, they may roam anywhere in the square. The other players act as line guards.

To score, the active players must kick the ball through the opposing team's line (beneath shoulder height). When a score is made, active players rotate to the sidelines, and new players take their places. Players on the sidelines may block the ball with their bodies but cannot use their hands. The team against which the point was scored starts the ball for the next point. Only active players may score. A point is scored for the opponents whenever any of the following occurs:

- A team allows the ball to go through its line below shoulder height.
- A team touches the ball illegally.
- A team kicks the ball over the other team's line above shoulder height.

Sideline Soccer

The teams line up on the sidelines of a large square with the end lines open. Three active players from each team are called from the end of the team line. These players remain active until a point is scored, and then they rotate to the other end of the line.

The object is to kick the ball over the end line, which has no defenders, between cones that define the scoring area. The active players on each team compete against each other, aided by their teammates on the sidelines.

To start play, a referee drops the ball between two opposing players at the center of the field. To score, the ball must be kicked last by an active player and must go over the end line at or below shoulder height. Regular rules prevail, with the restrictions of no pushing, holding, tripping, or other rough play. For out-of-bounds, the team on the side of the field where the ball went out-of-bounds is awarded a free kick near that spot. No score can result from a free kick. Violation of the touch rule also results in a free kick.

Line Soccer

Two goal lines are drawn 180 to 210 feet apart. A restraining line is drawn 15 feet in front of and parallel to each goal line. Field width can vary from 90 to 105 feet. Each team stands on one goal line, which it defends. The referee stands in the center of the field, holding a ball. At the whistle, three players (or more if the teams are large) run to the center from the right side of each line and become active players. The referee drops the ball to the ground, and the players try to kick it through the other team defending the goal line. The players in the field may advance by kicking only.

A score is made when an active player kicks the ball through the opposing team and over the end line, providing the kick was made from outside the restraining line. Place cones on the field corners to define the goal line. A player rotation system should be set up.

Line players act as goalies and are permitted to catch the ball. After being caught, the ball must be laid down immediately and either rolled or kicked. It cannot be punted or drop-kicked. One point is scored when the ball is kicked through the opponent's goal line below shoulder level. One point is also scored in cases of a personal foul involving pushing, kicking, tripping, or similar acts.

For illegal touching by the active players, a direct free kick is given from a point 12 yards in front of the penalized team's goal line. All active players on the defending team must be standing to one side until the ball is kicked; only goalies may defend. A time limit of 2 minutes should be set for any group of active players. When no goal is scored during this time, a halt is called at the end of 2 minutes, and players are changed.

An out-of-bounds ball is awarded to the opponents of the team last touching the ball. The regular soccer throw-in from out-of-bounds should be used. If the ball goes over the shoulders of the defenders at the end line, any end-line player may retrieve the ball and put it into play with a throw or kick.

Minisoccer

The playing area can be adjusted, depending on the size and skill of the players. A reasonable playing area is probably 150 by 225 feet. A goal, 24 feet wide, is on each end of the field, marked by jumping standards. A 12-foot semicircle on each end outlines the penalty area. The center of the semicircle is at the center of the goal.

The game follows the general rules of soccer, with one goalie for each side. The corner kick, not played in other lead-up games, needs to be introduced. This kick is used when the ball goes over the end line but not through the goal and was last touched by the defense. The ball is taken to the nearest corner for a direct free kick, and a goal can be scored from the kick. If the attacking team last touched the ball, a goalkeeper kick is awarded. The goalie puts the ball down and placekicks it forward. The players are designated as center forward, outside right halfback, fullback, and goalie. Players should rotate positions at regular intervals. The forwards play in the front half of the field and the guards in the back half, but neither positions are restricted to these areas entirely, and all may cross the center line without penalty.

A foul by the defense within its penalty area (semicircle) results in a penalty kick, taken from a point

12 yards distant, directly in front of the goal. Only the goalie is allowed to defend. The ball is in play, with others waiting outside the penalty area. Emphasize position play, and encourage the lines of three to spread out and hold their positions.

Suggested Performance Objectives

The following objectives are designed for three skill levels: introductory, intermediate, and advanced. The objectives can be used in intermediate or advanced soccer classes or in a heterogeneously grouped class to challenge students of varying abilities.

Introductory Unit: Core Objectives

Kicking

1. Execute a push pass, low drive, and lofted drive. Satisfy the instructor that these are understood and can be executed with the preferred foot. (All objectives may be performed with the preferred foot.)

Passing

2. Make three of five push passes from 10 yards to your partner.

3. Make three of five low-drive passes from 15 yards to your partner.

4. Make three of five loft-drive passes from 20 yards to your partner.

Dribbling

5. Dribble a distance of 20 yards twice with one or both feet. The ball must not be allowed to stray more than 5 yards.

Shooting

6. Shoot the ball with the preferred foot from 18 yards into an empty goal eight of 10 times.

Heading

7. Head the ball back to the tossing partner eight of 10 times over a distance of 5 yards. The partner must be able to catch the ball.

Control of the Ball

8. Control three of five passes on the ground using the feet only.

9. Control three of five passes in the air using the head, chest, or thigh.

Game Situation

10. Show an understanding of pass, run, and control in a minisoccer game situation.

Rules of the Game

11. Score 80 percent on a rules-of-the-game test. One retake is permissible.

Introductory Unit: Optional Objectives

Goalkeeping

1. Save six of 10 shots from 18 yards. The shots must be on target.

2. Punt the ball 25 yards four of five times.

Juggling

3. Keep the ball in the air with at least 10 consecutive touches. Hands or arms may not be used.

Field Dimensions

4. Diagram a full-size soccer field and give dimensions.

Grading

5. Achieve 13 passing grades for a unit pass. The instructor reserves the right to lower the number of required passing grades for the unit as necessary.

Intermediate Unit: Core Objectives

Kicking

1. Satisfy the instructor that the techniques of the push pass, low drive, and lofted drive are understood and can be executed with both feet.

Passing

2. Complete four of five push passes with the preferred foot from 10 yards. The passes must go between two cones placed 5 yards apart. Complete three of five passes with the nonpreferred foot.

3. Complete four of five low-drive passes with the preferred foot from 10 yards. The passes must go between two cones placed 8 yards apart. Complete three of five passes with the nonpreferred foot.

4. Complete four of five lofted-drive passes with the preferred foot from 10 yards. The passes must go over an obstacle 6 feet high. Complete three of five passes with the nonpreferred foot.

Dribbling

5. Dribble through six cones over 25 yards four times with no misses. Both feet must be used.

6. Dribble around an advancing goalkeeper, and score a goal three of five times.

Shooting

7. Shoot the ball with the preferred foot from 18 yards into an empty goal nine of 10 times.

8. Perform task 7, except with the nonpreferred foot, seven of 10 times.

Heading

9. Head the ball to a serving partner nine of 10 times over a distance of 10 yards. The partner must be able to catch the ball without its touching the ground.

Control of the Ball

10. Control four of five passes on the ground. Use the feet only.

11. Control four of five passes in the air. The head, chest, and thighs must be used.

Corner Kick

12. Propel three of five corner kicks inside the penalty area. The ball may not touch the ground between the corner and the penalty area.

Throw-In

13. Throw the ball with two hands to a partner 10 yards away four of five times. The partner must be able to catch the ball.

Juggling

14. Juggle the ball at least 10 consecutive times without allowing it to touch the ground.

Tackling

15. Successfully complete three of five block tackles on a partner dribbling a ball at a walking pace.

Goalkeeping

16. Kick goal kicks at least 20 yards in the air four of five times.

17. Punt the ball 25 yards, four of five times.

18. Save at least six of 10 on-target shots from the 18-yard line.

Rules of the Game

19. Score 80 percent on a rules-of-the-game test. One retest is allowed.

Intermediate Unit: Optional Objectives

Officiating

1. Help officiate at least two games.

2. Know the roles of the referee and linesmen.

3. Know the correct positioning of officials at corner kicks, goal kicks, and penalties.

Volleying

4. Volley four of five goals from outside the goal area with the preferred foot.

Swerving or Bending the Ball

5. Bend the ball into the goal from the goal line three of five times with the preferred foot.

Penalty Kicks

6. Score seven of 10 penalty kicks against a recognized peer goalkeeper.

Power and Distance Kicking

7. Score two of five goals into an empty goal from the halfway line.

Grading

8. Make 20 passing grades for a unit completion.

Advanced Unit: Basic Objectives

Passing

1. Make four of five push passes with the preferred foot from a distance of 10 yards between two cones, placed 5 yards apart, while running with the ball. Complete three of five passes with the preferred foot.

2. Make four of five low-drive passes with the preferred foot from a distance of 15 yards between two cones, placed 8 yards apart, while running with the ball. Complete three of five passes with the nonpreferred foot.

Dribbling

3. Dribble through nine cones over a distance of 40 yards and back to the start in 30 seconds or less. Both feet must be used, and no cones may be omitted.

4. Dribble around an advancing goalkeeper and score four of five times. The goalkeeper must be beaten to the left and to the right at least once.

Shooting

5. Score 10 of 10 shots into an empty goal from outside the 18-yard line with the preferred foot, and nine of 10 shots with the nonpreferred foot.

6. Score eight of 10 penalty kicks against a recognized peer goalkeeper.

7. Volley four of five goals from a serving partner, from outside the goal area, with the preferred foot, and three of five with the nonpreferred foot.

8. Serve or bend the ball from the goal line into the goal three of six times with the preferred foot. The ball must be placed within 1 foot of the line any distance from the post.

Heading

9. Head the ball back to a serving partner nine of 10 times over a distance of 10 yards. The partner must be able to catch the ball.

10. Head the ball back and forth with a partner a minimum of 10 times without touching the ground.

11. Head nine of 10 serves from a partner into an empty goal from a distance of 10 yards.

Control of the Ball

12. Control nine of 10 passes on the ground with the preferred foot.

13. Control eight of 10 passes on the ground with the nonpreferred foot.

14. Control nine of 10 passes from a partner with the head.

15. Control nine of 10 serves from a partner with the chest.

16. Control nine of 10 serves from a partner with the preferred thigh and eight of 10 with the nonpreferred thigh.

Corner Kick

17. Kick nine of 10 corner kicks into the penalty area with the preferred foot from the preferred side. The ball may not touch the ground between the corner and the penalty area.

18. Kick eight of 10 corner kicks into the penalty area from the nonpreferred side (same conditions as task 17).

Throw-In

19. Throw the ball with both hands to a partner 15 yards away, nine of 10 times. The throw must be placed so the partner is able to catch the ball with his or feet.

20. Throw the ball to a moving partner at least 10 yards away. The partner must be able to catch the ball with his or her feet.

Juggling

21. Juggle the ball at least 20 times without it touching the ground. The head, foot, and thigh must be used. Start with the ball on the ground and get it into the air using the feet.

22. Juggle the ball with a partner. At least 10 passes must be made. No restrictions are placed on the number of touches by each player.

Tackling

23. Use a block tackle on a partner jogging with the ball eight of 10 times successfully.

24. Use a slide tackle on a partner jogging with the ball three of five times successfully.

Goalkeeping

25. Kick four of five goal kicks at least 20 yards in the air before hitting the ground.

26. Punt the ball at least 30 yards four of five times.

27. Save seven of 10 shots on target from outside the 18-yard line.

Game Rules and Strategy

28. Demonstrate a thorough understanding of the rules of the game and principles of strategy.

Grading

29. Achieve a score of 80 percent or higher on a test covering the rules of the game. One retake is allowed.

Advanced Unit: Optional Objectives

Officiating

1. Officiate at least three games.

Grading

2. To successfully complete the unit, obtain 26 passing grades.

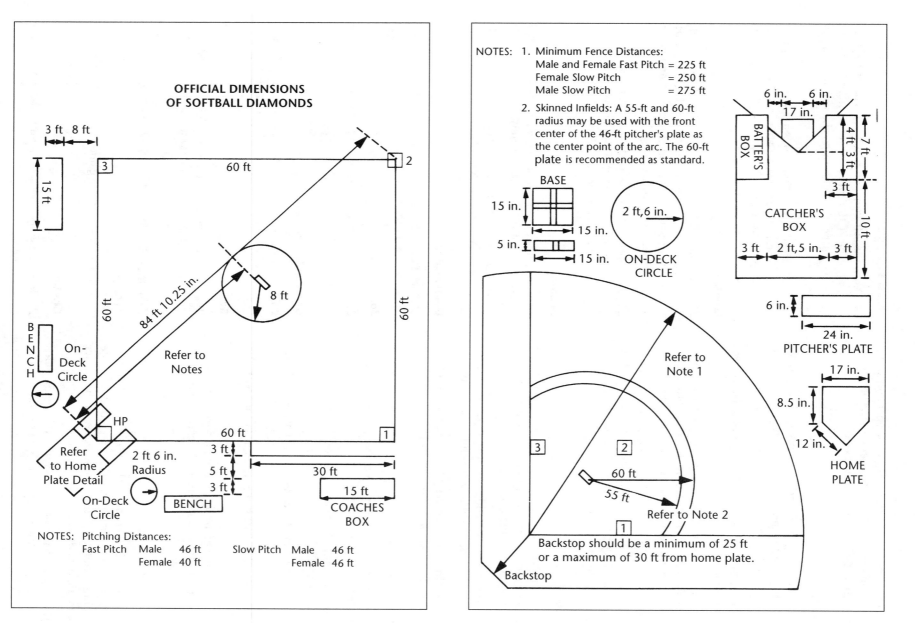

OFFICIAL DIMENSIONS OF SOFTBALL DIAMONDS

3 ft   8 ft

15 ft

3   60 ft   2

60 ft

60 ft

84 ft 10.25 in.

8 ft

Refer to Notes

B E N C H

On-Deck Circle

HP

Refer to Home Plate Detail

2 ft 6 in. Radius

On-Deck Circle

BENCH

60 ft

3 ft

5 ft

3 ft

30 ft

15 ft

COACHES BOX

1

NOTES: Pitching Distances:
Fast Pitch   Male   46 ft   Slow Pitch   Male   46 ft
             Female   40 ft   Female   46 ft

NOTES: 1. Minimum Fence Distances:
           Male and Female Fast Pitch = 225 ft
           Female Slow Pitch   = 250 ft
           Male Slow Pitch   = 275 ft

      2. Skinned Infields: A 55-ft and 60-ft radius may be used with the front center of the 46-ft pitcher's plate as the center point of the arc. The 60-ft plate is recommended as standard.

BASE

15 in.

15 in.

5 in.

15 in.

2 ft, 6 in.

ON-DECK CIRCLE

BATTER'S BOX

6 in.   6 in.

17 in.

4 ft   3 ft

7 ft

3 ft

10 ft

CATCHER'S BOX

3 ft   2 ft, 5 in.   3 ft

6 in.

24 in.

PITCHER'S PLATE

17 in.

8.5 in.

12 in.

HOME PLATE

Refer to Note 1

3

2

1

60 ft

55 ft

Refer to Note 2

Backstop should be a minimum of 25 ft or a maximum of 30 ft from home plate.

Backstop

FIGURE 19.8   Softball diamonds

SOFTBALL

Softball raises controversy among physical education teachers. Some instructors believe that it is a game in which one only catches "varicose veins" from standing around. On the other hand, because it is a less-active game, softball is often played by adults for many years. When the skill level of the participants is developed, the game can be enjoyable. If skill is lacking, emphasis should be placed on development skills and individual practice.

Softball can be taught effectively by using stations. This gives students ample practice in many different skills and avoids the situation in which students play only one position and specialize in skills. Softball can be played coeducationally, and many of the lead-up games make the activity enjoyable and suited to students' ability levels.

Sequence of Skills
Equipment and Facilities

Softball is played on a diamond with the dimensions shown in Figure 19.8. Lines can be applied to the field with chalk or can be burned into the grass with a solvent that kills the grass and leaves a brown line.

Softball requires some specialized equipment. When ordering gloves, about 20 percent should be left handed, and enough balls should be ordered so that each student has one. This allows many drills to be undertaken without waiting for the balls to be returned. Available equipment should include a set of bases for each diamond; bats of varying sizes (aluminum are the most durable); fielders' gloves; a catcher's glove, protector, and face mask; and batting tees. For less-experienced players, the soft softball is most desirable because it helps alleviate the fear of the ball that some players have. When a regulation softball is used, students often learn to dodge the ball, rather than catch it. Some teachers have had success with the large 16-inch ball. It moves slower, cannot be hit as far, and allows the game to be played in a smaller area. The drawback is that the large ball is difficult to throw because of its size.

Catching

Catching involves moving the body into the path of the ball. There are two ways to hold the hands for catching fly balls. For a low ball, the fielder keeps the fingers in and the thumbs turned outward. For a ball above waist level, the thumbs are turned inward and the fingers outward. The arms and hands extend and reach for the ball. As the ball comes into the glove, the

arms, hands, and body give to create a soft home for the ball.

When catching grounders, move into the path of the ball, then move toward the ball, and catch it on a "good" hop. Keep the eyes on the ball and follow it into the glove. The feet are spread, the seat is kept down, and the hands are carried low and in front. The weight is on the balls of the feet or on the toes, and the knees are bent to lower the body. As the ball is caught, the fielder straightens up, takes a step in the direction of the throw, and makes the throw.

Throwing

The ball is generally held with a three- or four-fingered grip. Smaller students usually have to use the four-fingered grip. The fingers should be spaced evenly, and the ball should be held with the fingertips.

Because throwing is a complex motor pattern, it is difficult to break the skill into component parts. At best, throwing skills can be slowed down about 10 percent in an effort to teach proper throwing technique. If a mature pattern of throwing has not been developed, students should focus on throwing for velocity rather than accuracy. After proper form has been learned, accuracy becomes a prime objective.

Overhand Throw. The player stands with the side opposite the throwing arm facing the target. The hand with the ball is brought back, over the head, at just above shoulder height. The nonthrowing hand is raised in front of the body. The weight is on the rear foot (away from the target), with the front foot advanced toward the target. The arm comes forward with the elbow leading, and the ball is thrown with a downward snap of the wrist. The weight of the body shifts simultaneously with the throw to the front foot. The rear foot rotates forward, and the throwing hand ends facing the ground during the follow-through. The eyes should be kept on the target throughout the throw.

Sidearm Throw. The sidearm throw is similar to the overhand throw, except that the entire motion is kept near a horizontal plane. The sidearm throw, which uses a quick, whiplike motion, is for shorter, quicker throws than the overhand. The sidearm throw should be used only for short infield throws because the sideways motion causes a spin on the ball, which results in a curved path.

Underhand Throw. The underhand throw is used for short distances, such as throwing to the pitcher covering first base or the person on second base throwing to the shortstop covering second base. The player faces the target, and the hand is swung backward with the palm facing forward. The arm is then moved forward in a pendulum swing with the elbow slightly bent. The weight shifts to the front foot during the toss.

Pitching

The pitcher must begin with both feet touching the rubber. The ball is held in front of the body with the pitcher facing home plate. The pitching hand is brought backward in a pendulum swing, and the wrist is cocked at the back of the swing. The pitcher steps forward on the opposite foot and swings the arm forward. The wrist is snapped, and the ball is released from the fingertips as the arm finishes moving in an upward, lifting fashion. The follow-through should be accompanied by a forward step of the foot on the throwing side so the player is in a fielding position.

Fielding Position

Infielders should assume the ready position in a semi-crouch, with the legs spread a shoulder width apart, knees bent slightly, and hands on or in front of the knees. The weight is distributed evenly on both feet so the player can move easily to the left or right. To field a grounder, the fielder moves as quickly as possible into the path of the ball, then moves forward, and plays the ball on a good hop. The glove should be kept near the ground and raised only as the ball rises. (A common mistake is to not put the glove down soon enough.) The eyes follow the ball into the glove, and the head is kept down. As the ball is caught, the fielder straightens up, takes a step in the direction of the throw, and releases the ball.

To catch a ground ball in the outfield, the player should employ the sure-stop method. This involves using the body as a barrier. The fielder drops to one knee in order to block the ball with the body if the catch is missed. This method should be used when runners are on base.

Batting

The bat is gripped with the dominant hand above and adjacent to the nondominant hand. The feet should be positioned comfortably apart, and the front of the body faces the plate. The knees are slightly bent, and the weight is distributed equally on both feet. The hands and the bat are held shoulder high and slightly behind the rear foot. The elbows are away from the body; the wrists cocked, and the bat held in an upward position. The bat should be followed with the eyes as long as possible. The stride begins by stepping toward the ball with the front foot. The hips are rotated, followed by the trunk and forward shoulder. The arms are extended, wrists snapped, and contact is made with the ball in front of the forward hip. Different grips on the bat can be tried, including the choke and long grip.

Batters should avoid using poor techniques such as lifting the front foot high off the ground, stepping back with the rear foot, dropping the elbows, or crouching or bending forward.

Base Running

After a hit, the batter should run hard with the head up and eyes looking down the base path. The runner moves past the bag, tagging it in the process, and turns out into foul territory, unless it is an extra base hit. If it is an extra base hit, the runner swings 5 to 6 feet to the right of the baseline, about two-thirds of the way down the base path, and makes the turn toward second.

Runners on base must stay in contact with the base until the pitcher releases the ball. The next base is faced, with one foot forward and the other foot touching the base in a push-off position. The knees are flexed, and the upper body leans toward the next base.

Ideas for Effective Instruction

Safety is important, and throwing the bat is a constant problem. The members of the batting team should stand behind the backstop or on the side opposite the batter. Techniques to make the batter think about the bat are requiring the player to carry the bat to first base, to change ends of the bat before dropping it, or to place the bat in a circle before running. It is usually best not to allow sliding because sliding can lead to injury if the proper equipment is not available. The catcher should always wear protective gear. In the early stages of practice, soft softballs can be used.

Many of the lead-up games were developed to increase the number of people who get to bat in each inning. One strategy for effective batting practice is to have a member of the batting team pitch so the ball is easy to hit. Players should rotate positions often. Another idea is to have players rotate to a new position each inning. This has the effect of making the players supportive of each other, considering the quality of the game depends on all of the participating players.

Station teaching is excellent for developing softball skills. It ensures that participants have the opportunity to practice a wide variety of activities. Players who are particularly skilled in an activity can help others. Teachers should position themselves at a different station each day to ensure that they have instructed all students at all stations over a 1- to 2-week period. The following stations can be used by placing task cards at each station so students know exactly what is expected of them.

Station 1. Catching Ground Balls

One person rolls and the other person catches the ball.

1. Roll the ball straight to the person.

2. Roll the ball to the left side. Increase the distance.

3. Roll the ball to the right side. Increase the distance.

4. Roll the ball in an unpredictable direction.

5. Bat the ball in different directions. Start at 5 yards and increase the distance up to 20 yards from the fielder.

Station 2. Batting

1. Work in groups of three with a batting tee. One person fields, one bats, and the other shags the ball. Hit 10 balls.

2. Perform item 1, except pitch the ball to the batter.

3. As the batter, try placing the ball. Call the direction where you are going to hit the ball, and then do so.

Station 3. Base Running

1. Run the bases using a circle technique. Have a partner time you.

2. Run the bases using a clover technique. Decide which you prefer and which allows you to run the bases faster.

3. Bunt and run to first. Have your partner time you.

4. Play "In a Pickle" in groups of three. (See game description in "Lead-Up Games and Learning Activities.")

Station 4. Throwing

1. One person stands at each base plus a catcher is behind home plate. Practice throwing to each of the bases from each position. Rotate positions after each person has had three throws.

2. Throw the ball from the outfield. Throw the ball through a cutoff person. Make five throws and rotate to catcher position.

3. If you are not throwing, back up the other positions and act as a cutoff person.

Station 5. Fly Balls

1. Throw fly balls back and forth.

2. Vary the height and direction of the throw so teammates have to move into the flight of the ball.

3. Make teammates move backward and forward to catch the ball.

4. Bat some flies and play the game "Five Hundred" (see next section for description).

Lead-Up Games and Learning Activities

Over-the-Line Softball

Over the line is a popular modified lead-up-type game incorporating softball skills. It is best as a three-versus-three game, but it can be modified to include more players. Offensive players try to hit the ball over a line about 20 yards from home plate and into a zone that is 20 yards wide and as long as possible. There is no running by the batters. The game can be started from a batting tee, a soft toss, or a pitch from a teammate, depending on the skill level of your students. The ball must land on the fly in the zone area to be a base hit. Three hits equals a run, and a ball hit over the head of all the fielders is a home run. Outs are made by hitting two fouls, one strike, a fly caught by a fielder, or a hit ball landing on any of the lines or being a ground ball. All of these rules can be modified for a local situation. A great area to play is on the marked football field because you can use the yard lines for the boundaries. The sideline of the field is the line to hit over, and home plate is backed up 20 yards. A fun variation is to divide the hitting zone into three areas with cones and award a single, a double, or a triple for landing the ball in the respective area.

Two-Pitch Softball

Two-pitch softball is played like regulation softball except that a member of the team at bat pitches. Every member of the team must have an opportunity to pitch. The batter receives only two pitched balls to hit, and the ball hit must be fair or it is an out. The pitcher does not field the ball, and no balls or strikes are called.

In a Pickle

A base runner is "in a pickle" when caught between two bases and in danger of being tagged out. To begin, both fielders are on a base with a runner in the middle. The goal is for the player in the middle to get to a base safely. If done, that person scores a point. In either case, rotation occurs.

Pepper

This is one of the older skill games in baseball. A line of four to six players is about 10 yards in front of and facing a batter. A player tosses the ball to the batter, who attempts to hit controlled grounders back to him or her. The next player pitches. The batter stays at bat for a period of time and then rotates to the field.

Five Hundred

A batter hits balls to a group of fielders. The goal is to score 500 points. When the total is reached, that person becomes the new batter. Fielders earn 100 points for catching a fly ball, 75 points for catching a ball on one bounce, 50 points for catching a ball after two bounces, and 25 points for any other ball. The points must total exactly 500 or the total immediately earned is subtracted from the fielder's score. Points are also subtracted if an error is made.

Home Run

The critical players are a batter, a catcher, a pitcher, and one fielder. All other players are fielders and take positions throughout the area. The batter hits a pitch and on a fair ball must run to first base and back home before the ball can be returned to the catcher. The batter is out whenever any of the following occur: a fly ball is caught; a strikeout occurs; or on a fair ball, the ball beats the batter back to home plate. The number of home runs per batter can be limited, and a rotation plan should be developed. The distance to first base may have to be varied, depending on the strength and skill of the players.

Work-Up

This is a game of rotating positions each time an out is made. The game is played using regulation softball rules. Three batters are up at bat. Each time there is an out, the players move up one position, and the player making the last out goes to right field. The pitcher moves up to catcher, the person on first base to pitcher, and all others move up one position. If a fly ball is caught, the batter and the person catching the ball exchange places.

Babe Ruth Ball

The outfield is divided into three sections: left, center, and right field. The batter calls the field to which the ball will be hit. The pitcher throws pitches that the batter can hit easily. The batter remains in position as long as the ball is hit to the designated field. Field choices are rotated. The batter gets only one swing but may let a pitch go by. There is no base running.

Speedy Baseball

Speedy baseball is played like regular softball with the following exceptions:

1. The pitcher is from the team at bat and must not interfere with or touch a batted ball on penalty of the batter being called out.

2. The team coming to bat does not wait for the fielding team to get set. Because it has its own pitcher, the pitcher gets the ball to the batter just as quickly as the batter can grab a bat and get ready. The fielding team members have to hustle to get to their places.

3. Only one pitch is allowed per batter. Batters must hit a fair ball or they are out. The pitch is made from about two-thirds of the normal pitching distance.

4. No stealing is permitted.

5. No bunting is permitted. The batter must take a full swing.

Suggested Performance Objectives

The following are performance objectives that might be used in a softball unit.

Contract Objectives

Throwing Tasks

1. Standing 45 feet from a partner who is inside a hoop, complete five consecutive underhand pitches to that person without causing him or her to move outside of the hoop.

2. Standing 60 feet from a partner who is inside a hoop, complete five overhand throws to that person without forcing him or her to move more than 1 foot outside the hoop.

3. Be able to demonstrate the proper stance, windup, and delivery of the windmill pitch to the instructor.

4. From a designated area of the outfield, situated 150 feet (boys) or 100 feet (girls) away, throw the softball through the air directly to a 10-foot-wide circle chalked in front of home plate. To count, the throw must bounce only once before landing or going through the circle. Student must make three of five throws to qualify for points.

5. Display pitching skills by striking out three or more batters or by allowing no more than five base hits in an actual game.

6. From an outfield or relay position, throw out a base runner at any base in an actual game.

Fielding Tasks

1. Demonstrating correct fielding stance, cleanly field five consecutive ground or fly balls hit by a partner.

2. Play a game of Pepper with a group of no more than six players, demonstrating good bat control, and hand–eye coordination, and fielding skills.

3. Play a game of Five Hundred with no more than five players and demonstrate skills in catching flies and line drives and in fielding ground balls.

4. In an actual game situation, participate in a successful double play.

5. Perform a diving or over-the-head catch in an actual game situation.

Hitting Tasks

1. Watch a film or read an article on hitting.

2. Using a batting tee, hit five consecutive softballs, on the fly or on the ground, past the 80-foot semicircle line marked off in chalk.

3. Execute proper bunting form and ability by dumping three of five attempts into designated bunting areas along the first or third baselines.

4. In an actual game, make two or more base hits.

5. Hit a triple or home run in an actual game.

6. During an actual game, observe an opponent or a teammate's swing. Write down the strong and weak points of that particular swing and bring them to the instructor's attention. The instructor will then match observations with your critique.

Optional Objectives

1. Make a diagram of an official softball diamond on posterboard. Illustrate proper field dimensions.

2. On a piece of paper, show how the batting average and earned run average are compiled.

3. Watch a college or fast-pitch softball game on television or at the actual setting. Record the score, place, teams, and date of the contest. List the strengths and weaknesses of each team, and note how weaknesses could be corrected.

4. Umpire a game for three or more innings.

5. Keep accurate score in an official score book for three or more innings.

SPEED-A-WAY

The game of speed-a-way was originated in 1950 by Marjorie Larsen, but it spent 10 years in experimental stages prior to its arrival on the field. It is a dynamic game that combines the challenges of soccer, basketball, speedball, fieldball, and field hockey. It was created in an effort to find a game that could serve as a lead-up for field hockey and bring enjoyment to participants without having to learn complicated rules and techniques.

Speed-a-way is intended for students from middle school through college. With the emphasis on student success, the game employs a great variety of fundamental movements such as running, throwing, catching, and kicking. This allows participants ample opportunities for vigorous activity, competition, and team cooperation.

The area in which speed-a-way is played is the same as for field hockey. The recommended size is 100 by 60 yards. This rectangle is divided into four parts with alleys and striking circles. There is an official speed-a-way ball, but a soccer or playground ball can be substituted. The game consists of four quarters of 8 minutes each, with a 2-minute rest period between quarters and a 10-minute rest period between halves. Substitutions can be made when the ball is dead.

Speed-a-way is played with two teams of 11 players. Each player wears a set of flags. Players line up on their half of the field at the beginning of each quarter and after each score. The ball is put into play by a "push-kick" backwards from the center of the field. The object of the game is to advance the ball through the opponent's territory by means of kicking, dribbling, heading, or shouldering a ground ball; by throwing an aerial ball; or by running with an aerial ball. A field goal (3 points) is scored by kicking the ball between the opponent's goalposts from within the striking circle. (If football or speedball goalposts are used, a dropkick over the bar scores 4 points.) A touchdown (2 points) is scored by running across the goal line with the ball or by passing it to a teammate who is already over the goal line but not between the goalposts. An aerial ball is one that has been converted from the ground with the feet.

Rules

1. The defense can only pull offensive players' flags when they are carrying the ball.

2. If flags are pulled before the ball leaves the offensive player's hand, the defensive team gains possession. Everyone moves 5 yards away before play can be continued.

3. In order for a player to carry the ball in his or her hands, the player must first legally lift the ball up and catch it. This is usually done with the feet. A teammate can lift the ball to another teammate, or a player can lift the ball to himself or herself with the feet.

4. If the ball goes out-of-bounds over the goal line (not between the goalposts) and is last touched by the offense, the goalie gets possession. The goalie may punt, place-kick, throw, or run the ball out of the

goal area. Once the goalie leaves the striking circle, the opposition can pull the goalie's flag. However, in the striking circle the goalie is "safe." Goalies may go anywhere on the field they desire, but they can only use their hands inside the striking circle.

5. If the ball goes out-of-bounds over the goal line (not between the posts) and is last touched by the defense, the offense receives a corner kick on the side where the ball went out.

6. When a ball goes out-of-bounds over a sideline, a player from the opposing team uses a two-handed overhead toss to put the ball in play.

7. A player holding the pivot foot in position cannot have their flag pulled for 3 seconds.

8. No contact is allowed during guarding. A player can be guarded by only one player.

Safety Precautions

Because the game of speed-a-way is fast moving, the safety of the game depends on the instruction players receive and the quality of officiating. A player should be taught that good position is an essential safety factor in speed-a-way. Good body control and skill in the fundamentals of running, starting, and stopping quickly should be encouraged to eliminate body contact. Players should be taught how to control the ball, to evade and dodge an opponent, to throw the ball, and to lift the ball to another teammate. The technique of guarding or tackling an opponent who is in possession of the ball is most important in the prevention of unnecessary body contact. Team play and its value in preventing injury should be emphasized. Players should be safety conscious and follow the rules at all times.

During the game, referees should be alert to the dangerous elements of the game. All harmful body contact, such as obstructing, pushing, charging, tripping, and dangerous kicking (kicking an opponent or kicking the ball directly into an opponent) should be called immediately. Speed-a-way can be a low-risk and nonthreatening game when taught and conducted with safety as a priority.

Lead-Up Games for Speed-A-Way

Circle Kickball

Ten to 20 players form a circle and use a speed-a-way, soccer, or playground ball. The skills used are kicking and trapping. Players kick the ball back and forth inside the circle. The object of the game is for a player to kick the ball out of the circle below the shoulder level of any other circle player. Each time a player achieves this, he or she collects a point. Any player who kicks the ball over the shoulders of a circle player will give back one of the points he or she has earned.

Croquet Ball

Students play in pairs or groups of three. Each student has a ball. The object of this game is for one ball to hit another. Each hit scores a point. The first player kicks his or her ball out 10 to 15 yards ahead. The next player kicks his or her ball and tries to hit the ball lying ahead. Alternate kicking continues until a hit is made. The game continues until a player scores a designated number of points. If three play, turns are taken in sequence. If a successful hit is made on one ball, the kicker gets an immediate try at the other.

Touch Ball

Eight to 10 students form a circle with one player in the center. One ball is used. The students are spaced around a circle about 10 yards in diameter. The ball is thrown or passed back and forth. If the center player touches the ball, the circle player who last touched the ball moves into the center.

Pin Kickball

Two teams of seven to 10 players face each other at 20 yards apart. Six or seven pins and two balls are needed. The object is to knock down the pins. Each pin is worth one point. Kicks should be made from the line behind which the team is standing. Players should concentrate on controlled traps and accurate kicks. Feel free to vary the amount of players per team and the number of pins used.

TEAM HANDBALL

Team handball is an exciting and challenging game that combines skills from basketball, soccer, water polo, and hockey. It involves running, dribbling, jumping, passing, catching, throwing, and goaltending. The object of the game is to move a small soccer ball down the field by passing and dribbling and then to throw the ball into a goal area that is 3 meters wide and 2 meters high. The game is relatively simple to learn and can be enjoyed by both sexes. It is inexpensive to add to the curriculum and can be played indoors, outdoors, or on a tennis court. Virtually any space can be adapted or modified for team handball. The play is rapid and involves continuous running, making the sport a good cardiovascular activity. Because the game is relatively new to the United States, many students will be inexperienced. A unit on team handball can provide students with a fresh challenge and increased motivation, and teachers should enjoy introducing a new activity.

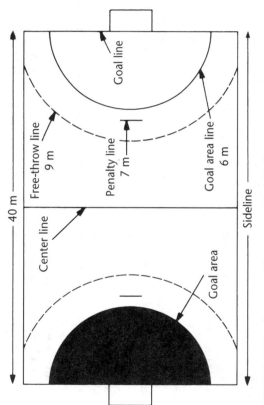

FIGURE 19.9 Court markings—team handball

Basic Rules

In regulation play, each team has six court players and one goalie. The six court players cover the entire court. A player is allowed three steps before and after dribbling the ball. There is no limit on the number of dribbles. Dribbling is, however, discouraged because passing is more effective. A double dribble is a violation. A player can hold the ball for 3 seconds only before passing, dribbling, or shooting. No player except the goalie can kick the ball in any way.

The court is marked (Figure 19.9) with a 6-meter goal area, a 7-meter penalty line, and a 9-meter free-throw line. The goal is 2 by 3 meters. The goal area inside the 6-meter line is only for the goalie. Other players are not allowed in this area. The 7-meter line is used for a major penalty shot, and the 9-meter line is used for a minor penalty shot. A regulation court is 20 by 40 meters.

One point is awarded for a goal. Violations and penalties are similar to basketball. A free throw is taken from the point of the violation, and defense must remain 3 meters away while protecting the goal. A penalty throw is awarded from the 7-meter line for a major violation. A major violation occurs when an offensive player who is inside the 9-meter line in a good shooting position is fouled. During a penalty throw, all players must be behind the 9-meter line.*

The official team handball looks like a small soccer ball. The men's ball is 23 inches in circumference, and the women's ball is 21 inches. A smaller minihandball

is available for younger students. Handballs are carried by most sporting goods dealers. Playground balls and small volleyballs can be substituted if necessary. The goals can be improvised by using boundary cones, tape on the wall, rope through a chain-link fence, soccer goals, field hockey goals, or homemade regulation goals. The floor lines can be established by marking the floor with tape or by putting boundary cones along the area where the lines should be. A basketball court can be easily modified for team handball by setting boundary cones along the goal area and by using the free-throw lane for the width of the goal.

Sequence of Skills

Team handball is a good unit to follow basketball, soccer, or water polo because it uses many of the same skills. The techniques and skill work are similar to those activities.

Passing

Team handball is a passing game, and many different passes can be used for short and medium ranges. The passing fundamentals are similar to those of basketball.

Chest, Bounce, and Overhead Passes. All are two-handed passes, similar to those in basketball.

One-Handed Shoulder or Baseball Pass. This is similar to an overhand throw in baseball. If the student cannot grip the ball, it can rest on a flexed hand with the fingers spread.

Sidearm Pass. This pass is similar to the shoulder pass except that the ball is released to the side of the body to avoid a defender.

---

* Specific rules of team handball are available from the United States Team Handball Federation, 1750 E. Boulder, Colorado Springs, CO 80909.

Shovel Pass. This one- or two-handed underhand pass is used for releasing the ball quickly and thus avoiding a defender.

Handoff Pass. This pass is similar to the one used by a quarterback handing off the ball to a running back. The receiver forms a pocket for the ball.

Roller Pass. The ball is simply rolled along the floor to a teammate when all other passing lanes are blocked.

Hook Pass. This pass is similar to the hook shot in basketball in which the passer hooks the ball over or around a defender. A jump may be added before the pass.

Jump Pass. Usually made with a shoulder pass, the jump pass occurs when the passer jumps over or around a defender and throws the ball.

Behind-the-Back Pass. Similar to the basketball pass, this can be effective because the smaller ball is easier to control than a basketball.

Dribbling

Dribbling in handball is the same as the basketball skill, but the ball is harder to control because it is small and the ball surface is uneven. Players need to get used to the legal three steps before and after dribbling, as well as the 3-second holding rule. Dribbling should be practiced some but in general should be discouraged in team handball.

Goal Shooting

All of the aforementioned passes can also be used for shots on goal. The following shots are the most popular.

Jump Shot. Because the offensive player can jump outside the goal area and land in the goal area after a shot, the jump shot is the most popular shot. Shooters run three steps, jump, and shoot, using the one-handed shoulder throw. This is the same as a one-handed shoulder pass, except that it is a shot on goal. The shot can be used with or without a defender.

Dive Shot. The dive shot is a good shot on either wing because the shooter can dive or fall away from an opponent.

Lob Shot. When a goalie comes out too far to defend, the shooter can lob the ball up and over the goalie's outstretched arms.

Penalty Shot. The penalty shot is the one-on-one free shot with only the goalie defending. The shooter must keep one foot stationary and cannot touch the 7-meter penalty line until the ball is thrown. The ball must be shot in 3 seconds. The goalie must be 3 meters or more away from the shooter. The shoulder or sidearm throw is usually most efficient for this shot.

Behind-the-Back. The shooter can fake a shot to the right and then bring the ball behind the back and the defender for a shot. The behind-the-back shot can be executed to either side.

Goal shooting involves the following general principles:

1. Attack the high or low corners on each shot.

2. Shoot primarily between the 6- and 9-meter line.

3. Find the open offensive player to take the shot.

4. Do not force a shot that is not open.

5. Do not shoot too far down on the wings because the angle is too extreme.

6. Use the floor or ground to bounce shots into the goal.

7. Try jump shots toward the goal, which are usually effective. The ball must be released before the shooter lands in the goal area.

8. Develop a wide variety of goal shots.

Goaltending

The position of goalie, the most important defender on the team, requires quick hands and feet and fast reaction time. All parts of the body can be used to deflect shots. The goalie also starts the offense after saving shots. The goalie needs to learn how to cut down shooting angles by moving out from the goal, depending on where the ball is located on the court. Goalies should practice saving shots in all four corners of the goal. They need to understand all of the rules governing the goalkeeper.

Defensive Strategy

The defensive strategy is similar to basketball in that person-to-person and zone defenses are popular. Beginning players should start with the person-to-person defense and learn how to stay with an offensive player. Zone defenses can be 6-0, 5-1, 4-2, and 3-3, with each person playing an area or zone. The back players in the zone are back against the goal line, while the front players are just inside the 9-meter line. The zone rotates with the ball as passes are made around the court.

Offensive Strategy

The offense starts the game with a throw-on (pass to a teammate) from the center line. A throw-on also initiates play after each goal. All six offensive players line up at the center line, and one teammate throws the ball to another. The defense is in position, using either a zone or person-to-person defense. Offensive strategy is similar to basketball with picks, screens, rolls, and movement to open up shots on goal. With a zone defense, short, quick passes are made in an overloaded portion of the zone.

Ideas for Effective Instruction

Set up learning stations for passing, shooting, goaltending, dribbling, and defensive work. The performance objectives in this section, for example, are useful for structuring practice time at each station. Students can play with Nerf or comparable foamrubber balls, playground balls, and volleyballs to get more practice attempts and to help beginning goalies perfect their skills. Group drills from basketball are applicable to team handball defense, offense, passing, and dribbling. Include various instructional devices for targets in passing, timing for dribbling through cones, or narrowing the goal area for shots to the corners. Penalty shots should be practiced daily. Competitive-type drills are enjoyable and motivating for most students.

Modified Games
No Bounce, No Steps, and No Contact

Students are forced to pass the ball rather than dribble. The walking or traveling rule from basketball is in effect because students are usually comfortable with this rule. The no-contact rule gives the offense an advantage. The 3-second rule should remain in effect to force quick passes and deter holding the ball.

Three Bounces, Three Steps, and No Contact

This game is closer to the regulation game and provides a gradual adjustment to the team handball rules. A variation would have the three-bounce and 3-second rules but with no steps allowed. Getting students used to the three-step rule is difficult.

Sideline Team Handball

Sideline handball can be played when space is limited and the class is crowded. Extra team members spread out along each sideline. These sideline players can receive passes from teammates and can help pass the ball down the court. Sideline members can only pass the ball, however, and the 3-second rule applies to them. One sideline can be devoted to one team, and the other sideline to the other team. A challenging variation is to have different team members on each sideline. This distribution forces the active players to sharpen their passing skills.

Suggested Performance Objectives

1. Dribble the ball with the right hand (standing position) for 10 consecutive times.

2. Perform task 1 but with the left hand.

3. Dribble the ball with the right hand (moving forward) from the center line to the goal line without losing the dribble.

4. Perform task 3 but with the left hand.

5. Pass the ball to a partner standing 10 feet away with a two-handed chest pass to the chest area (between chin and waist) eight of 10 times.

6. Pass the ball to a partner standing 10 feet away with a two-handed bounce pass to the waist area eight of 10 times.

7. Pass the ball to a partner standing 10 feet away with a two-handed overhead pass to the chest area eight of 10 times.

8. Pass the ball to a partner standing 10 feet away with a one-handed overhead pass to the chest area eight of 10 times.

9. While running from the center line, alternately pass a two-handed chest and bounce pass that can be caught by a partner running at a parallel distance of 12 feet, with three of four passes hitting the partner.

10. While standing 7 meters from the goal, hit three of five goals.

11. Defend three of five attempted shots taken by a partner from a distance of 7 meters.

12. Dribble the ball with the right hand (moving forward) from the center line to the goal area without losing the dribble. Jump up and make a goal three of five times.

13. From 6 meters, hit a target five consecutive times with the following passes: roller, hook, jump, shovel, one-handed shoulder, sidearm, and behind the back.

14. From 9 meters away, hit two of five goals.

15. From 9 meters away, defend four of five goal shots.

16. Dribble through a set of six cones in 25 seconds.

TRACK AND FIELD

Track and field events consist of running, jumping, weight throwing, and vaulting. Running events include sprinting short distances, running middle and longer distances, and hurdling over barriers. Relay races with four team members are run over various distances. The jumping events include the high jump, long jump, and triple jump. The throwing events are the shot put, discus, javelin, and hammer throws. The vaulting event is the pole vault.

In the United States, instruction in track and field activities as part of the physical education program began in the late 1890s. Both men and women have been interested in pursuing these events for various reasons. The tremendous variety of skills necessary for running, jumping, throwing, and vaulting provides people with an exciting challenge.

Track and field should continue to be an important part of the secondary school physical education program. Students with different body types are able to find success in some track and field activity. All students should have the opportunity to explore and experience the wide variety of challenges of this unit.

Secondary schools have changed to metric distances for the running events. These distances vary some from state to state and from men's events to women's events. The men's running events usually include the following: 100, 200, 400, 800, 1,600, and 3,200 meter; 400-, and 1,600-meter relay; 110-meter high hurdles, and 400-meter intermediate hurdles. The field events for men usually include the high jump, long jump, triple jump, pole vault, shot put, and discus, javelin, and hammer (only in certain states) throws. Women's running events are similar to the men's, but the women run only one hurdle race, which is 100 meters. The 1,600-meter relay race is sometimes replaced with a medley relay consisting of 100, 100, 200, and 400 meters. In the field events, the women do not pole-vault, triple jump, or throw the hammer. It is interesting to note that women are finally being allowed officially to run longer distances (such as 1,600 and 3,200 meters). The 1984 Olympic Games in Los Angeles marked the first Olympic marathon for women.

Sequence of Skills

Because track and field is a highly specialized area that includes many specific skills and techniques for each of the running, jumping, vaulting, and throwing events, it is difficult to adequately cover all of these activities in a limited space. Several good texts are available with in-depth information about specific events and the skills involved. Much of what should be taught will depend on the abilities of the students, the length of time allotted to the unit, and the equipment available for instruction. Teachers developing units for track and field should refer to the suggested readings.

Ideas for Instruction

Each event in track and field can serve as a learning station for students. After students are introduced to the events, they can rotate from station to station and work on each activity. Keep a clipboard at each station with records of each day's best performances in an activity. The day-to-day records can be used for motivation and as evidence of individual improvement. A class track meet is an enjoyable culminating activity. Teams can be organized and a regulation dual meet conducted.

VOLLEYBALL

Because volleyball was adopted as an Olympic sport in 1964, it has gained a great deal of visibility through the media. It continues to grow in popularity in the United States and throughout the world. Beach volleyball, the newest edition of the sport, is also in the Olympics and has added to the popularity of the sport. The sport has adopted a new rally-scoring technique where scoring occurs for either team on every serve. In the United States, volleyball is a vigorous sport that many pursue in school, club, and recreational leagues. Volleyball is challenging, lends itself to coeducational participation, and can be modified in several ways to suit the abilities of many students.

Most states offer competitive volleyball for girls in the secondary schools. Many states are adding volleyball for the boys. Secondary physical education programs should offer coeducational volleyball classes to encourage both boys and girls. With the increased recreational volleyball offerings in YMCAs, community centers, and city recreational programs, students will be able to participate in and enjoy this activity for many years.

Sequence of Skills

Volleyball is difficult to play without a basic skills foundation. Help students to master these skills before beginning regulation games. Devising modified games for beginning-level students is important because they will not be able to play a regulation game. (A few students would dominate, and the remaining students would become quickly frustrated.) The type of ball, the height of the net, and the rules of the game can all be adjusted to ensure a successful experience for beginning students.

Serving

Underhand Serve. The underhand serve position starts with the left leg forward and both knees bent slightly. The ball is held in the left hand about waist height. The right arm starts with a long backswing and then comes forward, the right hand striking the ball just below the midline. The striking hand can be open or slightly closed, and the heel of the hand should contact the ball. The body weight is transferred from the rear foot to the front foot as the ball is contacted. The arm swing follow-through should be in a straight line.

Overhand Serve. The overhand floater serve has no spin on the ball. The legs are staggered, with the left leg forward. The ball is held about shoulder height with the left hand under the ball and the right hand behind it. The ball is tossed 2 or 3 feet up above the right shoulder. The right arm is brought back, behind the ear, and then extended fully to hit the ball. The heel of the hand strikes the ball slightly below the midline. Little follow-through is used because the ball should float or wobble like a knuckle ball.

Students who lack the strength or ability to get the ball over the net can begin serving closer to the net, and the net can be lowered. As students develop skill, they should move back gradually to the regulation distance. Targets can be placed on the floor for work on accuracy as skill improves.

Passing and Setting

This skill involves moving the ball from one teammate to another. Forearm passes are used primarily for receiving a serve or a spike. Overhand set passes are used primarily for setting the ball into position for a spike. All passes require quick footwork while keeping a low center of gravity, which is necessary for getting under the ball.

Forearm Passes. In the forearm bump pass, the ball is hit off the forearms. The feet are about a shoulder width apart, and one foot is ahead of the other. The knees are bent, and the arms are extended forward. The forearms are rolled outward to provide a flat, parallel surface for the ball. The elbows must be locked together on contact with the ball. The upward movement of the arms and legs depends on the speed of the ball and on the required distance of the pass. Passers must watch the ball carefully. Forearm passes can be made in different directions and also with one arm if necessary.

Overhand or Set Passes. In overhand passes, the body is set up under the ball, which is directly above the passer's nose. The hands are cupped to form a triangle-shaped window. The knees are bent, and the legs are about a shoulder width apart and in a stride position. The ball is contacted simultaneously with the fingers and thumbs of both hands. The legs, body, and arms uncoil into the ball in one smooth movement. Sets can be made from a front position facing the target and from a back position with the back to the target.

Spiking

Spiking is an offensive maneuver, which involves hitting the ball above the net and downward into the opponent's court. A spiker usually takes three or four steps toward the net. A final step with the right foot followed by a close step with the left foot precedes takeoff. With both feet together, the spiker then jumps vertically straight up. The arms swing forward during the jump. As the arms come forward to about shoulder height, the back begins to arch, and the right arm is cocked behind the head. The left arm starts the forward motion downward, and the right arm uncoils and attacks the ball. The elbow leads the striking arm and shoulder. The striking hand is open and rigid, and the palm of the hand strikes the ball.

Blocking

Blocking is a defensive maneuver used to stop the ball from going over the net. Blocking can be done by any of the three players on the front line. Blockers can jump and reach over the net, as long as the ball has not been touched by the offensive player. Blockers should leave the floor slightly after the spiker. The takeoff starts with the legs bent at the knees. After the jump, the arms extend fully upward, as high as possible. The fingers are spread as wide as possible. The hands are held rigid and no wider apart than the width of the ball. As the blocker comes down, the arms are drawn back to the body, and the feet and legs absorb the landing.

Ideas for Effective Instruction

Volleyball lends itself to station work on passes, sets, serves, and spikes. The performance objectives listed at the end of this unit can be posted on task cards at the various stations. A class period could include work on the performance objectives, group skill work, and a modified game. It is important to adjust the height of the net, the rules of the game, and the type of ball used so that inexperienced students can keep the ball in play. Foam-rubber balls and beach balls are excellent for beginners.

Many passing, setting, and serving activities can be done with partners. Having one partner toss the ball and the other partner pass or set is a good introductory drill. A smooth wall is useful for passing and setting practice, and small groups in a circle can also be effective for passing and setting. For serving practice, several players can line up along both baselines of a court and serve several balls at a time. Servers can practice anywhere along the baseline. Beginning servers should always move closer to the net.

Setting and spiking drills can be arranged with a setter in the center forward position and a line of spikers in either the on-hand or off-hand position. The spiker tosses the ball to the setter and awaits a setup for a spike. Several ball chasers on the other side of the net can be useful. Net recovery shots can be practiced on a properly stretched net. One partner tosses the ball into the net, and the other player tries to recover the ball with a forearm pass.

Competitive situations are fun for drill work (e.g., sets in a row, passes with a partner, serves to a target area, or spikes to an area). These competitive challenges can be individual, with partners, or among small groups. The objectives included here offer many challenges that can be modified for students of different ability levels.

Lead-Up and Modified Games

Leader Ball

Organize students into several teams. The leader of each team stands about 5 yards away from teammates. The teammates can be in single file or standing side by side facing the leader. The leader uses a forearm pass or set and hits the ball to the first person in line. That person hits the ball back to the leader and goes quickly to the end of the line. The object is to hit the ball to all teammates quicker than the other teams.

Zigzag Relay

Half of the players on one team stand side by side about 2 to 3 yards apart and face the other half of their team. The ball is started at one end and passed or set, back and forth, down the line across a distance of 5 yards. The object is to control the ball and move it down the line quickly. The winning team is the fastest in getting the ball up and down the line to all team members. More than one ball can be added for variety.

Keep It Afloat

A group must keep the ball up in the air or against a wall for a specified amount of time. The group can be in a circle or arranged single file for the wall drill. Passes, sets, or both can be used.

Beach Ball or Nerf Ball Volleyball

Regulation rules are followed except that the server must move up close to the net. A beach ball or Nerf ball is easier to control than a regular volleyball.

One-Bounce Volleyball

Regular rules are followed except that the ball can bounce one time on each side. The bounce can occur after the serve, pass, or set. A variation of this game is to allow two or three bounces.

Volley Tennis

The game can be played on a tennis court or on a volleyball court. The net is put on the ground, as in tennis, and the ball is put in play with a serve. It may bounce once or can be passed directly to a teammate. The ball should be hit three times before going over the net. Spiking is common because of the low net.

Sitting or Kneeling Volleyball

Sitting or kneeling volleyball is a good indoor game to play on a mat or in the gym. The net is lowered according to the general size and ability level of the players. An overhead pass starts the game. Court size and number of players can vary.

Serve and Catch

Serve and catch is started with a ball on each side of the net. Several balls are served at the same time, and all balls must be caught on the other side. Once the balls are caught, they can be served from the opposing serving area. The object is to catch the ball and quickly serve so that your opponent cannot catch the ball. A scorer from each side is necessary.

Rotation Under the Net

The game, played with two, three, or four people on a team, is started with one team on each side of the net and with two or three other teams waiting in line to enter the game. The teacher begins the game by tossing the ball up on either side of the net. The ball must be hit three times, with the third hit going over the net. No spiking is allowed. The winning team rotates under the net, a new team rotates into its place, and the losing team rotates off the court and becomes the last team in line. The teacher throws the ball up in the air quickly as the teams are rotating. All teams must move quickly to the proper court. The game is fast moving and involves passing, setting, and court coverage. It is a good game for high school students who have developed passing and setting skills.

Three-Hit Volleyball

Three-hit volleyball is similar to regular volleyball, but the ball must be hit three times on a side with the third hit going over the net.

Minivolleyball

This is a modified game for students ages 9 to 12. The net is 6 feet, 10 inches, and the court is 15 by 40 feet. Three students are on a team, with two frontline players and one backline player. The rules are similar to regulation volleyball.

Blind-Man Volleyball

A cover is put over the net so that it is impossible to see what is happening on the other side. Regulation volleyball rules are followed. Teams must be ready because they never know when the ball is coming over the net. A scorer is necessary for both sides of the net.

Regulation Volleyball—Serves Modified

Regulation rules are followed, but the server can have two attempts, or the service distance is shortened.

Suggested Performance Objectives

Performance objectives have been used successfully with volleyball units at both the middle and high school levels. The following list can help structure a learning environment for volleyball activities. These can be modified according to the abilities of the students and the facilities available.

Core Objectives

Forearm Pass

1. Bump 12 consecutive forearm passes against the wall at a height of at least 10 feet.

2. Bump 12 consecutive forearm passes into the air at a height of at least 10 feet.

3. Bump 10 consecutive forearm passes over the net with the instructor or a classmate.

Overhead Set Pass

4. Hit 15 consecutive set passes against the wall at a height of at least 10 feet.

5. Hit 15 consecutive set passes into the air at a height of at least 10 feet.

6. Hit 12 consecutive set passes over the net with the instructor or a classmate.

Serves

7. Hit three consecutive underhand serves into the right half of the court.

8. Hit three of four underhand serves into the left half of the court.

9. Hit three consecutive overhand serves inbounds.

Attendance and Participation

10. Be dressed and ready to participate at 8:00 A.M.

11. Participate in 15 games.

12. Score 90 percent or better on a rules, strategies, and techniques test.

Optional Objectives

1. Standing 2 feet from the backline, bump three of five forearm passes into an 8-foot circle surrounding the setter's position. The height must be at least 10 feet. The ball will be thrown by the instructor or a classmate.

2. Bump three of five forearm passes over the net at a height of at least 12 feet that land inbounds and not more than 8 feet from the backline.

3. Standing in the setter's position (center forward), hit three consecutive overhead sets at least 10 feet high that land in a 5-foot circle where the spiker would be located. The ball will be thrown by the instructor or a classmate.

4. Hit three of five overhead passes over the net at least 12 feet high that land inbounds and not more than 8 feet from the backline.

5. Standing in the setter's position (center forward), hit three of five back sets at least 10 feet high that land in a 5-foot circle where the spiker would be located. The ball will be thrown by the instructor or a classmate.

6. Volley 12 consecutive times over the net with the instructor or a classmate by alternating forearm passes and overhead passes.

7. Alternate forearm passes and overhead passes in the air at a height of 10 feet or more, 12 consecutive times.

8. Spike three of four sets inbounds from an on-hand position—three-step approach, jump, extend arm, hand contact.

9. Spike three of five sets inbounds from an off-hand position.

10. Recover three consecutive balls from the net. Recoveries must be playable—that is, 8 feet high in the playing area.

11. Hit three consecutive overhand serves into the right half of the court.

12. Hit three of four overhand serves into the left half of the court.

13. Hit three of five overhand serves under a rope 15 feet high that land in the back half of the court.

14. Officiate at least three games, using proper calls and signals.

15. Coach a team for the class tournament, including planning strategy, making substitutions, and scheduling.

16. Devise and carry out a research project that deals with volleyball. Check with the instructor for ideas.

REFERENCES AND SUGGESTED READINGS

Lesson Plans

Casten, C. (2009). *Lesson plans for dynamic physical education for secondary school students* (6th ed.). San Francisco: Benjamin Cummings.

Archery

Fronske, H. (2008). *Teaching cues for sport skills* (4th ed.). San Francisco: Benjamin Cummings.

Haywood, K. M. (2002). Archery. In N. Dougherty (Ed.), *Physical activity and sport for the secondary school student* (5th ed.). Reston, VA: NASPE and American Association for Health, Physical Education, Recreation, and Dance (AAHPERD).

Haywood, K. M., & Lewis, C. S. (2006). *Archery: Steps to success* (3rd ed.). Champaign, IL: Human Kinetics Publishers.

Kentucky Department of Education. (2002). *Archery standards-based unit of study, Grades 6–8.* Frankfort, Kentucky: Author.

McCracken, B. (2001). *It's not just gym anymore: Teaching secondary students how to be active for life.* Champaign, IL: Human Kinetics Publishers.

McKinney, W. C., & McKinney, M. W. (1994). *Archery* (7th ed.). Dubuque, IA: Brown & Benchmark.

Mood, D. P., Musker, F. F., & Rink, J. E. (2007). *Sports and recreational activities* (14th ed.). Boston: McGraw-Hill.

Schmottlach, N., & McManama, J. (2006). *The physical education handbook* (11th ed.). San Francisco: Benjamin Cummings.

Badminton

Bloss, M. V. (2001). *Badminton.* Boston: McGraw-Hill.

Fronske, H. (2008). *Teaching cues for sport skills* (4th ed.). San Francisco: Benjamin Cummings.

Mood, D. P., Musker, F. F., & Rink, J. E. (2007). *Sports and recreational activities* (14th ed.). Boston: McGraw-Hill.

Schmottlach, N., & McManama, J. (2006). *The physical education handbook* (11th ed.). San Francisco: Benjamin Cummings.

Gymnastics

Feigley, D. A. (2002). Tumbling. In N. Dougherty (Ed.), *Physical activity and sport for the secondary school student* (5th ed.) Reston, VA: NASPE and AAHPERD.

Fronske, H. (2008). *Teaching cues for sport skills* (4th ed.). San Francisco: Benjamin Cummings.

Mood, D. P., Musker, F. F., & Rink, J. E. (2007). *Sports and recreational activities* (14th ed.). Boston: McGraw-Hill.

Schmottlach, N., & McManama, J. (2006). *The physical education handbook* (11th ed.). San Francisco: Benjamin Cummings.

Flag Football

Domitrovitz, M. (2002). Flag football. In N. Dougherty (Ed.), *Physical activity and sport for the secondary school student* (5th ed.). Reston, VA: NASPE and AAHPERD.

Fronske, H. (2008). *Teaching cues for sport skills* (4th ed.). San Francisco: Benjamin Cummings.

Mood, D. P., Musker, F. F., & Rink, J. E. (2007). *Sports and recreational activities* (14th ed.). Boston: McGraw-Hill.

Schmottlach, N., & McManama, J. (2006). *The physical education handbook* (11th ed.). San Francisco: Benjamin Cummings.

Field Hockey

Fronske, H. (2008). *Teaching cues for sport skills* (4th ed.). San Francisco: Benjamin Cummings.

Gray, G. R. (2002). Floor hockey. In N. Dougherty (Ed.), *Physical activity and sport for the secondary school student* (5th ed.). Reston, VA: NASPE and AAHPERD.

Mood, D. P., Musker, F. F., & Rink, J. E. (2007). *Sports and recreational activities* (14th ed.). Boston: McGraw-Hill.

Schmottlach, N., & McManama, J. (2006). *The physical education handbook* (11th ed.). San Francisco: Benjamin Cummings.

Whitney, M. G. (Ed.). *Eagle.* Colorado Springs, CO: United States Field Hockey Association (USFHA).

Basketball

Bryant, J. (2002). Basketball. In N. Dougherty (Ed.), *Physical activity and sport for the secondary school student* (5th ed.). Reston, VA: NASPE and AAHPERD.

Fronske, H. (2008). *Teaching Cues for Sport Skills* (4th ed.). San Francisco: Benjamin Cummings.

Mood, D. P., Musker, F. F., & Rink, J. E. (2007). *Sports and recreational activities* (14th ed.). Boston: McGraw-Hill.

Schmottlach, N., & McManama, J. (2006). *The physical education handbook* (11th ed.). San Francisco: Benjamin Cummings.

Summitt, P. H., & Jennings, D. (1991). *Basketball: Fundamentals and team play.* Dubuque, IA: Brown & Benchmark.

Wissel, H. (2004). *Basketball: Steps to success* (2nd ed.). Champaign, IL: Human Kinetics Publishers.

National Association for Girls and Women in Sport. (1982). *Tennis-badminton-squash guide.* Reston, VA: AAHPERD.

Paup, D. C. (2002). Badminton. In N. Dougherty (Ed.), *Physical activity and sport for the secondary school student* (5th ed.). Reston, VA: NASPE and AAHPERD.

Schmottlach, N., & McManama, J. (2006) *The physical education handbook* (11th ed.). San Francisco: Benjamin Cummings.

Lacrosse

Fronske, H. (2008). *Teaching cues for sport skills* (4th ed.). San Francisco: Benjamin Cummings.

Hutcherson, K. (2002). Lacrosse. In N. Dougherty (Ed.), *Physical activity and sport for the secondary school student* (5th ed.). Reston, VA: NASPE and AAHPERD.

Mood, D. P., Musker, F. F., & Rink, J. E. (2007). *Sports and recreational activities* (14th ed.). Boston: McGraw-Hill.

Soccer

Fronske, H. (2008). *Teaching cues for sport skills* (4th ed.). San Francisco: Benjamin Cummings.

Luxbacher, J. (2005). *Teaching soccer: Steps to success* (3rd ed.). Champaign, IL: Human Kinetics Publishers.

Mood, D. P., Musker, F. F., & Rink, J. E. (2007). *Sports and recreational activities* (14th ed.). Boston: McGraw-Hill.

Schmottlach, N., & McManama, J. (2006). *The physical education handbook* (11th ed.). San Francisco: Benjamin Cummings.

Weinberg, W. (2002). Soccer. In N. Dougherty (Ed.), *Physical activity and sport for the secondary school student* (5th ed.). Reston, VA: NASPE and AAHPERD.

Softball

Fronske, H. (2008). *Teaching cues for sport skills* (4th ed.). San Francisco: Benjamin Cummings.

Mood, D. P., Musker, F. F., & Rink, J. E. (2007). *Sports and recreational activities* (14th ed.). Boston: McGraw-Hill.

Potter, D. L. (2007). *Softball: Steps to success* (3rd ed.). Champaign, IL: Human Kinetics Publishers.

Ransdall, L. B., & Taylor, A. (2002). Softball. In N. Dougherty (Ed.), *Physical activity and sport for the secondary school student* (5th ed.). Reston, VA: NASPE and AAHPERD.

Schmottlach, N., & McManama, J. (2006). *The physical education handbook* (11th ed.). San Francisco: Benjamin Cummings.

Team Handball

Dwight, M. P., & Cavanaugh, M. (2002). Team handball. In N. Dougherty (Ed.), *Physical activity and sport for the secondary school student* (5th ed.). Reston, VA: NASPE and AAHPERD.

Fronske, H. (2008). *Teaching cues for sport skills* (4th ed.). San Francisco: Benjamin Cummings.

Mood, D. P., Musker, F. F., & Rink, J. E. (2007). *Sports and recreational activities* (14th ed.). Boston: McGraw-Hill.

Schmottlach, N., & McManama, J. (2006). *The physical education handbook* (11th ed.). San Francisco: Benjamin Cummings.

Track and Field

Bowerman, W. (1972). *Coaching track and field.* Boston, MA: Houghton Mifflin Co.

Doherty, J. (1976). *Track and field omnibook* (3rd ed.). Los Altos, CA: Track and Field News Press.

Fronske, H. (2008). *Teaching cues for sport skills* (4th ed.). San Francisco: Benjamin Cummings.

Knop, N. (2002). Track and field. In N. Dougherty (Ed.), *Physical activity and sport for the secondary school student* (5th ed.). Reston, VA: NASPE and AAHPERD.

National Federation of High School Associations. (2007). *Officiating track and field and cross country methods.* Champaign, IL: Human Kinetics Publishers.

Schmottlach, N., & McManama, J. (2006). *The physical education handbook* (11th ed.). San Francisco: Benjamin Cummings.

Volleyball

American Sport Education Program. (2007). *Coaching youth volleyball* (4th ed.). Champaign, IL: Human Kinetics Publishers.

Fronske, H. (2008). *Teaching cues for sport skills* (4th ed.). San Francisco: Benjamin Cummings.

Mood, D. P., Musker, F. F., & Rink, J. E. (2007). *Sports and recreational activities* (14th ed.). Boston: McGraw-Hill.

Schmottlach, N., & McManama, J. (2006). *The physical education handbook* (11th ed.). San Francisco: Benjamin Cummings.

Viera, B. L. (2002). Volleyball. In N. Dougherty (Ed.), *Physical activity and sport for the secondary school student* (5th ed.). Reston, VA: NASPE and AAHPERD.

WEB SITES

Archery
www.archery.org
www.usarchery.org

Badminton
www.usabadminton.org
www.worldbadminton.net

Basketball
www.basketballworldinc.com
www.yboa.org

Field Hockey
www.planetfieldhockey.com
www.usfieldhockey.com

Flag Football
www.goflagfootball.com
www.usffa.org

Lacrosse
www.lacrosse.org
www.lax.com

Softball
www.softball.mb.ca
www.usasoftball.org

Soccer
www.soccer.org
www.ussoccer.org

Team Handball
www.hickoksports.com
www.usateamhandball.org

Track and Field
www.hersheytrackandfield.com
www.usatf.org

Volleyball
www.avca.org
www.usavolleyball.org

NATIONAL STANDARDS FOR PHYSICAL EDUCATION*

STANDARD 1 Demonstrates competency in motor skills and movement patterns needed to perform a variety of physical activities.

STANDARD 2 Demonstrates understanding of movement concepts, principles, strategies, and tactics as they apply to the learning and performance of physical activities.

STANDARD 3 Participates regularly in physical activity.

STANDARD 4 Achieves and maintains a health-enhancing level of physical fitness.

STANDARD 5 Exhibits responsible personal and social behavior that respects self and others in physical activity settings.

STANDARD 6 Values physical activity for health, enjoyment, challenge, self-expression, and/or social interaction.

ESSENTIAL COMPONENTS OF A QUALITY PROGRAM

COMPONENT 1 A quality physical education program is organized around content standards that offer direction and continuity to instruction and evaluation.

COMPONENT 2 A quality program is student centered and based on the developmental urges, characteristics, and interests of students.

COMPONENT 3 Quality physical education makes physical activity and motor-skill development the core of the program.

COMPONENT 4 Physical education programs teach management skills and self-discipline.

COMPONENT 5 Quality programs emphasize inclusion of all students.

COMPONENT 6 In a quality physical education setting, instruction focuses on the process of learning skills rather than the product or outcome of the skill performance.

COMPONENT 7 A quality physical education program teaches lifetime activities that students can use to promote their health and personal wellness.

COMPONENT 8 Quality physical education teaches cooperative and responsibility skills and helps students develop sensitivity to diversity and gender issues.

*Reprinted from Moving Into the Future: National Standards for Physical Education, 2nd ed. (2004), with permission from the National Association for Sport and Physical Education (NASPE), 1900 Association Dr., Reston, VA 20191–1599.

20

Lifestyle Activities

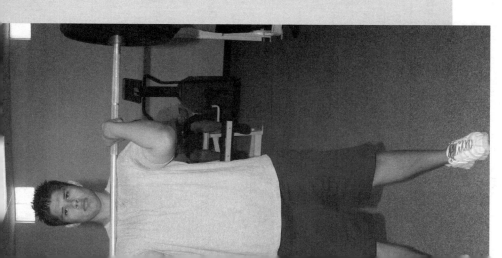

These lifestyle activities can easily be incorporated into students' lives, both now and in the future. Physical educators should try especially hard to offer as many of these activities as possible. These activities will become more important to students as they grow older and as they try to keep activity in their lifestyle.

BOWLING

The game of bowling today is a form of kingpins, the first bowling game to use finger holes in the ball. The sport has changed from a simple game played outdoors to a complex mechanized game played in large modern facilities. Bowling has become one of our most widely enjoyed recreational activities. Any family member may participate because the game is suitable for all ages and both sexes. Bowling can be played in any season, and facilities are usually available at most times of the day. Leagues are popular, and many businesses sponsor employee leagues. Schools have intramural leagues, and many bowling establishments organize leagues for children. These leagues are usually sanctioned by the proper national organization.

The play in bowling consists of rolling balls down a wooden alley with the object of knocking over 10 wooden pins positioned at the far end of the alley. The bowler stands any distance behind the foul line and takes three, four, or five steps before releasing the ball down the alley. If the player touches the alley beyond the foul line, a foul is called, and the ball counts as one ball bowled. No score is made on a foul, and the pins knocked down are immediately replaced. In bowling and duckpins, the pins knocked down after the first ball rolled are cleared away before the next ball is rolled. In candlepins, knocked-down pins are not cleared away. Each bowler has 10 frames in which to knock down as many pins as possible. If a bowler knocks down all of the pins in 10 frames of bowling, a perfect score of 300 is attained.

Sequence of Skills
Picking Up the Ball

If in an alley area, face the direction of the returning balls. Place the hands on opposite sides of the ball and lift the ball to a comfortable position in front of the body before placing the fingers and thumb in the holes. Avoid placing the thumb and fingers in the holes to pick up the ball as this places strain on the bowling hand.

Gripping the Ball

Holding the ball in the left hand (if right-handed), place the two middle fingers in the holes first and then slip the thumb in the thumbhole. Do not squeeze the ball with the fingertips, but maintain contact by slightly pressing the palm side of the fingers and thumb toward the palm area of the ball. The little finger and index finger are relaxed and flat on the ball.

Developing a Stance

The stance is the stationary position that the bowler holds before approaching the foul line. The development of a stance, which varies among bowlers, is essential for consistency in bowling. To locate the starting position, stand with the back to the foul line, walk four-and-a-half steps, stop, turn, and face the pins. The number of steps will vary with the three-, four-, or five-step approach. Standing erect, place the feet parallel to each other, or the left foot may be slightly in front of the right foot. The feet should be about 1½ inches apart. The weight is on the left foot, and the knees are slightly bent. The head is up, and the shoulders are level.

The ball is held at waist level and slightly to the right. The arm is straight from the shoulder to the wrist. The ball will be pushed out during the first step and will swing down directly below the shoulder. The wrist is kept straight and stiff during the pendulum swing. The elbow moves back alongside the body and should not be braced on the hip. The ball is supported by the nonbowling hand. The shoulders, hips, and feet are square with the pins when the stance is established.

After learning the basic stance, the bowler can develop a personal style. Some leading bowlers hold the ball approximately level with the chin and a few inches from the body. Proficient bowlers usually hold the ball at waist level and a few inches away from the body. The upper torso leans slightly forward. Taller bowlers sometimes use a half crouch and a shorter backswing.

Aiming

The method of aim should be decided after the footwork, timing, and method of rolling the ball have been established. The bowler should then experiment to find the preferable method of aim. Spot bowling (described as follows) is recommended.

1. **Pin bowling.** The bowler looks at the pins and draws an imaginary line between the point of delivery and the point on the pins at which the ball will be aimed. This line will be the route of the ball. The usual point to hit is the 1–3 pocket.

2. **Spot bowling.** The bowler draws an imaginary line from the point of delivery to some spot down the lane, usually at the division boards where the maple meets pine. Most lanes have triangular markings for spot bowlers.

Approaching and Making the Delivery

One-Step Delivery. The one-step delivery should be learned before the three-, four-, or five-step delivery. The stance for the one-step delivery differs from the general stance discussed previously. The foot opposite the bowling arm is behind. Extend the bowling hand, and after extension, drop the hand slowly to the side and simultaneously lean forward, bending the knees. Keep the arm relaxed and the wrist straight. Swing the arm forward to eye level, back to waist level, and forward again to eye level. The stance for the one-step delivery is assumed. The hands are at waist height as if gripping the ball. Push the arms forward, release the left hand, and complete the pendulum swing.

Repeat the push away and the pendulum swing, but as the arm swings forward (at the completion of the swing), slide ahead on the foot opposite the bowling arm. Keep the shoulders straight and the body facing straight ahead. Practice the simultaneous movement of arm and foot. No ball is necessary when first learning the approach and delivery. When the timing is learned, then add the ball.

Four-Step Delivery. The four-step delivery is the most popular. The stance is with the opposite foot forward, as presented earlier. Starting with the right foot, take four brisk walking strides forward. Repeat the four-step walk, making the fourth step a slide. At the completion of the slide, the full body weight should be on the sliding foot, knee bent, and shoulders parallel to the foul line. The forward foot should be pointed toward the pins.

To coordinate the delivery, the bowler should assume the stance, start the four-step walk, and push the ball out, down, back, and forward so that the arm movements coordinate with the steps (one, two, three, slide). As the foot slides, the ball comes forward and is released. At the release, the thumb is out, and the fingers and wrist are turning and lifting the ball. The right leg swings forward for balance, and the right arm, which was straight throughout the backswing, bends at the elbow for the follow-through. The body then straightens to get more lift on the ball.

Different types of balls can be thrown, depending on how the ball is released.

1. **Straight ball.** The wrist and forearm are kept straight throughout the entire delivery. The thumb

is on top of the ball, at a 12-o'clock position, and the index finger is at 2 o'clock.

2. *Hook ball.* The ball is held throughout the approach, delivery, and release, with the thumb at 10 o'clock and the index finger at 12 o'clock. If the ball hooks too much, move the thumb toward the 12-o'clock position.

Ideas for Effective Instruction

Gymnasium Bowling Sets

Gymnasium bowling sets are available through many equipment dealers. They usually contain 10 plastic pins, a triangular sheet for pin setup, score sheets, and a hard plastic ball. Sizes of the finger holes will vary and so may the weight of the ball.

Score Sheets

Score sheets can be drawn and duplicated. Sheets are included in gym sets, or an instructor can check with a local establishment about purchase or a possible donation.

General Rules and Scoring

1. A game consists of 10 frames. Each bowler is allowed two deliveries in each frame, with the exception of the 10th frame, in which three are allowed if a spare or strike is scored.

2. The score is an accumulated total of pins knocked down plus bonus points for spares and strikes.

3. If all 10 pins are knocked down on the first ball rolled, it is a strike. The scorer counts 10 plus the total of the next two balls rolled.

4. If all pins are knocked down with two balls rolled, it is a spare. The scorer counts 10 plus the number of pins knocked down on the next ball rolled.

5. If no pins are knocked down when a ball is rolled, the bowler is charged with an error. This includes gutter balls.

6. If pins left after the first ball constitute a split, a circle is made on the score sheet around the number of pins knocked down.

7. A foul results if the bowler steps across the foul line.

Etiquette

1. Take your turn promptly.

2. The bowler to the right has the right-of-way. Wait until the bowler on the right is finished before assuming a stance.

3. Continue your approach.

4. Step back off the approach after delivery.

5. Use your ball only, and use the same ball throughout the game.

6. Do not talk to a player who is on the approach.

7. Respect all equipment and the bowling establishment.

8. While competition is encouraged, be gracious in any case.

9. Return all equipment to its proper place.

Organization and Skill Work

Teach skills in sequence. Once the basic grip and stance have been taught (group situation), stations can be used for skill practice. Depending on the unit structure, students can work at stations on skills to be checked off, or they may be involved in lead-up games, minitournaments (using gym sets), or practice at a bowling facility. Because bowling skills are perfected through constant practice, the unit should be designed for maximum activity.

If space is available, mock lanes can be made. Using mock lanes can enhance the number of students involved in activity while using a smaller space. Students are able to practice approaching, releasing, and spotting without pins. They can work in pairs, taking turns practicing and rolling back the ball. Team games with the mock lanes and gymnasium bowling sets can be enjoyable. Hand out score sheets and have students record their scores. Scorers sign their names, and score sheets are checked for correct scoring procedure. Games with mock lanes and gymnasium sets can be used as a lead-up to bowling at a nearby facility.

Lead-Up Games and Learning Activities

Red Pin

Use regulation alleys or lanes set up on the gym floor. One pin is painted red (tape may be substituted). The bowler rolls one ball in each frame. The bowler scores only if the red pin is upset. The pinsetter makes no attempt to specifically place the red pin. It will occur in random placement. Because only one ball is rolled, no spares are scored. Strikes are possible and should be scored as in regulation bowling. This activity can be used for team or individual competition.

Scotch Bowling

This activity can be played on regulation lanes or in a gym with marked lanes. Students choose a partner and decide who will roll the first ball. Partners then alternate throughout the game, which is scored like regulation bowling.

Shuffle-Bowl

The game is played on a shuffleboard court, using shuffleboard cues, discs, and bowling pins or Indian clubs. The discs are slid at the pins. Play and scoring are carried out as in regulation bowling.

Skittles

Use an open area, wooden discs, and 10 small pins or Indian clubs. Slide or pitch the discs at the pins from a specified distance. Use regulation scoring.

Three Pins

Regulation equipment or the gymnasium with marked lanes can be used for play. The bowler attempts to knock down the 1–2–3 combination by hitting the 1–3 pocket (1–2, if left-handed). One ball is allowed for each turn. Players start with 20 points. Three pins down subtracts 3 points, two down subtracts 2 points, and one pin down subtracts 1 point. The first player to reach 0 points is the winner.

Soccer Bowling

Any open area, indoors or outdoors, is suitable for play. Soccer balls and wooden pins are used, and the game is scored like regulation bowling.

Basket Bowling

Play in an alley marked on the gym floor. Allow a 15-foot approach. Use two indoor softballs and a metal wastebasket propped up on its side with two bricks or similar objects facing the foul line. Five to 10 players and one retriever make up a team. Each player attempts to roll two balls into the wastebasket. Rotate and trade places with the retriever. One point is scored for each basket made, and the high scorer wins. If teams play against one another, use a time limit. Each player is allowed five turns. If the bowler steps over the foul line, 1 point is subtracted. If the ball is bounced on the alley, 1 point is subtracted. An official scorekeeper and judge are necessary.

Objectives, Tests, and Rating Form

Objectives

1. Bowl six games at any lane. Keep score and turn in the score sheet to the instructor. On a separate sheet, state the two basic rules for scoring. List and explain the symbols used in scoring.

2. Research and write a paper on the history of bowling using at least four sources. The paper should be typed and double-spaced with a bibliography.

3. Learn the correct way to pick up and hold the ball. Be able to demonstrate the hand positions, footwork, and release. Also be able to demonstrate the hand position that creates a hook, a straight ball, and a backup ball. Performance is evaluated on the basis of an oral explanation to the instructor.

4. Watch at least one tournament, either live or on television, for an hour, or observe an hour of league bowling. Report in writing about how this type of bowling differs from open bowling.

5. Obtain a rule book from the Women's International Bowling Congress (WIBC) and find out what special prizes are awarded in sanctioned leagues. Illustrate and explain the patches and award procedures.

6. Visit a lane and ask the operator for an inspection of an automatic pinsetter in operation. Find out how to operate the ball clearer, how to turn on the teleprompter, and how to reset the pins. Discover where the trouble bell and the foul-line indicator are located and how the foul line operates. When ready, take a short quiz from the instructor on this information.

7. Make a poster diagramming a lane. Enlarge and make offset drawings of the approach area and the pin-fall area. Write a short paper telling how one might use this information when bowling.

8. Compile a list of 15 bowling terms and a definition of each.

9. Take a written examination on bowling, covering etiquette, scoring, handicaps, averages, techniques, terminology, history, and rules.

10. Demonstrate the proper stance, the four-step delivery, and the position of the hands on each step.

11. Write a paper describing the following: moonlight bowling, headpin tournament, and 3–6–9 tournament.

Name _____

Bowler													

Approach

Push away on first step

Push away: out and down—elbow straight

Backswing: straight—in line with boards

Backswing: to shoulder level

Steps: smooth, gliding, even rhythm

Steps: length and speed increase

Slide on left foot

Release

Shoulders: parallel to foul line

Shoulders: level

Upper body: inclined forward

Left foot: in line with boards

Weight: balanced on left foot

Thumb: in 12-o'clock position

Ball: first strikes alley 1.5 ft in front of left foot

Follow-through: straight and to shoulder height

Aim

Approach: straight, in line with boards

Release: proper dot or dots at foul line

Route: crosses proper dart

Location where ball strikes pins? (e.g., 1–3, 1, 3, 1–2)

Place a (✓) in proper square if the item is peformed correctly

Place a (—) if it is not correct.

FIGURE 20.1 Bowling rating form

12. Practice spare bowling of a single pin until four out of 10 shots are made. (Have the proprietor take all but one pin out of the rack, and shoot at any set that the automatic pinspotter provides.) When ready, test yourself by trying 10 consecutive shots. Record the score as either a miss or a spare. Use any score sheet provided by the alley, and turn it in for credit.

Rating Form

A rating form (see Figure 20.1) is useful for partner work and when facilities are limited. The form enables students who are not participating actively to be cognitively involved. The instructor should spend some time helping students learn to use the form correctly.

FRISBEE

Playing with a Frisbee is an exciting lifetime physical activity that can offer success and challenge at all ability levels. It can be played on almost any size field or gymnasium area and can be used with individuals, small groups, or teams. The International Frisbee Disc

Association, which numbers more than 100,000 members, has statistics showing that more Frisbee discs are sold yearly in the United States than footballs and basketballs combined. An annual world championship held in the Rose Bowl draws large crowds to watch competitors focus on distance, accuracy, freestyle moves, and other games.

A number of factors make Frisbee disc sports an attractive new activity for physical education. A Frisbee costs only $4 to $8, depending on the type and quality of the disc. Frisbee provides excellent skills practice in throwing, catching, and eye-hand coordination, as well as offering many interesting individual challenges and team activities. The low injury risks and the attraction to students are positive factors. The sport can be effective in a coeducational environment and offers flexibility in terms of participants' ages and abilities and in terms of program space and time. Both team and individual skills can be learned with the Frisbee and used for a lifetime of enjoyment.

Sequence of Skills

Throws

Backhand Throw. The thumb is on the top of the disc, and the remaining fingers are under the rim. The index finger can also be placed on the outside lip of the disc. Coil the wrist and arm across the chest. Step forward and release the disc (keeping it level) with a snap of the wrist.

Backhand (Across-the-Chest) Curves. Use the same technique as the straight backhand but release the disc at an angle, with the lower side being the desired direction. Throw curves both left and right by tilting the disc.

Underhand or Bowling Throw. Use a backhand grip or put the index finger on the lip of the disc. Step with the opposite foot, bring the disc underhand past the body, and release it level, about waist height, with a wrist snap.

Thumber Throw. Hook the thumb under the disc and put the four fingers on top. Bring the disc down from the ear in a sidearm motion and release it when the disc is even with the body. Avoid a follow-through with the disc.

Sidearm Throw. Put the index and middle finger under the disc and the thumb on top. The two fingers can be together on the lip, or one can be on the lip and one in the middle of the disc. Release the disc in a motion similar to the thumber.

Overhand Wrist Flip. Grip the disc with the fingers on top and the thumb under the lip. Cock the wrist backward and start the throw behind the back at shoulder level. Flip the wrist forward to a point in line with the body.

Catches

Sandwich Catch. Catch the disc with one hand on top and the other on the bottom with the disc in the middle. Alternate hands from top to bottom on different occasions.

C-Catch. Make a C with the thumb and fingers. Watch the disc into the C and close the fingers on the disc. Throws below the waist should have the thumb up, and those above the waist should have thumb down.

Additional Skills

- *Skip-throwz off the ground.* Tip the forward edge down and throw the disc so it skips off the ground to a partner.
- *Tipping.* Use the finger, knee, head, toe, heel, or elbow. Watch the disc make contact with the various body parts and tip the disc in the air.
- *Catches.* Catch the disc with the finger, behind the back and head, between the legs, and with one hand.
- *Air brushing.* Hold the disc on one finger while striking the disc on its side to give it rotation.

Ideas for Effective Instruction

Frisbee discs are available from more than 30 different companies. Avoid the cheapest discs because they will not fly without turning over. Wham-O Manufacturing Company in San Gabriel, California, is the oldest and largest manufacturer of flying discs. They have an excellent World Class Series ranging from 97 to 165 grams. These discs are reasonably priced for secondary schools. Many companies use discs for advertising, and it is often possible to acquire promotional discs at a discount.

Instruction can begin by having partners, positioned about 5 yards apart, work on the basic backhand throw and sandwich catch. As students improve, have them move farther apart and use the backhand curves with the C-catch and the one-handed catch. Be sure to keep beginning students spread out and away from buildings, fences, and other obstacles, considering the disc is difficult to control. Next, the underhand throw, thumber, and sidearm can be introduced with several fancy catches.

After students have the basic idea, create four stations that focus on accuracy, distance, accuracy and distance combined, and loft time. Many station variations can be designed to challenge students. Check the following section on activities for specific ideas. Frisbee golf is a particularly good activity for beginners with few developed skills.

Lead-Up Games and Learning Activities

Throw for Distance

Set up five or six cones at varying distances and let students experiment with different throws for distance.

Throw for Distance and Accuracy

Mark a line with varying distances and have students throw as far as possible on the line. Subtract the distance of the Frisbee landing point away from the line from the total throw distance. Students should develop both distance and accuracy.

Throw for Accuracy

Make a large circular target, about 9 or 10 feet in diameter, on the ground with rope or jump ropes. Set cones at 10-, 15-, 20-, and 25-yard distances. Let students have five attempts at each distance, and record the number of accurate throws. Another variation is to hang a hula hoop from a tree or goalpost and have students throw through the hoop. Award one point for hitting the hoop and two points for going through the hoop.

Time Aloft

Record the time from release of the disc until it hits the ground.

Throw and Catch with Self

The object of this activity is to throw the disc as forward as possible and then to run and catch the Frisbee. A starting line is designated at which the disc must be released, and distance is measured from that line. The disc must be caught.

Follow the Leader

One player makes a specific throw, and the second player must try to make the same throw. The first player must match the catch of the second player.

Twenty-One

Players stand 10 yards apart and throw the disc back and forth. The throws must be accurate and catchable. One point is awarded for a two-handed catch and two points for a one-handed catch. A player must get 21 points and win by two points.

Frisbee Tennis

This is the same game as regular tennis, but the player must catch the Frisbee and throw from that spot. The serve starts to the right of the center mark and must go to the opposite backcourt, not into the service box.

Ultimate

Ultimate is a team game with seven or more on a side. The object is to move the Frisbee down the field by passing and to score by passing across the goal line to a teammate. The person with the disc can only pivot and pass to a teammate. If the Frisbee is grounded without being caught or intercepted, or if it goes out-of-bounds, the defending team gains possession.

Power Frisbee

Five to seven players on a team stand behind a line 15 yards from the opponents' line. The goal line is 10 yards wide. The object is to throw so hard that the opponents cannot make a one-handed catch. The Frisbee can be tipped by several people as long as a one-handed catch is used. The receiving team gets a point if the throw is too high, too wide, or too low. The height is determined by having team members stretch their arms straight up, usually 7 to 8 feet high. The first team to score 21 points wins. Use extra caution with beginners and younger students. Move the goals back a bit and match ability levels.

Frisbee Soccer

The game is played like soccer, but the disc is thrown to teammates and at the goal. If the disc is dropped, the defenders play offense. Rules can be modified to include two goalies and limitations on the number of steps possible.

Frisbee Softball

The game is similar to regular softball. The pitcher throws the disc to the batter, who must catch the disc and throw it into play past the pitcher. If the batter drops the pitch, it is a strike. No bunting or stealing is allowed. The other rules of softball apply.

FIGURE 20.2 Around Nine game

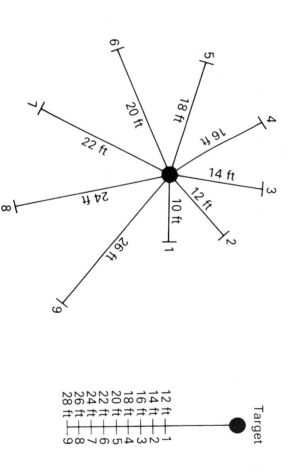

Frisbee Shuffleboard

Two players compete against two players. The game is played on a basketball court, and the goal is to score by throwing the Frisbee into the opponent's key. Throwers stand outside of the out-of-bounds line under the basket. The key is divided into two areas: the circular area around the free-throw line is worth two points, and the larger lane area is worth one point. Different-colored Frisbees are used to make scoring easier.

Frisbee Golf

Frisbee or disc golf is a favorite game of many students. Boundary cones with numbers can be used for tees, and holes can be boxes, hula hoops, trees, tires, garbage cans, or any other available equipment on the school grounds. Put the course together on a map for students and start them at different holes to decrease the time spent waiting to tee off. Regulation golf rules apply. The students can jog between throws for increased activity.

General Guidelines. Disc golf is played like regular golf. One stroke is counted each time the disc is thrown and when a penalty is incurred. The object is to acquire the lowest score.

T-Throws. T-throws must be completed within or behind the designated tee area.

Lie. The lie is the spot on or directly underneath the spot where the previous throw landed.

Throwing Order. The player whose disc is the farthest from the hole throws first. The player with the least number of throws on the previous hole tees off first.

Fairway Throws. Fairway throws must be made from behind the lie of the previous throw. A running approach to the throw is allowed.

Dog Leg. A dog leg is one or more designated trees or poles in the fairway that must be passed on the outside when approaching the hole. There is a two-stroke penalty for missing a dog leg.

Putt Throw. A putt throw is any throw within 10 feet of the hole. A player may not move past the point of the lie in making the putt throw. Falling or jumping putts are not allowed.

Unplayable Lies. Any disc that comes to rest 6 or more feet above the ground is unplayable. The next throw must be played from a new lie directly underneath the unplayable lie (one-stroke penalty).

Out-of-Bounds. A throw that lands out-of-bounds must be played from the point where the disc went out (one-stroke penalty).

Course Courtesy. Do not throw until the players ahead are out of range.

Completion of Hole. A disc that comes to rest in the hole (box or hoop) or strikes the designated hole (tree or pole) constitutes successful completion of that hole.

FIGURE 20.3 Students with Spinjammer Frisbees

Around Nine

A target is set up with nine different throwing positions around it, each 2 feet farther away (see Figure 20.2). The throwing positions can be clockwise or counterclockwise around the target. They can also be in a straight line from the target. Points are awarded based on the throwing position number (for example, number 7 means seven points for hitting the target). The game can be played indoors or outdoors.

One Step

This game is a variation of Power Frisbee. Opponents stand 20 to 30 yards apart. The object is to throw the disc accurately so the opponent can catch it while taking only one step. If the throw is off target, the thrower receives a point. If the throw is accurate and the receiver drops the disc, the receiver is awarded one point. The first player with five points loses the match.

Novel Frisbees

Spinjammer Activities. Spinjammer Frisbees have a special cone underneath the Frisbee for spinning the Frisbee on the index finger (see Figure 20.3). Many different spinning activities can be performed as an individual or with partners and small groups of students. Some examples include spinning the Frisbee and catching it on the index finger with either hand, passing it back and forth on the index finger with a partner, or passing it around a group of three students

to see how many passes can be made before the disc stalls out. See Figure 20.4 for an example of a programmed practice sheet for Spinjammer skills. Students will enjoy the change of pace and the ease in which they can learn to do a variety of tricks with the Spinjammer. The Spinjammers can also be used for all regular throws, catches, and games in this chapter.

Double-Disc Frisbees. This unique Frisbee is actually two frisbees that fit together and are designed so that they will separate during a proper throw after about 10 yards. It becomes a challenge for students to throw and catch both Frisbees without dropping one or both discs. Groups of three or four students can perform this challenging activity by having one student throw the Frisbees while two or three students try to catch one of the discs as they separate. This activity can become part of a Frisbee unit with a variety of Frisbees and different activities.

Suggested Performance Objectives

1. Throw 10 consecutive backhands through a hula hoop from 10 yards.

2. Perform same as objective 1, using underhand throws.

3. Perform same as objective 1, using sidearm throws.

4. Perform same as objective 1, using thumber throws.

Programmed Practice Sheet for Spinjammer Frisbee Skills

Name _____

Class Period _____

Date _____

Partner Name _____

Self	Peer	Teacher	Skills
			Spin and catch it 10 times. Right hand. Left hand.
			Pass the spinning Frisbee to a partner 10 times. Right hand. Left hand.
			Pop the spinning Frisbee and catch it 10 times. Right hand. Left hand.
			Pop the spinning Frisbee to a partner 10 times. Right hand. Left hand.
			Make a backhand throw to a partner 10 times, who uses a sandwich catch. Dominant hand.
			Make a bowling throw (underhand) to a partner 10 times, who uses a C-catch. Dominant hand.
			Make 10 backhand curves, left and right.
			Make 10 sidearm throws.
			Perform several types of fancy catches—one handed, left or right; under the leg, left or right; or behind the back, left or right. Perform at least five in a row of each.
			Make 10 thumber throws.

FIGURE 20.4   Example of a programmed practice sheet with a Spinjammer

Introduction	Review	Review	Review	Review
What is Frisbee? Types Activities Backhand throw Sandwich catch Backhand curves C-catch Underhand throw	Backhands—curves Underhands Catches **Teach** Frisbee golf **Activity** Play 6 holes of golf	Throws—catches **Teach** Thumber Sidearm Overhand wrist flip **Activites** 4 stations: Distance Accuracy Curves Partner work	Throws—catches **Teach** Fancy catches **Activities** Follow the leader Twenty-One One Step	Fancy catches **Teach** Throw to self **Activities** Frisbee softball Frisbee soccer
Review All throws **Teach** Skipping Tipping Brushing **Activites** 4 stations: Distance with accuracy Self-catch Accuracy Partner work	**Review** All catches **Teach** Freestyle **Activity** Ultimate	**Review** Skipping, tipping, brushing, freestyle **Activities** 4 stations: skill work Frisbee tennis Frisbee golf	**Activity** 9 holes of Frisbee golf	**Activities** 4 stations: Around Nine Follow the Leader Twenty-One One Step
Review Skills for station work **Activities** 4 Stations Frisbee softball	**Activities** Ultimate Frisbee soccer	**Activities** Station work Evaluation Around Nine Follow the leader Twenty-One One Step	**Activity** 9 holes of Frisbee golf	**Activities** Station work Evaluation Ultimate Frisbee softball

FIGURE 20.5 Frisbee block plan

5. Perform same as objective 1, using overhand wrist flips.
6. Throw a Frisbee 30 yards or more using two different throws.
7. Curve the disc around a tree so it lands in a designated target area three of five attempts.
8. Perform same as objective 7 but use the opposite curve.
9. Catch 10 consecutive sandwich catches.
10. Catch 10 consecutive thumbs-down catches above the waist.
11. Perform objective 10, with thumbs up below the waist.
12. Catch three of five discs behind the head, behind the back, or between the legs.
13. Make five consecutive, one-handed catches, both with the left and right hands.
14. Throw five consecutive skips into a target area.
15. Score 30 or less on a round of Frisbee golf.

These are just a few of the possibilities for challenging students with Frisbee performance objectives. The objectives could be combined with a grading scheme or used with learning stations for skill development. Activities need to be field-tested in order to establish fair distances and criterion levels for students of various ages and abilities. Figure 20.5 is a 3-week Frisbee unit block plan for middle school students.

Rainy-Day Activities

1. Review and teach rules and strategies for the various Frisbee games.

2. Set up a short putting (Frisbee golf) course in the gym, hallway, or locker room.

3. Review grips, throws, releases, and so forth.

4. Discuss Frisbee literature, and have students read and report on specific information.

5. Discuss the various types and sizes of discs and the purpose of each type.

6. Set up an indoor tossing accuracy test and let students work at improving their accuracy.

7. Develop a crossword puzzle or Frisbee word searches.

8. Assign a group of students to develop a crossword puzzle or a word search.

9. Devise and give a test on terminology.

10. Discuss with students the skills and activities associated with Frisbees and how playing with Frisbees can fit into their lifestyles.

11. Have students develop rules and regulations for a new game that will be played when the weather clears.

12. Invite a local Frisbee club or expert to class to give a demonstration and instruction on Frisbee techniques and skills.

GOLF

Each weekend millions of golfers everywhere try to obtain a tee-off time to hit and chase a little white ball around an 18-hole golf course. Golf may appear to be a simple sport, but it is actually a complex activity made up of many different shots or strokes (e.g., wood shots, long-iron shots, short-iron shots, pitching, chipping, and putting). It is quite challenging and proves to be fascinating to people of all abilities and ages, from 8 to 80. Golf is truly a lifetime sport that can be enjoyed by all people.

Sequence of Skills

The two primary methods of teaching golf are the swing or whole method and the position or part method. Both approaches lead to the same result—square ball contact with good acceleration. Both teaching methods can be effective, but the whole method seems easier and faster to learn, which makes it better suited to the limited time available for a physical education unit. The order of skills to be learned in a beginning class include: grip; stance; alignment; iron shots—half swing, three-quarter swing, and full swing; wood shots—half swing, three-quarter swing, and full swing; putting; chipping; pitching; and the bunker shot.

Grip

Encourage students to use the overlap grip (80 percent of all golfers use this grip). Place the left hand on the club in the following manner: First support the club with the right hand and let the left hand hang naturally at the side; then bring the left hand in until it contacts the grip of the club and wrap it around. (Checkpoint: The V formed by the thumb and index finger should point directly to the center of the body, and two knuckles should be visible on the left hand when looking straight down at the grip.) Place the right hand by letting it also hang naturally at the side. Bring it in to meet the club and wrap the fingers around the club so the little finger of the right hand lies over the index finger of the left hand. The thumb of the left hand should fit nicely into the palm of the right hand. (Checkpoint: The V formed by the thumb and index finger of the right hand should point to the center of the body or slightly to the right of center.) A final check on the grip is to extend all fingers and let the club fall to the ground. If the grip is correct, the club will fall straight down between the legs and feet.

Stance

The golf stance should be both comfortable and relaxed. There is a slight bend in the knees and at the waist. The arms and shoulders are relaxed. The feet are a shoulder width apart for the driver and closer together for the shorter clubs. The ball is positioned within a 6-inch span, starting inside the left heel for the driver and moving toward the center of the stance for the wedge.

Lift the club straight out in front of the body at waist level and swing it back and forth, similar to a baseball-bat swing. After three or four swings, return to a balanced position in the center. Bend forward from the waist until the club touches the ground. Now relax, and the club will move in slightly closer to the body. It is important that the waist bend lowers the club and not the arms. The relationship between arms and body remains the same until relaxation occurs. (Checkpoint: The preceding check can be applied to every club in the bag. It illustrates how far forward or back the ball must be played and the distance the student should stand from the ball.)

Alignment

A simple procedure for achieving alignment involves the following steps:

1. Stand about 10 feet behind the ball and draw an imaginary line from the flag to the ball.

2. Move to the side of the ball and set the clubface square to the target line. Both feet should be together with the ball centered.

3. Grip the club first and then spread the feet apart on a line parallel to the target line. The ball should be in line with the target, and the feet should be on a parallel line just left of the target. The distance between the toes and the ball is approximately 1½ feet.

Half Swing

Each student's swing will vary according to the person's stature, degree of relaxation, understanding of the swing, and natural ability. The half swing is started by bringing the club halfway back to a position parallel to the ground and then letting the club swing forward to the same position in front. The swing should be similar to the swing of a pendulum, and the grass should be brushed in both the backswing and forward swing. When the club is parallel to the ground in the backswing, the toe of the club should point straight up, and the grip end of the club should match the line of the feet. At the end of the forward swing, the toe of the club should point straight up again, and the far end of the club should match the line of the feet. After students can do a half swing, introduce the ball. Tell them to concentrate on swinging the club correctly and on the proper alignment procedures.

Three-Quarter Swing

The three-quarter swing is simply an extension of the half swing. The hands reach approximately shoulder height on the backswing and on the forward swing. Many students may be at this point already because most usually swing longer than they think.

Full Swing

A full swing is characterized by a club shaft that is almost parallel to, or parallel to, the ground at the top of the backswing. The full swing is a further extension of the half and three-quarter swings. At the top of the backswing, the clubhead should point to the ground, and the shaft should point toward the target. The club face will thus be square, and the plane will be correct.

The golf swing actually begins at the top of the backswing. The backswing is simply preparation. Students should visualize the full swing as a circle drawn in the air with the clubhead. The circle starts at the top of the backswing and is completed at the finish of the forward swing. Students should watch the clubhead draw the actual circle two or three times, always keeping the circle out in front. This will help them maintain one plane throughout the swing.

At this point, students should have the feel of the full swing, and it is time to experiment with different irons. Try the 5 iron, 9 iron, and finally the 3 iron. Concentration is still on the swing, for the same swing is used with every club. Once patterns of error have developed (such as slicing), students can begin to focus on changing a specific aspect of the total swing.

Woods

The same progression should be used to teach wood shots from the half to the full swing. The first wood hit should be the 3 wood from the tee. Next, move to the driver, or 1 wood, from the tee, and then experiment with the 3 wood off the ground. Students should move halfway down the club's grip to begin swinging. Tee the ball so the top edge of the club comes one-quarter to one-half of the way up the ball. The stance will be at its widest (a shoulder width), and the ball will automatically be positioned forward, inside the left heel.

Putting

Identical to the pendulum of a clock, the putter is an extension of the arms and shoulders and swings as one unit an equal distance back and forward. The feel is best obtained by having students grip as far down the shaft as they can reach. Square the putter to the target line and stroke straight back and straight through. Have students try the following putting techniques:

1. Use a reverse overlap grip in which the index finger of the left hand lies over the little finger of the right. This allows the whole right hand to be on the club for control.

2. The stance may be wide or narrow, and the ball may be centered in the stance or forward, remaining inside the left heel. If the ball is forward, a slight weight shift to the left must accompany this stance.

3. Place the dominant eye directly over the ball to improve visualization of the target line.

4. Feel the putter accelerating through contact. This may require shortening the backswing slightly.

5. If the ball misses the hole, overshooting the putt is preferable.

6. Keep the putter blade low to the ground to ensure good ball contact.

Learn to judge the break, or the roll of the green, by standing behind the ball and looking at the line between the ball and the hole and also at the slant of the entire green. Visualize throwing a pail of water toward the hole, and picture which way the water would run. For most putts (that is, 4 feet or less) play the ball to the hole, gradually move to the edge of the cup and eventually outside the cup as a point of aim. The point of aim may be a spot on the imaginary line to the hole or a point even with the hole but to one side. In both cases, the break takes the ball into the hole.

Chip, Pitch, and Bunker Shots

A chip shot is used when the ball is slightly off the green and there is room to hit the ball approximately halfway to the hole. The ball must land on the green and roll close to the hole. If there is not enough room to roll the ball to the hole, then a higher trajectory pitch shot is used. The pitch shot should land at the target. The bunker shot is used for coming out of a sand trap.

A chip shot usually requires a 7 iron and a putting-type stroke. A good technique is to have the students stand off the green and toss the ball underhand so that it rolls to within 4 feet of the hole. Students then place a tee in the green where the ball hit. The tee becomes the target for the chip shot.

The pitch shot should be practiced at different distances with different-sized targets (the greater the distance, the larger the target). Baskets, hula hoops, and parachutes are possibilities at 10, 30, and 50 yards. The 9 iron or wedge is used with a one-quarter, one-half, or three-quarter swing, depending on the distance and the circumstances. Students should learn to make a smooth swing and to let the loft of the club hit the ball. The ball should land at the target and roll slightly forward.

The long-jump landing pit can be used for bunker shot practice. Students should use a wedge or 9 iron and concentrate on the following:

1. Open the club face as you line up the shot.

2. Line up 2 inches behind the ball and focus on that spot, not on the ball.

3. Barely scrape the sand with a one-quarter through full swing, depending on the distance required to land the ball.

4. Always follow through with the club.

Ideas for Effective Instruction

Introduce and stress safety rules on the first day of class. A golf ball or club can cause serious damage, and thus, strict adherence to safety rules must be demanded. If the class is large and space is limited, safety officers may be appointed who can help manage ball retrieving, changing from station to station, and other responsibilities assigned by the instructor.

The following are safety suggestions that may help in class organization:

1. Allow ample swing space between students for any group formation.

2. Do not carry clubs while retrieving balls.

3. If space is limited, take students to the back of the line for individual correction.

4. Do not retrieve balls until instructed.

5. Group the left-handed players together at the far end of the hitting line, facing the right-handed players.

6. Be certain that equipment is in top condition at all times, and tell students to notify the instructor if equipment needs repair.

7. Caution students never to swing toward one another, even without a ball.

Start students with a high iron (7, 8, or 9) so they will experience success quicker. Students need to understand that developing a golf swing takes a lot of practice and is not an easy skill to master. Make sure that students are not overloaded with information and that they receive ample practice time. Depending on the amount of equipment available, teachers may want to assign partner work and to use a swing rating form. This motivates students without clubs to be more involved cognitively and improves their observation skills.

Learning stations can be arranged in the gymnasium or in outdoor fields. An example of an indoor facility, including irons, woods, chipping, pitching, and putting, is shown in Figure 20.6. An outdoor area could be arranged in a similar manner (e.g., around a football or baseball field).

Learning Activities
Modified Courses

Many teachers set up a short golf course in the field space they have available. Broomsticks, traffic cones, and hoops can serve as pins, tees, and holes. A power mower can be used to shape the fairways and greens. If it is impossible to dig holes, students can "hole out" when the ball strikes the target or when they are within a club's length of the target. Whiffle balls, plastic balls, or regular golf balls can be used, depending

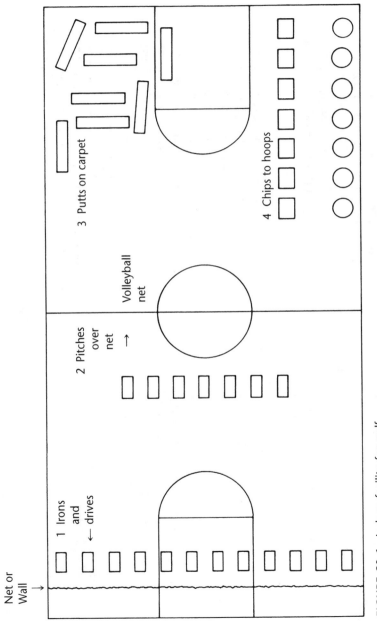

FIGURE 20.6 Indoor facility for golf

on what is available. All types of hazards can be set up using tires, hurdles, jump ropes, and cones. Specific course etiquette and rules can be taught with a modified course.

Putting

Miniature putting courses can be set up on smooth grass surfaces, carpeted areas, old carpet pieces, blankets, towels, mats, canvas, and even smooth floors if a whiffle ball is used. Paper cups, pieces of colored paper, shoe boxes, bleach containers, cans, and jars are possibilities for holes.

Partner Golf

Playing on a regular course or on a putting course, partners alternate hitting or putting toward the pin. If the class size is large, use groups of three or four.

Target Golf

Establish a number of concentric circles and point values around a target. Rope, jump ropes, or chalk can be used to mark the circles. The distance and size of the circles can vary according to the club used. This activity can be done with individuals or teams.

Rainy-Day Activities

Rainy days are a good time to have a "spell down" with questions on rules, fundamentals, etiquette, and types of matches. Crossword puzzles and word searches are available in the suggested readings. Short putting courses can be set up in the indoor space available.

Skill Tests

Many of the drills and game situations already mentioned can be used for evaluation. Here are a few other possibilities:

1. *Parachute.* Count the number of 7-, 8-, or 9-iron shots that land on the parachute in 10 trials.

2. *Putting.* Play 9 holes on a practice green and keep score. Ideally, each student would score two per hole or par the course.

3. *Chipping.* Count the number of balls that end up inside the 4-foot-radius circle.

4. *Pitching.* Pitch 10 balls at each station (10, 20, and 40 yards), and count the number of balls that land inside the target area.

5. *Bunker Shot.* Arrange a string in a circle with a 10-foot radius around one hole, and count the number of bunker shots that finish inside the circle after 10 trials.

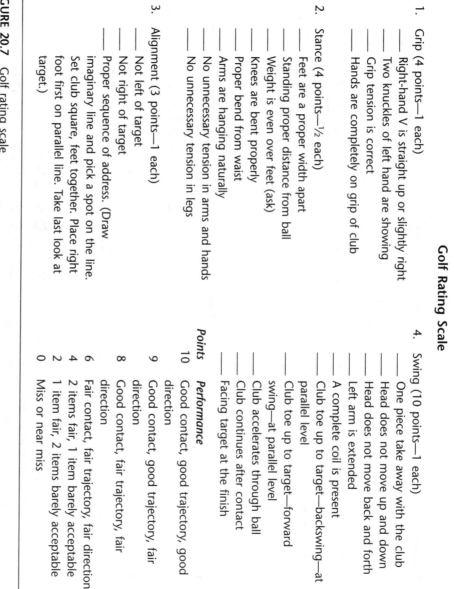

Golf Rating Scale

1. Grip (4 points—1 each)
   ___ Right-hand V is straight up or slightly right
   ___ Two knuckles of left hand are showing
   ___ Grip tension is correct
   ___ Hands are completely on grip of club

2. Stance (4 points—½ each)
   ___ Feet are a proper width apart
   ___ Standing proper distance from ball
   ___ Weight is even over feet (ask)
   ___ Knees are bent properly
   ___ Proper bend from waist
   ___ Arms are hanging naturally
   ___ No unnecessary tension in arms and hands
   ___ No unnecessary tension in legs

3. Alignment (3 points—1 each)
   ___ Not left of target
   ___ Not right of target
   ___ Proper sequence of address. (Draw imaginary line and pick a spot on the line. Set club square, feet together. Place right foot first on parallel line. Take last look at target.)

4. Swing (10 points—1 each)
   ___ One piece take away with the club
   ___ Head does not move up and down
   ___ Head does not move back and forth
   ___ Left arm is extended
   ___ A complete coil is present
   ___ Club toe up to target—backswing—at parallel level
   ___ Club toe up to target—forward swing—at parallel level
   ___ Club accelerates through ball
   ___ Club continues after contact
   ___ Facing target at the finish

Points	Performance
10	Good contact, good trajectory, good direction
9	Good contact, good trajectory, fair direction
8	Good contact, fair trajectory, fair direction
6	Fair contact, fair trajectory, fair direction
4	2 items fair, 1 item barely acceptable
2	1 item fair, 2 items barely acceptable
0	Miss or near miss

FIGURE 20.7 Golf rating scale

A rating scale can be used as part of an evaluation scheme or as a part of the learning activities done with partners (see Figure 20.7).

IN-LINE SKATING MINI-UNIT

In-line skating can be presented as a 1-week mini-unit. Many schools are able to rent the skates and safety gear for a reasonable fee for the unit. Fund-raising activities can provide the money for the rental. The following is an example of a daily agenda of lessons that could be presented in class for secondary students.

Day 1: The instructor goes over the class rules for the unit. The basic rules are as follows:

- Always wear the required equipment when skating.
- Never use the wall to stop.
- Always fall forward when falling.
- Never attempt to help keep someone from falling. This could lead to you falling as well.
- Always listen to the whistle commands.
- Enjoy skating and make it a part of your exercise regimen.

Students are then introduced to the equipment required for the unit. All students must wear wrist guards, elbow pads, and kneepads. NASPE guidelines state that helmets are not required if nonaggressive skates are used and the unit is done on an inside surface such as vinyl or wood gym floors. Students are shown where to get their equipment and how to put it on correctly. This is a great opportunity for those students who are proficient with in-line skating to help those who may be inexperienced. Once students have equipment on, the instructor leads the class through a daily stretch routine. This includes stretching both arms across the body and performing triceps stretches, wrist rotations, cross-legged oblique stretches, hurdler's stretches, sit-ups, and push-ups. Skills for the first day are getting up on your feet, skating slowly with body weight leaning forward, and performing the brake stop. Students are then shown the proper way to place equipment back in the proper bins as pairs.

Day 2: The instructor quickly reviews skills previously taught. Skills for the day are learning to fall properly and performing the T-stop. When falling, students should lean forward and fall on all fours with their chins up. Most of the body weight is taken on the kneepads while the wrist guards guide the student into a sprawl forward. This skill should be practiced frequently under control. Students should never fall backwards for obvious reasons. When teaching the T-stop, students drag one skate behind their body, which slows them to a stop. Students are encouraged to try both the T-stop and the brake stop and choose which one they like best.

Day 3: The instructor reviews the previous skills taught. Skills for the day include skating backwards and the crossover step when turning. When skating backwards, students work in pairs with one student pushing his or her partner slowly while the skater uses a figure-eight pattern with his or her skates to gain momentum. Partners switch roles and perform the activity again. When either skater feels confident enough, he or she may work on their own ability to skate backwards. The crossover step is simply stepping the right foot over the left foot while turning left and performing the opposite for turning right. Students are given tag games to play for the game segment of the lesson. Various adaptations of virtually any tag game can be used. Another game used is called "vanishing plates." There are enough paper plates or beanbags for all but one student. Students skate freely until the instructor signals to grab a plate. The student who does not get a plate is out and must skate around the perimeter until the next game begins. Each round, one plate is taken away from the field. Games usually last 1–2 minutes. If time allows, students are given time for free skating during parts of the period.

Day 4: The instructor begins with a review. The skill for the day is going from forward to backward skating without stopping and returning to forward skating again. Using a partial T-stop and turning the other skate does this. Not all if many students are able to perform this maneuver, so it is important that students are given a variety of choices. The period concludes with a limbo contest. Students are prohibited from leaning backwards. They must crouch and lean forward when going under the limbo bar. It is recommended to start the bar high and give students plenty of opportunities for practice and success. Each time the class goes through once, the bar is lowered. Students are not allowed to have anything other than their skates hit the floor as they pass under the bar. If so, they are eliminated and must skate freely around the area while the contest goes on. The last student that clears the bar is the winner. Limbo music really helps make this a fun event. A high-jump bar from track and field also works well for a limbo bar. This is also a good opportunity for any students who do not feel comfortable performing the limbo to assist in holding the bar.

Day 5: The instructor reviews previous skills taught. This day is a review of skills taught and any other new skills the instructor would like to add. An obstacle course is set up around the area, including tunnels made out of folding mats, figure eight's with large cones, small jumps with hula hoops, and beanbags and balls can be available for students to pick up and move to other areas without stopping. It is important to instruct students to be aware of others around them. The outside of the course is reserved for less accomplished skaters while the inside track is for more experienced skaters. This will help keep accidents from happening. To wrap up the day, the instructor reviews the week and talks with students about places to skate and skating as a lifetime activity.

JOGGING

Joggers and road races are probably the most visible form of the fitness renaissance. Millions take to the road regularly for fitness and sport reasons. Various types of distances for running events have become popular with men and women of all ages. Marathons, triathlons, and 15-k, 10-k, 5-k, and 2-mile fun runs are being offered virtually every weekend. People in all areas of the country run in all kinds of weather. Secondary students in physical education programs should have positive experiences with running because this is a potential lifetime activity that can contribute to fitness and be a form of play. Jogging is an easy, inexpensive activity that can be done individually or with a group.

Sequence of Skills

Jogging is simply slow running. It is different from walking in that both feet leave the ground during the flight or airborne phase. In walking, one foot is always in contact with the ground.

Running Form

Chapter 16 gives in-depth coverage to form running. Teachers should spend time working on running form, emphasizing one aspect of form with each drill. Students can overlearn the position of the head, hands, arms, knees, feet, and body lean. In distance running, the stride is shorter than in sprinting, and the heel of the foot should strike the ground before the ball of the foot. Breathing should be natural, through both the nose and mouth.

Program Design

Students need to understand how to design a jogging program to meet their individual objectives. Programs will differ according to those objectives. Some students want to lose weight, others may want to condition themselves for skiing, and others will want to improve their time in 10-k races. Program goals may vary, but students should all understand how the principles of frequency, intensity, and duration apply to a running program. Proper warm-up, cooldown, and stretching and strengthening activities must be taught. These are covered in Chapter 16.

Equipment

Runners must obtain adequate running shoes. Many are available at prices ranging from $40 to more than $300. They should have a well-cushioned, elevated heel, and a durable bottom surface. The toes should not rub the front of the shoe, and the tongue and lining should be padded. The sole must be flexible, with two layers for absorbing shock. An arch support should be built into running shoes.

The remaining equipment (shorts, socks, sweat suits, rain suits, jackets, hats, mittens, and so forth) is a matter of personal preference depending on the weather. Comfort is the key, with loose-fitting, nonirritating material. Extremely cold and warm weather can be dangerous. Students should understand how to prevent problems by dressing properly and avoiding certain weather conditions.

Ideas for Effective Instruction

Beginners should understand that jogging is an individual activity that can be noncompetitive. If students choose to be competitive runners, that is fine and is a personal choice. Teachers should reinforce this attitude by reducing the emphasis on running races in a jogging unit. The unit emphasis can be on personal improvement and individual goal accomplishment.

Jog–Walk–Jog

Beginners can be given a distance to cover by alternating jogging and walking. They progress by gradually reducing the walking and increasing the jogging. Various students can be assigned different distances, depending on their abilities. This technique can be used for jogging on a track. Students can jog the straightaways and walk the curves for 1 mile.

Timed Runs

Students can be given a set time of a certain number of minutes. They then try to jog continuously for the designated time. (Teachers blow a whistle every minute or half minute.)

Other Running Activities

Refer to Chapter 16 for descriptions of activities such as form running, file running, walk-sprint-jog, pace work, random running, and Fartlek. All can be modified for a jogging unit.

Group Runs

Divide students into small groups of similar ability. The group can run together for a certain time or distance. They should be encouraged to use the "talk test" during the run. This refers to the ability to comfortably carry on a conversation during a run as an indicator of proper jogging intensity.

Training Heart Rate

After students have learned about training heart rates (see Chapter 17), they can check their heart rates at rest before running, after running so many minutes, and again immediately after a run. This will help them to understand the concepts of training heart rate, recovery heart rate, and jogging at sufficient intensity.

Orienteering Runs

A jogging unit can include several orienteering meets emphasizing running from point to point on the school grounds. Draw a map with 10 checkpoints that must be found by the students. Each checkpoint has a secret clue, such as a letter, word, color, or team name. Students can work alone or with a partner. (See Chapter 21 for more orienteering ideas.)

Cross-Country Runs

Map out a cross-country course around the school grounds and in neighboring areas, and hold a meet with a chute for finishers and numbers distributed for the finishing positions. Arrange teams and establish categories for beginners, intermediates, and advanced runners. Set time limits, and allow students to run time trials to determine their category or team. Students can choose to be on a team or to run for individual improvement.

Exercise Trails

Set up an exercise trail around the school grounds with several stations for stretching and strengthening various muscle groups. Use a boundary cone with a sign to mark each station, and give students a rough map showing where each station is located. After completing a station activity, students should jog to the next station. The stations can be set up so the students get a total body workout. After a certain period of time, the trail can be modified.

Runs with Equipment

Some students with special interests may want to run with a piece of equipment (e.g., dribbling a soccer ball or a basketball). Others may want to carry a football or roll a hula hoop. Let students be creative, as long as they are engaged in a safe activity. Running with equipment adds variety to activities and is a good motivational device.

Mileage Cards and Maps

Many people enjoy keeping a record of the distances covered. Goals can be established for a given time period. Students can jog across the state by coloring in a route or moving a pin to a given point as they accumulate miles. Mileage cards or charts can be kept individually, or they can be posted in the locker room or on a bulletin board. Individual or group competitions can be set up based on the number of miles accumulated.

Rainy-Day Activities

Many of these activities (rating forms, pace work, timed runs) can be modified for running in the gymnasium. If the gym is also not available, there are many interesting running topics that teachers can discuss with students. These include training methods, safety, injuries, equipment, health benefits, exercise and calories, marathons, and the female runner. The suggested readings are filled with discussion topics.

RACQUETBALL

The game of racquetball is a direct descendant from the game of paddleball, which was first played in the 1920s. In the 1940s, a racquet with strings was introduced and became known as "paddle rackets." This sport grew in popularity, and in 1969, the International Racquetball Association was established, and racquetball was born. Within the last 10 years, the game has grown tremendously in popularity. This growth has brought about a comparable increase in the number of facilities, changes in racquet style, and a livelier ball. A Nielson Company survey found that racquetball was the fastest-growing participation sport from 1976 to 1979.

Racquetball can be played on a one-, three-, or four-walled court. The most popular is the enclosed four-wall court with a ceiling, but the other types of courts are more common at the middle and high school levels. The game can be played with two people (singles), three people (cutthroat), or four people (doubles). The object is to win each rally by serving or returning the ball so the opponent is unable to keep the ball in play. A rally is over when a side makes an error or is unable to return the ball to the front wall before it touches the floor twice. Note that one can score only when one is serving.

Sequence of Skills
Grip, Eastern Style

Forehand. Form a V on the top bevel of the handle with the thumb and index finger. Rest the thumb on the knuckle of the middle finger on the left side bevel of the handle. The palm of the hand should be approximately level with the bottom of the racquet. The index finger should be in a pistol-grip position.

Backhand. Rotate one-quarter turn to the left (counterclockwise). The V is now on the upper part of the left bevel.

Ready Position

The feet should be a shoulder width apart and the knees slightly flexed. The back is bent slightly forward, and the head is up. The weight is on the balls of the feet. The racquet should be in front of the body at about chest height. Stand in the middle of the court, approximately 4 feet behind the short line.

Forehand

From the ready position, pivot until facing the right sidewall with the left shoulder forward. Bring the wrist back beside the right ear, and point the racquet toward the ceiling. The weight is on the back foot. Start the forward swing with the racquet, and shift the weight from the back to the front foot. Rotate the shoulders and hips toward the front wall. Contact with the ball should be in line with the instep of the front foot. Keep the eyes on the ball and follow through across the body.

Backhand

Follow the same technique as the forehand, but contact the ball when it is about 6 inches from the lead foot.

Backwall Shot

Proper setup position is the key to any backwall shot. Watch the ball carefully and set up with the weight on the rear foot and the racquet by the ear. Step forward and stroke into the ball at the proper position, as stated in the previous discussion.

Serve

Drive. Hit the serve low and hard to the back corner where the back and sidewalls join. This usually goes to the receiver's backhand.

Crosscourt Z. Serve so that the ball strikes the front wall 3 to 4 feet from the sidewall and then rebounds to the sidewall and bounces deep in the opposite corner. The speed and height of the serve can be varied to create different angles for the opponent.

Lob. The lob is a change-of-pace serve that hits high on the front wall and stays close to the sidewall. It should land deep in the backcourt and drop straight down.

Ceiling Shot

The ceiling shot is a defensive shot to move the opponent back and to open up the front center court. The shot can be hit with a forehand, backhand, or overhead stroke, depending on the position of the ball. If the ball is above the head, an overhead shot can be used. A forehand or backhand can otherwise be used. The overhead shot is similar to a tennis serve. The elbow leads the movement, and the arm stretches overhead to contact the ball with an extended arm. The object is to place the shot close to the front wall on the ceiling. It is usually hit to the opponent's backhand side, tightly against the sidewall.

Passing Shot

The passing shot is an offensive shot that is hit low and hard to either side of the opponent, just out of reach. The object is to keep the ball close to the sidewall and low enough so the ball does not come off the back wall to any degree. The shot is a wise choice when the opponent is out of center position to either side of the court.

Kill Shot

The kill is an offensive shot hit low on the front wall. It is impossible to return if hit accurately. It can be hit straight into the front wall or can be hit off the sidewall into the front wall.

Ideas for Effective Instruction

Racquets are made of wood, fiberglass, aluminum, and various other combinations such as graphite and fiberglass. They have different weights, shapes, strings, and grip sizes. Wood racquets are cheaper but heavier; fiberglass racquets are lighter but less durable. Aluminum is lightweight and durable but quite expensive. Grips are usually leather or rubber. Leather seems to provide a better grip but is not as durable as the rubber. Grip size is the circumference of the handle in inches (such as 4⅛, 4⅝).

Racquetballs are quite lively and will break after some usage, so having extras is a good idea. Eye guards are available as a safety measure, and some players may want to wear a glove to provide a better grip.

It is usually best to have two students working in one court with one student on each side of the court. If more students must be placed on each court, then designate partners and have one hitting and one chasing balls or throwing setups. Have two hitters and two nonhitters per court. The nonhitter can perform a variety of functions, such as analyzing strokes, checking safety, or using a rating scale. Keep the hitters close to the sidewalls to give everyone more room.

Skill work can be accomplished easily by practicing performance objectives. It is best to start with a bounce-and-hit method and progress to a setup throw off the wall. Either of these methods can be done alone or with a partner. Some students need to practice bouncing the ball and throwing the ball off the wall. Take time to show students how to perform these skills.

Stress the importance of safety on the court because of the confined area and the dangerous implements. Players should be encouraged to wear eye guards and should be reminded never to turn around and expose the face to a person hitting from behind them. All players must tie the wrist strings snugly around the wrist to avoid losing control of the racquet and injuring others. Finally, players should be reminded that the rules of racquetball stress safety. Whenever there is any chance of endangering the opponent either by hitting with the racquet or by bodily contact, let the ball go and play the point over.

Lead-Up Games and Learning Activities

Ceiling Games

This is a change-of-pace game that requires students to use the ceiling shot. After the serve, a certain number of shots must hit the ceiling before or after hitting the front wall. If the ball does not hit the ceiling, it is a point or side-out. A useful variation is to change the required number of ceiling shots that a person must hit each time. For example, start with one and then increase the required number. Or, require all ceiling shots be hit after the serve.

Five Points and Out

This modified game allows five serves or less each time the serve changes hands. After five points are scored, the opponents change positions (server to receiver). The opponents change positions normally if a side-out is forced before the five points are scored. This modification keeps opponents from dominating the scoring through an exceptionally strong serve.

Eight-Ball Rally

After the serve, each person must hit the ball four times before a point can be scored. This forces a longer rally and encourages work on different shots.

Backhand Rally

After the serve, a player must hit a certain number of backhand shots before a point is scored or a side-out is forced. Start with one required backhand and then increase the number gradually.

Accuracy Drills

A challenging activity is to mark off the courts with targets on the floor and walls. Jump ropes, boundary cones, boxes, and masking tape are useful for constructing targets. Challenge the entire class to make five lob serves, five forehands, five backhands, five Z serves, and five drive serves to the target areas. Kill shots off the back wall and sidewalls can be practiced to marked areas on the front wall. Announce the winner in each category. Vary the size of the targets and the designated skills each day.

Cutthroat and Doubles

Cutthroat is played with three people. The server plays the other two players. Doubles is two players versus two.

Rotation

Rotation involves students playing a 5-minute game. A whistle is then blown, and students rotate to the court on the left if they are ahead and stay where they are if behind. The object of the game is to move up to the last court. Rotation is also enjoyable when playing doubles. Teammates move ahead a court if they are leading when the whistle blows.

Suggested Performance Objectives

These performance objectives can be used for skill work, as a motivational device, and as part of an evaluation scheme. Students can evaluate each other, or evaluation can be a combination of peer and teacher observation. A checklist can be used daily or weekly, and students can be required to complete a certain number of checklists before entering the class tournament.

Core Objectives

Forehand Drive

1. Standing 3 feet behind the short line and 3 feet from the sidewall, bounce the ball off the sidewall and execute a proper forehand drive, hitting the front wall below the 8-foot line, four consecutive times.

2. Standing 3 feet behind the receiving line and 3 feet from the sidewall, bounce the ball off the sidewall and execute a proper forehand drive, hitting the front wall below the 8-foot line, four consecutive times.

3. Standing 3 feet behind the service line and in the middle of the court, feed the ball to the front wall and then execute a proper forehand drive below the 8-foot line, three of four times.

4. Standing 3 feet behind the short line and in the middle of the court, feed the ball to the front wall and then execute a proper forehand drive below the 8-foot line, three of four times.

Backhand Drive

5. Repeat task 1, using a proper backhand drive.

6. Repeat task 2, using a proper backhand drive.

7. Repeat task 3, using a proper backhand drive.

8. Repeat task 4, using a proper backhand drive.

Back-wall Shot

9. Standing approximately 10 feet from the back wall, bounce the ball off the floor and then off the back wall and execute a forehand back-wall shot, hitting the front wall below the 8-foot line, three of four times.

10. Repeat task 9, using the backhand back-wall shot.

11. Standing approximately in the middle of the court, feed the ball to the front wall so it bounces off the floor and the back wall, and execute a forehand back-wall shot, hitting the front wall below the 8-foot line, three of four times.

12. Repeat task 11, using the backhand drive.

Serves

13. Hit three of five drive serves to the left court that land within 3 feet of the sidewall in the back court and are otherwise legal.

14. Hit three of five crosscourt serves to the left court that land within 3 feet of the sidewall and are otherwise legal.

15. Hit three of five lob serves to the left court that land within 3 feet of the sidewall, do not bounce out from the back more than 3 feet, and are otherwise legal.

16. Repeat task 13 to the right court.

17. Repeat task 14 to the right court.

18. Repeat task 15 to the right court.

Ceiling Shot

19. Standing in the backcourt, bounce the ball high enough to execute a proper overhand forehand ceiling shot so the ball hits the ceiling, front wall, floor, and the back wall low, three of four times.

20. Repeat task 19, using the regular forehand stroke.

Pinch Shot

21. Standing at midcourt, bounce the ball and execute a proper forehand pinch shot so the ball hits the sidewall and front wall, bounces at least two times, and hits the other sidewall, three of four times.

22. Repeat task 21, using the backhand stroke.

Intermediate and Advanced Skills

23. Repeat task 1, hitting the front wall below the 3-foot line.

24. Repeat task 2, hitting the front wall below the 3-foot line.

25. Repeat task 3, hitting the front wall below the 3-foot line.

26. Repeat task 4, hitting the front wall below the 3-foot line.

27. Repeat task 1, using a proper backhand drive and hitting the front wall below the 3-foot line.

28. Repeat task 2, using a proper backhand drive and hitting the front wall below the 3-foot line.

29. Repeat task 3, using a proper backhand drive and hitting the front wall below the 3-foot line.

30. Repeat task 4, using a proper backhand drive and hitting the front wall below the 3-foot line.

31. Repeat task 9, hitting the front wall below the 3-foot line.

32. Repeat task 9, using the backhand back-wall shot and hitting the front wall below the 3-foot line.

33. Repeat task 11, hitting the front wall below the 3-foot line.

34. Repeat task 11, using the backhand drive and hitting the front wall below the 3-foot line.

35. Repeat task 19, using the backhand stroke.

36. Repeat task 20, using the backhand stroke.

37. Repeat task 21 with feed off the front wall.

38. Repeat task 22 with feed off the front wall.

39. Repeat task 1, hitting the front wall below the 1-foot line (kill shot), three of four times.

40. Repeat task 3, hitting the front wall below the 1-foot line, three of four times.

41. Repeat task 14, using the backhand in the right court, three of four times.

42. Repeat task 15, using the backhand in the right court, three of four times.

Rainy-Day Activities

1. Review rules and strategies for serving, court position, passing shots, singles play, cutthroat, and doubles play.

2. Have students critique several racquetball articles or a chapter from an activity book.

3. Develop a crossword puzzle or word searches on racquetball.

4. Assign a group of students to develop a crossword puzzle or word search.

5. Work on serving against a wall indoors. Speed and distances can be modified according to the available space.

6. Have on hand a variety of racquets, balls, gloves, and eye guards, and discuss the advantages of each.

7. Show loop films on racquetball.

8. Devise and administer a test on terms and strategy.

9. Discuss caloric expenditure from playing racquetball.

10. Point out the health-related benefits of playing racquetball.

RHYTHMIC ACTIVITY

The urge to express oneself rhythmically has been characteristic of the human race throughout time. Dances have been done as religious rituals, as national and cultural customs, and as declarations of war. Current dances are borrowed from many cultures and groups, both ancient and modern. Because the United States is a melting pot of cultures, we have a broad and diverse range of folk dances representing many peoples.

Every generation dances. It is important that students learn the dances of the past as they develop new dances unique to their group. A wide variety of social skills can be learned through social dancing. Often, if people are not taught dance skills during the school-aged years, they are hesitant to participate in later years. The rhythmic program should thus be viewed as an integral part of the physical education program. If dance skills are not taught as part of the program, they probably will not be taught at all.

Sequence of Skills

The program should consist of four major parts: square dance, folk and round dances, social dance steps, and country swing and Western dance. Such a large number of skills and dances can be taught that it is impossible to list all of the activities here. Instead, refer to *Dance a While* (Pittman, Waller, & Dark, 2005), which offers supplementary and comprehensive coverage. Another concern is that different geographic areas have favorite dances and rhythmic activities peculiar to each. The authors of this book cannot offer activities that would be comprehensive enough in the rhythms area to suit all readers.

Square Dance

The text *Dance a While* (Pittman, Waller, & Dark, 2005) is an excellent source for square dancing. The basic movements of square dance are detailed in progression from Level 1A, beginner basics, to Level 5, intermediate basics. Fifty skills are listed and explained in clear and concise terms. A classified index of square dances is also provided, along with the basic skills that are developed in each dance and the level of difficulty. Each dance description contains the necessary performance instructions and recommended music.

Country Swing and Western Dance

Country swing and Western dance is popular with middle and high school students. The number of dance moves is limited only by the imagination of the dancers. An excellent source for a step-by-step approach to the moves can be found in the text *The Complete Book of Country Swing and Western Dance* by Livingston (1981). The text is illustrated in a step-by-step fashion with photographs and is easy to follow. The shuffle step is also included.

Folk and Round Dance

There are many folk and round dances of varying difficulty. When the dances are presented, the background and history of the dance should be shared with students. *Dance a While* (Pittman, Waller, & Dark, 2005) offers a rich repertoire of dances. A classified index detailing the basic steps, formations, and degree of difficulty is most useful. Directions for the dances are given, along with recommended tapes and CDs.

Social Dance Steps

Social dance steps should be developed in the rhythms unit. Steps most commonly taught are the waltz, foxtrot, swing, tango, rumba, samba, cha-cha, and bossa nova. Each can be presented with the basic steps taught first, followed by one or two variations. With middle school students, the dance steps can be learned individually and then with a partner. Emphasis should be placed on creating an enjoyable atmosphere because peer pressure to succeed is great. Instructors can develop a positive class attitude by demonstrating proper dance etiquette and by showing their enjoyment of the activity. *Dance a While* (Pittman, Waller, & Dark, 2005) is recommended as a valuable source.

ROPE JUMPING

Rope jumping can be a demanding activity enjoyed by all ages and ability levels. The American Heart Association has endorsed rope jumping for years because of its positive effects on cardiovascular endurance. It is an inexpensive activity that can be done in a limited amount of space, indoors or outside. Through rope jumping, students develop rhythm, timing, and coordination, as well as fitness. The numerous jumping activities can challenge all ability levels. The rope can be turned many ways at varying speeds, and the jumper can use a variety of foot patterns. Individual, partner, and small group activities are available.

Rope jumping is a useful carryover activity that can be enjoyed throughout one's life. Developing creative rope-jumping routines and skills can be a challenge to students. Because of the rhythmic aspect of jumping rope, teachers should add popular music to enhance everyone's motivational level.

Body Position and Rhythm

Jumping rope requires proper body position and alignment. The head should be up with the eyes looking ahead. Good balance is a must, with the feet, ankles, and legs close together. The body is erect during the jump. The knees flex and extend slightly with each jump. The elbows are kept close to the body at approximately a 90° angle. The basic jump should be straight up and down and about 1-inch high. The rope should be turned primarily with the wrists and forearms. Effective jumpers land on the balls of their feet and stay in one spot.

The speed at which the rope turns is referred to as the rhythm. Slow-time (half-time) rhythm involves turning the rope 60 to 90 revolutions per minute. The student jumps, rebounds, and then jumps again as the rope comes through. A rebound is a slight bend at the knee in order to carry or keep the rhythm. The student does not actually leave the ground during a rebound. Slow time is the easiest rhythm for beginners. Fast-time rhythm involves turning the rope 120 to 180 turns per minute. There is no rebound because the rope and the feet must move faster. In double-time rhythm, the rope is turned at the same speed as slow time, but instead of using a rebound, the performer executes a different type of step while the rope is coming around. Double-time rhythm is the most difficult to learn, because the feet and the turning of the rope must be coordinated. The feet must move quickly while the rope turns slowly.

Sequence of Skills

Several types of ropes are available that are useful for teaching the skill to secondary students. Sash cord and hard-weave synthetic ropes can be used, but the best jump ropes are made of plastic links with a plastic handle that turns. The rope should be heavy enough to maintain a rhythmic rotation. The length of the rope will vary according to the height of the student. Proper length can be determined by standing in the middle of the rope and pulling the ends up to the armpits or slightly higher. If the ends of the rope reach beyond that area, students can wrap the extra rope around the hands or get a longer rope if the one tested is too short. Most secondary students will need an 8-, 9-, or 10-foot jump rope.

Individual Steps

The following are foot patterns that can be used with all three rhythm patterns—slow time, fast time, and double time. Students should try the patterns in slow time before moving on to fast and double time.

Two-Foot Basic Step. The student jumps over the rope with both feet together. In slow time, there is a rebound in between each turn of the rope.

Alternate-Foot Step (Jog Step). The student alternates feet with every jump. The unweighted leg is bent slightly at the knee. A variation can have students jump a consecutive number of times on one foot before switching feet. For example, a student might jump five times on the right foot and then five on the left foot. With a fast-time rhythm, this step looks like jogging.

Swing Step Forward or Sideways. This is the same as the jog step, except the unweighted leg swings forward or sideways rather than backward. The student can alternate the forward swing with the side swing on each foot.

Side Swings—Left or Right. The student moves the rope to either side of the body and jumps off both feet in time with the rope. The student does not actually jump over the rope. This is a good technique to use to work on timing and cardiovascular fitness because it is demanding.

Rocker Step. The student starts with one leg in front of the other. As the rope comes around, the weight is shifted from the front leg to the back leg and alternates each time the rope goes around. The student rocks back and forth, from front foot to back foot.

Legs Spread Forward and Backward (Scissors). The student starts with one leg forward and one leg back, similar to the starting position for the rocker step. As the rope turns, the front leg is shifted back and the back leg is shifted forward. The position of the legs shifts each time the rope is turned.

Legs Crossed Sideways (Jumping Jack). The student starts with the legs straddled sideways. As the rope is turned, the legs are crossed with the right leg in front. Another straddle position is next, and then the legs are crossed again with the left leg in front. This sequence is repeated. The jump can also be executed with the feet coming together, instead of crossing each time, similar to the foot pattern of a jumping-jack exercise.

Toe Touches Forward or Backward. The student starts with one foot forward. The toe of the forward foot is pointed down and touches the ground. As the rope turns, the feet trade places, and the opposite toe touches the ground. For the backward toe touch, the foot starts in a backward position with the toe touching. The feet then alternate positions with each toe touching.

starts downward, the student executes a left or right side swing. A half-turn should be made in the same direction as the rope. As the rope is coming out of the side swing, the student must bring it up in a backwards motion. This motion can be completed to either side, as long as the turn is toward the rope side.

Another way to execute the shift is to make a half-turn while the rope is above the head with the arms extended upward. The rope will hesitate slightly and then should be brought down in the opposite direction. A final shifting strategy is from a cross-arm position. As the rope is going overhead, the student uncrosses the arms and makes a half-turn. This starts the rope turning in the opposite direction. The key is to uncross the arms and turn simultaneously.

Partner Activities

A wide variety of challenging combinations can be performed with partners using one rope. The partners can start jumping together, or one person can run into position after the other partner has started jumping. Partner activities can be fun with students the same size. They are more challenging when performed with students of varying sizes.

1. One person turns the rope forward or backward.
   a. The partner faces the turner for a specific number of jumps.
   b. Partners are back to back for a specific number of jumps.
   c. The partner turns in place—quarter turn, half-turn, and so on.
   d. The partner dribbles a basketball while jumping.
   e. Partners match foot patterns (e.g., jog step, swing step).
   f. Partners complete double turns.

2. Two students turn the rope forward or backward:
   a. Partners stand side by side, facing the same direction.
   b. Partners face opposite directions.
   c. Partners repeat activities 2a and 2b with elbows locked.
   d. Partners repeat 2a, 2b, and 2c while hopping on one foot.
   e. Partners are back to back turning one rope with the right or left hand.
   f. Partners repeat variation 2e while turning in a circle—both directions.

3. Three students jump together with one turning the rope, one in front, and the third in back. This can be done forward and backward.

4. Two students, each with a rope, face each other. One student turns the rope forward, and the other turns

Shuffle Step. The student starts with the weight on the left foot and the toe of the right foot touching the heel of the left foot. As the rope turns, the student steps to the right and the feet trade places. The left toe is now touching the right heel. The step is then repeated in the opposite direction.

Ski Jump. The student keeps both feet together and jumps to the left and right sideways over a line. This motion is similar to that of a skier. The jump can be performed with the rope going forward or backward.

Heel-Toe Jump. The student jumps off the right foot and extends the left leg forward, touching the heel to the ground. On the next jump the left foot is brought back beside the right foot with the toe touching the ground. The pattern is then repeated with the right foot touching the heel, then toe.

Heel Click. The student starts by completing several sideways swing steps in preparation for this pattern. As the leg swings out to the side, the opposite foot is brought up and the heels are touched together. The heel click can be completed on either side.

Crossing Arms. Crossing the arms can be added to all of the basic foot patterns. In crossing the arms, the hands must actually trade places. The hands must be brought all the way across the body and kept low. The upper body crouches forward slightly from the waist. Crossing can also be used for backward jumping. Students can learn to cross and uncross after a certain number of jumps.

Double Turns. A double turn occurs when the rope passes under the feet twice during the same jump. The student must jump higher and rotate the rope faster. The jump should be about 6 inches high, and a slight forward crouch is necessary to speed up the turn. Students should try consecutive double turns forward or backward. Various foot patterns can also be tried with double turns.

Sideways Jumping. The rope is turned sideways with one hand over the head and the other hand extended down between the legs in front of the body. As the rope is turned, the student jumps the rope one leg at a time. The weight is shifted back and forth between the legs as the rope turns around the body. Students can turn the rope either left or right, and either hand can be held overhead. Students should try the technique several ways.

Shifting from Forward to Backward Jumping. There are several ways to change jumping direction. The first way is to begin jumping forward. As the rope

backward, so the ropes are going in the same direction. Partners jump over both ropes on one jump. Students should then change their rope direction.

5. One student turns the rope. The partner comes in from the side, takes one handle of the rope, and begins turning. The partner's entrance must be timed so the rhythm of the rope remains constant. The partner then leaves and enters from the other side. This stunt can be performed with a forward or backward turn.

6. Partners face each other, turning one rope with the right hand. One partner turns to the left and exits from jumping while continuing to turn the rope for the other partner. After several turns, the partner who was out returns to the starting position. A variation can be tried with the partner turning to the right one-quarter turn.

Ideas for Effective Instruction

Rope jumping is a good example of an activity that can be improved with practice. Remind students constantly that these skills will be perfected only with regular practice. Such reminders help keep students from getting discouraged quickly.

Students should first try new jumping techniques without the rope to get the basic idea. They can then try the stunt with a slow-time rhythm with a rebound in between each movement. As they improve, fast time and double time can be tried. Some students may need to practice turning the rope in one hand to the side of the body to develop the necessary rhythm. Students should practice timing their jumps with the rope turning at the side. An instructor might do some partner jumping with a student who is having trouble with timing. Another effective instructional strategy is to use a movie, videotape, or loop film to give students a visual model of the skill. Several are listed in the suggested readings section of this chapter.

Students need plenty of room for practicing. Care should be taken because the ropes can be dangerous to a person's face and eyes. Horseplay with the jump ropes should not be tolerated. Ropes can be color-coded for various sizes. Students can help distribute and collect the ropes so they do not get tangled. Student helpers can hold their arms out to the sides, and the other students can place the ropes over their arms. Music with different tempos provides a challenge and motivates many students.

Learning Activities

In addition to the foot patterns, rhythms, turning patterns, and partner activities that have been men-

tioned, there are other effective learning activities that can be done individually, in small groups, or with the entire class.

Follow the Leader

Students can work with a partner, a small group, or the entire class—moving forward, backward, diagonally, or sideways—following a designated leader. Various foot patterns can also be used while moving.

Leader in the Circle

The students follow the leader who is in the center of a circle. This activity can be done with large or small circles. The leader calls the name of the next leader after a designated time period or after a certain number of foot patterns have been executed.

Relays

Many different jump-rope relays can be played with boundary cones and various types of jumps.

1. Jog-step down around the cone and back (forward turns).
2. Perform variation 1 but with backward turns.
3. Jog-step backward, using forward turns.
4. Perform variation 3 but with backward turns.
5. Hop to the cone on one foot, and hop back on the other.
6. Ski-jump down, and forward swing-step back.
7. Jog-step through a series of six cones, do 10 sit-ups, and jog-step back.
8. Use a two-foot basic step going down, do five rocker steps, five scissor steps, and come back with a two-foot basic step.
9. Partners (side by side with one rope, elbows locked, both facing forward) go down forward and come back backwards.
10. Partners (side by side with one rope, one person facing forward, the other facing backward) go down and back with a forward turn.

Routines

Various routines can be developed individually with guidelines for foot patterns, change of direction, crossing over, changing levels, rope speed, and routine length. Small groups can also make up routines, choose music, and perform together, and partner routines can be developed with two people using one rope. An example of the guidelines for a small-group routine follows:

- Two minutes or less—five members per group
- Two changes of direction (e.g., forward, backward, diagonal)
- Two changes of floor pattern (e.g., circle, square, back to back)
- Two changes of levels (e.g., high, low)
- Five changes of foot patterns (e.g., rocker, basic two-step)
- One change of rope direction
- One double turn

Rainy-Day Activities

All jump-rope activities are good for rainy days because they can be performed indoors in a limited space. Hallways and gymnasium foyers are possible areas for individual jump-rope activities. Students can work on individual skills if a limited space is available. A rotation schedule may have to be arranged so that some students are practicing while partners are observing and using a rating scale or checking off performance objectives. Students can also devote time to learning the appropriate terminology for foot patterns and rhythms.

STRENGTH TRAINING

Various forms of strength training have become extremely popular activities for general conditioning. Coaches and athletes involved in different sports are using extensive strength-training programs to improve performance. Adults and students of all ages are lifting weights and working on resistance machines in schools, health clubs, YMCAs, and in their homes. Current research has made women aware of the misconceptions about and benefits of resistance training. A properly developed strength-training program can produce positive changes in the body composition and in a person's performance. People engaged in strength training look better, feel better, and perform daily activities better. All of these results have contributed to the popularity of the sport.

Many different types of strength-training equipment are available. Machines such as the Hammer Strength, Smith Machines, Universal Gym, Nautilus equipment, the Orthotron, and the Cybex II are used commonly for training programs. Each machine offers a number of different advantages. Free weights, including different types of dumbbells and barbells, are still quite popular and are available in most weight rooms. Physical education teachers need to carefully analyze such factors as cost, space, objectives, and usage before purchasing strength-training equipment.

Sequence of Skills

Principles, Terminology, and Safety

Beginning strength trainers need to understand the basic principles of training relative to their specific objectives. Students must understand the definitions of strength, endurance, flexibility, warm-up, cooldown, sets, repetitions, frequency, rest intervals, and the various types of lifts for specific muscle groups. The type and number of lifts are determined by a student's objectives. Proper form must be understood in order to gain maximum benefits and to complete the activities safely. Spotting techniques are a necessity for certain lifts, especially with heavy weights. Safety in the weight-lifting area must be stressed constantly. Chapter 16 gives general information on these aspects of strength training. Additional specific information is available in the suggested readings listed at the end of this chapter.

Spotting

Spotters are people who stand by a lifter to provide help when necessary. Spotters are concerned about preventing a weight from falling or slipping if the lifter cannot control the weight. All students should understand the spotting procedures for a specific lift. They can check the equipment for proper alignment, tightened collars, and so forth, and they can be aware of the position of other students in the area. Specific attention should be paid to each lift, especially with heavier weights.

Breathing

Lifters should try to be consistent and natural in their breathing. Most experts agree that breathing should follow a pattern of exhaling during exertion and inhaling as the weight is returned to the starting position. With heavy weights, many lifters take a deep breath before the lift and hold the breath until the final exertion. The final exhalation helps complete the lift. Care is necessary, because holding the breath too long can make a person light headed and may even cause him or her to faint.

Grips

The three major grips are the overhand, underhand, and alternating. These grips are used with different types of lifts; for example, the overhand grip with the palms down is used for the bench press, the underhand grip with the palms up is used for curls, and the alternating grip with one palm up and the other down is used with the dead lift.

FIGURE 20.8   Bench press

Body Position

With free weights, it is especially important to get the feet, arms, and body aligned properly for lifting and removing weights from power racks or squat stands. Carelessness in alignment can result in an unbalanced position, which can, in turn, result in dropping the weights or in poor lifting technique. Each lift requires a different position, depending on whether the bar is being lifted from the floor or from a rack. Spotters must understand the type of lift to be executed and their specific responsibilities. For example, with a back squat, the following steps should be followed:

1. Check the collars to see that they are tightened.

2. Grip the bar and space the hands wider than the shoulders.

3. Align the middle of the back under the midpoint of the bar.

4. Use a pad or towel to cushion the bar against the back.

5. Bend the knees and align the body vertically under the bar.

6. Keep the head up and lift the weight straight up.

7. Move out from the rack and assume a comfortable foot position about a shoulder width apart.

8. Perform the lift with a spotter on either side of the bar.

Upper-Body Lifts

Bench Press. Use an overhand grip with the hands slightly wider than the shoulders. Bring the bar down to the chest and press up over the shoulders (Figure 20.8). Exhale on the press upward.

Curl. Use an underhand grip with the arms about a shoulder width apart. Curl the bar up the shoulders and extend downward slowly to a straight-arm position (Figure 20.9). A reverse curl can be used with an overhand grip.

Bent or Upright Rowing. Both lifts use an overhand grip about a shoulder width apart. The bent position starts with the barbell on the floor and the body bent at the hips (Figure 20.10). The knees are bent slightly. The bar is pulled to the chest while the back is stable. The upright position (Figure 20.11) starts with the bar across the thighs. The bar is pulled up to the chin area and returned slowly.

Military Press. An overhand grip slightly wider than the shoulders is used in a standing or sitting position. The bar is pressed upward from the chest and returned (Figure 20.12). A variation brings the bar down behind the head and then back up.

Bench Pullover. Lying on a bench, the lifter grips the bar overhand and pulls it straight up and over the face from the floor (Figure 20.13).

Shoulder Shrugs. With a straight barbell across the thighs or with two dumbbells at the sides of the body (Figure 20.14), the shoulders are raised or shrugged as high as possible and then returned to the starting position.

Triceps Extension. A barbell, two dumbbells, or a machine can be used. With the barbell, the weight bar is started overhead with an overhand grip and is then lowered slowly behind the head and extended back to the starting position. With a machine, the bar is brought down in front of the body.

Lateral Raises. Lateral raises are done using an overhand grip with dumbbells. A standing or bent position can be used. The weights start at the sides or on the floor and are raised laterally with straight arms.

Lower-Body Lifts

Front and Back Squat. Use an overhand grip with the bar across the front of the shoulders or across the upper-back muscles. The knees are bent to a position in which the thighs are parallel to the floor.

FIGURE 20.9   Curl

FIGURE 20.10   Bent rowing

FIGURE 20.11   Upright rowing

FIGURE 20.12   Military press

FIGURE 20.13 Bench pullover

FIGURE 20.14 Shoulder shrugs

Dead Lift. The lifter starts in a squat position with the weight on the floor, the feet about a shoulder width apart, and an alternating grip (Figure 20.15). The arms are kept straight and the back flat as the weight is lifted and the body comes to an erect position with the bar across the thighs.

Power Clean. The power clean is a complex lift that starts in the same position as the dead lift but with an overhand grip (Figure 20.16). The lift includes a start, an acceleration, and a catch phase. The bar is pulled up, past the waist (Figure 20.17), and ends up above the chest. The lifter must control both the weight and

the body as the weight moves through the starting position to the catch position.

Leg Curls and Extensions. These lifts call for a machine attached to a bench. The extension starts in a sitting position with the feet under a lower, padded section. The arms grip the sides of the bench, and the upper body is leaning slightly back. The legs are extended until they are parallel to the floor. The leg curl uses the upper padded section of the machine. The lifter is on the stomach, and the heels are hooked behind the pad. The heels are then pulled up toward the buttocks and lowered.

FIGURE 20.15 Dead lift

Heel Raises. The student begins on the balls of the feet and the toes over a stable board or step. The lifter holds a weight in each hand at the sides (Figure 20.18). The heels are then raised and lowered.

Learning Activities
Circuit Training

An effective strategy for organizing the activities in the weight room is to set up a circuit with a number of stations. The students can be divided into groups and rotated after a certain number of minutes. Students perform a specific number of sets and repetitions at each station.

FIGURE 20.16 Power clean—ready position

Each student should keep a daily log of the sets and repetitions and of the weights that were lifted. These records are important in organizing a progression and should help to motivate the students. Depending on the equipment and facilities available, a good approach is to develop a circuit for both lower-body exercises and upper-body exercises. Students can alternate upper- and lower-body workouts. Aerobic conditioning activities can also be alternated with the resistance training. Many teachers like to add variety to the circuit routines by changing stations regularly.

FIGURE 20.17 Power clean—intermediate position

FIGURE 20.18 Heel raises

Club Requirements

Requirements—To become a member, you must lift a combined total of 5.2 times your weight. The 3 required lifts are bench press, dead lift, and squat.

Weight	Required Total	Weight	Required Total
100–109	= 520	160–169	= 832
110–119	= 572	170–179	= 884
120–129	= 624	180–189	= 936
130–139	= 676	190–199	= 988
140–149	= 728	200–209	= 1040
150–159	= 780	210–219	= 1092
		220 and up	= 1144

Each participant is allowed 3 tries for each lift. Weight may be added to the previous lift, but it may not be subtracted from the previous lift.

Name _____ Date _____ Class 10, 11, 12

Body weight _____ Required total lift _____

	1st	2nd	3rd	Best of 3 lifts
Bench press	___	___	___	___
Dead lift	___	___	___	___
Squat	___	___	___	___
			Total	___

Coach's signature _____

FIGURE 20.19 Motivational club criteria for weight lifters

Partner Resistance Activities

Chapter 16 describes a number of partner resistance activities that can be used to supplement and add variety to a strength-training unit. These can also be added to a circuit or can be scheduled as an entire day's lesson. They are useful in situations in which equipment is limited. For example, while students are waiting their turns to use a weight machine, they can perform several resistance activities. Various stretch bands are also available for certain situations.

Muscle of the Day

Another good learning activity is to present students with information about one muscle at the end of each lesson. The name of the muscle and its functions are written on a card and placed on the wall of the weight room. A quick review of the muscles covered plus the addition of a new muscle takes place each day. This is a good concluding activity after each day's workout.

Specific information on the muscular system is available in Chapter 17.

Motivational Devices

Resistance training offers tangible evidence of improvement in the various lifts. This improvement can be tied to many different motivational devices: T-shirts, certificates, and membership in a club are popular examples of awards for lifting certain amounts of weight. These types of devices can be quite simple yet are effective and meaningful for many students. Figure 20.19 is a good example of motivational club criteria that could be used. The club could be available to students in the weight-training classes.

SWIMMING/AQUATICS

An aquatics instructional program in the secondary schools is an excellent addition to a balanced curriculum. Unfortunately, many school districts do not have

	Monday	Tuesday	Wednesday	Thursday	Friday
Introductory Warm-Up Activity	Pool Rules/EAP Practice EAP Pool Entry & Exit	Practice EAP	Marking	Partner Resistance Kicking	Lazy River
Fitness	Lazy River	Flutter Kick	Water Aerobics	Treading-Water Intervals	Racetrack Fitness in the Water
Lesson Focus	Water Safety: Treading Water Breathing Back Floating	Front Crawl Skills	Breathing Technique Front Crawl	Backstroke Skills	Partner Task Assessment Sheet
Game	Water Volleyball	Team relay: Kicking with Boards	Water Basketball	Five Passes	Water Frisbee

TABLE 20.1 Swimming/Aquatics Block Plan

the facilities necessary to implement swimming and related aquatics programs. It is, however, often possible to bus students to swimming pools outside the school. These may be municipal pools, YMCA and YWCA pools, or the facilities of various private organizations.

Swimming classes require teacher expertise in the area. Rotating teaching responsibilities is mandatory so that teachers with experience are used in the swimming instructional program, and those with less experience can teach aquatic games. The aquatic games component focuses on learning to adjust to the water. All aquatics teachers, regardless of assignment, should have the American Red Cross Water Safety Instruction certification.

The pool should be clean and warm. Nothing turns students off faster than having to swim in a pool that is inadequately heated. A pool with a uniform depth of 3 to 4 feet of water is often preferable for teaching nonswimmers because the students can stand up immediately if they have a problem. This offers beginning swimmers a measure of confidence. For intermediate and advanced swimmers, a standard pool, which can be used for diving as well as swimming, is preferable.

Keep lessons short in terms of time spent in the water. Students tire easily when learning new skills, and they can practice some skills out of the water. Considering swimming is an important lifetime skill, it is most desirable that students leave the class with a positive feeling about the instruction. Introducing students to any new activity is difficult, and most

students need extra encouragement and patience as they begin to overcome their fears of the water.

Sequence of Skills

A difficult aspect of teaching swimming to middle and high school students is the tremendous range of ability and experience that students bring to the class. Some students may not know how to swim, whereas others may have been swimming competitively since they were 3 years old. This necessitates homogeneous groupings according to ability. The skills to be taught may therefore range from drown proofing and survival skills to the criteria in American Red Cross Water Safety Instruction certification.

Because aquatics is a highly specialized activity involving specific skills that must be learned, it is challenging to develop meaningful lead-up activities. We recommend texts listed at the end of this section to teachers who are interested in creating a meaningful instructional program. They include chapters on developing a successful instructional program, which includes teaching essential aquatic skills, springboard diving skills, and lifesaving skills. Chapters are also offered on the evaluation of swimming skills. Of particular aid to the less-experienced teacher is a series of performance analysis sheets to help in evaluating various strokes and dives. We have included a section on swimming/aquatics safety, a suggested 5-day block plan for secondary students (Table 20.1) detailed lesson plans for those 5 days (Figure 20.20), and a Partner

AQUATICS LESSON—DAY 1

Performance Objectives (student outcomes)

Students will know the pool rules and be able to follow them.

Students will learn and demonstrate how to enter and exit the pool safely.

Students will demonstrate how to properly respond to the Emergency Action Plan (EAP).

Students will learn how to float and tread water to show movement skills and safety activities.

Introductory Activity: Pool Rules, EAP

(The EAP should be reviewed and practiced "prior" to the swim unit.)

Before entering the pool, students will be instructed on the pool rules, which will be posted in the aquatics area. The following pool rules include specific behavior in and out of the water.

- Follow all directions.
- No running in the pool area.
- No diving into the pool.
- Do not enter the pool until instructed.
- Enter the pool feet first in a cleared area.
- Stay off the lane line.
- When changing lanes, go under the lane lines, not over them.
- When the emergency sound airs, clear the pool immediately, go directly to the bleachers and sit quietly.

After reviewing pool rules, students will learn how to respond to an EAP and rehearse EAP requirements. Then they will practice pool entry and exit procedures.

Fitness: Lazy River

Students walk slowly in the shallow end of the pool, as if they are wading through a river. Students walk in their own personal space. Teacher calls out new directions every 30–60 seconds. Examples of student walking directions include normal steps, short steps, long steps, backward steps, side steps, and leg crossovers.

Lesson: Water Safety Skills—Treading Water, Breathing, Front Floating

Treading Water (water safety skill):

Teach students to tread in chest-high water. The objective is to teach students to keep the body upright and use a rhythmic motion. Begin with arm movements, with hands cupped and using a sculling motion. Hands must be in front of the student and submerged. Once arm movements have been practiced, teach two methods of leg movements: simulate bicycle leg pumping or a scissors kick.

Breathing: Teach breathing in waist-high water. Have students take a breath, fully submerge, and exhale, blowing bubbles. Have students reemerge for air and repeat the process.

Front Float (partner task): Using partner assistance, teach students how to float in waist-high water, keeping their faces in the water and spreading arms out to the side. Teach students how to recover by having them bring their knees to the chest and hands to their sides.

Activity: Water Volleyball

Divide students into two equal groups on each side of the net in the shallow end of the pool. Use a beach ball and have students focus on noncompetitive rallying.

Materials Needed:
- Pool rules sheets for each student
- Emergency Action Plan
- Pool volleyball net
- Beach balls

FIGURE 20.20 Aquatic lessons for five days (continues)

AQUATICS LESSON—DAY 2

Performance Objectives (student outcomes)

Students will perform an Emergency Action Plan (EAP) response (rehearsal).

Student will learn and demonstrate how to enter and exit the pool safely.

Students will demonstrate how to properly respond to the EAP.

Students will learn how to float and tread water to show movement skills and as a safety measure.

Students will show proper arm techniques in the crawl stroke (turning head to the side).

Introductory Activity: Practice EAP

Students will rehearse the EAP and understand its significance.

Fitness: Flutter Kick

Holding onto the edge of the pool with both hands, students will practice a flutter kick. The kicking motion originates from the hips, with a 12–15 inch range in kicking. Students will focus on keeping the legs straight and toes pointed. Students will then team with a partner and take turns practicing a flutter kick using a kickboard.

Lesson: Front Crawl Stroke

Teach proper breathing technique and arm movement in waist-high water in a stationary position before students attempt the front crawl stroke.

Arm Stroke: Arms alternate using the following movement skills: entry, down sweep, in sweep, upsweep, recovery. While one arm is in recovery, the other enters the water. This is done on the side of the pool, first using the wall for support. Then students will use kickboards with their hands extended to practice the skill.

Activity: Team Relay: Kicking with Boards

Divide students into teams of 4–6. Teams will do a relay of one lap of the pool, performing a flutter kick and using a kickboard. Students will start in the water (no diving).

Materials Needed:

- Kickboards
- Aids: An instructional video to demonstrate proper movement skills (optional)

AQUATICS LESSON—DAY 3

Performance Objectives (student outcomes)

Students will work cooperatively using the proper kicking technique.

Students will work on their cardiovascular fitness doing water aerobics.

Students will learn breathing and how to complete the front crawl.

Introductory Activity: Marking

Have students in waist-high water, grouped with a partner of similar ability. On "go," one partner walks, trying to lose his or her partner. On the signal, both stop. The chaser must try to reach out and touch their partner to mark them. If the partner can be marked, that player receives 1 point. If the chaser cannot mark their partner, the walking partner receives a point. Partners then switch, with the chaser becoming the leading walker.

Fitness: Water Aerobics

Students warm up with walking activities in the water. They will alternate periods of cardiovascular work (60 seconds) with resting or muscular strength activities (30 seconds).

Cardiovascular movements may include the following: walk forward, walk backward, jog forward, jog backward, march in place, jumping jacks, treading water, scissor kicks, jumping in place, side-to-side ski jumping. They may also perform the following rest or muscular strength movements: arm curls, calf raises, quadriceps stretches, hamstring stretches, back floating, practice of crawl-style breathing, triceps stretches.

FIGURE 20.20 Continued

Lesson: Breathing, Front Crawl Stroke

Breathing: With face in water, students exhale by blowing bubbles into the water, inhale by turning head sideways, taking a breath, and returning face to the water. For a breath, the head turns to the side of the recovering arm.

Leg Movement: Using the flutter kick, students work on breathing by using kickboards and turning heads to the side. When a breath is needed, one stoke is taken and heads turn to the side for a breath.

Front Crawl: Combine all the elements of front crawl and attempt the full stroke.

Activity: Water Basketball

Tie down flotation basketball hoops on each side of the shallow end of the pool. Divide class into two equal teams. Students will play noncontact water basketball. A student cannot hold the ball longer than 3 seconds. A team must make three passes before attempting to shoot a basket.

Materials Needed:

- Music interval tape for water aerobics
- Kickboards and other flotation devices for student assistance
- Two flotation basketball baskets
- One water basketball

AQUATICS LESSON—DAY 4

Performance Objectives (student outcomes)

Students will work cooperatively in a physical activity setting.

Students will demonstrate an ability to tread water.

Students will work on their cardiovascular fitness by learning backstroke skills.

Introductory Activity: Partner Resistance Kicking (out of water)

Students will be introduced to the flutter kick while lying on their backs, working outside of the pool on the deck. Students will work with a partner and take turns practicing a flutter kick. They will perform a flutter kick while a partner applies gentle resistance by holding their ankles.

Note: You may want to have students do this individually, sitting on the side of the pool kicking upward with their toes just breaking the surface of the water. This will give students the realistic feeling of resistance. This will not meet your objective of students working cooperatively for kicking, although they do work together in the skills section.

Fitness: Treading Water

Students will perform treading-water intervals in chest-high water. Begin by having students attempt 15 seconds of treading with 10-second rest intervals. Increase the treading time to 20 seconds with a 15-second rest interval. Music may be played during the treading portion, with mild stretching added to rest intervals.

Lesson: Backstroke Skills

Have students work with partners. Begin with a back float, keeping the head back with the water line at the tip of the chin and the middle of the top of the head with the ears in the water, while staying relaxed. Add a slow flutter kick to glide the body. Kicking movement originates from the hip, with power coming from the upward motion. At the end of the upbeat kick, the toes should reach the surface. Students may use kickboards for flotation assistance or keep their arms to their sides to help with body position.

Add arm movements, which alternate by using a power phase and recovery phase. In the power phase, the pinkie finger enters the water first and the hand sweeps outward and downward as the elbow bends; sweep the water past the thigh. In the recovery phase, the shoulder lifts from the water as the arm is lifted straight and relaxed from the water, thumb first. Rolling the body makes the recovery phase easier.

FIGURE 20.20 Aquatic lessons for five days, *continued*

Activity: Five Passes

Divide students into two teams. Scatter players across the shallow end of pool. The object of the game is for one team to make five consecutive passes to five different players using a flotation ball, without losing possession of the ball. Players may not hold the ball longer than 3 seconds. If a team successfully makes five consecutive passes, they score 1 point, and possession goes to the other team. If defense takes possession of the ball, they begin their five passing attempts.

Materials Needed:

- Kickboards
- Flotation ball

AQUATICS LESSON—DAY 5

Performance Objectives (student outcomes)

Students will work toward improving their fitness by participating in cardiovascular water activities.

Students will demonstrate their knowledge of basic swimming skills.

Students will work cooperatively in a partner task assessment.

Introductory Activity: Lazy River

Students walk slowly in the shallow end of the pool, as if they are wading through a river. Students walk in their own personal space. Teacher calls out new directions every 30–60 seconds. Examples of student walking directions include normal steps, short steps, long steps, backwards steps, sidesteps, and leg crossovers (carioca movements).

Fitness: Racetrack Fitness in Water

Task cards are in six posted locations of equal distance around pool. Students are divided into six teams and one team starts at each station. On the whistle, students swim to the next station and start their new task.

Stations include the following activities: jog in place; front crawl stroke, using arms only, with legs stationary; flutter kick with both hands on the pool edge; perform a breast stroke using arms only, with legs stationary; perform frog kick with both hands on edge of pool, treading water.

Lesson: Partner Task Assessment Sheet

Have students work with a partner to demonstrate learned aquatics skills. One partner will perform tasks, while the other partner will observe and check on a checklist if each task is performed. Once all tasks are attempted and assessed, the partners switch positions.

Activity: Water Frisbee

Divide class into two equal teams. Create a boundary in the shallow end of the pool, where students are able to play comfortably. Teams will attempt to maintain possession of the Frisbee by making five consecutive passes. Players may hold onto the Frisbee for no more than 5 seconds. If a team makes five consecutive passes to five different teammates, they will score 1 point and turn over possession to the other team. If the defense intercepts the Frisbee, then they will become offense and start their five consecutive passing attempts to score.

Materials Needed:

- Racetrack Fitness signs and cones
- Partner Task Assessment Sheets, clipboards, and pens
- Frisbees

FIGURE 20.20 End

Partner Task Assessment Sheet
Aquatics Skills

Student Name: _____

Student is a: _____ nonswimmer _____ beginning swimmer _____ experienced swimmer

Partner/Scorer Name: _____

Pool entry and exit:

_____ Enters shallow end using feet first

_____ Ensures no students are in path

_____ Exits shallow end using two hands

Floating on back:

_____ Holds head back and comfortably maintains a floating position.

_____ Is able to limit arm and leg movement while floating

Level of participation during fitness component:

_____ Participates fully

_____ Participates with reservations

Front crawl skills:

_____ Flutter kick movement starts from hips

_____ Arms alternate using power phase and recovery

Emergency Action Plan response:

_____ Exits pool; goes to bleachers quickly

_____ Sits in bleachers quietly

_____ Remains calm and follows directions

Breathing technique for front crawl stroke:

_____ With face in water, can exhale, blowing bubbles

_____ Turns head to side to take a breath, keeping side of head in water

Treading water:

_____ Able to tread water comfortably for 30 seconds

_____ Keeps body upright while treading

Backstroke skills:

_____ Flutter kick movement from hips

_____ Brings thumb out of the water first and submerges pinkie first

FIGURE 20.21 Partner Task Assessment Sheet—Aquatics Skills

Task Assessment Sheet to assess aquatics skills (Figure 20.21). We would like to thank teachers Mary Dean from the Kyrene Schools and Sean Jonaitis from the Gilbert Schools, both in Arizona, for their help.

Aquatics Safety

To ensure the safety of all individuals in an aquatics center, there must be clearly defined facility rules. Every staff member and student must strictly adhere to facility rules and safety responsibilities, which include identifying potential hazards and enforcing pool rules at all times. Rules should be posted in a highly visible location and clearly state student expectations. The students should be oriented on expectations and held accountable to strict adherence to ensure a safe environment. The rules should state both physical and behavioral expectations in and out of the pool, and they should encompass physical entry and exit of the pool, including diving regulations. In addition to pool rules, there must be an Emergency Action Plan (EAP).

An EAP is a well-written document that outlines systematic procedures in an emergency situation. An emergency includes any situation that may be of immediate threat or serious injury to one or more individuals. Emergency situations may include passive drowning; potential head, neck or back injuries; chlorine or chemical leakage; or other situations that are of immediate threat to human life or serious bodily injury. In such an emergency, the teacher must immediately activate the facility's EAP.

All school personnel and students in the aquatics facility should be familiar with the EAP and trained to activate the EAP in response to any emergency. When activated, student readiness is critical for a safe and timely response. The EAP should clearly outline specific actions and realistic expectations of teachers, staff, and students. While the teacher fully directs the plan, students may be designated for specific actions, such as contacting administrators and emergency services. Therefore, EAP practice drills should be conducted regularly with staff and students so that response actions are automatic and calmly executed.

The EAP should detail the activation of emergency sounds, immediate exit of all individuals from the pool, a designated location for students, the notification of school administration and emergency services, retrieval and/or use of lifesaving equipment, and escort of emergency personnel to and from the facility. It should contain emergency telephone numbers, dialing instructions, directions to and from the facility, and a diagram of an evacuation route.

While every emergency is unique, successful response actions in emergency situations require training readiness, student awareness, teamwork, and communication. Every staff member must strictly adhere to safety responsibilities, which include identifying potential hazards and enforcing pool rules at all times.

TENNIS

Developing from a crude handball game played in 14th-century France, the game of tennis became one of the most popular sports of the 1980s. Part of its popularity stems from the fact that it is truly a game for a lifetime. Children as young as 6 years old can learn to play. In fact, most of today's superstars began playing at very early ages. Tennis can also be played well by older age groups. The United States Tennis Association (USTA), which is the governing body for tennis in the United States, conducts national championships and has established national rankings for age groups beginning with the 12-year-old-and-under group and continuing through the 70-year-old-and-older group. Another reason for the popularity of tennis is that men and women

can compete on the same court at the same time (mixed doubles). Few other serious sports offer this possibility. The popularity of tennis is noticeable as one sees thousands of tennis courts across the country, usually with people waiting in line to play. The huge audiences at such classic tournaments as Wimbledon and the U.S. Open also attest to the game's popularity.

Although some tennis is played on grass courts (as at Wimbledon), and some is played on clay courts, most American tennis is played on hard surfaces such as asphalt or cement. The court is separated by a net, which is 3 feet high at the center and 3.5 feet high at the net posts.

In singles, one player is on each side of the net. In doubles, two players are on each side of the net. All players have a racquet. The ball is put into play with a serve. After the return of the serve, players may hit the ball before it bounces or may allow the ball to bounce once before hitting it. The object of the game is to legally hit the ball over the net into the opponent's court. Most coaches of the sport will say that to win, all you have to do is to hit the ball over the net one more time than the opponent does.

Sequence of Skills

Tennis skills fall into five basic categories. Some skills may not fit exactly into any one category, but for organizational purposes, these five will suffice: volley, ground strokes, lob, overhead, and serve.

Volley

The volley should be the first stroke learned because it is the simplest stroke. The eye–hand coordination involved is similar to that involved in catching a thrown ball, a skill most students have mastered by high school. The volley requires no backswing, and the ball does not bounce, so timing is simplified.

Ground Strokes

The forehand and backhand ground strokes are considered to be the foundation of a solid game. The forehand is the easier of the two for most people and should be learned first. The backhand is more difficult but not too difficult to learn with proper instruction.

Lob

After learning the ground strokes, the lob is relatively easy. It is basically a ground stroke, hit at a different angle. Backswing and body position are identical to those of the ground stroke.

Ideas for Effective Instruction

The Court

The game of tennis is played on a court as diagrammed in (Figure 20.22). A working knowledge of the court areas is vital to the student, not only for its importance in playing the game, but also for the following instructions.

Serve

The serve is a complicated stroke, and some tennis coaches prefer to introduce it as soon as possible to give students the maximum amount of time to master it. If the serve is the last skill taught, however, students are by then more familiar with the equipment, have a better feel for the game, and may be more successful with this skill.

Overhead

The overhead and serve are different from the other strokes and require learning new patterns. The overhead, or smash, should be taught first as this stroke resembles a simplified service motion. When the skill of hitting an overhead has been mastered, students will find it easier to learn to hit a serve.

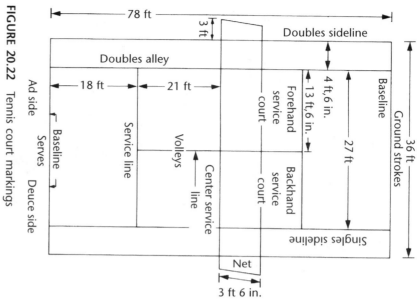

FIGURE 20.22 Tennis court markings

Singles Sideline. The singles sideline delineates the playing court for singles. A ball landing on the sideline is in play.

Doubles Sideline. The doubles sideline delineates the playing court for doubles. A ball landing on the doubles sideline is in play in doubles.

Doubles Alley. The doubles alley is the area of the court in play in doubles after the serve. It includes the doubles sideline.

Baseline. The baseline delineates the length of the court for both singles and doubles. When hitting a serve, the player must stand behind the baseline and may not touch it or step over it onto the court until the ball has left the racquet. A ball landing on the baseline is in play.

Service Line. The service line delineates the length of the service court. A serve must land between the net and the service line or on the service line to be in play.

Center Service Line. The center service line divides the service court into deuce and ad sides. A serve hitting the center service line is in play.

Ad Court. The ad court is the service court to the receiver's left. Any time an odd number of points has been played, the serve is made to this court (that is, 15–0, 30–40, ad in, or ad out).

Deuce Court. The deuce court is the service court to the receiver's right. Any time an even number of points has been played, the serve is made to this court (that is, 0–0, 15–15, 40–15, deuce).

The Match

Most people play tennis to try to win the match. To win a match, a player must win a predetermined number of sets (usually two out of three). To win a set, a player must win six games with at least a two-game margin. If a set ties at six games each, a tie breaker is played to determine the winner of the set. To win a game, a player must be the first to win four points. Each of these terms is explained in the following discussion.

Points and Games

A player wins a point if the opponent fails to legally return the ball, or if the opponent, while serving, fails to legally put the ball into play. The opponent will be awarded a point in any of these situations: the ball is allowed to bounce more than once before it is returned, the ball is returned so that it does not cross the net or land within the playing court, the ball is hit twice while it is being returned, the player is touched by the ball while it is in play, or the net is touched while the ball is in play.

Two methods are currently used for scoring games. The conventional scoring progression is love, 15, 30, 40, game. Both players start at love (0), and a player must win four points to win the game. The one exception is that a player must win by a two-point margin. If the server leads 40–30 and the receiver wins the next point, the score is deuce. The next player who wins two consecutive points wins the game. At deuce, if the server wins the following point, the score is advantage in (ad in). However, if the receiver wins the point, the score is advantage out (ad out). When a player with the advantage wins the next point, that player also wins the game.

Another scoring system, called no-ad, or VASS, simplifies this process, speeds the game along, and is better suited for physical education classes in which time limits are a factor. In this system, points are counted 0, 1, 2, 3, game. A two-point lead is not required because the first player to win a fourth point wins the game. Using this system, there is no ad or deuce.

Sets

The first player (or doubles team) to win six games wins the set if they have a two-game lead. A set might therefore last only six games (6–0), or might go to 10 or more games (6–4). If a set is tied at 5-all, the winner of the next game would go up 6–5, and would not have the necessary two-game margin to win the set. Should the leader win the next game, that player would also win the set, 7–5. If a set ties at six games each, however, a tiebreaker is used. The winner of the tiebreaker is the winner of the set, and the score is recorded at 7–6.

Tiebreaker

The USTA has established that the 12-point tiebreaker be used at 6-all. This occurs in the following manner:

1. The player who served the first game of the set serves the first point.

2. The receiver of point one serves points two and three, and the serve changes after every two points from that time.

3. Players change sides of the net at every six points (6–0, 3–3, 6–6).

4. The tiebreaker is won by the first player to reach seven points with at least a two-point margin. If the first player to reach seven does not have a two-point margin, play continues until one player establishes a two-point lead.

Match

In women's tennis and in almost all of men's tennis, the winner of a match is determined by the first player or team to win two sets. Some men's tennis is played to the best three of five sets, and thus if Smith defeated Jones (6–4, 3–6, 7–6, [9–7]), Smith won the first set 6–4, lost the second set 3–6, and won the third set in a tie breaker, the score of which was 9–7.

General Rules

The match usually begins with players spinning a racquet to determine who will serve the first game. The winner of the toss can choose to serve or to receive and can also choose which side of the net to begin from, or he or she can elect to have the opponent decide. After the initial choices are made, the opponent makes all other choices.

One player serves for a whole game. The first serve is hit from the right side of the court into the diagonal service area. The server has two chances to put the ball into play. If the serve is a fault, the second ball is served. If this serve is also a fault, the server loses the point. Any serve that touches the net but still lands in the proper service court is a "let," and the serve is hit again. After the first point of the game, the following serve takes place from the left side of the court. The serve alternates back and forth on each successive point throughout the game.

An exception to this rule applies to no-ad scoring. At 3–3 in a no-ad game, the receiver chooses the side into which the serve will be made. The serve is not automatically made to the deuce side, as might be expected, but the receiver may choose to receive from either side. The opponent then serves the next game in the same manner. The serve alternates after each successive game for the entire match. In doubles, each team may choose which player serves first for that team, and this alternates each time it is that team's serve.

At the conclusion of every odd-numbered game, players change sides of the net—after the first, third, and fifth game, and so forth, there is a court change.

Tennis is governed by a strict set of rules, which cover every imaginable situation. A thorough knowledge of these rules is important for the tennis instructor. A copy of the rules of tennis can be ordered from the USTA (see the suggested readings at the end of this unit).

Etiquette

Rules of etiquette are a vital part of tennis. Except for large tournaments and professional matches, referees and ball retrievers are seldom present at tennis matches. Rules of etiquette must be followed for the game of tennis to be enjoyable to all.

Most rules of etiquette can be summed up in this motto: "Do unto others as you would have them do unto you." For instance, if a ball was not seen clearly as being out or in, play it over. When the point is over, try to return the balls to the opponent, not merely in the general direction.

Never enter a court (or walk behind one) while a rally is in progress. If one must walk through a court, wait until there is a court change.

A rule of tennis states that any interference during play shall cause a "let," and the point will be replayed. If the opponent claims that there was a distraction during play, do not hesitate to play the point over.

Minimize verbal outbursts on the court. Not only is it distracting to the opponent, but it may be bothering players on other courts. Never throw racquets or slam balls around in anger. This is dangerous and unsportsmanlike.

Organization and Skill Work

Most tennis classes are organized along traditional lines—that is, the instructor shows groups of students proper grips, stances, backswings, and so forth, at the same time. Another method of organizing the class is to allow students to progress at their own rates. This can be accomplished through the use of a unit with performance objectives. Each student knows exactly what is expected and moves from one task to the next when able.

Prepare a unit for each student in the class. As the students come to class, give them a unit, give them access to balls and racquets, and encourage them to get started.

When the entire class has arrived, call them together for an organizational meeting. These meetings might include a "tennis tip" for the day, some comment about the unit, or some skill analysis. The meeting should be short so that most of the class time can be devoted to practicing and mastering skills.

If stations are used, each court can be designated for a particular skill (e.g., one court for volleys, one for ground strokes, and one for serving). Provide plenty of balls (beginners will fare as well with older balls as with newer ones) and racquets. Post the suggested skill tasks on the net or fence, and let the students progress at personalized rates. The instructor should be available for questions and feedback. Do not hesitate to intervene when a student is having difficulty.

Skill Work

The strength of the system is that it allows the teacher to help specific students with particular problems. Once the class has started, the teacher is free to roam the courts and to help students who are having problems. Key points to remember in teaching basic skills include the following:

Volley

1. Watch the ball hit the racquet.
2. Focus on footwork. Step across to hit the volley (a volley to the right should have a final step with the left foot).
3. Minimize backswing. Swing no farther back than the shoulder.
4. Punch the ball and follow through.
5. Never drop the racquet head below the wrist. Bend the knees instead.
6. Squeeze the racquet grip when making contact with the ball.

Ground Strokes

1. Change grips for the backhand and forehand.
2. Prepare for an early backswing; get the racquet back as soon as possible.
3. Set up with the side of the body to the net.
4. Contact the ball even with the front foot; do not wait until the ball gets into the body.
5. Contact the ball with the racquet perpendicular to the ground.
6. Follow through.
7. Keep the knees bent throughout the stroke.

Lobs

1. Set up exactly like you do for ground strokes.
2. Open the racquet face (approximately 45°).
3. Lift up through the swing and finish with a high follow-through.

Overheads

1. Get the racket in "back-scratcher" position as soon as possible.
2. Turn the side of the body toward the net.
3. Contact the ball in front of the body. Do not let it float overhead.

Serves

1. First and foremost, control the toss.
2. Use the continental or backhand grip (this will cause a slice serve, which is the most consistent).

3. "Throw" the racquet at the ball; use plenty of wrist and elbow.

4. Follow through; the back foot (from the stance) should end up on the court.

Safety

Tennis is a safe sport. Most injuries that occur are self-inflicted, such as ankle sprains, muscle sprains, or blisters. A few precautions can help prevent unnecessary injuries.

1. Warm up properly before beginning play.

2. Never leave loose balls lying around the court.

3. Never hit balls (especially serves) when the player opposite is not ready.

4. Communicate. Both players on a doubles team going for an overhead can cost the team a point and cause an injury.

5. Wear appropriate footwear.

Lead-Up Games, Modified Games, and Rainy-Day Activities

Practice is often enhanced, especially for advanced players, when stroke practice is conducted under gamelike conditions. Many students find it enjoyable to compete. The following drills can be done competitively.

Twenty-One

In the game of 21, both players must remain behind the baseline. The ball is put into play when either player drops the ball and hits a ground stroke. From that point on, the game uses the same rules as tennis, except that neither player may volley.

Advanced players can include the rule that any ball landing in front of the service line is out, or the ball may be approached from behind and volleyed. The first player to accrue 21 points wins.

Approach Game

To practice approaching the net, players use half of the court, from the doubles sideline to the center service line. After starting with a ground stroke, the first player moves halfway to the service line. After returning the first ball, player two moves halfway to the service line. After their next shots, players move to the service line and then continue to close in as far as possible, hitting volleys and half volleys. The game may be played to any total, usually 10 or 15.

Lob–Smash

Begin with one player at the net and the other at the baseline. Baseline players hit a lob, which is returned with an overhead. They play out the point and begin again. After 10 points, players change positions. The winner is the player with the most points after these 20 points have been played. Lob–smash can also be played with doubles.

Short Game

Players begin at the service lines and hit soft ground strokes. The ball may not land behind the service line. Regular tennis scoring can be used, or a point total can be set.

Return Drill

The return drill can be used to improve a player's return. One player practices returns while three to five players alternate serves. The receiver returns the serves from the court (either ad or deuce) for the entire time. Servers get two serves, just like the real game, and play the point. Only the server gets a point when a rally is won. When a server gets a designated number of points (usually four or five), the receiver and server exchange places, and all servers' scores return to 0. Each receiver thus gets at least 12 to 15 returns before rotating. The next time this same player becomes the receiver, returns are made from the opposite court. A variation is to have all servers serve and volley.

Half-Court Volleys

Divide the court into halves (as in the Approach Game). One player begins at the net, the other at the baseline. The volleyer puts the ball into play, and the player at the baseline must hit a passing shot (ground stroke). The ball must be kept in the half-court. Play to 10 points, switch places, and continue for 10 more points. As a variation, after the initial shot, the ground stroker may hit lobs and may approach the net if the opportunity arises.

Backboard Practice

If wall space is available in the gymnasium, ground strokes or volleys can be hit against the gym wall.

Service Practice

The gymnasium is an excellent place for beginners to practice the toss. Any line on the gym floor can be substituted for the baseline. Soft foam-rubber tennis balls are excellent for practice of the entire service motion in the gym.

Volleys

Without a net, players can practice volleys indoors. Have them stand 10 to 20 feet apart and hit soft volleys to each other.

Suggested Performance Objectives

Students should work with a partner. When an objective has been mastered to specification, have a partner (or instructor, where indicated) initial the task. The tasks are designed to be progressively more difficult. A student should therefore not proceed to a new task until all preliminary tasks have been completed. The court markings in Figure 20.22 will aid in the comprehension of many of the tasks. Students should refer to the diagram as needed until the markings are learned.

Volley

1. Without a racquet, assume a ready position (feet a shoulder width apart, knees bent, weight forward, hands in front of the body). Have a partner toss tennis balls to the dominant side. Stepping with the opposite foot, reach forward and catch five consecutive balls thrown from a distance of 15 feet. (Balls may not bounce.)

2. From the ready position, gripping the racquet at its head and using proper footwork (instructor will demonstrate), hit five consecutive forehand volleys to your partner who feeds the balls from a distance of 15 feet. (Balls may not bounce.)

3. Perform task 2, but grip the racquet just above the grip (five consecutive times).

4. Demonstrate to the instructor the continental grip—the grip with which volleys are hit.

5. Perform task 2, but use the continental grip, and grip the racquet on the grip (five consecutive times).

6. Perform task 2, but use the backhand side of racquet (five consecutive times).

7. Perform task 2, but grip the racquet just above the grip and use the backhand (five consecutive times).

8. Perform task 5, but use backhand (five consecutive times).

9. Stand halfway between the net and the service line. The partner or instructor will stand across the net at the baseline and drop and hit balls at you. Volley eight of 10 forehands across the net into the singles court.

10. Perform task 9, but use the backhand (eight of 10 times).

11. Standing as in task 9, your partner will randomly hit to your forehand and backhand side. Volley eight of 10 balls into the singles court.

12. Perform task 11, but balls must land in the singles court behind the service line (eight of 10 times).

13. From a distance of at least 6 feet from a wall, hit 15 consecutive volleys above a 3-foot mark. The ball may not touch the ground.

Ground Strokes

1. Demonstrate to the instructor the Eastern forehand and backhand grips.

2. Without a ball, practice 20 consecutive alternate forehand and backhand ground strokes, alternating the grip each time.

3. Standing behind the baseline, drop and hit 10 consecutive forehands across the net into the singles court.

4. Perform task 3, but use the backhand (10 consecutive times).

5. Stand behind the baseline. Your partner stands 20 feet away and bounces balls to your forehand. Hit five of seven forehands across the net into the singles court.

6. Perform task 5, but use the backhand (five of seven times).

7. Standing behind the baseline with a partner across the net, have your partner hit or toss balls to your forehand. Hit eight of 10 forehands across the net into the singles court.

8. Perform task 7, but use the backhand (eight of 10).

9. Perform tasks 7 and 8, but have your partner randomly toss balls to your forehand and backhand (eight of 10).

10. Standing behind a line 27 feet from the backboard, hit 10 consecutive ground strokes that strike the backboard on or above the white line, which is 3 feet above the ground.

11. Perform task 10, but hit 20 consecutive ground strokes.

12. With a partner (or instructor) at the opposite baseline, rally 20 consecutive ground strokes (ball may bounce more than once on each side of the net).

Lobs

1. From the baseline, drop and hit five consecutive forehand lobs into the opposite singles court behind the service line. Balls must be hit high enough so that your partner, from volley position, cannot touch them with the racquet.

2. Perform task 1, but hit backhand lobs (five consecutive times).

3. With partner tossing or hitting balls from the other side of the net, hit five consecutive forehand lobs into the opposite singles court behind the service line.

4. Perform task 3, but hit backhand lobs (five consecutive times).

Serves

1. Demonstrate to the teacher the proper service stance and grip for serving.

2. Using an overhead throwing motion, throw five consecutive balls into the service court from the baseline on both the deuce and ad sides (10 total).

3. Demonstrate the proper toss technique to the instructor.

4. Lay the racquet on the ground with the face 6 inches in front of your front foot. Using the nonracquet hand, toss balls approximately 2 feet higher than your head; three of five must hit the racquet face or frame.

5. Make your normal toss into the air, and using the racquet hand without a racquet, come through the service motion and hit five consecutive balls with the palm of your hand.

6. With a racquet in the "back-scratcher" position, hit five of seven serves into the proper service court.

7. Demonstrate to the instructor an acceptable full backswing for the service.

8. Perform task 6, but use the full backswing to hit five of seven serves into the forehand service court.

9. Place four empty tennis ball cans in the outside corner of the forehand service box. Serve until you have knocked over one can.

10. Perform task 9, but place cans in the inside corner.

11. Perform task 9, but place cans in the backhand court.

12. Perform task 9, but place cans in the inside corner of the backhand court.

Overheads

1. Using the service grip and standing in the service area (at the net), have a partner hit short lobs. Allow the ball to bounce. Hit three of five forehand overheads into the singles court.

2. Repeat task 1, but hit the ball before it bounces (three of five times).

3. Repeat task 1, but stand behind the baseline (three of five times).

4. Perform task 1, but hit six consecutive balls.

5. Perform task 2, but hit six consecutive balls.

6. Perform task 3, but hit six consecutive balls.

REFERENCES AND SUGGESTED READINGS

Lesson Plans

Casten, C. (2009). *Lesson plans for dynamic physical education for secondary school students* (5th ed.). San Francisco: Benjamin Cummings.

Bowling

Fronske, H. (2008). *Teaching cues for sport skills* (4th ed.). San Francisco: Benjamin Cummings.

Martin, J. L., Tandy, R. E., & Agne-Traub, C. (1994). *Bowling* (7th ed.). Dubuque, IA: Brown & Benchmark.

National Association for Girls and Women in Sport. (1979–1981). *Bowling-golf*. Reston, VA: AAHPERD.

Schmottlach, N., & McManama, J. (2006). *Physical education activity handbook* (11th ed.). San Francisco: Benjamin Cummings.

Strickland, R. H. (1989). *Bowling: Steps to Success*. Champaign, IL: Human Kinetics Publishers.

Frisbee

Caporali, J. M. (1988). The ultimate alternative. *Journal of Physical Education, Recreation, and Dance, 59*(9), 98–101.

Danna, M., & Poynter, D. (1978). *Frisbee players' handbook*. Santa Barbara, CA: Parachuting Publications.

Demas, K. (2002). Ultimate. In N. Dougherty (Ed.), *Physical activity and sport for the secondary school student* (5th ed.). Reston, VA: NASPE and AAHPERD.

Fronske, H. (2008). *Teaching cues for sport skills* (4th ed.). San Francisco: Benjamin Cummings.

Roddick, D., & Boda, T. (Eds.). (1986). *The discourse: A manual for students and teachers of the frisbee disc arts* (2nd ed.). San Gabriel, CA: Wham-O Sports Promotion.

Schmottlach, N., & McManama, J. (2006). *Physical education activity handbook* (11th ed.). San Francisco: Benjamin Cummings.

Golf

Fronske, H. (2008). *Teaching cues for sport skills* (4th ed.). San Francisco: Benjamin Cummings.

Mood, D. P., Musker, F. F., & Rink, J. E. (2007). *Sports and recreational activities* (14th ed.). Boston: McGraw-Hill.

Nance, V. L., Davis, E. C., & McMahon, K. E. (1994). *Golf* (7th ed.). Dubuque, IA: Brown & Benchmark.

Owens, B. B. (1989). *Golf: Steps to success.* Champaign, IL: Human Kinetics Publishers.

Owens, B. B. (1992). *Advanced golf: Steps to success.* Champaign, IL: Human Kinetics Publishers.

Schmottlach, N., & McManama, J. (2006). *Physical education activity handbook* (11th ed.). San Francisco: Benjamin Cummings.

White, H. (2002). Golf. In N. Dougherty (Ed.), *Physical activity and sport for the secondary school student* (5th ed.). Reston, VA: NASPE and AAHPERD.

In-line Skating

Fronske, H. (2008). *Teaching cues for sport skills* (4th ed.). San Francisco: Benjamin Cummings.

Schmottlach, N., & McManama, J. (2006). *Physical education activity handbook* (11th ed.). San Francisco: Benjamin Cummings.

Jogging

Fronske, H. (2008). *Teaching cues for sport skills* (4th ed.). San Francisco: Benjamin Cummings.

Mood, D. P., Musker, F. F., & Rink, J. E. (2007). *Sports and recreational activities* (14th ed.). Boston: McGraw-Hill.

Schmottlach, N., & McManama, J. (2006). *Physical education activity handbook* (11th ed.). San Francisco: Benjamin Cummings.

Racquetball

Allsen, P. E., & Witbeck, P. (1992). *Racquetball* (5th ed.). Dubuque, IA: Brown & Benchmark.

Fronske, H. (2008). *Teaching cues for sport skills* (4th ed.). San Francisco: Benjamin Cummings.

Kittleson, S. (1993). *Teaching racquetball: Steps to success.* Champaign, IL: Human Kinetics Publishers.

Liles, L., & Neimeyer, R. A. (1993). *Winning racquetball.* Dubuque, IA: Brown & Benchmark.

Mood, D. P., Musker, F. F., & Rink, J. E. (2007). *Sports and recreational activities* (14th ed.). Boston: McGraw-Hill.

Schmottlach, N., & McManama, J. (2006). *Physical education activity handbook* (11th ed.). San Francisco: Benjamin Cummings.

Rhythmic Activity

Hernandez, B. (2002). Dance education. In N. Dougherty (Ed.), *Physical activity and sport for the secondary school student* (5th ed.). Reston, VA: NASPE and AAHPERD.

Livingston, P. (1981). *The complete book of country swing and western dance.* Garden City, NY: Doubleday & Co.

Mood, D. P., Musker, F. F., & Rink, J. E. (2007). *Sports and recreational activities* (14th ed.). Boston: McGraw-Hill.

Pittman, A. M., Waller, M. S., & Dark, C. L. (2005). *Dance a while: Handbook for folk, square, contra, and social dance* (9th ed.). San Francisco: Benjamin Cummings.

Ray, O. M. (1992). *Encyclopedia of line dances: The steps that came and stayed.* Reston, VA: AAHPERD.

Rope Jumping

American Alliance for Health, Physical Education, Recreation, and Dance. (1992). *Jump rope for heart.* Reston, VA: AAHPERD. (Jump Rope for Heart materials can be obtained by contacting your local affiliate of the American Heart Association or by calling the AAHPERD Special Events Office at 703-476-3489.)

American Heart Association. (1984a). *Jump for the health of it: Basic skills.* Dallas, TX: Author.

American Heart Association. (1984b). *Jump for the health of it: Intermediate single- and double-dutch skills.* Dallas, TX: Author.

Melson, B., & Worrell, V. (1986). *Rope skipping for fun and fitness.* Wichita, KS: Woodlawn.

Poppen, J. D. (1989). *Action packet on jumping rope.* Puyallup, WA: Action Productions.

Sutherland, M., & Carnes, C. (1987). *Awesome jump rope activities book.* Carmichael, CA: Education Co.

Strength Training

Baechle, T. R. (1992). *Weight training.* Champaign, IL: Human Kinetics Publishers.

Fronske, H. (2008). *Teaching cues for sport skills* (4th ed.). San Francisco: Benjamin Cummings.

Groves, B. (2002). Weight training. In N. Dougherty (Ed.), *Physical activity and sport for the secondary school student* (5th ed.). Reston, VA: NASPE and AAHPERD.

Mood, D. P., Musker, F. F., & Rink, J. E. (2007). *Sports and recreational activities* (14th ed.). Boston: McGraw-Hill.

Moran, G., & McGlynn, G. (1990). *Dynamics of strength training.* Dubuque, IA: Brown & Benchmark.

Rasch, P. J. (1990). *Weight training* (5th ed.). Dubuque, IA: Brown & Benchmark.

Schmottlach, N., & McManama, J. (2006). *Physical education activity handbook* (11th ed.). San Francisco: Benjamin Cummings.

Westcott, W. L. (1995). *Strength fitness: Physiological principles and training techniques* (4th ed.). Dubuque, IA: Brown & Benchmark.

Swimming/Aquatics

American Red Cross. (1993). *Swimming and diving.* St. Louis: Mosby.

Fronske, H. (2008). *Teaching cues for sport skills* (4th ed.). San Francisco: Benjamin Cummings.

Hallett, B., & Clayton, R. D. (Eds.). (1980). *Course syllabus:*

Teacher of swimming. Reston, VA: American Alliance for Health, Physical Education, Recreation, and Dance (AAHPERD).

Johnson, R. (2002). Swimming. In N. Dougherty (Ed.), *Physical activity and sport for the secondary school student* (5th ed.). Reston, VA: NASPE and AAHPERD.

Mood, D. P., Musker, F. F., & Rink, J. E. (2007). *Sports and recreational activities* (14th ed.). Boston: McGraw-Hill.

Schmottlach, N., & McManama, J. (2006). *Physical education activity handbook* (11th ed.). San Francisco: Benjamin Cummings.

Thomas, D. B. (1989). *Teaching swimming: Steps to success.* Champaign, IL: Human Kinetics Publishers.

Vickers, B. J., & Vincent, W. (1994). *Swimming* (6th ed.). Dubuque, IA: Brown & Benchmark.

Tennis

The following publications contain material pertaining to rules and regulations: *The Rules of Tennis, Rules of Tennis and Cases and Decisions, A Friend at Court (Rules, Cases, Decisions, Officials, and Officiating),* and *The Code (Unwritten Rules Players Should Follow in Unofficiated Matches).* All may be purchased from the United States Tennis Association, Education and Research Center, Publications Department, 729 Alexander Road, Princeton, NJ 08540.

Brown, J. (1989). *Tennis, steps to success.* Champaign, IL: Human Kinetics Publishers.

Dusel, J. (2002). Tennis. In N. Dougherty (Ed.), *Physical activity and sport for the secondary school student* (5th ed.). Reston, VA: NASPE and AAHPERD.

Fronske, H. (2008). *Teaching cues for sport skills* (4th ed.). San Francisco: Benjamin Cummings.

Johnson, J. D. (1993). *Tennis* (6th ed.). Dubuque, IA: Brown & Benchmark.

Mood, D. P., Musker, F. F., & Rink, J. E. (2007). *Sports and recreational activities* (14th ed.). Boston: McGraw-Hill.

Schmottlach, N., & McManama, J. (2006). *Physical education activity handbook* (11th ed.). San Francisco: Benjamin Cummings.

WEB SITES

Bowling
www.bowlingindex.com

Frisbee
www.discgolf.com
www.pdga.org
www.upa.org

Golf
www.golfonline.com
www.teachkidsgolf.com

Racquetball
www.usra.org

Strength Training
www.biggerfasterstronger.com
www.hammerstrength.com
www.weiderfitness.com

Tennis
www.tennisserver.com
www.usta.com

NATIONAL STANDARDS FOR PHYSICAL EDUCATION*

STANDARD 1 Demonstrates competency in motor skills and movement patterns needed to perform a variety of physical activities.

STANDARD 2 Demonstrates understanding of movement concepts, principles, strategies, and tactics as they apply to the learning and performance of physical activities.

STANDARD 3 Participates regularly in physical activity.

STANDARD 4 Achieves and maintains a health-enhancing level of physical fitness.

STANDARD 5 Exhibits responsible personal and social behavior that respects self and others in physical activity settings.

STANDARD 6 Values physical activity for health, enjoyment, challenge, self-expression, and/or social interaction.

ESSENTIAL COMPONENTS OF A QUALITY PROGRAM

COMPONENT 1 A quality physical education program is organized around content standards that offer direction and continuity to instruction and evaluation.

COMPONENT 2 A quality program is student centered and based on the developmental urges, characteristics, and interests of students.

COMPONENT 3 Quality physical education makes physical activity and motor-skill development the core of the program.

COMPONENT 4 Physical education programs teach management skills and self-discipline.

COMPONENT 5 Quality programs emphasize inclusion of all students.

COMPONENT 6 In a quality physical education setting, instruction focuses on the process of learning skills rather than the product or outcome of the skill performance.

COMPONENT 7 A quality physical education program teaches lifetime activities that students can use to promote their health and personal wellness.

COMPONENT 8 Quality physical education teaches cooperative and responsibility skills and helps students develop sensitivity to diversity and gender issues.

*Reprinted from *Moving Into the Future: National Standards for Physical Education*, 2nd ed. (2004), with permission from the National Association for Sport and Physical Education (NASPE), 1900 Association Dr., Reston, VA 20191–1599.

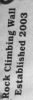

21

Outdoor
Adventure
Activities

Many physical education programs have added popular outdoor adventure activities to the curriculum. Rock climbing, caving, canoeing, fly-fishing, orienteering, and backpacking are just a few examples. Many students are interested in these activities, which are challenging and provide a sense of risk and adventure. These activities that can be added to the curriculum as stand-alone units or as a combination unit that provides introductory information in many of these areas. In addition to the detailed information on ropes course activities, orienteering, and group initiative games, we have added resources and Web sites in many other areas to help physical education teachers add these lifetime activities to the curriculum.

ROPES COURSE ACTIVITIES

Ropes course activities involve obstacles that use ropes, cables, logs, trees, ladders, tires, swings, cargo nets, rings, and other equipment to present students with a challenge that usually has a degree of controlled risk. These obstacles require students to climb, swing, crawl, and balance themselves. Beneath many of the obstacles are water, mud, people, cargo nets, and trees. All of the activities are completed with student spotters or a safety belay line of some type under the direct supervision of the teacher. The activities can be linked together in sequence, or they can be used as separate

challenges. Certain activities require strength and endurance, while others require balance and coordination. The ropes course activities can function as lead-up activities for rock climbing, caving, rappelling, or other adventure activities.

Teachers need to be certain that students begin with activities containing little risk. Student safety is always the most important factor. Generally, the beginning ropes course activities are situated close to the ground with many spotters available, thereby assuring students that little danger is involved. As they gain knowledge, experience, physical skill, and confidence, students can move to higher and more challenging obstacles. Teachers need to be aware of varying ability levels of students and not require all students to attempt the same activities unless they are ready for the obstacle. Some students will display fear of these types of activities and should be encouraged rather than pushed.

Ropes course activities, just like any other adventure activity, can be risky and have the potential for physical injury if safety factors are overlooked. We recommend that teachers seek the advice of experienced ropes course builders before constructing any of these activities (see the suggested readings at the end of this chapter). Ropes course activities can be built into the existing environment, or posts and logs can be placed in the ground. The following are examples of ropes course activities that could be used in this type of program.

Commando Crawl

In this activity, the student crawls across the top of a 2-inch Manila hawser rope by placing the chest on the rope and passing the rope under the body (Figure 21.1). One foot is hooked over the top of the rope and the other leg hangs down for balance. The student slowly pulls his or her way across the rope by using the arms and the top leg. The student should be spotted on both sides of the rope in case of a fall. If a fall does occur, the spotters should catch the student and slowly lower him or her to the ground. The rope should be secured to two trees, 4 to 5 feet above the ground. A bowline knot can be used on one side of the rope, and the opposite side should be wrapped around the tree and tied off with two half hitches. Wooden blocks may be secured to the trees below the rope to prevent the rope from slipping.

FIGURE 21.1 Commando crawl

Tire Swing

Students swing across a set of tires that are secured to a top rope or cable (Figure 21.2). The tires are set at varying heights above the ground, anywhere from 3 to 4 feet high. The tires should be 3 to 4 feet apart. The top cable should be 10 to 12 feet above the ground. To prevent a fall, spotters should be placed on both sides of the students as they proceed.

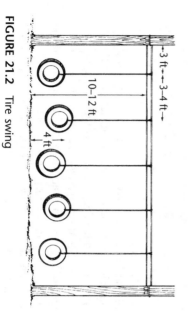

FIGURE 21.2 Tire swing

Kitten Crawl

Students crawl along two parallel inclined ropes that are secured at 5 feet high at one end and at 2 feet high at the other end. Students should be on all fours and can slowly crawl up or down the rope (Figure 21.3). Spotters should be aware that the participants can fall through the middle of the two ropes as well as over the sides. Wooden blocks can be used to prevent the rope from slipping down on the secured ends. The height of the ropes can be varied according to the ability levels of the participants.

Two-Rope Bridge

Two parallel ropes about 5 to 6 feet apart are secured to trees or posts. The students stand sideways on the bottom rope and hold on to the top rope with their hands. They slowly slide their way across the rope (Figure 21.4). The height of the bottom rope should be less than 5 to 6 feet for beginners. If the height of the bottom rope is higher than 6 feet, then a belay or safety system should be used. A 15-foot swami belt or waist loop of 1-inch tubular nylon flat rope can be wrapped around the student's waist and attached with a carabiner to a belay line. The top of the belay line can be attached with a

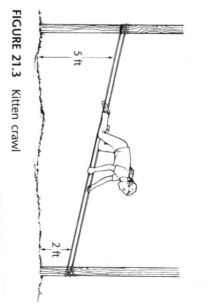

FIGURE 21.3 Kitten crawl

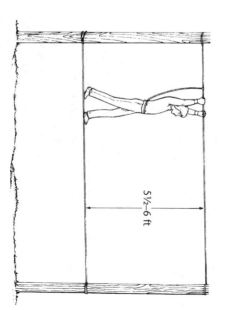

FIGURE 21.4 Two-rope bridge

carabiner to the top rope of the bridge. Spotters can be used for lower bridges, and they should follow the participant across the rope and be ready for a fall.

Three-Rope Bridge

The three-rope Burma bridge has been used in many areas for crossing various ravines, rivers, and mountain passes. It consists of two parallel ropes about waist high for handholds and a bottom rope to walk on (Figure 21.5). A number of V-shaped ropes should be placed about 2 feet apart along the bridge to support all three ropes. A rope or cable across the top of the bridge should be constructed for attaching a safety line. A swami belt can be attached to the student and then clipped to the top line with carabiners and a piece of nylon webbing. The height of the bridge can vary; it can be low or high depending on the local area. It is exciting to place the bridge over a natural obstacle if possible. It is important to use wooden blocks to prevent the ropes from slipping in order to ensure that the ropes are kept tight.

Tension Traverse

The student balances and moves across a rope suspended between two trees. A top support rope is attached to one tree, and the student applies tension on this rope for balance while sliding across the rope. The student should slide sideways across the rope. One hand should hold the support rope at the waist, and the other hand should hold the rope above the head (Figure 21.6). The bottom rope is 2 to 3 feet above the ground and should always be taut. Again, wooden blocks should be used to prevent the rope from slipping down. Spotters should be used for safety, and the students should be instructed to let go of the support rope and jump off if they are going to fall. If they hold on to the top rope while falling, they will swing into the tree or post.

Triangle Tension Traverse

This activity is similar to the tension traverse and adds two more sides to the activity. The bottom rope is placed in a triangle, and the student starts at one intersection of the triangle (Figure 21.7). The student balances and moves around the triangle with a top support rope similar to the straight tension traverse. Spotters should be used for safety as the students move around the triangle. The height of the bottom rope should be 4 to 5 feet and it should be taut and blocked to prevent slipping.

Balance Beam

The balance beam is a log attached between two trees or posts, anywhere from 5 to 10 feet high (Figure 21.8). It is a good obstacle that can be used as a bridge between two other rope activities. The students simply walk across the beam. If several beams are used in a course, they can be constructed at varying heights. If the beam is higher than 5 feet, a top safety belay line should be used. If the beam is lower than 5 feet, then student spotters are necessary for safety.

FIGURE 21.6 Tension traverse

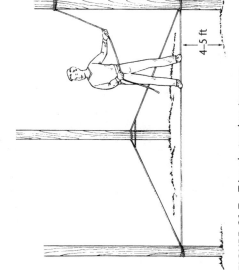

FIGURE 21.7 Triangle tension traverse

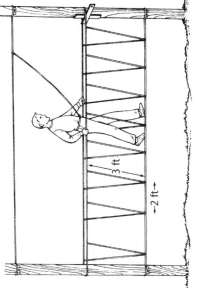

FIGURE 21.5 Three-rope bridge

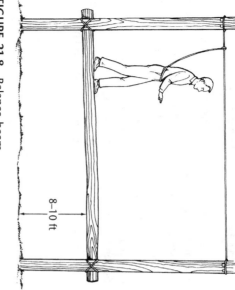

FIGURE 21.8 Balance beam

hold them in place. The upper attachment of the ropes should be blocked in order to prevent any slipping. Rubber tires can be nailed to the trees to prevent damage from the moving log. Participants need to move carefully to avoid falling on the log itself. Spotters can be used to help the students keep their balance.

Cargo Net Jump

Students move up an inclined log to a jumping platform and then jump into a cargo net in the tucked position. The cargo net should be made of 1-inch Manila rope with a small mesh (Figure 21.11). A rope ladder could be used to exit the net. The net can be secured 15 to 20 feet above the ground or lower, and the jumping platform should be about 5 feet higher than the net. The corners of the net should be secured and

Inclined Log

The inclined log is simply a balance beam that is placed at an angle (Figure 21.9). It is effective for beginners to walk on an obstacle that moves from the ground to a higher level. Students can walk up the log, bear crawl on all fours, or hug the log as they move up, depending on their comfort level. A moving belay should be set up slightly off-center from the log so that students will not fall into the log. As students move up the height of the log, the belay person or spotters should move with them. The log should be notched to enhance the footing and nailed and lashed to the trees or posts for support.

Swinging Log

Students walk along a moving log that is suspended from trees by ropes (Figure 21.10). The log should never be more than 1 foot above the ground because falls will be frequent in this activity. All rocks, stumps, and objects should be cleared away from the area. The log should be notched where the ropes are attached to

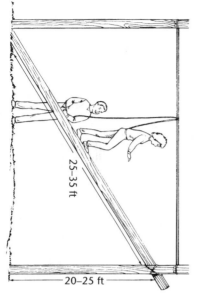

FIGURE 21.9 Inclined log

25–35 ft

20–25 ft

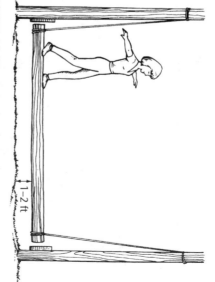

FIGURE 21.10 Swinging log

1–2 ft

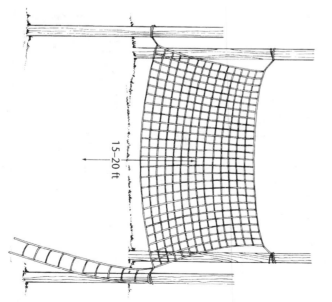

FIGURE 21.11 Cargo net jump

15–20 ft

blocked to avoid slipping. These secured corners should be inspected regularly before each use. The instructor needs to be careful with students on a jumping platform. Students should be instructed to jump into the center of the net, and only one student should be allowed in the net at a time.

Giant's Ladder

The students balance, jump, and swing up a giant ladder that is made of logs. The ladder encourages development of balance, strength, agility, and endurance. Students stand and balance on the first rung and then jump to the next rung and land on the chest or abdominal area (Figure 21.12). The feet swing free below the rung; students then pull upward onto the rung and get ready to move up to the next rung. The rungs get farther apart as the student moves higher on the ladder. The second rung is 4 to 5 feet from the first, and the third rung is 5 to 6 feet up the ladder. Students must be belayed throughout the climb. A top cable should be used to attach the belay rope. The instructor should keep a tight belay on students so they do not swing into any of the logs.

GROUP INITIATIVE ACTIVITIES

Group initiative activities are physical and mental challenges that require the cooperation and joint efforts of a group of students. They require the group to think, plan, and execute a strategy for solving the challenge. Teamwork and cooperation are necessary. These

activities force students to work together. Some of the activities involve risk, excitement, and adventure; thus, proper safety and supervision strategies must be implemented. These activities can be completed indoors or outdoors. They can be conducted in conjunction with ropes course activities or as totally separate activities. Many of them require a few special props in order to be effective.

Electric Fence

The object is to get a group of students over the "electric fence" without touching the fence (Figure 21.13). A piece of rope is stretched between two trees. The rope should be 5 feet off the ground. The students should be given a 4- by 4-inch beam that is about 8 feet long to help them. Students are not allowed to use the support trees, nor are they allowed to reach under the rope. They can reach over the top of the rope. There are many solutions. A good procedure is to have the group hold the beam on their shoulders and get a few stronger people over first. Then they can hold the beam on the opposite side for the others.

Boardwalk

This involves the use of four, 2- by 4-inch boards that are 10 to 12 feet long. Two sets of two boards are connected by ropes and eyebolts. About 10 students stand on two of the boards and then hold the other boards at about waist level (Figure 21.14). Working together, the students alternate lifting the boards and move forward as a group. All participants must keep their feet

FIGURE 21.13 Electric fence

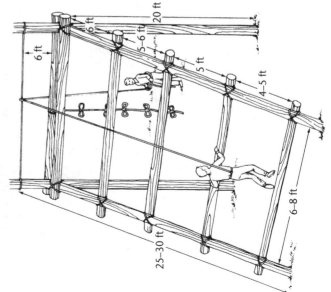

FIGURE 21.12 Giant's ladder

on the boards. It can be a race or just a challenge to work together.

FIGURE 21.14 Boardwalk

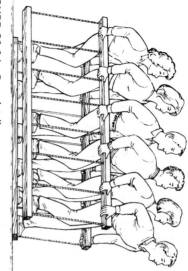

Platforms

A group of six to eight students stands on the first of three platforms. The platforms are 14 feet apart in a straight line. The students are given a 12-foot board and a 4-foot board. The challenge is to move the group from platform to platform without touching the ground with either the boards or any person in the group (Figure 21.15). The best solution is to extend the smaller board out from the platform about 2 feet and get the entire group to stand on this board. Then, a smaller person can walk out on the board and place the 12-foot board to the next platform and walk across. After three or four people have reached the second platform, the boards need to be switched so the smaller one is now on the second platform. This process continues until all students are on the third platform.

FIGURE 21.15 Platforms

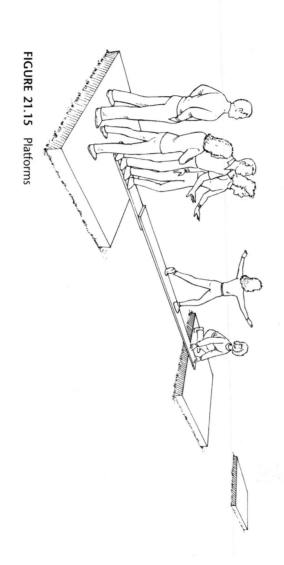

Nitro Crossing

The object is to get each member of a group to swing across an area with a bucket of "nitro" (water) without spilling it. The swing rope must be attached to some type of tree limb or cross board that provides a good swinging area. Two trip boards need to be placed about 1 foot off the ground on either side of the swing area (Figure 21.16). The trip boards can be on top of cones or blocks of wood. Half of the group starts on one side, and half starts on the other side. They try to swing their group members to the opposite side without spilling the nitro.

The Beam and the Wall

The object of this activity is to move a group of students over a log beam (Figure 21.17) about 8 feet above the ground or a solid wooden wall (Figure 21.18) that is 12 to 14 feet above the ground. Group members cannot use the support trees or posts. They must work together to support each member up and over the obstacle. The wall can be built with a walkway on the back side where students can stand. Once students get to the top, they can reach down and help others up.

Faith Fall and Trust Dive

The individual falls backward into the arms of a group of students. The individual stands on a balance beam or similar elevated object. The group lines up shoulder to shoulder in two opposite and facing lines (Figures 21.19 and 21.20). The arms are extended and alternated with the arms of the person directly across from them. Do not allow students to lock wrists because the

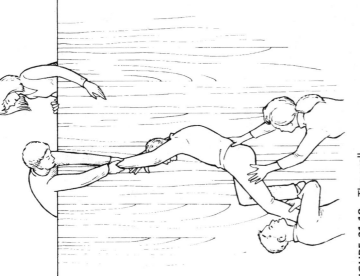

FIGURE 21.16 Nitro crossing

partners may bump heads. The individual falls when the catching line is ready.

Human Circle Pass

The group forms a tight circle about 6 feet in diameter, with the arms up in a catching position. One person is put in the middle and closes his or her eyes. When ready, the person falls backward, forward, or sideways into the hands of the group members. They support and pass the individual around the circle. Everyone takes a turn being in the center of the circle.

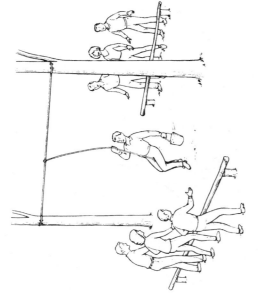

FIGURE 21.17 The beam

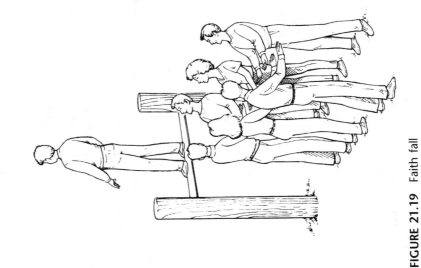

FIGURE 21.18 The wall

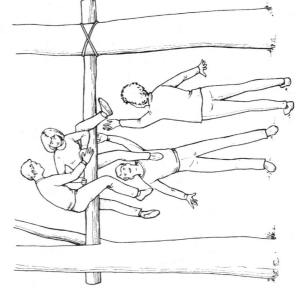

FIGURE 21.19 Faith fall

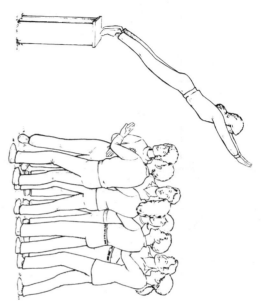

FIGURE 21.20 Trust dive

Human Line Pass

Students sit in a line on the ground with legs straight out, feet touching the person in front of them. The first person in line stands and sits back into the hands of the sitting people who pass the person backward over their heads. The process continues until all people have been passed. Spotters can be placed on each side of the line to ensure safety.

Lightbulb Change

The group is in the dark and cannot proceed until the lightbulb is changed. The goal is to form a pyramid high enough to reach the ceiling (13 to 15 feet) to change the bulb (Figure 21.21). A piece of tape can be used to show the highest spot reached by the group. A wall with no windows or protruding objects should be used. Spotters can also be used to make sure that no one falls backward.

High Water

This is similar to the lightbulb change, but the groups compete against one another to see which can make the highest mark on the wall with a piece of chalk or tape (Figure 21.21).

Sasquatch Race

Two groups are formed and are instructed to make a moving object with a specified number of feet and hands on the ground. Everybody must be part of the group and joined to the others. After the sasquatch is built, the two groups race to a finish line.

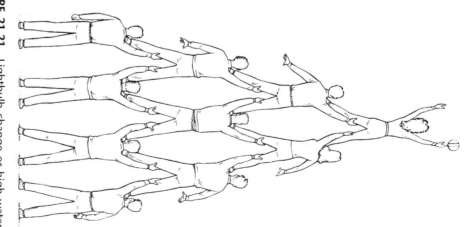

FIGURE 21.21 Lightbulb change or high water

Platform Stand

A platform with 20- to 24-inch sides can be used as the base of support. The object is to get as many people as possible standing on the platform simultaneously (Figure 21.22). The pose must be held for 8 seconds.

Stream Crossing

Students must move from one side of the area to the other without touching the floor. They are given small carpet squares on which to move across an imaginary stream. Fewer than the necessary number of squares are handed out, however, so students have to pass the squares back and forth in order to get their team across. The first team to move all members across the stream is declared the winner.

Height Alignment

Members of the group keep their eyes closed and are instructed to align themselves in a single-file line from shortest person to tallest person. The students cannot

can result in an enjoyable experience for all students and members of a family.

Orienteering activities can be easily modified and adapted to secondary physical education programs. Many activities can be completed in a classroom or gymnasium or on the school grounds. Teachers can use compasses and homemade maps of the school grounds to develop a challenging unit. A nearby park or a vacant lot can add great variety to orienteering courses.

Sequence of Skills

The basic skills involved in orienteering include reading a topographical map, using a compass, and pacing various distances. Considering many students have had little experience with these skills, it is important to introduce new information and terminology slowly. Students can perform many of the activities with a partner so there will be two heads working together on a problem. Teachers can include a variety of maps, a compass, and new pacing activities each day to keep the students challenged. Many types of activities and hands-on experiences should be incorporated in the unit. Competitive events can be added after students begin to understand the basic map and compass skills. The block plan at the end of this unit will provide some ideas for the sequencing of learning activities.

Learning Activities
Compass Activities

Parts of the Compass. Make the students aware of the basic parts of the compass and how the instrument works (Figure 21.23).

FIGURE 21.22 Platform stand

talk and can use only their hands to figure out the arrangement.

ORIENTEERING

Orienteering is a challenging outdoor adventure activity that combines cross-country running and the ability to read a map and use a compass. It has been called the thinking sport because rapid decisions need to be made in determining which route to follow so that a minimum of time and energy is used. Ideally, the orienteering competition should take place in a wilderness area that is not familiar to the participants. Orienteering events can be set up for beginners, novices, and experts, thus enabling people of all ages and abilities to take part and find success in these activities. The need for both physical and mental skills

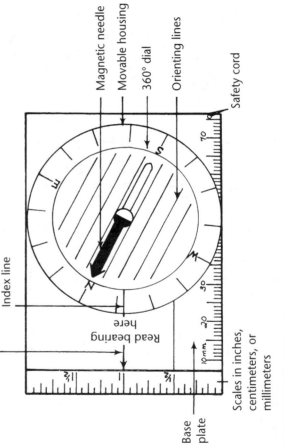

FIGURE 21.23 Parts of a compass

Forming a Triangle. Place a penny or other small object on the ground. Set any bearing less than 90°. Walk 10 paces on that bearing. Add 120° and walk another 10 paces. Repeat the procedure again and end up where you started. This drill can be repeated with another bearing and a different number of paces.

Forming a Square. Introduce the same basic game as "Forming a Triangle" except that 90° bearings are added each time, and four sides are formed. The distance must be the same each time.

Numbers and Numerals. Tape the numbers 1 to 10 on the floor in scattered positions around the gymnasium (Figure 21.25). Next, tape the Roman numerals I to X in scattered positions on the gymnasium walls. The students begin by standing on any of the numbers on the floor and shooting a bearing to the corresponding numeral on the wall. This drill can be made competitive by trying for the fastest time and correct bearing.

Forming a Christmas Tree. On a piece of graph paper, have students place a dot in the southeast quadrant of the paper. From this starting dot, have them draw a line the distances shown in Figure 21.26 and on the appropriate bearing.

Map Bearings. Teach students to determine the bearing between points on a map. The teacher puts several points on a map and then tells the students to find the bearing and distance between the points. Ten numbered points might be shown, and students can find the bearing and distance from 1 to 2, from 2 to 3,

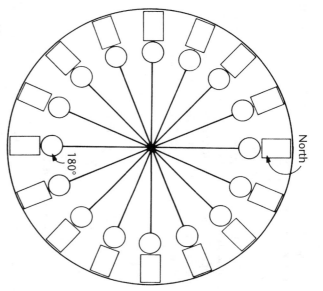

FIGURE 21.24   Compass bearings and directions

Following a Bearing. Discuss how to hold the compass properly. Give students a bearing to find and follow. Have them stand in one line facing the instructor. Call out a bearing and have them rotate their bodies in place until they are facing the bearing direction.

Compass Bearings and Directions. Have the students complete the directions and degrees in Figure 21.24.

Landmarks. Call out various visible landmarks, and have students shoot a bearing from where they are standing to the landmark.

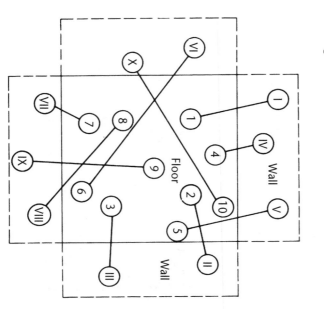

FIGURE 21.25   Numbers and numerals

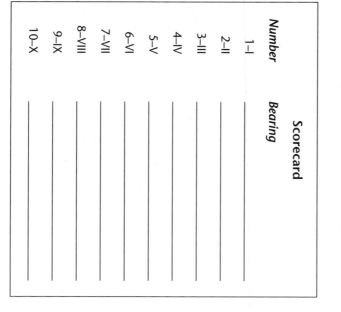

Scorecard	
Number	Bearing
1–I	
2–II	
3–III	
4–IV	
5–V	
6–VI	
7–VII	
8–VIII	
9–IX	
10–X	

and so forth. Advanced orienteering can include a discussion of magnetic declination and the addition or subtraction of declination.

Destination Unknown. Divide the class into four teams. Each team follows the given bearings and paces in Figure 21.27. All teams should end up at the same destination.

School-yard Compass Game and Competitive Compass Game. Consider setting up two challenging compass games that are available from The Silva Company (www.silva.se). The games are inexpensive and can be set up easily in a school situation.

Bearing	Distance (cm)	Bearing	Distance (cm)
1. 269	2.2	9. 136	6.3
2. 2	2.7	10. 293	1.9
3. 266	4.9	11. 141	5.2
4. 30	6.5	12. 284	2.4
5. 246	2.6	13. 125	5.2
6. 34	5.0	14. 271	5.1
7. 244	2.0	15. 179	2.7
8. 37	4.6		

FIGURE 21.26 Forming a Christmas tree

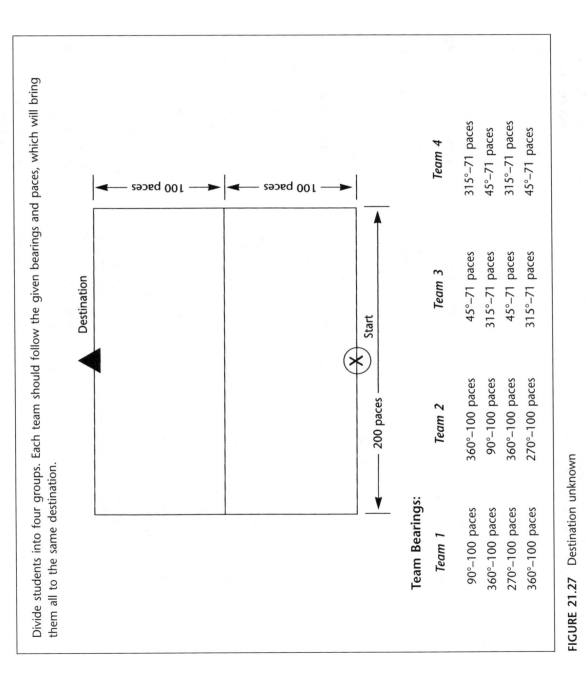

Divide students into four groups. Each team should follow the given bearings and paces, which will bring them all to the same destination.

Team Bearings:

Team 1	Team 2	Team 3	Team 4
90°–100 paces	360°–100 paces	45°–71 paces	315°–71 paces
360°–100 paces	90°–100 paces	315°–71 paces	45°–71 paces
270°–100 paces	360°–100 paces	45°–71 paces	315°–71 paces
360°–100 paces	270°–100 paces	315°–71 paces	45°–71 paces

FIGURE 21.27 Destination unknown

Map Activities

Mapping the School. Have students draw rough maps of the school grounds with all of the various buildings, fields, and identification points. These maps can later be used in orienteering competitions.

Map Squares. Cut up several topographical maps of the local area into small squares. Students try to locate the cut squares on an uncut map. Have the students identify points of interest, symbols, distances, contour lines, vegetation, roads, water, and so forth.

Map Symbol Relay. Draw a map symbol on one side of an index card and write the name of a different symbol on the back of the card. A duplicate set of cards is necessary for each team in the relay (four teams means four sets of cards). The game begins with the cards on one side of the gym and the teams on the opposite side. The teacher calls out the first symbol, such as a school. The first member of the team runs to the cards, finds the symbol, and then runs back to the team. The name of the next symbol to be found is on the back of the card with the school symbol. The game continues until all of the cards are played. Students waiting in line can be reviewing symbols. Students who select the wrong symbol must run back and find the correct symbol.

Taking a Trip. Label 10 to 15 points on several topographical maps, and have students calculate the actual distance between a certain number of points. They can calculate map distance and actual mileage. Next, have the students estimate how many days would be necessary to complete the trip. They should be able to describe what the terrain is like and where the water stops are located.

Contour Identification. Have students identify various mountainous and hilly areas from the way those areas look on a contour map. Figure 21.28 is an example of contour problems.

Map Problems. Make up map activities, such as those in Figure 21.29, for a local situation.

Dot-to-Dot Hike. Students start at the X in the northwest corner (Figure 21.30) and draw in the figure by following the directions. Students can develop their own dot-to-dot hike, making other figures.

Pacing Activities

Distance by Pace. Orienteers must be able to judge distance by their pace. One pace equals two steps. A good drill for determining the length of the pace is to set up a course that is 100 feet long. Students walk, jog,

or run the course and count the number of times that the right foot hits the ground. The length of the course (100 feet) is then divided by the number of paces in order to determine length of pace. Pace is usually rounded off to the nearest 6 inches. Pace will vary with walking, jogging, and running.

Contour Identification Problem

Have the students compare some actual terrain contours with the map representations. Training models are available from the Silva Co., and the teacher can develop a number of contour representations for learning activities. The following are a few examples:

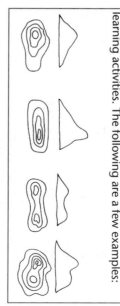

FIGURE 21.28 Contour problems

Distance by Time. One-mile courses can be set up in a variety of terrain, such as open road, open field, open woods, vegetated areas, dense woods, and mountainous areas. Students cover these areas by walking or jogging and record their times. The ability to cover a given distance at a consistent pace can be used later for competitive meets.

Competitive Orienteering Events

After students have received instruction in the use of the compass, maps, and pacing, competitive events can be introduced. Students should understand that they can compete against the environment, themselves, their peers, and elapsed time. It is not necessary to win the event to be successful.

Cross-Country or Point-to-Point Orienteering

Ten checkpoints are set up over the entire school grounds or park area. Teachers develop a map of the area to be covered, and duplicate maps are made up for all participants. Each participant uses a map and compass to find the checkpoints as quickly as possible. The compass is not necessary if unavailable. Decisions about the best route must be made quickly as participants begin. Several master maps should be set out with the locations of the checkpoints. Participants copy the locations of the checkpoints from the master map onto their own map. The time spent in copying down the checkpoints can be included in the overall accumulated time.

Each checkpoint should have a secret letter, word, or name that students must record on some type of

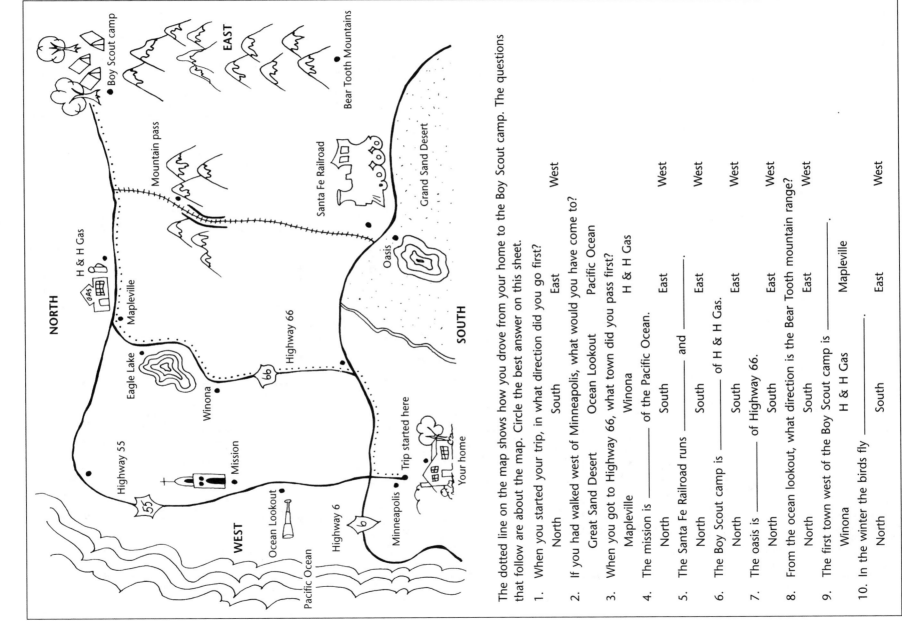

The dotted line on the map shows how you drove from your home to the Boy Scout camp. The questions that follow are about the map. Circle the best answer on this sheet.

1. When you started your trip, in what direction did you go first?
    North   South   East   West

2. If you had walked west of Minneapolis, what would you have come to?
    Great Sand Desert   Ocean Lookout   Pacific Ocean

3. When you got to Highway 66, what town did you pass first?
    Mapleville   Winona   H & H Gas

4. The mission is _____ of the Pacific Ocean.
    North   South   East   West

5. The Santa Fe Railroad runs _____ and _____ .
    North   South   East   West

6. The Boy Scout camp is _____ of H & H Gas.
    North   South   East   West

7. The oasis is _____ of Highway 66.
    North   South   East   West

8. From the ocean lookout, what direction is the Bear Tooth mountain range?
    North   South   East   West

9. The first town west of the Boy Scout camp is _____ .
    Winona   H & H Gas   Mapleville

10. In the winter the birds fly _____
    North   South   East   West

FIGURE 21.29   Map problems

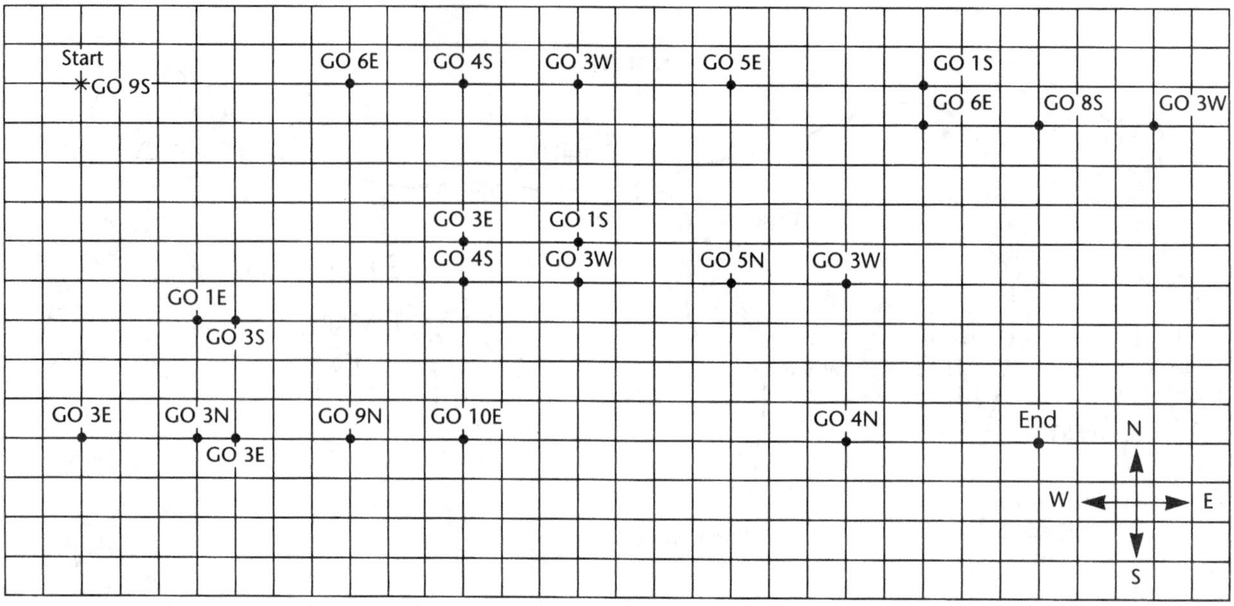

The grid shows:

Start *GO 9S, GO 6E, GO 4S, GO 3W, GO 5E, GO 1S, GO 6E, GO 8S, GO 3W

GO 3E, GO 3N, GO 3E, GO 1E, GO 3S, GO 3E, GO 4S, GO 1S, GO 3W, GO 5N, GO 3W, GO 4N, End

GO 9N, GO 10E

Compass: N, S, E, W

FIGURE 21.30 Dot-to-dot hike

card to show that they actually visited the checkpoint. In regulation meets, a coded punch with a number or letter is used at each control site. These punches are available from The Silva Company, but they are not a necessity. Checkpoints can be a boundary cone, an index card, an envelope, or something similar.

Score Orienteering

In score orienteering, each checkpoint has a designated point value. The checkpoints that are hardest to find and farthest away from the starting point are assigned the highest point totals. The object of the event

is to accumulate the most points within a set time. Students are given a map of the area on which they copy the locations of the checkpoints from a master map. Students must visit as many sites as possible within the time limit and then return to the starting point. If they are late, they can be disqualified or assessed a penalty. Students use some type of standard card to record the clue at each checkpoint that they visit.

Descriptive Orienteering

This type of event requires a compass and pacing skills instead of a map. Students attempt to find the

FIGURE 21.31 Descriptive orienteering sheet

In the Answers column, fill in the keyword or letter that you find at each checkpoint.

Orienteering

Checkpoint	Bearing	Description	Distance	Answers
1	90°	Backstop	50 yd	
2	180°	Goalpost	100 m	
3	230°	Cottonwood	200 ft	
4	160°	Irrigation	35 yd	
5	341°	Hoop	75 m	
6	45°	Palo Verde	400 ft	
7	106°	Trash barrel	150 yd	
8	270°	Power pole	250 ft	
9	78°	Fence post	350 yd	
10	200°	Jumping pit	40 m	

1.	2.	3.	4.	5.
Introduction	*Review*	*Review*	*Review*	*Review*
What is orienteering?	Directions and degrees	Maps, symbols, etc.	Compass and bearings	Map bearings
Brief history				Map symbols
Directions and degrees	*Teach*	*Teach*	*Teach*	*Teach*
Dot-to-dot problems	Maps, symbols scales, contours	Parts of compass	Landmark bearings	Pacing
Compass rose activity		How to hold	Map bearings	
	Activities	*Activities*	*Activities*	*Activities*
	Map the school	Taking a bearing	Boy Scout map problem	Distance by pace
	Map squares	Dial a bearing	Sea adventure	Triangle game
	Contour identification	Magnetic influence	Christmas tree	Square game
				Map symbol relay

6.	7.	8.	9.	10.
Review	*Review*	*Teach*	*Review*	*Review*
Pacing	Orienteering	Magnetic declination	Pacing	Declination
			Bearings	
Teach	*Activity*	*Activities*	Orienteering	*Activities*
Orienteering	Descriptive meet—	Declination problems		Descriptive meet
Point-to-point activity	Have students	Meridian map and	*Activity*	(short)
Score	return to master	compass fun	Point-to-point meet	Clues picked up at
Descriptive	table each time	Point-to-point activity		the next control
Relay	for the next	School-yard compass game		Competitive
Activites	bearing, clue,			compass game,
Taking a trip	and distance			or pacing by
Numbers and numerals				time and distance
Destination unknown				

11.	12.	13.	14.	15.
Review	*Activities*	Written examination	Final score orienteering exam meet	Final point-to-point orienteering meet
Materials for written exam	Relay orienteering meet			
	School-yard compass game and competitive compass game for skill test	Pacing—distance by time	(Off campus if possible)	(Off campus if possible)
Activities				
Score orienteering meet (20 min)				
Landmark bearings for skill test				

FIGURE 21.32 Orienteering block plan

checkpoints as quickly as possible by following a bearing (90°), a distance (50 yards), and a descriptive clue (small tree). The descriptive clue can be eliminated with more advanced participants. Students start at a designated master point and return to that point each time before starting toward the next point. In this way, teachers at the master point can monitor student progress throughout the meet. The checkpoints can all have letters, words, or team names. Each student is given a sheet similar to the one shown in Figure 21.31. A more challenging variation is to give students only the bearing and distance to one checkpoint. When

they find that checkpoint, they will find the bearing and distance posted for the next checkpoint. Students must find each checkpoint to get directions to the next point. Students can be started at different checkpoints.

Block Plan

Figure 21.32 is a sample block plan that offers a suggested 15-day unit for orienteering. The activities recommended in the block plan are available in this section or in *Outdoor Adventure Activities for School and Recreation Programs* (Darst & Armstrong, 1991).

Suggested Performance Objectives

These objectives could be used in a middle or high school unit on orienteering.

1. Identify the compass points.
2. Name the parts of a compass.
3. Find a compass bearing on a map.
4. Follow a compass bearing on a map.
5. Shoot bearings on key points.
6. Identify map symbols.
7. Identify map distances.
8. Determine the pace for 100 yards.
9. Form a triangle using three bearings.
10. Form a square using four bearings.
11. Complete an orienteering course in a time designated by the teacher.

Standard No. 1 = 5 points
Standard No. 2 = 3 points
Standard No. 3 = 1 point

12. Take a 10-question exam on orienteering.

Score: 100% = 5 points
90% = 4 points
80% = 3 points
70% = 2 points
60% = 1 point

TRANSVERSE CLIMBING WALL ACTIVITIES

Climbing walls are an excellent way to develop strength and coordination while solving climbing challenges. Students can learn to cooperate with others, and accomplishment of a climbing task contributes to student self-esteem. There is a certain amount of risk taking associated with climbing, but it is minimized by proper safety and minimal climbing heights. Most transverse walls in middle schools are about 10 feet high with a Red-Relief Line that keeps climbers close to the floor. Additional safety mats are placed along the base of the wall. High school walls can be much higher and more sophisticated. A typical wall may be 40-feet-or-more wide and have 200–300 handholds. The handholds are often color-coded for level of difficulty (see Figure 21.33).

Safety Rules

Climbing walls can be used safely in a physical education setting, but students must be made aware of and

FIGURE 21.33 High school students demonstrate a variety of handholds and footholds on a climbing wall

follow appropriate safety rules. Examples of rules include the following:

■ Climbing walls are only used when a teacher is directly supervising the activity.

■ Only soft-soled shoes are used during climbing activities.

■ Climbers must have a spotter—climbing alone is not allowed.

■ Climbing above the Red-Relief Line is not allowed. The climber's feet must stay below the red line at all times.

■ Climbers are not to touch or interfere with another climber on the wall.

■ Only climbers and spotters are allowed on the safety mats.

■ Participants must climb down from the wall—no jumping down is allowed.

Basic Holds

Students need to learn the basic ways to climb on the wall. Explain and practice handholds and footholds on the wall at a low level before proceeding to climb. The following are basic holds:

■ The Pinch—This basic hold is performed by simply squeezing the hold between the thumb and fingers.

■ Finger Grip—Just the fingers are used to hold a rock while adjusting the legs to a stable rock position.

■ The Crimp—Grasp the hold with the fingers at the middle joint and wrap the thumb over the first joint of the index finger.

- The Edge—This foothold uses the ball-to-toe part of the foot. Either side of the shoe can be used, i.e., the front with the toe pointing or the outside edge of the shoe.

- The Lock-Off—The crimp grip is used on the hold, and the arm is bent at the elbow and held close to the climber's body. This hold is used to stabilize the body close to the wall so the other arm can be used to reach for a new hold.

- Long Traverse—Students start at one end of the wall and move to the other end. Allow climbers to move at a pace suited to them. If some students are faster climbers, they can descend to the floor, pass slower moving students, and continue their climb.

Partner Activities

Partner activities are motivating because they bring a social and cooperative aspect to climbing. Allow students to change partners regularly so they learn to understand individual differences. Encourage students to be helpful but not to touch their partners while they are climbing.

- Point and Move—One partner is on the floor while the other partner assumes a four-point hold on the wall. The floor partner points to a hand-hold or foothold that is the next move the climber must take. The purpose is to challenge partners with reasonable moves, not impossible tasks. Change roles after five moves.

- Sightless Climbing—The climbing partner puts on a blindfold and is guided by his or her partner on the floor. Partners describe the direction and distance of the move to the climber.

- Keep in Touch—Partners are connected with a jump rope by tucking one end of the rope into each partner's pocket or waistband. Don't allow more than 6 inches of rope to be tucked so that this activity is challenging. Both partners begin climbing with the challenge to not lose contact (rope is pulled out).

- Obstacle Course—The object is to climb through and over objects without touching them while climbing. Special holds for hoops and sticks are made so these obstacles can be fastened to the wall.

- Gold and Silver—Climbers work together to transport treasure from one point to another across the wall. Once the climbers are on the wall, they cannot touch the floor or they have to start over. Treasure can be anything such as a wand, hoop, or a racquet. To increase the challenge have them move two or three pieces of treasure.

- Climb and Pass—The goal is for climbers to begin about 5 feet apart on the wall and then pass their partners to the opposite side without touching the floor. They must pass each other and cannot go below a climber to pass.

Individual Challenge Activities

A positive aspect of climbing walls is that students can use footholds to help them climb. This helps youngsters who are overweight find success. For students who are challenged, do not rush them. Give them activities to do that are near the floor and let them determine when they are ready to challenge themselves. Climbing challenges are individual in nature—each student strives to improve his or her performance without concern for how others are climbing. The following are examples of climbing activities that can be used to motivate students to stay on the wall and practice their skills.

- Four-Point Hold—Climbers take a four-point rock position (each hand and foot on a separate rock) and move to four new rocks.

- Red-Line Climb—Students climb high enough to get footholds on rocks above the red line.

- Red Line with Challenges—Similar to the previous climb except students are challenged to climb using only certain-colored rocks.

- Up and Down—Students climb above the red line and then return to the floor using the same pathway (same rocks).

- Three-Point Hold—Students climb off the floor and below the red line. They balance themselves and lift a limb from a hold, then try lifting a different limb.

- Catwalk—Climbers move without dragging their feet against the wall. The goal is to get them to place their feet accurately to their next foothold.

- Rotation—Climbers establish a four-point hold and then try to rotate their bodies (left or right) until their backs are to the wall. If successful, continue to rotate in the same direction until facing the wall.

- Move the Treasure—Stationary climbers move a beanbag or similar object from one rock to another. Also try picking up the treasure from the floor and placing it on a specified rock.

REFERENCES AND SUGGESTED READINGS

Casten, C. (2009). *Lesson plans for dynamic physical education for secondary school students* (6th ed.) San Francisco: Benjamin Cummings.

Darst, P., & Armstrong, G. (1991). *Outdoor adventure activities for school and recreation programs.* Prospect Heights, IL: Waveland Press.

Doody, A. J. (2002). Climbing and challenge course. In N. Dougherty (Ed.), *Physical activity and sport for the secondary school student* (5th ed.). Reston, VA: NASPE and AAHPERD.

Geary, D. (1995). *Using a map and compass.* Mechanicsburg, PA: Stackpole Books.

Hammes, R. (2007, May/June). Orienteering with adventure education: New games for the 21st century. *Strategies*, 7–13.

Ibrahim, H. (1993). *Outdoor education.* Dubuque, IA: Brown & Benchmark.

Kjellstrom, B. (1994). *Be expert with map and compass* (5th ed.). New York: Macmillan.

Mood, D. P., Musker, F. F., & Rink, J. E. (2007). *Sports and recreational activities* (14th ed.). Boston: McGraw-Hill.

O'Brien, J. (2002). Orienteering. In N. Dougherty (Ed.), *Physical activity and sport for the secondary school student* (5th ed.). Reston, VA: NASPE and AAHPERD.

Orlick, T. (1982). *The second cooperative sports and games book.* New York: Pantheon Books/Random House.

Renfrew, T. (1997). *Orienteering.* Champaign, IL: Human Kinetics Publishers.

Rohnke, K. (1984). *Silver bullets: A guide to initiative problems, adventure games, and trust activities.* Dubuque, IA: Kendall/Hunt Publishing Company.

Rohnke, K., Tait, C., Wall, J., & Rodgers, D. (2007). *The complete ropes course manual.* Dubuque, IA: Kendall/Hunt Publishing Company and Wall's Outdoor Associates.

Schmottlach, N., & McManama, J. (2006). *The physical education handbook* (11th ed.). San Francisco: Benjamin Cummings.

Webster, S. (1989). *Ropes course safety manual: An instructor's guide to initiatives and low and high elements.* Dubuque, IA: Kendall/Hunt Publishing Company.

WEB SITES

Adventure Activities
www.adventurehardware.com
www.humankinetics.com
www.pa.org
www.peakwear.com

Backpacking
www.aee.org
www.thebackpacker.com

Climbing and Climbing Walls
www.passemontagne.com/pdf/school-proposal.pdf
www.Rocklist.com
www.traversewall.com

Fly-Fishing
www.tu.org

Orienteering
www.orienteering.org
www.silva.se
www.uio.no/~kjetikj/compass/lesson1.html
www.us.orienteering.org

INDEX

Note: Page numbers followed by *f* indicate a figure or other illustrative material.

AAHPERD (American Alliance for Health, Physical Education, Recreation, and Dance), 21, 22, 231, 232, 233, 258, 344
AAHPERD basketball test, 233
AAHPERD Youth Fitness Test, 347
abdominal exercises
  cruncher, 355
  medicine balls, 377
  pilates, 378–379
  yoga, 379–380
abdominal strength, 234
academic achievement, 39
accident reports, 290, 291*fg*
accuracy drills (racquetball game), 493
Achilles tendon stretch, 352
act of God defense, 283
active aerobics activities, 328, 329*fg*, 330
active sports/recreational activities, 328, 329*fg*, 330, 419
active supervision
  Attention Analysis Form on, 219*fg*
  developing plan for, 131
  improving instruction through use of, 215–216, 218–220*fg*
  legal responsibilities regarding, 284
  maintaining student interest through, 130
  safety and liability checklist on, 290, 292
Activitygram program, 22
activity time, 333–335
Adams, R. S., 254
Adams, T. M., 86
addition tag, 320, 421
administrators. *See* school administrators
adolescents
  academic achievement, physical education, and, 39
  aerobic capacity of, 34–35
  benefits of physical activity for, 29–30

excessive weight and, 37–38
growth patterns of, 30, 31*fg*–32*fg*, 33*fg*
long-term effect of physical activity on, 39
physical education dropout by, 38–39
physical maturity of, 33–34
resistance (strength) training recommendations for, 41–42
type 2 diabetes in overweight, 38
types of appropriate physical activity for, 327*fg*–328
See also high school students; middle school students
adventure activities. *See* outdoor adventure activities
aerial ball (flag football game), 444–445
aerobic activities
  alternating partner resistance with, 367–368
  definition of, 391
  health club workouts, 368–369
  Physical Activity Pyramid on, 328, 329*fg*, 330
  See also endurance exercises
aerobic capacity
  Fitnessgram test on, 234
  impact of being overweight on, 35
  measuring, 34–35
affective domain
  assessment of the, 250, 253–254
  curriculum design inclusion of, 53
  teaching to enhance the, 115–116
aggressive communicators, 157
agility
  accommodating students with disabilities lacking, 273–274
  definition and testing of, 231
  as skill-related physical fitness component, 348
agility activities
  described, 312
  examples listed, 313–316

aides (teaching), 276
all-four pulls exercise, 361
all-fours circle, 315*fg*
ALT-PE (Academic Learning Time-Physical Education), 212
American Academy of Pediatrics, 40, 41, 347
American Alliance for Health, Physical Education, Recreation, and Dance (AAHPERD), 21, 22, 231, 232, 233, 258, 344
American College of Sports Medicine (ACSM), 329, 347
anecdotal record sheets, 244
animal walks and sport movements activity, 318
aquatics. *See* swimming/aquatics
archery instruction
  effective, 424–425
  lead-up games and learning activities, 425
  organization, skill work, and safety issues of, 425
  sequence of skills, 423–424
Arizona State University Observation Instrument (ASUOI), 224–227
Arkansas flip, 313
arm and should girdle stretches, 354
Armstrong, G., 535
Armstrong, M., 171
arm wrestling, 414
Arnold, R. K., 237
around nine game (frisbee game), 480*fg*, 481
around the world (basketball game), 435
arousal (excitement), 117
Ashworth, S., 176, 177, 193, 194, 195
assertive communicators, 157–158
Assessing Sport Skills (Strand & Wilson), 232
assessment. *See* evaluation; student performance assessment
assumption of risk defense, 283

astronaut drills, 358–359

AT (assistive technology), 270–271

athletic performance
 lack of predictive ability for, 38–39
 preseason conditioning and, 288
 See also motor performance; sports activities

attendance policies, 103–105

Attention Analysis Form, 219fig

Attitude Check Sheet, 253fig

attitudes
 assessment of student, 250, 253fig–254
 fostering student fitness, 349

attitudes/values assessment
 Attitude Check Sheet, 253fig
 Edgington Attitude Scale, 254
 overview of, 250, 253–254

Austin O'Brien High School (Canada), 82, 84fig

authentic assessment, 232, 246fig

Babe Ruth ball (softball game), 460

back builder exercise, 360–361

backhand rally (racquetball game), 493

back squat (strength training), 500

back stretches, 353

back-to-back takedown, 415

backwards running, 363

badminton instruction
 assessment for, 246fig
 court dimensions for, 428fig
 effective, 428–429
 lead-up games and learning activities for, 430–431
 organization and skill work for, 429–430fig
 reciprocal style sheet for forehand overhead clear, 194fig
 sequence of skills, 426–428

Bailey, B. A., 158

Bailey, D. A., 7, 34

Bain, L., 48

Bajema, C. J., 6

balance
 accommodating students with disabilities lacking, 273–274
 definition and testing of, 231
 as skill-related physical fitness component, 348

balance beam (ropes course), 523–524fig

balance beam stretch, 352

balance of curriculum, 61, 64

Baley, J. A., 282

ball activities, 317

ballistic stretching exercise, 351

Bar-Or, O., 7, 34, 35, 40

Baruth, L. G., 140

baseline and goal-setting, 333

base running (softball), 458

Basketball Dribbling Work Sheet, 87fig

basketball instruction
 AAHPERD basketball testing skills of, 233
 effective, 434–435
 guided discovery (convergent) teaching style for, 196
 lead-up games and learning activities, 435–436
 using multiple teaching styles for, 198–199
 peer feedback on, 181fig
 performance objectives for, 436–437
 sequence of skills, 432–434
 skills objectives for, 163fig
 tasks for, 180fig

basket bowling, 476

Bassett, D. R., Jr., 330, 331

batting (softball), 458, 459

beach ball (or nerf ball) volleyball, 468

Beals, K. A., 337

the beam (group initiative activity), 526, 527fig

beanbags activities, 317, 403–404

bear trap exercise, 361

Becker, W. C., 171, 172

behavior. See student behavior

Beighle, A., 330, 333, 335

bench press, 500fig

bench pullover (strength training), 500, 502fig

Benson, H., 399

bent or upright rowing (strength training), 500, 501fig

bibliography resources, 121

bicycle accidents, 398

Blair, S. N., 36, 234

Blakemore, C. L., 176

Blakemore Cook, C. L., 86

blind-man volleyball, 469

blob tag, 320

blocking
 flag football, 442
 volleyball, 467

block (or flexible) schedule example of frisbee instruction, 483fig
 orienteering, 535
 overview of using, 51–52fig, 121, 122fig
 swimming/aquatics, 505t

Blonna, R., 399

boardwalk (group initiative activity), 525–526fig

body bar exercises, 370–371

body composition
 definition of, 37
 physical fitness and, 37

body mass index (BMI), 344, 347
 testing, 234

body position (strength training), 500

Booth, M. L., 30

Bouchard, C., 336, 345

Boulay, M., 345

bounce pass (basketball), 433–434

bounce steps, 369

bowling instruction
 effective, 475
 lead-up games and learning activities, 475–476
 organization and skill work, 475
 overview of game, 473
 performance objectives of, 476–477
 pin relay, 419
 rating form for, 477fig
 rubric for, 240fig
 sequence of skills, 473–475

Braaten, J., 15

brainstorming conflict solutions, 156

breathing (strength training), 499

Brener, N. D., 36

broomstick balance, 416

Brynteson, P., 86

Buck, M. M., 86, 176

budget/funding factor, 52

builders/destroyers activity, 322

Bulger, S. M., 84

bulldozer, 421

bully or face-off (field hockey), 439

Burgeson, C. R., 36

Burke, B. S., 37

burpee-flip drill, 315

Butler, J., 198

butterfly exercise, 360fig

butt tug, 420

cageball games, 416–417

calorie expenditure
 specific physical activities and, 395fig
 by walking, 338fig

captain football (flag football game), 444

cardio-choice fitness, 366

cardio kickboxing, 371–373fig

cardiorespiratory system, 389–392

cardiovascular exercises
jogging, 357, 364, 367
medicine balls, 377
running activities, 314fig, 322, 356, 362–365, 368
cardiovascular fitness, 346–347
cargo net jump (ropes course), 524fig–525
caring (responsibility level), 154–155
carioca step running, 363
Carlson, T. B., 85
Carroll, M. D., 37
carrying the ball (flag football), 442
Casten, C. M., 73, 121, 186
catching
basketball, 434
flag football, 441
frisbee, 478
lacrosse, 446, 449
softball, 457, 459
ceiling games (racquetball), 492–493
centering (flag football), 442
Centers for Disease Control and Prevention (CDC)
on body composition, 347
on growth patterns, 30, 31fig–32fig
on Targeting Teenaged Girls project, 30
YRBSS conducted by, 6
challenge courses, 361, 362fig
checklists
for assessing performance outcomes, 239, 241fig–242fig
Corrective Feedback Checklist, 167fig
readiness checklist for performing tennis forehand, 183fig
safety and liability, 290, 292
Self-Responsibility Checklist, 95fig
Social Development Checklist, 94fig
softball peer assessment task, 241fig
volleyball skills peer assessment, 242fig
See also student performance outcome assessment
Chepko, S., 237
chest pass (basketball), 433
chicken baseball, 421
Chiogioji, E., 71
Chumlea, W. C., 6
circle dribble (field hockey game), 439

circle keep-away (field hockey game), 439
circle kickball
soccer game, 451
speed-a-way game, 462
circle sit, 420
circuit training, 358, 359fig, 503
circuit training fitness with a jog, 367
Clarke, H. H., 33, 38
classes
determining rules and procedures for, 158–159
integrating students with disabilities into, 275
using pedometers in, 331–332
See also lessons; schools
class management
cautious use of criticism for, 171
dealing with severe misbehavior, 169–171
decreasing unacceptable behavior, 164–169
using effective strategies for, 148–154
implementing proactive behavior approach to, 156–161
instruction vs., 134
know legal considerations of expulsion, 172
maintaining and promoting acceptable behavior, 161–164
making punishment a last resort, 171–172
striving for, 148
teaching responsible student behavior, 154–156
time spent on, 209–210fig, 217fig
class organization strategies
class size, 16–17
consistent stopping and starting, 149–150
effective grouping of students, 150–151
using equipment effectively, 153–154
establishing class procedures/expectations, 152–153
expediting instructional transitions in, 150
learning students' names, 152
makeup procedures, 105–106
using squads to expedite organization, 151fig–152
taking roll call, 153
class size, 16–17
Class Time Analysis Form, 217fig, 220–221

clothespin tag, 320
clothing
flag football uniforms, 443
motivating students to quickly dress into activity, 152–153
suitable for hot weather exercise, 40–41
uniforms/dress requirements, 102–103
coaching-teaching conflicts, 17
coeducational classes mandate, 13–14
coffee grinder square, 315fig
cognitive assessment, 247–250
cognitive domain
curriculum design inclusion of, 53
teaching for development of the, 114–115fig
Cohen, A., 250
combatives activities, 414–415
commanding/ordering, 133, 160
commando crawl (ropes course), 522fig
commonalities activities, 420
communication
on consequences of misbehavior, 159
examples of ineffective, 133
instruction effectiveness through effective, 133–134
listening skills and, 132–133
nonverbal, 136fig, 161–164, 215
communication styles
aggressive, 157
assertive, 157–158
passive, 157
community
as curriculum design factor, 50–51
using facilities in the, 16, 504–505
comparative negligence, 279, 282
compass
bearings and directions, 530fig–531fig
parts of a, 529fig
competition, desire for, 54–55
The Complete Book of Country Swing and Western Dance (Livingston), 495
computer services, 276
Concepts of Fitness and Wellness (Corbin and colleagues), 351
conceptual physical fitness programs, 14–15
conflict resolution, 155–156
Consalvi, A. R., 330

Conscious Discipline (Bailey), 158
consequences
  communicating misbehavior, 159
  removal of positive, 168
  See also discipline
content standards
  as curriculum design factor, 53
  definition of, 7-8
continuity exercises, 359-360, 359340
continuous movement activities, 357-358
contributory negligence, 279, 282, 283
cooperative activities, 420-421
cooperative learning style, 191-193*fig*
Cooper Institute, 10, 22, 74, 93, 233, 234, 346, 399
coordination
  accommodating students with disabilities lacking, 273
  definition and testing of, 231
  as skill-related physical fitness component, 348
Corbin, C. B., 14, 22, 29, 37, 73, 86, 92, 93, 163, 231, 234, 326, 331, 344, 345, 346, 351, 398, 399
Corbin, W. R., 231
core exercises
  abdominal, 355, 377-380
  pilates, 378-379
  stability balls, 374
  strength training, 371
  yoga, 379-380
Cornish, C., 232
Cornish handball test, 232-233
corrective feedback, 138-139, 166-167*fig* 214
Corrective Feedback Checklist, 167*fig*
counseling practices, 23
country swing and Western dance, 495
CPR (cardiopulmonary resuscitation), 398
crab walk exercise, 355
creative expression, 55
criterion-referenced evaluation, 255
criterion-referenced health standards, 234-235
criticism, 171, 213
Crobin, C. B., 385
croquet ball (speed-a-way game), 462
cross-country orienteering, 532, 534

cross-country runs, 490
crossover-step backward running, 363
crossover-step forward running, 363
Crouter, S. C., 330, 331
Cuddihy, T. F., 29, 86
cues
  instructional, 137-138
  prompting desired behavior with, 163-164
cultural-sports perspective, 12
curl (strength training), 500, 501*fig*
curl-up exercise, 355, 360, 361
curl-up with twist exercise, 355
curriculum
  an articulated K-12, 64-66
  description and value orientation of, 48
  designing a quality, 49-64
  mainstreaming students with disabilities and, 271-272
  scope, sequence, breadth, depth, and balance of, 61-64
  See also instruction; physical education programs
curriculum approaches
  fitness education, 86, 90-93
  knowledge concepts, 86, 87*fig*-90*fig*
  personal and social responsibility, 93-97*fig*
  skill development, 70-84
  sports education, 84-86
curriculum design steps
  1: develop guiding philosophy, 49
  2: define conceptual curriculum framework, 49-50
  3: consider environmental factors, 50-52*fig*
  4: determine content standards and student objectives, 53
  5: select student-centered activities, 53-59
  6: organize selected activities into instructional units, 59-64
  7: evaluate and modify the curriculum, 64
Cusimano, B., 215
cutthroat and doubles (racquetball game), 493

Dale, D., 29, 86, 92, 385
Dallal, G. E., 6
Dance a While (Pittman, Waller, & Dark), 495
DANGER, 391-392
Dark, C. L., 495

Darst, P., 20, 215, 224, 225, 226, 535
dead lift (strength training), 502, 503*fig*
deep-breathing exercises, 399
defensive squares drill (field hockey game), 439
departmental policies
  attendance and participation policies, 103-105
  class makeup procedures, 105-106
  development of, 102
  equipment, 108-110
  grading procedures, 110
  hygiene issues, 106-108
  uniforms and dress requirements, 102-103
descriptive orienteering, 534*fig*-535
desire to play, 54
developmental levels, 55-56
development (individualized teaching style), 191
diagnosis
  evaluation role in, 255-256
  individualized teaching style, 190
diagnostic practices, 23
diagonal soccer, 451-452
Dietz, W. H., 6
Dionne, E. T., 345
direct teaching style, 177
discipline
  communicating consequences of misbehavior, 159
  corrective feedback, 138-139, 166-167*fig*
  expulsion used as, 172
  individual vs. group, 160
  making punishment a last resort, 171-172
  removal from activity, 165
  removal of positive consequences as, 168
  reprimands, 165, 166-167
  strategies for dealing with unacceptable behavior, 164-166
  time-outs, 165, 168-169
  See also consequences; misbehavior; student behavior management

distance calculations, 333-335
distance running safety guidelines, 41*fig*
diversity issues
  improving instructional effectiveness, 140-143, 144*fig*
  teaching styles and, 197
Dobbins, D. A., 36

dodging
  field hockey, 438
  lacrosse, 446–447, 449
dorsal lift exercise, 361
double-disc frisbees, 481
dress codes, 102–103
dribble and hit for distance (field hockey game), 440
dribble keep-away (basketball game), 435
dribble tag (basketball game), 435
dribbling
  basketball, 434, 436
  field hockey, 438
  soccer, 183–184, 449–450, 453, 454–455
  team handball, 464
Dubowitz, V., 35
duration recording, 207, 212*fig*
Dynamic Physical Education for Secondary School Students (NASPE), 6
Dynamic Secondary School Curriculum Approach, 76

eclipse ball games, 418
Edgington Attitude Scale, 254
Edgington, C. W., 254
Education of All Handicapped Children Act (1975), 14, 51, 264
Education Amendments Act (Title IX) [1972], 12, 13–14, 51
eight-ball rally (racquetball game), 493
Eisenhower, D., 12
Eisenman, P., 37
electric fence (group initiative activity), 525*fig*
elementary school curriculum, 66
Emergency Action Plan (EAP), 510–511
emergency care plan, 289–290, 292
emergency telephone numbers, 290
endurance
  accommodating students with disabilities lacking, 272–273
  PACER (Progressive Aerobic Cardiovascular Endurance Run), 41, 333
  as physical fitness component, 347
endurance exercises
  definition of, 391
  jogging, 357, 364, 367
  walking, 336–340, 368
  See also aerobic activities
end zone hockey, 440
Ennis, C., 71

Ennis, K., 48
entanglement, 420–421
environment
  creating positive learning, 19–20
  creating a safe, 113–114
  curriculum design consideration of, 50–52*fig*
  determining use of space, 110–111
  least restrictive, 265
Epstein, L. H., 330
equipment
  archery, 424–425
  badminton, 428
  class rules on taking care of, 158
  as curriculum design factor, 51
  departmental policies regarding, 108–110
  effective class use of, 153–154
  gymnasium bowling sets, 475
  jogging, 490, 491
  lacrosse, 447
  legal responsibilities regarding, 286–287, 292
  lesson plan on, 120
  as physical education program issue, 16–17
  See also facilities; instructional devices
etiquette (tennis), 513–514
evaluation
  criterion-referenced, 255
  of effective teaching, 205–206
  improving teaching effectiveness through systematic, 205
  individualized teaching style step on, 191
  lesson plan on use of, 120–121
  norm-referenced, 254–255
  student performance, 254–257
  team member expectations (self-evaluation), 193
  See also grading; rating scales; rubrics; student performance assessment
event recording, 207, 221–222
Event Recording Form, 221*fig*
excessive weight. *See* overweight
exercise
  harmful practices and, 351
  heat/hot weather and, 40–41
  moderation in, 40
  See also physical activity; safety issues

exercises
  astronaut drills, 358–359
  calorie expenditures of specific, 338*fig*, 395*fig*
  cardio-choice fitness, 366
  challenge courses, 361
  circuit training, 358, 359*fig*
  circuit training fitness with a jog, 367
  continuity, 359–360
  continuous movement activities, 357–358
  deep-breathing, 399
  fitness cookie jar exchange, 366
  fitness scavenger hunt, 366
  flexibility and warm-up, 352–354
  health club workouts, 368–380*fig*
  interval training, 358
  isometric, 361, 416
  jump-bands circuit, 365–366
  jump and jog fitness, 367
  long jump-rope fitness routine, 367
  lower body development, 355–356, 376–378, 500, 502–503*fig*
  midsection, 355*fig*
  monopoly fitness, 365
  to music, 356–357
  parachute, 361–362
  partner racetrack fitness, 367
  partner resistance, 360–361
  running activities and drills, 362–365
  squad leader, 356
  teacher and student leader routines, 356
  track and field fitness, 365
  12 ways of fitness, 367
  upper-body development, 352, 354*fig*–355, 374, 376–380, 500–503*fig*
  See also physical activities; *specific exercises and activities*; strength training
exercise trails, 491
expulsion, 172
extrinsic social reinforcers, 162–163

face-off or bully (field hockey), 439
facilities
  using community, 16, 504–505
  as curriculum design factor, 51
  indoor golf, 487*fig*
  legal responsibilities regarding, 286–287, 292
  lesson plan on, 120
  as physical education program issue, 16–17

facilities (continued)
  softball, 457
  swimming, 504–505
  See also equipment
fading, 164
Faigenbaum, A. D., 42
faith fall (group initiative activity), 526, 527fig
Farrow, A., 250
fartlek training, 364–365
fastest tag, 320
Faulkner, R. A., 7, 34
feedback
  avoiding types that result in backlash, 160
  corrective, 138–139, 166–167fig, 214
  criticism, 171, 213
  form for tallying types of, 215fig
  general vs. specific, 213–214
  giving meaningful skill, 117–118
  giving positive group, 160
  giving students meaningful fitness, 348
  group vs. individual, 140
  how to present, 139–140
  improving teaching effectiveness through, 205
  nonverbal, 136fig, 161–164, 215
  using peer, 140, 141fig, 181fig
  positive, corrective, and negative, 138–139
  understanding different types of, 139
  See also instruction improvement
female growth patterns of, 30, 31fig–32fig, 33fig
Ferraro, K. F., 6
fetch relay, 419
field hockey instruction
  effective, 439
  lead-up games and learning activities, 439–440
  overview of sport, 437–438
  performance objectives for, 440–441
  rainy-day activities for, 441
  sequence of skills, 438–439
fielding
  field hockey, 438
  softball, 460–461
file running, 363–364
finger wrestle, 415
first-aid
  emergencies and, 289–290
  instruction on CPR and, 397–398
Fisher, C., 91
fist pull-apart exercise, 360

FIT (frequency, intensity, and time) formula, 347
Fitness/Activitygram K-12 program, 22
fitness cookie jar exchange, 366
fitness development activity, 124
FitnessGram, 333
Fitnessgram System
  described, 233–234
  my personal fitness record of, 236fig
Fitness for Life (Corbin & Lindsey), 14, 398, 399
Fitness for Life program, 86, 90–91, 92fig
Fitness for Life Teacher Resources and Materials CD-ROM (McConnell, Corbin, & Dale), 321
fitness routines
  ninth-grade skill development approach to, 78fig
  skill development approach to, 74–75fig
fitness scavenger hunt, 366
FitSmart Test User Manual (Zhu, Safrit, & Cohen), 250
five hundred (softball game), 460
five passes
  basketball game, 435
  flag football game, 444
five points and out (racquetball game), 493
five touch (lacrosse game), 449
flag football instruction
  effective, 442–443
  lead-up games and learning activities, 444–445
  using mastery learning instruction for, 188fig
  performance objectives for, 445
  sequence of skills, 441–442
flag grab combatives activity, 415
flag grab partner and small-group activity, 321
flash drill, 315–316fig
Flegal, K. M., 37
Fletcher, P., 37
flexibility
  activities to increase, 328, 329fig, 330
  ballistic and static stretching exercises for, 351
  as physical fitness component, 347
  testing, 234

flexibility exercises
  avoiding harmful, 351
  warm-up, 352–354
flexible (or block) schedule
  example of frisbee instruction, 483fig
  orienteering, 535
  overview of using, 51–52fig, 121, 122fig
  swimming/aquatics, 505t
flickerball games, 417–418
flip pass (basketball), 434
folk and round dance, 495
follow the leader
  frisbee game, 479
  partner and small-group activity, 321
football punting rubric, 238fig
forearm flex exercise, 360
foreseeability, 281
formal assessment, 230
formation rhythmic running activity, 321
form running, 362–363, 489–490
four corners activity, 317, 357–358
fourth down (flag football game), 444
Franks, B. D., 234
Freedson, P. S., 37, 333
Freedson, P. W., 345
frisbee golf, 480
frisbee instruction
  block plan for, 483fig
  double-disc, 481
  effective, 478–479
  lead-up games and learning activities for, 479–481fig
  overview of games, 477–478
  performance objectives of, 481, 483
  rainy-day activities, 484
  sequence of skills for, 478
  spinjammer, 481, 482fig
frisbee shuffleboard, 480
frisbee soccer, 479
frisbee softball, 479
frisbee tennis, 479
Fronske, H., 137
front-leg kick exercise, 356
front squat (strength training), 500
frozen tag, 320
FT (fast twitch) contracting, 35–36
fugitive tag, 320
Fuller, M. L., 142
Fulton, J. E., 28
functional fitness, 346
rope jumping, 498

games
  archery lead-up, 425
  badminton lead-up, 430–431
  basketball lead-up, 435–436
  bowling lead-in, 475–476
  cageball, 416–417
  eclipse ball, 418
  flickerball, 417–418
  frisbee lead-up, 479–481fig
  lacrosse lead-up, 449
  as lesson plan component, 124
  ninth-grade skill development
    approach to, 78–79fig
  potato ball, 418
  racquetball lead-up, 492–493
  scoops, 417, 418fig
  skill development approach to,
    75–76fig
  soccer lead-up, 451–453
  softball lead-up, 459–460
  speed-a-way, 461–462
  tag, 319–320
  Three-Person Volleyball, 85–86
  throtons, 417fig
  volleyball lead-in, 468–469
  See also introductory activities
Games Performance Assessment,
  247
Gardner, J. D., 6
gauntlet run activity, 317
gender differences
  avoiding biases in, 143–144
  growth patterns, 30, 31fig–32fig,
    33fig
  strength as, 35
genetic endowment, 344–345
giant's ladder (ropes course), 525fig
Gilbert High School super circuit
  class, 91fig
Gilliam, T. B., 37
Glasser, W., 349
Glass, W., 37
goalkeeping (goaltending)
  field hockey, 439
  lacrosse, 447
  soccer, 450
  team handball, 464
goal setting
  baseline and, 333
  differences between activity time
    and step, 333–335
  encouraging student, 155
  to improve teaching
    effectiveness, 205
  personalized activity goal, 333,
    334fig
  single standard goal, 333
  See also student performance
    objectives

goal shooting (team handball), 464
golf instruction
  effective, 486
  indoor facility and rainy-day
    activities for, 487
  learning activities for, 486–487
  sequence of skills, 484–486
  skill tests and rating scale for,
    487–488
grading
  arguments for and against,
    256–257
  educational objectives vs.
    administrative tasks of, 257
  establishing procedures for, 110
  evaluation used as part of, 255
  negative vs. positive, 259
  pass-fail vs. letter, 259–260
  on potential, 259
  process vs. product, 258
  relative improvement, 258
  See also evaluation; rating scales;
    rubrics
Graham, P., 91
"Grandma's law" (Premack
  Principle), 162–163
Gray, G. R., 289
Greenberg, J. S., 399
Greene, D., 163
Greenen, D. L., 37
Griffin, L. L., 198
Grimby, G., 39
grips
  golf, 484
  strength training, 499
group feedback
  giving positive, 160
  individual vs., 140
group initiative activities
  the beam and the wall, 526,
    527fig
  boardwalk, 525–526fig
  electric fence, 525fig
  faith fall, 526, 527fig
  height alignment, 528–529
  high water, 528fig
  human circle pass, 527
  human line pass, 528
  lightbulb change, 528fig
  nitro crossing, 526, 527fig
  overview of, 525
  platforms, 526fig
  platform stand, 528, 529fig
  sasquatch race, 528
  stream crossing, 528
  trust dive, 526, 528fig
group name juggling, 420
group runs, 490
group time sampling, 207–208

growth patterns
  effect of activity on, 34
  gender differences in, 30,
    31fig–32fig, 33fig
Grunbaum, J. A., 36
guided discovery (convergent)
  teaching style, 195–196
Guo, S. S., 6
gymnastics instruction
  effective, 446
  overview of, 445
  sequence of skills, 445

Haapasalo, H., 34
half-circle hockey, 440
half-court basketball, 436
half-court lacrosse, 449
handball instruction
  Cornish handball test for,
    232–233
  rating scale used for, 242–243fig
  team, 462–466
hands-and-tails tag, 320
Harrison, J. L., 176
Harrison, J. M., 86
Hastad, D. N., 232, 254, 256
Hastie, P. A., 84, 85
Haymes, E. M., 34
heading (soccer), 450, 453, 455
health
  impact of physical activity on,
    36–38
  as physical education outcome, 7
health club/fitness center
  aerobic workouts, 368–369
  cardio kickboxing, 371–373fig
  emphasis curriculum, 79–81
  medicine balls, 376–378
  pilates, 378–379fig
  stability balls, 373fig–376
  yoga, 379–380fig
  See also exercises; strength
    training
health foundations approach. See
  public health approach
health maintenance behaviors
  health-related fitness, 398–399
  self-evaluation and behavior self-
    control, 399–400
  stress reduction, 399
  three-pronged approach to, 398
health promotion, HELP
  philosophy on, 86
health-related physical activities,
  21–22fig
health-related physical fitness
  components of, 346–347
  described, 346
  instruction on, 398–399

healthy activity zone (HAZ), 333, 346

healthy eating habits
　good nutrition, 394-396
　MyPyramid and, 394fig
　as physical education outcome, 7

healthy fitness zone (HFZ), 333, 346

healthy lifestyle instruction
　on barriers to healthy living, 392-394
　on cardiorespiratory system, 389-392
　on health maintenance behaviors, 398-400
　importance of teaching, 384-385
　integrating health concepts, 385
　on muscular system, 387fig-389
　on nutrition and weight management, 394fig-396
　on safety and first aid, 397-398
　on skeletal system, 385-386
　on substance abuse, 396-397

healthy living barriers
　nutrition and weight management, 394fig-396
　stress as, 392-394
　substance abuse, 396-397

Healthy People 2000: National Health Promotion and Disease Objectives (U.S. Public Health Service), 12-13, 28

Healthy People 2010: National Health Promotion and Disease Objectives, 13, 21

heart
　basic concepts on the, 391
　structure of, 390fig
　training heart rate, 392, 490

Hedley, A. A., 344

heel raises (strength training), 503fig

height alignment (group initiative activity), 528-529

Hellison, D. R., 10, 93, 94, 96, 97

help-me tag, 320

HELP philosophy, 86

hierarchical analysis, 184-185

high-density lipoproteins (HDLs), 337

high school students
　curriculum for, 66
　health club/fitness center emphasis curriculum for, 79-81
　physical characteristics of, 57-58
　skill development approach for transition from middle school to, 76-79
　social, emotional, and intellectual development of, 58
　See also adolescents

high water (group initiative activity), 528fig

Hirst, C. C., 231

hitting (softball), 461

home base, 152

home run (softball game), 460

hoops activities
　hoops circle pass activity, 322
　hoops on the ground activity, 321

horse (basketball game), 435

hoops and plyometrics activity, for individual, partner, small-group units, 404

horizontal curricula
　definition of, 61
　skill development approach to, 75

Huang, I. W., 28

human circle pass (group initiative activity), 527

Human Kinetics, 22

human line pass (group initiative activity), 528

hurdler's stretch, 351

Huth, T., 91

hygiene issues, 106-108

IDEA (Individuals with Disabilities Education Act) [Public Law 105-17], 14, 264, 265

IEPs (individualized educational programs)
　assistive technology (AT) stipulated by the, 270-271
　described, 264
　development of, 267, 270
　example of, 268fig-269fig
　ignoring misbehavior, 165, 166
　improvement grading standard, 258

Imwold, C., 212

inactivity—sedentary living, 329

inclined log (ropes course), 524fig

inclined wall push-ups, 354

individual activities
　beanbags, 317, 403-404
　described, 312
　examples listed, 317-318
　hoops, 404
　individualized fitness workloads, 348
　juggling, 406fig-409fig
　jump bands, 404-406
　partner resistance exercise, 360-361, 367-368
　wands, 415-416

individualized teaching style, 190-191fig

individual skill instruction, 110

informal assessment, 230

in-line skating mini-unit, 488-489

in a pickle (softball game), 459

inquiry teaching style, 193-195

institutional evaluation programs, 236-237

instruction
　alternating practice episodes with, 149
　creating quality lesson plans for, 121-124
　defining effective, 204
　departmental policies governing issues of, 102-110
　designing comprehensive unit plans for, 120-121
　effective practice sessions as part of, 118-120
　on exercises for developing balanced fitness routines, 350-351
　expediting transitions in, 150
　giving meaningful skill feedback as part of, 149
　healthy lifestyle, 384-400
　improving quality of, 208-220
　maintaining focus of, 132
　observation of, 207-208, 220-227
　offering in-depth, 22-23
　planning for optimal skill learning, 116-117
　pre-instructional decisions related to, 110-114
　reflecting on completed lesson, 124-126
　responsibilities regarding, 284-286
　separating management from, 134
　students with disabilities and modifying, 272-274
　teaching each student as a whole person, 114-116
　See also curriculum; physical education programs

instructional cues, 137-138

instructional devices
　compass, 529fig-531fig
　description of, 112
　determining use of, 112-113fig

lesson plan on, 120
pedometers, 330–336
See also equipment
instructional formats, 110
instructional strategies
  alternating instruction with practice, 149
  archery, 423–425
  badminton, 194flg, 246flg, 426–431
  bowling, 240flg, 473–477flg
  field hockey, 437–441
  flag football, 188flg, 441–445
  frisbee, 477–484
  golf, 484–488flg
  group initiative, 525flg–529flg
  gymnastic, 445–446
  handball, 232–233, 242–243flg, 462–466
  individual skill, 110
  in-line skating mini-unit, 488–489
  lacrosse, 446–449
  large-group, 110
  orienteering, 529flg–537
  private sports, 16
  racquetball, 189flg, 248flg–249flg, 491–494
  rope jumping, 317, 357, 495–499
  ropes course activities, 521–525flg
  small-group (or station), 110, 111flg, 152, 175
  soccer, 183–184, 186flg, 195–196flg, 233, 449–455
  softball, 241flg, 456flg–461
  speed-a-way, 461–462
  swimming/aquatics, 398, 504–511
  tennis, 183flg, 233, 511–517
  track and field, 365, 466
  volleyball, 89flg, 184–187flg, 242flg, 466–470
  See also lessons; teaching; teaching styles
instruction effectiveness
  communicating effectively for, 133–134
  considering personal needs of students for, 140–145
  demonstrating a caring attitude toward students, 134–135
  demonstrating and modeling skills, 136–137flg
  developing effective listening skills for, 132–133
  using feedback as part of, 138–140
instructional cues for, 137–138

maintaining student interest for, 130–132
nonverbal communication used for, 136
instruction improvement factors
  active supervision and student contact, 130–131, 215, 218–220flg
  Attention Analysis Form, 219flg
  class management episodes, 209–210flg, 217flg
  instructional time/practice balance, 208–209flg
  instruction observation, 207–208, 218flg, 220flg–227
  practice and activity time, 212, 213flg
  response latency, 210–212
  student performance, 212–213, 214flg
  See also feedback
instruction observation
  methods used for, 207–208
  reflective observation comments, 218flg, 220flg
  for self-improvement, 208
  systems for research and supervision, 220–227
instruction observation systems
  Arizona State University Observation Instrument (ASUOI), 224–227
  Class Time Analysis Form, 217flg, 220–221
  event recording, 207, 221–222
  Oregon State University MS-PETE Supervision Coding Form, 222–224
integrated activity programs, 23–24
interdisciplinary courses approach, 15
International Athletics Association Federation (IAAF) Medical Committee, 41
interrogating, 133, 160
interval recording, 207
interval training, 358
introductory activities
  agility, 312, 313–316
  description and categories of, 312
  individual, 312, 317–318
  as lesson component, 124
  ninth-grade skill development approach to, 77–78flg
  partner and small-group, 312, 318–322
  skill development approach to, 73–74flg

sport movement challenges, 312, 316–317
See also games; lessons; physical activities
involvement (responsibility level), 154
irresponsibility, 154
isometric exercises
  parachute exercises as, 361
  wand activities as, 416
It's Not Just Gym Anymore (McCracken), 426

Jackson, A. W., 29
Jacobson, E., 399
Jacques, P. F., 6
Jensen, C. R., 231
Jewett, A., 48
jogging
  circuit training fitness using, 367
  as continuous movement activity, 357, 364
  effective instruction on, 490–491
  as potential lifetime activity, 489
  rainy-day activities using, 491
  sequence of skills for, 489–490
jog-walk-jog, 490
Johnson, C. L., 37
Johnson, J. R., 233
Johnson, M. L., 37
Johnson soccer test, 233
juggling activities, 406flg–409flg
jump bands activities
  for individual, partner, small-group units, 404–406
  jump-bands circuit, 365–366
  Jump Bands Work Sheet, 90flg
jumping jacks exercise, 356, 369
jump and jog fitness, 367, 368
jump rope. *See* rope jumping
jump shots (basketball), 434

K-12
  an articulated curriculum for, 64–66
  skill development approach articulation for, 81flg
Kannus, P., 34
Karabulut, M., 330, 331
Katch, V. L., 37
keep-away (basketball game), 435
keep it afloat (volleyball), 468
Kemp, J., 233
Kemp-Vincent tennis rally test, 233
kicking (soccer), 453, 454, 455
kick over (flag football game), 444
Kilanowski, C. K., 330
kitten crawl (ropes course), 522flg
knee bender exercise, 361

kneeling (or sitting) volleyball, 468
knee touch curl-up exercise, 355
knowledge activities, 106
    See also physical activities
Knowledge Analysis Sheet, 107fig
knowledge assessment
    overview of, 247–250
    pointers for effective written tests, 250
    rugby study guide and exam, 251fig–252fig
    sources of knowledge test questions, 250
knowledge concepts approaches
    Basketball Dribbling Work Sheet, 87fig
    Jump Bands Work Sheet, 90fig
    Orienteering Skills Practice Sheet, 88fig
    overview of, 86
    Volleyball Serves—Problem-solving Questions, 89fig
knowledge of performance, 117–118
knowledge of results, 117
Kounin, L. S., 159

Laakso, L., 7
labeling students, 133, 160
lacrosse instruction
    effective, 447–448
    lacrosse field, 447fig
    lead-up games for, 449
    organization and skill work of, 448–449
    overview of game, 446, 447–448
    sequence of skills, 446–447
Lacy, A. C., 232, 254, 256
LaMasurier, G., 73
Lambdin, D., 73
large-group instruction, 110
Larson, Y., 38
Larsen, M., 461
lateral passing (flag football), 441
lateral raises (strength training), 500
lateral shuffle, 314
Laurencelle, L., 6, 39
Lawrence, C. M., 183
Lawrence, G., 183
layup shots (basketball), 434
leader ball (volleyball), 468
leader in the circle (rope jumping), 498
leaping Lean with a forward roll, 315
learning
    ALT-PE (Academic Learning Time-Physical Education) on time spent, 212
    including instruction as part of each lesson, 116
    instructional cues to facilitate, 137–138
    integrating lesson with past/future instruction, 116–117
    knowing purpose of the lesson, 116
    major instructional components of, 123–124
    PBL (problem-based learning), 191, 196–197
    positive learning environment facilitating, 19–20
    providing practice sessions as part of, 118–120
    reflections on completed, 124–126
    teaching styles and, 197
    understanding role of arousal in, 117
    understanding role of arousal in learning, 117
learning center organization, 190–191fig
least restrictive environment, 265
Lee, T., 117, 118
legal issues
    areas of responsibilities, 283–290
    as curriculum design factor, 51
    expulsion and related, 172
    liability, 17, 280–281
    minimizing effects of a lawsuit, 290
    negligence, 279, 281–283
    torts, 281
legal responsibilities
    equipment and facilities, 286–287, 297
    instruction, 284–286, 290, 292
    safety, 40–42, 113–114, 288–291fig, 292
    sports programs, 287–288
    supervision, 283–284, 290, 292
leg curls and extensions (strength training), 502
leg extension exercise, 355
legislation
    as curriculum design factor, 51
    Education of All Handicapped Children Act of 1975 [Public Law (PL) 94-142], 14, 51, 264
    IDEA (Individuals with Disabilities Education Act) [Public Law (PL) 105-17], 14, 264, 265
    Title IX (Education Amendments Act) [1972], 12, 13–14, 51
leg wrestling, 414
Lepper, M. R., 163
lesson focus/games
    as lesson plan component, 124
    ninth-grade skill development approach to, 78–79fig
    skill development approach to, 75–76fig
lesson plans
    content of, 124
    creating quality, 121–123
    designing comprehensive unit, 120–121
    giving feedback as part of, 117–118
Lesson Plans for Dynamic Physical Education for Secondary School Students (Casten), 73, 121
lessons
    closing a, 153
    maintaining flow of, 131–132
    mastery learning units, 184–190fig
    planning, 116–126
    swimming/aquatics five-day, 506fig–509fig
    See also classes; instructional strategies; introductory activities
liability
    areas of responsibility of, 283–286
    checklist for safety and, 290, 292
    definition of, 280–281
    determination of, 281
    as physical education program issue, 17
liability insurance, 290
lifestyle physical activities
    bowling, 473–477fig
    frisbee, 477–484
    golf, 484–488fig
    in-line skating mini-unit, 488–489
    jogging, 357, 364, 367, 489–491
    Physical Activity Pyramid on, 328, 329fig, 330
    racquetball, 189fig, 248fig–249fig, 491–494
    rhythmic activity, 495–499
    rope jumping, 317, 357, 495–499
    strength training, 239fig, 358–361, 367–369, 499–504fig
    swimming/aquatics, 398, 504–511
    tennis, 183fig, 233, 511–517
    walking as "real," 336–337
    See also physical activities; sports activities

lifestyle sports/activities, 21
Lifetime Sports Education Project (LSEP), 21
lightbulb change (group initiative activity), 528fig
Lindsey, R., 14, 86, 93, 398, 399
line soccer, 452
listening
  refusing to engage in, 133, 160
  skills of, 132–133
Livingston, P., 495
locker room supervision, 108
locomotor skills, definition of, 8
log roll (three-person roll), 313
Lohman, T. G., 235
long jump-rope fitness routine, 367
loose caboose activity, 321
Lortie, G., 34
low-density lipoproteins (LDLs), 337
lower-back stretches, 352–353
lower body exercises
  medicine balls, 376–377
  pilates, 378–379
  strength training, 500–503fig
  stretches, 352–353
  types of, 355–356
  yoga, 379–380
lower-leg stretches, 352
Lukajic, O., 331
Lund, J. L., 86, 176, 230

McConnell, K., 92, 385
MacConnie, S. E., 37
McCracken, B., 426
Macfarlane, P. A., 351
McGee, R., 250
McGlynn, G., 37
McKay, H. A., 7, 34
McKenzie, T. L., 13, 28, 30, 36, 212
Mainland High School (Daytona Beach), 91
mainstreaming
  description of, 265fig–266
  systematic approach to successful, 271–275
male growth patterns of, 30, 31fig–32fig, 33fig
malfeasance, 279, 282
Malina, R. M., 30, 34
management. See class management
Mancini, V., 224, 225, 226
Mand, C., 85
manipulative skills, 8
Manning, M. L., 140
mapping activities, 532, 533fig–534
marking activity, 318
marking with addition or multiplication activity, 318

mass stand up, 420
mastery learning (outcomes-based) style
  described, 182–183
  designing units of instruction, 184–186
  dribbling soccer ball tasks, 183–184
  readiness checklist for performing tennis forehand, 183fig
  using units of instruction, 186–190fig
  worksheet for, 182fig
Matanin, M., 230
Matthews, D. L., 282
Mayer, J., 37
Measurement and Evaluation in Physical Education and Exercise Science (Lacy & Hastad), 232
medical examinations, 288
medicine balls exercises, 376–378
Melograno, V. J., 247
mental practice, 118
Merriman, J., 284
METs (metabolic equivalent of tasks), 327
Metzler, M. W., 176
middle school students
  curriculum for, 66
  developmental levels of, 55–56
  physical characteristics of, 56
  skill development approach for transition to high school, 76–79
  skill development approach used for, 73–76fig
  social, emotional, intellectual development of, 56–57
  See also adolescents
midsection exercises, 355fig
mileage cards/maps, 491
military press (strength training), 500, 501fig
minisoccer, 452–453
minivolleyball (volleyball), 469
Minneapolis Public Schools (MPS), 15
mirror drill in place activity, 321fig
misbehavior
  communicating consequences of, 159
  using criticism cautiously, 171
  dealing with severe, 169–171
  due to confusing instructions, 160–161
  expulsion due to, 172
  ignoring, 165, 166

making punishment a last resort, 171–172
strategies for decreasing, 164–169
See also discipline; student behavior
misfeasance, 279, 282
mismatched opponents error, 287
Mitchell, S. A., 198, 247
modeling
  being a positive role model, 349
  using correct and incorrect examples for, 134
  desirable behavior, 155
  desired behavior, 163
  student demonstrations and, 137fig
  teacher demonstrating and, 136–137
  See also teachers
moderate physical activity, 40
modified coed field hockey, 440
modified (or novel) team sports, 22
modifying personal behavior, 400
Mohr, D. J., 84
monopoly fitness, 365
moralizing, 133, 160
Morgan, C., 6
Morrow, J. R., 29
Morrow, J. R., Jr., 345
Mosston, M., 176, 177, 193, 194, 195
motivation
  evaluation role in, 255
  strength training, 504
motor performance
  impact of being overweight on, 36
  muscle fiber type and, 35–36
  strength and, 36
  See also athletic performance
motor skills
  competency in, 8–9
  fundamental, 8
  rhythmic, 8–9
  specialized, 9
movement activities
  move and change direction activity, 316
  move and change speed or level activity, 316
  move and change type of locomotion activity, 316
  movements on the floor, 368
  move and perform athletic movement activity, 316
  move and perform a fitness task activity, 316

movement activities *(continued)*
move and perform a stretch activity, 316–317
move, stop, and pivot activity, 316
move and quickly stop activity, 316
moving throw and catch activity, 322
movement patterns
competency in, 8–9
understanding concepts, principles, strategies, and tactics of, 9
multicultural education, 140–143, 144*fig*
muscle of the day activity, 504
muscle fiber type, 35–36
muscle fitness activities, 328–329*fig*, 330
muscular system, 387*fig*–389
musical hoops activity, 318
music (exercises to), 356–357
Must, A., 6
MVPA (moderate to vigorous physical activity), 327–328
My Personal Plan #1, 97*fig*
MyPyramid, 394*fig*

National Association for Sport and Physical Education (NASPE), 8, 53, 93, 116, 237, 250, 488
National Health and Nutrition Examination Survey (NHANES), 37
National Standards for Physical Education (NASPE), 250
National Strength and Conditioning Association (NSCA), 42
negative feedback, 138–139
negligence
common defenses against, 283
foreseeability issue of, 281
four elements of, 279, 281
types listed, 279, 282
nerf ball (or beach ball) volleyball, 468
new leader activity, 319
ninth-grade curriculum, 76–77
nitro crossing (group initiative activity), 526, 527*fig*
no bounce, no steps, and no contact (team handball), 465
no-goalie field hockey, 440
nonadversarial discussions, 155
nonconfrontational discussions, 155
nonfeasance, 279, 282

nonlocomotor skills, 8
nonparticipating students, 153
nonverbal communication improving instruction through, 215
prompting desired behavior with, 163–164
social reinforcers through, 136*fig*, 161–162
norm-referenced evaluation, 254–255
novel (or modified) team sports, 22
number challenges activity, 317
nutrition
importance of good, 394–396
MyPyramid and, 394*fig*
as physical education outcome, 7

obesity predictor, 6
observation. *See also* overweight observation. *See* instruction observation
Ogden, C. L., 6, 37
O'Hara, N. M., 36
Oja, P., 34
O'Leary, K. D., 172
Olsin, J. L., 247
one behind activity, 319
one-bounce volleyball, 468
one-hand push shots (basketball), 434
one step (frisbee game) 481
ordering/commanding, 133, 160
Oregon State University MS-PETE Supervision Coding Form, 222–224
orienteering
blocking plan for, 535*fig*
competitive events, 532, 534*fig*–535
descriptive, 534*fig*–535
jogging units using, 490
learning activities for, 529–531*fig*
map activities, 532
overview of, 529
pacing activities, 532
performance objectives for, 536
score, 534
sequence of skills for, 529
working a compass, 529*fig*–531*fig*
Orienteering Skills Practice Sheet, 88*fig*
Oslin, J. L., 198
outcomes
assessment of performance, 237–247
comparing physical fitness and physical activity, 29*fig*
definition of, 7

lesson plan on expected, 124
major physical education, 7
See also students
outdoor adventure activities described, 21*fig*
group initiative, 525*fig*–536
orienteering, 529*fig*–536
ropes course, 521–525
schedule for, 83*fig*
skill development approach using, 71*fig*, 81–84*fig*
transverse wall climbing, 536–537
Outdoor Adventure Activities for School and Recreation Programs (Darst & Armstrong), 535
"overlappingness," 159
over, under, and around #1 activity, 318, 319*fig*
over, under, and around #2 activity, 319
over and under ball relay, 419
overweight
elements and contributions to, 37–38
flexibility, trunk strength, and, 38
impact on aerobic capacity, 35
impact on motor performance, 36
type 2 diabetes and relationship to, 38
See also obesity predictor; weight management

pace chart
for 1-mile run, 365*fig*
for 40 and 100-yard dashes, 364*fig*
PACER (Progressive Aerobic Cardiovascular Endurance Run), 41, 333
pace work (running), 364
pacing activities (orienteering), 532
pacing/timing issues
ALT-PE (Academic Learning Time-Physical Education), 212
balancing instruction and practice times, 208–209*fig*
circuit training, 358
class management, 209–210*fig*
Class Time Analysis Form, 217*fig*, 220–221
collecting data on practice time, 213*fig*
maintaining instruction continuity through, 132
practice sessions, 119

pre-instructional decisions on, 112
response latency, 210–212
Pac-Man activity, 318
Paels, A. E., 37
palm wrestle, 415
Pangrazi, R. P., 5, 20, 22, 81, 109, 233, 234, 326, 330, 331, 332, 333, 335, 344, 345, 346
parachute exercises, 361–362
Parcell, G. S., 36
parents
  notified in case of emergency care, 290
  phone reports on misbehavior to, 165
  physical activity objectives of the, 54–55
  sample letter on policies and procedures to, 103*fig*
  students with disabilities and support from, 276
  See also students
Parker, M., 82
partner activities
  beanbags, 317, 403–404
  description of, 312
  examples of, 318–322
  hoops, 404
  juggling, 406*fig*–409*fig*
  jump bands, 404–406
  partner resistance exercise, 360–361, 367–368, 504
  rope jumping, 497–498
  sport stacking with speed stacks, 409–412
  wands, 415–416
partner golf, 487
partner passing (field hockey game), 439
partner racetrack fitness, 367
Partner Task Assessment Sheet—Aquatic Skills, 510*fig*
pass-and-squat relay, 419
passing
  basketball, 433, 436
  field hockey, 438
  flag football, 441, 443
  soccer, 453, 454
  team handball, 463–464
  volleyball, 467
passive communicators, 157
Pate, R. R., 36, 327, 333
Payne, V. G., 29
pec deck exercise, 360
Pedometer Power (Pangrazai, Beighle, & Sidman), 335
pedometers
  activities related to use of, 335–336

activity time measured by, 333–335
  used in class setting, 331–332
  considering accuracy of, 331
  description and uses of, 330
  measuring distance and stride length using, 335*fig*
  personal goal setting and use of, 333, 334*fig*
  program accountability and use of, 336
  teaching students how to use, 332
peer feedback
  basketball instruction, 181*fig*
  to increase quality performance, 140, 141*fig*
pelvis tilter exercise, 355
Pentabridge hustle activity, 318, 319*fig*
pepper (softball game), 459
Performance Analysis Sheet, 107*fig*
performance. *See* student performance
  personal best testing, 235–236
  personalized activity goal, 333, 334*fig*
  personal self-testing, 235
  personal and social responsibility approach, 93–97*fig*
  personal student interviews, 244
  phone calls home, 165
physical activities
  ALT-PE (Academic Learning Time-Physical Education) of, 212
  calorie expenditures of specific, 338*fig*, 395*fig*
  curriculum design of student-centered, 53–59
  involving the entire class, 159–160
  lesson plan on using, 120
  makeup work for missed, 106
  offering wide variety of, 20–22*fig*
  organizing into yearly instructional units, 59–64
  removing student from, 165
  safety guidelines for, 40–42
  student interests in specific, 58–59, 60*fig*
  students with disabilities and modifying, 272–274
  See also exercises; knowledge activities; lifestyle physical activities
physical activity
  for adolescents, 29–30, 327*fig*–328
  definition of, 326

effect on growth patterns, 34
HELP philosophy on lifetime, 86
  impact on health, 36–38
  levels of, 328–330
  long-term effect of, 39
  MVPA (moderate to vigorous physical activity), 327–328
  participation in regular, 9–10
  Physical Activity Pyramid, 328–329*fig*, 330
  as physical education outcome, 7
  physical fitness outcomes vs., 29*fig*
  public health approach on benefits of, 28–30
  relationship between fitness and, 345
  skill development approach to promoting, 70–84
  value of, 11–12
  weather guide on when to curtail, 40*fig*
  See also exercise; physical fitness
Physical Activity for Children: A Statement of Guidelines for Children Ages 5-12 (Corbin & Pangrazi), 22
Physical Activity and Health: A Report of the Surgeon General (USDHHS), 13, 21, 28, 330
Physical Activity Interest Survey, 60*fig*
Physical Activity Pyramid, 328–329*fig*, 330
physical education
  academic achievement relationship to, 39
  adolescent dropout of, 38–39
  benefits of, 4
  definitions of, 5–6
  diversity issues of, 140–143, 144*fig*
  major outcomes for, 7
  negative perception of, 4–5
  perspectives on, 12–13
  rationale for, 6–7
  physical education handbook areas covered by, 102
  attendance and participation policies, 103–105
  class makeup procedures, 105–106
  equipment, 108–110
  grading procedures, 110
  hygiene issues, 106–108
  uniforms and dress requirements, 102–103

physical education programs
  characteristics of successful,
    19–24
  coeducational classes of, 13–14fig
  conceptual, 14–15
  contributions to lives of students
    by, 5–6
  departmental policies of, 102
  equipment, facilities, and class
    size issues of, 16–17
  essential components of quality,
    16
  interdisciplinary courses of,
    15
  legal liability issue of, 17
  using pedometers for
    accountability of, 336
  private sports instruction as part
    of,
  role of evaluation in supporting,
    256
  state and local physical
    education requirements for, 13
  students with disabilities and, 14
  teaching and coaching conflicts
    issue of, 17
  virtual (online) physical
    education classes, 15–16
  See also curriculum; instruction;
    schools
physical education programs
    success factors
  all activity programs are
    integrated, 23–24
  diagnostic and counseling
    practices, 23
  positive learning environment,
    19–20
  student choice if offered, 20, 155
  students receive in-depth
    instruction, 22–23
  wide variety of activities
    available, 20–22
physical education standards
  1: motor skills/movement
    patterns competency, 8–9
  2: understanding movement, 9
  3: regular physical activity, 9–10
  4: physical fitness maintenance,
    10
  5: responsible personal and
    social behavior, 10–11
  6: valuing physical activity for
    many reasons, 11–12
physical fitness
  achieving/maintaining health-
    enhancing, 10

  assessment of health-related,
    233–237
  considerations for testing, 41
  creation of a positive experience
    with, 348–349
  current state of America's youth,
    344–345
  definition of, 326
  health-related and skill-related,
    346–348
  physical activity outcomes vs.,
    29fig
  relationship between physical
    activity and, 345
  stairway to, 91fig
  students with disabilities and,
    275–276
  See also physical activity
physical fitness development
  astronaut drills for, 358–359
  cardio-choice fitness for, 366
  challenge courses for, 361, 362fig
  circuit training fitness with a jog
    for, 367
  circuit training for, 358
  continuity exercises for, 359–360
  continuous movement activities
    for, 357–358
  exercises to music for, 356–357
  fitness cookie jar exchange for,
    366
  fitness scavenger hunt for, 366
  interval training for, 358
  jump-bands circuit for, 358
  jump and jog fitness for, 367
  long jump-rope fitness routine
    for, 367
  lower body, 355–356, 376–378,
    500, 502–503fig
  monopoly fitness for, 365
  parachute exercises for, 361–362
  partner racetrack fitness for, 367
  partner resistance exercises for,
    360–361, 367–368
  running activities and drills for,
    362–365fig
  squad leader exercises for, 356
  teacher and student leader
    exercise routines for, 356
  track and field fitness for, 365
  12 ways of fitness for, 367
  upper-body, 352, 354fig–355,
    374, 376–380, 500–503fig
physical fitness exercises
  avoidance of harmful practices
    and, 351–356
  balanced routines for, 350–351
  for developing fitness, 356–368
  encouraging addictive, 349

  flexibility and warm-up, 352–354
  health club workouts, 368–380fig
  for lower body development,
    355–356, 376–378, 500,
    502–503fig
  midsection, 355fig
  providing variety of, 348
  for upper-body development,
    352, 354fig–355, 374, 376–380,
    500–503fig
physical maturity, 33–34
Physician's Report Form, 105fig
picnic name game, 420
pilates, 378–379fig
pin kickball (speed-a-way game),
    462

pitching (softball), 458
Pittman, A. J., 288
Pittman, A. M., 495
placheck recording, 207–208
platforms (group initiative activity),
    526fig
platform stand (group initiative
    activity), 528, 529fig
Plowman, S. A., 38, 330
point-to-point orienteering, 532,
    534
portfolios, 247
positive feedback, 138–139, 213
positive learning environment,
    19–20
posture (students with disabilities),
    275–276
potato ball games, 418
potato relays, 419
potential grading standard,
    259
power
  definition and testing of, 232
  as skill-related physical fitness
    component, 348
power clean (strength training),
    502, 503fig
power frisbee, 479
power yoga, 379
practice sessions
  alternating instruction with,
    149
  ALT-PE (Academic Learning
    Time-Physical Education) and,
    212
  balancing instructional time
    with, 208–209fig
  collecting data on time spent on,
    213fig
  duration recording for, 212fig
  providing effective, 118–120
praise, 138–139, 213
preaching, 133, 160

pre-instructional decisions
  creating safe environment, 113–114
  determining instructional format, 110
  determining use of equipment, 111–112
  determining use of instructional devices, 112–113fig
  determining the use of space, 110–111
  determining use of time and pace, 112
Premack, D., 162
Premack Principle, 162–163
prescription (individualized teaching style), 191
preseason conditioning, 288
President's Challenge on Physical Fitness, 254, 334, 400
President's Council on Physical Fitness and Sports (PCPFS), 235, 254, 333
principals. See school administrators
private sports instruction, 16
problem-based learning (PBL), 191
problem solving (divergent) teaching style, 196–197
proficiency levels, 73
progressive relaxation, 399
Project Active Teen, 29
prompts (desired behavior), 163–164
proximate cause defense, 283
Prusak, K., 20
psychomotor domain, 53
public health approach
  on physical activity benefits, 28–30
  physical education perspective of, 12–13
  public statements issued on, 28
Public Law (PL) 94-142 [Education of All Handicapped Children Act of 1975], 14, 51, 264
Public Law (PL) 105-17 [IDEA Individuals with Disabilities Education Act], 14, 264, 265
punishment. See discipline
punting (flag football), 442
push-ups, 354fig
push-up tag, 320
putting (golf), 485–486, 487

quarter eagle, 313
quick hands with beanbags activity, 322
quick lineup activity, 322

racquetball instruction
  effective, 492
  knowledge test for, 248fig–249fig
  lead-up games and learning activities for, 492–493
  using mastery learning unit of instruction, 189fig
  performance objectives for, 493–494
  rainy-day activities for, 494
  sequence of skills for, 491–492
rainy-day activities
  archery, 426
  field hockey, 441
  frisbee, 484
  golf, 487
  jogging, 491
  racquetball, 494
  rope jumping, 499
  tennis, 515–516
Rairigh, R. M., 84
Raitakari, O. T., 7, 12
Rajic, M., 6, 39
Randall, L., 212
random running, 364
Rarick, L. G., 36
rating scales
  bowling rating form, 477fig
  golf, 488fig
  performance evaluation using, 242–244
  teaching effectiveness, 206fig
  team handball teacher, 243fig
  See also evaluation; grading; rubrics
reassigning students, 166
reciprocal teaching style, 193, 194fig
reclining partner pull-ups, 354
record keeping (accident reports), 290, 291fig
recreational and sports activities, 328, 329fig, 330, 419
redirecting student behavior, 155
red pin (bowling game), 475
reflections (teacher), 124–126
refusing to listen, 133, 160
regulation volleyball—serves modified, 469
reinforcement
  differential, 164
  as individualized teaching style, 191
  teaching caring through, 155
relays
  archery, 425
  rope jumping, 498
  suggested activities for, 419–420
  volleyball zigzag, 468

religious holidays, 104
removal of positive consequences, 168
reprimanding behavior, 165, 166–167
resistance push-up exercise, 361
resistance (strength) training. See strength training
respecting others rule, 158
respiratory system, 390fig–391
response latency, 210–212
responsibility levels, 154–155
Responsibility Rubric, 96fig
reverse curl exercise, 355
rhythmic activity, 495
rhythmic aerobic activity, 361–362
rhythmic expression, 55
Richardson, J., 88
Rink, J. E., 176
Roche, A. F., 6
rocking chair exercise, 354–355
roll call, 153
rooster hop drill, 314fig
rope jumping
  body position and rhythm for, 496
  as continuous movement activity, 357
  effective instruction for, 498
  as individual activity, 317
  learning activities for, 498–499
  partner activities for, 497–498
  as potential lifestyle activity, 495
  rainy-day activities for, 499
  sequence of skills for, 496–497
ropes course activities
  balance beam, 523–524fig
  cargo net jump, 524fig–525
  commando crawl, 522fig
  giant's ladder, 525fig
  inclined log, 524fig
  kitten crawl, 522fig
  overview of, 521
  swinging log, 524fig
  tension traverse, 523fig
  three-rope bridge, 523fig
  tire swing, 522fig
  triangle tension traverse, 523fig
  two-rope bridge, 522fig–523
Rose, K., 37
rotation (racquetball game), 493
rotation under the net (volleyball), 468–469
routines (rope jumping), 498–499
Rowland, T. W., 34, 35
rubber band activity, 317
rubrics
  bowling, 240fig
  Responsibility Rubric, 96fig

rubrics (continued)
  scoring, 238–239fig
  soccer dribbling, 186fig
  See also evaluation; grading;
    rating scales
rugby study guide/exam,
    251fig–252fig
running activities
  health club aerobic workouts,
    368
  jogging, 357, 364, 367, 489–491
  PACER (Progressive Aerobic
    Cardiovascular Endurance
    Run), 41, 333
  types of drills and, 314fig, 322,
    356, 362–365
running high fives activity, 322
running in place exercise, 356
running weave drill, 314fig

safety commission, 289
safety issues
  archery, 425
  Emergency Action Plan (EAP),
    510–511
  emergency care plan, 289–290
  guidelines for exercise and
    physical activity, 40–42
  guidelines for safety, 288–289
  instructing in a safe
    environment, 113–114
  instructions on first aid and,
    397–398
  major thrust of, 288
  resistance (strength) training,
    42
  safety and liability checklist,
    290, 292
  speed-a-way, 462
  strength training, 370
  swimming/aquatics, 398,
    510–511
  tennis, 515
  See also exercise
Safrit, M. J., 231, 250
Sallis, J. F., 7, 10, 13, 28, 36, 333
Saltin, B., 39
Samek, L. S., 183
sarcasm, 133
sasquatch race (group initiative
    activity), 528
scheduling
  as curriculum design factor,
    51–52fig
  flexible or block, 51–52fig, 121,
    122fig, 483fig, 505t, 535
  traditional, 52fig
Schmidt, R. A., 117, 118
Schneider, P. L., 330, 331

school administrators
  as curriculum design factor,
    50–51
  equipment and facilities
    responsibilities of, 286–287
  instruction responsibility of,
    284–285
  sending students to, 165
  supervision responsibility of,
    283–284
school districts
  departmental policies of,
    102–110
  Emergency Action Plan (EAP),
    510–511
  safety commission of, 289
School Nurse Excuse Form, 104fig
schools
  departmental policies of,
    102–110
  Emergency Action Plan (EAP),
    510–511
  expulsion from, 172
  implementing walking program
    by, 338–339
  mapping the, 532
  safety commission of, 289
  suspending or reassigning
    students, 166
  See also classes; physical
    education programs
scissors exercise, 361
scooping (lacrosse), 446, 449
scoops activities and games, 417,
    418fig
scope of curriculum, 61, 62fig–63fig
score orienteering, 534
scoring rubrics. See rubrics
scotch bowling, 476
seat pull-up, 415
seat roll, 313
sedentary living, 329
self-assessment logs, 244–247
self-control (responsibility level),
    154
self-evaluating, 399
Self-Evaluation form, 96fig
self-responsibility, 154
Self-Responsibility Checklist, 95fig
sequence of curriculum, 61,
    62fig–63fig
serve and catch (volleyball), 468
serving (volleyball), 89fig, 467
shaping desired behavior, 164
shared negligence, 279, 282
Shaw, J. M., 330
Shephard, R. J., 6, 39
Sherrill, A., 91

shooting
  basketball, 434, 436
  field hockey, 438
  soccer, 453, 454, 455
shoulder shrugs (strength training),
    500, 502fig
shuffle-bowl, 476
shuffle sideways running, 363
side-leg flex exercise, 356
sideline basketball, 435–436
sideline soccer, 452
sideline team handball, 465
side-of-the stretches, 353
Sidman, C. L., 333, 335
Siedentop, D., 19, 84, 85, 132, 176,
    184, 199, 205
Siervogel, R. M., 6
Sievanen, H., 34
Simoneau, J., 345
Simons-Morton, B. B., 28, 36
single standard goal, 333
sitting leg lift exercise, 361
sitting (or kneeling) volleyball,
    468
sitting pulls exercise, 361
sit-up sticks (field hockey game),
    439
skeletal system, 385–386
skill development approach
  articulation from K–12 grades,
    81fig
  choice element of, 72–73
  consideration of proficiency
    levels in, 73
  high school health club/fitness
    center emphasis curriculum,
    79–81
  outdoor adventure activity used
    in, 21fig, 71fig, 81–84fig
  overview of, 70–72
  suggested middle school
    curriculums using, 73–76fig
  suggested for transition from
    middle to high school, 76–79
skill practice
  using random, 119
  rubric for soccer dribbling, 186fig
  using variable, 119–120
skill-related physical fitness
  components of, 347–348
  described, 346
skills
  ALT-PE (Academic Learning
    Time–Physical Education) to
    learn, 212
  archery, 423–424
  badminton sequence of, 426–428
  basketball sequence of, 432–434
  bowling sequence of, 473–475

demonstrating and modeling, 134, 136–137fig
field hockey sequence of, 438–439
flag football sequence of, 441–442
general components of, 231–232
giving meaningful feedback on, 117–118
gymnastics sequence of, 445
jogging sequence of, 489–490
nonlocomotor, 8
objective assessment of physical, 231–237
objectives of basketball, 163fig
orienteering sequence of, 529
Partner Task Assessment Sheet—Aquatic Skills, 510fig
practicing, 119–120
racquetball sequence of, 491–492
rhythmic activity sequence of, 495
rope jumping sequence of, 496–497
sequence of frisbee, 478
soccer sequence of, 183–184, 186fig, 195fig, 223, 449–450
softball sequence of, 457–458
specific sport skills tests on, 232–233
strength training sequence of, 232–233
swimming/aquatics sequence of, 499–500
team handball sequence of, 463–465
tennis sequence of, 511–512
track and field sequence of, 466
volleyball sequence of, 466–467
skill tests
AAHPERD basketball test, 233
Cornish handball test, 232–233
for general skill components, 231–232
Johnson soccer test, 233
Kemp-Vincent tennis rally test, 233
skinfold test, 333
skittles (bowling game), 476
Slaughter, M. H., 235
small-group activities
beanbags, 403–404
description of, 312
examples of, 318–322
hoops, 404
juggling, 406fig–409fig
jump bands, 404–406
sport stacking with speed stacks, 409–412

stunts, pyramids, and combatives, 412–415
wands, 415–416
See also task (station) instruction
Smith, L. L., 351
Snider, S. A., 28
snorkeling instruction, 190fig
snowball relay, 419
Snow-Harter, C., 330
soccer bowling, 476
soccer croquet, 451
soccer instruction
dribbling tasks for, 183–184, 186fig, 449–450
effective, 450–451
guided discovery (convergent) teaching style for, 196
Johnson soccer test on skills, 233
lead-up games and learning activities, 451–453
performance objectives of, 453–455
reciprocal style sheet for long throw-in, 195fig
regulation soccer field, 451fig
sequence of skills for, 449–450
soccer keep-away, 451
social dance steps, 495
Social Development Checklist, 94fig
social-historical perspective, 12
social and personal responsibility approach, 93–97fig
social reinforces, 161–162
softball instruction
controversy over, 457
effective, 458–459
lead-up games and learning activities, 459–460
peer assessment task checklist, 241fig
performance objectives for, 460–461
sequence of skills, 457–458
softball diamonds, 456fig
Spain, C. G., 36
SPARK (Sports, Play and Active Recreation for Kids), 7
spectator activities, 106
Spectator Analysis Sheet, 108fig
speed-a-way, 461–462
speedy baseball, 460
speed and reaction time
definition and testing of, 231–232
as skill-related physical fitness component, 348
spider tag, 320
spiking (volleyball), 467
spinjammer frisbees, 482, 482fig

Sporting Goods Manufacturers Association survey (2000), 6
sport movement challenges
described, 312
examples listed, 316–317
sports activities
accidents and injuries related to, 398
archery, 423–426
badminton, 426–432
basketball, 163fig, 180fig–181fig, 196, 198–199, 233, 432–437
field hockey, 437fig–441
flag football, 188fig, 441–445
gymnastics, 445–446
handball, 232–233, 242–243fig, 462–466
lacrosse, 446–449
medical examinations, 288
mismatched opponents error in, 287
preseason conditioning, 288
soccer, 183–184, 186fig, 195–196fig, 233, 449–455
softball, 241fig, 456fig–461
speed-a-way, 461–462
sports and recreational, 328, 329fig, 330, 419
team handball, 462–466
track and field, 365, 466
transportation of students, 288
volleyball, 89fig, 184–187fig, 242fig, 466–470
waiver forms, 287–288
See also athletic performance; lifestyle physical activities
sport skill relays, 420
sport stacking with speed stacks, 409–412
spotting (strength training), 499
spread-eagle relay, 420
squads
exercises led by squad leaders, 356
guidelines for forming, 151fig–152
home base and station teaching using, 152
square dance, 495
square drill, 314
square hockey, 440
squat jumps exercise, 355
stability ball exercises, 373–376
staff
active supervision by, 130–131, 215–216, 218–220fig, 284, 290, 291
equipment and facilities responsibilities of, 287, 292

staff (continued)
- instruction responsibility of, 285–286
- See also teachers

stairway to lifetime fitness, 91fig

stance
- bowling, 474
- flag football, 442
- golf, 484

standards
- for assessing students with disabilities, 266–267
- as curriculum design factor, 53
- definition of content, 7–8
- physical education, 7–12

standing hand wrestle, 415

standing high fives activity, 322

standing movements, 368–369

star drill (field hockey game), 439

static stretching exercise, 351

station (or small-group) instruction. See task (station) instruction

Steen, T., 82

stepping-stone relay, 419

Stone, E. J., 30

stop, look, and listen rule, 158

Strand, B. N., 232, 255

stream crossing (group initiative activity), 528

strength
- abdominal, 234
- accommodating students with disabilities lacking, 272–273
- flexibility and trunk extensor, 234
- gender differences in, 35
- motor performance and, 36
- muscle fiber type, performance, and, 35–36
- as physical fitness component, 347
- upper-body, 234

strength training
- bench press used in, 500fig
- circuit training, 358, 359fig, 367, 503
- health club workouts for, 368–369
- learning activities for, 503–504
- motivational club criteria for weight lifters, 504fig
- overview of, 499
- partner resistance, 360–361, 367–368, 504
- recommendations for adolescents, 41–42
- safety issues related to, 370
- sequence of skills in, 499–503fig

strength yoga, 379
- See also exercises; health club/fitness center

stress, 392–394

stress reduction, 399

stretches
- avoiding harmful, 351
- warm-up, 352–354

stride length calculations, 335fig

student accident report, 290, 291fig

student behavior
- behavior contracts on, 169, 170fig
- conflict resolution element of, 155–156
- implementing plan for changing, 169
- modifying personal behavior, 400
- objectives related to NASPE content standards, 53
- ongoing process of promoting good, 161–164
- responsible personal and social, 10–11
- teaching responsible, 154–155
- See also misbehavior

student behavior contracts, 169, 170fig

student behavior management
- extrinsic reinforcers, 162–163
- nonverbal communication as, 136fig, 161–162
- prompting desired behavior, 163–164
- shaping desired behavior, 164
- social reinforcers, 161–162
- See also discipline

student choice
- as instruction approach, 20, 155
- responsible behavior as, 155
- skill development approach use of, 72–73

student interviews, 244

student leader exercise routines, 356

student performance
- assessment of, 230–254
- athletic, 38–39
- calculating, 212–213
- evaluation of, 254–257, 254–257
- feedback on knowledge of, 117–118
- genetic endowment and fitness, 344–345
- motor, 35–36
- weight training scoring rubric, 239fig
- See also exercises; health club/fitness center

student performance assessment
- of attitudes and values, 250–254
- cognitive assessment of knowledge, 247–250, 251fig
- formal and informal, 230
- objective physical skills, 231–237
- overview of, 230–231
- Partner Task Assessment Sheet—Aquatic Skills, 510fig
- peer feedback to increase quality, 140, 141fig
- performance outcomes, 237–247
- Performance Analysis Sheet, 107fig
- students with disabilities, 266–267
- See also evaluation

student performance evaluation
- criterion-referenced, 255
- grading for, 110, 255–260
- norm-referenced, 254–255
- rating scales used for, 242–244, 254–255
- rubrics used for, 96fig, 186fig, 477fig, 488fig
- uses for, 255–256
- See also goal setting

student performance objectives
- archery, 425–426
- badminton, 431–432
- basketball, 436–437
- beginning racquetball, 189fig
- bowling, 476–477
- field hockey, 440–441
- flag football, 445
- orienteering, 536
- soccer, 453–455
- softball, 460–461
- team handball, 465–466
- tennis, 516–517
- volleyball, 469–470
- See also goal setting

student performance outcome assessment
- anecdotal record sheets for, 244
- overview of, 237–238
- personal interviews for, 244
- portfolios for, 247
- rating scales for, 242–244
- scoring rubrics for, 238fig–239fig
- self-assessment logs for, 244–247
- tactical/game-play, 247
- See also checklists

students
- active supervision of, 130–131, 215–216, 218–220fig
- coed class, 14fig
- considering personal needs of, 140–144

curriculum design and developmental levels of, 55–56
dealing with nonparticipating, 153
diversity of, 140–143, 144*fig*
effective grouping of, 150–151*fig*
exercise routines led by, 356
high expectations communicated to, 159
labeling, 133, 160
learning names of, 152
maintaining interest of, 130–132
physical activity interests of, 58–59, 60*fig*
physical activity objectives of the, 54–55
physical education programs contributions to lives of, 5–6
skill demonstrations by, 137*fig*
teaching tolerance to all, 274–275
teaching the whole person, 114–116
transportation of, 288, 292
working cooperatively, 11*fig*
See also feedback; outcomes; parents

students with disabilities computer services available to, 276
designing curriculum appropriate for, 51
fitness and posture for, 275–276
IEPs (individualized educational programs) for, 264, 267–271
least restrictive environment for, 265
legislation covering rights of, 14, 51, 264, 265
mainstreaming, 265*fig*–266, 271–275
parental support of, 276
recruiting and training aides to work with, 276
screening and assessment of, 266–267

students with disabilities assessment
due process guidelines for, 266
procedures for ensuring standards, 266–267
student sharing, 155
stunts activities, 412–414
substance abuse instruction, 396–397
suspension, 166

swimming/aquatics accidents related, 398
block plan for, 505
overview of, 504–505
Partner Task Assessment Sheet—Aquatic Skills, 510*fig*
safety issues of, 510–511
sample lessons for five days, 506*fig*–509*fig*
sequence of skills for, 505, 510
swinging log (ropes course), 524*fig*

tackling
field hockey, 438
soccer, 450, 454, 455
tactical/game-play assessment, 247
tag games, 319–320
Taggart, A., 85
Tannehill, D., 19, 132, 176, 184, 199, 205, 230
Tanner, S. M., 42
tape shooting (archery game), 425
tardiness policy, 105
target golf, 587
Targeting Teenaged Girls project, 30
target work-up (archery game), 425
task (station) instruction basketball tasks, 180*fig*
benefits of, 177–180
description of, 110, 111*fig*, 175
desired student behavior facilitated by, 152
dribbling soccer balls, 183–184
guidelines for designing, 180–182
softball, 458–459
See also small-group activities
Taylor, J., 71
Taylor, W. C., 28, 333
"teachable moments," 132
teacher aids, 276
teacher leader exercise routine, 356
teachers
active supervision by, 130–131, 215–216, 218–220*fig*, 284, 290, 292
consultation between special education and physical education, 274
creating behavior plan for, 157–161
demonstrating caring attitude toward students, 134–135
demonstrating and modeling skills, 136–137
equipment and facilities responsibilities of, 287, 292
exercise routines led by, 356

instruction responsibility of, 285–286, 290, 292
learning students' names, 152
nonconfrontational and nonadversarial approach by, 155
using nonverbal communication, 136*fig*
teaching style matching abilities of, 197
"withitness" and "overlappingness" characteristics of, 159
See also modeling; staff

teaching
active supervision during, 130–131
avoiding gender biases, 143–144
conflicts between coaching and, 17
diversity issues of, 140–143, 144*fig*
effective listening and communication when, 132–134
physical skills and fitness, 349
responsible student behavior, 154–155
students how to use pedometer, 332
tolerance to students, 274–275
See also instructional strategies
teaching effectiveness defining, 204
evaluating, 205–206
goals and feedback on improving, 205
improving teaching skills for, 204
observing instruction to improve, 207–208, 220–227
rating scale for, 206
systematic evaluation to improve, 205
Teaching Games for Understanding (TGFU) (Griffin & Butler), 198
teaching skills improvement, 204
teaching styles
advantages of using different, 176–177
continuum of, 177*fig*
cooperative, 191–193*fig*
direct, 177
elements common to all, 199–200
framework for using multiple, 198*fig*–199*fig*
individualized, 190–191*fig*
inquiry, 193–197

teaching styles (*continued*)
mainstreaming students with disabilities and, 271
mastery learning (outcomes-based), 182–190*fig*
student learning and, 197
task (station), 110, 111*fig*, 152, 175, 177–182
See also instructional strategies
team activities
cageball games, 416–417
eclipse ball games, 418
flickerball games, 417–418
novel (or modified) sports, 22
potato ball games, 418
scoops games, 417, 418*fig*
team tug-of-war, 415
throton games, 417
See also instructional strategies

team handball instruction
court markings for, 463*fig*
effective, 465
modified games, 465
overview and rules of game, 462–463
performance objectives of, 465–466
sequence of skills for, 463–465
team member expectations (self-evaluation), 193
team paper, scissors, and rock, 421

Telama, R., 7
tennis instruction
effective, 512–514
on etiquette, 513–514
Kemp-Vincent tennis rally testing skills, 233
lead-up, modified, and rainy-day activities for, 515–516
organization and skill work, 514–515
overview of game, 511
performance objectives for, 516–517
readiness checklist for performing forehand, 183*fig*
safety issues of, 515
sequence of skills, 511–512
tennis court markings, 512*fig*
tension traverse (ropes course), 523*fig*

Thomas, D. R., 171
Thomas, J. R., 39
Thomas, K. T., 39
Thorland, W. G., 37
Thorpe, R. J., Jr., 6
thread the needle, 416
threatening communication, 133, 160

three bounces, three steps, and no contact (team handball), 465
three-hit volleyball, 469
Three-Person Volleyball, 85–86
three-person weave (field hockey game), 439
three pins (bowling game), 476
Three Rivers Study, 6
three-rope bridge (ropes course), 523*fig*
three-seconds, no steps (lacrosse game), 449
three on three (basketball game), 436
throton activities and games, 417*fig*
throw for accuracy (frisbee game), 479
throw for distance (frisbee game), 479
throw and catch with self (frisbee game), 479
throw for distance and accuracy (frisbee game), 479
throw for accuracy (frisbee game), 479

throwing
frisbee, 478
lacrosse, 446, 449
softball, 457–458, 459, 460
throw-in (soccer), 454, 455
tic-tac-toe or bingo (archery game), 479
time aloft (frisbee game), 479
timed runs, 490
time-outs, 165, 168–169
timing/pacing issues
ALT-PE (Academic Learning Time–Physical Education), 212
balancing instruction and practice time, 208–209*fig*
circuit training, 358
class management, 209–210*fig*
Class Time Analysis Form, 217*fig*, 220–221
collecting data on practice time, 213*fig*
maintaining instruction continuity through, 132
practice sessions, 119
pre-instructional decisions on, 112
response latency, 210–212
Title IX (Education Amendments Act) [1972], 12, 13–14, 51
toe dance, 415
toe toucher exercise, 361
tolerance, 274–275
touch ball (speed-a-way game), 462
Toward a Better Understanding of Physical Activity and Fitness: Selected Topics, Volume Two

(Corbin, Pangrazi, & Franks), 234
towels policy, 107–108
Townsend, J. S., 84
track and field instruction
fitness for, 365
skills and ideas for, 466
traffic accidents, 397–398
training heart rate, 392, 490
transportation of students, 288, 292
trapping (soccer), 450
treadmill exercise, 356
Treasure, J., 20
Trembley, J., 39
triangle-and-two tag, 320
triangle-plus-one tag, 320
triceps extension (strength training), 320
trust dive (group initiative activity), 500
"trigger story," 196
Trost, S. G., 333
Trudeau, F., 6, 39
true or false partner tag, 320
trunk extensor strength, 234
tug-of-war activities, 415
turkey shoot (archery game), 425
12 ways of fitness, 367
twenty-one (basketball game), 435
twenty-one (frisbee game), 479
two-handed overhead pass (basketball), 434
two-pitch softball, 459
two-rope bridge (ropes course), 522*fig*–523
type 2 diabetes
overweight and relationship to, 38
physical activity to reduce risk of, 337

ultimate (frisbee game), 479
uniforms/dress requirements, 102–103
United States Field Hockey Association, 437
United States Tennis Association (USTA), 511
upper-body exercises
medicine balls, 376–377
pilates, 378–379
stability balls, 374
strength training, 500–503*fig*
stretches, 352
types of, 354*fig*–355
yoga, 379–380
upper-body strength, 234
upper-leg stretches, 352

upright or bent rowing (strength training), 500, 501fig
U.S. Consumer Product Safety Commission, 288
U.S. Department of Health and Human Services (USDHHS), 6, 19, 28, 29, 326, 331
U.S. Public Health Service, 12–13, 21–22, 36
van der Mars, H., 84, 215, 217, 219, 222
vanishing beanbags activity, 317
vertical curricula
  definition of, 61
  skill development approach to, 75–76
Viikari, J., 7
Vincent-Graser, S. D., 332
Vincent, M. F., 233
Vincent, S. D., 330
Vincent, W., 332
virtual (online) physical education classes, 15–16
VO₂ max, 34
Vogler, W., 215
volleyball instruction
  designing mastery learning instruction for, 184–186
  effective, 467–468
  hierarchical analysis on spiking, 184–185
  lead-up and modified games for, 468–469
  using mastery learning unit of instruction, 187fig
  overview of game, 466
  performance objectives for, 469–470

sequence of skills, 466–467
Volleyball Serves—Problem-solving Questions, 89fig
volleyball skills peer assessment checklist, 242fig
volley tennis (volleyball), 468
volunteer aids, 276
Vouri, I., 34
waiver forms, 287–288
the walk (group initiative activity), 526, 527fig
walking activities
  calories burned by, 338fig
  health club aerobic workouts, 368
  implementing school walking program, 338–339
  jog-walk-jog, 490
  as "real" lifetime activity, 336–337
  suggested types of, 339–340
  as weight management, 337–338fig
walk-jog-sprint, 364
Waller, M. S., 495
wands activities, 415–416
Ward, D. S., 35
warm-up exercises
  medicine ball, 376
  types of, 352–354
Watson, E. R., 91
wave drill, 313fig
weave drill, 314fig
Wechsler, H., 36
wedging (soccer), 450
weekly physical activity log, 245fig
Weigand, B., 91
weight-lifting class, 22fig

weight management
  good nutrition for, 394fig–396
  walking for, 337–338fig
  See also overweight
weight training scoring rubric, 239fig
Welk, G. J., 30, 231
Welk, K. A., 231
Weltman, A. W., 37
Wham-O Manufacturing Company, 478
wheelbarrow relay, 419
Whitehead, J. R., 163
Whitiker, R. C., 6
Wilkinson, J. A., 6
Williams, D. P., 235
Williams, J. F., 12
Wilmore, J. H., 37, 38, 387
Wilson, R., 137, 232, 255
"withitness," 159
Women's International Bowling Congress (WIBC), 476
Wood, K., 91
word or team sounds, 420
work-up (softball game), 460
Yang, X., 7
YMCA/YWCA, 59, 449, 466, 499, 505
yoga, 379–380
Young, J. C., 36
Youth Risk Behavior Surveillance System (YRBSS), 6
Zakrajsek, D., 224, 225, 226
Zhu, W., 250
zigzag relay (volleyball), 468
zipper activity, 421